June 25–28, 2013
Taipei, Taiwan

Association for Computing Machinery

Advancing Computing as a Science & Profession

MobiSys'13

Proceedings of the 11th Annual International Conference on
Mobile Systems, Applications, and Services

Sponsored by:

ACM SIGMOBILE

Supported by:

NSF, Facebook, MediaTek, Intel, Microsoft Research, and Google

Association for
Computing Machinery

Advancing Computing as a Science & Profession

The Association for Computing Machinery
2 Penn Plaza, Suite 701
New York, New York 10121-0701

Notice to Past Authors of ACM-Published Articles
ACM intends to create a complete electronic archive of all articles and/or other material previously published by ACM. If you have written a work that has been previously published by ACM in any journal or conference proceedings prior to 1978, or any SIG Newsletter at any time, and you do NOT want this work to appear in the ACM Digital Library, please inform permissions@acm.org, stating the title of the work, the author(s), and where and when published.

ISBN: 978-1-4503-1672-9 (Digital)

ISBN: 978-1-4503-2288-1 (Print)

Additional copies may be ordered prepaid from:

ACM Order Department
PO Box 30777
New York, NY 10087-0777, USA

Phone: 1-800-342-6626 (USA and Canada)
+1-212-626-0500 (Global)
Fax: +1-212-944-1318
E-mail: acmhelp@acm.org
Hours of Operation: 8:30 am – 4:30 pm ET

Printed in the USA

Welcome from the General Chairs

On behalf of the entire organizing committee, it is our great pleasure to welcome you to the *11th International Conference on Mobile Systems, Applications and Services – MobiSys 2013* in Taipei, Taiwan. This is the first time the conference comes to Asia – marking MobiSys's ambition engaging the talent pool and the thriving mobile industry in the region. Expanded along are a few more 'firsts' in the conference's history: (1) Mobisys'13 is a 3-full-day event for the first time; (2) a panel is assembled, also for the first time, to foster discussions on a rather unusual, but treasured, community value – societal impact; (3) the first ever MobiSys tutorial is a comprehensive walk-through of localization technologies, a hot topic in the circle of start-ups; (4) a video program is installed for, we all know too well, a picture is more than a thousand words; (5) and finally, an exclusive geek's night in the renowned National Palace Museum.

In addition to the regular full paper sessions, this year also sees a high quality adjunct program of videos, demos and posters. To properly reflect the significance of the adjunct program, these submissions see a much tighter integration in the main program, with video presentations interspersed with the technical presentations of the main track, and posters and demos presented at the end of the first day. The workshop program has three workshops that cover exciting topics in mobile cloud computing, vehicular networking and cellular networking. The workshop program also includes a Ph.D. Forum that provides a friendly and supportive environment for doctoral students to present and discuss their dissertation work. Last but not least, Patrick Baudisch's keynote will provide an exciting and stimulating view of the future of mobile interactive devices.

Putting together MobiSys 2013 has been a team effort and we would like to thank a series of people. First of all, as the event coordinator, Patty Teng, has done an outstanding job making everything happen. As the Steering Committee Chair, Victor Bahl has been very supportive in putting the conference together and previous years' chair, Nigel Davies provided important and useful information. We are also very thankful to the people helping organizing the practical matters, including the Local Arrangement Chair Ling-Jyh Chen, the Web Chair Ted Tsung-Te Lai, and the Publicity Chair Kun-Chan Lan. A special thanks goes to the Student Travel Grants Chair, Tamer M. Nadeem for the hard work acquiring funds and making it possible for dozens of students to come to MobiSys'13.

We also want to thank the Technical Program Committee, including the Program Committee Chairs Romit Roy Choudhury and Feng Zhao, the Workshop Chairs Nic Lane and Junehwa Song, the Posters/Demos Chairs Ya-Yunn Su and Joy Ying Zhang, and the Videos Chairs Emiliano Miluzzo and Jitendra Padhye. A special thanks goes to our Publication Chair Shiao-Li (Charles) Tsao for compiling all of the proceedings.

We hope sincerely that you find your curiosity, as well as appetite, satisfied this week in Taipei!

Hao-Hua Chu & Polly Huang
MobiSys 2013 General Co-Chairs
National Taiwan University

Welcome from the Program Co-Chairs

Welcome to *MobiSys 2013: The Eleventh International Conference on Mobile Systems, Applications, and Services*. As the premier forum for presenting the latest research in mobile and wireless systems, this year's conference attracted a record number of 211 submissions, a sign of continuing vibrancy and increasing maturity of our community. In addition to the strong technical program covering virtually every major topic of mobile systems research, we've incorporated a new video program showcasing innovative ideas selected from submissions, and have continued the tradition of having an interactive demo and poster fest.

The Technical Program Committee and Industrial Reviewer Panel are to be lauded for their extraordinary effort in vetting each paper with care during the rigorous review process. Each paper was assigned to three Program Committee members for a first round of reviews. Each of the 211 papers with at least one positive review (weak accept) was assigned two additional reviewers from the Program Committee in the second round. A paper with potential industrial applications was further assigned to an Industrial Reviewer Committee member. In all, the Program Committee members and industrial reviewers generated 866 reviews and the top 60 papers received at least 5 reviews.

The Program Committee met for a full day at Jekyll Island, Georgia, USA. The Committee discussed the top 60 papers and accepted 33 papers for the program. Each of these 33 papers was shepherded by a member of the Program Committee, to ensure that recommendations made by the reviewers and during the Program Committee meeting were satisfactorily addressed.

The resulting technical program is the fruit of labor by many. We want to thank all the authors of submitted papers. We are indebted to the Technical Program Committee and Industry Reviewer Panel for their extraordinary work in reviewing papers and providing feedback for the authors, and the Video Program Committee for reviewing and selecting the short videos.

We hope you will find the program interesting and thought-provoking, and you will take this opportunity to share your ideas while also networking with other researchers and practitioners from around the world.

Romit Roy Choudhury
MobiSys'13 Program Chair
Duke University

Feng Zhao
MobiSys'13 Program Chair
Microsoft Research

Table of Contents

Session 8: Behavior and Activity Recognition

Session 9: Assorted Topics

Session 10: Videos

Session 11: Demonstrations

Session 12: Posters

MobiSys 2013 Organization

General Co-chairs: Hao-Hua Chu *(National Taiwan University)*
Polly Huang *(National Taiwan University)*

Program Co-chairs: Romit Roy Choudhury *(Duke University)*
Feng Zhao *(Microsoft Research)*

Video Program Co-chairs: Emiliano Miluzzo *(AT&T Labs)*
Jitendra Padhye *(Microsoft Research)*

Posters/Demos Co-chairs: Ya-Yunn Su *(National Taiwan University)*
Joy Ying Zhang *(Carnegie Mellon University)*

Workshop Co-chairs: Nic Lane *(Microsoft Research Asia)*
Junehwa Song *(Korea Advanced Institute of Science and Technology)*

Publication Chair: Shiao-Li (Charles) Tsao *(National Chiao Tung University)*

Web Chair: Ted Tsung-Te Lai *(National Taiwan University)*

Publicity Chair: Kun-Chan Lan *(National Cheng Kung University)*

Local Arrangements Chair: Ling-Jyh Chen *(Academic Sinica)*

Student Travel Grants Chair: Tamer M. Nadeem *(Old Dominion University)*

Steering Committee Chair: Victor Bahl *(Microsoft Research)*

Technical Program Committee: Sharad Agarwal *(Microsoft Research)*
Rajesh Balan *(Singapore Management University)*
Suman Banerjee *(University of Wisconsin-Madison)*
Gaetano Borriello *(University of Washington)*
Hojung Cha *(Yonsei University)*
Krishna Chintalapudi *(Microsoft Research India)*
Landon Cox *(Duke University)*
Prabal Dutta *(University of Michigan)*
Deborah Estrin *(Cornell Tech)*
Deepak Ganesan *(University of Massachusetts, Amherst)*
Shyam Gollakota *(University of Washington)*
Marco Gruteser *(Rutgers University)*
Jason Hong *(Carnegie Mellon University)*
David Kotz *(Dartmouth College)*

Technical Program Committee (continued):

Anthony LaMarca *(Intel Labs)*
Nic Lane *(Microsoft Research Asia)*
Koen Langendoen *(Delft University of Technology)*
Justin Manweiler *(IBM T.J. Watson Research Center)*
Z. Morley Mao *(University of Michigan)*
Jason Nieh *(Columbia University)*
Konstantina (Dina) Papagiannaki *(Telefonica)*
Mahadev Satyanarayanan *(Carnegie Mellon University)*
Junehwa Song *(Korea Advanced Institute of Science and Technology)*
Alexander Varshavsky *(AT&T Labs)*
Matt Welsh *(Google)*
Kamin Whitehouse *(University of Virginia)*
Guoliang Xing *(Michigan State University)*
Lin Zhong *(Rice University)*

Industry Reviewer Panel:

Suhrid Balakrishnan *(AT&T Labs)*
Saumitra Das *(Qualcomm Research, Silicon Valley)*
Fred Xiaofan Jiang *(Intel Labs)*
Ravi Kokku *(IBM Research India)*
Chun-Yu Lin *(HTC)*
Zhen Liu *(Microsoft)*
Fukumoto Masaaki *(NTT DoCoMo Labs)*
Xue Yang *(Intel Labs)*

Additional Reviewers:

Faisal Alquaddoomi
Shahriyar Amini
Justin Cranshaw
Sauvik Das
Afsaneh Doryab
Seungyeop Han
Eiji Hayashi
Andy Hsieh
Jinhakang Kang
Ilias Leontiadis
Jialiu Lin
Dionysios Logothetis
Brent Longstaff
Will Scott
Hongsuda Tangmunarunkit
Xiao Wang

MobiSys 2013 Sponsor & Supporters

Sponsor: sigmobile

Platinum Supporter: NSF

Gold Supporter: facebook

Silver Supporter: MEDIATEK; Microsoft Research

Bronze Supporter: Google

Co-Hosts: Academia Sinica; acm; Intel-NTU Connected Context Computing Center; Bureau of Foreign Trade; NSC; National Taiwan University; TAIPEI

AMC: Verifying User Interface Properties for Vehicular Applications

Kyungmin Lee*, Jason Flinn*, T.J. Giuli†, Brian Noble*, and Christopher Peplin†

University of Michigan* Ford Motor Company†

ABSTRACT

Vehicular environments require continuous awareness of the road ahead. It is critical that mobile applications used in such environments (e.g., GPS route planners and location-based search) do not distract drivers from the primary task of operating the vehicle. Fortunately, a large body of research on vehicular interfaces provides best practices that mobile application developers can follow. However, when we studied the most popular vehicular applications in the Android marketplace, no application followed these guidelines. In fact, vehicular applications were not substantially better at meeting best practice guidelines than non-vehicular applications.

To remedy this problem, we have developed a tool called AMC that uses model checking to automatically explore the graphical user interface (GUI) of Android applications and detect violations of vehicular design guidelines. AMC is designed to give developers early feedback on their application GUI and reduce the amount of time required by a human expert to assess an application's suitability for vehicular usage. We have evaluated AMC by comparing the violations that it reports with those reported by an industry expert for 12 applications. AMC generated a definitive assessment for 85% of the guidelines checked; for these cases, it had no false positives and a false negative rate of under 2%. For the remaining 15% of cases, AMC reduced the number of application screens that required manual verification by 95%.

General Terms

Human Factors, Verification

Categories and Subject Descriptors

D.2.2 [**Software Engineering**]: Design Tools and Techniques; D.2.4 [**Software Engineering**]: Software/Program Verification—*model checking*

Keywords

Model checking; Android; Vehicular user interfaces

MobiSys'13, June 25-28, 2013, Taipei, Taiwan

1. INTRODUCTION

Some mobile applications are often used in environments in which the user's attention must be focused on driving. For instance, drivers employ GPS route planners, music services, gas station locators, parking-spot finders, and similar tools. While well-designed applications that minimize driver distraction can improve the driving experience, poorly designed applications can too easily divert attention from the primary task of operating the vehicle. Although vehicular applications are currently the primary reason why mobile interfaces are currently designed with user distraction in mind, emerging technologies such as augmented reality are likely to increase the prevalence of such situations.

Unfortunately, as we show in a study of Android applications, many tools intended for vehicular usage today do not follow accepted industry guidelines. We argue that this problem does not arise from a lack of usability research; in fact, there exists a large body of detailed guidelines and standards for user interaction in vehicular environments [7, 10, 16, 19, 21]. Rather, the issue is that most mobile application developers simply do not have enough experience creating interfaces for automotive environments. They are not aware of the best practices in vehicular interface design, and they are not able to anticipate how drivers will interact with their applications in vehicular settings. This information gap results in applications that inappropriately demand too much attention from drivers.

Currently, there are several models for running mobile applications in vehicles. Some applications run on an in-vehicle *human-machine interface* (HMI) such as MyFord Touch or the Cadillac Cue system. Access to such platforms is closely controlled by vehicle manufacturers; any applications developed by third parties undergo strict testing in cooperation with manufacturers before they are deployed. Usability experts ensure that applications meet guidelines for in-vehicle use on a manufacturer's HMI platform. The advantage of this approach is that deployed applications meet a very high usability standard. The disadvantage is cost and speed of deployment; application testing can take many iterations between developers and usability experts. Developers must wait for feedback after each modification to the application interface, and each application evaluation requires a substantial amount of costly expert time.

A more recent class of in-vehicle applications run on smartphones. These applications are deployed through application marketplaces without the involvement of vehicular manufacturers. The advantage of the smartphone model is speed of deployment; mobile developers can often release a new application months after conceiving an initial idea. The disadvantages of this approach are two-fold. First, the input and output capabilities of a smartphone platform are not ideal for the vehicle; in contrast, vehicle HMIs have dashboard touchscreens, steering wheel controls, and other forms of interaction specifically designed for use in a vehicle. Second, as previously mentioned, mobile application developers are unaware of best practices for vehicular applications and often make poor design choices that lead to too much distraction when the application is used.

Recently, a hybrid model of application deployment has emerged in which an application running on a smartphone seamlessly interacts with in-vehicle HMIs by, for example, displaying the application graphical user interface (GUI) on the dashboard touchscreen and by enabling input via steering wheel controls. Ford's AppLink platform and the MirrorLink standard are two examples of this hybrid approach. While such platforms are a promising method for addressing the input and output limitations of smartphones, they provide little help to developers struggling to design applications appropriate for vehicular environments. Even if expert guidance were available to such developers, it is infeasible to have completely-manual testing scale to check the total number of vehicular applications in a marketplace such as iTunes or the Android store.

In this paper, we mitigate this dilemma with automated model checking of user interfaces. We have developed a tool, called AMC (Android Model Checker) that automatically explores the set of GUI screens displayed by an Android application and verifies that desired user interface properties hold over all such screens. AMC does not require application source code, nor does it require any application-specific knowledge. Instead, AMC develops a model of the application's GUI by executing the application. AMC regards each unique screen as a state, and it considers UI events (e.g., button presses) as transitions between those states. It explores the application state space (the GUI), until it has exhausted all reachable state transitions. It verifies properties such as minimal use of animation, appropriate color contrast, button closeness on the touchscreen, and task complexity as measured by the number of user actions required to complete an action. AMC outputs a list of violations of best practice guidelines for these properties along with snapshots that detail the specific violations.

The goal of AMC is not to completely eliminate the need for testing by human experts. Some issues defy automated judgment and are difficult to quantify. For instance, most experts would consider a moving graph of instantaneous gas mileage to be acceptable for vehicular usage, but would clearly consider a game with animation to be unacceptable. Automatic differentiation of the two animations can be difficult.

Instead, the goal of AMC is to substantially reduce the amount of work that a human expert must perform to help developers verify an application. AMC can check "easy" properties automatically, eliminating such tasks entirely from the expert's purview. For more challenging properties, AMC can prune large numbers of states and identify a small set of questionable screens that an expert must check manually. This helps the expert focus her time on the tasks that most require human judgment.

AMC also helps application developers by providing them with early feedback about usability violations. A developer can run AMC, generate a list of best practice violations, and fix those bugs without submitting the application for expert testing. After the application passes all AMC automated checks, expert checking can reveal any remaining problems.

To evaluate our tool, we studied 13 popular applications in the Android marketplace: 8 of these applications are designed for vehicular usage and 5 are not. Unsurprisingly, we found that applications that are not specifically intended for vehicular usage often do not follow accepted industry guidelines for vehicular interface design. However, we were surprised to find that *the Android applications intended for vehicular usage violated best practice guidelines at approximately the same rate as non-vehicular applications.* These results highlight the critical need for tools such as AMC that can help developers understand why their user interfaces may be inappropriate for use by the driver of a vehicle.

We evaluated AMC by comparing its results to those manually generated by an industry expert checking the same applications. AMC generated a definitive assessment for 85% of the application/property combinations that we studied. Compared to the expert assessment of these combinations, AMC had no false positives and a false negative rate of less than 2%. AMC deferred the remaining 15% of application/property combinations for further assessment by a human expert, but it reduced the number of screens that an expert must check in such cases by 95%. The median time for AMC to completely explore an application GUI is approximately 73 minutes; the most complex application that we studied (Twitter) required approximately 10 hours.

2. OVERVIEW

AMC automatically explores the GUI of an Android application. It checks the interface for violations of a set of pre-specified design properties. AMC uses a model-checking technique that attempts to exhaustively explore all screens that can possibly be displayed by the application. For each property, it may report that the property is upheld by the application (no violations were found), or it may output a list of violating screens annotated with screen snapshots that demonstrate each violation. Occasionally, AMC may be unable to automatically determine whether a property is upheld on a particular screen; in such cases, it reports a possible violation with an annotated snapshot.

While the properties that AMC checks are pre-configured, AMC contains no application-specific logic. Testing is fully automatic once started, so a user can leave AMC running and come back later to collect results. For applications with a cloud component, AMC requires that the testing computer have a working Internet connection; AMC also requires that any needed authentication be completed before testing starts. These requirements are minimal so as to make it trivial to apply AMC to testing a new application.

We envision two classes of users. Applications developers will use AMC to get early feedback on the distraction properties of their application GUI. A developer can run AMC in his own testing environment and get valuable insights without having to wait for feedback from a human expert.

We also envision that experts who control access to a vehicular application marketplace will use AMC to magnify their productivity. Many properties such as a maximum number of user actions per task and a minimum button size are tedious to check manually on each application screen, yet these properties are easy for a computer to verify automatically. We expect that an expert will simply rely on AMC to check these types of properties. Other properties, such as the acceptability of animation, require human judgment. AMC can classify some simple cases; for the remaining cases, it enumerates the specific screens that the expert should check further. Thus, even for properties that are hard to verify automatically, AMC can still substantially reduce the testing time required of a human expert.

3. DESIGN AND IMPLEMENTATION

AMC verifies user interface properties with a model checking approach similar to that used by CMC [15] in which it directly checks the implementation of an application. AMC starts with no information about the user interfaces states and the transitions among those states; instead, it discovers this information on the fly by triggering user actions and observing their effect on the application GUI.

Most prior model checkers operate by taking checkpoints of application states to allow the checker to deterministically revert to any past state by restoring a checkpoint. We initially planned to use this approach in AMC, but we quickly realized that checking mobile applications presents a substantial complication: the client typically only contains a portion of the application state, with the remainder contained in a cloud component. Restoring only the mobile component to a prior state is infeasible because the mobile and cloud components become out-of-sync. It is rare to see a mobile application in which the interaction between client and server is truly stateless (for instance, encrypted connections have inherent state, caching introduces state dependencies, and even simple identifiers often have constraints such as increasing monotonically).

AMC could potentially take a coordinated checkpoint on the mobile client and the cloud server. This is infeasible for third-party testers who do not have access to the cloud component. Even developers may lack the ability to checkpoint cloud state if the cloud component runs in an environment hosted by another organization.

For these reasons, AMC instead explores application state without the use of checkpoints. It uses the application GUI to return to desired states. This requires that AMC use its model of states and transitions among those states for navigation. It also requires that AMC discover when a new transition leads to a state that it has seen previously. This section discuss how AMC handles these and other challenges.

3.1 Modeling the user interface

AMC represents the graphical user interface of an Android application as a finite-state model. Intuitively, each distinct screen of the application is a state, and the user actions that transition between those screens are state transitions. AMC's model is therefore a directed graph in which the distinct screens are vertexes and the user actions are edges. In practice, the notion of what represents a "distinct" screen is open to interpretation, and AMC uses state equivalence heuristics, described in the next section, to determine whether two screens with different content and structure should be classified as the same state or as different states.

AMC constructs its state model on the fly. It begins with a single state that represents the initial screen displayed by the application. AMC adds a transition for each user action that may be performed on that screen such as a GUI button. Each of these transitions is initially marked as being unexplored.

AMC's basic state exploration algorithm works as follows. If there are no unexplored transitions left in the state model, AMC has fully explored the application GUI, and so it terminates. Otherwise, AMC chooses an unexplored transition. It orders the unexplored transitions by the number of actions required to reach that transition from the current application state. For instance, unexplored transitions on the screen currently being displayed are given top preference, transitions on any screen that can be reached using one user action are given the next highest preference, and so on. AMC determines the number of user actions to reach a particular state by executing a breadth-first search on the graphical representation of the state model starting at the current application state and terminating when the first unexplored transition is encountered.

After choosing an unexplored transition, AMC generates user events to navigate to the screen containing that transition (unless the transition is located on the current screen, in which case no navigation is required). AMC uses the Android monkey package [24] to send user actions such as touchscreen events and button presses to the Android screen. AMC determines the screen coordinates for such events by parsing the DOM tree, which describes all currently displayed widgets and their relative locations.

AMC next performs the user event necessary to effect the transition and observes the effect on the application GUI. Some actions do not cause the application to display a new screen; AMC models such actions as explored transitions that start and terminate in the same state. Some actions transition to a state that has already been observed by AMC (we defer the discussion of how AMC determines state equivalence to the next subsection). AMC simply adds the explored transition as a vertex from the old state to the new one. The remaining transitions generate a state previously unseen by AMC.

When AMC discovers a new state, it adds the state to its model, marks the transition it just took as explored, and sets the destination of the transition to the new state. It then takes a snapshot of the current screen using the screen capture feature of the Dalvik Debug Monitor Server, which is part of the Android SDK library. Snapshots are saved and may later be used to explain observed violations to the user. Next, AMC verifies user interface properties, as described in Section 3.5. Some properties, such as button size, pertain to individual states. For these properties, AMC highlights the violating region on the screen snapshot for that state in its report. Other properties, such as the number of user actions required to perform a task, are a property of multiple states and transitions. AMC generates a series of snapshots that illustrates the violation in such cases. We have found annotated snapshots to be an effective mechanism for quickly communicating violations to the user of our tool.

3.2 Determining state equivalence

AMC's model checking algorithm requires a good metric for determining state equivalence. To understand why this is crucial, consider a straw man equivalence function in which two GUI screens are considered to be the same state if and only if they have the exact same content.

AMC uses the Hierarchy Viewer tool [12] to extract the DOM information, expressed in XML format, for the currently displayed Android screen. The DOM tree contains all of the GUI widgets on a given screen along with any content within those widgets. For instance, the DOM tree will have a node for a list box element, as well as a node for each list item that describes the item contents. AMC generates a unique identifier for each screen, called the *content hash* by traversing the DOM tree in depth-first order and computing a hash over all nodes. Thus, AMC could potentially define two screens to be the same state if they have matching content hashes and declare them to be different states if their content hashes do not agree.

However, the proposed state equivalence function works poorly for most applications of reasonable complexity. Even simple actions, such as adding an item to a list or changing displayed text for an object will lead to a new state. For applications with cloud components, simply refreshing the same screen and downloading new content will lead to a new state. As a result, AMC state exploration will never terminate. Even worse, AMC may spend unnecessary time exploring "new" states that are essentially identical to states that it has seen previously. Thus, strict content equivalence is a poor choice for a state equivalence function.

Ideally, we would like to define state equivalence to match a user's intuitive notions of what constitutes the unique screens in an application. For instance, we would prefer that AMC treat the business and sports section screens of a newsreader application as the same state since both simply provide a list of articles that can be accessed. AMC therefore uses a state equivalence function that is based on structure, not content.

When a screen is displayed, AMC computes its *structure hash* by traversing the DOM tree in depth-first order and hashing the tag name, level, and sibling order of each XML node, omitting all other content. AMC uses the structure hash as a unique identifier for each state. Thus, if two screens have the same structure (layout of buttons, lists, text fields, custom views, etc.), but the screens have different content, AMC considers the two screens to be the same state.

From our initial experience using AMC, we learned that the structure hash is still too strict an equivalence check. As defined so far, the structure hash considers two screens to be different if a list or other container has a different number of elements. For instance, a screen that displays 3 gas stations would not be equivalent to another screen that is identical except for displaying 4 gas stations. This problem arises because individual list items are XML nodes and therefore affect the structure hash. Unfortunately, if this problem is not addressed, the AMC algorithm will sometimes fail to terminate (this is the familiar "state explosion" problem in model checking [25]).

On the other hand, we do not want to omit considering such list items entirely. Having one or two items in a list often enables actions that are not accessible if no items are in the list (for instance, one cannot click on a list item if none are present). Further, some lists such as menus do not contain items of homogeneous type; clicking on different items will have different effects.

AMC uses the following heuristic to handle lists and similar containers. If a list has more than one item, AMC checks whether those items are homogeneous. If the list items have registered different callback handlers, then they are considered heterogeneous (since clicking on different items is likely to have different effects). Since AMC does not require application source code, it distinguishes between two callback handlers by using the binary callback address passed to the GUI system.

Some applications multiplex many actions through the same handler. Therefore, if the callback handler is the same, AMC clicks on the first 2 items. If the items transition to different states, then the list items are deemed heterogeneous; otherwise, they are homogeneous. When AMC sees a list with more than 2 homogeneous items, it canonicalizes that state by considering only the first 2 items in the structure hash. This has the effect of making all instances of the same screen with two or more list items be the same state. Screens with different numbers of heterogeneous elements are always considered to be distinct states.

3.3 Non-deterministic transitions

From the point of view of AMC, user actions can sometimes appear to be non-deterministic. That is, taking the same action from the same state transitions to different states at different times. There are several reasons why this behavior can arise. In rare cases, the application may be truly non-deterministic. More often, the state transition is deterministic, but the resulting state depends on some aspect of application state that AMC cannot observe because it is unaware of application semantics. For instance, the back button may transition to a different state depending on the path that the user took to get to the current state. In another example, changing a configuration option in a menu may cause an action to transition to a new state. Mistakes in state classification can also lead to seemingly non-deterministic behavior. For instance, if AMC classifies two different screens as belonging to the same state, it is possible that performing the same action on each screen leads to a different state. While such misclassifications are rare, they will inevitably occur in any model-checking system like AMC that uses heuristics to avoid state explosion.

Seemingly non-deterministic behavior complicates the basic search strategy described in Section 3.1. When AMC performs user actions to transition to the nearest state with an unexplored transition, it may go astray and arrive at a different state than expected. Therefore, AMC must enhance its basic search algorithm to deal with such behavior.

AMC considers all transitions to be deterministic unless proven otherwise. AMC maintains a second graph of the application state model, called the *exploration graph* — this graph contains only deterministic edges. New edges are added to the exploration graph when AMC first explores the transition. However, if AMC retraverses an edge in the exploration graph and the transition leads to a state other than the one expected, it labels the transition as non-deterministic and removes the edge from the exploration graph.

AMC calculates the path to the nearest unexplored transition by applying the breadth-first search algorithm described in Section 3.1 to the exploration graph. Effectively, this finds the shortest path that traverses only deterministic edges. When the path traversal fails due to a newly-discovered non-deterministic edge, AMC re-runs the shortest path algorithm after the edge has been removed.

If too many edges are removed due to non-determinism, AMC may not be able to explore some transitions because it can no longer find a deterministic path to the state that contains the transition. However, we have observed that most seemingly non-deterministic transitions are fully deterministic if the application performs an identical sequence of n user actions (where n is greater than one). As a simple example, the back button often transitions to the state explored prior to the current state. Thus, clicking the back button on a given state appears to be non-deterministic if there exists two or more possible prior states. However, if one considers a 2-step sequence of actions, i.e., transitioning from the prior state to the current state and then clicking the back button, then the transition as a result of that sequence appears completely deterministic.

If after exploring all transitions that can be reached via deterministic transitions, AMC still has an unexplored transition, it uses the following algorithm to try to reach the state containing that transition, which we refer to the goal state. AMC keeps a log that contains the sequence of all states that it has visited along with each transition that it has triggered. It searches through the log to find all occurrences of the goal state. For each occurrence, it observes the past n actions that it took to reach the goal state (n is initially 2). It assumes this sequence is deterministic unless proven otherwise. So, it inserts in the exploration graph an edge from the starting state of the sequence to the goal state. The edge is given a weight of n since it contains n user actions. The edge remains in the graph until the sequence is demonstrated to be non-deterministic. AMC then restarts exploration and tries to reach the goal state via the new paths that it has added. If AMC again fails to reach the goal state, it tries again with $n = 4$ and $n = 8$. After $n = 8$, AMC gives up on exploring this particular transition and reports the state containing the transition as being only "partially explored". If there are multiple unexplored transitions, AMC proceeds until it either has explored or has given up on all such transitions.

3.4 Complications in state exploration

The Android platform has a few peculiarities that complicate AMC state exploration. First, Android does not provide a callback to an external observer when the display of a screen completes. Therefore, AMC has no means of knowing when to compute the structure hash. Initially, we used a simple timeout approach in which AMC waited 10 seconds for each screen to stabilize before computing the hash. However, this strategy substantially increased AMC's state exploration time since AMC waited after every transition. We could not reliably set the timeout to a lower value because some slow applications take several seconds to fetch data from a remote server and display results.

AMC currently uses a modified timeout-based approach. After exploring a transition, AMC continuously computes the new screen's structure hash. If the hash matches that of a previously explored state, then AMC considers the screen to have stabilized and waits no longer. With this approach, AMC waits for the full 10 second timeout only once for each new application state, and not once for every transition. This substantially decreases state exploration time because the number of states is much less than the number of transitions.

Many Android application screens have components that allow users to scroll down to view more items than can be displayed at one time. Depending on the specific method used by developers to implement scrolling, items not currently displayed may or may not appear in the DOM tree. For example, elements not currently displayed appear in the DOM Tree when the Android ScrollView widget is used, but not when the ListView widget is used. In the former case, AMC does not need to perform any extra actions. In the latter case, AMC sends events to the screen to cause the application to scroll down until all elements have been displayed. AMC identifies new elements that appear during scrolling by their unique row identifier; it adds these elements to its internal representation of the screen's DOM tree. Once the DOM tree is complete, AMC proceeds as described previously.

Some applications require text input to operate. The two examples we encountered were passwords and destination fields for GPS applications. In such cases, the AMC user must supply the appropriate text to enter and the associated text field's id prior to running AMC. With this information, AMC automatically inputs the supplied text on user's behalf whenever it encounters the associated text field on a screen.

3.5 Verifying user interface properties

User interface guidelines for vehicular settings are based on two key principles. First, vehicular application should not give rise to potentially hazardous behavior by the driver or other road users [21]. The driver's primary focus must be on the road and the driving task; the vehicular application's user interface should minimize its distraction level. This principle bounds the amount of time that the driver can spend on each action. For instance, as button size decreases, Fitts' Law [9] predicts that it will take longer for the user to position her finger to touch the button. Thus, overly small buttons require too much attention and distract driver focus from the road.

Additionally, actions should not have time limits since a driver should not be forced to divert his attention from the road at inappropriate moments. Many forms of animation violate this principle, since a user must watch the screen at a particular time to gather needed information.

Another principle is that that application must be consistent and limit state that the driver has to remember [10]. Being consistent includes maintaining the general look, feel, and layout of the application. For example, buttons should be placed in the same portion of the screen, with the same general functionality, so that the user can easily navigate. Limiting state bounds the maximum number of actions that can be required to perform a task.

AMC currently verifies seven properties: number of actions to perform a task, text contrast ratio, word count per screen, button size, button closeness, use of animation, and the amount of scrolling required per screen. AMC presents a modular interface for adding new properties, and it separates the verification code from the state exploration code. This design has made it easy to add new property verification modules as our experience with the tool has grown. We next discuss each property that AMC verifies in more detail.

3.5.1 User actions per task

Most vehicular interface guidelines suggest limiting the number of user actions (button presses, touchscreen events, etc.) that a driver must perform in order to complete a single task [7, 16, 19]. Excessive sequences of user actions increase the cognitive load on the driver and divert too much visual attention from the road. Since existing guidelines do not agree on a specific maximum number of actions that should be allowed, we consulted with an expert in Ford Motor Corporation's HMI lab, who suggested that no task should take more than 10 actions to complete.

While the notion of a task is somewhat application-specific, AMC can generate reasonable approximations of tasks using the graphical model created by state exploration. Given a starting state, a task is a series of actions that transitions to some destination state and then returns back to the starting state. For instance, a task could be navigating through menus and sub-menus, setting a configuration option, and then returning via the back button.

For every state in the graph, AMC finds the shortest round-trip path to and returning from every other state. If the length of this path is greater than the limit of 10 actions, AMC reports a violation. It appends annotated snapshots of all screens along the violating path and the transitions that move from one screen to another. This check is performed after state exploration finishes. Detecting violations does not require revisiting states since all necessary information is contained in the graphical state model.

AMC exhaustively considers all tasks rather than attempting to identify the set of tasks that are performed frequently. Such identification would require application-specific knowledge that AMC does not possess. Further, even infrequent tasks that violate guidelines should be avoided.

3.5.2 Text contrast ratio

Drivers should be able to discern screen elements with a quick glance. A poor contrast ratio between elements displayed on a screen increases the amount of time and attention required to understand the screen contents. Consequently, a contrast ratio of at least 3:1 between the luminance of the foreground and background is recommended [19]. AMC currently verifies this property for all text elements displayed by an application.

AMC uses the snapshot of each state to calculate contrast ratios for text elements. It parses the DOM tree to find all view objects that have text elements. It then extracts color information and screen locations for all such objects. AMC computes the background and foreground RGB values for each element, and it converts these values into luminance values using a conversion formula proposed by W3C's Web Content Accessibility Guidelines [6]. If the contrast ratio is below 3:1, AMC reports a violation and highlights the violating element on the state snapshot.

3.5.3 *Text word count*

Excessive text on a screen requires too much driver attention. According to industry-standard user interface guidelines [7], a task should take no longer than 20 seconds to finish. The average adult reads approximately 250 to 300 words per minute [27]. Thus, no screen should ever contain more than 100 words. Using this as a conservative upper bound (it is trivial to set the threshold to lower values), AMC counts the number of words in all text elements and reports a violation if there are more than 100 total words for any state.

Applications frequently embed text in images (for example, by displaying logos or using buttons with bitmap images). When text is embedded in an image, the DOM tree does not provide a description of that text. AMC handles these cases with Optical Character Recognition (OCR). When AMC encounters a leaf in the DOM tree that does not have a text element, it first calculates the screen region for that element. It then uses the Tesseract OCR tool [22] to identify any text within that region. If AMC discovers text, it adds the word count for that text to the total word count for the state.

If the screen has a scrolling component that hides some elements from view, AMC scrolls down to display more elements. This continues until all elements have been displayed or until the word count exceeds the specified limit.

3.5.4 *Button size*

Initiating touchscreen events should not be excessively distracting. If the surface area that initiates an event is too small, the driver must focus her attention on making sure that her finger contacts the screen at exactly the right location; this diverts attention from the road. Consequently, best practice guidelines say that the minimum contact surface area for a control such as a button is $80\,\text{mm}^2$ [19].

AMC verifies this property by first determining the height and width of a pixel on the test platform. In our evaluation, we assume a 9-inch dashboard touchscreen. This is conservative for Android applications since most smartphone screens are substantially smaller. For each clickable item on the screen, the DOM tree reveals the height and width of the item in terms of the number of pixels. By multiplying these values and scaling by the platform-specific conversion factors, AMC calculates the absolute button size. If this is less than $80\,\text{mm}^2$, it reports a violation and highlights the button on the application screen snapshot.

Android allows applications to add their own window element types; these application-specific types are referred to as *custom views*. For instance, many vehicular applications use a custom view to display a map element. Custom views often contain clickable button-like elements. Unlike standard buttons which are shown as elements in the DOM tree, individual clickable elements within an opaque custom view are hidden from AMC. AMC can detect the existence of a click handler function, but it cannot determine the size or location of clickable regions from the DOM tree. It cannot even determine the number of clickable regions in the custom view.

AMC uses empirical testing to learn more about clickable elements in a custom view. It sends click events to a custom view at $< x,y >$ coordinates that are laid out in a grid pattern such that the horizontal and vertical difference between clicks is slightly less than 50% of the minimum button size given a square button. For our 9-inch touchscreen, this works out to a grid with coordinates 20 pixels apart.

AMC then clicks on each grid coordinate. If the click causes the application to transition to a different state, AMC records the state at which it arrived, then returns to the original state to click on more grid coordinates.

AMC considers any set of contiguous grid coordinates that transition to the same state to be part of the same clickable region (button). For simplicity, it currently assumes that such regions are rectangular. Because the grid is regularly spaced, AMC can bound the minimum and maximum dimensions for a region. For instance, a region that is two clicks in width must have width between 21 and 59 pixels. AMC calculates the minimum and maximum button area from this information. If the maximum area is less than $80\,\text{mm}^2$, a violation is reported. If the minimum area is at least $80\,\text{mm}^2$, no violation exists. Otherwise, AMC needs more information to make a determination, since the button area could either be bigger or smaller than the minimum area. It therefore clicks on additional $< x,y >$ coordinates in a binary search pattern to determine the height and/or width of the region. The search terminates once a violation is detected or the button is determined to be at least as large as the guidelines require. In other words, AMC narrows its estimate of the button size until it can precisely determine whether or not the button violates the guideline.

This method of determining region size relies on the custom view not changing between clicks. Once the view changes, button locations may be added, removed, or moved; in other words, AMC can infer no useful information about region size. AMC checks to see if a custom view changes by comparing screen snapshots of the view region. It takes an initial snapshot before sending any click events. Five seconds after each click, it takes a new snapshot of the view region and compares that with the original snapshot. If the snapshots differ by more than 1%, AMC declares the view to have changed. In this case, AMC reports the view as a potential violation that requires further analysis because it cannot make a definitive judgment about the clickable regions contained within the view.

3.5.5 *Button distance*

For reasons similar to those cited for button size, the distance between the center of each pair of buttons should be at least 15 mm [19]. AMC determines the geographical center of each button on the screen, calculates the Euclidean distance in terms of the number of pixels, converts that value to a screen-specific absolute distance value, and reports a violation if the limit is exceeded.

For custom views, AMC uses a similar strategy to the one used to determine button size. It first uses the grid information to determine bounds on the center of each clickable region (again, assuming that such regions are rectangular). If all regions can be determined to be more than the maximum distance from each other, AMC terminates without reporting a violation. If any pair of regions are definitely too close to each other, AMC reports a violation. If the grid has insufficient granularity to determine whether a pair of regions are too close, AMC performs binary search to refine the bounds on the center of each button until it can determine whether or not a violation exists.

3.5.6 *Animation*

Drivers must be free to interact with the application at a time of their convenience. No application should ever demand that an action be performed within a time limit, since performing the action may force the driver to divert attention form the road at an inappropriate instance. A corollary of this guideline is that an application should never display animations, videos, and other highly-interactive visual elements [7].

Unlike the previous guidelines, human judgment is usually required to determine whether a visual artifact is acceptable. For instance, an animated graphical display of fuel efficiency in a hybrid vehicle is typically considered to be acceptable. On the other hand, interrupting a route display in a GPS application to pop-up an unsolicited chat message from a nearby vehicle would almost certainly be considered poor vehicular interface design (note: this is an actual application behavior that we observed!). AMC therefore detects *potential* violations of this property, but defers the actual evaluation to an expert tester. The goal of checking this property is therefore to substantially reduce the number of states that such an expert needs to examine.

When AMC discovers a new state, it pauses for four seconds to detect possible animations. During this interval, it takes several screen snapshots. It breaks each of the screen regions into blocks using a grid pattern and calculates the Sum of Absolute Differences (SAD) on each color channel to determine if a block has changed significantly between snapshots. Any block that has SAD value more than zero on any color channel is considered a potential violation. The changing regions on the screen snapshots are highlighted to illustrate the potential violation.

If an animation only affects a small portion of the screen, it is unlikely to be distracting. For instance, a blinking cursor can be helpful in drawing attention to an important screen region and may help reduce cognitive load.

When AMC detects animation on a screen, it divides the screen into 400 equally-sized blocks. It then compares each of these regions from the two snapshots. If content has changed in less than 10% of the blocks, AMC determines that there is no violation. If more than 10% of the content has changed, AMC reports the state as a potential violation. This rule substantially reduces the number of states that need to be manually examined and has not led to false negatives in any application.

3.5.7 Scrolling

Scrolling through many options commands too much attention from a driver. Usability guidelines therefore recommend eliminating scrolling or limiting the number of items in a list [19]. Alternative selection approaches such as voice recognition can be used when options are too numerous to include in a scrolling control.

AMC verifies that no list element contains more than 10 elements — we chose a limit of 10 based on a recommendation from an industry expert. For each list view object in a state's DOM tree, AMC reads the value of the 'mItemCount' field. If this value exceeds the limit, AMC reports a violation.

4. EVALUATION

We evaluated AMC by comparing its results to those of an industry expert evaluating 12 popular Android applications. We also calculated metrics for AMC such as state coverage and exploration time. Finally, we assessed the need for a tool such as AMC by examining how often current Android applications intended for vehicular settings violate best practice interface design guidelines.

4.1 Setup

We executed AMC on a Nexus One phone running Android 2.3.4. We have modified our Android system to enable AMC to extract event handler and text color information.

We assumed the existence of a phone-HMI hybrid interface that replicates the smartphone's display on a 9-inch vehicle touch screen. We further assumed that all user interactions with the application will take place using the vehicular touch screen.

Note that a 9-inch display is larger than that of almost all Android phones. Therefore, buttons and icons will be significantly larger on the touch screen. Any size-related violation we identify assuming the existence of a touch screen would also be a violation on most any Android phone.

Some applications support multiple input modalities for initiating an action, for example, UI events and voice commands. We check the UI in such instances because some set of users will opt for touch screen interaction, and so such interaction should meet best practice guidelines.

We selected 14 applications for our evaluation. These were selected because they were the most popular applications in their respective categories in the Android store as of November 2011. Five applications (Gmail, Google Finance, MyDays, eBay, and Twitter) are not targeted for use in vehicular environments. We expected that such applications would have numerous usability violations because they have not been designed for vehicular usage.

We defined eight of the applications (GasBuddy, Google Maps, Google Navigation, TomTom Navigation, Waze, iRadar, Beat the Traffic, and Best Parking) to be *vehicular applications*. Informally, a vehicular application is one that delivers information that may be particularly relevant to the driver of a vehicle, such as gas prices at nearby stations, recommended routes, police radar locations, and traffic information. Some applications, such as Waze, have specific mechanisms such as voice control for minimizing driver distraction. Although other applications, such as Google Maps, are not solely intended for use by a driver, our experience is that many people use such applications while driving because of the helpful information they provide. We expected that these applications would have considerably less violations than the first set (although our expectation turned out to be wrong).

Finally, we also selected an Android application called MPG that was developed as a demonstration application for the Ford OpenXC platform in conjunction with Ford experts who are well-versed in vehicular user-interface guidelines. This application was created specifically for a vehicle touch screen by a University of Michigan undergraduate student who was not involved in the AMC project.

4.2 Comparison with industry expert

We evaluated the quality of AMC's results by comparing them with the results of a manual evaluation by an industry expert. Since the expert had limited testing time available, we took several steps to reduce the manual testing time. First, we compared only 5 of the 7 categories reported by AMC (text word count, button size, button distance, animation, and scrolling). Manually evaluating the number of user actions per task was too time-consuming because the expert would have to reason about all possible paths through the application to evaluate each action. The expert did not evaluate contrast ratio because the measurement requires special software tools that were not available at the time.

Second, the expert evaluated only 12 of the 14 applications, omitting Gmail and Google Maps because they were too complex to evaluate thoroughly given a limited time budget. Finally, rather than ask the expert to exhaustively count all violations of each property in each application, we asked the expert to render only a binary decision: either the application upholds the property or it contains one or more violations.

Prior to manual testing, we informed the expert of the specific properties that we were checking for violations. However, we did not disclose AMC's results to the expert prior to testing. After the expert completed an independent assessment, we compared results for each application. In a few cases, AMC found violations that the expert did not discover (usually due to limited testing time), but which the expert agreed were indeed violations. We used this revised expert assessment as ground truth (i.e., we suspect the expert would have found these given unlimited testing time).

Table 1 compares the results of AMC and manual expert testing. For each form of testing, a check indicates no violation, and an x indicates that the application violates the best practice guideline. A triangle in the AMC column shows that AMC could not determine

	Text word count		Button size		Button distance		Animation		Scrolling	
Popular Apps	AMC	Expert	AMC	Expert	AMC	Expert	AMC	Expert	AMC	Expert
Google Finance	×	×	×	×	×	×	✓	✓	×	×
MyDays	×	×	✓	✓	×	×	✓	✓	×	×
eBay	✓	×	△	✓	△	✓	△	✓	×	×
Twitter	×	×	△	✓	×	×	✓	✓	×	×
Vehicular Apps	AMC	Expert	AMC	Expert	AMC	Expert	AMC	Expert	AMC	Expert
GasBuddy	×	×	✓	✓	×	×	✓	✓	×	×
Google Navigation	✓	✓	×	×	△	×	✓	✓	✓	✓
TomTom Navigation	×	×	×	×	✓	✓	✓	✓	×	×
Waze	✓	✓	△	×	×	×	△	✓	×	×
iRadar	×	×	×	×	×	×	✓	✓	✓	✓
Beat the Traffic	✓	✓	△	✓	×	×	△	✓	✓	✓
Best Parking	✓	✓	✓	✓	×	×	✓	✓	×	×
Industry App	AMC	Expert	AMC	Expert	AMC	Expert	AMC	Expert	AMC	Expert
MPG	✓	✓	✓	✓	✓	✓	✓	✓	✓	✓

This table compares AMC's results against those produced by manual testing by an industry expert. For each combination of application and usability property, the table shows AMC's result and the expert's result. A × indicates a violation, a ✓ indicates no violation, and a △ shows that AMC was not able to make a definitive judgment.

Table 1: Comparison of AMC testing with manual expert testing

on its own whether the application violated the user interface guideline. In these cases, one or more screens are flagged for subsequent manual analysis.

AMC reached a definitive judgment on 85% of the application/property combinations. Over 98% of these judgments were correct; i.e., they matched the ground truth expert assessment.

AMC had one false negative (word count for eBay). In this case, AMC was not able to visit the state that had the violation because of its state equivalence heuristic. The state is only reachable via multiple sub-menus that unfortunately all have the same structure. AMC incorrectly concludes that the sub-menu states are the same, and so it prematurely halts exploration of the sub-menu structure.

AMC cannot render a definitive judgment in 15% of the cases. Three of these cases are animations. Because this property is hard to assess, AMC defers any reasonably sized artifact for manual analysis. While the expert decided that all cases were not violations, AMC still substantially reduced the amount of manual analysis required. There are 381 total states discovered by AMC in the 12 applications. Of these, 49 states contain some form of animation, and AMC flagged only 4 of those states for manual analysis.

The remaining cases for which AMC cannot render a definitive judgment involve clickable regions in custom views. In these cases, AMC determined that view changed after clicking on a region, thereby rendering subsequent analysis useless. Again, although AMC cannot always provide a definitive judgment, it only flags a small set of states for manual analysis. There are 97 custom views in the 381 total states; AMC flagged only 13 of these for manual analysis. Across all five properties, AMC flagged less than 5% of application screens for manual analysis.

Although we did not compare results for 2 AMC properties, we believe that results for those properties will be similar to or better than the results for the other 5 properties. The violation criteria for both properties can be expressed quantitatively, and therefore AMC would not have to defer any checks for subsequent manual analysis.

4.2.1 Microbenchmarks

Table 2 shows more information about AMC's state exploration for the 14 programs. The second column shows AMC runtime. The median runtime is approximately 73 minutes, and the average runtime is slightly more than 2 hour and 33 minutes. There is clearly great variation in the time needed to explore an application, with the fastest application (Best Parking) taking about 10 minutes and the slowest (Twitter) taking a little over 10 hours.

Many factors contribute to exploration time. More complex applications that have more states and transitions naturally take longer to explore. The amount of seemingly non-deterministic behavior in an application has a large effect on exploration time. If AMC has difficulty reaching a particular target state with an unexplored transition, it may need to try many different routes before arriving at the target. Finally, applications with many custom views have longer exploration times because AMC must send many events to each custom view to discover the size and number of clickable regions within the view.

We believe AMC's exploration times are already quite reasonable since our tool executes offline, i.e., it requires no human supervision while it runs. Much of AMC's time is spent extracting the DOM tree for each state after a transition; this is a slow process on our older Nexus One phone, but it would run considerably faster on a modern phone. Additionally, exploration is potentially a highly parallelizable task. One can test multiple applications in parallel and potentially even test the same application on different computers with some minimal coordination among the test platforms.

The last three columns of Table 2 show the actual number of states in each application (which we computed by hand), the total number of states visited by AMC, and the total number of states that are visited by a purely random walk through the application. For the random walk, we configured our tool to select a random user action on each screen, wait for a transition, and then repeat. We terminated the random walk after it had been running for the exact same amount of time used by AMC for exploration. Since the random walk strategy can not easily handle custom views, we omitted checking such views for the purposes of this comparison.

Application	Total runtime	Number of states	States found by AMC	States found by random walk
Popular Apps				
Gmail	0:56:16	30	27	26
Google Finance	0:54:59	20	18	10
MyDays	1:55:03	41	26	15
eBay	0:50:29	29	24	19
Twitter	10:25:25	82	65	53
Vehicular Apps				
GasBuddy	4:28:06	67	59	50
Google Maps	1:59:26	47	31	27
Google Navigation	0:36:48	24	15	14
TomTom Navigation	4:05:13	50	36	20
Waze	6:09:15	98	81	70
iRadar	1:04:56	23	23	22
Beat the Traffic	0:19:02	18	18	16
Best Parking	0:10:26	15	11	8
Industry App				
MPG	1:22:31	5	5	4

Table 2: Time to evaluate applications and the number of states explored

For every application, AMC explores more states than the random walk strategy. However, AMC only visits 80% of the total states (as opposed to 65% for random walk). Some states are configuration-dependent: they can only be triggered by toggling application-specific menu items in the correct order. For instance, the MyDays application supports 7 different languages, but AMC explores only 2 of these languages (because of its heuristic of clicking on only 2 list items unless a significant difference in behavior is detected). It is possible, but unlikely, that the application will violate a user interface guideline in one language but not another; if so, AMC would fail to detect this.

For such applications, there exists a tradeoff between coverage and exploration time. Relaxing some of AMC's heuristics would lead to a larger number of states explored, but would likely give a poor return on the time spent in terms of finding new violations.

4.2.2 *Assessment of current Android applications*

After establishing that AMC is an effective tool for measuring vehicular user interface properties, we used AMC to assess the user interfaces of the 14 Android applications described in Section 4.1. Table 3 shows the total number of each type of violation detected for these applications. In the rare cases where the assessment of AMC and the industry expert differed, we use the expert's opinion after viewing the AMC results as the definitive judgment as to whether or not a violation exists.

Unsurprisingly, the results show that applications that are not designed for vehicular environments frequently violate the best practice design principles for which we tested. Since one would naturally expect the total number of violations to increase with application complexity, we normalize results by dividing the total number of violations by the number of unique application states. By this metric, the popular non-vehicular applications average 0.75 violations per state.

When we began our study, we expected the vehicular applications to more closely follow best practice guidelines. However, the 8 vehicular applications in the Android marketplace are only slightly better at following best practice guidelines and have a similar ratio of violations to total states (0.69).

The only application for which we found no violations was MPG. This application was developed with cooperation from Ford engineers to demonstrate the capabilities of the OpenXC platform. Although the primary developer was not familiar with vehicular user interface design, he likely benefited from feedback from engineers who had previously developed vehicular applications.

The best practice guidelines that were most often violated were user actions per task and text contrast ratio. This is unsurprising since these are the hardest two properties to check. Reasoning about the minimum number of actions to perform a task requires thinking about multiple states at once. Checking text contrast ratio requires special tools and/or doing complex calculations. On the other hand, we found no violations of the animation property: all instances of animation that AMC observed were judged by the industry expert to be acceptable.

Overall, these results support our conjecture that current vehicular application developers often make poor user interface design decisions. The most likely reasons for this are that they are unaware of best practices and they lack tools that can measure how their GUIs will perform in vehicular settings. AMC is designed to fill this gap.

4.3 Discussion

Since many mobile applications are supported by advertising, we had originally suspected that advertising would lead to many violations. Yet, no application that we studied had advertisements that directly triggered a violation. For instance, we did not encounter any advertisements with animation. Of course, advertisements may reduce the screen area available for application controls and indirectly lead to other violations.

AMC assumes that application behavior is mostly deterministic. If an application displays random pop-ups, for instance, AMC will only observe a violation if a pop-up occurs during exploration. Data retrieved from the cloud can also be non-deterministic. For instance, Waze displays nearby users on a map. If AMC exploration runs in the wee hours of the morning, then no users may be nearby; if exploration runs during rush hour, many users may be shown on the same map. AMC flags the map screen as an instance of animation that needs human judgment in the latter case, but not in the former case.

	Total states	User actions per task	Text contrast ratio	Text word count	Button size	Button distance	Animation	Scrolling
Popular Apps								
Gmail	30	17	2	2	0	0	0	3
Google Finance	20	0	1	3	1	4	0	3
MyDays	41	20	4	2	0	2	0	1
eBay	29	0	1	1	0	0	0	2
Twitter	82	24	28	7	0	14	0	9
Vehicular Apps								
GasBuddy	67	12	14	1	0	13	0	4
Google Maps	47	8	7	3	0	7	0	1
Google Navigation	24	0	0	0	2	1	0	0
TomTom Navigation	50	26	0	6	1	0	0	6
Waze	98	72	15	0	1	5	0	4
iRadar	23	0	2	1	5	4	0	0
Beat the Traffic	18	5	7	0	0	1	0	0
Best Parking	15	0	0	0	0	1	0	1
Industry App								
MPG	5	0	0	0	0	0	0	0

Table 3: Number of violations found for each application

AMC exploration currently only uses GUI buttons and Android built-in actions (e.g., the back button). Therefore, it does not yet find states that can only be reached by performing complex actions such as multi-touch.

5. RELATED WORK

To the best of our knowledge, AMC is the first tool to apply model checking to verify user interface properties for environments such as vehicles.

Model checking has been used to solve a diverse set of problems such as finding software bugs [4, 5, 26] and validating protocols [2, 23]. When model checking has been applied to testing application GUIs, it has been used both to discover the screens that a user would encounter and to check for faults such as GUI behavior that does not match an application specification.

Most GUI model checking systems require a pre-specified model of the GUI states and transitions [8, 17, 20]. For instance, the work of Takala et al. requires detailed definitions of GUI states and the locations of buttons within each state. Providing such a detailed model is an onerous task that requires substantial knowledge of the application's behavior.

Salvucci [18] created a cognitive model of using in-vehicle interfaces that predicts the time required by a driver to perform interactions with such interfaces. Such a model could be used to refine the heuristics (e.g., for maximum task length) that AMC uses to check for violations.

Several systems have attempted to reverse-engineer the GUI model using techniques similar to those employed by AMC. One such method is to transparently record a user's interactions with the application and generate a model based on those observations [3, 11]. The inferred model must be subsequently validated by the user. Thus, unlike AMC, which explores the GUI autonomously, these methods require a substantial amount of user time to generate the state model.

Similar to AMC's state exploration, a few methods do not require manual interaction to infer GUI states. GUI Ripping [14] infers the GUI model by automatically exploring the application in a depth-first manner. GUI Ripping defines the state by extracting all widgets, properties, and values of the window. Amalfitano et al. [1] apply a similar technique to Android applications, but their system requires application source code to detect all buttons in a state. AutoBlackTest [13] incrementally builds a GUI model as it explores by employing heuristics about what a state should be. None of these approaches deal well with applications that have both mobile and cloud components. It is challenging to checkpoint such applications, and they can exhibit the seemingly non-deterministic behavior discussed in Section 3.3.

AMC needs no external information to detect violations since the design principles it verifies are not application-specific. In contrast, most of the cited prior systems require some specification of the correct behavior of the program; for instance that a particular transition should cause the GUI to display a given state. Alternatively, systems such as AutoBlackTest generate test cases automatically, but leave it to the tester to manually verify the output of each test case. Thus, substantial manual effort is required either before or after exploration. AMC avoids this manual effort except in rare cases where it cannot make a definitive judgment.

There has been substantial effort in the usability community to determine best practices for vehicular interface design. This effort has resulted in quantitative best practice guidelines [7, 10, 16, 19, 21]. Currently, industry HMI experts use these and similar guidelines to manually verify the user interfaces of vehicular applications. AMC applies the same guidelines, but does so in an automated fashion. AMC is the first automated tool to validate vehicular interfaces.

6. CONCLUSION

Mobile computing systems are increasingly integrated with our day-to-day activities, moving beyond tablets and phones and into other devices and settings. In each new setting, different constraints on effective user interfaces will come into play. Application designers must target their products to these constraints, a difficult process even when designing an application specifically for one of these settings. Expert review can help with this process, but such review is costly and has long turnaround times, limiting its effectiveness—particularly early in the design cycle.

To reduce this pressure, we have developed a technique based on model checking that allows automatic exploration of an application's interface, verifying that particular elements of that interface meet the appropriate guidelines. This provides feedback in minutes or hours, and identifies most violations without false positives. The few remaining areas of concern can be the focus of human expert review or can be used to target the designer's efforts more efficiently, simplifying the design and verification process.

Acknowledgments

We thank the anonymous reviewers and our shepherd, Rajesh Balan, for comments that improved this paper. We also thank the vehicular HMI experts who provided advice during the design and implementation of AMC.

7. REFERENCES

[1] AMALFITANO, D., FASOLINO, A. R., AND TRAMONTANA, P. A GUI crawling-based technique for android mobile application testing. In *Proceedings of the 4th IEEE International Conference on Software Testing, Verification and Validation Workshops* (Berlin, Germany, March 2011), pp. 252–261.

[2] BLANCHET, B. Automatic verification of correspondences for security protocols. *Journal of Computer Security 17*, 4 (2009), 363–434.

[3] BROOKS, P. A., AND MEMON, A. M. Automated GUI testing guided by usage profiles. In *Proceedings of the 23rd IEEE/ACM international conference on Automated software engineering* (Atlanta, GA, November 2007), pp. 333–342.

[4] CADAR, C., DUNBAR, D., AND ENGLER, D. KLEE: Unassisted and automatic generation of high-coverage tests for complex systems programs. In *Proceedings of the 8th Symposium on Operating Systems Design and Implementation* (December 2008), pp. 209–224.

[5] CADAR, C., GANESH, V., PAWLOWSKI, P. M., DILL, D. L., AND ENGLER, D. R. EXE: Automatically generating inputs of death. In *Proceedings of the 13th ACM Conference on Computer and Communications Security* (2006).

[6] CALDWELL, B., COOPER, M., REID, L. G., AND VANDERHEIDEN, G. Web Content Accessibility Guidelines (WCAG) 2.0, 2008. `http://www.w3.org/TR/WCAG20/#contrast-ratiodef`.

[7] DRIVER FOCUS-TELEMATICS WORKING GROUP. Statement of principles, criteria and verification procedures on driver interactions with advanced in-vehicle information and communication systems. Tech. rep., Alliance of Automobile Manufacturers, June 2003.

[8] DWYER, M. B., CARR, V., AND HINES, L. Model checking graphical user interfaces using abstractions. In *Proceedings of the 6th European Software Engineering Conference* (Zurich, Switzerland, September 1997), pp. 244–261.

[9] FITTS, P. M. The information capacity of the human motor system in controlling the amplitude of movement. *Journal of Experimental Psychology 47* (1954), 381–391.

[10] GREEN, P., LEVISON, W., PAELKE, G., AND SERAFIN, C. Suggested human factors design guidelines for driver information systems. Tech. rep., The University of Michigan Transportation Research Institute (UMTRI), August 1994.

[11] GRILO, A., PAIVA, A., AND FARIA, J. Reverse engineering of GUI models for testing. In *Proceedings of the 5th Iberian Conference on Information Systems and Technologies* (Santiago de Compostela, Spain, June 2010), pp. 1–6.

[12] Hierarchy Viewer. `http://developer.android.com/tools/help/hierarchy-viewer.html`.

[13] MARIANI, L., PEZZÈ, M., RIGANELLI, O., AND SANTORO, M. Autoblacktest: a tool for automatic black-box testing. In *Proceedings of the 33rd International Conference on Software Engineering* (Waikiki, Honolulu, HI, May 2011), pp. 1013–1015.

[14] MEMON, A., BANERJEE, I., AND NAGARAJAN, A. GUI ripping: Reverse engineering of graphical user interfaces for testing. In *Proceedings of the 10th working conference on reverse engineering* (Victoria, B.C., Canada, November 2003), pp. 260–270.

[15] MUSUVATHI, M., PARK, D. Y., CHOU, A., ENGLER, D. R., AND DILL, D. L. CMC: A pragmatic approach to model checking real code. In *Proceedings of the 5th Symposium on Operating Systems Design and Implementation* (Boston, MA, December 2002), pp. 75–88.

[16] NAKAMURA, Y. JAMA guideline for in-vehicle display systems. Tech. rep., Japan Automobile Manufacturers Association, Oct 2008.

[17] PAIVA, A. C., FARIA, J. C., TILLMANN, N., AND VIDAL, R. A. A model-to-implementation mapping tool for automated model-based GUI testing. In *Proceedings of the 7th International Conference on Formal Engineering Methods* (Manchester, United Kingdom, November 2005), pp. 450–464.

[18] SALVUCCI, D. D. Predicting the effects of in-car interfaces on driver behavior using a cognitive architecture. In *Proceedings of the SIGCHI Conference on Human Factors in Computing Systems* (Seattle, Washington, March 2001), pp. 120–127.

[19] STEVENS, A., QUIMBY, A., BOARD, A., KERSLOOT, T., AND BURNS, P. Design guidelines for safety of in-vehicle information systems. Tech. rep., Transport Research Laboratory, Feb 2002.

[20] TAKALA, T., KATARA, M., AND HARTY, J. Experiences of system-level model-based GUI testing of an android application. In *Proceedings of the 4th IEEE International Conference on Software Testing, Verification, and Validation* (Berlin, Germany, March 2011), pp. 377–386.

[21] TASK FORCE HMI. European statement of principles on human machine interface for in-vehicle information and communication systems. Tech. rep., Commission of the European Communities, December 1998.

[22] Tesseract-ocr. `http://code.google.com/p/tesseract-ocr/`.

[23] TSUCHIYA, T., AND SCHIPER, A. Model checking of consensus algorithm. In *Proceedings of the 26th IEEE International Symposium on Reliable Distributed Systems* (Beijing, China, October 2007), pp. 137 –148.

[24] UI/Application Exerciser Monkey. `http://developer.android.com/tools/help/monkey.html`.

[25] VALMARI, A. A stubborn attack on state explosion. *Formal Methods in System Design 1*, 4 (1992), 297–322.

[26] YANG, J., SAR, C., AND ENGLER, D. eXplode: a lightweight, general system for finding serious storage system errors. In *Proceedings of the 7th Symposium on Operating Systems Design and Implementation* (Seattle, WA, November 2006), pp. 131–146.

[27] ZIEFLE, M. Effects of display resolution on visual performance. *Human Factors: The Journal of the Human Factors and Ergonomics Society 40*, 4 (1998), 554–568.

CarSafe App: Alerting Drowsy and Distracted Drivers using Dual Cameras on Smartphones

Chuang-Wen You[†*], Nicholas D. Lane[‡], Fanglin Chen[†], Rui Wang[†], Zhenyu Chen[†⊔], Thomas J. Bao[†]
Martha Montes-de-Oca[⋈], Yuting Cheng[†], Mu Lin[†], Lorenzo Torresani[†], Andrew T. Campbell[†]
[†]Dartmouth College, [‡]Microsoft Research Asia, [*]Academia Sinica
[⊔]Chinese Academy of Sciences, [⋈]National Autonomous University of Mexico
cwyou@citi.sinica.edu.tw, niclane@microsoft.com, {chentc, ruiwang, zhenyu}@cs.dartmouth.edu
thomas.j.bao@dartmouth.edu, martham@unam.mx, {yutingc, linmu, lorenzo, campbell}@cs.dartmouth.edu

ABSTRACT

We present CarSafe, a new driver safety app for Android phones that detects and alerts drivers to dangerous driving conditions and behavior. It uses computer vision and machine learning algorithms on the phone to monitor and detect whether the driver is tired or distracted using the front-facing camera while at the same time tracking road conditions using the rear-facing camera. Today's smartphones do not, however, have the capability to process video streams from both the front and rear cameras simultaneously. In response, CarSafe uses a context-aware algorithm that switches between the two cameras while processing the data in real-time with the goal of minimizing missed events inside (e.g., drowsy driving) and outside of the car (e.g., tailgating). Camera switching means that CarSafe technically has a "blind spot" in the front or rear at any given time. To address this, CarSafe uses other embedded sensors on the phone (i.e., inertial sensors) to generate soft hints regarding potential blind spot dangers. We present the design and implementation of CarSafe and discuss its evaluation using results from a 12-driver field trial. Results from the CarSafe deployment are promising – CarSafe can infer a common set of dangerous driving behaviors and road conditions with an overall precision and recall of 83% and 75%, respectively. CarSafe is the first dual-camera sensing app for smartphones and represents a new disruptive technology because it provides similar advanced safety features otherwise only found in expensive top-end cars.

Categories and Subject Descriptors

H.4 [**Information Systems Applications**]: Miscellaneous

General Terms

Design, Experimentation, Performance.

Keywords

Driver safety, dual-camera sensing, smartphone sensing.

1. INTRODUCTION

Driving while being tired or distracted is dangerous. In 2010, 3,092 people were killed and 416,000 injured in the United States alone during accidents directly attributed to distracted drivers [37]. Surprisingly, many people drive while being tired or drowsy [35] and according to experts, many drivers fail to recognize they are in a fatigued state. Tracking dangerous driving behavior can help raise drivers' awareness of their driving habits and associated risks, thus, helping reduce careless driving and promoting safe driving practices. Today's top-end cars come with a wealth of new safety features built-in. These include collision-avoidance, drowsy driver feedback (e.g., vibrating steering wheel), lane departure warning, lane weaving and pedestrian detection. By fitting advanced sensors into the vehicle (e.g., night cameras, radars, ultrasonic sensors), the car can infer dangerous driving behavior, such as drowsiness or distracted driving; some cars even trigger automatic steering when the car drifts into another lane or brake before getting dangerously close to the car in front. However, only a tiny percentage of cars on the road today have these driver alert systems; it will take a decade for this new technology to be commonplace in most cars across the globe. What do you do if you can't afford a top of the line car with advanced safety features?

We propose CarSafe, the first driver safety app that uses dual cameras on smartphones – shown conceptually in Figure 1 and in operation in Figure 2. CarSafe uses computer vision and machine learning algorithms on the phone to detect whether the driver is tired or distracted using the front-facing camera while at the same time tracking road conditions using the rear-facing camera. CarSafe focuses on five of the most commonly occurring dangerous driving events: drowsy driving, inattentive driving (e.g., when the driver is distracted and takes their eyes off the road), tailgating (i.e., getting too close to the car in front), lane weaving or drifting and ignoring blind spots during lane changes. CarSafe aims to mimic the safety features found in many of the top-end cars on the market today. However, the big advantage of CarSafe is that you do not need to drive a top-end car to get these safety features – all you need is a smartphone.

Several research projects are designing vision-based algorithms to detect drowsiness (using fixed mounted cameras in the car) or road conditions (using fixed or smartphone cameras [11]). These solutions usually detect driver states or road conditions limiting inference to either the road or driver side but not both. Today's smartphones do not, however, have the capability to process video streams from both the front and rear cameras simultaneously. To address this, CarSafe uses a context-based camera switching algorithm to schedule processing between two different camera classification pipelines at the "right time". The front camera pipeline

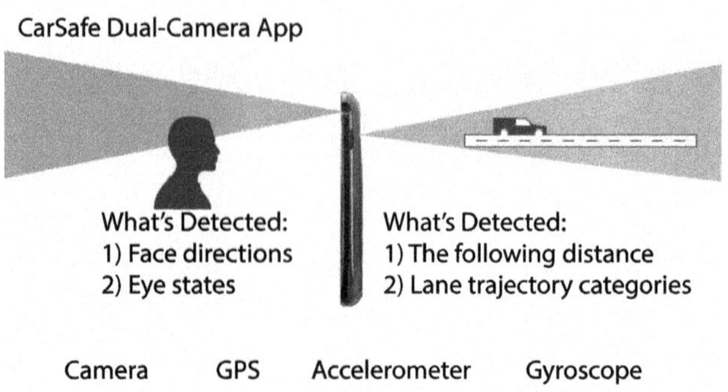

Figure 1: CarSafe exploits dual-camera sensing to track both driver and road-based events.

Figure 2: CarSafe, the first dual-camera sensing app, running on a Samsung Galaxy S3 mounted on the windshield of a car.

tracks the driver's head pose and direction as well as eyes and blinking rate as a means to infer drowsiness and distraction. If it detects drowsiness (or distraction), CarSafe alerts the driver by displaying a coffee cup icon (or an attention icon) on the phone's touch screen along with an audible alert. The rear camera pipeline monitors the distance between cars to determine if the driver is too close to the car in front as well as tracking lane change conditions. If it detects that the driver is too close to the car in front, a color status bar on the touch screen changes from green to red along with an audible alert. If CarSafe detects weaving across lanes on the road or other distracted or dangerous behavior, it alerts the driver by displaying an attention icon on the phone's touch screen along with an audible alert. The CarSafe UI shown in Figure 9 illustrates a number of these alerts.

CarSafe represents the first dual-camera sensing app, to the best of our knowledge, and therefore the design, insights and results provide a road map to others intent on building dual-camera apps in the future. The paper is structured as follows. §2 discusses the design considerations of implementing the CarSafe app on resource limited mobile phones that do not allow access to both cameras simultaneously. §3 presents the CarSafe architecture and detailed design based on three classification pipelines; that is, car, road, and driver classification pipelines. §4 describes the implementation details of CarSafe. This is followed in §5 by the evaluation of the CarSafe app. Results from a 12-person user study and system performance benchmarks are presented. The results look very promising – CarSafe can infer dangerous driving behavior and road conditions using context-driven camera switching with an overall precision and recall of 83% and 75%, respectively. Using blind spot hints and proximity information improves performance by up to 33% in terms of the F1 score. By adding intelligence into camera switching in comparison to a simple round robin approach boosts the F1 score by a further 16%. §6 discusses CarSafe in relation to related work. §7 presents some concluding remarks and future work.

2. DESIGN CONSIDERATIONS

In this section, we discuss the technical considerations that underpin the design of CarSafe while the detailed design is presented in §3.

2.1 Dangerous Driving Events

Drivers are faced with a multitude of road hazards and an increasing number of in-car distractions (e.g., music, conversation with passengers, phone calls, instrument panels, smartphone texting and browsing, etc.). CarSafe focuses on five of the most commonly occurring dangerous driving events [16].

Drowsy Driving (DD). Drivers who are fatigued are prone to episodes of microsleep [34]. Individuals are often unaware of these episodes; rather, people typically think they have been awake the whole time or have lost focus momentarily. As a result, drivers experiencing bouts of microsleep are at high risk of having an accident. While there has been work using static cameras [26] to infer microsleep, there has been no work on using smartphones to infer this with drivers. As a starting point, the smartphone's front camera should be able to monitor the prolonged and frequent blinks indicative of microsleep. There are many challenges to classifying microsleep including the diversity of people (e.g., glasses, facial expressions – such as smiling) and lighting conditions (e.g., overexposure, shadows).

Inattentive Driving (ID). Maintaining eye contact with the road is fundamental to safe driving. Again, by using the front camera of the phone, the head position of the driver can be used to determine an inattentive driving behavior when the driver is not looking at the road ahead. There is a broader set of distracted behavior that can also result in inattentive driving, such as, conversation with passengers, rubbernecking, texting, browsing, people watching and reading maps. Rather than attempting to infer specific scenarios, we treat all of these as examples of the driver being inattentive to the road; that is, not looking at the road ahead when the car is moving forward.

Tailgating (TG). Drivers should maintain a safe minimum distance with the car immediately ahead to ensure they can stop safely, if necessary. The danger level can be assessed by comparing the current following distance to an ideal safe distance based on DMV[1] guidelines (e.g.,[16]) and an estimate of the car speed. There are a number of commercial driving applications [11, 13] that use car-mounted smartphones and the rear camera to compute following distance and provide feedback to the driver (see §6); these applications are closed source and therefore it is not clear how they compute distances, in fact these applications often do not display the distance but a "following time" between cars. By developing this feature, our contribution is to offer a similar service but provide the technical details of how this is done – in addition we integrate this technique with a variety of others to provide more comprehensive protection.

Lane Weaving and Drifting (LW). Lane weaving happens when a driver performs one or more erratic lane changes. For example, frequent lane changing is an effort to maintain a high speed and

[1] Department of Motor Vehicles

avoid traffic congestion. Lane drifting is the inability of the driver to keep their vehicle within the lane markers. The CarSafe app should be capable of recognizing these unsafe car trajectories using both the inertial sensors and the rear camera of the phone when available. The rear camera monitors the car's trajectory by detecting and tracking lane markers. Similarly, inertial sensors observe changes in direction and acceleration. Top-end cars come with lane drifting and weaving detection as well as "real" blind spot monitoring (i.e., the car detects if another car is in a blind spot and flashes an icon). We aim to offer similar lane monitoring facilities using a commodity smartphone.

Careless Lane Change (CLC). Executing lane changes safely also requires a driver to check blind spots before proceeding. The driver does this by looking in the side and front mirrors of the car to check for unexpected vehicles. CarSafe should be capable of recognizing the head position of the driver using the phone's front camera, allowing the app to ensure the appropriate mirror checks are performed before each lane change. Lane changing itself can be detected using the rear camera and inertial sensors, as described above.

2.2 Dual Camera Processing

CarSafe fundamentally relies on the real-time processing of dual camera video streams. In what follows, we discuss the challenges and design considerations that arise.

Cross Stream Event Correlation. As shown in Figure 1 driving events can be independently monitored by each camera; for example, the front-facing camera detects the driver might be entering microsleep due to excessive long blinking; the rear-facing camera is watching the car ahead and is on the cusp of raising a tailgating alert. This is a likely event if a driver is entering microsleep. This example motivates the need for the simultaneously processing of video streams from the front and rear cameras. In addition, there may be strong correlation between events in and outside of the car, or causality: the driver is entering a drowsy state and because of that tailgating occurs. In contrast, there maybe no correlation between events on opposite sides of the camera streams – such as, the driver is attentive to the road but is driving too close to the car in front. In this example, there is no evidence of causality. Therefore, the app should be capable of fusing events detected from cameras and sensor readings to infer more complex behavior.

Limited Dual Camera Access. At the time of developing CarSafe, none of the mainstream smartphones provide simultaneous access to both the front and rear cameras. As a result, dual-camera sensing apps will be forced to switch periodically between the front and rear cameras. Motivated by this limitation, we conduct a series of experiments spanning a variety of high-end phone models and various manufacturers (viz. Nokia, Samsung, HTC, Apple). Not only did we verify that none of these platforms allow developers dual camera access but we also find that switching between cameras incurs a non-negligible delay. We refer to this delay as the *switching delay*. Table 1 presents the switching delay for the Samsung Galaxy S3 (Android 4.2), HTC One X (Android 4.2), Nokia Lumia 900 (Windows 7.5), iPhone 4S (iOS 5), and iPhone 5 (iOS 5) platforms. On average, delays across these platforms last 886 ms, with some platforms requiring more than 2000 ms to switch. Furthermore, we find the switching delay is asymmetric, and depends on the direction from which the switch is occurring (i.e., from the rear camera to the front camera or vice versa). All dual camera sensing apps must cope with the switching delay if they are to function on off-the-shelf hardware. In this paper, we implement CarSafe using the Android platform to investigate the challenges faced in building a dual camera app under a mainstream platform without assistance from specialized hardware, device drivers, or performing any OS hacking.

To further understand the reasons for this limitation, we study the source code of the Android Camera Architecture [3]. This framework employs three architectural layers to abstract away the complexity of directly manipulating camera hardware (e.g., via the Video4Linux (V4L) library [14]): (1) the application framework, (2) camera service, and (3) the hardware abstraction layer (HAL). By adopting a camera service layer to mediate between the application framework and the HAL, developers are isolated from the hardware. As a result, developers only need to interact with a standard Java interface. In contrast, platform engineers implementing the HAL on each smartphone require specialized hardware knowledge. This causes manufacturers to be resistant to significant architectural changes in existing HAL implementations. Because earlier smartphones only included a single camera, HALs are naturally designed with only single-camera access in mind. For example, the HAL for the Texas Instruments OMAP4460 chipset [17] used by the Samsung Galaxy Nexus limits the number of simultaneously connected camera streams to be one (i.e., the `MAX_SIMUL_CAMERAS_SUPPORTED` constant in the `CameraProperties.h` file is set to 1). Even though phone manufacturers have included multiple cameras along with the necessary hardware capabilities to process simultaneous streams, hardware vendors have yet to revise HAL implementations to expose this capability to developers. As a result, we find that if an app already has an opened camera stream, then all additional requests from an app to open additional camera streams (for example, through the Android Camera Service) are blocked at the HAL with runtime exceptions returned.

Phone manufacturers are beginning to react to this artificial dual-camera limitation [19]. For example, in April 2013 – after the CarSafe project was complete – Samsung announced support for dual camera access in the upcoming Samsung Galaxy S4. The Galaxy S4 will be equipped with Samsung's own Exynos 8-core processor, providing the necessary computational power to process multiple image streams at the same time. Samsung will redesign the HAL included with the Galaxy S4 to support dual camera access [19]. Because we design CarSafe to operate without native dual camera support it will operate even better on smartphones that offer zero switching delay (e.g., Galaxy S4). Furthermore, because the application framework layer remains unchanged, even under the S4, CarSafe will not require modifications to leverage new dual camera capabilities. CarSafe is an example of a dual camera sensing app that incorporates a unified implementation able to function correctly on both existing phones (e.g., Samsung Galaxy Nexus and S3) and future (e.g., Samsung Galaxy S4) dual-camera phones.

Blind Spot Processing. The fact that only one camera can be accessed at a time and the cost of switching – that is, the switching delay – results in blind spots and potentially missed events. Essentially, a switching solution implies that a dual camera app technically will have a blind spot in the front or rear at any given time.

Table 1: Camera switching overhead, including switching directions: front-to-rear (F-R) and rear-to-front (R-F).

Model \ Overhead	F-R (ms)	R-F (ms)	Face detection (ms)
Nokia Lumia 900	804	2856.3	2032.5
Samsung Galaxy S3	519	774	301.2
HTC One X	1030	939	680.3
iPhone 4S	446	503	70.92
iPhone 5	467	529	58.48

How do we determine the best time to switch cameras (e.g., the system is satisfied that an event is unlikely on one camera and switches to the other)? Furthermore, if the system has to switch, can it "fill in" in some capacity while in a blind spot? One way forward is to explore the use of other embedded sensors that are "always-on", and not subject to the limitations of camera switching. For example, CarSafe should be able to exploit inertial sensors, such as accelerometers, gyroscopes and digital compasses, to figure out what is occurring in the blind spot at any given time. In essence, CarSafe should be able to use other embedded sensors to compensate when the camera is looking at the wrong place. In addition, these "blind spot hints" can be used to enable intelligent camera switching.

2.3 Real-Time Performance

Table 1 shows the per-frame processing time for the same set of phone models described earlier. When running a representative workload (i.e., performing face detection on the phone) for an image analyzing task on Android [10], iOS [12] and Windows Phone [9] platforms, the processing time per frame ranges between 58 ms and 2032 ms. In comparison, the processing time is just 33 ms per frame when simply capturing frames without running any workload. As the phone executes more complex operations, it will require longer processing time for each frame, and therefore can not achieve real-time processing. However, with the availability of a multicore processor on these high-end phones, the amount of delay should be able to be further reduced if we can run tasks across multiple cores simultaneously. We will discuss how to boost the performance of image processing pipelines later in §3.5.

3. CARSAFE DETAILED DESIGN

In this section, we present a detailed discussion of the CarSafe architecture and algorithms, as illustrated in Figure 3. We begin with an overview of the architecture.

3.1 Overview

The key components include (1) driver, car and road classification pipelines; (2) dangerous driving event engine; (3) context-driven camera switching; (4) multi-core computation planner; and, (5) user interface.

Classification Pipelines. CarSafe comprises three sets of classifiers to infer driver behavior, car events and road conditions. Each component is designed and implemented as a classification pipeline operating on a different set of phone sensors.

Driver Classification Pipeline. Frames from the front camera are used to recognize (1) face direction – the turning angle, needed to track driver attention; and, (2) eye state – open/closed events, required for drowsiness detection.

Road Classification Pipeline. Frames from the rear camera are used to estimate (1) the following distance; and, (2) lane trajectory categories (i.e., lane change, and weaving).

Car Classification Pipeline. The GPS and inertial sensors are used to (1) estimate speed, (2) detect turns and (3) recognize lane trajectory categories. CarSafe exploits the continuous availability of these always-on sensors to make inferences when "the camera is looking the wrong way"; for example, inertial sensors can infer lane weaving when the camera is "watching" the driver.

Dangerous Driving Event Engine. Recognizing dangerous driving events requires the synthesis of the individual sensor-based inferences from the driver, car and road classification pipelines as overviewed above. CarSafe performs this cross stream event correlation (as discussed in the §2.2) by encoding each category of dangerous driving behavior listed in §2.1 as one or more rules. Rules are developed based on best practices for safe and defensive driving as outlined by DMVs [16, 8], traffic safety studies [7, 34] and through consultations with domain experts. The dangerous driving event engine evaluates each rule against the incoming stream of inferences (i.e., driver state, road conditions, and car events) made when sensor data is sampled.

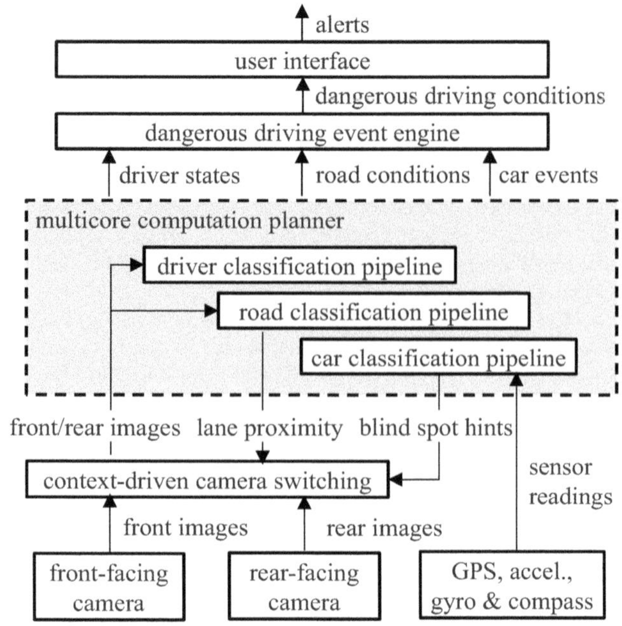

Figure 3: The CarSafe architecture.

Context-driven Camera Switching. Both driver and road conditions are subject to rapid and frequent changes demanding both the front and rear cameras to be continuously monitored. Because smartphones do not allow simultaneous access to both cameras CarSafe incorporates an adaptive context-driven camera switching policy. This mechanism is designed to minimize the number of events missed. It is also responsive to blind spot hints from the car classification pipeline.

Multi-core Computation Planner. Without carefully constructing and scheduling the computational workload necessary for CarSafe, user feedback can not be reliably generated in near real-time. As a result, for example – an alarm to alert a driver that they are frequently entering periods of microsleep may not be delivered in time. The planner enables CarSafe to more fully utilize the multi-core computational resources of the smartphone.

User Interface. Our CarSafe prototype can either be used by a driver as a stand-alone smartphone app, or as a transparent extension to an existing in-car app – for instance, car navigation. In all of these scenarios, the basic operation of CarSafe remains the same; whenever a dangerous driving event is detected a visual icon (e.g., a coffee cup indicating drowsy driving) is shown along with an audible alert. Icons are overlaid on the host app interface, as shown in Figure 9.

3.2 Classification Pipelines

We begin by describing the design of the three sensor-based classifiers used by CarSafe to track the state of the driver, road and car, respectively.

3.2.1 Driver Classification Pipeline

The driver classification pipeline, shown in Figure 4, comprises

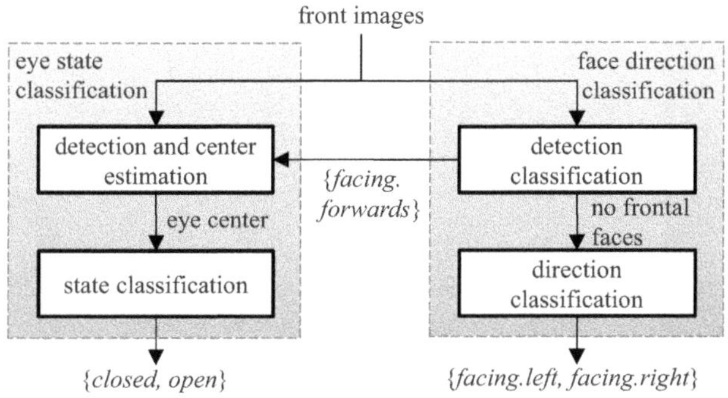

Figure 4: Data flow of driver classification pipeline.

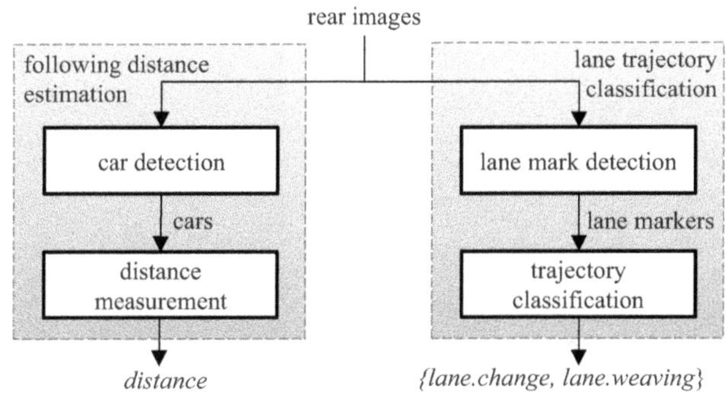

Figure 5: Data flow of the road classification pipeline.

two components: (1) face direction classification, and (2) eye state classification.

Face Direction Classification. Inferring the direction of the driver's face is divided into two steps: (1) detection classification and (2) direction classification.

Detection Classification. Images from the front camera are scanned to find the relative position of the driver's face. The scanning procedure is an iterative process. At each iteration a selected region of the overall image is provided to a classifier that determines if a face is present, and if so the face direction is classified. Initially, the size of the region is set to 200 x 200 pixels. If no face is found, the region is made smaller with the process terminated once a minimum region size is reached (70 x 70 pixels in the CarSafe prototype).

Direction Classification. To classify the direction of the driver's face we use two steps: (1) Haar-like features [41] that are extracted from image regions provided by the detection stage, after which (2) inference is performed using an Adaboost decision-stump classifier [33]. Haar-like features highlight differences between object classes (in this case faces) by aggregating pixel intensities for rectangular regions. We adopt this classifier design (i.e., combination of feature and model type) because it has been demonstrated to be effective in recognizing a variety of object types, including faces. The classifier is a cascade of decision-stumps (i.e., two-level decision trees). We train this model to recognize four face related categories that include: (1) no face is present; or the driver's face is either (2) facing forwards (defined as *facing.forwards* events), towards the road; (3) facing to the left, defined as *facing.left* events (i.e., a $\geq 15^\circ$ rotation relative to facing directly forward); and, (4) facing to the right, defined as *facing.right* events (another $\geq 15^\circ$ rotation but this time to the right).

Eye State Classification. The classification of driver's eye states (i.e., open and closed states) requires two steps: (1) detection and center estimation and (2) state classification. This stage is only performed if the driver's head is recognized as facing the road during face direction classification.

Detection and Center Estimation. This process is initialized by receiving the pixel co-ordinates of a region within the image that includes only the face of the driver from the face direction classifier. Similarly, two even smaller regions that enclose the eyes are searched for by exploiting a commonly used active shape model (available from [1]). This model uses 76 MUCT[2] pre-defined visual landmarks [21] that are fit to the image to estimate an eye bounding region. To find the eye center we calculate the vector field of image gradients with respect to the pixel intensities. By summing up the inner products of image gradients over each point within the iris, the eye center can be detected by finding the largest value.

State Classification. Eye classification is a two stage process comprising: (1) the extraction of SURF[3] features [25], followed by (2) inference using an SVM[4] classifier [28]. We compute 64-component SURF features to represent the two states (viz. open and closed) of the eye. Extracting features requires knowledge of the eye position and the pixel co-ordinates of the eye center, both of which are determined in the prior stage of the pipeline. SURF features are provided to a binary two-class SVM that is trained to classify eyes as either being open or closed (defined as an *open* or *closed* event). We train the SVM using the BioID face database [5]. Due to a limited number of examples of closed eyes in this database we recruit 30 volunteers to provide supplementary training data. In total our training set contains 160 open eye images and 160 closed eye images.

3.2.2 Road Classification Pipeline

As illustrated in Figure 5, the road classification pipeline comprises two components: (1) following distance estimation and (2) lane trajectory classification.

Following Distance Estimation. CarSafe estimates the following distance using a two stage process that begins with (1) the detection of the car immediately ahead, after which (2) the distance between the cars is estimated.

Car Detection. The recognition of a car within an image is essentially an identical process to the one performed by the face direction classifier; the iterative scanning process performed to detect cars is the same, as is the design of our car classifier (i.e., choice of features and classification model). In our prior work, WalkSafe [43], we verified this particular detector design is effective in recognizing cars. To train this classifier we use a labeled dataset where: positive examples (i.e., images containing cars captured from the rear) are sourced from the MIT CBCL[5] car dataset [38], and negative examples (i.e., images of cars taken at different angles along with various images containing road and urban settings) are collected from Google StreetView [20].

Distance Estimation. By applying a pin-hole camera projection we can estimate the following distance based on the pixel distance captured by the rear-camera image, such as Figure 6(a). To perform this projection requires the pixel co-ordinates within the image of

[2]Milborrow / University of Cape Town

[3]Speeded Up Robust Features

[4]Support Vector Machine

[5]Center for Biological & Computational Learning

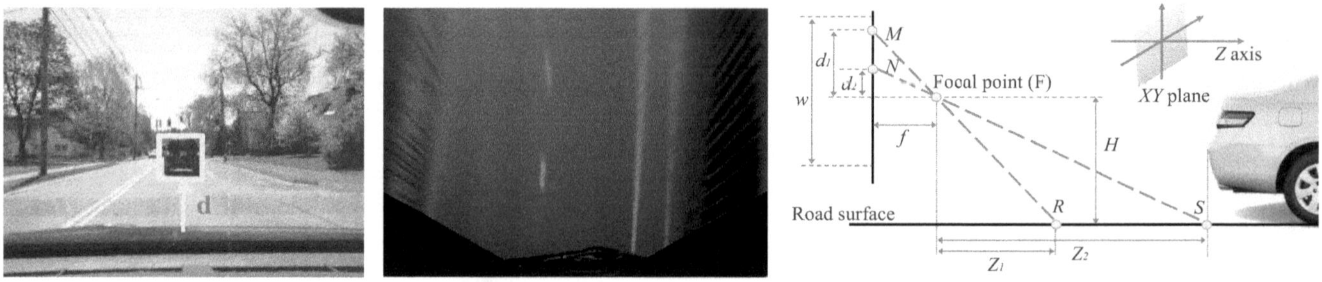

(a) Distance measurement **(b)** Bird's-eye view image **(c)** Pinhole model

Figure 6: Following distance measurement and lane detection steps. (a) The detected following distance (*d*, as indicated by the yellow arrow) in the gray-scale image. (b) The Bird's-eye view image is generated by applying inverse perspective mapping on the original gray-scaled image. (c) A pinhole model transforms in-image pixel distances between cars to real following distances.

(1) the car ahead and (2) the driver's car. The first co-ordinate pair (the car ahead) is provided by the previously described car detection stage; the second pair is detected with a simple threshold-based edge detector that identifies the front edge of the driver's car visible at the bottom of each image.

Figure 6(c) shows the pin-hole camera projection we perform. This figure illustrates how any road distance Z (e.g., Z_1 and Z_2) in the camera view is projected to an image pixel distance d (e.g., d_1 and d_2). As a result, the following distance can be computed by,

$$Z_2 - Z_1 = (\frac{1}{d_2} - \frac{1}{d_1}) \times f \times H \quad (1)$$

where Z_1 and Z_2 are the real-world distances between the smartphone and the front of the driver's car and the car immediately ahead respectively; d_1 and d_2 are the in-image pixel distance equivalents of Z_1 and Z_2; f is the rear-camera focal length; and finally, H is the smartphone mounting height.

Lane Trajectory Classification. This is a two stage process in which (1) lane markings are detected and tracked across multiple frames, after which (2) a classifier determines the trajectory category.

Lane Marker Detection. Detection of lane markers is performed in three stages: (1) perspective transformation, (2) vertical-edge detection, and (3) line detection. First, the perspective of each rear-camera image is transformed into a "bird's-eye view" by applying inverse perspective mapping [24]. The effect of the transformation can be seen by comparing Figure 6(a) and Figure 6(b). Second, possible lane marker edges are identified by a pixel-based search of the region of road immediately in front of the driver's car. For each pixel we compare it's gray-scale pixel value ($g(x, y)$) with that of pixels ($g(x - m, y)$ and $g(x + m, y)$) horizontally adjacent, where x and y are pixel co-ordinates and m is the lane marker width. As a result of this pixel search, we generate an edge-map in which pixels of potential lane markers are set as white and the remaining pixels as black. Third, we apply a Hough-line transformation [32] to the edge-map that will identify line segments and select lane markers. The Hough-line transformation we use first applies a Canny edge detector [29] before voting on line candidates using the RANdom SAmple Consensus (RANSAC) algorithm [32].

Trajectory Classification. Lane trajectory categories (including lane change (defined as *lane.change* events), and lane weaving (defined as *lane.weaving* events)) are distinguished by statistics that track lane marker crossing events. Crossing events are defined as when the intersection of the detected lane marker and the lower edge of the smartphone screen pass by the vertical center line of a frame. A decision tree [27] is trained based on (1) the duration and (2) the frequency of crossing events. We train the classifier using images collected during controlled driving maneuvers (see §5.1).

3.2.3 Car Classification Pipeline

Figure 7 shows the three components of the car classification pipeline: (1) speed estimation, (2) turn detection, and (3) lane trajectory classification.

Speed Estimation. Estimates of the vehicle's speed are based on time-series GPS positions. We first project the geodetic co-ordinates from the GPS (i.e., latitude and longitude) into a cartesian co-ordinate system. Speed is then estimated by dividing the sum of the distances between pairs of successive co-ordinates spanning a sliding window of five seconds.

Turn Detection. Similar to speed estimation, car turns are detected by observing significant changes in direction from time-series GPS positions. Again, GPS positions are first converted into cartesian co-ordinates after which vectors are formed from successive co-ordinates. Turns are detected by examining the change in angle between successive vectors within a sliding window of 10 seconds. A vehicle turn is inferred if the average change in angle exceeds a threshold, set to $\approx 50°$ in our experiments. The relative direction of the turn (i.e., left- or right-hand turn) is based on the polar coordinates of the average vector change. If the change in angle is positive the turn is to the right (defined as *turn.right* events) otherwise the turn is to the left (defined as *turn.left* events).

Trajectory Classification. This classifier recognizes the same set of classes as the road classification pipeline; however, it uses a completely different set of sensors – inertial sensor readings rather than the rear camera.

From three inertial sensors – the accelerometer, gyroscope and compass – a series of features are extracted that capture distinctive characteristics of the car trajectory as it moves within and between

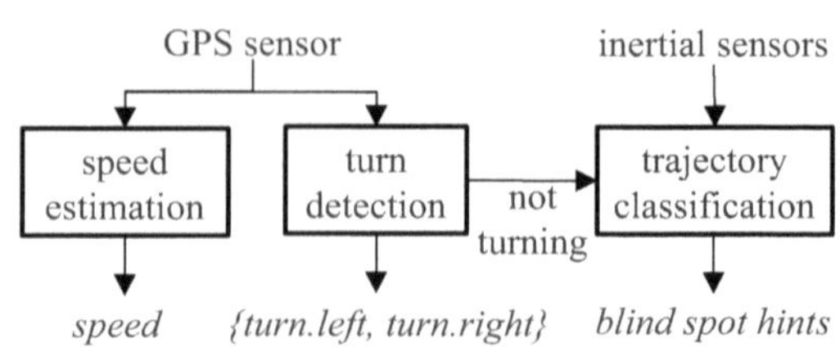

Figure 7: Data flow of the car classification pipeline.

the road lanes. We adopt a feature set and extraction algorithms previously developed in our own prior work [36]. Specifically, we use three time-domain features (mean, variance and mean-crossing rate) and five frequency-domain features (peak frequency, spectral entropy, spectrum sub-band energy, sub-band energy ratio, and spectrum correlation). These eight features are extracted for each sensor resulting in a 75-element feature vector. Prior experiments [36] have proven such features are effective in classifying physical activities (e.g., walking, running, standing) that have distinct time-series patterns within inertial sensor data – we now apply this same feature set to classifying car trajectories. In addition, the extraction algorithms used from [36] are robust to the precise position and orientation of the phone within the car.

Classification is performed using a binary bayesian classifier that represents classes as a multi-variate gaussian [27]. Two classes of trajectories are recognized – one "lane change/weaving" class for both types of lane trajectories (viz. lane change and weaving) and one "other" class that represents all other trajectories where the car largely remains in the same lane. Each feature vector is computed using a sliding window of 1.5 seconds of raw data ($\approx$ 128 raw data segments). Classification is performed over each input feature vector to recognize the current lane trajectory as being either the "lane change/weaving" or "other" class. To train the classifier, we use the driving data (see §5.1 for details) and manually label each data segment. Inferences (e.g., blind spot hints) can be use as input to context-driven camera switching.

3.3 Dangerous Driving Event Engine

CarSafe recognizes five types of dangerous driving events (detailed in §2.1). For each type, we describe the series of rules used to interpret the low-level state inferred by the classifiers described in §3.2 that allow dangerous events to be detected.

Drowsy Driving (DD). We adopt a standard metric for measuring alertness, PERcentage of CLOSure of the eyelid – called `PERCLOS` [44], which more formally represents the proportion of time within one minute that eyes are at least 80% closed [34]. This driver state information is provided by the driver classification pipeline detailed in §3.2.1. CarSafe continuously computes `PERCLOS` and declares the driver "drowsy" if `PERCLOS` exceeds a threshold (28%) guided by prior studies [44].

Inattentive Driving (ID). Two types of inattentive driving are monitored by CarSafe. In the first case, the output of the face direction classifier is tracked. If the driver's face is not facing forward for longer than three seconds while the car is moving forward (i.e., while a positive speed is reported by the car classification pipeline) and not turning as reported by the turn detector (also reported by car classification pipeline) then a dangerous driving event is inferred. We use a three second threshold based on the guidelines provided by [7]. In the second case, we monitor the turn detector. Each time a turn is detected the historical output of the face direction classifier is checked. If there is no a head turn corresponding to a car turning event then the driver did not check that the road is clear before turning – as a result, a dangerous event is inferred.

Tailgating (TG). We adopt the calculation for a minimum following distance from [16], which relies on the speed estimation made by the car classification pipeline. This estimate of a "safe following distance" is compared to the estimated current following distance also provided by the car classification pipeline. If CarSafe determines the safe following distance is not respected for a period longer than three seconds a dangerous driving event is inferred.

Lane Weaving and Drifting (LW). Detecting lane weaving or drifting relies on the trajectory classifier contained within the road classification pipeline. CarSafe reports a dangerous driving event if the classifier infers either lane weaving or lane drifting continuously for longer than two seconds, which would be significantly longer than the typical duration of a lane change maneuver [39].

Careless Lane Change (CLC). Each time the trajectory classifier associated with the road classification pipeline determines a lane change event has occurred the recent inferences made by face direction classification are examined. If there is no head turn corresponding to a lane change event (occurring within ϵ seconds prior to the lane change event detection) then a dangerous driving event is inferred. We set ϵ to three seconds based on the road safety findings provided in [31].

Algorithm 1: Context-driven Camera Switching

```
Input: B_min, F_min, B_add, and F_add
Output: Estimated time T_f or T_b
Connecting to the front camera initially (CurCamera = Front);
while TRUE do
    Waiting for the next frame from the CurCamera;
    Processing the received frame;
    if Close to a lane marker && CurCamera == Rear then
        switchTime = currentTime + 2 sec;
    if ((Received a blind spot hint) && CurCamera == Front) || (switchTime ≥ currentTime) then
        if CurCamera == Front then
            CurCamera = Rear;
            Estimate T_b based on Eq. 2;
            switchTime = currentTime + T_s^f + T_b;
        else
            CurCamera = Front;
            Estimate T_f based on Eq. 3;
            switchTime = currentTime + T_s^b + T_f;
        Switch to the other camera;
```

3.4 Context-driven Camera Switching

In what follows, we present the design of our context-driven camera switching.

Switching Algorithm. We provide the intuition that underpins the design of our camera switching mechanism; a formal description is provided in Algorithm 1.

Primarily, the switching between the front and rear cameras is regulated by two time intervals (i.e., T_e^f, and T_e^b). Each interval is associated with one of the two cameras. Once the time interval for a particular camera expires CarSafe switches to the other camera. The pair of time intervals are set by an event arrival prediction process, which seeks to dynamically adjust the time allocated to each camera based on the current driver, road or car conditions. For example, if the system determines that the driver is likely to enter a dangerously drowsy state more time is allocated to the front camera to monitor this situation closely. Figure 8 presents an example of the common case operation of the camera switching mechanism.

Scheduled camera switching based on a pair of timers is supplemented with temporary pre-emption of the switching plan driven by discrete events – we refer to this behavior as the pre-emption of the switching plan. For example, if the driver starts to drive close to the lane markers then a planned switch to the front camera can be delayed to allow further monitoring of the lane marker situation.

Event Arrival Prediction. We use two separate predictors that target two event types: (1) front-camera events, which focus on driver states; and (2) rear-camera events, which focus on car events and road conditions.

Front-Camera Events. The driver state event with the shortest time-scale is driver drowsiness (i.e., blink duration). We find for this reason the prediction of other driver state events are not needed and instead we focus on predicting driver drowsiness only. We again use PERCLOS to quantify drowsiness; the likelihood that a driver is drowsy increases inline with increases in PERCLOS. As a result, the time allocated to the rear camera is proportional to the most recent PERCLOS. More formally,

$$\mathrm{T}_e^f = \begin{cases} B_{add} \cdot (\frac{D_{TH} - \mathtt{PERCLOS}}{D_{TH}}) + B_{min}, & \text{if } \mathtt{PERCLOS} < D_{TH} \\ B_{min}, & \text{otherwise} \end{cases} \tag{2}$$

where D_{TH} is the threshold for PERCLOS, that determines if the driver is in a drowsy state; B_{add} is a scaler that regulates the relationship between PERCLOS and T_e^f; finally, B_{min} sets a floor for the prediction of T_e^f – to cope with the switching delay between cameras, B_{min} must be be greater than the switching delay ($\mathrm{T}_s^f + \mathrm{T}_s^b$).

Rear-Camera Events. Similar to the design of front camera event prediction, rear camera events also focus on a single key event type; that is, the following distance between cars. When the following distance is decreasing, we predict when this distance will be equal to – or smaller than – the minimum safe following distance (detailed in §3.3). In cases where the following distance is constant or increasing we enforce a maximum time between expected events. More formally,

$$\mathrm{T}_e^r = \begin{cases} F_{add} + F_{min}, & \text{if } \frac{D - D_s}{V} > (F_{add} + F_{min}) \\ max(\frac{D - D_s}{V}, F_{min}\}, & \text{otherwise} \end{cases} \tag{3}$$

where D_s is the minimum safe following distance; D is the current following distance, as estimated by CarSafe; F_{add} controls the varying range of T_e^r – to limit the maximum value of T_e^r when CarSafe detects no front cars and F_{min} sets a floor for the prediction of T_e^r. Similarly, F_{min} should be set greater than the switching delay ($\mathrm{T}_s^f + \mathrm{T}_s^b$).

Switching Plan Pre-emption. Planned switching events can be pre-empted by hints from sensors or current car context. We now describe two examples of pre-emption due to (1) proximity to lane markers and (2) expected trajectory changes based on sensor data observations.

Lane Proximity. When the car is close to lane markers a lane event (e.g., lane change) is more likely to occur. As a result, we introduce the following camera switching pre-emption heuristic. If the car is closer than 0.6 meters from the nearest lane marker then any planned camera switching is delayed (≈ 2.0 seconds), allowing an immediately occurring lane event to be captured.

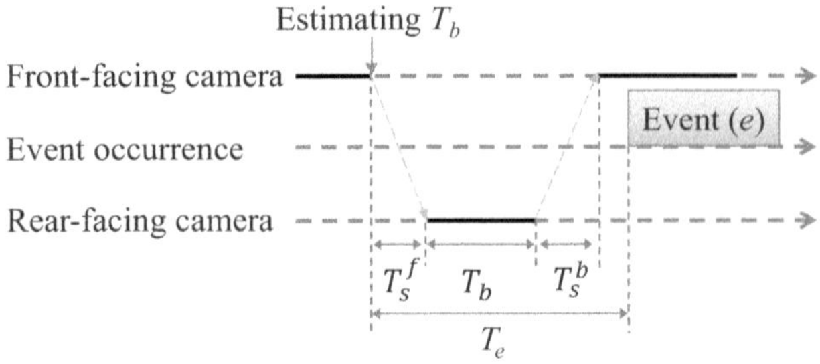

Figure 8: Context-driven Camera Switching algorithm in action. Here, an event (e) is monitored with the rear-facing camera. Although switching occurs roughly at the same time the event begins it is only monitored once the switching delay overhead (T_s^f) has past.

Lane Trajectory – Blind Spot Hints. If lane trajectory changes happen while the front camera is active (rather than the rear camera), an event, such as a lane change or weaving, can go unobserved (i.e., missed events). As a result, we incorporate another pre-emption heuristic based on blind spot hints from the always-on inertial sensors, as discussed in §3.2.3. If the trajectory classifier (which uses blind spot hints) determines that changes in the car trajectory occur then the rear camera is immediately activated. By switching to the rear camera the road classification pipeline can immediately verify the car trajectory inference, after which camera switching returns to the timer based policy.

3.5 Multi-core Computation Planner

We determined experimentally in §2.3 that processing dual image streams from the front and rear cameras can overwhelm the smartphone's computational resources. To maintain near real-time user feedback CarSafe relies on a computational planner, which aims to effectively leverage the multi-core architecture of new smartphones to perform classification, as discussed in §3.2. The multi-core computation planner is comprised of three components: (1) dispatcher, (2) queue manager, and (3) de-multiplexer.

Dispatcher. A pool of threads is maintained by dispatcher. Each thread contains one single classifier, of the three described in §3.2. The dispatcher allocates new camera frames or other data to unused threads. Because frames do not have dependencies with other frames being processed, the allocation of data to threads is greatly simplified. For example, multiple threads each running the same road classification pipeline can operate on different captured image frames.

Queue Manager. The dispatcher may find no available threads when new data arrives to be processed. In such cases this data is placed in a queue to wait until a thread becomes available. When a thread does become available the most recent data (e.g., image frame) is used rather than the data that has been in the queue the longest. This allows the most recent data to always be processed as soon as possible. Any frames waiting that are older than the one selected are dropped from the queue and go unprocessed.

De-multiplexer. The processing time for frames is variable, even for identical classifiers. As a result, it is possible for the output of frame processing to arrive out of order. In other words, a new frame may be completed before an older frame even though the new frame may have started processing later than the older frame. To cope with this problem each frame is timestamped with the time when processing began. Upon computation being completed the results of multiple frames can be re-ordered based on these timestamps.

3.6 User Interface

Figure 9 illustrates CarSafe integrated into OsmAnd [18], an open-source car navigation application. The user interface overlays simple icons to the map screen that correspond to particular dangerous driving events. A different method is used for the following distance alert. A small rectangular border is placed around the conventional GUI. This frame changes color based on the following distance; that is, green for safe and red for unsafe.

CarSafe can also operate independently as a stand-alone application. The same GUI events and icons are displayed along with con-

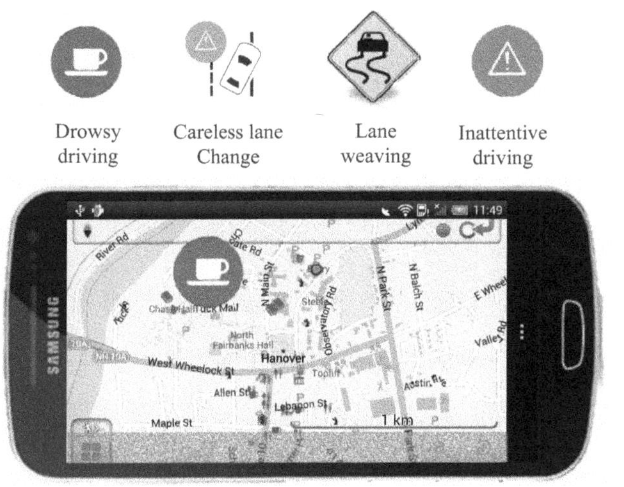

Figure 9: The example UI screenshot of CarSafe which indicates drowsy driving and tailgating conditions. The red rectangle at the bottom edge of the screen indicates the tailgating condition. The top row shows four icons representing for the rest of dangerous driving conditions.

tinually updating driver safety statistics (e.g., total time the driver has been inattentive of the road).

4. CARSAFE IMPLEMENTATION

We implement CarSafe on the multi-core Galaxy S3 Android phone. The driver, road and car classification pipelines, which represent the most computationally demanding modules, are written in C and C++ based on the OpenCV libraries and interfaced with Java using JNI wrappers. Other CafeSafe architectural components (viz. dangerous driving event engine, context-driven camera switching, and multi-core computation planner) are implemented using pure Java. To validate the prototype, we integrate the CarSafe modules with the OsmAnd navigation app. Because of privacy concerns, only Android programs running in the foreground can capture images from a camera through an Android image preview surface (e.g., SurfaceView). However, by overlaying an "invisible" dedicated drawing surface (shrinking it an extremely small size) on top of the original view hierarchy of OsmAnd, CarSafe modules can be easily embedded into, and seamlessly work with, OsmAnd without modifying the original navigation UI (e.g., the navigation map in Figure 9). The embedded drawing surface can receive preview images from either the front or rear camera at a rate of 30 fps. To boost the frame processing performance, we first set the resolution of preview images to 320 x 240 pixels. Because CarSafe classification pipelines represent computationally demanding models, single core phones have difficulty processing frames in real-time. To gain better performance we exploit new multi-core phones and target our first implementation to the Samsung Galaxy S3 with a 1.4 GHz quad-core Cortex-A9 CPU. We replicate the complete processing pipelines for the three classification pipelines (viz. driver, road and car classifiers) across four parallel threads on multiple CPU cores. When CarSafe is fully operational, the CPU usage is 64% for the Samsung Galaxy S3 (four CPU cores). While this represents a high continuous load on the phone, we argue that increased cores and advances in the development of more efficient computer vision and machine learning algorithms will allow the CarSafe pipelines to run at higher frame rates while riding the technology curve of more and more cores.

5. EVALUATION

In this section, we evaluate CarSafe under real-world conditions where people use the application in the wild. Specifically, we discuss results from a user study where participants use CarSafe while commuting around the Hanover (New Hampshire, USA) area. In addition, we present results from a set of system performance benchmarks. Our findings include: (1) CarSafe can detect a range of dangerous driving conditions with acceptable levels of accuracy; (2) CarSafe's classification pipelines cope with a majority of everyday road conditions; (3) context-based camera switching is effective, and allows CarSafe to operate on existing phones given that today's phones do not allow simultaneous access to both cameras; and, (4) the multi-core computation planner improves system utilization when supporting the CarSafe workload, enabling higher frame rate throughput.

5.1 Datasets

Collecting datasets to adequately evaluate CarSafe is challenging. This is because dangerous driving events are not guaranteed to happen during everyday driving for small scale trials of the app. In contrast, car manufacturers go to great lengths to ensure that there is a strong likelihood of observing dangerous driving events when evaluating new car safety technologies. For example, scientists working for Mercedes-Benz [15] evaluating safety features (e.g., weaving, drowsy driving) use specialized cars with dual steering wheels where participants of these drowsy driving studies are physically tired prior to the start of the experiment or simulation, hence increasing the probability of dangerous driving events occurring. Such an approach is beyond our means. As mentioned, only collecting data from normal/routine driving experiences is not viable on its own, simply because we can not accumulate enough examples of poor or dangerous driving to fully evaluate CarSafe. Furthermore, it would be irresponsible to run an experiment that promoted dangerous behavior without taking the sort of measures that the car manufacturers take.

For these reasons, we evaluate CarSafe using two distinct experiments and datasets: that is (1) *controlled car maneuvers*, where we safely "stage" dangerous driving events under controlled conditions using six study participants (6 males) – each driver is accompanied by a "co-pilot" who orchestrates the controlled maneuvers only when external conditions on the road and around the car are safe (e.g., where the co-pilot instructs the driver to weave when no other cars are on the road); and (2) *normal daily driving*, which only contains data collected during drivers' (using six study participants - 5 males and 1 female) everyday driving routines (e.g., commuting to and from work, going to the stores, etc.) without any controlled maneuvers or participation of a co-pilot. Note, that while participants in the controlled car maneuvers experiments all conduct the same set of controlled maneuvers they also conduct their normal driving between controlled maneuvers. We argue that this combination of experiments provide the necessary driving events required to evaluate CarSafe while minimizing the risks to participants.

We recruit a total of 12 participants (11 males and 1 female) with ages ranging from 23 to 53 years to collect their driving data under controlled car maneuvers and normal daily driving conditions. There are 6 participants in each of the study groups – 6 in the controlled car maneuvers group and 6 in the normal daily driving group. Participants are comprised of undergraduates, graduates, postdoctoral researchers, and faculty members of Computer Sci-

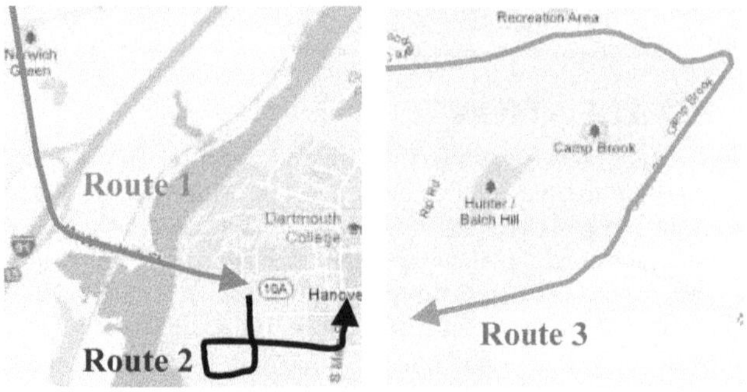

(a) Routes 1 and 2 (b) Route 3

Figure 10: Routes for the controlled car maneuvers dataset.

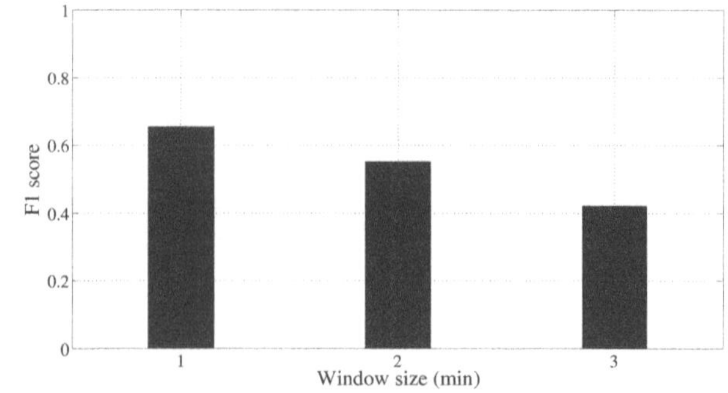

Figure 11: The F1 scores of the drowsy driving detection using different detection window sizes.

ence, Dartmouth College. A wide variety of different cars are used in the study including but not limited to: Dodge Stratus, Volkswagen Tiguan, Honda Civic, Subaru Forester, Subaru Outback, Nissan Camry, Volvo 850 and Mazda Familia. Both datasets combine to provide 300 minutes of driving data and include a total of 164 dangerous driving events. Under normal daily driving conditions, participants tend to drive their cars carefully, and therefore perform few dangerous driving events. Among these events, 121 dangerous driving events come from the controlled dataset and 43 events come from the normal daily driving dataset. The most common dangerous driving event found in the normal daily driving dataset is tailgating, where 22 tailgating events are detected.

Controlled Car Maneuvers Dataset. We recruit six participants to perform the role of drivers during our controlled experiments. All maneuvers are staged in one of three pre-defined routes (see Figure 10) selected for their lack of traffic. We use the participant's own vehicle during experiments, which is instrumented with three smartphones – one runs CarSafe, and two others capture frames from either the front or rear camera as well as capture sensor data (i.e., GPS, accelerometer, compass, gyroscope). After the experiments are completed we manually label dangerous driving events by replaying recorded video and segmenting the sensor and video streams as required. The labeling of such video is laborious, it requires multiple passes by different researchers to verify the ground-truth driving events are correct. Subjects repeat each of the following four maneuvers four times.

Scenario #1 (Careless lane change). Participants perform lane changes without checking their blind spots (i.e., not turning their heads to check the lane is clear). This scenario is performed along route 1 shown in Figure 10(a).

Scenario #2 (Tailgating). Participants drive along route 3 (shown in Figure 10(b)) behind another car driven by a researcher involved in the CarSafe project. The subject then periodically drives close to the car in front.

Scenario #3 (Driving while drowsy and lane weaving). Participants follow route 3, as shown in Figure 10(b). During the first half of the route, we ask drivers to periodically blink for an increasing period of time between 1 and 5 seconds, emulating microsleep. The other maneuver requires the drivers to weave between lanes erratically during the second part of the route.

Scenario #4 (Inattentive driving). While following route 2 (shown Figure 10(a)) participants are asked to periodically look away from the road while driving, as well as during left and right stationary turns.

Daily Driving Dataset. Six participants (5 males, 1 female) who drive daily are recruited to provide completely natural driving data that occurs as part of their everyday routine. Typically, most data comes from the subject's daily commute between home and work. We instrument the participants' cars just as we did for the prior dataset; that is, three smartphones are installed in each car, one running CarSafe and two others constantly capturing data; specifically, from the front- and rear-facing cameras. All videos from the front- and rear-facing cameras are manually labeled with ground-truth events which include all driving maneuvers, both normal and dangerous.

5.2 Overall CarSafe Accuracy

The key metric in CarSafe performance is its ability to detect instances of dangerous driving under real-world conditions. Table 2 provides the precision (*PR*) and recall (*RC*) results across all tested dangerous driving scenarios – including both controlled and normal daily driving groups. We find the mean precision and recall for all scenarios are 83% and 75%, respectively. Among these dangerous conditions, the cases related to detecting drowsy driving have a lower precision of 60%. To understand the cause of these particular false positive cases, we first analyze how the detection window size impacts the accuracy of the drowsy driving detection as follows.

Window Size Tuning – Drowsy Driving Detection. To determine the optimal value of the detection window size (described in §3.3), we develop a computer based simulator that includes the same CarSafe implementation that runs on Android smartphones (due to the portability of Java and by cross-compiling C++). We replay, through the simulator, the continuous image streams from the raw front- and rear-facing cameras captured during our experiments described earlier, along with all collected sensor data. As a result our simulator can test any possible switching behavior.

Table 2: The overall accuracy for detecting dangerous driving conditions. The columns provide: true positives (*TPs*), false positives (*FPs*), ground truth (*GT*), precision (*PR*), and recall (*RC*).

Condition	# of *TPs*	# of *FPs*	# of *GT*	*PR*	*RC*
Drowsy driving (DD)	18	12	25	0.60	0.72
Tailgating (TG)	62	8	78	0.89	0.79
Careless lane change (CLC)	12	2	14	0.86	0.86
Lane weaving (LW)	16	0	22	1.00	0.72
Inattentive driving (ID)	16	4	25	0.80	0.64
Overall	-	-	164	0.83	0.75

Figure 11 shows the F1 score[6] for drowsy driving detection when the window size is set to 1, 2, and 3 minutes. Before analyzing these window sizes, we run a pilot study to determine empirical thresholds of PERCLOS as 0.28, 0.31, 0.42 for detecting drowsy driving conditions using 1, 2, and 3 minute windows, respectively. Then, the F1 scores of different window sizes are obtained by running collected data using the simulator. We set the window size as 1 minute and the threshold for detecting drowsy driving conditions as 0.28, which results in a higher number of false positives. To further confirm the cause of these false positive cases, we manually analyze each false positive case and find that this is the result of poor lighting conditions (e.g., a shadowed or bleached out face) and facial expressions (e.g., smiling, squinting) that confuse the classifier, which are challenging scenarios for many vision-based algorithms. If we exclude these cases precision increases to 75%.

5.3 Driver, Road, and Car Classification Pipeline Benchmarks

We now evaluate each of the three classifiers responsible for monitoring driver, road and car states.

Driver Classification Pipeline. Table 3 reports the precision and recall for face direction events (i.e., *facing.right* (FR) and *facing.left* (FL)). We find for FR precision is 68% and recall is 68%; similarly, for FL the precision and recall are 79% and 88%, respectively. After studying these errors we identified two primary causes: (1) event loss (i.e., missing events) due to camera switching (39%); and, (2) "shallow face turnings", which are difficult to detect (17%). Errors in these face-based events (i.e., FR and FL) can also propagate to the process of recognizing driver inattention (i.e., ID) because these inferences are inputs used to detect this particular dangerous driving event. We find 71% of false negatives that occur when detecting driver inattention are due to errors in face direction inference. This is much larger than the fraction of false negatives caused by camera switching (14%) or due to failing to detect a car turn (14%). However, 66% of false positives (also for driver inattention) are due to undetected car turn events (discussed later) with the remainder caused by camera switching (33%).

As part of future work, we plan to incorporate other information (e.g., detecting the relative locations of the eyes in the detected face region) to filter out false positives when detecting face direction events.

To test the accuracy of eye state recognition within the driver classification pipeline we use a test dataset of front-camera frames. This dataset includes 1780 frames from six individuals. We hand label eye state for each frame. Table 4 provides the confusion matrix for the test dataset using the driver classifier. We find accuracy, precision and the false positive rates are 92%, 93% and 18%, respectively. The majority of false positives are due to challenging lighting conditions (5%) and reflections on driver's glasses (41%). These errors represent the limitations of vision algorithms when dealing with shadows, very bright light and reflections. However, the key use of eye states is for drowsy driver detection which uses an accumulation of prolonged blinks and eye closed events observed over a time window; therefore, the impact of errors in individual frames is diminished.

[6]F1 score is the harmonic mean of precision and recall [27]

Table 3: The overall accuracy for detecting individual low-level events. The rows are: *facing.right* (FR), *facing.left* (FL), *lane.change* (LC), *lane.weaving* (LW), *turn.right* (TR), and *turn.left* (TL).

Event	# of *TPs*	# of *FPs*	# of *GT*	*PR*	*RC*
Part 1: events detected from the driver classifier					
FR	21	10	31	0.68	0.68
FL	23	6	26	0.79	0.88
Part 2: events detected from the road classifier					
LC	21	1	24	0.95	0.88
LW	16	2	22	1.00	0.73
Part 3: events detected from the car classifier					
TR	31	0	35	1.00	0.89
TL	22	2	25	0.92	0.88
Overall	-	-	-	0.89	0.82

Table 4: Confusion matrix for the eye state classifying error.

# of frames		Detected	
		Open	*Closed*
Actual	*Open*	**1266**	41
	Closed	89	**384**

Road Classification Pipeline. Table 3 reports the detection accuracy of lane trajectory events (i.e., *lane.weaving* (LW), and *lane.change* (LC)) for the road classification pipeline. The table shows precision – 95% (LC) and 100% (LW) – is close to or higher than recall – 88% (LC) and 73% (LW). We investigate the cause of low recall for LW events and find this is due to the car being close to the lane markers for very brief periods during lane weaving – especially compared to the more controlled slower trajectory when performing a lane change (LC). To isolate the accuracy of lane marker detection state within the road classification pipeline (ignoring trajectory classification) we compile a test dataset of rear-camera images containing lane markers. This dataset contains 814 frames. For each frame we label (by hand) the position of the lane markers. We then provide these frames as input to the road classification pipeline directly. This experiment finds that lane markers are detected accurately in 85% of frames.

We perform a specific experiment to quantify the accuracy of following distance estimation. First, we instrument a stationary car with CarSafe. Next, another car is driven so it is positioned in front of the first car. We repeat the experiment 5 times with various distances between the two cars ranging between 5 and 35 meters. At each distance, manual measurements provide ground truth which is compared to the CarSafe distance estimate. Figure 12 reports the results from this experiment. We find that the mean error is 2.0 meters. We further find that following distance estimation is not possible beyond 35 meters. This is because the size of the front car in the image frame becomes too small and noisy for the estimation process to function correctly.

Car Classification Pipeline. Table 3 shows the turn detection performance of the car classification pipeline. Recognition of turn events (i.e., *turn.right* (TR) and *turn.left* (TL)) is 100% (precision) and 89% (recall) for TR events and 92% (precision) and 88% (recall) for TL events, respectively. We find all false positives (100%) are caused when driving along curved roads. The majority of false negative misclassifications (69%) are due to noisy GPS samples collected when the car stops for a long time before turning; other false negatives (31%) occur during turns that are $\leq 90^\circ$ (i.e., shallow turns). Our results show many of these errors may be removed by using existing map-matching algorithms [30] combined with the GPS. Table 5 provides a confusion matrix for the lane trajectory events inferred by the car classification pipeline. Mean precision and recall are 84% and 76%, respectively. Although both precision and recall appear to perform well, this component is primarily used to provide bind spot hints that are used to enable pre-emptive

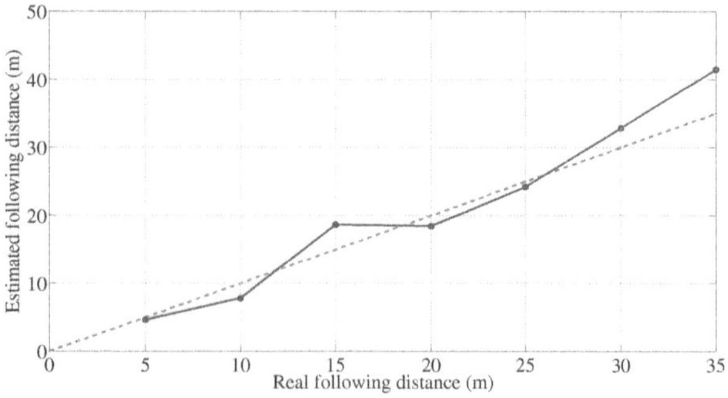

Figure 12: The accuracy of the estimated following distance (from 5 ~ 35 meters). The red dotted line indicates the ground truth of following distance, and the blue real line indicates the estimated following distance.

switching. For example, if the car classification pipeline detects a change in the car trajectory, CarSafe will immediately switch to the rear camera to verify the car trajectory inference.

5.4 Context-driven Camera Switching

In the following experiments, we perform parameter sensitivity analysis for context-driven camera switching and compare its performance to a baseline switching solution.

Methodology. Based on the same simulator described in subsection 5.2, we can test any possible switching behavior used during the experiment.

Baseline Switching Scheme. We compare our adaptive context-aware switching strategy (`carsafe`) to a static strategy (`baseline`) that gives equal time to both cameras in a simple round robing manner, but does not adjust to the environment (e.g., blind spot hints).

Parameter Tuning. Figure 13 shows the precision and recall for different parameter combinations for both `carsafe` and `baseline` switching schemes. During this experiment we perform a conventional grid parameter search with intervals of 1 sec within a parameter range of 1 to 30 seconds, for each parameter. The simulator provides both recall and precision values. Figure 13 shows that `baseline` performance is clustered at the bottom left hand side of the graph, compared to the top right hand side clustering for `carsafe`. In other words, across the majority of parameter combinations `carsafe` outperforms `baseline` – on average this margin is 25% (precision) and 14% (recall). By consulting Figure 13 we find for `carsafe` the optimal mean precision and recall (83% and 75%) respectively, is achieved when $\{F_{min}, B_{min}, F_{add}, B_{add}\}$ are set to 4, 4, 1, and 1 seconds. This combination represents the equilibrium when balancing two competing factors: (1) shorter switching times allow for more frequent updates from both cameras, but a larger fraction of camera time is lost to the overhead of camera switching; and (2), longer switching times miss fewer events on average, but compromise dangerous event detection since the information from one camera is frequently stale (out-of-date). In comparison, we find the optimal `baseline` configuration is 12 seconds.

Switching Strategy Comparison. Figure 14 illustrates the F1 score when detecting each dangerous driving event (viz. DD, ID, CLC, LW, and TG) assuming both the `carsafe` and `baseline` schemes. For this experiment we use the optimal parameter configuration for both techniques, determined by our earlier experiment. On average `carsafe` has a 16% higher F1 score than `baseline`. One of the largest differences is when detecting CLC, which shows `carsafe` provides a 33% increase over `baseline`.

Table 5: Confusion matrix for detecting lane change/weaving through the car classifier. "Lane change/weaving" class represents either lane change or weaving trajectory while the "other" class represents all other trajectories where the car largely remains in the same lane.

# of data segments		Detected	
		Lane change / weaving	*Other*
Actual	*Lane change / weaving*	**190**	30
	Other	109	**1127**

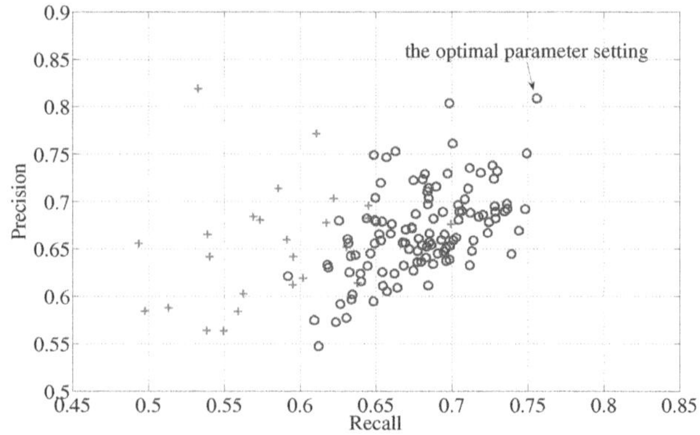

Figure 13: The precision-recall graph of different parameter settings for the `carsafe` and `baseline` schemes. A red cross (blue circle) indicates the precision and recall of the `baseline` (`carsafe`) scheme based on a particular set of parameters.

5.5 Multi-core Computation Planner Benchmarks

A set of experiments is conducted to estimate the average image processing rate of CarSafe. These experiments are carried out on a Samsung Galaxy S3 with an Android 4.2 OS.

Figure 15 presents CarSafe's processing time for both driver- and

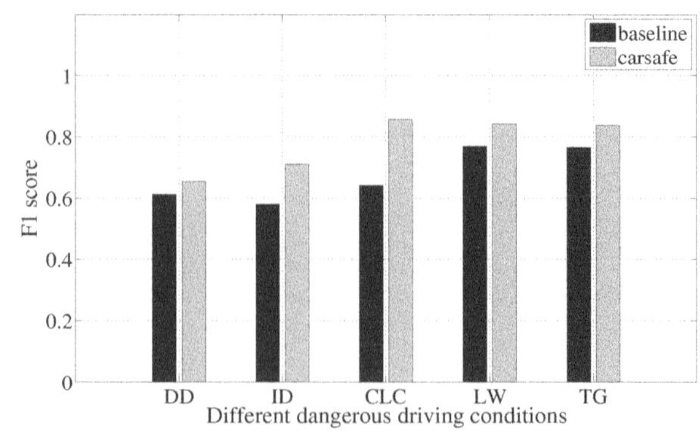

Figure 14: The F1 scores for detecting dangerous driving conditions using `baseline` (dark-color) and `carsafe` (bright-color) schemes.

road-based events. In CarSafe, multiple threads are dispatched in the multi-core computation planner component to boost the image processing performance. The frame rate of CarSafe image processing is boosted from 4.95 (running one thread) to 9.87 (running four concurrent threads) fps for the driver classification pipeline, and from 3.82 (running one thread) to 10.86 (running four concurrent threads) fps for the road classification pipeline. The standard deviation of the frame processing time is 7.88 (7.71) seconds for the driver (road) classification pipeline, which helps reduce the jitter in the frame processing latency. The figure shows that the processing time will not decrease when there are more than 4 threads concurrently processing. In order to boost the frame rate of image processing while maintaining an overall short waiting time, CarSafe concurrently maintains four threads within the multi-core computation planner.

6. RELATED WORK

Recognizing driving behavior (i.e., driver drowsiness, lane departure, and following distance) using fixed vehicle-mounted devices is an active area of research. In the case of drowsy driving, Bhowmick *et al.* [26] identifies driver drowsiness by detecting eyes and classifying eye states (viz. open and closed states) using an infra-red camera. By illuminating facial landmarks the nose and eyes are easily recognized, and by finding the eye shape the state of the eye can be classified. Vural *et al.* [42] predicts sleep episodes by monitoring facial actions (e.g., blinking, and yawning) using cameras and head movement – here the driver wears a head-mounted accelerometer. Aly [24] presents a real-time lane marker detector, which relies on a vehicle-mounted camera, bird's-eye view transformation and a gaussian filter. After transforming vehicle-mounted camera images to a bird's-eye view through inverse perspective transformation, the system filters the images via a 2D selective-orientation gaussian filter and thresholds the filtered images by zeroing all values below a set threshold. Finally, the system fits lines to the thresholded images, that identify lane markers, by using a RANSAC algorithm. Stein *et al.* [40] measures the following distance using a monocular camera mounted near the rear-view mirror. They design a vision-based Adaptive Cruise Control (ACC) system to determine the following distance by transforming the measured distances, i.e., the distances between the driving and preceding cars in the camera coordinate system, to real following distances in the world coordinate system based on a simple pinhole model. However, none of these examples of existing studies into driver behavior detection consider the limitations and challenges of a smartphone-based implementation. In developing CarSafe, we re-examine this family of techniques in light of real-world phone-in-car scenarios and investigate how they can be adapted to run on multi-core smartphones.

By integrating powerful sensors into top-end cars (e.g., cameras, radar, and ultrasonic sensors), manufacturers are bringing similar forms of driver behavior monitoring to the consumer market. These systems [15, 23, 6] warn the driver using acoustic (e.g., playing a voice recording [6]), tactile (e.g., seat and steering wheel vibration [23]) and visual (e.g., a blinking coffee-cup icon on the dashboard [15]) alerts when dangerous driving conditions are detected. Although the cost of safety technology is dropping, most safety technologies are not available in entry-level vehicles; it will be a decade before the vast majority of cars on the road today have these safety features built-in. In contrast, smartphone solutions such as CarSafe can be used in all cars (new or old) and represent a cheap and disruptive technology. Several commercial smartphone apps [11, 4, 13] are emerging. iOnRoad [11] and Augmented Driving [4] for example focus on monitoring the following distance using the back camera and LDWS [13] offers warning sounds when the vehicle departs a lane marker. To the best of our knowledge, none of these apps detect dangerous driving behavior using the front- and rear-facing cameras – they typically are only watching conditions on the road.

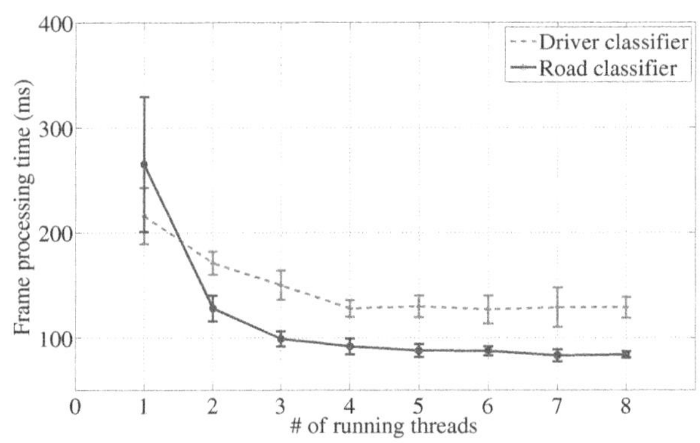

Figure 15: The frame processing time and time variance of the driver and road classifiers when replicating 1 ~ 8 running threads.

7. CONCLUSION

This paper describes the design, implementation and evaluation of CarSafe and presents results from a small-scale deployment of the app in the wild. The performance of the overall system looks very promising given the real challenges of different drivers, context and road conditions. Our future plans are to improve the current prototype with the goals of advancing the UI design (which was not a focus of this paper) in addition to gaining further improvements in the real-time performance of the CarSafe classification pipelines. We also plan to release CarSafe on Google Play [2] to get further input from the broader app user community. Finally, we plan to develop a set of open APIs enabling full access to the front and rear cameras and will start by studying more experimental open source platforms, such as, Tizen [22]. Our goal is to stimulate interest in dual camera sensing apps to encourage major platform vendors to solve this problem.

8. REFERENCES

[1] Active Shape Model. `http://code.google.com/p/asmlib-opencv/`.

[2] Android Apps on Google Play. `https://play.google.com/store`.

[3] Android Open Source Project. `http://source.android.com`.

[4] Augmented Driving. `https://itunes.apple.com/tw/app/augmented-driving/id366841514?mt=8`.

[5] BioID Face Database. `http://www.bioid.com/`.

[6] Bosch Debuts Low-Cost Drowsy Driver Alert System. `http://editorial.autos.msn.com/blogs/autosblogpost.aspx?post=caac1a6c-af18-43ae-8fda-244305f449ec`.

[7] Breakthrough Research on Real-World Driver Behavior Released. `http://www.nhtsa.gov/Driving+Safety/Distracted+Driving/Breakthrough+Research+on+Real-World+Driver+Behavior+Released`.

[8] Driver's Handbook - Lane change. http://www.mto.gov.on.ca/english/dandv/driver/handbook/section6.5.0.shtml.

[9] Face Detection for Windows Phone 7. http://facedetectwp7.codeplex.com/.

[10] FaceDetect - OpenCV. http://opencv.willowgarage.com/wiki/FaceDetection.

[11] iOnRoad. http://www.ionroad.com/.

[12] iOS 5 Face Detection with Core Image. http://www.bobmccune.com/2012/03/22/ios-5-face-detection-with-core-image/.

[13] LDWS 2.1. http://www.androidzoom.com/android_applications/tools/ldws-21_ljrs.html.

[14] Linux Media Infrastructure API. http://linuxtv.org/downloads/v4l-dvb-apis.

[15] No Doze: Mercedes E-Class Alerts Drowsy Drivers. http://www.autoweek.com/article/20081224/free/812249991.

[16] NYS DMV - Driver's Manual - Chapter 8: Defensive Driving. http://dmv.ny.gov/dmanual/chapter08-manual.htm.

[17] OMAP™ Processors - OMAP™ 4 Processors - OMAP4460. http://www.ti.com/product/omap4460.

[18] OsmAnd (OSM Automated Navigation Directions) - Navigation and Routing based on Open Street Maps for Android Devices. http://osmand.net/.

[19] Samsung Galaxy S4 - Captuers All The Fun. http://www.samsung.com/global/microsite/galaxys4/fun.html.

[20] Street View – Google Maps. www.google.com/streetview.

[21] The MUCT Face Database. http://www.milbo.org/muct/.

[22] Tizen: An Open Source, Standards-based Software Platform. https://tizen.org/.

[23] Volvo's Work within Active Safety. http://www.crp.pt/docs/A18S104-6_3_MariaFlink.pdf.

[24] M. Aly. Real Time Detection of Lane Markers in Urban Streets. In *IEEE IV '08*, pages 7–12, 2008.

[25] H. Bay, A. Ess, T. Tuytelaars, and L. Van Gool. Speeded-Up Robust Features (SURF). *Comput. Vis. Image Underst.*, 110(3):346–359, June 2008.

[26] B. Bhowmick and K. Chidanand Kumar. Detection and Classification of Eye State in IR Camera for Driver Drowsiness Identification. In *IEEE ICSIPA '09*, pages 340–345, 2009.

[27] C. M. Bishop. *Pattern Recognition and Machine Learning (Information Science and Statistics)*. Springer-Verlag New York, Inc., Secaucus, NJ, USA, 2006.

[28] C. J. C. Burges. A Tutorial on Support Vector Machines for Pattern Recognition. *Data Min. Knowl. Discov.*, 2(2):121–167, June 1998.

[29] J. Canny. A Computational Approach to Edge Detection. *IEEE Trans. Pattern Anal. Mach. Intell.*, 8(6):679–698, June 1986.

[30] Y.-Y. Chiang and C. A. Knoblock. Automatic Extraction of Road Intersection Position, Connectivity, and Orientations from Raster Maps. In *ACM GIS '08*, pages 22:1–22:10, 2008.

[31] P. Finnegan and P. Green. The Time to Change Lanes: A Literature Review. Technical Report IVHS-TR-90-13, National Technical Information Service, Sep. 1990.

[32] D. A. Forsyth and J. Ponce. *Computer Vision: A Modern Approach*. Prentice Hall Professional Technical Reference, 2002.

[33] Y. Freund, R. Schapire, and N. Abe. A Short Introduction to Boosting. *Journal-Japanese Society For Artificial Intelligence*, 14(5):771–780, 1999.

[34] R. Knipling. PERCLOS, A Valid Psychophysiological Measure of Alertness as Assessed by Psychomotor Vigilance. Technical Report FHWA-MCRT-98-006, Federal Highway Administration, Office of Motor Carrier Research and Standards, October 1998.

[35] C. C. Liu, S. G. Hosking, and M. G. Lenne. Predicting Driver Drowsiness using Vehicle Measures: Recent Insights and Future Challenges. *Journal of Safety Research*, 40(4):239–245, 2009.

[36] H. Lu, J. Yang, Z. Liu, N. D. Lane, T. Choudhury, and A. T. Campbell. The Jigsaw Continuous Sensing Engine for Mobile Phone Applications. In *ACM Sensys '10*, pages 71–84, 2010.

[37] NHTSA's National Center for Statistics and Analysis. Distracted Driving 2010. Technical Report DOT-HS-811-650, National Highway Traffic Safety Administration, Sep. 2012.

[38] C. Papageorgiou and T. Poggio. A Trainable Object Detection System: Car Detection in Static Images. Technical Report 1673, October 1999.

[39] D. D. Salvucci and A. Liu. The Time Course of a Lane Change: Driver Control and Eye-movement Behavior. *Transportation Research Part F: Traffic Psychology and Behaviour*, 5(2):123–132, 2002.

[40] G. P. Stein, O. Mano, and A. Shashua. Vision-based ACC with a Single Camera: Bounds on Range and Range Rate Accuracy. In *IEEE IV '03*, pages 120–125, 2003.

[41] P. Viola and M. Jones. Rapid Object Detection using a Boosted Cascade of Simple Features. In *IEEE CVPR '01*, volume 1, pages I–511 – I–518 vol.1, 2001.

[42] E. Vural, M. Cetin, A. Ercil, G. Littlewort, M. Bartlett, and J. Movellan. Drowsy driver detection through facial movement analysis. In *HCI '07*, pages 6–18, 2007.

[43] T. Wang, G. Cardone, A. Corradi, L. Torresani, and A. T. Campbell. WalkSafe: A Pedestrian Safety App for Mobile Phone Users who Walk and Talk while Crossing Roads. In *ACM HotMobile '12*, pages 5:1–5:6, 2012.

[44] W. W. Wierwille, S. S. Wreggit, C. L. Kirn, L. A. Ellsworth, and R. J. Fairbanks. Research on Vehicle-Based Driver Status/Performance Monitoring: Development, Validation, and Refinement of Algorithms for Detection of Driver Drowsiness. Technical Report DOT-HS-808-247, National Highway Traffic Safety Administration, 1994.

CrowdAtlas: Self-Updating Maps for Cloud and Personal Use

Yin Wang
HP Labs, Palo Alto
yin.wang@hp.com

Xuemei Liu*
Baidu Inc., Shanghai
liuxuemei01@baidu.com

Hong Wei
Shanghai Jiao Tong University
keith.collens@sjtu.edu.cn

George Forman
HP Labs, Palo Alto
george.forman@hp.com

Chao Chen
Shanghai Jiao Tong University
chaochen@sjtu.edu.cn

Yanmin Zhu
Shanghai Jiao Tong University
yzhu@sjtu.edu.cn

ABSTRACT

The inaccuracy of manually created digital road maps is a persistent problem, despite their high economic value. We present CrowdAtlas, which automates map update based on people's travels, either individually or crowdsourced. Its mobile navigation app detects significant portions of GPS traces that do not conform to the existing map, as determined by state-of-the-art Viterbi map matching. When there is sufficient evidence collected, map inference algorithms can automatically update the map. The CrowdAtlas server aggregates exceptional traces from users with the navigation app as well as from other, large-scale data sources. From these it automatically generates high quality map updates, which can be propagated to its navigation app and other interested applications. Using CrowdAtlas app, we mapped out a 4.5 km^2 street block in Shanghai in less than half an hour and built a walking/cycling map of the SJTU campus. Using taxi traces collected from Beijing, we contributed 61 km of missing roads to OpenStreetMap, the first set of completely computer-generated roads for this large, open-source map community.

Categories and Subject Descriptors

C.2.4 [**Distributed Systems**]: Distributed applications; H.2.8 [**Database Management**]: Database Applications—*Data mining; Spatial databases and GIS*; H.4 [**Information Systems Applications**]: Miscellaneous; I.5.4 [**Pattern Recognition**]: Applications

Keywords

mobile systems; spatial data mining; GPS; map matching; map inference; road maps

*The work was performed during an internship at HP Labs.

MobiSys'13, June 25-28, 2013, Taipei, Taiwan

1. INTRODUCTION

Year 2012 marks the 500th anniversary of cartographer Gerardus Mercator's birth, who introduced the term "atlas" for maps and invented the Mercator projection widely used today. Nautical charts and terrain maps have long been precisely plotted with modern cartography technologies. However, digital road maps remain surprisingly inaccurate and incomplete. Both keynote talks of the recent ACM GIS conference mentioned persistent map accuracy problems with Google, Apple, etc., and emphasized auto map correction as one of the top open problems [35, 39]. Since people increasingly rely on navigation using smart phones for everyday activities, inaccurate maps can have substantial economic consequences, as evidenced by the recent iOS map incident [19]. A British insurance survey found 26% of drivers had been directed by their GPS to go through no-entry signs or prohibited areas [33], and the news periodically reports car accidents caused by or related to digital maps [29,52,54].

The U.S. maps of Google, Waze, and OpenStreetMap all stem from the TIGER products of the U.S. Census Bureau, which have various quality issues such as road disconnections and misalignments [1, 36, 56]. In addition to correcting existing maps, updating them promptly and consistently can be more challenging. TomTom estimates that up to 15% of roads change each year in some way [5]. The map situation is worse in developing countries where there is more new construction and roads more often degrade beyond use. We show later that commercial maps of central Shanghai have missing roads and incorrect road types. While inaccurate maps rarely create problems for daily commuting, they cause plenty of frustration for travelers in unfamiliar areas, especially in foreign countries because of the additional language barrier.

In addition to heavy demand for updating road maps, there are also growing needs for additional types of maps for non-motorist traffic. Fueled by the green transportation movement, many cities are ramping up the rate of bike path development [25]. Unfortunately, most cycling maps rely on crowdsourcing and are far from complete [22]. In addition, personalized maps are increasingly popular. There are many applications and online services that customize maps to include personal points of interest. Customized road networks can help navigate private or personal routes not on existing maps, e.g., off-road driving or cycling, and backcountry hiking or skiing.

Existing commercial and public maps are created manually, which is costly, error-prone, and cannot keep up with the aggregate rate of change. For example, NAVTEQ (now Nokia) employs more than 7,000 employees worldwide in its Location Content team to update its maps [2]. Google, TomTom, and Waze also encourage users to submit map edits online, pending manual review by their teams of content editors. The largest crowdsourced mapping project is OpenStreetMap (OSM), which has more than 600,000 registered contributors. However, due to the skills and effort needed for map creation, user-contributed maps on OSM are limited in detail, freshness and accuracy. For example, its street-level maps in China are currently limited to a few tourist locations and have various quality issues, as we will illustrate. There is no automated map update system.

Automated road inference using GPS probes has gained much attention recently [12,15,17,20,23,32], partly because large-scale GPS traces are increasingly abundant from systems that track user locations, such as fleet management, telematics systems, and online navigation apps [9,10,37,55]. Most existing map inference methods rely on low-noise, densely-sampled, and uniformly distributed GPS traces. With high-noise, sparsely-sampled, and highly-disparate data, calculating road geometry, inferring road connectivity, and gaining high map coverage all become very challenging. A few recent studies try to address some of the challenges but not all of them simultaneously [12, 32]. In addition, tunnels, plane-separated roads, and road metadata cannot be inferred from longitude/latitude data alone. By contrast, completing and updating a reasonably accurate base map is much more practical than generating a new map from scratch. For example, some work has demonstrated refining the road geometry in a base map using densely sampled GPS traces [44,45].

Leveraging the latest GPS map inferencing techniques, we built CrowdAtlas, a system that automatically and continuously rectifies existing maps using data collected from mobile probes. CrowdAtlas employs a *Hidden Markov Model* (HMM)-based *map matching* algorithm [40,56] to detect the discrepancies between GPS samples and roads, and applies a clustering-based map inferencing algorithm [32] to the discrepant traces to update maps. CrowdAtlas can utilize large-scale GPS data from existing location tracking systems and provide reciprocal benefits back to such systems. We also built CrowdAtlas app, a *map-inaccuracy*-aware navigation app, for users without access to these systems or even without internet connection, and for users who want to create and use customized maps.

We make the following contributions.

- An automatic map update system that consists of a server and/or a navigation app. The server attains coverage and accuracy by leveraging large-scale, noisy GPS streams from existing location-tracking systems. The app can add new roads in a standalone mode.

- The novel combination of map inference with navigation map matching for practical, highly-accurate, and real-time map update, including heavy customization of our prior state-of-the-art map inference and map matching algorithms.

- Implementation and evaluation of CrowdAtlas, completing roads in a 4.5 km^2 street block in the Shanghai Pudong district, creating a cycling/walking campus map of Shanghai Jiao Tong University, and contributing 61 km of roads for the Beijing map on OSM. The latter is based on 8 days of GPS data from 70 taxis, obtained from a fleet management system. To the best of our knowledge, this is the first set of computer-generated roads uploaded to OSM. We make our datasets available for public use [1].

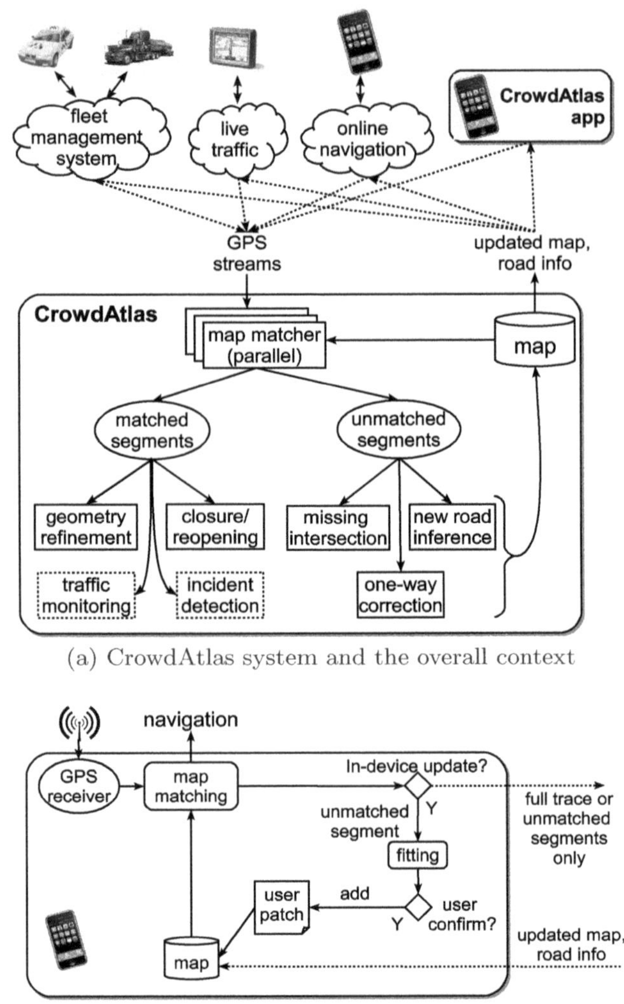

(a) CrowdAtlas system and the overall context

(b) CrowdAtlas navigation app

Figure 1: CrowdAtlas architecture

Section 2 gives an architectural description of CrowdAtlas. Sections 3 and 4 describe the algorithms for map matching and map updates, respectively, and Section 5 gives implementation details. Section 6 contains evaluations for standalone and server updates. Section 7 discusses related work, and Section 8 concludes.

2. OVERVIEW

We discuss the CrowdAtlas server and its mobile navigation app in turn.

2.1 CrowdAtlas Service

Figure 1a shows the overall system. At a high level, CrowdAtlas consumes GPS streams from various sources and offers map services with real-time updates. The idea is like *crowdsourcing*; however, compared with other crowdsourced map services, updates can be automated without requiring skilled users or user attention. Because of this automation, it can also leverage a variety of large-scale GPS trace sources from existing services or applications that do location tracking, e.g., fleet management systems for service or delivery [13, 55], live traffic estimation such as by TomTom or Garmin, and online navigation such as by Apple or Google maps.

CrowdAtlas consists of a series of stream processing tasks. First, the GPS traces go through a *map matching* procedure using the current map data. This is a common procedure used in location tracking and navigation, which matches a series of GPS coordinates to the most likely passable route on the given map. We customized a reliable map matching algorithm [40, 56] so it can recognize map inaccuracy during the matching process, and thereby we separate matched and unmatched trace segments. Map matching is the most time-consuming step. Fortunately, it can be run independently for different traces. CrowdAtlas parallelizes map matching using multithreading for city- or state-scale map update, or distributed computing for global-scale map update. After map matching, CrowdAtlas infers new roads from unmatched segments, using a streaming variant of our prior map inference algorithm [32]. We also extend this algorithm to infer other missing map features, including intersections, new turn possibilities, and one-way road directions and corrections. In addition to inferring new map features, CrowdAtlas uses the matched segments to refine road geometry and to detect road closures and reopenings. The scalable and reliable map matcher also enables other GPS-based analysis tasks, such as traffic monitoring [27, 59] and incident detection [49]. For example, each GPS sample typically includes the travel speed measurement, or we can estimate it from the time interval and the map matched path between consecutive samples. The median speed of samples matched to a road segment is the current travel speed of the road. While CrowdAtlas can provide these additional information services to users, we focus on inference of missing roads in this paper, which is the most challenging task among all updates CrowdAtlas provides.

Figure 2 illustrates the overall stream processing flow for new road inference on the server. Figure 2a shows 8 days of data from 70 taxis in Beijing, with a sampling interval of 10 seconds. This area has few high-rise buildings, but noise still exists. After map matching, Figure 2b shows unmatched sub-traces (red) with a few matched samples (black) before and after. (The short green line segments in the figure connect matched samples to their road locations.) The unmatched sub-traces are then aggregated with a stream clustering algorithm. Once a cluster exceeds a support threshold, CrowdAtlas invokes a *polygonal principal curve* algorithm [31] to extract the road centerline from the cluster. With one week of data and a threshold of four sub-traces, there are three clusters in the area, shown with distinct colors in Figure 2c, and their three inferred roads are shown in Figure 2d, overlaid on a Bing aerial image. Judging from the image, these line segments are well aligned with the centerlines of the actual roads. The server can infer other missing roads in the area as more unmatched GPS traces accumulate over time. One could lower the support threshold to achieve greater recall of missing roads, but this

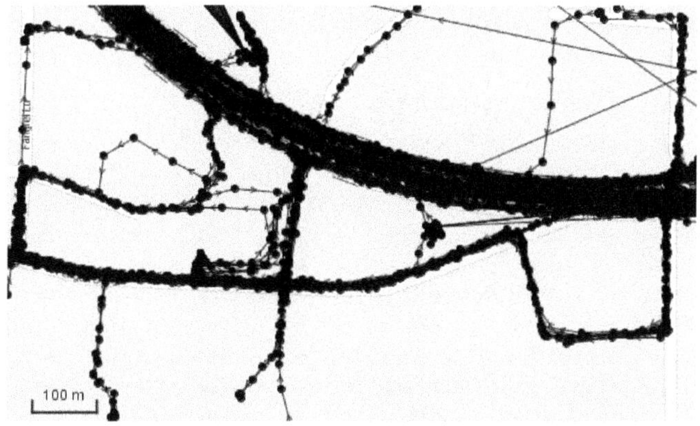

(a) Input GPS traces (70 taxis in Beijing, 8 days)

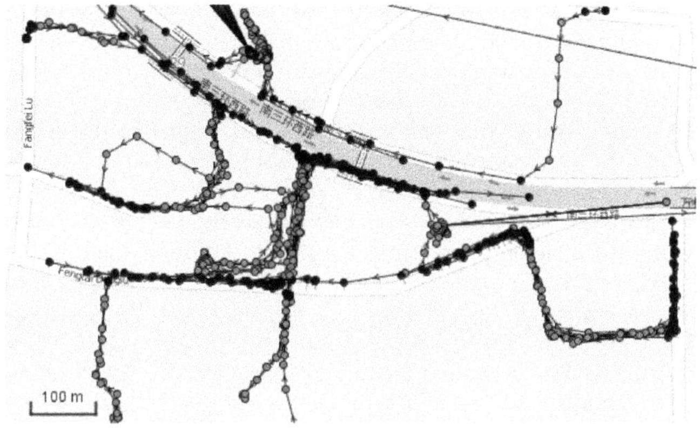

(b) Extracting unmatched segments (red) after map matching

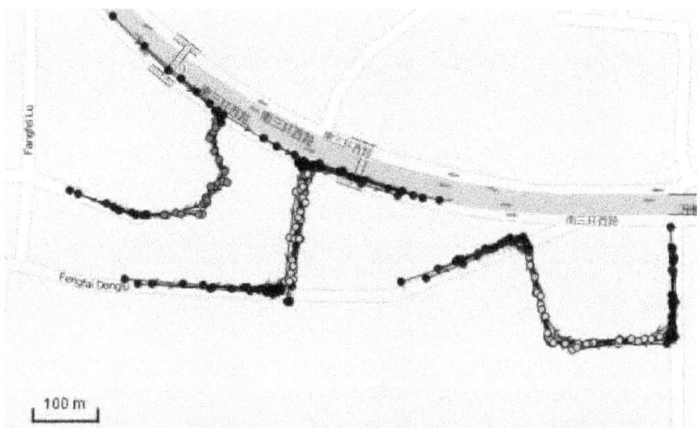

(c) Extracting clusters with sufficient unmatched segments

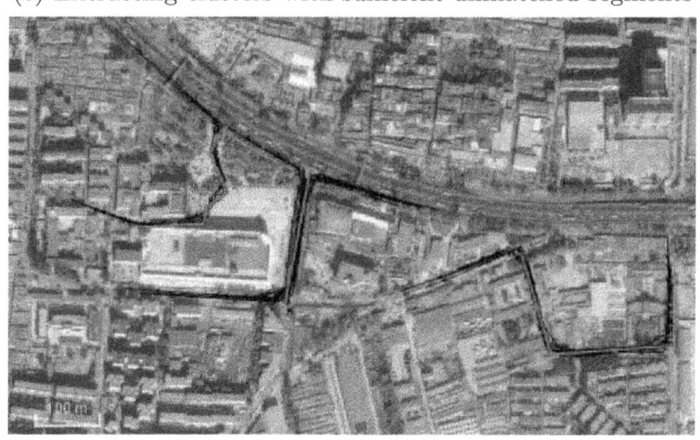

(d) Fitting new roads to clusters (red, arrows for one-way)

Figure 2: Stream processing flow on CrowdAtlas server

increases the possibility of inferring roads from noise and leads to greater position error.

2.2 CrowdAtlas App

CrowdAtlas can leverage existing GPS data from location tracking systems and services. In addition, we built our own navigation app that can either upload GPS traces to the server and receive aggregated map updates, or else update in-device maps based on personal travel habits using our software in a standalone mode. The app has several key benefits over other navigation apps or services that could use CrowdAtlas as a map provider. First, it can build personalized maps for an individual, e.g., trail, cycling, or off-road driving maps. Second, its navigation is aware of map-inaccuracy and is optimized for the purpose of map update. It dynamically adjusts the sampling rate transmitted to the server to reduce the data volume for known roads, while providing dense sampling for unmatched traces. Communication cost is of great economic concern to location tracking systems, and many use low sampling rates for this reason [55], which impair map update efficiency and accuracy. Using CrowdAtlas app guarantees high-quality map updates while incurring negligible extra communication—proportional to the number of missing roads on the map, not the size of the fleet. This provides dense sampling only where the server needs it, which is far better for map update than sending all traces at a uniformly low sampling rate. The user can also opt to send only unmatched segments to the server, reducing privacy exposure somewhat but losing the opportunity to correct existing roads. Standalone operation further avoids data upload and internet connection altogether.

Figure 1b shows the architecture of the navigation app. From the user's perspective, it can be viewed as a navigation system integrated with a mini CrowdAtlas server for standalone use. It has an interactive mode of operation to enable users to map out an area or a road system themselves. The clustering step is omitted, so that one need not retrace a road multiple times to generate sufficient data. Instead, it fits a road right away after detecting an unmatched subtrace and asks for user confirmation. Standalone updates can only add new roads and other map features; it would be risky to reposition roads based on a single user's trace. Updating known roads is only enabled on the server, as it should require evidence from multiple users to justify.

3. MAP MATCHING

We first introduce the basics of the Viterbi map matching algorithm and then discuss our customization for the purpose of map update.

3.1 Background

Almost all map matching algorithms consist of two steps: i) finding a set of candidate road match locations within the error radius of a sample, and ii) selecting a sequence of candidates to form the matched path maximizing some criterion. Various algorithms differ in the second step on the selection criteria, which can be largely divided into two groups: incremental methods [38, 53, 57], where the algorithm picks the current best candidate based on previous observations only, and global methods [34, 40, 51], where the algorithm picks a whole sequence at once, typically using Viterbi dynamic programming. In general, real-time

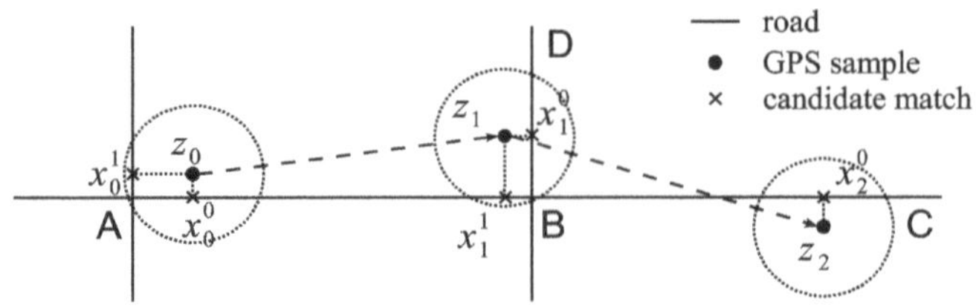

Figure 3: Map matching illustration

(online) map matching requires incremental algorithms, while global algorithms are more accurate for offline map matching.

Figure 3 shows an example. GPS samples z_0, z_1, and z_2 have candidate sets $\{x_0^0, x_0^1\}$, $\{x_1^0, x_1^1\}$, and $\{x_2^0\}$ in their error circles, respectively. Upon observing z_1, the most likely drive path is ABD since they are closest to the samples. However, after observing z_2, the most likely path should be ABC.

In our prior comparative study [56], global algorithms based on *Hidden Markov Models* (HMM) are the most accurate for offline map matching. In particular, the best performers are the HMMs whose transition probability incorporates the length of the shortest path between two consecutive candidates [34,40]. These models are especially robust against long sampling intervals, even up to a minute between samples.

The CrowdAtlas server requires only offline map matching. We use the HMM-based Viterbi dynamic programming algorithm described in [56], which improves upon [40] and is the most accurate in our prior comparative study. In a nutshell, taking a sequence of GPS samples as input, the Viterbi algorithm calculates the probabilities for all candidate matches of each sample in a forward loop. Next, starting from the candidate with the maximum probability of the last sample, a backward loop recovers the most likely path taken by the host generating the GPS sequence. CrowdAtlas server breaks incoming GPS streams by time windows and matches the streams section by section. By contrast, the CrowdAtlas navigation app requires real-time map matching. In this case, we simply let Viterbi output the candidate match with the highest probability immediately during the forward loop. The result is identical to a *Bayes filter* applied to the same HMM formulation. Map matching using a Bayes filter applied to a different HMM formulation has been proposed previously [38]. After a mismatch between the map and the GPS is detected, as discussed in the next subsection, the CrowdAtlas app invokes the backward loop of the Viterbi algorithm to more accurately recover the unmatched segment. For this purpose, it keeps a window of previous observations in case it needs to go back for a mismatch.

3.2 Extracting Unmatched Segments

The HMM-based map matching algorithm discussed in the previous subsection can detect two types of mismatches between GPS traces and road maps. Type I mismatch is when a sample's error radius does not intersect any road. Type II mismatch is when two consecutive matches are disconnected on the existing map or the shortest path between them is too long to be traversed by the host within the sampling interval. In CrowdAtlas we set the maximum travel speed to 180 km/h; therefore, any consecutive samples matched to locations beyond $50t$ meters from each other are considered a mismatch, where t is the sampling interval.

GPS signals are inherently noisy. In addition, roads vary in width, and maps can be misaligned. Ideally, we want to match GPS samples to the right roads even in these cases, but not miss any unmatched segments. To achieve these two opposing goals, we develop a novel technique of applying different error radius thresholds to matched and unmatched segments. The error radius for candidate search in the map matching algorithm is 50 m, which doubles the maximum error in a Seattle dataset [56] and is used by other map matching algorithms [40]. On the other hand, when mismatches are detected, we extend the mismatched segment both ways in a postprocessing step until the samples are within 15 m of roads, a threshold needed to cover road width based on our visual inspection as well as empirical evaluation in Section 6.

Applying different error radii to matched and unmatched segments separately, CrowdAtlas can accurately differentiate new roads from noise. On one hand, noisy GPS samples within 50 m of the road are always matched, which well covers Gaussian GPS noise and map misalignment problems. On the other hand, a new road is not missed as long as a section of it is more than 50 m away from existing roads (because GPS samples generated from that section are Type I mismatches, and we extend them to cover the rest of the new road until within 15 m of the connecting roads). Even if the entire new road is within 50 m of existing roads, there is often a Type II mismatch detected, because connecting the start and end locations using existing roads would be very circuitous.

In our experimental study, CrowdAtlas never missed any new road traveled by the probe, but there are outlier samples and traces well beyond 50 m to the path taken, e.g., the long line segments in Figure 2a. Compared to normal GPS noise or noise due to misaligned maps, these outliers are very sparse and never formed a cluster.

3.3 Map Matching in the CrowdAtlas App

As discussed in Section 3.1, CrowdAtlas app employs the same Viterbi algorithm for map matching and unmatched segment extraction, but it also outputs the most likely candidate immediately after each observation for navigation.

Another important feature we implement in CrowdAtlas app is dynamic sampling, which applies a high sampling rate to unmatched segments and a low sampling rate to matched ones. Without sacrificing map update efficiency and accuracy, dynamic rates significantly reduce the data communicated over the network, saving both energy and communication fees. The latter is a crucial concern for many location tracking services, which typically sample at one minute or longer just to save cost [55]. The extra cost CrowdAtlas incurs is proportional to the number of new roads generated (modulo noisy samples) and is not affected by fleet size or drive distance if server updates propagate frequently.

We apply dynamic rates only to the data transmitted to the CrowdAtlas server. For the purpose of navigation, low sampling rates would degrade the user experience and would not save energy since existing mobile phones do not turn off their GPS units for short duty cycles [42,51]. However, many people use smart phones for navigation already. In this case, the additional power needed is for new road inference in standalone mode or data transmission in server mode. The former is negligible since the inference typically takes less than half a second. The latter is also immaterial because dynamic sampling significantly reduces the data to be transmitted, eliminating the bulk of the points on existing roads.

Most GPS-equipped phones provide the accuracy estimate of the sample, e.g., `getAccuracy()` in Android returns the standard deviation of the GPS measurement in the current location, assuming Gaussian noise. We use this information to better adjust the error radius dynamically. More specifically, instead of using two fixed error radii as in the server, our app sets the radius to be twice the standard deviation returned by `getAccuracy()`, with a lower bound of 15 m to cover road width, the same used in the server. If twice of the standard deviation is beyond 50 m, we simply discard the sample since it is likely noise. This dynamic error radius feature is crucial for detecting walking/cycling trails, which often closely parallel drive roads.

4. MAP UPDATE

We describe new road inference, other map updates, and challenges and limitations of CrowdAtlas.

4.1 New Road Inference

CrowdAtlas infers new roads using our prior clustering-based map inference algorithm, which has been shown to achieve good road coverage even for noisy and sparse data [32]. In this algorithm, each cluster contains line segments of consecutive samples that are likely generated from one road, judged by their location proximity and direction similarity. The road centerline is extracted from each cluster using B-spline fitting. We customize this algorithm for the goal of map update rather than new map inference, described below.

Trace clustering: In CrowdAtlas, the element in each cluster is an entire unmatched segment, i.e., a sequence of unmatched samples, rather than a line segment of a consecutive pair. The distance between two unmatched segments is the *Hausdorff distance* of the two trajectories, i.e., the longest distance between a sample of one segment and the trajectory of the other. Clustering whole unmatched segments filters out noise effectively, since multiple traces have to follow the same trajectory to form clusters, which does not happen for erratic, noisy samples. In our prior work, as well as other popular *Kernel Density Estimation* (KDE) based approaches, portions of noisy traces sometimes locate together and lead to false positive roads [12,32]. Hausdorff distance considers only the longest distance between two traces, which is rather aggressive in noise filtering. A softer distance measurement that considers percentile or probability may include traces with a few noisy samples in the cluster, in which case we would need more robust centerline fitting algorithms. This is a typical tradeoff between road coverage and precision. We prefer the latter for the purpose of automated road update. We apply a streaming variant of the *single linkage clustering* algorithm [48]. Each newly extracted unmatched segment is compared with existing segments to calculate the Hausdorff distance. For those segments within a distance threshold to the new one, their respective clusters are merged and augmented with the new segment.

Centerline fitting: CrowdAtlas fits a road to a cluster once its number of traces exceeds a support threshold. We apply a *polygonal principal curve* algorithm to fit the set of samples in the cluster [31], which generates a polyline to minimize its mean square error to the samples. In our experiments using real taxi traces from Beijing, this algorithm is more accurate and more compatible with existing maps than alternative methods such as B-spline fitting [45] and KDE [12, 20]. B-spline fitting models roads by smooth polynomial functions, which is often overly smooth for straight roads or sharp turns. Even for curved freeways, B-spline fitting is overkill since almost all digital maps approximate curves by polygonal lines, and CrowdAtlas must be compatible with these maps in order to update them. KDE is good at approximating road centerlines from samples with Gaussian noise. However, it requires sufficient samples evenly distributed over the road, which requires substantially more data for the same degree of road coverage [32]. After polyline fitting, we apply the Douglas-Peucker algorithm [21] that is widely used in *cartographic generalization* and other map inference work [12] to remove unnecessary intermediate nodes.

Connection: After fitting a centerline to a cluster, the connectivity between the new road and existing ones is determined by the matched samples immediately before and after the unmatched segments in the cluster. These samples indicate which roads the new road connects to, called *anchor roads*, but not the exact intersection location unless the sampling rate is sufficiently high, e.g., 1 Hz. Instead of using the matched locations of these samples, we find the intersection via a set of rules. First, if there is already an intersection near the end node of the new road, CrowdAtlas connects the new road to this existing intersection. If there is no intersection nearby, CrowdAtlas extends the last line segment of the new road until it intersects with the nearest anchor road. We use the nearest anchor road because there can be multiple anchor roads at low sampling rates, e.g., the trace completely skips a short road after the unmatched segment. However, it is also common that a new road connects to a major road represented by two one-way roads of opposite directions on map. Therefore, if there is an anchor road parallel to the nearest one, CrowdAtlas further extends the last line segment to intersect the parallel road of opposite direction.

Iteration: Once a new road is generated and added to the map, future GPS traces following the road will be matched and no new unmatched segment will be extracted. However, existing unmatched segments in other clusters may partially overlap with the new road. We rematch and re-cluster these segments for iteratively more road inference. Figure 4 shows an example, where a whole block of roads is missing from OSM in an urban canyon area. The cluster corresponding to Road 1 first exceeds the support threshold of three and the road is added. Unmatched segments overlapping Road 1 are rematched and re-clustered. Road 2 is generated next. Upon its inference, Road 3 is immediately added after rematching and re-clustering because it exceeds the threshold. The unmatched segments corresponding to Road 3 did not form a single cluster earlier because they do not follow the same road beyond Road 3. Road 4 is added next. The rest of the unmatched segments do not form clusters of sufficient support because they do not fully overlap or are too noisy to be within the Hausdorff distance to another trace, which

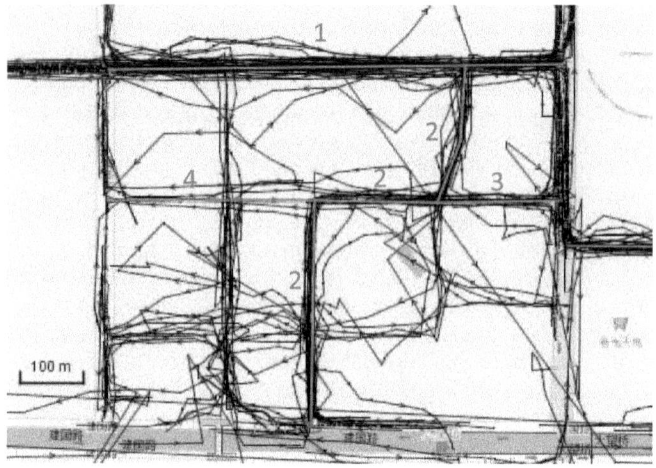

Figure 4: Iteratively inferring a block of missing roads

we set to 20 m based on our empirical study. All missing roads in the block will be added eventually with more data.

Road attributes: CrowdAtlas infers the directionality of the new road by checking whether all unmatched segments of the cluster follow the same direction. It infers the type of the road (e.g., freeway, primary, or residential) by comparing the speed profile and traffic frequency of the new road with those of the existing roads, and picks the most similar type. The number of lanes could be inferred from GPS traces as well [18]. Finally, there are computer vision techniques that could extract road names and traffic signs from street views [36], which could complement CrowdAtlas to produce fully-fledged digital maps.

Standalone mode: CrowdAtlas app follows a similar procedure to infer new roads in its standalone mode. However, instead of aggregating multiple GPS traces for high confidence, this app adds each new road immediately, given user confirmation. The road type (e.g., driveway, cycling way, or footpath) is determined by the travel mode set by the user in the app. There are techniques that infer road types in more comprehensive ways [61], which CrowdAtlas could exploit.

4.2 Other Map Updates

In addition to new roads, CrowdAtlas infers other missing map features from unmatched segments. Even in commercial-grade maps, missing intersections are quite common [56]; i.e., the map data fails to connect two roads with a connecting node, preventing navigation aids from considering any route from one to the other. These errors are not visually detectable on the rendered raster map if the roads overlap or come extremely close. Fortunately, CrowdAtlas reliably detects missing intersections as Type II mismatches in its map matching process. When the number of such mismatches between two close roads exceeds a threshold, CrowdAtlas connects them at the corresponding location, typically using the existing intersecting point of the two road polylines. Similarly, new turn possibilities of an existing intersection can be inferred. Incorrectly marked one-way roads also incur Type II mismatches. If the inferred road does not overlap with an existing one-way road—indicating that the two opposite ways are well separated as typical of major roads—then we add the inferred road. Otherwise we simply change the one-way mark of the existing road to two-way.

In order to update the geometry of existing roads, CrowdAtlas keeps for each a limited buffer of recently matched traces. Periodically (e.g. daily), if the buffer has enough newly accumulated traces and the median signed offset from the road centerline exceeds a threshold, a revised geometry is generated by the same centerline fitting algorithm as for new road inference. Whether to refine an existing road or to generate a new road is determined by the error radius in map matching, discussed in Section 3.2. A road constantly within the radius to the correct location is refined, otherwise a new road is generated.

A closure of a road segment between intersections is detected by a surprising lack of newly matched traces. Each segment establishes an appropriate timeout proportionate (3x) to the maximum time between vehicles in a training window. No timeout is set for a segment until it has accumulated at least a week of data and at least five traces. Thus, most residential roads have no timeout established. A reopening event is detected by a matched trace arriving for a road segment believed closed.

Merging new roads generated by both standalone operation and the server could result in near-duplicates. To avoid this, CrowdAtlas app employs the iterative rematching and fitting process used by the server. Roads created in the app save the original unmatched trace that generated the road; later these are matched against the updated map from the server. Standalone updates can be removed or updated if these traces fully or partially match in the new map.

4.3 Challenges and Limitations

Inferring new roads in an existing map is significantly easier than building from an empty map, since we only need to focus on unmatched trace segments, which are relatively short and easy to locate. However, CrowdAtlas still faces several challenges and limitations. First, the base map must have a reasonably accurate skeleton of arterial roads. Without a base map or if the base map is too sketchy, unmatched segments become lengthy, and it takes a long time for them to form clusters with sufficient support. These clusters tend to cross multiple roads in a real map, which reduces readability. Road 2 in Figure 4 is an example; it would likely be covered by three different roads in a manually created map.

In the introduction, we listed tunnels and plane separated roads as inherent limitations for map inference using only latitude and longitude. Hopefully these road features are already covered in the base map, since they are typically on major roads. In practice, accurate maps of arterial roads are relatively easy to obtain. For example, in OSM, developed countries are relatively well covered by public or out-of-copyright data, and a commercial donation from Automotive Navigation Data covers major truck roads in China and India.

Another major challenge for GPS-based map inference is user-friendly map presentation. Road names and address numbers cannot be added automatically. A more serious problem is whether to represent a major road by one two-way polyline or two one-way polylines in the map data. Four or more separate polylines are common for parallel expressways and freeways. Existing map inference work always makes a single representation choice for all roads.

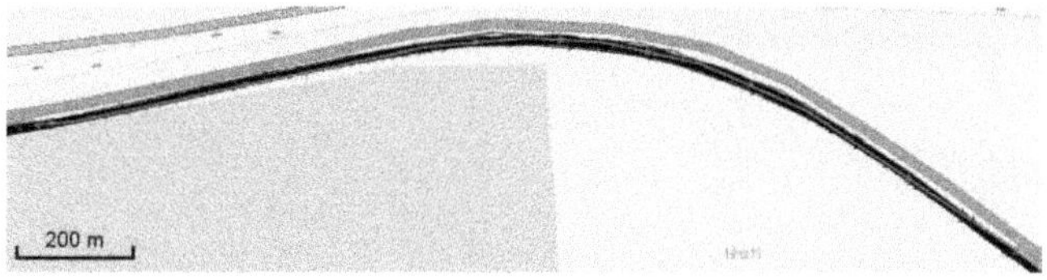

(a) CrowdAtlas infers a missing segment of a divided freeway

(b) A double-polyline major road with both wrong direction marks and missing segments on OSM

Figure 5: Double-polyline roads are a challenge

However, map updates must be compatible with existing manually created maps, which commonly contain different choices in different places. Figure 5a shows an example where CrowdAtlas correctly inferred a missing segment in one direction of a divided freeway. Figure 5b, however, is a difficult case because it is missing a segment in one direction, the direction mark of the other is backwards, and the two opposite ways are much closer. Without both high-precision and high-frequency data CrowdAtlas may connect the inferred eastbound missing segment to the existing upper polyline since it is consistent in direction, and it is closer than the lower road stub. Fortunately, direction errors of arterial roads are rare and easy to detect because they quickly incur many unmatched traces. Figure 5b is the only error of this type we found on the Beijing OSM map. Using CrowdAtlas app for trace collection can also solve the problem with its dynamic error radius feature, discussed in Section 3.3, which can emit unmatched segments covering the whole missing eastbound segment like Figure 5a, under normal GPS measurement conditions (small error radius).

5. IMPLEMENTATION

We implemented CrowdAtlas and its app in Java. Our implementation leverages many open source tools. We use OSM and its tool suite for the base map and its relevant read/write, database import/export operations. We also use JMapView, a GUI of OSM, to visualize and verify the results, as well as capture the screenshots in this paper. Our road fitting algorithm leverages the implementation of the polygonal principal curve algorithm by permission of its author [31]. Our software development focused on the algorithms, described in Sections 3 and 4, and scalability, described below.

Map matching is the bottleneck of CrowdAtlas, because it involves the Viterbi dynamic programming algorithm with a complexity of $O(nm^2)$, where n is the number of observations and m is the number of states of the HMM. This algorithm further invokes the costly shortest-path calculation for each match candidate of each sample. We have heavily optimized our implementation in our prior work [56], and it is one of the best performers in the 2012 GIS Cup competition for both speed and accuracy [7]. Nevertheless, it is still orders of magnitude slower than the other processing steps of CrowdAtlas. Furthermore, map

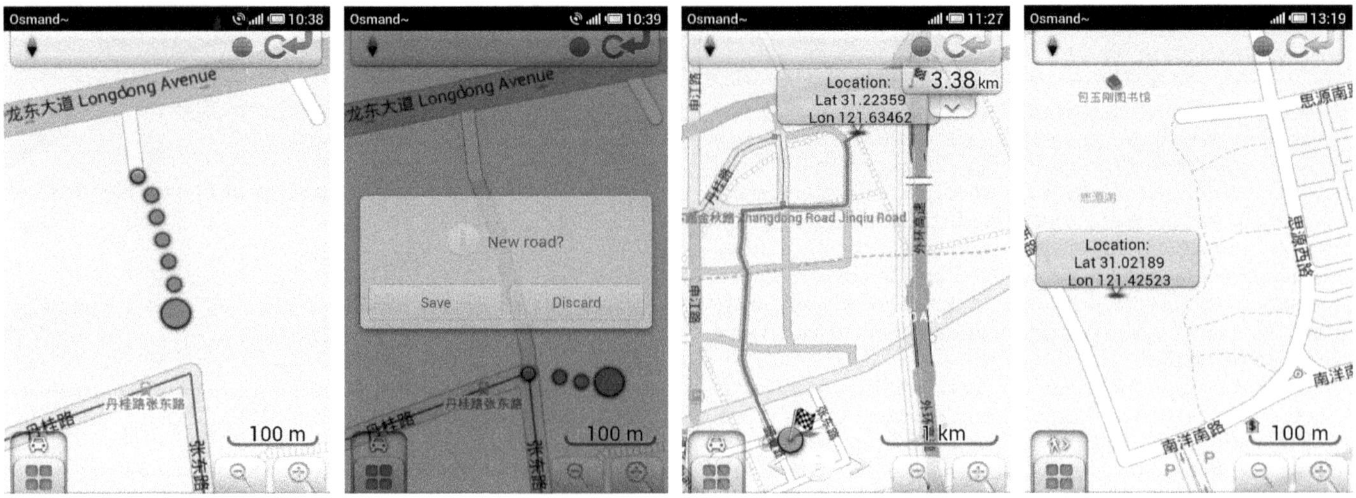

Figure 6: Screenshots of CrowdAtlas app: i) OsmAnd map missing roads in an area of Shanghai Pudong (plus unmatched GPS track overlaid); ii) user confirmation after traversing the new road (cyan, new red dots are shown as the user continues on another missing road); iii) map after generating multiple roads, plus navigation path (dark blue) showing the use of these new roads; iv) building a walking/cycling map of SJTU campus, where the lower left icon indicates the transportation mode.

matching must scale as more GPS data becomes available, while the other tasks only need to scale with the map, which is relatively stable.

Fortunately, map matching can be easily parallelized by partitioning the input GPS streams using a spatial grid or political boundaries. We implement both multithreaded and distributed map matching for different scales of data. The latter is based on Storm [4], a scalable distributed stream processing platform. By contrast, only a single workstation is needed for all the map update nodes in Figure 1a. Having only a single map writer simplifies our implementation.

Each map matcher node caches the map in memory for fast spatial indexing and shortest-path calculation. The cache in map matcher can be slightly outdated because of the delay between the inference of a new road and its propagation back to map matcher through the map database. Outdated caches may only produce extra unmatched segments for already inferred roads. CrowdAtlas uses the road version number in OSM to detect possibly outdated unmatched segments, and rematches them using the latest map in the new road inference node. When a new road is inserted, the version numbers of its anchor roads on both ends are incremented. An unmatched segment is rematched if at least one of its anchor roads is not current. This rematching step piggybacks on the existing iterative fitting process of new road inference, discussed in Section 4.1, which indexes new roads and unmatched segments for fast computation.

CrowdAtlas does not store its input GPS streams in persistent storage, and data loss is possible upon failure, which includes both the input and intermediate results. However, each node can always restart independently, and the map updates will eventually occur as new evidence builds up over time.

CrowdAtlas app is based on OsmAnd, an open source navigation app for Android using OSM maps [3]. There are many map editing tools available for OSM map formats, allowing users to add road attributes and other information. Based on the dynamic sampling feature discussed in Section 3.3, when the trace is matched to the map, CrowdAtlas app samples sparsely and sends each one to the server right away to facilitate real-time applications such as traffic monitoring. This is similar to many fleet management systems where the vehicle location is transmitted periodically through SMS. On the other hand, unmatched trace segments are densely sampled and buffered until they again match to an existing road, triggering batch transmission. Alternately, it could buffer all samples and transmit only when a 3G connection is available. In standalone mode, a popup window asks for user confirmation when a new road is detected. We simply set a timeout for the popup window, in which case the new road is discarded.

6. EVALUATION

We evaluate the standalone and server map updates of CrowdAtlas separately.

6.1 Standalone Map Update

Figure 6 shows a series of screenshots from the CrowdAtlas app. The first three were captured during an experiment in a recently developed area of the Pudong district where a block of roads are largely missing. We took a drive to complete the map systematically. The first screenshot was captured while driving a missing road. The second screenshot is the confirmation pop-up after generating the road (cyan). The third screenshot is the final result with all the roads completed. We picked a pair of locations for navigation to confirm that the roads generated are navigable, as shown by the dark blue line. There are nine roads inferred in total, with lengths ranging from 171 m to 1534 m. The inference and map save time added together for each road is between 110ms and 459ms, a minor delay for a smooth user experience, and negligible extra energy consumption for those who use navigation apps already. While waiting for user confirmation, CrowdAtlas app continues to infer new roads if there are more unmatched segments, as illustrated in the second screenshot. Therefore, the user can drive around

Figure 7: Photo of the shortcut footway from the entrance to the library in SJTU.

an area to map out missing roads and then confirm them in a batch.

The whole process took only 27 minutes. In comparison, other offline navigation apps or devices typically have an annual map update cycle, and there is no guarantee you get the update you want in your area. Google map in the area has a few quality issues. Its satellite view is misaligned, and one of the roads we generated is shown as only a road stub. It was probably surveyed before construction was complete. The Baidu map is more consistent with our result. Interested readers can verify using the lat/lon provided in the third screenshot.

In another experiment we aimed to build a cycling/walking map for the campus of Shanghai Jiao Tong University. The campus has an area of 3.2 km^2, and it is gated to limit motorist traffic. However, there is no cycling/walking map, and almost every student has been asked for directions by visitors numerous times. We mapped the campus on foot by setting the travel mode to *pedestrian* in OsmAnd, indicated by the icon in the lower left of the rightmost screenshot of Figure 6. There is a large amount of work on automated travel mode detection [43,61], which OsmAnd could leverage to automatically change the travel mode. The screenshot shows a small part of the campus, from its main entrance (southern end) to the library (northern end). The OSM map includes only the driveway connecting the entrance to the library, which is a detour compared to the shortcut footway used by most students, shown in Figure 7. The screenshot shows this vertical shortcut, which saves walking time by 34%, as well as another four horizontal footways connecting it to the vertical driveway on the right. CrowdAtlas app inferred these roads correctly after we walked them. The samples along all horizontal footways are within 50 m to either the driveway or the shortcut inferred earlier. Without the dynamic error radius feature, samples would have always matched to either road and no new footway would be detected. Comparing with commercial maps, Google map is also missing these footways. While Baidu map contains some of these footways, they are incorrectly marked as driveways that can be used for vehicle navigation.

6.2 Server Map Update

Our evaluation of server map update uses taxi traces collected from 70 taxis in Beijing for 8 days in December 2008, a total of 4,351,977 samples. The dataset was sampled at 10 second intervals, which is relatively frequent and helps in the verification of map matching results. We also sub-

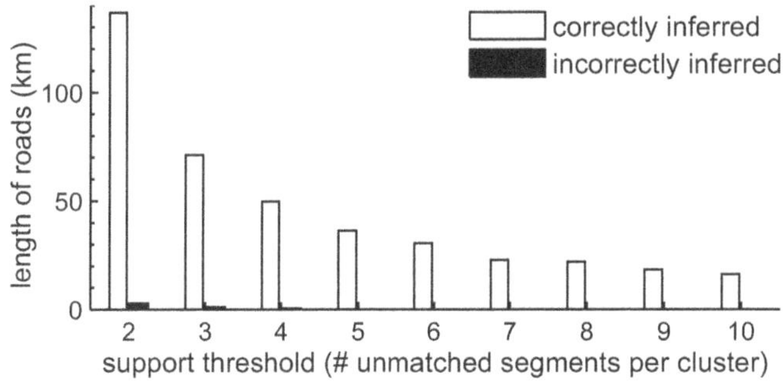

(a) New roads inferred vs. different support thresholds

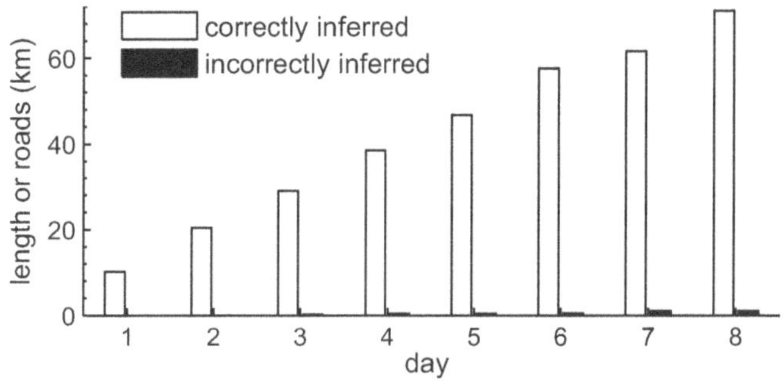

(b) New roads accumulated by day (support = 3)

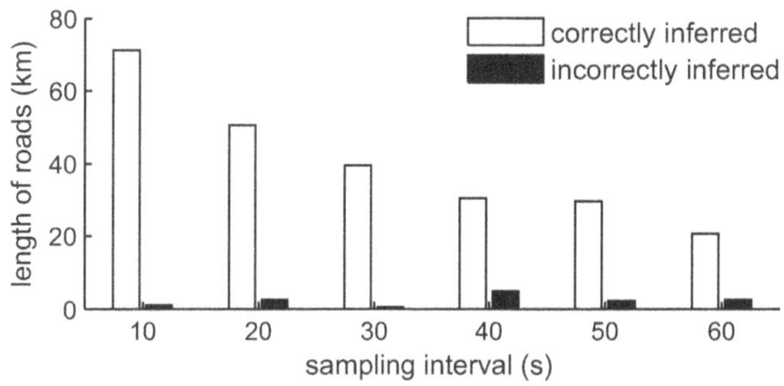

(c) Using sub-sampled data (support = 3)

Figure 8: New road inference

sample the data to evaluate the performance of CrowdAtlas under long-sampling-interval data. The standard deviation of the Gaussian GPS noise is within 10 m under normal conditions, but typical outliers exist, especially in urban canyon areas, e.g. Figure 4 (detailed characteristics of the dataset are available in [55]). We use the OSM map of 10/31/2012 to evaluate our map update results, and compare them with an earlier map and the latest map to understand how the manually created OSM map evolves.

After map matching, only 37,355 unmatched samples remain in 4,968 unmatched segments. Thus the CrowdAtlas app could have reduced the amount of data communicated to less than 1%. Figure 8 shows the new road inference results. We verified our generated roads manually using both Bing aerial images and Google maps (which agree with each other in most cases except for two inferred roads, which are consistent with the aerial image but still missing from Google maps). Figure 8a shows that increasing the support threshold can eliminate incorrectly inferred roads, mostly due to noise or insufficient data, leading to errors

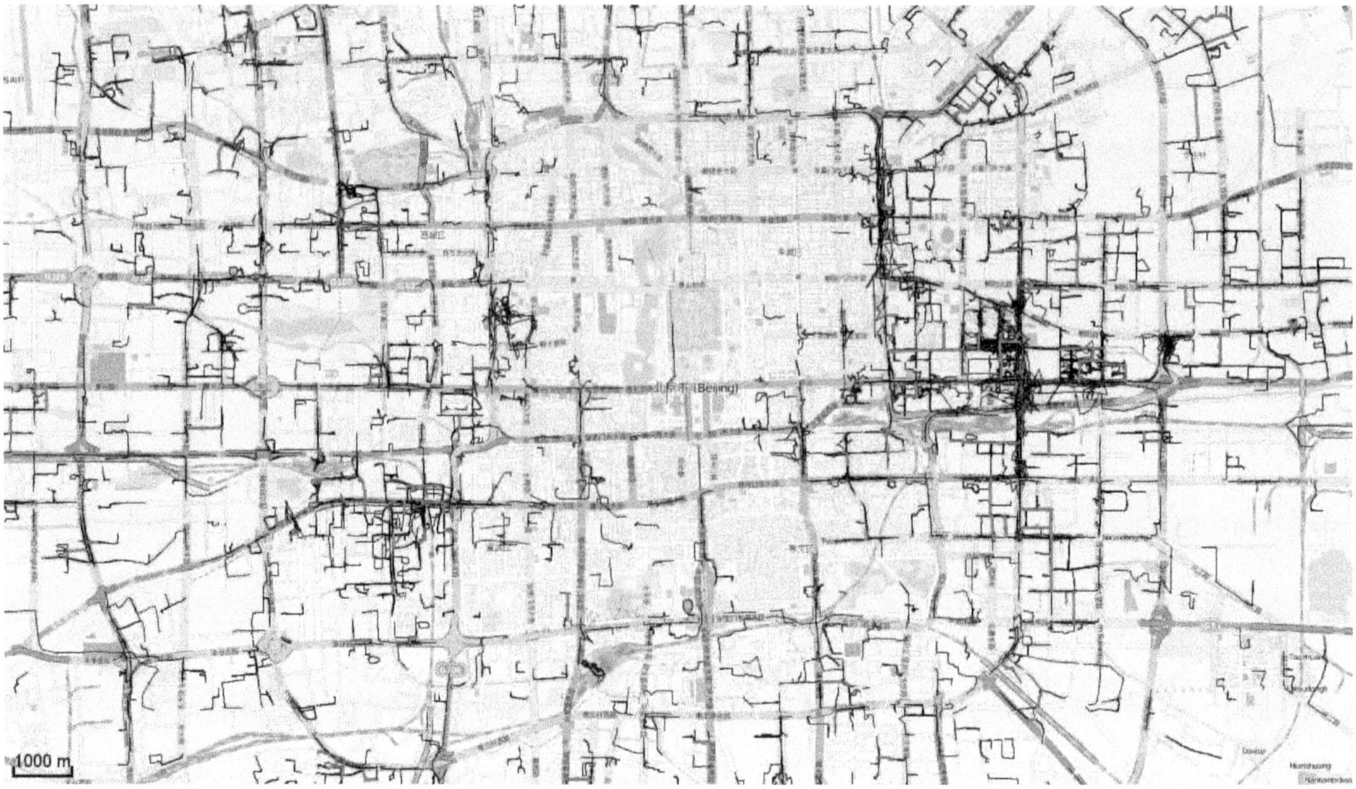

Figure 9: New roads (red) inferred from unmatched trace segments (black) overlaid on the latest OSM base map

in road geometry. At the support threshold of three (or four) traces, there are only six (or three) incorrectly inferred roads, totaling less than 1 km in length in either case; a support threshold of five or more eliminates false positives altogether. Given our limited data volume, we also considered even lower thresholds that would not be viable in production. Using a threshold of two almost doubles the length of roads inferred, albeit with more false roads. Figure 8b shows that new roads increase linearly as time progresses, which indicates that our dataset is not sufficient to complete the whole city map. Finally, Figure 8c shows that longer sampling intervals can reduce the number of roads inferred and increase noise. Up to 30-second intervals CrowdAtlas works reasonably well and the false roads can be eliminated by slightly increasing the support threshold. Beyond 30-seconds, the ratio between correct and incorrect roads significantly decreases, because of the increasing errors in map matching and trajectory-based clustering.

Figure 9 shows all unmatched segments and new roads inferred in central Beijing using all eight days of data, with a support threshold of three. There are a few urban canyon pockets where unmatched traces are quite noisy, but the clustering step finds the right traces to infer new roads. The rest of the unmatched segments, especially further from central Beijing, are indeed from missing roads but lack the support to trigger the fitting process. In summary, the inferred roads showed good accuracy as well as reasonable coverage considering the volume of data, which naturally would grow over time.

Note that the backdrop raster map in Figure 9 was retrieved from OSM in early December, which includes manual edits people had entered online after the date of our map. We compared our inferred roads to these online edits, noting that Beijing is one of the most actively updated areas in OSM. Their map of 12/3/2012 with over a month of additional edits includes 17 of our inferred roads, a total length of 8.5 km—a modest subset of our ~71 km using a small dataset. However, compared with an earlier map of 5/8/2012, we find several correct roads that have since been removed and not re-entered; each of these was correctly inferred by CrowdAtlas. In general, manual edits are error-prone and may not converge. There are also five inferred roads that existed back in 2008 but are not in the latest map, a total length of 1.8 km. But instead of being false positives, we verified from dated satellite images by Google Earth that most were actually detours used during construction. In addition to new roads, CrowdAtlas detected 11 incorrectly marked one-way roads, a total of 3.2 km. We have submitted 156 inferred roads not on the latest map to OSM (by userID "CrowdAtlas"), a total length of 61 km.

Next we use the matched segments to refine road geometry. Among all 25,555 roads in the map of 10/31/2012, 13,303 have no sample matched, partly because of the limited data volume. There are also many roads for non-motorist traffic only, and roads in rural areas of Beijing not frequently visited by taxis. Finally, some of the roads are constructed after 2008. For the rest of the matched roads, we consider those visited by at least three different taxis, with at least ten samples matched, and at least five samples matched to locations more than 10 m apart from each other. The last requirement ensures that samples are spread out for correct centerline fitting. There are 6,568 roads satisfying

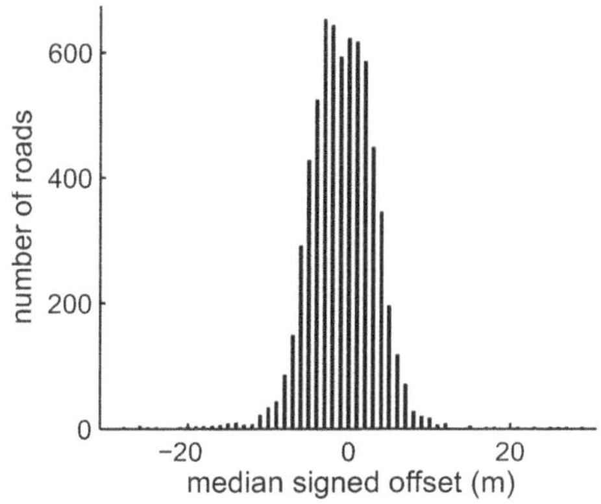

(a) Histogram

(b) Example

Figure 10: Geometry refinement of existing road

	map matching	new road	refinement
time (s)	1,544	67	2

(a) Baseline computation time using a single thread

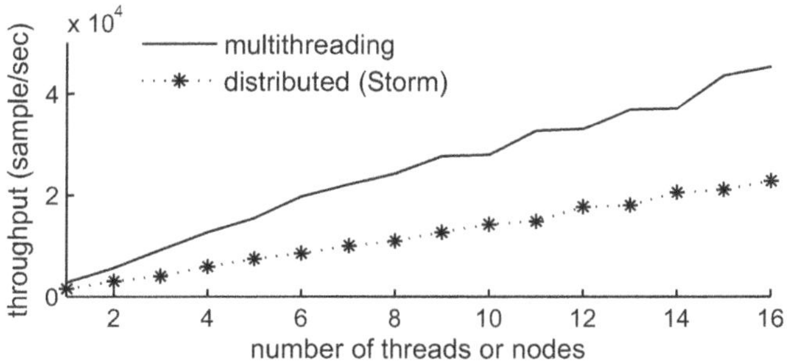

(b) Parallel map matching with memory-cached maps

Figure 11: Computation time and scalability

these requirements, and Figure 10a is the histogram of the median signed offset from the centerline. There are only 32 roads with the absolute median larger than 15 m. Our visual inspection suggests that 15 m is a reasonable cutoff threshold for well aligned roads. Within 15 m it is hard to judge which is more accurate: the samples, the vector map, or the aerial image. We manually inspected these 32 roads and found 19 of them are due to missing parallel roads or missing connections between parallel roads. For example, if the express freeway is included in the map without representing the local freeway by separate polylines, samples generated from local freeways are matched to express freeways, since they are typically within our error radius of 50 m for map matching. These samples would exhibit a significant offset. Using CrowdAtlas app for data collection can solve the problem with its dynamic error radius feature, which would extract the trace segment as unmatched rather than matched under good GPS measurements. Another 8 roads are due to insufficient data such that the whole matched sample set is dominated by noise, caused by high-rise buildings or covers, e.g., elevated roads and airport driveways. The remaining five roads are indeed misaligned; three of them are due to earlier construction; one of them has been manually corrected in the latest map of 12/03/2012. The last one is shown on Figure 10b, where the vertical road shown in white is clearly misaligned with both the samples and the aerial image. Without CrowdAtlasit would be very challenging to detect one misaligned road in a city-scale map.

Finally, we examine the computation time and the scalability of CrowdAtlas. Figure 11a shows the baseline computation time of different tasks using a single core on a dual Xeon E5 2650L 1.8G Hz workstation. We used the full Beijing dataset, and the support threshold for new road inference is again three. Map matching is orders of magnitude slower than new road inference and geometry refinement. New road inference takes much longer than refinement because there are lots of missing roads. Inferring each road takes less than half a second on average. Therefore with stable maps, new road inference should be lightweight, and one server ought to be able to handle global updates. Figure 11b shows the scalability of map matching by multithreading, using the same Xeon workstation, or distributed computing, using 16 PCs. In each case, the map is fully cached in memory so there is no communication cost or database overhead with the map server. Not surprisingly, the throughput scales almost linearly since each thread or node operates on the input trace independently. Using the Xeon workstation, the throughput is roughly 2,800 samples per second per thread. At the sampling interval of 10 seconds, this throughput implies the scale of 28k vehicles per core, or 448k vehicles in total for the workstation. Longer sampling intervals may require more processing time for the shortest-path calculation. Nevertheless one workstation is more than sufficient for map matching city- or state-scale data.

7. RELATED WORK

Map matching: Section 3.1 mentioned incremental map matching algorithms using only previous observations [38, 53, 57], and global algorithms using Viterbi dynamic programming [34, 40, 51]. Incremental algorithms perform poorly at narrow Y-splits or close parallel roads, where future observations are often needed to correctly match the current sample to one of the two extremely close roads. There are also map matching algorithms that minimize the geometric measure of *Fréchet distance* between a GPS trace and a path on map [8, 14]. These algorithms are inaccurate at long sampling intervals, when there are too many alternative paths with the same Fréchet distance to the input trace, making it difficult for the algorithm to choose the right one [56].

Map Inference: There are three categories of methods for GPS-based map inference: K-means [6, 23, 45, 58], *Kernel Density Estimation* (KDE) [12, 16, 20, 47, 50], and trace merging or clustering [15, 30, 32, 41]. Most of these algorithms have various unrealistic assumptions of the GPS data, including low noise (e.g., only Gaussian noise with a standard deviation less than 5 m [24, 40]), high sampling frequency (e.g., 1 Hz), and uniform distribution (e.g., passing through each road to be inferred exactly once). Their performance deteriorates rapidly if any of these assumptions does not hold; see the comparative studies for detailed analyses [11, 32]. The only exceptions are the trace clustering algorithm [32], which CrowdAtlas improves upon, and a variant of a KDE-based algorithm [32] and its recent extension [12]. The KDE-based methods estimate road centerlines from GPS samples alone, which is particularly good for sparse and noisy data. Road connectivity and attributes are inferred by map matching GPS traces to the inferred roads. Our clustering-based method is simpler since each cluster contains all the information needed to infer a new road and insert it into the map. Furthermore, our trace-based clustering is more robust against random noise since traces have to tightly overlap to form clusters, while KDE would infer roads from noise samples if they accumulate in one area. Finally, it is straightforward to adapt our clustering algorithm to streams, while the KDE-based methods are designed for offline processing. Our road fitting step, however, could use KDE as an alternative, which may be more robust than principal curve estimation but requires full coverage of samples on the road.

Another category of automated map inference is based on aerial imagery [28, 46]. Roads covered by tree canopy and road connectivity are very challenging for these methods. Currently most contributors of OSM create maps from aerial imagery manually, and missing connections are frequently identified by CrowdAtlas in our experiments. Also, obtaining frequently updated, high-resolution aerial images is very expensive, so updating maps periodically using aerial imagery is not economical. Valuable future work could combine CrowdAtlas with aerial imagery analysis to increase the confidence of map updates.

Relevant Systems: Google, TomTom, and Waze leverage crowdsourcing for map update, where user-submitted changes can be integrated into their map products after manual review [39]. OpenStreetMap is the largest crowdsourcing map community. All of its user-contributed maps so far are manually created using its GUI tools. There are also numerous services, mobile apps, and GPS devices that allow users to store and share their GPS traces, but they do not create navigable maps. There is considerable interest in mining large-scale GPS trace sources for various transportation related tasks, e.g., traffic monitoring [27, 59], incident detection [49], empirical shortest-time route calculation [60], and empirical taxi fare calculation [10]. It is straightforward to incorporate these systems into CrowdAtlas and benefit from its scalable and reliable map matching engine. There are also systems designed to store, compare, and query GPS traces [26]. CrowdAtlas currently does not store traces after map update, but can use these systems to do so, and augment each trace with the map matching result to benefit other applications.

8. CONCLUSION

CrowdAtlas offers a solution to the ongoing problem of digital road map inaccuracy—automation to fix errors, reduce lag times for changed roadways, and keep up with the growing demand for specialized maps. By transmitting high frequency samples to the server only when off the known road network, our mobile app enables new roads to be accurately inferred with a minimum of communication overhead. Because the server only infers roads when several unmatched vehicle traces cluster tightly together, the roads produced have high precision and do not require a specialist to edit and integrate them, yielding a high level of automation.

9. ACKNOWLEDGMENTS

We thank our shepherd Gaetano Borriello and anonymous reviewers for helping us improve the paper. Yang Yue provided us the taxi dataset from Beijing, for which we are grateful. We also acknowledge the support of the HP Labs Innovation Research Program (CW267311), the Shanghai Pu Jiang Talents Program (10PJ1405800), NSFC (61170238, 60903190, and 61027009), the Doctoral Fund of the Ministry of Education of China (20100073120021), and the 863 Program (2009AA012201 and 2011AA010500).

10. REFERENCES

[1] GPS dataset. `grid.sjtu.edu.cn/mapupdate/`.

[2] NAVTEQ. `navteq.com/company_history.htm`.

[3] OsmAnd: OSM Automated Navigation Directions Android app. `www.osmand.net`.

[4] Storm: Distributed and fault-tolerant realtime computation. `storm-project.net/`.

[5] TomTom Map Update Service. `www.tomtom.com/en_gb/maps/map-update-service/`.

[6] G. Agamennoni, J. I. Nieto, and E. M. Nebot. Robust inference of principal road paths for intelligent transportation systems. *IEEE Trans. on Intelligent Transportation Systems*, 12(1):298–308, 2011.

[7] M. Ali, T. Rautman, J. Krumm, and A. Teredesai. ACM SIGSPATIAL Cup 2012. In *GIS*, 2012.

[8] H. Alt, A. Efrat, G. Rote, and C. Wenk. Matching planar maps. *Journal of Algorithms*, 49(2):262–283, 2003.

[9] J. Angwin and J. V.-Devries. Apple, Google collect user data. *Wall Street Journal*, April 2011.

[10] R. K. Balan, K. X. Nguyen, and L. Jiang. Real-time trip information service for a large taxi fleet. In *MobiSys*, 2011.

[11] J. Biagioni and J. Eriksson. Inferring road maps from GPS traces: Survey and comparative evaluation. In *Transportation Research Board*, 2012.

[12] J. Biagioni and J. Eriksson. Map inference in the face of noise and disparity. In *ACM GIS*, 2012.

[13] A. Biem, E. Bouillet, H. Feng, A. Ranganathan, A. Riabov, O. Verscheure, H. N. Koutsopoulos, and C. Moran. IBM Infosphere streams for scalable, real-time, intelligent transportation services. In *SIGMOD*, 2010.

[14] S. Brakatsoulas, D. Pfoser, R. Salas, and C. Wenk. On map-matching vehicle tracking data. In *VLDB*, 2005.

[15] L. Cao and J. Krumm. From GPS traces to a routable road map. In *ACM GIS*, 2009.

[16] C. Chen and Y. Cheng. Roads digital map generation with multi-track GPS data. In *International Workshop on Geoscience and Remote Sensing*, 2008.

[17] D. Chen, D. Chen, L. J. Guibas, J. Hershberger, and J. Sun. Road network reconstruction for organizing paths. In *SODA*, 2010.

[18] Y. Chen and J. Krumm. Probabilistic modeling of traffic lanes from GPS traces. In *ACM GIS*, 2010.

[19] T. Cook. A letter from Tim Cook on maps, 2012. `apple.com/letter-from-tim-cook-on-maps`.

[20] J. J. Davies, A. R. Beresford, and A. Hopper. Scalable, distributed, real-time map generation. *IEEE Pervasive Computing*, 5(4):47–54, 2006.

[21] D. H. Douglas and T. K. Peucker. Algorithms for the reduction of the number of points required to represent a digitized line or its caricature. *Cartographica*, 10(2):112–122, Oct. 1973.

[22] B. Dudley. Google Maps gets bike routes, built in Fremont. *The Seattle Times*, March 2011.

[23] S. Edelkamp and S. Schrödl. Route planning and map inference with global positioning traces. In *Computer Science in Perspective*, p.128–151, 2003.

[24] J. Eriksson et al. The pothole patrol: using a mobile sensor network for road surface monitoring. In *MobiSys*, 2008.

[25] R. Gordon and J. Tucker. Ruling paves way for San Francisco bike lanes. *San Francisco Chronicle*, August 2010.

[26] M. Haridasan, I. Mohomed, D. Terry, C. A. Thekkath, and L. Zhang. Startrack next generation: A scalable infrastructure for track-based applications. In *OSDI*, 2010.

[27] B. Hoh, M. Gruteser, R. Herring, J. Ban, D. B. Work, J. C. Herrera, A. M. Bayen, M. Annavaram, and Q. Jacobson. Virtual trip lines for distributed privacy-preserving traffic monitoring. In *MobiSys*, 2008.

[28] J. Hu, A. Razdan, J. Femiani, M. Cui, and P. Wonka. Road network extraction and intersection detection from aerial images by tracking road footprints. *IEEE T. Geoscience and Remote Sensing*, 45(12-2):4144–4157, 2007.

[29] C. Johnson, C. Shea, and C. Holloway. The role of trust and interaction in GPS related accidents. In *Int'l Conference on Systems Safety*, 2008.

[30] S. Karagiorgou and D. Pfoser. On vehicle tracking data-based road network generation. In *Proceedings of the 20th International Conference on Advances in Geographic Information Systems*, SIGSPATIAL '12, pages 89–98, 2012.

[31] B. Kégl, A. Krzyzak, T. Linder, and K. Zeger. Learning and design of principal curves. *IEEE Trans. Pattern Anal. Mach. Intell.*, 22(3):281–297, 2000.

[32] X. Liu, J. Biagioni, J. Eriksson, Y. Wang, G. Forman, and Y. Zhu. Mining large-scale, sparse GPS traces for map inference: Comparison of approaches. In *KDD*, 2012.

[33] N. Lomas. GPS driving British motorists to distraction. *Bloomberg Businessweek*, July 2008.

[34] Y. Lou, C. Zhang, Y. Zheng, X. Xie, W. Wang, and Y. Huang. Map-matching for low-sampling-rate GPS trajectories. In *ACM GIS*, 2009.

[35] S. Madden. Keynote: Going big on spatial data. In *ACM GIS*, 2012.

[36] A. C. Madrigal. How Google builds its maps. *The Atlantic*, Sept 2012.

[37] S. Mathur, T. Jin, N. Kasturirangan, J. Chandrasekaran, W. Xue, M. Gruteser, and W. Trappe. Parknet: drive-by sensing of road-side parking statistics. In *MobiSys*, 2010.

[38] O. Mazhelis. Using recursive Bayesian estimation for matching GPS measurements to imperfect road network data. In *IEEE Conference on Intelligent Transportation Systems*, 2010.

[39] B. McClendon (Google VP). Keynote: The path from paper to product: How spatial research reaches users. In *ACM GIS*, 2012.

[40] P. Newson and J. Krumm. Hidden markov map matching through noise and sparseness. In *ACM GIS*, 2009.

[41] B. Niehoefer, R. Burda, C. Wietfeld, F. Bauer, and O. Lueert. GPS community map generation for enhanced routing methods based on trace-collection by mobile phones. In *Advances in Satellite and Space Communications*, 2009.

[42] J. Paek, J. Kim, and R. Govindan. Energy-efficient rate-adaptive GPS-based positioning for smartphones. In *MobiSys*, 2010.

[43] S. Reddy, M. Mun, J. Burke, D. Estrin, M. H. Hansen, and M. B. Srivastava. Using mobile phones to determine transportation modes. *TOSN*, 6(2), 2010.

[44] S. Rogers, P. Langley, and C. Wilson. Mining gps data to augment road models. In *KDD*, 1999.

[45] S. Schrödl, S. Schrödl, K. Wagstaff, S. Rogers, P. Langley, and C. Wilson. Mining GPS traces for map refinement. *Data Min. Knowl. Discov.*, 9(1):59–87, 2004.

[46] Y.-W. Seo, C. Urmson, and D. Wettergreen. Exploiting publicly available cartographic resources for aerial image analysis. In *GIS*, 2012.

[47] W. Shi, S. Shen, and Y. Liu. Automatic generation of road network map from massive GPS, vehicle trajectories. In *IEEE Conf. on Intelligent Transportation Systems*, 2009.

[48] R. Sibson. Slink: An optimally efficient algorithm for the single-link cluster method. *The Computer Journal*, 16(1):30–34, 1973.

[49] A. Skabardonis, T. Chira-Chavala, and D. Rydzewski. The I-880 field experiment: Effectiveness of incident detection using cellular phones. Technical Report UCB-ITS-PRR-98-1, University of California, Berkeley, 1998.

[50] A. Steiner and A. Leonhardt. A map generation algorithm using low frequency vehicle position data. In *Transportation Research Board*, 2011.

[51] A. Thiagarajan et al. Accurate, low-energy trajectory mapping for mobile devices. In *NSDI*, 2011.

[52] T. Vanderbilt. It wasn't me, officer! It was my GPS. *Slate*, June 2010. `www.slate.com`.

[53] N. R. Velaga, N. R. Velaga, M. A. Quddus, and A. L. Bristow. Developing an enhanced weight-based topological map-matching algorithm for intelligent transport systems. *Transportation Research Part C: Emerging Technologies*, 17(6):672–683, 2009.

[54] R. Wabash. 9 car accidents caused by Google Maps & GPS. *Ranker*, April 2012. `ranker.com`.

[55] Y. Wang, Y. Zhu, Z. He, Y. Yue, and Q. Li. Challenges and opportunities in exploiting large-scale GPS probe data. Technical Report HPL-2011-109, HP Labs, 2011.

[56] H. Wei, Y. Wang, G. Forman, Y. Zhu, and H. Guan. Fast Viterbi map matching with tunable weight functions. In *GIS*, 2012. (SIGSPATIAL Cup).

[57] C. E. White, D. Bernstein, and A. L. Kornhauser. Some map matching algorithms for personal

navigation assistants. *Transportation Research Part C*, 8(1–6):91–108, 2000.

[58] S. Worrall and E. Nebot. Automated process for generating digitised maps through GPS data compression. In *Australasian Conference on Robotics and Automation*, 2007.

[59] J. Yoon, B. Noble, and M. Liu. Surface street traffic estimation. In *MobiSys*, 2007.

[60] J. Yuan, Y. Zheng, X. Xie, and G. Sun. T-Drive: Enhancing driving directions with taxi drivers' intelligence. *IEEE Trans. Knowl. Data Eng.*, 25(1):220–232, 2013.

[61] Y. Zheng, L. Liu, L. Wang, and X. Xie. Learning transportation mode from raw GPS data for geographic applications on the web. In *WWW*, 2008.

Sensing Vehicle Dynamics for Determining Driver Phone Use

Yan Wang
Stevens Institute of Technology
Hoboken, NJ 07030, USA
ywang48@stevens.edu

Jie Yang
Oakland University
Rochester, MI 48309, USA
yang@oakland.edu

Hongbo Liu
Stevens Institute of Technology
Hoboken, NJ 07030, USA
hliu3@stevens.edu

Yingying Chen
Stevens Institute of Technology
Hoboken, NJ 07030, USA
yingying.chen@stevens.edu

Marco Gruteser
Rutgers University
North Brunswick, NJ 08902, USA
gruteser@rutgers.edu

Richard P. Martin
Rutgers University
North Brunswick, NJ 08902, USA
rmartin@rutgers.edu

ABSTRACT

This paper utilizes smartphone sensing of vehicle dynamics to determine driver phone use, which can facilitate many traffic safety applications. Our system uses embedded sensors in smartphones, i.e., accelerometers and gyroscopes, to capture differences in centripetal acceleration due to vehicle dynamics. These differences combined with angular speed can determine whether the phone is on the left or right side of the vehicle. Our low infrastructure approach is flexible with different turn sizes and driving speeds. Extensive experiments conducted with two vehicles in two different cities demonstrate that our system is robust to real driving environments. Despite noisy sensor readings from smartphones, our approach can achieve a classification accuracy of over 90% with a false positive rate of a few percent. We also find that by combining sensing results in a few turns, we can achieve better accuracy (e.g., 95%) with a lower false positive rate.

Categories and Subject Descriptors

H.4 [**Information Systems**]: Miscellaneous

Keywords

Driving Safety, Driver Phone Detection, Smartphone, Accelerometer, Gyroscope

1. INTRODUCTION

Distracted driving due to mobile devices contributes to nearly one thousand fatalities per year [4] and is now receiving attention not only from government regulators but also within the highest executive levels of the mobile industry [2]. Indeed, the National Transportation Safety Board has called for a nationwide ban on mobile devices behind the wheel [11], while the mobile industry has adopted a subtler approach with apps that seek to manage distraction. The AT&T DriveSafe app [3], for example, silences the phone for incoming text messages while in driving mode as discussed in [26, 36].

Such approaches depend on the phone being able to sense when the user is driving, since experience with a phone's silent mode and instant message status has shown that users are not very reliable at setting the status manually. Several known approaches exist for detecting whether a phone user is in a vehicle. More difficult, however, is determining whether a user is actually driving or is simply a passenger in the vehicle. In our prior work, we addressed this problem by exploiting built-in Bluetooth handsfree systems in vehicles for audio localization of the phone. While it is expected that the fraction of Bluetooth handsfree equipped vehicle will rise significantly over the coming years, there is also considerable interest in techniques that are less dependent on such infrastructure, so that they can be more easily retrofitted into existing vehicles without Bluetooth.

In this paper, we explore a low-infrastructure approach that senses acceleration due to vehicle dynamics to decide a phone's position. As in prior work, we seek to determine the in-vehicle location of the phone and use that as a heuristic to determine whether the phone is used by the driver or passenger. It uses a fundamentally different sensing approach, however, to determine this location. The key insight is that the centripetal acceleration varies depending on the position in the car. By comparing the measured acceleration from the phone with the acceleration measured at a reference point inside the car, the phone can decide whether it is located left or right of the reference (i.e. on the driver or passenger side). This technique can operate in conjunction with our bump sensing technique for determining front or rear location [37]. We refer to this approach as low-infrastructure since it can more easily be retrofitted in existing cars by plugging in a small OBD-II or cigarette light adapter. It does not require having a handsfree bluetooth kit wired into the existing car audio system.

While the idea of utilizing centripetal acceleration differentials between the target phone and the reference point seems simple, many challenges arise in practice. First, the embedded sensors are noisy and affected by unpredictable driving environments. A second challenge is minimizing the additional infrastructure needed beyond the phone. Third, the sensor readings in smartphones are pose dependent, thus cannot be directly used to represent the vehicle's dynamics. To address these issues, we propose a centripetal acceleration based driver phone use sensing algorithm that mitigates the noise of the sensor readings and unpredictable geometries, such as different size of turns, driving speed, and driving styles. Extensive experimental results in both parking lots and roads confirm the effectiveness and efficiency of our proposed algorithm which requires no built-in infrastructure. Specifically, we make the following contributions:

- Proposing a method for distinguishing driver and passenger phone use that is less dependent on built-in vehicle infrastructure than the audio-ranging approach. It determines the in-vehicle position of a phone by using its sensors to monitor position dependent differences in acceleration forces and comparing them with a vehicle reference reading.

- Describing and evaluating multiple possible designs for providing a vehicle reference reading, including a cigarette lighter adapter with accelerometer sensor, an OBD-II port adapter that provides vehicle speed reference readings to the phone over Bluetooth, and opportunistically using other phones as a reference.

- Designing algorithms that can use these various reference inputs and can compensate for bias in the reference measurements by taking into account data from both left and right turns of a vehicle.

- Demonstrating through extensive experiments in a parking lot and through real-world driving in two cities with different phone models and vehicles that it is feasible to determine phone position with high accuracy after the vehicle has passed through a few curves.

The experimental results show that by relying only on the plug-in adapters, our proposed algorithm can achieve high detection rates and low false positive rate in both parking lot and real driving environments. By making use of a few turns, a more reliable result can be obtained. Our results show that position can often be determined after the vehicle drives out of a parking lot or before it reaches a main road. We therefore believe that the detection latency is acceptable. Our prototype implementation also shows that current Android smartphones have adequate computational capabilities to perform the signal processing needed in a standard programming environment.

The rest of the paper is organized as follows. In Section 2, we place our work in the broader context of reducing driver distraction and using sensors on smartphones to facilitate driving safety and vehicle monitoring applications. We provide the system overview and core detection algorithm in Section 3. We then present our system implementation by leveraging different infrastructures in Section 4. In Section 5, we perform extensive evaluation of our system in real-road driving environments involving two types of phones and two vehicles in two cities. We discuss about a possible infrastructure-free approach of determining driver phone use by adding a phone's GPS in Section 6. Finally, we conclude our work in Section 7.

2. RELATED WORK

There has been active research work in detecting dangerous behavior while operating an automobile [18,20,24], especially for the driver distraction problem caused by hand-held devices. Some recent work dedicated to mitigate driver phone distraction includes Quiet Calls [31], Blind Sight [25], Negotiator [35], and Lindqvist's systems [26]. Furthermore, some apps are developed to block incoming or outgoing calls and texts for the phones inside a moving vehicle [5, 12, 14]. Apps such as [9] require special devices installed inside the vehicle to enable blocking cellular communications of a specific phone based on the readings from the vehicle's speedometer, or even rely on a radio jammer [7]. These studies either require prior knowledge of the phone use by the driver (e.g., user activates the system indicating himself as the driver) or blindly block calls/text of all the cellphones inside the vehicle. These solutions, however, cannot automatically distinguish a driver's cell phone from a passenger's.

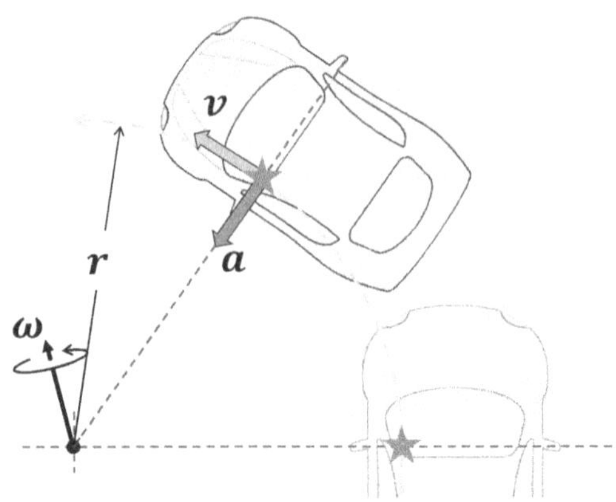

Figure 1: Illustration of centripetal acceleration, tangential speed, angular speed, and the radius of the circular movement.

Since diverse sensors have been integrated in smartphones, they are endowed with powerful capabilities that can be used to sense vehicle dynamics and facilitate a broad array of applications related to driving safety and road monitoring. The moving vehicle can be detected based on the embedded smartphone sensors and the cellular signal, for example, accelerations and cellular signal strength [15, 23, 30, 33]. Other studies use smartphone embedded sensors to alert dangerous driving, monitor road conditions, and detect traffic accidents [17,24,29,34]. Dai et.al. [17] propose a system to detect and alert dangerous vehicle maneuvers by utilizing the accelerometer and the orientation sensor. WreckWatch [34] detects traffic accidents using the accelerometer and microphone. Johnson et.al. [24] present a system using Dynamic Time Warping (DTW) and smartphone based sensor-fusion to detect and recognize vehicular motions. Furthermore, smartphone sensors are also used to monitor the road conditions [19, 28, 29], e.g., the accelerometer in a smartphone is able to detect a large acceleration perpendicular to the road surface when the vehicle passes bumps or potholes on the road. These studies confirm the feasibility of utilizing sensors on smartphones to sense the vehicle dynamics, which may be further used to automatically determine the driver phone use.

Towards the most related work in detecting driver phone use, Chu et.al. [16] present a driver detection system (DDS) by utilizing multiple sensors (including accelerometer, gyroscope, and microphone) in smartphones to capture the features of driver's movement. However, this approach is sensitive to the behavior of each individual, and highly depends on the position where drivers carry the phone, which is less practical. Yang et.al. [36, 37] introduce an acoustic relative-ranging system that classifies on which car seat a phone is being used leveraging the car's audio infrastructure. This approach relies on the vehicle's audio system. Different from the above work, in this project we explore a low-infrastructure approach that senses acceleration forces from vehicle dynamics to determine the phone's position inside the car.

3. SYSTEM DESIGN

To build a low-infrastructure solution leveraging embedded sensors on smartphones, we devise an approach that senses position-

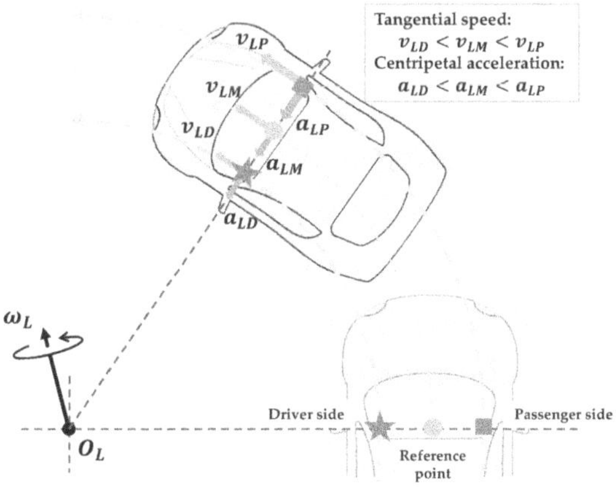

Figure 2: Illustration of different centripetal accelerations at different in-vehicle positions.

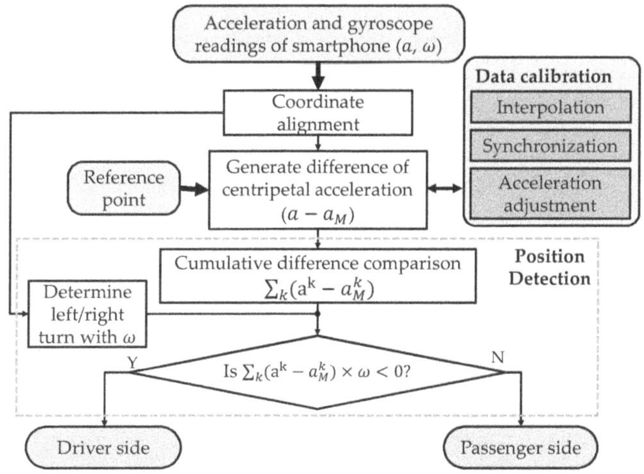

Figure 3: Overview of system flow.

dependent acceleration forces when a vehicle turns. In this section, we provide background information, system challenges, overview of our system design, and a driver phone use sensing algorithm.

3.1 Background

When a vehicle makes a turn, it experiences a centripetal force, which has its direction orthogonal to the direction of movement of the vehicle and toward the center of the turn. This centripetal force generates a centripetal acceleration a also pointing toward the center of the curve. Assuming a turn following a perfect circle, the centripetal acceleration (a) can be obtained by using the angular speed (ω), the tangential velocity (v) and the radius (r) of the turn [32]:

$$a = \omega v = \omega^2 r = \frac{v^2}{r}. \quad (1)$$

The relationship of these parameters are illustrated in Figure 1. Phones located on passenger- and driver-side positions inside the vehicle will have the same angular speed but follow circles of different radii. Based on Equation (1), it can be seen that different radii at constant angular speed will lead to differences in centripetal acceleration on these positions.

Inspired by this simple yet useful physics observation, we seek to measure such centripetal acceleration differences with smartphone sensors to design a low-infrastructure solution for determining driver phone use.

3.2 Challenges and Goals

Building such a system involves a number of challenges in both design and implementation:

Robustness to Real-Road Driving Environments. The centripetal acceleration is affected by a number of factors including the different size of turns, driving speed, and driving style. Furthermore, vibrations from the vehicle (e.g., a running engine) and environment (e.g., wind) all contribute to noisy sensor readings. Thus, the algorithm to obtain the centripetal acceleration has to be robust to deal with real road driving environments.

Achieving Single Phone Sensing. The approach should work even when only a single phone is present in the vehicle, since it is not always clear that this phone belongs to the driver.

Determining the Pose of the Phone. The measured sensor readings from smartphones can not be directly applied to produce vehicle dynamics (e.g., centripetal acceleration) without knowing the pose of the phone inside the vehicle. An effective re-orientation mechanism is needed to align the phone's pose with the vehicle's coordinate system.

Computational Feasibility on Smartphones. The driver phone sensing process should complete in a short time on standard smartphone platforms.

3.3 System Overview

The basic idea of our system is to examine the centripetal acceleration (sensed by the smartphones during a turn) at different positions inside the vehicle. Figure 2 shows when a vehicle making a left turn, the driver side has smaller centripetal acceleration (a_{LD}) than that at the vehicle's center (a_{LM}), which in turn has smaller centripetal acceleration than that at the passenger side (a_{LP}). In general, compared to the center of the vehicle the driver phone always has a smaller radius (and thus experiences smaller centripetal acceleration) when the vehicle makes a left turn and a larger radius (corresponding to larger centripetal acceleration) when the vehicle makes a right turn. Therefore, if the phone's centripetal acceleration is smaller than that at the center in a left turn, or larger in the case of a right turn, then the phone is on the left side of the vehicle. Our system can thus utilize the difference of the centripetal acceleration experienced at different positions within the vehicle to distinguish the driver phone use from passengers'.

A vehicle usually undergoes multiple turns at the beginning of a trip (e.g., pulling out of a parking lot or driving in local streets before getting onto main roads). The difference of the phone's centripetal acceleration obtained by comparing left and right turns can help to determine whether the phone is at the driver side or passenger side. However, this approach requires turns made by the vehicle have the same radii, which is not practical in real-road driving environments. Our system seeks to find a solution that can exploit the difference of centripetal acceleration from *the same turn* to sense the driver phone use. The advantage of this solution is that our system can work under real-world driving scenarios with various turn sizes and driving speeds.

In particular, our system can obtain the difference of the centripetal acceleration within a turn by employing a reference centripetal acceleration, such as that at the vehicle's center or from a second phone. There are three ways of utilizing a reference centripetal acceleration that we implement in our system: 1) A low-cost cigarette lighter adapter containing an accelerometer acting as a reference point. Our system can directly compare the centripetal acceleration of the phone in the vehicle to that obtained from the cigarette lighter adapter to determine the driver phone use. 2) The speed of the vehicle obtained from the OBD-II port adapter can be used to calculate the centripetal acceleration at the vehicle's center, which is compared to the centripetal acceleration of the smartphone to detect the driver phone use. The OBD-II interface has been made mandatory for all vehicles sold in the United States since 1996. 3) When there are multiple occupants in the car, a passenger phone in the same vehicle can be employed. Our system can compare the centripetal acceleration of the passenger phone and that of the driver phone. This approach, however, relies on the presence of (and communicating to) a second phone in the vehicle. In this work, we focus on solutions (i.e., solutions 1 and 2) that a single phone can perform self-determination of the driver phone use through sensing. The plug-in adapters could share the reference readings with the phone over Bluetooth.

Realizing our approach requires three sub-tasks: *Coordinate Alignment*, *Data Calibration*, and *Position Detection*. The flow of our system is illustrated in Figure 3. When the target phone detects the Bluetooth connection (e.g. from the cigarette lighter adapter when the driver enters the car), it starts collecting readings from its accelerometer and gyroscope, which are used to derive the phone's acceleration and angular speed. Our system performs *Coordinate Alignment* so that the centripetal acceleration and angular speed derived from the phone sensors are aligned with the vehicle's. The coordinate alignment is only performed when our system starts or when the system detects the gyroscope readings crossing certain thresholds, which is caused by the change of phone's position. Once the vehicle is detected to start making a turn, the target phone collects the information from the reference point (e.g., acceleration from cigarette lighter adapter or speed from the OBD-II port adapter). The phone further conducts calibration on the data collected by itself as well as the data reported by the reference point. Our data calibration process includes three steps: *Data Interpolation*, *Trace Synchronization*, and *Acceleration Adjustment*, which aims to synchronize the traces from different sources and reduce the hardware bias caused by different phone models. Finally, *Position Detection* determines the phone's position in car leveraging the cumulative difference of centripetal acceleration (e.g., k samples around the maximum angular speed) and combining the turn direction determined from the sign of the angular speed. We next describe how to sense vehicle dynamics using smartphones and present the core component, *Detection Algorithm*, in our system. We leave the detailed presentation of *Coordinate Alignment* and *Data Calibration* to the next section (Section 4).

3.4 Sensing Vehicle Dynamics

Phone and Vehicle Alignment. We utilize the 3-axis accelerometer and 3-axis gyroscope embedded in the smartphone to obtain the centripetal acceleration while the vehicle makes a turn. There are two coordinate systems, one for the smartphone ($\{X_p, Y_p, Z_p\}$) and the other for the vehicle ($\{X_c, Y_c, Z_c\}$), as illustrated in Figure 4. To simplify the description of our approach, we assume the smartphone's coordinate system is already aligned with the vehicle's (i.e., *aligned*). We will describe how to align the phone's coordinate system in Section 4.2.

Deriving Centripetal Acceleration via Accelerometers. As illustrated in Figure 4, X_c points to the passenger side of the vehicle (i.e., opposite side of the driver). The X-axis acceleration reading on the phone reflects the centripetal acceleration (i.e., a) when the vehicle makes a turn. As illustrated in Figure 5, the X-axis reading is zero when the vehicle is driving along a straight line and reaches its positive or negative peak when the vehicle goes into the middle of a turn. The sign of the acceleration on the X-axis is determined by the turn direction due to that the centripetal acceleration is always pointing to the center of a turn. Thus, the X-axis acceleration is negative when the vehicle is making a left turn, and vice versa. Additionally, the Y_c points to the head of the vehicle. Thus, the Y-axis acceleration reading of the phone indicates the acceleration of the tangential speed (i.e., v) of the vehicle in a turn.

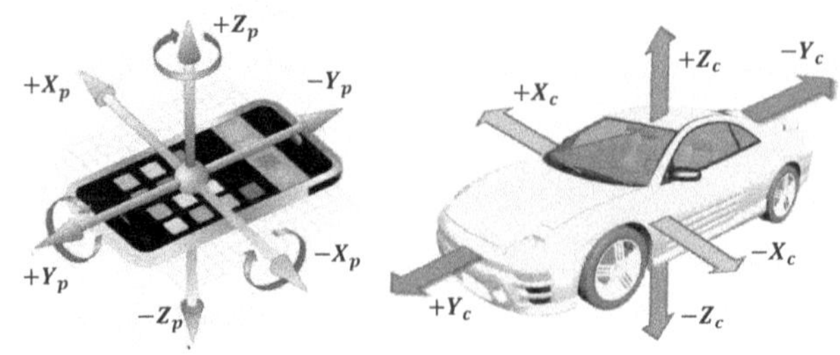

Figure 4: Coordinate systems of a smartphone and a vehicle.

Determining Turn Directions using the Gyroscope. To compare the centripetal acceleration at different positions inside the vehicle, we need to determine the turn direction, i.e., whether the vehicle is making a right turn or a left turn. The Z-axis gyroscope reading on the phone can be utilized to represent the vehicle angular speed of the turn. Figure 5 illustrates the rotation rate on Z-axis of a gyroscope on the phone during a left and right turn respectively. A counter clockwise rotation around Z-axis generates positive reading, which indicates the vehicle is making a left turn; otherwise, the gyroscope generates negative reading, indicating the vehicle is making a right turn. We note that the power consumption is only $1.5mW$ [8] for a accelerometer sensor and $10mW$ [8,21] for a gyroscope sensor. Whereas the power consumption of a smartphone is significantly higher (for example, the average power of HTC EVO is about $450mW$ [27]).

3.5 Algorithm for Sensing Driver Phone Use

It is essential to understand what are the important factors affecting the difference of the centripetal acceleration between two different positions inside the vehicle. We have the following lemma to capture such factors:

LEMMA 1. *The difference of centripetal acceleration between two in-vehicle positions is determined by the angular speed and relative distance between these two positions.*

PROOF. Assume there are two positions in the vehicle, one is the target position which is unknown, and the other is a known reference position, e.g., the center of the vehicle. When the vehicle is making a left turn, assume the radius of the target phone is r_L, and the radius of the reference position is thus $r_{LM} = r_L + \Delta r$, where Δr is the relative distance between the target position and the reference position. The difference of centripetal acceleration between these two positions can then be represented as

$$\Delta a_L = a_L - a_{LM} = \omega_L^2 r_L - \omega_L^2 (r_L + \Delta r) = -\omega_L^2 \Delta r. \quad (2)$$

Similarly, when the vehicle is making a right turn, the difference of centripetal acceleration between the target phone and the reference position is $\Delta a_R = \omega_R^2 \Delta r$. Based on the equations above, it is clear that the difference of the centripetal acceleration between two positions inside the vehicle is determined by the angular speed of the vehicle and the distance between these two positions. □

The above analysis shows that the difference of centripetal acceleration only depends on the relative distance between two positions inside the vehicle and angular speed during the turn. Thus,

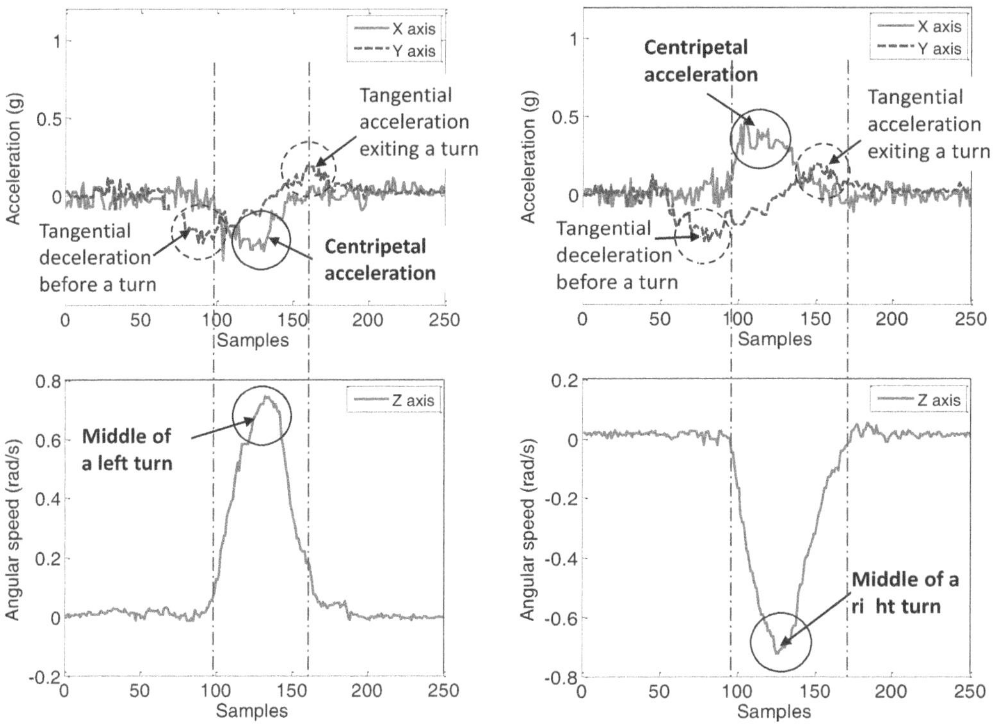

Left turns

Right turns

Figure 5: Accelerometer and Gyroscope readings when a smartphone is aligned with the vehicle who undergoes a left and a right turn respectively.

our approach of using the difference of centripetal acceleration is scalable to handle any turns with different radii. The larger the angular speed is, the more powerful the discrimination becomes in the centripetal acceleration when sensing driver phone use. Moreover, when undergoing left turns, the centripetal acceleration of the driver phone is smaller than that at the reference point (such as the cigarette lighter adapter and OBD-II port adapter), whereas it is larger than that of the reference point when going through right turns. Therefore, given the difference of the centripetal acceleration and the turning direction, our system is able to determine whether the phone is a driver phone or passenger one. Specifically, our algorithm determines the driver phone use within a single turn using the following hypothesis test:

$$\begin{cases} (a - a_M)\omega > 0, \mathcal{H}_0 : \text{passenger phone} \\ (a - a_M)\omega < 0, \mathcal{H}_1 : \text{driver phone}, \end{cases} \tag{3}$$

where a is the centripetal acceleration of the smartphone measured from its X-axis accelerometer, a_M is the centripetal acceleration of the reference position, and ω denotes the angular speed measured from smartphone's Z-axis gyroscope sensor. The sign of ω reflects the turn direction, e.g., ω is positive when the vehicle is making a left turn.

Cumulative Difference Comparison. Finally, the differences of centripetal acceleration within the turning period are accumulated in our algorithm so that to improve the detection robustness. Particularly, our algorithm utilizes 21 samples of acceleration readings at the time when the angular speed reaches its maximum value. The cumulative difference of centripetal acceleration is then combined together with the turning direction to decide whether the target phone is on the driver side or the passenger side.

Feasibility Study. Figure 6 depicts the difference of centripetal acceleration between driver's phone and passenger's when our vehicle went through 57 left turns and 60 right turns respectively. The results are categorized in three ways: *angular speed*, *car speed* and *turn radius*. It is encouraging that there is an obvious trend that increasing angular speed results in a larger value of difference of centripetal acceleration (as observed in Figure 6 (a)). Whereas the difference does not change much when increasing the vehicular driving speed and turn radius as shown in Figure 6 (b) and (c).

Utilizing Multiple Turns. Our algorithm can further improve the detection performance by combining multiple single turn results (e.g., N turns) through a simple majority voting process:

$$\begin{cases} \sum_{i=1}^{N} \dfrac{(a^i - a_M^i)\omega^i}{|(a^i - a_M^i)\omega^i|} > 0, \mathcal{H}_0 : \text{passenger phone} \\ \sum_{i=1}^{N} \dfrac{(a^i - a_M^i)\omega^i}{|(a^i - a_M^i)\omega^i|} < 0, \mathcal{H}_1 : \text{driver phone}, \end{cases} \tag{4}$$

where a^i, a_M^i, and ω^i are the smartphone's centripetal acceleration, reference centripetal acceleration, and smartphone's angular speed in i^{th} turn.

3.6 Detection Using Mixed Turns

The accuracy of the reference point affects the performance of our sensing algorithm. We find that observations from the reference point can be biased. For example, the vehicle speed provided by OBD-II is an overestimation possibly due to worn tires. Such a bias affects the algorithm accuracy when using the difference of centripetal acceleration within the same turn. Since a vehicle usually undergoes multiple turns during a trip, we exploit the centripetal acceleration obtained from *mixed turns*, i.e., comparing the normalized centripetal acceleration of the phone under a left turn to that of a right turn. The *normalized centripetal acceleration*

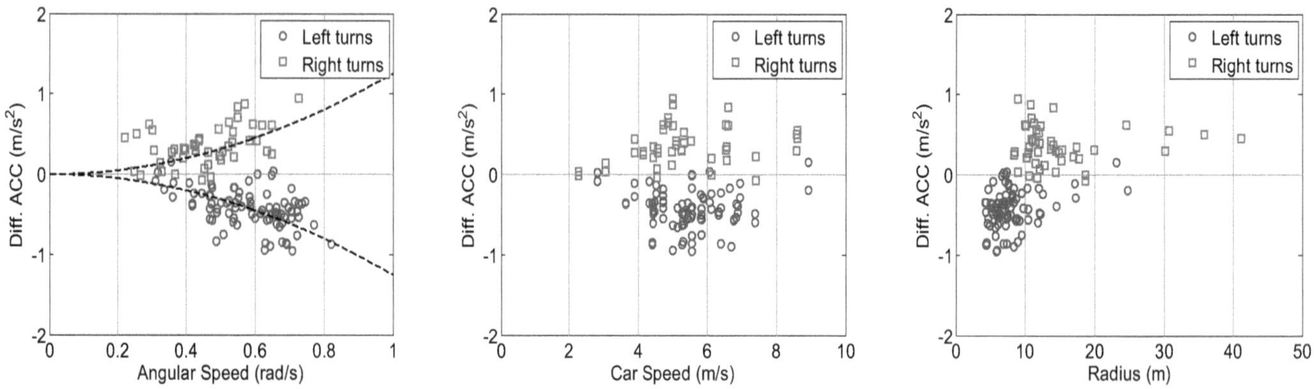

(a) Categorized with angular speed

(b) Categorized with car speed (obtained from OBD-II)

(c) Categorized with turn radius

Figure 6: Difference of centripetal acceleration between driver's phone and passenger's categorized in three ways (angular speed, car speed, and turn radius) when the vehicle undergoes 57 left turns and 60 right turns in the parking lot.

is defined as the ratio of the measured centripetal acceleration of the phone to the centripetal acceleration derived from the reference point. Using normalized centripetal acceleration enables our algorithm to work with mixed turns with different turn sizes and driving speeds encountered under real-road driving environments. The system can automatically launch this detection once a left turn and a right turn are identified based on gyroscope readings, irrespective of the sequence of these turns.

Impact of Bias. The reference centripetal acceleration a'_{LM} (for example under the left turn) can be expressed as:

$$a'_{LM} = a_{LM}\beta \tag{5}$$

where a_{LM} is unbiased centripetal acceleration of the reference point and β is the bias. When the OBD-II port adapter is used as the reference point, β comes from the biased estimate of the vehicle speed. Then the difference in centripetal acceleration becomes:

$$\Delta a_L = a_L - a'_{LM} = (1-\beta)a_L - \beta\omega_L^2\Delta r. \tag{6}$$

When there is no bias (i.e., $\beta = 1$), the above expression becomes Equation (2). However, the existence of bias ($\beta \neq 1$) can arbitrarily change the sign of the difference in centripetal acceleration, making the detection result inaccurate.

Working with Mixed Turns. Our algorithm compares the normalized centripetal acceleration of the phone under a left turn to that of a right turn to eliminate the impact of bias coming from the reference point. We denote the normalized centripetal acceleration of the phone under a left and right turn as $\hat{a}_L = \frac{a_L}{a'_{LM}}$ and $\hat{a}_R = \frac{a_R}{a'_{RM}}$, respectively. The difference of the normalized centripetal acceleration under the left and right turn can then be expressed as:

$$\begin{aligned}\Delta\hat{a}_r = \hat{a}_L - \hat{a}_R &= \frac{a_L}{a'_{LM}} - \frac{a_R}{a'_{RM}} = \frac{a_L}{a_{LM}\beta} - \frac{a_R}{a_{RM}\beta} \\ &= \frac{1}{\beta}\left(\frac{a_L}{a_{LM}} - \frac{a_R}{a_{RM}}\right).\end{aligned} \tag{7}$$

If the phone is at the driver side, a_{LM} is always larger than a_L (i.e., $\frac{a_L}{a_{LM}} < 1$), whereas a_{RM} is always smaller than a_R (i.e., $\frac{a_R}{a_{RM}} > 1$). Thus, we always have $\Delta\hat{a}_r < 0$. Similarly, if the phone is at the passenger side, we always have $\Delta\hat{a}_r > 0$. Thus, the sign of $\Delta\hat{a}_r$ becomes independent of the bias, turn size and driving speed. Our driver phone sensing with mixed turns can be further formulated as the following hypothesis test:

$$\begin{cases} \hat{a}_L - \hat{a}_R > 0, \mathcal{H}_0 : \text{passenger phone} \\ \hat{a}_L - \hat{a}_R < 0, \mathcal{H}_1 : \text{driver phone}. \end{cases} \tag{8}$$

We envision that our system can intelligently perform driver phone detection based on the availability of turns. This means that when a single turn is available, our system applies the algorithm involves the single turn. When multiple/mixed turns are available, our system performs more accurate driver phone detection using the accumulative multiple/mixed turns.

4. SYSTEM IMPLEMENTATION

In this section, we present the *Data Calibration* and *Coordinate Alignment* sub-tasks in our system. We then describe two system approaches, one using the cigarette lighter adapter with an accelerometer sensor and the other using the OBD-II port adapter as the reference points.

4.1 Data Calibration for Enhanced Reliability

In real-road driving environments, many factors (such as running engines and wind) affect the readings from the accelerometers and gyroscopes on smartphones. The sensor readings obtained can be noisy and unreliable. To address this issue, we develop several steps in our system to perform data calibration for robust detection. Our data calibration sub-task has the following capability: filter noise from sensor readings, ensure the synchronization between sensor readings from different sources, and reduce bias caused by hardware difference in smartphones.

4.1.1 *Data Interpolation*

To reduce the noise in readings obtained from the accelerometers, we apply a moving average filter to the sensor readings. However, we observe that although a fixed sampling rate is used, the real sampling interval has a small variation. Therefore, before applying the moving average filter, we interpolate to estimate the samples at evenly spaced time series points, i.e. $[t_0, t_0+\delta, t_0+2\delta, \ldots]$, where δ is the interpolation step and t_0 is the starting time stamps for the

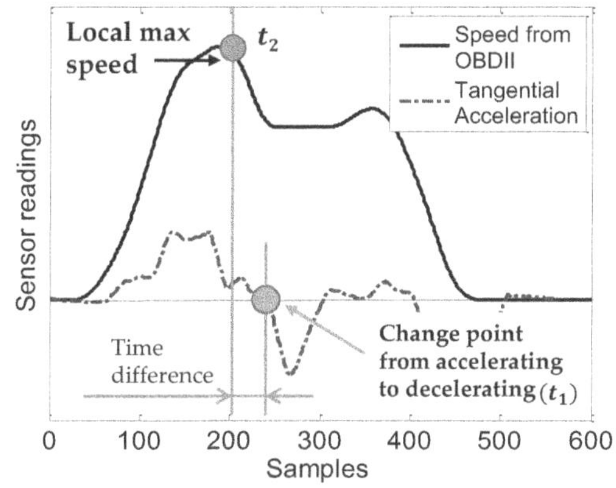

(a) Before synchronization

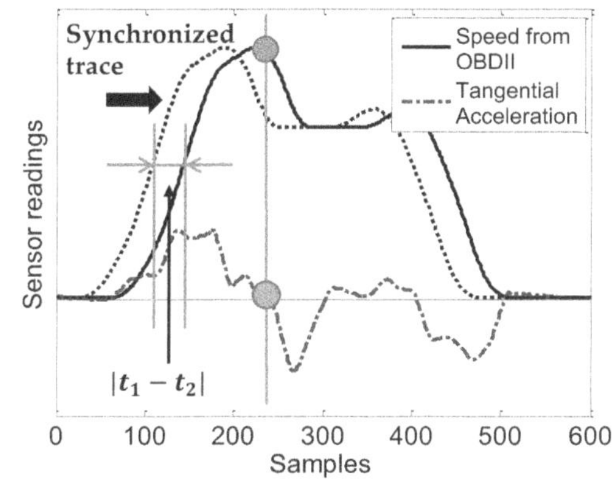

(b) After synchronization

Figure 7: Illustration of trace synchronization mechanism via tangential acceleration.

readings. Similarly, we also apply interpolation to readings from the gyroscope to obtain a uniform time interval between consecutive samples for comparison. In our experiments, we observe that a small time window of 5 samples for the moving average filter and a δ of $0.05s$ for the interpolation step are good enough to produce reliable sensing results.

4.1.2 Trace Synchronization

This procedure is used to synchronize the sensor readings from the phone and the readings at the reference point (e.g., the cigarette lighter adapter or OBD-II port adapter) since these readings come from two sources with different clocks. In our approach, two types of reference data are involved, one is the centripetal acceleration of the vehicle (reference acceleration from the cigarette lighter adapter), and the other is the speed of the vehicle (reference speed from OBD-II port adapter). To synchronize the phone's centripetal acceleration readings with the ones from the reference acceleration we calculate the cross correlation between these two sequence of readings in time series. When the cross correlation reaches the maximum, these two sequence of readings are synchronized because both sequences reflect vehicle's movement.

However, when the speed obtained from the OBD-II port adapter is used as the reference point, synchronization becomes more challenging. We develop a synchronization mechanism utilizing vehicle's acceleration, leveraging the change point in the tangential acceleration during normal driving, to synchronize the trace of reference speed from OBD-II with the acceleration reading trace from

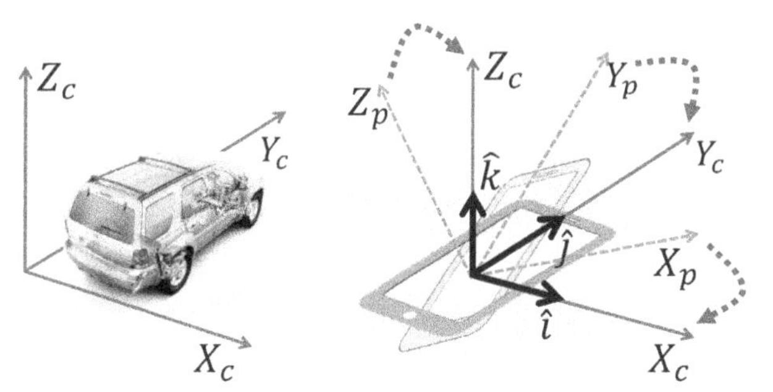

Figure 8: Illustration of how the phone's coordinate system is aligned to the vehicle's coordinate system.

smartphone in time series. The rationale behind this mechanism is that the time point that the vehicle changes from acceleration to deceleration during normal driving is the point that the vehicle reaches its maximum speed. Figure 7 illustrates how the tangential acceleration value change facilitates the synchronization with the reference speed trace. The time (t_2) that the reference speed from OBD-II reaches its local maximum should match the time (t_1) that the vehicle's tangential acceleration (i.e. the acceleration on the Y axis) changes from positive to negative. Thus, for the reference speed trace (from OBD-II), we can perform synchronization by subtracting the time difference ($t_2 - t_1$) from all its time stamps.

4.1.3 Acceleration Adjustment

Acceleration adjustment is used to reduce the bias caused by hardware differences in smartphones through adjusting the centripetal acceleration of the phone. Because the centripetal acceleration only exists during a turn, the readings on the X-axis accelerometer of the phone should be zero when the vehicle is moving along a straight line. Nevertheless, the acceleration on the X-axis may have a constant value different from zero due to different hardware characteristics in different phone models. To reduce such a bias, our system performs the following adjustment: 1) use the phone's gyroscope to determine the time period that the vehicle is driving along a straight line, i.e., the time period with no rotation rate on the Z-axis gyroscope; 2) calculate the mean value of the X-axis acceleration during this time period; and (3) subtract the calculated mean value from all the X-axis acceleration readings to remove the constant bias.

4.2 Coordinate Alignment

Our system cannot derive meaningful vehicle dynamics from sensor readings on the smartphone unless the phone's coordinate system is aligned with the vehicle's. The *Coordinate Alignment* sub-task aligns the phone's coordinate system with the vehicle's by utilizing the accelerometers and gyroscopes on smartphones. As illustrated in Figure 8, the phone's coordinate system ($\{X_p, Y_p, Z_p\}$) is determined by the pose of the phone inside the vehicle. Our coordinate alignment aims to find a rotation matrix R to rotate the phone's coordinate system to match with the vehicle's ($\{X_c, Y_c, Z_c\}$). We define three unit coordinate vectors under the vehicle's coordinate system as $\hat{\imath}, \hat{\jmath}$ and $\hat{k}$ for X_c, Y_c and Z_c axis respectively (i.e., $\hat{\imath} = [1, 0, 0]^T$ in vehicle's coordinate system). We denote the corresponding coordinates of these three unit vectors in the phone's coordinate system as:

$$\hat{q} = [x_q, y_q, z_q]^T, \tag{9}$$

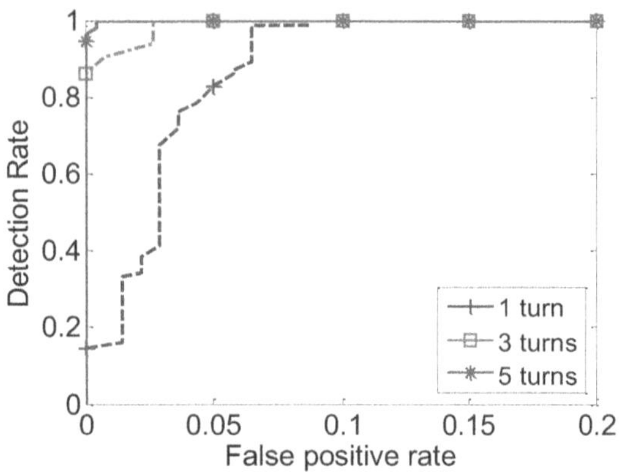

Figure 9: ROC curve when using single or multiple turns and the acceleration of adapter phone as the reference acceleration in parking lot.

where $q \in i, j, k$, and the rotation matrix is given by [22]:

$$R = \begin{Bmatrix} x_i & x_j & x_k \\ y_i & y_j & y_k \\ z_i & z_j & z_k \end{Bmatrix} \tag{10}$$

Our coordinate alignment sub-task utilizing smartphone's accelerometer and gyroscope readings to obtain each element in the rotation matrix R consists of three steps:

Deriving $\hat{k}$. We can apply a low pass filter (e.g., exponential smoothing) on the three axes accelerometer readings on the phone to obtain the constant components from these three accelerations and derive the gravity acceleration [1], which is then be normalized to generate the unit vector $\hat{k} = [x_k, y_k, z_k]^T$.

Deriving $\hat{j}$. To obtain $\hat{j}$, we utilize the fact that the three-axes accelerometer readings of the phone are caused by vehicle's acceleration or deceleration when driving straight. For example, we can obtain $\hat{j} = [x_j, y_j, z_j]^T$ through extracting the accelerometer readings when the vehicle decelerates (e.g., the vehicle usually decelerates before making turns or encountering traffic lights and stop sign). The gyroscope is used to determine whether the vehicle is driving straight (i.e., with zero rotation rate). We note the gravity component needs to be excluded because it distributes on all three axes of the phone when the phone's coordinate system is not aligned with the vehicle's.

Obtaining $\hat{i}$. Since the coordinate system follows the right hand rule, we can determine the unit vector $\hat{i} = \hat{j} \times \hat{k} = [x_i, y_i, z_i]^T$.

After obtaining the rotation matrix R, given the sensor reading vector in the phone's coordinate system $\mathbf{s}$, we can obtain the rotated sensor reading vector $\mathbf{s}'$ aligned with vehicle's coordinate system by applying a rotation matrix R as: $\mathbf{s}' = \mathbf{s} \times R$. We note that there are existing studies utilizing the sensors embedded in smartphones to calibrate the coordinate systems between the phone and the vehicle [29]. Different from the previous study, our coordinate alignment mechanism does not require working with the GPS on the phone, and thus is more accurate and energy efficient.

4.3 Reference Using a Cigarette Lighter Adapter

We next show how a low-cost cigarette lighter adapter containing an accelerometer can be employed as a reference point in our system. The location of the cigarette lighter charger is ideal for the reference point since it is located at the center of the front seats.

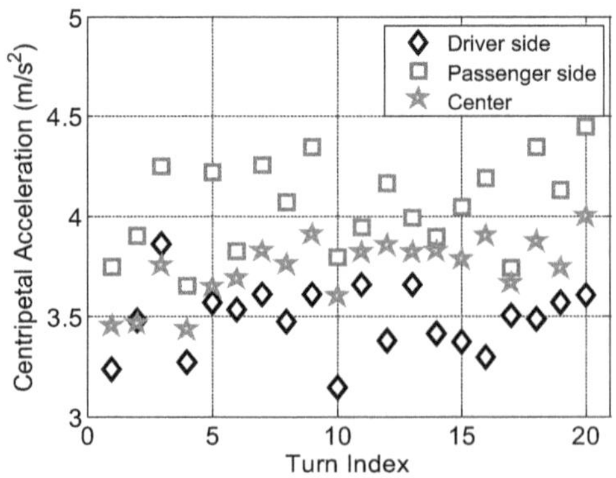

(a) 20 left turns

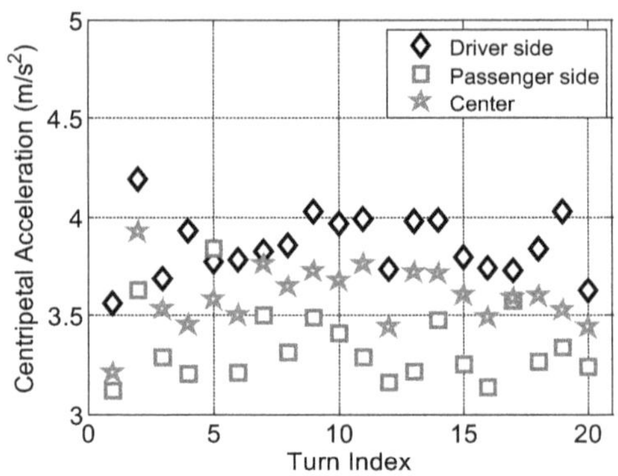

(b) 20 right turns

Figure 10: Centripetal acceleration at different positions inside the vehicle under 20 left and 20 right turns in parking lot.

Our system can thus distinguish driver phone use from passenger's by comparing the centripetal acceleration of the phone to that of the reference point. The centripetal acceleration of the reference point can be obtained from the cigarette lighter adapter's accelerometer. The measured centripetal acceleration from the cigarette lighter adapter is then transmitted to the target phone via Bluetooth for comparison.

Since at the beginning of a trip, a vehicle usually makes multiple turns to pull out of a parking lot or drive on local streets before getting onto main roads, we demonstrate the feasibility of the cigarette-lighter-adapter-based approach by driving a car in the parking lot of Babbio Center at Stevens Institute of Technology for over a one month time period. During our experiments, we utilize a smartphone (the *adapter phone*) and place it at the location of the cigarette lighter charger to simulate the cigarette lighter adapter containing an accelerometer. To distinguish the driver phone use from the passenger's, we place two iPhone4s at driver and passenger side respectively. We have 65 turns in total including both left and right turns at the parking lot. Each turn has about 90 degrees and lasts for about 20 seconds (which includes the time period when driving straight and turning). The radii of the turns are approximately 10 meters and the speed of the turns is around $10mph$. Note that without notice, the sensor readings we are referring to are after coordinate alignment.

Figure 9 presents the detection rate versus false positive rate when applying driver phone sensing algorithm within the same turn. The detection rate indicates how many cases of driver phone use are correctly detected, whereas the false positive rate shows

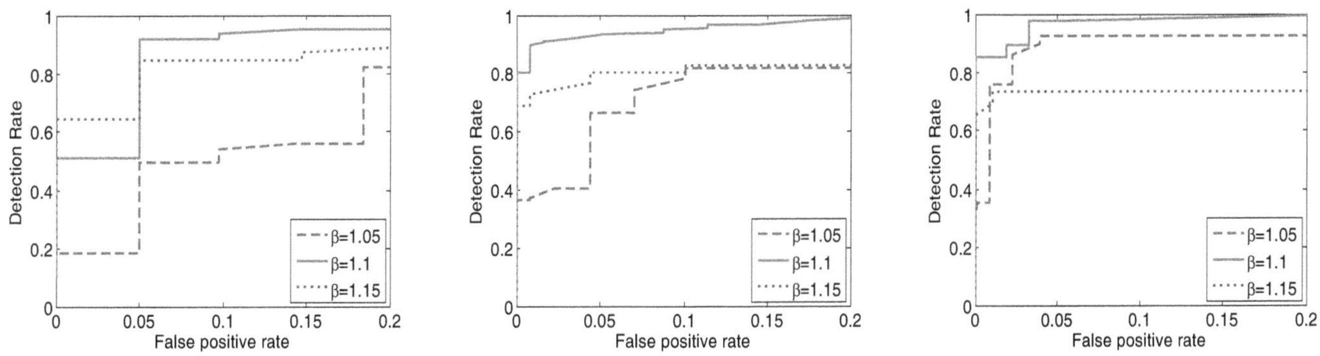

(a) 2 turns (b) 3 turns (c) 5 turns

Figure 11: ROC curve when using multiple turns and OBD-II speed in parking lot.

how many cases of passenger phone use are mistakenly classified as driver phone use. It is encouraging that our system can achieve above a 90% detection rate with about a 6% false positive rate using a single turn. Once the algorithm is applied when the vehicle undergoes multiple turns, the performance has a substantial improvement. For example, with 3 turns, the detection rate can be improved to 99.7% with much less false positive (3%), whereas with 5 turns, our system can reach 100% detection rate with less than 1% false positive (0.4% to be exact). These results confirms the feasibility of sensing vehicle dynamics to determine driver phone use.

4.4 Reference Using an OBD-II Port Adapter

The OBD-II interface has been made mandatory for all vehicles sold in the United States after 1996, and inexpensive OBD-II port adapters with Bluetooth connection are readily available in the market. We can forward the speed of the vehicle from the OBD-II port adapter to the smartphone via a Bluetooth connection. In our system implementation, we utilize a low cost OBD-II port adapter, which allows us to collect the vehicle's speed from the OBD-II port adapter via a USB connection, to use the speed of the vehicle as the reference point. The centripetal acceleration of the car's center (i.e., reference point) is the product of the OBD-II speed and the angular speed measured by the target phone. The driver phone use can be detected by comparing the phone's centripetal acceleration to that of the vehicle's center.

4.4.1 OBD-II Speed

We use the ElmScan 5 compact OBD-II scan toolkit (about 30 dollars) to obtain the OBD-II speed, which has a sampling rate of about 20 samples/s. The OBD-II speed represents the speed of the car's center since it is calculated based on the averaged distance traversed by four tires. Thus, the calculated centripetal acceleration based on the OBD-II speed and the angular speed is for the center of the vehicle. However, the OBD-II speed estimation is a conservative overestimation to allow for changes in tires' circumferences. We assume the reported speed is proportional to the true speed: $v'_M = v_M \times \beta$, where v'_M and v_M are the estimated and true speed respectively. We also assume that the value of β is constant per vehicle, even though there is a slight variation in practice due to the change of tire pressure. We study the impact of the bias (β) on the performance of our algorithm in our experiments.

4.4.2 Evaluation

We use the same experiment setup as we had in the parking lot in Section 4.3. Figure 10 shows the scatter plot on the centripetal accelerations from three sources: smartphone at driver seat, smartphone at passenger seat, and the calculated one for the vehicle's center based on the OBD-II speed, under 20 left turns and 20 right turns respectively. Note that we did the OBD-II speed adjustment by setting the speed adjustment coefficient $\beta = 1.1$. We observe that the centripetal acceleration calculated based on OBD-II speed is in between the centripetal acceleration of the driver phone and passenger phone. This indicates that employing the centripetal acceleration derived from the OBD-II speed is an effective reference point for determining driver phone use.

Figure 11 depicts the detection rate versus false positive rate by applying our algorithm when using multiple turns under different bias β. With a small bias $\beta = 1.1$, we can achieve 91% detection rate with 5% false positive rate under two turns. By increasing the number of turns, the performance can be significantly improved. For example, with 3 and 5 turns, the detection rate is improved to 93% with 5% false positive rate and 97% detection rate with only 3% false positive rate, respectively. We find that the bias β is critical to the detection performance when only data for few turns is available, but the sensitivity to β decreases with the increasing number of turns, as shown in Figure 11. When data for multiple turns is available, our approach does not rely on a careful calibration of β, rather, a simple approximation is sufficient. Note that the bias can be learned offline. Alternatively, our algorithm based on mixed turns (Section 3.6) can eliminate the impact of the biased OBD-II speed. We present the results from using mixed turns tested from real-road driving environments in the next section.

5. EVALUATION IN REAL-ROAD DRIVING ENVIRONMENTS

In this section, we evaluate our proposed driver phone use sensing system in real road driving environments using two types of phones in two different cities.

5.1 Experimental Setup

5.1.1 Phones and Vehicles

We conduct our experiments with two types of phones: iphone4 and HTC 3D. Both phones have a Bluetooth radio, 3-axis accelerometer and gyroscope. The iphone4 is equipped with a 1GHz ARM Cortex-A8 CPU and 512M RAM running with iOS5.2, whereas the HTC 3D has a Qualcomm MSM8660 1.2GHz CPU and 1G RAM running with Android 2.4. Both the accelerometer and gyroscope sampling rate are 20 samples/s. There are two vehicles used in our experiments: a Honda Accord (*Car A*) and an Acura sedan (*Car B*).

(a) Driving trajectory in Hoboken, NJ

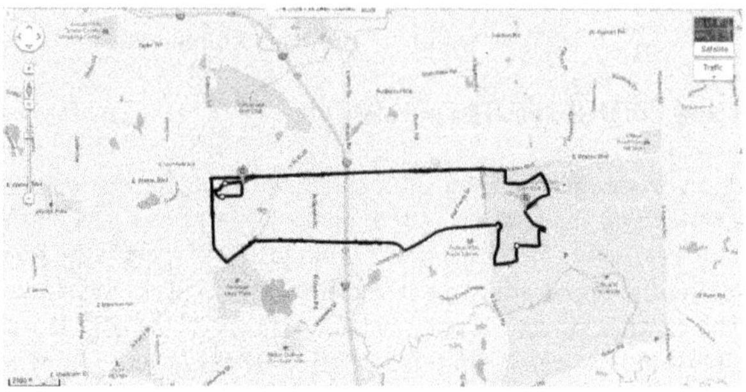

(b) Driving trajectory in Pontiac, MI

Figure 12: Daily commute routes used for real-road driving evaluation in Hoboken, NJ and Pontiac, MI.

5.1.2 Real Road Driving Scenarios

To evaluate our proposed system, we conduct experiments using the iphone4 for over one month when Car A is used as the daily commute vehicle in Hoboken, NJ. Hoboken has a typical urban setting. To test the generality of our system, we further experiment with the HTC 3D using Car B to commute to work in Pontiac, MI for over one week. Pontiac presents a suburban environment. The driving routes are depicted in Figure 12. The phones are placed in either the driver or passenger seat/door during the experiments. Each of the traces contains 10 to 20-minute of driving. Table 1 summarizes the details on the traces collected in these two cities. In total, we have 292 left turns and 278 right turns in Hoboken, NJ, and 211 left turns and 219 right turns in Pontiac, MI.

5.1.3 Prototype

We implement our sensing driver phone use system using the Android platform. The prototype runs as an Android App and collects readings from the accelerometer and gyroscope in the smartphone. It then runs through the detection algorithm using either single or multiple turns to determine whether the phone is at the driver or passenger side. Our prototype also works with the OBD-II port adapter via Bluetooth. We also present the results using iPhone 4 by applying trace driven off-line analysis.

5.1.4 Metrics

Location	Left turns	Right turns	Car	Phone
Hoboken,NJ	292	278	Car A	iphone4
Pontiac,MI	211	219	Car B	HTC 3D

Table 1: Traces collected in Hoboken, NJ and Pontiac, MI.

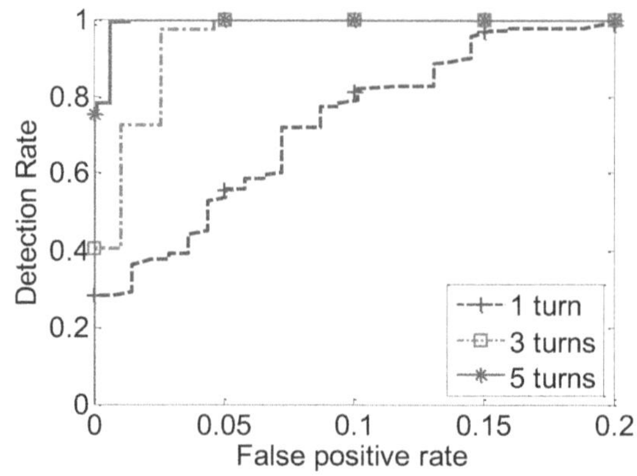

(a) Car A, iPhone4, Hoboken, NJ

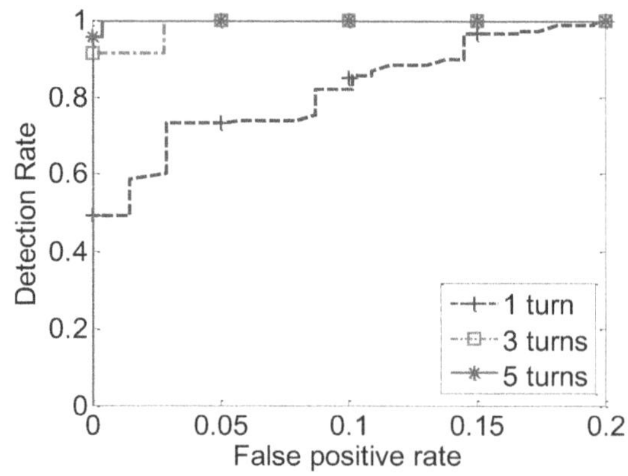

(b) Car B, HTC 3D, Pontiac, MI

Figure 13: ROC curve when using the adapter phone as the reference point.

To evaluate the performance of our system, we define the following metrics:

Accuracy. Accuracy is defined as the percentage of the trials that were correctly classified as driver phone use or passenger phone use.

Detection Rate (DR) and False Positive Rate (FPR). Detection rate is defined as the percentage of driver phone use that are correctly identified by our system, whereas the False positive rate is defined as the percentage of passenger phone use that are classified as driver phone use.

Detection Latency. We define the detection delay as the time needed to make a decision on whether it's a driver phone use or passenger use starting from driving a vehicle.

5.2 Evaluation Using a Cigarette Lighter Adapter

We evaluate the effectiveness of using the adapter phone placed at the cigarette lighter charger as the reference when driving Car A in Hoboken, NJ and Car B in Pontiac, MI. Figure 13 presents the detection rate versus false positive rate when applying our algorithm to determine the driver phone use. We observe that within one turn, our system achieves over a 80% detection rate with less than a 10% false positive rate for both traces in Hoboken and Pontiac. By utilizing multiple turns for detection, the performance is further improved. Specifically, for the experiments in Hoboken, the detection rate goes up to 97% with a 3% false positive rate with 3 turns. And with 5 turns, our system can achieve a 99.1% detection rate with less than a 1% false positive rate (0.3% to be

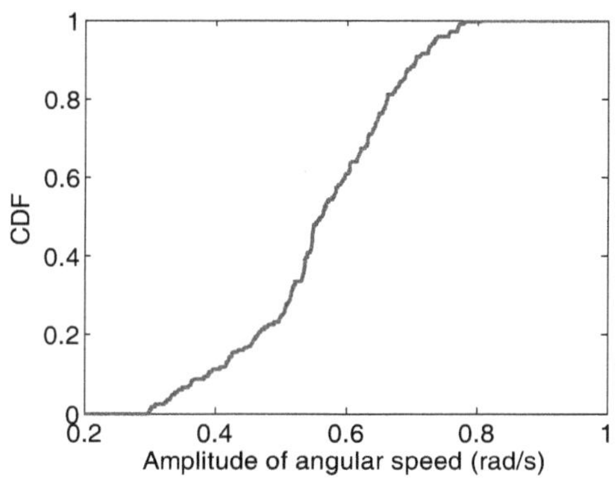

Figure 14: Cumulative distribution function of the angular speed in 570 turns collected from driving in Hoboken, NJ over one month time frame.

exact) in Hoboken. Similarly, for the experiments in Pontiac, we can achieve a 91.4% detection rate with a 2.4% false positive rate by using 3 turns, and a 98.42% detection rate with a 0.92% false positive rate by using 5 turns. This indicates that our system can achieve very high detection accuracy when the vehicle undergoes only a few turns. We note that the best performance in the ROC curves is achieved when the threshold (for the hypothesis testing as described in Equation (8)) is about $10cm$ away from the center of the car to the passenger side.

5.3 Evaluation Using an OBD-II Port Adapter

We further evaluate using the OBD-II speed as reference by applying mixed turns detection, which eliminates the dependence on the bias caused by using the OBD-II.

Filtering Turns with Angular Speed. The noise in the sensing data affects the results of the hypothesis test. Our system adopts a strategy to select turns with a large angular speed so that to get a larger difference of acceleration, thus making our algorithm more robust to noisy sensor readings. As shown in Equation (2), the larger the angular speed is, the more powerful the discrimination becomes in the centripetal acceleration. Given the certain noise level presented in the sensing data, we can thus filter out the turns with small angular speed to improve the detection performance. Our strategy is to choose the turns based on the maximum angular speed and filter out those with the maximum angular speed below a threshold. Figure 14 shows that through our study with 570 turns collected from real-road driving in Hoboken, NJ over one month time period, over 80% of the turns have maximum angular speed larger than 0.5 rad/s. This suggests that applying our turn selection strategy to cope with the noisy sensing data will only sacrifice a small portion of the data. We thus choose 0.5 rad/s as the threshold in our study.

Results. Figure 15 presents the system performance when using mixed turns with and without turn selection based on driving traces in Hoboken, NJ. We observe that the performance under turn selection is 20% better than that without turn selection. In particular, with the turn selection strategy, the detection rate is about 80% with a false positive rate of 20% under only 1 set of mixed turns, whereas the detection rate goes up to 91% with only a 5% false positive rate based on 3 sets of mixed turns.

5.4 Evaluation Using Dual Phones

When there are passengers in the vehicle, our system can leverage a second phone instead of an adapter on the car to determine

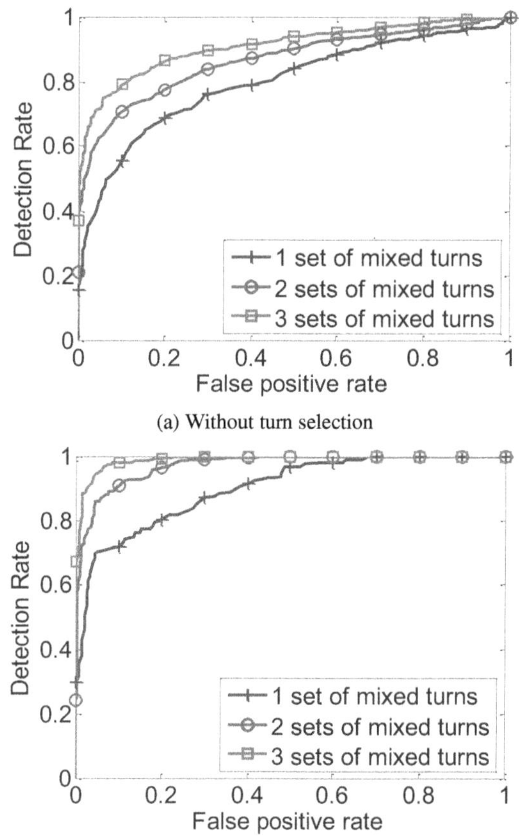

(a) Without turn selection

(b) With turn selection

Figure 15: ROC curve when using OBD-II port adapter as the reference point under mixed turns using iPhone4, Car A in Hoboken NJ.

the driver phone. While we have not found any detailed statistics on driver versus passenger cell phone use in vehicles, a federal accident database (FARS) [10] reveals that about 38% of automobile trips include passengers. Basically, our system can directly compare the centripetal acceleration of these two phones to determine the one on the left side is the driver's phone. These two phones can exchange their centripetal acceleration via Bluetooth. To evaluate such an approach, we carry out a series of experiments by putting one phone at two driver's locations: driver's left pocket (*position A*), driver's right pocket (*position B*), and the other phone at two passenger's locations: passenger's left pocket (*position C*), and passenger's right pocket (*position D*).

Figure 16 shows the detection accuracy of employing the second phone as reference when driving in two cities when undergoing 1, 2, and 3 turns. We observe that when undergoing one turn the scenario A-D achieves the best detection accuracy, which is over 95% because the two phones have the largest distance between each other in the vehicle, while the scenario B-C with two phones located in the closest positions achieves about 70% accuracy under one turn. This is because the significance of the difference of centripetal acceleration between two phones is only affected by the relative distance between them. We find that the accuracy for B-C scenario can go up to 90% when undergoing 3 turns. We observe similar detection accuracy in Pontiac, for instance, the scenario A-D can achieve the detection accuracy over 95.6% and 99.8% for 1 and 3 turns respectively. These results show that using the ac-

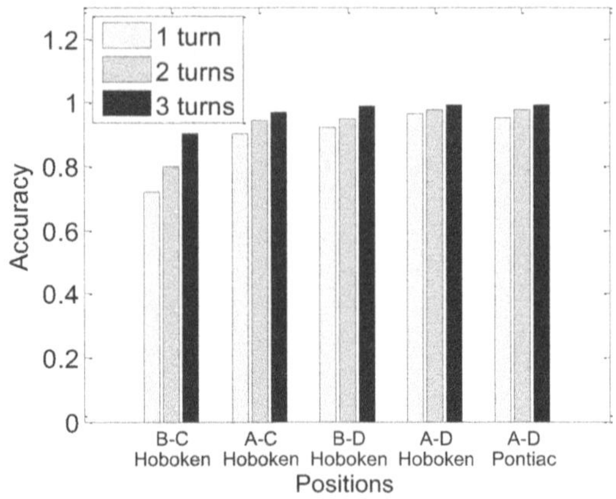

Figure 16: Detection accuracy of using a second phone inside the vehicle as the reference.

celeration from the second phone as the reference generally has good performance in real-world driving tests. Moreover, by using multiple turns, the detection accuracy can be further improved, especially for the phones that are placed very close to each other (i.e. the B-C scenario).

5.5 Detection Latency

In reality, it is common that a vehicle experiences more turns at the beginning of a trip before getting onto main roads, such as driving the vehicle out of the parking lot and then driving on local streets. These turns make our system able to determine whether the phone is driver's or passenger's. When sensing driver phone use is conducted using a single turn, the detection latency consists of the algorithm execution time and the turning time (which includes time for sensing data collection). In our system prototype, we find that the algorithm execution time is at the level of sub-millisecond. Thus, the detection latency is determined by the turning time. Based on our experiments summarized in Table 1, the average turning time is about $10s$ in both Hoboken, NJ and Pontiac, MI.

When multiple turns are employed in our detection algorithm, the time interval between two turns, measured between two maximum angular speeds, dominates the total detection latency. We observe that the average time interval between two turns in Hoboken, NJ is about $28s$, while it is $18s$ in Pontiac, MI. Therefore, the latency of our algorithm is the sum of turning times and the time between turns. For instance, when we use two turns with the cigarette lighter adapter, the latency is about $48s$ and $38s$ in Hoboken and Pontiac respectively. This indicates that our driver phone sensing algorithm has an acceptable detection latency in environments including both urban and suburban. The time delay in Hoboken city is longer than that in Pontiac. This is because Hoboken has the urban city setting and the driving routes involve more traffic lights and stop signs. Therefore, vehicles experience longer waiting time before making turns.

6. DISCUSSION

In this section, we first discuss how this technique can be extended with front-rear detection based on acceleration forces created when the vehicle passes over bumps. We then discuss our initial attempts and results towards a completely phone-based solution, that is a solution that also eliminates the requirement for the plugin adapter. Finally, we speculate about other vehicle sensors

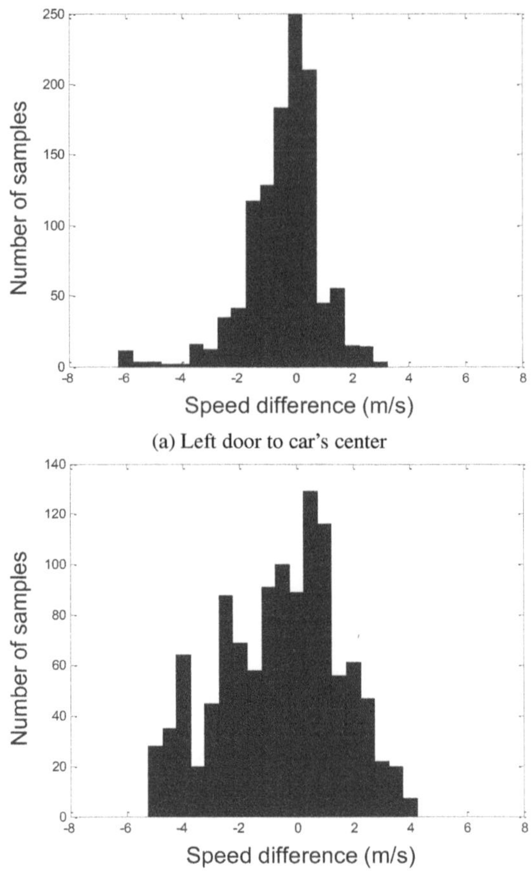

(a) Left door to car's center

(b) Right door to car's center

Figure 17: Histogram of differential speed between the phone's position on left/right door and at the center of the vehicle.

that could be used as a reference point, when vehicles become a more open platform.

6.1 Extended System with Front-Rear Detection

While left-right classification is able to disambiguate the majority of in-vehicle phone use situations, a complete system for driver phone detection involves both left-right and front-rear classifications of phone position. The left-right classification approach proposed in this study can be integrated with the front-rear accelerometer classification described in our previous work [37]. The basic idea of this front-rear classification is that the acceleration forces on a vehicle when passing over speed bumps, potholes, or other uneven surfaces are also position dependent. Consider that the front wheels will hit the bump first, followed by the rear wheels a short time later. Since the front seats are closer to the front wheels, phones at this position will observe a stronger effect from this bump than phones on the rear seats. Our prior experiment show that it could achieve as high as 90% accuracy when passing two bumps and 94% when passing three bumps.

6.2 Towards Infrastructure-Free Driver Phone Use Detection

One possible infrastructure-free approach is to use the smartphone's GPS speed measurement as a reference. At the first glance,

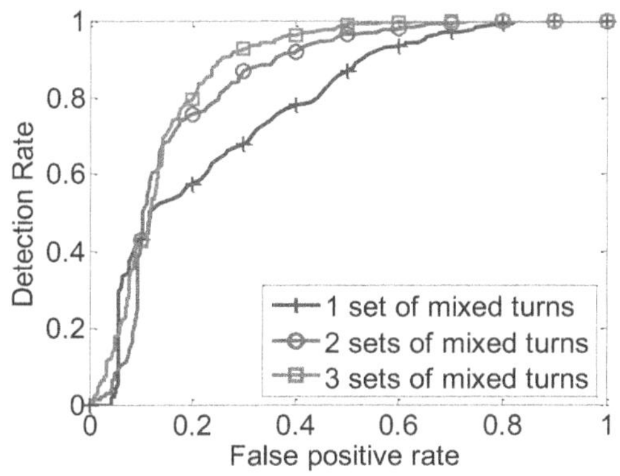

(a) Without turn selection

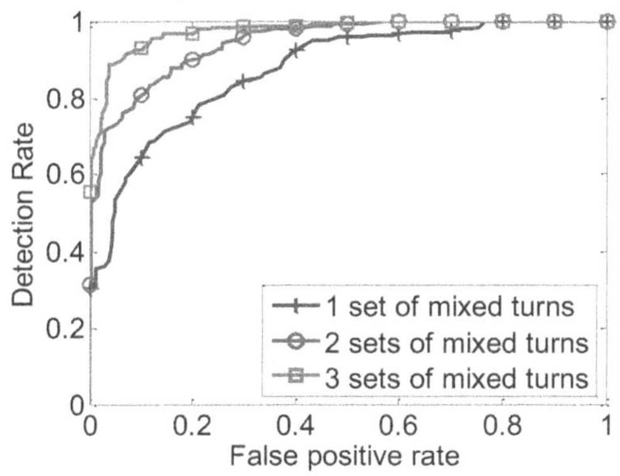

(b) With turn selection

Figure 18: ROC of driver phone use sensing in Hoboken with mixed turns algorithm and GPS speed.

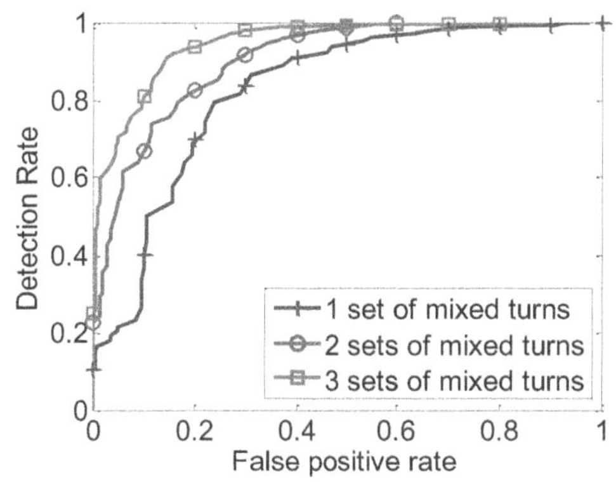

(a) Without turn selection

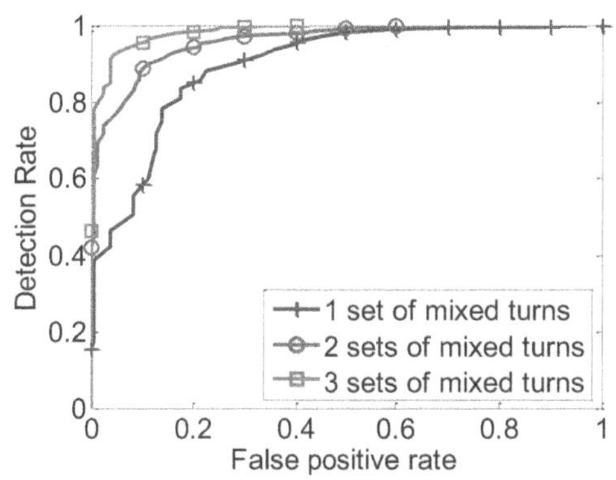

(b) With turn selection

Figure 19: ROC of driver phone use sensing in Pontiac with mixed turns algorithm and GPS speed.

using a speed measurement at the phone position does not seem suitable as a reference. This is less clear however when taking, for example, the GPS chip's internal processing and smoothing into account. Consider a phone on one side and a vehicle moving in a straight line with a constant velocity. In this case, both the instantaneous and smoothed velocities will be the same. When the vehicle turns, the value of the smoothed velocity will lag closer to the center velocity. Assuming the phone's gyroscopes and accelerometers are closer to the instantaneous values, the difference could be used to discriminate the side of the vehicle.

The filters used on GPS chipsets are often proprietary, so we perform experiments to test this hypothesis. We place two iPhone4s on two front doors, and also employ a third iPhone4 in a center cup holder to collect the tangential speed of the center of the vehicle. We then compare the GPS speed from the center phone to those obtained from the front doors. Figure 17 presents the histogram of the differences between the GPS speed of the center phone and the two phones on two front doors. We observe that both histogram of the difference centered at around $0m/s$, which indicates that the GPS speed is not sensitive to the in-vehicle position, thus making using the smartphone's GPS speed tractable as a replacement of the OBD-II speed.

We further use real road driving experiments to validate the use of phone's GPS. The results presented in Figure 18 and Figure 19 show that for both traces in Hoboken, NJ and Pontiac, MI, our algorithm can achieve over 80% detection rate with 3 sets of mixed turns without turn selection. Based on turns with $\omega > 0.5rad/s$, our algorithm can achieve much better detection rate, that is 90% and 95% in Hoboken and Pontiac respectively. These results show some promise in using the GPS speed measured by the phone to derive the vehicle reference and possible achieve completely infrastructure-free driver detection. While cannot fully explain these observations, we believe these results warrant further study.

6.3 Integration with Additional Vehicle Sensors

Our work also points to a more intriguing possibility of vehicular smartphone applications where all the vehicle's sensors are available to an authorized smartphone. While ODB-II to Bluetooth is a first step in this direction, much richer interfaces with additional information are possible and have been realized in select vehicles. For example, the Open-XC interfaces [13] provides additional vehicle parameters to Android phones. Of particular interest, is the steering wheel angle measured by a steering wheel position sensor [6] (this sensor normal provides information for electronic stability control). Having such information available would provide additional and potentially more accurate means for determining the turn radius of the vehicle and estimating acceleration forces at a vehicle reference point.

7. CONCLUSION

In this paper we demonstrate a low-infrastructure approach for discriminating between a phone in the driver or passenger position of a moving vehicle by sensing vehicle dynamics. It does not rely on a built-in handsfree Bluetooth system in the car but only on the phone's embedded sensors and a simple plug-in reference module for the cigarette lighter or OBD-II port. The insight that the centripetal acceleration varies depending on the position in the car enables us to build a system that exploits the difference of centripetal acceleration at different positions inside the vehicle to determine the driver phone when turning. Our system accomplishes the task by comparing the measured centripetal acceleration at the phone with that from a reference point in the vehicle. Instead of such a reference point, the system could also leverage a second phone in the car to perform detection when available.

We demonstrate the generality of our approach through extensive experiments with two different phone types and two different cars in two cities over a month-long time period. Our findings show that our approach yields close to 100% accuracy using only a few turns with less than 3% false positive rate. While the system has to wait until the vehicle has passed through one or more turns, our experiments show that detection is often possible by the time a vehicle leaves a parking lot or before it reaches a main road, so the determination is available for the vast majority of trips.

8. ACKNOWLEDGEMENT

This work is supported in part by the National Science Foundation Grants CNS-0954020, CNS-1016303, CNS-1040735 and CNS-0845896.

9. REFERENCES

[1] Android Developers. http://developer.android.com/reference/android/hardware/SensorEvent.html.
[2] AT&T chief speaks out on texting at the wheel. http://www.nytimes.com/2012/09/20/technology/att-chief-speaks-out-on-texting-while-driving.html.
[3] AT&T driver safety app. http://www.theverge.com/2012/8/15/3243963/att-texting-driving-safety-app.
[4] Distracted driving and driver, roadway, and environmental factors. http://www.distraction.gov/download/research-pdf/Distracted-Driving-and-Driver-Roadway-Environmental-Factors.pdf.
[5] Drivesmart plus. http://tinyurl.com/4v7oygy.
[6] Electronic stability control. http://en.wikipedia.org/wiki/Electronic_stability_control.
[7] Guardian angel vehicle platform. http://www.trinitynoble.com/.
[8] InvenSense MPU-6000/6050 Six-Axis (Gyro + Accelerometer) MEMS Motion Tracking Devices. http://www.invensense.com/mems/gyro/mpu6050.html.
[9] Key2safedriving app. http://www.key2safedriving.com/.
[10] National highway traffic safety administration:Fatality analysis reporting system. http://tinyurl.com/24h2t7.
[11] No call, no text, no update behind the wheel: NTSB calls for nationwide ban on PEDs while driving. http://www.ntsb.gov/news/2011/111213.html.
[12] Textecution. http://www.textecution.com/.
[13] The OpenXC Platform. http://openxcplatform.com/.
[14] Txtblocker. http://www.txtblocker.com/.
[15] G. Chandrasekaran and et.al. Tracking vehicular speed variations by warping mobile phone signal strengths. In *IEEE PerCom*, 2011.
[16] H. Chu, V. Raman, J. Shen, R. Choudhury, A. Kansal, and V. Bahl. Poster: You driving? talk to you later. In *ACM MobiSys*, 2011.
[17] J. Dai, J. Teng, X. Bai, Z. Shen, and D. Xuan. Mobile phone based drunk driving detection. In *PervasiveHealth*, 2010.
[18] H. Eren, S. Makinist, E. Akin, and A. Yilmaz. Estimating driving behavior by a smartphone. In *Proceedings of IEEE Intelligent Vehicles Symposium (IV)*, 2012.
[19] J. Eriksson, L. Girod, B. Hull, R. Newton, S. Madden, and H. Balakrishnan. The pothole patrol: Using a mobile sensor network for road surface monitoring. In *ACM MobiSys*, 2008.
[20] M. Fazeen, B. Gozick, R. Dantu, M. Bhukhiya, and M. C. Gonzalez. Safe driving using mobile phones. *IEEE Transactions on Intelligent Transportation Systems (TITS)*, 2012.
[21] J. A. Geen. Very low cost gyroscopes. In *IEEE Sensors*, 2005.
[22] A. Glassner. *Graphics Gems*. Morgan Kaufmann, 1990.
[23] D. Gundlegard and J. Karlsson. Handover location accuracy for travel time estimation in GSM and UMTS. In *IEEE ITSC*, 2009.
[24] D. Johnson and M. Trivedi. Driving style recognition using a smartphone as a sensor platform. In *Proceedings of the 14th IEEE International Conference on Intelligent Transportation Systems (ITSC)*, 2011.
[25] K. A. Li, P. Baudisch, and K. Hinckley. Blindsight: Eyes-free access to mobile phones. In *ACM CHI*, 2008.
[26] J. Lindqvist and J. Hong. Undistracted driving: A mobile phone that doesn't distract. In *HotMobile*, 2011.
[27] H. Liu, Y. Gan, J. Yang, S. Sidhom, Y. Wang, Y. Chen, and F. Ye. Push the limit of wifi based localization for smartphones. In *ACM Mobicom*, 2012.
[28] A. Mednis, G. Strazdins, R. Zviedris, G. Kanonirs, and L. Selavo. Real time pothole detection using android smartphones with accelerometers. In *IEEE DCOSS*, 2011.
[29] P. Mohan, V. Padmanabhan, and R. Ramjee. Nericell: Rich monitoring of road and traffic conditions using mobile smartphones. In *ACM SenSys*, 2008.
[30] M. Mun and et.al. PEIR, the personal environmental impact report, as a platform for participatory sensing systems research. In *ACM MobiSys*, 2009.
[31] L. Nelson, S. Bly, and T. Sokoler. Quiet calls: Talking silently on mobile phones. In *ACM CHI*, 2001.
[32] R. Serway and J. Jewett. *Physics for scientists and engineers*. Brooks/Cole Publishing Company, 2009.
[33] A. Thiagarajan, J. Biagioni, T. Gerlich, and J. Eriksson. Cooperative transit tracking using smart-phones. In *ACM SenSys*, 2010.
[34] J. White, C. Thompson, H. Turner, B. Dougherty, and D. C. Schmidt. WreckWatch: Automatic traffic accident detection and notification with smartphones. *Mobile Networks and Applications*, 2011.
[35] M. Wiberg and S. Whittaker. Managing availability: Supporting lightweight negotiations to handle interruptions. *ACM Transactions on Computer-Human Interaction*, 2005.
[36] J. Yang, S. Sidhom, G. Chandrasekaran, T. Vu, H. Liu, N. Cecan, Y. Chen, M. Gruteser, and R. Martin. Detecting driver phone use leveraging car speakers. In *ACM MobiCom*, 2011.
[37] J. Yang, S. Sidhom, G. Chandrasekaran, T. Vu, H. Liu, N. Cecan, Y. Chen, M. Gruteser, and R. Martin. Sensing driver phone use with acoustic ranging through car speakers. *IEEE Transactions on Mobile Computing (TMC)*, 2012.

Optimizing Background Email Sync on Smartphones

Fengyuan Xu[1,3], Yunxin Liu[1], Thomas Moscibroda[1], Ranveer Chandra[2], Long Jin[1,4], Yongguang Zhang[1], Qun Li[3]

[1]Microsoft Research Asia, Beijing, China [2]Microsoft Research, Redmond, WA, USA

[3]College of William and Mary, Williamsburg, VA, USA [4]Tsinghua University, Beijing, China

ABSTRACT

Email is a key application used on smartphones. Even when the phone is in stand-by mode, users expect the phone to continue syncing with an email server to receive new messages. Each such sync operation wakes up the smartphone for data reception and processing. In this paper, we show that this "cost of email sync" in stand-by mode constitutes a significant source of energy consumption, and thus reduces battery life. We quantify the power performance of different existing email clients on two smartphone platforms, Android and Windows Phone, and study the impact of system parameters such as email size, inbox size, and pull vs. push. Our results show that existing email clients do not handle email sync in an energy efficient way. This is because the underlying protocols and architectures are not designed for the specific needs of operating in stand-by mode. Based on our findings, we derive general design principles for energy-efficient event handling on smartphones, and apply these principles to the case of email sync and implement our techniques on commercial smartphones. Experimental results show that our techniques are able to significantly reduce energy cost of email sync by 49.9% on average with our experiment settings.

Categories and Subject Descriptors

C.2.2 **[Computer-communication Networks]**: Network Protocols - *Applications*

General Terms

Experimentation, Measurement, Performance

Keywords

Energy Efficiency, Smartphone, Email, Cellular Network

1. INTRODUCTION

Standby time, a battery's life in standby mode, is important for smartphones to provide good power performance to users. Even though many smartphones claim a standby time of more than 10 days in their technical specifications, in practice their standby times are often much shorter, e.g., only two or three days or even less. The main reason for such a big gap is that when a smartphone remains in standby mode, it stays connected to the Internet through its cellular data interface (e.g., 3G), waiting for various incoming events, such as emails, short messages, instant messages, notifications of social applications (e.g., Twitter and Facebook), and many other push notifications.

This *connected standby* state, in which the screen is off while the network connectivity stays active, is of fundamental importance for mobile devices. Most users keep their phone in connected standby for a large fraction of time during the day. In this state, the reception of an incoming event (email, instant message...) wakes up the cellular data interface as well as the phone's operating system (OS), to receive the set of packets over the network and process received data. Collectively, these operations consume a significant amount of power. For example, our measurements show that the energy cost of receiving a small email on an Android smartphone is more than 14,000mJ, which is as high as the energy consumed by a typical smartphone in standby mode for 10 minutes. In other words, the reception of a single email reduces the standby time of a smartphone by 10 minutes. Assuming the phone has a standby time of 10 days without receiving any events, its standby time will be reduced to less than 6 days (a reduction of more than 40%), if it receives 100 emails per day. This is despite the screen being off during the entire duration, and without any user interaction.

In this paper, we study the power performance of email sync in connected standby on smartphones. Email is a killer application on smartphones for most users, who expect their email clients to keep synchronized with one or more email servers even when the phone is in standby mode. We measure the energy consumption of existing email clients on two major smartphone platforms: Android and Windows Phone (WP). Our results show that email sync is indeed a major drain on existing platforms, and we observe that existing mobile email clients do not handle incoming emails in an energy-efficient way. The reason is that the underlying protocols, and the overall design of today's mobile email clients do not take into account the specific characteristics and needs of operation in connected standby mode: data processing is not sufficiently de-coupled from network communication (thus preventing the 3G interface from quickly going to sleep), memory management and storage input/output (I/O) are un-optimized, and network protocols and interface operations are tailored for operations other than event reception.

Based on our findings, we formulate new design principles for energy-efficient event handling (and specifically email sync) on smartphones in connected standby. Applying these principles to the case of email sync, we develop 5 new techniques, each one addressing one of the shortcomings we have identified in existing systems.

- In current systems, long 3G tail times keep the 3G interface on for longer than is necessary. We advocate fast dormancy and adaptive 3G tail times based on email arrival patterns, to reduce the energy cost of the 3G tail.
- In current email clients, data transmission and data processing are coupled together, e.g., a final ACK packet is sent to the email server once the received email has been completely processed. Depending on the amount of processing time required to handle an incoming email, this coupling can prevent the 3G interface from going to sleep for a long time. We propose decoupling the data transmission from data processing to improve energy efficiency.
- In some email clients, the amount of data processing and memory/storage I/O required to handle an incoming email depends on the *size of the inbox*, leading to a particularly high energy cost for receiving emails when there are many of them in the email client's inbox. We mitigate this problem by using a small cache for incoming emails, to enable fast email processing.
- Flash storage operations on smartphones are slow, which leads to long data processing times, thus keeping the OS awake longer. We show that in connected standby, it therefore makes sense as a design principle to perform email reception *entirely in-memory*.
- Finally, in some clients, a new secure network connection is established for receiving every new incoming email, resulting in repeated TCP and SSL handshakes and a waste of energy. We solve this problem by reusing network connections across the reception of multiple emails.

Collectively, these techniques achieve significant reductions in the energy cost of email syncing. Specifically, we have implemented them by modifying an existing email client on commercial smartphones. Experimental results show that our revised email client is able to significantly improve email sync's energy efficiency, reducing the average energy cost by 49.9% and up to 77.9% if we put the 3G interface into sleep immediately after an email is received.

In summary, the main contributions of this paper are:

- We show that email sync in a connected standby state is a major source of energy consumption in today's smartphones, and that existing email clients are not optimized for operation in this mode.
- We derive design principles for energy-efficient event handling in connected standby, and propose techniques for reducing the energy required per email sync.
- We implement a new email client on smartphones and show that it is significantly more energy efficient.

The paper is organized as follows. Section 2 gives background information on email sync in smartphones. In Section 3, we present a measurement study on the email-sync energy cost of existing smartphone email clients, and derive general guidelines to make event reception energy-efficient in connected standby. Section 4 describes our novel techniques. We describe our implementation and evaluation results in Sections 5 and 6, respectively. In Section 7, we demonstrate that our techniques can also be used to improve energy efficiency when receiving events in other event-triggered applications. Section 8 surveys related work before we conclude in Section 9.

2. BACKGROUND ON EMAIL SYNC

Similar to desktop or laptop PCs, smartphones usually use a client application to sync email from a server. Typically email sync can be done in one of two ways: *polling* or *pushing*. In polling, a client proactively connects to a server to check for new emails. The client can be configured to automatically poll the server periodically (e.g., every 10 minutes), or the user can manually start a polling operation. Polling has two disadvantages. First, it wastes energy if a server does not have any new emails, particularly if polling is too frequent. Second, because a new email may arrive before a client polls its server, polling causes a delay in receiving the email, in the worst case as long as the polling time interval. As a result, users may find it hard to set a proper polling time interval to balance the energy cost and email receiving delay. For these reasons, push email is widely used on smartphones. Most popular email services, such as Microsoft Exchange, Gmail and Hotmail, support push email. The Gmail application on Android supports push email, but not poll email.

In push email, instead of polling from a client, emails are received by pushing from a server. Once a server receives a new email for a client, it pushes the new email to the client through a previously established TCP connection. Consequently, the client is able to immediately receive new emails as soon as they arrive. Push email not only has minimal delay but in some cases also saves energy since a client does not need to poll a server when there is no new email. As smartphones are usually behind a Network Address Translator (NAT) and a firewall, they often use a private IP address rather than a public one. As a result, an email server cannot initialize a TCP connection to a smartphone. Therefore, push email requires a persistent TCP connection between a client and a server so that the server can send new emails to the client over the persistent TCP connection. For example, Microsoft Exchange supports push email by Direct Push [1]. A client first connects to a server using TCP. To receive push emails, the client uses a long-standing HTTP POST (the protocol used by smartphones to talk to a Microsoft Exchange server is called Exchange ActiveSync [2] which is on top of HTTP) request to ask the server to respond within a time period, e.g., 15 minutes. Then the smartphone can go to sleep or standby mode. If the server has new emails within the 15 minutes, it pushes the emails to the client. Otherwise, the server will send a HTTP 200 OK message to the client who then sends another long-standing HTTP POST to the server.

Push email usually works only on cellular networks (e.g., 3G) but not on Wi-Fi. This is because the coverage of cellular networks is pervasive, and the cellular module of a smartphone can work independently from the smartphone's Operating System. When the OS is in sleep mode, the cellular module remains connected and can receive data from the cellular network. After receiving a data packet from an email server (or any other servers), the cellular module will generate an interrupt to wake up the OS. The execution of the email client is resumed, and the email can be pushed from the server. In contrast, Wi-Fi networks usually have a small amount of coverage and roaming between different Wi-Fi networks breaks the persistent connection required by push email. Furthermore, on some smartphones, the Wi-Fi interface is usually turned off when the OS is asleep, and hence the Wi-Fi interface cannot receive any data. Therefore, in this paper, we focus on studying email sync on cellular networks. Even on a cellular network, the carrier operator may tear down a TCP connection if it is idle for too long (a common timeout threshold is 10 minutes), to release the resources allocated for the TCP connection in the NAT and firewall. Email clients on smartphones handle this issue by sending a keep-alive message to the server before the timeout is reached, e.g., a PING message used in Direct Push [1].

3. PROFILING ENERGY COST OF EMAIL SYNC

In this section we measure and analyze the power performance of existing email clients on smartphones. We first describe the experimental setup and then report the results and findings.

3.1 Experimental Setup

We have studied email sync behaviors on two smartphone platforms: Windows Phone and Android. For the WP platform, we used a Samsung Omnia 7 smartphone running Windows Phone 7.5. We used the built-in email client provided by WP. For the Android platform, we used a Samsung Nexus S smartphone running Android ICS 4.0.4. We also used the built-in email client provided by Android. Both email clients support different email services.

Our study uses two popular email services: Microsoft Exchange and Google's Gmail, examining both push email and poll email. All experiments were conducted in Beijing, China, using the 3G network of China Unicom. Monsoon Power Monitor [3] was utilized to measure the power consumption of smartphones. We focused on the power consumption of the connected standby mode. That is, we measured the energy cost of receiving emails without any user interaction and the screens of the smartphones were off while receiving email. The disruption from other concurrent operations is rare in this situation, so we do not consider it in this work.

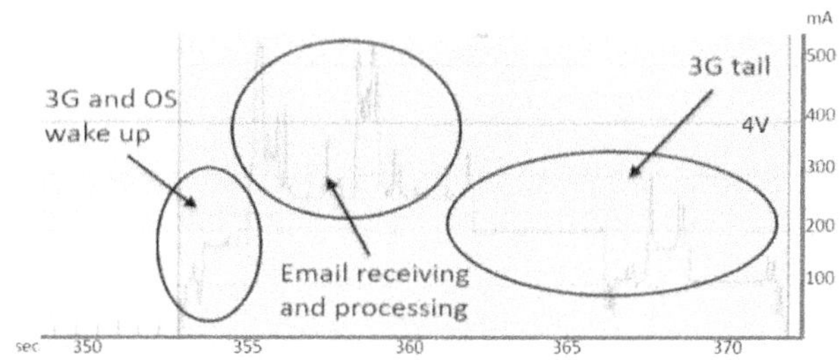

Figure 1: Power trace of receiving a push email on Android using Exchange email service

3.2 Measurement Results

3.2.1 Stages of receiving an email

We measured the power traces of receiving an email on the two platforms. Figure 1 shows the power trace of receiving a small-push email using the Exchange email service on Android. This email consisted of 2 KB random text content and the total data received was 10 KB including all headers and metadata. We can see there are several major stages in receiving this email. At the beginning, the smartphone was in sleep mode with little power consumption (about 30 mW). When the server pushed the email to the smartphone over the 3G network, the 3G interface and operating system of the smartphone woke up. We call this the *Wakeup* stage. Then the email client received and processed this email, which is called the *Receive* stage. The last stage was 3G tail time when the 3G interface stayed in a high power state but no network traffic was occurring. We call this the *Tail* stage. After the Tail stage, the 3G interface and the operating system went back to sleep. The total time duration of receiving the email is 18.42 seconds.

The 3G tail time is controlled by the cellular module using a timer. When there is no data packet transmission, the timer starts to count down. If the network remains idle after the timer expires (e.g., after 10 seconds), the 3G interface goes to sleep. If there is a data packet that is sent or received, the timer is reset. The 3G tail time is designed to reduce network latency. From Figure 1, we can see that it takes about two seconds for the 3G interface to wake up from sleep mode. During the 3G tail time, the 3G interface can keep active for continuous network traffic, avoiding wakeup latency.

We also measured the power trace in receiving the same email on Android through polling. The overall procedure is very similar to the pushing case and consists of the same three major stages (i.e., Wakeup, Receive and Tail). The difference is that, in the polling case, the operating system first wakes up itself (via a timer based on the email polling interval) and then proactively wakes up the 3G interface for querying the email server instead of being interrupted by the 3G interface passively. The total time duration of receiving the email is 18.54 seconds, similar to the push email scenario.

We further measured the power trace when receiving the same email on WP through pushing. Again it consists of the same three major stages. However, compared to the Android cases, the total time for receiving the email on the WP device is much shorter, taking only 7.24 seconds. One reason is that the WP smartphone we used has a much shorter 3G tail time than the Android smartphone. To confirm this, we conducted experiments to measure the 3G tail time on the two smartphones. We found that the WP smartphone has a 3G tail time of about 5 seconds but the Android smartphone has a 3G tail time of 10 seconds. This shows that the WP smartphone enables fast dormancy (see more details in Section 4), a technique to shorten 3G tail time, but the Android smartphone does not.

We also measured power traces of other combinations for receiving email. For example, using Gmail email service and pulling on WP, we observed the same three major stages in all the other power trace curves. We conclude that it is a common pattern of receiving an email.

Note that the stage markers in Figure 1 are just for illustration purposes, used instead of showing the exact duration of each stage. In particular the Tail stage and the Receive stage may be overlapped. For example, the 3G tail time may start immediately after all data transmissions are finished but before the data processing is done. In addition, in all the above experiments, when the email was received, the email clients on both Android and WP had already stored 200 other emails. Later in this Section we will see that the energy cost of receiving an email may depend on inbox size, particularly with WP.

3.2.2 *Energy cost of receiving an email*

To study the email receiving performance of different configurations, we measured the energy cost of receiving the same 10 KB email using various combinations of the two platforms (WP and Android), two email services (Microsoft Exchange and Google Gmail) and two email receiving approaches (push and poll), with an inbox of 200 messages. Table 1 shows the average results.

Our first observation was that we can see that the energy cost on Android is much higher than the one on WP. Aside from hardware differences, one reason is that the WP smartphone has a shorter 3G tail time than the Android smartphone as aforementioned. The 3G tail time is five seconds shorter on WP, leading to about 2,736 mJ energy saving. In addition, as we will show later, WP has low energy cost of email receiving when the inbox size is small.

Table 1: Average energy cost of receiving a small email with various configurations

Configuration	Energy Cost (mJ)
Android + Exchange + Push	14,976
Android + Exchange + Poll	14,674
Android + Gmail + Push	N/A
Android + Gmail + Poll	20,750
WP + Exchange + Push	5,429
WP + Exchange + Poll	5,659
WP + Gmail + Push	6,235
WP + Gmail + Poll	7,027
Android + Gmail App (Push)	12,931

Second, we could see that push email and poll email have very similar energy costs given the same email service and platform. On Android, the difference between push and poll is only 2% for the Exchange service, while this difference is less than 4% on WP. For Gmail, the difference on WP is 13%. This is reasonable because push email and poll email are fundamentally very similar: they receive the same emails and do the same data processing work. On Android, the default email client does not support push email for Gmail service and thus we do not have the number in Table 1.

We also found that the energy costs of two email services are similar on the same platform, although the Exchange service always consumes less. For example, polling-based Gmail on Android takes 20,750mJ energy, but Exchange service with polling consumes 14,674 mJ. On WP, push-based Gmail service takes 6,235mJ energy but the same service of Exchange requires 5,429 mJ energy. Despite this, different email services might be different in implementation details; they are expected to have similar patterns due to the nature of the email service. In fact, Microsoft Exchange ActiveSync (EAS) protocol has been widely used for the synchronization of emails, contacts, calendar, tasks and notes from a messaging server to a mobile device. Many companies, including Google [11] and Apple [12], have licensed and adopted EAS in their own email services for mail sync on mobile devices.

We also evaluated the Gmail application that is specifically designed for the Gmail service by Google on Android, which only supports push email. The last row of Table 1 shows the result. We can see that it requires less energy, compared to the default email client on Android. This suggests that Google does some Gmail specific optimizations, probably on both the client side and the server side. However, we do not know the technical details because the Gmail application is not open source.

Due to the similarity of push email and poll email, and the similarity of Exchange service and Gmail service, in the rest of this section, we focus more on Exchange push email.

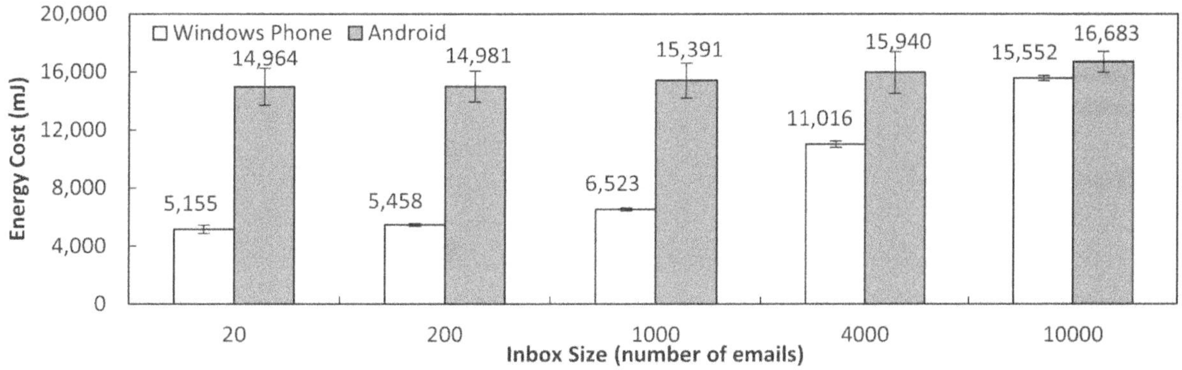

Figure 2: Energy cost of receiving a push email of 10 KB using Exchange service with different inbox sizes (five trials per experiment)

3.2.3 Energy cost vs. inbox size

We measured the energy cost of receiving the same email in different inbox sizes. Inbox size is measured in terms of the number of emails already received in the inbox on a smartphone. We used the same small email of 10 KB that we used in the aforementioned experiments.

Figure 2 shows the results using Exchange push email. Interestingly, we can see that the energy cost of receiving the same email on WP highly depends on the inbox size. When the inbox size is small, the energy cost is small and increases with the inbox size significantly. For example, the energy cost when the inbox has 10,000 emails is more than three times the energy cost when the inbox is as small as 20 emails. This is probably found by updating the metadata of the inbox database. For example, to support "conversation view", the email client needs to group all the emails of a conversation thread together.

Compared to WP, Android has a much flatter energy cost in different inbox sizes. However, when the inbox size is small, the energy cost on Android is much higher than WP. For example, when the inbox size is 20 emails, Android consumes 190% more energy than WP. Even if we exclude the extra energy cost (2,736 mJ) of the long 3G tail time on Android, Android still needs 137% more energy than WP. For large inbox size like 10,000 emails, Android and WP have similar energy cost, with a small difference of 7%.

One may argue that 10,000 emails are too many for smartphones as many users only download a small part of their whole inbox onto their smartphones, e.g., only the recent emails in the last few weeks. However, with an informal survey, we found that some people do download a large number of emails or even all their emails onto their smartphones. The main reason is that they can easily search emails on smartphones, particularly when their smartphones do not have a data connection. Furthermore, email clients on smartphones usually store only email headers and limited text

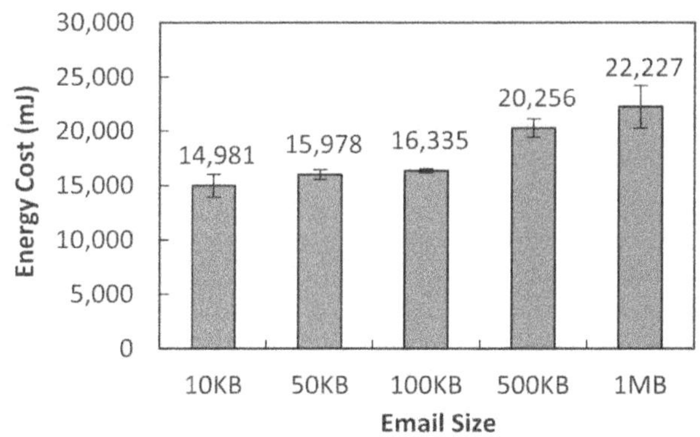

Figure 3: Energy cost of receiving an email with various email sizes (five trials per experiment)

content of email bodies (e.g., up to 5 KB bytes text). By default, attachments or embedded images are excluded. Thus, today's smartphones have enough storage space to store a large number of emails.

3.2.4 Energy cost vs. email size

We measured the energy cost of receiving an email with different email sizes. As previously mentioned, smartphone email clients usually download the email header and a limited amount of the email body for a new email. Users cannot specify the amount of data to be downloaded in both built-in email clients on the two platforms. Based on our observation, the email client on WP receives very limited email data, about only 10 KB including all email headers. The email client on Android can receive up-to several hundred KB of data (see more details in Section 3.2.6), more suitable for testing. Consequently, we only measured the energy cost of receiving an email with different sizes on Android.

Figure 3 shows the results with an inbox of 200 emails. The email size is defined as the total received data size if the email is completely received, including email content, headers and metadata. We decided the size of an email using Outlook

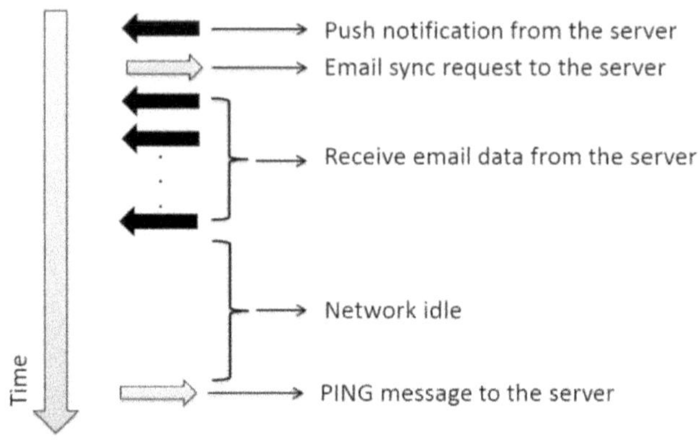

Figure 4: Network packets transmitted in receiving a push email using Exchange service on WP

email client on a PC. Outlook email client can download all the email data and show the received data size. We can see that the energy cost increases as the email size gets larger but the difference is small, not proportional to the difference in email sizes. For example, when the email size is changed from 11KB to 107KB, an increase of 873%, the increase in energy cost is only 31%. This is for two reasons. First, the email size mainly contributes to the energy cost of receiving and processing the data, which is only a small part of the total energy consumption. Second, for large emails the Android email client does not receive all the email data. For instance, an email with a size of 500 KB and an email with a size of 1,000 KB have similar amounts of data written to the flash storage (336 KB vs. 340 KB).

3.2.5 Network activities in receiving an email

To find out what happened behind the energy cost, we profiled the network activities of the email clients when receiving an email. To do that, we captured the network data packets received and sent by the email clients. On Android, we used Tcpdump [4] to save all the network packets for offline analysis. For WP, we did not have a tool to capture packets. Thus, instead of using 3G, we conducted experiments on receiving emails over Wi-Fi. To make push email work over Wi-Fi, we kept the smartphone on at all times so that it could receive emails pushed from the email server. Then we used Wireshark [5] on a laptop to capture all network packets of the smartphone transmitted in the air.

Figure 4 shows the packets (excluding TCP ACKs) transmitted in receiving the small email sized 10KB on WP pushed from the Exchange server. Basically, the email client first received notification of the new incoming email from the server over the previously established TCP connection. Then it started to fetch the email from the server and processed it. After that, the client sent out a PING message packet to the server to wait for the next incoming new email.

We can see that there is a network-idle time period between the PING packet and the prior burst data transmission. During this time period, the email client is processing the received

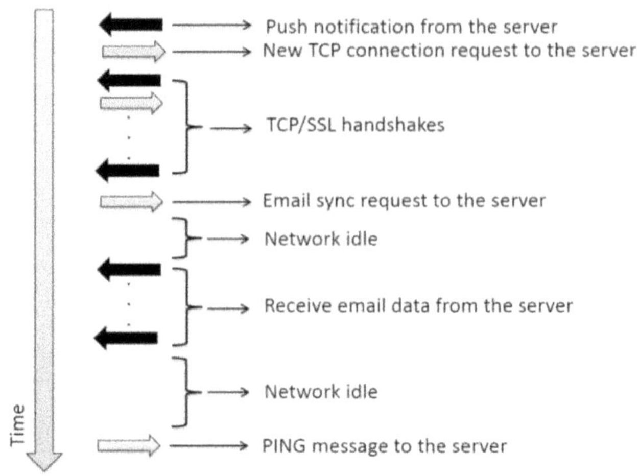

Figure 5: Network packets transmitted in receiving a push email using Exchange service (the same one used for Fig. 4) on Android

email. We found that this processing time increases with inbox size. As shown in Table 2, with an inbox size of 200 emails, it was 0.5 seconds but increased to 10 seconds when the inbox had 10,000 emails.

Figure 5 shows the network packets transmitted on Android when receiving the same push email from the same Exchange server. Compared to WP, the network activities on Android are different as follows. First, instead of using the same TCP connection to fetch a new email, after receiving a notification over the existing TCP connection, the Android email client establishes a new TCP connection to the email server to receive the new email. Doing so introduces some overhead on TCP and SSL handshakes between the client and the server, where 12data packets (6.9KB in total) are transmitted. Second, on Android there are two network-idle time periods. One is between the email sync request sent from the client to the server and the server's reply. The other one is after receiving the burst event data and before the final PING message sent from the client to the server. However, unlike WP, the network-idle time periods do not depend on inbox size. Table 2 also shows the total network-idle time on Android. It bears no obvious relationship to the inbox size, ranging from 3 seconds to 4.6 seconds (3.6 seconds on average).

3.2.6 Storage activities in receiving an email

Besides the network activities, we also profiled the storage activities in receiving an email. For Android, we developed a tool to intercept the storage access APIs (e.g., file reading and writing) to capture all the flash-storage operations of the email client. For WP, we couldn't develop such a tool due to the limited programmability offered by Windows Phone. Therefore, we only conducted the flash-storage experiments on Android.

Table 3 shows the total amount of data written to flash storage for different incoming email sizes. We can see that the

Table 2: Network idle time during email receiving

Inbox size (number of emails)	Network idle time (seconds)	
	WP	Android
20	0.4	3.5
200	0.5	4.6
1,000	0.9	3.0
4,000	3.5	3.4
10,000	10.0	3.5

Table 3: Data size written to flash in email receiving

Email size (KB)	10	50	100	500	1,000
Data size (KB)	139	156	188	336	340

amount of data written to flash storage increases with email size. This is because the email client needs to write the received email data into the inbox database. Thus, more data were written to flash storage for larger email. However, when the email is very large, the data amount written to flash storage does not increase any more. This is because the Android email client limits the maximum data received for emails. Unfortunately it does not provide an option for users to configure such a behavior.

The results show that the Android email client immediately writes received email data onto flash storage. All flash operations in receiving an email were distributed in a time period of one to two seconds, each writing a small amount of data. As we will show in Section 4.3, small flash writes are time and energy expensive and should be avoided in receiving emails.

3.2.7 *Energy distribution*

Finally we studied how the total energy cost of receiving an email is distributed in the three stages of the power curves: *Wakeup* stage for the 3G interface and operating system to wake up, *Receive* stage for the email receiving and processing, and *Tail* stage for the 3G tail time. We denote the time duration of the Wakeup stage as the time period between the time when the smartphone wakes up and the time before receiving the notification packet from the server. We define the time duration of the Tail stage as the time period between the time when the last packet is transmitted and the time when the smartphone goes to sleep again. We treat the rest of time as the time duration of the Receive stage.

Figure 6 shows the results. We can see that the Wakeup stage takes stable and fixed energy costs on both WP (907-936 mJ) and Android (979-1,022 mJ) no matter how big the inbox is. The energy cost of the Tail stage is also quite stable on the two platforms. On WP, the Tail stage takes 2,419-3,427 mJ (2,866 mJ on average) of energy but on Android it takes 5,832-6,307 mJ (5,962 mJ on average) of energy, due to the difference of 3G tail time on the two platforms. Different from the Wakeup stage and the Tail stage, the energy cost of Receive stage depends on the inbox size. Particularly for WP, the energy cost increases significantly with the inbox size,

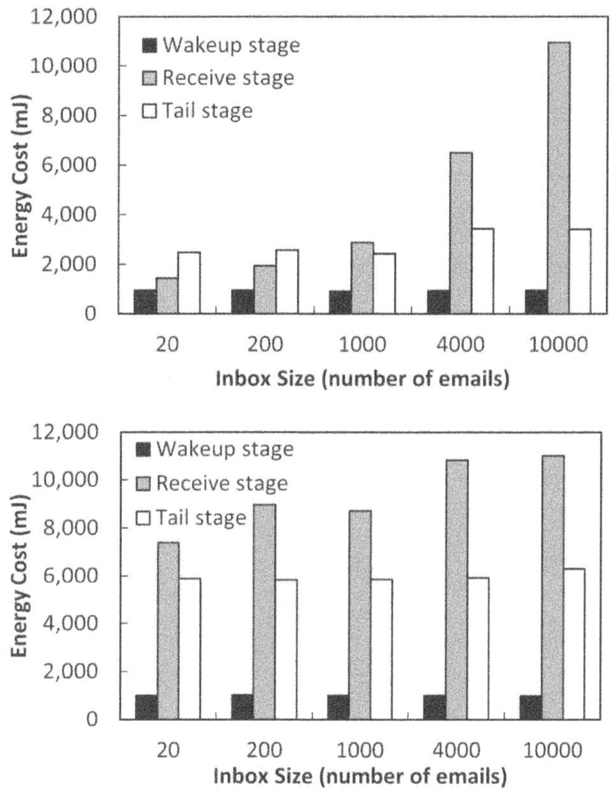

Figure 6: Energy distribution among the three stages in receiving an email with different inbox sizes. Top: on WP. Bottom: on Android.

from only 144mJwhen the inbox size is 20 to 10,944 mJ when the inbox size is 10,000. For Android, the numbers are relatively flat: 7,387 mJ for inbox of 20 and 11,002 mJ for inbox of 10,000.

In addition, we can see that the Receive stage and Tail stage take more energy than the Wakeup stage. The Receive stage takes 30% - 71% (49% on average) of the total energy cost on WP, and takes 52% - 61% (57% on average) of the total energy cost on Android. For the Tail stage, it takes 22% - 51% (38% on average) of the total energy on WP, and takes 33% - 42% (37% on average) of the total energy cost on Android. Therefore, to reduce the energy cost of receiving emails, we should focus on optimizing these two stages.

3.3 Summary of Findings

Based on above measurement results in Section 3.2, we can see that the existing smartphone email clients are not energy efficient in following aspects.

First, the 3G tail time takes a large part of the total time of receiving an email. The 3G tail time is designed to reduce the network latency for burst data transmissions. However, the inter-arrival time of incoming events is not short in the connected standby mode. Occasional transmissions make the 3G tail time unnecessary in most cases. Therefore, the energy is wasted on the 3G interface.

Second, the data transmission and processing are coupled together, leading to more wasted energy. Receiving an email is composed of the following steps: first is communicating with the server to receive some data, processing the received data locally, and then communicating with the server again. The second step of the communication resets the 3G tail timer, causing the 3G interface on for longer time and thus wasting energy.

Third, the email clients write data onto the flash storage when receiving an email. As we will show in Section 4.3, flash operations are energy-expensive and should be batched together to save energy.

Fourth, when the inbox size is large, receiving an email costs more energy than small inbox case. It is desirable to reduce the energy cost for a large inbox size.

Finally, on Android, the email client always initializes a new TCP connection to the server to receive an email. Doing so wastes energy due to the duplicated TCP and SSL handshakes.

Next in Section 4 we propose techniques to address above energy inefficiency and reduce the energy cost of receiving email. Those techniques can also be used as general design guidelines to improve power performance of other applications on smartphones.

4. REDUCING ENERGY COST OF EMAIL SYNC

From Figure 1, we can see that the baseline power, when the system is active but idle (e.g., during the 3G tail time), can reach over 200 mW. This means that once the 3G interface and the OS wake up, the smartphone will consume a large amount of energy even without doing any tasks. Therefore, to reduce the energy cost of receiving an email, one effective way is to shorten the total time period of email receiving as much as possible. In this section we show how we achieve it with five techniques, each of them addressing one energy inefficiency issue we observed in Section 3.

4.1 Reducing 3G Tail Time

The 3G tail time causes a lot of energy to be wasted in receiving emails. After a new email is received and processed, the 3G interface enters the tail state in which the whole smartphone does nothing but consume energy. While the 3G tail is designed to save energy and reduce latency in continuous network data transmissions, it is not suitable for the connected standby mode. In the connected standby mode, the events received by a smartphone are pretty sparse, often arriving at a time period much longer than 3G tail time. Thus, it is likely that the 3G tail time cannot cover multiple events. To verify it, we measured the inter-arrival time of the emails of four researchers at Microsoft Research Asia. In total 31,303 emails, only 1.3% emails come within a ten-second time frame of previous one. Therefore, a 3G tail time of ten seconds rarely covers more than one incoming emails and thus wastes a considerable amount of energy.

The problem of wasted energy caused by the 3G tail time has already been identified recently. To solve the problem, a technique called fast dormancy [7] has been proposed to force the 3G interface to quickly sleep faster than before, e.g., five seconds rather than ten seconds. However, rapid dormancy increases the signaling overhead of cellular networks if the sleep timers are too short. In fact, in the early days of fast dormancy, some popular smartphones using aggressive timers have led to severe signaling channel congestions [25]. Later the network-controlled fast dormancy was adopted by 3GPP in Release 8 [16] to reduce the signaling overhead caused by the fast dormancy. Researchers have proposed to adaptively use the fast dormancy based on application traffic patterns [8, 9, 14, 18]. For example, in [8] the authors proposed a tail optimization protocol based on fast dormancy. In [9] a system has been built to predict the end of communication to invoke the fast dormancy without increasing the network signaling load.

We advocate for the fast dormancy to be used in connected standby. As shown by our measurement results in Section 3, the WP smartphone we used enables fast dormancy and thus has a shorter 3G tail time than the Android smartphone. We also agree with the authors in [8] and [9] for adaptive 3G tail time based on application traffic patterns.

In particular, because that network events are very sparse in the connected standby, 3G tail time still wastes energy even if fast dormancy is enabled. In an ideal case, the 3G interface should go to sleep immediately after the event receiving is finished. However, to avoid interference with other applications, individual applications must not directly control the 3G tail time. Instead, we propose that the OS should provide a global service that collects the network usage information of all the applications running in connected standby, decides the shortest length of 3G tail time, and collaborates with the cellular network to put the 3G interface into sleep mode as quickly as possible, minimizing the energy waste of 3G tail time. Due to the long inter-arrival time of network events in the connected standby, the signaling overhead is small.

4.2 Decoupling Data Transmission from Data Processing

Due to the 3G tail effect, data transmission should be decoupled from data processing to save energy. In an ideal case, an email client should first finish all network communication with a server and then process the received data, so that the 3G interface is able to go to sleep as soon as possible. In receiving a push email, there are three steps: 1) fetching the email content from the server, 2) processing the received

Table 4: Energy and time cost of databasewriting

	Energy cost per email (mJ)		Time cost per email (ms)	
	Database in memory	Database on flash	Database in memory	Database on flash
Individual writes	1	32	1	55
Batch writes	0.59	0.64	0.58	0.65

email locally (e.g., updating the inbox database), and 3) telling the server that it is ready to receive the next push email and then go to sleep. As we show in Section 3, in such a "transmission-processing-transmission" process, existing email clients do the second transmission part after the processing part is finished, which seems a natural design choice due to the sequential nature but is not energy efficient. During the data processing part, the 3G interface stays awake unnecessarily and the second data transmission resets the 3G tail timer, wasting energy. For example, assume that the data processing needs two seconds and the power is 200 mW, 400 mJ energy will be wasted. Therefore, to save energy, an email client should batch all its data transmissions together. It should first fetch new email content and immediately tell the server that it is ready to receive the next push email before waiting for the email processing to be finished.

Batching all data transmissions together may be difficult if a network protocol depends on the result of data processing. For example, if an email server requires an email client to tell whether the email processing is successful or not, the email client cannot start the second data transmission part before the data processing part is finished. We propose to solve this problem using speculative execution [6]. That is, we predict the result of the data processing part and send the predicted result to the server without waiting for the data processing part to be finished. If we find that the predicted result is wrong after the data processing part is finished, we can re-sync with the server. If we can correctly predict the data processing results with a high probability, we can still batch data transmissions together to reduce the 3G tail effect. To determine feasibility, we conducted an experiment to measure the failure rate of receiving and processing 10,000 emails. We found that all the 10,000 emails were successfully processed without any error. This indicates that the email receiving is reliable and we can correctly predict the email processing results with a high probability. Therefore, it is possible to leverage speculative execution to save energy. Furthermore, for Microsoft Exchange and Gmail services on smartphones, they do not depend on the email processing results. Thus, we can easily batch data transmissions and decouple them from data processing.

4.3 In-Memory Data Processing

Writing data to flash storage is slower than writing data to memory, particularly for small, random data writes [13, 14, 19]. We conducted experiments to measure the performance difference of the flash storage and memory. We used a Nexus S smartphone running Android 4.0.4. We inserted an email of 270 bytes into a SQLite database for 1,000 times and measured averaged energy and time cost of inserting one email. We used the SQLite database because the Gmail client and the default email client on Android use SQLite to store emails. The SQLite library provides two types of APIs to write data into a database: individual writes and batching multiple writes together as a transaction. Thus, we measured the performance of writing the 1,000 emails one by one and batching the 1,000 email writes together.

Table 4 shows the results. For individual writing, when the entire database was loaded in memory, the average energy and time cost per email was just 1 mJ and 1 ms. When the database was stored on the flash storage, the corresponding energy and time costs increased to 32 mJ and 55 ms. For batching writes, when the database was loaded in memory, the average energy and time costs were 0.59 mJ and 0.58 ms. When the database was stored on flash storage, the corresponding figures were 0.64 mJ and 0.65 ms. Those results show that for small writes, flash storage costs much more energy (32 times) and takes much more time (55 times) than memory. However, for writing a large amount of data together, the flash storage and memory have similar performance in terms of the energy and time costs.

Therefore, to reduce the energy and time cost in email receiving, an email client should not issue many small flash writes. Instead, it should batch multiple small writes together and commit them to flash in a batch. As mentioned before, email clients on smartphones only download email headers and up to several kilobytes of email bodies. Thus, the data received for a new email is small. However, as we show in Section 3, existing email clients write received data of every email to the flash storage immediately, which is not energy efficient. Therefore, when an email client receives a new email, it should cache the received data in memory rather than writing them to flash immediately. Once the client has received a sufficient number of emails (e.g., 10 emails) or the cached data are larger than a threshold, it can flush all the data to flash storage together. Furthermore, the client may also piggyback data writes with other activities. For example, when the user turns on the smartphone to check emails or use other applications, the client can write its cached data to flash. As those flash writes share the same baseline power with other activities of the user, they will not introduce much extra energy or time overhead.

Delaying flash writes may cause data loss if the email client or the smartphone crashes before the cached data are written to flash storage. However, modern smartphone operating systems including Windows Phone, Android and iOS all run each application in a separate protection domain (i.e., the so called "application based security model"). Failures of one application will not affect other running applications. As a result, today's smartphones are more reliable and crash less than before. Even when running out of battery, the operating system will terminate applications gracefully, to give them chance to save data onto flash. Smartphone email clients are also pretty reliable. We measured the default email client on Android by receiving 10,000 emails and did not observe any failure or crash. In addition, even if the email client crashes before writing the cached data to flash storage, it can re-sync the emails with the server. Therefore, in-memory data processing is able to reduce the energy cost of email receiving.

4.4 Reusing Existing Network Connections

In receiving emails, email clients should reuse existing network connections rather than making new ones. In particular, for the push email, because an email client already maintains a persistent network connection with a server to receive notification of new incoming emails, it should receive a new email over the continuous network connection to save energy. Even for a poll email, when an email client does a second polling before the network connection of the last polling times out, it should also reuse the previous network connection.

While it may be easy and natural to make a new network connection to receive every new email, the energy cost may not be negligible. As most email services require a secure network connection, making a new network connection includes not only TCP layer handshakes but also SSL layer handshakes to negotiate the encryption method and exchange security keys. As shown in our experiments on Android in Section 3, the overhead of making a secure TCP connection is not negligible. Without transmitting any application data packets, it consumed 1,757 mJ energy to make a TCP/SSL connection. In total 6.9 KB data were transmitted between the client and server. WP is more energy efficient. It always reuses the same TCP connection to receive new emails.

4.5 Data Structure Partitioning

One interesting finding on WP is that the energy cost of receiving the same email increases significantly when the inbox size is large. On Android, the energy cost also increases with inbox size but the increase is not as significant as WP. The possible reason is that when storing a new email into the database of an inbox, it takes more time to update the metadata. For example, the email client needs to search the whole inbox to associate the new email with the right conversation thread. The cost of doing so depends on the inbox size. In addition, when the inbox is too large to be loaded into the memory of the email client, searching the inbox takes more energy and time due to the frequent flash operations.

To solve this problem and reduce the energy cost of receiving an email, we propose partitioning a large inbox into two parts:

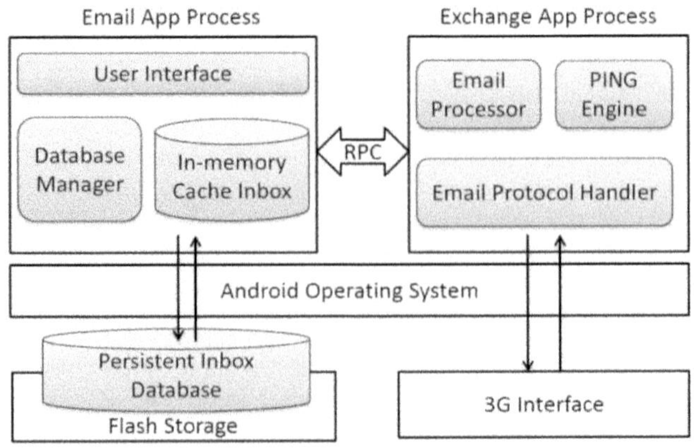

Figure 7: Implementation architecture

one small inbox with recently received emails (e.g., emails received in last two weeks) and one large inbox containing all remaining emails. The email client only uses the small inbox to handling email receiving. That is, when receiving an email, the client only inserts it into the small inbox and updates the metadata without using the large inbox. Thus, the energy cost of receiving emails is reduced even if a smartphone stores many emails. This approach is based on a key observation: most of the time users only need to check recent emails on their smartphones. Therefore, it is not necessary to touch all the emails already stored in a smartphone in receiving new emails. When a user does need to access all the emails, e.g., in searching the whole inbox, the client can search both the small inbox and the large one to return the combined results. As searching a whole inbox happens much more rarely than receiving emails, inbox partitioning is able to save energy.

5. IMPLEMENTATION

Implementing the techniques proposed in Section 4 only requires modifications on the email client side. Since the Gmail application on Android and the built-in email client on WP are not open source, implementation is done on the built-in email client of Android, which is accessible and widely used. The source code we used is vanilla Android 4.0.4 with kernel 3.0.8.

Figure 7 illustrates the architecture of our implementation, focusing on email syncing and processing. On Android the built-in email client consists of two parts, each running in a separate process. The first part is the network communication part which implements the email protocol and handles all the communication details with the email server to receive and send emails. For Exchange email service, this part runs as an app named "Exchange". It runs in the background without a UI. The other part is the data processing which processes received emails and provides user interfaces to handle all the interaction details with users including reading emails and

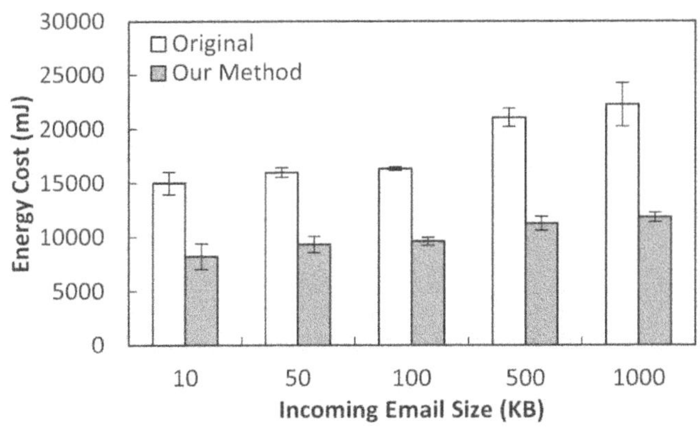

Figure 8: Energy saving with different email sizes

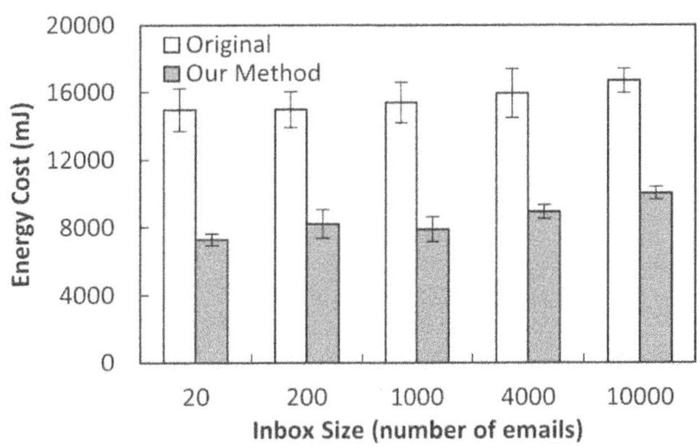

Figure 9: Energy saving with different inbox sizes

composing emails to send out. It also deals with email storage, saving emails to and loading emails from the SQLite database. This part runs as an app named "Email". The Email app process and the Exchange app process exchange data through Remote Procedure Calls (RPCs).

To decouple data transmission from data processing, we revised the Email Protocol Handler in the Exchange application to do all data transmissions without waiting for the Email Processor to finish processing a received email. Specifically, PING messages are sent via the PING Engine in Figure 7. In the original client, the PING Engine checks up in a two-second interval whether the Email Protocol Handler allows it to resume PING messaging after an email-receiving event ends. So there is a delay between the completion of receiving an email and the start of PING. The energy is wasted because the cellular module has to delay its sleep mode. We improved the signaling between the Email Protocol Hander and the PING Engine so that a PING message can be sent out immediately. Thus, all data transmissions are batched together to save energy. We also revised the Email Processor to report an error if anything is wrong in processing an email so that the Email Protocol Handler can re-sync with the email server. In addition, we revised the Email Protocol Handler to receive emails by re-using the existing TCP connection rather than making a new one, avoiding energy waste of TCP/SSL handshakes.

In the Email application, we added a new Database Manager, loading a small cache inbox into the memory to implement in-memory email receiving. On the flash storage, all the emails are stored in a big database. The Database Manager manages the data sync between the in-memory cache inbox and the persistent one on the flash storage. When the user interacts with the smartphone or we receive more than a customized number of emails, the Database Manager commits the new email data onto the flash storage.

Android does not provide an API for fast dormancy and we cannot control the 3G tail time on the fly. We have managed

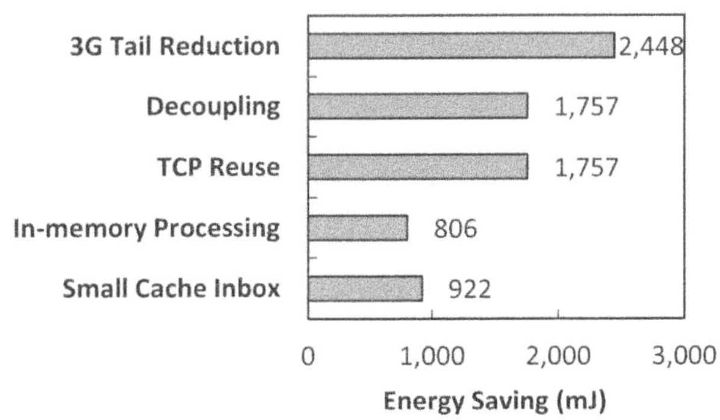

Figure 10: Anatomy of total energy saving

to enable fast dormancy on the Nexus S smartphone by flashing a new baseband firmware.

6. EVALUATION

We evaluate our implementation by measuring the total energy saved in receiving an email and the individual ones contributed by each technique we proposed and implemented. For all the experiments, we used Exchange push email service with the original built-in email client provided by Android and our revised one on a Nexus S smartphone. For each experiment, we repeated for the procedure five times and report the average results with standard deviations.

Total energy saving. Figure 8 shows the total energy saving of our revised email client, compared to the original one when the inbox size is 200 emails but the new incoming email has different sizes. On average the total energy saving is 44.3%, with a narrow range from 41.2% to 46.9%. These results demonstrate that our proposed techniques are able to significantly reduce the energy cost of email receiving. The energy savings mainly come from the shortened email receiving time. On average our revised email client reduces the time period of receiving the emails by 47.6%, compared to the original one.

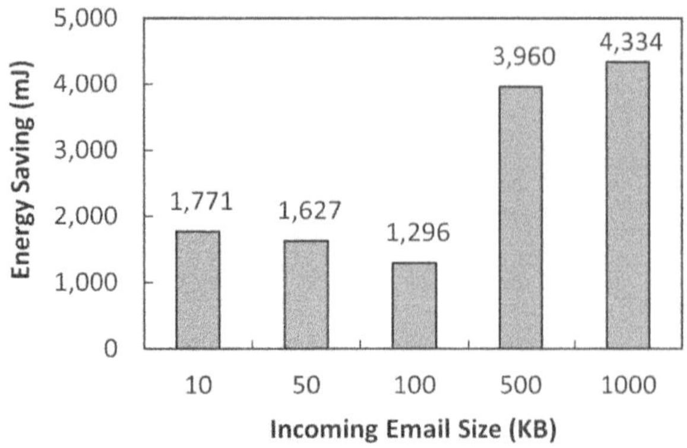

Figure 11: Energy saving of decoupling data transmission from data processing in different email sizes

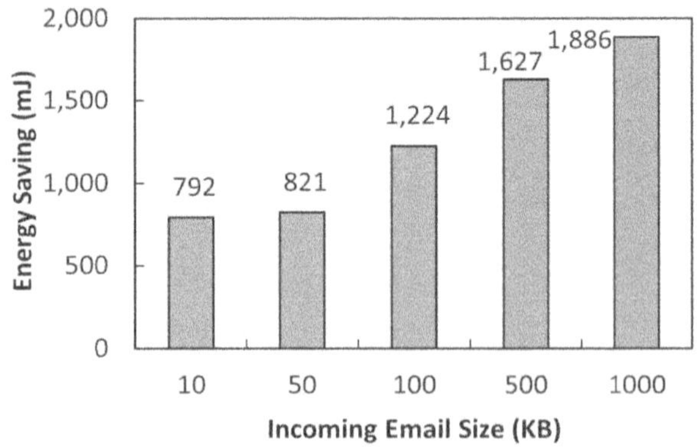

Figure 12: Energy saving of in-memory data processing in different email sizes

Figure 9 shows the total energy savings of our revised email client in receiving a small email of 10 KB with different inbox sizes. Similar to Figure 8, we can see that our revised email client is able to effectively reduce the total energy cost of email receiving no matter how many emails the inbox has. The average energy saving is 45.8%, also with a small range from 39.9% to 51.3%. Compared to Figure 8, the average energy saving is higher because when the email is large, the received data volume becomes large and more energy will be saved by our proposed techniques, as shown later in this Section.

Energy saving of each technique. Figure 10 shows the anatomy of the total energy saving in receiving the 10 KB email with an inbox of 200 emails. For the total energy savings of 7,690 mJ, the largest part comes from reducing 3G tail time which saves 2,448 mJ (32%) energy. Decoupling data transmission from data processing part and reusing TCP connections also save a significant energy cost, each with 1,757 mJ (23%). The in-memory processing part and using small cache inbox part reduce relatively less energy, saving 806 mJ (10%) and 922 mJ (12%)energy, respectively.

Reducing the 3G tail time and reusing the TCP connections have fixed energy savings, independent from incoming email size and inbox size. However, the energy saving of other techniques may depend on the email size or inbox size. Figure 11 shows how much energy can be saved by decoupling data transmission from data processing for different email sizes. We can see that generally the energy saving increases when the email size becomes large. The decoupling technique tries to batch all data transmissions together. When the email is large, more data is transmitted over the network and thus the energy saved by batching becomes large.

Similarly, Figure 12 shows how much energy can be saved by in-memory processing for different email sizes. We can see that the energy saving is high for large emails. This is because the processing cost (e.g., writing operation) heavily depends on email size. Thus, when the email size is large, processing the email entirely with memory operations will save more energy.

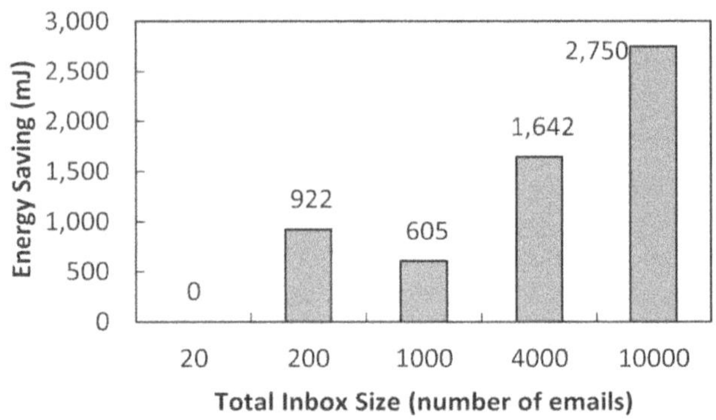

Figure 13: Energy saving of using a small cache inbox for email receiving with different total inbox sizes

Figure 13 shows the benefit of using a small cache inbox for email receiving when the total inbox size is different. The size of the small cache inbox we used is 20. Thus, the benefit for the inbox size of 20 in Figure 13 is zero. For a larger inbox size, we can see that the extra energy saving caused by using the small cache inbox increase as the total inbox size becomes large. For the total inbox size of 10,000 emails, the extra energy saving is 2,750 mJ. These results demonstrate the effectiveness of using the small cache inbox.

Note that in all the above experiments, we measured the energy cost of receiving individual emails without counting the energy saving of batch writing multiple emails onto flash. In our implementation we batch 20 emails together for writing their data onto flash. By doing so, we can further save 634 mJ energy per email. On average this increases the total energy saving of receiving a 10 KB email to 49.9% in different inbox sizes.

Furthermore, we also calculate how much extra energy can be saved if we can put 3G interface into sleep immediately after the end of receiving an email. Doing so we can further save 2,448 mJ of energy. For receiving a 10 KB email with an inbox size of 200, this will increase the total energy saving by 77.9%.

7. EVENT RECEIVING IN OTHER APPLICATIONS

Despite this paper focusing only on email receiving, the techniques we proposed may also be applied to other applications. Example applications include various social network applications such as Facebook and Twitter, locations based applications which receive notifications upon location changes, and many other applications which receive push notifications when new updates or new in-application content are available. Similar to email, when in standby mode, those applications maintain their own persistent connection or use a separate push notification service like Google client notification service [15] to keep connected to a server for receiving various events or poll changes from a server. Such event receiving is very similar to email receiving and follows the "transmission-processing-transmission" pattern. Each event receiving also wakes up the 3G interface and a smartphone's entire operating system for a small amount of data transmission and processing. Due to the similarity between receiving emails and receiving other events, those applications may also have the issues with energy inefficiency we found in email receiving, such as sparse data transmissions resetting 3G tail timer, frequent small flash writes, and making new network connections unnecessarily. Therefore, our proposed techniques can be used as general design guidelines for those applications rather than specific techniques designed for email receiving only.

We plan to investigate more applications to further study how the techniques we proposed in this paper may be used to reduce the energy cost of receiving events in connected standby. In addition, recent tablet devices and other types of mobile devices have started to function like smartphones, keeping connected in standby mode to receive various network events including emails. For example, Windows 8 introduces a new connected standby power mode [17] to provide such support. We also plan to study the power performance of applications on those devices and look for potential improvements.

8. RELATED WORK

System power management. Power management is important to mobile devices including smartphones due to the limited power supply of batteries. All smartphone operating systems come with components to leverage hardware capabilities and manage system activities to save power, e.g., adjusting screen backlight levels, running CPU at low frequency, putting network interfaces into sleep or killing power-hungry applications in low battery mode. Various techniques have been proposed to reduce the power consumption of each key component of a smartphone such as the screen [22], CPU [24] and network communication [20, 23]. However, even with good system-level and component-level power management, applications that are not well designed can still cause high energy consumption.

Finding energy bugs of applications. Recently researchers have started to study how to improve the power performance of mobile applications by finding energy bugs. Energy bugs are not real program bugs causing failures but they lead to unnecessarily high energy consumption. For example, in [10] the authors proposed techniques for automatically finding non-sleep energy bugs in applications. However, such a tool depends on pre-configured program patterns to find energy problems, e.g., requiring a Wakelock to prevent the system from sleeping without releasing it, and only works for serious non-sleep bugs. Authors in [21] built tools for developers to estimate the energy consumption of their applications and find potential energy inefficiency issues. Our work focuses on finding energy inefficiency when receiving email by measuring the energy performance of existing email clients. The techniques we proposed are complimentary with existing work and can be used as general design guidelines for other applications.

Fast dormancy. The problem of the cellular data network tail has drawn a lot of attention. Smartphone manufacturers have developed their own and inconsistent ways to reduce the energy cost of a cellular tail, which results in the standard approach called network-controlled fast dormancy in 3GPP [7, 8]. Researcher also proposed schemes to reduce the power consumption of applications by using fast dormancy adaptively [8, 9]. We believe that fast dormancy should be used in connected standby. However, even with fast dormancy, there is still wasted energy in the event receiving during the connected standby due to very sparse network activities. We propose that the OS should provide a global service to collect the network usage information of all the applications running in the connected standby. When all the applications finish their event receiving, the service works with the cellular network to immediately put the 3G interface into sleep mode and thus minimizes the energy waste of the 3G tail time in connected standby.

9. CONCLUSIONS

In this paper we have studied the power performance of email sync on the Windows Phone and Android operating systems. We conducted experiments to measure the energy cost of email receiving in existing email clients, using both push and poll emails, with different email services, email sizes and inbox sizes. Together with our analysis of the network and flash storage activities, the measured results indicate that existing email clients are not energy-efficient in several aspects. Besides 3G tail time, the main source of inefficiency stems from the coupling of the data transmission and data processing, which is a bad design choice in connected standby mode. Frequent storage access, making new TCP connections to receive new emails and updating a large inbox are further components that increase the time duration of email sync and lead to energy waste.

Based on the experiment, we advocate that the fast dormancy should be used in the connected standby and propose other techniques to address the energy inefficiency of existing email clients, including the decoupling of data transmission from data processing, in-memory processing, reusing existing network connections and using a small cache inbox to handle the email sync. We have implemented these techniques and evaluation results show that average energy savings reach 49.9%. If we can put the 3G interface into sleep mode immediately after receiving an email, the total energy savings can be increased to 77.9%.

ACKNOWLEDGEMENTS

We thank our shepherd, Mahadev Satyanarayanan, and anonymous reviewers for their valuable comments and insightful feedback. This project was supported in part by US National Science Foundation grants CNS-1117412 and CA-REER Award CNS-0747108.

REFERENCES

[1] Microsoft Direct Push.http://technet.microsoft.com/en-us/library/cc539119.aspx.

[2] Microsoft ActiveSync Command Reference Protocol Specification.http://msdn.microsoft.com/en-us/library/dd299441(v=exchg.80).aspx.

[3] Monsoon Power Monitor. http://www.msoon.com/LabEquipment/PowerMonitor/.

[4] Tcpdump. http://www.tcpdump.org/.

[5] Wireshark.http://www.wireshark.org/.

[6] B. W. Lampson. Lazy and Speculative Execution, talk at *OPODIS*, 2006.

[7] UE "Fast Dormancy" behavior. 3GPP discussion and decision note RP-090960, 2009.

[8] F. Qian, Z. Wang, A. Gerber, Z. M. Mao, S. Sen and O. Spatscheck. TOP: Tail Optimization Protocol for Cellular Radio Resource Allocation, In *ICNP*, 2010.

[9] P. K. Athivarapu, R. Bhagwan, S. Guha, V. Navda, R. Ramjee, D Arora, V. N. Padmanabhan and G. Varghese. RadioJockey: Mining Program Execution to Optimize Cellular Radio Usage. In *Mobicom*, 2012.

[10] A. Pathak, A. Jindal, Y. C. Hu and S. P. Midkiff. What is keeping my phone awake? Characterizing and Detecting No-Sleep Energy Bugs in Smartphone Apps. In *MobiSys*, 2012.

[11] Google adopts Microsoft sync protocol, http://www.windowsfordevices.com/c/a/News/Google-adopts-Microsoft-sync-protocol/.

[12] Apple finally acknowledges iPhone's Exchange support, http://www.zdnet.com/blog/microsoft/apple-finally-acknowledges-iphones-exchange-support/1246.

[13] A. Carroll and G. Heiser. An Analysis of Power Consumption in a Smartphone. In *Usenix ATC*, 2010.

[14] S. Deng and H. Balakrishnan. Traffic-Aware Techniques to Reduce 3G/LTE Energy Consumption. In *CoNEXT*, 2012.

[15] A. Adya, G. Cooper, D. Myers and M. Piatek. Thialfi: A Client Notification Service for Internet-Scale Applications. In *SOSP*, 2011.

[16] 3GPP Release 8, http://www.3gpp.org/Release-8.

[17] P. Stemen and S. Berard. Understanding Connected Standby.*Microsoft Build* conference talk, 2011.

[18] F. Qian, Z. Wang, A. Gerber, Z. M. Mao, S. Sen and O. Spatscheck. Profiling Resource Usage for Mobile Applications: A Cross-layer Approach. In *Mobisys*, 2011.

[19] H. Kim, N. Agrawal and C. Ungureanu. Revisiting Storage for Smartphones. In *FAST*, 2012.

[20] H. Han, Y. Liu, G. Shen, Y. Zhang and Q. Li. DozyAP: Power-Efficient Wi-Fi Tethering. In *MobiSys*, 2012.

[21] R. Mittal, A. Kansal, and R. Chandra. Empoweringdevelopers to estimate app energy consumption. In*MobiCom*, 2012.

[22] M. Dong and L. Zhong. Chameleon: a color-adaptive-web browser for mobile oled displays. In*MobiSys*, 2011.

[23] F. Dogar, P. Steenkiste and K. Papagiannaki. Catnap: Exploit High Bandwidth Wireless Interfaces to Save Energy for Mobile Devices. In *Mobisys*, 2010.

[24] M. Ra, B. Priyantha, A. Kansal and J. Liu. Improving Energy Efficiency of Personal Sensing Applications with Heterogeneous Multi-Processors. In *UbiComp*, 2012.

[25] How smartphones are bogging down some wireless carriers. http://arstechnica.com/gadgets/2010/02/how-smartphones-are-bogging-down-some-wireless-carriers/.

Energy Characterization and Optimization of Image Sensing Toward Continuous Mobile Vision

Robert LiKamWa[†,‡], Bodhi Priyantha[‡], Matthai Philipose[‡], Lin Zhong[†,‡], and Paramvir Bahl[‡]

[†]Rice University, Houston, TX [‡]Microsoft Research, Redmond, WA

ABSTRACT

A major hurdle to frequently performing mobile computer vision tasks is the high power consumption of image sensing. In this work, we report the first publicly known experimental and analytical characterization of CMOS image sensors. We find that modern image sensors are not energy-proportional: energy per pixel is in fact inversely proportional to frame rate and resolution of image capture, and thus image sensor systems fail to provide an important principle of energy-aware system design: trading quality for energy efficiency.

We reveal two energy-proportional mechanisms, supported by current image sensors but unused by mobile systems: (*i*) using an optimal clock frequency reduces the power up to 50% or 30% for low-quality single frame (photo) and sequential frame (video) capturing, respectively; (*ii*) by entering low-power standby mode between frames, an image sensor achieves almost constant energy per pixel for video capture at low frame rates, resulting in an additional 40% power reduction. We also propose architectural modifications to the image sensor that would further improve operational efficiency. Finally, we use computer vision benchmarks to show the performance and efficiency tradeoffs that can be achieved with existing image sensors. For image registration, a key primitive for image mosaicking and depth estimation, we can achieve a 96% success rate at 3 FPS and 0.1 MP resolution. At these quality metrics, an optimal clock frequency reduces image sensor power consumption by 36% and aggressive standby mode reduces power consumption by 95%.

Categories and Subject Descriptors

I.4.m [**Image Processing and Computer Vision**]: Miscellaneous; I.5.4 [**Performance of Systems**]: Modeling techniques, Performance attributes

General Terms

Design, Experimentation, Measurement, Performance

MobiSys'13, June 25-28, 2013, Taipei, Taiwan

Keywords

Image sensor; energy efficiency; mobile systems; computer vision; energy proportionality

1 Introduction

Cameras are ubiquitous on mobile systems, from laptops, tablets, smartphones, to wearable devices, such as Google Project Glass or GoPro Helmet Cameras. Originally intended for capturing photo or video, cameras have inspired many to provide new mobile computer vision services, including marker-identification, gesture-based interaction, and object recognition. Many researchers, including ourselves [2], also envisage that by showing computers what we see on the go, we will see a new generation of personal computing coming, or *continuous mobile vision*. Unfortunately, image sensing, the very first stage of any vision-based application, is power-hungry, consuming hundreds of milliWatts. As a result, users and developers refrain from using the camera extensively. For example, most computer vision applications for smartphones are intended for occasional, instead of continuous, use; wearable cameras are designed for on-demand capture rather than continuous on-the-go capture.

Modern mobile systems employ CMOS image sensors [5] due to their low power and low cost. CMOS image sensors are an active area of circuit research where power consumption, image quality and cost of fabrication have been the main focuses of improvement. However, mobile systems integrate these image sensors with such a narrowly defined hardware and software interface that typically only the frame resolution and sometimes the frame rate can be changed in software. Furthermore, as we show later, reducing the image quality does not currently provide significant power reduction. The image sensor remains a black box to system and application developers with its system behavior, in particular power consumption, not well understood.

In this work, we provide a comprehensive treatment of the energy characteristics of image sensors in the context of computer vision applications. In particular, we consider (*i*) how the energy consumption of an image sensor is related to its image quality requirements, i.e., frame rate and resolution, (*ii*) how the energy consumption can be reduced from a systems perspective, and (*iii*) how the energy consumption can be reduced through image sensor hardware improvements. Our study includes fine-grained power measurement, modeling, prototyping, and model-driven simulation.

First, in Section 3, we report a detailed power characterization of five CMOS image sensors from two major vendors in the mobile market, breaking down the power consumption by major components and by operational modes. Based on the measurements and our understanding of image sensor internals, we construct power models that relate energy consumption to image quality requirements such as frame rate, resolution, and exposure time. By varying frame rate and resolution, we study the *energy proportionality* of image sensors; in particular, we consider how the energy cost for collecting a constant number of pixels changes when the frame rate and resolution changes. We observe that while power consumption decreases when frame rate or resolution drops, the energy per pixel increases significantly, up to 100 times more when reducing frame rate from 30 frames per second (FPS) to 1 FPS, which suggests poor energy proportionality. This observation suggests a key barrier in applying a well-known principle in energy-aware system design [6]: sacrifice quality (in this case, via frame rate and resolution reduction) for energy efficiency. Our characterization also reveals that the analog part of image sensors not only consumes a large portion of the power consumption (33-85% of sensor power) but also constitutes the bottleneck of energy proportionality.

Second, in Section 4, our investigation reveals two unexplored hardware mechanisms for improving energy proportionality: clock scaling and standby mode. Modern image sensors allow a wide range of external clock frequencies, but mobile systems often supply a clock of fixed frequency. We show that given the image requirement, there exists a frequency at which an image sensor consumes the lowest energy per pixel. Modern image sensors also provide a *standby mode* in which the entire image sensor is put into a non-functional, low-power mode. We show that standby mode can be applied between frames when the frame rate and resolution are sufficiently low. We call this optimization *aggressive standby*. We show that by combining clock scaling and aggressive standby, the energy proportionality of image sensing can be significantly improved, leading to almost constant energy per pixel across a wide range of image quality requirements and over 40% efficiency improvement when image quality requirement is low, e.g., one megapixel per frame and 5 FPS. In Section 5, we suggest several hardware modifications to further improve energy efficiency, in particular that of the analog parts.

Finally, in Section 6, using computer vision benchmarks and the data collected from the characterization, we demonstrate the quality vs. energy tradeoffs of image sensors with and without applying the optimizations described above. For continuous image registration on video, useful for image mosaicking and depth estimation, we can achieve a 36% power reduction by choosing an optimal clock frequency, and a 95% power reduction by using aggressive standby. Our suggested architectural modifications of image sensors can further reduce power. For example, by putting components in standby during exposure the power can be further reduced by 30%.

2 Background

We first provide an overview of the CMOS image sensor, the core of the camera on mobile systems. While cameras use optical and mechanical elements to focus light to the plane of the image sensor, we specifically discuss various electronic components and controls related to the image quality and power consumption after the light reaches the sensor.

2.1 Major Components of Image Sensor

A typical image sensor is a single chip that includes the following components as illustrated by Figure 1. The *pixel array* consists of an array of pixels; each pixel employs a photodetector and several transistors to convert light into charge stored in a capacitor. The *analog signal chain* employs active amplifiers and Analog-to-Digital-Converters (ADC) to convert the voltage of the capacitor into a digital output. Serial readout sensors employ a single analog signal chain for the sensor, while column-parallel readout sensors use one analog signal chain for each pixel column. The *image processor* performs basic digital image processing, such as demosaicking, denoising and white-balancing. The *I/O controller* interfaces the image sensor with the external world, usually the application processor in a mobile system. Along with streaming frame data, the I/O controller also receives instructions used to set the internal registers of the image sensor that determine the sensor's operational mode and parameters including frame rate and resolution. The *digital controller* manages the timed execution of the operations of the image sensor.

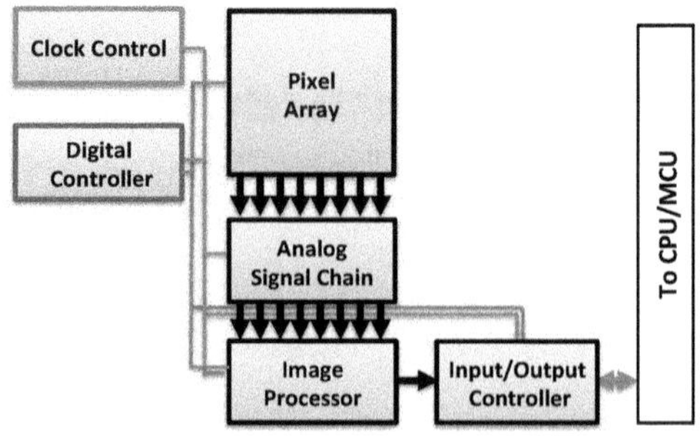

Figure 1: General image sensor architecture

2.2 Electronic Shutter (Exposure Control)

CMOS image sensors employ an *electronic shutter* to control the *exposure time*, T_{exp}, the length of time during which light can enter the sensor before a pixel capacitor is read out. Long exposures are used for low-light indoors scenes, while short exposures are used for bright outdoors scenes. There are two types of electronic shutters. (*i*) A *rolling shutter*, as shown in Figure 2, clears a row of pixels T_{exp} before it is to be read out. The rolling shutter then waits to clear the next row to prepare another row for exposure. The rolling nature allows the readout of some rows to overlap with exposure of other rows. However, with moving scenes, this causes temporal problems; although each row is exposed for a duration of T_{exp}, the top row of the frame is exposed much earlier than the bottom row of the sensor. (*ii*) A *global shutter* clears all rows of the pixel array simultaneously. After T_{exp} of exposure, the charge is transferred to a *shielded area*, a memory that maintains the state of the captured frame and frees the pixel array to subsequent exposure. As rows are read out from the shielded area, they do not face the moving effects suffered from rolling shutter operation. However, global shutters require memory for all pixels, and thus require expensive and complicated designs.

A programmable *shutter width* dictates the exposure time allotted by the electronic shutter. This allows systems developers to program the camera to operate in different ambient light environments. The shutter width is held as a register value and is implemented by the digital controller, which resets the charge of the pixel array capacitors appropriately.

2.3 Power, Clock, & Operational Modes

On mobile devices, the sensor is powered by multiple voltage rails, supplying the pixel array, the analog signal chain, the image processor, and the digital controller independently. We exploit these separate power rails to measure the power consumption of the various image sensor components and provide a characterization of the chip in Section 3.

An image sensor also uses an external *clock*. The clock controls the speed of the digital logic. Typically, an image sensor outputs

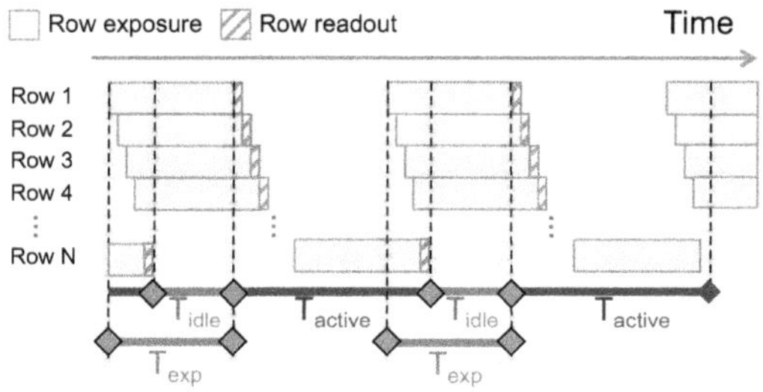

Figure 2: Streaming mode with rolling shutter

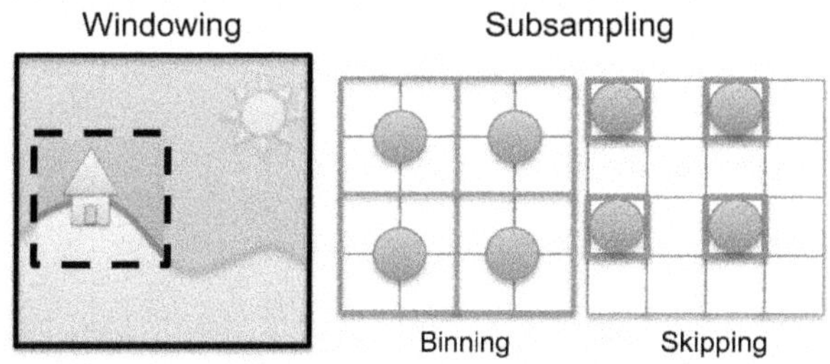

Figure 3: Image windowing and subsampling techniques

one pixel per clock period. Higher clock speeds allow sensors to process frames at different speeds, but consume significantly more power.

An image sensor typically provides two operational modes: streaming and standby. In *streaming* mode, the sensor alternates between two states: an idle state and an active state. During the *idle* state, the sensor is on and may be undergoing exposure, but the analog signal chain is not yet active to read out the pixel array. In the *active* state, the analog signal chain reads out the pixel array, the digital elements process the image and the I/O controller streams the frame out from the sensor. In Figure 2, the image sensor is in the streaming mode, alternating between T_{active} and T_{idle}. Because of the rolling shutter operation, T_{exp} can expose rows while rows are being read out during the T_{active} state.

In *standby* mode, much of the image sensor chip is put in a low-power mode with clock and/or power gated, but all register states are maintained, which allows for rapid wakeup. Standby mode consumes minimal power (0.5 - 1.5 mW). This mode is intended for taking snapshots where preview is not required; the sensor can remain in standby mode, wakeup to take a picture, and then return to standby.

2.4 Quality Controls

Typical image sensors provide controls to vary the quality of the frame, allowing for tradeoffs between frame resolution, field-of-view, frame rate, and power consumption. These are maintained by register values set through the I/O controller and controlled with the digital controller. We detail these operations below.

Frame rate R: The frame rate is the number of frames per second in the output stream. It is usually dictated by the system developer. The frame time, $T_{frame} = 1/R$, is the inverse of the frame rate. The minimum frame time is limited by the number of pixels in the image and the clock frequency. However, the frame time can be elongated by programming *Vertical Blanking*, which adds a number of "blank rows" to the image for timing purposes. Each blank row takes the same amount of time as reading a row out from the frame, but many components may be idle during the blanking time. The vertical blanking is manifested as rows of zeros in the image stream, and can be discarded by the processor receiving the output stream. Increased vertical blanking thus effectively raises the frame time, lowering the frame rate.

Frame resolution N: The frame resolution N indicates the number of pixels in the image, and directly influences the data transfer, processing, and storage requirements of the image sensor system. N can be reduced with two mechanisms: *windowing* and *subsampling*.*Windowing* directs the image sensor to output a smaller rectangular window of the frame, as shown in Figure 3. By specifying the size and location of the window, the system can request outputs with reduced fields-of-view. In contrast, *subsampling* preserves the field-of-view, but produces a "resized" lower resolution image. Image sensors use one of two techniques to achieve subsampling: (i) *Row/Column Skipping* skips sampling every other row or column of pixels. As a result, many pixels are not sent to the image processor, leading to rapid subsampled readout of an image. On the other hand, (ii) *Row/Column Binning* combines the values of adjacent pixels in the image processor after the analog signal chain. Groups of adjacent pixels create a single pixel value, reducing high-frequency aliasing effects and noise in the subsampled image. These techniques are shown in Figure 3.

2.5 Integration inside Mobile Systems

The image sensor is usually directly connected with the main application processor in a mobile device. Because large image sensors used in modern mobile devices require high data transfer speeds that cause synchronization issues on parallel buses, current devices use a serial interface between the image sensor and the application processor. For example, the Qualcomm Snapdragon S4 and Nvidia Tegra 3 use serial MIPI interfaces that consist of a clock to transfer data, one or more serial data paths, and a serial control bus [19].

Due to lack of hardware access, user applications on mobile devices resort to using the camera APIs provided by the operating system. The typical actions include control (e.g., focus the camera), image and video capture, and configuration (e.g., set resolution) of the camera. For example, the Windows Phone 8 native API provides `StartRecordingToSinkAsync()` for capturing an image and `StartRecordingToStreamAsync()` for recording a video, while the `AudioVideoCaptureDevice` maintains properties such as autofocus regions and exposure time. Control over frame rate and subsampling (but not windowing) parameters are also provided. Android and iOS SDKs provide similar APIs.

3 Energy Characterization

In this section, we report a characterization study of the energy consumption of several state-of-the-art CMOS image sensors. In particular, we evaluate the *energy per pixel* under various image quality requirements in terms of frame rate and resolution, which are relevant to computer vision applications. We have three objectives. First, we want a thorough understanding of how image sensors consume power in their major components. Second, we want to identify effective mechanisms to achieve the same quality with the lowest energy per pixel. And finally, we want to identify problems in the energy proportionality of existing and emerging image sensors: why does the energy-per-pixel increase as quality requirements decrease?

3.1 Apparatus and Image Sensors

We use a National Instruments USB-6212 16-Bit, 400 kilosample/second DAQ device for power measurements. We characterize five image sensors from two major vendors of CMOS image

Table 1: Important notations

Symbol	Description	Model (Source)
R	Framerate	
N	Number of pixels in a frame	
f	Clock frequency	
T_{frame}	Frame time	$T_{frame} = 1/R$
T_{active}	Time in active state	$T_{active} \approx N/f$
T_{idle}	Time in idle state	$T_{idle} = T_{frame} - T_{active}$
P_{idle}	Power consumption in idle state	$P_{idle} = a_1 \cdot f + a_2$ (Equation 10)
P_{active}	Power consumption in active state	$P_{active} = (b_1 \cdot N + b_2) \cdot f + b_3$ (Equation 12)
E_{frame}	Energy per frame	$E_{frame} = P_{idle}T_{idle} + P_{active}T_{active}$ (Equation 1)
P_{seq}	Power consumption for sequential frame capturing	$P_{seq} = \frac{P_{idle} \cdot (T_{frame} - T_{active}) + P_{active} \cdot T_{active}}{T_{frame}}$ (Equation 4)

sensors for the mobile market, as summarized by Table 2. By concurrently measuring the current into various voltage rails we are able to infer the power characteristics of the internal components of modern image sensors.

Table 2: Image sensors characterized in our study and power consumption at 24 MHz

	Max. Res.	P_{active}	P_{idle}	Market
A1	2592x1944	163.5 mW	161.9 mW	Snapshot
A2	768x506	189.5 mW	141.8 mW	Automotive
B1	3264x2448	338.6 mW	225.4 mW	Mobile
B2	2592x1944	225.1 mW	218.6 mW	Mobile
B3	752x480	137.1 mW	105.9 mW	Security

3.2 Breakdown by Components

We next provide our measurement results regarding the power consumption of the image sensors in idle and active modes, i.e., P_{idle} and P_{active}, and their breakdown into major components.

P_{active} Breakdown: We find that in the active state, the analog read-out circuitry consumes 70-85% of the total power, except for in B3, where it consumes only 33%, due to the column-parallel readout of its analog signal chain. The digital controller and image processing consumes 5%. The I/O controller that manages external communication consumes 10-15%. The breakdowns are shown for each sensor in Figure 4. As the bulk of the power is consumed by the analog signal chain, due to numerous power-hungry ADCs, this provides the greatest opportunity for new power-saving techniques, which we explore in Section 5.

P_{idle} Breakdown: Between frame captures, the sensors enter the idle state, where they still consume considerable power. The analog signal chain and image processor are powered during the idle state, but do not actively process pixels. In addition, I/O chains typically remain active during the idle state in order to communicate with the sensor to output blank rows or wait for register changes. As a result, the power of many components is typically reduced during the idle state. However, the amount of disparity depends on the image sensor architecture. For A2, B1 and B3, the analog power drops 15-45%. For A1 and B2, the analog components reduce their power minimally, less than 1%. The digital components for all of the sensors drop 10-55% and 3% for A1 and B2. For B2, the I/O power drops 40% and for A1 the I/O power drops 8%.

3.3 Energy Consumption Per Frame

We next examine the energy consumption per frame. Modern image sensors are programmed to capture a single frame (single shot) or to capture sequentially (video). For sequential frame capture, energy consumption per frame can be equivalently evaluated by the average power consumption in tandem with the frame rate.

In both cases, the energy consumption per frame depends on the power consumption of the operational modes and how much time the sensor spends in each mode. That is,

$$E_{frame} = P_{idle}T_{idle} + P_{active}T_{active} \tag{1}$$

From measurements and data sheets, we find that T_{active} is determined by the clock frequency, as one pixel is read out for every clock period. As the readout is pipelined with the digital processing and output of the image sensor, we can estimate:

$$T_{active} \approx N/f \tag{2}$$

The idle time T_{idle} is determined by the exposure time for single frame captures and the frame rate for sequential frame captures. Figure 6 shows the power traces measured from the power rails of all of the sensors under sequential capture. The typical power consumption waveform clearly shows that the sensor alternately undergoes the active and idle states.

Single Frame Capture: For capturing a single photo, we care about the energy consumption for capturing a frame, E^{single}_{frame}. Figure 5(a) shows the power behavior of capturing a single image. The sensor must undergo exposure for T_{exp}, which ranges from 0.1 ms to 70 ms, depending on the lighting environment of the scene and the aperture size of the camera system (f/2.8 for typical smartphone cameras). The frame is then read out during T_{active}, after which the sensor may turn off. Thus, the energy consumption of a single frame capture can be simply modeled by inserting $T_{idle} = T_{exp}$ into Equation (1):

$$E^{single}_{frame} = P_{idle}T_{exp} + P_{active}T_{active} \tag{3}$$

Sequential Frame Capture: For sequentially capturing images, such as for video, we care about the average power consumption, P_{seq}. Figure 5(b) shows the power behavior of capturing sequential

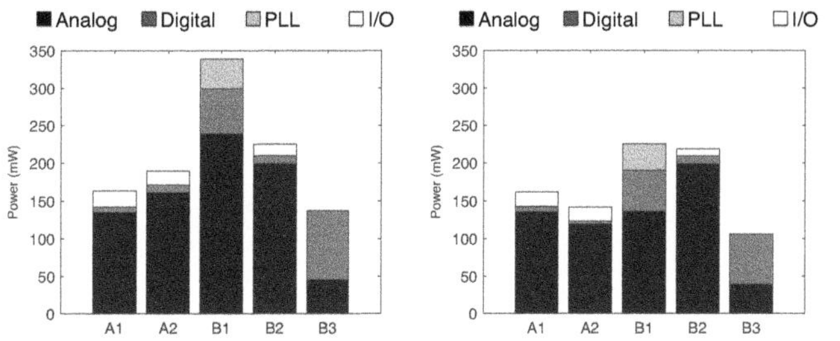

(a) P_{active} (b) P_{idle}

Figure 4: Average power of various rails in active state (a) and idle state (b), at 24 MHz

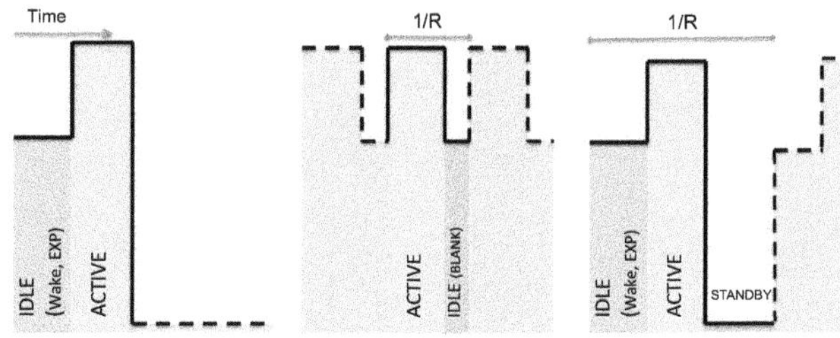

(a) (b) (c)

Figure 5: Power behavior for single capture (a), standard sequential capture (b) and sequential capture with aggressive standby mode (c)

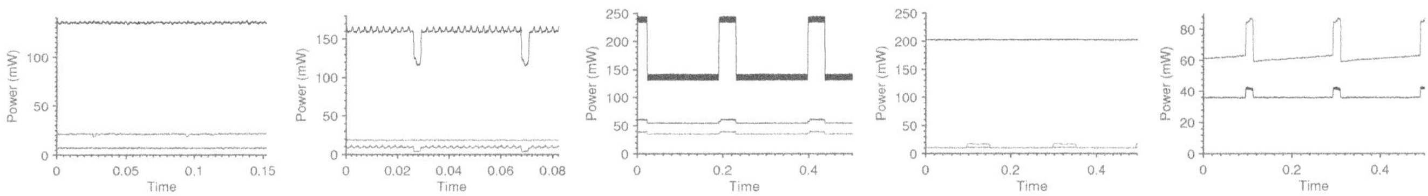

(a) A1 (1 MP, 15 FPS) (b) A2 (1 MP, 20 FPS) (c) B1 (1 MP, 5 FPS) (d) B2 (1 MP, 5 FPS) (e) B3 (0.3 MP, 5 FPS)

Figure 6: Power waveform of image sensors. Analog (blue), digital (green), and I/O (red) voltage rails. For (c), the magenta line is the PLL voltage rail.

frames at a frame rate of R. Exposure can occur in either the active and idle states but because the exposure itself does not consume much power, this does not affect the overall power consumption. A cycle of capturing a frame can be clearly broken into two parts: the active state and the idle state, i.e., $T_{frame} = T_{idle} + T_{active}$. When the frame rate R is low, T_{idle} can be significant. The average power of sequential frame capture can be modeled as follows:

$$P_{seq} = \frac{P_{idle} \cdot (T_{frame} - T_{active}) + P_{active} \cdot T_{active}}{T_{frame}} \quad (4)$$

3.4 Energy Proportionality

In this section, we explore the energy implications of varying the quality parameters of frame capture. In particular, we vary the frame rate and resolution of the frame capture, model the power implications, and perform measurements for verification. Our measurements indicate that current image sensors are not energy proportional, as the energy consumption per pixel increases as the quality requirement decreases.

3.4.1 Frame rate

With a fixed clock frequency, the maximum frame rate of the sensor is the inverse of T_{active}. However, as explained in Section 2.4, the frame rate can be reduced by inserting blanking time. Then, for a given frame rate R, the energy per frame is:

$$\begin{aligned} E^{seq}_{frame}(R) &= P_{idle}(1/R - T_{active}) + P_{active}T_{active} \\ &= P_{idle}/R + (P_{active} - P_{idle})T_{active} \end{aligned} \quad (5)$$

Thus, we expect the energy per frame to increase as the frame rate decreases, as the power consumption becomes dominated by the idle power consumption. This is shown in Figure 7 by inserting measured P_{active} and P_{idle} values into the above equation. For each of the sensors, as the framerate drops from 20 FPS to 1 FPS, the energy per frame increases by an order of magnitude. Thus, image sensors are not energy proportional to frame rate. Instead, their energy per pixel increases as the performance requirement in terms of frame rate drops. In Section 4, we will show how the energy proportionality can be significantly improved by aggressively applying a power-saving standby mode during the idle state.

3.4.2 Resolution

When changing the resolution of the frame through subsampling or windowing techniques, fewer pixels are read out. Equation 2 indicates that T_{active} is proportional to the number of pixels and so a lower resolution will result in a shorter active time. Conversely, our measurements indicate that P_{active} and P_{idle} are only minimally influenced by the number of pixels, and thus remain unchanged for the purposes of our model. Then, we can model the energy for a single frame capture by plugging the numbers into Equation 1:

$$E^{single}_{frame}(N) = P_{active}N/f + P_{idle}T_{exp} \quad (6)$$

$$E^{single}_{frame}(N)/N = P_{active}/f + \frac{P_{idle}T_{exp}}{N} \quad (7)$$

For small T_{exp}, the second term is negligible. In this case, the energy per frame is reduced proportionally to N, as shown in Figure 8, and the energy per megapixel is nearly constant, as shown in Figure 9. Among sensors A1, A2, B1, and B2, the energy per megapixel is around 6 - 8 mJ/MP. B3 consumes lower energy per megapixel (3 mJ/MP), due to the low-analog-power nature of its column-parallel readout.

For sequential frame capture at constant frame rate, a shorter T_{active} requires a longer T_{idle} to keep T_{frame} constant. Then, building on Equation 5, with R fixed, we can model the energy of a frame and energy per megapixel as:

$$E^{seq}_{frame}(N) = (P_{active} - P_{idle})N/f + \frac{P_{idle}}{R} \quad (8)$$

$$E^{seq}_{frame}(N)/N = (P_{active} - P_{idle})/f + \frac{P_{idle}}{RN} \quad (9)$$

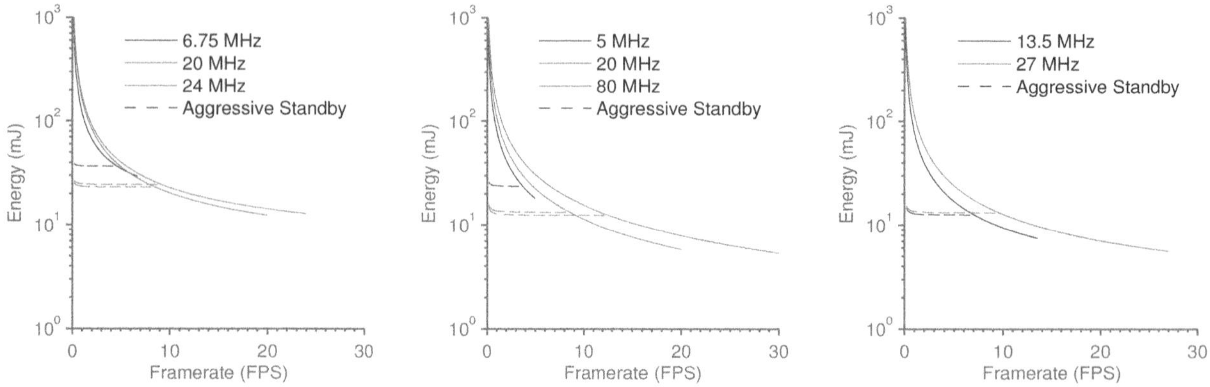

(a) B1 (b) B2 (c) B3

Figure 7: Modeled energy per frame in sequential frame capture without and with aggressive standby (1 MP frame)

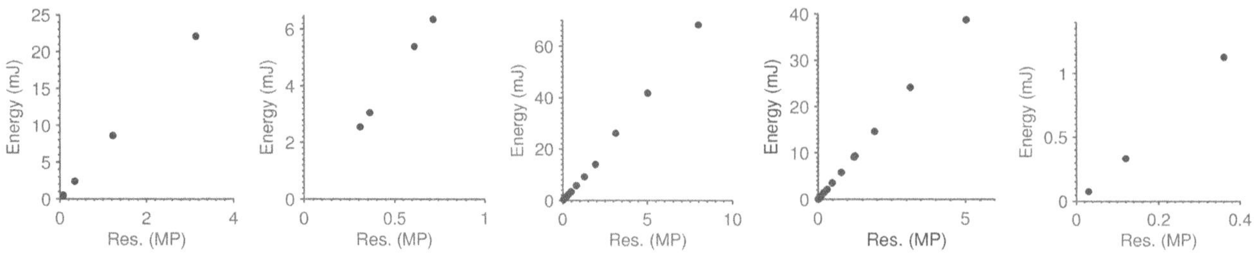

(a) A1 (b) A2 (c) B1 (d) B2 (e) B3

Figure 8: Modeled energy per frame for subsampled single frame capture (with short T_{exp}, i.e., $E^{single}_{frame}(N) \approx P_{active}N/f$)

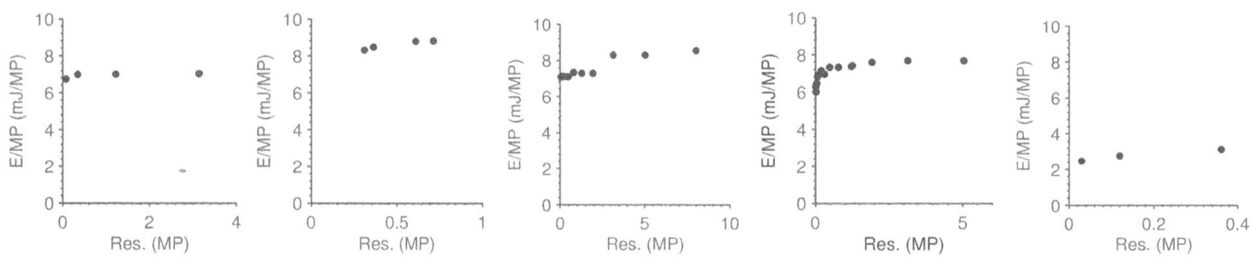

(a) A1 (b) A2 (c) B1 (d) B2 (e) B3

Figure 9: Measured energy per megapixel for subsampled single frame capture (with short T_{exp}, i.e., $E^{single}_{frame}(N)/N \approx P_{active}/f$)

Given a constant frame rate R and a small resolution N, the energy per megapixel is dominated by the second term and is thus inversely related to the resolution of the subsampled frame, as shown in Figures 10 and 11, generated by simulating various framerate and resolution combinations with measured P_{active} and P_{idle} values. For example, for A1 at 1 FPS, the energy per megapixel rises by an order of magnitude as the resolution is dropped from 3 MP to 0.3 MP. Thus, as resolution is decreased, the energy per megapixel increases.

Our models and measurements indicate that current image sensors are not energy proportional to image quality reductions in framerate and resolution. In almost all cases, reducing the quality results in drastically higher energy per megapixel. The exception is the energy per megapixel of a subsampled single image capture, which remains relatively constant as resolution is decreased. In the next two sections, we explore existing mechanisms and propose future mechanisms to push towards energy proportionality.

4 Exploiting Existing Mechanisms

In this section, we exploit hardware mechanisms supported by modern CMOS image sensors to improve their energy efficiency. The key question we try to answer is: *given the frame rate (R) and resolution (N), what is the optimal configuration of an image sensor to achieve the lowest energy per frame?* The answer to this question can be implemented by the mobile system's image sensor driver to configure the sensor for energy efficiency when receiving requests from computer vision applications.

We identify two important existing power-saving mechanisms, *clock scaling* and *standby mode*, and answer the question by exploiting them. Modern mobile systems do not change the clock frequency of their image sensors nor do they apply standby mode to

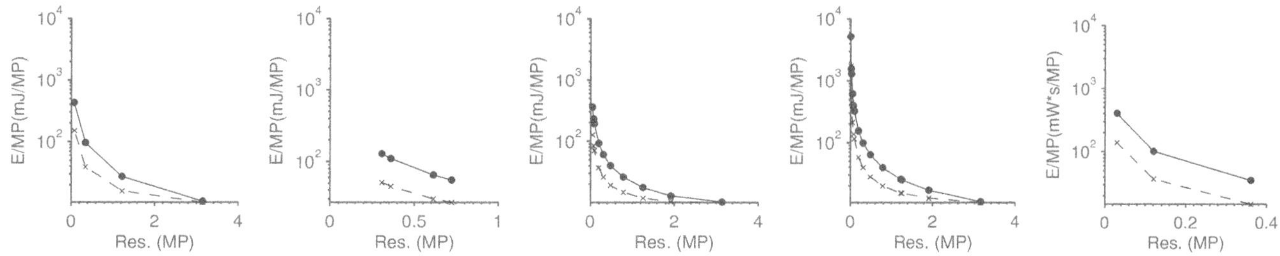

(a) A1 (b) A2 (c) B1 (d) B2 (e) B3

Figure 10: Modeled energy per megapixel for subsampled sequential capture based on P_{active} and P_{idle} measurements at 5 FPS. Aggressive standby (from Section 4) is represented by the dashed line.

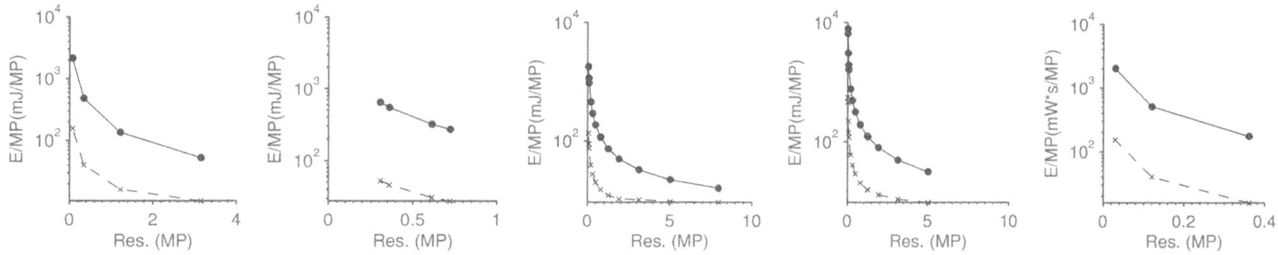

(a) A1 (b) A2 (c) B1 (d) B2 (e) B3

Figure 11: Modeled energy per megapixel for subsampled sequential capture based on P_{active} and P_{idle} measurements at 1 FPS. Aggressive standby (from Section 4) is represented by dashed line.

image capture because they intend the image sensors to be used for capturing high-resolution photo and fixed frame rate video, where clock scaling and standby mode bring little benefit. These mechanisms offer significant power efficiency when frame rate or resolution is low, which is sufficient for many computer vision tasks and for video streaming over networks. For 1 MP readouts, up to 50% of the power consumption of single frame capture and 30% of the power consumption of sequential frame capture can be eliminated by choosing the correct clock frequency. Further, by aggressively applying standby between frame captures, one can largely remove the idle energy consumption, leading to significant average power reduction, e.g., 40% for B1 at 5 FPS at 24 MHz.

4.1 Clock Scaling

Modern mobile systems do not change the clock frequency (f) of their image sensors. However, since the clock is supplied externally, its change only requires simple additional hardware, such as a programmable oscillator. For our experiments, we used a DS1077 oscillator, programmable over I^{2}C, and connected it to the external clock input on the B1, B2, and B3 image sensors.

Changing the clock frequency has significant implications on the image sensor's efficiency. We employ measurements with our understanding of the image sensor internals to quantify the relationship between f and the power consumption of an image sensor.

Our measurements, as summarized by Figure 12, show that both P_{idle} and P_{active} increase with f almost linearly. This is not surprising, since increasing the clock frequency linearly increases the switching power consumption of the digital and I/O parts of the circuit. (The clock frequency does not affect the analog signal chain power consumption, as these largely consume static power.)

We have:

$$P_{idle} = a_1 \cdot f + a_2 \qquad (10)$$

$$P_{active} = c_1 \cdot f + c_2 \qquad (11)$$

Table 3 summarizes the power model parameters for B1 to B3 according to our power vs. clock frequency measurements. Based on our understanding of how the clock works internally, we can further relate P_{active} to N as:

$$P_{active} = (b_1 \cdot N + b_2) \cdot f + b_3 \qquad (12)$$

$b_1 \cdot N \cdot f$ denotes the power consumption by the analog signal chain, which reads out N pixels in each cycle of the clock. $b_2 \cdot f$ denotes the switching power consumption by the rest of the sensor, driven by the clock.

We make a few important notes about the above power models. First, b_3 is equivalent to c_2 and denotes the static power consumption of the sensor, independent of the clock. Second, a_1, a_2, and c_2 are intrinsic to the sensor and are independent of the frame rate or resolution. In contrast, c_1 increases as the number of pixels increases. Third, we have $c_1 \gg a_1$ and $c_2 \geq a_2$ because the digital circuitry stops switching in the idle state and the analog circuitry, while not driven by the clock, does not do additional work in the idle state.

Using measurements and the models derived above, we next seek to answer the opening question by setting clock frequencies optimally.

4.1.1 *Single Frame Capture*

If we plug the models described above into the energy for a single frame capture, Equation 3, we can derive the energy consumption by single frame capture as:

$$E_{frame}^{single} = a_1 \cdot T_{exp} \cdot f + \frac{c_2 \cdot N}{f} + C \qquad (13)$$

E_{frame}^{single} achieves the minimum when $f_{best}^{single} = (\frac{c_2 \cdot N}{a_1 \cdot T_{exp}})^{\frac{1}{2}}$.

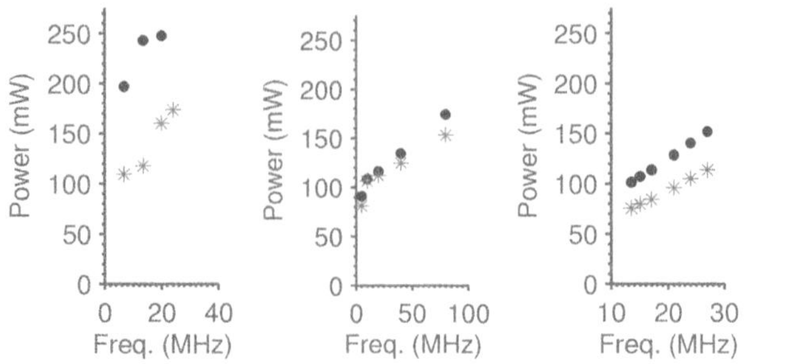

(a) B1 (b) B2 (c) B3

Figure 12: Clock frequency f vs. P_{active} (blue dot) and P_{idle} (red stars)

Table 3 gives the f_{best}^{single} for B1-B3 under both indoor and outdoor exposure times and $N = 10^6$. Figure 13 also displays the energy for single frame captures for our measurements and the power model at different frequencies. As is evident from the table and the figure, the optimal frequency choice depends heavily on the exposure time. For outdoor usage, f_{best}^{single}, the optimal frequency choice, is typically higher than the sensor typically allows.

REMARK 1. *For single frame capture, the sensor's optimal clock frequency depends on the resolution (N) and exposure time (T_{exp}). For bright outdoors scenes, with short exposure times, the clock frequency should be set as fast as the sensor can handle.*

4.1.2 *Sequential Capture*

If we plug the frequency models above into our equation for sequential capture, Equation 4, we can derive the power consumption by sequential frame capture as:

$$P_{seq} = a_1 \cdot f + \frac{R \cdot N \cdot (c_2 - a_2)}{f} + B \quad (14)$$

P_{seq} reaches its minimum when $f_{best}^{seq} = (\frac{R \cdot N \cdot (c_2 - a_2)}{a_1})^{\frac{1}{2}}$. Table 3 gives f_{best}^{seq} when $N = 10^6$ and $R = 5$ for B1 and B2. The optimal frequencies are within the range of clock frequencies allowed by the sensors. Therefore we have the following remark.

REMARK 2. *Without considering standby mode, the lowest power consumption for sequential frame capture can be achieved by carefully selecting the clock frequency depending on the frame rate (R) and the frame resolution (N).*

4.2 Aggressive Standby

We can also apply standby mode to idle time between two frames in sequential frame capturing as illustrated by Figure 5(c). During standby mode, the sensor consumes minimal power (e.g., 10 μW in standby mode vs. >100 mW in idle state). For simplicity, we ignore the wakeup time from standby mode, which occupies only tens of μs. The sensor performs no operation during standby mode, so a full T_{exp} cannot pipeline with the readout of the image pixels. As such, the duration of standby mode is $T_{standby} = T_{frame} - T_{exp} - T_{active}$. Therefore, we can calculate the average power consumption as

$$P_{seq}^{aggr} \approx \frac{P_{standby}(T_{frame} - T_{active} - T_{exp}) + P_{idle}T_{exp} + P_{active}T_{active}}{T_{frame}} \quad (15)$$

Table 3: Parameters relating clock frequency f to power consumption. We assume 0.05ms and 50ms for T_{exp} outdoors and indoors, respectively. $N = 10^6$ and $R = 5$. All frequencies in MHz.

	B1	B2	B3
a_1	4.0E-06	8.2E-07	3.35E-06
a_2	76.2	90.1	4.4
c_1	5.6E-06	1.0E-06	5.1E-06
c_2	159.0	93.0	13.1
f_{best}^{single} (indoor)	28.2	47.6	19.0
f_{best}^{single} (outdoor)	564.4	951.9	379.2
$f_{best}^{seq}(5\ FPS)$	10.2	4.2	3.6

For clarity and simplicity, we ignore the standby power, i.e., $P_{standby} \approx 0$, since it is very small compared to P_{idle} and P_{active}. We have

$$P_{seq}^{aggr} \approx \frac{P_{idle}T_{exp} + P_{active}T_{active}}{T_{frame}} \quad (16)$$

$$P_{seq}^{aggr} \approx a_1 \cdot R \cdot T_{exp} \cdot f + \frac{R \cdot c_2 \cdot N}{f} + D \quad (17)$$

We note P_{seq} achieves its minimum when $f = f_{best}^{single} = (\frac{c_2 \cdot N}{a_1 \cdot T_{exp}})^{\frac{1}{2}}$. As we see above, the best frequency depends on the exposure time, given the quality requirement.

REMARK 3. *With aggressive standby, the sensor's optimal clock frequency for sequential frame capture depends on the resolution (N) and exposure time (T_{exp}). For bright outdoors scenes, with short exposure times, the clock frequency should be set as fast as the sensor can handle.*

We also note that in aggressive standby mode with a fixed clock rate and resolution size, the energy per frame remains constant as frame rate changes, as shown in Figure 7. This is due to the fact that frame rate is changed by extending the standby time, where the sensor consumes minimal power.

Hence, significant power reductions can result from application of clock scaling and aggressive standby. In our measurements, choosing an optimal clock frequency can reduce the power consumption of single frame capture by up to 50%. An optimal clock frequency can also reduce the power consumption of sequential frame capture by up to 30%. Additionally, by applying standby aggressively between frames, one can further reduce power consumption, e.g., 40% for B1 at 5 FPS at 24MHz.

5 New Power-Saving Mechanisms

Based on our findings, we next discuss a number of hardware modifications that further improve the energy efficiency of image sensors. Since the analog signal chain is the dominant power consumer in both idle and standby states and analog circuits are known to improve much slower than their digital counterparts, we focus on improving the efficiency of the analog signal chain without requiring a new design of analog circuitry.

5.1 Heterogenous Analog Signal Chains

Existing image sensors employ analog signal chains provisioned for the peak performance in terms of pixel per second supported by the image sensor. Because of this, while the pixel per second can be

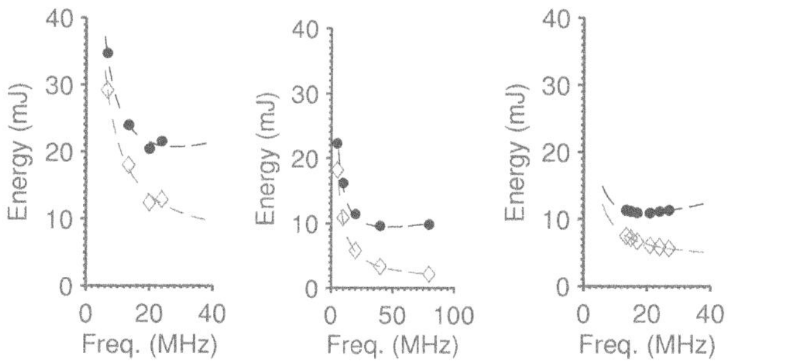

(a) B1 (b) B2 (c) B3

Figure 13: Energy measurements of single frame capture at 1 MP with T_{exp}=50 ms (blue dot) and T_{exp}=0.125 ms (red diamond) at different f with theoretical models (dashed lines)

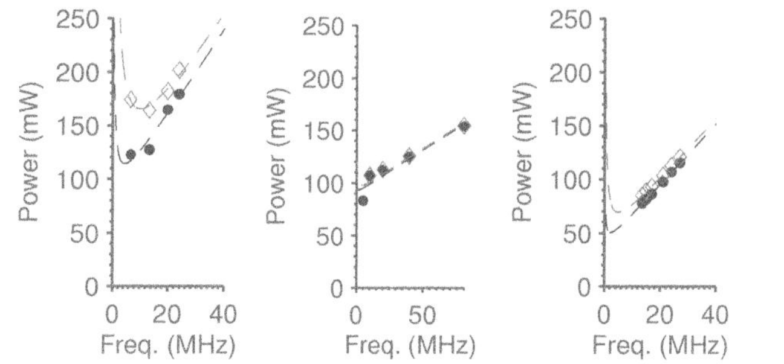

(a) B1 (b) B2 (c) B3

Figure 14: Power for sequential capture of 1 MP frames at 1 FPS (blue dot) and 5 FPS (red diamond) at different f with theoretical models (dashed lines)

orders of magnitude lower in practice for continuous applications, the energy per pixel remains almost constant as shown in Figure 9. By using a much simpler analog signal chain for low performance capture, a much lower energy per pixel can be achieved in these situations.

We suggest that an image sensor should include a heterogeneous collection of analog signal chains each optimized for certain bitrates. For example, one sophisticated chain could be active for full resolution, e.g., high-quality video taking, while another could be used when a much lower resolution is needed for computer vision applications. In both cases, the idle analog signal chain should be powered off.

To implement heterogeneous analog chains, extra but not duplicated circuitry is needed because the heterogeneous chains are not operational at the same time. For example, many complex modules of the analog signal chain, such as analog to digital converters (ADCs), will require only a small increase in hardware resources, since submodules of these modules can be shared between different implementations. For example, at lower resolutions, successive approximation (SAR) ADCs can be implemented by simple modifications to control logic to ignore least significant bits; similarly, lower resolution pipelined ADCs can be implemented by disabling the last pipeline stages that generate the least significant bits. Hence, image sensor designs with multiple analog chains require a careful balance between the increased cost due to extra hardware resources and the power savings achieved.

5.2 Fine-grained Power Management of Sensor Components

Existing image sensors provide a standby mode for the entire sensor. In Section 4.2, we showed how this mode can be aggressively applied to reduce the power consumption during the idle state. Now we explore the opportunity to apply power management (gating the power supply or clock) in a more fine-grained manner to reduce the power consumption during the active state.

Per Column Power Management of Analog Signal Chain: During readout, all column parallel analog signal subchains operate in parallel to read out a row of pixels simultaneously. However, during column skipping and windowing operations, not all pixels of a row need to be read out. The analog signal subchains for the skipped columns are left on in modern image sensors. As fewer pixels are addressed, these components should be shut off to save power. If only 1/2 of the columns are addressed, this would lead to substantial power savings, dropping the analog power by 50% and the total power by 30-40%.

Power Management during Exposure: For single frame capture and sequential frame capture with aggressive standby applied, the power consumption during exposure time can contribute significantly to the total energy per frame or average power consumption, respectively. During the exposure time (T_{exp}), which can be long (e.g., 50 ms) under low illumination, most parts, including the digital components, the analog signal chain's amplifiers and ADC's, and the I/O, are in idle state, which still consumes substantial power. By putting these parts into the standby mode with either power or clock gated, the sensor would reduce the energy consumption of taking a single frame, i.e., Equation 3, and the power consumption of sequential capture, i.e., Equation 4. This has the effect of nullifying P_{idle}. It is easy to show that *when the power management is applied to the exposure time, the best clock frequency is always the highest possible regardless of the exposure time.* At this point, for long exposures, the sensor can consume fractions of the original energy cost of single frame capture; at T_{exp}=50 ms, B1, B2, and B3 would consume 19%, 83% and 50% less energy, respectively.

6 Energy Optimization for Continuous Vision Scenarios

Toward understanding the quality vs. efficiency tradeoffs possible for computer vision applications, we next specifically consider the power consumption of the image sensor during the execution of two fundamental computer vision problems: *image registration* and *object detection*.

Using the power models derived in Sections 3 and 4, we can model the image sensor power consumption when reducing the frame rate, reducing the window (field-of-view), and capturing the image at a lower resolution. In this section, we also apply the two power-saving mechanisms and gauge the impact on the performance of image registration and object detection. In doing so, we demonstrate that these mechanisms can reduce the energy consumption by 95% without sacrificing application performance. We also estimate the impact of suggested modifications from Section 5, reducing the energy consumption by 98% of the original.

Dataset

Our dataset consists of 90 seconds of 270x480, 30 FPS video from a smartphone mounted at chest level. The video was captured by a user walking around an outside path. We compute our machine vision tasks on adjacent pairs of frames of the video.

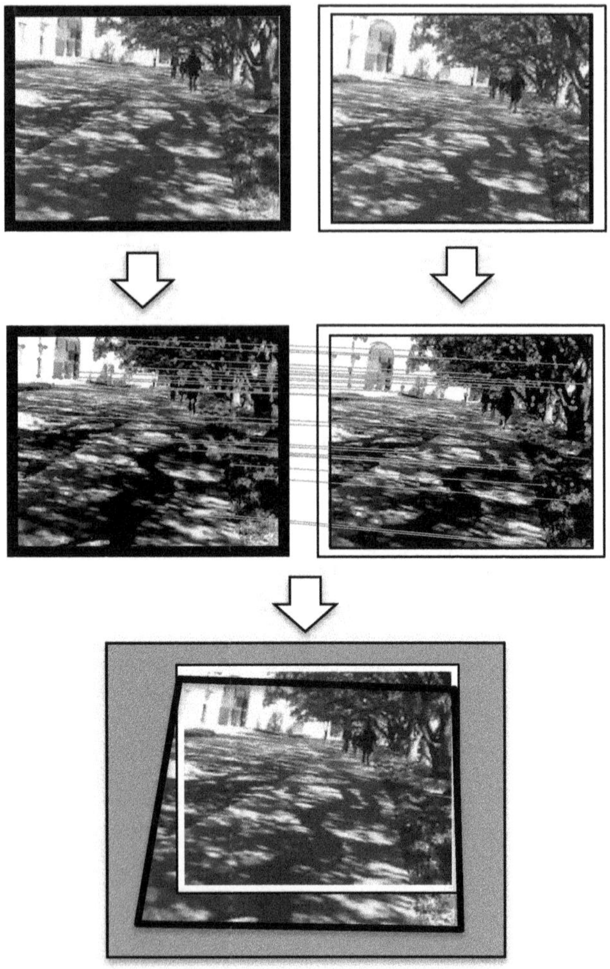

Figure 15: Image registration at 3 FPS. Corners (red dots) and homography inlier matches (green lines), along with image-mosaicked result.

To simulate low-resolution frame capture, we created image pyramids of the dataset by subsampling the resolution of the original frames. Each subsampled layer of the pyramid is constructed by taking the previous layer, convolving it with a Gaussian blur kernel, and removing multiples of rows. Subsampling by n is then defined by keeping every nth row. We also created windowed versions of our datasets: for a parameter W, we discard $W\%$ of the rows and $W\%$ of the columns from the borders of the image, effectively reducing the field of view. To simulate a reduction of frame rate to R FPS, we performed our vision tasks on pairs separated by $30/R$ frames.

6.1 Image Registration

Image registration – determining the correspondence points between two images – is a common problem in computer vision. Registration can be used to stitch images of a scene together, i.e., image mosaicking, to estimate the depth of objects, i.e., structure from motion, and to reduce shaking in video, i.e., image stabilization [8].

6.1.1 Algorithm

The registration algorithm involves finding corners in each image, matching corners in pairs of images, discarding outliers, and computing plane-to-plane transforms of the pair of images [7]. In this section, we describe the image operations necessary to compute the algorithm.

The Harris & Stephens corner detector [7] locates corners and edges in images by autocorrelating local patches around each pixel in an image. Where the autocorrelation value returns above a threshold, the algorithm detects a corner in the image. The patches around the corners in each image must then be matched with each other to generate correspondence pairs. This is done by correlating all possible pairs of corner patches. Where a corner in Image B is the maximum match of a corner in Image A and vice-versa, the pair of corners are determined to be a match.

With 4 or more corner matches, a plane-to-plane homography transform can be determined by fitting a 3x3 transform matrix to the set of corner pairs, e.g., using least squares. Because matches may be inaccurate, common homography algorithms use a Random Sample Consensus (RANSAC) to remove outliers from the list of matches. With a sufficient number of inliers, the homography is considered a success. In our implementation, we consider the existence of 25 inliers as the criterion for success.

6.1.2 Results

On our original dataset, the image registration process succeeded on 2783 frame pairs and failed on 7 pairs, for a success rate of 99.9%. Image registration also performs well with downscaled datasets. Frame rate reduction to 3 FPS still returned 95.7% success, 30% Windowing returned 96.5% success, and a downsampling to a resolution of 135x240 returned 91.8% success. Table 4 shows these quality parameters alongside their power consumption implications.

As shown in Figure 16, standard sequential capture does not significantly reduce the power consumption with lower quality requirements. However, by implementing clock scaling and aggressive standby modes, we can dramatically reduce the power by lowering the frame rate, window size, and subsampled resolution. For example, at 3 FPS, where image registration can still perform with 95.6% accuracy, the average power consumptions of B1, B2, and B3 are 185, 112, and 114 mW, respectively, using default configurations. By appropriately selecting the clock frequency, we can reduce the power consumptions to 106, 95, and 55 mW, giving a power savings of 36%. Aggressive standby further reduces the power consumptions to 9.9, 5.1, and 5.2 mW, or 5% of the original power consumption. Our proposed hardware modifications from Section 5 have significant power-impact when performing subsampling and windowing tasks, as columns of analog-signal chain are switched off. For W=30%, the modifications carry an estimated 75% reduction in power over aggressive standby mode, while for subsampling by 2, the modifications can reduce the power by an estimated 81%.

6.2 Object Detection

Detecting objects in frames is another fundamental and useful machine vision technique for understanding captured scenes. We apply the Viola-Jones Object Detection Framework [28], a widely-used platform for object detection, to detect the presence of human figures in our datasets.

6.2.1 Viola-Jones Object Detection Framework

The Viola-Jones framework detects objects in images based on their "Haar-like" rectangular features. A cascaded set of Adaboost-trained classifiers based on such features allows the framework to rapidly and robustly search image frames for objects from the library. While the original paper's example uses human faces as the subject, the

Table 4: Power consumption (in mW) for image registration (IR) success and person detection (PD) recall, for sequential capture P_{seq}, with optimal clock frequency $P_{seq}(f)$, with aggressive standby P_{aggr}, and with estimated architectural modifications P_{arch} for sensor B1

	IR Success %	PD Recall %	N pix.	P_{seq}	$P_{seq}(f)$	P_{aggr}	P_{arch}
Full Resolution	99.9%	94.4%	129600	202.2	154.2	99.1	32.7
Frame rate = 3 FPS	95.7%	83.3%	129600	185.8	106.1	9.91	3.27
Window, W = 30%	96.5%	77.8%	63504	192.9	129.5	71.6	17.8
Subsample by 2	91.8%	72.2%	32400	188.6	115.1	55.5	10.2

framework is robust to using other types of objects. We use it to detect human figures, using the `PeopleDetector` classifier from the Computer Vision Toolbox of MATLAB 2012b.

6.2.2 Results

Object Detection has fundamental challenges when objects in a scene are in unexpected poses or are occluded from view. However, in a continuous mobile vision scenario, the detection only needs to find an object once over all the frames in which the object is in view. Additionally, in such a continuous scenario, a preliminary detection at low quality could be followed by a high quality frame capture, which would check the validity of an object detection. Because we are primarily concerned with energy proportionality, we are most concerned with the low quality *recall* frame, ensuring that we detect an object when it is present in a scene.

To accommodate these relaxed expectations, we use a metric in which we count the number of false negatives on an instance basis rather than on a frame-by-frame basis. Then, our recall rate is (# of detected people)/(# of people).

Table 4 and Figure 16 shows the performance of Person Detection at various quality parameters on our 90-second dataset with 18 people in the scene. At full 270x480 resolution, Viola-Jones detects 17 of the people. As with image registration, scaling the frame rate offers the largest opportunity for energy proportionality, while still maintaining high performance. At 3 FPS, People Detection can detect 15 people, performing with 83.3% accuracy. The Viola-Jones performance weakens at lower resolutions, and low framerates reduce the chance that a person is detected. However, the balance between success rate and power offers computer vision developers the ability to carefully trade power for algorithmic performance, enabling low-power computer vision.

7 Related Work

To the best of our knowledge, our work is the first publicly known study of the energy efficiency of image sensing from a system perspective. We next discuss related work in improving the energy consumption of cameras and image sensors.

CMOS Image Sensor Design: In this work, we study CMOS image sensors from a *system* perspective. We examine the power implications of sacrificing quality, which vision applications are likely to make, reveal inefficiency in the quality-power tradeoffs made by existing mobile image sensors, and suggest architectural modifications to improve the tradeoff. Our approach is complementary to that taken by the vibrant image sensor community, whose focus has been on improving image sensors through better circuit design. We refer the readers to textbooks on image sensor design for this approach, e.g., [22, 23]. It is well-known to image sensor designers that ADCs are often the power and performance bottleneck of high-speed, high-resolution image sensors, e.g., [3]. As the ADC is the interface between the physical and digital worlds in multiple domains, e.g., in sensors and wireless receivers, its performance and power efficiency has been extensively studied. We refer the readers to textbooks, e.g., [25] and survey papers, e.g., [13, 21] for recent development in ADC design.

Often, proposed techniques to address the ADC bottleneck involve many forms of compression, from temporal compression [17, 16, 11, 14, 4] to DCT [10] to predictive coding [15] to compressive sensing [26, 24]. These new architectures require significant modifications to the system and to camera applications. As a result, they are often intended for application-specific systems, e.g., surveillance camera networks [11]. In contrast, our presented techniques and modifications are evolutionary changes that can be easily incorporated into image sensors without any change to the system hardware designs or applications. Additionally, the goal of these sensor designs is orthogonal to ours: they target at reducing the power consumption of high-resolution capture, while we target at making the energy consumption proportional to image quality for efficient low-resolution capture.

Other Work Toward Efficient Vision Systems: Because image sensing is power-hungry, many have investigated the energy efficiency of a camera system at a high level for various platforms, but do not examine the internals of current image sensors for sources of inefficiency and mechanisms for software-based optimization as we do in this paper. Wireless visual sensor networks have tried both commercial-off-the-shelf image sensors and research prototypes like the ones discussed above [27] but are limited to much simpler applications like surveillance, due to an extremely tight power constraint. Many have made cameras wearable and a few have adventured to optimize the battery lifetime of the wearable cameras beyond simply duty cycling, e.g., [18, 9], and mobile phone designers are extraordinary careful not to quickly drain the battery, e.g., [1, 12]. The general approach has been to employ low-power sensors to manage the operations of the power-hungry image sensor. Without examining the internals of image sensors and their interface with the system and software, such work brings complementary benefits to our solutions.

We also note that power-saving mode and clock scaling have been extensively studied for microprocessors and digital circuits in general. Usually, clock scaling is combined with voltage scaling for maximal energy saving. For example, the authors of [20] show that given a processor, a workload and its deadline, there is an optimal way to apply clock/voltage scaling and power-saving mode jointly. For some processors, it is efficient to run as fast as possible and then enter a low-power mode, while for others, it can be most efficient to run as slow as possible. Our results in Section 4 show that image sensors have similar power-saving modes and allow clock scaling to reduce power consumption of the digital circuitry. Moreover, single and sequential frame captures can be considered as real-time workloads for image sensors. Image sen-

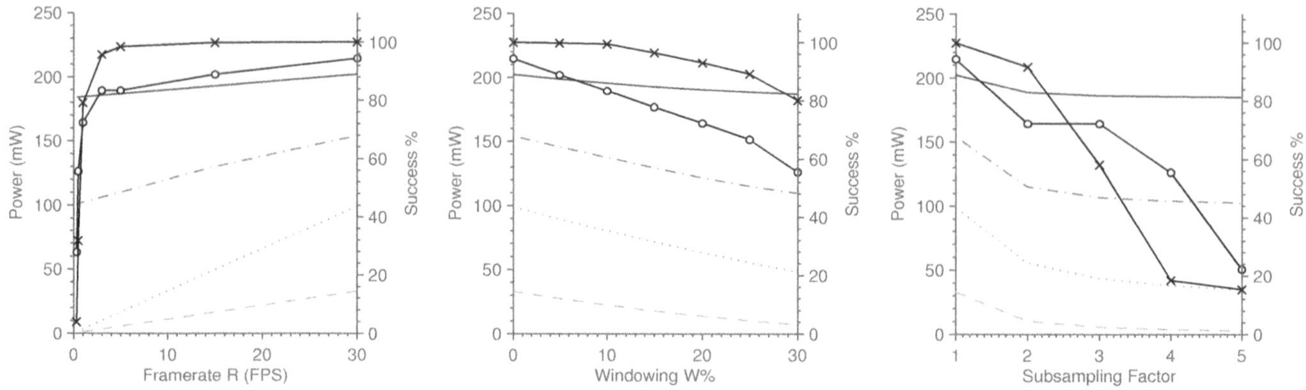

(a) Frame rate (b) Windowing (c) Subsampling

Figure 16: B1 Power consumption, image registration success (X) and person detection recall (O) at various quality parameters for sequential capture (blue solid), with optimal clock frequency (magenta dashed-dotted), with aggressive standby (red dotted), and with architectural modifications (green dashed)

sors, however, are distinct from microprocessors because the analog circuitry, which dominates power consumption, is not affected by clock or voltage scaling; a supply voltage change can ruin the accuracy of an analog-to-digital converter. Thus, power management and clock scaling solutions for microprocessors are not directly applicable to image sensors.

8 Discussion

System and API Support for Power-Saving Mechanisms: As we have demonstrated, clock scaling and aggressive standby power models described in Section 4 provide an opportunity to reduce the power consumption of the camera for tasks that do not require high frame rates and/or high resolutions. However, current mobile systems do not provide any system or API support for applications to adjust the clock frequency or apply standby mode. We hope our work will motivate platform and system vendors to consider such support.

Energy-Aware Computer Vision: Energy-proportional image capture opens the possibility of a new class of algorithms which carefully balance the tradeoff between accuracy metrics and power performance. With our power models, scaling the frame rate and resolution of an image has direct impact on the power consumption of a system. We plan to devise hierarchical/cascaded algorithms, using low-power image sensor modes to sense when to turn on progressively higher-power modes to detect information from a scene with low energy consumption. Other such algorithms from the vision community could leverage the quality-energy tradeoff to understand captured images and video on a continuous basis at low power.

9 Conclusion

Current image sensor operation is power-hungry and not energy-proportional. To explore this problem, we perform an experimental and analytical characterization of image and video capture on CMOS image sensors. We show two mechanisms for improving energy efficiency: (*i*) optimal clock scaling, which reduces power by up to 50% or 30% for one mega-pixel photos and videos, respectively; (*ii*) aggressive standby mode, which results in 40% power reduction for 1 MP, 5 FPS capture. We also suggest architectural modifications that further improve the energy efficiency of low-quality capture.

We use computer vision benchmarks to show application quality and energy efficiency tradeoffs that can be achieved with existing image sensors. For continuous image registration, a key primitive for image mosaicking and depth estimation, we achieve a 36% power reduction with an optimal clock frequency, and a 95% power reduction by using aggressive standby. Image sensor architectural modifications can further scale down the power consumption by an additional 30%. The quality-energy tradeoffs our work offers create new opportunities for continuous mobile vision under a power budget.

ACKNOWLEDGMENTS

The authors thank Eddie Reyes for his assistance in MATLAB programming for image registration and person detection benchmarks. The authors also thank the scientists at Aptina Imaging for corroborating our observations about the capabilities of modern day image sensor architectures and for answering our technical questions. The authors are grateful for the useful comments made by the anonymous reviewers and the paper shepherd, Dr. Shyamnath Gollakota. This work was supported in part by NSF Awards #0923479, #1012831, and #1054693.

REFERENCES

[1] M. Azizyan, I. Constandache, and R. Roy Choudhury. SurroundSense: mobile phone localization via ambience fingerprinting. In *Proc. ACM Int'l Conf. on Mobile Computing and Networking (MobiCom)*, 2009.

[2] P. Bahl, M. Philipose, and L. Zhong. Vision: cloud-powered sight for all: showing the cloud what you see. In *Proc. ACM Wrkshp. Mobile Cloud Computing and Services (MCS)*, pages 53–60, 2012.

[3] Y. Chae, J. Cheon, S. Lim, M. Kwon, K. Yoo, W. Jung, D.H. Lee, S. Ham, and G. Han. A 2.1 M pixels, 120 frame/s CMOS image sensor with column-parallel $\Delta\Sigma$ ADC architecture. *IEEE Journal of Solid-State Circuits*, 46(1):236–247, 2011.

[4] N. Cottini, L. Gasparini, M. De Nicola, N. Massari, and M. Gottardi. A CMOS ultra-low power vision sensor with image compression and embedded event-driven energy-management. *IEEE Journal of Emerging and Selected Topics in Circuits and Systems*, 1(3):299–307, 2011.

[5] A. El Gamal and H. Eltoukhy. Cmos image sensors. *IEEE Circuits and Devices Magazine*, 21(3):6–20, 2005.

[6] J. Flinn and M. Satyanarayanan. Energy-aware adaptation for mobile applications. *ACM SIGOPS Operating Systems Review*, 33(5):48–63, 1999.

[7] C. Harris and M. Stephens. A combined corner and edge detector. In *Alvey Vision Conference*, volume 15, page 50. Manchester, UK, 1988.

[8] Richard Hartley. *Multiple view geometry in computer vision*. Cambridge University Press, Cambridge, UK New York, 2003.

[9] S. Hodges, L. Williams, E. Berry, S. Izadi, J. Srinivasan, A. Butler, G. Smyth, N. Kapur, and K. Wood. SenseCam: A retrospective memory aid. In *Proc. ACM Int'l Conf. on Ubiquitous Computing (UbiComp)*, 2006.

[10] S. Kawahito, M. Yoshida, M. Sasaki, K. Umehara, D. Miyazaki, Y. Tadokoro, K. Murata, S. Doushou, and A. Matsuzawa. A CMOS image sensor with analog two-dimensional DCT-based compression circuits for one-chip cameras. *IEEE Journal of Solid-State Circuits*, 32(12):2030–2041, 1997.

[11] D. Kim, Z. Fu, J.H. Park, and E. Culurciello. A 1-mW CMOS temporal-difference AER sensor for wireless sensor networks. *IEEE Transactions on Electron Devices*, 56(11):2586–2593, 2009.

[12] N.D. Lane, E. Miluzzo, H. Lu, D. Peebles, T. Choudhury, and A.T. Campbell. A survey of mobile phone sensing. *IEEE Communications Magazine*, 9, 2010.

[13] B. Le, T.W. Rondeau, J.H. Reed, and C.W. Bostian. Analog-to-digital converters. *IEEE Signal Processing Magazine*, 22(6):69–77, 2005.

[14] J.A. Leñero-Bardallo, T. Serrano-Gotarredona, and B. Linares-Barranco. A 3.6 s latency asynchronous frame-free event-driven dynamic-vision-sensor. *IEEE Journal of Solid-State Circuits*, 46(6):1443, 2011.

[15] W.D. León-Salas, S. Balkir, K. Sayood, N. Schemm, and M.W. Hoffman. A CMOS imager with focal plane compression using predictive coding. *IEEE Journal of Solid-State Circuits*, 42(11):2555–2572, 2007.

[16] P. Lichtsteiner, C. Posch, and T. Delbruck. A 128$\times$ 128 120 dB 15 μs latency asynchronous temporal contrast vision sensor. *IEEE Journal of Solid-State Circuits*, 43(2):566–576, 2008.

[17] U. Mallik, M. Clapp, E. Choi, G. Cauwenberghs, and R. Etienne-Cummings. Temporal change threshold detection imager. In *Digest of Technical Papers from IEEE Int. Solid-State Circuits Conference*, pages 362–603, 2005.

[18] WW Mayol, B. Tordoff, and DW Murray. Towards wearable active vision platforms. In *Proc. IEEE Int.Conf. Systems, Man, and Cybernetics*, 2000.

[19] MIPI camera interface specifications. http://www.mipi.org/specifications/camera-interface.

[20] A. Miyoshi, C. Lefurgy, E. Van Hensbergen, R. Rajamony, and R. Rajkumar. Critical power slope: understanding the runtime effects of frequency scaling. In *Proc. ACM Int'l. Conf. Supercomputing*, pages 35–44, 2002.

[21] B. Murmann. A/D converter trends: Power dissipation, scaling and digitally assisted architectures. In *Proc. IEEE. Custom Integrated Circuits Conference*, pages 105–112, 2008.

[22] J. Nakamura. *Image sensors and signal processing for digital still cameras*. CRC, 2005.

[23] J. Ohta. *Smart CMOS image sensors and applications*, volume 129. CRC, 2007.

[24] Y. Oike and A. El Gamal. CMOS image sensor with per-column $\Sigma\Delta$ ADC and programmable compressed sensing. *IEEE Journal of Solid-State Circuits*, 48(1), 2013.

[25] M.J.M. Pelgrom. *Analog-to-Digital Conversion*. Springer, 2010.

[26] R. Robucci, J.D. Gray, L.K. Chiu, J. Romberg, and P. Hasler. Compressive sensing on a CMOS separable-transform image sensor. *Proceedings of the IEEE*, 98(6):1089–1101, 2010.

[27] S. Soro and W. Heinzelman. A survey of visual sensor networks. *Advances in Multimedia*, 2009.

[28] Paul A. Viola and Michael J. Jones. Robust real-time face detection. In *Proc. Int'l. Conf. Computer Vision (ICCV)*, 2001.

Leveraging Graphical Models to Improve Accuracy and Reduce Privacy Risks of Mobile Sensing

Abhinav Parate Meng-Chieh Chiu

Deepak Ganesan Benjamin M. Marlin

Department of Computer Science
University of Massachusetts, Amherst
Amherst, MA 01003-9264
{aparate,joechiu,dganesan,marlin}@cs.umass.edu

ABSTRACT

The proliferation of sensors on mobile phones and wearables has led to a plethora of context classifiers designed to sense the individual's context. We argue that a key missing piece in mobile inference is a layer that fuses the outputs of several classifiers to learn deeper insights into an individual's habitual patterns and associated correlations between contexts, thereby enabling new systems optimizations and opportunities. In this paper, we design *CQue*, a dynamic bayesian network that operates over classifiers for individual contexts, observes relations across these outputs across time, and identifies opportunities for improving energy-efficiency and accuracy by taking advantage of relations. In addition, such a layer provides insights into privacy leakage that might occur when seemingly innocuous user context revealed to different applications on a phone may be combined to reveal more information than originally intended. In terms of system architecture, our key contribution is a clean separation between the detection layer and the fusion layer, enabling classifiers to solely focus on detecting the context, and leverage temporal smoothing and fusion mechanisms to further boost performance by just connecting to our higher-level inference engine. To applications and users, *CQue* provides a query interface, allowing a) applications to obtain more accurate context results while remaining agnostic of what classifiers/sensors are used and when, and b) users to specify what contexts they wish to keep private, and only allow information that has low leakage with the private context to be revealed. We implemented *CQue* in Android, and our results show that *CQue* can i) improve activity classification accuracy up to 42%, ii) reduce energy consumption in classifying social, location and activity contexts with high accuracy(>90%) by reducing the number of required classifiers by at least 33%, and iii) effectively detect and suppress contexts that reveal private information.

Keywords

Continuous context-sensing; Energy-Accuracy-Privacy optimizations; Mobile computing

Categories and Subject Descriptors

C.5.3 [**Computer System Implementation**]: Microcomputers—*Portable devices*; D.4.8 [**Operating Systems**]: [Performance Modeling and prediction]; K.8 [**Personal Computing**]: [General]

1. INTRODUCTION

The past decade has seen unprecedented growth in sensor-rich mobile phones and wearable accessories such as fitness monitors, sleep monitors, heart monitors and others. With the proliferation of such devices, there has been significant emphasis on techniques to draw higher-level inferences from continuous sensor data as we move around in our day-to-day lives. Research has shown that several aspects of our behavior can be inferred including physical activity, sleep behavior, social context, movement patterns, emotional or affective context, and mental disorders, with varying degrees of accuracy.

The growing landscape of high-level inferences presents an interesting opportunity: *can we combine these inferences to obtain deeper insights into individual behavior?* Intuition suggests that the outputs of individual inference algorithms must be correlated across space and time; after all, they sense various dimensions of an individual's habits, behaviors and physiology all of which are inter-linked. As a simple example, take the case of an individual's mobility patterns and how much of it can be inferred without using any location sensor such as GPS, cell tower or WiFi. Location is often correlated to social context — the fact that phones of colleagues are in proximity (detected via bluetooth) can indicate that the likely location is the workplace whereas the fact that a family member's phone is nearby means that one is likely at home. Similarly, location relates to activity context — a user may be more sedentary at work than at other times during the day, therefore one could infer that the most likely location is the workplace by observing the level of activity. More broadly, almost all inferences are related in one way or another — studies have shown that sleep (or lack of it) affects our mood and productivity, social interactions influence our emotional context, addictive behavior is correlated to specific locations and social interactions, and so on

The existence of a rich interaction graph between inferences presents an opportunity and a challenge. On one hand, a model of the relations across the different inferences can be leveraged to gain insights into individual behavior, thereby enabling new systems optimization opportunities. For example, a high level inference framework might observe relations between semantic location and activity levels, and learn that an individual has mostly sedentary behavior at the workplace. This provides two opportunities to optimize inference of the location context, "work": a) energy-efficiency can be improved by relying primarily on activity inference rather than expensive GPS, and b) accuracy can be improved when there is significant error (e.g. indoor settings) by fusing it with activity levels.

On the other hand, the ability to leverage relations across inferences comes with a steep price tag — loss of privacy. A mobile application that purports to merely be using the accelerometer to detect activity levels may indeed be inferring your location. More disturbing is the possibility that a single application developer may have several applications, one that monitors sensors for activity level, and perhaps another that uses bluetooth, which may be leveraged in conjunction to reveal much more than from the seemingly innocuous individual applications. Compounding this issue is the fact that we do not have tools that allow us to reason about how much of privacy exposure occurs from revealing seemingly innocuous sensor data if the adversary were to have a good model of the relations across contexts.

In this paper, we present a mobile "big data" inference framework, *CQue*, that takes as input streams of inferences from diverse on-body and smartphone-based sensors, and provides a unified way for exploiting and exploring relations across these inferences. *CQue* can be used in several ways: a) an inference algorithm can leverage *CQue* to improve accuracy and/or energy-efficiency, while remaining agnostic of how this is achieved, b) a user can issue "what if" queries that explore the extent of privacy leakage of sensitive information that might be possible if certain sensor data were revealed to one or more applications, and c) a user can specify privacy policies to provide a first order protection against privacy leakage of sensitive information to the untrusted applications.

In terms of system architecture, the key benefit of *CQue* is that it separates *detection* from *fusion*. Existing classifiers are largely designed in a stovepipe manner to address a specific context sensing goal as best as possible. While they start with detection of the specific activity (e.g. conversation, walking, etc), real-world vagaries often result in spurious state transitions due to several confounding factors. To address these issues, classifiers often rely on other sensor sources that can identify confounders and reduce errors. *CQue* provides a clean separation between the detection layer and the fusion layer — in this way, a classifier can be designed to just focus on detecting the phenomena of interest, and leverage fusion mechanisms to further boost performance by just hooking into *CQue*.

To users and applications, *CQue* offers a simple context querying interface with support for several types of queries. A "context query" can request different contexts, while optionally specifying constraints such as confidence requirements and delay bounds. For example, a query might request sedentary activity context with 90% certainty and a maximum notification delay of two minutes. *CQue* uses the query constraints to reason about how to duty-cycle inference algorithms, and how much temporal history to leverage to improve accuracy and confidence. A "what if" query provides a measure of potential leakage of sensitive information if applications were allowed access to specific sensor sources. For example, a query can request the expected leakage of "home" location context if an application had access to accelerometer and bluetooth data. Internally, *CQue* would execute such a query by providing a measure of the correlation between the outputs of inference algorithms that operate on accelerometer and bluetooth data, and the specific location context that the user does not wish to reveal. Finally, through privacy policies, a user can specify a context as private that should not be revealed, and suppress the non-private contexts in real-time that can be used to infer private context using correlations among these contexts. A user can specify this policy specific to an application or a group of applications that can potentially collude.

Our results show that:

- *CQue* can answer context queries with high confidence and improve accuracy up to 42% by performing fusion of information from multiple context-inference algorithms
- When energy is limited, *CQue* can lower execution costs for multiple context queries by exploiting context relations to run fewer inference algorithms. If energy is plentiful, *CQue* can decide what context algorithms in addition to the query set should be executed to improve accuracy.
- *CQue* is effective in assessing privacy risks and provides privacy while ensuring high utility to the applications.

The rest of the paper is organized as follows. §2 describes the prior work done in the related research areas. In §3, we provide an high-level overview of the *CQue* query engine along with the description of how a context query can be specified in our framework. In §4.1, we describe the relationship model used by *CQue*. Rest of §4 describes the components of *CQue* query engine in detail that are responsible for optimizing multiple context queries and addressing privacy. We describe the implementation details and the experimental evaluation of *CQue* in §5 and §6 respectively. We discuss possible extensions of this work in §7. Finally, the conclusions are provided in §8.

2. RELATED WORK

In this section, we describe three areas of related work — model-driven sensor data acquisition, context inference for mobile phones and privacy in temporal data.

Graphical models for sensor data acquisition: There has been substantial work on leveraging spatial and temporal models of correlations between distributed sensor sources to optimize sampling and communication in a sensor network [3, 5, 6, 12, 14]. For example, BBQ [6] uses a Dynamic Bayesian Network to select the minimum number of sensor nodes for data acquisition such that it can answer range queries within query-desired confidence bounds. Meliou et al [14] extend this work to sensor network routing where a query can be answered with desired confidence bounds while traversing the minimum number of nodes in a network spanning tree. Graphical models are also used in [5], which explored the problem of answering range queries while minimizing the energy cost of sampling sensors, and in [3], where sensors use models to reduce the communication costs by transmitting samples to a base station only when the ground truth is significantly different from the prediction made by the model. The similarities with prior efforts are only in that they leverage DBNs — we use DBNs in a novel application context which is for real-time inference on a mobile phone to enable energy-accuracy-delay tradeoffs and protect privacy.

Context-Sensing: Our work is closest to ACE [15] that proposes a context sensing engine that exploits relationships among contexts to infer an energy-expensive context from a cheaper context. The central difference between ACE and *CQue* is that the former uses Associate Rule Mining to learn rules among contexts (e.g. *Driving* $\Rightarrow \neg$*At Home*), but such mining approaches cannot take a context classifier's uncertainty into account. The ability to take uncertainty into account is critical when using classifiers that operate on raw sensor data — for example, if a classifier may detect *Driving* with a low confidence, say 0.7, GPS may detect *At Home* with an error radius of 100m, and so on. In these cases, the rules would assume perfect context information whereas *CQue* would use the uncertainty in inferring the relations. Thus, a probabilistic approach is strictly superior to a rule based one.

Also related to *CQue* are efforts to develop a context-sensing engine for phone that can be used by applications to request contexts [4, 13]. The Jigsaw context sensing engine [13] comprises of a set of sensing pipelines for accelerometer, microphone and GPS. More recently, Kobe [4] proposed a context querying engine for mobile phones that can be used to plugin different classifiers, and that balances energy consumption, latency and accuracy of the classifiers by offloading computation to the cloud. Unlike these approaches, *CQue* can leverage probabilistic relations across contexts.

CQue is complementary to prior work on context sensing engines which have largely explored optimizations of individual classifiers (e.g. [2, 11, 13, 20]). *CQue* allows individual classifiers to be easily integrated without worrying about how to leverage other contexts to improve performance and efficiency.

Privacy in temporal data: There has been some work in addressing privacy where the adversary is aware of the temporal correlations [8, 17, 19]. MaskIT [8] presents a privacy-preserving mechanism to filter a stream of contexts that can be used to answer context queries requested by the phone applications. It presents two privacy checks to decide when a user context can be released while providing privacy guarantees against an adversary knowing temporal correlations modeled as a Hidden Markov model(HMM) of user contexts.

Our goal in this work is not to to prove privacy guarantees or design new privacy metrics, rather our argument is that the use of DBN enables considerably more flexible privacy policies in comparison with an HMM-based approach. When MaskIT identifies that a privacy breach might occur, it suppresses all contexts at that time without considering which subset of them might contribute to the breach. In contrast, *CQue* enables more fine-grained reasoning of which specific context(s) lead to a privacy breach such that only that information can be suppressed.

3. CQUE OVERVIEW

The *CQue* framework has been designed with the goal of providing an easy-to-use abstraction to application developers and end users, both for exploiting correlations across inference to improve energy-efficiency and accuracy, as well as to use these correlations to ascertain privacy leakage or contextual insights. This goal is accomplished using a high level query language and an underlying execution environment running as a service on the phone. In the following, we provide an high-level overview of the *CQue* framework.

Context Query Interface. At the top level of *CQue* are applications that issue context queries using a high-level declarative query language. *CQue* provides a simple query language for the applications to request contexts. Consider the following three queries:

```
Q1. (drive | accel+gyro+gps, 240s, 0.8)
Q2. (home? | accel+gyro)
Q3. (home? | with friends)
```

The first query requests the context *drive*, and includes three other optional fields. The keywords *accel*, *gyro* and *gps* suggest that

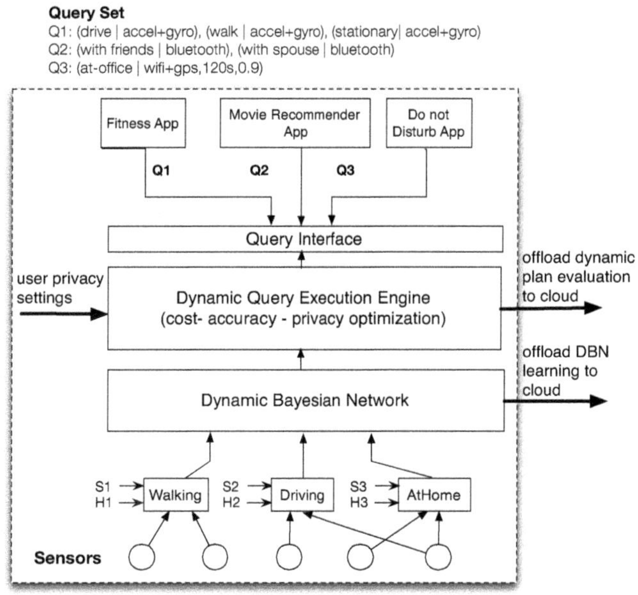

Figure 1: High-level overview of the framework describing the workflow

any combination of classifiers that use those sensors may be used in answering the query (to ensure that the app only uses sensors for which it has approval from the user). These keywords could also refer to other inferences, if the application needs more explicit control over other contexts that should be fused. Finally, the query can also replace this with a '*' which would let *CQue* automatically choose sensors and classifiers to optimize the system. The value '240s' in the query is the *delay tolerance* and denotes that the application can tolerate the maximum delay of 240 seconds for each record in the query response. The query processor uses this delay window to improve the confidence in the output context value. The query can also provide a *confidence threshold.* In the above example, the query processor will output context as soon as it reaches confidence of '0.8', provided it is within the delay tolerance period. If confidence values associated with the context output are lower than the query-desired *confidence threshold*, the context is reported as 'unknown'.

The next two queries marked by '?' are privacy queries and provide a measure of *information gain* in queried context "home" if any inference algorithm operating over accelerometer and gyroscope sensors were used (Q2) or if *with friends* inference algorithm was used (Q3). In turn, this measure provides a *privacy score*, an indicator of privacy leakage. Note that in providing a *privacy score*, *CQue* is limited to using inference algorithms that are available in its library.

CQue Architecture. The central tenet of *CQue* is an architectural separation between the mechanisms that inference algorithms use to improve performance. Inference algorithms are often designed in a stovepipe manner and integrate a combination of the following components: a) *feature extraction*, which involves extracting time-domain or frequency-domain features from the raw sensor data, b) *classification*, where they look at a short temporal sequence and detect a particular event or state, for example, walking, running, cycling, smoking, etc, c) *temporal consistency* mechanisms such as Hidden Markov Models (HMMs) to correct mis-classifications that occur in the classification, and d) *context fusion* where they leverage other information such as location or time to provide additional input to correct classification errors.

In contrast to the stovepipe approach, our design separates these components into a cleaner, layered architecture where any classifier can simply hook into *CQue*, and leverage temporal consistency and context fusion mechanisms to improve performance. *CQue* models temporal consistency with a time-series of previous observations, and uses active learning mechanisms to automatically determine when user input is needed to improve this model. *CQue* also automatically determines the relationships between a classifier output and all other observations from other classifiers/sensors that it has access to, and determines when and how to use additional observations to improve accuracy. In short, it can make the process of designing a new inference algorithm a lot easier for a designer.

Execution Environment. The execution environment of *CQue* is shown in Figure 1 and consists of following core components: (i) a graphical model, namely, Dynamic Bayesian Network, and (ii) a query processor. The *Dynamic Bayesian Network* (DBN) is the at the core of *CQue* and plays an important role in making various decisions during query processing. The DBN provides a model of the relationships across multiple contexts for the phone user and keeps track of the time-series of observations for various contexts. It then uses context relationships to boost confidence in observations made by individual classifiers or to correct them. The second component is a *query processor* which is responsible for interaction with applications including receiving context queries and generating the responses to the queries. In addition, depending on the current state of the DBN and the time-series of observations, the query processor needs to determine which context-inference algorithms should be executed such that it can provide best answers for the queries within the specified constraints. These decisions are made by the query processor at every time step during execution. As shown in Figure 1, the result of these decisions are the signals $S_1, S_2, ..., S_n$ indicating which context-algorithms be executed. Finally, upon observing the output of selected context-inference algorithms, *query processor* enforces user-specified privacy policies (defined in §4.2) by deciding a maximal set of queried contexts whose values can be released to the applications without violating the privacy policies.

In addition to the query execution, the query processor is responsible for sampling human-provided context values during the learning phase of the DBN. Such human input can be minimized through active learning to only obtain input at appropriate times to improve the structure of the DBN. These human inputs shown as signals $H_1, H_2, ..., H_n$ in Figure 1 are provided to the context-inference algorithms that can use it to retrain themselves to personalize for the phone user.

4. THE EXECUTION ENVIRONMENT

The execution environment of *CQue* is responsible for i) modeling and learning the relationships across contexts, ii) multi-query optimization such that uncertainty in queried contexts is minimized while operating within the budget and delay constraints of a query, and iii) executing privacy queries and enforcing privacy policies. In the following, we describe each component of the execution environment in detail.

4.1 Inference Framework

The core learning framework in *CQue* is a Dynamic Bayesian network (DBN), which is a class of Bayesian networks that can represent a time-series of random variables to model temporal consistency. A DBN can describe both temporal and static relationships

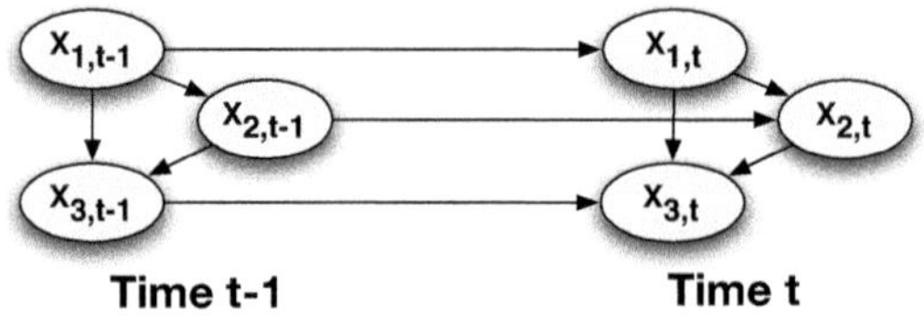

Figure 2: An example of 2-step Dynamic Bayesian Network. The nodes in the graph model the set of random variables $\mathbf{X} = \{X_1, X_2, X_3\}$.

among random variables at different time instances. This model is represented as a directed acyclic graph consisting of nodes corresponding to each random variable at each time instance. The static dependencies across random variables at time instance t are represented by edges connecting nodes corresponding to these random variables. The temporal dependencies are represented by transition edges connecting nodes at time instance $t-1$ with nodes at time instance t. Each node in this graph has a conditional probability table (CPT) describing dependencies on its parent nodes. Figure 2 shows an example of 2-step DBN for two time slices which can be unrolled to accommodate a time-series of any length by duplicating the time-slices and transition edges. We use notation $\mathbf{X}$ to denote the set of random variables. We use $\mathbf{X_t}$ to denote set of nodes representing random variables $\mathbf{X}$ at time instance t and use $\mathbf{X_{1...t}}$ as short notation to describe time series of nodes $\mathbf{X_1}, ..., \mathbf{X_t}$. With this notation, the joint probability distribution for a time series of nodes is given by

$$Pr(\mathbf{X_{1...t}}) = Pr(\mathbf{X_1}) \prod_{t=2}^{t} Pr(\mathbf{X_t}|\mathbf{X_{t-1}})$$

In the above equation, probability $Pr(\mathbf{X_t}|\mathbf{X_{t-1}})$ is computed using the DBN.

DBN Model for CQue. In *CQue*, we have three types of DBN nodes — sensors, classifier-provided context, and real-world context. The goal of the DBN is to model relationships across real-world contexts while taking into account the uncertainty associated with the classifier-provided contexts. We considered two criteria in constructing the DBN model: a) classifiers are black boxes, and we do not assume knowledge of what sensors they utilize, what sampling rates they use, how they duty-cycle sensors to save energy, and what features they extract, and b) we wish to keep the model simple and low complexity so that DBN inference can be performed in real-time on the mobile phone.

To address these considerations, classifiers and sensors are separated from the DBN into a different layer. Figure 3 shows an example where classifiers provide the probability of a context through observation nodes called virtual evidences, $\mathbf{O}$, to the DBN. The uncertainty in evidence is accounted in these observation nodes using Pearl's method [18]. In this method, for some context X_i and corresponding observation node O_i, if $L(x)$ gives the likelihood of classifier stating that $X_i = x$ if X_i is actually in state x and if $\overline{L(x)}$ gives the likelihood of a classifier stating that $X_i = x$ if X_i is not in state x, then the conditional probabilities for observation node O_i given the current state for real world context X_i satisfies:

$$Pr(O_i = x|X_i = x) : Pr(O_i = x|X_i \neq x) = L(x) : \overline{L(x)}$$

With these conditional probabilities and given a series of virtual evidences $\mathbf{O_{1...t}}$, we can compute the joint probabilities for time series of real world contexts $\mathbf{X_{1...t}}$ as follows:

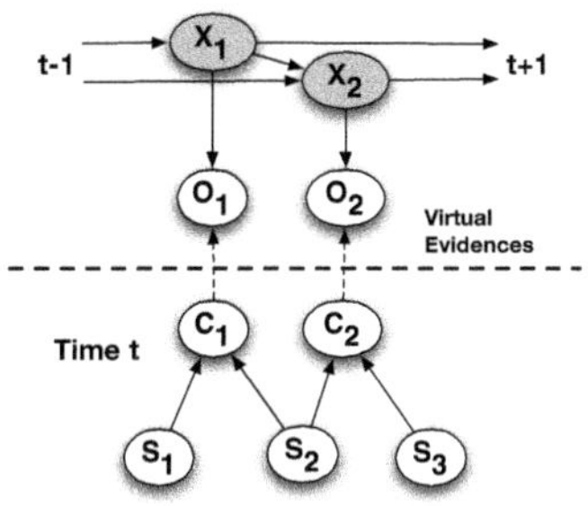

Figure 3: A model separating DBN from the layer of sensors and classifiers, where classifiers provide virtual evidences to the DBN.

$$Pr(\mathbf{X_{1...t}}, \mathbf{O_{1...t}}) = Pr(\mathbf{X_1}|\mathbf{O_1}) \prod_{t=2}^{t} Pr(\mathbf{X_t}|\mathbf{X_{t-1}})Pr(\mathbf{O_t}|\mathbf{X_t})$$

This model has several benefits: a) it is computationally cheap both when classifiers are turned on or off since it avoids the complexity of modeling sensor and classifier variables in the DBN itself, b) it requires no additional human labels for modeling these variables while training the DBN, and c) it can easily be extended to handle multiple classifier implementations for the same context without changing the DBN structure.

DBN usage in CQue. The output of the DBN is used in several ways by *CQue*.

1. **Filtering/Smoothing** Most of the contexts that we observe in the real world have some temporal consistency i.e they last for some time period. Such temporal relationships can be used to correct intermittent misclassifications made by context-inference algorithms. Since a DBN models temporal consistency with the time-series of previous observations, a DBN can correct the current output and reduce the probability of a context taking an incorrect value. Apart from the temporal consistency, a misclassification can be corrected using relationships with other contexts if the observations are available for them.

2. **HindSight** The previous case described using history to correct output at the current time. Similarly, a DBN can be used to improve the confidences in historical observations, which perhaps had low confidence. Future observations with high confidence can be used to improve the confidence of previous observations. This capability can be exploited when queries specify a higher delay tolerance threshold.

3. **Value of Information** The DBN can also be used to assess the value of a context-inference algorithm. *Value of information* (VOI) is defined as the expected gain in certainty for the random variables in DBN if an additional observation is made. This is useful for the query processor, which can decide what context observation can provide highest utility.

4.2 Query Processor

The query processor is responsible for i) multi-query optimization i.e. achieving the confidence requirements of context queries while operating within query constraints, ii) execution of privacy leakage queries, and iii) enforcement of user-defined privacy policies. Multi-query optimization in *CQue* raises following challenges: a) how to choose the inference algorithms to execute given the budget?, and b) how to handle different delay tolerance requirements of queries? In addition, privacy queries and policies require us to answer: a) how to execute privacy queries?, and how to enforce privacy policies? We address these question in the rest of this section.

Which inferences to execute given a budget?

The *CQue* query processor needs to execute the set of inference algorithms that provides maximum value of information (VOI) for the queried contexts within the budget constraints. The budget is typically in the form of energy since inference algorithms consume energy, but in cases where the user is interrupted to provide labels, the budget may be the number of interruptions allowed per day.

Due to the relationships across contexts, the set providing maximum VOI may be larger than the query set as some contexts that are not part of the query set may be useful to improve the inference accuracy for contexts that are in the query set. Similarly, this set can be smaller than the query set if some of the queried contexts are strongly implied by other contexts in the query. In addition, the set of inferences that provides the maximum VOI can change over time, depending on the user's current context as well as dynamics in the user's behavior patterns. In this section, we describe an adaptive approach to deciding the set of inferences that need to be executed to satisfy query demands while remaining within the budget.

The problem of selecting the optimal set of context-algorithms to execute given a budget and the set of queries can be formalized as follows. Let Q be the set of context queries, let E_{t-1} be the set of context classifiers undergoing execution currently and v be the corresponding classifier outputs. Let $\mathcal{F}(Q, E, E_{t-1}, v)$ be the utility function giving the VOI of the contexts, E, for the query set where E is the subset of observation nodes $\mathbf{O}$ in the DBN. Let $C(E)$ give the cost of executing algorithms for contexts in E. If $\mathcal{B}$ is the maximum budget, then our goal can be defined as identifying a set E_t i.e. the set of context classifiers to be executed next such that:

$$E_t = \underset{E \subseteq \mathbf{O_t}: C(E) \leq \mathcal{B}}{\arg\max} \mathcal{F}(Q, E, E_{t-1}, v) \tag{1}$$

Since our goal is to have high certainty for query set Q, we consider the information gain for query set Q (also called VOI) as the utility function which is given by:

$$\mathcal{F}(Q, E, E_{t-1}, v) = H(Q|E_{t-1} = v) - H(Q|E, E_{t-1} = v) \tag{2}$$

where $H(.)$ is the entropy function. We must note that computing optimal-set of classifiers to be executed at the next iteration is an **NP**-hard problem[10]. We solve this optimization problem using a greedy approach as described in Algorithm 1. The results by Nemhauser et al. [16] and Krause et al. [10] have shown that a greedy algorithm provides a solution within the constant factor $(1 - \frac{1}{e})$ of the optimal solution for a general bayesian network.

Our extension of optimization problem to the DBN does not change the results as long as we select nodes E_t from a set S such that the nodes corresponding to S in DBN are independent to each other given the query set Q. In a DBN, we select E_t from a set of observation nodes O_t where each observation node is connected to the DBN only through a parent hidden node. Hence, any path between any two observation nodes is always blocked by one of the parent hidden nodes. Thus, any two observation nodes in DBN are **d**-separated [21] and hence, independent of each other.

We note that Algorithm 1 gives near-optimal solution when each classifier is assigned a unit cost. In a specific scenario, there may be several considerations in determining the cost, which depends on the cost of sensing, processing, or obtaining human input. If the resulting costs are non-uniform in nature, we refer the readers to an algorithm as described in [10].

Algorithm 1 Compute Optimal Set

Input: Budget k; query set Q; set $\mathbf{O_t}$ from DBN;
utility function $\mathcal{F}$; previous observed set E_{t-1} and corresponding set of classifier outputs v; Cost function C.
Output: Set of observations $E \subseteq \mathbf{O_t}$
Let $E = \phi$
for $i = 1$ to k **do**
  $o^* = \arg\max_{o \in \mathbf{O_t} \setminus E} \mathcal{F}(Q, E \cup \{o\}, E_{t-1}, v)$
  $E = E \cup \{o^*\}$
end for
return E

How to handle delay requirements of queries?

In *CQue*, we unroll the DBN such that it can accommodate a series of observations of length W. At each time-step, we slide the DBN window over observations such that the oldest observations are dropped and the latest observations are added to the DBN. As a result of this sliding window, any context observation resides in DBN for exactly W time-steps. Hence, we can compute the probability for queried contexts W times, corresponding to having $0, 1, 2, ..., W - 1$ observations from the future. This allows our framework to answer a query with a delay upto $W - 1$ time-steps. Our framework can use this delay period in three cases: i) if the sequence of historical observations have low confidence resulting in low confidence for the latest observation, ii) if the sequence of historical observations have fluctuating values for the contexts indicating low confidence in the output of context inference algorithms, and iii) if the latest observation is different from the historical observations. In the first two cases, we wait for the future observations and hope that these observations are consistent and have high confidence. If this happens, we boost the probability of queried context in hindsight. In the third case where the latest observation is different from the historical observations, it can happen either because of intermittent misclassification by the classifier or because the context value has actually changed. Any future observation can help in distinguishing these cases and improve the certainty in the context.

How to execute privacy queries?

Unlike queries that request current state of an individual, *privacy queries* look for aggregate information regarding the mutual information shared between a context and sensor data or other contexts available in *CQue*. In our framework, we provide two types of privacy queries: i) user specifies a query context, Q and wants to know information revealed about the queried context from a specified list of sensors (S) and contexts (C); and ii) user specifies a query context Q and wants to know ranked list of contexts along with a *privacy score* that indicates how much information is revealed by a ranked context about the queried context. Thus, these queries help user understand how much information can be revealed about certain context from other contexts. Together, these two query types enable users to make a decision regarding their own privacy.

For the first query type, given a user specified sensor list S we identify context classifiers C^S that can execute given sensors S. In addition to S, user can provide a set of contexts C. Now, we want to have an uncertainty measure in queried context Q if contexts in $C' = C \cup C^S$ are observed. We use a normalized variant of mutual information based on information theory that gives a distance metric between Q and C' and is given as follows :

$$D(Q|C') = 1 - \frac{H(Q) - H(Q|C')}{H(Q)}$$

This metric takes value 1 if Q is independent of C' and takes value 0 if Q is fully determined by C'. We use this measure as a *privacy score* where a higher score indicates less information leakage.

For the second query type, a user is interested in identifying ordered list of contexts that reveal most information about queried context Q. For each context c supported in *CQue*, we use *privacy score* $D(Q|c)$ as described above to measure information leaked about queried context Q. We rank contexts based on this metric.

How to enforce privacy policies?

As described in §2, one of the benefits of *CQue* is that the DBN provides in-depth and real-time information about correlations between different context outputs in contrast with HMMs and other techniques that have been leveraged in prior work. *Our focus is not on identifying the best privacy exposure policy or proving its privacy properties; rather it is to demonstrate that CQue can be used to develop such methods.*

To demonstrate these benefits, *CQue* supports a privacy policy that can suppress context values that leads to change in confidence or the probabilistic belief about a private context greater than threshold δ. Such a policy can provide greater privacy control than a simpler policy that just blocks a specific private context from being revealed. In *CQue*, a user can define these policies specific to a potential adversarial entity where this entity can be an application or a group of applications or all the applications on the user's phone. A policy for a group of applications can be useful to protect against information collusion among these applications in a group.

In *CQue*, we assume a strong adversary having access to the user's DBN. Now, we enforce user policy by using the DBN to calculate the confidence or the posterior probability for the private context using the output for the set of contexts, requested by the adversarial entity, as observations in DBN. Also, we compute prior probability for the private context without using any observations in the DBN. If the difference between posterior probability and the prior probability is greater than δ, then we suppress the value of the context that causes the maximum change in probabilities. If the change in probabilities is still high with the remaining context outputs, we repeat the process of removing context value that causes maximum change until we reach the threshold limit δ. We release the remaining contexts to the adversarial entity.

4.3 Learning the Graphical Model

Now, we describe the challenges involved in learning the DBN model for the phone user. There are two challenges in learning the DBN: a) how to learn structure without executing all sensors and context inference algorithms continuously on the phone since this consumes significant energy, and b) how to minimize interruptions of the phone user to obtain ground truth labels for learning.

Context relationship hints: The learning process can degrade user experience due to the energy cost of running several context inference algorithms concurrently on the phone. While it is possible to randomly sample a few contexts at a time, this can slow down the learning process as the random approach may not always sample related contexts together. To perform efficient sampling and facilitate faster learning of personalized relationships, we maintain, for each context, a list of contexts to be sampled together that may possibly have soft relationships. The soft relationships may or may not hold for individual users and it does not necessarily result in edges in DBN connecting softly-related contexts. As it may not be possible to envision all the soft relationships, we still perform random sampling and bias the sampling for contexts that seem to be related.

While the use of soft relationships can address the efficient sampling problem, we can speed up the learning process and parameter estimation in DBN by the use of *hints* that can be provided by the context-inference algorithm developers. A context developer can include hints for each context that identify positive causes and negative causes for it. As an example, *driving* is a direct positive cause for user's location being *on street* whereas user's location being *at home* is a negative cause for *on street*. These hints can be directly utilized in setting the parameters for relationships that are true for a majority of users.

Minimizing human-provided labels: One of the challenges in learning the dynamic bayesian network is that we do not have access to ground truth for contexts. While ground truth can be obtained by having the user provide ground truth for an initial training period, we wish to minimize interruptions and hence use this option sparingly. Instead, we can sample the contexts inferred by the algorithms along with the confidence value associated with the output. The inferred context values provide us with the partial observations of the underlying Markovian process. We use the Structural EM algorithm described in [7] to learn the structure of the DBN from the partial observations. In this algorithm, the structure of the DBN is improved iteratively until the MDL score of the structure B given a training data set D converges. Let us suppose a structure B consisting of n random variables $X_1, ..., X_n$. We use the notation x_i and Π_{x_i} to denote an assignment for X_i and its parent set $\mathbf{Pa}(X_i)$ respectively. Also, $N(x_i, \Pi_{x_i})$ denotes number of instances in the training data D where $X_i = x_i$ and $\mathbf{Pa}(X_i) = \Pi_{x_i}$. Let N be the total number of instances in training data. Then, the MDL score for a DBN structure B given data set D is given as:

$$\sum_i \{ \sum_{x_i, \Pi_{x_i}} E[N(x_i, \Pi_{x_i})|D] \log \theta(x_i, \Pi_{x_i}) - \frac{\log N}{2} \#(X_i, \mathbf{Pa}(X_i)\}$$

where $\theta(x_i, \Pi_{x_i}) = \frac{E[N(x_i)|D]}{E[N(x_i, \Pi_{x_i})|D]}$ and $\#(X_i, \mathbf{Pa}(X_i)$ is the number of parameters needed to represent $Pr(X_i|\mathbf{Pa}(X_i))$. We need to take expected counts as we have access to only partial observations. We simplify the learning process by first learning the static network of the DBN followed by learning the transition edges of the network. This process is suboptimal in nature but it has been shown in practice to yield parameters estimates close to optimal.

While learning the DBN without any human input is ideal, this can lead to errors particularly if the training and test context distributions are very different. Thus, there is a need for at least some corrective human input. We randomly sample human input for a small fraction of contexts in-order to correct DBN parameters, and assign these human-provided contexts higher weight over the instances obtained using context-inference algorithms.

4.4 Classifier Personalization

So far, our discussion has assumed that the underlying context classifiers are black-boxes *i.e.* they do not expose their internal behavior or allow changes. Thus, the DBN is limited to the context output and uncertainty provided by the classifiers. A natural question is whether we can do better if we were able provide *feedback* from the DBN to the classifier in-order to improve its performance further.

In *CQue*, any human input provided to the DBN can not only be used to correct DBN parameters, but also be used to personalize the classifiers. A classifier personalized for an individual user is beneficial as it provides higher classification accuracy and better uncertainty estimates. The use of personalized classifiers also benefits the DBN — with personalized classifiers, the correct DBN parameters can be learnt using fewer future human input resulting in shorter training period. *CQue* provides an API to the developers of context classifiers to receive human-provided labels that can be leveraged for personalization.

5. IMPLEMENTATION

We now describe the implementation of *CQue* on Android smartphones running Android OS version 2.2 or higher.

Inference Engine: The *CQue* inference engine is designed to run in real-time on a mobile phone to avoid any delays incurred in accessing the cloud. The query processor maintains a model of a DBN that is personalized to the phone user. This model is stored as a file in an XMLBIF format which is an interchange format that is recognized by most bayesian inference softwares. In our implementation, we use the well known variable-elimination algorithm's implementation for probabilistic inference provided by the Java Bayes package [1]. One downside is that accurate inference using variable-elimination can take exponential time in the number of variables in the bayesian network. While this was not an issue for the number of contexts in our current implementation, this may be a bottleneck as the number of contexts increase. Future implementations of *CQue* will use fast approximate inference algorithms such as importance sampling and MCMC simulation to optimize inference performance on the phone [21].

Query Plan: As discussed in §4.2, *CQue* uses a dynamic query plan where the decision regarding what contexts to execute given a certain energy budget is periodically re-visited to capture dynamics in the incoming context stream. Such dynamic adaptation can be expensive to perform on the phone since it depends on the number of contexts in the DBN. So, for infrequent plan evaluation or if the size of the DBN is small, our implementation performs such planning on the phone, but otherwise offloads the computation to the cloud.

DBN Learning: While the execution engine can execute on a mobile phone, learning the DBN is more computationally intensive and requires cloud support. We implemented the DBN learning algorithm using partial observations by modifying the WEKA package [9]. *CQue* offloads the process of learning the DBN to the cloud by sending the appropriate context instances to the server at the end of each day. The DBN is learnt at the end of every day in the cloud and is sent back to the *CQue* framework in XMLBIF format. Over time, the frequency of updating the DBN reduces as its structure and parameters stabilize. Also, to facilitate faster learning of DBN parameters, we maintain a configuration file that provides initial parameter estimates for the DBN, based on average numbers from a general population. The configuration file has entries for each context containing a list of positive and negative causes for it along with the conditional probability. For example, the negative cause list for the context *at office* looks like: *at home,0.99; at store,0.85; at restaurant,0.93; driving,1.0.*

Query Processor: We implemented the context engine as a background service running on android phones. This service is responsible for activating context-inference algorithms and appropriate sensors, and providing the context values generated by the algorithms to the query processor. Communication between the query processor and the context engine uses Android IPC. Our implementation currently supports semantic location contexts, social contexts and activity contexts: a) **Activity contexts**: *walking*, *driving* and *stationary*, b) **Social contexts:** *with friends*, *with colleagues* and *alone*, and c) **Location contexts:** *at restaurant*, *at home*, *at office*, *at store* and *on street*.

Our implementation uses decision-tree classifiers for activity recognition. We used well-known set of features extracted from the 3-axis accelerometer and gyroscope readings. The following features were computed for accelerometer readings along each of the three axis: mean, standard deviation, mean-crossing rate, energy given as normalized sum of squared discrete FFT component, peak frequency in FFT and peak energy. In addition, we computed correlation between each pair of axes. The gyroscope readings were used to compute mean and standard deviation of angular velocity around each of the three axis. For classifying social and location contexts, we used a user-provided mapping from bluetooth devices to the social context and a mapping from WiFi access points to the corresponding semantic location (either user provided or using publicly available databases). Unlike activity contexts, the classified social and location contexts have higher confidence associated with them. While we restricted ourselves to the above contexts due to the nature of our datasets, our architecture is general is designed to accommodate other context-engines that may be added by practitioners.

User Interface: The *CQue* framework provides an interface to the user to specify an energy budget and preferences for interruption (during training) and privacy. The energy budget can be specified as a fraction of a full battery that may be used for running *CQue* and a battery threshold below which *CQue* should be stopped. For interruption preferences, a user can specify the total interrupts permitted per day while training the DBN. For privacy preferences, a user can select private contexts, select a level of protection against adversary from low, medium and high where these values map to values for threshold for change in adversarial confidence $\delta = 0.4$, $\delta = 0.25$ and $\delta = 0.05$ respectively. Additionally, user can select the applications for which these preferences apply.

6. EXPERIMENTAL RESULTS

In this section, we describe the set of experiments performed to evaluate our framework. We first describe the data sets and the evaluation metrics used for the experimental evaluation. Next, we present our analysis of privacy for various contexts.We then look at the energy-accuracy tradeoffs and demonstrate the benefits of using DBN over context-classifiers using a set of experiments, and conclude with an evaluation of how various parameters such as delay, and interruption budget impact results.

6.1 Data Sets and Evaluation Metrics

Datasets.

In order to conduct our experiments, we used following two datasets:

Reality Mining Dataset: This data set contains data collected continuously for 100 students and staff at MIT over academic year 2004-2005. This data provides various contexts like user's location (work, home, other) based on cell-tower observations, social contexts based on proximity of bluetooth devices and physical activities like stationary, walking and driving based on self-reports. The duration of user traces varied from 30 days to 269 days. In our evaluation, we used data from 37 users who had data for at least 10 weeks. The traces for each of these users contains 3 location contexts and 3 activity contexts. In addition, we derive social contexts using clustering of bluetooth devices that appear closer in time, thus the number of social contexts varied from user to user and there were at least 2 such contexts.

Activity Dataset: While the reality mining dataset has rich multi-sensor data, it relies on self-reports for activity classification, hence it does not allow us to understand how accuracy of activity classifiers can be improved through the use of *CQue*. To address this, we collected a trace of user contexts for two weeks from seven users. Each of the seven users provided about 50 context labels per day. Since there could be labeling error, we corrected activity context information using GPS information and manual correction at the end of each day. All users providing data were graduate students. We used data from four users to train the activity classifiers. For testing, we used these classifiers to classify activities for the remaining three users. For each user in the test set, we divided their data into two weeks — in the first week, a personalized user-specific DBN is trained using the outputs of the classifier algorithms, and a few human labels obtained from the ground-truth set (depending on the interruption limits, and label selection scheme), and the data in the second week is used to evaluate *CQue*.

Set of Contexts.

In both the datasets, we have a set of contexts that includes location contexts like *at home*, *at office*, *on street* and three activity contexts, namely, *walking, driving* and *stationary*. For social contexts, we use the groups of bluetooth devices in the close proximity of a user as the social context. In Activity dataset, we have these groups explicitly labeled as *friends, colleagues, roommates, spouse* whereas in Reality mining dataset, we do not have explicit labels but we identify these groups as *group-1, group-2* and so on. For each context, the corresponding classifier outputs *true* or *false* value along with the confidence value associated with the classification output. We use these values as input in DBN.

Evaluation metrics.

We use three performance metrics in our evaluation: 1) **Accuracy**, which is computed as the fraction of these contexts that are correctly classified, 2) **Confidence**, or the probability of the most likely value for the context provided by the DBN, and 3) **F-Measure** which gives the harmonic mean of recall and precision (higher score is better)

6.2 Cost-Accuracy Tradeoffs using DBN

One of the benefits of a DBN is that it allows a tradeoff cost for accuracy — by understanding the relations across different contexts, an inference algorithm can be turned off to reduce overhead. While the "cost" can be different depending on the sensing and communication needs of the inference algorithm, or the burden of user input, we use a simplistic model where we assume that all classifiers have equal cost. This model provides an intuitive understanding of the cost-accuracy tradeoffs.

Classifiers < Queries. We first look at the case where the system runs fewer classifiers than the number of queries and exploits the context-relationships to answer context queries for which there are no observations coming from the classifier. This case demonstrates that the DBN can be used to answer the context queries in expectation which is not possible otherwise using classifiers alone. We evaluate this model using the Reality Mining dataset.

In this experiment, we consider all the contexts that we support to be in the query set. We then vary the budget such that it can execute between 1 to 5 classifiers. Based on the budget, the set of classifiers are chosen that can provide maximum information gain as described in §4.2.

Figure 4 shows the accuracy and F-measure averaged over 37 users as the number of classifiers increases. We see that both these

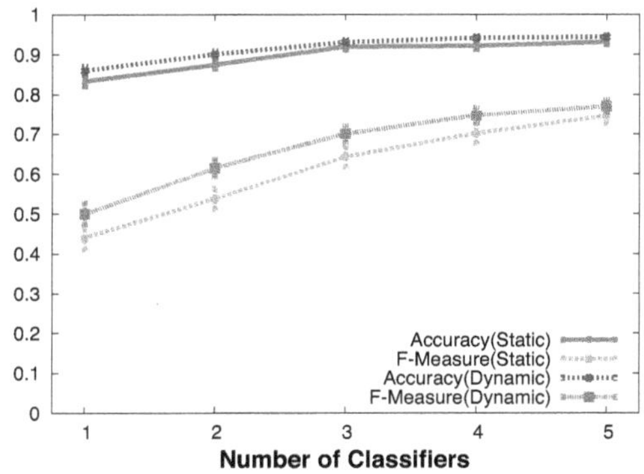

Figure 4: Effect of varying number of executing context classifiers when number of queries (≥ 6) is higher than the number of executing contexts. The figure shows aggregate accuracy and F-measure over 37 users for static and dynamic plan execution.

metrics improve as we increase the number of classifiers, and even with two classifiers executing, we get fairly good accuracy and F-measure. Thus, significant benefits can be obtained with only a small number of classifiers by leveraging a DBN model of the relations across contexts.

It might seem surprising that very high accuracy can be achieved even with a single classifier. In fact, this is because most contexts have biased distribution (e.g. the stationary state is true ($> 90\%$) of the time), hence high accuracy can be achieved by just using the model in expectation with no classifiers executing! But this gives poor recall, precision and consequently the F-measure is low, and more context input is required to improve these metrics. Figure 4 shows that DBN achieves 75% F-measure and 94% accuracy using only 4 classifiers resulting in at least 33% cost reduction.

Figure 4 also compares the use of a dynamic plan where the query plan is re-evaluated every 20 minutes vs a static plan where the query plan is evaluated once. The dynamic plan provides better accuracy and F-measure than static plan across the board. This is because the dynamic plan selects appropriate set of classifiers using value of information provided by the observed classifier outputs in real-time whereas static plan selects the set of classifiers without considering the real-time classifier outputs.

Classifiers > Queries. We now look at the benefits of using a DBN when the number of classifers that execute are greater than the number of queries. We use the Activity dataset in this study, since we have raw data for activity inferences, which are typically the contexts with highest inaccuracy. We look at the performance for the three activity contexts (walking, driving and stationary), which have highest uncertainty. We compare two mechanisms: a) using just the activity recognition classifiers, and b) using all the context classifiers with DBN. We show results for three representative users in the dataset.

Figure 5(a) shows that accuracy is worst when we use only classifiers alone, and the use of DBN improves improve accuracy significantly. The improvement in accuracy by using DBN for users U1 and U2 is above 24% for both *stationary* and *driving* contexts. Improvements are small for *walking* activity (2%) since DBN neither observed any context strongly related with *walking* nor the temporal consistency. This was because *walking* was a rare context and rarely lasted for longer than a few minutes.

Figure 5 (b) shows F-measure for various classes. We see that this metric generally improves since the main role of the DBN is to correct the outputs provided by the classifiers and hence, improve recall and precision. Since the DBN performs corrections using the temporal consistency, the recall value for a certain context may drop if the context is rarely seen and lasts for a very short duration. In our traces, we observed that the *walking* activity was infrequent. In such a case, if the classifier does not generate output with high confidence the DBN can smooth out the walking context resulting in reduced recall but higher precision. As a result, F-measure does not see significant gain. In contrast, the *driving* context though rarely seen as compared to *stationary* lasts longer and hence, sees improvement in recall and hence, improves F-measure.

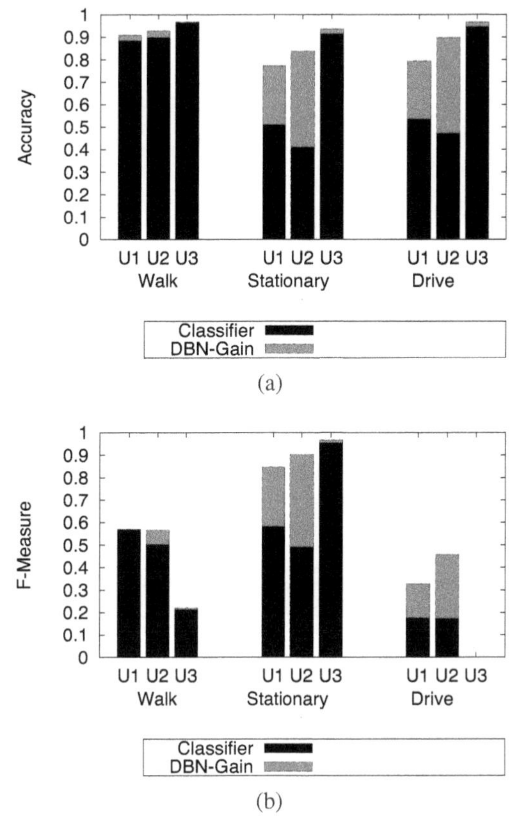

Figure 5: Accuracy and F-Measure for various activity classes for Classifier only and gain provided by Classifier+DBN mechanism on data from 3 users. Results show that using the DBN is beneficial in most cases, except in the case of rarely occurring contexts.

6.3 Evaluating Privacy

In this section, we evaluate two aspects of how *CQue* can be useful in dealing with privacy breaches due to correlations across contexts.

Location-Social Relations: In our first experiment, we look at a two sensor scenario and understand the correlations between these contexts across different datasets. Recall that location is obtained through GPS and social interactions through bluetooth. We use *CQue* to understand how a privacy breach can occur for a *privacy-sensitive* context through indirect observations. Here, we assume a *strong adversary* that has access to the personalized DBN for a user. Potentially, this is possible if various apps on a phone that observe different contexts decide to collude and combine their data to generate a complete DBN.

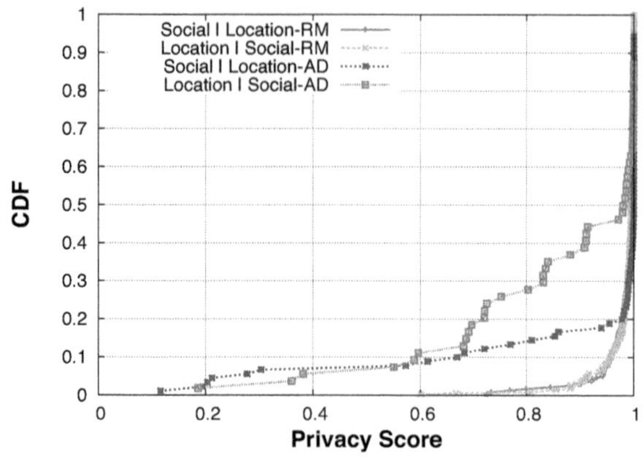

Figure 6: Cumulative distribution of privacy scores for cross-context pairs in i)Reality Mining dataset (RM), and ii)Activity dataset(AD). From the distribution of privacy scores, we can conclude that there is significant cross-context privacy leakage in Activity dataset whereas no such leakage is observed in Reality Mining dataset. This emphasizes the importance of personalized DBN to evaluate privacy for a user.

Given such an adversary, a *privacy-sensitive* context can be inferred by observing one or more other contexts. Using our *privacy score*, we can rank contexts in the decreasing order of its capability to infer *privacy-sensitive* context. In this experiment, we look two scenarios: a) all cases where we use one location context as a private context (p) and a social context o as observation, and b) the reverse scenario where a social context are private and location is observed. We evaluate *privacy score* $D(p|o)$ for each pair $\langle p, o \rangle$ of contexts. Figure 6 gives distribution of privacy scores for these scenarios for the Reality Mining and Activity Datasets.

The results are interesting — we see that there is considerably higher correlation across location and social context in the case of the activity dataset than in the reality mining data. This is also reflected in Table 1, which shows the accuracy of inferring location/social only based on the prior distribution of these contexts v.s. observing the other context. The results show that there is only a small change in the case of the RM dataset, but the accuracy increases by more than 25% in the case of the AD dataset. In other words, an adversary would be able to infer an individual's location with substantial accuracy if they only had access to the bluetooth information on the AD dataset. Our explanation for these results is that bluetooth usage is far more prevalent in recent times, therefore the correlations have increased. Overall, our results show that *CQue* can be used to provide intuition about the correlations across contexts, thereby enabling more informed decision about what to expose.

Suppression Policy for Privacy: In our second experiment, we look at how *CQue* can be used to implement a real-time suppression policy for protecting privacy. Our policy is intended to be representative and illustrate how the DBN may be used, and we make no formal claims regarding its privacy properties. In our experiment, the user can define a policy that permits releasing a maximal set of context observations such that the change in adversarial confidence for private context upon observing this set is less than threshold δ. As a result, some of the non-private contexts can be suppressed in real-time to control the change in adversarial confidence. Thus, it results in lower utility for the applications seeking contexts. Figure 7 gives an example showing the fraction of context data that can be released as a result of this suppression for various values of δ where we chose *at home* as the private context and rest of the contexts as queries. A smaller value of δ results in much tighter privacy control but releases too few contexts.

(a) Privacy leakage in All Location Contexts

Metric	Observation	
	None	All social contexts
Accuracy (RM)	73.9±3.0	74.81±2.73
Accuracy (AD)	61.11±5.55	88.9±6.26

(b) Privacy leakage in All Social Contexts

Metric	Observation	
	None	All location contexts
Accuracy (RM)	73.86±2.9	74.18±2.82
Accuracy (AD)	64.01±15.29	87.3±5.94

Table 1: Cross-context privacy leakage in location and social contexts for i)Reality Mining dataset(RM), and ii)Activity dataset(AD). For activity dataset, we see significant increase in accuracy for all the location contexts when all the social contexts are observed and vice versa. For reality mining dataset, accuracies do not change with cross-context observations.

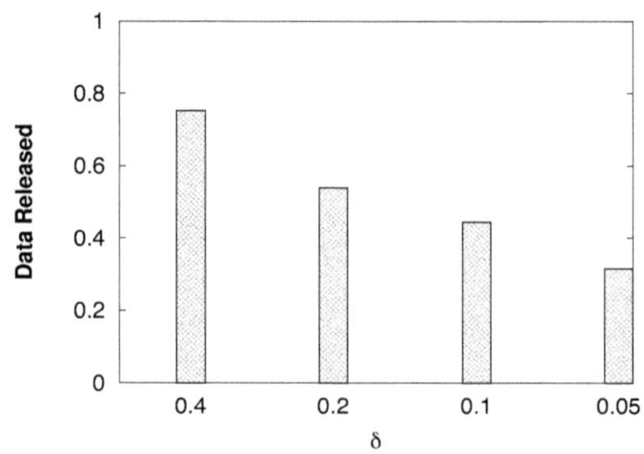

Figure 7: Fraction of data that can be released to prevent change in adversarial confidence greater than δ for a private context *at home*.

Table 2 shows the fraction of data suppressed in context of each category: *social, location,* and *activity* for value of threshold $\delta \in \{0.1, 0.4\}$. In this case, we choose *at friend's place* as a private context available in Activity dataset. We can see that *CQue* suppresses in an intelligent manner where it suppresses highly correlated social context more frequently than the less correlated location or activity contexts. If we were to use a mechanism like MaskIT [8], it would suppress every context at the same level. Since *CQue* releases more contexts, it results in higher utility for the applications and the users who use these applications.

In conjunction, these experiments demonstrate the potential use of *CQue* both for understanding privacy implications of releasing a context, as well as to implement privacy policies that leverage relations across contexts.

6.4 DBN with Personalized Classifiers

While all our previous results have assumed classifiers to be black-box code that cannot be modified, we now look at the case where we can personalize the classifiers using the human input ob-

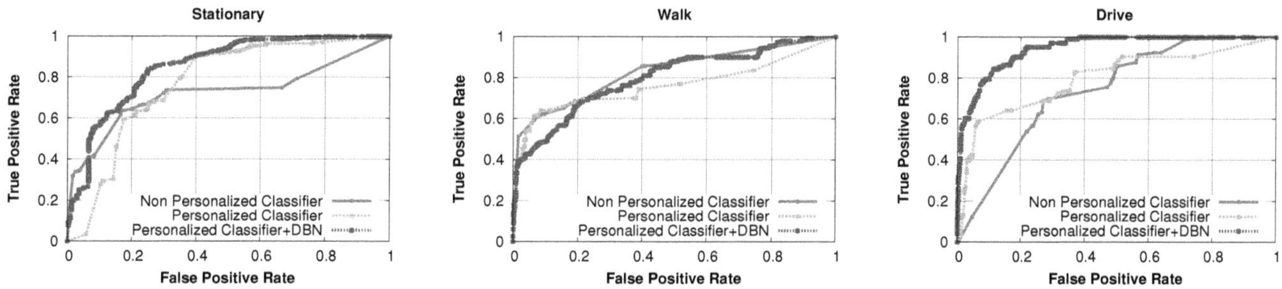

(a) (b) (c)

Figure 8: ROC curve for each activity class for i) non-personalized classifier, ii) personalized classifier, and iii) DBN using personalized classifier.

Threshold δ	Social Context	Location Context	Activity Context
0.4	27.67%	13.99%	17.52%
0.1	26.81%	16.01%	17.35%

Table 2: Table showing fraction of data suppressed in contexts of each category to prevent change in adversarial confidence greater than δ for a private context *at friend's place*.

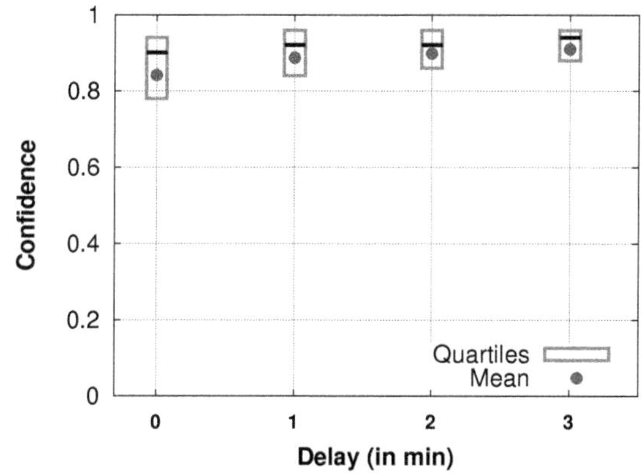

Figure 9: Effect of delay on confidence distribution, as we increase delay-tolerance for queries from zero to three minutes. We consider all the query results that had conf$<$ 0.98 when DBN was used with 0 delay in response (35% of the results), and show how summary statistics for this group improves as we increase the delay-tolerance for the queries from 0 to 3.

tained by the DBN during its learning phase. This feature leverages the fact that contexts like user activity can see significant benefit with personalization as there are differences across individuals.

In our experiment, we personalize the classifiers for activity contexts in AD dataset by training it with additional user-specific labels obtained from the user's data for training DBN i.e. the first week of user's trace. Figure 8 gives ROC curves for each activity class for both personalized and non-personalized classifiers. The ROC curve shows the performance of the classification mechanism when the discrimination threshold is varied. A classification mechanism with a larger area under the ROC curve indicates that it is a better mechanism. In figure 8, it can be seen that the personalized classifier tends to have larger area under the ROC curve compared to the non-personalized classifiers. Moreover, the area under ROC curve for DBN is always larger than the area for either of the classifier-based schemes. Except for *walking* which has a small operating region where the classifier performs better than DBN, the DBN clearly dominates the classifiers over all operating regions in the ROC. This shows that classifier personalization together with a DBN can provide the best method to improve accuracy.

6.5 Impact of Delay

The delay tolerance period provided by queries provides a tuning knob that can influence results provided by the query engine. In this experimental setup, we study the impact of increasing value of this parameter on activity contexts in AD dataset. In general, whenever the DBN observes a change in context value output by the classifiers, the confidence of the DBN may drop. This confidence improves with more observations obtained in the future. Thus, the main role of using a delay-tolerance period is to improve confidence in the DBN output. Figure 9 shows the distribution of confidence when delay-tolerance is increased. Apart from boosting confidence, the use of a delay-tolerance window reduces the intermittent misclassifications by the classifiers.

6.6 Implementation Benchmarks

We benchmark our implementation on Samsung Galaxy Nexus phone running Android OS version 4.1.2. This device has 700MB RAM and 1.2 GHz dual-core processor. In this evaluation, we look at the following two metrics: i) *inference time* i.e. the time required to make a probabilistic inference about a context given a set of evidences from the classifiers, and ii) *plan evaluation time* i.e. the time required to generate a dynamic plan for a given set of queries. All experiments are done using the Reality Mining dataset.

Inference Time: Since the computational complexity of an accurate inference algorithm to infer a context is exponential in number of parent nodes for the context in DBN, the actual required time for probabilistic inference varies from context to context and from user to user due to variations in the personalized DBN model structure. Thus, we measure *inference time* using traces from multiple users with varying size of the DBN model. In this experiment, we select one context as a query and use rest of the contexts as observations. We repeat this experiment for all the available contexts for each user. The user traces consisted of 5-11 contexts. Upon evaluation on Galaxy Nexus phone, we observed an average *inference time* across all the contexts and the users to be 9.31 ± 0.71ms. Also, the fastest context had an average *inference time* of 2.13ms for a user trace consisting of 7 contexts whereas the slowest context had an average *inference time* of 21ms for a user with DBN model consisting of 11 contexts.

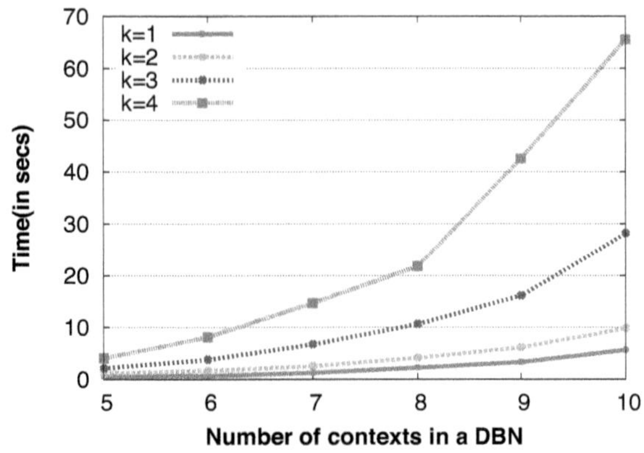

Figure 10: Time to generate a dynamic plan selecting best k classifiers where k varies from 1 to 4 and the query set consists of all the contexts available in a DBN. The figure shows the variation in time as the number of contexts in a DBN, N is varied from 5 to10. The plan evaluation time increases linearly in k and exponentially in N.

Plan Evaluation time: We evaluate *plan evaluation time* on Galaxy Nexus phone for multiple user traces consisting of 5-11 contexts. In this evaluation, we set all the contexts as queries and measure time to generate dynamic plan selecting best k classifiers where $k = 1, 2, 3, 4$. We note that the time complexity of generating dynamic plan with best k classifiers is linear in k and exponential in N where N is the number of contexts in the DBN. We show the results in Figure 10. From the figure, we can see that the *plan evaluation time* increases quickly with the number of contexts in DBN and requires more than a minute to evaluate best 4 classifiers for a DBN consisting 10 contexts. This might still be practical if we generate a plan only when the set of queries change, which might be infrequent. However, if the plan is re-evaluated every few minutes, this approach quickly becomes infeasible. This problem can be addressed in two ways: i) using an approximate inference algorithm with better time complexity, which is part of our ongoing work, or ii) evaluating the plan in the cloud when its complexity exceeds a certain threshold. Of course, dynamic plan evaluation on the cloud has the overhead of data transfer of the current classifier outputs with the appropriate confidence values. However, the DBN model itself is not required to be sent to the cloud as it is already trained on the cloud.

7. DISCUSSION

In our results, we have demonstrated the utility of *CQue* framework for energy-efficient and accurate continuous sensing of user context while understanding the privacy implications. In this section, we discuss potential opportunities for improvement and various interesting questions posed by our framework for further exploration.

Feature-level DBN structure: Our current implementation of the DBN supports fusion of high-level categorical contexts that are the outputs of classifiers. While this is beneficial in that we can take advantage of extensive work on the design of individual activity or behavior classifiers, the downside is that if a classifier outputs inaccurate uncertainty estimates, we may have incorrect inferences that can impact the accuracy of all the related contexts. One way to address this issue may be to use both categorical contexts from classifiers as well as low-level signal features extracted from the sensor data (e.g. spectral features, mean, variance, etc), and to use combination of these different inputs towards information fusion for context inference.

Privacy leakage: We have touched upon the issue of privacy leakage by leveraging correlations across contexts, but *CQue* does not capture all possible attacks that can use multi-sensor inference techniques. The privacy leak detection in *CQue* for a sensitive context is based on a model of adversary who is aware of the context relationships in DBN, but it is possible to have an undetected privacy leak if there are relationships that cannot be modeled by the DBN. For example, the DBN can model and evaluate privacy leakage over a short window of W adjacent time steps but it cannot detect privacy leaks before W time steps. A powerful adversary with alternative long-term models may still be able to execute privacy attacks. Thus, much work remains before we fully understand how to effectively understand the extent of privacy leakage that is possible using sophisticated multi-sensor inference techniques.

Duty-cycling classifiers: One question that we have not fully explored is the interaction between duty-cycled classifiers and the DBN. Several techniques have been proposed to leverage temporal consistency in classifiers for duty-cycling *i.e.* if the context value is not expected to change for some time period, then reduce the sampling rate of the sensor. *CQue* does not currently take advantage of such approaches to duty-cycle classifiers. One method to incorporate such approaches is to use the last observed classifier output as evidence in DBN for next few time-steps while the classifier is inactive. Another interesting question is whether the DBN can be used to learn the duty-cycle for each classifier. Intuitively, if the current state of DBN indicates that some context, say c, is unlikely to change soon then we can have a lower duty-cycle for context c where its classifier will remain inactive for a long time.

DBN learning time: How much training data is needed to fully learn an accurate DBN structure? Although one week of trace proved to be sufficient to learn good structures in our experiments, it might not be the case in general since there may be some longer-range patterns that cannot be captured, and the patterns may change over time. To answer this question, we need larger-scale datasets across more individuals that can help us understand how to learn the DBN effectively across a population while limiting burden to provide labels, as well as the learning period.

8. CONCLUSIONS

Context awareness distinguishes smartphones from traditional computing platforms and can play a key role in creating smart mobile applications. We argue that user contexts across several dimensions are correlated, and if we can learn these correlations in a personalized manner, we can leverage it to improve performance as well as understand the privacy implications of revealing seemingly unrelated contexts. In this paper, we described our context querying framework, *CQue*, that exploits probabilistic relationships across contexts for each individual user to improve energy-efficiency, accuracy and reliability of context sensing, as well as the ability to understand privacy implications.

The ability to understand relations across contexts can have far-reaching consequences. A growing area of healthcare is personalized behavioral monitoring using smartphones and on-body sensors, where behavioral scientists seek to understand relations between addictive or unhealthy behavior, and the individual's state in the real world (activities, social interactions, location, etc) . Our work can enable such understanding, and is a step towards a "big data inference toolkit" for mobile sensing.

9. ACKNOWLEDGEMENTS

We thank our shepherd, Nicholas Lane, and the anonymous reviewers for their comments. This research was supported by UMass S&T award and NSF grants CNS-0910900 and CNS-0855128.

10. REFERENCES

[1] Java bayes. *http://www.cs.cmu.edu/ javabayes/.*

[2] L. Bao and S. S. Intille. Activity Recognition from User-Annotated Acceleration Data. *Pervasive Computing*, pages 1–17, 2004.

[3] D. Chu, A. Deshpande, J. M. Hellerstein, and W. Hong. Approximate Data Collection in Sensor Networks using Probabilistic Models. In *ICDE*, page 48, 2006.

[4] D. Chu, N. Lane, T. Lai, C. Pang, F. Li, X. Meng, Q. Guo, and F. Zhao. Balancing energy, latency and accuracy for mobile sensor data classification. In *SenSys*, pages 54–67, 2011.

[5] A. Deshpande, C. Guestrin, W. Hong, and S. Madden. Exploiting correlated attributes in acquisitional query processing. In *ICDE*, pages 143–154, 2005.

[6] A. Deshpande, C. Guestrin, S. Madden, J. Hellerstein, and W. Hong. Model-driven data acquisition in sensor networks. In *VLDB*, pages 588–599, 2004.

[7] N. Friedman, K. Murphy, and S. Russell. Learning the Structure of Dynamic Probabilistic Networks. In *UAI*, pages 139–147, 1999.

[8] M. Götz, S. Nath, and J. Gehrke. Maskit: privately releasing user context streams for personalized mobile applications. In *SIGMOD*, pages 289–300, 2012. ACM.

[9] M. Hall, E. Frank, G. Holmes, B. Pfahringer, P. Reutemann, and I. H. Witten. The weka data mining software: An update. In *SIGKDD Explorations*, pages 10–18, 2009.

[10] A. Krause and C. Guestrin. Near-optimal Nonmyopic Value of Information in Graphical Models. In *UAI*, pages 324–331, 2005.

[11] J. Lester, T. Choudhury, N. Kern, G. Borriello, and B. Hannaford. A hybrid discriminative/generative approach for modeling human activities. In *IJCAI*, pages 766–772, 2005.

[12] M. Li, D. Ganesan, and P. Shenoy. Presto: feedback-driven data management in sensor networks. In *NSDI*, page 23, 2006.

[13] H. Lu, J. Yang, Z. Liu, N. D. Lane, T. Choudhury, and A. Campbell. The jigsaw continuous sensing engine for mobile phone applications. In *SenSys*, pages 71–84, 2010.

[14] A. Meliou, C. Guestrin, and J. M. Hellerstein. Approximating sensor network queries using in-network summaries. In *IPSN*, pages 229–240. IEEE, 2009.

[15] S. Nath. Ace: exploiting correlation for energy-efficient and continuous context sensing. In *Proceedings of the 10th international conference on Mobile systems, applications, and services*, MobiSys '12, pages 29–42, New York, NY, USA, 2012. ACM.

[16] G. L. Nemhauser, L. A. Wolsey, and M. L. Fisher. An analysis of approximations for maximizing submodular set functions-I. *Mathematical Programming*, 14(1):265–294, Dec. 1978.

[17] A. Parate and G. Miklau. A framework for safely publishing communication traces. In *Proceedings of the 18th ACM conference on Information and knowledge management*, CIKM '09, pages 1469–1472, New York, NY, USA, 2009. ACM.

[18] J. Pearl. *Probabilistic Reasoning in Intelligent Systems: Networks of Plausible Inference*. Morgan Kaufmann, San Francisco, USA, 1988.

[19] R. A. Popa, H. Balakrishnan, and A. J. Blumberg. Vpriv: protecting privacy in location-based vehicular services. In *Proceedings of the 18th conference on USENIX security symposium*, SSYM'09, pages 335–350, Berkeley, CA, USA, 2009. USENIX Association.

[20] N. Ravi, N. Dandekar, P. Mysore, and M. L. Littman. Activity recognition from accelerometer data. In *IAAI*, pages 1541–1546, 2005.

[21] S. J. Russell and P. Norvig. *Artificial Intelligence: A Modern Approach*. Prentice Hall, second edition, 2002.

ProtectMyPrivacy: Detecting and Mitigating Privacy Leaks on iOS Devices Using Crowdsourcing

Yuvraj Agarwal
University of California, San Diego
yuvraj@cs.ucsd.edu

Malcolm Hall
University of California, San Diego
mhall@cs.ucsd.edu

ABSTRACT

In this paper we present the design and implementation of ProtectMyPrivacy (PMP), a system for iOS devices to detect access to private data and protect users by substituting anonymized data in its place if users decide. We developed a novel crowdsourced recommendation engine driven by users who contribute their protection decisions, which provides app specific privacy recommendations. PMP has been in use for over nine months by 90,621 real users, and we present a detailed evaluation based on the data we collected for 225,685 unique apps. We show that access to the device identifier (48.4% of apps), location (13.2% of apps), address book (6.2% of apps) and music library (1.6% of apps) is indeed widespread in iOS. We show that based on the protection decisions contributed by our users we can recommend protection settings for over 97.1% of the 10,000 most popular apps. We show the effectiveness of our recommendation engine with users accepting 67.1% of all recommendations provide to them, thereby helping them make informed privacy choices. Finally, we show that as few as 1% of our users, classified as experts, make enough decisions to drive our crowdsourced privacy recommendation engine.

Categories and Subject Descriptors

C.2.4 [**Computer-Communication Networks**]: Distributed Systems; D.4.6 [**Operating Systems**]: Security and Protection—*Privacy*;

General Terms

Design, Measurement, Experimentation, Human Factors

Keywords

Privacy, Mobile Apps, Crowdsourcing, Recommendations, Apple iOS

MobiSys'13, June 25-28, 2013, Taipei, Taiwan

1. INTRODUCTION

Smartphones are rapidly becoming the mobile platform of choice for users worldwide. While there are several factors behind this growth, one key driver is the "App Store" model of software distribution introduced by Apple, Google, Microsoft and others. Using standardized APIs third-party developers can build applications for platforms such as iOS and Android, which has enabled even those with limited programming experience to release Apps. The phenomenal impact of this model is clear – Apple surpassed 40 billion App downloads in Jan 2013 with over 775,000 iOS Apps in their App Store.

However, the popularity of this model is also a cause for concern, especially from a privacy perspective. In order to build apps with rich functionality, some of the APIs provided by smartphone platforms provide access to potentially private user data. For example, access to the users location, address book, music, photos and unique identifiers (UDID, IMEI,Wi-Fi MAC etc) can be used to track users across applications. Managing access to this private data has become more important given the change in the development model. Until a few years ago, mobile apps were written by a few trusted companies. In contrast, they are now implemented by many individual developers, small companies and large entities alike - not all of whom can be trusted. Furthermore, a large fraction of apps are free, where developers try and supplement their income by incorporating third party advertisement frameworks such as Apple's iAd or Google's Admob. Rather than the app's code, often it is the ad frameworks that access private user data to show targeted ads [14, 27].

The two popular smartphone platforms, Android and iOS, have different approaches towards tackling this problem and for reviewing apps in general. Android does not specifically review apps for the data they access, and instead requires developers to specify the permissions their application needs, notifying the user about them at install time. As a result users bear the responsibility of looking at the permissions and either accepting *all*, or opting not to use the app. In contrast, Apple does review each app submission to make sure that it meets the App Store Review guidelines and any violations lead to rejection. Until recently, iOS did not notify users of apps accessing private information. iOS 5 added notification and control over apps accessing location, while iOS 6 (releasing in September 2012) adds it for contacts, calendars and photos.

Despite these provisions, it has been shown that access to privacy sensitive information by 3rd party apps is rampant in both Android [3, 7, 8, 14, 26, 31] and even in iOS[6]. While in some cases these accesses are indeed warranted for the functionality of the app, in others there may not be an apparent reason. A recent incident causing public outcry was when Path, a social networking app on iOS, was found to access and upload users address books unknown to them. In a few cases, apps access private data and transmit it for downright malicious reasons [19, 29, 28]. Recognizing these privacy breaches, researchers have utilized static analysis [6, 30], or run time checks on suitably modified versions of the Android OS [7, 14, 31] to detect access to private data. Recently, researchers have proposed substituting shadow data in place of private data [3, 31], or blocking the transmission of sensitive information over the network [14].

Unfortunately, almost all of the prior research focuses on the Android platform due to its open source nature as well as the number of restrictions on iOS (Section 2 provides background on iOS). The sole exception is PiOS[6] which utilizes static analysis to show that numerous iOS apps do access private user information. Furthermore, its still not clear how users react to prompts or cues about privacy and whether the protections provided by smartphone OSes are effective in enabling users to make informed choices. In a recent study, Felt et al. [11] observed and interviewed users to evaluate their understanding of Android permissions noting that very few users actually looked at, or even understood, the permissions requested by applications while others just accepted them by default.

In this paper we present **ProtectMyPrivacy** (PMP), a system that detects access to private data at runtime by apps on iOS devices. Similar to prior work on Android, PMP enables users to decide fine grained privacy protection settings on a per app basis by allowing suitably anonymized data to be sent instead of privacy sensitive information [3, 14, 31]. However, a crucial differentiator of PMP as compared to prior work is that we have developed a crowd-sourced system to collect and analyze users protection decisions to help make privacy recommendations to users. The key issue addressed by our crowdsourcing feature is to determine if a clear consensus emerges among the users of an app whether it *should* be granted access to private user data for its functionality, or for a user visible feature or a clear need. We show that our crowd sourced recommendations help our users make more informed privacy choices. Our hope is that with the fine grained privacy control enabled with PMP the balance of power on what private information apps have access to will shift from being in the hands of developers, to the users. As a result, developers will have increased incentives to educate and inform the user about the information they collect and why the users should agree to provide it.

In this paper we make the following contributions:

- The design and implementation of ProtectMyPrivacy, a system for iOS devices to detect access to private information and protect users by substituting anonymized data based on user decisions. A central component of ProtectMyPrivacy is a crowdsourced recommendation engine to analyze manual protection decisions, and use them to provide app privacy recommendations.

- We deployed PMP to real users via the Cydia Store and have collected data on their protection decisions over the past nine months. We present a large scale characterization of access to private data by over 225,685 iOS apps used by 90,621 users of PMP (as of Dec 10th, 2012). Our data shows that 48.4% of apps access the identifier, 13.2% user location, 6.2% user contacts and 1.6% the user's music library.

- We further evaluate PMP by analyzing over 5.97 million protection decisions made by our users, with an average user making 66 decisions. Based on these decisions, we can provide privacy recommendations for 97.1% of the most popular apps (top 10,000). Finally, we show that our recommendations are effective with over 67.1% of all recommendations presented to our users being accepted by them.

2. IOS SECURITY MODEL AND 'JAILBREAKING'

Before describing ProtectMyPrivacy, we briefly discuss Apple iOS, focusing on its security model and privacy features. iOS uses code-signing, encryption and sandboxing to secure the platform. Code-signing ensures only executables reviewed and distributed by Apple are allowed to run. Encryption ensures apps can't be reverse-engineered, protecting the app developer's investment, and that only the purchaser can launch the app. Sandboxing ensures that individual apps cannot access others' data or other parts of the file system. Apple provides various APIs to communicate with the OS and allow apps to register a URL handler that allows them to communicate with each other using parameters. Apps can access shared resources, including privacy sensitive data such as contacts, location, photos using well defined iOS APIs. Recognizing the need for protecting user privacy, Apple introduced pop up notifications in iOS 5 for when an app requests the user's location allowing users to also deny access. In iOS 6, this privacy notifications has been expanded to include contacts, calendars and photos however it is yet to be seen if these many notifications will become obtrusive.

Apps are normally distributed via the Apple controlled App Store and they are subject to a review process to make sure they adhere to strict guidelines. The review includes static analysis to ensure only the published API methods are used and runtime analysis to check apps don't attempt to read outside of the sandbox. However, due to the sheer number of apps submitted, apps that secretly circumvent guidelines sometimes pass review and go on sale; however these are often later removed.

A point of some discussion is the level of control Apple places on the App Store and on the iOS platform. For an app to be distributed in the App Store, developers must use only the published APIs in the Apple SDK, or risk the app being rejected. In response to this an alternative distribution channel has become popular - known as the Cydia Store - which also supports the distribution of apps that function outside of Apple's guidelines, for example those that use lower level capabilities than the public SDK offers in addition to OS 'tweaks' and customizations. The Cydia community actually began before there was even an official App Store, and since has become quite popular, with 4.5 million active users in April 2011[15] which increased to 14 Million active users on iOS6 alone in March 2013 [24] with an estimated 23 Million total jailbroken iOS devices. The use of Cydia requires modification of an iOS device using a process called *jailbreaking* which removes Apple's code-signing requirement, such that apps can be installed from other sources, *in addition to* installing standard apps from the regular App Store.

While jailbreaking has been deemed legal in the US, it is not supported by Apple since it is often used to install pirated apps and more importantly circumvent iOS protection features. It is therefore possible that jailbreaking may leave users vulnerable to other attacks if they install untrusted apps from unknown sources rather than just from the App Store. As we will describe later in this paper, PMP requires the ability to intercept calls to official iOS APIs that apps use to access private information such as user location or contacts. Unfortunately, there is no way to do this on non-jailbroken devices due to the platform security. Therefore, in order for us to do this large scale app privacy study we had to develop PMP on jailbroken devices and leverage the Cydia store to distribute PMP.

The overall implications and the security discussion of jailbreaking are beyond the scope of our paper. We also do not advocate jailbreaking as a method to protect user privacy, although a number of our users did contact us to say that they jailbroke their devices just to use PMP. We also note that for the purpose of our study, we considered apps that users install from the App Store and not any of the Cydia apps. Although it's possible that some of the apps we have tracked have been pirated, these are essentially decrypted, but identical, versions of purchased apps, and so far no apps have been seen that have been tampered with further. As a result, we believe our findings generalize to the apps that normal non-jailbroken users would install from the App Store.

3. RELATED WORK

Related work on smartphone privacy falls into four general categories: mechanisms of data access control, studies of privacy issues, mechanisms to mitigate privacy issues, and finally user perceptions about app privacy.

Most research into data access control has been explicitly developed for the Android OS in which apps explicitly ask for permissions from the user at install time. Avik [5], ScanDroid [13] and Kirin [9] look at expressing the security properties of Android Apps formally [5], reason about whether extracted permissions are upheld [13], or analyze them for cases when combined permissions can be dangerous [9]. Barrera et al. [1] analyze over a thousand Android apps showing that only a small fraction of requested permissions are used widely. Stowaway [10] similarly analyzes over a thousand Apps statically to show that a third request one or more extra permissions than they really need. Note, the above papers explore retrofitting the Android permission model to determine extraneous permissions but do not explicitly protect user privacy from malicious applications.

A first step towards protecting user privacy is detecting apps that access sensitive data. TaintDroid [7] proposes modifying the Android OS such that 'taint' values can be assigned to sensitive data and their flow can be continuously tracked through each app execution, raising alerts when they flow to the network interface. TaintDroid imposes a runtime overhead because it runs continuously for all applications and hence the authors tested it on a set of thirty popular Android apps reporting that many of them leak privacy sensitive data. In contrast, PiOS [6] employs static analysis techniques to detect privacy leaks. The authors of PiOS construct a CFG of downloaded and decrypted iOS apps, to determine if there is a path from 'sources' of sensitive data to 'sinks' where the information can leave the device. Their analysis on 1400 iOS apps detected over a hundreds apps accessing and sending the UDID, and less often the location and the address book. The Spyphone project [22] reported a number of private data elements accessible by apps, however we chose to study the ones that seemed most privacy intrusive as the basis for our work. The Wall Street Journal also did a study in 2010 on fifty popular iPhone and Android applications each and analyzed their network traffic to detect privacy leaks [25, 26] (as has also been done by others [23]). While these approaches detect privacy breaches by apps, they do not provide mechanisms to actually protect the user from them.

To protect user privacy, it is important to understand when apps access private user data for legitimate reasons such as to provide location based services, and distinguish it with questionable reasons such as sending data to ad networks [6, 27] or downright malicious reasons [19, 29, 28]. Researchers have therefore proposed methods to prevent privacy sensitive data from being acquired by apps in the first place. The Apex system [20] extends Android to enable users to selectively allow, deny or constrain access to the specific permissions requested by applications. A side effect of denying access to resources is that an app may throw an exception and terminate. Mockdroid [3] proposes modifying the Android OS so as to substitute private data with *mock* data – such as constant values or null values – when apps request it. The authors ran MockDroid on the same set of 27 apps used by the TaintDroid [7] system and showed that most of them continued to function, but with reduced functionality in some cases. Zhou et al. [31] similarly developed TISSA for Android that provides various types of mock data in place of private data at runtime to untrusted apps based on user preferences. The authors evaluated TISSA on 24 free Android apps showing that it imposes minimal overhead on a modified Android OS [31]. Appfence [14] builds upon the TaintDroid system [7] to provide shadow data to untrusted apps as well as perform exfiltration blocking to prevent sensitive data from leaving the device. Appfence focuses on the user visible side-effects of giving shadow data, and their evaluation on fifty Android apps showed that two thirds of the effective permissions could be reduced without affecting the app functionality. A limitation of the prior approaches is that they need a modified version of the Android OS. To address this criticism Jeon et al.[16] developed two tools, "Dr. Android" and "Mr. Hide", that run on stock Android phones. Mr. Hide is a service that provides access to private data, while Dr. Android is a Dalvik Rewriter tool that retrofits existing Android apps to use the interface exported by Mr. Hide. Their analysis of this on a set of 19 apps demonstrated that these techniques worked well, although for certain applications the rewriting did change the behavior of the app itself. Finally, the PrivacyBlocker application [30] uses static analysis on application binaries and replaces calls for private data with hard coded shadow data. This approach however requires target applications to be re-written and reinstalled and cannot be done at runtime.

Researchers have begun to explore user perceptions of privacy on smartphones. Felt et al. [11] interviewed Android users on their understanding of Android permissions noting that very few users actually looked at them and often accept

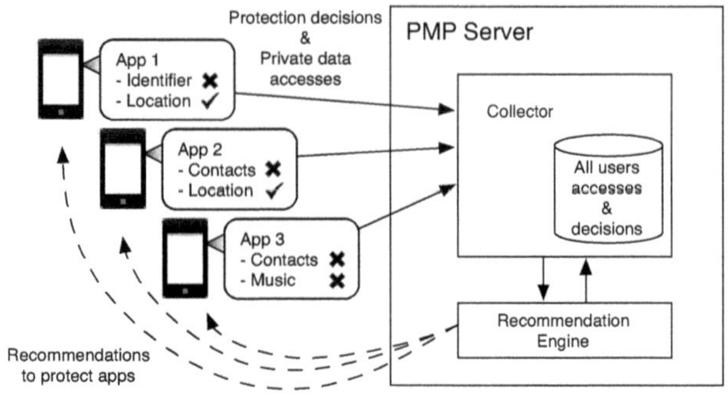

Figure 1: ProtectMyPrivacy architecture based on crowd sourcing. Participating devices transmit their protection decisions for individual applications to our server, which processes the data and uses that to provide recommendations to other devices and users.

them by default. In a project contemporary to ours, Lin et al. [17] collect users expectations of the permissions that particular apps may require, and then measure the users responses to the actual private data access by the same apps using Taintdroid. The authors recruited 179 Amazon Mechanical Turk users to crowdsource these decisions for the top 100 Android apps, observing that users were often surprised about the accesses to their private data and unable to determine why it was needed. In a similar vein to PMP, the paper proposes a new privacy summary screen to give users additional privacy context about apps during installation. While PMP also employs crowdsourcing for app privacy decisions, we focus on building and deploying a scalable recommendation system and evaluating its efficacy on a large number of real users.

PMP differs from the prior work in several key areas. First, as far as we know, except PiOS [6] all of the prior work has been for Android. Android, or the Dalvik VM it uses, being open source is amenable to modification while iOS is more complicated because of its closed source nature and native compiled code. Second, most prior work has been tested on a somewhat limited set of apps, and more importantly not on real users in the wild. In contrast, PMP has been deployed to 90,621 users with over 225,685 unique apps. This paper is therefore the first large scale study showing the actual extent of access to private data by iOS apps as well as our users' response to it by protecting and allowing these accesses. Finally, all of the prior works, which propose replacing privacy sensitive data by shadow data, rely on users to make the appropriate decisions. While PMP also provide users a similar ability to make these decisions on their own, our recommendation engine feature that employs crowd sourcing to suggest protection settings to users is novel and has not been used before, or evaluated at scale, in this context.

4. ARCHITECTURAL DESIGN

We had a number of goals in mind when designing ProtectMyPrivacy (PMP). First, PMP should be architected such that it can be evaluated by a large population of real smartphone users, despite its technical complexity. Second, PMP should be able to detect runtime access to private information, and determine whether to allow or deny the access (either by prompting the user or automatically). Third, PMP should have an easily accessible user interface (UI) for configuring privacy settings across apps. Finally, we wanted to design PMP such that we can collect protection decisions made by users and feed this data into a recommendation engine so that future users benefit from crowdsourced protection decisions.

Most of the prior work on smartphone privacy for Android proposed either using modified versions of Android running on a few test devices or using static analysis on a set of downloaded apps. The number of apps that can be tested are limited in both cases since new apps and updated versions are released often. In contrast, we designed PMP to be fully dynamic in nature, running in the hands of real iOS users "in the wild". Standard iOS apps from the App Store are self-contained and sandboxed, that is they can only access data and settings created by that particular app. However, PMP should run transparently as a plug-in to any unmodified app that the user runs, whilst communicating with its own database to store settings.

PMP detects access to private data and allows the user to protect or allow these accesses, as illustrated in Figure 1. The first information type we protect is the smartphone's unique device identifier (UDID), which is a SHA1 hash of a concatenated string of unique hardware id's including the serial number, International Mobile Equipment Identity (IMEI), Wi-Fi MAC and Bluetooth MAC. Developers can utilize the UDID to monitor app usage, advertising networks can utilize it for cross-app tracking, associating the identifiers with user location and behavior [27]. The number is also linked by the carrier to personally identifiable billing information such as name and address.

The next private data type that PMP protects is the user's address book stored in a database on the device, containing contact information such as names, addresses, phone numbers and emails. Recently, the Path social networking app was found to read the users' entire address book and upload it to a server without their permission, causing significant backlash. It is not certain if Path, or other apps that do this, profit from the sale of personal information, but it is possible that this information (such as address books) could be sold by unscrupulous developers. PMP should empower users to allow access to their address book, or protect it by redirecting the access to an alternative address book, filled with fictitious entries (names, emails and phone numbers) on a per app basis. Sending fictitious information not only protects the user but also reduces the integrity of the rogue developers' remote database, making it difficult to distinguish between genuine and fictitious data, reducing the value and potentially preventing a sale.

A long standing concern is location privacy. If an app does not require location for an obvious or needed feature then PMP should allow the user to protect their location. For the same reason, as with the UDID, PMP should provide a random location or allow users to choose a fake location to prevent profiling. We note that Apple has indeed recognized the need for protecting user privacy and added notifications for access to contacts, calendar and photos in iOS 6 (released Oct 2012). However, since the list of private data items that apps can access may increase, PMP should be extensible in the data types it protects, so that our system can simply be updated to accommodate them. These include apps accessing photos, music libraries, and other ways of tracking user identity such as the MAC addresses, device name, user email address and phone number.

An important aspect of detecting and manipulating runtime access to private information is that PMP needs to have a very low overhead such that it does not affect app or device performance or reduce battery life. Furthermore, since apps may access private data at any point during execution, PMP should pause the app's runtime when access first happens and prompt the user to make a decision.

The third aspect of PMP's design is an easy to understand UI. When prompting the user to make a privacy protection decision, it should be done in a manner that is consistent with other notifications, for example mimicking the location access prompts in iOS 5. PMP prompts should therefore simply be an extension of any existing iOS privacy prompts. Next, since users may want to *temporarily* disable protection to use a specific app feature, for example location based search on an app, PMP should allow this without necessarily exiting the app. Finally, users should be able to view the privacy settings for all installed apps in one place, so they can browse and keep track of what decisions have been made.

The final design goal of PMP is the creation of a crowd-sourced recommendation engine to help users make more informed protection decisions, perhaps even automatically. The basic idea is to leverage the manual protection decisions made by users of a particular app, and use it to generate recommendations for other users of the same app as shown in Figure 1. The recommendation algorithm that PMP uses should account for developers trying to potentially game the system by providing initial recommendations, as well as give preference to users who make a lot of manual decisions while discounting users who make a handful of decisions. PMP should allow the recommendation algorithm, and hence the recommendations, to be changed on the fly as additional data and decisions are made. Using crowd-sourcing for recommendations on privacy settings was in part inspired by prior work which shows that less-experienced users can benefit from customizations decided by experts [18].

5. IMPLEMENTATION

In this section we describe our implementation of ProtectMyPrivacy on the iOS platform, highlighting how we support our design goals mentioned in Section 4. We first describe the features of iOS and the capabilities provided by jailbreaking that we utilize for PMP. Next we describe the PMP app itself that users install on their devices. Finally, we describe the back end infrastructure supporting PMP and our crowd sourced recommendation system.

5.1 iOS Platform Features

A background of iOS, its design and security features was provided in Section 2. iOS apps run as native binaries in an XNU environment which improves performance and also gives programmers access to familiar C++ APIs. One of the design goals of PMP was to support unmodified apps, which for iOS requires adding functionality to running processes. As mentioned in Section 2 it is not possible to do this due to iOS security features, without "jailbreaking" the device. On a jailbroken device, however, there is support for the Mac OS X DYLD_INSERT_LIBRARIES environment variable (similar to LD_PRELOAD on Linux) which allows plugins to be loaded before apps execute. This has enabled the creation of an open-source project MobileSubstrate (MSub) to standardize the iOS plugin API [12].

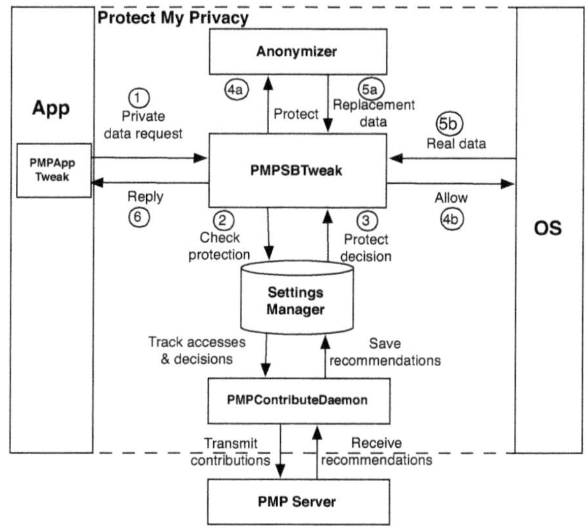

Figure 2: ProtectMyPrivacy acts as a layer between apps and the OS – the labels (1) through (6) denote the different steps taken when private information is accessed.

MSub allows developers to inject code into the address space of other iOS apps, replacing the existing implementation of specific classes. There are currently 100+ MSub powered customizations or 'tweaks' available for iOS in the Cydia Store. A popular one, for example, allows modification of the visual theme of applications such as changing color schemes and icons. MSub supports filters, which restrict what apps will be modified by a specified code injection. For example we specified that our dynamic libraries are only loaded into executables that link to the UIKit, the iOS UI framework; thus it is only loaded into executables that users actually interact with.

iOS APIs are a mixture of Obj C and C. The UDID and location APIs are in an Obj C framework, while contacts and music are in C; MSub provides method replacement APIs for both languages, however it still took a significant amount of effort on our part to determine which methods should be replaced to detect access to the various potentially privacy invasive APIs. For C, MSub uses a technique called *hooking* that works at the assembly level, and for Obj C, it uses *method swizzling* that uses the built-in `class_replaceMethod` function. PMP requires the plugins loaded into existing apps to communicate with a centralized PMP module for which we use the CPDistributedMessagingCenter, a wrapper on top of the Mach Interface Generator (MIG) generated Remote Procedure Call (RPC) subsystem. It uses a publish/subscribe API for transmitting hash-tables containing strings, with an synchronous mode to allow message senders to await replies.

5.2 PMP iOS App

We designed the PMP app which runs on an iOS device to be modular, with five components that communicate with each other via RPC. These are *PMPAppTweak*, *PMPSBTweak*, *PMPContributeDaemon*, *PMPWeeApp* and *PMPSettings*. Figure 2 illustrates the different PMP modules at a high level, as well as how they communicate with each other and the server.

Using MSub we implemented *PMPAppTweak*, a dynamic library that is loaded into all apps launched by the user. When this dynamic library is launched it replaces various methods used to access private information. In the case of the Address Book Framework (AB), for example, it uses `MSHookFunction` to replace `ABRecordCopyValue(...)` which is essentially a public API around a directly inaccessible SQLite database and returns the data for a particular property in an AB record. We monitor this method call for properties of interest, such as `kABLastNameProperty`, `kABPhoneProperty` or `kABEmailProperty`, and when detected, we activate our alternate version of the method. First, we check with the PMPSBTweak (see below) by means of RPC, on whether this app should have AB information protected. If so, we first invoke the original method call to retrieve the real AB information, then pass it to an anonymizer. Our anonymizer takes into account the dynamic nature of the AB where records do change, and rather than build a default fictitious address book, we randomly move around characters and the numbers in each record. Since we keep the same record count, our system is more robust to potentially serious array out of range errors as the application tries to access address book data. Furthermore, when we anonymize the data at runtime we use the same seed generated once per device which ensures the same modified value is passed to all apps, to give any cross-app tracking the illusion of consistent and valid data. We replace all other ABRecord methods in the same way so that the entire API is covered for providing replacement information. We note that it may be possible by a determined hacker to reverse engineer the original values by observing anonymized data from many devices. For those circumstances stronger anonymization schemes such as format-preserving encryption [2] may be better and we plan to explore them further. We are also considering the option of returning a set of preset names with random data for the address book. We currently protect the identifier, location and music in an identical way by replacing the appropriate method calls that provide access to these private data items. Our method is easily extensible to other private data types that may be accessed using iOS method calls and is not limited to the ones we currently protect. For example, we have recently added protection for the photo library but did not include it in this paper because we have not evaluated it yet.

We have implemented another MSub dynamic library, our *PMPSBTweak* module, that is loaded into the Springboard, the iOS home screen application that displays app icons and manages their launches, comparable to the desktop application in a PC environment. This module allows us to access the list of apps that are currently installed, look up their identifier and version numbers, and allow us to respond to notification when new apps are upgraded or installed. For example, on this notification we query our PMP server for updated recommendations. This module also acts as a central store for the PMP settings database. That is, it loads the settings on device boot, and ensures they are saved correctly. This module also listens for RPC messages from apps asking if private information of each type should be protected, and handles them as follows. First it checks to see if the user has previously decided to use recommendations for this particular app. If they have not and recommendations are available for the app, we prompt the user to check if they would like to use them (Figure 3c). This prompt enables the user to configure all the protection settings for this app at once. Alternatively, if no recommendation is available, then the user must respond to the privacy prompt by tapping "Protect" or "Allow" as shown in Figure 3a. The RPC message call from the source app causes it to pause while it waits for a response.

The third module is *PMPContributeDaemon*, a background daemon which persists across reboots. It can be started (or stopped) by the PMPSettings app if the user opts-in or out of contributing their PMP activity including protection decisions. When started this module listens for RPC messages from PMPSBTweak denoting changes to protection settings, as well as what private data each app is attempting to access – which are sent to our PMP server. Users that contribute their protection decisions are rewarded with recommendations for their other apps. Based on our modular design, all communication with the PMP server is confined to this daemon. As a result, if a user turns off contributions, this daemon is stopped and thus there is no server communication. If recommendations had been previously received, we leave them on the device although they do not get updated any further. Therefore, due to the way our system is designed, it is in the users interest to leave the contribute feature on in order to benefit from the recommendations feature.

PMPSettings, as shown in Figure 3b, is where PMP can be configured. When the PMP app is launched it displays the privacy settings of all apps configured so far. Users can review their previous protect or allow decisions, update them, or decide to start using the automatic recommendations as shown in Figure 3e. We also provide options to configure the replacement data, for example generating a new random unique identifier, and allowing the user to choose a replacement fake location on a map.

PMPWeeApp is a Notification Center (NC) WeeApp (or plug-in) that offers quick access to protection settings while an app is running. On iOS (v5.0 and later) users can drag their finger down from the top of the screen and they are presented with NC, which displays status information such as current weather, or new emails. NC supports plugins, although only unofficially at present, which enabled us to add an area to NC to manipulate the protection settings manually or switch to using recommendations without exiting the app (Figure 3d). *PMPWeeApp* is designed for users to temporarily allow access to their private data such as their location, while using a particular feature of an app, and then protecting it again afterwards. Of course, it is entirely possible for applications to cache private data as soon as access is granted and use it later.

Overall, we have implemented three places where users can configure PMP privacy settings: in the target app when the access is detected at runtime (InApp), in the Notification Center (NC) while the app is running, and in the PMP Settings app (Settings).

We have ensured that our implementation of the PMP app and its components do not impose any perceptible overheads in terms of performance by measuring the interactiveness and latency of different apps with and without PMP installed. Additional delay does occur when an app accesses a protected feature and the user is shown a popup to make a protection decision, however these are only to solicit user input on first access. It is also important to consider the

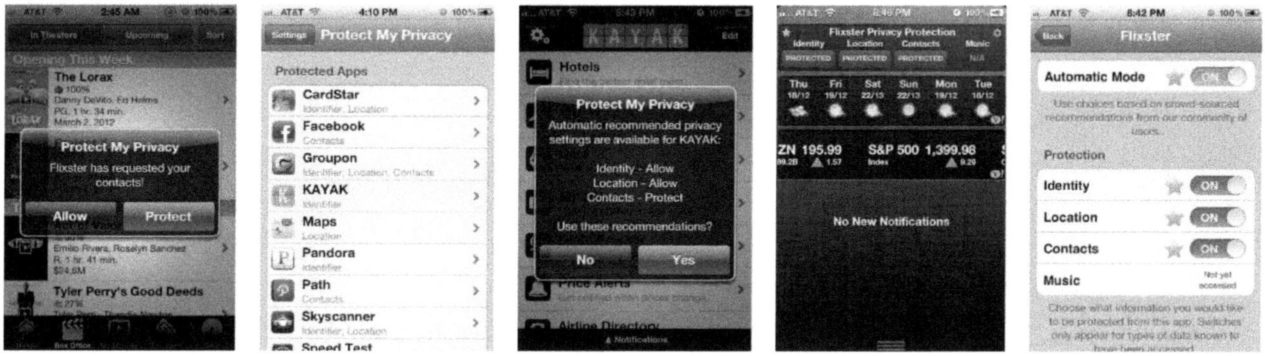

(a) (b) (c) (d) (e)

Figure 3: Screenshots of the ProtectMyPrivacy iOS application, from left to right: (a) in-app popup for a contacts access, (b) settings showing different applications and what features they have accessed, (c) Pop-up showing that a recommendation is available, (d) Notification Center showing which recommendations are in use (in yellow) for the Flixster app, and (e) Flixster settings in the settings app, showing stars for what is recommended, and also displaying if one of the privacy protected features has not been accessed yet.

impact of the PMP app on the battery lifetime of a device. While we have not yet performed detailed battery lifetime measurements, we do note that we have implemented PMP with energy efficiency in mind. For example, we measured the CPU usage of our *PMPContributeDaemon* which runs in the background to periodically upload data periodically to be negligible. Furthermore, to reduce the energy used by this daemon for network transfers we batch and compress data to reduce the frequency and the size of these uploads.

5.2.1 PMP App Security Analysis

By building PMP upon jailbroken devices and MSub, we lose compatibility with iOS code-signing enforcement which prevents runtime attacks, as covered earlier in Section 2. Hence when using PMP, users will have stronger protection against privacy-focused attacks, but lose protection against runtime attacks. Furthermore, it may be possible for an App Store app to detect jailbreak, download, then execute an unreviewed payload, which could potentially replace PMP's overridden methods back to their originals form. However, in that scenario an attacker could circumvent PMP entirely by reading files outside of the sandbox normally detected by Apple's runtime review. To limit these risks we added various integrity checks to PMP, and we recommend our users only install trusted apps from the App Store. The fact is, a jailbroken phone may be open to new security issues, a complete security analysis is beyond the scope of this paper. We merely use jailbroken devices as a method to experiment, develop, and collect data for our research.

5.3 PMP Server Software

We have installed a dedicated PMP server to collect users' PMP activity, run various back end analysis and finally to deliver recommendations. We first developed a generic logging framework, called Leo, that utilizes the Doctrine ORM, MySQL, PHP and Apache. Leo allows storage and retrieval of data in an extensible format using simple insert and query APIs, with transmissions optimized for minimizing mobile data use and secured using SSL. Leo uses 'layers' for app data types, for example, protection decisions, access detections, and recommendations, each stored in distinct layers that correspond to individual MySQL database tables. Access to layers is secured with individual read and write keys.

When the PMP app sends data to be stored in a layer, it is sent as an Apple Property List (PList), a serialized dictionary containing standard fields such as the title, subtitle and app version, along with created and updated timestamps. It also has a properties dictionary for custom fields - layers have the capability to draw out these custom property fields and insert them into database table fields, and optionally add indexes for faster queries. The Leo client library for iOS that we have implemented has a simple API for logging system data, and this is cached locally on the device and uploaded whenever an Internet connection is available, so no data is lost. Leo also features a default app stats layer that allows us to track app usage, device types and OS versions. In PMP, the Protect layer is for storing users protection decisions and has custom fields for *feature* (string for identifier, contacts, etc.), *protect* (boolean for user protected or allowed) and *recommended* (boolean for if this was a recommended decision). Note that all communication between iOS clients and our server is done over SSL encrypted HTTP messages.

5.3.1 Generating Recommendations

Once we receive the protection decisions from our contributing users, we use them to generate recommendations based on the following parameters. First, we only consider apps with a minimum number of users ($n > 5$). Second, we include decisions from only active users of an app (used for more than a week). Third, we include decisions only from users who have made decisions for a minimum number of other apps ($n > 10$ apps). We use these conditions to prevent developers from gaming the recommendation system and improve the quality of recommendations by factoring out naive users and users who stopped using the app. We then process the resulting decisions to calculate the percentage of users who protect/allow each feature, for example, identity or location, within each app. If 55%-100% of valid decisions are to protect, we will recommended protect, while if only 0%-45% of valid decisions protect, we will recommended allow. In this example, we call the 10% range between 45% and 55% a *deadband*, where a recommendation to protect or allow is too close to call. We chose a 10%

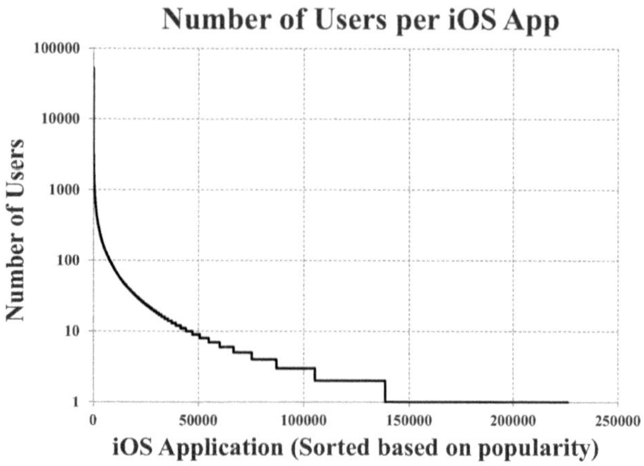

Figure 4: Number of Users per iOS app. Applications are sorted with the most popular app first.

Line	Features Accessed	Apps	Percentage
	Access **at least** 1		
1	– Identifier (I)	109,300	48.43%
2	– Location (L)	29,952	13.27%
3	– Contacts (C)	14,041	6.22%
4	– Music (M)	3655	1.62%
	Access **at least** 2		
5	– Identifier & Location	19,596	8.68%
6	– Identifier & Contacts	10,100	4.48%
7	– Identifier & Music	2,566	1.14%
8	– Location & Contacts	4,446	1.97%
9	– Location & Music	1,035	0.46%
10	– Contacts & Music	805	0.36%
11	Access All 4 (I,L,C,M)	94	.04%
12	Don't Access Anything	101,784	45.10%
13	Total Apps	225,685	100%

Table 1: Number of iOS apps that access certain protected features such as identifier, location, contacts or the music library.

deadband since it provided a good tradeoff between being able to provide recommendations for around 70% of the total apps, while reducing ones for which we were unsure about the right choice. For example, based on our current data, a 10% deadband provides recommendations for 69.6% of the total apps. Based on these calculations we created a recommendation layer in Leo (app & version) which our PMP app on iOS devices queries for recommendations.

For use in our evaluation later, we also generate an `expert` set of recommendations. While experts can be chosen in multiple ways, including perhaps even a set of paid 'certificate experts', we chose to designate users of our system who make a large number of protect or allow decisions, across a large number of apps used as experts. The intuition is that these users are active across many apps, and use apps often, to make better privacy decisions. We first identified the minimum number of decisions the top 2% of users of our system made (364) and also the the minimum number of applications the top 2% users of our system made decisions for (163). As a heuristic, we then define experts as ones who meet both criteria, i.e. they make a minimum of 364 decisions across at least 163 different apps, which results in 1133 users (1.2%) from our current user base of 90,621 users. We then use the same 10% deadband used for the general recommendation table, to create our `expert` recommendation layer in Leo based on these experts decisions. In Section 6 we evaluate the user acceptance rates of both the general and the expert recommendations.

6. EVALUATION

We released PMP via the Cydia Store for free in February 2012. Over the past nine months we have continued to iterate the design; releasing new versions with refinements and bug fixes as shown on our project website [21]. The first set of versions of our app (V1.x) did not deliver recommendations as we focused on scaling our system and collecting data about user choices on what they protected or allowed. In the third week of April we released an updated version with the crowd sourcing based recommendation feature enabled (V2.x). Subsequently, on Dec 3rd, 2012 we released another version (V 2.3.x) that included user surveys to help us analyze our users privacy choices and gather their feedback on recommendations.

In the rest of this section we present observations from our extensive dataset, as well as evaluate the effectiveness of PMP in protecting user privacy. We first describe the different user statistics we collect which form the basis of our quantitative analysis. We then present user and app statistics with a breakdown on what private pieces of data apps access, using this to evaluate the protect or allow decisions made by users. Lastly, we evaluate our recommendation engine and show its effectiveness.

6.1 Data Collected from Users

The PMP server receives data only from users who have contribute enabled in the PMP app. This data includes the app name, ID and version, what types of private information each app tries to access, and how many such requests happen. These statistics are collected on every app invocation and then batched and sent to our server. We also receive statistics from users about the decisions they make, either to protect or to allow, for each of the privacy sensitive information types. These protection statistics are collected for each app and also let us know where the decision was made, for example, in the in-app alert (InApp), in the PMP settings app (Settings) or using the iOS Notification Center (NC). These pieces of information are used by our recommendation engine feature.

6.2 User and Application Breakdown

Based on our analysis of the data we have collected at the time of writing this paper, we have 90,621 unique users. We determine the number of users based on the unique hashed UDIDs recorded in our database and also corroborated that with the number of downloads of our PMP software. Note that we account for users upgrading or resetting their device, and only count the number of unique hardware devices. Based on our dataset, we have observed 225,685 unique apps across all our users (considering multiple versions of an app as a single app). This number is less than a third of the estimated 775,000 total apps in the iOS App Store (as of January 2013), which suggests that two thirds of the App Store apps are not downloaded by our sample set of users, although we are confident that our dataset from 90,621 users

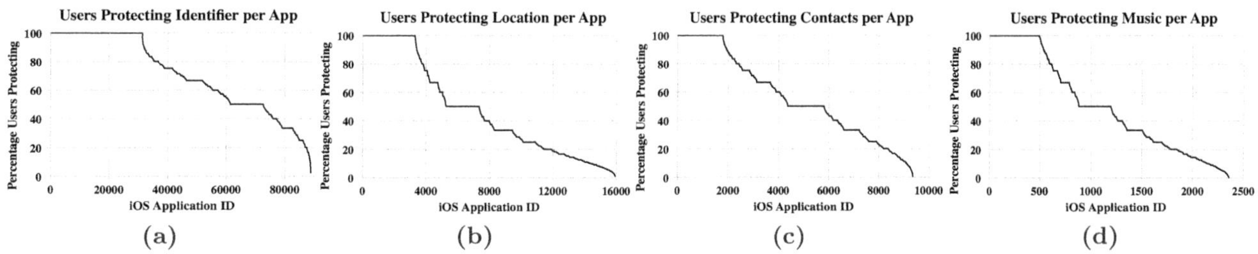

Figure 5: Percentage of users per app that protect access to (a) Identifier, (b) Location, (c) Contacts or (d) Music. The graphs are sorted by apps which have the highest percentage of users protecting access to the particular feature first.

statistically accounts for the most popular apps. Furthermore we noticed that within the 225,685 apps we observe, only 75,284 (33.3%) of them had at least five users, while the rest don't seem very popular.

In Figure 4 we plot the number of users (Y-axis in log scale) per unique app using PMP, showing the apps with the most users first. The distribution here follows a broadly log-linear distribution, correlating with other studies of smartphone application usage [4]. A few apps are very popular, with large number of users: 41 apps have over 10,000 users, 520 apps have between 1,000 - 10,000 users, while 7,134 apps have between 100 - 1,000 users. We see that there is a very long tail in the distribution: 39,365 apps have between 10 - 100 users, and finally 178,626 apps have less than 10 users each. Although our data is collected from jailbroken users, we nevertheless believe it is representative of regular non-jailbroken users for the reasons mentioned in Section 2. For instance, our 90,621 users install the same apps (particularly free apps) as users of non-jailbroken devices, which are only available in the regular iOS App Store. Note that while jailbreaking has become increasingly trivial, leading to an estimated 23 Million users jailbreaking their devices as of March 2013[24], it still requires an additional step and therefore our user population is likely biased towards more power users. Furthermore, our users who found and installed the PMP app from the Cydia jailbreak store are likely to be more privacy conscious than perhaps the average user.

6.2.1 *Applications Accessing Protected Features*

Next we analyze which apps accesses what privacy sensitive information types. Table 1 summarizes the breakdown for the number of apps that access at least one feature, ones that access at least two features, and ones that access all of the protected features. Our data shows some interesting trends. We see that 48.4% of the total apps access the identifier, 13.2% access location, 6.2% access contacts and only 1.6% access the music library (Line 1 to 4). When looking at the data for apps that access at least two protected features we observed that identifier and location (Line 5) are accessed together by 8.6% of apps while the identifier and the contacts (Line 6) are accessed by 4.5% of the total apps. This data points to the possibility that some of these apps may be legitimately accessing contacts, location and the identifier to provide a specific features such as "email friends" or to provide location-based services. As shown in prior work, a large number of apps often include third party ad frameworks which access privacy sensitive information to provide targeted ads [6, 14]. We present a specific app case study in Section 6.5. The focus of our work is not to identify

Statistic	Number
Users making 1 to 10 decisions	18,757 Users
Users making 10 to 100 decisions	44,260 Users
Users making 100 to 363 decisions	16,729 Users
Users making > 363 decisions (Top 2%)	1,865 Users
Users making decisions on 1 - 10 Apps	24,344 Users
Users making decisions on 10 - 50 Apps	36,907 Users
Users making decisions on 50 - 162 Apps	19,731 Users
Users making decisions on > 162 Apps (Top 2%)	1,854 Users
Average Number of decision across all our users	66 Decisions
Expert Users (> 363 Decisions & > 162 Apps)	1,133 Users

Table 2: Summary table showing the breakdown of the number of users making protect or allow decisions. A large number of our users make between 10 and 100 decisions.

which of these apps legitimately require access to the private data types. Instead, we rely on our users decision to protect or allow access, based on whether they think that an app should be granted access for its functionality, a user visible feature, or a clearly communicated need.

6.3 Breakdown of Protection Decisions

As mentioned earlier, as PMP users make decisions to either protect or allow an app access to any privacy data, the PMP contribute daemon sends us that decision. Based on this collected data, on our server we can determine the distribution of the protect or allow decisions across different apps. Figure 5 (a) shows the percentage of users that decide to protect access to the identifier (I) across all the apps that access it. Note, the apps are sorted based on the percentage of users protecting access, thus the apps for which 100% of our users choose to protect are shown first. Figure 5 (b), (c) and (d) similarly show the percentage of users protecting access to location (L), contacts (C) and the music library (M) respectively across the apps that access these features. We make two key observations from these figures. First, we can see that for a significant fraction of apps, users unanimously choose to protect access to one or more of the four protected features (I,L,C,M). This behavior indicates that none of the users of these apps thought there was a reason for them to have access to their private data. Second, there are in general more apps for which users choose to protect, rather than allow access to three of the four features (I,C,M) except location where its the opposite with more apps being allowed access.

Table 2 provides a breakdown in terms of the number of users that make decisions, binned into different categories based on how often they make protect (or allow) decisions. These decisions are ones that users made themselves (be-

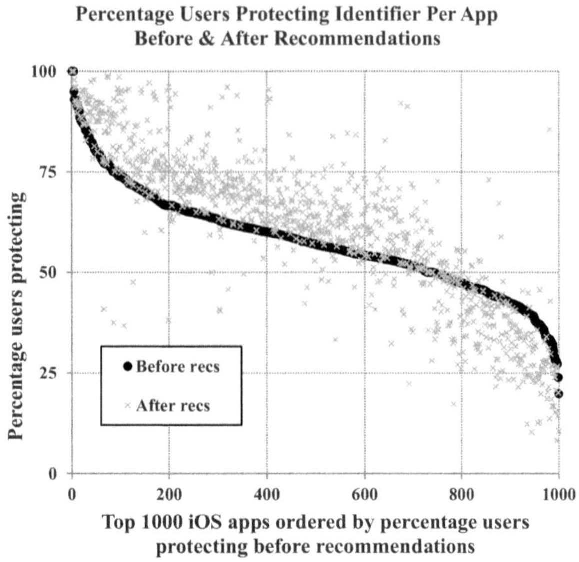

Figure 6: Percentage of users protecting (or allowing) access to their **identifier** before and after recommendations per app. Overall, after recommendations the percentage protected goes up for most apps since a large fraction of them have a protect recommendation for identifier.

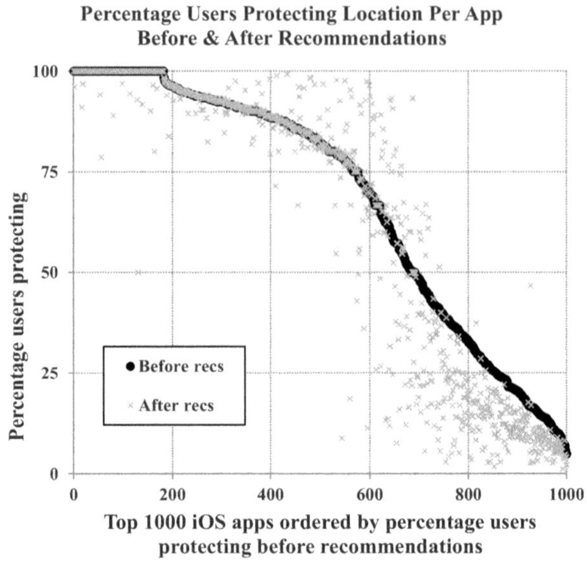

Figure 7: Percentage of users protecting (or allowing) access to their **location** before and after recommendations per app. As expected, the percentage protected goes up for apps with a protect recommendations and goes down for apps with an allow recommendation.

fore seeing recommendations) across all their apps and for accesses to either of the private data items, for example, identity or location. The users that make less than 10 decisions (18,757) are those who may have installed PMP and subsequently uninstall it after use, or users who turned contribute off so that we do not get their decisions. However, as can be observed from the table, an average user of PMP makes over 66 decisions, while a large number of our user population makes 10 to 100 (44,260 users) and 100 to 363 (16,729 users) decisions. Table 2 shows the benefit of allowing users to contribute their protection decisions, and their willingness to do so, since it is that drives our ability to provide recommendations.

6.4 Recommendation Feature

In the previous section we showed that many of our users manually make decisions to protect and allow individual apps access to privacy features using the PMP UI on their device. However, not all users necessarily want to make these individual decisions for each app they have installed. Furthermore, in some cases, users may not be convinced whether certain apps *should* have access to their private data, and whether that private data is essential for the app's functionality. We implemented our crowd sourced recommendations engine especially for these users and we next evaluate its effectiveness.

In order to observe the effect of our recommendations on the protection settings of apps, we considered the 1000 most popular apps which access the identifier including only those apps for which we have recommendations. Our intuition was that if our recommendations were having their desired effect, the number of users protecting their identifier for an app should increase if we recommend protecting, and correspondingly decrease if we recommend allowing. To validate this hypothesis, Figure 6 plots the percentage of users protecting access to the identifier before and after receiving recommendations for the top 1000 apps. For ease of understanding, we sorted the apps in decreasing order of the percentage of users that were protecting access before recommendations were available. As can be observed from Figure 6, for most of the apps the percentage of users protecting (or allowing) access to their identifier does indeed follow the recommendations. The percentage protected for apps with a recommend protect increases, while the percentage protected for apps with a recommend allow decreases after recommendations. There are few cases where this does not happen, for example, if the app has a sudden increase in the number of users who make manual decisions against the recommendations. We note that the next time the recommendations are generated those particular apps will likely see a change in their recommended settings. Figure 7 shows a similar plot for location before and after recommendations are available. We did not include plots for contacts or music in the interest of space.

Total Number of Apps (With at least 5 users)	52,386
Total Apps with Recommendations Available	36,442
Top 10K apps with Recommendations Available	9,709
Top 1K apps with Recommendations Available	966
Total Recommendations Shown to Users	1,935,213
Total Recommendations Accepted by Users	1,297,614
Percent Apps with Rec. Available	69.6%
Percent Top 10K Apps with Rec. Available	97.1%
Percent Top 1K Apps with Rec. Available	96.6%
Percent User Acceptance of Rec. Shown	67.1%

Table 3: Summarizing the effectiveness of our recommendation feature. Over 67% of almost two million recommendations offered to our users are accepted by them. We can also recommend protection settings for 97.1% of the 10,000 most popular apps.

	General	Expert	Matching Recs.
Apps with Recs. for Identity	85.0%	85.4%	74.2%
Apps with Recs. for Location	24.9%	25.2%	90.9%
Apps with Recs. for Contacts	9.7%	10.1%	86.1%
Apps with Recs. for Music	2.9%	2.9%	89.6%

Table 4: Comparing **General** and **Expert** recommendations. Overall, the recommendations are similar with 74.2% - 90.9% of the app recommendations matching for different features.

Next, we evaluate the overall efficacy of our recommendation feature by looking at the number of recommendations available and the overall acceptance of those recommendations by our users. Table 3 provides a summary of the recommendation feature based on data collected for V2 of our PMP app (all data before Nov 3rd, 2012). As can be observed, PMP can provide recommendations for 69.6% of the apps with at least 10 users, 97.1% of the top 10K Apps, and 96.6% of the top 1K most popular apps. As we gather more data for less popular apps (less than 10 users) we will be able to provide more recommendations. Furthermore, as can be seen from the table, the acceptance rate of all recommendations (almost two Million) shown to our users is 67.1% giving us confidence that the feature is indeed successful and liked by our users. Finally, we observe that over 99% of our users do have the recommendation feature turned on, denoting that they are indeed interested in receiving recommendations and find them useful.

6.4.1 *General and Expert Recommendations*

As described in Section 5.3.1 earlier, we generate an expert set of recommendations based on the data from the top 1% of our users in terms of the number of decisions and the number of apps they make decisions for. On December 3rd, 2012 we released V3 of our PMP App that uses these expert recommendations in addition to the general recommendations. Half of the users who have upgraded to this version of our app are shown general recommendations while the others are shown the expert recommendations. In addition, when users do not accept PMP recommendations we briefly asked them to select the reason for doing so. The goal of collecting this information was to identify *why* users reject recommendations coming from the crowd.

Table 4 shows a comparison of the general and expert recommendations. The first column shows the percentage of apps that have recommendations for protecting (or allowing) identity, location, contacts or music based on the general recommendations. Similarly, the second column shows the same values for the expert recommendations. The third column shows the actual overlap, or matching recommendations, for the applications for each feature. As can be observed from the table, a large fraction of the recommendations indeed match (74.2% to 89.6%) across the two sets of recommendations.

While our users do accept a majority of recommendations (67.1%), a natural question is why they don't accept the rest of the recommendations. Another related question is whether expert recommendations are accepted more than the general recommendations. As mentioned earlier, in the current version of PMP (V3), we show half of our users general recommendations while the other half are shown the expert recommendations. Furthermore, we asked the users to

	General	Expert
Accept Recommendations	75%	73.8%
Reject Recommendations	25%	26.2%
Total	100%	100%
− > Reason: Recommendation incorrect	2.9%	3.2%
− > Reason: Prefer manual choice	7%	7.2%
− > Reason: Prefer to respond on access	1%	1.4%
− > Reason: Other / Don't say	14%	14.6%

Table 5: User responses for general and expert recommendations. Both recommendations are accepted around 75% of the time. 2.9% of the time users reject recommendations since they are incorrect, while 7% of the time it looks like they view the recommendations although still make manual decisions.

	Everyone	Non-Experts	Experts
Very Low - Low	11 (0.6%)	10 (0.6%)	1 (0.7%)
Low - Neutral	63 (3.7%)	60 (3.8%)	3 (2%)
Neutral	867 (50.4%)	798 (50.8%)	69 (46%)
Neutral to high	340 (19.8%)	313 (19.9%)	27 (18%)
High - Very High	440 (25.6%)	390 (24.8%)	50 (33.3%)
Total	1721 (100%)	1571 (100%)	150 (100%)

Table 6: User Responses to the question about iOS expertise on a scale of -10 to 10, 0 being neutral (or no response).

	Everyone	Non-Experts	Experts
Very Low - Low	5 (0.2%)	4 (0.2%)	1 (0.7%)
Low - Neutral	23 (1.1%)	23 (1.2%)	0 (0%)
Neutral	973 (46.3%)	911 (46.7%)	62 (41.3%)
Neutral - High	354 (16.9%)	325 (16.7%)	29 (19.3%)
High to Very High	745 (35.5%)	687 (35.2%)	58 (38.7%)
Total	2100 (100%)	1950 (100%)	150 (100%)

Table 7: User Responses to the question about their privacy consciousness on a scale of -10 to 10, 0 being neutral (or no response).

provide some context about why they reject a recommendation, also allowing them to click "Other Reason/Skip" if they did not want to give a reason. Table 5 provides a breakdown of the 10,000 or so recommendations that have been shown in the current version of the PMP app over over week of Dec 3rd - Dec 10th, 2012. As we can see, users receiving either set of recommendations are as likely to accept them (75%). Our users reject around 3% of the recommendations since they do not match what they want, showing that our recommendations are most likely correct. Finally, around 7% of our users marked that they prefer to make manual decisions, although since they have the recommendation feature turned on, they do view the recommendations. We believe that these users are in fact influenced by our recommendations but like to have manual control over their settings.

To perform a deeper analysis of the responses collected from our users, in the latest version of our app we also asked our users to rate themselves on a scale of -10 (Very Low) to 10 (Very High) on their iOS expertise and also their privacy consciousness. We allowed them to be neutral, or give no response, by entering zero on both the questions. We then split the responses into those that came from our top-1% experts and those that came from the set of non-experts to see whether there was an bias or a clear observable trends in how users rated themselves. Table 6 reports the responses for the iOS expertise question while Table 7 reports it for the privacy question. There are several interesting observations from these responses. First, our data shows that consistent with the popular belief, jailbreakers are indeed more privacy conscious and rate themselves high on level of iOS expertise. Second, many of the users who we do not rate in our 1% expert group still rate themselves high on both the survey questions. Therefore, relying on self-reporting for the choice of experts to drive our recommendation system is not optimal. We believe our mechanism of choosing these experts based on their contributed decisions work very well in practice.

6.5 Application Case Study: Flixster

When we released PMP, we noticed that several popular apps were being detected and reported for accessing private data. One of those is Flixster, a popular app that provides users reviews and recommendations for movies. Within a few weeks we had the developers of Flixster contact us that their users complained that PMP flagged their app as accessing their address book. The developers claimed that they did not access the address book, as verified by an internal code review. They claimed that their app was being incorrectly flagged by PMP and that we should immediately fix the problem. We performed a detailed analysis of Flixster version 5.2 on our end, using tools such as an intermediate web proxy and TCPDump to observe the data transmitted. Based on these forensics, we determined that it was a 3rd party ad library that iterated over all the contacts in the user's address book and sent back privacy sensitive information about the user such as the contacts, location and various pieces of demographic information such as education, age, gender, zip code and race. After we provided feedback to Flixster about our findings, we did not hear back from them, however, an updated version 5.3 of the app uses a different ad library that no longer invades privacy in this way.

7. DISCUSSION

In this paper we chose to generate recommendations based on either the privacy decisions of all our users or those made only by experts that we identified from our dataset. Another alternative to generating recommendations is to personalize them somewhat by segmenting users into different categories based on their privacy preferences. These preferences could be captured based on their past privacy decisions or based on survey questions. ProtectMyPrivacy could in that case provide a different set of recommendations for users that are more paranoid about their privacy as opposed to those that are less concerned. We plan to explore different strategies of generating personalized recommendations as part of our future work, however we note that its not yet clear whether they will have higher acceptance than our current strategy of considering all the decisions together.

A natural question about ProtectMyPrivacy is its utility to the general, non-jailbroken, users of iOS. Ideally, we would have liked to develop PMP in a way such that it could be released in the App Store. However, this is not possible without working closely with Apple themselves since some of the extensions we have made to the OS, e.g. hooking method calls that access private data, are not allowed under the App Store guidelines. Therefore, in September 2012 we developed a 'lite' version of PMP that provided non-jailbroken users an audit of their apps, and alert them if particular apps were known to access any private data items as well as display our recommendations for those apps. We designed PMP Lite to simply query our database and while it was not be able to protect users by substituting fake data, it could still help non-jailbroken users make decisions about which apps to use, and ones to avoid. Furthermore, users could even leverage our crowd sourced recommendations to make more informed privacy choices using the additional privacy controls introduced in iOS 6 (released Oct 2012) for contacts and location. We submitted PMP Lite to the App Store for review, and after several weeks of waiting we received a phone call from the Apple App review team that our PMP Lite application would not be accepted. After filing a formal request for the reason for rejection, we received another phone call from Apple which essentially said that no form of our app would be accepted since the review team had trouble with the "basic concept of your privacy app". This experience underscores the benefit of doing our research project on jailbroken users first.

We do believe that regular users of iOS can indeed benefit from knowing which apps are known to access privacy protected data, and whether other users of the app think those accesses are warranted. In the near term we are looking to implement a HTML5 based web application that can be accessed on any iOS device using a web browser. Users can then enter the name of any application that they are interested in and view its privacy summary based on crowd-sourced data from users of PMP.

8. CONCLUSION

In this paper we show that access to privacy sensitive information such as the unique identifier, or user location or even the address book is commonplace in iOS apps. We then present PMP, a privacy protecting architecture for iOS that not only notifies users of access to this sensitive information by individual apps, but also provides a mechanism to allow such accesses or deny them by substituting anonymized shadow data in its place. Next, PMP allows users to contribute their privacy decisions, based on which we have developed a novel recommendation feature to suggest protection settings to other users of the same apps. Our data shows that within a period of just nine months our community of users has grown to 90,621 people and they have contributed their protection decisions for 225,685 unique apps. Our analysis on our collected data shows several interesting findings. We observe that 48.4% of the total applications access the identifier, 13.2% access location, 6.2% access contacts and 1.6% access the music library. Next we find that a large number of our users actively make privacy decisions: 44,260 users make 10-100 decisions while 16,729 users make 100-363 decisions. We show that we can make recommendations for over 97.1% of the most popular (Top 10,000) apps, and over 69.6% of all apps with at least five users. Finally, we report that 67.1% of all recommendations given to users of our system were accepted by them. Our data also shows that as few as 1% of our users, classified as experts, make enough decisions to drive our crowd-sourced privacy recommendation engine. We believe that our data clearly points to the value and feasibility of using crowd sourcing as a method to help smartphone users make privacy decisions.

9. ACKNOWLEDGEMENTS

We would like to thank Barry Brown, and Sivasankar Radhakrishnan, Panagiotis Vekris and Thomas Weng, for their comments on the early version of this paper. We would also like to thank our shepherd and our anonymous reviewers for their comments to help improve the paper. This work was supported in part by NSF grant SHF-1018632.

10. REFERENCES

[1] D. Barrera, H. Kayacik, P. van Oorschot, and A. Somayaji. A Methodology for Empirical Analysis of Permission-based Security Models and its Application to Android. In *Proceedings of the 17th ACM Conference on Computer and Communications Security (CCS)*, pages 73–84. ACM, 2010.

[2] M. Bellare, T. Ristenpart, P. Rogaway, and T. Stegers. Format-preserving Encryption. In *Selected Areas in Cryptography*, pages 295–312. Springer, 2009.

[3] A. R. Beresford, A. Rice, N. Skehin, and R. Sohan. MockDroid: Trading Privacy for Application Functionality on Smartphones. In *Proceedings of the 12th Workshop on Mobile Computing Systems and Applications (HotMobile)*, 2011.

[4] M. Böhmer, B. Hecht, J. Schöning, A. Krüger, and G. Gernot Bauer. Falling Asleep with Angry Birds, Facebook and Kindle: A Large Scale Study on Mobile Application Usage. In *Proceedings of the International Conference on Human Computer Interaction with Mobile Devices and Services (MobileHCI)*, 2011.

[5] A. Chaudhuri. Language-based Security on Android. In *Proceedings of the ACM SIGPLAN fourth workshop on Programming Languages and Analysis for Security (PLAS)*, pages 1–7. ACM, 2009.

[6] M. Egele, C. Kruegely, E. Kirdaz, and G. Vigna. PiOS: Detecting Privacy Leaks in iOS Applications. In *Proceedings of the Network and Distributed System Security Symposium(NDSS)*, 2011.

[7] W. Enck, P. Gilbert, B.-G. Chun, L. P. Cox, J. Jung, P. McDaniel, and A. Sheth. TaintDroid: An Information-Flow Tracking System for Realtime Privacy Monitoring on Smartphones. In *Proceedings of the 9th USENIX conference on Operating Systems Design and Implementation (OSDI)*, 2010.

[8] W. Enck, D. Octeau, P. McDaniel, and S. Chaudhuri. A Study of Android Application Security. In *Proceedings of the 20th USENIX Security Symposium*, 2011.

[9] W. Enck, M. Ongtang, and P. McDaniel. On Lightweight Mobile Phone Application Certification. In *Proceedings of the 16th ACM conference on Computer and Communications Security (CCS)*, 2009.

[10] A. Felt, E. Chin, S. Hanna, D. Song, and D. Wagner. Android Permissions Demystified. In *Proceedings of the 18th ACM conference on Computer and communications security*, pages 627–638. ACM, 2011.

[11] A. Felt, E. Ha, S. Egelman, A. Haney, E. Chin, and D. Wagner. Android Permissions: User Attention, Comprehension, and Behavior. Technical report, University of California, Berkeley, 2012.

[12] J. Freeman. Mobile Substrate. `http://iphonedevwiki.net/index.php/MobileSubstrate`.

[13] A. P. Fuchs, A. Chaudhuri, and J. S. Foster. SCanDroid: Automated security certification of Android applications. *Manuscript, Univ. of Maryland, http://www.cs.umd.edu/~avik/projects/scandroidascaa*, 2009.

[14] P. Hornyack, S. Han, J. Jung, S. Schechter, and D. Wetherall. These Aren't the Droids you're Looking For: Retrofitting Android to Protect Data from Imperious Applications. In *Proceedings of the 18th ACM conference on Computer and Communications Security (CCS)*, pages 639–652. ACM, 2011.

[15] Ian Shapira, The Washington Post. Once the Hobby of Tech Geeks, iPhone Jailbreaking now a Lucrative Industry, 2011.

[16] J. Jeon, K. Micinski, J. Vaughan, N. Reddy, Y. Zhu, J. Foster, and T. Millstein. Dr. Android and Mr. Hide: Fine-grained Security Policies on Unmodified Android. Technical report, University of Maryland, 2011.

[17] J. Lin, S. Amini, J. Hong, N. Sadeh, J. Lindqvist, and J. Zhang. Expectation and Purpose: Understanding Users Mental Models of Mobile App Privacy Through Crowdsourcing. In *Proceedings of the 14th ACM International Conference on Ubiquitous Computing (Ubicomp)*, 2012.

[18] W. Mackay. Patterns of Sharing Customizable Software. In *Proceedings of the 1990 ACM conference on Computer-supported cooperative work*, pages 209–221. ACM, 1990.

[19] MobiStealth. `http://www.mobistealth.com/`.

[20] M. Nauman, S. Khan, and X. Zhang. Apex: Extending Android Permission Model and Enforcement with User-defined Runtime Constraints. In *Proceedings of the 5th ACM Symposium on Information, Computer and Communications Security (CCS)*, pages 328–332. ACM, 2010.

[21] Protect My Privacy (PmP). iOS Privacy App. `http://www.protectmyprivacy.org`.

[22] N. Seriot. iPhone Privacy. In *Black Hat DC*, 2010.

[23] E. Smith. iPhone Applications & Privacy Issues: An Analysis of Application Transmission of iPhone Unique Device Identifiers (UDIDs). Technical report, Technical Report, 2010.

[24] The Next Web. Popular Jailbreak Software Cydia hits 14m Monthly Users on iOS 6, 23m on All Devices, March 2013.

[25] S. Thurm and Y. Kane. The Journal's Cellphone Testing Methodology. *The Wall Street Journal*, 2010.

[26] S. Thurm and Y. Kane. Your Apps Are Watching You. *The Wall Street Journal*, 2010.

[27] N. Y. Times. Mobile Apps Take Data Without Permission. http://bits.blogs.nytimes.com/2012/02/15/google-and-mobile-apps-take-data-books-without-permission/.

[28] M. T. Vennon. Android Malware: Spyware in the Android Market. Technical report, SMobile Systems, 2010.

[29] T. Vennon. Android Malware. A Study of Known and Potential Malware Threats. Technical report, SMobile Global Threat Center, 2010.

[30] XEUDOXUS. Privacy Blocker and Inspector. `http://privacytools.xeudoxus.com/`.

[31] Y. Zhou, X. Zhang, X. Jiang, and V. W. Freeh. Taming Information-Stealing Smartphone Applications (on Android). *Trust and Trustworthy Computing (TRUST)*, pages 93–107, 2011.

SmartAds: Bringing Contextual Ads to Mobile Apps

Suman Nath
Microsoft Research
sumann@microsoft.com

Felix Xiaozhu Lin*
Rice University
xzl@rice.edu

Lenin Ravindranath
Microsoft Research
lenin@csail.mit.edu

Jitendra Padhye
Microsoft Research
padhye@microsoft.com

ABSTRACT

A recent study showed that while US consumers spent 30% more time on mobile apps than on traditional web, advertisers spent 1600% less money on mobile ads. One key reason is that unlike most web ad providers, today's mobile ads are not *contextual*—they do not take into account the content of the page they are displayed on. Thus, most mobile ads are irrelevant to what the user is interested in. For example, it is not uncommon to see gambling ads being displayed in a Bible app. This irrelevance results in low clickthrough rates, and hence advertisers shy away from the mobile platform.

Using data from top 1200 apps in Windows Phone marketplace, and a one-week trace of ad keywords from Microsoft's ad network, we show that content displayed by mobile apps is a potential goldmine of keywords that advertisers are interested in.

However, unlike web pages, which can be crawled and indexed offline for contextual advertising, content shown on mobile apps is often either generated dynamically, or is embedded in the apps themselves; and hence cannot be crawled. The only solution is to scrape the content at runtime, extract keywords and fetch contextually relevant ads. The challenge is to do this without excessive overhead and without violating user privacy. In this paper, we describe a system called SmartAds to address this challenge.

We have built a prototype of SmartAds for Windows Phone apps. In a large user study with over 5000 ad impressions, we found that SmartAds nearly doubles the relevance score, while consuming minimal additional resources and preserving user privacy.

Categories and Subject Descriptors

H.4 [**Information Systems Applications**]: Communications Applications

*Work done while at Microsoft Research.

General Terms

Design, Experimentation, Performance

Keywords

Mobile, Apps, Contextual, Advertisements

1. INTRODUCTION

Recently, an interesting study pointed out that advertising market shares of dominant media such as TV, radio, and Web are proportional to the average number of minutes consumers spend on the media per day [13].

The mobile market is one prominent exception to this rule. In 2011, US consumers spent 1.3× more time within mobile apps alone than on the Web (through desktop or mobile browsers). In 2012, the gap was 1.8× and it is expected to grow in coming years. However, the mobile advertising market today is very small compared to TV, radio, and Web advertising. In 2011, advertisers spent less than 1% of their overall advertising budget for mobile advertising; in contrast, they spent 16% for Web advertising [13].

This striking gap between the opportunity and the reality of mobile advertising has been particularly damaging for companies such as Facebook and Google that derive bulk of their revenues from ads and whose services can be accessed from mobile apps as well. It also impacts amateur app developers, many of whom rely solely on advertising revenue from ads shown in their apps.

One key reason behind this gap is that unlike traditional web ads, *today's mobile ads are mostly irrelevant.* The screen capture in the left of Figure 1 starkly illustrates this. With such irrelevant ads being shown, today's mobile advertising is justly derided as taking a "spray and pray" [25] approach. It should come as no surprise that this approach does not yield expected revenue. In order to fully exploit the potential of mobile advertising, we must strive to show more relevant ads to the consumers.

For traditional web, the relevancy problem is addressed in part, by *contextual advertising*[1], wherein the ads displayed on the page are based on the content of the page. For example, when a user visits an astronomy blog, the contextual advertising network shows him an ad on a telescope. Contextual advertising was pioneered by Google AdSense [3].

[1]Contextual advertising is different from *context-aware advertising* where ads are shown depending on the user's physical context such as location. These two can be combined, but in this paper we focus on contextual advertising only.

The crucial fact that enables contextual advertising is that web pages can be crawled by a bot and indexed offline. We will describe this process in more detail in §2.

Can we use the same approach to deliver relevant ads within mobile apps? Unfortunately, this is not straightforward. The fundamental reason is that *unlike a web page, the content shown by a mobile app cannot be easily crawled and indexed.* For example, certain news outlets provide mobile-only content, which is not available via standard web interface. Other content is embedded within the mobile app itself (e.g. large collections of reference material). This makes it difficult, if not impossible, to show contextual ads in mobile apps. We will describe this in more detail in §2.

Some adhoc solutions for providing contextual mobile ads have been tried. For example, some ad systems try to glean contextual information from app metadata such as the name of the app and the category. We will discuss these solutions in more detail later in the paper. However, our study (§3) of over 1200 top apps from Windows Phone marketplace unambiguously shows that these adhoc measures are not sufficient.

What is needed is a system that can extract ad keywords from content displayed by mobile apps at runtime, and fetch relevant ads based on those keywords. Furthermore, this task must be accomplished with minimal overhead (memory, network bandwidth etc.) and without violating user's privacy.

To fulfill this need, we have built SmartAds. SmartAds dynamically scrapes page contents as a user uses an app, extracts relevant ad keywords and fetches and displays relevant ads. SmartAds architecture (§4) strikes the right balance between utility (how relevant ads are), efficiency (memory, network, battery and computation overhead), and user privacy. SmartAds achieves this with a novel client-server based keyword extraction technique, with various systems parameters carefully chosen based on a 1-week long trace of bidding keywords on Microsoft's ad network.

SmartAds consists of a client library that the developer includes in the app, and a server that the library communicates with. At runtime, the client and the server work together to extract keywords from the content being seen by the user. The server then fetches relevant ads from a third-party ad provider and sends it to the client library. The client library is responsible for displaying the ad.

SmartAds currently focuses on contextual advertising only. We note that there are various other techniques for delivering relevant ads. For example, physical context-aware advertising (such as AdNext [19] and CAMEO [18]) delivers ads based on users' locations, activities, and other physical contexts. Behavioral targeting [33] (such as Yahoo! Smart Ads [31]) delivers ads to targeted users based on information collected on each individual user's past web usage history. Contextual targeting of SmartAds is complimentary to, and can be combined with, these other types of targeting. Relative effectiveness of specific targeting techniques and their combinations within mobile apps are topics of future research.

We have built a prototype of the SmartAds system for Windows Phone apps. Using this prototype, and a large-scale user study, we show (§5) that SmartAds more than doubles the relevance score of mobile advertisements. We also show that the user privacy is not violated, and the resource overhead is minimal. An example of a *relevant* ad fetched by SmartAds is shown in Figure 1 (right).

Figure 1: Left: Irrelevant mobile ad. The mobile app shows a list of nearby restaurants, while the ad (the box at the bottom) is about real estate agents. Right: Relevant mobile ad about restaurant coupons delivered by SmartAds.

In summary, this paper makes the following two contributions. First, using data culled from 1200 top Windows Phone apps, we demonstrate the need for a online, contextual mobile advertising system. We believe that this is the first study of its kind. Second, we design, build and evaluate SmartAds, a contextual mobile advertising system that strikes the right balance between utility, efficiency and privacy. To best of our knowledge, this is the first such system.

The rest of the paper is organized as follows. We survey the state of the art in web contextual advertising in Section 2. In Section 3, we characterize contents of mobile apps based on data culled from 1200 top Windows Phone apps. We describe SmartAds design and implementation in Section 4 and evaluate it in Section 5. We discuss various extensions of SmartAds in Section 6, discuss related work in Section 7, and conclude in Section 8.

2. BACKGROUND

In this section, we discuss the state of the art in web contextual advertising, and contrast it with the state of the art in mobile advertising.

2.1 Contextual Advertising

Contextual advertising is a form of targeted advertising for ads displayed on websites or other media, such as content displayed in mobile devices. The ads themselves are selected and served by automated systems based on the content displayed to the user. For example, if a user visits an astronomy blog and sees an ad on a telescope, that's contextual advertising.

We stress that the web advertising community uses the word `context` *in a narrow sense.* In the ad community, *context* typically implies only the content displayed on the page. The ad providers typically take many signals (e.g. location, prior history) besides the page content into account while selecting the ad, but the term *contextual advertising* refers specifically to the idea of taking page content into account.

Contextual advertising for the web was pioneered by Google AdSense [3]. Many other ad providers such as Yahoo! Publisher Network [32], Microsoft AdCenter [21] and Advertising.com [4] followed in Google's footsteps. These advertising networks typically work by providing webmasters with JavaScript code that, when inserted into web pages, displays relevant ads from the ad network's ad inventory. The core task of matching ads to web pages consists of the following steps.

Offline ad labeling. Ads in ad network's inventory are labeled with keywords, called *bidding keywords*, which are provided by advertisers.

Offline keyword extraction. Ad network employs a bot (e.g., Google's MediaBot) that crawls web pages and uses machine learning algorithms (such as KEX [34]) to extract prominent keywords and concepts in them. Note that the bot can parse dynamically rendered web pages as well, as long as it does not require human input, such as solving Captchas.

Online web page to ad matching. When a user visits a website, the ad network selects an available ad whose bidding keywords best match the keywords/concepts in the web page.

Contextual advertising has been very successful on the web. Because the ads are more targeted, users are more likely to click on them, thus generating revenue for the owner of the website and the ad network.

2.2 Mobile Ads

Many mobile app developers use mobile advertisements within their apps as their only source of revenue. More than 50% of the apps in the major mobile app stores show ads [14].

To embed ads in an app, the app developer typically registers with a third-party mobile ad network such as AdMob [1], iAd [16], Microsoft Mobile Advertising [24] etc. The ad networks supply the developer with an ad control (i.e. library with some visual elements embedded within). The developer includes this ad control in his app, and assigns it some screen "real estate". When the app runs, the ad control is loaded, and it fetches ads from the ad network and displays it to the user.

Different ad networks use different signals to serve relevant ads. One of the main signals that mobile ad networks use today is the app metadata [24]. As part of the registration process, most ad networks ask the developer to provide metadata information about the app (for e.g. category of the app, link to the app store description etc.). This allows the ad network to serve ads related to the app metadata.

Ad networks also receive dynamic signals sent by the ad control every time it fetches a new ad. Depending on the privacy policies and the security architecture of the platform, these signals can include the location, user identity, etc. Note that unlike JavaScript embedded in the browsers, the ad controls are integral parts of the application, and have access to the all the APIs provided by the platform.

Our focus in this paper is contextual advertising, where the signal is the content of the app page that the user is viewing. We are not aware of any ad control that provides such contextual advertising for mobile apps.

This is because building contextual advertising systems for mobile apps is quite challenging. Unlike web pages, content displayed by mobile apps cannot be crawled and indexed by a bot in an offline manner, and hence existing contextual ad systems cannot perform the offline keyword extraction phase mentioned before. While some mobile apps fetch web content that is crawlable by bots (e.g. apps that fetch and display Wikipedia content), the apps often transform this content in a variety of ways, sometimes combining content from multiple sources.

For example, a news aggregator app, such as `News 360`, uses web API to pull news items from several web services and displays it. Many of these web services do not have any traditional web front-end that a web bot can discover and crawl. Furthermore, the content fetched from the web is modified before being shown to the user. Other apps have sizable amounts of content embedded in them (e.g. reference data or large religious texts).

Thus, the only surefire way of providing contextual ads to a mobile app is to parse the content in an online manner (i.e. as it is displayed), and to extract keywords. However, this is a challenging task for two reasons. First, the mobile platform has limited resources. Dynamically scraping the displayed content, extracting keywords and sending it through the network, without incurring unacceptable overhead is a non-trivial task. Second, sending the content of the page to the ad network can seriously compromise user privacy.

Note that our goal is related to recently proposed techniques for "just-in-time" contextual advertising in dynamic web pages [5, 20]. These techniques aim to deliver relevant ads to dynamic web pages based on useful signals extracted from them during runtime. In general, these techniques rely on various properties of web pages and are not directly applicable for mobile apps. For example, [5] uses page URL as well as referrer URL, which do not exist for mobile apps. It also sends short excerpts of the page to backend server, and hence violates privacy. [20] uses previously recorded traffic to the page that, again, does not generally exist for mobile apps. We therefore seek for alternative techniques that work for mobile apps.

We have built SmartAds to address the aforementioned challenges for mobile apps. Before we explain the design of SmartAds, we first characterize the content of existing mobile apps to motivate the need to deliver ads based on the app page content.

3. CHARACTERIZATION OF MOBILE APPS

Like websites, mobile apps typically display content in different screens (*App Pages*) that users can navigate between. In most platforms, only one app page is displayed to user at a time. Each of these app pages can contain different set of UI controls displaying different content. We will call the content displayed by an app page as *Page Data*. In Figure 1, page data consists of a list of restaurant names and their addresses.

An online system to extract keywords from page data is needed only if a significant fraction of mobile apps possess the following three characteristics.

First, the page data displayed by the app should be a rich source of ad keywords. If it turns out that most apps display content that do not contain keywords that advertisers bid on, there is no need for our system.

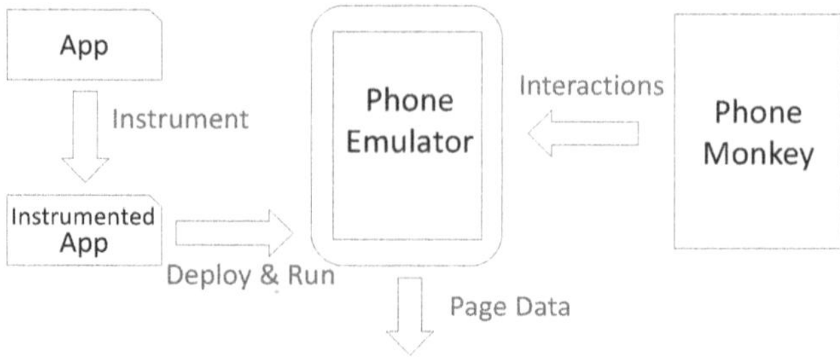

Figure 2: Schematics of page data logging

Second, the page data should provide significantly more keywords than the metadata about the app. As we described in §2.2, many ad providers today take metadata into account while selecting ads to display. Page data needs to do substantially better.

Third, the page data should change significantly over a period of time - i.e. between different invocations of the same app. Otherwise, one could build a system that runs the app in an emulator and extract the keywords (essentially, an offline system).

Consider, for example, the `Around Me` app that allows a user to search for local business around his location. If a user uses the app for finding local restaurants, he should be shown restaurant related ads (based on extracted keyword `restaurant`), but if he uses it for searching for nearby parking lots, he should be shown parking related ads. In other words, as the page data can change over time and location, offline extraction is not sufficient. Another example is a news aggregator app, where the content always changes with time.

To verify whether these conditions hold true for a significant fraction of mobile apps, we collected and analyzed page data from a large number of apps from the Windows Phone marketplace, as follows.

3.1 Methodology

To capture page data from a large number of apps in a scalable manner, we developed a UI automation tool called PhoneMonkey. The PhoneMonkey can emulate various user interactions (touch, swipe etc.) to navigate through various pages of the app. To capture the page contents, we leverage the binary instrumentation framework described in [28]. We instrument the app binary to insert custom logging code that logs the contents of each page as it is rendered. We then load the instrumented app in a phone emulator (e.g., Windows Phone Emulator for running Windows Phone apps) and use the PhoneMonkey to emulate various user interactions (e.g., by clicking a button, by selecting an item in a drop-down list box, etc.). As various app pages are rendered, their contents are logged, which we retrieve for later analysis. The overall architecture is shown in Figure 2.

Apps. Our binary instrumentation framework is designed for Silverlight [27] apps, which constitute a vast majority of the apps in the Windows Phone marketplace today. We focus on top 1200 Silverlight apps in the Windows Phone marketplace that do not require username and password for an external service (e.g. the Facebook app). We run each of these 1200 app 30 times with the PhoneMonkey. In each run, the PhoneMonkey starts the app, selects a random UI navigational control (such as a button) in the current page, acts on it to navigate to the next app page, and repeats the process until it reaches a page without any UI control or until it goes outside the app (e.g., a web page). We call each run an *app session*. Each session represents a random execution path through the app. For each session we vary the location and other sensor inputs fed to the emulator.

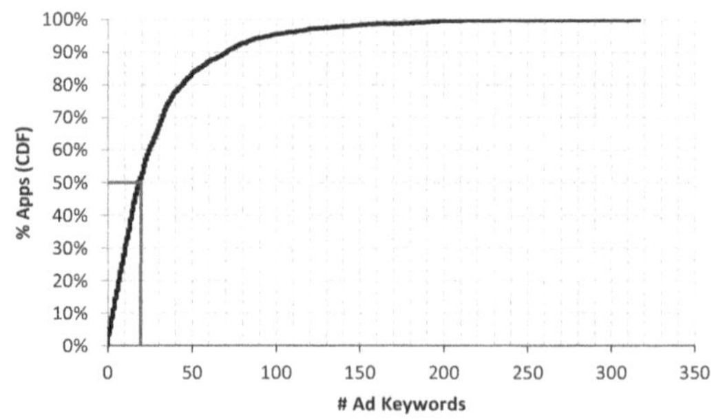

Figure 3: CDF of ad keyword counts extracted from page data. Page data of half the apps contain more than 20 ad keywords that could be targeted with contextual ads.

Keyword Extraction. Our logging instrumentation captures the complete contents of all pages rendered during each session. For advertising purpose, we need to extract a small number of keywords that are prominent in these pages. Ads for these pages will be chosen based on these keywords. Keyword extraction from a webpage is a well-studied area. We use a modified version of the well-known KEX [34] keyword extractor[2] that was originally designed for webpages. KEX uses document features (such as where in the page a word appears, whether it is bolded) and some global information (how many advertisers are interested in the word) to assign each word in the document a weight. We will discuss KEX in more detail in Section 4. For the purpose of this section we treat KEX as a blackbox. The blackbox takes in the page data and a one week trace of bidding keywords from Microsoft's advertising network collected during the first week of July 2012, and assigns each word on the page a weight between 0 and 1 that indicates how "useful" the word is as keyword to base the ad upon. For example, the words "is" and "zebra" may both get a low score: the former because it is too common, while the latter because no one is bidding on it. On the other hand, the word "pipe" may get higher weight because a number of plumbing business have bid upon it.

For the results described below, we consider all words with score higher than 0.1. Using other thresholds changes the absolute numbers, but our conclusions will still hold.

3.2 Results

Page data is a good source of ad keywords. Figure 3 shows the CDF of ad keywords extracted from page data of various apps after running each app 30 times. As shown, most apps contain a good number (> 20) of ad keywords that ad networks can exploit to select contextual ads. This

[2]For convenience, we use the term KEX to refer to [34]; authors did not use any specific name of their system.

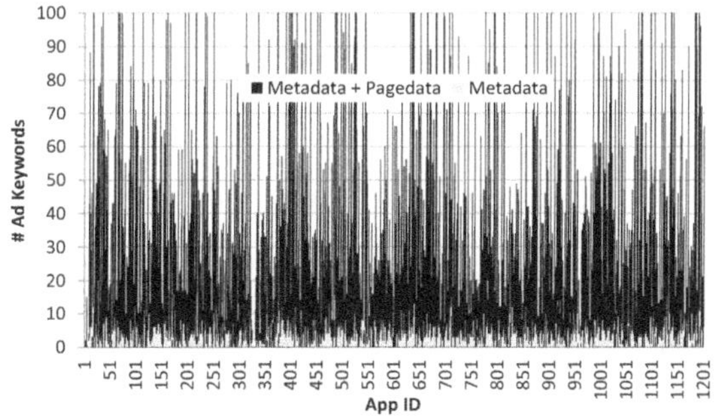

Figure 4: Number of ad keywords extracted from page data and metadata. (The y-axis, with a max value of 317, is clipped at 100 for clarity.) For most apps, page data contains more ad keywords than metadata.

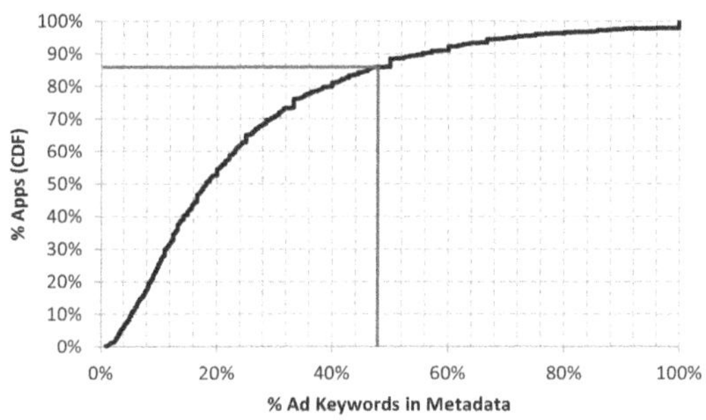

Figure 5: CDF of fraction of ad keywords extracted from app metadata alone. For $>85\%$ apps, metadata contains $<50\%$ ad keywords.

demonstrates the unique opportunity of delivering contextual ads based on page data. We stress that this result is a conservative estimate and the true potential for contextual ads based on page data is likely to be bigger. This is because the PhoneMonkey fails to explore certain execution paths of an app if they require textual inputs (such as a search query) or are behind app-specific UI control that the PhoneMonkey does not know how to interact with (such as an image acting as a button). Thus, in hands of human users, the app is likely to generate more keywords.

Page data yields more keywords than metadata. While page data may be a rich source of ad keywords, we need to show that it yields substantially more keywords than app metadata (such as the name, category and description) – today's mobile ad networks already take metadata into account.

To this end, we separately extract keywords from app metadata and from page data. Figure 4 shows the number of keywords we learn from page data and from app metadata of all 1200 apps. We see that for most apps, page data contains more ad keywords than app metadata. In Figure 5 we show CDF of what fraction of total ad keywords extracted from an app indeed come from metadata alone (i.e., if an app's metadata contains 5 keywords and its page data contains 15 additional ad keywords *that do not appear in metadata*, 25% of its ad keywords come from metadata). The graph shows

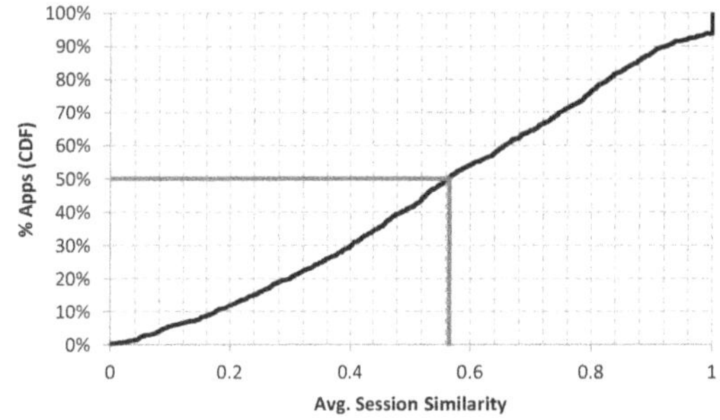

Figure 6: CDF of session similarities of apps. Half the apps have session similarity <0.55.

that more than 85% of the apps have more ad keywords in page data than in metadata. These numbers clearly show the value of extracting ad keywords from page data.

Page data is dynamic, and requires online keyword extraction. Our results so far demonstrate that extracting ad keywords from page data can be helpful in selecting contextual ads for apps. But we need to decide whether collecting this data at runtime (i.e. online) is necessary.

To understand how important online extraction is, we measure *average session similarity* of various apps. To compute session similarity of an app, we generate $n = 30$ app sessions of an app, where each session is a random execution path from the start page of the app. For each session x, we extract the set K_x of ad keywords in all pages in the session. For each pair of sessions x and y, we compute their Jackard similarity $S_{xy} = |K_x \cap K_y|/|K_x \cup K_y|$, which denotes the fraction of keywords common between x and y. Finally, we compute session similarity of the app as the average similarities of all session pairs. Note that the value of session similarity lies within the range $[0, 1]$. Intuitively, a small value of average session similarity implies that two random sessions of the app have diverse set of ad keywords and hence they should be shown different ads.

Figure 6 shows the CDF of session similarities of various apps. Median session similarity is 0.55. This means that half the apps have average session similarity less than 0.55. For these apps, each session looks significantly different from other sessions of the same app (with almost half new keywords compared to the other session). This highlights the fact that an offline keyword extraction process is unlikely to work well for all user sessions.

The above result is a conservative one. Recall that for each app we use $n = 30$ sessions, which are supposed to be random samples of execution paths in the app. For some apps, however, PhoneMonkey explores only a small number of execution paths. For those apps, many of our sampled sessions look exactly same or very similar, boosting their average session similarity values. With a better PhoneMonkey that can explore more execution paths, app sessions will exhibit even less similarities, further strengthening our argument for online keyword extraction.

Note that another important argument behind the need of online keyword extraction is that a PhoneMonkey may not be able to explore many important pages inside an app. This can happen for many reasons: e.g., if a page can be reached only after some human inputs (e.g., username/password)

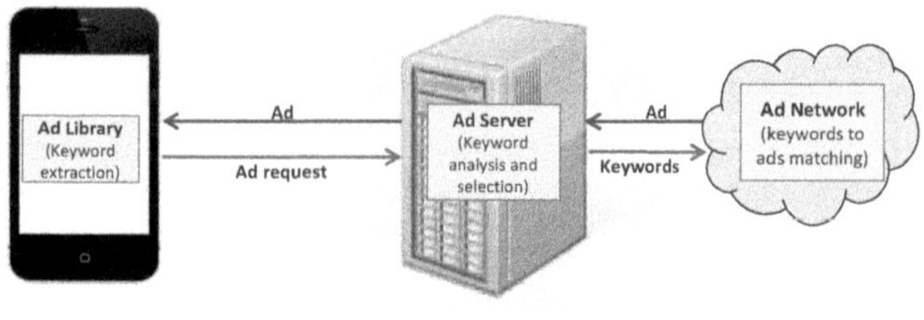

Figure 7: SmartAds Architecture

that the PhoneMonkey cannot emulate, if a page is behind a custom UI control that the PhoneMonkey does not know how to interact with, if the app contains a large number of pages and the PhoneMonkey explores only a fraction of them due to time constraints, etc. With online extraction, we can leave navigation within an app to its user, making sure that we extract keywords from the page the user is currently consuming.

3.3 Summary

The results in this section show that page data provides a rich set of ad keywords, and it is a substantially richer source of ad keywords than the app metadata. Finally, we also showed that page content of the app varies significantly between sessions, and thus, online extraction of keywords from page data is necessary.

4. SmartAds ARCHITECTURE

SmartAds consists of a client-side ad library and an ad server (Figure 7).

The developer includes the ad client within his app. When a user uses the app, the ad client periodically extracts prominent keywords from the current app page and requests an ad from the ad server. The ad server analyzes the keywords sent by the client and ranks them. It then requests an ad network for ads matching these keywords. The ad network is a third-party entity that accepts bids and ads from a variety of sources (e.g. a plumber may create an ad for his business and bid on the word "pipe"). The ad network returns any ads that it may have for the keywords sent by the ad server. The ad server selects the ad matching the highest-ranked keyword, and returns it to the client for displaying.

In this section, we focus on how the ad client and the ad server selects the best keyword to request ads from the ad network. The process that the ad network uses to pick ads that match the keywords is outside the scope of this paper. Our ad server can use any ad network that can return an ad for a given keyword.

The design of SmartAds is guided by the following concerns:

Utility. SmartAds should be able to extract keywords that are prominent on the current app page, while relevant to available mobile ads.

Efficiency. The SmartAds client should have minimal impact on memory consumption of the app, as well as on its network, CPU and energy footprint.

Privacy. SmartAds should not violate user's privacy, e.g., by sending sensitive words such as user's bank account number from an app page to the ad server.

The core functionality of SmartAds is keyword extraction. Given an app's page data, SmartAds extracts prominent keywords that describe the theme of the app page and can be matched with available ads. One might consider using existing keyword extractors, such as the well-known KEX [34], designed for extracting ad keywords from web pages. They can offer good utility, but they pose a tradeoff between efficiency and privacy depending on where the extraction is done.

Extracting keywords entirely on the client is infeasible, because good keyword extractors uses some *global* knowledge that can be too big to fit on the client's memory. For example, an important component of SmartAds's keyword extractor is a dictionary of bidding keywords and their global popularity among ads. However, the database of all keywords that advertisers are bidding on can be several hundred MBs (§4.2.2). This database needs to be in the RAM for fast lookup. Most mobile platforms limit the amount of RAM the app can consume to avoid memory pressure. For example, the Windows Phone limits apps to consume only 90MB of RAM at runtime. Android and iOS also impose a similar restriction.

Running KEX at the server is also problematic. This is because the client would have to upload the entire content and layout information of the page, to allow KEX to extract all the necessary features. This not only wastes communication bandwidth (average page size, including their layout information, is several KBs in the 1200 apps we studied), but can also compromise user privacy, since sensitive information such as a user's name or bank account number, could be sent to the server.

To address these concerns, SmartAds uses a novel keyword extraction architecture. In the rest of the section, we describe various components of the architecture and how they achieve good utility, efficiency, and privacy.

4.1 Achieving Good Utility

To extract prominent keywords from an app page, we start with KEX that has been found effective for web pages and modify it to address efficiency and privacy concern. Given a page, it produces a ranked list of keywords with scores between 0 and 1, indicating how useful each keywords is, to base the ad on.

The core of KEX is a classifier. Given a feature vector of a word W in document D, it determines the likelihood score of W being an advertising keyword. More formally, it predicts an output variable Y given a set of input features $\overline{X}$ associated with a word W. Y is 1 if W is a relevant keyword, and 0 otherwise. The classifier returns the estimated probability, $P(Y = 1|\overline{X} = \overline{x})$:

$$P(Y = 1|\overline{X} = \overline{x}) = \frac{\exp(\overline{x} \cdot \overline{w})}{1 + \exp(\overline{x} \cdot \overline{w})} \quad (1)$$

where the vector of weights is $\overline{w}$, w_i is the weight of input feature x_i.

The original KEX implementation was designed to extract keywords from web pages. We now describe how we modified it for SmartAds.

4.1.1 Local features

KEX uses many document features that are specific to web pages. We exclude features that do not apply to app pages. For example, KEX assigns higher weight to a word that appears in the HTML header. This does not apply for app pages. We retained the following KEX local features that are applicable to app pages.

- `AnywhereCount`: The total number of times the word appears in the page
- `NearBeginningCount`: The total number of times the word appears in the beginning of the page. Beginning is defined as the top 33% of the screen.
- `SentenceBeginningCount`: The number of times the word starts a sentence.
- `PhraseLengthInWord`: Number of words in the phrase.
- `PhraseLengthInChar`: Number of characters in the phrase.
- `MessageLength`: The length of the line, in characters, containing the word.
- `Capitalization`: Number of times the word is capitalized in the page. It indicates whether the word is a proper noun or an important word.
- `Font size`: Font size of the word.

In addition, app pages have features that are not found in HTML pages. For example, based on the data collected in §3, we found that the UI element (e.g. TextBox) containing user input is a good indicator of the word's importance. Thus, we needed to include the UI element containing a word to the list of document features that KEX considers in its ranking function. However, we used a somewhat ad hoc approach to determine the weights of various UI controls to be used in KEX's model: we mapped various UI controls to existing KEX features. For example, if a word appeared in a user input `TextBox`, it is considered to be `Capitalized` and `NearBeginning`.

In principle, one should train KEX's machine learning model with a large corpus of labeled page data to determine the weight of various UI elements. However, innovating on core machine learning techniques for keyword extraction is outside the scope of this paper; our aim in this paper is to build an end-to-end system for delivering contextual ads to mobile apps while striking a right balance between relevance, efficiency and privacy. We therefore leave such training as future work. Once such weights are learned from training data, they can be readily incorporated into SmartAds to further improve its relevance.

4.1.2 Global knowledge

KEX is designed to use a large English dictionary that ascribes relative importance to words, based on how common they are in the English language. For example, words such as "the" are assigned a lower weight.

In our setting, we instead use the knowledge about how often advertisers bid on a keyword. To learn this, we use a 1-week bidding keyword trace collected from Microsoft's Bing ad network during the first week of July 2012. As we show in Section 4.2.2, using a longer trace has negligible impact. Having this trace, we assign each word a weight equal to $\log(1 + frequency)$, where $frequency$ is how many times the word appears in the bidding keyword trace. This reflects the distribution of the keywords advertisers are most interested in.

Using the above local features and global knowledge, our modified KEX produces a good set of ad keywords from an app page (as is evident in our evaluation results in §5). However, an ad network can have millions of bidding keywords, making the global knowledge too large to fit in a mobile device's memory. Therefore, KEX cannot be run entirely on the client. On the other hand, running KEX entirely on the server poses network overhead and privacy concerns. We now discuss how SmartAds addresses these concerns.

4.2 Achieving Efficiency

4.2.1 Addressing memory overhead

The large memory overhead of keyword extraction comes from the large global knowledge. To avoid this overhead at the client side, we split the KEX functionality between the client and the server such that the global knowledge (and associated computation) is maintained at the server and the client does only as much as is possible without the global knowledge. Observe that the scoring function as shown in Equation 1, is based on dot products of the feature vector $\overline{x}$ and the weight vector $\overline{w}$. Dot product is *partitionable*: it can be computed partially at the client and partially at the server. Thus, we partition $\overline{x}$ into a vector of local features $\overline{x_l}$ (e.g., `AnywhereCount`) and a vector of global features $\overline{x_g}$ (e.g, global knowledge of a keyword), with weight vectors $\overline{w_l}$ and $\overline{w_g}$ respectively. For each word w in a given page, the client computes its local score $L_w = \overline{x_l} \cdot \overline{w_l}$ and sends (w, L_w) to the server.[3] The server uses the global knowledge to compute w's global score $G_w = \overline{x_g} \cdot \overline{w_g}$. Finally, the server computes the overall score of the word w as $S_w = L_w + G_w$. The score S_w is then used in Equation 1 to compute w's probability of being an advertising keyword.

4.2.2 Addressing communication overhead

Note however, that uploading all words on the page to the server is both wasteful, and can potentially violate privacy. We now describe how we tackle these problems.

Intuitively, the client does not need to send a word if it does not have any chance of being selected as one of the extracted keywords at the server. *How can the ad client locally prune unnecessary keywords?*

We exploit knowledge about the keywords that advertisers bid on to achieve such pruning. The client keeps a list of all bidding keywords and sends a word to the server only if it is one of the bidding keywords. However, there can be too many bidding keywords (typically hundreds of millions) to fit in client's memory. Moreover, merely checking bidding keywords is not sufficient; we also need to consider words that are *related* to the bidding keywords, further increasing the memory overhead. (See §6.1 on a discussion on how SmartAds gets related words).

To address this challenge, we compress the list of bidding keywords and related keywords using a *Bloom filter* [6]. A Bloom filter is a space-efficient probabilistic data structure, that can be used to test whether an element is a member of a set. False positive retrieval results are possible, but false negatives are not. The Bloom filter is constructed by the server, from its knowledge of bidding keywords, and sent to the ad client. The ad client uses the Bloom filter to check whether a candidate word is included in the list of bidding keywords or not. The client sends a word to the ad server only if it passes the Bloom filter.

[3] If the page does not contain enough ad keywords (e.g. a page with just images), we fall back to ad keywords in previous app pages in the same session or to ad keywords in app metadata. We discuss this in detail in (§6.1).

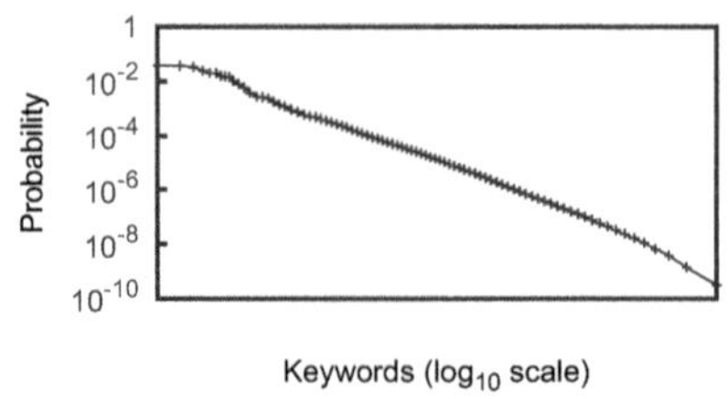

Figure 8: PDF of bidding keyword frequencies in a 1-week long Bing ad trace

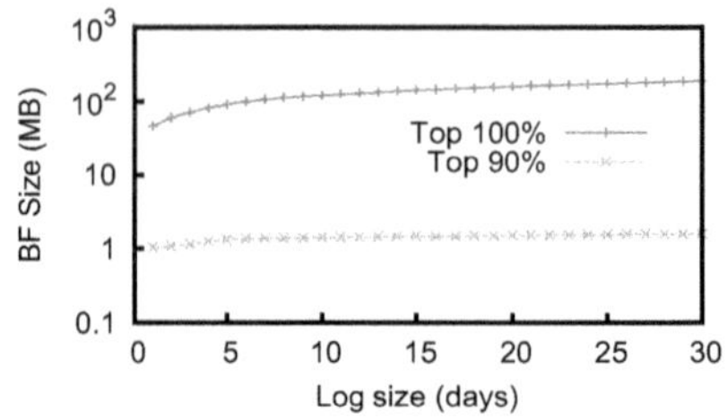

Figure 9: Bloom filter size for top x% and related keywords, for various trace length

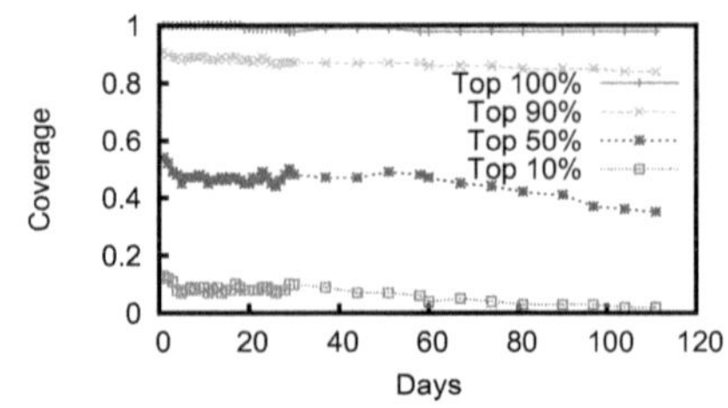

Figure 10: Coverage of top x% and related keywords from 1-week trace over time

There can be tens of millions of bidding keywords in an ad network and hence a Bloom filter can be very large if we include all bidding keywords. Therefore, we use the second optimization of including only a relatively small number of bidding keywords that cover most of ads in the ad network.

To see whether the above techniques are feasible, we need to answer two important questions: (1) what is the memory footprint of the Bloom filter? (2) how often does the Bloom filter change? We answer these questions with a 1-week trace of bidding keywords collected from Microsoft's ad network within the first week of July 2012.

Bloom filter size at the client. The size of a Bloom filter depends on the number of items and false positive rates of lookups one is willing to tolerate. Simple mathematical analysis shows that for n items and a false positive rate of p, the optimal size of a Bloom filter is $-\frac{n \ln p}{(\ln 2)^2}$ bits [8].

Ideally, we would like to use all bidding keywords. Our bidding keyword trace shows that this size can be prohibitively large to fit in a smartphone. Fortunately, there are many popular bidding keywords each of which appears in labels of a large number of ads. In particular, frequencies of bidding keywords follow a power law distribution, as shown by the pdf of bidding keywords in our one week trace in Figure 8. (The units on the x-axis are omitted as it is sensitive to Microsoft's business.) This implies that a small number of bidding keywords appear in most of the ads. More precisely, in the 1-week trace, 2.2% most frequent bidding keywords can fit in a smartphone's memory and yet cover 90% of the ads. We can therefore use this small fraction of bidding keywords and yet achieve a high coverage of ads.[4]

Figure 9 shows the size of the Bloom filter maintained at the client, for various lengths of Bing traces. The size of the Bloom filter is chosen to be optimal to bound the false positive rate to $< 1\%$. We show numbers for two cases when we consider (a) all unique keywords in the trace and (b) only the most frequent unique keywords covering 90% of the ads. As shown, the Bloom filter size is small (around 1MB) when we consider keywords covering 90% of the ads. The graph also shows that Bloom filter size is not much sensitive to how long a trace we use.

Dynamics of bidding keywords. A Bloom filter is not incrementally updatable: even though new items can be added dynamically, items cannot be deleted[5]. Therefore, if the set of bidding keywords that we use for local pruning changes dramatically, the client needs to download the entire Bloom filter from the server. For practical reasons, this should happen rarely.

To see how frequently bidding keywords change, we do the following experiments with our trace. We first build a Bloom filter with a base keyword set S_x, which consists of top keywords covering x% of the ads in a 1-week long trace. Then, on each subsequent day, we compute what fraction of ads available on that day on Microsoft's ad network are labeled with the keywords in S_x. If there are too much churns of bidding keywords, the coverage should drop down quickly. Figure 10 shows the results for various value of x. It shows that coverage is relatively stable for higher values of x. For example, starting with keywords covering $x = 90\%$ of the ads, coverage remains higher than 85% even after three months. This suggests that the Bloom filter at the client does not need to be updated very often. Bloom filter's small size and infrequent update rate make it practical to be used in our application.

4.3 Achieving Privacy

Privacy and contextual ads are at odds with each other since for the ad server to select an ad relevant to an app page, it needs to know the page content. The solution we have presented so far already provides some form of privacy: *the ad server knows only the ad keywords in the page and nothing else.* Since ad keywords are essentially popular keywords bid by advertisers, they are likely to be non-sensitive keywords. This also raises the bar of an adversarial advertiser to exploit the system: since we pick only popular bidding keywords, an adversary is unlikely to make a sensitive word into our list of popular keywords without making a large number of bids for the same keyword. Finally, the ad server makes the list of popular keywords public so that a third party can audit if the list contains any sensitive keywords.

Note that SmartAds does not guarantee absolute privacy, where no information about the client is disclosed to the server. In fact, as shown in [15], *it is impossible to guarantee such absolute privacy* in a client-server contextual ad system without sacrificing ad quality or system efficiency. The only guarantee SmartAds provides is that the ad server does not know the existence of any word in a user's app page unless the word is an ad keyword.

Even achieving this guarantee is not straightforward while using Bloom filter as it can have false positives. Therefore, the ad client may occasionally send to the ad server sensitive words (such as his SSN or a name of a disease) that appear in an app page but are not ad keywords. This can violate user's privacy.

To avoid potential privacy breach, the ad client and the

[4]We discuss in Section 6.2 how the remaining 10% ads actually get served to clients.

[5]Deletion is supported in counting Bloom filter that has more memory footprint and therefore we do not use this.

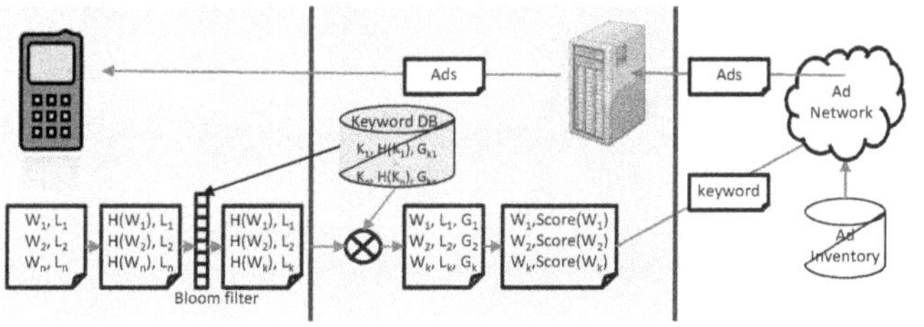

Figure 11: Keyword extraction in SmartAds

ad server use a one-way hash function and operate on hash values of all keywords instead of their plaintexts. The server builds the Bloom filter of hashvalues of all ad keywords. The client hashes all candidate keywords on the current page and sends only the hashvalues if they exist in the Bloom filter. The server maintains a dictionary of all ad keywords and their hashvalues; hence it can map a hashvalue to its plaintext only if it is an ad keyword. The server ignores all hashvalues that do not appear in its dictionary, without knowing their plaintexts. In this way, SmartAds achieves our target privacy goal that the ad server knows plaintexts of only the words that are popular ad keywords.

4.4 End-to-end workflow in SmartAds

Figure 11 shows the overall operation of the SmartAds system. It works as follows.

Offline Processing. The ad server maintains a database containing all ad keywords. For each keyword k, the database maintains k, a hashvalue $H(k)$ of k, and a global feature value G_k of K. The value G_k is used by the keyword extraction algorithm for computing overall ranking of a keyword. For our KEX-based keyword extractor, G_k is computed as $\log(1 + freq_k)$, where $freq_k$ is the number of times K is used to label any ad in the ad inventory. The database is updated as the ad inventory is updated.

Periodically (e.g., once in every three months) the server computes a Bloom filter from all the $H(k)$ values in the keyword database and sends it to mobile phone clients. The size of the Bloom filter is optimally selected based on the number of keywords in the keyword database and a target false positive rate.

Online Processing. The ad client works as follows. After an app page is loaded, it "scrapes" the current page content to generate a list of candidate keywords. Typical app pages are organized as a hierarchy of UI controls (e.g., text box, images, list box); scraping is done by traversing the hierarchy and extracting texts in all UI controls. For each scraped word W, the client module computes its hash $H(W)$ (using the same hash function the server uses to generate the keyword database) and its local feature vector L_w. If $H(W)$ passes the Bloom filter, the pair $(H(W), L_w)$ is sent to the server. If a $H(W)$ value does not appear in the server's keyword database (i.e., a false positive in the client's Bloom filter), it discards the value, without knowing the corresponding word W. Otherwise, it retrieves G_w from the keyword database and combines it with L_w to compute the overall score of the word W. Keywords with scores above a threshold are selected as extracted keywords.

Our Implementation. We have implemented SmartAds system for Windows Phone apps. The ad client is a DLL that developers can include in an app page programmatically or by dragging and dropping from Microsoft Visual Studio control toolbox. We have also implemented a tool that can insert the ad client into existing apps with binary rewriting techniques [28]. The ad server runs in Windows Azure. We use Microsoft Bing's ad network for retrieving suitable ads matching a given keyword.

5. RESULTS

In this section, we evaluate the performance of SmartAds. The most important metric for evaluating the performance of any ad selection system is the relevance of the ads shown. As shown in Figure 1, SmartAds can display a more contextually relevant ads, compared to other ad controls. Since relevance is subjective, we quantify relevance of ads shown by SmartAds via a large user study described in §5.1. The next important metric is the delay incurred in fetching and showing the ad. Users of mobile apps typically have short attention spans [12] and the best time to draw a user's attention is during or as soon as he moves from one page to another [17]. So, ads must be fetched and displayed as soon as possible after the page loads. Our results (§5.2) show that the SmartAds system is responsive and is able to fetch relevant ads quickly. Finally, in §5.3, we evaluate the impact of the ad control on the mobile phone, in terms of CPU, memory, network and battery consumption. If this overhead is excessive, app developers may not use the ad control. Our results show that the overhead is minimal.

5.1 Relevance

SmartAds dynamically retrieves ads based on the keywords extracted from the content of the app page and hence delivers ads that are contextual and more relevant. We evaluate the increase in relevance via a user study.

As a baseline for our comparison, we consider the relevance of the ads delivered by a major ad control for Windows Phone. We refer to the ad control as the *baseline ad control* and the ads shown by it as *baseline ads*. The baseline ad control uses a number of useful signals such as app metadata (e.g., app description and category in the marketplace) and user's location to choose relevant ads.Based on official documentation, other ad controls use the same or a subset of signals as the baseline ad control uses: some use location only, some use location plus metadata, etc. (No ad control for Windows Phone uses page data for choosing ads.) Therefore, we believe ads from our baseline ad control is a reasonable comparison point for our study.

The user study was based on top 353 apps from Windows Phone marketplace that used the baseline ad control. We ran these 353 apps using the PhoneMonkey (§3.1). Each app was run for 10 minutes. As the PhoneMonkey visited various pages in the application, it captured and logged the XML used to render the page. Various heuristics were used to ensure that the XML was captured only after the page was fully loaded. The contents included the ad displayed by the baseline ad control. We captured no more than 10 unique pages per app. In total, we captured a total of 2500 unique pages from the 353 apps.

Next, we removed the existing ad (provided by the baseline ad control) from these pages and ran SmartAds offline on the page content. SmartAds extracted keywords from the page and fetched suitable ads for the given keywords from the Microsoft Bing's ad network. At this point, for each page we had an ad served by the baseline ad control and by the SmartAds ad control.

Then, using this data we generated two different screenshots for each page, an original one showing the ad from the baseline ad control and the other showing the ad obtained by SmartAds. Hence, in total, we had a database of 5000 app screenshots showing ad either from baseline ad control or from SmartAds.

The user study was based on these 5000 screenshots. We created a website where users could indicate how relevant the ad in the screenshot is to the content of the screenshot. The user study website is shown in Figure 12. We provided users with three score levels[6] (i) Very relevant (ii) Somewhat relevant and (iii) Not relevant. Users were not told the source of the ad in the image. After a user labeled an image, he/she was shown another randomly selected image.

We asked users in a mailing group consisting of 400 people in our organization to visit the website and label the images. The responses were completely voluntary and anonymous. The website was accessible only from our corporate intranet.

In total, we obtained 6230 labels. Each screenshot got at least one label and a random subset of them got more than one. There were 3105 labels for baseline ads and 3125 labels for SmartAds.

The results from the user study are shown in Figure 13. When the ad was generated by SmartAds, over 75% of the ads were labeled either "Very relevant" or "Somewhat relevant". In contrast, only 41% of the ads generated by the baseline ad control were labeled "Very relevant" or "Somewhat relevant". This result clearly demonstrates the importance of using the content of the page while generating the ad.

From the results we also see that about 25% of the ads generated by SmartAds were labeled non-relevant. We investigated these pages further and found that the non-relevancy stems from two major factors. First, there are apps which display minimal text content in the screen and mostly show images or controls (for e.g. games). Second, in certain apps, the keywords on the screen does not match any bidding keyword i.e. there are no ad providers bidding for content (keyword) related to the app. In both these cases, SmartAds falls back to retrieving keywords from the metadata of the app (See §6.1) which in many cases are not relevant to the content on the screen.

Note that in practice Windows Phone ads are likely to be more relevant than our study shows. This is because Microsoft Ad Control, which is used by > 80% ad supported apps, uses behavioral and location-based targeting as well. With behavioral targeting, a user is shown ads relevant to his search history in Bing (if he is signed in to Bing by using the same Microsoft ID he uses in his Windows Phone). With location-based targeting, a user is shown ads on near-by business. We disabled these targeting in our study (i.e., we disabled phone's GPS and the PhoneMonkey did not have any Bing history) as we wanted to demonstrate benefits of using page data over metadata in choosing ads. Behavioral and location-based targeting are orthogonal to contextual targeting, and they can be combined. We leave studying the effectiveness of such combined targeting as part of our future research.

[6]We experimented with the number of levels in smaller settings, and discovered that three levels struck the right balance between useful granularity and user irritation.

Figure 12: User Study Website

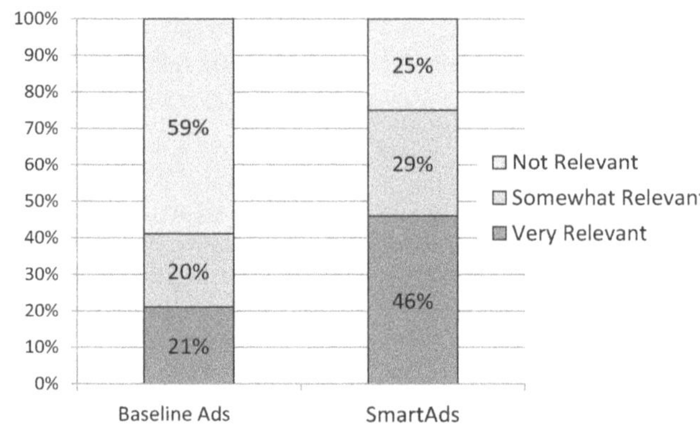

Figure 13: Ad relevance results from the user study

5.2 End-to-end performance

Mobile app users are impatient, and in many cases spend only tens of seconds on each app [12]. Moreover, the best time to draw a user's attention is during or as soon as he moves from one page to another [17]. is not fetched and displayed sufficiently quickly after a page is loaded, the user may never notice it. To characterize this end-to-end performance, we measure the time to deliver an ad starting from Page Load. This is the time that elapses between the instance the user navigates to a page, and before he sees the ad.

To measure the end-to-end performance and overhead, we inserted SmartAds client into a set of existing apps by rewriting app binaries [28]. These apps already had the baseline ad control and binary rewriting simply replaced the the ad control library with ours. We asked 5 volunteers to run these apps over a period of 5 days. All users had a Samsung Focus phone running Windows Phone 7.1. We instrumented both the ad client and the ad server to measure the end-to-end performance and the performance of different components.

When a page loads, SmartAds scrapes the page, does key-

Component	Average Runtime (ms)
Page Scraping	30
KEX Local	20
KEX Server	<1
Ad network query	500

Table 1: Average runtime of various components in the SmartAds implementation.

word extraction, runs them through the bloom filter and sends the filtered keywords to the ad server. The ad server in turn queries the ad provider for a relevant ad and sends the ad back to the app.

In our deployment, the average end-to-end time to deliver an ad after the page loads is 650ms. SmartAds performance is comparable to the performance of other ad controls.

The breakdown of the time consumed by the different components of the SmartAds system is shown in Table 1. We see that the keyword extraction at the client and the server are implemented efficiently and takes only 20ms on average. Page scraping takes only 30ms on average. Our biggest bottleneck is the time to query the ad network from the ad server. This delay is not under our control, although if we were to deploy SmartAds in production, we could work with the ad network to reduce this delay.

5.3 Overheads

Our distributed keyword extraction technique significantly reduces the amount of resources consumed at the mobile device. In this section, we show the end-to-end performance of SmartAds and the overhead across various resources including compute, memory, network and battery.

CPU Overhead. SmartAds runs asynchronously and does not affect the performance of the app. Even so, the CPU overhead is minimal. The combined runtime of page scraping and local keyword extraction represents the computation overhead at the mobile device. As seen from Table 1, this overhead is minimal.

Memory Overhead. As mentioned is Section 4, SmartAds uses a compact bloom filter to check for ad keywords instead of storing all ad keywords in memory. The size of our bloom filter is 1MB. To measure the memory overhead of our ad control, we run apps with and without the ad control and measure the average peak memory load. Based on our measurements, SmartAds control consumes around 2.8MB of memory on an average. This overhead is low compared to the typical amount of memory consumed by apps today.

Network Overhead. In comparison to existing mobile ad controls, the extra data that SmartAds control sends are the keywords and their weights to the ad server. We send 12 bytes of data per keyword (8 bytes for keyword hash and 4 bytes for weight). From our analysis of 1200 apps, we find that the average number of keywords extracted per page is 7.6. Hence, the average extra bytes sent is 91.

We also measured how much existing ad controls upload and download each time they fetch ads. The number varies across ad controls; but on average various ad controls upload 1.5KB and download 5KB of data. Thus, even if SmartAds functionality are incorporated into existing ad controls, the additional overhead ($<$ 100 bytes) would be negligible.

Battery Overhead. To measure the battery overhead, we use a software power meter [22]. We run apps with and without the ad control through the power meter and measure the average power consumed. The increase in power consumed was less than 1% and well within experimental noise.

5.4 Summary

The results in this section show that the SmartAds system delivers relevant ads. Compared to the baseline ad control, which takes into account only the application description, SmartAds significantly improves relevance score. The results also show that SmartAds is efficient and consumes minimal resources.

6. DISCUSSION

6.1 Optimizations

In §4.2, we briefly mentioned two optimizations, without discussing them in detail. Specifically, we mentioned that we rely on metadata if the page data does not contain any keywords. We also mentioned that we augment ad keywords with related words. We now describe these two optimizations in more detail.

Addressing lack of text. One problem of extracting ad keywords from app pages is that some pages do not contain enough texts and hence keyword extractor do not produce any advertising keywords. To show relevant ads even on those pages, we use three levels of keywords. Level 1 keywords are the ones dynamically learned from the current page. Level 2 keywords are the ones dynamically learned from all the pages the user has viewed in the current session. Additionally, the ad server maintains Level 3 keywords for each app, learned offline from that app's metadata. If Level 1 keywords are empty, we fall back to Level 2 keywords. If both Level 1 and Level 2 keywords are empty, we fall back to Level 3 keywords to select relevant ads. Intuitively this means that we always give preference to the current page to show ads. If current page does not contain any advertising keywords, we consider all the pages the user has visited in the current session. Finally we consider app descriptions and content of all app pages (including the ones the user has not visited in this session) to extract keywords.

Handling related keywords. Suppose, the set of bidding keywords contains only one keyword {`HDTV`} and the current app page contains the words `LED TVs are cool`. Clearly, after filtering based on bidding keywords, the ad client will not extract any keywords even though it could show an ad for `HDTV` on this page because `LED TVs` and `HDTV` are related. Typical keyword extraction tools (including KEX) ignore such related words. However, we would like to capture such relations because a typical app page contains small amounts of texts, and hence capturing related words would give us opportunities to show more relevant ads. We therefore extend the set of original bidding keywords with their related words: {`HDTV`, `LED TV`, `LCD TV`}. We call this extended set of bidding keywords and their related words as *ad keywords*.

We use two data sources to find related words. The first source is a database of related keywords automatically extracted by analyzing Bing web queries and click logs. The degree of relationship between two keywords is computed based on how often Bing users searching for those two keywords click on the same URL. The second source is a web service provided by `http://veryrelated.com` that, given a keyword, returns a list of related keywords. Based on a WWW snapshot from Yahoo, it automatically discovers related words and concepts. The degree of relationship between two keywords is computed based on how often they appear in the same web page and how popular they are on the Internet.

Our experiments show that such keyword expansion is useful. For example, starting with a list of 1.3 million most frequent bidding keywords, the first and the second source above expanded the list to 1.96 million and 2.06 keywords respectively. We also found that around 25% of the keywords we extracted from app pages are these related keywords, which means we would have lost the opportunities of delivering relevant ads had we not considered these related keywords.

6.2 Dealing with Tail Bidding Keywords

Recall that we have configured SmartAds's client-side Bloom filter to include a small number ($\approx 2\%$) of popular bidding keywords that cover around 90% of the ads. The reader might worry that ads with bidding keywords in the tail of the distribution (i.e., remaining 10% of the ads) may never get served to users.

In practice, however, contextual signal (i.e., ad keywords extracted from current page) is only one of many signals used by a real ad system; in many occasions the ad system would use other signals such as a user's location (for context-aware targeting), his web or app usage history (for behavioral targeting), etc. The remaining 10% of the ads can be served in these situations, by matching their keywords with a user's search history for example. Even if the ad server decides to use the contextual signal to serve ad, it can occasionally serve these 10% tail ads in multiple ways: (1) by serving them when their keywords are semantically related to any keyword in the Bloom filter, (2) by prioritizing them when the current page does not contain any important ad keywords, or (3) by occasionally serving them even if the contextual signals do not match them.

Our design of SmartAds exposes a tradeoff between ad coverage and memory/network overhead, and the ad system can operate at a desirable sweet spot by tuning the size of the Bloom filter. The smaller the Bloom filter, the smaller the memory and network overhead and the larger the fraction of uncovered tail ads. SmartAds could also disable the Bloom filter at the client, in which case the client would send local features of *all* words in the current page to the server. This would increase network overhead compared to our current Bloom-filter-based design, but would still be cheaper than sending the raw text and metadata of the whole page.

6.3 Developer provided keywords

The reader may have wondered whether app developers could supply the right keywords to ad controls at run time, obviating the need for SmartAds. A few mobile ad controls do have this option [2]. For example, the developer of a recipe app can specify appropriate keywords, allowing the ad server to deliver ads on food ingredients or groceries. One might argue that an app developer could hard-code static ad keywords for every page of his app. He could also implement some logic to dynamically generate them during runtime. However, such logic is hard to implement in practice because the quality of an ad keyword depends on information the developer might not have access to (e.g., how popular a keyword is among advertisers). SmartAds automates the whole process *with zero developer effort*. Note also that for certain apps such as news aggregator, the developer simply does not know what content may be displayed at runtime. Finally, allowing app developers to specify keywords opens up the possibility of *keyword pollution*, where a developer intentionally provides popular keywords that do not appear in the page, in an attempt to increase the chance of getting matching ads from the ad network. Therefore, some ad networks simply ignore developer-provided keywords.

7. RELATED WORK

There is very little research literature specifically related to improving the relevance of mobile advertisements, and most of that has focused on using location to increase the relevancy of the advertisements shown. In the AdNext system [19], authors propose to use mobility patterns to predict which store the user is likely to visit next, and show him advertisements related to that store. In [15], authors consider using various physical contexts such as location and user activities to serve ads. These works are orthogonal to SmartAds; SmartAds could incorporate such additional signals to further increase ad relevance.

The CAMEO framework [18] and the study in [23] consider pre-fetching advertisements and displaying relevant ads at the right time. The focus of these works is on saving bandwidth by pre-fetching ad — not on increasing relevance. CAMEO considers location and app name as the only relevance signal. We have not considered the possibility of prefetching the ads in SmartAds design, since we want to adapt the ads dynamically to the content being displayed to the user.

Many researchers have focused on power consumption and privacy issues raised by mobile apps, and by advertisement controls. While we are indeed concerned about resource utilization and privacy, these issues are not the primary focus of our paper. However, we will discuss representative papers for sake of completeness. In [26], authors have shown that much of the energy consumed by mobile apps is used by third-party ad controls. The SmartAds control is designed to consume as few resources as possible. A number of researchers have looked at privacy violations by mobile apps [11, 10, 15] and especially those of third-party ad controls [14]. SmartAds protects app user's privacy by leaking only which ad keywords occur on the screen.

Delivering relevant ads to web pages has been well studied. In achieving the goal, one of the most popular approaches is keyword extraction. Riberio-Neto *et al.* [29] propose a series of strategies to match ads with web pages, based on keywords extracted from both the ad body and the web page content. Centering on keyword extraction, many methods have been proposed to better describe both advertisements and web pages, in order to match them more accurately. For instance, eBay uses their custom features (such as merchandise categories) to depict their advertisements, in matching their ads with numerous 3rd-party web pages [30]. KEX [34] uses additional web-specific features (e.g., HTML tags, URL, etc.) to identify keywords that carry more weights from any given web page. Inspired by them, SmartAds further employs features that are specific to mobile application UI in order to improve the quality of extracted keywords.

"Just-in-time" contextual advertising dynamically extracts keywords and other signals from dynamic web pages for selecting relevant ads [5, 20]; however, as mentioned in Section 2, they use web page-related features and are not directly applicable to mobile apps. Beyond keywords, several 'deeper' features have been employed for delivering relevant ads, including semantics mined from web pages (e.g., topics) [7] and user interactions in browsing [9]. However, such in-depth understanding requires to run intensive algorithms (usually in the cloud) over full page contents or user inputs, making them infeasible in the case of mobile Ads due to privacy concerns.

8. CONCLUSION

Our focus in this paper was to bring contextual advertising to mobile ads. Using data crawled from 1200 top Windows Phone apps, we demonstrated the need for a system that delivers contextual ads. We designed and built SmartAds, a contextual mobile advertising system that strikes a right balance between ad relevance, efficiency and privacy.

Through a large user study, we showed that SmartAds significantly improves the relevance of mobile ads compared to systems that rely only on the metadata information of the app. We also analyzed the performance of SmartAds end-to-end and showed that SmartAds is efficient, consumes minimal resources and incurs low overhead.

9. REFERENCES

[1] Admob. `http://www.google.com/ads/admob`.

[2] Admob. keyword-targeted ads. `http://support.google.com/admob/bin/answer.py?hl=en&answer=1307264`.

[3] Google adsense. `http://www.google.com/adsense`.

[4] Advertising.com. `http://www.advertising.com/`.

[5] A. Anagnostopoulos, A. Z. Broder, E. Gabrilovich, V. Josifovski, and L. Riedel. Web page summarization for just-in-time contextual advertising. *ACM Trans. Intell. Syst. Technol.*, 3(1):14:1–14:32, 2011.

[6] B. H. Bloom. Space/time trade-offs in hash coding with allowable errors. *Commun. ACM*, 13(7):422–426, 1970.

[7] A. Broder, M. Fontoura, V. Josifovski, and L. Riedel. A semantic approach to contextual advertising. In *SIGIR*, 2007.

[8] A. Broder and M. Mitzenmacher. Network applications of bloom filters: A survey. *Internet Mathematics*, 1(4):485–509, 2002.

[9] K. S. Dave. Computational advertising: leveraging user interaction and contextual factors for improved ad retrieval and ranking. In *WWW*, 2011.

[10] D. Davidson and B. Livshits. Morepriv: Mobile os support for application personalization and privacy. Technical report, Microsoft Research, 2012.

[11] W. Enck, P. Gilbert, B.-G. Chun, L. P. Cox, J. Jung, P. McDaniel, and A. Seth. TaintDroid: An Information-Flow Tracking System for Realtime Privacy Monitoring on Smartphones. In *OSDI*, 2010.

[12] H. Falaki, R. Mahajan, S. Kandula, D. Lymberopoulos, R. Govindan, and D. Estrin. Diversity in smartphone usage. In *MobiSys*, 2010.

[13] Flurry Blog. The great mobile ad spending gap. `http://blog.flurry.com`, February 2012.

[14] M. Grace, W. Zhou, X. Jiang, and A.-R. Sadeghi. Unsafe Exposure Analysis of Mobile In-App Advertisements. In *WiSec*, 2012.

[15] M. Hardt and S. Nath. Privacy-aware personalization for mobile advertising. In *ACM CCS*, 2012.

[16] iAd. `http://advertising.apple.com/`.

[17] S. Iqbal and B. Bailey. Effects of intelligent notification management on users and their tasks. In *ACM CHI*, 2008.

[18] A. J. Khan, K. Jayarajah, D. Han, A. Misra, R. Balan, and S. Seshan. CAMEO: A middleware for mobile advertisement delivery. In *ACM MobiSys*, 2013.

[19] B. Kim, S. Kang, J.-Y. Ha, Y. Rhee, and J. Song. AdNext: A Visit-Pattern-Aware Mobile Advertising System for Urban Commercial Complexes. In *HotMobile*, 2012.

[20] L. Li, W. Chu, J. Langford, and R. E. Schapire. A contextual-bandit approach to personalized news article recommendation. In *WWW*, 2010.

[21] Microsoft advertising. `http://advertising.microsoft.com/`.

[22] R. Mittal, A. Kansal, and R. Chandra. Empowering developers to estimate app energy consumption. In *MobiCom*, 2012.

[23] P. Mohan, S. Nath, , and O. Riva. Prefetching mobile ads: Can advertising systems afford it? In *EuroSys*, 2013.

[24] Microsoft mobile ad control. `http://advertising.microsoft.com/mobile-apps`.

[25] S. Ovide and G. Bensinger. Mobile ads: Here's what works and what doesn't. `http://online.wsj.com/article/SB10000872396390444083304578016373342878556.html?mod=WSJ_hp_EditorsPicks`, September 2012.

[26] A. Pathak, Y. C. Hu, and M. Zhang. Where is the energy spent inside my app? Fine Grained Energy Accounting on Smartphones with Eprof. In *EuroSys*, 2012.

[27] C. Perzold. *Microsoft Silverlight Edition: Programming Windows Phone 7*. Microsoft Press, 2010.

[28] L. Ravindranath, J. Padhye, S. Agarwal, R. Mahajan, I. Obermiller, and S. Shayandeh. AppInsight: Mobile App Performance Monitoring in the Wild. In *OSDI*, 2012.

[29] B. Ribeiro-Neto, M. Cristo, P. Golgher, and E. de Moura. Impedance coupling in content-targeted advertising. In *SIGIR*, 2005.

[30] X. Wu and A. Bolivar. Keyword extraction for contextual advertisement. In *WWW*, 2008.

[31] Yahoo! Smart Ads. `ttp://advertising.`yaoo.com/marketing/smartads/.

[32] Yahoo publisher network. `http://advertisingcentral.yahoo.com/publisher/index`.

[33] J. Yan, N. Liu, G. Wang, W. Zhang, Y. Jiang, and Z. Chen. How much can behavioral targeting help online advertising? In *WWW*, 2009.

[34] W.-t. Yih, J. Goodman, and V. R. Carvalho. Finding advertising keywords on web pages. In *WWW*, 2006.

CAMEO: A Middleware for Mobile Advertisement Delivery

Azeem J. Khan*
Oriental Institute of Management
University of Mumbai
azeem@oes.ac.in

Kasthuri Jayarajah
School of Information Systems
Singapore Management University
kasthurij@smu.edu.sg

Dongsu Han
Department of Electrical Engineering
KAIST
dongsu.han@gmail.com

Archan Misra
School of Information Systems
Singapore Management University
archanm@smu.edu.sg

Rajesh Balan
School of Information Systems
Singapore Management University
rajesh@smu.edu.sg

Srinivasan Seshan
Department of Computer Science
Carnegie Mellon University
srini@cs.cmu.edu

Abstract

Advertisements are the de-facto currency of the Internet with many popular applications (e.g. Angry Birds) and online services (e.g., YouTube) relying on advertisement generated revenue. However, the current economic models and mechanisms for mobile advertising are fundamentally not sustainable and far from ideal. In particular, as we show, applications which use mobile advertising are capable of using significant amounts of a mobile users' critical resources without being controlled or held accountable. This paper seeks to redress this situation by enabling advertisement supported applications to become significantly more "user-friendly". To this end, we present the design and implementation of CAMEO, a new framework for mobile advertising that 1) employs intelligent and proactive retrieval of advertisements, using context prediction, to significantly reduce the bandwidth and energy overheads of advertising, and 2) provides a negotiation protocol and framework that empowers applications to subsidize their data traffic costs by "bartering" their advertisement rights for access bandwidth from mobile ISPs. Our evaluation, that uses real mobile advertising data collected from around the globe, demonstrates that CAMEO effectively reduces the resource consumption caused by mobile advertising.

Categories and Subject Descriptors

C.2.1 [**Network Architecture and Design**]: Wireless Communication

*Research performed by author as a Research Fellow at Singapore Management University.

General Terms

Design, Experimentation, Performance

Keywords

Wireless; Mobile; Advertising

1. INTRODUCTION

As per Gartner forecasts, over 85% of the applications to be downloaded from the mobile application marketplaces in 2012 will be free and principally supported by advertising revenue, even though the same applications are often available in both advertisement-supported and paid-for, advertisement-free versions. This points to the fact that users are happy to "pay" for applications with their *attention*, but not with their pocketbooks. The end result is that "Advertisements" have become the de-facto mechanism that mobile applications use to generate revenues. There are clear indicators that this "payment" model is here to stay, with mobile advertising revenues growing by 149% in 2011 [1].

Unfortunately, the current advertisement delivery framework has certain limitations that are likely to make consumers increasingly hostile to such advertising traffic. From a conceptual viewpoint, an ideal advertising framework is one that *only monetizes user* ***attention****, without incurring the user any additional monetary or resource costs (such as network bandwidth or device energy).* However, as mobile ISPs universally move towards metered wireless data plans, consumers are progressively growing wary of the hidden costs of such advertising traffic, both in terms of *bandwidth consumption* [12, 28], and *energy overheads* [19]. To circumvent such costs, savvy consumers often end up installing ad-blocking software or turning off their cellular data

[0]This research is supported by the National Research Foundation Singapore under its International Research Centre @ Singapore Funding Initiative and administered by the IDM Programme Office.
This research is supported by the National Research Foundation Singapore under its IDM Futures Funding Initiative, and administered by the Interactive & Digital Media Program Office, Media Development Authority.

connections when executing an application with a heavy advertising footprint.

In this paper, we present a new mobile advertisement delivery framework,called CAMEO[1]. CAMEO's main goal is to significantly lower the overheads, as perceived by the consumer, of delivering advertisements to mobile applications, thereby making the business model of advertisement-supported free applications much more "consumer-friendly". To achieve this objective, the CAMEO middleware component on a mobile device provides two new features:

1. *Reducing Costs*: CAMEO allows advertisement networks to proactively place a corpus of context-driven advertisements on a mobile device, by exploiting time windows when the consumer is connected to a cheap or free network (e.g., Wi-Fi@home), and then serve advertisements locally using this on-device corpus. Such proactive retrieval benefits consumers by significantly reducing the bandwidth and energy overheads associated with advertising traffic.

2. *Bartering of Advertisements for Access Connectivity*: CAMEO enables individual mobile applications to use "advertising rights" as a form of implicit & universal currency to negotiate free or subsidized data bandwidth from different mobile ISPs. While this doesn't reduce the energy or bandwidth demands for an application, it can reduce the users' costs associated with connectivity (e.g., when on metered data plans or attaching to pay-per-use Wi-Fi hotspots). Note that other studies have proposed the explicit monetization of users' information [22], while applications such as Facebook Zero[2] have negotiated directly with large ISPs to make their application data consumption free to end consumers [15]. Unlike these past designs and alternatives where the user must explicitly allocate bandwidth across multiple applications, CAMEO minimizes user distraction by avoiding direct user involvement, and lets an individual application dynamically tailor the use of advertising slots (as the medium of exchange between users' attention and bandwidth).

Note that the above two components are independent but symbiotic. By making costs for advertising content more explicit to application developers through the negotiation component, our model provides developers and their advertisement network partners stronger incentives to perform advertisement prefetching and display more efficiently.

To explore the challenges in supporting more efficient ad delivery and support ad negotiation, we have designed and built a prototype user-space implementation of CAMEO for the Android OS. Through our implementation and associated empirical studies, we make the following key contributions:

1. **Use context prediction to prefetch advertisements and reduce the network 'cost' of advertisement delivery:** We propose, in Section 4.1, a bulk ad prefetching model that first predicts future user context by mining past context history, and then leverages this context prediction to retrieve a comprehensive corpus of relevant advertisements. This on-device corpus can then be used by CAMEO to serve advertisements locally. Through extensive empirical studies in multiple geographies (North and South America, Europe, and Asia), we establish, in Sections 5.2 and Section 6.1 respectively, the key contexts that drive the selection of context-aware mobile advertisements and that an appropriately selected corpus can indeed be prefetched periodically with negligible cost.

2. **Allow on-device serving of advertisements while preserving different advertisement selection and pricing models:** In Section 4.2, we show how CAMEO allows different advertisement networks to apply their advertisement-selection logic over prefetched advertisements stored locally on the mobile device. Subsequently, in Section 4.4, we show how CAMEO also supports different popular models of real-time pricing. CAMEO achieves this flexibility by effectively decoupling the tasks of advertisement *selection* and *delivery*.

3. **Demonstrate significant savings in bandwidth and energy overheads:** Using empirical data of consumer application behavior and micro-benchmarks of CAMEO's performance on mobile devices, we show, in Section 7.2, that CAMEO's bulk prefetching provides substantial savings in both advertisement-related traffic and energy consumption. Most importantly, such bandwidth savings are realized though CAMEO performs bulk prefetching of advertisements.

4. **Flexible model for negotiation between individual applications and mobile ISP:** In Section 4.3, we present CAMEO's proposed use of a simple, but generic, slot-based advertising model (borrowed from television advertising) to negotiate preferences and constraints between an application and an ISP. This model also allows applications using CAMEO-compatible applications to effectively intersperse advertising content from conventional advertisement networks and the mobile ISP.

2. BACKGROUND AND ISSUES

We first review the current interaction model for mobile advertising and highlight a few of the drawbacks that motivated our proposed research on CAMEO.

2.1 The Current Model

Main players: The mobile advertising eco-system consists of 4 players: applications, advertisement networks, mobile ISPs, and consumers. At present, advertisements are retrieved "over the top" (directly by an application from the advertising content provider, without any direct involvement of the mobile ISP): Ad-supported *applications*, such as AccuWeather and Angry Birds, use advertisement libraries provided by *advertisement networks* (**AN**) to fetch and display advertisements. An individual application specifies the layout of an advertisement and supplies the relevant user contexts, such as gender, age group, and keywords, using the library. By interacting with the AN's servers, the advertisement library then retrieves and displays an ad that best matches the context and the AN's business interest. ANs thus provide an online marketplace for brokering matches

[1]Context-Aware **A**dvertising **M**ediator and **O**ptimizer

[2]Facebook Zero is a text-only version of Facebook for the developing world.

between advertisers and the application developers. *Mobile ISPs* presently provide the underlying connectivity substrate that allows mobile applications to access online services (including ANs). ISPs worldwide have increasingly migrated to metered data plans, where the cost of connectivity for a *consumer* is a function of the amount of data consumed in a billing cycle.

Economic Model: Advertisers pay for advertising to the AN, which in turn shares a fraction of the revenue with the application developer. Currently, the most dominant payment models are 'cost-per-click' (CPC), 'cost-per-impression' (CPM), and 'cost-per-acquisition' (CPA). In CPC and CPA, payments accrue when users click on an advertisement or makes a specific action (e.g., updating on-line shopping carts). In CPM, advertisers are charged whenever an advertisement is *displayed* on the mobile device. As different models have different strengths, we consider all three models in this paper[3]. The AN's selection of advertisements are driven by two criteria: 1) matching of the user context to the context triggers that advertisers may have specified (e.g., at a specific location), and 2) the price they are willing to pay (which is often decided through real-time auctions [8]).

2.2 Problems

CAMEO is predicated on the belief that mobile advertising can become significantly more *consumer-friendly* by tacking the following problems associated with today's advertisement delivery framework.

High Overheads of Advertisement Delivery: Mobile applications presently engage in multiple network transactions to fetch and display a single advertisement, leading to a significant consumption [12] of often-precious data bandwidth. When operating under metered-data plans (e.g., on almost all 4G/LTE networks), users effectively end up 'paying' for the advertising-related traffic generated from their mobile devices. As an example, Khan [12] reported that the retrieval of a 5–8KB image advertisement on the *Angry Birds* application generates almost 30KB of network traffic. This is particularly troublesome for applications that are otherwise 'standalone' (e.g., mobile games), whose network traffic is almost *entirely* advertising related. Likewise, the frequent signaling overhead generated by such intermittent advertisement retrieval also consume a significant amount of energy on the mobile device [28, 19].

Limited Ability to use Ads as a Means to Monetize Connectivity: Presently, mobile ISPs have no role in the economics of advertising and view advertising content merely as 'application data'. Accordingly, the present model fails to capitalize on a possible convergence of interests, where *a)* mobile ISPs (e.g., Wi-Fi hotspots at public venues such as shopping malls and train stations) might be interested to offer free or subsidized connectivity in return for the prerogative to insert their own advertisements, *on existing applications preferred by the consumer*, and *b)* applications might make themselves more appealing by continuing to operate even when the consumer does not have an explicit pre-existing ISP subscription (e.g., at hotspots or while roaming).

[3]Facebook offers all three, and Google's Adwords offers CPC and CPA on their search network and all three on their display network. A market survey shows that, for video advertising, all payment models are equally preferred by the advertisers [2].

3. DESIGN GOALS

CAMEO's mobile advertising-related middleware aims to *a)* reduce the bandwidth and energy overheads of fetching and displaying advertisements from individual ANs, and *b)* promote the flexible use of advertisements as a universal currency for bartering network connectivity. The design goals for CAMEO are as follows:

1. **Support lower cost of advertisement delivery without modifying the AN's advertisement selection logic:** Given the high signaling traffic overhead involved in retrieving an individual advertisement, and the energy overheads of activating a radio interface intermittently to interactively fetch such advertisements, CAMEO's design should allow retrieval of advertisements in bulk, especially during periods of connectivity to 'cheap' access networks (e.g., opportunistic association with home or office Wi-Fi networks), to amortize these traffic and energy costs. However, it is essential that such bulk retrieval does not impact the AN's desire to control the selection, in real time, of each individual advertisement displayed.

2. **Minimize user involvement:** CAMEO should require only minimal, or preferably zero, user involvement in the process of optimizing advertisement delivery or negotiating an "advertisements for subsidized connectivity" barter with a mobile ISP. Mobile devices typically run a variety of concurrent applications (usually many background applications and a foreground one), which vary significantly in their network traffic demands, and in the types and frequency of advertisements shown. Accordingly, we believe that users would find it very challenging to determine a suitable apportioning of the (bandwidth, advertisement) budget among competing applications—user-involved adaptation has proven to be a major challenge in prior mobile systems, such as Odyssey [18].

3. **Incentivize developers to make their applications "consumer-friendly":** CAMEO should effectively empower each application developer to *independently* find the best way for the application to 'spend' the virtual currency of advertisements (reflected in the tradeoffs the application makes between the application's bandwidth requirements and its frequency of displaying ads), so as to maximize the application's "consumer friendliness".

4. **Require minimal modifications to applications and ANs:** The design for prefetching bulk advertisements should be *minimally disruptive*, requiring, at best, only minor changes to application code or AN interfaces. Moreover, while enabling the dynamic exchange of advertisements in return for subsidized connectivity, CAMEO should isolate applications from the complexity of mobile ISPs, by having the middleware bear the brunt of responsibility for functions such as ISP selection, negotiation of bartering agreements and traffic & advertising contract enforcement.

To achieve efficient, AN logic-compliant advertisement delivery, we will show (in Section 4.1) how CAMEO selects advertisements locally from a corpus of prefetched advertisements during periods of cheap network connectivity, and

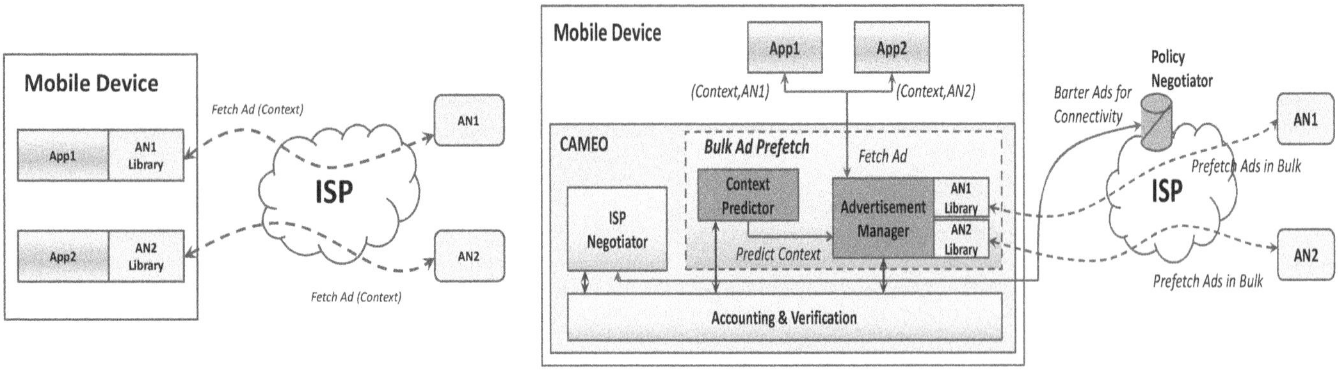

a) Current Ad Retrieval

b) Modified Ad Retrieval via CAMEO

Figure 1: The key components of CAMEO

how applications can use this feature of CAMEO via simple API calls. To minimize user involvement while incentivizing each application to maximize its "customer friendliness", we will develop (in Section 6.3) CAMEO's *per-App* negotiation model, where each application dynamically and opportunistically negotiates network access from ISPs that might be willing to offer such subsidized access in return for the privilege of inserting their own advertising content in the application's ad-stream. We prefer such a "per-App" negotiation model over possible alternatives for such preferred connectivity, as this model provides finer *granularity* (applications can tune their own behavior based on individual-specific usage patterns), greater *dynamicity* (the connectivity is negotiated on-the-fly and does not require long-term contracts) and lower *user involvement* (negotiations for access connectivity are transparent to the user).

4. CAMEO ARCHITECTURE

CAMEO sits as a middleware on the mobile device, performing three functions that effectively mediate the interactions between individual applications and the ANs/ISPs:

1. It pre-fetches a corpus of advertisements from multiple ANs without application intervention.
2. It serves advertisements from the locally-stored corpus to the mobile application.
3. It negotiates with the ISP (bandwidth in exchange of advertisements) on behalf of the mobile applications.

Figure 1 illustrates the key functional components of the CAMEO framework, and shows how the new advertisement retrieval and negotiation models differ from current practices. As explained in Section 2.2, and illustrated in Figure 1.a), applications presently treat the ISP as a bit-pipe, and use AN-specific libraries to directly fetch individual advertisements from the corresponding AN. In contrast, Figure 1.b) shows the CAMEO-enhanced interaction model, where the various components of the CAMEO client middleware mediate the interaction between applications and ANs by exposing APIs to each individual application. The advertisement prefetch and local serving functionalities are provided by the combination of the **Context Predictor** and **Advertisement Manager** components. The logically-separate functionality of bartering advertisement privileges in return for access bandwidth is performed by the **ISP Negotiator**. Each of these three components interact with the **Accounting and Verification** module, which assures ANs that the local advertisements are being served "correctly" and enforces the bartering agreements set up with an ISP. We now describe each of the key functions individually.

4.1 Predictive Bulk Ad-Prefetch

CAMEO's design seeks to reduce the high bandwidth and energy overheads associated with the current model of interactive and intermittent retrieval of individual advertisements, by serving the vast majority of advertisements *locally*, i.e., from an intelligently managed local corpus prefetched to the mobile device. However, as we will see in Section 5, the advertisements on mobile devices are highly context-sensitive, i.e., the selection of an advertisement depends on the real-time context of the mobile user/device. Prefetching relevant advertisements, thus, requires predicting the future contexts of the mobile device/user. CAMEO realizes such predictive prefetching by having our Context Predictor monitor the user context and apply machine learning techniques on past context history to predict the future context.[4]. Subsequently, to retrieve relevant advertisements for the future, the Advertisement Manager supplies this predicted context to an AN and asks it to provide an appropriate corpus of advertisements. At the time of ad display, the Advertisement Manager performs a local lookup to select an advertisement matching the current context, and serves this advertisement to the requesting application.

In Section 7, we demonstrate that this prefetching technique is indeed effective in supporting context-dependent advertisements and realizes significant bandwidth and energy savings.

4.2 Advertisement Selection

CAMEO supports three different models for advertisement selection on the mobile device, each of which assumes that the AN has already dispatched a corpus of relevant advertisements that are then stored locally. In the order of decreasing overhead, we present the three models that vary in their level of real-time interaction with the AN:

1. **AN Advertisement Selection (ANAS):** In ANAS, CAMEO contacts the AN and provides the current context. We assume that the AN is already aware of the contents of the corpus that it has previously

[4]In practice, such context profiling and prediction can even be performed on an infrastructure server.

pushed to the mobile device. The AN then applies its custom-selection logic, and delivers CAMEO a unique ID corresponding to the selected advertisement. Note that the advertisement itself is not downloaded again. The ANAS model focuses on eliminating redundant ad transmissions and is particularly suited for mobile applications that provide utility only when connected to the network—e.g., an application that retrieves arrival times of buses in real-time. We observe in Section 7.2 that ANAS can reduce the bandwidth consumption by up to 4.6 times when displaying 100 advertisements.

2. **Local Advertisement Selection (LAS):** In LAS, CAMEO allows each AN to send over a static set of rules along with the relevant ad corpus. Upon request for an ad from an application, CAMEO operates on the rules locally to return an ID corresponding to an ad to be displayed. This model eliminates real-time signaling and transmission associated with advertising. LAS is thus appropriate for standalone applications that only require network connectivity for ad display. Our results in Section 7.2 shows that this method can reduce the energy consumption by an order of magnitude, when displaying 100 advertisements. An unintended but perhaps useful consequence of LAS is the ability to show advertisements on an *offline* device.

3. **Best Effort Advertisement Selection (BEAS):** In this model, the selection logic is performed locally by CAMEO, in a *statistical* fashion. Under the BEAS approach, the AN specifies multiple constraints that are specific to each advertisement. Our current CAMEO implementation allows ANs to specify two constraints: (1) f_i: how frequently an advertisement, ad_i, can be displayed, and (2) Max_i: the maximum number of times an ad can be shown. Given these specifications, CAMEO can apply a randomized selection procedure that adheres to these constraints. For example, if there is no limit on the maximum number of times an ad can be shown and f_i is identical for all advertisements, the CAMEO can simply select the advertisements in round-robin fashion.

4.3 Bartering Ads for Connectivity

CAMEO utilizes a *slot-based* model for negotiating and specifying the agreement by which applications can allow ISPs to insert their advertisements in exchange for access connectivity. This model is inspired by the television industry, where advertisements (and associated revenue) are shown at specific timeslots (e.g., five 30-second slots every eight minutes) and are apportioned between a regional and national broadcaster, the local affiliate TV station and the last-mile access provider (e.g., the local cable company). In CAMEO, we propose a similar design. Most advertisement-supported mobile applications show advertisements at fixed intervals or when a specific event is triggered (e.g., the user reaches the next level of a game). We consider each such display of advertisement as a *slot*. When a mobile application barters for free bandwidth with the ISP, it can choose to fill some of these *slots* with advertisements from the ISP (or more likely the ISP's preferred AN). A detailed design of the protocol for the negotiation between the mobile application and the ISP is described in Section 6.3.

4.4 Accounting and Verification

To ensure that ANs and ISPs can trust this new model of CAMEO-mediated advertisement selection and display, CAMEO must provide certain accounting and verification functionality. While click spams and other fraudulent behavior are a concern for mobile advertising even today [3], CAMEO's unique features of *a)* local selection from the prefetched advertisements and *b)* dynamic interleaving of ISP-provided advertisements, introduce some additional requirements and concerns. Note that our current implementation of CAMEO does *not* provide this support: we believe that eventually CAMEO will become a part of the base OS and a combination of previously-studied software and hardware innovations (e.g., TPMs) will make such accounting a default capability. In this section, we thus describe the accounting functionality that CAMEO requires and possible techniques that we can leverage to provide this support.

CAMEO's model of displaying prefetched advertisements creates two accounting challenges:

- *C1):* If the context prediction is inaccurate, CAMEO does not have the correct prefetched ads to display. As a result, CAMEO must make a decision to contact the AN again to fetch a new ad or instead display a sub-optimal ad.
- *C2):* CAMEO's decentralized advertisement selection makes it harder for advertisers to enforce total or daily global budget constraints, if we use the BEAS or LAS models.

To address challenge C1, CAMEO could periodically report its mispredictions to the AN and allow it to estimate potential loss in revenue. Both ANs and applications could use this information to decide whether to obtain a new corpus of advertisements proactively. To address C2, CAMEO could rely on statistical techniques to estimate the number of ad impressions that are occurring at any time. This estimate could be used be clients to tune the probabilistic selection of ads on any client.

In Section 4.2, we alluded to the possibility of displaying ads when the device is offline. If this was implemented it would created additional challenges related to tracking ads shown. However it would also create a challenge similar to the problem of click and impression fraud in today's systems which is an ongoing research problem [23, 4].

5. EMPIRICAL STUDY

To demonstrate the real-world potential of context prediction based prefetching, we perform an empirical study of mobile advertisements. In addition, to get an in-depth understanding of average user behaviors and connectivity, we analyze the mobile usage patterns of twenty users with an instrumented Android phone that monitored user activity and network connectivity for more than a month.

5.1 Data Collection Procedure

Mobile advertisements study: We fetched advertisements from Google's AdMob network with different contexts using a custom script deployed on 100+ PlanetLab nodes and machines in Singapore and Pittsburgh. We vary all five context variables supported by the AdMob's library. The different context attributes that were varied are as follows: 4 Android OS versions including tablets and smartphones; 3 international and 3 US mobile carriers; gender; age group; 5 different key words: no keyword, music, game, language, business; and 4 popular and non-popular applications (SoundHound (SH), Plume (PL), Hanping Chinese Dictionary (HD) and a custom demo app (DM)). Note that we also vary the location implicitly by geographically distributing the clients.

The advertisements were fetched every minute to abide by Google's recommendation. At this rate, in our fetching process, the same context repeats every 840 minutes. For the PlanetLab nodes, we generated a corpus of more than 1 million advertisements over 14 days. For Singapore and USA locations, we generated a corpus of 60K advertisements over a period of two months. The advertisements fetched were observed to be mainly of non-interactive HTML (with AdMob's standard Javascript), HTML with banner images, and creatives (interactive text or image) rendered using JavaScript.

User study: A custom developed monitoring application was installed onto 20 Android-based smartphones at our Singapore campus. 12 of them belonged to students and the rest to office staff on-campus. The monitoring application tracks and records almost every Android event related to user interaction as well as system information such as battery level. For a subset of users, we also monitored their bandwidth usage.

5.2 Opportunities for Prefetching and Caching

We analyze the data to answer three key questions:
(1) Which context determines the ads to be displayed?
(2) Are some ads displayed more frequently than others?
(3) What's the average lifetime and size of ads?

Some contexts are more important. We see that ads are far more dependant on certain contexts. To analyze the importance of different context, we quantify the information contained in each context using mutual information (MI) from information theory. The entropy is a measure of uncertainty for a random variable, and the mutual information of two random variables measures the amount of uncertainty reduced by knowing one of the two. We take an ad as a random variable whose value is its content and calculate its entropy and the mutual information of ads and different contexts with general statistics (Table 1). We make two important observations. First, the number of unique ads are relatively small. Across different fetches same ads reappear many times, which suggest that prefetching and caching can be effective. Second, location and app names give much more information than other contexts.

We studied the overlap of advertisements across different locations and applications. In Table 2, we quantify the overlap across 10 countries and 10 states in the US for the SH application over a period of 14 days. We found that ads served in different countries as well as across cities of the same country were different. A similar computation for ads seen across three different applications from Pittsburgh, US also shows differences in the ads served reaffirming the MI results .

These results show that the prediction of context is critical in prefetching relevant advertisements. If the prediction is not accurate, bandwidth will be wasted and our solution will have little benefit. However, as we shall see in Section 6.1 below, these important contexts can be predicted with relatively high accuracy.

Table 1: Location and app names are important contexts.

total # of ads	1.8M
# of unique ads	17178 (0.9%)
Entropy(ad)	**9.45 bits**
MI(ad, (location, app name))	**3.61 bits**
MI(ad, location)	**2.54 bits**
MI(ad, app name)	1.01 bit
MI(ad, OS)	0.54 bit
MI(ad, carrier)	0.14 bit
MI(ad, age)	0.11 bit
MI(ad, gender)	0.03 bit
MI(ad, keyword)	0.03 bit

Table 2: Fraction of overlap between advertisements across location and application context changes.

Change in context	Average overlap	Std. Dev.
Across 10 different countries	5.41%	8.9%
Across 10 states in US	41.7%	9.57%
Across three applications	4.86%	3.4%

Ad display distribution is skewed. We also observed that the distribution of ads is heavily skewed towards a small number of popular ads. Figure 2 shows this distribution. The top 100 ads are fetched more than 50% of times across all users and contexts. On average, they are fetched more than 82 times each at each device. This suggests that caching of ads can be very effective in reducing the bandwidth consumption of advertising. Previous measurements at the mobile infrastructure [28] and on the handsets [12] show that the same ads are repeatedly fetched as they are not cached.

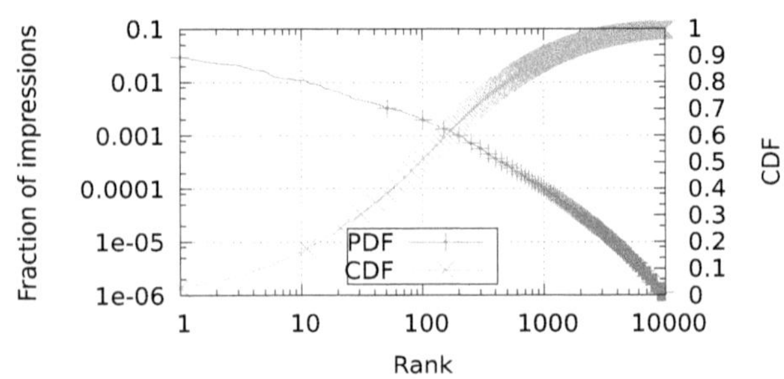

Figure 2: Top 100 ads (0.58%) are fetched for more than 50% of the times.

Some ads have a long life. Figure 3 shows the complementary CDF of ads' lifetime. The lifetime of an ad is the time for which it appears on devices before it is not seen anymore. The ad lifetime reflects advertisers' constraints, such as the budget and the duration of ad campaigns. We see that about 37% of the advertisements are still served by the advertisement network after 24 hours. In fact, 14% of ads continue to be served even after a week. This implies that a significant fraction of the ads can be cached for a relatively long time on mobile devices. For example, if CAMEO's prefetched bulk-ad refresh interval is once per

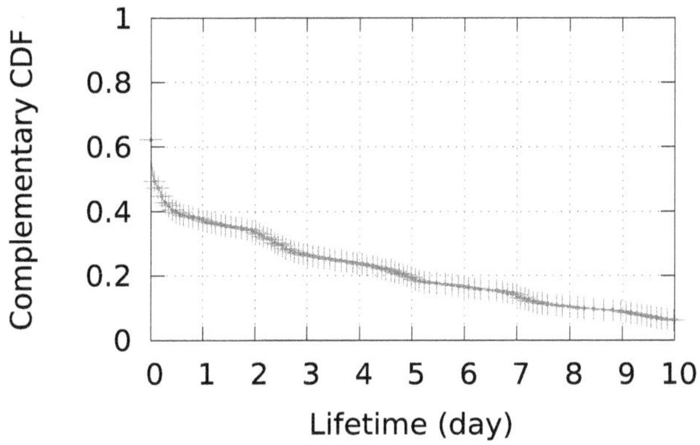

Figure 3: CCDF of ad lifetime

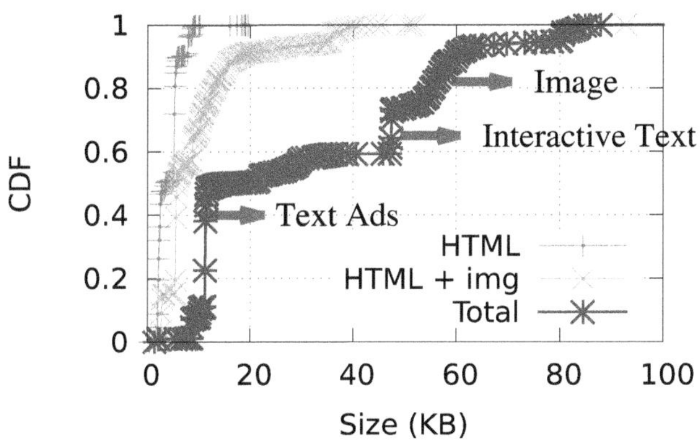

Figure 4: CDF of the size of advertisement

day, on average approximately 63% of all ads will get replaced every day. Note that CAMEO can still prefetch all ads regardless of their lifetime.

Figure 4 shows the size distribution of the ads. The figure shows the total size and the breakdown of an ad's components. All ads are HTML based and they contain references to Javascript code, icons, and/or images. We see that ad-specific components (ad HTML and images) only take up a fraction (median = 5.8 KB) of the total size (median = 15 KB). On closer inspection of the HTML files, we observed that even the ad-specific HTML contains large amounts of redundancy as it is generated from a template. Moreover, we see that the same Javascript code is repeatedly downloaded every time to the mobile. In Section 7, we show that significant bandwidth savings are achievable by exploiting these redundancies.

5.3 Network Usage Patterns

We characterize two aspects of user behavior that are closely related to CAMEO's approach:
(1) How much bandwidth do people consume, and how often do people use ad-supported apps?
(2) How often are users connected to cheap networks?

Figure 5 shows us the average daily bandwidth consumption for different users in our user study. Average users consume ≈30 MB of upload and download data. 44% of the data was consumed while on a metered bandwidth network.

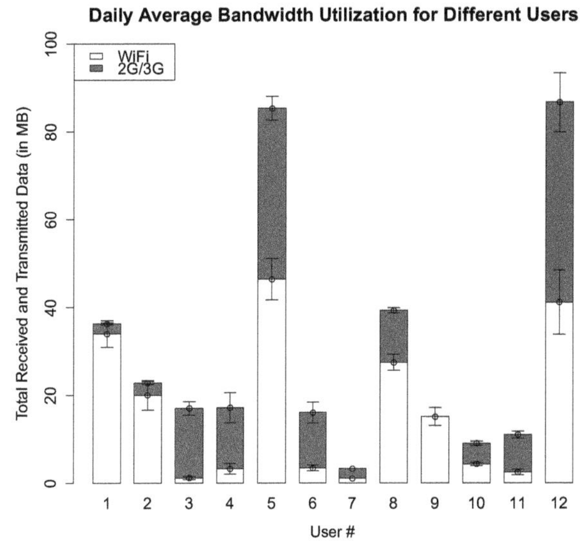

Figure 5: Typical bandwidth utilization of different users

We also calculated that the fraction of time the users spent on ad-supported applications was about 11%. The most actively used apps (more than 60%) were social networking and instant messaging related mobile apps which as of now do not contain advertisements.

Next we analyzed the average times per day that users had different types of connectivity. Figure 6 reports the number of hours in a day (averaged over 30 days) that ten users are connected to different networks. We observe that for both populations, the users were connected to cellular networks for most parts of the day. (For the remaining users we did not have the data for the entire 30 days but the results are similar.)

We must point out that this reported result is our best estimate due to inherent limitations in the Android OS and our own measurement software. We label the user as 'not connected' when the phone is turned off or the airplane mode is set on the phone. We label a user having WiFi only when they obtained an IP from a WiFi network. Note that when a user is on WiFi s/he may still have no Internet connectivity. If the user was 'not connected' and not on WiFi, we assumed that the user had cellular connectivity since cellular data coverage in Singapore is 100%.

6. IMPLEMENTATION OF CAMEO

We now describe, in greater detail, our implementation of each of the different components of CAMEO.

6.1 Context Prediction for Ad Prefetching

In Section 5.2, we showed that *location* and *application* contexts appear to be the two most important determinants of the advertisement selection logic. For prefetching to be successful, CAMEO must predict these two contexts for a user accurately. CAMEO's current implementation uses a simple profile-based predictor to predict such context. Location prediction is fairly well studied (e.g., [25, 24, 6, 20, 17]); moreover, in our study, city-level location granularity was sufficient, as finer-grained location did not result in any statistical differences in the advertisements selected.

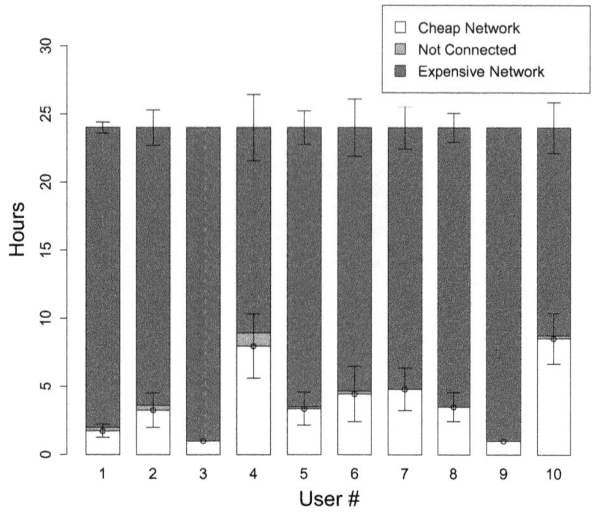

Figure 6: Avg. user hrs. on different networks

We thus focus on predicting the set of applications that individual users will execute in the future. Presently, for any specified future interval, CAMEO determines the set of *possible applications* as the union of all applications that have a non-zero access probability over *any 'bin' (explained shortly) within that interval.* In other words, if the user has a non-zero likelihood of using any particular application, then CAMEO assumes that it must prefetch advertisements associated with that application context as well.

To build a predictive profile, our implementation divides each day into smaller time intervals termed *bins* (currently, each bin is 15 minutes long) and considers tuples of the form *(day of week, bin)* for prediction. For each such tuple, the algorithm computes the fraction of time spent interacting with different applications. Figure 7 illustrates the computation process. For example, for the bin (Monday, 9:30-9:45am), the algorithm computes the probability for using *App*1 by calculating the fraction of time the user spent accessing *App*1 between 9:30–9:45am over the past few Mondays. In Section 7.1, we shall evaluate three different strategies for using these per-bin probabilities to determine the set of applications likely to be used by the user over any given time period.

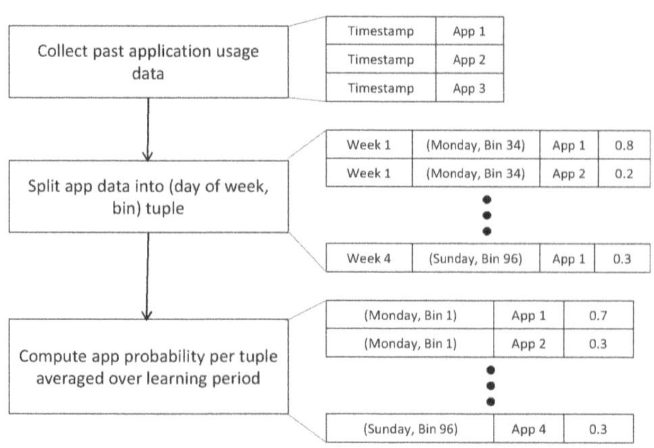

Figure 7: Simplified context prediction flow.

6.2 Local Advertisement Selection

The CAMEO implementation supports all three advertisement selection models discussed in Section 4.2. In CAMEO, the corpus of advertisements is currently identified by a unique device-specific ID, and the corpus contains the advertisements as well as an index of the hashes of each advertisement. In the ANAS model, CAMEO issues a *FetchAd*() request, containing the corpus ID and receives back the ID (hash) of the advertisement selected for display. To support LAS, CAMEO downloads a simple XML-based ruleset that dictates the advertisement selection logic. This ruleset is used in the *FetchAd*() method, taking the local corpus as input and returning the ID of the selected advertisement. CAMEO's implementation of BEAS currently uses a weighted selection logic where an advertisement from the corpus is selected randomly in proportion to its *display frequency* value, f_i. CAMEO also maintains a per-ad counter, as well as the list of timestamps, to ensure that the BEAS limits (on f_i and Max_i) are not violated. For all three models, the selection history is also logged in our currently primitive version of the Accounting and Verification component.

6.3 ISP Negotiation

We now describe the implementation of CAMEO's ISP negotiator that enables on-the-spot exchange between advertising rights of apps and subsidized connectivity to mobile ISPs.

Pricing and negotiation model: While CAMEO can support any number of ad-based charging models with ISPs, the present implementation supports two of the most common pricing models for access connectivity: 'per unit time' and 'per byte transferred'. In the first model, time is partitioned in slots of t seconds, and the ISP obtains the right to show one advertisement in each slot. In the second model, the ISP is allowed to show a total of x advertisements (of maximum size S) in exchange for y bytes of data traffic.

CAMEO's Accounting and Verification module then cooperates with the ISP infrastructure to monitor the data consumed by each individual application (possible alternative approaches for such monitoring are suggested in Section 9), and subsequently enforce its agreed-upon barter model. The CAMEO API alerts each individual application that its negotiated traffic contract is about to expire, either because sufficient time has elapsed since the display of the last ISP-provided advertisement or because the application traffic volume is approaching the specified limit but has not yet displayed enough ISP advertisements. To accommodate background applications (which clearly cannot use advertising views as a currency), CAMEO also implements an inter-Application request model, where a background application (e.g., an email client) can request the foreground application (via CAMEO) for a portion of its traffic quota. While CAMEO can mediate these requests, the acceptance or rejection by the foreground application would depend entirely on prior business/partnering arrangements among the respective developers.

Overview of the process: When an application starts up and the device does not have pre-existing connectivity, CAMEO searches local ISPs that supports the negotiation and identifies a negotiator address for each ISP. Such information can be exchanged as part of the selection and association, similar to protocols such as GSM MAP and 802.11u

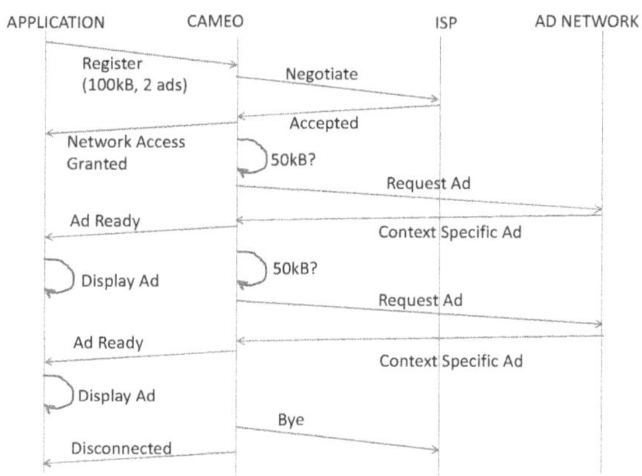

Figure 8: A CAMEO-ISP negotiation example

ANQP. Our current implementation uses a DHCP option field.

CAMEO then performs negotiations on behalf of the application and then accepts the best 'deal' it can find with an agreeable ISP. Note CAMEO can be used in conjunction with users' existing data plans for ad-subsidized connectivity. However, if all negotiations fail, CAMEO informs the user and allows the user to fallback to other data plans, such as a micropayments option. CAMEO also supports re-negotiation to reach an agreement. For example, the mobile application may offer to display ISP-provided ads more frequently. Conversely, the application may re-negotiate and lower its bandwidth requirements. For example, it may choose to change the richness of the content (fetching only text instead of both images and text) in order to obtain free connectivity to the Internet.

Negotiation protocol: Figure 8 illustrates a typical negotiation process, based on a per-byte model, where the negotiated agreement would require the ISP to transfer y bytes of network traffic in exchange for the ability to select and display x advertisements.

On initialization, the CAMEO-enabled mobile application registers with CAMEO with its expected bandwidth usage and maximum available 'slots'. (The application also registers other details such as the different ANs used by the application.) For negotiating network access, CAMEO contacts the ISP's negotiation server with the offer of the application (y = 100KB and $x = 2$.) In our example, once the ISP accepts this offer, CAMEO informs the application of the approved access.

Next, the application specifies the source ports (and the type—TCP/UDP) it will use for its traffic and also registers a callback function with CAMEO to receive notifications when ISP's advertisements are to be shown. CAMEO then interacts with the ISP network elements to set up the monitoring and enforcement of these flows. At appropriate intervals (in our example, once after every 50KB of data transfer), CAMEO fetches new advertisements from the ISP and asks the application to display them.

7. EVALUATION

Using our prototype implementation, we evaluate the following three aspects of CAMEO:

1. How accurately can we predict users' future context? In Section 7.1, we show that our prediction algorithm achieves 84% accuracy on average.
2. How much energy and bandwidth savings does it achieve? In Section 7.2, we show that we reduce the energy consumption by 25 to 37 times and bandwidth by up to 4.8 times when displaying 100 advertisements while incurring very little overhead.
3. Is CAMEO's ISP negotiation feasible? We show that the negotiation protocol introduces little overhead and ISPs may actually benefit from switching to an ad-supported model.

7.1 Context Prediction

We measure the accuracy of prediction using two metrics—time period of prediction and the fraction of time an application was used. We divide each day into time bins. Using past history (training set), each bin has a list of applications that were observed as being used in that bin and we know the number of bins they appeared in. (i.e. fractional use). We observe future usage (test set) to compute the prediction accuracy.

1. Binary prediction with short bins: To measure the accuracy over short periods, each bin is set to be 15 minutes long (total 96 bins/day). For each bin in the test set, we compute the fraction of applications in the test set that were also part of the training set. If all applications in the bin remain the remain, we count that as a successful prediction. The prediction accuracy is now defined as the fraction of bins that were predicted correctly.
2. Binary prediction of long bins: To measure accuracy over a day, each bin is set to be a day. We perform a binary test of whether an application was used on the same day. The prediction accuracy is now simply the fraction of applications that were predicted correctly.
3. Weighted prediction: To measure how often an application context appears in a day, the difference in the fraction of time (δ_i) an application i was used in the test set versus the training set is computed. The accuracy is then computed as $100 - \sum \delta_i \cdot 100$

We divided the one-month period of the users' logs into two sets of two weeks each. The first two weeks' data is used as the training set. The next two weeks' data is used as the test set. Table 3 summarizes the accuracy results obtained using the above three approaches for three random users on a Monday. Figure 9 summarizes the mean accuracy of the different approaches (for the two week data set) for each day of the week (for user #3).

Table 3: App. Prediction Results for Monday

User #	Approach #1	Approach #2	Approach #3
1	75%	30.77%	82.70%
2	51.07%	81.25%	90.05%
3	67.86%	90.90%	76.41%

We make two observations here:

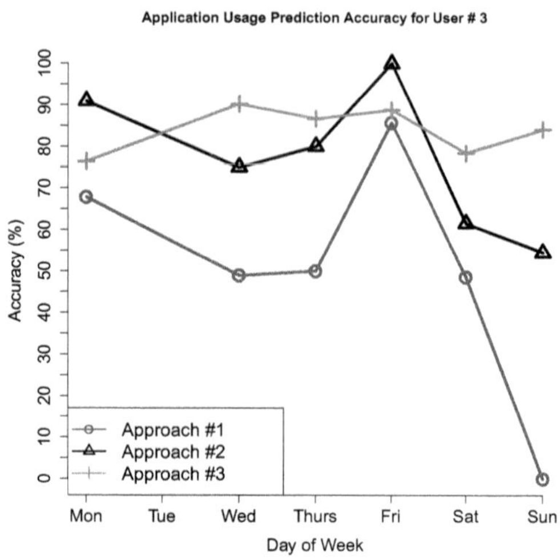

Figure 9: Prediction Accuracy.

Table 4: Bandwidth usage (in MB) with and without CAMEO prefetching

No. of ads	Without CAMEO	With CAMEO pre-fetch	
		ANAS	LAS & BEAS
10	0.646	0.321	0.322
100	6.334	1.375	1.324
1000	61.129	5.439	4.754

1. Predicting application context over shorter time periods was difficult with the simple approaches but was much easier for longer time periods.

2. Users operate phones inconsistently over weekends.

7.2 Resource savings on the mobile

We demonstrate that CAMEO can significantly reduce the bandwidth and energy consumption while incurring very little overhead. We compare the performance and overhead (size of cache needed and latency) of delivering mobile advertisements with and without CAMEO.

Bandwidth savings: We estimate the bandwidth usage with and without CAMEO.

Without CAMEO each advertisement is fetched on demand without being cached at the mobile device [12, 28]. However, when using CAMEO, each unique advertisement is sent only once during the bulk ad pre-fetch phase. We generate the cache for advertisements using the corpus and the context from the user data. Table 4 lists the amount of network traffic that is created for displaying 10, 100 and 1000 advertisements for our demo application. This includes all network traffic including DNS lookups but it assumes that the mobile device is already connected to the network.

We observe that when CAMEO is used, significant bandwidth savings are achieved even with a moderate number of displayed advertisements, regardless of its local ad selection methods (ANAS, LAS, and BEAS). These savings occur because CAMEO removes (1) significant repetitions of advertisements (see Figure 2) by sending each unique advertisement once and (2) overhead of DNS lookups and repeated Javascript code [12, 28]. We believe that compression can gain further savings since most of the advertisements share templates and are pure text (HTML) (refer Section 5.2).

Table 5: Energy consumption (in Joules) for fetching different no. of advertisements with and without CAMEO prefetching

No. of ads	Current Systems		With CAMEO pre-fetch			
			ANAS		LAS & BEAS	
	3G	WiFi	3G	WiFi	3G	WiFi
10	140.53	21.16	138.17	20.17	29.41	4.78
100	1403.25	210.73	1369.02	196.31	36.33	7.70
1000	14017.2	2100.87	13632.8	1938.96	60.02	17.67

Table 6: Size of cache in MB as a function of the number of advertisements displayed to the user for different apps. DM=demo, HD=Hanping, PL=Plume, SH=SoundHound

Ad impressions	DM	HD	PL	SH
10	0.27	0.18	0.22	0.27
100	1.06	0.44	0.82	0.86
1000	3.25	0.75	2.36	2.06

Energy savings:

Table 5 reports the energy consumption for fetching advertisements using CAMEO. We measured the energy consumption using the Monsoon power measurement tool on a Samsung Galaxy SIII phone running Android OS v4.0.4, on Singapore's SingTel network and the Singapore Management University's WiFi network in Singapore. We use the same cache described above for the bulk ad pre-fetch. The results show that CAMEO provides significant energy savings only when the ad selection is completely done locally (LAS and BEAS). We observe no significant difference in energy consumption between the current system (w/o CAMEO) and CAMEO's ANAS, which contacts the ad network every time an ad is displayed. CAMEO reduces the energy consumption by 38 times on 3G and 30 times on WiFi when 100 advertisements are displayed using the LAS or BEAS logic. Note that CAMEO's energy consumption includes the energy consumed in the prefetch phase. This may increase as corpus size increases. However, since CAMEO can be configured to prefetch only when the mobile device is on a cheap network and connected to a power source, the actual impact on energy consumption for a large corpus may be negligible.

Storage overhead: The storage overhead of the advertisement corpus can be very user specific. It depends on a number of factors such as the prediction accuracy, the time which an advertisement supported application spends in the foreground, the desired hit-rate in the cache, and the advertising network's priorities. To get a rough estimate on the *minimum* size of the cache needed for serving ads, we make a simplifying assumption—we are able to predict context perfectly. We compute the statistical frequency with each unique advertisement is shown for the different contexts and typical time spent in each of these contexts.

Table 6 lists the minimum size of cache needed to show different number of advertisements for each app in our study. The cache size will increase if the advertisement network wishes to cover more contexts than the ones that have been predicted. It will also increase because context-prediction can never be 100% accurate. Since each user typically uses multiple ad-supported apps, the total storage requirements

Table 7: Network changes and the corresponding signaling messages for different users

User	N/w Changes	Apps	Negotiations	Messages	Bytes
1	1.6	1.75	3	34	1863
2	2.2	1.09	3	29	1863
3	3.7	1.54	6	68	3726
4	2.4	2.5	6	72	3726
5	4.1	2.3	10	114	6210

will be much higher. Nevertheless, the storage required is a very small fraction of the total space seen on most mobile devices.

Latency for advertisement display: We measure the latency of invoking the API to get an advertisement for display. To measure this, we record the timestamps on the mobile just before and just after the code for fetching the advertisement is executed, i.e. before the advertisement is displayed on screen. For LAS and BEAS, the advertisements are fetched locally and the latency is about 0.1ms. For ANAS, fetching an advertisement over the existing 3G networks took approximately 6.1 seconds for an advertisement, almost 60% of which was spent turning ON the 3G radio. This represents the worst case when there is no pre-existing connectivity. On the WiFi network, the latency was closer to 3.8 seconds, which was also spent mostly on turning ON the WiFi radio. For ANAS, we observed similar latency values when fetching advertisements without CAMEO. Fetching very large advertisements with ANAS was slightly faster by about 20ms.

7.3 ISP Negotiation

We first show that our ISP negotiation introduces minimal overhead and that this can be seamlessly integrated into the association and connection establishment process. Then, we explore whether ISPs would have any financial incentives to provide an ad-subsidized plan through CAMEO.

Signaling load: We first evaluate the signaling overhead of our negotiation protocol. We deployed our prototype on a campus network, placing a mobile device on the campus WiFi network and the ISP negotiator on a different (wired) subnet. For the negotiation process described in Section 6.3, a total of 621 bytes were exchanged employing 12 messages (excluding the TCP handshakes).

We analyzed our user data set to determine how many times a user switches between two networks in a day (averaged over a one-month period). Every time a user changes a network, all the CAMEO enabled applications that are in use will need to re-negotiate thereby creating a flurry of messages on the network. Table 7 shows the mean number of times (per day) five different users switched between networks, the mean number of advertisement supported applications in use (per day) and the corresponding number of messages that are generated on the network for each network switch. (The rest of the users fell between the extremes and their data is not reported here.) For Table 7, we assumed that each user used the ad-supported application on every network.

Financial Feasibility: We explore whether it is feasible for the ISP to financially break even the cost of giving free bandwidth with advertisements. We consider two different

Table 8: Mean application network traffic data rate and frequency of advertisements for popular advertisement-supported free applications

Application	Ad fetch interval	Ads/second	Ads/MB
Angry Birds	45 sec	0.022	50
Sound Hound	45 sec	0.022	7
SG Buses	37 sec	0.027	36
The Weather Channel	60 sec	0.016	30

charging models for connectivity: 1) where a user is charged by time and 2) where the user pays for a bandwidth budget. Boingo follows the first model and plans that charge \$8 for 24 hours access ($\approx$0.01 cents/second) and \$10 for a month ($\approx$ 0.0004 cents/second) . AT&T follows the second model and offers 300 MB for \$20 (6.7 cents/MB) and 5 GB for \$50 (1 cent/MB).

According to KPCB's Internet Trends report [14], the effective CPM (cost per 1000 impressions) on mobile devices was \$0.75. At this rate, Boingo will break even for showing ads every 8.1 seconds and every 3.2 minutes for its two different rate plans. AT&T will break even for showing 88.8 ads/MB (or an ad per every 11.25 KB data) delivered on its lower tier plan and 13.3 ads/MB (or an add per 75 KB data) on its higher tier plan.

Although the rate of advertisements may be too high for applications that generate large amount of traffic (such as a web browser fetching 1 MB web pages), we find that this model is feasible for applications that generate relatively small amount of traffic (such as an email application). For example, Table 8 shows the rates of advertisements displayed for some popular "free" applications. From the data, we observe that both ISPs (offering different pricing models) can break even for some applications with users subscribing the higher tier plans.

8. RELATED WORK

Monetization of personal information: Many studies [22, 13, 5] propose monetization of users private information through an open market where users directly get paid for the information they choose to expose to targeted advertising. They propose various auction-like mechanisms that allow user's control and trade-off in the amount of information they expose. Rather than directly compensating users, CAMEO propose the use of ad slots as the medium of exchange between users attention and bandwidth by extending the existing model.

Resource use of mobile advertising: Eprof [19] analyzed the energy consumed in smartphone apps and revealed that mobile advertising library is responsible for 65 to 75% of the energy consumed by free apps. Khan et al. [12] show that free apps are actually free because they bear cost to most users who are on a metered data plan. Vallina-Rodriguez et al. [28] presented a comprehensive measurement study of the traffic generated by mobile advertising. Analyzing a trace of a mobile carrier with more than 3 million subscribers, they show that ads account non-significant fraction of the data traffic. Advertising account for 1% of all mobile traffic, and for 50% of Android users, more than 5% of the traffic is related to advertising. They also suggest that prefetching can be an effective solution. However, they do not address how context-dependant ads can be prefetched. Mohan et al. [16] also propose pre-fetching of advertisements to reduce energy consumption. They use similar techniques as ours to prefetch advertisements. However their focus is less on predicting future context and more on selecting the set of advertisements that will preserve the future deadlines for displaying advertisements.

Security and privacy in advertising: Many studies have pointed out the potential user privacy risks and security problems. AdRisk [9] showed that ad libraries collect private information ranging from user's location to more private information such as call logs, browser bookmarks, and list of apps installed. To address such privacy problems, many system have been proposed. For example, AdDroid [21], AppFence [11], Adnostic [26], and Privad [10] provide users with better control over the information transmitted from their mobile device.

Prevention or mitigation of click and impression fraud has also been an important area of study. While detection of click frauds or spams have primarily been the interest of advertisement networks for many years [7, 27], recent studies [3] characterized the behavior of click-spammers. Systems, such as AdSplit [23] and Quire [4], propose remote attestation-based verification of advertisement related events as a solution for click-spams.

We take the same view as many of these studies that support for advertising should be incorporated into the mobile operating system. Therefore, many of the studies are complementary to CAMEO.

Protocols for seamless roaming: Mobile networks provide standard protocols for roaming. GSM's Mobile Application Part (MAP) supports dynamic authentication of a roaming user and assignment of a roaming number. Similarly, 802.11u also supports seamless roaming and cellular to Wi-Fi offload. In the network selection process, 802.11u's Access Network Query Protocol (ANQP) allows mobile devices to query information such as hotspot provider's name and roaming agreements in place. We envision that CAMEO's negotiation protocols will be part of network discovery and selection protocols, such as GSM MAP and 802.11u ANQP.

9. DISCUSSION AND FUTURE WORK

While this paper describes the basic mechanisms that enable optimized advertisement delivery and advertisement bartering for connectivity, there are many repercussions of this design on the advertising and mobile application ecosystem that we leave for future work. For example, Section 4.4 describes some of the issues associated with accounting and verification of ad delivery/display. Below, we discuss some of the issues associated with network traffic policing, privacy, content management and revenue generation.

Traffic Policing.

One of CAMEO's core goals is to enable applications to use ad bartering to pay for the connectivity that they use. This will require the creation of a contract between the application and the ISP regarding the terms of the exchange; that must then be enforced! Section 4.4 describes techniques that can be used to verify the ad display part of the contract; however, we also need to enforce the network usage part. For example, the ISP could perform per-flow accounting on the edge router to police the contract. However, some edge routers may not have the memory or CPU resources to perform the necessary flow accounting — especially if hundreds of mobile devices are connected and their applications keep shifting between foreground (where they can see advertisements) and background (where they cannot and the mobile OS closes the open ports) states. One hybrid solution would be for the ISP to perform per-device (i.e., aggregate) accounting but for the CAMEO service on each mobile device to perform per-flow accounting. Note that the CAMEO service must already implement per-flow accounting to alert applications when either a) sufficient time has elapsed since the display of the last ISP-provided advertisement or b) their traffic volume is approaching the specified limit without enough ISP advertisements being displayed on the client. However, the aggregate accounting solution does raise issues related to ISPs trusting the end device accounting; we defer solutions to these issues to future work.

Privacy.

CAMEO relies heavily on accessing user context to enable targeted advertising. However, the user should be able to specify which context data can be used by CAMEO. However, it is likely that better context data will result in carefully targeted advertisements that could produce more revenue per ad. Hence, CAMEO could incorporate consumer friendly negotiation mechanisms that allow more interesting context to be traded off for fewer ads.

Content Management.

CAMEO's support for both ad developer and network provider advertising raises issues related to regulation and fairness. When a mobile application developer signs up today with an AN, there are clear rules and agreements on what type of advertisements can be shown. In future work, we plan to explore mechanisms to ensure that local ISPs use the same content policies that developers have with ANs. For example, an ISP should not show an inappropriate advertisement in applications meant for children.

Revenue Maximization.

One of CAMEO's key features is that it allows ISPs, app developers, ad networks, and users to engage in revenue exchange associated with advertising. However, in response, each of these players is likely to develop new revenue maximizing strategies. For example, we are currently investigating better context prediction and pre-fetching strategies that ad network could use to improve ad targeting and minimize the number of ads they must deliver (and "pay" for using ad slots) over expensive connectivity. We also plan to explore the tradeoffs of using pre-fetched advertisements instead of the dynamic auctions that ad networks use to select ads today. In addition to exploring the best strategies for each player, we also plan to explore the interaction of these strategies and their impact on the whole systems behavior.

10. CONCLUSION

Mobile advertising is a rapidly growing industry [1] that has a significant impact on the business models of the mobile Internet. However, the mechanisms that support sending advertising to mobiles devices have not been well though out. In particular, the mechanisms disenfranchise key stakeholders including end users and the mobile ISPs. In particular, the current model unfairly imposes cost to these stakeholders without providing a flexible business model for them. While many studies have addressed piecemeal solutions for the various problems with the current mobile advertising ecosystem, the core thesis of CAMEO is that the mobile advertising ecosystem should be redesigned to allow win-win interactions between all the key stakeholders. This paper explored key designs of such an architecture. CAMEO employs predictive prefetching that effectively decouples the tasks of advertisement selection and delivery. The resulting flexibility allows CAMEO to schedule proactive bulk advertisement retrieval in a way that minimizes the cost associated with fetching those advertisements. In addition, CAMEO provides a flexible negotiation model that allows individual applications to negotiate with mobile ISP for bandwidth access; opening up new business models and opportunities.

11. REFERENCES

[1] US online ad revenues continue growth, set Q1 peak. http://www.marketingcharts.com/wp/direct/online-ad-revenues-hit-record-317b-in-2011-surpass-cable-tv-21842/, June 2012.

[2] Digital video advertising trends: 2012. http://www.breakmedia.com/digitalvideoadstudy, 2012.

[3] V. Dave, S. Guha, and Y. Zhang. Measuring and fingerprinting click-spam in ad networks. In *Proc. ACM SIGCOMM*, pages 175–186, 2012.

[4] M. Dietz, S. Shekhar, Y. Pisetsky, A. Shu, and D. S. Wallach. Quire: Lightweight provenance for smart phone operating systems. In *Proceedings of the 20th USENIX conference on Security*, 2011.

[5] A. Ghosh and A. Roth. Selling privacy at auction. In *Proc. ACM conference on Electronic Commerce*, 2011.

[6] J. Ghosh, M. J. Beal, H. Q. Ngo, and C. Qiao. On profiling mobility and predicting locations of wireless users. In *Proc. international workshop on Multi-hop ad hoc networks: from theory to reality*, REALMAN '06, 2006.

[7] Google ads: Ad traffic quality resource center. `http://www.google.com/intl/en_ALL/ads/adtrafficquality/index.html`.

[8] How cost are calculated in adwords. `http://support.google.com/adwords/bin/answer.py?hl=en&answer=1704424`.

[9] M. C. Grace, W. Zhou, X. Jiang, and A.-R. Sadeghi. Unsafe exposure analysis of mobile in-app advertisements. In *Proc. ACM conference on Security and Privacy in Wireless and Mobile Networks*, pages 101–112, 2012.

[10] S. Guha, B. Cheng, and P. Francis. Privad: Practical Privacy in Online Advertising. In *Proc. Symposium on Networked Systems Design and Implementation (NSDI)*, Boston, MA, Mar 2011.

[11] P. Hornyack, S. Han, J. Jung, S. Schechter, and D. Wetherall. These aren't the droids you're looking for: Retrofitting android to protect data from imperious applications. In *Proc. ACM CCS*, pages 639–652, 2011.

[12] A. J. Khan, V. Subbaraju, A. Misra, and S. Seshan. Mitigating the true cost of advertisement-supported "free" mobile applications. In *Proc. Workshop on Mobile Computing Systems & Applications*, 2012.

[13] K. C. Laudon. Markets and privacy. *Communications of the ACM*, 39(9):92–104, Sept. 1996.

[14] M. Meeker and L. Wu. Kpcb internet trends 2012, May 2012. `http://www.kpcb.com/insights/2012-internet-trends`.

[15] C. Mims. Facebook's plan to find its next billion users: convince them the internet and Facebook are the same. `http://qz.com/5180/facebooks-plan-to-find-its-next-billion-users-convince-them-the-internet-and-facebook-are-the-same/`, Sept. 2012.

[16] P. Mohan, S. Nath, and O. Riva. Prefetching Mobile Ads: Can advertising systems afford it? In *Proceedings of the Eighth European Conference on Computer Systems, Eurosys'13*, 2013.

[17] A. J. Nicholson and B. D. Noble. Breadcrumbs: forecasting mobile connectivity. In *Proc. ACM MobiCom*, pages 46–57, 2008.

[18] B. D. Noble, M. Satyanarayanan, D. Narayanan, J. E. Tilton, J. Flinn, and K. R. Walker. Agile application-aware adaptation for mobility. In *Proc. ACM Symp. on Operating Sys. Principles*, Oct. 1997.

[19] A. Pathak, Y. C. Hu, and M. Zhang. Where is the energy spent inside my app?: Fine grained energy accounting on smartphones with eprof. In *Proc. ACM european conference on Computer Systems*, EuroSys, pages 29–42, 2012.

[20] P. N. Pathirana, A. V. Savkin, and S. Jha. Mobility modelling and trajectory prediction for cellular networks with mobile base stations. In *Proc. ACM MobiHoc*, 2003.

[21] P. Pearce, A. Felt, G. Nunez, and D. Wagner. Addroid: Privilege separation for applications and advertisers in android. In *Proc. AsiaCCS*, 2012.

[22] C. Riederer, V. Erramilli, A. Chaintreau, B. Krishnamurthy, and P. Rodriguez. For sale : Your data: By : you. In *Proc. ACM HotNets*, 2011.

[23] S. Shekhar, M. Dietz, and D. S. Wallach. Adsplit: Separating smartphone advertising from applications. In *Proceedings of the USENIX Security Symposium*, 2012.

[24] L. Song, D. Kotz, R. Jain, and X. He. Evaluating next-cell predictors with extensive wi-fi mobility data. *IEEE Transactions on Mobile Computing*, 5(12), Dec. 2006.

[25] M. H. Sun and D. M. Blough. Mobility prediction using future knowledge. In *Proceedings of the 10th ACM Symposium on Modeling, analysis, and simulation of wireless and mobile systems*, MSWiM '07, 2007.

[26] V. Toubiana, A. Narayanan, D. Boneh, H. Nissenbaum, and S. Barocas. Adnostic: Privacy preserving targeted advertising. In *Proc. NDSS*, 2010.

[27] A. Tuzhilin. The Lane's Gifts v. Google Report. `http://googleblog.blogspot.com/pdf/Tuzhilin_Report.pdf`.

[28] N. Vallina-Rodriguez, J. Shah, A. Finamore, Y. Grunenberger, K. Papagiannaki, H. Haddadi, and J. Crowcroft. Breaking for commercials: Characterizing mobile advertising. In *Proc. ACM IMC*, pages 343–356, 2012.

Scalable Crowd-Sourcing of Video from Mobile Devices

Pieter Simoens
Ghent University - iMinds
Gaston Crommenlaan 8/201
9050 Gent, Belgium
psimoens@intec.ugent.be

Yu Xiao
Aalto University
Konemiehentie 2
02150 Espoo, Finland
yu.xiao@aalto.fi

Padmanabhan Pillai
Intel Labs
4720 Forbes Avenue
Suite 410
Pittsburgh, PA 15213, USA
padmanabhan.s.pillai@intel.com

Zhuo Chen
Carnegie Mellon University
5000 Forbes Ave
Pittsburgh, PA 15213, USA
zhuoc@cs.cmu.edu

Kiryong Ha
Carnegie Mellon University
5000 Forbes Ave
Pittsburgh, PA 15213, USA
krha@cmu.edu

Mahadev Satyanarayanan
Carnegie Mellon University
5000 Forbes Ave
Pittsburgh, PA 15213, USA
satya@cs.cmu.edu

ABSTRACT

We propose a scalable Internet system for continuous collection of crowd-sourced video from devices such as Google Glass. Our hybrid cloud architecture, *GigaSight,* is effectively a Content Delivery Network (CDN) in reverse. It achieves scalability by decentralizing the collection infrastructure using cloudlets based on virtual machines (VMs). Based on time, location, and content, privacy sensitive information is automatically removed from the video. This process, which we refer to as *denaturing,* is executed in a user-specific VM on the cloudlet. Users can perform content-based searches on the total catalog of denatured videos. Our experiments reveal the bottlenecks for video upload, denaturing, indexing, and content-based search. They also provide insight on how parameters such as frame rate and resolution impact scalability.

Categories and Subject Descriptors

C.2.4 [**Computer-Communication Networks**]: Distributed Systems; I.4.0 [**Image Processing and Computer Vision**]: Image processing software; I.5.4 [**Pattern Recognition**]: Applications

Keywords

mobile computing, cloud computing, denaturing, cloudlet, computer vision, virtual machines, Google Glass, smartphone

1. INTRODUCTION

Head-up displays (HUDs) have been used for more than a decade in military and maintenance tasks. In these challenging domains, the primary design goal was to provide hands-free user assistance. Comfort and style were only second order design considerations, hence limiting mainstream adoption by the public. Today, we are on the verge of a disruptive generation of HUDs that target daily use by the general public. Google Glass is the most well-known example, but others are also being developed. For example, the NSF Quality of Life Technology Center has created a first-person vision system for disabled veterans [25].

When equipped with a front-end camera, HUDs enable *near-effortless capture of first-person viewpoint video.* Recording a video will merely require you to press a button on the shank of your glasses, rather than taking your smartphone out of your pocket and performing a number of touch screen interactions. Easy video capture will greatly increase the number of videos shared with the world (e.g. by uploading to YouTube). A good example of the videos we might expect was recently provided by designer Diane von Furstenberg, who wore Google Glass to capture and share her experience at the Spring 2013 Fashion Show in New York City [4]. As of today, YouTube already contains thousands of first-person videos captured with less elegant commercial products such as the Contour+2 [10]. Integrating video capture with correlated sensor information such as gaze tracking, audio, geolocation, acceleration, and biodata (e.g., heartrate) is only a matter of time.

In this paper, we focus on the gathering, cataloging, and access of first-person video from many contributors. By automatic tagging of this rich data collection, and by enabling deep content-based search of any subset of that data, we create a valuable public resource much like the Web itself. Even simple uses of this resource can transform today's applications in imaginative ways:

Imagine Google Street View Live, allowing you to see live video that was recently captured by someone walking down that street. You see the same things that the user saw, and linger over the scenes that caught the user's attention. You are effectively reliving his walk down the street. Parts of some scenes are blurred because the user did not want to share them with you. You can click on "Winter", and the video stream changes to one captured by a user walking down that street last winter. You can click on "multiview" and see the street from the viewpoints of multiple users simultaneously.

Figure 1 speculates on many other use cases that could be enabled by a large-scale searchable video repository.

Enabling this futuristic vision poses technical challenges at many levels. It also creates many policy-related challenges, such as those pertaining to privacy and user incentives. Our focus is on technical issues, but policy issues are relevant to the extent that they require supporting mechanisms in the implementation. This paper makes the following contributions:

MobiSys'13, June 25–28, 2013, Taipei, Taiwan

Marketing and Advertising: Crowd-sourced videos can provide observational data for questions that are difficult to answer today. For example, which are the billboards that attract the most user attention? How successful is a new store window display in attracting interest? Which are the clothing colors and patterns that attract most interest in viewers? How regional are these preferences?

Locating people, pets and things: A missing child was last seen walking home from school. A search of crowd-sourced videos from the area shows that the child was near a particular spot an hour ago. The parent remembers that the child has a friend close to that location. She is able to call the friend's home and locates the child there.

Public safety: Which are the most dangerous intersections, where an accident is waiting to happen? Although no accident has happened yet, it is only a matter of time before a tragedy occurs. Crowd-sourced videos can reveal dangerous intersections, for timely installation of traffic lights.

Fraud detection: A driver reports that his car was hit while it was parked at a restaurant. However, his insurance claims adjuster finds a crowd-sourced video in which the car is intact when leaving the restaurant.

Figure 1: Example Use Cases

- It describes the potential benefits of crowd-sourced first-person video collection, offers an incentive model for such a system, identifies the key challenges in realizing such a capability at global scale, and derives the technical requirements for a viable implementation.
- It presents *GigaSight,* a hybrid cloud architecture for scalable crowd-sourcing of video from mobile devices. This architecture is effectively a Content Distribution Network (CDN) in reverse, and achieves scalability by decentralizing the cloud computing infrastructure using VM-based cloudlets at the edges of the Internet.
- It introduces the concept of *denaturing* for privacy, and shows how contributor-specific privacy policies can be automatically enforced on captured video through contributor-specific algorithms.
- It shows how captured video content can be automatically tagged for future searches, both using meta-data such as location and time, as well as image content tags extracted by computer vision algorithms. For image content that is not tagged, we also show how to perform interactive content search of video segments.
- It evaluates a proof-of-concept prototype implementation of the GigaSight architecture to expose its scalability bottlenecks. Based on these measurements, the paper proposes mechanisms to improve scalability in future implementations.
- It presents a model for the scalability of GigaSight, based on cloudlet capacity and location.

It is important to keep in mind that this work describes a proof of concept rather than a mature, fully-deployed system with a large user base. There are many technical challenges in realizing this vision, as discussed in the rest of this paper. Our goal is to expose and quantify the design tradeoffs in building such a system. This work also exposes new public policy challenges in areas such as privacy. A full understanding of these issues will have to await real experience from a deployed system.

2. INCENTIVE MODEL AND PRIVACY

2.1 Continuous Capture and Sharing

Today, users manually select and tag the video fragments they upload to YouTube. Their videos are typically of personal achievements (e.g., first person viewpoint sports), or special occasions that they want to share. The content thus has enough personal value to serve as an incentive for the user to spend time on editing, selection, and tagging. This self-interest is absent in continuously captured scenes of everyday life. The value of sharing such scenes lies in the fact that they may have high value to someone else. For example, a recent CNN news article [12] reported the arrest of a thief whose act of stealing appeared in the background of the photo shown in Figure 2. The tiny figure in the background would normally be ignored by anyone who views this image. It is only the context of a theft that makes it relevant. This is only one of many real-world examples in which an image captured for one reason proves valuable to someone else in a completely different context. Stieg Larsson's fictional work "The Girl with the Dragon Tattoo" embodies exactly this theme: a clue to the murderer's identity is embedded in the backgrounds of old crowd-sourced photographs [18]. While individual frames from continuous video capture can substitute for photographs in these examples, use of video segments can lead to even richer insights. In the use cases of Figure 1, the public safety example requires video: humans find it easy to detect a near-miss in the motion captured by a video segment, but hard to detect it from a single photograph or frame. More generally, content-based video search algorithms from the computer vision community have greatly increased in sophistication and accuracy in the past decade [15, 27]. They are now capable of reliably detecting human-meaningful actions such as clapping, hugging, bending down to pick up an object, tripping, falling, slipping, and sliding.

Figure 2: Theft captured in photo (Source: CNN [12])

These examples reveal two different requirements. First, in the absence of personal motivation, there needs to be an explicit incentive model for sharing continuously captured videos. We believe that any realistic incentive model must be accompanied by a privacy preserving mechanism that is as effortless as the capturing of the video itself. No economically viable incentive will be high enough to convince large numbers of users to go through their continuously-captured videos and manually remove sensitive scenes. Second, tags added by the user who captured a video are unlikely to be sufficient as the basis of search. Content-based search using computer vision algorithms that embody a search query will be needed. This processing can be done in advance for frequently-searched objects, thus producing an index for the video collection. However, some searches may involve queries about objects or scenes that were not anticipated during indexing. For these, a search mechanism that is better than brute force viewing of video segments is required.

2.2 Author-Publisher Model

Our goal here is only to describe a *plausible* incentive model. We recognize that a pilot deployment of the proposed system will be necessary to validate the proposed model and to explore other incentive models. We propose that crowd-sourced video be treated as *authored content*. What you see and capture effortlessly through your Google Glass is yours. By looking at some people rather than others, by gazing longer at some window displays rather than others, by averting your gaze from a street scene, and so on, you are implicitly exercising taste and judgment. A video capture embodies that taste and judgment. Good will or peer recognition may suffice to encourage sharing in some use cases (e.g. Google Streetview Live), but they are fragile incentives. A more robust and scalable approach is to create a business relationship with the service provider that invests in the video capture infrastructure. Like a book publisher, the service provider monetizes your authored content and shares the revenue with you. This leads to a simple incentive model: *you reap financial rewards for capturing and sharing scenes that others find to be of value.*

2.3 Denaturing

Unfortunately, always-on video capture is much less deliberate and controlled than authoring text. You can't help capturing scenes, but specific objects/people in them may not be what you (or they) want published. It is therefore crucial to edit out frames and/or blur individual objects in scenes. What needs to be removed is highly user-specific, but no user can afford the time to go through and edit video captured on a continuous basis. One therefore needs a process that continuously performs this editing as video is submitted for sharing. If a user is confident that the editing process accurately reflects his personal preferences, he is likely to share his captured video without further review. We refer to this user-specific lowering of fidelity as *denaturing*.

Denaturing has to strike a balance between privacy and value. At one extreme of denaturing is a blank video: perfect privacy, but zero value. At the other extreme is the original video at its capture resolution and frame rate. This has the highest value for potential customers, but also incurs the highest exposure of privacy. Where to strike the balance is a difficult question that is best answered individually, by each user. This decision will most probably be context-sensitive.

Denaturing is a complex process that requires careful analysis of the captured frames. From a technical viewpoint, state-of-the-art computer vision algorithms enable face detection, face recognition, and object recognition in individual frames. In addition, activity recognition in video sequences is also possible [27].

However, preserving privacy involves more than blurring (or completely removing) frames with specific faces, objects, or scenes. From other objects in the scene, or by comparing with videos taken at the same place and/or time from other users with different privacy settings, one might still deduce which object was blurred and is hence of value to the person who captured the video. In its full generality, denaturing may not only involve content modification but may also involve meta-data modification. For example, the accuracy of location meta-data associated with a sequence of video frames may be lowered to meet the needs of *k-anonymity* in location privacy [28, 36]. Whether the contents of the video sequence will also have to be blurred depends on its visual distinctiveness — a scene with the Eiffel Tower in the background is obviously locatable even without explicit location meta-data.

Guidance for denaturing may also be conveyed through social mores that deprecate video capture in certain locations and of certain types of scenes. In addition, a system of tagging locations or objects with visual markers (such as QR codes) could indicate that video capture is unwelcome. One can imagine video capture devices that automatically refrain from recording when they recognize an appropriate QR code in the scene. In addition, denaturing algorithms on a cloudlet may also strip out scenes that contain such a code. In the long run, one can envision the emergence of an ethics of video capture in public. A starting point might be the work of Kelly et al. [16] on an ethical framework for image capture in health care contexts. Many broader societal issues, such as the ability to subpoena captured but encrypted video, add further complexity.

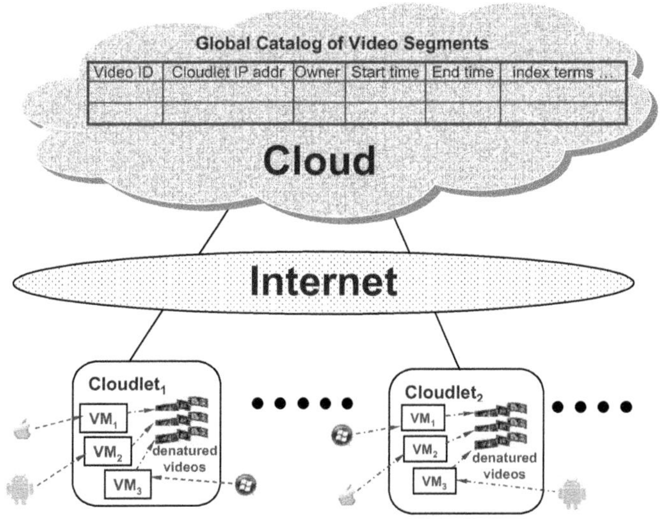

Figure 3: GigaSight Architecture.

Clearly, denaturing is a very deep concept that will need time, effort and deployment experience to fully understand. We restrict the scope of this paper to understanding the architectural and performance implications of denaturing, and leave the development of widely-accepted denaturing algorithms as future work. For evaluating the impact of denaturing on scalability in Section 5, we use conceptually simple but compute-intensive denaturing algorithms such as blurring all faces or blurring only a subset of faces from a user-specific list.

3. ARCHITECTURE: A CDN IN REVERSE

A key challenge is the high cumulative data rate of incoming videos from many users. Without careful design, this could easily overwhelm the capacity of metro area networks or the ingress Internet paths into centralized cloud infrastructure such as Google's large data centers or Amazon's EC2 sites. Today, 1 hour of video is uploaded to YouTube each second [35], which is the equivalent of only 3600 users simultaneously streaming. When the usage of HUDs becomes mainstream, this number will rapidly increase. Verizon recently announced an upgrade to 100 Gbps links in their metro area networks [24], yet one such link is capable of supporting 1080p streams from only 12000 users at YouTube's recommended upload rate of 8.5 Mbps. Supporting a million users will require 8.5 Tbps.

To solve this problem, we propose Gigasight, a *hybrid cloud architecture* that is effectively a CDN in reverse. This architecture, shown in Figure 3, uses decentralized cloud computing infrastructure in the form of VM-based *cloudlets* [29]. A cloudlet is a new architectural element that arises from the convergence of mobile computing and cloud computing. It represents the middle tier of a 3-tier hierarchy: mobile device – cloudlet – cloud. A cloudlet can be viewed as a "data center in a box" that "brings the cloud closer." While cloudlets were originally motivated by reasons of end-to-end latency for interactive applications, our use of cloudlets

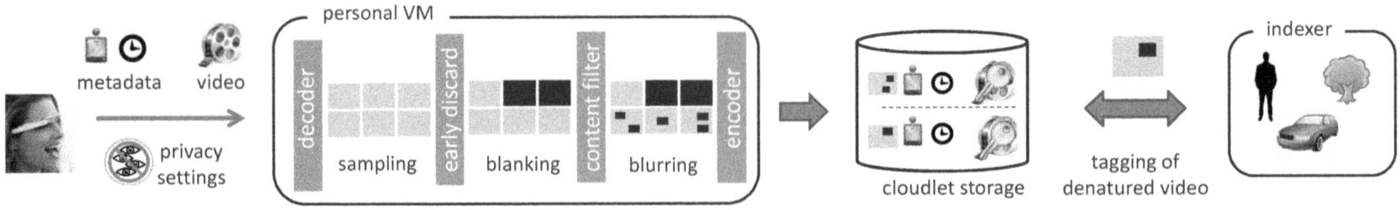

Figure 4: Overview of the GigaSight implementation.

here is based solely on bandwidth considerations. Today, "micro data centers" from companies such as Myoonet [22] and AOL [21] are already available for repurposing as cloudlets. To achieve good performance and extend battery life, tasks such as image processing for denaturing are offloaded from mobile devices to cloudlets. Zhu et al. [37] propose a media-edge cloud architecture in which storage, CPUs, and GPU clusters are presented at the edge of the network to provide sufficient QoS and QoE. This architecture aligns with our cloudlet-based 3-tier approach.

It is important to note in Figure 3 that cloudlets are not just temporary staging points for denatured video data en route to the cloud. With a large enough user base and continuous video capture, the constant influx of data at the edges will be a permanent stress on the ingress paths to the cloud. Just buffering data at cloudlets for later transmission to the cloud won't do — because users will be streaming 24/7, there will never be a "later" when ingress paths are unloaded. The potential bandwidth bottleneck is at the access and aggregation network, and not in the core network with its high-speed links. Preprocessing videos on cloudlets also offers the potential of using content-based storage optimization algorithms to retain only one of many similar videos from co-located users.

Cloudlets are the true home of denatured videos. Only meta-data about these videos (such as owner (anonymized), location of capture, start and end time of capture, cloudlet where stored, and index terms) is stored in a global catalog in the cloud. In a small number of cases, based on popularity or other metrics of importance, some videos may be copied to the cloud for archiving or replicated in the cloud and other cloudlets for scalable access. But most videos reside only at a single cloudlet. How long they are kept around depends on the storage reclamation and replication policy.

Although denaturing directly on smartphones may be more reassuring to users, our results in Section 6.1 show that the negative impact on battery life is unacceptable. We therefore perform denaturing on a cloudlet as video is being streamed into it. For each mobile user who is currently associated with a cloudlet, there is a "personal" VM that performs the customized denaturing for that user. When a user moves a significant distance, this VM migrates to another cloudlet that is now closer. This process is analogous to Wi-Fi handoff. Although the use of VMs incurs additional overhead relative to denaturing by a cloudlet-wide process, our approach supports user-specific denaturing and is likely to give the user greater confidence in the process.

Other cloudlet VMs (not shown in Figure 3) encapsulate image processing code to perform background indexing of recently-captured videos. Users can also manually add tags to their videos. To handle searches that are time-sensitive (such as locating a lost child) or to search for content that is not indexed, custom search code encapsulated in a VM can directly examine denatured videos.

Notice that Figure 3 is agnostic regarding the exact positioning of the cloudlets in the network. One option could be to place numerous small cloudlets at the very network edge. An alternative is to place fewer but larger cloudlets deeper in the network, e.g., at metropolitan scale. Our analysis in Section 6.2 suggests that placement close to the edge is preferable.

4. PROTOTYPE IMPLEMENTATION

We have implemented a complete prototype of the GigaSight architecture presented in Figure 4. The prototype comprises the complete chain of functionality from uploading video, over denaturing and indexing to the final step of searching through the available video segments.

4.1 Mobile client

Given the stringent limitations on weight and size to keep HUDs comfortable, it can be expected that their storage and processing power will be limited. We therefore use a smartphone as a HUD proxy that buffers video segments en route to the rest of the GigaSight framework. Our GigaSight mobile app was developed for Android Ice Cream Sandwich (4.0.4). Its functionality includes the configuration of user-specific privacy rules and the buffering of video segments. Figure 5 shows two screenshots of our app. In our current prototype, the mobile device camera acts as a complete surrogate for the HUD, including the actual video capture.

The user defines a default policy to publish or to blank all of his video segments. He can specify rules to deviate from this policy. Each rule is a chain of filters that scope time, location or objects. We apply a logical OR between rules, and a logical AND between the filters of a single rule, giving the user sufficient semantic possibilities to specify privacy settings. Time filters allow the user to specify, for example, that no video captured between 9 AM and 5 PM can be shared. Location conditions allow the user to specify geographical regions by simply tapping on a map. The object-based filters are currently limited to the faces present in the training set of our face recognition algorithms.

Captured videos are cached and uploaded as soon as a Wi-Fi connection becomes available. Through a REST-based API, the mobile device registers new segments and updates the associated metadata

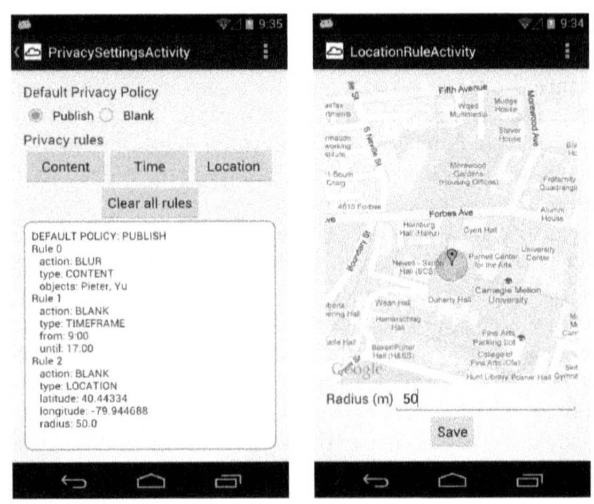

(a) Example privacy rule (b) Example location filter

Figure 5: Screenshots of the GigaSight frontend app.

Figure 6: Example of a denatured video frame.

information. At present, we capture video in MP4 format, as well as time-stamped GPS information. In future versions, more information streams can be associated with the video when additional sensors become available on HUDs.

4.2 Personal VM

The personal VM denatures the video uploaded by the mobile client following the user-defined privacy rules discussed in the previous section. It is the only component in the GigaSight entity, apart from the mobile device itself, that accesses the original, non-denatured video. As such, it forms the cloud-based counterpart of the mobile device: an entity that the user trusts to store personal content, but with much more computational and storage resources. When a mobile client signals that it has a segment ready for upload, the personal VM requests the Data Manager to allocate space for storing the processed video. The Data Manager, running as a cloudlet-wide service in a separate VM, organizes the cloudlet storage and metadata database.

Figure 4 illustrates how uploaded video is denatured inside the personal VM before being stored on the cloudlet. For the sake of clarity, the components interfacing with the mobile client and the Data Manager are not shown in this figure. The denaturing process is implemented using C++ and OpenCV 2.4.2.

Denaturing is implemented as a multi-step pipeline. In the first step, a subset of the video frames is selected for actual denaturing. As the results presented in section 5.2.2 will clearly indicate, video denaturing is too compute-intensive to perform at the native video frame rate. Then, metadata-based filters with low computational complexity are applied. This early-discard step is a binary process: based on the time and location, the frame is either completely blanked or passed through unmodified. In the third step, we apply more complex content-based filters. Currently, our prototype only supports face detection: any detected face will be blurred, as shown in Figure 6. The video frames are first decoded to raw RGB frames and converted to gray scale. Histogram equalization is applied to improve the contrast of the frame in order to increase the face detection accuracy. For each frame, the algorithm gives an array with the bounding boxes of the detected faces.

We combined a profile face detector with two variants of frontal face detection. The profile face detector and one of the frontal face detectors are based on Haar-like features [19, 34]. The classifiers for these algorithms are both included in the OpenCV distribution. The second frontal face detector uses the Local Binary Pattern (LBP) [6]. The LBP classifier we use [1] was trained from the PUT Vein Pattern Database [2].

The output of the denaturing process is a low-framerate video file that is stored on the cloudlet storage system. This provides a representative overview of video content for the indexing and search operations. The frames of the denatured video act as thumbnails for the full fidelity video.

Along with the denatured version, we also store an encrypted version of the original video. In the current version of our prototype, the personal VM encrypts video based on the Advanced Encryption Standard (AES) implementation that is included in the OpenSSL library. Each encrypted video can only be decrypted with a unique private key that is generated during encryption. If a user wants to see the complete video, the original must be decrypted and denatured inside the personal VM of the user that originally captured the video. Of course, if a video has been completely denatured as the result of a previous search, the ad-hoc denaturing will not be repeated.

4.3 Data Manager

The Data Manager runs in a separate VM on the cloudlet. It manages the storage of the video segments and the database with the associated metadata. The data is logically organized as a collection of segments. We define a segment as a record of the reality during a continuous period in time and space. Each segment contains one or more streams, each representing a single informational dimension of the reality. Streams can be audio, video, GPS coordinates, or any other sensor information captured.

All video and metadata are stored on local disk storage in the cloudlet. This is exported as an NFS volume for concurrent access by multiple local VMs. When a personal VM or the indexer wants to write or read a stream, the Data Manager provides a NFS pathname for the stream. Access to the Data Manager is mediated through a REST-interface implemented using TastyPie, Django and Python.

The metadata describing the different streams is stored in a MySQL database and initially includes the segment ID of the stream, capture time, duration, access control rights, and a geographical bounding box of the GPS coordinates, delineating the area in which the video has been captured. The GPS fixes are stored as a separate stream of the same segment. When the thumbnails of a video stream are processed by a specific indexer, the results are stored in a separate table of the database. These tags describe the detected objects and their positions in the video.

4.4 Video Content Indexer

The indexing of denatured video content is a background activity that is performed by a separate VM on the cloudlet. In our current implementation, each denatured frame is analyzed individually by computer vision code to obtain tags for that frame. A future version of our prototype will be able to analyze sequences of denatured frames in order to tag human-meaningful actions such as clapping, falling, etc. For each tag produced by the indexer, an entry is created in a dedicated tag table of the cloudlet database. Each entry contains the tag, the ID of the video segment, and a confidence score. For example, an entry "dog, `zoo.mp4`, 328, 95" indicates that our indexer detected with 95% confidence a dog in frame 328 of the video `zoo.mp4`. After extraction, these tags are also propagated to the catalog of video segments in the cloud. The global search workflow using these tags is described in Section 4.5.

As a proof of concept, we use a Python-based implementation of Shotton et al.'s image categorization and segmentation algorithm [30] with classifiers trained on the MSRC21 data set mentioned in that work. This enables us to identify, with acceptable levels of false positives and false negatives, the 21 classes of common objects

Table 1: Hardware used for the experiments.

smartphone	Samsung Google Galaxy Nexus I9250 Dual-core 1.2 GHz Cortex-A9 Android v4.0.4 Wi-Fi 802.11 a/g/n 1 GB RAM, 16 GB internal memory
cloudlet	Intel® Core™ i7-3770 CPU 3.40 GHz, 4 cores Linux 3.2.0 x86_64 32 GB RAM, 900 GB hard disk
Wi-Fi AP	Belkin N750 DB Wi-Fi Dual-Band N+ 2.4 GHz / 5 GHz (link rate up to 450 Mbps)

such as aeroplanes, bicycles, birds, etc., that are listed in the first column of Table 2.

An additional source of information about image content can come from the denaturing step. Since denaturing is performed before indexing, some important features of an image may not be available to downstream image processing algorithms. For example, a face detection algorithm may not correctly tag an image with faces because they are blurred. The obvious solution of indexing before denaturing is not acceptable because users expect their videos to be denatured first, before they are exposed to the cloudlet's image processing code. We, therefore, allow the denaturing step to export tags that are discovered in the course of denaturing. In the example above, the tag "face" would have been exported as an attribute of a frame with faces. Thus, the tags for a frame are the union of those obtained during denaturing by the user's image processing code within his personal VM, and those obtained during indexing by the cloudlet's image processing code.

4.5 Search Workflow

GigaSight uses a two-step hierarchical workflow to help a user find video segments relevant to a specific context. First, the user performs a conventional SQL search on the cloud-wide catalog. His query may involve metadata such as time and location, as well as tags extracted by indexing. Our prototype uses a Django-based webserver that supports these queries on a MySQL database. A production version of GigaSight would likely use a distributed cloud database such as BigTable to ensure a scalable global service. The result of this step is a list of video segments and their denatured thumbnails. The identity (i.e., the IP addresses) of the cloudlets on which those video segments are located can also be obtained from the catalog.

Viewing all the video segments identified by the first step may overwhelm the user. We therefore perform a second search step that filters on actual content to reduce the returned results to a more relevant set. This step is very computationally intensive but can be run in parallel on the cloudlets. This step uses *early discard*, as described by Huston et al. [14], to increase the selectivity of a result stream. Using a plugin interface, image processing code fragments called *filters* can be inserted into the result stream. These code fragments allow user-defined classifiers to examine video segments and to discard irrelevant parts of them, thus reducing the volume of data presented to the user. We provide a suite of filters for common search attributes such as color patches and texture patches. For more complex image content (such as the 21 classes shown in Table 2) the user can train his own STF filters offline and insert them into the result stream.

To illustrate this two-step workflow, consider a search for *"any images taken yesterday between 2pm and 4pm during a school outing to the Carnegie Science Center in Pittsburgh, showing two children in a room full of yellow balls and one of the children wearing his favorite blue plaid shirt."* The first step of the search would use the time and location information and the "face" tag to narrow the search. The result is a potentially large set of thumbnails from denatured videos that cover the specified location. From a multi-hour period of video capture by all visitors, this may only narrow the search to a few hundred or few thousand thumbnails. Using a color filter tuned to yellow, followed by a composite color/texture filter tuned to blue and plaid, most of these thumbnails may be discarded. Only the few thumbnails that pass this entire bank of filters are presented to the user. From this (hopefully) small set of thumbnails, it is easy for the user to pick the result shown in Figure 6.

5. EVALUATION

In exploring the limits to scaling GigaSight, we seek to identify the key bottlenecks in the system through experiments on our prototype. After the description of our experimental testbed in Section 5.1, we characterize separately the load incurred by video upload, denaturing and indexing in Section 5.2. Based on the insights gathered, we study in Section 5.3 how the available compute capacity on a cloudlet should be allocated between the personal VMs and the indexer in a set-up with multiple users.

5.1 Experimental Setup

To evaluate our prototype, we built a set-up consisting of smartphones and quad-core desktop machines emulating cloudlet and cloud hardware. Table 1 lists the details of this hardware. The state-of-the-art dual-core smartphones were connected to the cloudlets over a private 5 GHz 802.11n access point (AP), to minimize interference and collisions caused by other devices not participating in the experiment. The AP was connected via a private 1 Gbps LAN network to the cloudlet. The results reported in this section are used in Section 6.2 to study the scaling of GigaSight with larger infrastructures.

Lacking HUDs representative of devices such as Google Glass, we manually captured 10 minute videos with a smartphone while walking in downtown Pittsburgh. The videos were captured with resolutions set to 480p@30fps and 1080p@24fps, the representative formats available on action cameras such as the Contour+2, and encoded through an H.264 codec in a MP4 container.

To expand and diversify our video database, especially for the denaturing and indexing performance evaluation, we crawled 36 videos from YouTube, in the resolutions 360p (including 8 at 480x360 and 4 at 640x360), 720p (1080x720), and 1080p (1920x1080). When selecting the videos on YouTube, we ensured that they represented first-person viewpoints, and excluded music clips and other professionally edited content. We classified the selected YouTube videos into 4 categories: first-person viewpoint sport, in-vehicle viewpoint, public events (e.g., street parades), and public places (including holiday reports).

5.2 Scaling and Throughput

The scalability of this architecture, in terms of the number of users that can be served relative to cloudlet compute capacity and wireless network bandwidth, is the most important question that we explore. Our system performs video collection, denaturing, and indexing. Our goal is to understand which of these steps poses the scalability bottleneck with our current hardware.

5.2.1 Video Upload: The Cost of Capture

The goal of our first experiment is to quantify the capacity of the Wi-Fi channel in terms of the number of concurrent video uploads by multiple phones in GigaSight. Furthermore, we evaluate the individual throughput and energy consumption of each phone.

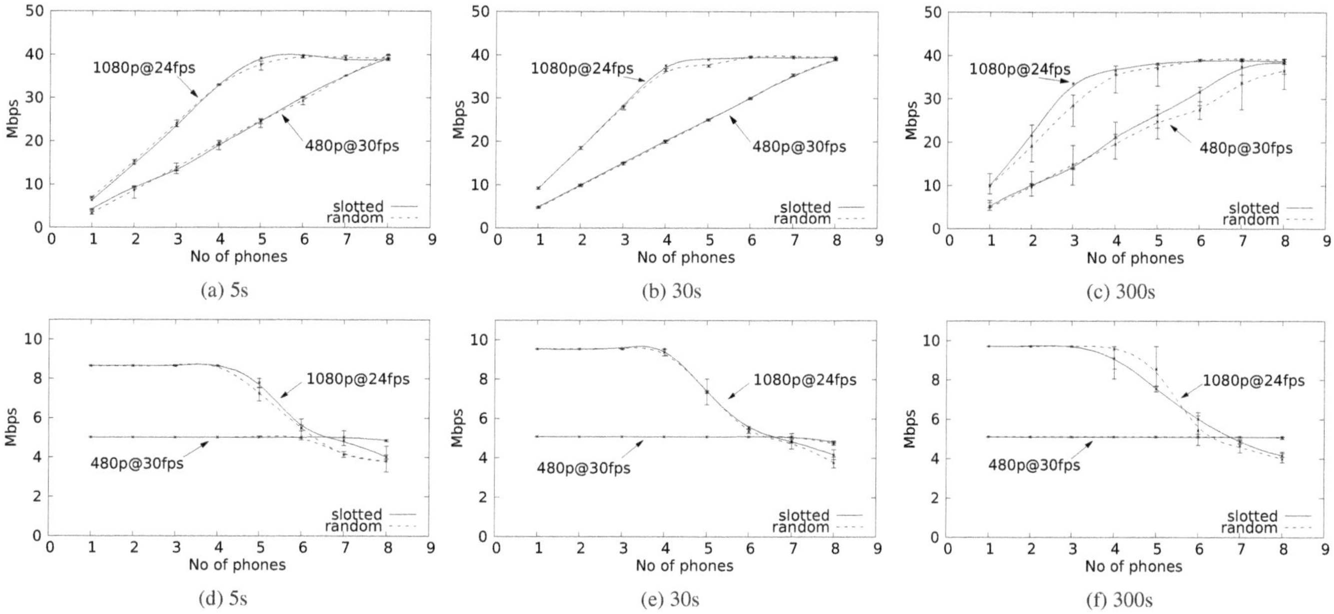

(a) 5s (b) 30s (c) 300s

(d) 5s (e) 30s (f) 300s

Figure 7: Throughput [Mbps] for different resolutions and video framerates. The figures on the top row show the cumulative throughput of the AP, the bottom row shows the net throughput achieved by each phone.

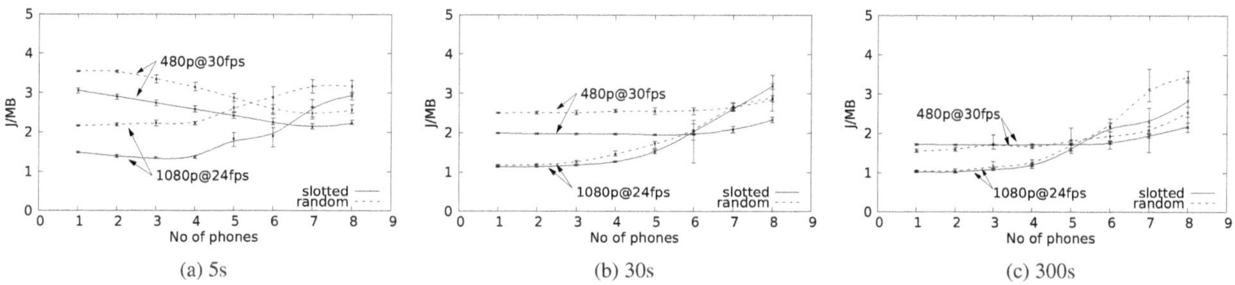

(a) 5s (b) 30s (c) 300s

Figure 8: Energy consumption of video upload from Nexus I9250 via 802.11n.

We first validated the maximum TCP throughput of our Wi-Fi channel using iPerf, a bandwidth measurement tool. When running the iPerf client on our laptop, the average throughput was around 160 Mbps, in line with what can be realistically expected from a dedicated 802.11n channel. However, when running the iPerf client on our Android phone, the measured throughput dropped to 25 Mbps. Clearly, the maximum throughput for a single device is limited by the processing capacity of the device and/or the implementation of the TCP stack and Wi-Fi driver.

We then moved on to experiments with actual video upload, where we gradually increased the number of phones uploading to the cloudlet. To avoid any potential overhead of virtualization, denaturing, or indexing, we only ran a lean Python server on the cloudlet that measures the total throughput received and the throughput per phone. This experiment allows us to set the baseline of how many users can be supported by our current cloudlet and Wi-Fi AP.

We envision the smartphone as a cache-in-your-pocket, temporarily buffering the captured video before sending it in a burst to the cloudlet, instead of continuously streaming to the cloudlet. To allow for repeatability of the experiments, we use a set of captured videos that we divided into fragments of 5 s, 30 s or 300 s using the FFmpeg tool [8]. These fragments were stored on the smartphones beforehand and reused during the experiments.

We compare two types of upload patterns: random and slotted. In the random case, the smartphones start the upload of the first segment after a delay randomly selected in the interval [0, n], where n equals the length of the video segments used (5 s, 30 s or 300 s). Each subsequent segment becomes available for upload every n seconds.

In the slotted case, the interval of n seconds is divided into a number of slots equal to the number of participating phones. For example, with 5 s segments and 2 phones, one phone uploads its first segment at t = 0 s, 5 s, and so on, whereas the other device uploads at t = 2.5 s, 7.5 s, and so on. This mechanism tries to avoid as much as possible transmission collisions with other phones. With more phones, the individual slots become shorter and it becomes more likely that the upload of a video segment is still in progress when the next phone starts transmitting. At this point, the individual throughput of each phone will start degrading.

We conducted experiments for the 480p and 1080p videos. The results, averaged over 5 iterations, are shown in Figure 7. The figures in the top row show the cumulative throughput received by the cloudlet and are indicative of the total load on the system. The bottom row shows average throughput per phone.

For both resolutions, the overall throughput to the cloudlet increases linearly with the number of phones, until the maximum

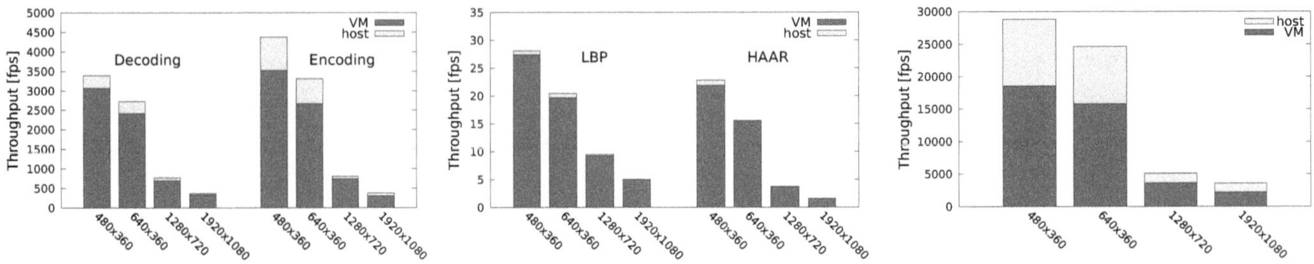

(a) Video Decoding and Encoding (b) Face Detection and Blurring (c) AES Encryption

Figure 9: Performance of Video Denaturing.

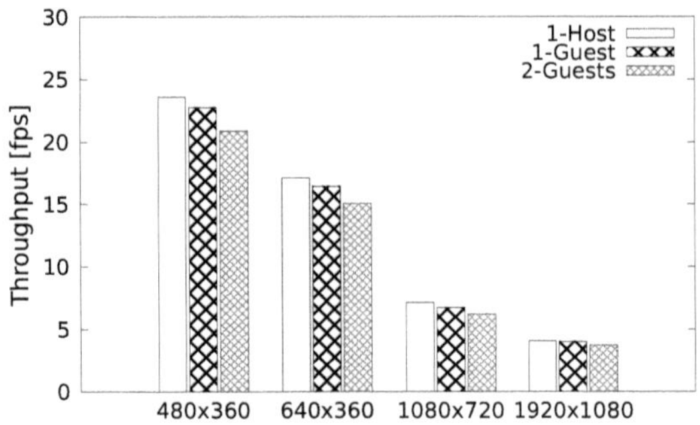

Figure 10: Overall throughput of the personal VM.

channel throughput (approx. 40 Mbps) is reached. The bitrate of video upload is around 5 Mbps for 480p@30fps and 10 Mbps for 1080p@24fps. We observed that the throughput per phone starts to drop when there were more than 8 phones uploading 480p videos or 5 phones uploading 1080p videos at the same time.

The overall throughput does not increase significantly with the use of slotted transmission mechanism. We attribute this to the fact that the transmission speed of a smartphone is limited. Even when a phone has the full channel capacity at its disposal, it will not reach the maximum theoretical bitrate. As a result, the duration of the upload of a single segment overspills the length of the slot even with few other phones and relatively long segment sizes. We expect that the performance of the slotted transmission will increase with better hardware and software implementations. Notably, the Android 4.2 update to the Google Nexus phone might bring improvements.

Another observation is that uploading shorter segments results in a lower average individual throughput, due to some discrepancies in the bitrates produced by FFmpeg when dividing videos into very short segments. The cumulative size of six 5 s-long video segments is *smaller* than when the same 30 s are encoded as a single segment.

Figure 8 shows how much energy it takes for a phone to send one unit of data. We measured the energy by means of the Monsoon Power Monitor [5]. In general, the energy consumption increases drastically when the Wi-Fi channel is saturated, and it is more energy efficient to upload larger video segments.

Uploading longer segments requires the device to wake up less frequently from the sleep state, while the total number of bytes transmitted remains constant. Interestingly, the energy consumption per byte for 5 s 480p video upload decreases with the number of nodes until the Wi-Fi channel is saturated. Careful analysis of the power measurement traces indicated that the smartphone applies two power states for transmission. In the experiments with one and two smartphones, the transmission starts in the highest power state before switching to the lower power state. When more smartphones are involved in the experiment, the smartphone immediately starts in the lower power state, presumably because it senses more collisions on the network. Transmitting in a lower power state results in longer transmission durations. In the 5 s 480p case, the increased energy cost of the longer transmission duration does not exceed the energy savings realized by sending at a lower rate because there is relatively little data to send. In all other cases, the longer transmission duration results in an increase in the average power consumption. Also note that the smartphone requires less energy per byte for 1080p resolution, presumably because the smartphone sends at lower rates. Overall, the slotted approach results in significant energy gains only for low-traffic scenarios.

5.2.2 *Denaturing: The Cost of Preserving Privacy*

In this section, we provide answers to two questions with respect to the scalability of denaturing. First, what is the throughput of each step of the denaturing pipeline presented in Figure 4, expressed in terms of video frames processed per second? Second, what is the overhead of virtualization in terms of the degradation of the throughput of the denaturing process?

As listed in Table 1, each cloudlet machine has 4 cores. By enabling hyperthreading, each machine can provide up to 8 virtual CPUs (vCPUs) that must be distributed between the VMs running on the host. We used KVM as the VMM. The video denaturing pipeline consists of 4 stages: video decoding, early-discard of frames based on metadata and sampling rate, content-based blurring, and video encoding. Along with a denatured, low-framerate version, the entire original video is stored in encrypted form on the cloudlet. To measure the individual throughput of each step, we ran each stage individually, either on the host or inside a VM with 8 vCPUs. The results are shown in Figure 9. We omitted the results of the early-discard, since this is a computationally trivial step. Note that the content-based filtering is the only step in the pipeline that can be parallelized: decoding, encoding and encryption rely on the sequential order of the frames. Hence, to obtain the results we ran 8 threads for face detection and blurring, while we used one thread for each of the other steps. The tests were conducted with the 36 videos crawled from YouTube, representing a wide diversity in content.

As shown in Figure 9, the throughput decreases with the video resolution for each step in the denaturing pipeline. Even for the highest resolution (1080p), a personal VM with 8 virtual CPUs can decode/encode over 300 fps and encrypt over 2200 fps. This is much higher than the load that can be expected on a single personal VM: users will typically upload not more than 30 fps. However, the throughput of face detection is much lower. In our experiments, we combined the HAAR-based profile detector with both the LBP and the HAAR frontal face detector. Clearly, the HAAR frontal face detector is more computationally intensive: the throughput drops from 21.93 fps to 1.61 fps when the resolution increases from 360p to 1080p. The LBP-based frontal face detector achieves relatively

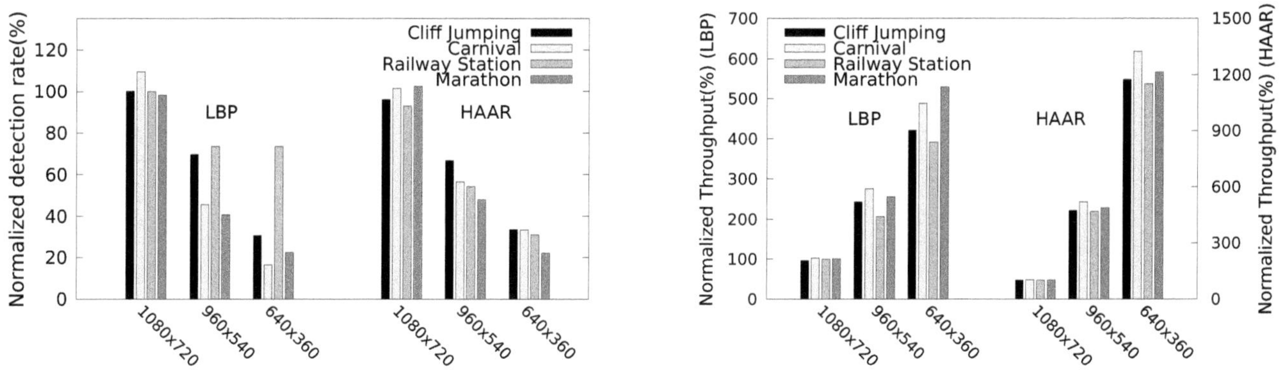

(a) Accuracy vs. Resolution (b) Throughput vs. Resolution

Figure 11: Accuracy and Throughput, normalized to the original 1080p resolution.

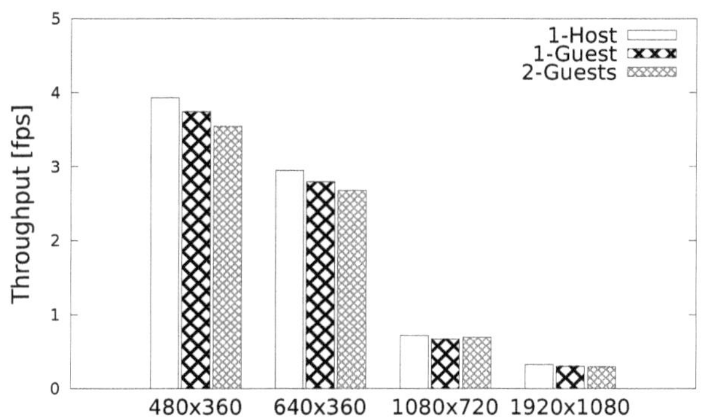

Figure 12: Throughput of the indexing process.

higher throughput: it processes up to 27.42 fps for 360p videos and 5.04 fps for 1080p videos. Obviously, the major bottleneck is the computer vision algorithms used for face detection.

In practice, the decoding, encoding, and denaturing routines are running in parallel. Upon the arrival of a video segment, the decoding thread converts the video into raw frames and pushes them into a shared queue. Meanwhile, a number of parallel denaturing threads fetch the raw frames and apply the meta-data and content-based filtering. The processed frames are forwarded to an encoding thread to be written into a new MP4 video file. This new video file contains only denatured frames and is indexable. Its framerate depends on the number of frames selected per second of video for denaturing. Typically, this selection rate will be much lower than the original frame rate because of computational constraints. As explained in Section 4, the video at original frame rate can be denatured on an ad-hoc basis.

We measured the overall throughput of the personal VM in three scenarios: running as a native process, inside a personal VM with 8 vCPUs, or running in 2 personal VMs with 4 vCPUs each. The latter scenario reflects the case with two users. The number of parallel denaturing threads is equal to 8 in the native scenario, and equal to the number of vCPUs in the virtualized scenarios.

The results are shown in Figure 10, including the cumulative throughput of both VMs in the 2-Guests scenario. Denaturing the video in a native process on the host results in an overall throughput of 4.06 fps for 1080p videos, 7.16 fps for 720p and up to 23.61 fps for 360p. This processing throughput drops by 1 % to 6 % when using virtualization. Due to scheduling overhead, the cumulative throughput of the cloudlet drops by an additional 7 % to 8 % in the scenario with 2 VMs. We can conclude that given the computational requirements of denaturing, the penalty of virtualization on the total throughput is limited.

Reducing the resolution is a clear path to increasing the throughput of the personal VM, but might negatively impact the detection accuracy of the denaturing process. We are convinced that the privacy preserving algorithms must be close to perfect for users to trust the system. To investigate this trade-off between throughput and accuracy, we selected one 1080p video from each of the 4 categories in our YouTube video database and created lower-resolution copies. We randomly chose 50 frames of the complete video and manually counted the number of detected faces in each of the resolutions. The results shown in Figure 11(a) are relative to the number of correctly detected faces we counted in the original resolution, while the results shown in Figure 11(b) are relative to the throughput when processing at the original resolution.

Scaling down the resolution prior to denaturing results in a higher throughput but has a clear impact on the accuracy. Interestingly, scaling down from 1080p to 720p does not result in a significant decrease in detection accuracy, but neither does it significantly improve throughput. For some videos, the accuracy is even higher than in the original, 1080p resolution. Further lowering the resolution, however, is detrimental to accuracy, mainly because relatively small faces in a video are no longer detectable. Note that the classifiers we used were trained with images of faces no larger than 20x20 pixels, and should in principle be able to detect such small faces.

Our results suggest that denaturing should be performed at resolutions of at least 720p, otherwise users may loose their trust in the denaturing process. On the other hand, one might argue that small faces are already unrecognizable at lower resolutions even without denaturing. More in-depth study of this trade-off is required.

5.2.3 Indexing: The Cost of Content Search

The process of content-based indexing is conceptually very similar to denaturing: it involves running computer vision algorithms inside a VM on the cloudlet. Hence, the main research questions involving the indexer are similar to the ones posed in the previous section: what is the throughput of the indexer in frames per second, and what is the penalty of virtualization? To evaluate the impact of the resolution on the accuracy, we indexed 12 YouTube videos in 1080p resolution and their scaled-down versions.

We compare the throughput of the indexing process for the same scenarios: running as a native process, or inside a VM with either 8 or 4 vCPUs. The frames are indexed using the STF filter for the MSRC21 dataset [30], generating a score for each of the 21 tags.

Table 2: Accuracy of the indexing process for different resolutions.

Classes	Total Tags	720p		480p		360p	
		TP (rate)	FP	TP (rate)	FP	TP (rate)	FP
aeroplane	4	4(100.0%)	0	4(100.0%)	0	4(100.0%)	0
bicycle	0	0 (N/A)	2	0 (N/A)	2	0 (N/A)	11
bird	68	63 (92.6%)	4	59 (86.8%)	7	57 (83.8%)	15
boat	0	0 (N/A)	0	0 (N/A)	0	0 (N/A)	0
body	2408	2352 (97.7%)	19	2284 (94.9%)	24	2185 (90.7%)	23
book	74	74(100.0%)	20	74(100.0%)	60	74(100.0%)	92
building	875	870 (99.4%)	137	856 (97.8%)	219	836 (95.5%)	273
car	122	118 (96.7%)	52	111 (91.0%)	136	108 (88.5%)	176
cat	573	560 (97.7%)	10	552 (96.3%)	15	546 (95.3%)	24
chair	22	22 (100.0%)	1	20 (90.9%)	2	19 (86.4%)	5
cow	0	0 (N/A)	0	0 (N/A)	0	0 (N/A)	0
dog	1004	965 (96.1%)	14	921 (91.7%)	25	882 (87.8%)	35
face	523	504 (96.4%)	32	468 (89.5%)	59	464 (88.7%)	65
flower	12	11 (91.7%)	0	10 (83.3%)	0	10 (83.3%)	0
grass	131	126 (96.2%)	0	120 (91.6%)	0	116 (88.5%)	0
road	370	351 (94.9%)	24	317 (85.7%)	41	291 (78.6%)	50
sheep	2	2(100.0%)	0	2(100.0%)	0	1 (50.0%)	0
sign	125	124 (99.2%)	10	120 (96.0%)	12	115 (92.0%)	17
sky	1409	1338 (95.0%)	1	1210 (85.9%)	1	1074 (76.2%)	3
tree	1080	1066 (98.7%)	97	1040 (96.3%)	189	984 (91.1%)	234
water	1290	1208 (93.6%)	4	1145 (88.8%)	6	1102 (85.4%)	8
total	10092	9758 (96.7%)	427	9313 (92.3%)	798	8868 (87.9%)	1031

Results are based on the indexing of 3583 frames obtained by sampling 1 frame per 2 seconds from 12 video segments scaled down to different resolutions. "Total Tags" refers to the number of frames classified to have certain tags by the indexing algorithm at 1080p, which we assume to be ground truth. The number of True Positives (TP) represents how many of these frames were also found in the same video at lower resolution. The rate in parentheses is TP divided by total tags. False Positives (FP) are frames not found in the 1080p resolution. Non-denatured frames were used, as is evident from the results of the face detection.

Figure 12 shows how the indexing throughput decreases from 4 fps for the lowest resolution to less than 1 fps for the highest resolution. Table 2 shows the trade-off between resolution and indexing accuracy for each of the 21 classes. We considered the frames detected by the filter in the original 1080p video as the ground truth (perfect accuracy) and compared how many of those frames are found in the same video at lower resolution. When compared to the denaturing, the detection accuracy of the STF filters is more robust to lowering the resolution. Overall, we can conclude that in our current prototype we can perform the indexing on the lowest (360p) resolution without sacrificing too much accuracy.

5.3 Cloudlet Capacity Allocation

The previous sections indicated how denaturing and indexing are extremely computationally intensive. In this section, we study how the available cloudlet hardware should be allocated between the indexer and the personal VMs of multiple users. Allocating more vCPUs to the personal VMs rather than to the indexer allows us to increase the number of denatured frames per second of video for each user, but the non-indexed denatured videos will keep accumulating if the indexer cannot keep up. Conversely, overdimensioning the indexer might result in idle CPU cycles because it is waiting for new denatured videos from the personal VMs.

We combined 4 quad-core machines into a larger cloudlet and dedicated two of them to the indexer. The resources on the other two machines were distributed over a number of personal VMs for the denaturing process. The Data Manager was running on one of the machines used for denaturing. Videos were uploaded in chunks of 30 s at 1080p resolution and processed through the complete GigaSight chain: registering in the database, decoding, denaturing, encryption, and indexing. We followed our conclusions of the previous sections: denaturing is performed at the original 1080p resolution for maximum accuracy, while the indexer will first transcode the denatured video to 360p before running the actual content detection algorithms.

Table 3: Multi-user system performance.

vCPUs per personal VM	# users	selection rate [fps]	denaturing throughput [fps]	indexer throughput [fps]
2	4	0.5	**1.9**	1.9
	6	0.5	2.8	**2.2**
	8	0.5	3.7	**2.4**
4	2	1.5	**2.7**	2.7
	3	1.5	4.2	**3.7**
	3	1	**2.9**	2.9
	4	1	3.8	**3.5**
8	1	3	**2.9**	2.9
	2	2	3.9	**3.5**
	2	3	5.8	**4.1**

We varied the number of vCPUs of the personal VM, the number of users, and the selection rate: the number of frames per second of video that is forwarded to the early-discard and content-based filtering steps of Figure 4. These two parameters jointly determine the load on the GigaSight system. For example, if there are two users uploading at 24fps and each personal VM selects 1 out of 24 frames for processing, the personal VMs are expected to produce 2 denatured frames every second. The indexer must operate at the same rate or higher.

Table 3 provides an overview of workable system configurations and the throughput of the denaturing and indexing VMs. The bottleneck on the overall system throughput is indicated in bold. When the indexer is indicated as the bottleneck, it means we had to reduce the selection rate of the personal VMs and hence not fully utilize the resources allocated to the personal VM. Conversely, when the denaturing is the bottleneck, it means that the indexer has spare resources and that the configured selection rate is the maximı can be achieved with the given size of the personal VMs. N the number of users and the number of video segments in the overhead of virtualization and the overhead of database t tions, respectively. All of these factors must be taken into ꞓ when allocating cloudlet resources.

6. ALTERNATIVE ARCHITECTURES

A key goal of GigaSight is to support a large number graphically distributed users. Only then does a globally able video catalog become a truly valuable asset. Many aı tural and deployment decisions can greatly affect this scalab this section, we explore key design alternatives for the archi First, we investigate the feasibility of moving denaturing cloudlet to mobile devices. Next, we weigh the scalability ployment scenario with numerous edge cloudlets against ꞓ larger cloudlet at metropolitan scale.

6.1 Denaturing on the smartphone

With 8-core smartphones entering the market, mobile have enough processing power on board for compute-intensi such as denaturing. Some mobile OS now natively offer an face detection. However, improvements in battery capaci not followed the pace of the innovations in computing haı In this section, we evaluate the battery drain caused by con face detection, the most compute-intensive part of denaturiı

We have written two face detection applications for Andr deployed them on our Nexus smartphones. The two appli are respectively built on the OpenCV for Android SDK ꞓ FaceDetector classifier of the Android SDK. The OpenCV ...p.. mentation is identical to the one used in the personal VM, whereas the second version is included to exploit potential optimizations by directly accessing native Android API's. We use the same videos as for the evaluation of denaturing on cloudlets.

Our results show that performing face detection in one 1080p frame using OpenCV for Android consumes on average 50.46 J, with a throughput of only 0.05 fps. The face detector provided by Android SDK is much more efficient compared with the one based on OpenCV SDK. It can produce 0.31 fps at the price of 9.0 J per frame. The energy demand of face detection drains a fully charged battery in 2.96 to 3.33 hours. Notice that the energy cost of video upload is agnostic to the location of the denaturing, as the same number of frames must be uploaded.

Obviously, in terms of both throughput and battery life, denaturing on mobile devices is unattractive — offloading is the only viable option. An added benefit of uploading non-denatured video is that it can be reused by other vision-based applications on the cloudlet that are working on behalf of the user.

6.2 Cloudlet size and location

The scalability of GigaSight depends on the specific configurations of cloudlets and their locations in the network. System architects must balance the cloudlet computational capacity with the number of cloudlets, to maximize both the number N of simultaneous users per cloudlet, and the number F of (denatured and indexed) frames that each user contributes per unit of time. We build a first-order model to estimate the performace, based on cloudlet capabilities and cloudlet ingress bandwidth. We assume that neither the cloudlet storage throughput nor the wireless channel capacity is a bottleneck. The Wi-Fi bandwidth can be easily expanded by deploying more access points, and even a single hard drive provides two orders of magnitude higher bandwidth than today's video bitrates.

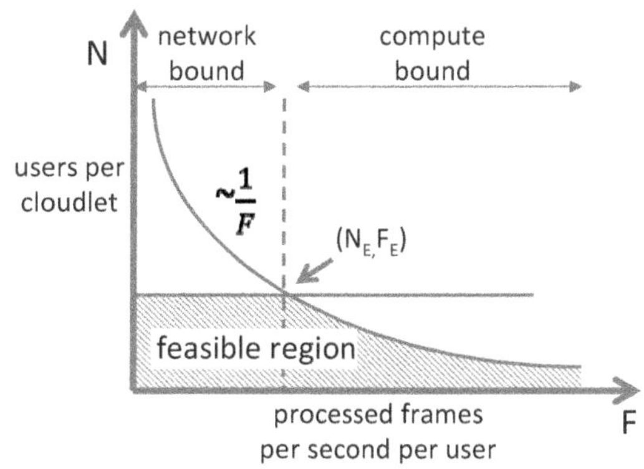

Figure 13: Model of tradeoff between number of users (N) and processed framerate per user (F). The shaded region represents the range of feasible choices with fixed network and processing capacity.

The value of F reflects the throughput of the denaturing-indexing pipeline. From Figure 10, we derive that denaturing 5 frames of 1080p video per second requires 8 virtual cores (VC). For indexing, we need 8 VCs to index 4 frames per second, including the initial transcoding to 360p. Assuming that virtualization overhead does not significantly hurt the performance, we need the following number of VCs to support N users on one cloudlet:

$$\begin{aligned} \#VC &= N\left(\tfrac{5}{8}F + \tfrac{4}{8}F\right) \\ \#VC &= 1.125\,N\,F \end{aligned} \tag{1}$$

The number of users supported by one cloudlet is bound either by the ingress bandwidth I to the cloudlet infrastructure, or by the number of available cores C. If each user uploads video at rate R, this trade-off is expressed as follows:

$$N \leq min\left(\frac{I}{R}, \frac{C}{1.125\,F}\right) \tag{2}$$

As illustrated in Figure 13, for values of $F < F_E$, the number of users supported is limited to N_E users. For values $F > F_E$, the architecture is compute bound and $N < N_E$.

Using this model, we can compare the two alternative design strategies that are illustrated in Figure 14. In the first model, many LAN-connected cloudlets are deployed at the network edge. Cloudlets may be co-located with one or more Wi-Fi access points, as initially proposed in the seminal paper on cloudlets [29], but newer mobile broadband variants are appearing. Femtocells will be gradually deployed in home networks, and Nokia Siemens Networks recently unveiled a LTE base station including service hosting infrastructure [23]. In the second model, one larger cloudlet is deployed at metropolitan scale, such as a campus or a city [3]. This model with MAN-cloudlets forms a middle ground between the first model with edge cloudlets, and the traditional clouds in the core network cloud model.

We can compare both models by estimating the evolution of video rates and hardware capabilities over the next 5 years. Our assumptions are listed in Table 4. The video captured by mobile devices is assumed to scale from HD (1080p) to Ultra-HD (4k). These cameras will capture 4 times more pixels than today, but at the same time the coding efficiency of the related H.265 codec will increase by 50 % compared to H.264 [20]. Consequently, we model the video bandwidth to double between now and 2018. With respect to the network bandwidth, we assume typical local LAN ingress bandwidths for edge cloudlets. We use 1 Gbps and 10 Gps

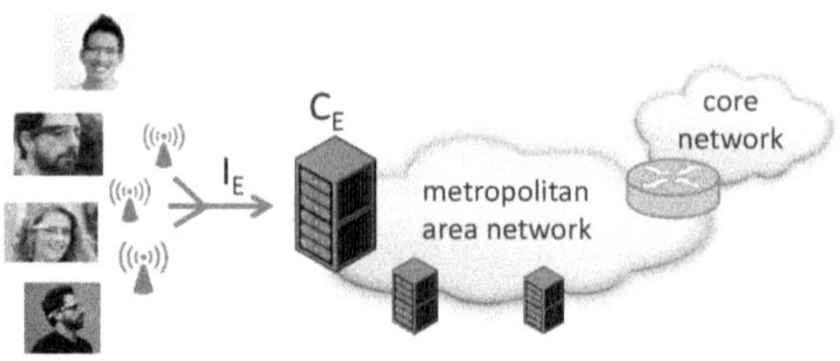

(a) Smaller edge cloudlets

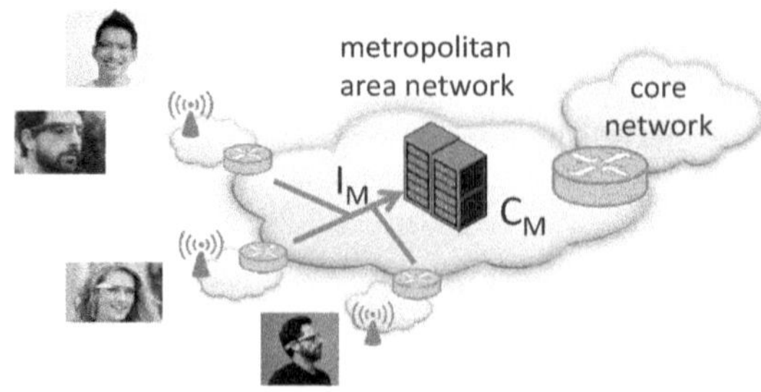

(b) Larger cloudlet in the metropolitan area network

Figure 14: Two possible deployment models for GigaSight infrastructure.

Table 4: Technical specifications of GigaSight infrastructure.

	Parameter	2013	2018
video	bitrate (R)	8.5 Mbps	17 Mbps
edge cloudlet	ingress BW	1 Gbps	10 Gbps
	CPU cores	128	2048
MAN cloudlet	ingress BW	100 Gbps	1000 Gbps
	CPU cores	1024	16384

Table 5: Number of users and attainable framerates

	2013		2018	
	N_E	F_E	N_E	F_E
edge cloudlet (Fig. 14a)	118	1.9	588	6.2
MAN cloudlet (Fig. 14b)	11765	0.2	58824	0.5

for 2013 and 2018, respectively. For MAN cloudlets, we assume ingress link capacity of 100 Gbps based on a recent Verizon announcement [24], and (optimistically) project a 10 fold improvement in the future. Cloudlets are modeled as mini-datacenters, e.g. Myoonet [22]. The computational capacity of the cloudlets is expressed in terms of the number of CPU cores. We model an edge cloudlet as a single, fully populated blade chassis. For the MAN case, we assume a full rack with similarly dense servers. The 2013 figures in Table 4 are based on technical specifications of actual HP blades [13]. We assume a 16-fold increase in capacity for 2018.

Based on the hardware specifications of Table 4 and Equation 2, we can calculate the number of users N_E and the framerate per user F_E at which computational and network resources are balanced. The results are presented in Table 5. Since our models were based on hyperthreaded cores, we account for this by assuming twice the virtual cores as physical cores in our calculations.

From a technical viewpoint, we can conclude that edge cloudlets perform much better than MAN cloudlets. With one larger cloudlet per MAN, both the number of users and the framerate per user is surprisingly low. Such a cloudlet should support all users in a region the size of a city or campus. Typically, this will involve at least 100k users. It is clear that transmitting all videos to a single cloudlet creates a bottleneck at the ingress of the cloudlet. However, even if we are underestimating the capacity of the MAN network, there are practical restrictions (cost, cooling) on the size of the MAN cloudlet. This model requires one data center per MAN with the size of a traditional cloud-based data center. With edge cloudlets, much higher framerates can be achieved. Given our assumptions, in 5 years one edge cloudlet is able to support 121 users with real-time denaturing and indexing at the full rate of 30 fps. Of course, this analysis only takes into account technical parameters. Managing a distributed infrastructure with edge clouds might lead to increased total cost of ownership. These parameters must be considered when designing the architecture of GigaSight.

7. RELATED WORK

Privacy. Computer vision algorithms have been widely used for preserving the user's privacy in video sharing. PrivacyCam [9] is a framework developed for CCTV channels for public safety. Introducing different layers of privacy protection, it allows users with higher clearance levels to see more information than daily CCTV operators. Using the hardware contemporary at the time of writing, the authors report a throughput of approx. 4 fps of 320x240 JPEG frames. Hardware has noticeably improved since the publication of the paper, and we achieve approximately the same throughput for higher resolution frames. PrivacyCam is complementary to our work, as it aims to protect the privacy of the persons being filmed, whereas we are primarily concerned with protecting the privacy of the video creators. The creators are given full control about which scenes are made public.

The privacy risks emerging from innocuous wearable sensors have been extensively studied by [26]. The results highlight an overall lack of awareness of the actual information contained in personal data sets and the privacy threats associated with them. On the other hand, the study reveals that participants have significant concerns with sharing sensed data with the general public, especially when released with their identities. We aim to tackle this concern by our concept of denaturing in personal VMs.

Visual content tagging. A substantial amount of work has been performed on the use of metadata for automated tagging and highlight selection in video segments. This metadata is typically derived either directly from other smartphone sensors, or from social network activity. In [33], video highlights in live broadcasts of sports events are automatically selected by analyzing sudden bursts in Twitter activity. Bao et al. [7] correlate sensor information of nearby smartphones to detect event highlights, such as acoustic information (e.g., cheering) or common orientation (e.g., all people looking at the same person making a toast).

We have used purely vision-based algorithms to categorize and tag video segments. Our prototype uses Semantic Texton Forests, but other detectors have been created, typically in specific areas where the number of common concepts is more or less fixed. For example, Snoek et al. [31] proposed visual detectors for analyzing videos of rock concerts. They created detectors for 12 common concert concepts such as a guitar and the logo of the festival. By comparing an expert's opinion with the automatically suggested labels, they report an accuracy of approximately 85%.

Crowd-sourcing of video. An interesting use case of video crowdsourcing was presented in [17]. The video captured by smartphones mounted on the windshield is analyzed to detect traffic signals ahead. The information is shared with other drivers in the vicinity. This allows the system to advise the driver on the optimal speed they should maintain so that the signal is green when they arrive at the next intersection.

8. FUTURE WORK

The work described here is only a first step towards scalable content-based search on crowd-sourced, denatured videos. There are several important directions for future research.

Performance of Computer Vision Algorithms. GigaSight relies heavily on computer vision algorithms for denaturing and content-based indexing. These algorithms are extremely resource intensive. We believe that the throughput might drastically improve when GPU virtualization matures and advanced, highly optimized GPU routines become available inside VMs.

Another challenge is the detection accuracy of computer vision algorithms. Today's algorithms tend to work best on images captured under well-controlled lighting and exposure conditions. Our experience shows that the quality of individual frames of a video captured by a smartphone are much poorer than expected by these algorithms. Lighting variations, semi-occlusion of faces and objects, and detection of small faces are other challenges. Snoek et al. [32] have evaluated the progress of the accuracy of visual-search engines between 2006 and 2009. They conclude that the progress is substantial, with accuracy doubling in just three years.

Storage management and reclamation. We have currently left open the question of how much storage capacity a cloudlet needs to have. This capacity will be a function of the average retention period of a video segment and of the observed mobility patterns of typical users from historical traces. Many algorithms published in the context of CDNs can be reused in GigaSight, such as the distribution and duplication of popular video segments.

In contrast to YouTube, where videos are never deleted, the major goal of GigaSight is to provide a global view on the world. Hence, another interesting concept we plan to focus on is *semantic deduplication*: how can "largely similar" video segments, e.g. captured by two users walking next to each other, be reduced to just a single representative one? What are the storage savings that can be realized from semantic deduplication, and what is the impact of its computational cost on scalability?

Apart from storing the videos, the related metadata must also be handled properly. In our current implementation, we used off-the-shelf MySQL databases on the cloudlet and the cloud. Metadata is synchronized over a REST-interface. Although this provided enough performance for our experiments, to truly scale up the system we will look into more advanced distributed databases such as Spanner [11].

9. CONCLUSION

Having a searchable catalog of crowd-sourced videos provides a unique hindsight view on the world that potentially leverages many existing and future applications. We have presented GigaSight, a framework integrating the complete chain of processing from the initial capture of video to the visual content search. Uploaded videos are denatured inside personal VMs running on cloudlets: sensitive scenes are automatically removed based on time, location, and content. As denaturing is a near effortless way for users to protect their privacy, this effectively lowers the barrier to share first-person video. The personal VMs establish a clear demarcation line where the original videos can be processed.

We have investigated both frame rate and resolution as parameters to scale up the system. Denaturing only a subset of the video frames results in a linear reduction of the system load, and still allows the user to guess the content of a video from a limited set of frames. This measure, however, cannot be applied to an infinite extent, especially for *inter*-frame action detection. Our experiments indicate that the effect of scaling down the resolution depends on the specific computer vision algorithm used. In our prototype, lowering the resolution does not reduce the accuracy of object detection in our indexer, but dramatically reduces the accuracy of the face detection algorithm in the denaturing process.

As HUDs such as Google Glass enter the mainstream, people will have the ability to effortlessly and continuously capture video. GigaSight offers an approach to transforming this capability into a truly disruptive force.

10. ACKNOWLEDGEMENTS

We thank our shepherd Kamin Whitehouse and the anonymous reviewers for their valuable comments and suggestions. This research was supported by the National Science Foundation (NSF) under grant numbers CNS-0833882 and IIS-1065336, by an Intel Science and Technology Center grant, and by the Department of Defense (DoD) under Contract No. FA8721-05-C-0003 for the operation of the Software Engineering Institute (SEI), a federally funded research and development center. This material has been approved for public release and unlimited distribution (DM-0000276). Additional support for cloudlet-related research was provided by IBM, Google, and Bosch.

11. REFERENCES

[1] http://www.visionopen.com/cv/cascadePUT.xml.

[2] https://biometrics.cie.put.poznan.pl/.

[3] Ieee standard for local and metropolitan area networks: Overview and architecture. *IEEE Std 802-2001*, 2002.

[4] DVF through Google's Glass. http://www.thedailybeast.com/videos/2012/09/13/dvf-through-google-s-glass.html, SEP 2012.

[5] Monsoon power monitor. http://www.msoon.com, 2012.

[6] T. Ahonen, A. Hadid, and M. Pietikainen. Face description with local binary patterns: Application to face recognition. *IEEE Trans. Pattern Anal. Mach. Intell.*, 28(12):2037–2041, 2006.

[7] X. Bao and R. Roy Choudhury. Movi: Mobile phone based video highlights via collaborative sensing. In *Proc. of 8th Int. Conf. on Mobile Syst., Appl., and Services*, pages 357–370. ACM, 2010.

[8] F. Bellard et al. Ffmpeg. http://www.ffmpeg.org, 2012.

[9] A. Chattopadhyay and T. Boult. Privacycam: A privacy preserving camera using uclinux on the blackfin dsp. In *Proc. of IEEE Conf. on Computer Vision and Pattern Recognition*, pages 1–8, 2007.

[10] Contour+2. http://contour.com/products/contour-plus-2, 2012.

[11] J. C. Corbett, J. Dean, et al. Spanner: Google's globally-distributed database. In *Proc. of the 10th USENIX Conf. on Operating Syst. Design and Impl.*, pages 251–264, 2012.

[12] J. Guzzardo. CNN report: New Jersey family's picture catches theft in the making. http://www.cnn.com/2010/CRIME/08/24/new.jersey.theft.photo/index.html?hpt=C1, AUG 2010.

[13] HP. Eight steps to building a bladesystem. http://h20195.www2.hp.com/v2/GetPDF.aspx/4AA1-4286ENW.pdf.

[14] L. Huston, R. Sukthankar, R. Wickremesinghe, M. Satyanarayanan, G. R. Ganger, E. Riedel, and A. Ailamaki. Diamond: A storage architecture for early

discard in interactive search. In *Proc. of the 3rd USENIX Conf. on File and Storage Technol.*, pages 73–86, 2004.

[15] Y. Ke, R. Sukthankar, and M. Hebert. Event detection in crowded videos. In *Proc. of IEEE 11th Int. Conf. on Computer Vision*, pages 1–8, 2007.

[16] P. Kelly, S. J. Marshall, H. Badland, J. Kerr, M. Oliver, A. R. Doherty, and C. Foster. An ethical framework for automated, wearable cameras in health behavior research. *American J. Preventive Med.*, 44(3):314–319, 2013.

[17] E. Koukoumidis, M. Martonosi, and L.-S. Peh. Leveraging smartphone cameras for collaborative road advisories. *IEEE Trans. Mobile Comput.*, 11(5):707 –723, MAY 2012.

[18] S. Larsson. *The girl with the dragon tattoo*. Afred A. Knopf, 2010.

[19] R. Lienhart and J. Maydt. An extended set of haar-like features for rapid object detection. In *Proc. of Int. Conf. on Image Processing*, volume 1, pages I–900 – I–903, 2002.

[20] L. Liu, R. Cohen, H. Sun, A. Vetro, and X. Zhuang. New techniques for next generation video coding. In *Proc. of 2010 IEEE Int. Symp. on Broadband Multimedia Syst. and Broadcast.*, pages 1–6, 2010.

[21] R. Miller. AOL brings micro data center indoors, adds wheels. `http://www.datacenterknowledge.com/archives/2012/08/13/aol-brings-micro-data-center-indoors-adds-wheels`, AUG 2012.

[22] Myoonet. Unique scalable data centers, December 2011. `http://www.myoonet.com/unique.html`.

[23] Nokia Siemens Networks. Nokia Siemens revolutionizes the mobile base station. `http://www.nokiasiemensnetworks.com/sites/default/files/document/nokiasiemensnetworks_2013_02_25_en_liquid_apps_launch_0.pdf`, FEB 2013.

[24] PC world. `http://www.pcworld.com/article/255519/verizon_to_offer_100g_links_resilient_mesh_on_optical_networks.html`, 2012.

[25] Quality of life technology center. `http://www.cmu.edu/qolt/AboutQoLTCenter/PressRoom/ces-2012/first-person-vision.html`, 2012.

[26] A. Raij, A. Ghosh, S. Kumar, and M. Srivastava. Privacy risks emerging from the adoption of innocuous wearable sensors in the mobile environment. In *Proc. of the SIGCHI Conf. on Human Factors in Comput. Syst.*, pages 11–20, 2011.

[27] S. Sadanand and J. Corso. Action bank: A high-level representation of activity in video. In *Proc. of IEEE Conf. on Comput. Vision and Pattern Recognition*, pages 1234 –1241, JUN 2012.

[28] P. Samarati and L. Sweeney. Protecting privacy when disclosing information: k-Anonymity and its enforcement through generalization and suppression. Technical Report SRI-CSL-98-04, SRI Int., 1998.

[29] M. Satyanarayanan, P. Bahl, R. Caceres, and N. Davies. The case for VM-based cloudlets in mobile computing. *IEEE Pervasive Comput.*, 8(4), OCT 2009.

[30] J. Shotton, M. Johnson, and R. Cipolla. Semantic texton forests for image categorization and segmentation. In *Proc. of IEEE Conf. on Computer Vision and Pattern Recognition*, pages 1–8, June 2008.

[31] C. G. Snoek, B. Freiburg, J. Oomen, and R. Ordelman. Crowdsourcing rock n'roll multimedia retrieval. In *Proc. of Int. Conf. on Multimedia*, pages 1535–1538, 2010.

[32] C. G. Snoek and A. W. Smeulders. Visual-concept search solved? *Comput.*, 43(6):76 –78, JUN 2010.

[33] A. Tang and S. Boring. #epicplay: Crowd-sourcing sports video highlights. In *Proc. of ACM Conf. on Human Factors in Computing Syst.*, pages 1569–1572. ACM, 2012.

[34] P. Viola and M. Jones. Rapid object detection using a boosted cascade of simple features. In *Proc. of the IEEE CS Conf. on Comput. Vision and Pattern Recognition*, volume 1, pages I–511 – I–518, 2001.

[35] YouTube statistics. `http://www.youtube.com/t/press_statistics`, 2012.

[36] G. Zhong and U. Hengartner. A distributed k-anonymity protocol for location privacy. In *Proc. of IEEE Int. Conf. on Pervasive Computing and Communications*, pages 1–10, 2009.

[37] W. Zhu, C. Luo, J. Wang, and S. Li. Multimedia cloud computing. *IEEE Signal Process. Mag.*, 28(3):59–69, MAY 2011.

Just-in-Time Provisioning for Cyber Foraging

Kiryong Ha
Carnegie Mellon University
5000 Forbes Ave
Pittsburgh, PA 15213, USA
krha@cmu.edu

Padmanabhan Pillai
Intel Labs
4720 Forbes Ave, Suite 410
Pittsburgh, PA 15213, USA
padmanabhan.s.pillai@intel.com

Wolfgang Richter
Carnegie Mellon University
5000 Forbes Ave
Pittsburgh, PA 15213, USA
wolf@cs.cmu.edu

Yoshihisa Abe
Carnegie Mellon University
5000 Forbes Ave
Pittsburgh, PA 15213, USA
yoshiabe@cs.cmu.edu

Mahadev Satyanarayanan
Carnegie Mellon University
5000 Forbes Ave
Pittsburgh, PA 15213, USA
satya@cs.cmu.edu

ABSTRACT

Cloud offload is an important technique in mobile computing. VM-based cloudlets have been proposed as offload sites for the resource-intensive and latency-sensitive computations typically associated with mobile multimedia applications. Since cloud offload relies on precisely-configured back-end software, it is difficult to support at global scale across cloudlets in multiple domains. To address this problem, we describe just-in-time (JIT) provisioning of cloudlets under the control of an associated mobile device. Using a suite of five representative mobile applications, we demonstrate a prototype system that is capable of provisioning a cloudlet with a non-trivial VM image in 10 seconds. This speed is achieved through dynamic VM synthesis and a series of optimizations to aggressively reduce transfer costs and startup latency.

Categories and Subject Descriptors

D.4.7 [**Software**]: Operating System – Organization and Design

General Terms

Experimentation, Measurement, Performance

Keywords

mobile computing, cloud computing, cloudlet, cloud offload, virtual machine, Amazon EC2, VM synthesis, Wi-Fi, wireless

1. INTRODUCTION

Cloud offload from mobile devices has been the subject of many recent papers [5, 7, 21, 35]. These efforts are rooted in work stretching back over a decade on the theme of *cyber foraging* [41], whose goal is to overcome the resource limitations of wireless mobile devices. Flinn [8] traces the evolution of this technique and gives a comprehensive review of work in this area. For reasons discussed in Section 2.1, it will remain an important technique for the future despite mobile hardware improvements. *VM-based cloudlets* that are dispersed at the edges of the Internet and located just one WiFi hop away from associated mobile devices have been proposed as cyber foraging sites for cloud offload [42].

Mobile computing today spans many device operating systems and application environments (e.g., Android, iOS, Windows 8), as well as diverse approaches to partitioning and offloading computation. The latter range from language-specific approaches such as MAUI to legacy implementations that depend on specific back-end operating systems and runtime support [1]. There is churn in this space from new OS versions, patches to existing OS versions, new libraries, new versions of cyber foraging tools, new language runtime systems, and so on. VMs cleanly encapsulate this messy complexity, but create the problem of precisely provisioning a cloudlet from a large and continuously evolving space of VM images.

The large size of VM images complicates dynamic provisioning of cloudlets. At the same time, the presumption of *ubiquity* in mobile computing deprecates a static provisioning strategy. A mobile user expects good service for all his applications at any place and time. Wide-area physical mobility (e.g., an international traveler stepping off his flight) makes it difficult to always guarantee that a nearby cloudlet will have the precise VM image needed for cyber foraging (e.g., natural language translation with customized vocabulary and speaker-trained voice recognition via the traveler's smartphone). The VM guest state space is simply too large and too volatile for static provisioning of cloudlets at global scale. A different provisioning challenge involves the deployment of new cloudlets for load balancing, hardware upgrades, or recovery from disasters. Dynamic self-provisioning of cloudlets will greatly simplify such deployments.

Rapid just-in-time provisioning of cloudlets is the focus of this paper. We show how a cloudlet can be provisioned in as little as 10 seconds with a complete copy of a new VM image that is the back-end of an offloaded application such as face recognition, object recognition, or augmented reality. The compressed sizes of these VM images can range from 400 MB for a stripped-down Linux guest, to well over 2 GB for typical Windows based images. The key to rapid provisioning is the recognition that a large part of a VM image is devoted to the guest OS, software libraries, and supporting software packages. The customizations of a base system needed for a particular application are usually relatively small. Therefore, if the *base VM* already exists on the cloudlet, only its difference relative to the desired custom VM, called a *VM overlay*, needs to be transferred. This concept of a VM overlay bears resemblance to copy-on-write virtual disk files [25] or VM image hierarchies [3], but extends to both disk and memory snapshots.

MobiSys'13, June 25–28, 2013, Taipei, Taiwan

Year	Typical Server Processor	Speed	Typical Handheld Device	Speed
1997	Pentium® II	266 MHz	Palm Pilot	16 MHz
2002	Itanium®	1 GHz	Blackberry 5810	133 MHz
2007	Intel® Core™ 2	9.6 GHz (2.4 Ghz x 4 cores)	Apple iPhone	412 MHz
2011	Intel® Xeon® X5	32 GHz (2.7 GHz x 6 cores x 2 sockets)	Samsung Galaxy S2	2.4 GHz (1.2 GHz x 2 cores)

Table 1: Hardware Performance (adapted from Flinn [8])

Our approach of using VM overlays to provision cloudlets is called *dynamic VM synthesis*. Proof-of-concept experiments [42] showed provisioning times of 1–2 minutes using this approach. In this paper, we present a series of optimizations that reduces this time by an order of magnitude.

Although motivated by mobile computing, dynamic VM synthesis has broader relevance. Today, public clouds such as Amazon's EC2 service are well-optimized for launching images that already exist in their storage tier, but do not provide fast options for provisioning that tier with a new, custom image. One must either launch an existing image and laboriously modify it, or suffer the long, tedious upload of the custom image. For really large images, Amazon recommends mailing a hard drive! We show that dynamic VM synthesis can rapidly provision public clouds such as EC2.

2. BACKGROUND

2.1 Need for Cyber Foraging

The initial observation that mobile devices are resource-poor relative to server hardware of comparable vintage dates back to the mid-1990s [40]. Table 1, adapted from Flinn [8], illustrates the consistent large gap in the processing power of typical server and mobile device hardware between 1997 and 2011. This stubborn gap reflects a fundamental reality of user preferences: Moore's Law has to be leveraged differently on hardware that people carry or wear for extended periods of time. This is not just a temporary limitation of current mobile hardware technology, but is intrinsic to mobility. The most sought-after features of a mobile device always include light weight, small size, long battery life, comfortable ergonomics, and tolerable heat dissipation. Processor speed, memory size, and disk capacity are secondary. For as long as our appetite for resource-intensive applications exceeds what mobile devices can sustain, cyber foraging will continue to be relevant.

Today, tasks such as free-form speech recognition, natural language translation, face recognition, object recognition, dynamic action interpretation from video, and body language interpretation lie beyond the limits of standalone mobile computing technology. Table 2, from Ha et al. [16], shows the median and 99th percentile response times for speech recognition and face recognition on typical mobile hardware in 2012, with and without offloading. The results show that cloud offload improves both the absolute response times and their variance. Looking further into the future, one can imagine cognitive assistance applications built from these primitives (such as an advanced version of IBM's Watson [51]) seamlessly augmenting human perception and cognition, and assisting attention-challenged mobile users in their real-world and cyber-world interactions. Cyber foraging will be essential to realizing such a futuristic world.

Application	No Offload median	No Offload 99%	Offload median	Offload 99%
SPEECH	1.22 s	6.69 s	0.23 s	1.25 s
FACE	0.42 s	4.12 s	0.16 s	1.47 s

Table 2: Speech and Face Recognition Today (Source: [16])

2.2 VM-based Cloudlets

Which specific part of the infrastructure should one leverage for cyber foraging? The obvious answer today is "the cloud." Public cloud infrastructure such as Amazon EC2 data centers are natural offload sites for resource-intensive computations triggered by mobile devices. Unfortunately, these large consolidated data centers are suboptimal offload sites for a growing number of resource-intensive yet latency-sensitive mobile applications. In the course of its travels, a roaming mobile device often sees multiple network hops to such a data center [49]. The resulting end-to-end latency can be large enough to seriously affect many emerging mobile applications [16]. In hostile environments such as military operations and disaster recovery, physical distance also increases vulnerability to network disruptions [44].

A cloudlet is a new architectural element for cyber foraging that represents the middle tier of a 3-tier hierarchy: mobile device – cloudlet – cloud. To serve as shared infrastructure, a cloudlet must provide safety and strong isolation between untrusted computations from different mobile devices. To sustain viable business models, it has to incorporate authentication, access control, and metering mechanisms, and has to meet service level expectations/guarantees through dynamic resource management. To be cost-effective, cloudlet deployments need to support the widest possible range of user-level computations, with minimal restrictions on their process structure, programming languages or operating systems.

In public and private clouds, these requirements are met using the VM abstraction. For precisely the same reasons, VMs are also valuable as the organizing principle of cloudlets. An important difference is that cloudlets only contain soft state that is cached or otherwise re-creatable, while clouds contain both hard and soft state. In the context of this paper, the most important components of "state" are VM images. A cloudlet can thus be viewed as a "data center in a box" that "brings the cloud closer." Today, "micro data centers" from companies such as Myoonet [28] and AOL [26] are already available and can be repurposed as cloudlets.

3. DYNAMIC VM SYNTHESIS

3.1 Basic Approach

The intuition behind dynamic VM synthesis is that although each VM customization is unique, it is typically derived from a small set of common base systems such as a freshly-installed Windows 7 guest or Linux guest. We refer to the VM image used for offloading as a *launch VM*. It is created by installing relevant software into a *base VM*. The compressed binary difference between the base VM image and the launch VM image is called a *VM overlay*. This idea of a binary difference between VM images to reduce storage and network transfer costs has been successfully used before [3, 25, 57]. We, therefore, extensively use this overlay concept for both VM disk and memory snapshots in this work.

At run-time, *dynamic VM synthesis* (sometimes shortened to "VM synthesis" or just "synthesis") reverses the process of overlay creation. Figure 1 shows the relevant steps. A mobile device delivers the VM overlay to a cloudlet that already possesses the base VM from which this overlay was derived. The cloudlet decompresses the overlay, applies it to the base to derive the launch VM, and then

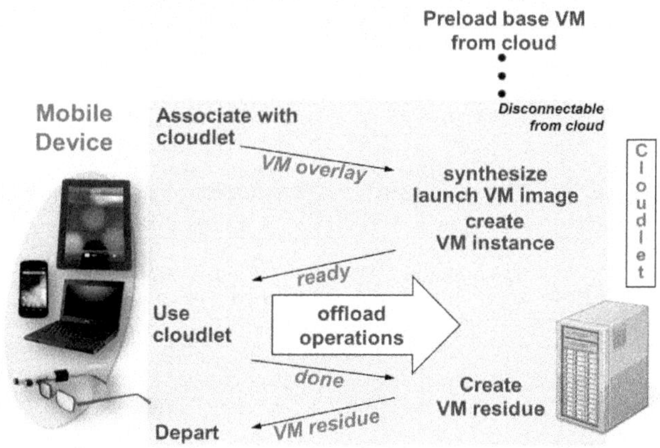

Figure 1: Dynamic VM Synthesis from Mobile Device

creates a VM instance from it. The mobile device can now begin performing offload operations on this instance. The instance is destroyed at the end of the session, but the launch VM image can be retained in a persistent cache for future sessions. As a slight variant of this process, a mobile device can ask the cloudlet to obtain the overlay from the cloud. This indirection reduces the energy used for wireless data transmission, but can improve transfer time only when WAN bandwidth to the cloud exceeds local WiFi bandwidth.

Note that the cloudlet and mobile device can have different hardware architectures: the mobile device is merely serving as transport for the VM overlay. Normally, each offload session starts with a pristine instance of the launch VM. However, there are some use cases where modified state in the launch VM needs to be preserved for future offloads. For example, the launch VM may incorporate a machine learning model that adapts to a specific user over time. Each offload session then generates training data for an improved model that needs to be incorporated into the VM overlay for future offload sessions. This is achieved in Figure 1 by generating a *VM residue* that can be sent back to the mobile device and incorporated into its overlay.

There are no constraints on the guest OS of the base VM; our prototype works with both Linux and Windows. We anticipate that a relatively small number of base VMs will be popular on cloudlets at any given time. To increase the chances of successful synthesis, a mobile device can carry overlays for multiple base VMs and discover the best one to use through negotiation with the cloudlet. Keep in mind that the VMs here are virtual appliances that are specifically configured for serving as the back-ends of mobile applications. Although these virtual appliances are generated on top of conventional operating systems such as Linux or Windows, they are focused and dedicated to serve a particular mobile application, rather than general-purpose desktop environments that need a wider range of functionality.

It is useful to contrast dynamic VM synthesis with demand paging the launch VM from the mobile device or cloud using a mechanism such as the Internet Suspend/Resume system® [43]. Synthesis requires the base VM to be available on the cloudlet. In contrast, demand paging works even for a freshly-created VM image that has no ancestral state on the cloudlet. Synthesis can use efficient streaming to transmit the overlay, while demand paging incurs the overhead of many small data transfers. However, some of the state that is proactively transferred in an overlay may be wasted if the launch VM includes substantial state that is not accessed. Synthesis incurs a longer startup delay before VM launch. However, once launched, the VM incurs no stalls. This may be valuable for soft real-time mobile applications such as augmented reality.

OBJECT: identifies known objects and their positions in an image. Originally intended for a robotics application [48], it computes SIFT features [24] to match objects from a database, and computes position based on geometry of matched features. The back-end of this application runs in a Linux environment.

FACE: detects and attempts to identify faces in an image from a prepopulated database. The algorithm uses Haar Cascades of classifiers for detection and the Eigenfaces method [52] for identification. The application backend is based on OpenCV [32] computer vision routines, and runs on Microsoft Windows 7.

SPEECH: performs speech-to-text conversion of spoken English sentences using a Hidden Markov Model (HMM) recognition system [47]. The Java-based application backend runs on Linux.

AR: [50] is an augmented reality application that identifies buildings and landmarks in a scene captured by a phone's camera, and labels them precisely in the live view. An 80 GB database constructed from over 1000 images of 200 buildings is used to perform identification. The application backend uses multiple threads, OpenCV [32] libraries, and runs on Microsoft Windows 7.

FLUID: is an interactive fluid dynamics simulation, that renders a liquid sloshing in a container on the screen of a phone based on accelerometer inputs. The application backend runs on Linux and performs a smoothed particle hydrodynamics [46] physics simulation using 2218 particles, generating up to 50 frames per second. The structure of this application is representative of real-time (i.e., not turn-based) games.

Figure 2: Example Mobile Multimedia Applications

It is also useful to contrast VM synthesis with launching the base VM and then performing package installations and configuration modifications to transform it into the launch VM. This is, of course, exactly what happens offline when creating the overlay; the difference is that the steps are now being performed at runtime on each association with a cloudlet. On the one hand, this approach can be attractive because the total size of install packages is often smaller than the corresponding VM overlay (e.g., Table 3) and, therefore, involves less transmission overhead. On the other hand, the time delay of installing the packages and performing configuration is incurred at run time. Unlike optimization of VM synthesis, which is fully under our control even if the guest is closed-source, speeding up the package installation and configuration process requires individual optimizations to many external software components. Some of those may be closed-source, proprietary components. Of even greater significance is the concern that installing a sequence of packages and then performing post-installation configuration is a fragile and error-prone task even when scripted. Defensive engineering suggests that these fragile steps be performed only once, during offline overlay creation. Once a launch VM image is correctly created offline, the synthesis process ensures that precisely the same image is re-created on each cloudlet use. This bit-exact precision of cloudlet provisioning is valuable to a mobile user, giving him high confidence that his applications will work as expected no matter where he is in the world. Finally, the installation approach requires the application to be started fresh every time. Execution state is lost between subsequent uses, destroying any sense of seamless continuity of the user experience.

3.2 Baseline Performance

We have built an instantiation of the basic VM synthesis approach, using the KVM virtual machine monitor. In our prototype, the overlay is created using the `xdelta3` binary differencing tool. Our experience has been that `xdelta3` generates smaller overlays than the native VM differencing mechanism provided by KVM. The VM overlay is then compressed using the Lempel-Ziv-Markov algorithm (LZMA), which is optimized for high compression ra-

App name	Install size (MB)	Overlay Size (MB) disk	memory	Synthesis time (s)
OBJECT	39.5	92.8	113.3	62.8
FACE	8.3	21.8	99.2	37.0
SPEECH	64.8	106.2	111.5	63.0
AR	97.5	192.3	287.9	140.2
FLUID	0.5	1.8	14.1	7.3

Table 3: Baseline performance (8 GB disk, 1 GB memory)

tios and fast decompression at the price of relatively slow compression [54]. This is an appropriate trade-off because decompression takes place in the critical path of execution at run-time and contributes to user-perceived delay. Further, compression is only done once offline but decompression occurs on each VM synthesis.

We test the efficacy of VM synthesis in reducing data transfer costs and application launch times on the VM back-ends of five mobile applications, summarized in Figure 2. In each case, user interaction occurs on a mobile device while the compute-intensive back-end processing of each interaction occurs in a VM instance on a cloudlet. These applications, written by various researchers and described in recent literature, are the building blocks of futuristic applications that seamlessly augment human perception and cognition. Three of the five back-ends run on Linux, while the other two run on Windows 7. These compute-intensive yet latency-sensitive applications are used in all the experiments reported in this paper.

We first construct base VM images using standard builds of Linux (Ubuntu 12.04 server) and Windows 7. These VMs are configured with 8 GB of disk and 1 GB of memory. An instance of each image is booted and then paused; the resulting VM disk image and memory snapshot serve as *base disk* and *base memory* respectively. To construct a launch VM, we resume an instance of the appropriate base image, install and configure the application binaries, and launch the application. At that point, we pause the VM. The resulting disk image and memory snapshot constitute the launch VM image. As soon as an instance is resumed from this image, the application will be in a state ready to respond to offload requests from the mobile device — there will be no reboot delay.

The overlay for each application is the compressed binary difference between the launch VM image and its base VM image, produced using `xdelta3` and LZMA compression. The sizes of the overlays, divided into disk and memory components, are reported in Table 3. For comparison, the sizes of the compressed application installation packages are also reported. Relative to VM image sizes, the VM synthesis approach greatly reduces the amount of data that must be transferred to create VM instances. Compared to the launch VM images (nominal 8 GB disk image plus memory snapshot), Table 3 shows that overlays are an order of magnitude smaller. While they are larger than the install packages from which they were derived, VM synthesis eliminates the fragile and error-prone process of runtime package installation and configuration as discussed in Section 3.1. In fact, as we show later in Section 8.1, provisioning using the most optimized version of VM synthesis is faster than runtime installation and configuration.

The total time to perform VM synthesis is also reported in Table 3. These times were measured using a netbook (client) and a virtual machine (server) hosted in a cloudlet described in Table 4. The client serves the application overlays to the cloudlet, which performs synthesis and executes the application VMs. For each application, the total time reported includes the time needed to transfer the overlay across WiFi, decompress it, apply the overlay to the base image, and resume the constructed application image. We note that the netbook used here is not significantly more capable

	Mobile	Cloudlet
Model	Dell™ Latitude 2120 Netbook	Dell™ Optiplex 9010 Desktop
CPU	Intel® Atom™ N550 1.5 GHz, 2 cores	Intel® Core® i7-3770 3.4 GHz, 4 cores, 8 threads (4 VCPUs for VM)
RAM	2 GB	32 GB (1 GB VM RAM)
Disk	250 GB HDD	1 TB HDD (8 GB VM disk)
Network	802.11a/g/n WiFi*	1 Gbps Ethernet
OS	Ubuntu 12.04 64bit (Linux kernel 3.2.0)	Ubuntu 12.04 64bit (Linux kernel 3.2.0)
VMM	—	QEMU/KVM-1.1.1†
misc	Belkin N750 Router (802.11n, GigE)	

*2.4 GHz 802.11n used here; 38 Mbps measured average BW
†modified for some experiments, as described in Sect. 7.2

Table 4: System configuration for experiments

than smartphones today, and achieves the same network bandwidth (38 Mbps) on 802.11n as the Samsung Galaxy 2 in our tests. Since most computation is done offline or on the cloudlet, and the data transfer is network limited, we do not expect significantly different results using a smartphone. However, for our prototype implementation, the netbook was convenient as it allowed us to use a full complement of x86 tools and libraries for the front-ends of our five applications. We use this configuration for all of the experiments in this paper.

Although this baseline implementation of VM synthesis achieves bit-exact provisioning without transferring full VM images, its performance falls short for ad-hoc, on-demand use in mobile offload scenarios. Table 3 shows that only one of the applications, FLUID, completes synthesis within 10 seconds. A synthesis time of 60 to 150 seconds is more typical for the other applications. That is too large for good user experience.

In the rest of this paper, we present a multi-pronged approach to accelerating VM synthesis. We first reduce the size of the overlay using aggressive deduplication (Section 4) and by bridging the semantic gap between the VMM and guest OS (Section 5). We then accelerate the launch of the VM image by pipelining its synthesis (Section 6), and by optimistically launching before synthesis is complete (Section 7). The results presented in each of these sections shows the speedup attributable to that optimization.

4. DEDUPLICATION

4.1 Concept

Our first optimization leverages the fact that there are many sources of data redundancy in a VM overlay. Through deduplication we can eliminate this redundancy and thus shrink the overlay. A smaller overlay incurs less transmission delay and also consumes less energy on the mobile device for transmission. Deduplication is very effective at reducing redundant data, and has been used widely in a variety of fields. In the virtualization space, it has been applied to reduce memory footprints of concurrent VMs [53], and in accelerating VM migration [57]. It is particularly well suited to VM overlays, since the significant expense of deduplication is only incurred offline during overlay construction. The overhead of re-inflating deduplicated data during synthesis is trivial, especially because the cloudlet is a powerful machine that is not energy-constrained. From a number of sources, we can anticipate some duplication of data between the memory snapshot and the disk image of the launch VM. For example, at the moment the launch VM is suspended during overlay construction, the I/O buffer cache of the guest OS contains some data that is also present in its virtual disk. Additionally, data from some files on the virtual disk may

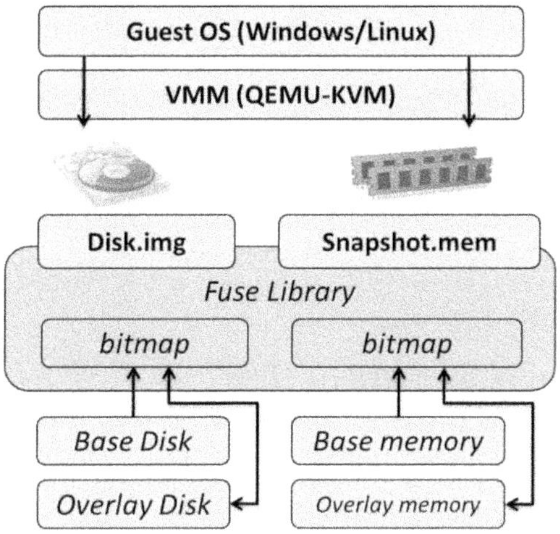

Figure 3: FUSE Interpositioning for Deduplication

have been read by the application back-end into its virtual memory during initialization. Further, depending on the runtime specifics of the programming language in which the application is written, there may be copies of variable initialization data both in memory and on disk. These are only a few of the many sources of data duplication between the memory snapshot and the disk image of the launch VM.

Separately, we can also expect some duplication of data between the overlay and the base VM (which is already on the cloudlet). Recall that the baseline implementation in Section 3.1 creates a VM overlay by constructing a binary delta between a launch VM and the base VM from which it is derived. This binary delta may contain duplicate data that has been copied or relocated within the memory or disk image. Indeed, the baseline system cannot take advantage of the fact that many parts of memory should be identical to disk because they are loaded from disk originally, e.g., executables, shared libraries, etc. An efficient approach to capturing this begins with a list of modifications within the launch VM and then performs deduplication to further reduce this list to the minimal set of information needed to transform a base VM into the launch VM. If we could find this minimal set, then we could construct smaller VM overlays.

4.2 Implementation

The choice of the granularity at which comparisons are performed is a key design decision for deduplication. Too large a granularity will tend to miss many small regions that are identical. Very small granularity will detect these small regions, but incur large overhead in the data representation. Our choice is a chunk size of 4 KB because it is a widely-used page size for many popular operating systems today. For example, current versions of Linux, Mac OS X, and Windows all use a 4 KB page size. An additional benefit of deduplicating at this granularity is that most operating systems use Direct Memory Access (DMA) for I/O, which means the disk is accessed with memory page size granularity. Thus, the 4 KB chunk size is likely to work well for both memory and disk deduplication.

To discover the portions of disk and memory modified during the process of creating a launch VM, we introduce a shim layer between the VMM and the backing files for virtual disk and memory using FUSE, as shown in Figure 3. During the installation and configuration steps of launch VM construction, the shim layer exposes I/O requests from the VMM to the virtual disk file and memory snapshot file. On every write to either the virtual disk or memory snapshot, we redirect the write to the corresponding overlay file and mark a bitmap indicating this chunk has changed. When reads occur at a later point in time, we consult this bitmap to determine if the read should be serviced from the original base files, or from the new overlay files. As in [30], we have found that FUSE has minimal impacts on virtual disk accesses, despite the fact that it is on the critical read and write paths from the VM to its disk. However, memory operations would become prohibitively expensive with this additional component. We therefore do not use FUSE to capture memory changes. Rather, we capture the entire memory snapshot only after we finish customizing the launch VM. We then interpret this memory snapshot, and compare it with *base memory* to obtain the modified memory chunks and corresponding bitmap.

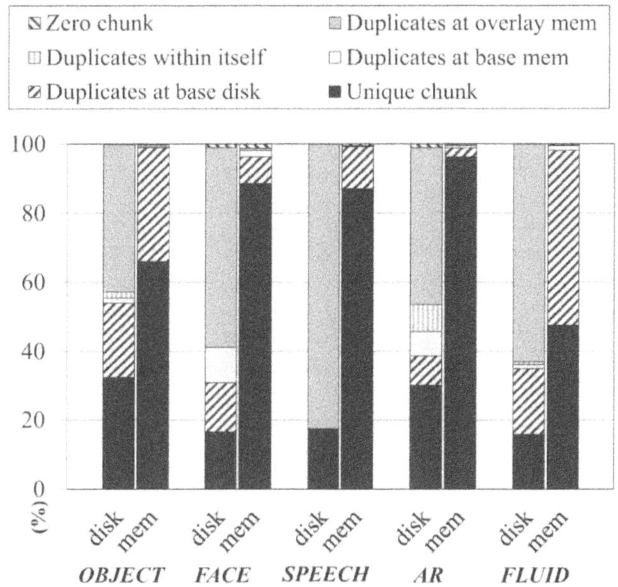

Figure 4: Benefit of Deduplication

We reuse this FUSE shim layer at VM synthesis time to avoid the data copying that would be required to explicitly merge the overlay virtual disk/memory with the base to reconstruct the launch VM. Instead, we redirect VM disk/memory access to either the overlay or the base image based on the bitmap. This approach to just-in-time reconstruction of a launch image has been used previously in systems such as ISR [20] and the Collective [3], though only for VM disk.

Once we have a list of modified disk and memory chunks, we perform deduplication by computing SHA-256 hashes [12] of their contents. We use these hashes to construct a unique set of pages which are not contained within the base VM and must be included in the transmitted overlay. We construct the set of unique modified disk and memory chunks using five comparison rules: (1) compare to base VM disk chunks, (2) compare to base VM memory chunks, (3) compare to other chunks within itself (within modified disk or modified memory respectively), (4) compare to a zero-filled chunk, and (5) compare between modified memory and modified disk. These five comparison rules capture various scenarios that are frequent sources of data redundancy, as discussed in Section 4.1.

For each unique chunk, we compare it to the corresponding chunk (same position on disk or in memory) in the base VM. We use the `xdelta3` algorithm to compute a binary delta of the chunk and transmit only the delta if it is smaller in size than the chunk. The idea behind this is that even if the hashes do not match, there may still be significant overlap at a finer byte granularity which a binary delta algorithm can leverage.

4.3 Evaluation

Figure 4 shows the benefit of deduplication for the overlay of each application. For any deduplication between memory and disk, we choose to only retain the duplicated chunks within memory. For deduplication purposes, it does not matter if the canonical chunk resides within disk or memory; we chose the memory snapshot as the canonical source of chunks.

Averaged across the five applications, only 22% of the modified disk and 77% of the modified memory is unique. The biggest source of redundancy is between modified memory and modified disk: each application exhibits greater than 58% duplication, with SPEECH exhibiting 83% duplication. The base disk is the second biggest source of duplication. On average, 13% of the modified disk and 21% of the modified memory are identical with chunks in the base disk. We analyzed files associated with the duplicated chunks for the OBJECT application. Our findings are consistent with our intuition: most of the associated files in the modified disk are shared resources located within the `/usr/shared/`, `/usr/lib/`, and `/var/lib/` directories, and a large portion of the files are shared libraries such as `libgdk-x11`, `libX11-xcb`, and `libjpeg`. The overlay memory shows similar results, but it also includes copies of executed binaries such as `wget`, `sudo`, `xz`, `dpkg-trigger`, and `dpkg-deb` in addition to shared libraries.

5. BRIDGING THE SEMANTIC GAP

5.1 Concept

The strong boundary enforced by VM technology between the guest and host environments is a double-edged sword. On the one hand, this strong boundary ensures isolation between the host, the guest, and other guests. On the other hand, it forces the host to view each guest as a black box, whose disk and memory contents cannot be interpreted in terms of higher-level abstractions such as files or application-level data structures. This challenge was first recognized by Chen and Noble [4]. Various attempts to bridge the semantic gap between VMM and the guest include VM introspection for intrusion and malware detection [13, 18] and memory classification [2] for improving prefetcher performance.

The semantic gap between low-level representations of memory and disk, and higher-level abstractions is also problematic when constructing VM overlays. For example, suppose a guest application downloads a 100 MB file, and later deletes it. Ideally, this should result in no increase in the size of the VM overlay. However, the VMM will see up to 200 MB of modifications: 100 MB of changed disk state, and 100 MB of changed memory state. This is because the file data moves through the in-memory I/O buffer cache of the guest OS before reaching the disk, effectively modifying both memory state and disk state. When the file is deleted, the guest OS marks the disk blocks and corresponding page cache entries as free, but their (now garbage) contents remain. To the VMM, this is indistinguishable from important state modifications that need to be preserved. Deduplication (described in Section 4) can cut this state in half, but we would still unnecessarily add 100 MB to the overlay.

Ideally, only the state that actually matters to the guest should be included in the overlay. When files are deleted or memory pages freed, none of their contents should be incorporated into the overlay. In essence, we need semantic knowledge from the guest regarding what state needs to be preserved and what can be discarded. When constructing the launch VM, a user (or application developer) installs a back-end application server on the base VM. This installation process typically involves several steps including downloading installation packages, creating temporary files, and moving executable binaries to target directories. Also, it is likely that all unneeded files will be deleted after finishing the installation process. We note that there is nothing unusual about this procedure for constructing custom VMs; it is identical to how custom VMs are typically generated in Amazon EC2, for example. We wish to fully leverage the user's intent when producing the overlay. We discard chunks containing semantically unnecessary footprint of the installation process by bridging the semantic gap between the VMM and guest in a manner that is transparent to guests.

In separate sections below, we show how this semantic gap can bridged for disk and memory state.

5.2 Implementation: Disk

To accurately account for disk blocks that are garbage, we need either (1) a method of communicating this information from the guest OS to the host, or (2) a method of scanning the contents of the file system on the virtual disk to glean this OS-level information. The first approach requires guest support, and may not be possible for every guest OS. The second approach requires no guest support, but does require an understanding of the on-disk file system format. Both approaches may be used in tandem to cross-check their results.

Exploiting TRIM support: The TRIM command in the ATA standard enables an OS to inform a disk which sectors are no longer in use. This command is important for modern devices such as Solid State Drives (SSDs) which implement logic to aggressively remap writes to unused sectors. Wear-leveling algorithms and garbage collection inside of SSDs use this knowledge to increase write performance and device life.

The TRIM command provides precisely the mechanism we desire — an industry-standard mechanism for communicating semantic information about unused sectors from an OS to the underlying hardware. We can exploit this mechanism to communicate free disk block information from the guest OS to the host to reduce VM overlay size. We modify the VMM (KVM/QEMU) to capture TRIM events and to log these over a named pipe to our overlay generation code. When generating the overlay, we merge this TRIM log with a trace of sector writes by timestamp to determine which blocks are free when the VM is suspended; these blocks can be safely omitted from the overlay. To make use of this technique, we simply need to ensure that TRIM support is enabled in the guest OS. As TRIM is an industry standard, it is supported by almost all modern operating systems, including recent Linux distributions and Windows 7.

Introspecting the file system: An alternative approach is to use knowledge of the on-disk file system format to directly inspect the contents of a virtual disk [19, 37] and determine which blocks are currently unused. Many file systems maintain lists of free blocks forming a canonical set of blocks which should not be included in an overlay. In the worst case, the entire file system can be crawled to determine which blocks are in use by files within the file system. Although this approach is file-system-specific, it avoids the need to communicate information from a running guest, or to carefully trace TRIM and write events.

We identify free disk blocks using the tool described by Richter et al. [37]. This tool reads and interprets a virtual disk image and produces a list of free blocks. It supports the `ext2/3/4` family of Linux file systems and the `NTFS` file system for Windows.

5.3 Implementation: Memory

It is difficult to determine which memory pages are considered free by a guest OS. Although the VMM can inspect the page tables, this is not sufficient to determine if a page is in use because unmapped pages are not necessarily free [2]. Inspecting page contents is also not good enough, because free pages normally contain random data and are not zeroed.

To bridge this gap, there are two natural approaches: (1) communicate free page information from the guest OS to the host, or (2) interpret memory layout data structures maintained by the guest OS. Unfortunately, there is no standard way of accomplishing the first approach (i.e., no memory counterpart to TRIM support), so we focus our efforts on the second approach. In order to obtain the list of free memory pages we first introduce a tiny kernel module into Linux guests. This module exposes the memory addresses of two data structures for memory management through the `/proc` file system in the guest. We suspend the VM, and feed these addresses and the memory snapshot to an offline scanning program. This scanning program reads the memory snapshot and parses the memory management data structures at the specified addresses to identify the free pages.

Since our approach requires modifying the guest OS, it is not usable on closed-source OSs such as Windows. Further, in-memory data formats tend to be highly volatile across OS releases, and to evolve much more rapidly than file system formats. Even an open-source kernel such as Linux will require significant maintenance effort to track these changes.

Other techniques could be employed to infer free pages without the need for guest support. For example, a VMM could monitor memory accesses since the guest's boot and keep track of pages that have been touched. This would avoid guest modification at the cost of lower fidelity—some of the pages reported as used could have been touched, but later freed. Perhaps with the advent of Non-Volatile Memories (NVMs), which provide persistent storage with memory-like, byte-addressable interfaces, there may be a need to introduce a standardized TRIM-like feature for memory. Such support would make it possible to bridge the memory semantic gap in an OS-agnostic way in the future.

5.4 Evaluation

For the disk semantic gap, our experiments show that the TRIM and introspection approaches produce nearly identical results. Just a few additional free blocks are found by the introspection approach that were not captured by TRIM. We therefore present only the results for the TRIM approach.

Figure 5 shows how much we gain by closing the disk semantic gap. For each application we construct the VM image by downloading its installation package, installing it, and then deleting the installation package. We therefore expect our approach to find and discard the blocks that held the installation package, reducing overlay size by approximately the installation package size. Our results confirm this for all of the applications except one: for FACE, the semantically discarded disk blocks together were smaller than the installation package. On investigation, we found that this was due to the freed blocks being reused post-install. On average, across the five applications, bridging the disk semantic gap allows 25% of modified disk chunks to be omitted from the overlay.

Figure 5 also shows the savings we can achieve by discarding free memory pages from the VM overlay. We can discard on average 18% of modified memory chunks for the Linux applications OBJECT, SPEECH, and FLUID. Since our implementation is limited to Linux, we cannot reduce the memory overlays for the two Windows-based applications (FACE and AR).

Combining deduplication and bridging of the semantic gap can be highly effective in reducing the VM overlay size. Figure 6 shows VM overlay size with each optimization individually represented, and also combined together. The "baseline" represents VM overlay size using the approach described in Section 3. The bar labeled "deduped" is the VM overlay with deduplication applied; "semantics" is the VM overlay with semantic knowledge applied (only disk for Windows applications); and, "combined" is the VM overlay size with both optimizations applied. On average compared to the baseline implementation, the deduplication optimization reduces the VM overlay size to 44%. Using semantic knowledge reduces the VM overlay size to 55% of its baseline size. Both optimizations applied together reduce overlay size to 28% of baseline.

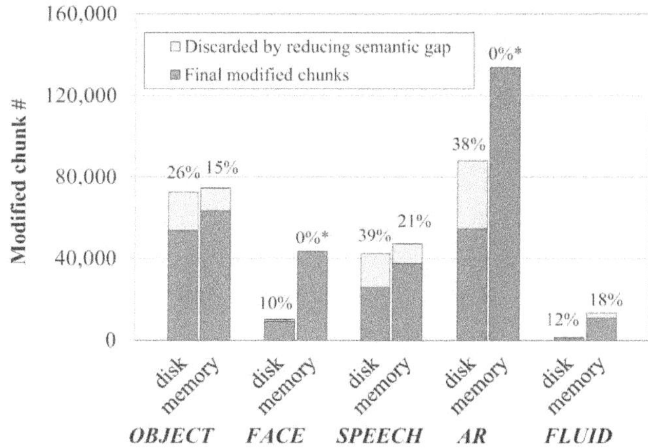

*Our implementation cannot determine free memory pages for Windows guests.
*Percentage represents the fraction of discarded chunks.

Figure 5: Savings by Closing the Semantic Gap

The final overlay disk almost disappears when we combine both optimizations. This is because a large portion of disk chunks are associated with installation packages. Recall that to install each application, we first download an installation package in the VM and remove it later when it finishes installation. This installation file is already compressed, so further compression does little. In addition, this newly introduced data is less likely to be duplicated inside the base VM. Therefore, applying semantic knowledge removes most of the unique chunks not found by deduplication. For example in AR, 25,887 unique chunks remained after deduplication, but 96% of them are discarded by applying semantic knowledge.

6. PIPELINING

6.1 Concept

There are three time-consuming steps in VM synthesis. First, the VM overlay is transferred. Next, the VM overlay is decompressed. Finally, the decompressed VM overlay is applied to the base VM (i.e., `xdelta3` in reverse). These steps are serialized because we need the output of the preceding step as input to the next one, as shown in Figure 7. This serialization adds significantly to the VM start latency on a cloudlet. If we could begin the later steps before the preceding ones complete, we could shrink the total time for synthesis as shown in Figure 8.

6.2 Implementation

The implementation follows directly from the pipelining concept. We split the VM overlay into a set of segments and operate on each segment independently. The VM synthesis steps can now be pipelined. The decompression of a segment starts as soon as it is transferred, and happens in parallel with the transfer of the next segment. Likewise, the application of an overlay segment to the base VM proceeds in parallel with the decompression of the next

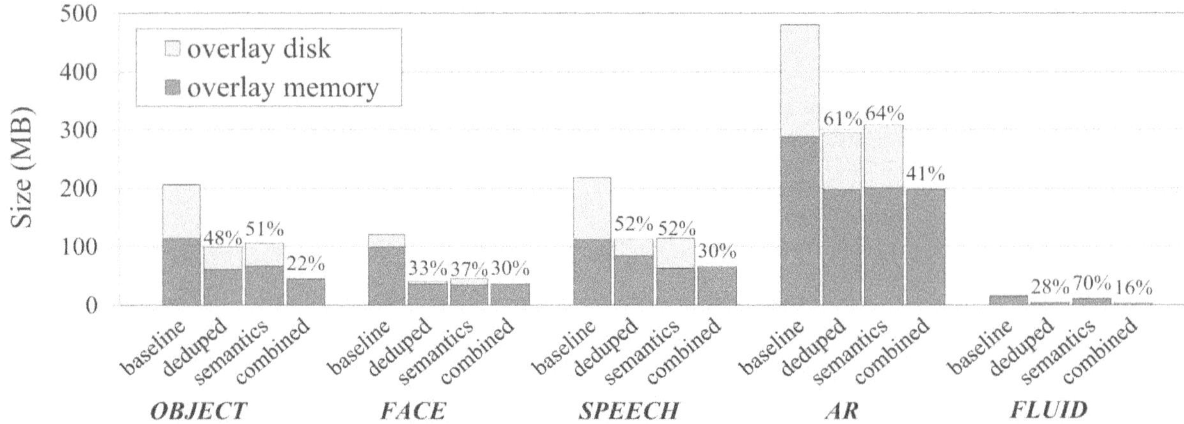

Figure 6: Overlay Size Compared to Baseline (Percentage represents relative overlay size compared to baseline)

Figure 7: Baseline VM Synthesis

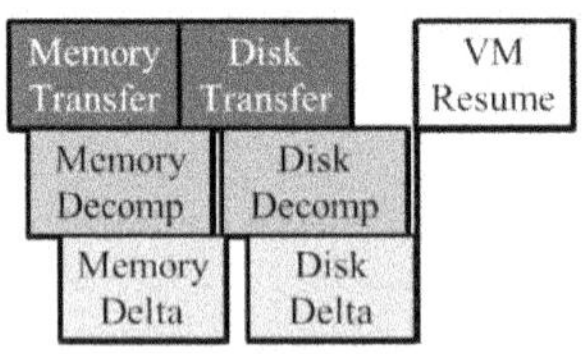

Figure 8: Pipelined VM Synthesis

segment. Given sufficiently small segment size, the total time will approach that of the bottleneck step (typically the transfer time), plus any serial steps such as VM instance creation and launch.

6.3 Evaluation

Figure 9 compares the performance of the baseline synthesis approach to an optimized one that combines deduplication, semantic gap closing, and pipelining. The results confirm that once pipelining is introduced, transfer time becomes the dominant contributor to the total synthesis time. The synthesis time shown in Figure 9 includes all of the time needed to get the VM to the point where it is fully resumed and ready to accept offload requests from the mobile device. Two applications now launch within 10 seconds (FACE and FLUID), while two others launch within 15 seconds (OBJECT and SPEECH). Only AR takes much longer (44 seconds), but this is because its overlay size and, therefore, transfer time remains high. On average, we observe a 3x–5x speedup compared to the baseline VM synthesis approach from Section 3.

7. EARLY START

7.1 Concept

We have shown that the optimizations described in the previous sections greatly reduce the size of overlays and streamline their transfer and processing. For several of the applications, the optimized overlay size is close to the size of the install image. Hence, there is little scope for further reducing size to improve launch times. Instead, we consider whether one really needs to transfer the entire overlay before launching the VM instance. This may not be necessary for a number of reasons. For example, during

	OBJECT	FACE	SPEECH	AR	FLUID
% chunks	17.4	56.9	26.8	65.2	27.1
% size	30.6	63.0	33.0	87.9	50.3

Percentage of the overlay accessed between VM launch and completion of first request, in terms of chunks and compressed overlay size.

Table 5: Percentage of Overlay Accessed

the overlay creation process, the guest OS was already booted up and the application was already launched at the point when the VM was suspended. Any state that is used only during guest boot-up or application initialization will not be needed again. As another example, some VM state may only be accessed during exception handling or other rare events and are unlikely to be accessed immediately after VM instance creation.

The potential benefits of optimism can be significant. Table 5 shows the percentage of chunks in the overlay that are actually accessed by the five benchmark applications between VM launch and completion of the first request. A substantial number of chunks are not used immediately. We can speed up VM launch by transferring just the needed chunks first, synthesizing only those parts of the launch VM, and then creating the VM instance. The transfer of the missing parts of the overlay and synthesis of the rest of the launch VM can continue in the background until it is completed.

7.2 Implementation

We explored a number of alternatives in translating the concept of early start into a viable implementation. One option is to profile the resume of the launch VM, and order the chunks in the overlay accordingly. When offloading, the VM is resumed concurrently with the synthesis operations. If the VM attempts to access chunks that have not yet been synthesized, it will be blocked until the chunk becomes available. If the order of chunks is correct, the VM can begin running significantly before the VM synthesis completes.

Unfortunately, it is difficult to get this order perfectly right. In our early experiments, multiple profiling runs produced slightly different chunk access patterns. In particular a small number of chunks may be accessed early in one run, but not at all in another. With a large number of chunks, it is unlikely that every chunk that is needed early in an actual VM resume will have been picked up in the profiling. More likely, one or more of these chunks will be missed in profiling, and will be placed near the end of the overlay. Getting even one chunk wrong can force the VM to wait for all chunks to be transferred and VM synthesis to complete.

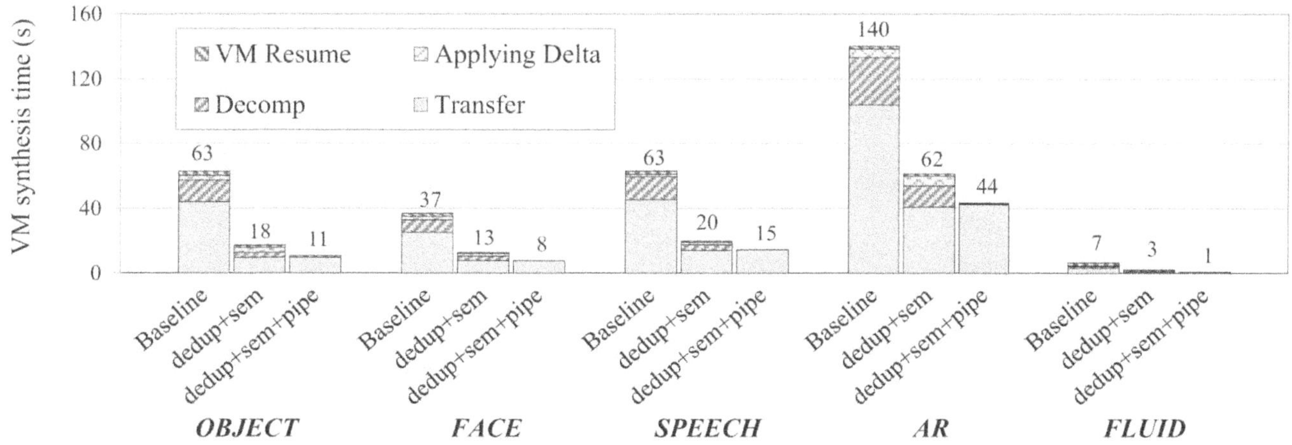

Figure 9: VM Synthesis Acceleration by Pipelining

Alternatively, we can avoid trying to predict the chunk access order by using a demand fetching approach, as done in [20], [39], and many subsequent efforts. Here, the VM is started first, and the portions of the overlay needed to synthesize accessed chunks are fetched on demand from the mobile device. Unfortunately, this approach, too, has some issues. Demand fetching individual chunks (which can be very small due to deduplication and delta encoding) requires many small network transfers, with a round trip penalty imposed on each, resulting in poor effective bandwidth and slow transfers. To alleviate this, we can cut the overlay into larger segments comprised of many chunks, and perform demand fetching at segment granularities. This will help amortize the demand fetching costs, but leaves open the question of sizing the segments. Smaller segments let one fetch more closely just the needed chunks. Larger segments, in addition to being more bandwidth friendly, can achieve better compression ratios, but will be less selective in transferring just what is needed. Finally, how chunks are grouped into segments can also significantly influence performance. For example, if needed chunks are randomly distributed among segments, one will likely need to transfer the entire overlay to run the VM.

Our implementation uses a hybrid approach that combines profiling and demand paging, similar to VMTorrent [36] though applied to VM overlays rather than VM images. We make a reasonable attempt to order the chunks according to a profiled access pattern computed offline. We then break the overlay into segments. During offload, we start the VM and begin streaming the segments in order, but also allow out-of-order demand fetches of segments to preempt the original ordering. Thus, we use demand fetching to retrieve chunks that were not predicted by the profiling, but unlike [36], we simultaneously bulk-stream segments in a work-conserving manner to quickly transfer and synthesize all chunks. While this approach bears some resemblance to classic prefetching with out-of-band handling of demand misses, these concepts are being applied to an overlay rather than a VM image.

Figure 10 illustrates our implementation of this hybrid approach. A critical issue is that all of the widely used VMMs, including KVM, Xen, VirtualBox, and VMware, require the entire memory snapshot before resuming a VM, hindering early start. So, we first modify the VMM (KVM in our case) to resume a VM without first reading in the entire memory snapshot. Rather, it now memory maps the snapshot file, so portions are implicitly loaded when accessed. We then implement a FUSE file system that hosts the VM disk image and memory snapshot. This routes disk accesses of the VMM to our user-level code that can perform just-in-time VM synthesis on the accessed chunks (disk or memory). Our code consults

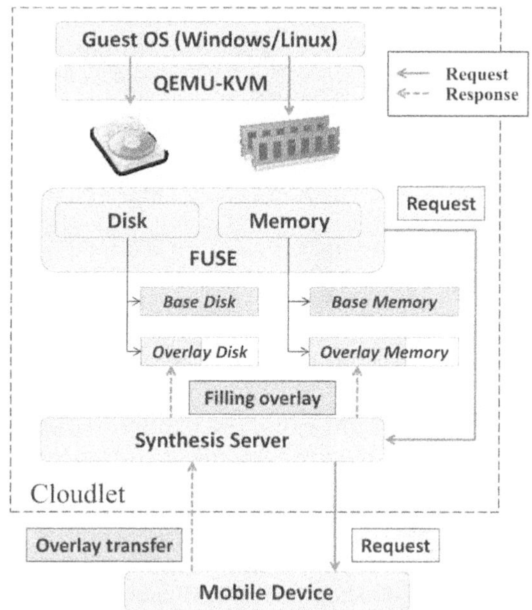

Figure 10: System Implementation for Early Start

a small bitmap that indicates whether the particular chunk needs to be served from the base image or the overlay. If the overlay is needed, then a local cache of processed chunks is checked. If the chunk is not available, a demand-fetch of the needed overlay segment is issued to the mobile device. Concurrently, in the background, the code processes the stream of overlay segments as it is received from the mobile device. With this implementation, only the small bitmap assigning chunks to overlay or base image needs to be transferred before the VM is launched.

7.3 Evaluation

We evaluate our early start approach with a few different combinations of segment size and chunk order. We test with small (approx. 64KB) and medium (approx. 1MB) sized segments, as well as with just a single segment comprising the entire overlay. (The latter effectively disables demand-fetching). We also test with chunks sorted by access-order (based on a single profiling run of each application) and offset-order (with memory before disk chunks). We slightly modify the ordering so that duplicate chunks are contained within the same segment, avoiding any need for pointer-chasing between segments when handling deduplication.

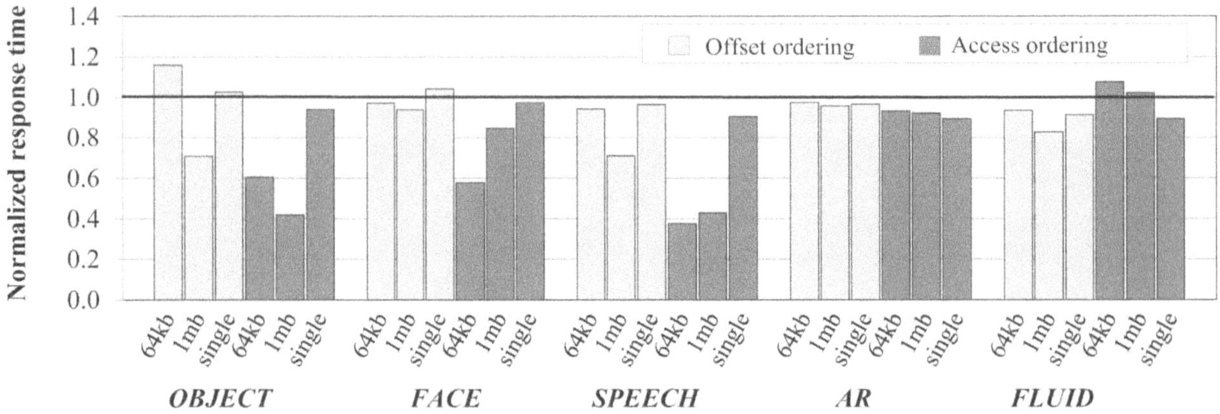

Figure 11: Normalized First Response Time for Early start

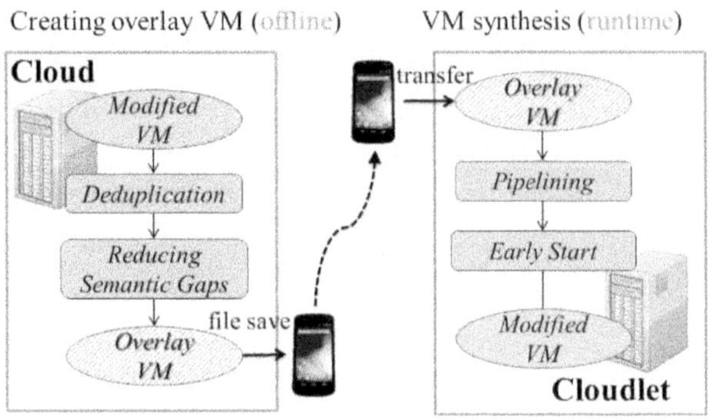

Figure 12: Fully Optimized VM Synthesis

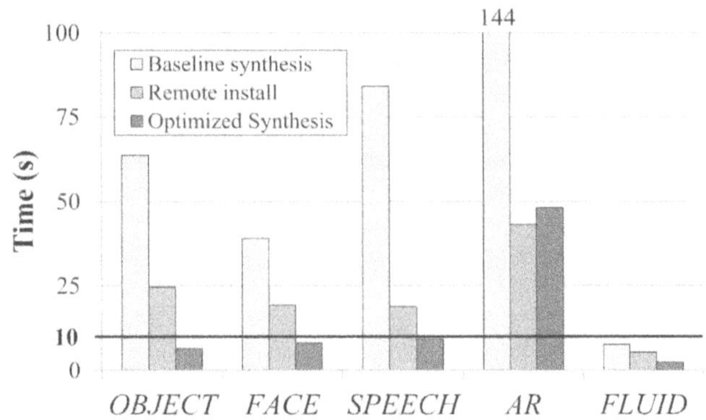

Figure 13: First response times

With early-start, the VM synthesis time itself is less relevant. Rather, the metric we use is the first response time of the application. This is measured by having the mobile device initiate the synthesis of the application VM, and then repeatedly attempt to send it queries. The response time is measured from the initial VM start request to when the first reply returns to the client, thus including the overlapped transfer time, synthesis time, and application execution time. Figure 11 compares performance of early start for different chunk ordering policies and segment sizes. The values are normalized to the first response time when the VM begins execution once VM synthesis (including all of the other optimizations discussed previously) completes. Access ordering alone does not help significantly due to the inaccuracies of the single profiling runs. However, access-ordered chunks with demand fetching with 64 KB or 1 MB segments can significantly reduce first response times. We see up to 60% reduction for *SPEECH* and *OBJECT*. For *FLUID*, the response time without early start is already so short that small fluctuations due to compression and network affect the normalized response time adversely. *AR*, which requires 90% of the data in its overlay, does not benefit much from early start.

8. FINAL RESULTS AND DISCUSSIONS

8.1 Fully Optimized VM Synthesis

We have shown that all of the various techniques for improving VM synthesis described in this paper work quite well on their own. One may wonder: how effective are these techniques when combined? In this section we evaluate a complete, fully-optimized implementation of VM synthesis incorporating all of the improvements described in this paper. The figure of merit here is the total latency as perceived by the user, from the beginning of the application offload process to when the first reply is returned. This first response metric is dependent on the time consumed by the offloading operation and launch of the application VM.

Figure 12 illustrates the fully-optimized process of VM synthesis as we intend it to be used with mobile devices and cloudlet infrastructure. We first construct minimal application overlays via deduplication and by preserving only the semantically meaningful chunks. We store and serve these overlays to the cloudlet from the mobile device (a netbook in our experiments). To minimize the time required to perform VM synthesis, we pipelined the synthesis steps, and then applied early start on the cloudlet.

Figure 13 shows the improvement in first-response times with our fully-optimized VM synthesis over the baseline version described in Section 3. In this experiment, we used an overlay segment size of 1 MB, which provides a good tradeoff between demand fetch granularity and good compression. Overall, we improved performance of VM synthesis by a factor of 3 to 8 across these applications. Except for *AR*, the first responses for all of the other applications come within 10 s. A combination of multiple factors causes significantly longer synthesis times for the *AR* application. First, it has the largest installation size among all five applications and a significant portion of the installation is a database file that is less likely to be deduplicated. In addition, we could not close the memory semantic gap for *AR* since our implementation cannot determine free memory pages for Windows guests. Further, as depicted in Table 5, *AR* requires almost all of the overlay to serve the initial request, and, thus, it does not benefit from the early start optimization.

We also compare our results to the first-response time for a remote installation approach to running a custom VM image. This

1. Create a new EC2 VM instance from an existing Amazon VM image,
2. Attach a cloud block device with VM synthesis tools and base VM image,
3. Change the root file system of the instance to the attached block device,
4. Perform **VM synthesis** over the WAN to construct the modified VM disk,
5. Mount the modified VM disk,
6. Synchronize / copy the modified file system with the instance's original,
7. Detach block device,
8. Reboot with the customized file system.

Figure 14: Steps in VM Synthesis for EC2

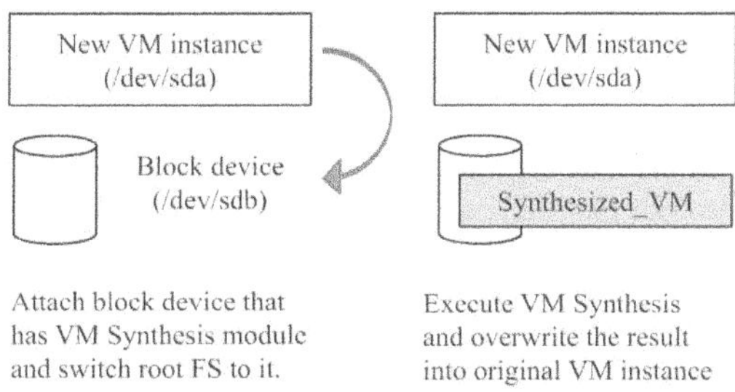

Figure 15: VM Synthesis for EC2

involves resuming a standard VM, uploading and installing the application packages, and then executing the custom applications. In Section 3.2, we have already dismissed this approach on qualitative grounds; in particular, even scripted install can be fragile, the resulting configuration is not identical every time, and the application is restarted every time so execution state is not preserved. The only redeeming quality of this approach is that the install packages tend to be smaller than the baseline VM overlays, potentially making the remote install faster. Here, we use highly optimized application packages that are self-contained (including needed libraries, or statically-compiled binaries), and fully-scripted installation to show the remote install approach at its fastest.

As we can see from Figure 13, however, our optimized VM synthesis approach produces significantly better first-response times than remote install in all but one case. In that case, the two approaches are basically a tie. Thus, our optimized VM synthesis approach can achieve very fast offload and execution of custom application VMs on cloudlets, yet maintain strong guarantees on their reconstructed state.

8.2 Improved WiFi Bandwidth

All of the experiments in this paper were conducted using 802.11n WiFi at 2.4 GHz (38 Mbps measured average bandwidth). We expect these times to improve in the future as new wireless technologies and network optimizations are introduced, increasing the bandwidth of WiFi networks. In other words, VM synthesis time is now directly correlated to network bandwidth. While WAN bandwidth improvements require large infrastructure changes, mobile bandwidth to the wireless AP at a cloudlet only requires localized hardware and software changes. New WiFi standards such as 802.11ac promise up to 500 Mbps and are actively being deployed [55]. Recent research [14] also demonstrates methods of increasing bandwidth up to 700% with software-level changes for WiFi networks facing contention. Thus, both industry and research are focused on increasing WiFi bandwidth. This directly translates into faster VM synthesis. Based on our measurements, until actual transfer times improve by 3x, the transfer stage will remain the bottleneck (assuming the cloudlet processor remains constant). Beyond this, we will need to parallelize the decompression and overlay application stages across multiple cores to benefit from further improvements in network bandwidth.

	10 Mbps		100 Mbps	
	Synthesis	Amazon	Synthesis	Amazon
Synthesis Setup	44 s	—	46 s	—
Uploading†	36 s	607 s	8 s	204 s
Post-processing	96 s	139 s	97 s	105 s
Total	180 s	746 s	154 s	310 s

† Upload time for VM synthesis includes all synthesis steps (overlay transfer, decompression, and applying delta).

Table 6: Time for Instantiating Custom VM at Amazon EC2

9. VM SYNTHESIS ON AMAZON EC2

In this paper, we have presented VM synthesis as a technique to rapidly offload customized application VMs to cloudlet infrastructure near a mobile device. However, the technique is much more general than this, and can help whenever one wishes to transfer VM state across a bottleneck network. In particular, VM synthesis can significantly speed up the upload and launch of a custom VM on commercial cloud services across a WAN. Here, we describe our VM synthesis solution for Amazon's public EC2 cloud.

The normal cloud workflow to launch a customized VM involves three steps: (1) construct the VM image, including installing custom software and libraries, and making requisite configuration changes; (2) upload the VM image to the cloud, a step largely limited by the client-to-cloud bandwidth; and (3) launch and execute a VM instance based on the uploaded VM image, a step that depends on the cloud provider's backend scheduling and resources. VM synthesis promises to speed up the second step by reducing the amount of state uploaded to a cloud.

Today, no cloud supports VM synthesis as a primitive operation. In our EC2 implementation, we perform VM synthesis entirely within a running VM instance. EC2 does not allow external access to the disk or memory image of an instance, so we cannot manipulate the saved state of a paused instance to effect synthesis. We also cannot generate a data file, treat it as a VM image, and launch an instance based on it. We work around these limitations by performing VM synthesis within a live instance, which modifies its own state and then reboots into the custom VM environment. Assuming that the base VM image and synthesis tools have already been installed in an EC2 block device, synthesis proceeds in the eight steps shown in Figure 14. Steps 1-3 occur on the left hand side of Figure 15, while steps 4-8 occur on the right hand side. We do not handle the memory portion of a VM in EC2 because we do not have access to the raw memory image. This requires an unnecessary reboot and wasted time in synchronizing file systems. If EC2 had a VM synthesis primitive, the memory image and VM disk could be directly exposed by their infrastructure and only step 4 would remain; the VM overlay would be transmitted, applied, and then the VM could be directly resumed without reboot.

We compare the time it takes to perform VM synthesis to the time required in the normal cloud workflow to deploy and execute a custom VM with the OBJECT application. The results are shown in Table 6. For VM synthesis, synthesis setup corresponds to steps 1-3, uploading to step 4, and post-processing corresponds to steps 5-8. With the normal Amazon workflow, there is no analog to synthesis setup. However, after upload, Amazon takes time to provision resources and to boot a VM within EC2; this is included in the total post-processing time. We present results for two WAN bandwidths, 10 Mbps and 100 Mbps, in Table 6. In both cases, VM synthesis wins over the normal cloud workflow with a 4x improvement in the 10 Mbps case and a 2x improvement in the 100 Mbps case. The normal cloud workflow is bottlenecked on bandwidth because it must upload the full 514 MB compressed VM image, but VM synthesis reduces this to a much more compact 42 MB VM overlay. It is important to note here that pre- and post-processing for VM synthesis are artificially inflated because of the lack of native VM synthesis support and the convoluted mechanisms we needed to employ to work around limitations imposed by EC2.

10. RELATED WORK

Offloading computation has a long history in mobile computing, especially to improve application performance and battery life [11, 31, 38]. The broader concept of cyber foraging, or "living off the land" by leveraging nearby computational and data storage resources, was first articulated in 2001 [41]. In that work, the proximity of the helper resources, known as "surrogates," to the mobile device was intuitively assumed, but how to provision them was left as future work. Since then, different aspects of cyber foraging have been explored by a number of researchers. Some of these efforts have looked at the tradeoffs between different goals such as execution speed and energy usage based on adaptive resource-based decisions on local versus remote execution [9, 10]. Other efforts have looked at the problem of estimating resource usage of a future operation based on past observations, and used this estimate to pick the optimal execution site and fidelity setting [15, 29]. Many researchers have explored the partitioning of applications between local and remote execution, along with language-level and runtime tools to support this partitioning [1, 5, 7].

Since 2008, offloading computation from a mobile device over the Internet to a cloud computing service such as Amazon EC2 [45] has become possible. But, cloud computing places surrogates far away across a multi-hop WAN rather than nearby on a single-hop WLAN. A 2009 position paper [42] introduced VM-based surrogate infrastructure called "cloudlets." Proximity of offload infrastructure was deemed essential for deeply immersive applications where crisp interactive response requires end-to-end latency to be as low as possible. Recent application studies [6, 16] have confirmed the need for proximity of offload infrastructure when a mobile device runs interactive and resource intensive applications.

Aspects of the VM overlay concept can be seen in copy-on-write (COW) mechanisms. Sapuntzakis et al. [39] showed how COW could be applied hierarchically to VMs to create an efficient representation of a family of virtual appliances. Their following work, the Collective [3], advanced this approach and proposed a cache-based system to cope with various network conditions. Similarly, QCOW2, a widely used virtual disk file format, uses a read-only base image and stores modified data in a separate file [25]. Strata [34] combined union file system and package management semantics to easily create and deploy virtual appliances and to dynamically compose them. VM overlays, as articulated in [42], extend the base and modifications concept to both VM disk and memory state, and focuses on a mobile, cyber-foraging use case.

Some aspects of the optimization techniques proposed in this work have been individually investigated in other domains. Deduplication has been widely adopted in file systems, network storage, and virtualization. In file systems, it is used to reclaim storage space by detecting duplicated files or blocks. LBFS (Low Bandwidth File System) [27] is an example of a network file system that uses deduplication to reduce bandwidth demand. It introduced the use of Rabin fingerprints for defining content-based chunk boundaries that are edit-resistant. REBL (Redundancy Elimination at the Block Level) [22] applied deduplication along with compression and delta-encoding to achieve effective storage reduction. It introduced the concept of super-fingerprints to reduce the computational effort of deduplication. Deduplication has also been used in the virtual machine space. Waldspurger removed duplicated memory pages and shared identical memory pages across multiple virtual machines to conserve memory on the host machine [53]. Several recent works have also used deduplication to reduce the cost of VM migration both within datacenters [57] and across WANs [56]. As our work uses deduplication in an offline stage, we can apply it aggressively across both disk and memory images.

Demand fetching of VM disk state was introduced by Kozuch et al. [20] and Sapuntzakis et al. [39]. Both leveraged the fact that only a small portion of a VM disk is typically accessed in a session. Post-copy migration [17] applied demand fetching of VM memory to live VM migration to reduce network transmission costs and the total migration time. Post-copy migration immediately started the VM at the target destination instead of pre-copying a VM's memory state over mulitiple iterations. SnowFlock [23] combined demand fetching and packet multicasting to provide highly efficient and scalable cloning of VMs. It started VM execution on a remote site with only critical metadata and performed memory-on-demand, where clones lazily fetch portions of VM state as it is accessed. VM image Distribution Network (VDN) [33] used demand fetching of content-addressed chunks in the datacenter. VMTorrent [36] enabled scalable VM disk streaming by combining block prioritization, profile-based execution prefetch, and on-demand fetch. Our work also uses profiled prefetching and demand-fetching.

The significance of the semantic gap between VMMs and guest OSes was first articulated by Chen and Noble [4]. Later, Garfinkel and Rosenblum [13] coined the term virtual machine introspection and developed an architecture focusing on analyzing memory. Another effort to bridge this gap is VMWatcher [18], which enabled malware detection by introducing a technique called guest view casting to systematically reconstruct internal semantic views of a VM, such as files, processes, and kernel modules, in a non-intrusive manner. Kaleidoscope [2] exploited x86 architectural information (e.g. page table entries) to classify VM memory into sets of semantically-related regions and used this for better prefetching and faster cloning of a VM into many transient fractional workers. Our work bridges the semantic gap to minimize VM overlay size by identifying freed pages and blocks, and, to the best of our knowledge, is the first to use TRIM support for this purpose.

11. FUTURE WORK

Our experiments used a netbook as a surrogate for a powerful mobile device of the future. Although we expect hardware specifications of smartphones will soon catch up with today's netbooks, we plan to repeat our experiments on an Android-based smartphone to verify the feasibility of our optimizations on these platforms. We do not anticipate major differences in the results, since most of the processing in our system is done offline or on the cloudlet, and the mobile device mostly acts as a sensing, user interaction, and data storage device.

We also plan to re-engineer our software as an extension to the widely used OpenStack platform for cloud computing. With this in mind, we have carefully designed and implemented our system to support backward compatibility with OpenStack. Acceptance of our code into OpenStack would simplify the deployment and widespread use of VM synthesis, especially since some of our optimizations require modifications to KVM.

An important aspect of practical cloudlet usage is leveraging temporal locality of user mobility. In daily life, most users are likely to follow repeated routines and to frequently revisit a few locations. Hence, there is high value in caching the results of previous VM synthesis operations. By reusing cached launch VMs, the synthesis step can be completely avoided. This can be especially valuable if the overlay is large.

12. CONCLUSION

Beyond today's familiar desktop, laptop and smartphone applications is a new genre of software seamlessly augmenting human perception and cognition. Supporting the compute-intensive and latency-sensitive applications typical of this genre requires the ability to offload computation from mobile devices to widely dispersed cloud infrastructure, a.k.a., cloudlets. Physical dispersion of cloudlets makes their provisioning a challenge. In this paper, we have shown how cloudlets can be rapidly and precisely provisioned by a mobile device to meet its exact needs just before use. We have also shown that although our solution, dynamic VM synthesis, was inspired by the specific demands of mobile computing, it also has broader relevance to public cloud computing infrastructure.

We have made our source code available for download at our project site: `http://elijah.cs.cmu.edu/`.

13. ACKNOWLEDGEMENTS

We thank our shepherd Jason Nieh and the anonymous reviewers for their valuable comments and suggestions. We thank Gene Cahill and Soumya Simanta for implementing the SPEECH and FACE applications, Alvaro Collet for implementing the OBJECT application, and Doyub Kim for implementing the FLUID application. We also thank Benjamin Gilbert and Jan Harkes for their valuable discussions throughout the work.

This research was supported by the National Science Foundation (NSF) under grant numbers CNS-0833882 and IIS-1065336, by an Intel Science and Technology Center grant, and by the Department of Defense (DoD) under Contract No. FA8721-05-C-0003 for the operation of the Software Engineering Institute (SEI), a federally funded research and development center. This material has been approved for public release and unlimited distribution (DM-0000276). Additional support for cloudlet-related research was provided by IBM, Google, and Bosch.

14. REFERENCES

[1] R. K. Balan, D. Gergle, M. Satyanarayanan, and J. Herbsleb. Simplifying cyber foraging for mobile devices. In *Proceedings of the 5th International Conference on Mobile Systems, Applications and Services*, San Juan, Puerto Rico, 2007. ACM.

[2] R. Bryant, A. Tumanov, O. Irzak, A. Scannell, K. Joshi, M. Hiltunen, A. Lagar-Cavilla, and E. de Lara. Kaleidoscope: Cloud micro-elasticity via VM state coloring. In *Proceedings of the Sixth Conference on Computer Systems*, Salzburg, Austria, 2011. ACM.

[3] R. Chandra, N. Zeldovich, C. Sapuntzakis, and M. S. Lam. The Collective: A cache-based system management architecture. In *Proceedings of the 2nd Symposium on Networked Systems Design & Implementation*, Boston, MA, 2005.

[4] P. M. Chen and B. D. Noble. When virtual is better than real. In *Proceedings of the Eighth Workshop on Hot Topics in Operating Systems*, Elmau/Oberbayern, Germany, 2001. IEEE Computer Society.

[5] B.-G. Chun, S. Ihm, P. Maniatis, M. Naik, and A. Patti. CloneCloud: Elastic execution between mobile device and cloud. In *Proceedings of the Sixth ACM European Conference on Computer Systems*, Salzburg, Austria, 2011. ACM.

[6] S. Clinch, J. Harkes, A. Friday, N. Davies, and M. Satyanarayanan. How close is close enough? Understanding the role of cloudlets in supporting display appropriation by mobile users. In *Proceedings of the IEEE International Conference on Pervasive Computing and Communications*, Lugano, Switzerland, Mar. 2012.

[7] E. Cuervo, A. Balasubramanian, D.-k. Cho, A. Wolman, S. Saroiu, R. Chandra, and P. Bahl. MAUI: Making smartphones last longer with code offload. In *Proceedings of the 8th International Conference on Mobile Systems, Applications, and Services*, San Francisco, California, USA, 2010. ACM.

[8] J. Flinn. *Cyber Foraging: Bridging mobile and cloud computing via opportunistic offload.* Morgan & Claypool Publishers, 2012.

[9] J. Flinn, D. Narayanan, and M. Satyanarayanan. Self-tuned remote execution for pervasive computing. In *Proceedings of the Eighth Workshop on Hot Topics in Operating Systems*, Elmau/Oberbayern, Germany, 2001. IEEE Computer Society.

[10] J. Flinn, S. Park, and M. Satyanarayanan. Balancing performance, energy, and quality in pervasive computing. In *Proceedings of the 22nd International Conference on Distributed Computing Systems*, Vienna, Austria, 2002. IEEE Computer Society.

[11] J. Flinn and M. Satyanarayanan. Energy-aware adaptation for mobile applications. In *Proceedings of the Seventeenth ACM Symposium on Operating Systems Principles*, Charleston, South Carolina, USA, 1999. ACM.

[12] Gallagher, P. Secure Hash Standard (SHS), 2008. `http://csrc.nist.gov/publications/fips/fips180-3/fips180-3_final.pdf`.

[13] T. Garfinkel and M. Rosenblum. A virtual machine introspection based architecture for intrusion detection. In *In Proceedings Network and Distributed Systems Security Symposium*, San Diego, California, USA, 2003.

[14] A. Gupta, J. Min, and I. Rhee. WiFox: Scaling WiFi performance for large audience environments. In *Proceedings of the 8th International Conference on Emerging Networking Experiments and Technologies*, Nice, France, 2012. ACM.

[15] S. Gurun, C. Krintz, and R. Wolski. NWSLite: A light-weight prediction utility for mobile devices. In *Proceedings of the Second International Conference on Mobile Systems, Applications, and Services*, Boston, MA, USA, June 2004.

[16] K. Ha, P. Pillai, G. Lewis, S. Simanta, S. Clinch, N. Davies, and M. Satyanarayanan. The impact of mobile multimedia applications on data center consolidation. In *Proceedings of the IEEE International Conference on Cloud Engineering*, San Francisco, CA, Mar. 2013.

[17] M. R. Hines and K. Gopalan. Post-copy based live virtual machine migration using adaptive pre-paging and dynamic self-ballooning. In *Proceedings of the 2009 ACM SIGPLAN/SIGOPS International Conference on Virtual Execution Environments*, pages 51–60, Washington, DC, USA, 2009. ACM.

[18] X. Jiang, X. Wang, and D. Xu. Stealthy malware detection through VMM-based out-of-the-box semantic view reconstruction. In *Proceedings of the 14th ACM Conference on Computer and Communications Security*, Alexandria, Virginia, USA, 2007. ACM.

[19] R. W. Jones. Libguestfs tools for accessing and modifying virtual machine disk images, Dec. 2012. `http://http://libguestfs.org/`.

[20] M. Kozuch and M. Satyanarayanan. Internet Suspend/Resume. In *Proceedings of the Fourth IEEE Workshop on Mobile Computing Systems and Applications*, Callicoon, NY, USA, 2002. IEEE Computer Society.

[21] M. D. Kristensen. Execution plans for cyber foraging. In *Proceedings of the 1st Workshop on Mobile Middleware: Embracing the Personal Communication Device*, Leuven, Belgium, 2008. ACM.

[22] P. Kulkarni, F. Douglis, J. LaVoie, and J. M. Tracey. Redundancy elimination within large collections of files. In *Proceedings of the USENIX Annual Technical Conference*, Boston, MA, USA, 2004. USENIX Association.

[23] H. A. Lagar-Cavilla, J. A. Whitney, A. M. Scannell,

P. Patchin, S. M. Rumble, E. De Lara, M. Brudno, and M. Satyanarayanan. SnowFlock: Rapid virtual machine cloning for cloud computing. In *Proceedings of the 4th ACM European Conference on Computer Systems*, Nuremberg, Germany, 2009. ACM.

[24] D. G. Lowe. Distinctive image features from scale-invariant keypoints. *International Journal of Computer Vision*, 60(2):91–110, Nov. 2004.

[25] M. McLoughlin. The QCOW2 image format, Sep. 2008. `http://people.gnome.org/~markmc/qcow-image-format.html`.

[26] R. Miller, Aug. 2012. `http://www.datacenterknowledge.com/archives/2012/08/13/aol-brings-micro-data-center-indoors-adds-wheels`.

[27] A. Muthitacharoen, B. Chen, and D. Mazières. A low-bandwidth network file system. In *Proceedings of the eighteenth ACM symposium on Operating Systems principles*, Banff, Alberta, Canada, 2001. ACM.

[28] Myoonet. Unique scalable data centers, Dec. 2011. `http://www.myoonet.com/unique.html`.

[29] D. Narayanan and M. Satyanarayanan. Predictive resource management for wearable computing. In *Proceedings of the 1st International Conference on Mobile Systems Applications, and Services*, San Francisco, CA, May 2003.

[30] B. Nicolae, J. Bresnahan, K. Keahey, and G. Antoniu. Going back and forth: Efficient multideployment and multisnapshotting on clouds. In *Proceedings of the 20th International Symposium on High Performance Distributed Computing*, San Jose, California, USA, 2011. ACM.

[31] B. D. Noble, M. Satyanarayanan, D. Narayanan, J. E. Tilton, J. Flinn, and K. R. Walker. Agile application-aware adaptation for mobility. In *Proceedings of the 16th ACM Symposium on Operating Systems and Principles*, Saint-Malo, France, Oct. 1997.

[32] OpenCV. OpenCV Wiki. `http://opencv.willowgarage.com/wiki/`.

[33] C. Peng, M. Kim, Z. Zhang, and H. Lei. VDN: Virtual machine image distribution network for cloud data centers. In *Proceedings of the 32nd IEEE International Conference on Computer Communications*, Orlando, FL, USA, 2012. IEEE.

[34] S. Potter and J. Nieh. Improving virtual appliance management through virtual layered file systems. In *Proceedings of the 25th International Conference on Large Installation System Administration*, pages 3–3, Boston, MA, 2011. USENIX Association.

[35] M.-R. Ra, A. Sheth, L. Mummert, P. Pillai, D. Wetherall, and R. Govindan. Odessa: enabling interactive perception applications on mobile devices. In *Proceedings of the 9th International Conference on Mobile systems, Applications, and Services*, Bethesda, Maryland, USA, 2011. ACM.

[36] J. Reich, O. Laadan, E. Brosh, A. Sherman, V. Misra, J. Nieh, and D. Rubenstein. VMTorrent: Scalable P2P virtual machine streaming. In *Proceedings of the 8th International Conference on Emerging Networking Experiments and Technologies*, Nice, France, 2012. ACM.

[37] W. Richter, M. Satyanarayanan, J. Harkes, and B. Gilbert. Near-real-time inference of file-level mutations from virtual disk writes. Technical Report CMU-CS-12-103, Carnegie Mellon University, School of Computer Science, Feb. 2012.

[38] A. Rudenko, P. Reiher, G. J. Popek, and G. H. Kuenning. Saving portable computer battery power through remote process execution. *Mobile Computing and Communications Review*, 2(1), Jan.

[39] C. P. Sapuntzakis, R. Chandra, B. Pfaff, J. Chow, M. S. Lam, and M. Rosenblum. Optimizing the migration of virtual computers. In *In Proceedings of the 5th Symposium on Operating Systems Design and Implementation*, Boston, MA, USA, 2002.

[40] M. Satyanarayanan. Fundamental challenges in mobile computing. In *Proceedings of the ACM Symposium on Principles of Distributed Computing*, Ottawa, Canada, 1996.

[41] M. Satyanarayanan. Pervasive computing: vision and challenges. *Personal Communications, IEEE*, 8(4):10–17, 2001.

[42] M. Satyanarayanan, V. Bahl, R. Caceres, and N. Davies. The case for VM-based cloudlets in mobile computing. *IEEE Pervasive Computing*, 8(4), Oct. 2009.

[43] M. Satyanarayanan, B. Gilbert, M. Toups, N. Tolia, A. Surie, D. R. O'Hallaron, A. Wolbach, J. Harkes, A. Perrig, D. J. Farber, M. A. Kozuch, C. J. Helfrich, P. Nath, and H. A. Lagar-Cavilla. Pervasive personal computing in an Internet Suspend/Resume system. *IEEE Internet Computing*, 11(2), 2007.

[44] M. Satyanarayanan, G. Lewis, E. Morris, S. Simanta, J. Boleng, and K. Ha. The role of cloudlets in hostile environments. *IEEE Pervasive Computing*, 12(4), Oct-Dec 2013.

[45] A. W. Services. Overview of Amazon Web Services, Dec. 2010. `http://d36cz9buwru1tt.cloudfront.net/AWS_Overview.pdf`.

[46] B. Solenthaler and R. Pajarola. Predictive-corrective incompressible SPH. *ACM Trans. Graph.*, 28(3):40:1–40:6, July 2009.

[47] Sphinx-4. Sphinx-4: A speech recognizer written entirely in the java programming language. `http://cmusphinx.sourceforge.net/sphinx4/`.

[48] S. Srinivasa, D. Ferguson, C. Helfrich, D. Berenson, A. Collet Romea, R. Diankov, G. Gallagher, G. Hollinger, J. Kuffner, and J. M. Vandeweghe. HERB: A home exploring robotic butler. *Autonomous Robots*, 28(1):5–20, Jan. 2010.

[49] S. Sundaresan, W. de Donato, N. Feamster, R. Teixeira, S. Crawford, and A. Pescapè. Broadband Internet performance: A view from the gateway. In *Proceedings of the ACM SIGCOMM 2011 Conference*, Toronto, Ontario, Canada, 2011. ACM.

[50] G. Takacs, M. E. Choubassi, Y. Wu, and I. Kozintsev. 3D mobile augmented reality in urban scenes. In *Proceedings of IEEE International Conference on Multimedia and Expo*, Barcelona, Spain, July 2011.

[51] C. Thompson. What is I.B.M.'s Watson? *New York Times Magazine*, June 2011. `http://www.nytimes.com/2010/06/20/magazine/20Computer-t.html`.

[52] M. Turk and A. Pentland. Eigenfaces for recognition. *Journal of Cognitive Neuroscience*, 3(1):71–86, 1991.

[53] C. A. Waldspurger. Memory resource management in VMWare ESX server. In *Proceedings of the 5th Symposium on Operating Systems Design and Implementation*, Boston, Massachusetts, 2002. ACM.

[54] Wikipedia. Lempel-Ziv-Markov chain algorithm, 2008. `http://en.wikipedia.org/w/index.php?title=Lempel-Ziv-Markov_chain_algorithm&oldid=206469040`.

[55] Wikipedia. List of 802.11ac Hardware, 2012. `http://csrc.nist.gov/publications/fips/fips180-3/fips180-3_final.pdf`.

[56] T. Wood, K. K. Ramakrishnan, P. Shenoy, and J. van der Merwe. CloudNet: Dynamic pooling of cloud resources by live WAN migration of virtual machines. In *Proceedings of the 7th ACM SIGPLAN/SIGOPS International Conference on Virtual Execution Environments*, Newport Beach, California, USA, 2011. ACM.

[57] X. Zhang, Z. Huo, J. Ma, and D. Meng. Exploiting data deduplication to accelerate live virtual machine migration. In *Cluster Computing (CLUSTER), 2010 IEEE International Conference on*, Heraklion, Greece, 2010. IEEE.

SIF: A Selective Instrumentation Framework for Mobile Applications*

Shuai Hao, Ding Li, William G.J. Halfond, Ramesh Govindan
Computer Science Department, University of Southern California
{shuaihao, dingli, halfond, ramesh}@usc.edu

ABSTRACT

Mobile app ecosystems have experienced tremendous growth in the last five years. As researchers and developers turn their attention to understanding the ecosystem and its different apps, instrumentation of mobile apps is a much needed emerging capability. In this paper, we explore a selective instrumentation capability that allows users to express instrumentation specifications at a high level of abstraction; these specifications are then used to automatically insert instrumentation into binaries. The challenge in our work is to develop expressive abstractions for instrumentation that can also be implemented efficiently. Designed using requirements derived from recent research that has used instrumented apps, our selective instrumentation framework, SIF, contains abstractions that allow users to compactly express precisely which parts of the app need to be instrumented. It also contains a novel path inspection capability, and provides users feedback on the approximate overhead of the instrumentation specification. Using experiments on our SIF implementation for Android, we show that SIF can be used to compactly (in 20-30 lines of code in most cases) specify instrumentation tasks previously reported in the literature. SIF's overhead is under 2% in most cases, and its instrumentation overhead feedback is within 15% in many cases. As such, we expect that SIF can accelerate studies of the mobile app ecosystem.

Categories and Subject Descriptors

D.3.3 [**Programming Languages**]: Language Constructs and Features—*Frameworks*

General Terms

Design, Experimentation, Languages, Performance

*The first author, Shuai Hao, was supported by Annenberg Graduate Fellowship. This material is based upon work supported by the National Science Foundation under Grant No. CNS-905596. Any opinions, findings and conclusions or recommendations expressed in this material are those of the author(s) and do not necessarily reflect the views of the National Science Foundation (NSF).

Keywords

App Instrumentation; Programming Framework; Smartphone; Separation of Concerns

1. INTRODUCTION

Mobile app ecosystems, such as the iPhone App Store and Google Play, have experienced tremendous growth in the last five years. Relative to ecosystems for desktop applications, mobile device app ecosystems are fast growing and have a large number of users, an evolving base of smartphone and tablet platforms, a large number of contributors and developers, as well as a wide range of functionality made possible by ubiquitous Internet access and the availability of various kinds of sensors (GPS, cameras *etc.*).

These factors, together with rapid growth in the use of mobile devices, have sparked an interest in understanding the properties of mobile apps. Recent research has developed methods to study performance properties [25, 29] and security properties [15, 30, 22, 26] of mobile apps. A common thread through this line of research is *instrumentation*: each work has developed customized ways to insert instrumentation for studying app behavior. More generally, app instrumentation is a crucial emerging capability that will facilitate future studies of the mobile app ecosystem.

Traditionally, instrumentation frameworks for programming languages have permitted some degree of flexibility in instrumenting software (Section 5). However, these are insufficient for mobile apps which rely on concurrency, event handling, access to sensors, and (on some mobile platforms) resource usage permissions integrated with the app. These differences, together with the constraints of mobile devices, motivate the need for an instrumentation framework with qualitatively different requirements from that considered in prior work.

A careful analysis of prior research that has used custom instrumentation reveals several interesting requirements of an instrumentation framework for mobile apps (Section 2). We find that the framework must permit *selective* instrumentation since the processing constraints on mobile devices preclude pervasive instrumentation. Furthermore, this capability must permit arbitrary user-level instrumentation that can alter the functionality of the app and not just measure performance. Moreover, the instrumentation framework must permit path inspection between specified codepoints, a capability motivated by device access control capabilities in some mobile OSs. Finally, because user-level instrumentation can add significant overhead, the framework must be able to accurately estimate the overhead of the specified instrumentation.

The paper describes the design and implementation of a Selective Instrumentation Framework (SIF) for mobile apps that satisfies these novel requirements (Section 3). Our first contribution is identifying the smallest set of instrumentation primitives that permit expressivity while admitting efficient implementation. SIF allows users to specify instrumentation locations using *codepoint sets* (collections of locations in the code) that can be selected at various levels of granularity from class hierarchy specifications down to individual bytecodes, and then specify user-defined instrumentation for each set. It also defines a *path set* abstraction, which allows users to dynamically trace inter-procedural paths between two arbitrary codepoints in the app. This capability is novel in an instrumentation framework, and can be used to explore privacy leakage and permissions violations in mobile apps. Taken together, these two abstractions can be used to express all instrumentation tasks considered in the literature. A second contribution is SIF's use of static and dynamic program analysis to derive instrumentation locations, minimize instrumentation overhead, and estimate instrumentation cost. In particular, implementing the path set abstraction requires sophisticated stitching of intra-procedural path segments to derive inter-procedural paths.

SIF's abstractions and implementation methods are, for the most part, independent of the underlying mobile app ecosystem, but we have implemented SIF for the Android platform. Using this implementation, we have evaluated SIF's expressivity and efficiency (Section 4). We demonstrate that SIF's abstractions can express many of the instrumentation tasks previously proposed in the literature, as well as other common tasks. Moreover, the SIF specifications are compact, requiring fewer than 100 lines of code even for the most complicated instrumentation tasks. Finally, SIF can often reduce instrumentation cost significantly, requires less than half a minute to instrument binaries, and provides accurate (within 15%) overhead feedback in many cases.

While much work remains (Section 6), we believe that SIF can accelerate studies of the mobile app ecosystem and lead to an improved understanding of app behavior and usage.

2. BACKGROUND AND MOTIVATION

In this section, we motivate the need for an instrumentation framework for mobile apps, and articulate the unique requirements posed by these apps. We then describe the challenges associated with satisfying these requirements; this discussion lays the groundwork for the design of SIF, described Section 3.

Instrumentation Frameworks. *Instrumentation* refers to the process of inserting code into an application, often by an entity (software or user) other than the original developer. An *instrumentation framework* is a software system that allows an entity to insert instrumentation at specific points in a program. In traditional software systems, instrumentation frameworks are widely used for a variety of tasks [18, 16], but, as we discuss in Section 5, these do not satisfy one or more of the requirements of mobile app instrumentation that we identify below.

Instrumentation frameworks are generally based on one of three different mechanisms. The first mechanism is to instrument the source code, an approach which requires source to be available to the instrumentor. A more general mechanism instruments the runtime system responsible for program execution; for example, an instrumented operating system or virtual machine can record every executed method. The drawback to this is that a customized runtime system must be developed for every platform on which an entity will want to perform instrumentation. Furthermore, once developed, it can be very difficult to modify the runtime system instrumentation.

The third mechanism, and the one we choose, is binary instrumentation, in which instrumentation code is directly inserted into the compiled binary or bytecodes. This does not require source code and is more portable and flexible than customized runtime systems. More broadly, the use of binary instrumentation also enables users to instrument and analyze apps after they have been released. This is an especially important capability in the mobile app ecosystem because its growth has spurred a number of independent efforts in understanding the performance and behavior of mobile apps. For example, AppInsight [25] developed a way to instrument apps for a specific purpose, namely, critical path monitoring. The code for doing this instrumentation was done manually, and was targeted for the purpose of critical path monitoring. In our work, we seek to provide a programming framework that can specify, at a high-level, the instrumentation required for AppInsight and other tasks, leaving the task of generating the low-level instrumentation to a compiler.

Framework Requirements. We conducted a survey of recent research work that has developed customized instrumentation, and have used these to develop a set of requirements for a binary instrumentation framework. We discuss three specific examples; Section 4 presents a more comprehensive discussion of these pieces of research.

- Many mobile apps, in response to a user action, perform multiple concurrent operations, and the user-perceived latency is dominated by the *critical path* (the concurrent operation which takes the most time) through the code. AppInsight [25] has attempted to develop general methods to instrument apps for critical path analysis.

- Some existing mobile operating systems provide coarse-grain access control to sensors and other system facilities: *e.g.*, Android requires app developers to explicitly require permission to access the network or GPS. Researchers [22] have developed methods to instrument apps to enable more *fine-grained permissions* checking: *e.g.*, preventing third-party libraries, often used to develop applications, from using the permitted resources.

- We have been developing a *sensor auditing* capability to instrument an app to understand what processing it performs on the sensor (*e.g.*, GPS or camera), and whether, after acquiring location sensor readings, the app uploads the sensor readings to a website.

Many of these studies are motivated by novel features of mobile app platforms: concurrent execution and event handling, per-app restrictions on resource usage, and the availability of novel sensors on mobile devices.

These studies drive the requirements for our binary instrumentation framework. A strawman approach to solving these problems is to instrument every method call or execution path. However, this can incur significant overhead on modern smartphones, to the point where app usability can be impacted. In some preliminary experiments, we have observed up to 2.5x greater CPU usage when using Android's Traceview [5] to instrument every method and system API invocation. Accordingly, the first requirement of a binary instrumentation framework for mobile apps is *selectivity*: users should be able to instrument only the code of interest to their study.

To support AppInsight and the fine-grained permissions study, our framework needs to provide selectivity by allowing users to *flexibly specify locations* for inserting instrumentation. Specifically, in these studies, the authors inserted instrumentation at specific points in the program: event handlers, API calls with certain permission capabilities, etc.

Many instrumentation frameworks permit selectivity of method calls or APIs. Our sensor auditing study motivates another requirement for a binary instrumentation framework that prior work lacks (Section 5), the ability to *inspect dynamic execution paths*. This capability would allow a user to determine which code paths were traversed between two points in the code, and examine what transformations might have been done on data along these paths.

Instrumentation frameworks differ in the kinds of instrumentation they allow a user to insert. To support AppInsight, a binary instrumentation framework that provides basic instrumentation primitives (such as timing or counting procedure invocations) would suffice. However, the fine-grained permissions study alters the functionality of an app. To support instrumentation for functional modifications, a binary instrumentation framework must allow arbitrary *user-specified instrumentation*, since it cannot anticipate the kinds of instrumentation that might be needed.

Finally, *efficiency* is an important requirement of instrumentation frameworks; the instrumentation overhead must be minimal and must preserve the usability of the mobile app. This is particularly difficult to achieve in a framework which permits user-specified instrumentation, since the framework has no control over the complexity of that instrumentation. Accordingly, we add one additional requirement for binary app instrumentation, *overhead feedback*. If the instrumentation framework can estimate the overhead of user-specified instrumentation, users can quickly adapt the instrumentation (*e.g.,* by being more selective) in order to reduce the overhead, without actually needing to run the instrumented binary.

These requirements raise significant research questions and challenges. What are the appropriate abstractions for specifying *where* instrumentation should be inserted? This is particularly challenging for path inspection since some apps are highly complex and contain several million distinct paths (a static analysis of the code paths involved in composing email using the Gmail app reveals nearly 0.15 million path segments). Additionally, how do we provide a flexible mechanism for allowing the user to provide *any instrumentation* without introducing extra overhead and complications? Finally, how do we minimize and report guidance on *overhead* in a way that can help users? In particular, how do we accurately predict the overheard of arbitrary instrumentation?

Our SIF instrumentation framework provides functionality to meet all of these challenges. SIF provides a domain-specific programming language and support libraries that allow users to selectively instrument an app with arbitrary user-specified code along any path or codepoint based location. The framework uses sophisticated program analysis techniques to introduce minimal overhead during instrumentation and provide overhead feedback for the user-specified instrumentation. We describe how SIF provides all of this functionality in the next section.

3. A SELECTIVE INSTRUMENTATION FRAMEWORK

In this section, we describe SIF, our binary instrumentation framework for mobile apps that satisfies the requirements listed in the previous section. We begin with an overview that describes how a user interacts with SIF and the instrumentation workflow within SIF. We then discuss the instrumentation specification language abstractions, and describe how we overcome some of the challenges listed in Section 2. We conclude the section by describing our implementation of SIF for Android.

3.1 Overview of SIF

Figure 1 describes the overall workflow for SIF. A user provides three pieces of information as input to SIF. The first is the original app binary to be instrumented. The second is the user-specified instrumentation code, written in a language called SIFScript[1]. We say that a SIFScript codifies an *instrumentation task*. The third input to SIF is a *workload description*. Intuitively, a workload description captures the app use-cases that the user is interested in instrumenting. For example, in the critical path analysis example above, the user may be interested in knowing the user-perceived latency for posting to Facebook. This use-case (posting to Facebook) is encapsulated in a workload description obtained from a *workload generator* (Figure 1). We describe later how a user provides a workload descriptor. The workload description is used by SIF to provide accurate overhead feedback, as described in Section 3.3.

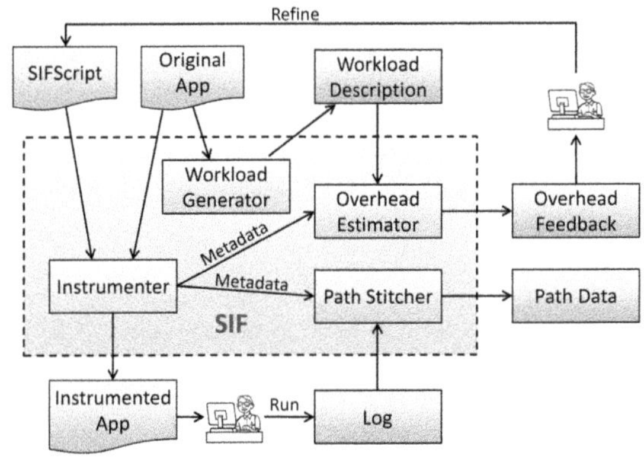

Figure 1: Overview of SIF

In the first step of SIF's workflow, the *instrumenter* component interprets the SIFScript specification and generates an instrumented version of the app. This *instrumenter* realizes the user-level specification and path inspection capabilities in SIF by inserting the user-specified instrumentation code at the appropriate locations. The instrumenter also outputs some additional metadata used in later stages. In our current instantiation of SIF, all instrumentation output is stored locally on the mobile device, then extracted for post-processing. In future work, we plan to explore automatic export of instrumentation output to a cloud server, a capability that can enable large-scale debugging and app analytics in the wild.

The metadata generated by the instrumenter, together with the workload information input by the user, is fed to an *overhead estimator*. That component calculates the impact of the instrumentation for the given workload description. Impact may be measured in terms of the extra execution time or additional resource usage (*e.g.,* CPU cycles, memory, energy) incurred as a result of the instrumentation. If the estimated impact is unacceptable, users can refine their instrumentation specifications.

When the instrumented application is run, the instrumentation outputs either log data generated by SIF defaults or the data collected by the user-specified instrumentation. An example of the latter is execution timings generated by user-specified instrumentation. In addition, SIF produces output whenever the user employs its path inspection capability. This output is an intermediate description of paths traversed; a SIF module called the *path stitcher* component is automatically invoked on this output to generate user readable path information. In the remainder of this section, we describe the components of SIF.

Before we do so, a word about the potential users of SIF. In our

[1]In what follows, we will use SIFScript to denote both the language and the specification program; the usage will be clear from the context.

	Syntax	Description
CPFinder	setClass	class name and hierarchy filter
	setMethod	method name filter
	setBytecode	bytecode filters (e.g. position, opcode, type, name)
	setPermission	permission filter matched with all API invokes
	setLoops	filter to select loop structures
	init	reset all filters
	apply	scan app binary, apply specified filters, return a set of matching codepoints
Instrumenter	place	insert user code before/after/at target codepoint
	placeLoops	insert user code before/after/at backedge
UserCode	constructor	carry class and method names, list of operands of interest (e.g. method/invoke arguments)
PathFinder	contains	shortlist paths that may contain specified codepoint set
	sequence	shortlist methods that may appear on any path that sequences the list of codepoint sets
	report	insert logging instructions to target methods and call sites

Figure 2: Operations on SIF abstractions

view, SIF is an instrumentation tool at an intermediate level of abstraction. It is intended for an expert user, such as a researcher or a software engineer, who understands the app code and/or the mobile OS API well, and who might, without SIF, have manually instrumented apps for whatever task he/she is interested in (or developing custom software for this instrumentation). It can be made more broadly available to other users by adding front-end code that provides a higher-level of abstraction: for example, a security researcher can make available a web page which takes a binary and instruments it for some purpose (say to block ads), and users wishing an ad-free version of their app can upload a binary, retrieve the instrumented binary and run it. Finally, it is not unreasonable to expect developers to use SIF even when they have access to app source code: instrumentation is a programming concern that is separable from application logic, and a tool like SIF, which allows developers to treat instrumentation as a separate concern rather than having to weave instrumentation into application logic, might be helpful in many cases.

3.2 The SIFScript Language

Our first design choice for SIF was to either define a new domain-specific language for SIFScript or to realize SIFScript as an extension to an existing language. A new language is more general since it can be compiled to run on multiple mobile platforms, but it also incurs a higher learning curve. Instead, we chose to instantiate SIFScript as a Java extension. This design option has the advantage of familiarity, but may limit SIF's applicability to some mobile OS platforms. However, we emphasize that the abstractions and the underlying instrumentation methods based on program analysis are independent of specific mobile app programming platforms, and are extensible to multiple platforms.

The next design challenge for SIF was to identify abstractions that provided sufficient expressivity and enabled a variety of instrumentation tasks. In addressing this challenge, we were guided by the requirements identified in Section 2 and the instrumentation tasks described in Section 4.

An instrumentation specification language should permit instrumenting code according to different attributes, such as method invocations, specific bytecodes, or classes. The language should also allow for combining these attributes in different ways to build up sophisticated instrumentation specifications. To permit maximum flexibility and cover the use cases discussed in Section 2 and Section 4, SIFScript incorporates two qualitatively different instrumentation abstractions, codepoint sets and path sets. These abstractions

```
class TimingProfiler implements SIFTask {
  public void run() {
    CPFinder.setBytecode("invoke.*", ".* native .*");
    UserCode code;
    for (CP cp in CPFinder.apply()) {
      code = new UserCode("Logger", "start", CPARG);
      Instrumenter.place(code, BEFORE, cp);
      code = new UserCode("Logger", "end", CPARG);
      Instrumenter.place(code, AFTER, cp);
    }
  }
}
class Logger {
  private static Map map = new HashMap();
  public static void start(int mid, int pos) {
    long id = Thread.currentThread().getId();
    String k = mid + "," + pos + "," + id;
    long start = System.nanoTime();
    map.put(k, start);
  }
  public static void end(int mid, int pos) {
    long end = System.nanoTime();
    long id = Thread.currentThread().getId();
    String k = mid + "," + pos + "," + id;
    long start = map.get(k);
    Log.v(TAG, k + "," + (end - start));
  }
}
```

Listing 1: Timing profiler for native invokes

```
class LocationAuditor implements SIFTask {
  public void run() {
    CPFinder.setPermission(LOCATION);
    Set<CP> X = CPFinder.apply();
    CPFinder.setPermission(INTERNET);
    Set<CP> Y = CPFinder.apply();
    PathFinder.sequence(X, Y);
    PathFinder.report();
  }
}
```

Listing 2: Location auditor

specify *where* in a binary program the user wishes to insert instrumentation.

Codepoint Set This abstraction encapsulates a *set* of instructions (*e.g.,* bytecodes or invocations of arbitrary functions) in the binary program that share one or more *attributes*. For example, a user might define a codepoint set that consists of all invocations to a specified library (we discuss other attributes below).

Path Set This abstraction encapsulates the set of dynamically traversed paths that satisfy a user-specified *constraint*. Currently, SIF supports two forms of constraints: paths traversing any codepoint in a codepoint set or paths containing at least one codepoint from each of two or more codepoint sets.

Figure 2 documents the operations on these abstractions; these operations are discussed in greater detail below.

3.2.1 Codepoint Sets

We now discuss the semantics of SIFScript abstractions using a simple example instrumentation task. Listing 1 shows the complete SIFScript listing of a *timing profiler*, which selectively profiles the execution time of *native code* invocations. Modern smartphone OSs (e.g., iOS and Android) permit apps to implement part of their functionality at a lower-level in native code (usually C) for performance reasons. Native code is used in many apps such as browsers, video display and gaming.

SIFScript allows users to specify instrumentation tasks by defining separate classes for each task; each instrumentation task inherits from a `SIFTask` base class. Users can *select* arbitrary codepoints, *define* user-specified instrumentation, and specify *where* to place instrumentation. Line 3 of Listing 1 is an example of a SIFScript construct for selecting codepoints. `CPFinder` is a class that provides methods to specify *codepoint attributes* and iterate on the identified codepoint sets. In line 3, the `setBytecode()` method selects all points in the binary that are invocations to native methods. More generally, `setBytecode()` takes as its first argument a regular expression that specifies the kind of bytecode (in this example, invocations), followed by an optional argument that specifies a regular expression matching the name (in this example, native invocations).

Although not shown in our example, SIFScript contains a hierarchy of attribute specifications, which users may use to progressively narrow codepoint selections. The `setClass()` method of `CPFinder` selects classes whose name or whose class hierarchy matches specified regular expressions. If this method is invoked, only codepoints within matching classes are considered for inclusion in a codepoint set. Within these classes, users may narrow down the scope of codepoint selection by using `setMethod`, which takes, as an argument, a regular expression for the method names. Only codepoints within the matching methods are considered. Thereafter, users may invoke `setBytecode()` to specify codepoints inside the relevant classes and methods. Users may also use `setPermissions()` to refine the selection to those codepoints that require resource access permissions (e.g., network or location access) and `setLoops()`, which allows users to instrument loop edges.

If any of these attributes are not defined, the effect is equivalent to specifying *no* refinement. For example, if `setClass()` is omitted, all classes are considered when selecting codepoints. Thus, in Listing 1, line 3 selects native methods in *all* classes.

The `CPFinder` class also contains two other methods. `init()` resets a selection, since a SIFScript might contain multiple instrumentation steps, with each step instrumenting a different selection of codepoints. `apply()` (line 5) analyzes the specified attribute and computes the resulting codepoint set.

Once a codepoint set has been defined (as in line 3), the next step in writing a SIFScript is to specify what instrumentation to insert, and where to insert instrumentation. For the former, SIFScript defines a `UserCode` type which declares a code block; a new code block can be specified in the constructor to `UserCode` which takes as arguments a class name, a method name, and arguments to the method. Thus, an instance of `UserCode` effectively specifies arbitrary user-specified instrumentation. For example, in line 6, the SIFScript defines `code` to be the `start` method of the `Logger` class, and in line 8, the `end` method. Lines 13-27 provide the definitions of these methods. The `start` method generates and stores a timestamp along with a thread specific key. The `end` method computes the invocation time and writes it out to a log.

To specify where to insert instrumentation, SIF provides an `Instrumenter.place()` method. This method takes three arguments: a `UserCode` instance, a *location specification*, and a codepoint. The semantics of `place()` are as follows: it places the `UserCode` code block instance at the specified codepoint. SIF currently supports three location specifications: `BEFORE` inserts the code block before a codepoint, `AFTER` inserts it after the codepoint, and `AT` replaces the codepoint. In Listing 1, line 7 shows the `start` method of `Logger` being inserted before the codepoint, and line 9 shows the `end` method being inserted after the codepoint. The `Instrumenter` also supports a `placeLoops()` method to instrument loop back-edges; this is discussed in Section 3.3.

3.2.2 Path Sets

In Section 2, we motivated the need for a path inspection capability in a mobile app instrumentation framework. To illustrate SIF's abstraction for path inspection, consider the context-aware app `aroundme`, which searches for points of interest near a mobile device's current location. To achieve this, the app requests access permissions for both location data and the Internet. But, since it displays advertisements in the free version, privacy-conscious users may be interested in knowing whether the app leaks their location information. To audit how their location information is used, users can write a *location auditor* instrumentation task in SIF using the path inspection abstraction, as shown in Listing 2. This auditor provides the user with a listing of all sub-paths that access location data and then access the Internet.

The basic abstraction for path inspection in SIF is the *path set* provided by the `PathFinder` class. Conceptually, a path set consists of a collection of *paths traversed by the app when it is executed*. Thus, unlike the codepoint set abstraction, the set of paths belonging to a path set cannot be enumerated statically (i.e., before execution).

As with codepoint sets, path sets are specified by describing attributes of paths for interest. SIF currently supports two forms of attribute specifications. The `contains`(C) method of `PathFinder` takes as an argument a codepoint set, and returns all *intra-procedural* paths (i.e., paths that begin and terminate within the same procedure) that contain at least one of the codepoints in the argument. `sequence`$(C_1, C_2, \ldots, C_n)$ specifies all inter-procedural paths that contain, in sequence, a member of each of the n codepoint sets. Thus, a path in this set contains a codepoint $c_i \in C_1$ followed by a $c_j \in C_2$, and eventually $c_k \in C_n$. The path starts in the method containing c_i and ends in the method containing c_k.

SIF supports one *action* on path sets, `report()`, which logs all paths in a path set, so a human can inspect them. This log contains every instruction in the path, so a user can understand what operations are performed along a path.

In the location auditor (Listing 2), the user defines two codepoint sets, the first is all invocations (e.g., API calls) with permission to access location data and the second is all invocations with permission to perform network operations. At runtime, the location auditor logs all paths between an invocation in the first codepoint set and an invocation in the second codepoint set. If the output is empty, the user knows that there is no direct leakage of location information, for the tested use cases. If the output is non-empty, the user can examine the processing done on the location data before a network operation occurs, for example, to determine whether the location granularity was coarsened to the zip code level.

3.3 SIF Component Design

In this section, we describe how various components of SIF are designed and how they collectively realize the abstractions described above. SIF's design borrows from program analysis techniques and abstractions. Before we discuss the SIF design, we introduce some of these techniques and abstractions.

3.3.1 Preliminaries

A *control flow graph* (CFG) represents the flow of control (branching, looping, procedure calls) in a program or within a method. Nodes in the graph represent basic blocks of code and edges represents jumps or branches. CFGs are often used in many static analysis applications.

A *call graph* captures the invocation relationship among methods within a program. A static call graph can be constructed by analyzing a program and constructing relationships between callers and callees. A dynamic call graph depicts the sub-graph of the static call graph that is encountered during an execution and can be constructed by instrumenting and logging invocations.

SIF uses a technique called *efficient path profiling* [8] proposed by Ball and Larus. This technique instruments programs to accurately, but with minimal overhead, measure path execution statistics. The Ball-Larus profiler assigns weights to edges of a method's control-flow graph (CFG) such that the sum of the edge weights along each unique path through the CFG results in a unique path identifier; a single instrumentation counter per method then suffices to record the path traversed during each invocation of the method. When a program instrumented with these counters is executed, the output is a count, for each path, of the number of times the path is executed.

More precisely, the Ball-Larus profiler instruments *path segments*. For example, in methods with two branches, there are two path segments, the *then* and *else* branches. In methods with a single loop, there are four acyclic path segments: one that runs through the method without executing the loop body, a second that starts at the beginning and terminates at the end of the loop body, a third containing the execution of the loop body to the end of the method, and a fourth containing only the loop body. Intuitively, any loop execution can be described using a linear combination of these path segments. An execution that does not execute the loop body will result in a count vector $\langle 1, 0, 0, 0\rangle$; one iteration will result in $\langle 0, 1, 1, 0\rangle$ and k iterations in $\langle 0, 1, 1, k-1\rangle$. The complete path can be reconstructed *post facto* by correlating the outputs of the Ball-Larus profiler with the CFG.

We extend the Ball-Larus profiler to handle nested method calls, exceptions, and concurrency. We identify and discard paths that result in exceptions, since their catch blocks may cause control-flow to jump outside of the method, a behavior for which the Ball-Larus profiler is undefined. Concurrency is handled by using the thread's ID to identify the counter that must be updated to track the path ID.

3.3.2 Realizing the Codepoint Set Abstraction

There are three distinct parts to realizing the codepoint set abstraction: finding target instrumentation positions, enabling access to local data variables, and inserting user-defined action code.

Finding the target instrumentation positions is performed by the method `CPFinder.apply()`. This method first combines the regular expression based attribute specifications for class hierarchy, classes, methods, bytecodes and permissions into a set of constraints. Then, the method hierarchically applies these constraints during successive scans of the code, ultimately identifying the set of instructions that need to be instrumented.

A challenge for SIF is to provide user-defined instrumentation with access to program state that is available at each instrumentation codepoint. For example, consider a codepoint `invoke-bar(x,y)` inside method `foo(a,b)`. User-specified instrumentation code should be able to access the method signature (`foo(int,int)`), method arguments `(a,b)`, and operands of the instruction (*i.e.,* the method reference to `bar`, invocation arguments `(x,y)`, and the return value, if any). This type of access to the program state is necessary, for example, in code that tracks the values of arguments supplied to `bar`.

For method signatures, SIF scans the binary to extract these signatures, then inserts instructions to load at runtime the corresponding signature at the appropriate locations, so that they will be accessible to user-specified instrumentation code. SIF also provides users with access to other information discussed above. To access this information, SIF makes special symbols available to users that notify SIF to instrument in such a way so that this data is provided to the inserted instrumentation code as arguments. When SIF encounters these special symbols, it inserts additional instrumentation to make this data available to the user-specified instrumentation code.

SIF inserts the user-specified instrumentation at all of the identified codepoints via the `Instrumenter.apply()` method. There are two approaches to this: one is to inline the instrumentation code at each codepoint, and the other is to insert an invocation to the instrumentation code. SIF employs the latter approach, which results in more compact instrumentation if there is more than one codepoint that must be instrumented with the same code.

As an aside, we note that code obfuscation frameworks, which obfuscate binaries without affecting functionality, can limit the applicability of SIF's codepoint abstraction. These frameworks cannot obfuscate invocations to system APIs and methods, so SIF will still be able to instrument those codepoints.

Supporting Distinguished Codepoints. Apps contain distinguished codepoints that correspond to higher-level program constructs of interest to users. These codepoints are method entry and exit, CFG branch edges, exception entry points, and loop back-edges. Our current instantiation of SIF supports only the subset required to achieve the instrumentation tasks discussed in Section 4, but the remainder are straightforward to support using CFG analysis. To instrument method entry and exit, a user would first identify codepoints that define a method using the `CPFinder` then use the `Instrumenter.place()` method with the location specification of either `ENTRY` or `EXIT`. To identify codepoints related to loop "back-edges" (jumps back to the beginning of the loop), SIF provides the `CPFinder.setLoops()` method. This method uses a depth-first search of the CFG to identify back-edges. Then the `Instrumenter`'s `placeLoops()` function inserts instrumentation `before` a back-edge (at the loop exit), `after` a back-edge (at the loop entry), and `at` a back-edge.

3.3.3 Realizing the Path Set Abstraction

In SIF, path sets support path inspection capabilities. The methods to support path inspection take codepoint sets as arguments; the techniques discussed above can be used for identifying the relevant codepoints. The remainder of this section discusses how SIF realizes path inspection. In general, SIF provides path inspection capabilities by appropriately adapting the Ball-Larus path profiling method discussed above, and using a *path stitcher* as a post-processing step to aggregate the path segments produced by path profiling into method-level or inter-procedural paths. SIF's adaptations reduce the overhead of path profiling.

Implementing the `contains(`C`)` method of `PathFinder` is conceptually straightforward. One could simply instrument all path segments of all methods in an app using the Ball-Larus profiler, then `report` only those path segments containing the specified codepoints (these can be identified in a post-processing step). Instead, in SIF, we use each $c \in C$ to identify the methods that contain c, and only instrument those methods.

Implementing `sequence()` is a little bit more involved. Extending Ball-Larus profiling to inter-procedural paths is known to be a hard problem, and it is not one we solve in this paper. Our approach relies on the observation that we know which inter-procedural paths are of interest, namely, the ones that traverse specified codepoint sets. We can use the Ball-Larus profiler, together with additional instrumentation, to find these inter-procedural paths.

We discuss the algorithm for the case when the input to `sequen-`

`ce()` contains two codepoint sets C_1 and C_2. The extension of this algorithm to multiple codepoint sets follows in a straightforward manner.

For `sequence(`C_1, C_2`)`, we wish to record all paths at runtime that execute a $c_i \in C_1$ followed by a $c_j \in C_2$. We could instrument every method in the app using the Ball-Larus profiler, but this approach adds unnecessary instrumentation and does not give us enough information to determine inter-procedural paths between each c_i and c_j.

Instead, we use a more sophisticated program analysis to statically determine an over-approximation of all the methods invoked between the codepoints in C_1 and C_2. To identify these methods that could be invoked between codepoints, we perform a standard reachability analysis (with some additional inputs to specify concurrency and event handling constraints) between all $c_i \in C_1$ and $c_j \in C_2$. All intervening methods in the call graph are marked for instrumentation. We then add additional instrumentation beyond that required by the Ball-Larus profiler, described below, to instrument these methods. This approach trades off slightly higher instrumentation costs for a much more compact instrumented binary.

The additional instrumentation identifies the identifier of the path segments and ordering of the path segments, so that the path stitcher can reconstruct the intra-procedural path. For example, suppose that codepoint c_i is invoked in procedure A along path $p_{l,A}$ (where l is an identifier for the path). One approach to obtaining the inter-procedural path is to record l, A and the timestamp at which that path was executed. Then, when codepoint c_j is invoked in procedure B along path $p_{m,B}$, m, B is also output by the instrumentation. If l, A and m, B occur successively in the output, then we can infer that B was called by A and the corresponding inter-procedural path consists of l followed by m. In SIF, a *path stitcher* performs this analysis of paths.

Rather than output timestamps and path segment identifiers, we note that it suffices to simply output the sequence of path segment identifiers encountered during the execution. From this sequence, and by logging all call sites encountered during execution[2] and every method entry and exit, it is possible to stitch together inter-procedural paths. We optimize this logging by run-length encoding the path identifier sequence and compactly encoding the call site information.

Finally, the path stitcher performs a *call stack simulation* in order to determine the calling sequence of the path segments from the executed methods. To do this, it uses the logged records from path profiling and simulates the call stack encountered during execution. The output of this step is the set of all inter-procedural paths between each $c_i \in C_1$ and $c_j \in C_2$.

Dealing with Exceptions and Concurrency. Mobile apps may throw exceptions and contain concurrent threads. To handle exceptions, we conservatively include every exception handler when performing the reachability analysis. To handle concurrency, we log thread identifiers so the path stitcher can separate path segments executed by different threads. Our path stitcher can also splice thread paths when one thread creates another (by searching for a thread fork call) and identify thread identifier reuse (by determining when the thread has exited).

3.3.4 Overhead Feedback

The final component of SIF is the overhead feedback estimator. In SIF, overhead can come from two sources: instructions inserted by SIF components (*e.g.,* instructions to load method templates or perform path logging) and user-specified instrumentation code. As we show in Section 4, the former component is small. However, as in any programming framework that provides flexibility, users can insert instrumentation that adds significant processing overhead to an app, making the app unusable. To give the user approximate feedback on the overhead introduced by their instrumentation, SIF provides an overhead feedback estimator.

The overhead of instrumentation is difficult to define statically (*i.e.,* without running the app) since, in many cases, execution time is dependent on code structures that can execute a variable number of times. So, SIF provides users with a way to provide a *workload* as input. Intuitively, a workload captures the dynamic execution statistics for a given use of the app (*e.g.,* playing one instance of a game or sending an email). To translate the workload into paths that can be analyzed, SIF provides the user with a version of the app instrumented only with the Ball-Larus profiler (*i.e.,* the version does not contain the user-specified instrumentation). The user can execute the workload on this instrumented app and obtain the frequency of execution of every path segment in the app. This constitutes the workload.

Based on this information, the overhead estimator knows precisely which instructions inserted by SIF are executed and how many times each is executed. In addition, the overhead estimator can determine how many times user-specified instrumentation is invoked, and can account for the overhead of this as well. This estimation works well if user-specified instrumentation's CFG is acyclic; extending overhead estimation to more complex user-specified instrumentation is left to future work.

The overhead estimator combines the instruction counts derived from the workflow description and profiled estimates of execution time for each instruction to provide an estimate of the total execution time incurred by instrumentation (feedback based on other measures of overhead, such as energy, is left for future work). With this estimate, users can refine their instrumentation specification in order to reduce overhead.

We emphasize that, to determine overhead, the overhead estimator runs a version of the app instrumented using the Ball-Larus profiler (to generate the workload description), but does not need to run a version of the app that includes user-specified instrumentation. In this sense, the feedback provided to the user is an estimate. This is convenient because the user has to generate the workload description once, but may iteratively refine instrumentation several times.

3.4 Implementation of SIF for Android

We have designed SIF to be broadly applicable to different mobile computing platforms. The abstractions on which SIF depends are general in that they are based on standard programming constructs (instructions, invocations and paths). Furthermore, the components use program analysis techniques common to imperative programming, but not specific to a given programming language. We have chosen to instantiate SIF for the Android platform because of the platform's popularity and active research targeting the platform. That said, it should be conceptually straightforward to instantiate SIF on other platforms like Windows, iOS and we have left this to future work.

We made two exceptions to the generalizability goal of SIF. The first is that, along with handling concurrent execution, we implemented path set abstractions to handle Android-specific asynchronous tasks that can be executed in the background. Second, permissions support is closely modeled on Android's permissions model. The reason for this is that prior work [6] has identified, for a given per-

[2]Within a given method, another method m may be invoked at several points. Logging the call sites helps disambiguate these during path stitching.

mission capability, a list of APIs which match that capability, for example, the set of API calls that require INTERNET permission to use the network. SIF uses this list to implement permissions-based codepoint selection. We have left it to future work to identify the permission mappings of other platforms.

Although Android uses a dialect of Java, our specification language abstractions are implemented as an extension of Java. We do this because there are robust tools for Java bytecode manipulation. To manipulate Android programs, we first convert Dalvik bytecode to Java. To achieve this translation, we use apktool [1] to unpack and extract app binaries and resource files, and dex2jar [3] to convert Dalvik bytecode to Java bytecode. The BCEL [2] library is used for reading and modifying Java bytecode. Finally, Android SDK tools convert Java bytecode back to Dalvik and repack the instrumented app. We have implemented EPP [8] in Java. The total implementation of SIF is about 5,000 lines of code.

Our implementation does not handle Java reflection and dynamically loaded code instantiated by the Java class loader. Program analysis techniques for handling reflection and dynamic class loading have not progressed to the point where it is possible to accurately analyze a broad range of code. Furthermore, SIF has no visibility inside native code, which is used by several applications, but can instrument invocations to native methods. We have left these issues to future work. Finally, we note that SIF can also be used, with minor modifications to instrument arbitrary Java programs, not just mobile apps. We have left an exploration of this capability to future work also.

4. EVALUATION

The primary research question with SIF is its applicability for instrumentation. There are several aspects to this applicability: is SIF expressive enough to express a variety of instrumentation tasks, is its language compact enough to permit rapid instrumentation, is its framework efficient enough to be usable, and is its overhead feedback accurate enough for users to rely on its estimates. In this section, we address these aspects using our Android instantiation of SIF. All our experiments are conducted on Galaxy Nexus smartphones running Android 4.1.2.

4.1 Expressivity of SIF

To demonstrate the expressivity of SIF, we have implemented ten different instrumentation tasks, shown in Table 1, which demonstrate different facets of SIF. These tasks exhibit variety along several dimensions. First, they range from a simple timing profiler task that requires a single instrumentation step to sophisticated multi-step tasks, such as injecting privacy leaks and performing critical path analysis in the presence of concurrent events. Second, some of these tasks illustrate traditional uses of instrumentation, such as performance monitoring or dynamic tracing, while others are more specific to mobile apps, focusing on sensor usage and sensor data security. Third, while some of these instrumentation tasks are common, a majority of them have been motivated by recent research. Finally, these tasks use different combinations of the SIF abstractions: path sets or codepoint sets specified at different granularities (class hierarchy, method, bytecode); permissions; and the ability to instrument loops.

As Table 2 shows, the SIFScript for each instrumentation task is very compact. No SIFScript exceeds 100 lines; if we exclude FreeMarket, AlgoProf and AppInsight, the remaining tasks require less than 30 lines. This demonstrates the conciseness of the abstractions; as we shall discuss later, the larger tasks, AlgoProf and AppInsight, are approaches that use extensive instrumentation to study application behavior.

Task	Description	#Steps	Granularity	Reference
Timing Profiler	collects timing profile of native method invokes	1	bytecode	-
Call Graph Profiler	builds runtime call graph between two app methods	4	method	-
Flurry-like Analytics	collects and uploads user-specific analytics data for some methods	2	class hierarchy, method	[4]
Fine-grain Permission	allows user to decide on Internet usage for third-party library code	2	class hierarchy, class name, permission	[15] [30]
AdCleaner	removes ads from an app	1	bytecode	[24]
Privacy Leakage	exploits permission privilege to collect and upload sensor data	1	class hierarchy, method, permission	-
FreeMarket	exploits Google IAB vulnerabilities	3	bytecode	[26]
AlgoProf	estimates programs' cost function	10	method, bytecode, loop	[29]
AppInsight	profiles upcalls and critical paths	12	method, bytecode	[25]
Location Auditor	collects all execution paths between location and internet use	3	permission path set	-

Table 1: Implemented instrumentation tasks

	LOC* (SIF)	LOC (user)	LOC (total)
Timing Profiler	12	16	28
Call Graph Profiler	30	22	52
Flurry-like Analytics	13	18	31
Fine-grained Permission	20	44	64
AdCleaner	10	4	14
Privacy Leakage	12	44	56
FreeMarket	22	-	-
AlgoProf	61	-	-
AppInsight	91	-	-
Location Auditor	10	0	10

Table 2: Implemented SIF tasks (*Line Of Code)

Timing Profiler. The Timing Profiler shown in Listing 1 profiles the timing of native method invocations. For space reasons, instead of showing SIF code for subsequent instrumentation tasks, we use a pictorial representation of these tasks. Figure 3 shows this representation for the timing profiler. Attribute specifications for codepoint sets (line 3 in Listing 1) are represented as boxes with a gray background. User-specified instrumentation (lines 13-27 in Listing 1) is represented as a blue box with a brief description of the instrumentation code. The relative positioning of these boxes indicates whether the user-specified instrumentation is inserted before (top left), after (bottom right), or replaces (middle) the corresponding codepoints. Double arrows between filter boxes indicate multiple instrumentation steps (the Timing Profiler has only one step, but subsequent instrumentation tasks have more than one).

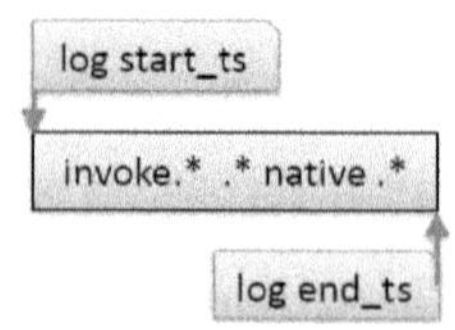

Figure 3: Timing profiler

To demonstrate the timing profiler, we have applied it to the Angry Birds app and measured the app's native method invokes. Angry Birds uses native methods to optimize UI event handling. As an aside, we note that we cannot instrument entry and exit of the Java definitions of the native methods, since these methods always have an empty body. Instead, we have to select all invoke instruction types (Android permits several invocation types), refine this codepoint set to native method invocations, and then insert the timestamp logging code before and after each such invoke.

We ran the instrumented app with a common use case (for this application, playing a single game). The results show a mismatch between the static and dynamic view of native method usage in the app. While a static analysis of the binary shows 18 distinct native method invocations, only 7 are actually involved in our use case. As Table 3 shows, some of these are used significantly more than others but exhibit significant variability in execution time (*e.g.,* update). Other are computationally expensive (*e.g.,* init and pause) and infrequently invoked.

The total size of the SIF implementation of the Timing Profiler is 28 lines of code. This illustrates the conciseness of SIFScript; even small and simple programs are able to provide meaningful and useful insights into app behavior.

	#invokes	Avg (ms)	Min (ms)	Max (ms)
setVideoReady	1	0.061	0.061	0.061
nativeInit	1	507.996	507.996	507.996
nativeInput	156	0.046	0.031	0.336
nativeKeyInput	10	0.027	0.031	0.061
nativePause	1	182.007	182.007	182.007
nativeResize	1	0.031	0.031	0.031
nativeUpdate	3696	5.605	0.366	3894.928

Table 3: Native methods invoked during a game run

Call Graph Profiler. Another common use of instrumentation is to log the dynamic call graph of an application. This task is different from the timing profiler in two ways. First, rather than instrumenting invocations, it instruments method entries and exits. Second, while the timing profiler uses a single instrumentation step, the call graph profiler uses multiple steps, where each step refers to instrumenting a distinct codepoint set or reporting a distinct path set.

Figure 4 illustrates the SIF steps to construct a call graph for all methods invoked between `X.foo()` and `Y.bar()`. The first step instruments every method entry to check a global variable that controls call graph generation. If this variable is set, the instrumentation increments a global variable that tracks the *level* of the current method in the call graph, and logs both the level and method identifier. The second step performs analogous actions for the exit of every method. In these two steps, the instrumentation location is specified by indicating a bytecode position; by default, SIF applies this to every method in every class. Finally, the last two steps instrument the entry and exit points of the target methods to (respectively) enable and disable the global variable that controls call graph generation. From the sequence of log records and level indicators, it becomes easy to infer the dynamic call graph. The SIFScript for this instrumentation task is 52 lines of code.

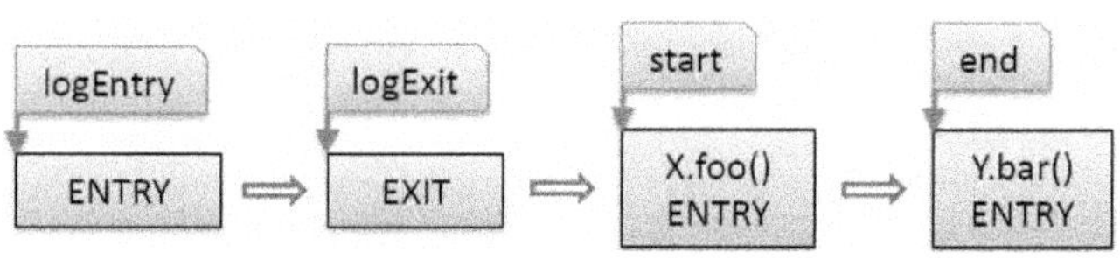

Figure 4: Call graph profiler

We verified our call graph profiler on `Angry Birds`, instrumenting the app to identify the dynamic call graph generated between calls to the app's `onCreate()` and `onDestroy()` methods. This logs 100 distinct app methods out of a total of 1958 methods in the app. The call graph has over 22K edges and a max depth of 10, with 90% of the calls being 5-6 methods deep. This example demonstrates how one can use SIF to develop insights about app structure and complexity.

An alternative implementation could use the path set `sequence` method to find all paths between `X.foo()` and `Y.bar()`, then post-process the returned paths to determine invocations and entry/exit pairs. The relative performance of these approaches depends on the app and the inputs; SIF's feedback estimator can be used to determine which approach might be better for a given workload.

Flurry-like App Usage Analytics. In mobile apps, it is common practice for developers to collect data about post-deployment app usage. In fact, there are several services, Flurry [4] being the most popular, which provide developers with an API for logging app usage information. When users use an app, these logs are uploaded to the service's site and made available to developers. This capability enables developers to refine their apps or introduce new features based on customer preferences, expertise, or other factors.

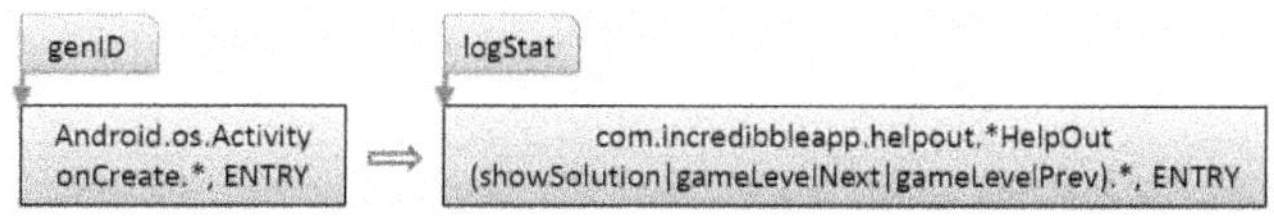

Figure 5: Flurry-like analytics

We now show how SIF can provide usage statistics for apps whose developers have not used the analytics API while developing the app. Our code is specific to `helpout`, a multi-level puzzle game app. In this game, users advance levels when they successfully complete a level, and can choose to move down a level or have the app display a solution. We develop instrumentation to count how many times a user advances levels, chooses to move down a level, or displays a solution.

To do this in SIF requires only two steps (Figure 5) and 31 lines of code. In the first step, the SIFScript loads a unique identifier for the game player from storage (generating one if necessary) when a game starts. The SIFScript identifies the game start codepoints by create a class hierarchy based attribute specification that selects all app-defined classes derived from the Android `Activity` class and all `onCreate` methods of those classes. Then, it instruments these codepoints by inserting code for loading and generating the user identifier. This identifier is used to distinguish between multiple game users.

In the second step, the SIFScript instruments the methods that implement the functionality discussed above: going up a level, going down a level, and asking for help. Whenever one of these methods is invoked, the user-specified instrumentation sends a message to a server that includes the method name and the user identifier.

App usage analytics can help developers of `helpout` understand the distribution of expertise among their users. We had three users play an instrumented version of this game, and recorded their usage. As Table 4 clearly shows, user C has the least expertise in this game, going down a level twice and asking many times for the solution, while user B has the highest expertise, going up to level 22.

Beyond illustrating SIF's ability to support application diagnostics, this instrumentation task demonstrates how SIF allows scripts to perform more sophisticated actions beyond simply counting or timing method usage (*e.g.,* uploading data to a server).

	showSolution	gameLevelNext	gameLevelPrev
user A	2	10	0
user B	0	22	0
user C	5	7	2

Table 4: Analytics results collected from 3 users

Fine-grained Permissions. In Android, permissions to access resources, such as sensors and devices, are granted and enforced at the granularity of an entire app. However, many apps are composed of multiple "packages" obtained from different developers. For example, `aroundme` is an app that returns context-sensitive results, and its free version uses two additional packages developed by `ads` and `flurry`. The Android security model does not distinguish between the developer of the app and the developers of other packages, and treats them all as identical principals from a security perspective.

Motivated by this observation, some recent work [15, 30] has proposed finer-grained permissions granting and enforcement. This work analyzes the app to infer the right set of permissions needed for each package, then instruments the app to enforce those permissions. We now show how SIF can be used to develop functionality analogous to fine-grained permissions enforcement.

Our SIFScript code pops up a dialog box to obtain explicit permission the first time that a method in a given package invokes a certain permission. In our example, the SIFScript checks methods in the `flurry` API that require INTERNET permission. Thereafter it remembers the user's choice and only invokes the API if the user has granted the necessary permission.

Our SIFScript for this task (Figure 6(a)) contains two steps. The first step of our SIFScript selects the `onCreate` method of the entry activity and stores a reference to `Context` in the user-specified instrumentation class. Most UI actions in Android, such as popping up a dialog box, require a pointer to a UI `Context`. The second step illustrates the use of codepoint set selection based on permissions capabilities and the ability of SIF to *replace* codepoints. In this step, the SIFScript replaces all API invokes that need INTERNET permission in the `flurry` module with another method that has the same signature as the replaced method, but displays a dialog box (Figure 7) that asks for the user's choice. Subsequent invocations to any method in `flurry` will result in network traffic only if the user has granted access.

We have instrumented the `aroundme` app with this capability. Our SIFScript is 64 lines of code, and can be easily extended to enforce fine-grained permissions for modules other than `flurry` or permissions other than network access. This would require a different codepoint set definition and additional code to track different types of permissions.

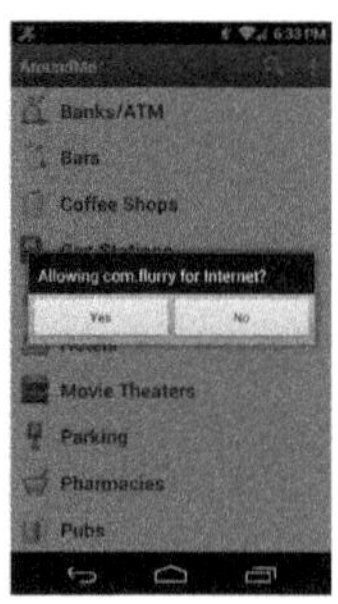

Figure 7: Dialog asking for user's choice

AdCleaner. Free versions of many mobile apps come with advertisement displays. In fact, this feature is so pervasive that there exist third-party libraries that app developers can use to include ad displays. Ads can consume Internet bandwidth, affect energy usage, and take up valuable screen real estate. Analogous to Web-based ad blockers, mobile app users can add a blacklist of domain names for ad hosting servers in their local name resolvers, but this requires root access. Recent research [24] has explored using library interposition techniques to block ads.

This capability is simple to implement in SIF, and requires only

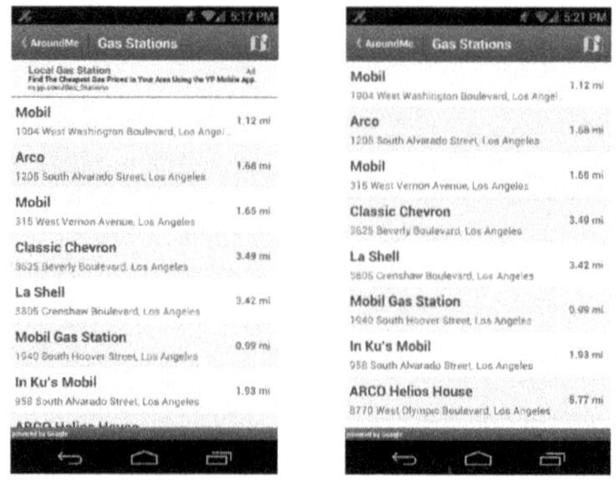

(a) Before (b) After

Figure 8: Screenshot before and after AdCleaner

14 lines of code and a single instrumentation step. Our implementation simply replaces the `loadAd()` method invocation of a popular ad library with a null method. Figure 8 shows the screenshots of `aroundme` before and after our instrumentation is applied.

Privacy Leakage. As with many tools that have significant expressive power, SIF can also be used for malicious purposes. With this instrumentation task, we illustrate how easy it is in SIF to innocuously insert a significant privacy leak. In this example, this capability is achieved as a result of SIF's support for arbitrary user-specified instrumentation.

We have been able to instrument the `Skype` app, which is permitted to use both the camera and the network, to periodically take a picture with the camera and upload it to a website. This can, of course, significantly leak privacy by exposing the physical context of a given user. The SIFScript for this (Figure 6(c)) is 56 lines of code and requires only a single step, which instruments the `onCreate` method of the entry activity and stores a reference to the `Context` object. The inserted code *starts a background task* that periodically takes a photo and uploads it to a user server.

Figure 9 shows an experiment in which a user first uses a phone outdoors, puts the phone in his pocket, then removes the phone indoors. The photos clearly reveal these place transitions in addition to several details about the locations.

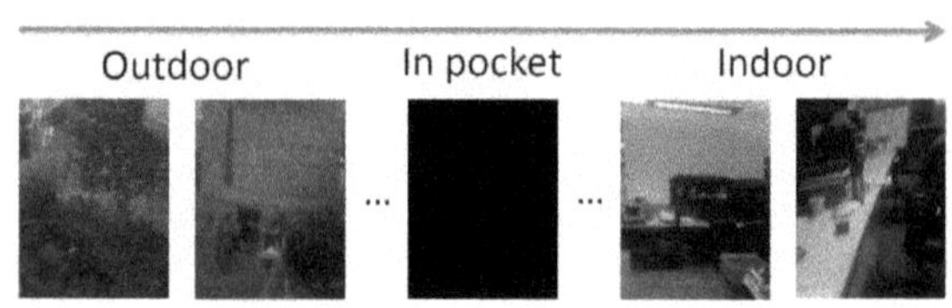

Figure 9: Photos taken and uploaded by instrumented app

FreeMarket. A recent study [26] has explored vulnerabilities in the process of in-app Android purchases. Specifically, the work proposes an attack on Google's In-App Billing service protocol that allows for users to pay for purchases from within an app. This attack instruments an app to modify its behavior to (a) bypass access to Google's billing servers, (b) redirect these calls to a local Android service (instantiated by instrumentation code) that always returns successfully, and (c) bypassing a key verification step. These instrumentation steps have been documented in [26] and we have been able to devise SIF code that replicates these instrumentation steps.

The SIFScript for this task consists of 22 lines of codepoint set specifications. The first step finds invokes to Android's `bindService` API in `Context` class and replace that binding with one to

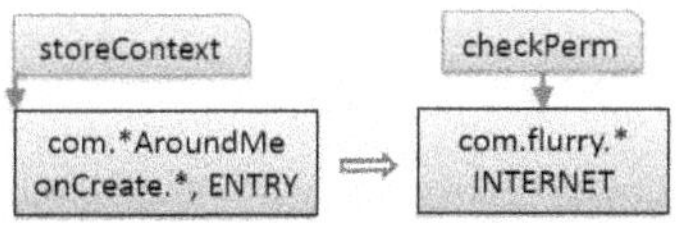

(a) Fine-grained permission control

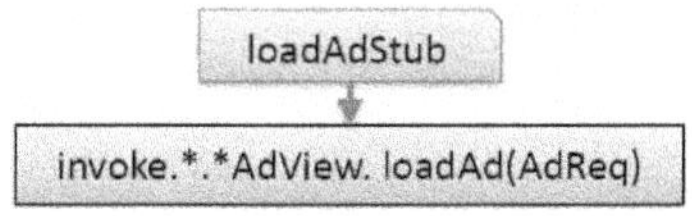

(b) AdCleaner

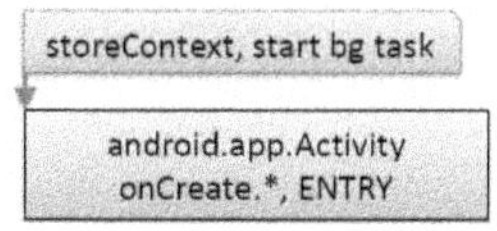

(c) Privacy leakage study

Figure 6: SIFScript descriptions for some tasks

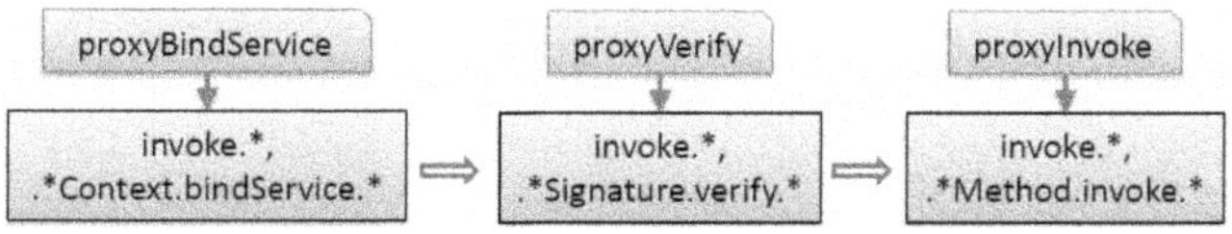

Figure 10: FreeMarket attacker

a local service. The second step replaces invocations to the signature verification Java API call with a null method that is always successful. A final step adds some instrumentation to deal with the case where in-app billing is invoked through Java reflection.

We have re-created the instrumentation steps necessary to mount the attack described in [26], but have not validated that attack because (a) the actions of the local service are not described in detail in the paper, and (b) the attack is successful only on some applications whose identities are not revealed in the paper (so we would have to search for a vulnerable app).

AlgoProf. A recent work [29] has explored methods to estimate an application's asymptotic complexity as a function of input size. Their prototype, AlgoProf, instruments Java bytecode in order to collect extensive profiling information, and then post-processes the output to produce a complexity estimate. Specifically, they instrument every method entry and exit, array access, field access, object allocation, and loop entry and exit. Although this work did not target mobile apps (its focus is on Java apps in general), it nicely demonstrates features of SIF that might be exploited in future instrumentation-based studies of mobile apps.

We have written a SIFScript to replicate the instrumentation required by AlgoProf. For space reasons, we omit a pictorial description of the code. The SIFScript has *ten* steps which require 61 lines of code (not including the user-specified instrumentation), and uses a wide range of SIF's codepoint set capabilities. Unlike previous examples that have only instrumented method entry and exit or invocations, this SIFScript also instruments Java bytecodes (*e.g.,* for field accesses) and is the only one of our examples that also instruments loops. Although our SIFScript easily duplicated the instrumentation part of the approach in only 61 lines of code, we could not verify the results of executing the instrumented apps without also duplicating AlgoProf's complexity inference algorithms, which was beyond the scope of this paper.

AppInsight. By far the most complex instrumentation task that we have applied SIF to is AppInsight [25], which analyzes latency-critical paths in mobile apps. Based on the observation that many UI actions require multiple concurrent operations, this work identifies *upcalls* and then adds instrumentation code to match upcalls with asynchronous callers.

The SIFScript for AppInsight requires *twelve* instrumentation steps requiring 91 lines of code (not including user-specified instrumentation). These steps run the gamut of location specifications and actions, instrumenting individual bytecodes and invocations, replacing invocations with user-defined instrumentation, and inserting new handlers for specified events. It was not possible to compare the output of our implementation against the original AppInsight because SIF works for Android platforms and AppInsight leverages certain opcodes and functions that are only present in Silverlight (Windows Phone). Nonetheless, our SIFScript implementation demonstrates that even complex state of the art instrumentation based approaches can be easily implemented in SIF.

Location Auditor. Finally, we have previously described another instrumentation task, location auditing (Listing 2) on the `aroundme` app. This task demonstrated the use of the pathset abstractions. An experiment involving this instrumented app is discussed below.

4.2 Efficiency of SIF

The second major aspect of SIF's design is its efficiency, which we quantify in four distinct ways. First, SIF uses program analysis to minimize the instrumentation of path sets, and we quantify these savings. Second, we demonstrate that SIF's user-perceived time to instrument a binary is moderate. Third, we quantify the runtime overhead due to SIF. Finally, we quantify the accuracy of our feedback estimator. With an accurate estimator, users can iteratively refine their instrumentation to achieve acceptable overhead.

Program Analysis for Path Sets. SIF analyzes the program binary in order to minimize the instrumentation for the `sequence` operation on path sets. To evaluate its performance, we instrumented the `aroundme` app with the location auditor task (Listing 2). `CPFinder` was able to find 10 codepoints with LOCATION permission and 12 with INTERNET permissions. Using program analysis, SIF determined that only 25 methods (out of about 560 methods in the app) needed to be instrumented, or fewer than 5% of the total number of methods. This demonstrates the benefit of sophisticated program analysis for path sets.

We also ran a simple use case that searched for nearby gas stations and restaurants. SIF reported three suspicious paths: two from the `aroundme` package and one from `ads`. As expected, `aroundme` read the location and sent it over the network. Unexpectedly, we found that the `ads` package also appeared to send a user's location over the network, presumably for location-targeted advertising.

No path was reported for the `flurry` package, indicating that, at least for this use case, there were no paths that read the GPS sensor then accessed the network. However, by analyzing network traffic, we found that `flurry` *did* leak location information. An analysis of the binary revealed that it read and stored the location in memory or storage, and later transmitted that location over the network. To detect such leaks, taint analysis or other forms of information flow analysis are necessary; SIF's path inspection capabilities can help narrow the search scope of leakage.

Time to Instrument Apps. In this section, we quantify the CPU time taken to instrument binaries for seven of the tasks presented above; in each case, we instrument the corresponding apps used to demonstrate the instrumentation tasks. Our measurements are performed on a ThinkPad T400 laptop with 3GB RAM. As shown in Table 5, the search for relevant codepoints is fast; `CPFinder` takes at most 4.6s to finish. The time to apply the instrumentation is at most 6s. Notice that the cost depends on the app binary size as well as the complexity of the relevant SIFScript. Instrumentation time is dominated by the the cost of packing and unpacking the

	Finding Codepoint	Placing Instrumentation	Unpacking + Packing	Total
Timing Profiler	2.236	3.458	18.491	24.185
Call Graph Profiler	4.532	5.972	19.371	29.875
Flurry-like Analytics	0.975	1.269	17.452	19.696
Fine-grained Permission	1.261	1.597	8.873	11.731
AdCleaner	1.093	1.325	8.755	11.173
Privacy Leakage	0.864	1.421	23.92	26.205
Location Auditor	1.569	2.093	9.014	12.676

Table 5: Time to instrument SIF tasks

app. All tasks can finish within half a minute; we consider this to be reasonable, especially since SIF itself only contributes to a small fraction of these times.

Runtime Overhead. There are two sources of overhead that affect the performance of an instrumented app: user-defined instrumentation, and instructions inserted by SIF. We now quantify the latter by replacing all user-defined code with empty stub so that the functionality of the original app is unchanged; this allows us to measure the overhead attributable to SIF. We run the same workload on both original and instrumented app and compare their running time. Table 6 shows the duration of original app and the overhead introduced by SIF. Overall, SIF introduces less than 2% overhead except for the call graph profiler, where the overhead is 4.41%. This is because SIF overhead depends on the number of codepoints to be instrumented and the call graph profiler has to instrument many more codepoints than the rest.

	Original app (sec)	Overhead by SIF (sec)
Timing Profiler	59.473	0.452 (0.76%)
Call Graph Profiler	59.729	2.637 (4.41%)
Flurry-like Analytics	115.384	0.679 (0.59%)
Fine-grained Permission	11.862	0.153 (1.29%)
AdCleaner	11.721	0.114 (0.97%)
Privacy Leakage	35.230	0.137 (0.39%)

Table 6: Runtime overhead of SIF

Accuracy of Overhead Feedback. We evaluate the accuracy of SIF's overhead estimates by comparing them with measured ground truth values. Our experiments measure execution times with and without instrumentation. The difference between these two numbers is the ground truth cost of the instrumentation. The experiments were averaged over ten runs and controlled for most types of non-deterministic behavior seen between successive runs [3].

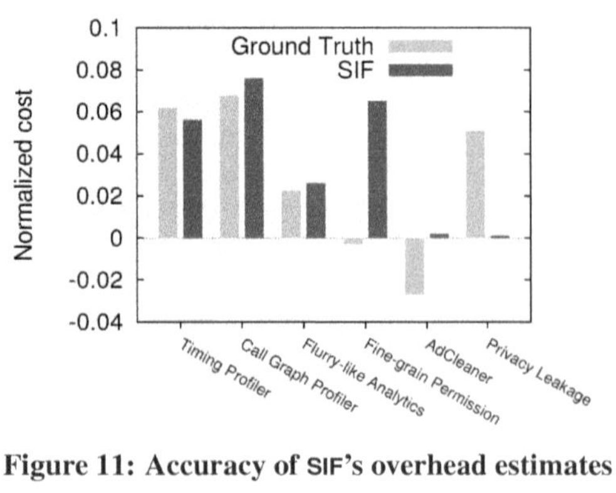

Figure 11: Accuracy of SIF's overhead estimates

Figure 11 plots the SIF estimates and measured ground truth for the six tasks we have tested completely that also involve user-specified instrumentation. The y-axis represents the instrumentation overhead measured as a fraction of the total execution time. SIF's overhead estimate is very close to ground truth, within 15%, for all tasks but privacy leakage. For fine-grained permission control and AdCleaner, the measured ground-truth has *lower* execution time after the instrumentation; that is because, in both cases, SIF replaces invocations with null methods. Our overhead estimator currently does not account for *replaced* invocations, so it over-estimates overhead. However the estimate in these situations will always provide a conservative upper bound estimate, which is appropriate, since the goal is to give the user an approximate indication of potential overhead. The one case that requires significant future work is the privacy leakage study. Its estimate is significantly off because its user-defined instrumentation is complex (the code fires a periodic timer which uploads a photo) and we have not developed analysis methods for such code.

[3] For example, we modified the `Angry Birds` binary to set its random number seed to a fixed value (by default, it uses the current local time.

5. RELATED WORK

Instrumentation frameworks have been widely used for traditional software. Adaptive Programming [18] provides a language to systematically alter classes, but does not support instrumentation of particular methods or paths. Aspect-Oriented Programming (AOP) [16] allows for instrumentation of user-defined programming points that match certain conditions, and has spawned many derivative pieces of work [19, 14, 21]. However, these pieces of work focus on specific problems and do not provide a general purpose framework for instrumentation. More general frameworks that are based on AOP include AspectJ [17], AspectC++ [28], and LMP [10]. Compared to SIF, these approaches are limited by the underlying representation of codepoints; they do not include loops [16] and are limited to method invocation, entry, and exit points. In comparison, SIF is able to arbitrarily instrument any codepoint or path-based location.

More broadly, SIF differs from AOP based instrumentation frameworks in four ways. First, it provides mechanisms for identifying and utilizing path-based information. Second, although AOP allows for loop structures to be used as codepoints, this is not adequate for extracting complete path information; SIF's instrumentation mechanisms allow for a more complete handling of language constructs such as loops and exceptions. Third, unlike AOP, SIF provides inter-procedural instrumentation mechanisms in addition to intra-procedural instrumentation. Finally, SIF provides support for multi-threaded path information reporting; in AOP it is difficult to distinguish thread information at local codepoints, but SIF can distinguish paths that belong to different threads by taking advantage of global path variables.

An earlier binary instrumentation framework, Metric Description Language (MDL) [12], allows users to dynamically record information for x86 instructions. MDL is tightly coupled with x86, restricts the instrumentation that can be inserted to either counter or timers, and does not support path-based structures, such as loops and branches. In contrast, SIF permits arbitrary user-specified instrumentation, and supports path-based structures like loops and branches.

DynamoRio[7] and Pin[20] are dynamic code manipulation frameworks. They run x86 instructions on interpreters using Just In Time Translation (JIT) and perform instrumentation while executing the programs. In contrast, SIF uses static instrumentation techniques, which avoids the runtime cost of interpretation and instrumentation of these two approaches. Also, SIF can analyze the structure of an entire application during instrumentation, so it can have a global view that allows for optimization and more sophisticated instrumentation. For example, it can more readily identify subsets of relevant paths and loop structures than these approaches. Similarly, Valgrind [23] provides a Shadow Value recording, a form of instrumentation, for assembly code. Unlike SIF, however, it does not support user-defined instrumentation.

There have also been instrumentation frameworks proposed for Java or Android applications. InsECTJ [27] can record runtime information for Java applications. It can trace bytecode execution at specified points, such as method entry, and record information, such as method arguments, at these points; unlike SIF, it does not support the insertion of arbitrary user-specified instrumentation at these points. Davis *et al.* [9] have built a framework to rewrite methods in Android applications. Their framework cannot, unlike SIF, exploit the path information for more sophisticated instrumentation.

Several other pieces of work have instrumented binaries to study various kinds of application behavior: dynamic memory allocation [11], data flow anomalies [13], app billing [26], workload characterization [29], dynamic permissions checking [22], and critical path latency [25]. Although these approaches make extensive use of instrumentation, they do not provide general code instrumentation capabilities that SIF does. We have shown that SIF is expressive enough to realize the instrumentation used in many of these papers.

6. CONCLUSION

In this paper, we have described the design and implementation of SIF, a binary instrumentation framework for mobile apps whose codepoint set abstractions are able to specify instrumentation location at different granularities and incorporate resource usage permissions. Its path set abstractions allow dynamic path inspection between arbitrary codepoints, and its program analysis techniques can reduce the overhead of instrumentation. SIF is expressive enough to incorporate a variety of instrumentation tasks previously proposed in the literature, and is quite efficient.

Much work remains, however, including validating SIF on other instrumentation tasks, porting SIF to other platforms and integrating their access permissions methods into SIF, supporting advanced language features such as reflection in its path set abstractions, evaluating the effectiveness of path sets for studying privacy leakage and comparing path-sensitive analysis with more expensive information-flow style analyses, studying the usability of overhead feedback, and improving the accuracy of feedback estimation for advanced forms of user-specified instrumentation.

Acknowledgements

We would like to thank our shepherd, Z. Morley Mao, and the anonymous reviewers, for their insightful suggestions for improving the technical content and presentation of the paper.

7. REFERENCES

[1] apktool. http://code.google.com/p/android-apktool.

[2] BCEL. http://commons.apache.org/bcel.

[3] dex2jar. http://code.google.com/p/dex2jar.

[4] flurry. http://www.flurry.com.

[5] traceview. http://developer.android.com/guide/developing/debugging/debugging-tracing.html.

[6] K. W. Y. Au, Y. F. Zhou, Z. Huang, and D. Lie. Pscout: analyzing the android permission specification. In *Proc. of ACM CCS*, 2012.

[7] V. Bala, E. Duesterwald, and S. Banerjia. Dynamo: a transparent dynamic optimization system. In *ACM SIGPLAN Notices*, 2000.

[8] T. Ball and J. R. Larus. Efficient path profiling. In *Proc. of ACM/IEEE MICRO*, 1996.

[9] B. Davis, B. Sanders, A. Khodaverdian, and H. Chen. I-arm-droid: A rewriting framework for in-app reference monitors for android applications. *MoST*, 2012.

[10] K. De Volder and T. D'Hondt. Aspect-oriented logic meta programming. In *Proc. of ACM Reflection*, 1999.

[11] D. Garbervetsky, C. Nakhli, S. Yovine, and H. Zorgati. Program instrumentation and run-time analysis of scoped memory in java. *Electronic Notes in Theoretical Computer Science*, 2005.

[12] J. Hollingsworth, B. Miller, and J. Cargille. Dynamic program instrumentation for scalable performance tools. In *Proc. of IEEE SHPCC*, 1994.

[13] J. Huang. Detection of data flow anomaly through program instrumentation. *IEEE TOSE*, 1979.

[14] J. Irwin, J. Loingtier, J. Gilbert, G. Kiczales, J. Lamping, A. Mendhekar, and T. Shpeisman. Aspect-oriented programming of sparse matrix code. In *Proc. of ISCOPE*, 1997.

[15] J. Jeon, K. K. Micinski, J. A. Vaughan, A. Fogel, N. Reddy, J. S. Foster, and T. Millstein. Dr. android and mr. hide: fine-grained permissions in android applications. In *Proc. of CCS SPSM*, 2012.

[16] G. Kiczales, J. Lamping, A. Mendhekar, C. Maeda, C. Lopes, J. Loingtier, and J. Irwin. Aspect-oriented programming. *Proc. of ECOOP*, 1997.

[17] R. Laddad. *AspectJ in action: practical aspect-oriented programming*. Manning, 2003.

[18] K. Lieberherr. Adaptive object-oriented software the demeter method. *PWS Boston*, 1996.

[19] C. Lopes. *D: A language framework for distributed programming*. PhD thesis, Northeastern University, 1997.

[20] C. Luk, R. Cohn, R. Muth, H. Patil, A. Klauser, G. Lowney, S. Wallace, V. Reddi, and K. Hazelwood. Pin: building customized program analysis tools with dynamic instrumentation. In *Proc. of ACM SIGPLAN Notices*, 2005.

[21] A. Mendhekar, G. Kiczales, and J. Lamping. Rg: A case-study for aspect-oriented programming. Technical report, SPL97-009, 1997.

[22] M. Nauman, S. Khan, and X. Zhang. Apex: extending android permission model and enforcement with user-defined runtime constraints. In *Proc. of CCS SPSM*, 2010.

[23] N. Nethercote and J. Seward. Valgrind: a framework for heavyweight dynamic binary instrumentation. In *Proc. of ACM PLDI*, 2007.

[24] P. Pearce, P. A. Felt, G. Nunez, and D. Wagner. AdDroid: Privilege Separation for Applications and Advertisers in Android. In *Proc. of ACM ASIACCS*, 2011.

[25] L. Ravindranath, J. Padhye, S. Agarwal, R. Mahajan, I. Obermiller, and S. Shayandeh. AppInsight: mobile app performance monitoring in the wild. In *Proc. of ACM OSDI*, 2012.

[26] D. Reynaud, T. Song, E. Magrino, R. Wu, and Shin. Freemarket: Shopping for free in android applications. *NDSS*, 2012.

[27] A. Seesing and A. Orso. Insectj: a generic instrumentation framework for collecting dynamic information within eclipse. In *Proc. of OOPSLA on Eclipse Technology eXchange*, 2005.

[28] O. Spinczyk, A. Gal, and W. Schröder-Preikschat.

Aspectc++: an aspect-oriented extension to the c++ programming language. In *Proc. of ACM TOOLS Pacific*, 2002.

[29] D. Zaparanuks and M. Hauswirth. Algorithmic profiling. In *Proc. of ACM PLDI*, 2012.

[30] Y. Zhou, X. Zhang, X. Jiang, and V. W. Freeh. Taming information-stealing smartphone applications (on android). In *Proc. of TRUST*, 2011.

APPENDIX

A. MORE SIFSCRIPT PROGRAMS

```
class FineGrainPerm implements SIFTask {
  public void run() {
    CPFinder.init();
    CPFinder.setClass("com.tweakersoft.aroundme.
         AroundMe", "android.app.Activity");
    CPFinder.setMethod("onCreate:\\(Landroid\\/os\\/
         Bundle;\\)V");
    CPFinder.setBytecode(ENTRY);
    UserCode code;
    for (CP cp : CPFinder.apply()) {
      code = new UserCode("Logger", "storeContext",
         THIS);
      Instrumenter.place(code, BEFORE, cp);
    }
    CPFinder.init();
    CPFinder.setClass("com.flurry.*", null);
    CPFinder.setPermission(INTERNET);
    for (CP cp : CPFinder.apply()) {
      code = new UserCode("Logger", "checkPerm",
         ALL_ARGS);
      Instrumenter.place(code, AT, cp);
    }
  }
}
class Logger {
  private static Activity act;
  private static short allow = -1;
  public static void storeContext(Object obj) {
    act = (Activity) obj;
  }
  public static Object checkPerm(Object obj, String
       name, Object... args) {
    if (allow < 0) {
      create_dialog(act);
    }
    Object ret = null;
    if (allow > 0) {
      List<Class> params = new ArrayList<Class>();
      for (Object arg : args) {
        params.add(arg.getClass());
      }
      try {
        Method mthd = obj.getClass().getMethod(name,
           params);
        ret = mthd.invoke(obj, args);
      } catch (Exception e) {}
    }
    return ret;
  }
  private static void create_dialog(Context con) {
    AlertDialog.Builder builder = new AlertDialog.
         Builder(con);
    builder.setCancelable(true);
    builder.setTitle("Allowing com.flurry for
         Internet?");
    builder.setInverseBackgroundForced(true);
    builder.setPositiveButton("Yes", new
         DialogInterface.OnClickListener() {
      public void onClick(DialogInterface dialog, int
           which) {
        allow = 1;
        dialog.dismiss();
      }
    });
    builder.setNegativeButton("No", new
         DialogInterface.OnClickListener() {
      public void onClick(DialogInterface dialog, int
           which) {
        allow = 0;
        dialog.dismiss();
      }
    });
    AlertDialog alert = builder.create();
    alert.show();
  }
}
```

Listing 3: Fine-grained permission control

```
class PermLeakage implements SIFTask {
  public void run() {
    CPFinder.init();
    CPFinder.setClass(null, "android.app.Activity");
    CPFinder.setMethod("onCreate:\\(Landroid\\/os\\/
         Bundle;\\)V");
    CPFinder.setBytecode(ENTRY);
    for (CP cp : CPFinder.apply()) {
      UserCode code = new UserCode("Logger", "start",
           THIS);
      Instrumenter.place(code, BEFORE, cp);
    }
  }
}
class Logger {
  public static void start(Object obj) {
    Activity act = (Activity) obj;
    Context context = act.getApplicationContext();
    new Timer().schedule(new MyTask(context), 0,
         10000);
  }
}
class MyTask extends TimerTask {
  private SurfaceView view;
  private Camera cam;
  private PictureCallback jpegPictureCallback = new
       PictureCallback() {
    public void onPictureTaken(byte[] data, Camera
         camera) {
      FileOutputStream fos = null;
      String fname = String.format("/sdcard/%d.jpg",
           System.currentTimeMillis());
      try {
        fos = new FileOutputStream(fname);
        fos.write(data);
        fos.close();
      } catch (Exception e) {}
      HttpClient httpClient = new DefaultHttpClient()
          ;
      HttpPost httpPost = new HttpPost("http://enl.
           usc.edu/upload.php");
      MultipartEntity multiPart = new MultipartEntity
           ();
      multiPart.addPart("my_pic", new FileBody(new
           File(fname)));
      httpPost.setEntity(multiPart);
      try {
        httpClient.execute(httpPost);
      } catch (Exception e) {}
    }
  };
  public MyTask(Context context) {
    view = new SurfaceView(context);
    cam = Camera.open();
    try {
      cam.setPreviewDisplay(view.getHolder());
    } catch (IOException e) {}
  }
  public void run() {
    cam.startPreview();
    cam.takePicture(null, null, jpegPictureCallback);
    try {
      Thread.sleep(500);
    } catch (InterruptedException e) {}
  }
}
```

Listing 4: Privacy leakage

RetroSkeleton: Retrofitting Android Apps

Benjamin Davis
University of California, Davis
bendavis@ucdavis.edu

Hao Chen
University of California, Davis
chen@ucdavis.edu

ABSTRACT

An obvious asset of the Android platform is the tremendous number and variety of available apps. There is a less obvious, but potentially even more important, benefit to the fact that nearly all apps are developed using a common platform. We can leverage the relatively uniform nature of Android apps to allow users to tweak applications for improved security, usability, and functionality with relative ease (compared to desktop applications). We design and implement an Android app rewriting framework for customizing behavior of existing applications without requiring source code or app-specific guidance. Following app-agnostic transformation policies, our system rewrites applications to insert, remove, or modify behavior. The rewritten application can run on any unmodified Android device, without requiring rooting or other custom software.

This paper describes RetroSkeleton, our app rewriting framework, including static and dynamic interception of method invocations, and creating policies that integrate with each target app. We show that our system is capable of supporting a variety of useful policies, including providing flexible fine-grained network access control, building *HTTPS-Everywhere* functionality into apps, implementing automatic app localization, informing users of hidden behavior in apps, and updating apps depending on outdated APIs. We evaluate these policies by rewriting and testing more than one thousand real-world apps from Google Play.

Categories and Subject Descriptors

D.4.6 [**Operating Systems**]: Security and Protection

Keywords

Android; Dalvik; VM; bytecode; rewriting

1. INTRODUCTION

Android is now the dominant smartphone platform for new devices sold, with a 68.1% market share of smartphones shipped in the second quarter of 2012 according to the International Data Corporation Worldwide Quarterly Mobile Phone Tracker [20]. A major feature of the Android platform is the tremendous number of third-party Android apps available for users to install on their devices, with more than 700,000 Android apps [26] available on Google Play [5] alone.

Many Android apps have access to a wide variety of sensitive information, including banking and payment details, email and messaging content, photos, and browsing history. It may be difficult for a user to determine exactly what an app may do, so the user must rely on their limited assessment of the trustworthiness of the developers of the app, and of any included third-party libraries. Most users with devices associated with a telecommunication provider either can not or do not root their devices, which can be a risky and unsupported operation. Without access to privileged and low-level functionality, these users are left with even less control over what apps may do on their device than on traditional desktop systems. For these reasons, commonplace practices on traditional desktop PCs, such as installing a third-party firewall to monitor incoming and outgoing connections, cannot be performed on most stock devices. The controls provided by the Android platform, such as the permission system, are extremely limited, coarse-grained and inflexible. For example, if a user installs an apps that requests the INTERNET permission, then the app is granted permanent, unlimited access to the network.

Our work is based on the observation that the vast majority of Android apps (estimated over 95% [28]) are entirely compiled into Dalvik bytecode (i.e., containing no native code). Not only are most apps built on the same framework, but the Dalvik bytecode does not include the ambiguity that frequently makes analysis of other compiled software (e.g. x86 machine code) impractical. We take advantage of the consistency in app implementation to design and implement an Android app rewriting framework for customizing behavior of existing applications without requiring source code or app-specific guidance. We call our app rewriting system RetroSkeleton after the ability to retrofit apps with new behavior by modifying their internals.

RetroSkeleton can be used to provide users with more control over the security, usability, and functionality of apps, even compared to desktop applications. We provide a system for automatically embedding policies completely into applications via automated app rewriting to insert, remove, or modify app behavior. Our system is capable of supporting a wide range of flexible, customizable transformation policies that can be written and applied to apps automatically without any app-specific knowledge or guidance. In this paper we describe several different policies we have implemented and applied to real apps, providing features such as fine-grained network access control, HTTPS-Everywhere features, or on-the-fly localization of app UI elements. Apps transformed

MobiSys'13, June 25–28, 2013, Taipei, Taiwan

by our rewriting system can be installed on stock, unmodified and unrooted Android devices.

Our Android app rewriting system was designed to have four important properties:

- **Complete**: intercept all target method invocations, including dynamic invocation via reflection
- **Flexible**: powerful enough to support a variety of complex transformation policies
- **App-Independent**: no manual app-specific guidance needed to create or apply transformation policies
- **Deployable**: rewritten apps work on unrooted, unmodified Android devices, no additional software required

1.1 Threat Model

We assume that the user of a rewritten app trusts the Android platform, the transformation policy writer and rewriting process, but not the original app code. We do not attempt to hide the fact that the app has been modified from the rewritten app.

1.2 Contributions

In this paper, we make the following contributions.

- Design and implementation of an Android app rewriting system capable of replacing arbitrary method calls with custom handlers
- Flexible framework supporting the application of app-agnostic transformation policies to arbitrary Android apps
- Sample transformation policies, including the integration of fine-grained access control, improved security of network communications, and automatic localization of UI elements
- Application and evaluation of these polices to over one thousand real-world apps available via Google Play

A major contribution of our system is the ability for policy-writers to specify high-level policies that can be applied to arbitrary apps automatically without any app-specific guidance. Policy writers identify the Java methods of interest and write Java source code, or higher level functions that generate Java source, for the bytecode operations they wish to embed into rewritten apps. Our system automatically generates all handler classes, methods, and supporting code to intercept all method calls of interest, even those invoked via reflection. Our system can apply a single policy to any real-world app automatically without requiring app-specific guidance.

2. DESIGN

We change application behavior by intercepting method invocations in Android apps. In our system, we call the methods we intercept the *target methods*. Wherever the original app would have invoked a target method, our rewritten app instead calls a new method we've added to the app. We call these new methods we add to rewritten apps method *handlers*. Generally, each target method has its own corresponding handler. The *transformation policy* includes the list of target methods and the Java source code for each associated handler method. A person we call the *policy writer* creates a transformation policy that can be applied to any arbitrary app (these policies are app-agnostic). A *user of our rewriting system* provides a transformation policy and an Android app as input to our rewriting system. Our rewriting system analyzes the app, augments and applies the transformation policy without any user guidance, and produces a new, stand-alone Android app suitable for deployment to an unmodified Android device. We include a high level view of the components of our rewriting system design in Figure 1.

2.1 Approach: Method Interception

Typical policies regulate how apps interact with the sensors, data and other resources of the system. We intercept method calls because they are the primary mechanism that Android apps use to interact with the underlying device. For example, apps use method calls into the Android platform API to send and receive data over the network, access the GPS and other sensor data, read and write data to the address book and other stores, and manage the UI. Policy writers can take advantage of existing knowledge of the Android platform when designing transformation policies, rather than building policies around the implementation details of how certain app behavior may manifest itself in low-level system calls invoked by the Dalvik virtual machine.

2.2 Identifying Method Invocations

Most Android apps are written in Java, and compiled down to bytecode that runs on Android's Dalvik virtual machine. While the architecture is different, Dalvik bytecode is at a similar level of abstraction to that of the Java virtual machine. Specifically, instructions in Dalvik bytecode are clearly defined by the specification and can be interpreted without the ambiguities that complicate the analysis some other platforms such as x86 machine-code.

In Dalvik bytecode there are several instructions for method invocation. Method call instructions include the invocation type (e.g. static, direct, virtual, super), the method signature (which includes the parent class, method name, and parameter types), and the registers associated with the call. It is not always possible to identify the exact method that will be executed at runtime, due to virtual method invocation, inheritance and related concepts. For example, a method call instruction may specify a method signature for the parent class of the object on which the instruction is invoked at runtime. If the object is the instance of a class that extends the parent class and overrides the method in question, a virtual method invocation specifying `Parent->method` will execute `Child->method` at runtime. There are many cases that much be addressed when building a general system for identifying and intercepting method calls of any type, which are complicated with issues such as protected methods, final methods, and so on. So while it is easy to identify method-invocation instructions, we must adopt a number of strategies to ensure that we intercept all target method invocations despite these challenges.

2.3 Method Handler Design

Our strategy for method interception is based on our previous work for a system called I-ARM-Droid [11]. This previous work describes method interception as a means for implementing inline reference monitors in Android apps. We leverage the method interception strategy from this earlier work to build our generalized and complete rewriting system. In this section we give an overview of the strategies involved with intercepting different types of method invocations.

We intercept method invocations by identifying all of the instructions that may invoke a target method, and replace them with instructions to invoke one of our handler method and store the result in the appropriate register. These method handlers may perform any operations described in the transformation policy, which may include invoking the original method call and returning the result (e.g. after notifying or asking the user). To support this kind of dy-

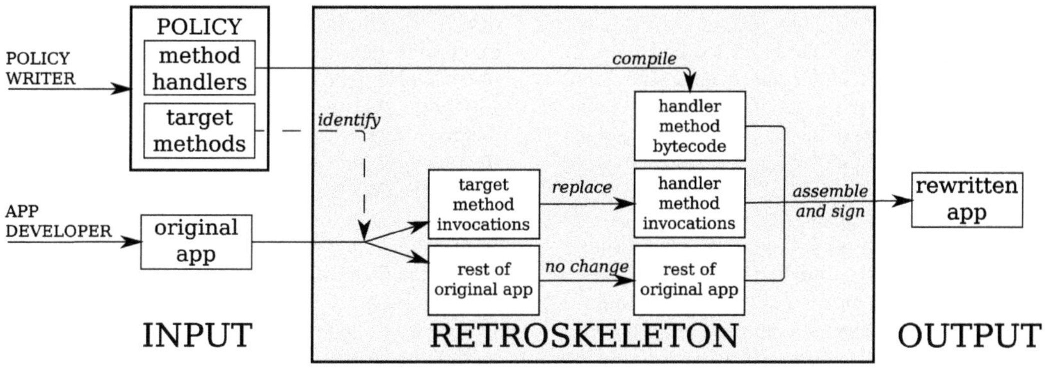

Figure 1: RetroSkeleton System Diagram

namic runtime introspection in our method handlers, our rewritten applications pass all of the original instance objects and parameters involved in the target method call to our handler methods. We require a number of different approaches to handle all of the ways target methods may be invoked.

2.3.1 Stub Methods

Static Methods We replace calls to a public, static target method (such as the `loadLibrary` method in `java.lang.System`) with a call to a static, public handler method that takes the same parameters. We call these static, public handlers *stub* methods. Our stub methods receive all of the same parameters as the original target method would have, and returns a value of the same return type. Because the stub methods receive all of the original parameters, the handler may invoke the original target method from within the handler if desired.

Instance Methods Normal instance method invocations can also be replaced with calls to stub methods. For example, imagine an app invoking the `openStream` method on a `java.net.URL` object instance. Because the `openStream` method is final, we know that the object must be a `URL` object (as opposed to some child class that has overridden the method). We replace this method invocation with an invocation of a static stub method. However, we also pass the instance on which the target method is invoked to the stub method handlers for instance target methods. In our example, our static stub handler for `openStream` receives the `URL` object as a parameter, which it may inspect and perhaps invoke the original target method from within the handler, as specified by the transformation policy.

Constructors We replace invocations of target constructors with calls to our associated static stub "factory" methods that receive the same parameters as the original target constructor. Inside these static handlers, we create an object of the appropriate type and return the object back to the original application. We also insert a move instruction that copies the reference to the new object returned from the static handler into the register on which the constructor was originally invoked.

Occasionally, this approach can result in bytecode that does not pass verification. Dalvik bytecode is register-based, with "virtual" registers local to each method. Constructors are invoked on registers containing uninitialized references to an object, and the object is initialized in place. However, with our approach, bytecode restrictions prevent us from passing uninitialized references to our factory methods, so we create a new object and return the new reference. If two registers contain the same reference to an uninitialized object, and we replace the constructor invoked on one with a call to our stub method, we update one register with the new object but the other register still refers to the uninitialized object. The bytcode verifier can detect when later instructions in the method may refer to the uninitialized object and will prevent the app from executing on an Android device.

While this issue is responsible for the majority of app failures in our evaluation (see Section 5.2.2), it is still relatively rare in practice (detected in less than 7% of apps tested with our policies). We could resolve this issue by analyzing the register usage in the same way as the bytecode verifier and copying our new object into all necessary registers, but we have not yet implemented this functionality.

2.3.2 Wedge Classes

While the simple stub-method-based approaches described above cover many cases, we need a separate technique to handle the use of inheritance and virtual method invocations frequently found in Android apps. We handle the remaining cases by analyzing the classes declared in each Android app during rewriting, and injecting classes providing handler methods into the object hierarchy of the original app.

Developers of Android apps often create new classes that extend existing classes. Assume we wish to intercept the `bind` method for the `DatagramSocket` class in the `java.net` package. Consider the case when an app developer creates a `DevSocket` class that extends `DatagramSocket`. The way we handle the invocation of the `bind` method on an instance of the developer's class depends on the goals of our policy.

Full-hierarchy interception Our system supports full-hierarchy interception, which means that for any class A with target method m in our transformation policy, our rewritten app should also intercept all invocations of m on objects of type B where B extends A. Our rewriting system analyzes all classes in an app and identifies all classes that extend target classes specified in the transformation policy. For these cases, our system can automatically add B's m to the list of target methods and generate the associated handler code and rewrite as normal.

Partial-hierarchy interception In practice, however, we find that it is often more useful to only intercept method calls that invoke the method in the parent class. For example, many Android platform methods provide the API to low-level interactions with the underlying device, such as sensor, network, and file system access. Many useful transformation policies control the app's ability to interact with the API in the framework, but are not concerned with intercepting developer methods that override target methods without invoking the original target method.

For example, if the developer creates a `DevSocket` class that extends `DatagramSocket` and overrides the `bind` method with an implementation that performs no network operations, a transformation policy controlling network access would not want to intercept this method. On the other hand, if the developer overrides `toString` with code that invokes `super.bind` then we would want to intercept this request.

We provide this functionality by generating *wedge classes* that extend non-final classes containing target methods, and include *wedge method* handlers for each target method in the parent class. In our example, our wedge class would extend `DatagramSocket` and override `bind`, implementing the handler method behavior. Our rewriting system also identifies all classes extending the target class, and modifies them to instead extend our wedge class, and replace all internal calls (e.g. via `super`) as appropriate.

In our rewritten app, invoking the `bind` method on an instance of `DevSocket` only invokes our handler when `DevSocket` has not overridden `bind`, or if the developer's class calls `super.bind` from within the class. This allows us to properly intercept all and only calls to the platform target methods, without intercepting developer methods that do not invoke our target methods. This approach is also useful for target methods that cannot be directly invoked, such as methods marked with the `protected` access modifier.

2.3.3 Use of Stub Methods and Wedge Classes

We use both the stub and wedge class approach together so all target methods are intercepted however they are invoked in the rewritten app. Static, direct, and virtual method invocations on target methods are rewritten to stub method calls. Virtual and super invocations on non-target methods that resolve to target methods are intercepted by wedge methods. We do not generate stub or wedge methods in cases where they are unnecessary. Specifically, we do not wedge final or abstract methods or create stub methods for target methods that cannot be called publicly. Section 3 will describe how we handle special cases, such as reflection.

2.4 Method Handler Behavior

As described above, transformation policies primarily contain two types of information. First, they contain a list of all target methods, identified by method name, containing class, parameter types, along with their associated data such as the return type, attributes (protected, final, etc.) and checked exceptions declared. Second, transfer policies describe the method handlers, which is what executes whenever the original app would have invoked a target method.

In order to preserve application functionality as much as possible, our handler methods return values matching the return type of the associated target method. When the target methods are replaced, the parameters (and instance object, when applicable) normally passed to the target method will be passed as parameters to the handler. Because the parameter and return types of the target methods are specified in the transformation policy, along with the appropriate attributes of the method (e.g. static, protected, final), our system generates the appropriate signatures for all stub and wedge methods. The policy writer only needs to specify the body of these handler methods.

The method handler bodies are written in Java source code. This design allows policy writers to work at the level of abstraction Android apps are normally implemented, and apply existing platform knowledge, experience and tools to guide policy development. In order to preserve app behavior when possible, we require and confirm as part of the handler method compilation process that handler methods return a value of the type the target method originally returned. We also recommend that handler methods do not throw new exceptions that the original app would not expect from an invocation of the target method, though we do not enforce this.

While policy writers may specify the source code for handler methods directly as a string, we also allow policy writers to specify functions that generate the appropriate Java source to alleviate the tedium of writing similar handlers for many methods (e.g. logging a set of target methods to the Android logging system). In many policies, method handlers may invoke the original target method, perhaps after logging the request or performing an access control check. We call the expression for invoking the original target method from within the handler method (using the handler method parameters) the *passthrough* behavior. Similarly, method handlers may wish to avoid calling the original target method, but must return a value to the application in order to preserve app behavior. Our system can also generate a reasonable default "deny" expression based on the attributes of the target method. For target methods that return void, the handler may simply `return`. A handler method could create and throw a new exception matching a type declared by the target method. If there are no better alternatives, the handler could simply return `null`. Our system allows policy writers to specify handler-generator functions that receive a map of the target method properties, auto-generated passthrough source, and auto-generated deny source at rewrite-time, and return Java source. Policy writers are free to use or ignore the default passthrough and deny behavior.

We also provide a separate namespace for policy writers to create support classes for code outside of the handler method classes. This allows policy writers to centralize and avoid duplication of code across multiple handler methods.

2.5 Generating Support Code

In Android apps, all of the Dalvik bytecode is combined into a single `classes.dex` file. All of our handler methods are specified in Java source, but without the source code for the app we cannot use the standard Android app development tools to recompile the entire app. Instead, we generate the Dalvik bytecode for our classes containing handler methods, then merge the bytecode with the rewritten application bytecode before assembling the rewritten app.

We use the Android development tools to create a new, nearly empty Android project. We generate the source code for the classes containing our handler methods into this project directory. All of our handler classes are placed into a unique namespace that will not collide with any classes in the original app. In each of our wedge classes, we also generate constructors corresponding to each constructor in the parent (target) class. Constructors are not automatically inherited, so if a wedged class is expecting a particular constructor to be present in the parent class, we must provide it in our wedge class. These constructors simply invoke the associated target classes' constructor unless otherwise specified in the transformation policy.

If the transformation policy has been augmented with target methods found in the original app, then the handler methods may have developer classes used in the parameters or return type of these target methods. If these developer classes do not exist in our support project, then the handler methods will fail to compile as the types referenced will not be found. We do not have source code for the original app's classes, so instead we simply generate *skeleton classes* with the necessary types and methods. These skeleton classes will not be included in the rewritten app, and are only used so the Android build tools can compile the source for the handlers

```
(def mytargets
 (merge
  (mktarget
   ["Ljava/net/URL;" "openStream" []]
   {:return "Ljava/io/InputStream;"
    :exceptions ["java.io.IOException"]
    :attributes #{:final}
    :stub-policy policy-logcat})

  (mktarget
   ["Landroid/app/Activity;"
    "onResume" ["Landroid/os/Bundle;"]]
   {:return "V"
    :attributes #{:protected}
    :wedge-policy policy-activity-update})))
```

Figure 2: Example Target Method Specification

```
(defn policy-logcat
  [[contain-cls method-name param-types] _]
  passthrough]

  (str "android.util.Log.i(\"RWAPP\", \""
       contain-cls "->" method-name
       "(" (join param-types) ")"
       "\";\n")
       passthrough))

(defn policy-activity-update
  [target passthrough]

  (str "rs.ActivityMon.setActivity(this);\n"
       (policy-logcat target passthrough)))
```

Figure 3: Example Policy Implementations

and generate valid Dalvik bytecode with the appropriate type signatures.

We use the official Android development tools to compile and build an app containing Dalvik bytecode for all of our handler classes. We disassemble the bytecode of this app and extract the bytecode for all of the stub, wedge and other support classes included in the policy. These classes exist in a package that will not conflict with existing code in the app being rewritten. We merge the bytecode for these classes into the app we are rewriting, and then assemble the result into a new `classes.dex` file including all of the rewritten versions of the original app code and our handler classes. We use the smali [18] Dalvik bytecode assembler/disassembler to build our modified bytecode.

2.6 Transformation Policy Design

Policy writers specify policies in Clojure [3] (a Lisp dialect). The main part of the policy is the description of the target methods and method handler generators. The targets are specified as a map of the tuple of the containing class, method name, and parameter types of the target method, to a hashmap of various attributes including the return type, checked exceptions (if any), non-default attributes (if any) and the stub and wedge policies. We include a very simple definition in Figure 2. This policy logs every time the `URL->openStream` method is invoked, and logs and updates a global reference to the current Activity whenever `Activity->onResume` is invoked. Note that `URL` class is final so its target methods are not wedged, and the `onResume` method in `Activity` is protected, so it does not have a static stub method.

The `mktarget` function generates the stub and wedge class names and other default values. While policy writers can create custom `mktarget` functions to set and automatically apply default stub and wedge policies, we specify them explicitly in our example. Stub and wedge policies are specified as functions that receive the tuple describing the target method and the passthrough source and produce the Java source code for the method handler. We also provide a helper function that passes the automatic deny code as well, though we do not show this here.

The `policy-logcat` function produces the Java source to log the containing class, method name, and parameter types to the Android logcat logging facility with the tag "RWAPP" before invoking the passthrough code. The `policy-activity-update` function produces the Java source to update global reference to the current Activity by passing the value of `this` to some of our support code, before logging the request and invoking the passthrough code. See Figure 3 for the code listing for these two policies.

3. CHALLENGES

3.1 Reflection

Android apps can invoke methods specified dynamically via Java's reflection API. While the precise methods invoked via reflection cannot always be identified statically, we *can* identify the calls to the reflection API statically. For example, we statically identify and rewrite calls to Java's `Method->invoke` reflection method even though the parameters may be determined at runtime.

Our handler methods for the reflection API perform dynamic inspection of the parameters to determine at runtime the method the app is attempting to invoke via reflection. If it matches one of our target methods, we instead invoke the associated target handler and return the result, otherwise our handler performs the requested invocation as expected. Our reflection handlers are recursive in the sense that they can handle attempts to invoke the reflection API via reflection.

3.2 Native Code

While it is relatively uncommon (estimated less than 5% by Zhou et al. [28]), Android applications may also include native code. Native code is compiled into machine-code specific to a particular architecture, and the techniques for analyzing and instrumenting this kind of code is outside the scope of this work. While we do not attempt to make any guarantees about what native code may do once invoked, we detect and prevent the invocation of native code in rewritten apps by identifying the invocations of native code. Before rewriting an app, we analyze the bytecode and extract signatures for all of the native methods. We augment the transformation policy by adding these native methods to our targets list and generate method handlers for each. For example, in our fine-grained network access control policy we automatically generate handlers that log these calls and ask the user whether to allow or deny the call to native code at runtime. We do not attempt to rewrite Android apps written entirely in native code.

3.3 Intercepting Unexamined Code

Android apps have several mechanisms for dynamically generating or loading classes, bytecode, or libraries. We include signatures for the methods that provide these capabilities to prevent rewritten apps from executing unexamined code. Policy writers can specify handlers for these methods that can block or allow these requests dynamically based on runtime decisions (e.g. input from the user).

3.4 Integration with App UI

By embedding our policies directly into our rewritten apps, we have the ability to achieve deep integration with the operation of the rewritten app. It is particularly useful to be able to integrate into the UI of the rewritten app. In Android, most operations involving the UI must be made within the main (UI) thread, with a reference to the current Context (such as the foreground Activity, Android's name for a GUI frame). These features may not be easily accessible within all method handlers (e.g. invoked from a background thread).

In order to simplify UI-based operations made from within method handlers invoked from a variety of contexts, we have implemented a small support class and set of method handlers for various Activity lifecycle methods (e.g. the `onCreate` and `onResume` methods) that maintain a globally accessible model of the current Activity displayed to the user. This context can be used to execute events on the UI thread, which we use to display notifications to the user via dialog boxes, popup messages, and integration with app UI elements in our example policies described below.

We build on this to provide a general mechanism that blocks handler methods invoked from a background thread and performing some task in the UI thread before returning. Normally, dialog boxes are requested asynchronously in Android, but we used this mechanism to allow the user to make a decision about how to handle a request in our fine-grained network access control policy. As a convenience, these UI support methods are available to all policy writers, who are also free to implement their own.

4. APPLICATIONS OF REWRITING

To demonstrate the power, flexibility and practicality of our rewriting system, we have developed several example transformation policies. In this section we describe the design and implementation of these policies. We evaluate the application of these policies to real-world apps in Section 5.

4.1 Fine-Grained Network Access Control

In Android if a user installs an app that requests the INTERNET permission then the app is granted unlimited access to make network requests. To provide users with the ability to specify more fine-grained control over the network connections an app can make, we created a transformation policy that intercepts, logs, and prevents apps from making unapproved network operations.

Target Methods Our transformation policy includes target methods for Android platform methods that perform network operations, including methods in the URL, URLConnection, Socket and related classes. Any time the original application would have made a network request, the rewritten version checks to determine if the request should be automatically allowed, denied, or if the user should be asked to decide. If the user is asked, the rewritten app presents a dialog box to the user asking whether to allow or deny the given request. If the network request is attempted in a background thread, the background thread is blocked until the user responds to the dialog window presented in the UI thread. If any request is denied (either automatically by policy, or by user decision) then our handler throws an appropriate exception (e.g. `java.io.IOException`), or returns `null` if the target method would not normally throw an exception. Rewritten apps also log all network access attempts to Android's built-in logging system `logcat`, along with the allow/deny decisions made for each request.

We also intercept network requests made via reflection (see Section 3.1), and prevent unauthorized network access by prompting the user for permission before executing any native or unexamined code (as described in Sections 3.2 and 3.3).

Support Methods We use the mechanisms described in Section 3.4 to present the user with a dialog box when needed to request permission for network requests and the execution of native and dynamically loaded code. To notify the user of requests that were automatically allowed or denied, we display a message via `Toast` message (simple, brief, noninteractive popup message).

4.2 HTTPS-Everywhere

Many popular web services support both HTTP and HTTPS connections. Unfortunately, many of these services, and apps that use these services, default to the HTTP version of these sites. This can leave users vulnerable to sniffing, session-hijacking attacks like Firesheep [9], SSL-stripping and other attacks.

The HTTPS-Everywhere [12] project provides browser extensions that rewrite HTTP web URLs to HTTPS alternatives for many popular services. Often the URL rewriting involves more than simply changing the protocol to `https`. For example, some sites serve static content from Amazon's S3 storage service. While original domain may only serve content via HTTP, the same content can be retrieved via HTTPS from the Amazon S3 servers. The HTTPS-Everywhere contributors maintain a set of manually-specified rewriting rules for many major websites that map resources offered over HTTP to known HTTPS alternatives.

HTTPS-Everywhere is implemented in a browser context where there are well-defined extension systems capable of rewriting URLs. However, this does not help Android apps that make requests directly to these web services, and to our knowledge no such feature is available for Android apps. Researchers such as Fahl et al. [16] show that many Android apps fail to use HTTPS even when it is available. We can use our rewriting system to produce apps that use the HTTPS version of URLs when available using the URL-rewriting rules from the HTTPS-Everywhere project.

Target Method Handlers We have ported popular URL-rewriting rules from the HTTPS-Everywhere project into support methods we add to rewritten apps. We created a transformation policy that intercepts many platform methods for creating network connections to a URL. In the handlers for these network API methods, we replace (at runtime) the destination with the HTTPS alternative when we have an applicable HTTPS-Everywhere rule.

4.3 User Notification of Background Activity

We can write transformation policies that make use of our deep integration with the rewritten app. We have written a transformation policy designed to inform users of background network requests by augmenting the app UI itself.

Target Methods Handlers In this transformation policy, when we intercept a network request we update the count of requests and display the new total in the title of the current Activity on the screen. We use the network target methods from the fine-grained access control policy and keep track of the current Activity using the mechanism described in Section 3.4. After updating the total, our handler methods create a new Runnable task to execute in the main thread and update the app UI.

4.4 Automatic App Localization

Our rewriting system can also be used to perform some forms of localization and internationalization automatically. We have created a policy that rewrites apps to translate text in app UI widgets via an online web translation service.

Target Methods This transformation policy targets the `setText` and similar methods in some common Android UI classes, including `TextView`, `Button`, `CheckBox`. We intercept `setText` API calls that take strings as well as string asset resource identifiers. We pass the specified string, looking up the string resource if required, to our translation code in our method handlers. One benefit of our approach, as opposed to simply translating all strings found within an Android app, is that our rewritten apps will also translate content generated dynamically, or retrieved from external sources such as the network.

Method Handlers Whenever the original app would normally set the text in one of these widgets, we intercept these calls and translate the text via a web-based translation service, updating the widget with the translated text. Apps usually set the text in UI widgets from within the Android UI (main) thread, so rewritten apps will invoke our handlers in the UI thread. Regular `setText` calls finish quickly, but delaying the UI thread while translating each string via network request would impact the responsiveness of the app. Our system allows us to specify handlers that handle this gracefully.

Asynchronous Design In order to maintain UI responsiveness, our handlers return immediately after creating a new background task to perform the translation. After receiving the translation from the web service, this background task updates the widget with the new text asynchronously, queuing the update task to run back in the UI thread. This means that the app will remain responsive to user and other events while the translation occurs, and the UI will be updated asynchronously as translation results are received.

Our current implementation performs the translation using a simple web service we have created to test our functionality, though the handlers could be updated to function with an existing provider such as Google or Bing. Of course, the translations will only be as good as can be provided by the translation service. We note that when applying a transformation policy that includes network requests, the rewritten app must include the Android INTERNET permission, so this permission must be added if it is not already included in the original manifest.

4.5 Auto-Patching Apps

Our rewriting system can also be used to automatically update apps to run on an updated or different environment. For example, we can write a transformation policy that replaces calls to one API with another. To demonstrate this capability, we created a simple policy that replaces calls to some of the Wallpaper API deprecated in Android version 2.0 to the equivalent functionality provided by the new WallpaperManager. We applied this policy to apps written for the old API and observed that the rewritten apps used the new API. Our system makes it very easy to write these simple policies and have confidence that the target methods will be intercepted, no matter whether the methods are invoked directly or via reflection.

5. EVALUATION

5.1 Evaluation Set Selection

We evaluated the feasibility of our rewriting system for use with real-world apps by testing with randomly selected apps downloaded from Google Play. We have an automated system that crawls and downloads free apps from Google Play, and we selected our apps for evaluation from this set. Some apps available on Google Play fail to install or run, or require specific hardware, so to ensure we would have at least one thousand working apps in our evaluation set we first selected 1200 apps at random. We then discarded apps that were invalid, incompatible or otherwise failed to install or launch on an Android emulator running Android version 4.2. This left us with 1119 apps for our evaluation set. Upon examination we found that of these 1119 apps, only 49 (less than 4.4%) contain native code.

Policy	Total Apps	Failure		Success	
		#	%	#	%
Network	1119	27	2.4%	1092	97.6%
Notify	1119	0	0%	1119	100%
HTTPS	1119	0	0%	1119	100%
Localization	1119	0	0%	1119	100%

Table 1: Successfully rewritten apps

5.2 Rewriting Real-World Apps

We rewrote and tested each of the 1119 apps four different times: once for each of the four general transformation policies described in Section 4. While we confirmed the functionality of our Wallpaper API replacement transformation policy on a few apps known to use the deprecated API, this API was not commonly used in our set of apps so we do not further explore its application here. In this section, we abbreviate the names of the four general transformation policies as follows:

- **Network**: fine-grained network access control
- **HTTPS**: apply HTTPS-Everywhere rules to replace http requests with https equivalents when possible
- **Notify**: display background network activity in app
- **Localization**: translate UI widget content via web service

5.2.1 Rewriting Evaluation

We applied each of our four general sample transformation policies to all of these apps to produce four sets of rewritten apps. Table 1 includes the number of apps that were successfully rewritten when applying each transformation policy. Success at this stage means that the support and handler methods were able to be compiled and integrated into the new app, producing a complete, installable Android Package file (APK).

The Notify, HTTPS, and Localization policies were successfully applied to all apps. The only issues detected in the rewriting stage were when applying the network transformation policy to apps that included native code. Because our network policy is designed to prevent any unauthorized network request, applying this policy automatically adds target methods for each native method in the app. When compiling the handler methods our system generates skeleton classes for the necessary developer classes, as described in Section 2.5. All of the errors in rewriting occur because the target app containing native methods has been obfuscated so that the class and package names in the app are no longer valid Java identifiers (e.g. naming collisions between package and class names). We detect this error and halt the rewriting process, rather than producing a rewritten app that we cannot guarantee has captured all app-specific native methods.

In theory we could detect and resolve these collisions and rewrite our handler code after compilation to match the names used in the rewritten app. We have not yet implemented this feature as it is only necessary when rewriting apps obfuscated in this way with policies that augment the target method list with developer methods. In our evaluation set occurs rarely (2.4% of apps), so we simply detect this case so our system will not produce apps that appear complete but have not been completely rewritten.

Policy	Total Apps	Failure #	Failure %	Success #	Success %
Network	1092	6	0.5%	1086	99.5%
Notify	1119	7	0.6%	1112	99.4%
HTTPS	1119	76	6.8%	1043	93.2%
Localization	1119	4	0.4%	1115	99.6%

Table 2: Rewritten apps that successfully verify and run

5.2.2 *App Usage Evaluation*

We ran each rewritten app in the Android emulator and manually verified whether rewritten apps pass the bytecode verification stage, launch and begin to execute as expected. We ran each app using the Android monkeyrunner tool and took a screenshot of the running app. In this test, "success" means that the app passed the bytecode verification and ran without crashing, which we confirmed by examining the system and application logs and the screenshot of the running app. While we do not attempt to achieve full code coverage, during testing each successfully rewritten app executed at least one of our added handler methods. General techniques for automatically verifying the behavior of Android apps is an open and difficult problem [23] and may depend on the desired outcome of rewriting. For example, should blocking network access in an app that requires be considered "breaking" the app?

The Network, Notify and Localization policies each had a success rate of over 99%, and the HTTPS policy had a success rate of over 93%. The exact results for each policy can be found in Table 2.

The majority (82%) of the failures occur when Android performs the bytecode verification across the entire app at launch and detects the issue described in Section 2.3.1, when multiple registers in the same method reference the same uninitialized object and a target constructor is invoked on one of these registers. The Android verifier detects this condition in the bytecode before running the application, preventing the rewritten applications with uninitialized registers from executing. It would be possible to perform the same bytecode checks as the verifier at rewrite time and handle this condition by updating both register references, though we have not yet implemented this functionality.

In our evaluation set we observed that the HTTPS policy has the highest failure rate due to its many, frequently-used constructors in the list of target methods. The Network, Notify and Localization policies perform better in our tests as they intercept fewer frequently-used constructors, with mostly non-constructor target methods. For example, these policies intercept the `openStream` method rather than the `java.net.URL` constructor.

The remaining (18%) run failures came from issues involving the application of our transformation policies on apps with unusual characteristics. For example, our localization policy creates a new background thread for each new translation task. While this makes the transformation policy simple to write, apps that attempt to set a large number of widgets at once may cause our rewritten apps to hit the thread pool limit. In our tests our sample policies work well in most cases, and their designs could be made more robust to further improve the success rate.

5.2.3 *Transformation Policy Evaluation*

In addition to evaluating the rewriting and execution of each app, we also manually verified the functionality of the transformation policies in the rewritten apps.

Network For the network policy, we observed the interception of network requests, dialog boxes presented to the user, and policy decisions applied to network requests.

Policy	Original Size	Mean Increase	
Network	515.3 KiB	38.9 KiB	7.54%
Notify	526.3 KiB	30.8 KiB	5.85%
HTTPS	526.3 KiB	29.6 KiB	5.62%
Localization	526.3 KiB	19.6 KiB	3.72%

Table 3: Mean impact on uncompressed `classes.dex`

Notify For the policy notifying the user of background network requests we ran and confirmed the integration and display of this information in the title bar of the current Activity.

HTTPS In our policy we include the URL-rewriting rules from the HTTPS-Everywhere project for several popular sites, including AdMob, Blogger, Google App Engine, Foursquare, Doubleclick, Reddit and related domains. We confirmed the rewriting of http network destinations to https requests via tcpdump when running the apps in the emulator. We transformed http requests to associated https requests in 226 apps (20.2%).

Localization To simplify testing and avoid being tied to any particular provider, we created a simple web service with a to simulate an online translation service. This service receives a string via POST message and returns a translated string. In deployment situations this could pass the string to a web translation service such as those provided by Google or Bing. However, for testing our service returns the string with sentinel prefix and suffix values for easy identification in rewritten apps. We observed our transformed strings in the expected widgets in the rewritten apps, and confirmed the operation of our transformation policy by logging the requests made to our web service.

5.2.4 *Impact on App Code Size*

We add our handler code as separate methods, rather than injecting our custom behavior inline at every point the original application invoked a target method. This means that even if our handlers are complex and large, they are only included in the app once. Whenever the original app invokes a target method, we replace this single instruction with only one or two instructions to invoke our handler instead (depending on the invocation type). So, the app code increases linearly with the number of handlers in the policy rather than with the number of times an app invokes a target method.

Android apps are packaged in APK files, which contain all of the bytecode and assets for the application. Inside this compressed archive, the `classes.dex` file contains all of the Dalvik bytecode for the application. We measure the impact of the policies described in this paper on the size of an app by measuring the size increase of the uncompressed `classes.dex` file. We note that the `classes.dex` file is compressed in the rewritten APK, further minimizing the impact of our added code.

Table 3 lists the mean size of the `classes.dex` file when extracted from the original (compressed) APKs, and the sizes of the new `classes.dex` files after rewriting but before recompression. Our system successfully applied the Network policy to only 97.6% of the apps, so we compare the sizes of the rewritten `classes.dex` files only to those in apps that were successfully rewritten. The bytecode added scales linearly with the number of target methods specified in the policy and the sizes of the method handlers. This means that a policy that has little variance in the number of target methods specified or handler sizes will add approximately the same amount of bytecode to each app.

Table 4 lists the size analysis on the complete APKs produced by our rewriting system. These APKs are the actual files that are

Policy	Original Size	Mean Increase	
Network	1915.4 KiB	11.03 KiB	0.58%
Notify	1987.1 KiB	9.19 KiB	0.46%
HTTPS	1987.1 KiB	9.66 KiB	0.49%
Localization	1987.1 KiB	7.09 KiB	0.36%

Table 4: Overall impact on APK size (compared to mean size of recompressed original APKs)

deployed to Android devices. We discovered that because several APKs in our evaluation set had been poorly compressed, our system actually produced some rewritten APKs that were smaller than their originals. To discount the effect of different compressions, Table 4 compares the sizes of APKs before and after rewriting both of which were compressed in the same way by us. As in Table 3, we compare our rewritten APKs only to those in the original set that were successfully rewritten.

5.3 App Performance

The impact of our modifications of the performance of a rewritten app depends greatly on the behavior of the handler methods. However, the only overhead required by our design is the addition of one new method call for each target method invocation in the original app. In [11] we describe our method interception strategy in more detail and perform a microbenchmark test to measure the overhead of adding an additional method invocation for each target method call. We applied a very simple transformation policy that intercepts the `StringBuilder->append` method, with a handler that only invokes the original method, to an app we created that performs one million appends. We ran the original and rewritten versions of the app on a HTC Thunderbolt phone running Android 2.3.4. We measured the run time of each and in this test executing our method handler for each target method invocation adds an average of less than 0.2 microseconds per call. Due to the minor impact on resource usage, this overhead is also unlikely to make a measurable impact on power consumption on the device. Rewritten apps only pay this performance penalty when executing a target method, as the remainder of the app code is left unmodified.

While the inherent overhead of our method interception is low, the overall impact on app performance depends on the functionality of the handler methods and the target methods intercepted. The overhead added by many of our handlers is marginal relative to the original target method call (e.g. logging a network request method). When more time-consuming handlers are required, our deep integration into the app allows for sophisticated policies that minimize the impact on app performance (e.g. our localization policy translates UI text in background threads and updates the UI asynchronously). In general, well-written method handlers will not impact the app performance more than if the original app had implemented the desired behavior. Policy writers can weigh the performance impact against the value of the added functionality.

5.4 Rewriting Speed

Apps can be rewritten quickly on a normal desktop PC. On average, a normal desktop machine with a 2.66 GHz Intel Core 2 Quad CPU (Q9450) with 4 GB of RAM and a single 7200 RPM hard disk our system can rewrite an apk in less than 5 seconds. This is the time required for the entire end-to-end rewriting process, which includes disassembling the original app, analyzing the contents of the target app, generating the Java source for all target method handlers, compiling the handler code, rewriting the app bytecode and merging in the handler code, reassembling and signing the rewritten app. The bytecode rewriting is performed in a single pass, which scales linearly with the size of the app bytecode.

6. DISCUSSION

6.1 Transformation Policy Development

While users may develop transformation policies themselves, it seems more likely that most users will use community developed, vetted, and maintained policies, much in the way that communities have evolved to produce and maintain policies for Adblock Plus [1], NoScript [6], HTTPS-Everywhere [12], and similar security-focused browser extensions. Policy writers can use static and dynamic techniques to analyze the Android platform (such as those described in by Felt et al. [17]) to ensure proper coverage of functionality across the Android platform.

Our system only requires handler methods to declare the same checked exceptions and return type as the target methods, leaving policy writers with the power to modify the state and operation of the app in dramatic ways. This allows for powerful transformations to app behavior, but policy writers must carefully consider the effects of their modifications. It is possible for transformation policies to change the internal state of an app in ways the app does not expect or handle gracefully (e.g. by throwing an unexpected runtime exception). We leave it to the policy writers and users of the rewriting system to decide what changes to app behavior are appropriate and necessary to achieve their rewriting goals.

6.2 Transformation Policy Application

Our system could be deployed in a number of ways. Users may download Android apps and run the rewriting tools themselves to produce a new app to install on their device. Alternatively, this rewriting system may be provided as part of an online service that rewrites Android apps on the fly as requested by a user. Corporate environments may rewrite apps before allowing installation on a device (e.g. via a proxy as apps are downloaded to the device, or by providing a private "market" of rewritten apps).

Imagine an enterprise that requires all apps to be rewritten before installed on a corporate device. This rewriting process could allow the enterprise to mitigate the risk of installing apps developed by untrusted third parties. This enterprise could provide a trusted rewriting service that applies a trusted transformation policy to any arbitrary app requested by a user. This trusted policy can be applied to many apps, so it seems more feasible for an enterprise to maintain a single trusted transformation policy than to develop all of the apps that users desire.

Android apps include a digital signature from the developer over the contents of the app. Of course, because rewriting the app changes the content, the original signature will not be valid for the rewritten version of the app. The rewriting system can generate a new signature for the rewritten app. In this way, users can verify that the rewritten app was created by a trusted rewriting service and was delivered by without tampering.

Rewriting requires just a few seconds on a normal desktop PC, which is fast enough to support on-line rewriting before installation on users devices. While our current rewriting system runs on traditional PCs, it may be possible to perform the rewriting entirely on the Android device itself.

6.3 Advanced Policies

Except when replacing calls to parent classes in wedged classes, our current policies replace each target method with the same handler globally. However, it is possible for us to use our system to differentiate method calls by call site. For example, given the ability to identify ad libraries in apps, either by package name or class properties, we could rewrite apps to block all network requests made from an ad library and allow all network requests made from the rest of the app. This functionality cannot be provided by solutions lacking the deep app integration provided by our rewriting system (e.g. an ad-blocking proxy cannot distinguish between requests made from ad vs. app code). The blocking of ad requests could be performed as in our fine-grained network access control policy, as well-written ad libraries should gracefully handle what it sees as a failed network request. We leave the exploration of policies that distinguish based on call site to future work.

6.4 Legal and Ethical Discussion

We designed RetroSkeleton to be a powerful tool to enable flexible rewriting of apps. Like many other tools, RetroSkeleton may be used for a variety of purposes. While many uses benefit app markets, developers, and users, some may not. The legality of reverse engineering, modifying, and redistributing apps depends on the jurisdiction and contract (e.g., EULA) of the involved parties. Technically savvy users could disassemble, modify, and repackage Android apps without RetroSkeleton, so all the operations performed by RetroSkeleton could be applied manually when RetroSkeleton is unavailable. Furthermore, many effects of RetroSkeleton can also be achieved by other means, such as blocking network requests with a proxy instead of the Fine-Grained Network Access Control policy described in Section 4.1.

Currently, even markets that vet apps before admission make only a binary decision between accepting or rejecting an app. Markets could improve by using automated app rewriting to enforce policies on submitted apps, thus acquiring an additional level of control over the quality of the apps that they distribute to their users. Developers may benefit if app rewriting adds functionality that their users desire without having to implement those features themselves, or in ways that their users find more trustworthy. Users may be more likely to install an app if it has been rewritten using a policy provided by a trusted party to give them additional control or guarantees about its behavior.

On the downside, rewritten apps may restrict behavior that developers or ad providers depend on for revenue (e.g. delivering targeted advertisements). As a result, developers may refuse to distribute their apps on markets that rewrite apps. Users of rewritten apps may not know if undesirable behavior in apps results from rewriting.

While developers may not bypass the interception mechanisms of RetroSkeleton, they are free to detect modifications and change the behavior of their apps (e.g., refusing to run) when rewritten. We make no attempt to hide our modifications from rewritten apps (Section 1.1). Developers can easily check if their apps have been rewritten, e.g. by comparing a checksum of the code with the expected value. Also rewritten apps are signed by the rewriter, rather than the original developer.

7. RELATED WORK

7.1 Modifying the Android Platform

Android includes a permission system that limits apps to categories of functionality declared at install time. Android apps declare the coarse-grained categories of functionality they wish to use in their application manifest. If the user installs the app, the app is granted unlimited access to all data and functionality requested in the manifest. These permissions are very coarse-grained (e.g. a single "INTERNET" permission for network access), and once installed, the user cannot control or constrain what the app does with the granted permissions.

Finding the Android permission system lacking, many researchers modified the open-source Android platform to develop custom builds of Android [19, 29, 22, 8]. Many of these, such as Apex [22] and TISSA [29], are designed to improve the security and privacy controls on Android, modeled around the permission-based methods. While the Android platform is open source, many drivers for hardware support are not, and installing custom Android builds may require rooting the device, voiding the warranty, and/or violating the carrier's terms of service. This makes it infeasible for most normal users to update or modify the firmware or platform to provide additional controls or functionality.

It is also difficult for these custom builds to keep up with new versions to the Android platform, and to support all hardware devices, as open-source versions of device drivers may not be available. In contrast, using our system rewritten apps may be deployed to any stock Android device. In addition to these deployment issues, policies integrated into the platform are far less flexible than our app-specific approach. It is relatively difficult to extend platform-based policies to add new capabilities, and policies in the platform will apply to all apps on the device. Our approach can apply different policies to different apps, and we can easily add and apply new policies at any point.

7.2 Rewriting Android Apps

Jeon et al. [21] developed a system to provide finer-grained permissions for Android. Their work is based on a specialized replacement for some privacy-sensitive APIs and use Dalvik bytecode rewriting to modify apps to use their replacement API. Their replacement APIs fulfill the requests using inter-process communication to shuttle the request to an independent service, also installed and running on the device, which contains all permissions. Their approach shares many advantages with ours, in that it requires no modifications to the underlying Android platform. While their goals are focused on providing these fine-grained permission methods, our work is a more general system capable of replacing any methods of interest with any other custom behavior. We provide a new policy language for high-level app-agnostic transformation policies as well as the analysis and rewriting infrastructure to apply them without manual guidance. We believe our system could be used to implement their approach by targeting the same API calls and providing handlers that perform the inter-process communication to their separate service. Of course, our system is flexible enough to also support other kinds of policies, such as those in Section 4, that embed new behavior into the app itself and do not require inter-process communication to handle intercepted calls.

Other researchers have used app rewriting for even more specialized transformations. Reynaud et al. [24] discovered vulnerabilities in Google In-App Billing by rewriting applications that communicated with the Google Market app to bind to their own fake Market app instead. We believe that RetroSkeleton is general and flexible enough for future researchers to use to perform these interesting investigations without having to develop independent, specialized rewriting systems.

7.3 Alternate Android Approaches

Xu et al. [27] have developed Aurasium, which provides reference monitor capabilities by repackaging Android apps to use a custom version of libc. Their system can enforce security policies by interposing on low-level system calls, and performing their security checks from within the replaced libc call. In contrast, our approach allows policy writers to specify what they want to intercept at the method call level, rather than requiring knowledge of how these operations manifest themselves as low-level libc calls. Furthermore, policy writers specify the new behavior they wish to add as Java code that operates on the Java objects passed to their target method, rather than on the low-level data available within libc functions. Aurasium is designed for reference-monitor capabilities, and we can achieve similar results by intercepting calls to sensitive methods, such as those that require the "INTERNET" permission. However, RetroSkeleton can be used for many other ways, such as app UI augmentation or behavior modification like our auto-localization functionality, which would be far more difficult to achieve from within a replaced libc.

Adblock Plus for Android [2] has recently been released and provides a mechanism for blocking many ads from being retrieved by Android apps. Adblock Plus for Android works by installing an Android service on the device that runs a local proxy server in the background at all times. Then the Android device is configured to use the Adblock Plus local proxy server as the proxy for network connections. This local proxy server blocks requests to known ad services. Our rewriting system may be used to similarly provide ad blocking capabilities, with a number of advantages. First, we can apply different ad-blocking policies for each app, while the Adblock Plus proxy cannot distinguish between call sites. We can rewrite and redistribute apps without Adblock Plus's requirements of a system with manual proxy-specification support (Android 3.1 or newer, custom Android build or a rooted device). Rewritten apps also would not require a proxy service running in the background consuming resources as we can integrate the blocking decisions into the new app. We may be able to provide more advanced blocking, such as blocking network requests from ad libraries but permitting requests made from within the main app, as discussed in Section 6.3.

7.4 Java-based Approaches

While Dalvik bytecode differs from Java bytecode, Dalvik bytecode is created from Java. As a result, tools such as ded [13] and dex2jar [4] have been created to convert Dalvik bytecode into Java bytecode. This approach allows for the use of Java-based analysis tools such as WALA [7] on the resulting Java bytecode. This conversion is nontrivial and frequently produces code that can not be assembled back into a functional Android app, as reported in [24]. While this does not matter for pure analysis-based studies, our goal is to produce valid Android apps after rewriting so we operate on the Dalvik bytecode without conversion.

While the Dalvik and Java virtual machines differ in many ways (e.g. register-based instead of stack-based), some techniques used to rewrite Java bytecode apply to our approach to Dalvik rewriting. Java bytecode instrumentation by Chander et al. [10] involves invocation and class substitution to produce modified Java programs. While our rewriting system works on Dalvik rather than Java bytecode, our stub and wedge class approach for low-level method interception is similar to their Java-based system with respect to the class hierarchy of the rewritten software. RetroSkeleton uses this low-level mechanism to perform aspects of the method interception, and provides a new high-level abstraction that allows policy writers to create policies that can be applied to any app. Without a system automating this work, rewriters must identify and create new and different wedge classes for each rewritten app, depending on the classes used and defined by the original app developer. RetroSkeleton analyzes the app and target methods in the policy to automatically generate the appropriate stub and wedge classes with the necessary properties, and modifies the app class hierarchy as needed. This automated analysis and generation is critical for real-world use given the tremendous number and variety of Android apps available.

Rudys and Wallach [25] apply many of these ideas to develop a more complete reference monitor capable of preventing infinite loops and providing transactional rollback to revert changes made in an aborted operation. While our goals are different, their work demonstrates the power and flexibility of bytecode rewriting to provide advanced functionality to existing apps.

Erlingsson and Schneider used inline reference monitors (IRM) for enforcing security properties in Java applications [15]. The Java IRM design detailed in [14] highlights the many benefits of integrating code into the target application itself, such as easier observation of the internal state of the application. Because our approach embeds all changes entirely into the rewritten apps, our system provides these same benefits to policy writers. Because RetroSkeleton can interpose on method calls of interest, it can be used to embed reference monitor functionality into Android apps, but this is only one potential application of our system. Our system allows policy writers to just as easily write policies that add functionality other than security checks, such as adding new UI behavior.

8. CONCLUSION

In this paper, we have presented the design and implementation of a flexible Android app rewriting framework. This framework leverages the relatively uniform way that Android apps are implemented to provide users with the capability to apply powerful and complex policies to arbitrary apps without any app-specific guidance. Our system rewrites apps to insert, remove and modify app behavior, producing rewritten apps that can be deployed to stock Android devices.

We have demonstrated the power of this approach by implementing policies including fine-grained network access control, HTTPS-Everywhere-like capabilities, informing users of hidden app behavior, and automated UI-element localization. We applied these policies to more than one thousand real-world apps from Google Play with a more than 93% success rate for all policies.

9. ACKNOWLEDGMENTS

This paper is based upon work supported by the National Science Foundation under Grant No. 1018964.

10. REFERENCES

[1] Adblock Plus. `http://adblockplus.org`. Accessed: 2012/12/10.

[2] Adblock Plus for Android. `http://adblockplus.org/en/android-about`. Accessed: 2012/12/10.

[3] Clojure. `http://clojure.org`. Accessed: 2012/12/10.

[4] dex2jar: Tools to work with Android .dex and Java .class files. `http://code.google.com/p/dex2jar/`. Accessed: 2012/12/10.

[5] Google Play. `https://play.google.com/store`. Accessed: 2012/12/10.

[6] NoScript Firefox Extension. `http://noscript.net`. Accessed: 2012/12/10.

[7] T.J. Watson Libraries for Analysis (WALA). `http://wala.sourceforge.net`, 2012. Accessed: 2012/12/10.

[8] A. R. Beresford, A. Rice, N. Skehin, and R. Sohan. MockDroid: Trading Privacy for Application Functionality on Smartphones. In *HotMobile*, 2011.

[9] E. Butler. Firesheep. `http://codebutler.com/firesheep/`. Accessed: 2012/12/10.

[10] A. Chander, J. Mitchell, and I. Shin. Mobile Code Security by Java Bytecode Instrumentation. In *DARPA Information Survivability Conference & Exposition II, 2001. DISCEX'01. Proceedings*, volume 2, pages 27–40. IEEE, 2001.

[11] B. Davis, B. Sanders, A. Khodaverdian, and H. Chen. I-ARM-Droid: A Rewriting Framework for In-App Reference Monitors for Android Applications. In *IEEE Mobile Security Technologies (MoST)*, May 2012.

[12] EFF. HTTPS-Everywhere. `https://www.eff.org/https-everywhere/`. Accessed: 2012/12/10.

[13] W. Enck, D. Octeau, P. McDaniel, and S. Chaudhuri. A Study of Android Application Security. In *Proceedings of the 20th USENIX Security Symposium*, August 2011.

[14] U. Erlingsson. *The Inlined Reference Monitor Approach to Security Policy Enforcement*. PhD thesis, Cornell University, 2003.

[15] U. Erlingsson and F. Schneider. IRM Enforcement of Java Stack Inspection. In *Security and Privacy, 2000. S P 2000. Proceedings. 2000 IEEE Symposium on*, pages 246 –255, 2000.

[16] S. Fahl, M. Harbach, T. Muders, L. Baumgärtner, B. Freisleben, and M. Smith. Why Eve and Mallory Love Android: An Analysis of Android SSL (In)Security. In *Proceedings of the 2012 ACM Conference on Computer and Communications Security*, CCS '12, pages 50–61. ACM, 2012.

[17] A. Felt, E. Chin, S. Hanna, D. Song, and D. Wagner. Android Permissions Demystified. In *Proceedings of the 18th ACM Conference on Computer and Communications Security*, pages 627–638. ACM, 2011.

[18] B. Gruver. smali: An Assembler/Disassembler for Android's dex Format. `https://code.google.com/p/smali/`. Accessed: 2012/12/10.

[19] P. Hornyack, S. Han, J. Jung, S. Schechter, and D. Wetherall. These Aren't the Droids You're Looking For: Retrofitting Android to Protect Data from Imperious Applications. In *Proceedings of the 18th ACM Conference on Computer and Communications Security*, CCS '11, pages 639–652. ACM, 2011.

[20] IDC. International Data Corporation Worldwide Quarterly Mobile Phone Tracker. `http://www.idc.com/getdoc.jsp?containerId=prUS23638712`. Accessed: 2012/12/10.

[21] J. Jeon, K. K. Micinski, J. A. Vaughan, A. Fogel, N. Reddy, J. S. Foster, and T. Millstein. Dr. Android and Mr. Hide: Fine-Grained Permissions in Android Applications. In *Proceedings of the Second ACM Workshop on Security and Privacy in Smartphones and Mobile Devices*, SPSM '12, pages 3–14. ACM, 2012.

[22] M. Nauman, S. Khan, and X. Zhang. Apex: Extending Android Permission Model and Enforcement with User-Defined Runtime Constraints. In *Proceedings of the 5th ACM Symposium on Information, Computer and Communications Security*, pages 328–332. ACM, 2010.

[23] V. Rastogi, Y. Chen, and W. Enck. AppsPlayground: Automatic Security Analysis of Smartphone Applications. In *Proceedings of the Third ACM Conference on Data and Application Security and Privacy*, CODASPY '13, pages 209–220, New York, NY, USA, 2013. ACM.

[24] D. Reynaud, D. Song, T. Magrino, and R. S. Edward Wu. FreeMarket: Shopping for Free in Android Applications. In *Proceedings of the 19th Annual Network & Distributed System Security Symposium*, Feb. 2012.

[25] A. Rudys and D. Wallach. Enforcing Java Run-Time Properties Using Bytecode Rewriting. *Software Security Theories and Systems*, pages 271–276, 2003.

[26] B. Womack. Google Says 700,000 Applications Available for Android. `http://buswk.co/PDb2tm`. Accessed: 2012/12/10.

[27] R. Xu, H. Saïdi, and R. Anderson. Aurasium: Practical Policy Enforcement for Android Applications. In *Proceedings of the 21st USENIX Conference on Security Symposium*, Security'12, pages 27–27. USENIX Association, 2012.

[28] Y. Zhou, Z. Wang, W. Zhou, and X. Jiang. Hey, You, Get Off of My Market: Detecting Malicious Apps in Official and Alternative Android Markets. In *Proceedings of the 19th Annual Network & Distributed System Security Symposium*, Feb. 2012.

[29] Y. Zhou, X. Zhang, X. Jiang, and V. Freeh. Taming Information-Stealing Smartphone Applications (on Android). *Trust and Trustworthy Computing*, pages 93–107, 2011.

SmartSynth: Synthesizing Smartphone Automation Scripts from Natural Language

Vu Le
Univ. of California at Davis
vmle@ucdavis.edu

Sumit Gulwani
Microsoft Research, Redmond
sumitg@microsoft.com

Zhendong Su
Univ. of California at Davis
su@cs.ucdavis.edu

ABSTRACT

This paper presents SmartSynth, a novel end-to-end programming system for synthesizing smartphone automation scripts from natural language descriptions. Our approach is unique in two key aspects. First, it involves a carefully designed domain-specific language that incorporates standard constructs from smartphone programming platforms to balance its expressivity and the ability to synthesize scripts from natural language. Second, our synthesis algorithm integrates techniques from two research areas: (1) It infers the set of components and their partial dataflow relations from the natural language description using techniques from the Natural Language Processing community; and (2) It uses techniques from the Program Synthesis community to infer missing dataflow relations via type-based synthesis and constructs scripts in a process akin to reverse parsing. SmartSynth also performs conversational interactions with the user when multiple top-ranked scripts exist or it cannot map part of the description to any component. Evaluated on 50 tasks collected from smartphone help forums, our system produces the intended scripts in real time for over 90% of the 640 natural language descriptions obtained from a user study for those tasks. SmartSynth has also been adapted to TouchDevelop, an end user-targeted programming environment on mobile platforms, with very promising results (see `http://www.cs.ucdavis.edu/~su/smartsynth.mp4` for a video demo). We believe that SmartSynth is a step toward fully personalized use of smartphones' increasingly rich functionalities.

Categories and Subject Descriptors

D.1.2 [**Programming Techniques**]: Automatic Programming; D.3.2 [**Programming Languages**]: Language Classifications—*Design languages*; H.5.2 [**Information Interfaces and Presentation**]: User Interfaces—*Natural language*

General Terms

Algorithms, Design, Languages, Human Factors

Keywords

Program synthesis, natural language processing, smartphone, automation script

1. INTRODUCTION

We have entered a new era for computing in recent years with the sharp increase in availability and popularity of multi-functional mobile devices. These devices are equipped with more and more sensors, which radically multiplies the ways people interact with them. Indeed, they have led to an enormous number of novel applications and interesting challenges for programming [34] and finding personalized applications [42].

In this paper, we study the problem of developing smartphone automation scripts, those that execute some tasks automatically under certain conditions (*e.g.*, the phone turns off network connections automatically when its battery is low, or the phone sends the user's spouse a text saying "Kids are dropped" when she is at the location of their kids' school). The abundance of such scripts on popular smartphone platforms like Locale [39], Tasker [7], and On{x} [29] motivate our problem domain.

The current state of the art in end-user programming of smartphones is far from satisfactory. General-purpose languages such as Java, C#, and Objective C are clearly not suitable for most end user. The other alternative is visual programming systems such as App Inventor [30] and Tasker [7], which visualize programming constructs into building blocks. Users program by identifying blocks and composing them visually. Although these systems are more user-friendly, they still require end users to consciously think about programming like typical programmers, such as introducing variables and deciding when/how to use conditionals, loops, or events.

Because of the deluge of mobile devices and their underlying systems, we believe in the promising direction toward *general* programming systems with *natural* interfaces for meeting end users' needs. Two notable examples are VoiceActions [10] and Siri [5] for controlling smartphones via speech. However, they only provide support for limited smartphone features. Siri, for example, only matches speech to pre-defined patterns. Our goal is to be (1) *natural* so that users can interact with the system through natural language (NL) and (2) *general* so that, unlike Siri, our system does not simply match NL descriptions to pre-defined patterns.

SmartSynth To this end, we introduce SmartSynth, a new end-to-end *NL-based programming system* for synthesizing smartphone scripts. The key ***conceptual novelty*** of SmartSynth is the methodology to decompose the problem into: (1) designing a domain-specific language (DSL) to capture automation scripts users commonly need, and (2) combining natural language processing (NLP) and program synthesis [11] techniques to synthesize scripts in the DSL from NL. Our ***technical novelties*** include: (1) a carefully designed DSL that incorporates standard constructs from smartphone programming platforms and balances its expressivity and the feasibility for automatic script synthesis from NL descriptions, (2) techniques adapted from the NLP community to translate English descriptions into rele-

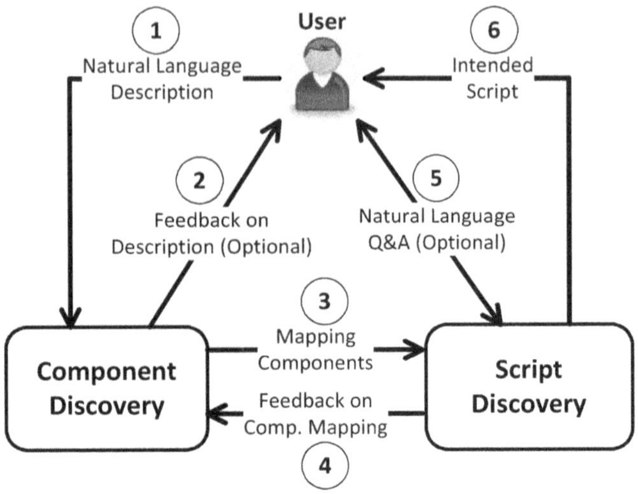

Figure 1: SmartSynth's system architecture.

vant components (*i.e.* script constructs) and a partial set of dataflow relations among the components, and (3) techniques inspired by the program synthesis community to complete the partial set of dataflow relations via type-based program synthesis [15,27,32] and construct the desired scripts via reverse parsing [2].

Indeed, we combine and refine recent advances in both the NLP and program synthesis areas. A recent, emerging trend in NLP is semantic understanding of natural languages. There have been recent, although limited, successes in translating structured English into database queries [4] and translating NL statements into logic in specific domains [9,20]. As for program synthesis, the traditional goal has been to discover new or complicated algorithms from *complete logical specifications*. There is recent, renewed interest in this area of synthesis because of (1) interesting applications (such as end-user programming [14] and intelligent tutoring systems [13]), and (2) the ability to deal with under-specifications (such as examples [14], and a set of APIs or keywords [15,24]). Our combination of NLP and program synthesis is synergistic since NLP is used to "partially understand" natural language and program synthesis is then used to refine this understanding and generate the intended script.

Figure 1 illustrates SmartSynth's process of synthesizing scripts. The user communicates her intent via natural language (Step 1). The "Component Discovery" box contains two algorithms that are inspired by the NLP area: (i) a mapping algorithm that maps the description into script components such as APIs and literals (Step 3), and (ii) an algorithm that asks the user to refine parts of the description that SmartSynth does not understand (Step 2). The "Script Discovery" box first uses an NLP-based algorithm to detect dataflow relations among the identified components. If these relations do not fully specify the dataflow relationships between components, SmartSynth invokes our algorithm (inspired by type-based synthesis) to complete the missing dataflow relations. If there are multiple equally high-ranked relations, SmartSynth initiates an interactive conversation with the user to resolve the ambiguities (Step 5). As the final step, it constructs the intended script from the identified components and relations using an algorithm akin to reverse parsing.

An interesting feature of SmartSynth is the NLP-Synthesis feedback loop in Steps 3-4. Although our NLP algorithm has its own mapping feature set to perform component mapping, it might not precisely capture the mapping in some cases, due to irregularities of natural language. SmartSynth uses program synthesis technique to gain confidence about the quality of the generated script and as another metric for the quality of NLP mapping. In particular, SmartSynth repeatedly requests the NLP-based algorithm for the next likely interpretation of the description, if the current interpretation is deemed unlikely (*i.e.*, the interpretation does not translate to a high-confidence script).

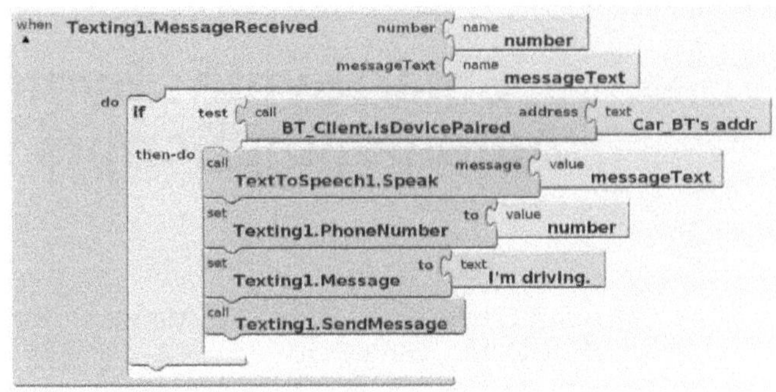

Figure 2: A visual program for Example 1 written in AppInventor.

Contributions We make the following contributions:

- We introduce an automation language `SmartScript` that is expressive enough to represent a wide variety of automation scripts discussed on online forums, while at the same time restrictive enough to enable efficient search over the program space (Section 3).
- We present an algorithm for generating likely `SmartScript` scripts from natural language descriptions (Section 4). Our algorithm involves three key technical steps: (1) generation of script components, (2) generation of dataflow relations among those components, and (3) constructing the script from the components and dataflow relations. The first and second steps leverage techniques from NLP, while the second and third steps leverage techniques from program synthesis.
- We have implemented our technique and evaluated it on 50 different tasks collected from smartphone help forums. Our results show that SmartSynth is effective — it can generate the intended scripts in real time for over 90% of the 640 NL descriptions collected via a user study (Section 5). We have also extended SmartSynth to TouchDevelop, which has a much larger grammar and API set, with similar positive results. A video demo of the extended system is available at `http://www.cs.ucdavis.edu/~su/smartsynth.mp4`.

Paper Organization The rest of the paper is structured as follows. We first use a concrete example to motivate and illustrate SmartSynth (Section 2). Section 3 introduces our DSL `SmartScript` and defines the notion of script components. Sections 4 presents three key steps of SmartSynth— mapping NL descriptions to components, detecting dataflow relations among the identified components, and synthesizing scripts from these components and relations. We then present our detailed evaluation of SmartSynth (Section 5). We discuss related work in Section 6 and conclude in Section 7.

2. EXAMPLE

We motivate our system via the following running example, taken from a help forum for Tasker [7].

EXAMPLE 1. *The user wants to create a script to do the following when she receives an SMS while driving: (1) read the content*

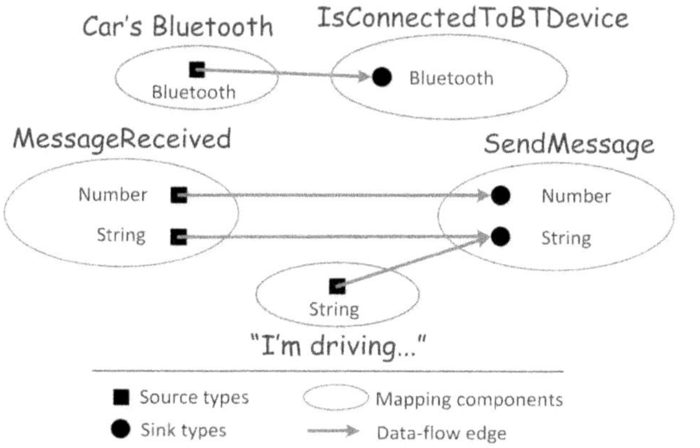

Figure 3: The graph showing all possible dataflow relations among components identified by the Component Discovery algorithms.

Description	Possible Mappings
When I receive a new SMS	`MessageReceived`
if the phone is connected to	`IsConnectedToBTDevice` `IsConnectedToWifiNetwork` `IsConnectedToDataService`
my car's bluetooth	`Car_BT`
reads out loud	`Speak`
the message content	`MessageReceived.Text`$_O$
replies	`SendMessage` `SendEmail`
the sender	`MessageReceived.Number`$_O$
"I'm driving"	`"I'm driving"`

Table 1: Possible mappings from text chunks to components in Ex. 1. `Text`$_O$ and `Number`$_O$ are return values of `MessageReceived`.

of the message and (2) send a message "I'm driving" to the sender. Since the user always connects her car's bluetooth to the phone when she is in the car, she uses this fact to denote that she is driving[1]*. One possible description of this script is:*

> "When I receive a new SMS, if the phone is connected to my car's bluetooth, it reads out loud the message content and replies the sender *"I'm driving."*."

Users of both conventional and visual programming systems have to deal with all the low-level details and make several decisions, often unintuitive to them, during the process of creating a new program. In contrast, users of SmartSynth only need to give the system their problem description in NL, and interact with it, if necessary, in natural language. Below we compare traditional programming systems with SmartSynth using our example.

Identifying Components Users of conventional and visual programming systems have to conceptualize their ideas into script components (*i.e.*, script constructs such as APIs), potentially under several refinement steps [40]. This is a non-trivial task as it assumes that users should understand all script constructs' specifications. As shown in Figure 2, users of AppInventor have to conceptualize and identify various components while transforming the idea in Example 1 into a running script.

In comparison, SmartSynth automatically decomposes the description into disjoint text chunks and matches each chunk to its supported components (details in Section 4.1). For the description in Example 1, SmartSynth is able to decompose and match the description to the components shown in Table 1. When any chunk of the description cannot be mapped to a component, SmartSynth will ask the user to refine the chunk.

However, as is often the case in NLP, mapping a chunk to components can be ambiguous. For example, we can map *"if the phone is connected to"* to any of the three candidates shown in Table 1. Similarly, we can map *"replies"* to either `SendMessage` or `SendEmail`. One can look at API arguments to resolve these ambiguities. In the first case, since the argument is a bluetooth device, it is very likely that the mapping component is `IsConnectedToBTDevice`. But this approach does not work as well for the second case, where the ambiguity can only be resolved by considering the global context that may indicate receipt or sending of an SMS.

SmartSynth takes a different approach. Instead of manually encoding many disambiguation rules, it relies on the techniques inspired by type-based synthesis to automatically disambiguate mapping candidates. Specifically, from each mapping candidate that needs to be resolved, SmartSynth generates a script and assigns it a score indicating how likely the script is. The best mapping is associated with the script that has the highest score. In Example 1, SmartSynth is able to select the right mapping set (`IsConnectedToBTDevice`, `SendMessage` and the others) because together they form the highest ranked script.

Synthesizing Scripts Besides identifying all necessary components, users of conventional systems also need to understand the components' low-level details in order to assemble them meaningfully.

To create the script in Figure 2, the users must understand that `MessageReceived` is an event and returns a phone number and a message content, which may be stored in two temporary variables. They need to understand that `IsDevicePaired` is the guard of the conditional and it must be linked with the car's bluetooth. Also, the APIs `Speak` and `SendMessage` must be configured with arguments of types `Text` and `Number` & `Text` respectively. Finally, the users need to pass the temporary variables/literals to those APIs and arrange them in the correct order.

In contrast, users of SmartSynth are not required to understand those low-level details because the system knows the signatures of all those APIs. The challenge is to generate additional script constructs such as loops, conditionals and assignments to combine these components together into a script reflecting the user's intent. SmartSynth solves this challenge in the following steps (details in Section 4.2). First, it builds a special data structure that represents all possible dataflow relations among the components. We call each of them a (dataflow) *relation*. Figure 3 shows the data structure for the right component mapping set. An edge in this figure represents a relation, which specifies a possible dataflow from a value (source) to an API's parameter (sink). The value from a source might be assigned to multiple sinks (if they have the same type), and a sink might receive a value from different sources (also of the same type). For example, the sink denoting the message content in `SendMessage` can be assigned to the argument from either the received message of `MessageReceived`, or the string literal "I'm driving" because they have the same type `String`.

Next, SmartSynth uses classic NLP techniques [19] to detect likely relations from the NL description. These relations must be derived from the set of all possible relations embedded in the graph. Table 2 shows the relations that SmartSynth has detected from the description. A row in this table represents a relation defining which source is assigned to a sink. For example, the last row states that

[1] In fact, this is a clever workaround to avoid using the GPS sensor, which drains the battery power very quickly.

Return value or Literal	API Parameter
Car_BT	IsConnectedToBT-Device.Bluetooth$_I$
MessageReceived.Text$_O$	ReadText.Text$_I$
MessageReceived.Number$_O$	SendMessage.Number$_I$
"I'm driving"	SendMessage.Text$_I$

Table 2: Relations detected from Example 1's description. Subscripts I/O characterize the field of an API as a parameter or a return value.

the message content to be sent by `SendMessage` is the string literal "I'm driving". SmartSynth generates and returns the final script to the user if it is able to detect all necessary relations from the NL description (Figure 4).

```
when (number, content) := MessageReceived()
  if (IsConnectedToBTDevice(Car_BT) then
    Speak(content);
    SendMessage(number, "I'm␣driving");
```

Figure 4: The script for Example 1.

However, since users can give free-form descriptions, SmartSynth may often detect only a *subset* of the necessary relations. In these cases where the intent is under-specified, SmartSynth uses techniques inspired by type-based synthesis to find the missing relations. It performs searching over the dataflow graph for missing relations and uses a special ranking scheme to prioritize more likely relations. SmartSynth then uses these newly discovered relations to generate the most likely script and returns it to the user.

As an example, suppose that the user had given a slightly different description "*... and send back...*" (instead of "*... and replies the sender...*") and also suppose that SmartSynth does not model this mapping and thus is unable to extract the third relation between MessageReceived.Number$_O$ and SendMessage.Number$_I$ in Table 2. Nonetheless, SmartSynth can discover this missing relation and generate the same script as in Figure 4.

3. AUTOMATION SCRIPT LANGUAGE

In this paper, we use a scripting language `SmartScript` (Figure 5) with representative features of the current smartphone generation. Since `SmartScript` is an intermediate language, we can port it to other mobile platforms via simple syntax-directed translation [2].

3.1 Language Features

We have designed `SmartScript` from an extensive study of the scripts from various smartphone help forums. This design process is an interesting exercise to balance the trade-offs between the expressiveness of `SmartScript` and the effectiveness of SmartSynth. The restrictions that we place in `SmartScript` (event and conditionals only appear at the top of the script) allow SmartSynth to perform type-based synthesis more effectively under the uncertainties in NL processing.

A script P in `SmartScript` represents a task that executes a sequence of actions under a certain condition. It has some parameters I (which will be entered by users when the script runs) and may be triggered by an event E. When the event occurs, it generates some variables. The conversions T converts these variables into new types that are used in the condition C. The condition is then evaluated and if it holds, the main body M is executed.

Script P	$::=$	$I\ E\ T\ C\ M$
Parameter I	$::=$	$\mathbf{input}(\mathbf{i}_1, \ldots, \mathbf{i}_n) \mid \epsilon$
Event E	$::=$	$(\underline{r_1}, \ldots, \underline{r_n}) := \mathbf{when}\ \underline{\mathtt{Event}}() \mid \epsilon$
Conversions T	$::=$	$F_1; \ldots; F_n;$
Condition C	$::=$	$\mathbf{if}\ (\Pi_1 \wedge \cdots \wedge \Pi_n)\ \mathbf{then}$
Body M	$::=$	$Stmt_1; \ldots; Stmt_n;$
Conversion F	$::=$	$\mathbf{x} := \mathtt{Convert}(a)$
Predicate Π	$::=$	$\underline{\mathtt{Predicate}}(a_1, \ldots, a_n)$
Stmt. $Stmt$	$::=$	S
	$\mid$	$\mathbf{foreach}\ \mathbf{x} \in a$ $\mathbf{do}\ S_1; \ldots; S_n;\ \mathbf{od}$
Atom. Stmt. S	$::=$	$A \mid F$
Action A	$::=$	$(\underline{r_1}, \ldots, \underline{r_n}) := \underline{\mathtt{Action}}(a_1, \ldots, a_n)$
Argument a	$::=$	$\mathbf{x} \mid \mathbf{i} \mid \underline{r} \mid \underline{l}$

Figure 5: The syntax of automation language: **x**, **i**, $\underline{r}$, $\underline{l}$ refer to a temporary variable, an argument of the script, a return value, and a literal, respectively. The essential components identified by the NLP techniques are underlined.

We use a few examples, each of which contains an NL description and the synthesized script, to illustrate our key language constructs.

Event and Conditional

EXAMPLE 2. [Phone Locator] *When the phone receive a new text message, reply with my current location if the message content is "Secret code".*

```
when (number, text) := MessageReceived
  if (text = "Secret␣code") then
    text2 := LocationToString(CurrentLocation);
    SendMessage(number, text2);
```

API Composition

EXAMPLE 3. [Picture Uploader] *Take a picture, add to it the current location and upload to Facebook.*

```
pic := TakePhoto();
text := LocationToString(CurrentLocation);
pic2 := AddTextToPhoto(pic, text);
UploadPhotoToFacebook(pic2);
```

Loops

EXAMPLE 4. [Group Texting] *Send my current location to 111-1111 and 222-2222.*

```
text := LocationToString(CurrentLocation);
foreach number in {111-1111, 222-2222} do
  SendMessage(number, text);
od
```

3.2 Essential Components

Script components (constructs) in `SmartScript` are not equally important. A component is essential to the semantics of the script if we cannot reconstruct the script once we have removed the component from it. On the other hand, a component is not essential if we are still able to reconstruct the script if the component is removed. In order to successfully generate the intended script, SmartSynth must be able to identify all essential components from an NL description.

In Figure 5, we underline all `SmartScript`'s essential components. An essential component in `SmartScript` is either an API or an entity. While APIs are pre-defined and related to smartphone functionalities, entities correspond to personal data. This mixture enables the easy creation of personalized automation scripts.

APIs We have created a representative set of 106 APIs that cover most of the available functionalities of the current generation of smartphones. We annotate each API with a set of weighted tags (used by the mapping algorithm to map text chunks to appropriate components), and a type signature (used by the synthesis algorithm to generate only type-safe scripts). The tag set is weighted since some tags are more indicative of a component than others.

We classify the APIs into the following categories to match the constructs in `SmartScript`:

- **Events:** These represent events that occur on the phone. For example, the event of receiving a new text message (`MessageReceived`), or the event of receiving a phone call (`IncomingCall`). These events trigger script execution.
- **Predicates:** These denote conditions on the state of the phone. For example, there are text messages that the user has not read (`HasUnreadMessages`), or the phone is in landscape orientation (`IsInLandscapeMode`). They also include comparison operators (*e.g.*, $<$, $>$, and $=$). Predicates restrict the condition under which the script is executed.
- **Actions:** These are normal phone operations, such as turning off wifi or bluetooth connection (`TurnWifiOff`, `TurnBluetoothOff`), muting the phone (`MutePhone`), taking a picture (`TakePhoto`), or sending a text message (`SendMessage`). SmartSynth executes a sequence of actions in a script's body when its event is triggered and the predicates are satisfied.

Entities Entities represent values that are passed among APIs inside a script. An entity is one of the following:

- **Return values:** These are return values of our representative APIs. For example, the content of the received message ($\texttt{MessageReceived.Text}_O$), the caller of incoming call ($\texttt{IncomingCall.Number}_O$).
- **Literals:** These are personal data items from the user's phone (*e.g.*, a contact in her address book, her bluetooth headset, her music collection, her current location) or generic values (*e.g.*, a string "I'm driving", the time 10pm).

The purpose of identifying APIs is to form the script's skeleton, while that of capturing entities is to prepare for building the dataflow relations among these identified APIs in a later step. We discuss the details of our algorithm next.

4. SYNTHESIS ALGORITHM

The key observation behind our synthesis algorithm is that a `SmartScript` script can be constructed from its constituent set of essential components and the dataflow relations among those components. This observation allows us to reduce our original problem of synthesizing a `SmartScript` script from an NL description to the following three sub-problems: (a) identifying essential components (Section 4.1), (b) identifying their dataflow relations (Section 4.2.1), and (c) constructing the script from the components and their dataflow relations (Section 4.2.2). We use techniques inspired from both the NLP and program synthesis communities to solve these sub-problems.

We first use an algorithm inspired by NLP techniques to map the given NL description to a set of essential components. We then use rule-based relation detection algorithm (a classic NLP technique) to extract dataflow relations among the identified components. Since this algorithm may not be able to extract all relations, we use a technique inspired by type-based synthesis to find the likely missing relations. Finally, we use the components and their relations to construct the script and return it to the user. We explain these algorithms in detail next.

4.1 Component Discovery

We assume that for every NL description, there exists a decomposition of that description into disjoint text chunks, where each of the text chunks can be mapped to a component. It is expected that there are many possible ways to decompose a given description into chunks. Furthermore, each of the chunks can be mapped to many possible components. Thus, the space of all possible mappings from an NL description to a set of components is large. ***The key high-level insight*** of our component discovery algorithm is to consider all possible mappings (to gain high recall) in a ranked order (to gain high precision).

To this end, we have developed an effective data structure that efficiently stores all possible description decompositions, and the supportive and refutative features used to map these decompositions into components. We then find the best component mapping from this data structure.

Mapping Data Structure Our data structure is a weighted directed graph $\langle V, E\rangle$ where

- V is a set of vertices. Each vertex represents a *cut* between two consecutive words in the description.
- E is a set of edges. An edge (v_i, v_j) denotes a chunk of text that starts from the vertex v_i and ends at the vertex v_j.

For each edge in E, we need to calculate the confidence of mapping its text chunk to a particular component. We use mapping features to calculate this score.

Mapping Features A *feature* h is a function that returns the confidence score of mapping an edge in our data structure to a component. In other words, it indicates how likely a text chunk (represented by the edge) is mapped to a certain component, among all possible components.

Currently, our system uses the following features:

- **Regular expressions:** We use a set of regular expressions to extract entities. A chunk is likely mapped to an entity if it matches the corresponding regular expression. For each entity that is an API's return value, we create a set of common terms that people might call it. For example, we associate $\texttt{MessageReceived.Text}_O$ with "message content", "received content", and "received message". To extract literal entities (*e.g.*, the time "10pm", the number "123-4567"), we define regular expressions for all data types used in SmartSynth.

- **Bags-of-words:** We use the bags-of-words model [19] to categorize a chunk as representing some APIs. A chunk is more likely mapped to an API if it contains more words that are related to the API's tags. For example, it is more likely to map "send a text" to `SendMessage` than to map the single word "send" to the same API, because the tag set of `SendMessage` contains both "send" and "text".

- **Phrase length:** This feature gives a negative score to a mapping (between a chunk and a component) if the chunk is either too long or too short.

- **Punctuation:** A punctuation is an indication of the start or end of a chunk. Therefore, chunks that start or end with punctuations have higher scores.

- **Parse tree:** Although NLP parsers may not provide precise parse trees, they are still useful because these parse trees are partially correct, and we can exploit them to gain higher mapping confidence. For example, if a parse tree indicates that a text chunk is a noun phrase, it increases the confidence of mapping this chunk to entities. Also, if the main verb in a chunk matches a verb in an action API, it is more likely to map the chunk to this API. In our implementation, we use the Stanford NLP parser [21].

The above features give different scores for mapping a text chunk to a component. The *aggregate function* combines these scores into a single score. In our implementation, the aggregate function is a weighted sum of all feature scores. It is formally defined as follows:

$$f(e, c) = \sum_{h_i \in F} w_i * h_i(e, c)$$

where e is the edge that contains the text chunk, c is the component that e maps to, F is the feature set, w_i is the feature weight.

For each edge, we select the mapped component whose aggregate score is the highest. This score becomes the edge's weight in the data structure.

$$mapping(e) = \{\langle c, f(e, c)\rangle \mid c \in \operatorname*{argmax}_{c \in C} f(e, c)\}$$

where argmax returns the components that maximize the value of the function f.

We store all related information in the data structure to make a *global* decision based on all the features. The next step is to extract the best mappings for the whole NL description from the data structure.

Finding the Best Mapping A path from the start node to the end node decomposes the descriptions into several disjoint text chunks. Each chunk is mapped to a component with a confidence score represented by the weight of its corresponding edge. The total confidence score of mapping the whole description to a component set is the total weight of the corresponding path. Thus, the best mapping (which has the highest total confidence score) corresponds to the longest path in the graph.

4.2 Script Discovery

Once SmartSynth has discovered the set of essential components, it uses the following ingredients to synthesize the intended script: (1) type signature of the components, (2) structural constraints imposed by the automation script language, (3) spatial locality of the components in the natural language description, and (4) an effective ranking scheme.

C_1	typeof (C_2)	typeof (C_3)	Relations
`IsConnected-ToBTDevice`	`BT`		$\langle C_2, C_1.\texttt{BT}_I\rangle$
`ReadText`	`Text`		$\langle C_2, C_1.\texttt{Text}_I\rangle$
`SendMessage`	`Number`	`Text`	$\langle C_2, C_1.\texttt{Number}_I\rangle$ $\langle C_3, C_1.\texttt{Text}_I\rangle$

Table 3: Some rules to detect relations in Example 1. C_1, C_2, C_3 is a sequence of identified components.

The overall process works as follows. Using typing information, SmartSynth builds a dataflow graph to capture all possible dataflow relations among the provided components. It uses a classic NLP technique to extract dataflow relations from the relative orders of the identified components. If the set of extracted relations is *incomplete*, SmartSynth utilizes the dataflow graph and a ranking scheme to identify the most likely missing relations. SmartSynth then constructs the intended script from the identified components and relations via a process akin to reverse parsing, and returns the script to the user. Next, we discuss these steps in detail.

4.2.1 Dataflow Relations Discovery

Dataflows are essential in determining the intended script. If components are building bricks, dataflows are the cement to glue the bricks together to form scripts. ***The key insight*** in this process is to use an NLP technique to detect a (partial) set of (high-confidence) dataflow relations followed by a type-based synthesis technique to complete this set using type signatures of components and a ranking scheme.

DEFINITION 1 (DATAFLOW RELATION). *A dataflow relation is an ordered pair of a* source *(i.e., an API return value or a literal) and a* sink *(i.e., an API parameter), representing a value assignment from the source to the sink.*

Dataflow Graph We build the graph $G_C = \langle V, E\rangle$ that concisely captures all dataflow relations among the identified components C as follows:

- V is the set of all sources and sinks in C.

- E is the set of all directed dataflow edges from sources to sinks, such that they are type-compatible. Each edge in E represents a dataflow relation between a source and a sink.

A source type τ_1 is type-compatible with a sink type τ_2 if they have the same type or τ_1 is a list of type τ_2 (we use the later case to generate loops).

The task of SmartSynth is to determine which relations are most relevant in G_C. It does this in two steps. First, it detects dataflow relations among components from their relative locations in the description. When necessary, it uses type-based synthesis techniques to infer additional relations from the dataflow graph.

Detecting Partial Dataflow Relations We use rule-based relation detection algorithm, a standard NLP technique, to detect dataflow relations among the identified components. Since all of our APIs are pre-defined and structured (each API is annotated with its type signature), we are able to manually compile a set of rules to extract relations based on the order of how components appear in the sentence. Specifically, if an API component is followed by entities having types that match its signature, those entities are likely to be the API's arguments.

Algorithm 1: Discovering the most likely complete dataflow set

```
   Input  : component set C, partial relation set R̃
   Output: the most likely complete dataflow set R_top
1  begin
2      G_C ← BuildDataFlowGraph(C)
3      T_all ← {t | t is sink in G_C.V}
4      T_conc ← {t | ⟨s,t⟩ ∈ R̃}
5      T̃ ← T_all \ T_conc          // to be concret'd sinks
6      𝓡 ← {ArbitraryRelationSet(R̃)}
7      𝒬 ← {⟨R̃, T̃⟩}
8      while 𝒬 ≠ {} do
9          ⟨R, T⟩ ← 𝒬.Dequeue()
10         if MinCost(R) ≤ MaxCost(𝓡) then
11             if T = ∅ & GenCode(R) ∈ SmartScript then
12                 if Cost(R) < MaxCost(𝓡) then
13                     𝓡 ← {R}
14                 else if Cost(R) = MaxCost(𝓡) then
15                     𝓡 ← 𝓡 ∪ {R}
16             else          /* explore child spaces */
17                 t ← choose(T)
18                 foreach (s, t) ∈ G_C.E_v do
19                     𝒬.Enqueue(⟨R ∪ ⟨s,t⟩, T \ t⟩)
20         else ; /* prune this branch */
21     if 𝓡 = ∅ then R_top ← ⊥
22     else if 𝓡 = {R} then R_top ← R
23     else R_top ← PerformConversation(𝓡)
24     return R_top
```

Table 3 shows three rules for detecting all relations in Example 1. The first rule states that if the entity following IsConnectedToBT-Device has type BT, there is a relation between those two.

We remark that these rules can be learned automatically using supervised learning [19, 20]. However, in a manageable domain like ours, expert rules work quite well. The Stanford NLP parser also uses hand-written rules to extract typed dependencies (grammatical relations between words) [28].

Even though our algorithm works fairly effectively, it is unable to detect all relations within a description, as is typically the case with NLP algorithms. In these cases, SmartSynth relies on recent advances in modern program synthesis to complete the relation set and generates the final script. Without the synthesis algorithm, SmartSynth would halt here and ask the user to refine the description despite that it might be entirely correct.

Completing the Relation Set The goal here is to discover missing relations to form a complete *dataflow set* that can be turned into a script in a later phase. We use a specialized ranking scheme to find the most likely complete dataflow set among all possible sets.

DEFINITION 2 (COMPLETE DATAFLOW SET). *A set $G_{\mathcal{C}}$ of dataflow relations among components in $\mathcal{C}$ is* complete *if every sink of a component in $\mathcal{C}$ has one and only one relation associated with it. This dataflow set fully specifies how arguments are passed to all the sinks in $\mathcal{C}$.*

Algorithm 1 describes the process of completing the dataflow set. At the high-level, SmartSynth performs search over the dataflow graph to find the best dataflow sets $\mathcal{R}$ for the sinks $\tilde{T}$ that have not been assigned any values (line 5). SmartSynth uses the ranking scheme (represented by Cost) to guide the search towards more likely relations (lines 12, 14). It enforces structural constraints imposed by SmartScript by eliminating dataflow sets that do not conform to the language (line 11). To speed up the discovery process, our algorithm implements the general branch-and-bound algorithm. It ignores a search sub-space if the minimum cost (MinCost) of all dataflow sets in that space is greater than that of the current set (lines 10 and 20).

Algorithm 2: Script Construction

```
Input  : component set C, dataflow set R
Output: an automation script
begin
    /* generate temporary variables */
    foreach source τ ∈ C do
        SymTable[τ] ← new variable
    /* assign sources' vars to sinks */
    foreach (τ_s, τ_t) ∈ C.E do
        SymTable[τ_t] ← SymTable[τ_s]
    I ← live input variables in C
    E ← ⊥
    if ∃e ∈ C : e is event then E ← e
    C ← ⋀_i Π_i where Π_i is a predicate in C
    T ← conversion functions used by C
    M ← the rest of actions and conversion functions in g
    /* generate the foreach loop */
    foreach (τ_s, τ_t) ∈ g.E_v s.t. τ_s = List⟨τ_t⟩ do
        s ← the subgraph reachable from τ_t
        SymTable[τ_t] ← new variable
        /* replace s by foreach stmt */
        M ← M[(foreach SymTable[τ_t] ∈ SymTable[τ_s]
              do s od) / s]
    P ← ⟨I, E, T, C, M⟩
    return P
```

One important aspect of Algorithm 1 is our specialized ranking scheme, which helps prioritize the search process toward the script that most likely matches the user's intention. We next discuss the ranking scheme.

Ranking Scheme Our high-level insight behind the ranking scheme is to give preferences to those scripts (1) that have greater coupling among the components, (2) that are more generally applicable, or (3) that require fewer user inputs.

We define a set of (negative) cost metrics to realize the above insight, each of which defines a less likely or less preferred feature of a script. The Cost function is simply the sum of the costs given by each of them:

- **Unused Variable Cost**: This metric gives a unit cost to each unused variable generated by SmartSynth. It promotes scripts that have better coupling among components.
- **Parameter Cost**: This metric gives a unit cost for each of parameters the script uses. This is because users normally do not want to configure the script when it runs. They often want fully automatic scripts.
- **Domain-Specific Cost**: This metric contains expert rules that capture what people usually do in practice. For example, in the messaging domain, we punish the script if the replied message is the same as the content of the received message.

Algorithm 3: The overall algorithm of SmartSynth.

Input : NL description d
Output: script P, or request to refine (parts of) d

```
1  begin
2    G_d ← BuildDataFlowGraph(d)
3    if G_d is connected then
4      C ← BestMapping(G_d)
5      R̃ ← DetectRelations(C)
6      while MappingScore(⟨C, R̃⟩) < δ do
         /* mapping score too low */
7        C ← NextBestMapping()
8        R̃ ← DetectRelations(C)
9      if C ≠ ∅ then                    /* mapping exists */
10       𝓡 ← CompleteRelations(⟨C, R̃⟩)
11       if 𝓡 > 1 then
           /* equally ranked sets */
12         R ← QuestionAnswering(𝓡)
13       else R ← 𝓡.First()
14       return GenerateCode(⟨C, R⟩)
       /* refine the whole desc. */
15     return AskForRefinement(d)
16   else               /* refine nonmappable phrases */
17     l ← DisconnectedSubGraphs(G_d)
18     return AskForRefinement(l)
```

This ranking scheme work quite effectively for our problem domain. However, in the presence of a large amount of user data, we can build a probabilistic ranking model. We are investigating this option for the TouchDevelop domain from its thousands of scripts contributed by its users.

4.2.2 *Script Construction*

At this point, SmartSynth has found a set of components and a complete set of dataflow relations. It now uses Algorithm 2 to construct the intended script. This process is the reverse of the normal parsing process in a compiler. A compiler breaks down a program into components and dataflow relations to enable optimizations and low-level code generation. In contrast, the SmartSynth synthesizes the script structure from its building pieces, namely the components and their dataflow relations. During this synthesis process, SmartSynth needs to: (1) generate code to pass arguments to APIs, (2) generate conditionals, and (3) generate loops.

SmartSynth generates a temporary variable for each API return value, and, based on the dataflow set identified in the previous steps, passes these variables as arguments to other APIs (line 2-5). Next, it extracts the event and conditionals from the event and predicate components to form the guard of the script (lines 8-9). The remaining action APIs form the body.

The ***most interesting aspect*** of the script construction process is loop generation. SmartSynth generates a looping construct if there is a relation from a collection to an API parameter (lines 12-16). For example, the user may say "send Joe and John my current location." Although the user does not explicitly mention the word "loop", it would be her intention to use a loop. In particular, SmartSynth detects that there is a relation between the group {Joe, John} and `SendMessage.Number`$_I$, and generates a loop to send messages to both Joe and John.

4.3 SmartSynth

Having described the two technical components (namely Component Discovery and Script Discovery), we now ready to formally describe the rest of SmartSynth's architecture in Figure 1.

Algorithm 3 implements all the components in the architecture. It realizes our observation that a `SmartScript` script can be identified from its essential components and their dataflow relations. Specifically, it uses NLP techniques to find components from the provided NL description (line 4) and to detect some of relations (line 5). It then invokes the synthesis algorithm to complete the dataflow relations (line 10), and to synthesize the final script in line 14. If nothing goes wrong, those steps correspond to the simplest possible workflow in SmartSynth.

However, since it is dealing with end users and natural language, SmartSynth faces many uncertainties. For example, users might give irrelevant and/or ambiguous descriptions. We discuss SmartSynth's error handling mechanism next.

Handling Descriptions with Unsupported Functionalities Due to their high expectation (and sometimes ignorance), users might ask for functionalities that are not supported by SmartSynth.

If the given description is in-scope, there exists a meaningful decomposition of the description into several chunks, and SmartSynth is able to map each of these chunks to a component. The graph in this case is a *connected* graph. On the other hand, if one or more parts of the description are out-of-scope, these parts cannot be mapped to any component(s). The graph in this case is *disconnected*. SmartSynth asks the user to refine the phrases corresponding to the disconnected subgraphs that cannot be mapped to anything (line 17 in Algorithm 3, step 2 in Figure 1). Figure 6 visualizes this case.

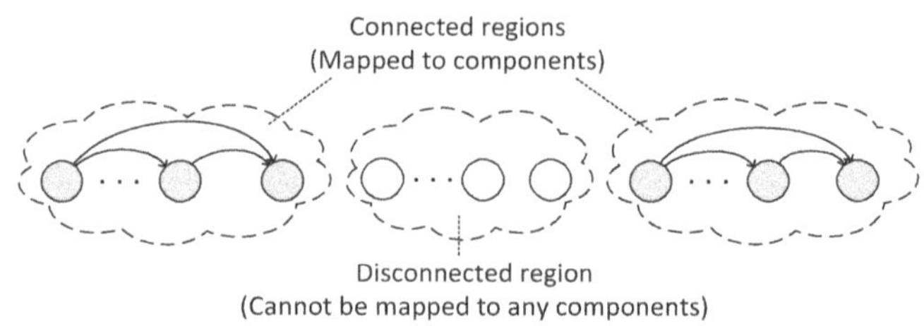

Figure 6: A region in the description that cannot be mapped to any component. SmartSynth reports its phrase to the user to clarify.

Handling Ambiguous NL Descriptions Although SmartSynth uses multiple mapping features to increase the precision of the component mapping process, there are cases where these features cannot promote the best component mapping properly. This is unavoidable because we cannot precisely model natural language (due to its irregular nature).

SmartSynth resolves such cases via the feedback loop on lines 6-8 in Algorithm 3 (and Steps 3-4 in Figure 1). SmartSynth evaluates the quality of the component mapping provided by the mapping algorithm and repeatedly generates other interpretations of the NL description, if the current one is unsatisfactory.

Handling Equally Likely Scripts When the ranking scheme cannot differentiate the top dataflow sets, SmartSynth has multiple equally ranked scripts at the top. In such cases, SmartSynth performs interactive conversation with the user to eliminate undesired scripts (line 12 in Algorithm 3, and Step 5 in Figure 1). It generates a sequence of *distinguishing* multiple-choice questions based on these candidates and presents them to the user, one question at a time. Her answers help SmartSynth capture more constraints and eliminate unintended dataflow sets.

The intuition behind the algorithm is that each question corresponds to a sink that receives different values in those dataflow sets, and the answer choices are those values that can be assigned to the sink. When the user selects an answer, SmartSynth eliminates those dataflow sets that do not correspond to the selected value.

Because the sink set is finite and known *a priori* (sinks are parameters of pre-defined APIs), we are able to build a database that stores an NL question for each of the sinks. Similarly, we define NL representations for all the sources. SmartSynth generates questions and answers by looking up the values of the corresponding sinks and sources in the database. For example, for the sink `SendMessage.Number`$_I$, SmartSynth generates the question *"Who do you want to send the SMS to?"*. Suppose this sink is related to two sources, `MessageReceived.Number`$_O$ and `111-1111`. They will be presented as two answer choices *"(A) The sender of the received SMS"* and *"(B) The phone number 111-1111"*.

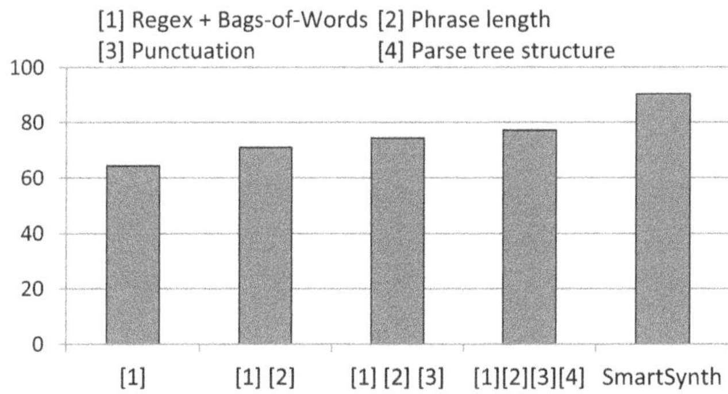

Figure 7: The result of mapping phrases to components under increasingly sophisticated configurations.

5. EVALUATION

In this section, we evaluate the effectiveness of SmartSynth in discovering the right set of components and their dataflow relations. We also compare the overall performance of SmartSynth and the system that employs only NLP techniques. We implemented SmartSynth in C#. All our experiments were run on a machine with an Intel® i7 2.66 GHz CPU and 4 GB of RAM. We use the Stanford NLP parser [21] wrapped under a public web service [1].

We compile the benchmark from task descriptions found in help forums of Tasker [7], App Inventor [30], and TouchDevelop [38]. Among the 70 found descriptions, seven cannot be expressed in our language `SmartScript`. Therefore, we remark that `SmartScript` was able to express 90% of the kind of real-life examples that it was designed for. All the inexpressible descriptions that we found required synchronization between different tasks, possibly through the use of some shared global variables or control-flow among events. To illustrate, we describe below one of them; the other ones are similar.

EXAMPLE 5. [Inexpressible in `SmartScript`] *If there is an unread SMS and the user has not turned the screen on, remind her every 5 minutes.*

This script has two synchronized tasks, which may be synchronized using a global status variable denoting whether or not the screen has been turned on. We plan to extend our language to allow task synchronization as future work.

Of the remaining 63 task descriptions that are expressible in `SmartScript`, 13 are similar to another one in the set. Table 4 shows the distinct 50 tasks. To collect NL descriptions for those benchmark tasks, we conducted an online user study involving freshman students. We provided a one page document describing their task. We divided the benchmark into two sets that are roughly equivalent in terms of complexity. The system randomly assigned a student to one set. For each problem in an assigned set, we gave the student its desired script in `SmartScript` as the specification, and asked the student to give several NL descriptions that match the given script.

Eleven students participated in the study, giving a total of 725 distinct descriptions for our 50 benchmark tasks. Among these given descriptions, 640 match their respective specifications. We used these 640 descriptions to evaluate SmartSynth.

In Table 4, column "Compnts" shows, for each task, the total number of components that are identified from the description. The next two columns divide these components into APIs and entities. Column "Relations" corresponds to the number of dataflow relations for each task, and "Detected Relations" shows how many relations on average the NLP-based algorithm can extract from various descriptions. The last two columns show the average parsing time by the Stanford NLP parser and the average total synthesis time under ten runs. Note that the parsing time includes the communication overhead to the web service provider. It dominates the total time by SmartSynth.

Component Discovery We first evaluate the effectiveness of SmartSynth in mapping descriptions into components. Figure 7 shows the precision of this process under increasingly sophisticated configurations. The baseline algorithm (regular expression for entities and bag-of-words for APIs) produces the right component set 64.3% of the time. The algorithm combining all features achieves a 77.1% precision (the fourth column). These results indicate that the considered features work harmoniously to improve the overall precision.

Component Discovery (with Feedback Loop) Since mapping from descriptions to components tends to be ambiguous, SmartSynth utilizes the feedback from the synthesis algorithm (see Section 4.3) to gain higher mapping confidence. The last column of Figure 7 shows that the aid from the feedback loop helps improve the mapping precision to 90.3%. This proves that the synthesis feedback is very effective in disambiguating mapping candidates. Note that we measure precision by counting the number of sets that are mapped *entirely* correctly, while in other settings, *individual* components are counted. Their performance might be reduced when measured in our context.

Dataflow Relation Detection (with NLP Technique) We now evaluate the capability of SmartSynth in finding dataflow relations among APIs and entities under the ideal case, *i.e.* when the components are mapped correctly. Figure 8 shows some statistics on the number of dataflow relations that the rule-based relation detection algorithm can detect on benchmark tasks that are grouped by the number of relations.

These results indicate that the rule-based relation detection algorithm works quite effectively for tasks that have few relations. Specifically, it found almost all relations in the 1-relation tasks and nearly 86% relations in those having four. However, the rule-based algorithm faces problems when the tasks contain more relations. In particular, it could not detect nearly half of the relations in tasks having 7 or more relations. In order to resolve this, SmartSynth needs further support. Next, we measure the effectiveness of the

Test	Brief description of the benchmark	Compnts	APIs	Entities	Relations	Detected Relations	t_{NLP} (ms)	t_{total} (ms)
1	Reply current location, read sender's number and msg's content	12	6	6	7	4.13	3,151	3,325
2	Reply current loc. and batt. level upon receiving a secret code	11	5	6	7	3.75	2,705	3,206
3	Phone locator by SMS	10	5	5	8	4.6	4,376	5,737
4	Text a friend when come nearby	8	3	5	4	2	1,102	1,137
5	Silent at night but ring for important contacts	8	3	5	4	3.14	2,544	2,617
6	Speak weather in the morning	7	3	4	3	1.67	388	405
7	Take a picture, add the location and upload to Facebook	7	4	3	4	3	837	875
8	Auto response to SMS at night	7	3	4	4	3.61	2,071	2,134
9	Alert and turn off connections when battery is low	7	6	1	1	1	2,402	2,878
10	Text wife when nearly finish a long commute	6	2	4	3	2.94	1,439	1,481
11	Send SMS at a particular time	6	2	4	3	2.60	1,173	1,210
12	Send an email when leaving the office	6	2	4	3	2.67	1,077	1,108
13	Send a message when kids are dropped at school	6	2	4	3	2.88	1,644	1,689
14	Send to a list of friends current location every 15 minutes	6	3	3	4	4	788	817
15	Reply busy message if connected to car's bluetooth	6	3	3	3	2.19	2,723	2,811
16	Turn off GPS when connected to home wifi	5	2	3	1	1	737	779
17	Increase display timeout while running some apps	5	2	3	3	2	948	983
18	Auto answer calls when headset is connected	5	3	2	1	1	1,339	1,395
19	Block calls from a group of users	5	2	3	2	1.42	715	744
20	Connect to home wifi when disconnected from car's bluetooth	5	2	3	2	2	1,234	1,292
21	Find direction from current loc. to the place a photo is taken	5	3	2	3	2.07	759	787
22	Turn off wifi and GPS at night	5	3	2	2	2	653	688
23	Ring loudly for important contacts	5	2	3	3	3	1,090	1,128
24	Lower volume when a loud friend is calling	5	2	3	3	3	1,539	1,584
25	Take a picture and add current time to it	5	3	2	3	1.88	486	507
26	Handsfree texting	5	3	2	2	1.36	1,246	1,290
27	Broadcast the received message from a group	5	2	3	4	3	827	859
28	Read the received message while connected to car's bluetooth	5	3	2	2	1.90	1,122	1,176
29	Mute the phone if is in the theater	4	2	2	1	0.89	467	485
30	Disable screen rotation at night	4	2	2	2	2	413	436
31	Mute the phone if is in meeting	4	2	2	1	0.92	344	359
32	Turn on data service for apps that require data	4	2	2	2	1.76	1,501	1,547
33	Turn on GPS when apps requiried GPS are run	4	2	2	2	1	752	781
34	Send current location to a friend via SMS	4	2	2	3	2	272	284
35	Send an SMS with a secret code to trigger an alarm	4	2	2	1	1	912	947
36	Repeat caller name	4	3	1	2	1	441	459
37	Alert when receive an email with important subject	4	2	2	1	1	759	788
38	No text while driving	4	2	2	2	1.55	1,824	1,879
39	Ask to take the call if connected to car's bluetooth	4	3	1	1	1	1,702	1,776
40	Launch Pandora when the headphone is plugged	3	2	1	1	1	310	327
41	Reduce the volume when headset is plugged in	3	2	1	1	1	361	379
42	Keep screen awake when using the keyboard	3	2	1	1	1	414	434
43	Maximize screen brightness for calls	3	2	1	1	1	406	424
44	Turn off ringer by turning the phone down	3	3	0	0	0	718	757
45	Lay the phone down to switch to speaker	3	3	0	0	0	792	827
46	Show direction from current loc. to previously saved loc.	3	2	1	2	2	661	696
47	Open the keyboard and start texting	2	2	0	0	0	199	211
48	Unplug headset to pause media player	2	2	0	0	0	219	231
49	Play alert sound when battery is full	2	2	0	0	0	221	233
50	Send a text message to a group	2	1	1	3	2	387	402

Table 4: Characteristics of the benchmark set extracted from smartphone help forums.

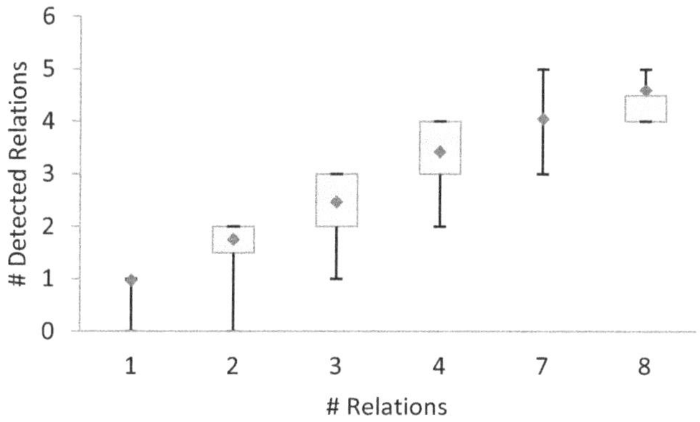

Figure 8: The number of dataflow relations detected by the rule-based algorithm for various tasks grouped by relation number.

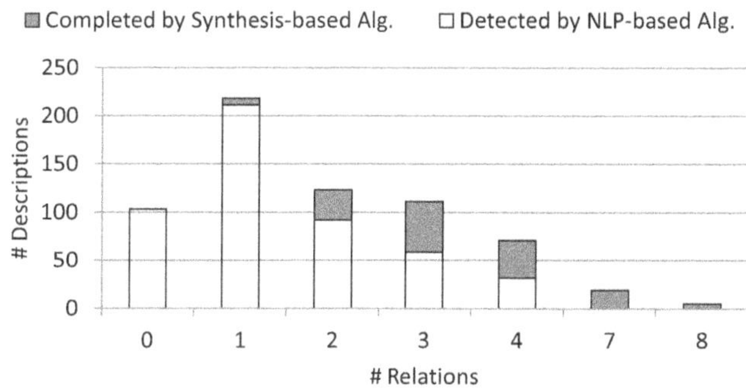

Figure 9: The number of descriptions whose dataflow relations are entirely detected by the rule-based algorithm (total 487) vs. those that require completion by the completion algorithm (total 153), grouped by the number of relations.

synthesis-based algorithm in assisting the rule-based algorithm to complete those missing relations.

Dataflow Relation Completion (with Synthesis Technique) Figure 9 shows that in nearly a quarter of the cases, the rule-based algorithm failed to detect all the dataflow relations in the solution set. Furthermore, the failure rate is proportional to the number of dataflow relations in the task descriptions. These indicates that pure NLP techniques do not scale well with complicated tasks. By employing the relation completion algorithm inspired by program synthesis area, SmartSynth was able to complete the dataflow sets and synthesize the desired scripts. In general, the synthesis-inspired algorithm is more useful with more complicated scripts, where the failure rate of detecting all relations using only NLP techniques is close to 100%.

Overall Performance Should SmartSynth only use NLP techniques and not employ the synthesis-inspired algorithm, it would suffer from the ambiguity of mapping descriptions to components and the uncertainty of extracting their relations. As a result, it might not be able to generate the user's intended script. Evaluated on our data, such system only returns the intended script 58.7% of the time (mostly with simple descriptions).

With the appearance of techniques inspired by program synthesis area, SmartSynth both improves its component identification (from the feedback loop) as well as its relation discovery (from additional relations found using the relation completion algorithm). SmartSynth achieves the 90% accuracy by combining the strength of the two research areas.

SmartSynth works quite well once it combines the strength of both NLP and synthesis communities. However, it might fail to generate the intended script sometimes. We discuss such cases next.

Discussion Given the NL description is grammatically correct and in-scope, there are two possibilities for SmartSynth to fail in generating the intended script. The first possibility is when users ask for a script that is not expressible in `SmartScript`. When designing `SmartScript`, we carefully balanced the trade-offs between language expressiveness and synthesis effectiveness. We can extend `SmartScript` to cover more scripts, but this also expands the search space, and may make the completion algorithm less scalable and the ranking scheme less effective. Nonetheless, `SmartScript` is able to express 90% of automation scripts that users care about (see Section 5).

The second possibility is when SmartSynth captures the intent from the NL description incorrectly. This is a common problem for any system that handles NL. Although it cannot completely avoid incorrect mappings, SmartSynth alleviates this problem by empowering the feedback loop, which estimates script likelihood and repeatedly generates alternative interpretations of the provided description, if the current script is not likely.

As with any programming paradigms that use examples or natural language descriptions, the correctness of the synthesized script in SmartSynth needs to be checked by the user. Another limitation of SmartSynth is its tight integration with the API set and the English language. To support any new APIs (or new languages), we have to add new rules and possibly new ranking metrics. Interesting future work is to learn these rules and ranking metrics automatically from training data. Currently, we only support small tasks that can be described in one-liners. We are considering expanding `SmartScript` to support task descriptions that use multiple sentences.

6. RELATED WORK

We discuss related work from both NL understanding and program synthesis.

Natural Language Interfaces (NLIs) There have been numerous attempts to build NLIs for many other application domains such as controlling robots [9], performing navigation [36], processing XML [22], and most notably for querying databases (NLIDBs) [4]. To solve the NL ambiguity problem, NLIDBs normally accept only a restricted subset of natural language [8, 18]. For example, in [8], relative clauses must follow their noun phrases. In contrast, users of SmartSynth can give free-form descriptions.

Another challenge in implementing NLIDBs is the capability to perform conversations with users, where they can give anaphora (referring to previous objects) and elliptical (incomplete) sentences based on the context and previous query results [4]. Because of its nature, SmartSynth does not have this problem. However, it does provide feedback on the scope of queries and performs interactive conversations with the user to resolve query ambiguities.

The main difference between SmartSynth and other NLIs is its use of type-based synthesis algorithms. While other systems have difficulties in extracting *all* necessary constraints, SmartSynth overcomes this problem by exploiting the capabilities of working with under-specifications of synthesis algorithms to complete the missing dataflow relations. We believe that our approach is applicable for building natural language interfaces for other domains as well.

Specification Extraction From NL Extracting specifications automatically from NL has long been a research dream. Kate *et al.*

propose an approach to transform NL to formal languages [20]. Xiao *et al.* develop a template-based method to extract security policies from NL software documentations [41]. Pandita *et al.* analyze API descriptions to infer their method specifications [31]. Our approach complements these existing approaches on specification extraction. SmartSynth can also leverage advances in this area to improve its NLP engine's capability of identifying components and detecting dataflow relations, which may reduce the burden on its synthesis engine to complete the relations.

General-purpose Programming Using NL and Keywords NaturalJava [33] is an attempt to bridge the gap between NL and general-purpose programming languages. It performs translation from a restricted form of NL, which is centralized around Java's programming concepts, to Java statements. It requires the user to think and give descriptions at the syntactical level of Java. Little and Miller propose a code completion tool that synthesizes the most likely Java expression in a code context from a set of keywords [23]. SmartSynth is different, in that it synthesizes a complete script and does not require extra contextual information.

Metafor [25, 26] considers the programming task as telling a story. It automatically generates the program structure from a given NL description. It can extract classes and method names from the description, but the paper is unclear about how to extract the constraints to form sequences of statements inside the methods.

Digital Assistants Siri [5] is a virtual personal assistant that allows users to ask questions and give verbal commands. It originated from the CALO project [37], the "largest known artificial intelligence project in U.S. history" [2]. Siri can handle a wide range of queries, but only those that are simple and relate to a single phone functionality [6]. In other words, users cannot give complicated commands that combine different phone features. Voice Action [10] is another personal assistant application targeting Android phones. However, it requires its users to give queries that fit pre-defined patterns. It also does not allow compositions of supported functionalities.

In contrast, users of SmartSynth can give commands containing events, conditions, and actions without any restrictions. Thus, SmartSynth provides users with greater flexibility and control over their smartphones.

Program Synthesis Program synthesis is the task of automatically synthesizing a program in some underlying domain-specific language from a given specification using some search techniques [11]. It has been applied to various domains [11], including bit-vector algorithms [15], graph algorithms, mutual exclusion algorithms, intellisense for auto completion [17,27], and spreadsheet macros [12, 14,35]. In this paper, we apply program synthesis to a new end-user programming domain of smartphone scripts. The traditional intent specification mechanisms based on logical specifications or examples are not useful here: Logical specifications are beyond the expertise of end-users and not worth the effort for small scripts. The by-example paradigm [13] does not apply since smartphone scripts are not functional programs: they are event-based and have side-effects. In contrast, we use natural language.

Our synthesis algorithm performs *type-based synthesis* that refers to a class of search techniques that use typing information/abstraction to perform search and produces a ranked set of results. Type-based synthesis has been used for various applications: synthesizing snippets that can convert a given source type into a given target type [17,27], completing partial expressions [32]. , assembling a given set of APIs into a program [15]. In each of these cases, the programmer starts out with (incomplete) program structures and the underlying synthesis engine generates ranked completions/assemblies of these structures. SmartSynth is different from these systems in two key ways: (i) SmartSynth does not require the user to start out with program structures — these are automatically inferred from NL descriptions; (ii) SmartSynth extracts relational information from NL descriptions, which helps disambiguate between multiple solutions and significantly improves the effectiveness of ranking.

[2] `http://sri.com/about/siri.html`

7. CONCLUSION

There is a proliferation of programmable mobile systems, thanks to the market for devices with various form factors and the competition. Natural user interfaces for programming are important for two reasons. First, standard programming is beyond the expertise of hundreds of millions of end-users or non-programmers. Second, even programmers find it difficult to keep pace with new syntax and APIs supported by new systems. To this end, we have proposed SmartSynth for synthesizing smartphone automation scripts from natural language descriptions. SmartSynth combines and refines techniques from two different research areas, namely Natural Language Processing and Program Synthesis. It is able to synthesize the intended scripts, in real time, for over 90% of the 640 NL descriptions obtained from a user study (involving 50 different tasks collected from smartphone help forums).

We believe that our NL translation techniques can also be useful for structured logical domains in education, such as elementary geometry [16] and automata theory [3]. This can pave the way for exciting advances in computer-aided education, such as automated grading [3] and solution generation [16] given NL descriptions of word problems.

Acknowledgments

We would like to thank our shepherd, Deepak Ganesan, and the anonymous MobiSys reviewers for valuable feedback on earlier drafts of this paper. This research was supported in part by NSF grants 0917392 and 1117603, and a Microsoft SEIF award. The information presented here does not necessarily reflect the position or the policy of the government and no official endorsement should be inferred.

8. REFERENCES

[1] `http://nlp.naturalparsing.com/`.

[2] A. V. Aho, M. S. Lam, R. Sethi, and J. D. Ullman. *Compilers: Principles, Techniques, and Tools (2nd Edition)*. Addison Wesley, August 2006.

[3] R. Alur, L. D'Antoni, S. Gulwani, D. Kini, and M. Viswanathan. Automated grading of dfa constructions. In *IJCAI*, 2013.

[4] L. Androutsopoulos. Natural language interfaces to databases - an introduction. *Journal of Natural Language Engineering*, 1, 1995.

[5] Apple. Siri for iPhone. `http://www.apple.com/iphone/features/siri.html`.

[6] J. Aron. How innovative is Apple's new voice assistant, Siri? *The New Scientist*, 2011.

[7] Crafty Apps. Tasker for Android. `http://tasker.dinglisch.net/`.

[8] S. S. Epstein. Transportable natural language processing through simplicity–the PRE system. *ACM Transactions on Information Systems (TOIS)*, 3(2), 1985.

[9] C. Finucane, G. Jing, and H. Kress-Gazit. LTLMoP: Experimenting with language, temporal logic and robot control. In *IEEE/RSJ ICIRS*, 2010.

[10] Google. Voice Actions for Android. `http://www.google.com/mobile/voice-actions/`.

[11] S. Gulwani. Dimensions in program synthesis. In *PPDP*, 2010.

[12] S. Gulwani. Automating string processing in spreadsheets using input-output examples. In *POPL*, 2011.

[13] S. Gulwani. Synthesis from examples: Interaction models and algorithms. *SYNASC*, 2012. Invited talk paper.

[14] S. Gulwani, W. Harris, and R. Singh. Spreadsheet data manipulation using examples. *Communication of the ACM*, 2012.

[15] S. Gulwani, S. Jha, A. Tiwari, and R. Venkatesan. Synthesis of loop-free programs. In *PLDI*, 2011.

[16] S. Gulwani, V. Korthikanti, and A. Tiwari. Synthesizing geometry constructions. In *PLDI*, 2011.

[17] T. Gvero, V. Kuncak, and R. Piskac. Interactive Synthesis of Code Snippets. In *CAV*, 2011.

[18] G. Hendrix, E. Sacerdoti, D. Sagalowicz, and J. Slocum. Developing a natural language interface to complex data. *ACM Transactions on Database Systems (TODS)*, 3(2), 1978.

[19] D. Jurafsky and J. H. Martin. Speech and Language Processing: An Introduction to Natural Language Processing, Computational Linguistics and Speech Recognition. Prentice Hall, 2nd edition, 2008.

[20] R. J. Kate, Y. W. Wong, and R. J. Mooney. Learning to transform natural to formal languages. In *AAAI*, 2005.

[21] D. Klein and C. D. Manning. Accurate unlexicalized parsing. In *ACL*, 2003.

[22] Y. Li, H. Yang, and H. V. Jagadish. NaLIX: an interactive natural language interface for querying XML. In *ICMD*, 2005.

[23] G. Little and R. C. Miller. Keyword programming in Java. In *ASE*, 2007.

[24] G. Little and R. C. Miller. Keyword programming in Java. *ASE*, 2009.

[25] H. Liu and H. Lieberman. Metafor: visualizing stories as code. In *IEEE IUI*, 2005.

[26] H. Liu and H. Lieberman. Programmatic semantics for natural language interfaces. In *Extended Abstracts on Human Factors in Computing Systems*, 2005.

[27] D. Mandelin, L. Xu, R. Bodík, and D. Kimelman. Jungloid mining: helping to navigate the api jungle. In *PLDI*, 2005.

[28] M. D. Marneffe, B. MacCartney, and C. D. Manning. Generating typed dependency parses from phrase structure parses. In *LREC*, 2006.

[29] Microsoft Research. on{X}. `http://onx.ms/`.

[30] MIT Center for Mobile Learning. MIT App Inventor for Android. `http://appinventor.mit.edu/`.

[31] R. Pandita, X. Xiao, H. Zhong, T. Xie, S. Oney, and A. Paradkar. Inferring method specifications from natural language api descriptions. In *ICSE*, 2012.

[32] D. Perelman, S. Gulwani, T. Ball, and D. Grossman. Type-directed completion of partial expressions. In *PLDI*, 2012.

[33] D. Price, E. Riloff, J. Zachary, and B. Harvey. NaturalJava: a natural language interface for programming in Java. In *IEEE IUI*, 2000.

[34] M.-R. Ra, B. Liu, T. L. Porta, and R. Govindan. Medusa: A Programming Framework for Crowd-Sensing Applications. In *MobiSys*, 2012.

[35] R. Singh and S. Gulwani. Learning semantic string transformations from examples. *VLDB*, 2012.

[36] I. Song, F. Guedea, F. Karray, Y. Dai, and I. El Khalil. Natural language interface for mobile robot navigation control. In *ISIC*, 2004.

[37] SRI International. Cognitive Assistant that Learns and Organizes. `http://www.ai.sri.com/project/CALO`.

[38] N. Tillmann, M. Moskal, J. de Halleux, and M. Fahndrich. TouchDevelop: programming cloud-connected mobile devices via touchscreen. In *ONWARD*, 2011.

[39] Two forty four a.m. LLC. Locale. `http://www.twofortyfouram.com/`.

[40] N. Wirth. Program development by stepwise refinement. *Communication of the ACM*, 14(4), 1971.

[41] X. Xiao, A. Paradkar, S. Thummalapenta, and T. Xie. Automated extraction of security policies from natural-language software documents. In *FSE*, 2012.

[42] B. Yan and G. Chen. AppJoy: Appjoy: Personalized mobile application discovery. In *MobiSys*, 2011.

FM-based Indoor Localization via Automatic Fingerprint DB Construction and Matching

Sungro Yoon†, Kyunghan Lee°, and Injong Rhee†

† Department of Computer Science
North Carolina State University
Raleigh, NC, USA
{syoon4, rhee}@ncsu.edu

°School of Electrical and Computer Engineering
Ulsan National Institute of Science and Technology
Ulsan, Republic of Korea
khlee@unist.ac.kr

ABSTRACT

We present ACMI, an FM-based indoor localization that does not require proactive site profiling. ACMI constructs the fingerprint database based on the pure estimation of indoor RSS distribution, where the signals transmitted from commercial FM radio stations are used. For this, ACMI makes use of our signal model harnessing public transmission information of FM stations in a combination with a floorplan of a building. Using the fingerprint database as the knowledge base, ACMI actively performs multi-level online signal matching to infer the current location of a mobile user. ACMI achieves good indoor localization accuracy even without site profiling efforts. We evaluate ACMI with extensive indoor experiments in 7 different locations with over 1,100 indoor spots. The results show that ACMI achieves up to 89% room identification and accuracy of 6 m localization error on average using 8 FM broadcast signals.

Categories and Subject Descriptors

C.2.1 [**Network Architecture and Design**]: Wireless communication; H.4.m [**Information Systems Applications**]: Miscellaneous

Keywords

FM, indoor localization, automation

1. INTRODUCTION

The prevalence of smart devices has triggered the recent emergence of location-based services. While *anywhere* services is expected, however, satellite signals do not reach inside the buildings and therefore the GPS (global positioning system) is not available indoors. To address this issue, there has been an urgent call for an accurate indoor localization technique.

Received signal strength (RSS) based techniques have been actively discussed among several branches of studies. They are known to provide robust and accurate indoor localization [1, 29]. The RSSs from various signal sources form a position-specific signature. Thus given the signature DB, a mobile user can query the current location based on the sampled RSSs. The merit is that this technique achieves good accuracy without the need for an installation of any new infrastructure nor any complicated hardware and software. But the difficulty is with an exhaustive preprocess of site profiling, where every single spot in a building should be probed to store the corresponding RSS samples. This process is labor-intensive and time-consuming, thus becoming the major bottleneck that hinders the technique from being widely deployed in the real world.

Crowdsourcing is an alternative way to the manual site profiling. Crowdsourcing distributes the heavy load by asking each mobile user contribute to build the fingerprint database collaboratively. But in this approach it is hard to expect that a mobile user can label the sampled RSSs with precise location, because the current location is not known to the user a priori at the moment. Therefore inputs with at most room-level accuracy might be expected [9, 17]. Recent innovations [19, 23, 27] solve this problem with dead-reckoning powered by motion sensors (e.g., accelerometer, compass, etc.) and the knowledge of floorplans or landmarks. Therefore the mobile users, unawarely, can report the current location with measured RSS samples. Although this alleviates the issue, still, some non-negligible time duration might be required to stabilize the database and to start the localization service.

Another challenge with the current RSS fingerprint based localization is the vulnerability of the signal source itself. WiFi is being commonly used for the RSS-based techniques because of its abundance in the availability. It has been reported however that the WiFi signals, around 2.4 GHz or 5 GHz, are very susceptible to human presence or orientation of mobile devices [2, 30]. Moreover the WiFi APs are de-

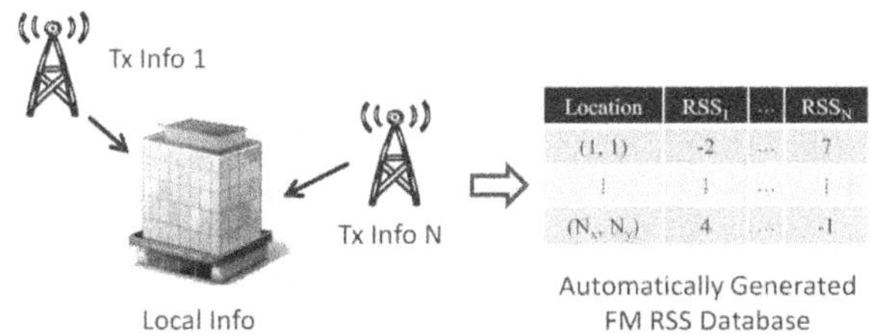

Figure 1: Example scenario of ACMI.

MobiSys'13, June 25-28, 2013, Taipei, Taiwan

ployed without careful planning in many cases and therefore their configuration might be easily changed by individuals. This means that even with the extensive site profiling efforts, after some time, it is highly probable that the RSSs sampled by mobile users do not match accurately with pre-surveyed RSSs.

In this paper, we present ACMI, a system named after Automatic Construction and Matching of Indoor RSS fingerprint database. We choose FM broadcasts as the signal source. Enabled by the excellent stability of this medium [2] we build the fingerprint database purely based on the indoor signal propagation model. Thus the site profiling efforts can be saved. Consider a scenario, as illustrated in Figure 1, where an IT technician sends necessary information to a third party service provider. Based on the model and the given information, the service provider can immediately generate and offer the RSS fingerprint database.

There have been such model-based approaches [5, 12, 16] in the literature. These proposals use WiFi signal to achieve good accuracy, but we strongly believe that the model-based technique can better be realized with FM signals. The major benefit is that FM signals are stable and have a city-wide coverage. Also the essential information for the model, such as global coordinate of transmission antenna, transmission power, etc., is readily available [8]. Unless manually surveyed, such information about WiFi APs is not known beforehand. WiFi coverage is small and there are a number of APs heterogeneously deployed with such unknown characteristics even in a single building. Finally, it has been recently shown that FM-based localization can provide very good accuracy. Chen et al. showed that FM fingerprint-based indoor localization can achieve 92% room identification and up to 1 ft. localization accuracy [2].

The challenge we face is that, to the best of our knowledge, there does not exist a model that estimates the indoor RSS distribution of FM signals, transmitted from remote stations usually tens of miles away. Through extensive in-building measurements we have found that a few dominating rules exist, which determine the RSS at a certain indoor spot. We develop an empirical model conforming to the rules. The evaluation shows the impressive similarity between the model-based estimation and the actual measurements. Using this model and signals from 8 FM stations, simple minimum squared error (MSE) match shows the accuracy between 10m and 18m without any calibration. We further demonstrate that the accuracy can be improved with online operations. We perform least mean square (LMS) based runtime parameter calibration, and then perform path matching based positioning. Extensive evaluation performed in 7 different sites over 1,100 spots shows that our system can achieve average 89% room identification and 6 m localization accuracy.

We outline our contributions as follow. (1) We propose a novel FM-model based indoor localization that can avoid the site profiling. (2) For this we perform extensive indoor measurements and suggest a practical model that predicts the RSS distribution only using the publicly available FM transmission information and the floorplan of a building. (3) We propose an online calibration and inference technique that can improve the localization accuracy. (4) Finally we perform extensive evaluation and show that the system achieves good accuracy in real-world scenarios.

The rest of this paper is organized as follows. In Section 2, we discuss relevant studies. Then we describe our findings from indoor measurements in Section 3 and establish an empirical model in Section 4. The system is described in Section 5 and we further discuss several issues in Section 6. The performance is evaluated in Section 7 and finally Section 8 concludes the paper.

2. RELATED WORK

2.1 Fingerprint-based Techniques

RADAR [1] has pioneered the RSS fingerprint-based indoor localization. At each indoor location, broadcast packets from WiFi APs are overheard. The RSSs from multiple APs form a single vector representing the specific location and by performing look-ups within the pre-built database the current location can be found. Horus [29] advances the technique by introducing a probability based inference model, where the RSS from an AP is modeled into a random variable that varies according to time and location. Apart from the RSS, a recent technique [21] utilizes the channel impulse response of WiFi as the location-specific signature and achieves highly accurate indoor localization. While these techniques are very accurate, they require the labor and time intensive site profiling where every indoor spot should be manually matched with corresponding fingerprints. In case WiFi is used as the signal source, this site profiling should be performed repetitively due to the significant temporal variances of WiFi signals.

Crowdsourcing is an alternative way for sharing the load among multiple users. The problem is that it is difficult for such mobile users to label the collected RSS samples with accurate location information [9, 17]. Recent innovations [19, 27] solve this problem by the use of the floorplan and the movement detector. Still, it takes time for convergence of the fingerprint DB.

2.2 Model-based Techniques

To avoid the manual profiling processes researchers suggested to automatically generate the look-up DB, based on known radio wave propagation characteristics [5, 12, 16]. Lim et al. proposed a technique [16] that, by observing WiFi RSSs and finding the linear relationship with geographic distances, builds the signal-distance map. This signal-distance map can be used to locate a mobile user's location. Ez [5] also builds RSS-distance equations, but exploits genetic algorithm to solve the equations. These two techniques basically base upon log-distance propagation model but do not explicitly assume any prior knowledge about infrastructures or deployments. They automatically obtain essential information from a few initial measurements. ARIADNE [12] uses floorplan together with sophisticated ray tracing method. By using known locations of WiFi APs and transmission powers, it can automatically generate the look-up DB.

Modeling approaches other than RSS also exist such as time of arrival [24], time difference of arrival [3] and angle of arrival [25]. They achieve highly accurate localization. However, these techniques require complicated processing in either software or hardware.

2.3 FM-based Localization

There have been growing research interests regarding FM-based *outdoor* localization. The advantage is that FM signals cover very wide area (up to 300 km), they have good availability of signal sources and FM radios consume less power compared to GPS or WiFi. FM signal can be used to detect a mobile user [15] or a passing object [11] outdoors. Youssef et al. showed the feasibility of the FM-modeling-based technique in an outdoor setup [28]. Based on the signal strength model and the calibration, 8 km accuracy has been achieved. But the main difficulty with the RSS-based approach is that the RSSs of FM signals do not significantly vary within nearby outdoor locations because of the strong transmission power. Therefore, close-by areas within small distances are often indifferentiable with FM RSSs. The linear relationship between the displacement and the signal phase of FM pilot tone can be considered [14] but it has not been verified experimentally.

Recently, Chen et al. inspired the research community by experimentally showing the feasibility of FM RSS-based indoor localization [2]. Unlike the outdoor environment, indoor structures create various shadow-like attenuation patterns that can be preferably used as signatures for the positioning. With FM RSS alone, they achieved up to 92% room level identification. In the meanwhile, they showed that the FM signals are robust to fading, human presences and changes in mobile devices' orientations unlike WiFi. It has been also shown that FM signals do not experience much temporal variations as WiFi signals.

2.4 Indoor Propagation Models

The well-known log-distance propagation model estimates the signal strengths of radio signals as

$$P(d) = P(d_0) - 10 \cdot n \cdot log_{10}(\frac{d}{d_0}) \;\; [dBm],$$

where $P(d)$, the received power at distance d is given by subtracting the attenuation factor from $P(d_0)$, the signal strength at reference distance d_0, usually set to 1m. Here n is the path loss exponent that is obtained experimentally. This simple log-distance model is not accurate indoors for following reasons. First, there could be obstacles between the transmitter and the receiver that further attenuate the signals. Second, this model assumes that the transmission power is equal (isotropic) in all directions, while nowadays many WiFi APs occupy antenna arrays or directional antennas and therefore they are non-isotropic. Finally, this model does not take into consideration the non-line-of-sight indirect signals that traverse longer paths than the direct signals.

To overcome the inaccuracy of log-distance model with indoor signal propagation, empirical models have been proposed [4, 7, 20]. While these models accurately estimate the indoor signal strengths, most of them considered only high signal frequencies ($\geq$ 900 MHz) that are commonly used for the wireless communication. These frequency bands have significantly different characteristics compared to FM signals at very high frequency (VHF) that range from 30 MHz to 300 MHz; the propagation of higher frequency signals is very rectilinear, while VHF signals around 100 MHz experience severe diffraction. Also, those studies only consider the case where a transmitter is inside the building. In our model, we consider the indoor propagation of FM broadcast signal where the transmitters are usually tens of miles away.

Another line of study [13, 22, 26] is to build a mathematical model. The ray tracing technique was originally used in 3D graphics analysis. It tracks virtually infinite number of very small *ray tubes* that stem out from the transmitter. Direct propagation, reflection and diffusion of a radio wave can be accurately modeled by the ray tube. Accumulating the ray tubes at each spot on the floor, the ray tracing can accurately predict the indoor RSS distribution. But the ray tracing cannot be used in our system for the following two reasons. First, the transmitter is too far away, which makes it impossible to model the traversal path of ray tubes. It is not known which obstacles are in between the building and FM transmitters. Second, the ray tracing technique is computationally complex. Computation of a scenario where the transmitter is just tens of meters away takes several hours [26]. Therefore, in our case the heavy computation may kill the practicality of our system. But we can consider this as one of future work.

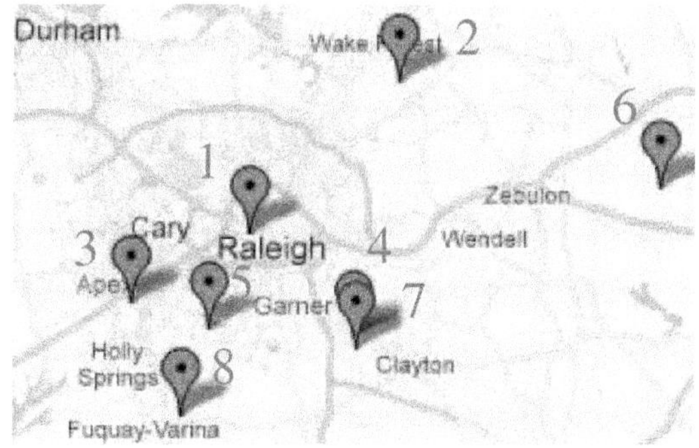

Figure 2: Locations of 8 available FM stations in the vicinity.

ID	Freq.(MHz)	P_{Tx}(kW)	Height(m)	Dist.(km)
1	88.1	25	79	2.1
2	89.7	100	359	29.3
3	93.9	100	453	16.6
4	94.7	95	511	18.9
5	96.1	98	300	10.4
6	100.7	4.3	489	59.6
7	101.5	96	555	19.8
8	105.1	73	339	21.0

Table 1: Information of FM stations that we used for our measurements.

3. MEASUREMENT AND OBSERVATION

In this section, we describe our findings from experimentations. The findings will be used to design the empirical indoor propagation model in the next section. Note that we do not make any assumption or adjustment to existing *outdoor* path loss models. We adopt one of outdoor path loss models [18] to estimate the RSSs at outer walls of a building and use the values as the basis of our indoor propagation model.

3.1 Measurement Methodology

We separately perform measurements outside and inside the building. We use USRP1 assembled with basic-RX daughterboard and FM Terk Pro antenna. RSSs of broadcast signals from 8 FM stations are measured in a round-robin way at each position. The locations of those FM stations are

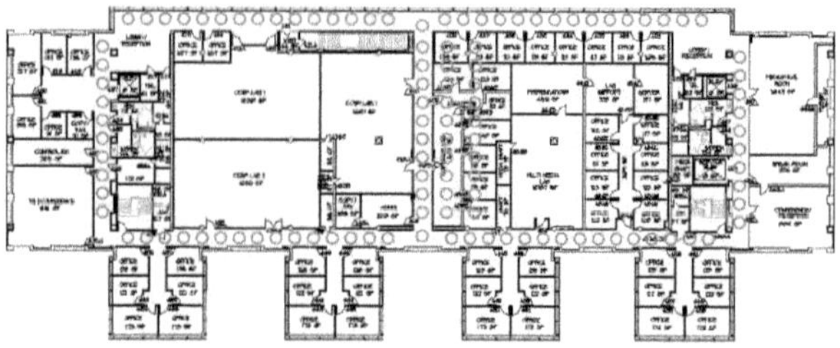

Figure 3: Floorplan of building. Red dots represent the spots where RSSs have been sampled.

shown in Figure 2 and other information is listed in Table 1. While there are a few more stations in the vicinity, we only select these stations based on the availability of signals in buildings.

3.2 Outside the Building

The purpose of this measurement is to test the accuracy of outdoor RSS estimation. In other words, we would like to see if we can accurately estimate the RSSs at the surface of a building given only the public information. These outdoor RSSs will naturally define the maximum of indoor RSS values. We measure the RSS of FM signals at the roof top of a building and compare with estimated values.

The RSS outside the building is estimated to be

$$RSS = Net\ Tx\ Power - Path\ Loss\ [dBm],$$

where the net transmission power indicates the actual transmitted power from the transmission antenna to the direction towards the local building. Usually an FM transmission antenna is *directional* and so the field strength of an FM transmission antenna differs at each direction. The net transmission power is calculated by multiplying *normalized relative field strength* to the original transmission power (See Figure 11 (b)). Thus it is required to calculate the actual direction from the transmission tower to the local building using the global coordinates (longitude and latitude).

We refer a technique from previous studies [18], which takes transmission power, antenna height and distance between a transmitter and a receiver. The RSSs outside the building are estimated based on this path loss model and compared with the actual measurements in Figure 4. The average estimation error is 3.8 dB for all FM stations. Note that the estimation error for the station 1 is significantly larger than those of other stations. We analyze that the reason should be the lower height of the transmission tower. The height of the this transmission tower is 79 m while other towers are 430 m in average. Therefore the signals might be frequently blocked by obstacles during the traversal path. With the similar reason, we find that signals from remote stations tend to experience larger path loss compared to adjacent stations (e.g., station 2, 6 and 8).

3.3 Inside the Building

We perform indoor measurements to observe how internal structures of a building create various RSS patterns. We measure RSSs in 375 spots within a 35 m by 95 m office building shown in Figure 3. Each spot is around 2 feet away from each other. Below, we list the findings that we observed from the measurement data.

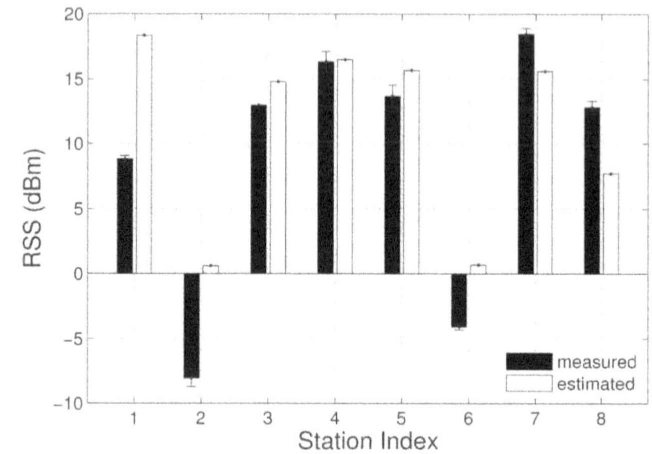

Figure 4: The measured and estimated RSSs outside the building. Average error is 3.8 dB.

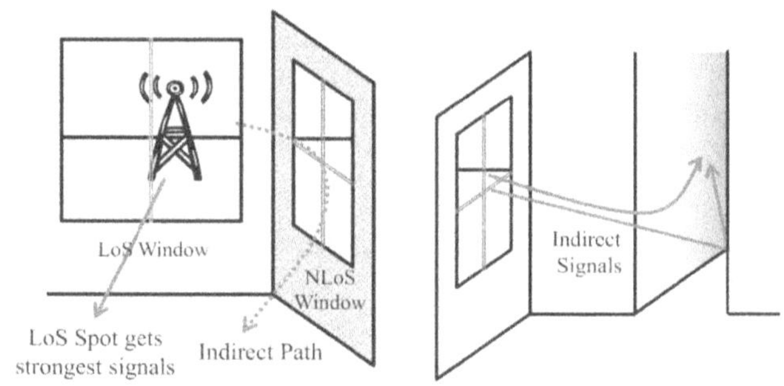

(a) Windows are the major entrance of signals.

(b) Signals often reach to isolated areas that has no direct path to windows.

Figure 5: Indoor propagation characteristics of FM broadcast signals.

3.3.1 *"Windows are the main entrances of FM signals into a building."*

VHF signals cannot usually penetrate through the surface of a building. They experience huge attenuation when blocked by the exterior walls. On the other hand, the signals can pass through windows and enter into the building with relatively small attenuation. Interestingly, we found that the amount of attenuation depends upon the direction that the window is facing.

Line of Sight (LoS) Window: If an FM transmission tower is in the direction that a window is facing, at a certain indoor spot, we call each as the *LoS window* and the *LoS spot* as shown in Figure 5 (a). LoS windows are the main source of FM signals in the building and the LoS spot located right beside the LoS window gets the strongest RSS of that FM broadcast. While there could be many windows in a building, the RSSs near the LoS windows are almost same with only negligible variances. Figure 6 compares RSSs at building surface, LoS windows, NLoS windows and the average RSSs. We see that an LoS spot beside LoS windows gets the strong RSSs, almost comparable to the RSS outside the building.

Non-LoS Window: Even though an indoor spot does not have an LoS path to the transmission tower, if that spot has

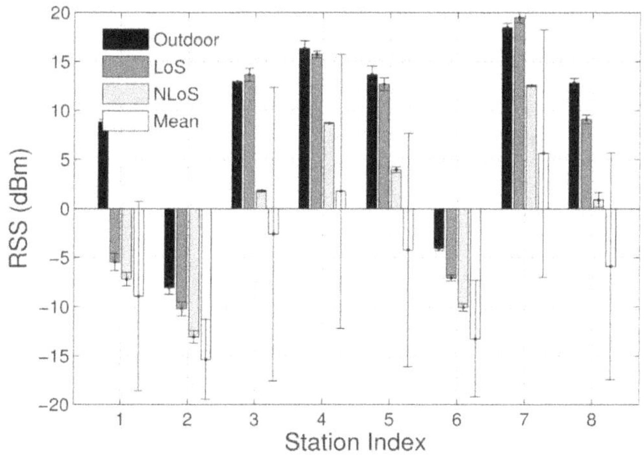

Figure 6: The RSSs at outside the building, windows with LoS, without LoS and average values are compared and averaged at 60 different spots.

a rectilinear path to *any other window* the spot also gets relatively strong signals. The reason is that VHF signals, after being blocked by exterior walls, can still enter the *Non-LoS windows* from other sides via indirect paths. The indirect paths are shown as a dotted line in Figure 5 (a). Unlike the LoS window case, Figure 6 shows that the RSSs at the NLoS windows are not regular. This is mainly because the traversal paths of NLoS signals are affected by the outer structures of a building. But we observe that the RSSs at NLoS windows are still stronger than average indoor RSSs.

Size of Window: A radio wave can freely pass through a hole only when diameter of the hole is larger than its wavelength. Recall a microwave oven; while one can see inside the oven via visible rays, the microwave radiation still cannot pass through the metal mesh since the diameter of the mesh is smaller than the wavelength. From our observation, the FM signals are significantly attenuated when the size of a window is less than half the wavelength, which is around 1.5 meters with 100MHz signals.

3.3.2 *"Indoor walls significantly attenuate the signals."*

Indoor walls block the direct propagation of signals and significantly attenuate the RSS. Empirical studies [7, 20] report that the amount of attenuation increases linearly proportional (in log-scale) to the number of obstacles during the path. We also observe the similar trends. We performed measurements to see the RSS attenuation when signals propagate across walls. In order to accurately measure the attenuation caused only by walls, we chose 30 LoS spots and 30 nearby spots right behind the walls. The actual distance between each pair is less than 2 m. Then we measured the RSS at those spots. For signals from 8 stations, the attenuation was 6.9 dB in average. But this depends on the material of the wall and can vary across buildings.

3.3.3 *"Signals experience significant indoor path loss."*

Indoor attenuation of FM signals is much larger than outside. We measure the amount of path loss, while varying the distance to the LoS window. To accurately measure the impact of path loss we choose a different building for this

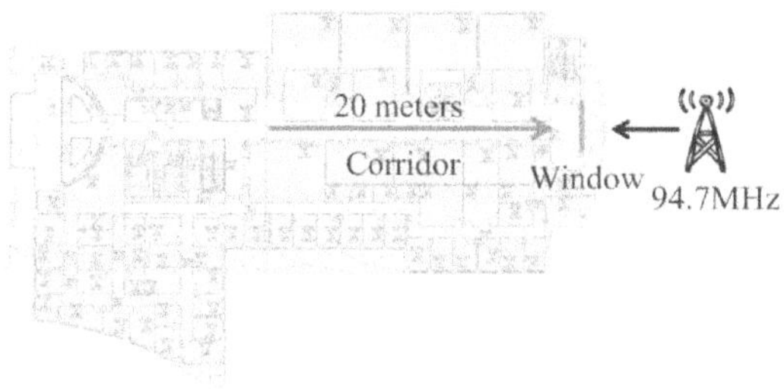

(a) Path loss measurement methodology.

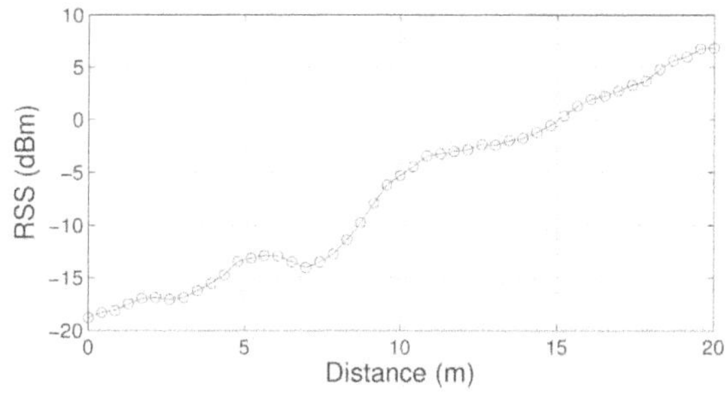

(b) Indoor path loss measurement results.

Figure 7: Pass loss measurement at an indoor corridor shows the path loss exponent of 2.16.

measurement only. The building has a corridor with a large window at one end as shown in Figure 7 (a). We measure the RSSs of LoS signals while moving 20 meters. The result is shown in Figure 7 (b) and the average path loss exponent is 2.16. But as previous studies show [7, 20], the path loss exponent widely varies with environments.

3.3.4 *"Signals frequently take indirect paths to reach isolated areas."*

An isolated spot, which does not have a direct path to any window, still gets signals. The reason is that VHF signals can detour when facing obstacles and often reach to isolated areas, as illustrated in Figure 5 (b). Such signals would include diffraction, diffusion and reflection. But we just refer them as indirect signals since they arrive simultaneously and thus are not differentiable.

Large portion of VHF signals takes indirect paths. So the isolated spots often exhibit higher RSSs at VHF than they should at higher carrier frequencies. We refer an indoor spot, which has a direct path to any window and no obstacle in-between, as *direct spot*. The direct spot includes both the LoS and the NLoS spots. We find that the isolated spots exhibiting higher RSSs usually have clear paths to those direct spots. As a result, the RSSs at those isolated spots never exceed those of the nearest direct spots and decrease with the distance to those direct spots. We perform the similar experiment as above to see the path loss of the indirect signals and the result was similar. So we omit the result here.

4. MODEL AND VERIFICATION

We suggest an empirical model based on our observation. The model is given as follows:

$$RSS(s,t) = \max[RSS_{LoS}(s,t), RSS_{NLoS}(s,t), RSS_{ind}(s,t)], \quad (1)$$

Algorithm 1: BuildRSSDatabase(S, T, W, R)

```
Input: set S, coordinates of all indoor spots
Input: set T, coordinates of all FM stations
Input: set W, coordinates of all windows
Output: RSS(s, t) for ∀s ∈ S, ∀t ∈ T
for t ∈ T do
    for s ∈ S do
        RSS_LoS ← 0, RSS_NLoS ← 0;
        if ∃w ∈ W such that w, s and t are on a straight line then
            d ← distance to the nearest w;
            n ← number of walls between s and w;
            RSS_LoS ←
            max(RSS(t)) − 10αlog(d/d0) − n · f;
            if size of w < λ/2 then
                RSS_LoS = RSS_LoS − C2;
            end
        end
        if ∃w ∈ W such that w = NLoS window then
            d ← distance to the nearest w;
            n ← number of walls between s and w;
            RSS_NLoS ←
            max(RSS(t)) − 10αlog(d/d0) − n · f − C1;
            if size of w < λ/2 then
                RSS_NLoS = RSS_NLoS − C2;
            end
        end
        RSS(s, t) ← max(RSS_LoS, RSS_NLoS);
    end
end
for t ∈ T do
    U: set of spots with direct paths to any w ∈ W;
    for s ∈ S do
        RSS_ind ← 0;
        if s has a direct path to any u ∈ U then
            d ← distance to u;
            RSS_ind ← RSS(u, t) − 10αlog(d/d0);
        end
        RSS(s, t) ← max(RSS(s, t), RSS_ind);
    end
end
```

where $RSS(s,t)$ is the estimated RSS of signals from FM station t, at an indoor spot s and the rests are RSSs received via three different paths. While each RSS via the different path should be summed up in reality, we rather choose to take the maximum out of three for the following reasons. First, we want to keep the linearity of RSS equation in logarithm scale, which is preferable for the online calibration. The summation process will require the conversion of each RSS component into linear scale and therefore include exponential terms such as $RSS = 10 \cdot log_{10}(10^{RSS_{LoS}/10} + 10^{RSS_{NLoS}/10} + 10^{RSS_{ind}/10})$. Those exponential terms hinder the use of linear algorithm that we will adapt for the calibration. Second, there is no great difference between maximum and summation, in dB scale, since one of the RSS components is usually significantly larger than others.

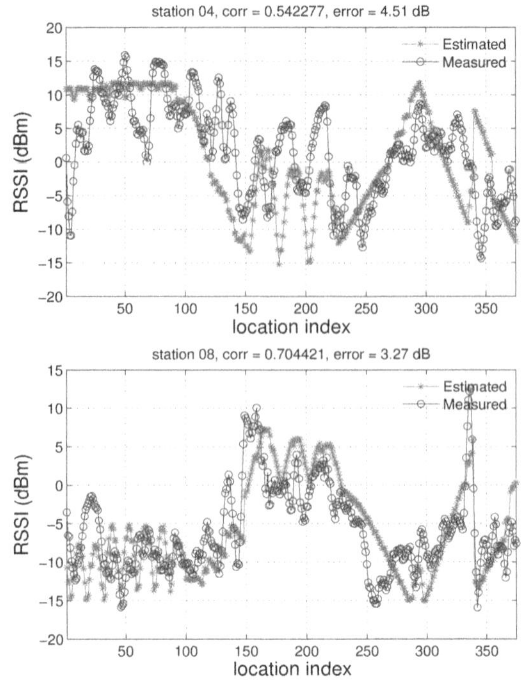

Figure 8: Comparison between model-generated RSS estimation with actual measurements, for FM station 4 and 8, respectively. The cross-correlation is 0.54 and 0.70, and the median error is 4.5 dB and 3.3 dB, respectively.

RSS_{LoS} is the portion received via the LoS path:

$$RSS_{LoS}(s,t) = max(RSS(t)) - \alpha \cdot 10 \cdot log_{10}(d/d_0) - n \cdot f, \quad (2)$$

where $max(RSS(t))$ is the maximum indoor RSS of signals from station t. The term is derived from the outdoor path loss model described in Section 3.2. α is the path loss exponent, d is the distance from s to the source of signal (e,g., LoS window in this case), d_0 is the reference distance (1 m), n is the number of walls between the spot and the LoS window and f is the wall attenuation factor. In the same manner, RSS_{NLoS} is the RSS via NLoS windows given as

$$RSS_{NLoS}(s,t) = max(RSS(t)) - \alpha \cdot 10 \cdot log_{10}(d/d_0) - n \cdot f - C_1, \quad (3)$$

where C_1 is the constant attenuation factor of LNoS signals. As described in Section 3.3.1, C_1 is hard to model since the amount of attenuation is not regular. For now we bear the modeling error that arises by setting this value into constant and try to alleviate via online techniques.

In case the size of either an LoS window or an NLoS window is smaller than half the wavelength, around 1.5 m with VHF signals, we subtract the small window attenuation factor, C_2 from the RSS.

Finally, RSS_{ind} is the RSS of signals delivered from other direct spots via an indirect path:

$$RSS_{ind}(s,t) = RSS(u,t) - \alpha \cdot 10 \cdot log_{10}(d/d_0), \quad (4)$$

where u is the nearest direct spot from s and d is the distance to u. Note that any of RSS_{LoS}, RSS_{NLoS} and RSS_{ind} can have zero value according to the indoor structure. Algorithm 1 is based on this model and generates the RSS

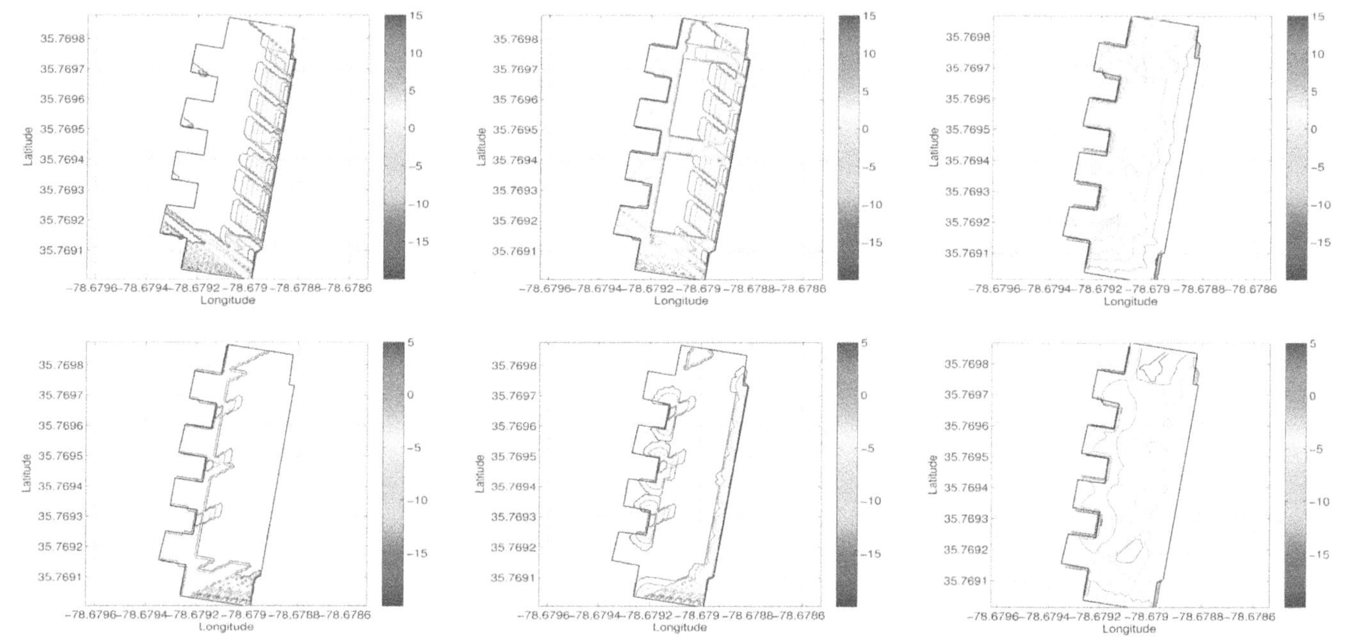

Figure 9: Model-generated RSS distributions over the floor. Each column demonstrates each algorithm step: (1) LoS signals only (2) NLoS signals added and (3) indirect signals added, respectively. Each row is the distribution of signals from station 4 and 8. The FM stations are located south east and south west of the building, respectively. For the floorplan of the building, please see Figure 3.

database. Figure 9 shows the step by step RSS output of the algorithm for the signals from station 4 and 8. The floorplan and the transmission information are given as an input to the model (see Figure 3, Figure 11 and Table 1).

4.1 Modeling Parameters

There are parameters α, f and C_1 used in the model. We basically use the values measured from our experiment. For example, we use measured indoor path loss exponents 2.16 for α. But we observe that the values vary at different environments. We use the measured values as seeds for the online training algorithm and calibrate the parameters during the runtime. The training algorithm is described in Section 5.3.1.

For C_2, we just regard as if there is a wall right in front of the window. Therefore we subtract a constant value f from the expected RSS. So C_2 and f are same.

4.2 Verification

To see the accuracy, we compare the estimation with actual measurements. We choose 375 actual spots within the building and measure the RSSs at each of them. Figure 8 shows the RSS estimations together with actual measurements at those spots. While the estimation does not perfectly match with the measurements, we can visually see the similarity between the two. For further verification of the modeling accuracy, please see Section 7.2.

5. SYSTEM DESCRIPTION

5.1 Overview

ACMI runs in two separate modes. Figure 10 depicts the overall architecture. During the offline phase ACMI

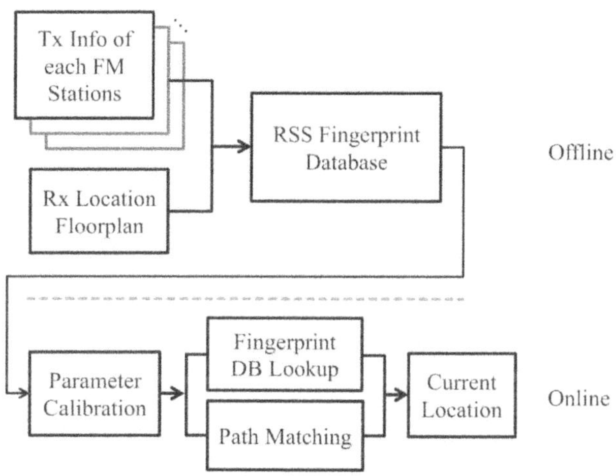

Figure 10: Architecture of ACMI.

builds the FM fingerprint DB using the proposed propagation model. This offline operation is one-time process which is performed autonomously without any participation from users. The output of this offline phase, fingerprint DB, is provided to mobile users who want to navigate through the building. As the innate discrepancy exists between the model and the actual RSS distribution, a mobile user can perform online adjustment phase in order to further improve the accuracy. The online phase comprises runtime parameter calibration and path matching.

5.2 Offline Phase

FM fingerprint database is built offline. Because we already described the procedure in the previous section we

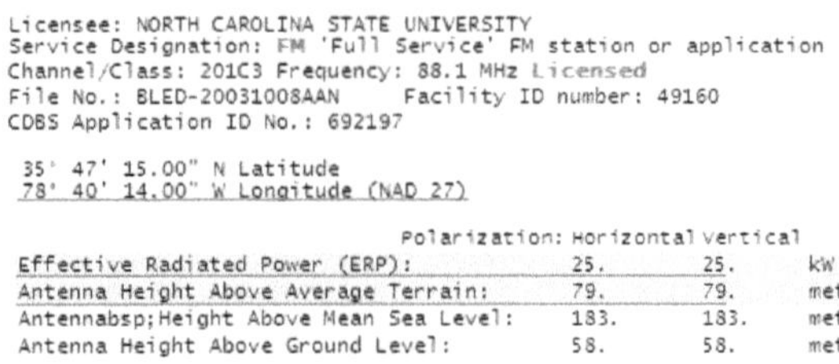

Licensee: NORTH CAROLINA STATE UNIVERSITY
Service Designation: FM 'Full Service' FM station or application
Channel/Class: 201C3 Frequency: 88.1 MHz Licensed
File No.: BLED-20031008AAN Facility ID number: 49160
CDBS Application ID No.: 692197

35' 47' 15.00" N Latitude
78' 40' 14.00" W Longitude (NAD 27)

Polarization:	Horizontal	Vertical	
Effective Radiated Power (ERP):	25.	25.	kW ERP
Antenna Height Above Average Terrain:	79.	79.	meters HAAT
Antennabsp;Height Above Mean Sea Level:	183.	183.	meters AMSL
Antenna Height Above Ground Level:	58.	58.	meters AGL

(a) Coordinate & height of Tx tower.

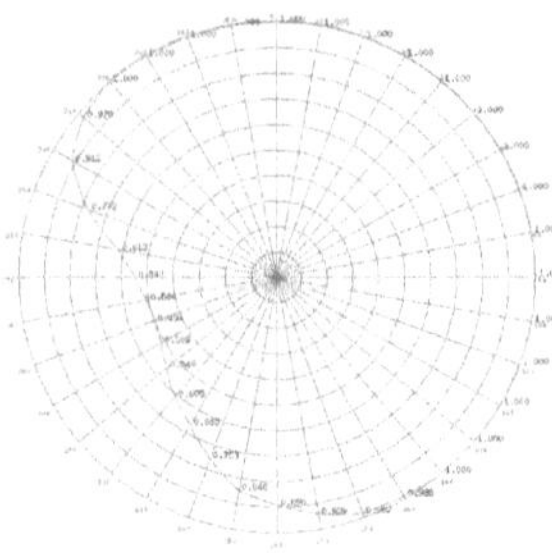

(b) Relative field polar plot of transmission antenna.

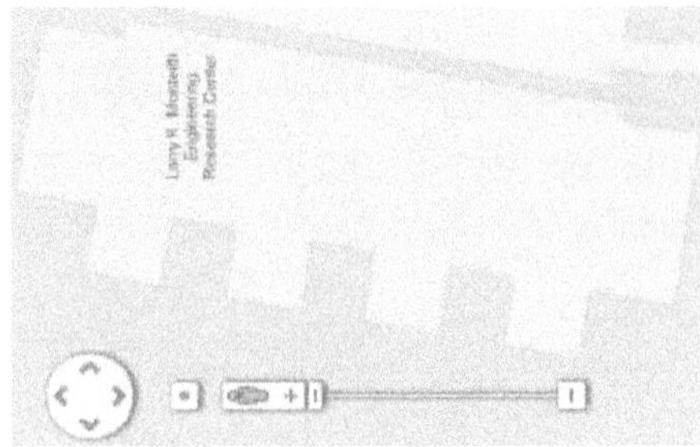

(c) Coordinate of building.

Figure 11: Required information for building the fingerprint DB.

just explain the information required for the offline phase and omit any further detail.

5.2.1 Source Information

The transmission information of FM radio includes coordinates of FM towers, transmission power, antenna direction and height. The information is managed by FCC. FCC provides a query database which is accessible via web interface [8]. Local information includes the coordinates of a building and the floorplan.

Coordinate of FM Tower: The coordinates of an FM tower is provided as Figure 11 (a) shows. The global longitude and latitude information is required to calculate (1) distance and (2) direction toward the local building. The distance is used to estimate the outdoor path loss. The direction is required to calculate the net transmission power and also to analyze the indoor RSS distribution (e.g., to figure out LoS and NLoS windows).

Transmission Power and Antenna Direction: As an FM transmission tower is usually installed outside a city, the antenna is commonly directed towards the inner city for the power efficiency. So both the transmission power and antenna direction is required together to obtain the net transmission power. The transmission power is shown in Figure 11 (a). FCC provides antenna direction information in the form of relative field plot, as Figure 11 (b) shows.

Antenna Height: Antenna height has an impact on the outdoor path loss. Signals from higher antenna experience less obstacles and thus less path loss [18]. The height of a transmission tower is given in Figure 11 (a).

Coordinates of Local Building: This is required to compute the distance and the direction between the transmission tower and the local building. Today's map applications (e.g., Bing Map) provides high-resolution coordinates of buildings in most of major cities.

Floor Plan: Floor plan has the internal structure information of a building and therefore is essential for the estimation of RSS distribution over the floor. Our model needs the topology information of exterior walls, interior walls, and windows. We import the structural information in our software and process such that each object (e.g., wall and window) is assigned its own global coordinate. Finally, the transmission towers and the indoor structures are organized in a single data structure representing the global topology, shown in Figure 9.

5.3 Online Phase

ACMI performs DB look-up to find out the current indoor position. This look-up is based on simple minimum squared error (MSE) matching. Current position L is estimated to be a location in DB of which the RSS vector has the smallest Euclidean distance with the measurement. L is formally given as $\arg\min_s ||\overrightarrow{RSS_{DB}}(s) - \overrightarrow{RSS_M}||$ where $\overrightarrow{RSS_{DB}}(s)$ is the estimated RSS vector in DB at an indoor spot s and $\overrightarrow{RSS_M}$ is the measured RSS vector at the mobile user's current location.

At this point the room identification shows large deviation ranging between 59% and 89%. The main cause is the errors in the outdoor path loss estimation. This estimation is not always accurate because of weather or unknown surrounding obstacles. Variability of antenna gains in mobile devices can also have some impact on this. The site-specific model parameters are another reason. The parameters are not uniform across buildings because of diversity in building materials. Therefore the runtime calibration is essential to correct these values.

But the calibration still does not guarantee the perfect capture of real RSS distribution. Ambiguity arises when multiple spots across the fingerprint DB exhibit similar RSS signatures. This causes localization error. One easiest remedy is to crosscheck as many signal sources as possible, e.g., 32 FM signals as in [2]. But such abundance might not be always available.

We perform path matching to improve the localization accuracy. The path matching *clusters* multiple indoor spots along the walking path of a mobile user. The basic motivation of path matching is that, even though the RSS estimation at each individual spot is not perfectly accurate, the *RSS changing pattern* over the broader area can be unique with much higher probability. For instance, imagine a scenario where a mobile user moves away from one of windows toward the inner part of a building. It is natural that the RSS gradually decreases with the distance to the window while slope of the curve might vary. The accuracy can be substantially improved by matching between a cluster of measured RSSs along the walking path and the estimated RSSs. The final result is 89% room identification and 6 m localization accuracy.

5.3.1 Runtime Calibration

The runtime calibration is a two-step process where the unknown parameters are derived first and then RSS DB is refined. $max(RSS(t))$, α, f and C_1 in Equation (3) are

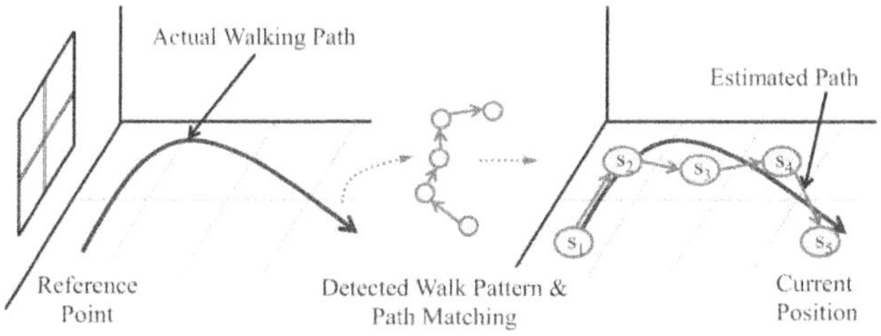

Figure 12: Indoor positions along the walking path are recognized by walk detection. The detected positions are used to (1) calibrate the model parameters and to (2) perform the path matching.

the parameters to be calibrated. ACMI mainly performs the calibration at known reference points e.g., a building entrance. The reference point is defined a priori and its exact location is readily known to the system.

The calibration process is triggered when a mobile user walks into the reference point. Starting from the reference point, RSSs are sampled at multiple spots as the mobile user takes steps. The sampled RSSs are compared with the estimated RSSs at the same locations to calibrate the parameters. Exact location of each step is indeed hard to know, but we rely on the walk detector that uses motion sensors in a smart device to infer the approximate location. We further describe this in Section 5.3.2. In our setup, we use 5 nearby spots for the calibration, as shown in Figure 12.

At each spot the largest RSS component should be decided among RSS_{LoS}, RSS_{NLoS} and RSS_{ind} according to Equation (1). Usually either LoS or NLoS signal component dominates at the building entrance. The stronger component of the two is decided based on the following simple rule; if a transmission tower is visible the LoS signal will dominate; otherwise the NLoS signal will. Only in case a certain reference point is isolated and does not have direct path to any source of signals, then the indirect component should be selected.

Once the strongest component has been determined the simple solution should be to directly solve the linear equations for the parameters since we have only a fixed number of unknowns. However, the RSS samples in real world always include measurement noises for various reasons, e.g., changes in the orientation of antennas or existence of surrounding objects. It is therefore required to choose optimal values that minimize the estimation errors.

LMS-based Calibration: Assume that the NLoS signal is strongest at a certain reference point. Then equation (3) is re-written as

$$Y = H \cdot X + W,$$

where Y is l-rank measurement vector $[y_1 \cdots y_l]$ with y_i the measured RSS at location $i = 1 \cdots l$, H is the array of parameters $[max(RSS(t)), \alpha, f, C_1]$ to be calibrated, X is l-rank vector $[x_1, \cdots, x_l]$ such that each x_i is $[1, -10 \cdot log_{10}(d_i/d_0), -n_i, 1]^T$ and W is the measurement noise. Here H and X are defined to reformulate equation (3). The minimum mean squared error (MMSE) is known to provide optimal solution when the measurement noise exists. But it requires the knowledge of C_X, the auto-covariance matrix of X, that is not available in our case.

We use the least mean square (LMS) filter. The LMS filter does not require the knowledge of C_X but is proven to converge to a solution equivalent to MMSE [10]. In LMS, the parameter vector H is updated as:

$$H_{i+1} = H_i + \mu \cdot e_i \cdot x_i,$$

where μ is a small constant and e_i is defined as $e_i = Y_i - H_i \cdot x_i$. RSS vector Y_i is measured at step i where each measurement step is notified by the walk detector. H_i is then iteratively updated to minimize the error term e_i. We expedite the computation by assigning the measured values from experiments as an initial seed for H_0. In our implementation, it took measurements at less than 5 locations to converge.

So far we only described the NLoS case but the same steps apply for RSS_{LoS} and RSS_{ind}. The elements in H and X are replaced with corresponding ones accordingly.

Refinement of Fingerprint DB: With the calibrated parameters, the fingerprint DB should be re-generated and offered to the user. The user can simply report the parameters to the service provider, where the DB is automatically refined based on the parameters.

5.3.2 Path Matching

ACMI samples and keeps l-recent RSS measurement vectors in the buffer. While performing the localization, ACMI continuously checks for ambiguity. We define that estimation is *ambiguous* when the matching error at a spot s is large, formally given as:

$$||\overrightarrow{RSS_{DB}}(s) - \overrightarrow{RSS_M}|| \quad > \quad \theta_{amb}.$$

When the ambiguity is detected ACMI starts looking into the buffer to find a path $P = [s_0, ..., s_{l-1}]$ such that

$$P \quad = \quad \arg\min_{s_i \in S} \sum_{j=0}^{l-1} ||\overrightarrow{RSS_{DB}}(s_j) - \overrightarrow{RSS_M}(j)||,$$

where $\overrightarrow{RSS_M}(j)$ is the jth measured RSS vector in the buffer and l is the maximum buffer length. After the path is chosen, s_{l-1}, the last spot in the matched path, is finally estimated to be the current location.

Then the question is how to choose the candidate spots $\hat{s_0}, ..., \hat{s_{l-1}}$. Given that the total number of indoor spots is $|S|$, to find the best match among all the possible combinations will incur $|S|^l$ computations. To reduce the search space, we extract the user walking pattern. Each $\hat{s_{i+1}}$ is dead-reckoned from $\hat{s_i}$ based on the motion sensors in the smart device. We regulate the distance between two successive spots such that $||\hat{s_i} - \hat{s_{i+1}}|| = d_{const}$ to relate only neighboring spots with the pre-defined fixed interval. The two conditions are forced by the walk detector. The result is $O(|S|)$ number of candidate spots that meet the detected walking pattern.

Walk Detector: Walk detector reports the topology of indoor spots along the user walking path. Walk detector combines dead-reckoning and footstep detection together. Accelerometers in smartphones detect the acceleration in 3 dimensions along with compass information. The information can be used to calculate the displacement of a mobile user. As UnLoc [23] shows, this dead-reckoning can provide moving direction with reasonable accuracy within a short distance.

But note that we do not directly use the dead-reckoning to infer the indoor position itself. In the long run, the dead-reckoning based localization is inaccurate if without periodic calibration because sensing errors are cumulated. Rather, the primary goal of dead-reckoning is to obtain the short-term walking pattern of a mobile user. The detected pattern is only used to reduce the search space in performing the path matching.

In the meanwhile the accelerometers can effectively detect the number of footsteps that a user takes. This is because the human walk introduces the significant jolt orthogonal to the ground (i.e., z-axis). From this it is possible to estimate the distance that the user has moved. The footstep detection has been actively used in recent proposals [6, 19, 23, 27], so we do not describe in more detail. In our experiment we use 3 steps (around 2 m) displacement between the spots.

6. DISCUSSIONS

General Applicability: There are a few limiting factors that might hinder the use of ACMI. First, obstacles around the building, e.g., trees, hills or other buildings, can block the FM signals and therefore incur the estimation error of outdoor RSSs. This can disturb the accurate RSS estimation. If online parameter calibration is performed, however, this case does not pose a fundamental limit. The path loss estimation error can be corrected via the calibration.

Second, if a floorplan itself does not properly reveal the sufficient structural information it is difficult to estimate the indoor RSS. This case is more complicated. For instance, consider a building of which the ceiling itself is a large window. Our approach cannot effectively deal with the case since we only utilize 2-D information obtained from the floorplan. However, this is also not the fundamental challenge. We can extend our 2-D floorplan-based model into 3-D one once the whole set of information about the building is provided.

Reference Point Recognition: A mobile user can manually notify ACMI, of the current location, when she visits a reference point. Reference points can be chosen from frequently visited landmarks. But it may true that users cannot always accurately pin-point their positions.

ACMI can try to automatically recognize reference points. It is achieved by detecting the distinctive RSS characteristic at a spot. During the runtime ACMI keeps looking for an indoor spot s where any element of the measured RSS becomes the maximum, i.e., $RSS_M(s,t) = max(RSS(t))$ for any $t \in T$. This indicates that a mobile user is near one of LoS windows and greatly reduces the ambiguity in inferring the user's location. As the false positive detection will lead to ill calibration of parameters, we trigger the reference point detection when $|RSS_M(s,t) - max(RSS(t))|$ is small.

Alternatively, an assistive signal from bluetooth emitters installed at a few reference points can explicitly notify the mobile device when to calibrate. The measured signal at the position can be used to calibrate the model parameters, and to correct the estimation of the current location as well.

Complexity: We discuss how to further reduce the complexity of online path matching. If it is detected that a user has come back to the previously visited location there is no reason to continue the matching operations. In this case ACMI resets the path matching. ACMI continuously checks if the following condition is met whenever a new RSS is sampled:

$$||\overrightarrow{RSS_M} - \overrightarrow{RSS_M}(i)|| \;<\; \theta_{dup} \;\; for\; i = 1 \cdots l,$$

Location (floor)	# of spots	Area (m^2)	# of rooms
MRC (2nd)	36	2,990	46
MRC (3rd)	86	2,990	55
MRC (4th)	375	2,990	69
EB-E (1st)	147	4,550	28
EB-E (2nd)	129	4,550	59
EB-E (3rd)	119	4,550	69
EB-W (1st)	217	4,550	23

Table 2: Locations where RSS measurements were performed.

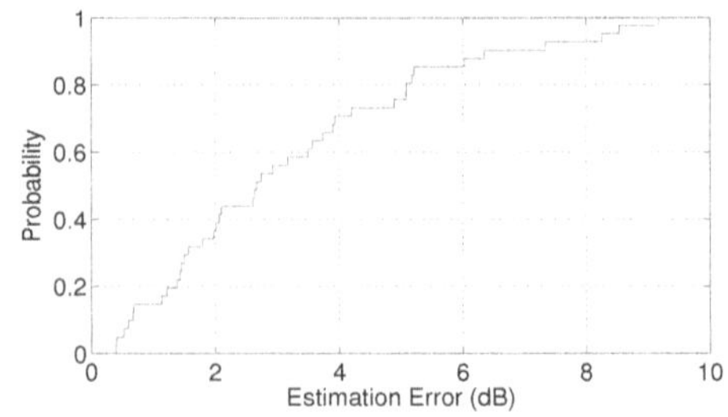

Figure 13: Estimation error distribution in dB.

where θ_{dup} is pre-defined threshold. When the condition is met, ACMI determines that the user came back to the previous location, empty the buffer and restart the path matching from the next step.

Another way to reduce the computation is to filter out the erroneous candidates earlier while performing the path matching. In path matching, ACMI traces back the buffered RSS samples to find the path $P = s_0, ..., s_{l-1}$ that shows the minimum RSS difference. If a segment of a certain path shows large RSS difference, there is no need to further look into remaining candidate spots along the path. For example, if $RSS_M(s_{l-1}) > \theta$, all the paths $P = ..., s_{l-1}$, ending at s_{l-1} can be immediately ignored.

7. EVALUATION

In this section, we first verify the similarity of our indoor signal propagation model with the actual RSS measurements. Then we see the localization accuracy of the model combined with the proposed online processing.

7.1 Experiment Setup

We perform measurements and collect RSSs at 1,109 spots in 7 different locations, shown in Table 2. These are the department buildings in campus with 35m×85m (MRC) and 55m×85m (EB-E and EB-W) area and each floor has different indoor structures. We use USRP1 with a laptop computer to collect the data. Signals from 8 FM stations are used as formerly described in Section 3.

We also implement the walk detector on Android platform. The walk detector reports the topology of 5 most recently visited indoor spots, where each spot is separated by 2 m from the previous one. In our test, after taking 10 m movement, the estimated position of the very last spot had 60th percentile error of 0.97 m and 80th percentile error of 1.95 m. We use the path and distance information reported by the walk detector together with the RSS log to obtain the indoor position.

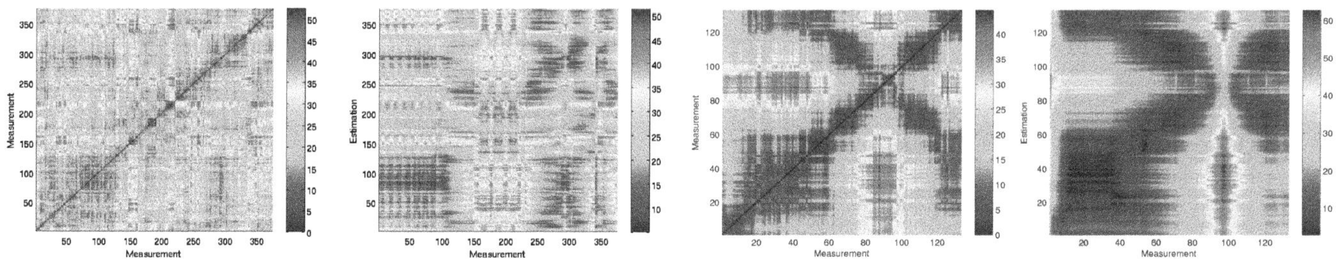

(a) MRC 4th floor.

(b) EB-E 2nd floor.

Figure 14: Euclidean distance representation of RSS vectors where X and Y axis represent the indoor spot index. Left figures show the Euclidean distance between measurement vectors and right figures show measured and estimated vectors. The area in blue shows more similarity between two vectors than red.

7.2 Modeling Accuracy

Figure 13 shows the distribution of estimation error of signals from 8 stations in all location. The calibration has been performed and so the outdoor path loss estimation error is not included. It is shown that our model achieves the 70th percentile error of 4 dB. Figure 14 demonstrates the modeling accuracy more intuitively. It shows the Euclidean distance between RSS vectors in two different locations, MRC 4th floor and EB-E 2nd floor. The left figures of each set show the self-distance of RSS measurement vectors. The diagonal line is clearly shown in blue, which means that the Euclidean distance is zero between same set of RSS vectors. The RSS measurement and estimation vectors (without calibration) are compared in the right figures. While the diagonal line is not visible at a glance, we can still observe bluish area in both figures along the diagonal line. This means that even though not perfectly accurate as the real measurements, the model captures the way signals are propagated indoors. The information is a useful hint to estimate the current location of a user.

The impact of the modeling accuracy can be read from black bars in Figure 15, which demonstrate the performance of the simple MSE matching purely based on the RSS DB. We observe there is a wide variance in the modeling accuracy, ranging between 10m and 18m.

In our observation, there are three reasons with the variance in the accuracy. The first reason is the internal structures of a building. If the internal structure does not create distinct RSS signatures, e.g., an open space without many obstacles, there is not much differentiation in RSSs between nearby spots. Then the localization accuracy will drop. The second reason is with the initial modeling parameters. We observe that the runtime calibration improves the accuracy around 6 meters at engineering buildings (EB-E-1,2,3 and EB-W-1). This is mainly because the initial parameters were measured in MRC 4th floor and quite different at other locations. On the other hand MRC data shows no significant improvement in accuracy after the calibration. The third reason is more fundamental. If there are structures that do not appear in the floorplan, the RSS distribution cannot be correctly modeled. Even with online calibration, there will still be some modeling errors. Per our observation, metal objects such as steel desks or shelves induce path loss almost comparable to indoor walls. This can be indeed mitigated using more signal sources. If there are signals from various directions, the unexpected obstruction that some signals experience will have less impact on the RSS vector.

Location(floor)	Ref.	α	f (dB)	C (dB)
MRC (2nd)	1	2.15	6.2	7.7
MRC (3rd)	3	2.15	7.0	7.3
MRC (4th)	8	2.16	6.3	7.5
EB-E (1st)	3	2.58	6.4	6.9
EB-E (2nd)	2	2.56	6.9	6.5
EB-E (3rd)	3	2.56	6.2	6.5
EB-W (1st)	3	2.63	5.4	6.1

Table 3: The number of detected reference points and the trained parameters at each location.

7.3 Localization Performance

We test the localization performance of ACMI at different locations. Three cases, (1) simple DB look-up with no additional online processing (None), (2) online calibration and (3) online path matching after the calibration (Calib.+PM), are shown. For the online calibration we first notified ACMI of the initial location at the entrance of buildings. As we roam around within the buildings, ACMI automatically recognized additional reference points and performed further calibration and correction of the estimated locations. Since the false positive is more harmful we made it conservative such that ACMI detects the reference point only when it is very certain. The parameters are shown in Table 3.

Figure 15 shows the evaluation results. Without any online operation, the localization accuracy entirely depends on the modeling accuracy and it varies from 10 to 18 meters. Online calibration reduces the error in places where the model parameters have the significant difference with initial values. After the path matching the accuracy becomes around 6 meters. For the path matching, we used the maximum path length of 5. Figure 16 shows the error distribution after the path patching. In all of dataset, the error is less that 10 m with 60% probability.

The room identification ranges between 59% and 89% between any online operation and improves up to average 89% after the path matching. Note that the room identification accuracy does not align with the localization accuracy since it also depends on the size of rooms. For example, in MRC-4 there are many small private offices with area less than 12 m^2 so the accuracy is around only 60%.

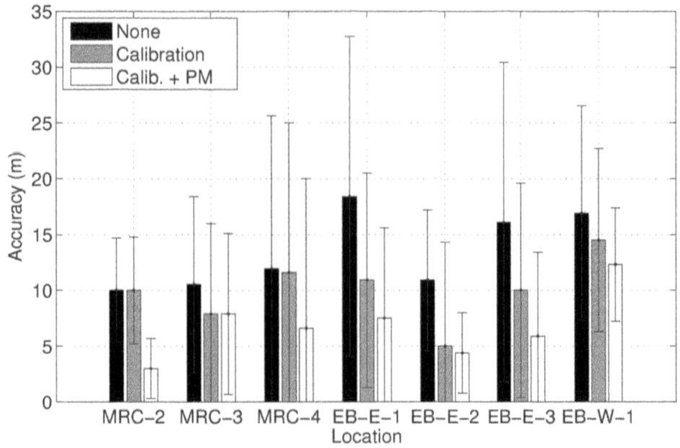

(a) Average localization accuracy with 95% confidence interval.

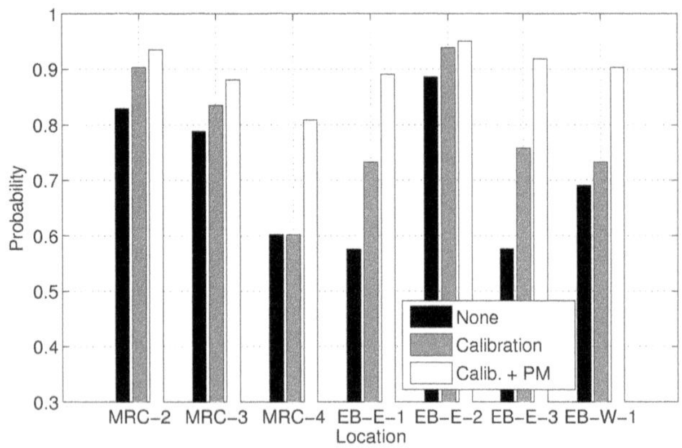

(b) Room level identification accuracy.

Figure 15: Localization accuracy.

7.3.1 *Scaling with Number of FM Stations*

We use signals from only 8 stations due to the limited availability in our area. As we would like to see the system performance when there are more FM stations, we perform simulations in the following way. In addition to the existing RSS traces we generate signals from virtual FM stations. The virtual FM stations are assigned the average values of transmission power and antenna height calculated from the real FM stations. Then they are distributed around the building with random distances and directions. To make it realistic, we manually add random measurement errors that amount to the modeling errors measured from our earlier experiments. We run the simulations 30 times for each number of stations. Figure 17 shows the simulation results where up to 24 virtual FM stations are introduced. It is shown that with signals from 32 stations the localization accuracy improves up to 3 m without any online operations and below 1 m with runtime calibration and path matching.

8. CONCLUSION

In this paper, we try to build an indoor localization system that does not require site survey. While there have been innovative proposals in the literature, we take a new approach that, by modeling the FM signal distribution over the floors, performs fingerprint-based indoor localization. While our empirical model is simple, we show that the model is effective and catches well RSS variations within a building with

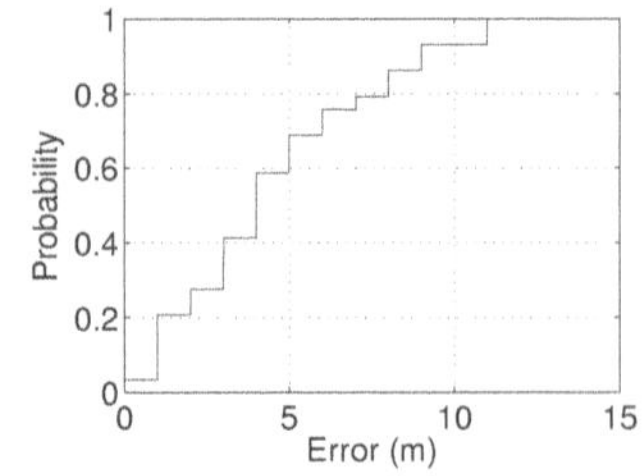

(a) MRC-2.

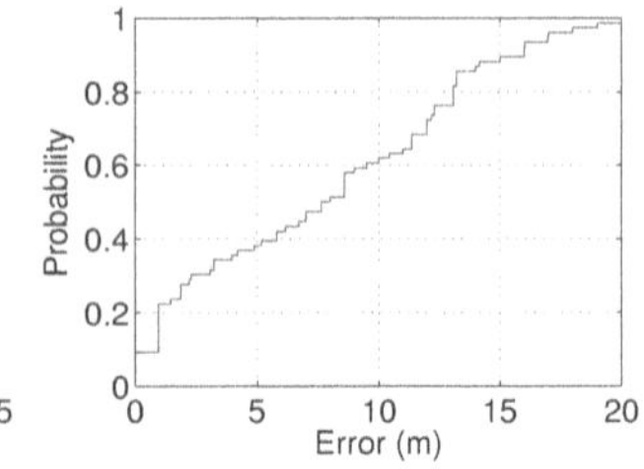

(b) MRC-3.

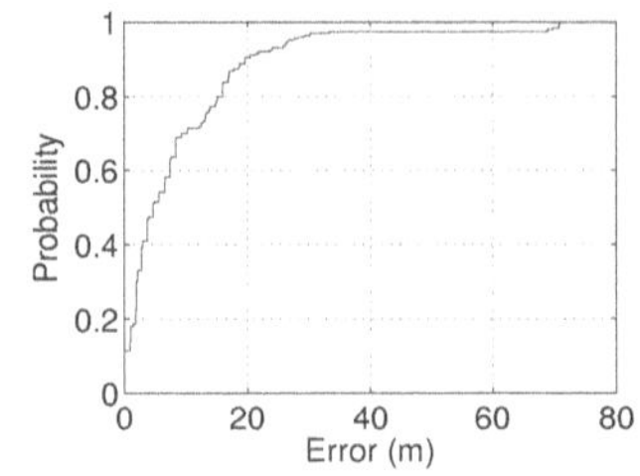

(c) MRC-4.

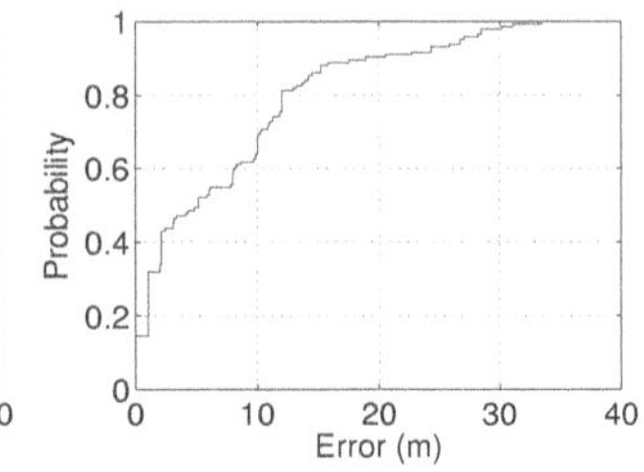

(d) EB-E-1.

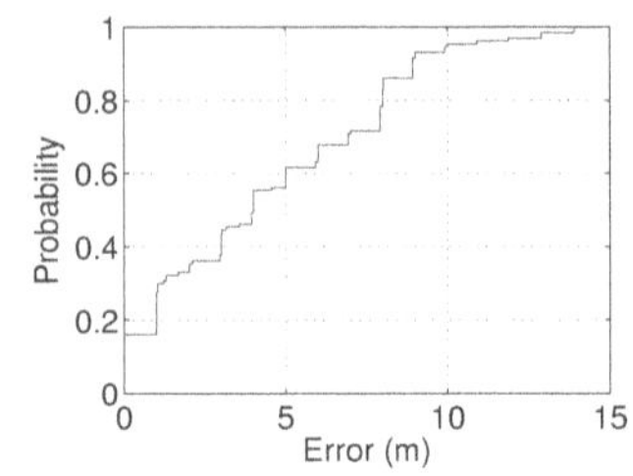

(e) EB-E-2.

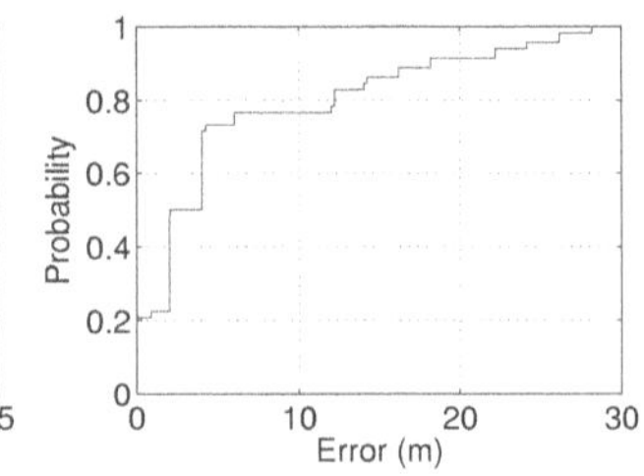

(f) EB-E-3.

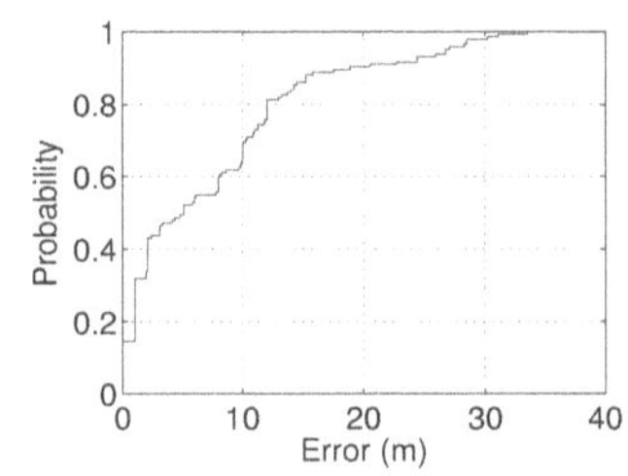

(g) EB-W-1.

Figure 16: Distribution of localization errors of ACMI, after path matching.

reasonably good accuracy. We further improve the accuracy using the online calibration and the path matching technique. In all of the processes, there is not much expenditure in time and cost for installation and running of this system. We believe that this proposal can suggest a new direction to the indoor localization research.

9. ACKNOWLEDGEMENT

We appreciate our shepherd Dr. Prabal Dutta for his sincere guidance. We also thank anonymous reviewers for their precious comments and suggestions.

10. REFERENCES

[1] Bahl, P., and Padmanabhan, V. RADAR: an in-building RF-based user location and tracking system. In *Proceedings of IEEE INFOCOM, 2000.*

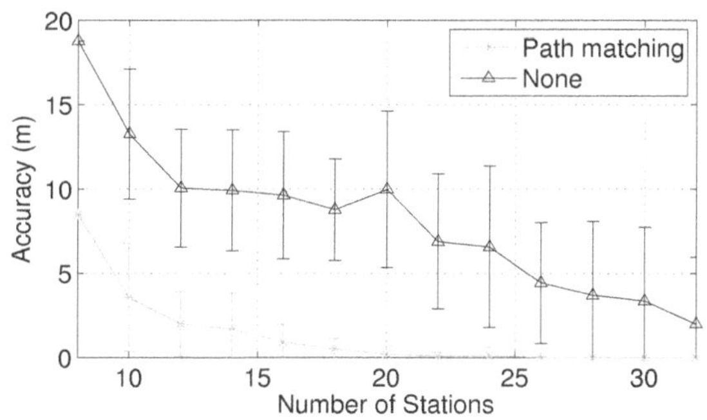

Figure 17: Simulation results show that the performance of ACMI scales with number of FM stations.

[2] CHEN, Y., LYMBEROPOULOS, D., LIU, J., AND PRIYANTHA, B. FM-based indoor localization. In *Proceedings of ACM MobiSys, 2012.*

[3] CHENG, X., THAELER, A., XUE, G., AND CHEN, D. TPS: a time-based positioning scheme for outdoor wireless sensor networks. In *Proceedings of IEEE INFOCOM, 2004.*

[4] CHEUNG, K.-W., SAU, J.-M., AND MURCH, R. A new empirical model for indoor propagation prediction. *Vehicular Technology, IEEE Transactions on 47*, 3 (aug 1998), 996 –1001.

[5] CHINTALAPUDI, K., PADMANABHA IYER, A., AND PADMANABHAN, V. N. Indoor localization without the pain. In *Proceedings of ACM MobiCom, 2010.*

[6] CONSTANDACHE, I., CHOUDHURY, R., AND RHEE, I. Towards mobile phone localization without war-driving. In *Proceedings of IEEE INFOCOM, 2010.*

[7] DURGIN, G., RAPPAPORT, T., AND XU, H. Measurements and models for radio path loss and penetration loss in and around homes and trees at 5.85 GHz. *Communications, IEEE Transactions on 46*, 11 (nov 1998), 1484 –1496.

[8] FEDERAL COMMUNICATIONS COMMISSION. FM Database. `http://transition.fcc.gov/fcc-bin/fmq?call=WKNC`.

[9] GEUN PARK, J., CURTIS, D., TELLER, S., AND LEDLIE, J. Implications of device diversity for organic localization. In *Proceedings of IEEE INFOCOM, 2011.*

[10] HAYKIN, S. *Adaptive Filter Theory, 4th Ed.* Prentice Hall, 2001.

[11] HOWLAND, P., MAKSIMIUK, D., AND REITSMA, G. FM radio based bistatic radar. *IEE Proceedings of Radar, Sonar and Navigation 152*, 3 (june 2005), 107 – 115.

[12] JI, Y., BIAZ, S., PANDEY, S., AND AGRAWAL, P. ARIADNE: a dynamic indoor signal map construction and localization system. In *Proceedings of ACM MobiSys, 2006.*

[13] JI, Z., LI, B.-H., WANG, H.-X., CHEN, H.-Y., AND SARKAR, T. Efficient ray-tracing methods for propagation prediction for indoor wireless communications. *Antennas and Propagation Magazine, IEEE 43*, 2 (apr 2001), 41 –49.

[14] KELLY, D. C., RACKLEY, D. T., AND BERGLUND, V. P. Navigation and positioning system and method using uncoordinated beacon signals. *US Patent* (1994).

[15] KRUMM, J., CERMAK, G., AND HORVITZ, E. RightSPOT: A novel sense of location for a smart personal object. In *Proceedings of UbiComp, 2003.*

[16] LIM, H., KUNG, L.-C., HOU, J. C., AND LUO, H. Zero-configuration, robust indoor localization: Theory and experimentation. In *Proceedings of IEEE INFOCOM, 2006.*

[17] PARK, J.-G., CHARROW, B., CURTIS, D., BATTAT, J., MINKOV, E., HICKS, J., TELLER, S., AND LEDLIE, J. Growing an organic indoor location system. In *Proceedings of ACM MobiSys, 2010.*

[18] PEREZ-VEGA, C., AND ZAMANILLO, J. Path-loss model for broadcasting applications and outdoor communication systems in the VHF and UHF bands. *Broadcasting, IEEE Transactions on 48*, 2 (jun 2002), 91 – 96.

[19] RAI, A., CHINTALAPUDI, K. K., PADMANABHAN, V. N., AND SEN, R. Zee: zero-effort crowdsourcing for indoor localization. In *Proceedings of ACM MobiCom, 2012.*

[20] SEIDEL, S., AND RAPPAPORT, T. 914 MHz path loss prediction models for indoor wireless communications in multifloored buildings. *Antennas and Propagation, IEEE Transactions on 40*, 2 (feb 1992), 207 –217.

[21] SEN, S., RADUNOVIC, B., CHOUDHURY, R. R., AND MINKA, T. You are facing the Mona Lisa: spot localization using PHY layer information. In *Proceedings of ACM MobiSys, 2012.*

[22] VALENZUELA, R. A ray tracing approach to predicting indoor wireless transmission. In *Proceedings of IEEE VTC, 1993.*

[23] WANG, H., SEN, S., ELGOHARY, A., FARID, M., YOUSSEF, M., AND CHOUDHURY, R. R. No need to war-drive: unsupervised indoor localization. In *Proceedings of ACM MobiSys, 2012.*

[24] WERB, J., AND LANZL, C. Designing a positioning system for finding things and people indoors. *Spectrum, IEEE 35*, 9 (sep 1998), 71 –78.

[25] XIONG, J., AND JAMIESON, K. SecureAngle: improving wireless security using angle-of-arrival information. ACM Hotnets-IX, 2010.

[26] YANG, C.-F., WU, B.-C., AND KO, C.-J. A ray-tracing method for modeling indoor wave propagation and penetration. *Antennas and Propagation, IEEE Transactions on 46*, 6 (jun 1998), 907 –919.

[27] YANG, Z., WU, C., AND LIU, Y. Locating in fingerprint space: wireless indoor localization with little human intervention. In *Proceedings of ACM MobiCom, 2012.*

[28] YOUSSEF, A., KRUMM, J., MILLER, E., CERMAK, G., AND HORVITZ, E. Computing location from ambient FM radio signals [commercial radio station signals]. In *Proceedings of IEEE WCNC, 2005.*

[29] YOUSSEF, M., AND AGRAWALA, A. The Horus WLAN location determination system. In *Proceedings of ACM MobiSys, 2005.*

[30] ZHANG, Z., ZHOU, X., ZHANG, W., ZHANG, Y., WANG, G., ZHAO, B. Y., AND ZHENG, H. I am the antenna: accurate outdoor AP location using smartphones. In *Proceedings of ACM MobiCom, 2011.*

High-Accuracy Differential Tracking of Low-Cost GPS Receivers

Will Hedgecock
will.hedgecock@vanderbilt.edu

Miklos Maroti
miklos.maroti@vanderbilt.edu

Janos Sallai
janos.sallai@vanderbilt.edu

Peter Volgyesi
peter.volgyesi@vanderbilt.edu

Akos Ledeczi
akos.ledeczi@vanderbilt.edu

Institute for Software Integrated Systems, Vanderbilt University
Nashville, TN, USA

ABSTRACT

In many mobile wireless applications such as the automated driving of cars, formation flying of unmanned air vehicles, and source localization or target tracking with wireless sensor networks, it is more important to know the precise relative locations of nodes than their absolute coordinates. GPS, the most ubiquitous localization system available, generally provides only absolute coordinates. Furthermore, low-cost receivers can exhibit tens of meters of error or worse in challenging RF environments. This paper presents an approach that uses GPS to derive relative location information for multiple receivers. Nodes in a network share their raw satellite measurements and use this data to track the relative motions of neighboring nodes as opposed to computing their own absolute coordinates. The system has been implemented using a network of Android phones equipped with a custom Bluetooth headset and integrated GPS chip to provide raw measurement data. Our evaluation shows that centimeter-scale tracking accuracy at an update rate of 1 Hz is possible under various conditions with the presented technique. This is more than an order of magnitude more accurate than simply taking the difference of reported absolute node coordinates or other simplistic approaches due to the presence of uncorrelated measurement errors.

Categories and Subject Descriptors

C.3 [**Special-Purpose and Application-Based Systems**]: Real-time and Embedded Systems

General Terms

Algorithms, Measurement, Performance

Keywords

GPS, localization, differential tracking, relative localization

MobiSys'13 June 25–28, 2013, Taipei, Taiwan

1. INTRODUCTION

Precise node location information is highly important for many mobile systems. For outdoor applications, GPS is quickly becoming the de-facto standard for location determination; however, low-cost receivers, such as those found in smartphones, can exhibit large errors on the order of tens of meters, especially in urban areas or under dense foliage. Higher quality devices provide much better accuracy, but can cost hundreds of dollars, and commercial-grade surveying deployments can reach into the thousands while requiring extensive setup and calibration before they are usable.

While GPS is remarkable in its ability to provide absolute coordinates anywhere on Earth, many applications, including typical wireless sensor network (WSN) deployments, do not need precise *absolute* locations. In fact, most of today's WSN localization methods rely on estimating the range between nodes to derive their locations in a *relative* coordinate system. Furthermore, numerous applications beyond WSNs also need accurate relative locations, such as formation flying of UAVs and other robotic applications, precision agriculture, land surveying, autonomous driving (e.g. platoon formation and collision avoidance), and others. Existing solutions in use today are based on absolute GPS coordinates (e.g. Differential GPS) or additional sensors such as LIDAR or gyroscopes, but these are typically very costly.

The main question this paper seeks to answer is whether it is feasible to build a localization service that provides highly accurate (centimeter-scale) relative positions for a set of mobile nodes relying on pure GPS alone. We introduce **RegTrack** (Relative GPS Tracking), a novel approach for using a network of two or more traditional, low-cost, single-frequency GPS receivers to derive highly accurate tracking vectors between them in a relative coordinate system. One might argue that since most GPS error sources are highly correlated in the same geographic region, simply taking the difference of the reported absolute locations from two GPS devices over time would result in very accurate pairwise location estimates. There are very specific conditions under which this may be true, but due to inherently uncorrelated errors such as minuscule receiver clock biases from GPS time, it is almost never the case. Additionally, substantial errors can accumulate in the presence of multipath due to signal reflections, especially in urban areas or in the likely case that the receivers cannot see the exact same set of satellites. We believe that an increase in GPS accuracy (in the relative sense) without a corresponding increase in cost will enable the production of novel applications that are either not economical today or are out of reach altogether.

The underlying idea of our approach is simple: let a network of cooperating GPS receivers share their raw satellite measurements with one another to solve for the 3D pairwise relative changes in position between them as opposed to absolute locations. These vector solutions are derived locally on each node with the resulting tracks of all other nodes computed using the local node's location as a reference position. As such, the relative locations of all nodes in a region will be known accurately, regardless of whether the given node is stationary (as in surveying applications) or moving (as in vehicle-based applications). The only caveat is that *the initial relative positions of the sensor nodes must be known* to make the tracking results useful.

While a procedure to automatically determine initial relative positions is a significant missing piece in our goal of a complete localization system, this paper will show that our novel method is already usable for highly accurate tracking in applications such as land surveying or precision agriculture, where the initial node locations are already well-known. It can also be used in its current state for applications involving temporal feature extraction, such as the mapping of certain events (e.g. a lane change or a left turn in a vehicle's track) to a specific time tag, or in applications in which additional sensing modalities may enable periodic re-initialization of any of the participating nodes' relative locations. More importantly, however, we will conclude this paper with an outline on how we plan to definitively solve the location initialization problem without imposing the requirement of the stationary calibration phase present in all existing methods that are able to achieve centimeter-scale localization precision, tracking or otherwise.

An in-depth discussion and evaluation of RegTrack, along with its relevant error sources and corrections, is the subject of the rest of this paper. We show that simple approaches to GPS relative localization do not work well, and our novel tracking approach provides significantly better results than existing methods. In a benign environment with clear views of the sky, our technique showed as much as a 20x improvement over standard GPS positioning algorithms, with relative precision on the scale of centimeters. Additionally, our method produced results ranging from a 3-7x improvement in moderately obstructed and highly dynamic environments, with precision on the order of decimeters, regardless of the baseline length between a pair of receivers which, in our experiments, varied from 0 m all the way up to 3.5 km.

We also show that RegTrack is unlike Differential GPS or Real-Time Kinematic Surveying, both of which require precise knowledge of the absolute locations of one or more of the nodes and can costs thousands of dollars. On the other hand, our baseline accuracy is currently dependent on the initial relative location estimates of the participating nodes, but our methodology requires only instantaneous relative location information for initialization and can be used with low-cost, single-frequency (L1) GPS receivers.

The rest of the paper is organized as follows. We start with a brief overview of GPS and related work. We then continue with an in-depth discussion of the error and observation models necessary to make our algorithm work, as well as the actual methodology used in RegTrack. This is followed by a short description of the hardware platform and software implementation used to carry out this work. We continue with an evaluation of the system and an analysis of the experimental results, and conclude by describing our ideas for the continuation of the work.

2. BACKGROUND AND RELATED WORK

The Global Positioning System (GPS) is a satellite-based navigation system developed by the U.S. Department of Defense in the 1970s for military and civilian applications. Currently, it consists of 31 satellites on six orbital planes about 20,000 km above the Earth's surface. This constellation enables accurate location information to be computed at any place, any time on Earth using trilateration with range measurements between an observer and a few visible satellites.

Range estimation is performed using the times-of-flight of radio signals transmitted by the satellites. Although each satellite is equipped with a highly accurate and synchronized atomic clock, receivers are driven by much less accurate crystal oscillators. This design decision allowed for a truly ubiquitous localization service, but makes it impossible to directly measure the times-of-flight of radio signals traveling at the speed of light with acceptable accuracy. (Note that in GPS research, distance estimates based on an imprecise and arbitrary local clock are called pseudoranges). Instead, the receiver's clock offset from true absolute time becomes another unknown in addition to its 3D position coordinates. Thus, at least four independent measurements (satellites) are needed for a position fix to be computed. For the same reason, a low-cost GPS receiver can provide a highly accurate global time reference (tens of nanoseconds of accuracy) when locked onto the minimum number of satellites [5].

Many high-accuracy GPS algorithms make use of an additional signal observation, called the *carrier phase* or *carrier range* of a satellite signal, to increase positioning accuracy. These values are very precise (centimeter-scale) measurements of the change in range between a satellite and receiver over time, and are sometimes referred to as the *integrated Doppler shift*. Since the initial phase or range at the start of integration is unknown, however, these measurements are ambiguous and must be used in conjunction with other observations, such as the pseudorange, to be of use in localization.

GPS satellites continuously transmit messages using a Code Division Multiple Access (CDMA) spread spectrum technique, which allows them to share the exact same carrier frequency and, more importantly, use a single local oscillator (LO) at the receiver; thus, the phase noise and frequency instability of the LO affect all received signals in the same way. The GPS signal has a rich hierarchical structure with each signal derived from the same atomic clock source. All satellites transmit on at least two carrier frequencies (L1: 1.57542 GHz and L2: 1.2276 GHz) which are modulated by a pseudo-random noise (PRN) sequence. For civilian applications, each satellite uses a unique sequence of 1023 bits (known as the Course Acquisition, or C/A code) transmitted continuously at 1.023 million bits/s, whereas military applications make use of a much longer sequence (the Precision, or P code) at 10.23 million bits/s. Receivers need to know the assigned sequences *a priori* to lock onto the signals and separate them from noise and from each other. At the top of the signal hierarchy, each satellite transmits a low speed navigation message at 50 bits/s that contains its own clock and location (ephemeris) information.

A typical GPS receiver consists of a low-noise *analog frontend* for amplifying, filtering, and down-converting the antenna signal (~1.5 GHz), an *analog-to-digital converter* (ADC) for digitizing the quadrature IF signal (~2 MHz), and a *highly parallel digital signal processor* implemented in an ASIC along with a traditional processor core. The key element of this architecture is the custom digital signal processor, operating on tens of independent signal paths (channels) in parallel. Each channel uses a digital correlator (assigned to one of the known satellite codes) to find, track, and correlate a PRN sequence in the received data with the expected PRN signal, shifted and scaled in time. The tracked shift and scale values that give the maximum correlation value represent the signal time-of-flight and Doppler shift (arising from the relative motions of the satellites, with orbital velocities of ~4000 m/s), respectively.

Each standalone GPS receiver is prone to several sources of measurement error, and understanding the error budget is essential to enhancing accuracy. First, the propagation speed of radio signals in the ionosphere and troposphere is different than in free space; thus, both refract GPS signals differently, potentially causing significant error in the overall result. Second, each GPS satellite broadcasts its orbital position (ephemeris) and clock correction data in the navigation message, as described above. Both pieces of information are based on a predictive model and are, therefore, inaccurate. These errors however, along with the atmospheric effects, are correlated within a bounded geographic region and can be compensated later when more accurate information is available. Other sources of error include multipath and measurement noise in the GPS receiver. It is much more difficult to mitigate these (using more refined antennas or higher precision receivers that increase the cost, size, and power requirements of the unit); fortunately, these effects represent a much smaller percentage of the total error.

Consumer GPS receivers—used mainly for navigational and recreational applications—represent the standalone class and are affected by all error sources described above. The prevalence of these receivers has dramatically driven down cost, size, and power requirements over the past decade. However, for applications where standalone accuracy may be insufficient, the huge price gap to a more precise system can be prohibitive. Our work aims at bridging this gap when only accurate *relative* locations are needed.

High-precision GPS receivers and receiver systems employ a variety of techniques to mitigate these errors. Atmospheric effects can be corrected by using both L1 and L2 carrier frequencies, as refraction is frequency dependent. In fact, as part of the GPS modernization program, there is an additional proposed L5 carrier frequency for civilian receivers. In military-grade GPS, receivers can use the faster P(Y) code for more precise time-of-arrival measurements. Carrier phase measurements and tracking can provide even higher accuracy (comparable to the wavelength of the carrier signal), but generally require extensive post-processing.

Finally, there are several solutions based on differential corrections. While all of these approaches employ more than one receiver, they differ widely in geographic scale, real-time properties, complexity, and their effectiveness in mitigating atmospheric, ephemeris, and satellite clock errors. One end of the spectrum is represented by Satellite-Based Augmentation Systems (SBAS), like the Wide Area Augmentation System (WAAS) used in the U.S., which broadcasts real-time correction information via geostationary satellites based on measurements from several ground reference stations. Most consumer-grade GPS receivers are capable of using this coarse correction information. The other extreme is based on offline post-processing, where highly accurate correction data is calculated at a reference station with a precise clock (such as an atomic clock source) and a well-known location.

Most similar to our work is Differential GPS (DGPS), which also uses multiple receivers to increase GPS accuracy. In DGPS, mobile receivers can calculate their absolute positions with increased accuracy by altering their received satellite measurements according to corrections sent out by one or more static base stations which have been well-calibrated and know their own positions and clock biases to a high degree of accuracy [15]. This method, while providing absolute instead of relative coordinates, requires preliminary setup of expensive, stationary base stations which precludes it from being used in everyday mobile system deployments.

Another class of methods which has been gaining popularity and increasing in accuracy over recent years is called Real Time Kinematic (RTK) satellite navigation [13, 11], which works in a similar fashion to DGPS, except that all coordinates are found using carrier phase measurements with respect to a dedicated sensing station. Again, the sensing station is located at a well-known, pre-defined location and transmits its own position and raw carrier phase measurements to other receivers in the vicinity. As such, participating nodes can calculate their coordinates *relative to a base receiver* with a high degree of accuracy. In RegTrack, there is no dedicated base station or reference node. Every receiver considers itself to be the reference when computing the relative locations of its neighbors. Hence, the architecture is symmetric and there is no single point of failure.

Another drawback of RTK is that the carrier phase measurements it uses are exclusively relative measurements which require knowledge of an unknown (but constant) number of carrier signal wavelengths between a satellite and receiver at an arbitrary point in time to be of any use in absolute positioning; thus, the system must either:

1. Have extremely accurate knowledge of the absolute base station position,

2. Use dual-frequency receivers to minimize single-point errors such as atmospheric delay or measurement noise, or

3. Spend a considerable amount of time solving for the carrier ambiguities in the system - a very active area of research itself [16, 12].

Even after taking these steps into consideration, the system breaks down readily in the face of difficult multipath environments, moderate to severe line of sight obstructions to satellite visibility, satellite losses of lock, or cycle slips, making it most appropriate for use in low-dynamic situations with a clear, broad view of the sky such as nautical navigation or land surveying [9].

There is also ongoing research in enhancing the core methods and algorithms used in standard GPS positioning techniques. Researchers from several Brazilian universities have tried to improve upon the RTK positioning algorithm by using wavelets as the foundation for a mathematical model of the GPS system [4]. Additionally, there has been research into better methods of DGPS base station design [6], as well as the use of relative positioning in automotive safety applications [2]. The advantage of our research, however, is that it is general and extensible to most any type of mobile sensing network, whereas these papers present very application-specific results which do not provide a means of building upon them or extending them to other areas.

Finally, there are active research efforts in the mobile systems community centered around GPS with the focus of reducing power consumption. Jurdak et al. [8] and Paek et al. [3] explore various duty cycling strategies. Liu et al. [10] go one step further and offload location determination to a remote server, trading off GPS usage for increased communication overhead. These efforts are orthogonal to our approach, as we are focusing on increasing positioning accuracy and disregarding the associated cost in power in this first phase of our project.

3. ERROR MODELING

A significant amount of research has been undertaken to characterize the various sources of error that may affect a GPS radio signal as it propagates from satellite to receiver. The generally accepted error sources include both the satellite and receiver's clock synchronization biases from actual GPS system time, delays due to propagation speed retardation as the signal traverses the Earth's atmosphere, multipath interference, antenna phase center offsets, satellite orbital errors, and receiver noise. From these errors, we obtain generally-accepted pseudorange and carrier phase observation models for a single receiver:

$$P_r^s(t) = \rho_r^s(t) + c\tau_r(t) - c\tau^s(t) + d_{iono}^s + d_{tropo}^s + M_{r,\rho}^s(t) + \phi_r^s(t) + E^s + \epsilon_P \tag{1}$$

$$\lambda_{L1}\Phi_r^s(t) = \rho_r^s(t) + c\tau_r(t) - c\tau^s(t) - d_{iono}^s + d_{tropo}^s + B_r^s + M_{r,\Phi}^s(t) + \phi_r^s(t) + E^s + \epsilon_\Phi \tag{2}$$

where P denotes pseudorange, λ_{L1} is the wavelength of the carrier signal in a vacuum (~19.05 cm), Φ is the carrier phase observation, ρ is the geometric range traveled by the radio signal from receiver to satellite, c is the speed of light, τ is clock bias, d is an atmospheric delay, M denotes multipath, ϕ is any antenna phase center offset, E is the satellite orbital error, B is a constant ambiguity term, and ϵ is receiver noise. Additionally, any subscripts refer to a receiver, superscripts refer to specific satellites, and t values indicate that the corresponding term is dependent on time. These conventions hold throughout the rest of this paper.

In addition to these explicit error sources, there also exists an implicit effect known as the Sagnac effect due to the rotation of the Earth during the time of signal transmission [1]. Once a GPS signal leaves a satellite, it must travel a finite amount of time before it reaches a receiver. Since the Earth is rotating during this time, the propagation time (and hence the raw observations) will either grow or shrink as the receiver rotates away from or toward the incoming signal. If receiver and satellite positions were calculated in a non-rotating, Earth-Centered Inertial (ECI) frame, this would not cause a problem since the receiver position at the time of reception would indicate the correct propagation distance from the satellite at the time of transmission. In GPS, however, satellites transmit their ephemeris data to allow users to calculate their positions in an Earth-Centered,

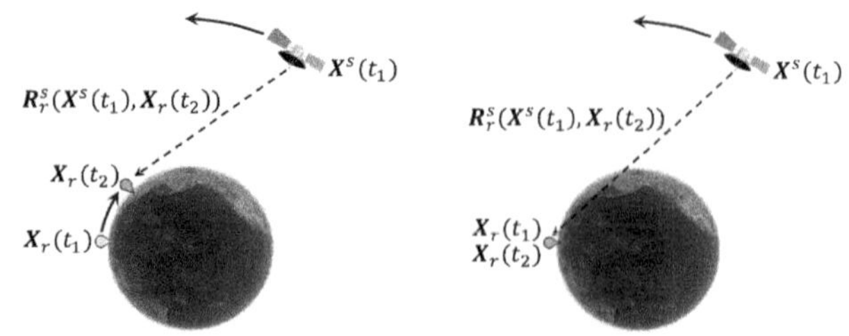

(a) ECI Frame: Since the coordinate system is fixed in space, the receiver position, $\mathbf{X}_r(t_1)$, at the time of signal transmission, t_1, is not equal to its position, $\mathbf{X}_r(t_2)$, at the time of signal reception.

(b) ECEF Frame: Since the coordinate system rotates with the Earth, the receiver positions at the time of signal transmission and reception appear identical, $\mathbf{X}_r(t_1) = \mathbf{X}_r(t_2)$

Figure 1: **The Sagnac Effect**

Earth-Fixed (ECEF) coordinate frame which rotates along with the Earth. As such, any changes in propagation delay induced by the rotation of the Earth are not taken into account in the calculation of the satellite positions. Figure 1 explains this phenomenon.

Since the ECEF coordinate system rotates along with the Earth, it is clear from Figure 1b that the signal propagation range from satellite to receiver, $\mathbf{R}_r^s = ||\mathbf{X}^s(t_1) - \mathbf{X}_r(t_2)||$, computed under the assumption that the coordinate system has remained stationary between t_1 and t_2 will be incorrect and will not coincide with the observed pseudorange and carrier phase measurements. In order to account for this problem, the user must correct the computed satellite positions for the amount of rotation the receiver experienced during the time of signal transmission. Corrections for this effect are commonly referred to as Earth rotation corrections and a number of algorithms exist for computing them. Left uncorrected, the Sagnac effect can contribute to satellite position errors on the order of 30 m, so this type of effect cannot be ignored.

3.1 Dual-Receiver Error Sources

There exist several subtleties regarding the Sagnac effect that do not seem to appear in literature at this time of writing, stemming from the fact that the Earth continues to rotate in the presence of time delay errors such as atmospheric perturbations or clock biases:

1. Most Earth rotation corrections are calculated using raw pseudorange observations that include two types of errors: signal errors (which directly affect the actual propagation time of the satellite signal) and bias errors (which appear in the observation but are not due to signal delays). Due to the *bias* errors, we cannot know the exact time of reception of the satellite signals, which means we do not know the real propagation time of the signal, and hence cannot accurately estimate how far the Earth has rotated during this time.
2. In the two-receiver case, if measurements are made at two slightly different times, the satellite positions at the time of each signal transmission will have *actually* been different.
3. Also in the two-receiver case, the change in satellite positions during any measurement time discrepancy

will result in an error analogous to the motion of the receivers described earlier in this section; namely, the signal propagation times will have been different, and thus, the Earth will have experienced differing amounts of rotation.

Due to these subtleties, two receivers making observations at apparently the same time (according to their local clocks) may calculate satellite positions that are up to ~9 m apart from one another. In reality, these two combined error sources typically amount to 1-3 meters of error per satellite.

Ideally, we'd like to take the satellite geometry "snapshots" according to both receivers and extrapolate the measurement data to correspond to what the observations and satellite positions *should* have been if taken exactly at the GPS epoch in the absence of any clock errors. Unfortunately, this requires a slight increase in computational complexity, and extrapolation of measurement data to a specific *reception* time is not quite as simple as it may seem.

4. TECHNICAL APPROACH

Our approach to solving the localization problem posed in this paper involves:

- the addition of a new data conditioning algorithm to remove the two-receiver error sources mentioned in the previous section,
- a new observation model that leverages the time-varying constellation of a set of mutually visible satellites into a single set of equations that we call the *Dual-Epoch, Double-Differenced Model*, and
- the application of a novel tracking algorithm through time to produce accurate 3D pairwise mappings of all the relative node locations in a network of receivers.

4.1 Data Conditioning

As mentioned in the previous section, the optimal way to overcome the error subtleties arising from the two-receiver case is to extrapolate the data from two or more receivers to the exact common point in time when the receivers *should* have made their measurements, namely the GPS epoch. In order to begin the extrapolation procedure, it is necessary to first determine the clock bias of each receiver so that we know how far forward or backward to extrapolate the data. This step can be as simple as solving for the standalone 3D position and bias of each receiver using a simple least-squares optimization routine as described in [5].

Once the receiver clock bias is known, the obvious next step would be to simply rotate each of the receivers' coordinate frames and data sets to coincide with the nominal GPS epoch. This will not result in a satisfactory solution however, especially in the multiple receiver case, because although the receivers themselves can be rotated into a cohesive frame, the satellite positions do not "rotate" with the Earth, but rather follow their own orbits. This means that errors due to the discrepancies between satellite positions at actually different transmit times will still be present. Additionally, the amount of Earth rotation experienced during the measured signal propagation interval cannot be assumed to be identical to the amount of rotation that would have been experienced at the extrapolated time.

In order to correctly extrapolate the data, we need to determine the change in signal propagation time (and by extension, the propagation range, R_r^s) if the measurement had been correctly made at the GPS epoch. Fortunately, the instantaneous change in range can be inferred quite accurately using the Doppler shift observable (necessarily computed by all GPS chips), which directly indicates the line-of-sight *range rate* between a satellite and receiver at any given time:

$$\Delta R_r^s = f_D^s(t) * \lambda_{L1} * t_{bias} \tag{3}$$

where $f_D^s(t)$ is the instantaneous Doppler frequency to satellite s reported by the receiver, λ_{L1} is the vacuum wavelength of the carrier signal, and t_{bias} is the receiver clock bias from GPS system time. Assuming a Doppler shift accuracy of ±1 Hz, this change in range is guaranteed to be accurate to better than 191 μm.

Since we know both the receiver clock bias and what the measurement observables should have been, we can iteratively calculate the satellite positions, $\mathbf{X}^s$, and Earth rotation corrections to find the updated transmit times of each GPS signal that would have been received at the exact GPS epoch. Essentially, we are using the ΔR_r^s results from Equation 3 to minimize the non-linear function:

$$\epsilon = \Delta R_r^s - (R_r^s(t_t') - R_r^s(t_t)) \tag{4}$$

where t_t is the transmit time of the signal we actually received, t_t' is the updated transmit time corresponding to the signal that would have been received at the exact GPS epoch, $R_r^s(t_t) = ||\mathbf{X}^s(t_t) - \mathbf{X}_r||$ is a constant equal to the satellite-receiver range at the actual time of reception, and $R_r^s(t_t') = ||\mathbf{X}^s(t_t') - \mathbf{X}_r||$ is the calculated range at the exact GPS epoch. Put another way, we are trying to find the corrected transmit time, t_t', which would result in an $R_r^s(t_t')$ that minimizes Equation 4. The following procedure explains how this can be done:

1. Calculate the range at the actual time of reception: $R_r^s(t_t) = ||\mathbf{X}^s(t_t) - \mathbf{X}_r||$,
2. Update the measurement observables by the computed ΔR_r^s value,
3. Correct the signal transmit time according to: $t_t' = t_t - t_{bias}$,
4. Calculate the satellite position at the new transmit time, t_t',
5. Translate the satellite positions into the receiver's ECEF frame using Givens Rotations (see [5]),
6. Calculate the corrected range according to the new satellite positions: $R_r^s(t_t') = ||\mathbf{X}^s(t_t') - \mathbf{X}_r||$,
7. Compute the range error (Equation 4),
8. Iterate through the following until the magnitude of the new range error exceeds that of the previous:
   - Update the possible transmit time, t_t', by either $\pm 1\mu$s,
   - Calculate the new satellite position at this time and translate into the receiver's ECEF frame.
   - Compute the updated range and calculate the corresponding range error.

Luckily, the propagation biases are small enough that only 1-3 iterations of the above algorithm are usually required to find a solution that extrapolates satellite positions to μm accuracy. This can be verified by examining the apparent satellite positions according to two co-located receivers at the same epoch and noting that the positions should now be identical. Table 1 summarizes actual results using this algorithm.

Satellite #	Mean Difference without Extrapolation	Mean Difference with Extrapolation
6	1.7 m	< 1 mm
14	2.0 m	< 1 mm
15	1.4 m	< 1 mm
18	1.4 m	< 1 mm
21	1.9 m	< 1 mm
22	2.1 m	< 1 mm
27	1.8 m	< 1 mm

Table 1: **Average satellite positional differences as seen from three receivers at the same GPS epoch over the course of 30 minutes.**

4.2 Dual-Epoch, Double-Differenced Model

With the independent rotational effects removed and the data extrapolated to the proper GPS epoch, it is now possible to introduce a new set of observation models involving two receivers and a single satellite that contain a minimum amount of residual error while maintaining a stronger geometry than similar triple differencing models. This new set of equations (See Equations 5 and 6) constitutes the Dual-Epoch (dual-receiver, single-satellite), Double-Differenced model.

Unlike the standard double-differenced equations that use data from a single epoch by necessitating the inclusion of a "reference satellite," (see [5]), this model uses two single-differenced observations from consecutive epochs to generate a new observation. The effect of this alteration is twofold:

1. No reference satellite is required; therefore, individual satellites observations are, in fact, independent of one another and do not require additional manipulations in situations when a reference satellite would have changed or disappeared, and
2. Traditional double-differenced carrier range models result in an integer ambiguity that is dependent on the satellite, receiver, and reference satellite; whereas, in the dual-epoch, double-differenced model, this ambiguity term completely cancels out.

The following describes this new model (where $\nabla\Delta$ denotes the double-differencing operation between satellite s and receivers j and k over two epochs):

$$\nabla\Delta P^s_{jk} = \nabla\Delta\rho^s_{jk} + c\nabla\Delta\tau_{jk} + \nabla\Delta M^s_{jk} + \nabla\Delta\phi^s_{jk} + \nabla\Delta\epsilon_P \tag{5}$$

$$\nabla\Delta\lambda\Phi^s_{jk} = \nabla\Delta\rho^s_{jk} + c\nabla\Delta\tau_{jk} + \nabla\Delta M^s_{jk} + \nabla\Delta\phi^s_{jk} + \nabla\Delta\epsilon_\Phi \tag{6}$$

We can see here that the carrier phase model (Equation 6) no longer includes an ambiguity term. If we assume that the multipath, antenna phase center offsets, and receiver noise are negligible, this equation can be re-written:

$$\nabla\Delta\lambda\Phi^s_{jk} = \nabla\Delta\rho^s_{jk} + c\nabla\Delta\tau_{jk} \tag{7}$$

where the result includes only the difference between the change in ranges of two receivers over the course of one epoch and the difference between the two receivers' clock drifts. Equation 7 is unique in that it uses highly accurate carrier phase observations to produce unambiguous estimates of the change in relative ranges between a satellite and two receivers through time without requiring any sort of reference satellite or node.

4.3 Tracking Algorithm

This new observation model can be used directly in the creation of a novel tracking algorithm with the potential for centimeter-scale precision through time. We can note that by subtracting one receiver's carrier phase observation to satellite s from a second receiver's similar observation, the result is the range difference between the two receivers to that satellite, which is equal to the baseline between the two receivers projected onto the line-of-sight unit vector from receiver to satellite. Note that the GPS satellites are such a great distance from the surface of the Earth that the unit direction vectors can be assumed to be identical for both receivers with little effect on the result as long as the two receivers are located in the same geographic region. We perform the same operation at the next time epoch, $t+1$, and then subtract the two results to create the dual-epoch, double-differenced value through time, with model corresponding to Equation 7.

Since $\nabla\Delta\rho^s_{jk}$ represents how much the projected baseline described above has changed over the course of one epoch, the model can be expanded as follows:

$$\nabla\Delta\lambda\Phi^s_{jk}(t) = R^s_k(t) - R^s_j(t) - R^s_k(t-1) + R^s_j(t-1) + c\nabla\Delta\tau_{jk} \tag{8}$$

When the range is written recursively, we see that:

$$\begin{aligned}\nabla\Delta\lambda\Phi^s_{jk}(t) &= (R^s_k(t-1) + \Delta R^s_k) - \\ &\quad (R^s_j(t-1) + \Delta R^s_j) - R^s_k(t-1) + \\ &\quad R^s_j(t-1) + c\nabla\Delta\tau_{jk} \\ &= \Delta R^s_k - \Delta R^s_j + c\nabla\Delta\tau_{jk}\end{aligned} \tag{9}$$

This shows that the dual-epoch, double-differenced result is actually a measure of the change in range between two nodes and a satellite (plus the difference in relative clock drifts). Geometrically, this corresponds to the change in receiver-receiver baseline ($\Delta\mathbf{b}$) projected onto the unit direction vector from receiver to satellite ($\mathbf{a}^s_r$):

$$\nabla\Delta\lambda\Phi^s_{jk}(t) = \Delta\mathbf{b}\cdot\mathbf{a}^s_r + c\nabla\Delta\tau_{jk} \tag{10}$$

It is clear from this result that neither of the initial positions of the receivers must be precisely known in order for the relative motions between them to be accurately tracked. Additionally, it is unnecessary to solve for the motions of *both* of the receivers, since Equation 10 allows for a direct solution of the change in baseline based on our general knowledge of the unit direction vector to satellite s. Thus, the assumption that one node is stationary ($\Delta R^s_j = 0$), even when it is not, causes all of the relative motion to be attributed to the second node ($\Delta R^s_k = \Delta\mathbf{b}\cdot\mathbf{a}^s_r$), which is exactly what is desired, even though it is incorrect in the *absolute* sense.

In order to solve a system of tracking Equations 9 or 10, a simple least-squares optimization routine can be set up to estimate the tracked 3D coordinates through time along with the clock drift difference. As long as consistent satellite locks are maintained with at least four satellites, the relative positions of any node after initialization can be determined via simple dead reckoning (i.e. adding the current tracking result to the last relative position estimate).

We should note here that our implementation does carry out a small amount of *preprocessing* to filter bad data and minimize the effects of multipath and random outliers. To begin, data from satellites appearing lower than 12° on the horizon are disregarded, as signals from such satellites have significantly more atmosphere to traverse than higher-elevated satellites. This has been shown to significantly decrease the accuracy of the signals, not to mention the fact that lower-angled satellites are more likely to be intermittently blocked by obstructions and influenced by multipath reflections. Next, carrier phase data is tested at each epoch to ensure that no cycle slips (sub-millisecond losses of satellite lock) have occurred, as a slip of only one cycle will introduce ~19 cm of error into the satellite observation.

Cycle slips are detected by comparison of the received carrier phase observation ($\Phi(t)$) to a prediction of what the observation is expected to be ($\Phi'(t)$), calculated by extrapolating the carrier phase from the previous epoch forward in time using the instantaneous Doppler shift observation ($f_D(t)$), which is immune to such cycle slips. Recall that Doppler shift tells us the frequency offset of a received carrier signal from that of the transmitted signal. The carrier phase observable is obtained by counting the number of cycles that pass in a beat signal formed by mixing the transmitted carrier with a sine wave equal to the frequency of the received signal. Thus, the two observations are linked mathematically, with the Doppler shift giving a direct estimate of the number of additional carrier cycles that should pass over the next second. Thus, the error between the received carrier phase and the predicted carrier phase, where $\Phi'(t) = \Phi(t-1) + f_D(t-1)$, can be used to detect cycle slips. Currently, any error over the threshold of one-half a carrier cycle is deemed to be a cycle slip, and the corresponding measurement is disregarded.

Finally, a rudimentary form of multipath detection is carried out by disregarding satellite observations which maintain a residual error of greater than one-quarter the wavelength of a carrier cycle after the tracking solution has been found. If such an observation exists, the offending satellite is removed and the tracking algorithm is repeated until no further residuals of this magnitude are present.

In addition to allowing for the tracking of relative motions without requiring precise *a priori* knowledge of any node locations, our tracking methodology has the added advantage that neither of the nodes must remain stationary during the tracking procedure due to the fact that:

- Any absolute changes in position are irrelevant since all motion gets attributed to the "relative" receiver, and
- The unit direction vectors are virtually identical for a node that has only moved an order of meters in one epoch.

Note that the only components in tracking Equation 10 are the change-in-baseline term and the double-differenced clock bias (which in this case, equals the difference between the two receivers' clock drifts). We can analyze the error introduced by the assumption that the unit direction vector to a satellite does not change between consecutive epochs numerically for the worst case by noting that a satellite completes a full orbit every 11 hours and 58 minutes. In other words, the largest angle it could trace out in the sky over one second would occur when it passes through the zenith directly overhead. At the standard orbital period, 1 second equates to 0.008357°. This means that the most influence the change in unit direction could have would be $1.0 - (1.0 \times \cos 0.008357) = 10.636 \times 10^{-9}$ times the baseline. This is such a small number that it can be disregarded, but it is very important to note that the error due to this effect increases with increasing baseline lengths. Anything over 1,000 km will start to introduce errors on the centimeter level so our method should only be used for so-called *short baselines* less than 1,000 km.

5. IMPLEMENTATION DETAILS

In order to test the aforementioned algorithms, we implemented a combined version of the error correction procedure and tracking algorithm (called **RegTrack**) as a mobile smartphone app using standard Java. We chose a network of HTC Desire Android smartphones to experimentally evaluate RegTrack. Each phone was paired with exactly one custom Bluetooth-headset [14] that includes a μblox LEA-6T GPS receiver. We chose this particular L1 receiver because it supplies raw measurement data, whereas many low-cost receivers do not. We do not see this as a significant roadblock since the data is necessarily available internally; it is simply a question of providing it directly as an output. The standalone accuracy of the LEA-6T is around 2.5 m with an unobstructed view of the sky.

In our setup, the headset streamed raw GPS data (pseudorange, carrier phase, ephemeris, etc.) over a virtual COM port to the phone, using the UBX protocol of the μblox GPS receiver. The GPS coordinates computed and reported by the GPS receiver were also streamed to the phone to allow for comparison between RegTrack and the built-in algorithm supplied by μblox.

To avoid having a single point of failure, we opted for a distributed, symmetric software architecture where each smartphone shares its raw GPS data with the entire network and runs the localization algorithm independently on the GPS data received from its peers, as well as from the local GPS receiver. We relied on an Android port of the JGroups reliable group communication protocol stack for network-wide broadcast of raw GPS readings [7]. JGroups provides group membership management, guarantees atomic multicast messages (all or none message delivery), maintains packet ordering, and handles retransmissions of lost packets – a variety of features that are required to ensure that all smartphones in our network operate on the same input data set. In our prototype, we configured JGroups to use UDP (IP Multicast) over WiFi as the underlying transport protocol. Essentially, each phone was set up to act as a Bluetooth-to-JGroups bridge that receives raw GPS data via the Bluetooth link and disseminates it to the network, as well as a network receiver, accepting JGroups messages from the network and forwarding them to the solver, which, in turn, computes the relative coordinates of the nodes in the network.

6. EVALUATION

Our evaluation approach compares the accuracy of RegTrack to the ground truth. However, to put the results into context, we also need another methodology to create a reference. We decided to use a simple method we call Absolute-to-Relative (A2R) coordinate determination. In this technique, we simply subtract the absolute positions of one or more receivers from the absolute position of a reference receiver, creating a map of relative locations with respect to the reference receiver's coordinate system. If, by extension, we would like to find the baseline between two mobile nodes that are moving relative to the stationary reference (and to one another) using A2R, we would simply subtract the relative position vectors (from the reference to each of the

Figure 2: **Experiment with three nodes exactly 9 feet apart moving around a running track, relative to an additional stationary node.**

mobile nodes) from one another, which would result in a position vector from one mobile node to the other *as seen from the reference node.*

This method, while simple and easy to implement, is limited by the uncorrelated errors present in the absolute positioning technique used. On the other hand, the μblox chip represents the top-end of several low-cost, L1 receiver lines, so if we are able to demonstrate improvements over it, this shows a useful contribution to localization research.

6.1 Experiment: Running Track

Establishing the ground truth for localization experiments is always difficult, even more so when mobility is involved. The site for our first set of experiments, a running track with precisely marked lanes, helped greatly in this regard; hence, we tried out multiple different scenarios. The first experiment was a stationary setup with four nodes placed on the track at the corners of a rectangle approximately 100x50 m in size. The second experiment utilized a 9-foot long pole. We placed one receiver at each end of the pole and walked around the track multiple times in the middle of lane 4. The pole was kept perpendicular to the direction of movement; hence, the nodes were moving approximately on the border between lanes 2 and 3, and between 5 and 6, respectively. We also placed an additional stationary node on the track. Finally, we constructed an equilateral triangle of three 9-foot long poles and put a node at each corner. This setup was similar to the single pole configuration with an additional node moving along the center of lane 4 ahead of the other two nodes (see Figure 2). Once again, a stationary node was also used.

These experiments are useful because the relative distances of the nodes attached to the poles are precisely known at all times, with only the relative directions changing. As such, they provide us with a way to measure the performance of the technique in the "free mobility" case with extreme precision. The additional static node adds range mobility to the experiment, since both the relative directions **and** distances to the nodes are changing continuously when viewed from this receiver. This provides performance statistics on the technique when used with baselines of varying lengths.

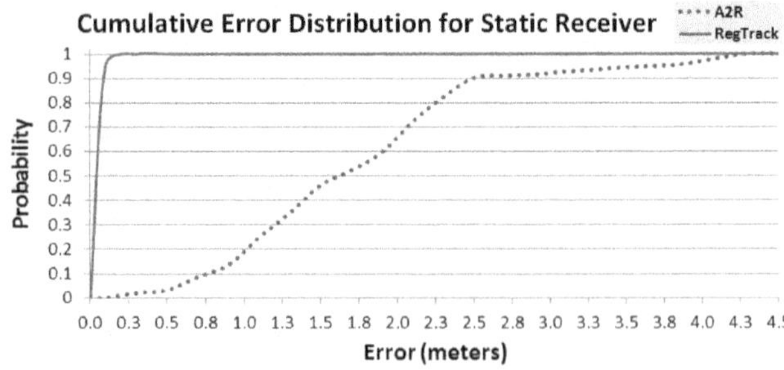

Figure 3: **Cumulative error distributions for a stationary receiver.**

Finally, the stationary node gives us the ability to create absolute ground truth maps for easier visualization, such as using Google Earth as shown in Figure 5.

6.1.1 *Stationary Setup*

In this setup, we had four nodes placed at the corners of a rectangle approximately 100x50m in size. The track had trees and a building next to it, so the nodes had a partially obstructed view of the sky. Nevertheless, this can still be considered a benign GPS environment. To test system stability, we let the system run for more than 25 minutes. Note that RegTrack made no assumptions that the nodes were stationary.

To evaluate the accuracy of the system, we set the absolute initial position of each node to be equal to the reported absolute location from the GPS chip (from which the RegTrack algorithm can deduce the initial relative positions of each receiver). This gives a fair comparison since both the A2R and RegTrack algorithms start with identical views of all of the node positions in the network. Each receiver then tracks the motions of the other nodes through time using the pairwise relative tracking vectors between the remote node and itself. The error is determined from the distance between the computed relative location at any point in time and the ground truth. Since the nodes are completely stationary, the ground truth is simply the starting location of each node. In other words, the position of a node in the network relative to any of the other nodes should be identical to its relative position when tracking was initialized for both A2R and RegTrack.

The results shown in Figure 3 indicate the cumulative error distribution for one of the three remote nodes as viewed from an arbitrarily chosen reference receiver. Note that different choices of reference and/or remote node result in almost identical distributions, so only one of the 12 possible options is shown here. In every case, RegTrack produced very accurate results with mean errors ranging from 7.5-10.3 cm (with standard deviations of 4.9-6.8 cm). The errors using A2R were significantly worse, with mean errors ranging from 1.46-1.82 m and standard deviations from 0.7-0.84 m. This is almost a 20-time improvement in average error, with an extremely substantial increase in stability as evinced by the low standard deviations. Figure 4, taken from an actual track experiment, shows what this type of improvement looks like graphically over a 25-minute period. Note that RegTrack resulted in both significantly slower and smaller error accumulations than A2R; however, the errors in A2R appear to be zero-mean, whereas the RegTrack errors indicate a slow bias over time.

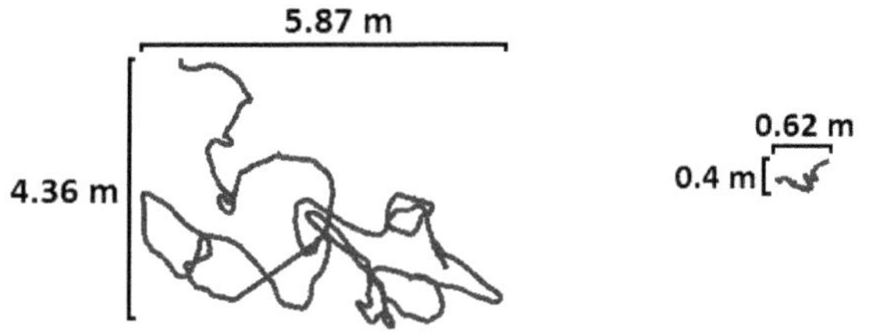

(a) A2R (b) RegTrack

Figure 4: **Static tracks using A2R vs. RegTrack.**

6.1.2 *Fixed 9-foot distance*

The results of the experiment with two mobile nodes on a 9-foot (2.74 m) pole and a single stationary node are probably the easiest to visualize. Figure 5 shows the ground truth of this experiment—the tracks of the two mobile nodes in Google Earth. Figure 6 shows the tracks estimated by A2R *as seen by the stationary node*, under the assumption that its precise absolute location is known. Finally, Figure 7 shows the tracks computed by RegTrack, indicating the relative location vectors between the stationary node and the two mobile nodes through time (and again assuming that the stationary node is perfectly localized and the starting positions are known). In other words, these results indicate the tracks of the two mobile nodes as seen from the reference with relative ranges varying from 0 to ~125 m. In the latter two figures, the ground truth is shown using a dashed line, and the background image is removed for clarity.

As the figures show, the tracks reported by RegTrack are generally closer to the ground truth. For example, the two nodes are always perpendicular to the track and finish almost exactly where they started. This is also apparent in Figure 8, which shows the estimated distance between the mobile node pair (as seen from the stationary reference) as it moved around the lap. Notice by comparing Figure 6 to Figure 8 that the A2R tracks are not only inconsistent in their ability to stay in the correct lane position, the nodes also frequently move in an orientation that is not perfectly parallel to the track, as indicated by the greater than 9-ft range errors in Figure 8 that correspond to track locations in Figure 6 at times when they visually appear to be *less* than 9-ft, and also in the starting locations of the two nodes in Figure 6 (with a range of close to 5 m as opposed to the expected 2.74 m).

Knowing the ground truth between the two mobile nodes to be a fixed 9 feet, or 2.74 m, the mean error using A2R (as seen from the stationary reference node) was 89 cm with a standard deviation of 68.5 cm. Taking the *difference of the vectors* provided by RegTrack between each mobile node and the reference, the mean error was 16.8 cm with a standard deviation of 8.4 cm.

Note that we can also track the relative distance of the two mobile nodes without an explicit reference node. Each of the mobile nodes can consider itself to be the reference and track the relative location of the other. (This is the default operating mode of RegTrack, and we refer to it as "RegTrack-Direct" in the rest of this paper. The stationary reference node was only necessary to give results over changing baseline ranges and to show the absolute track in

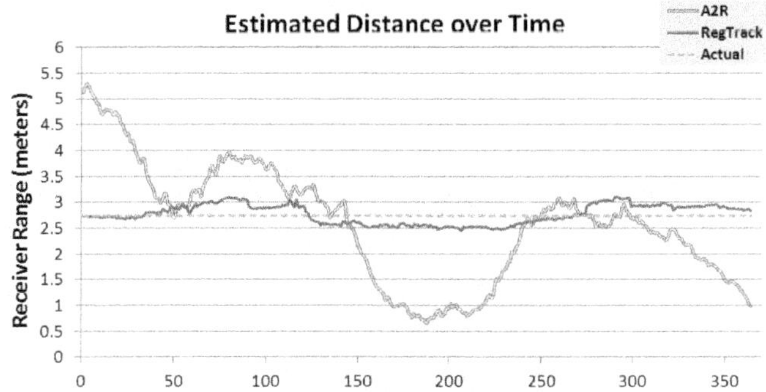

Figure 8: **Estimated distance between the mobile nodes (as seen by the stationary node) as a function of time as they moved around the track.**

Figures 6 and 7.) This method provides a mean error of 14.2 cm according to both receivers, with a standard deviation of 7.8 cm. It is interesting to note that the relative errors are very similar whether we use a reference node up to 125 m away or just the two mobile nodes that are less than 3 m apart. In conclusion, this experiment showed a factor of 6 improvement over the A2R approach, with almost a 10-time improvement in stability as indicated by the standard deviation values.

6.1.3 *9-foot equilateral triangle*

This experiment was very similar to the previous one with the addition of an extra mobile node. Again, our approach is compared to A2R; that is, the value computed by taking the difference of the absolute positions reported by the three μblox receivers involved and the stationary reference. The combined mean error of RegTrack for all three baselines was 23.2 cm, and the standard deviation came to 17.6 cm, which was a 3.5-time improvement over the A2R standard deviation of 63.2 cm. The mean error of A2R was 1.12 m, giving us a 6.6x improvement in overall mean error.

Notice that in this setup, each mobile node sees the other two at a 60-degree angle. Since RegTrack computes location vectors, we can estimate this angle easily. It is also straightforward to do with A2R. Figure 9 shows the distribution of all three angle estimates throughout the lap. These results show a marked improvement over A2R, with a clear spike in the distribution curve around the 60-degree mark. The standard deviation of the RegTrack results was 8°, while the standard deviation of the A2R results was 33°. Note, however, that due to the close proximity of the receivers, a small error in range can result in significant angular errors.

6.2 Experiment: Automobile

Since multiple experiments in a fairly benign environment all produced marked improvements over A2R, we decided to test the limits of our system by running experiments in both a partially-obstructed area and under high-dynamic conditions, namely driving in a car. We should note here that the data for the following experiments was, by necessity, logged and then processed after the experiment instead of in real-time, due to the fact that we were driving in an area far wider than a single wireless router was able to cover. In the future, we may investigate alternate means of data dissemination to

Figure 5: **Ground truth**

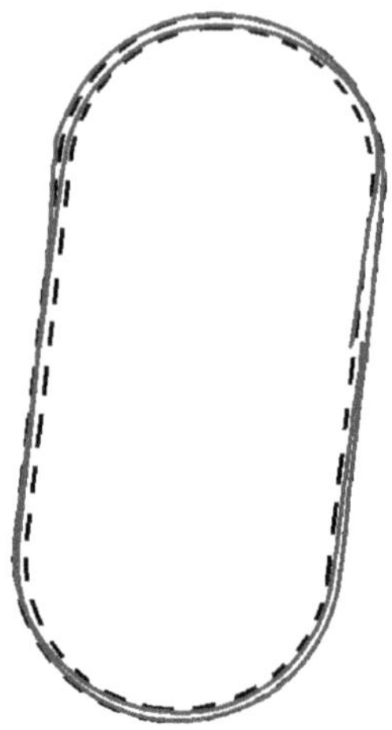

Figure 6: **A2R.**

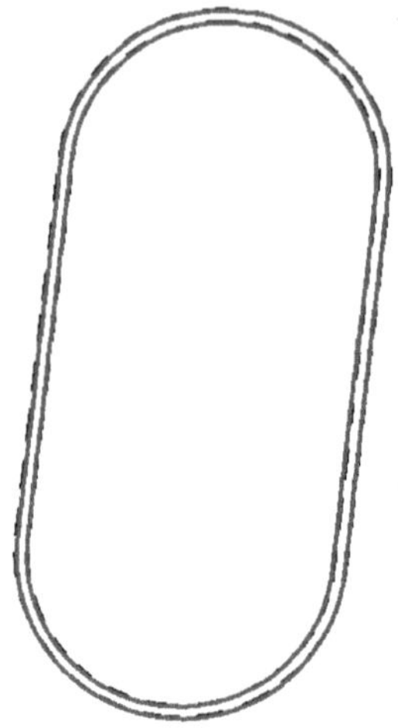

Figure 7: **RegTrack**

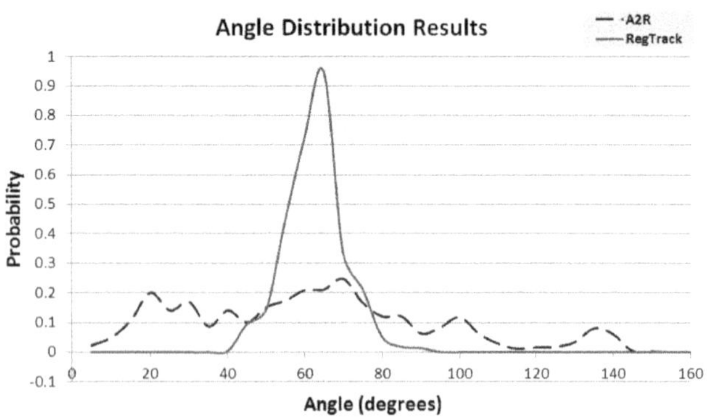

Figure 9: **Angle distributions for one lap.**

overcome this problem, such as ad-hoc phone-to-phone networks or even a cellular data implementation.

In carrying out the following experiments, we noted (as expected) that there were times when one or more of the receivers could not maintain enough satellite locks to continue using RegTrack. Since re-calibration was out of the question in such dynamic experiments, we overcame this problem by simply extrapolating the node tracks based on the most recent velocity estimates of the receiver. So long as the velocity did not change abruptly during an outage, this solution worked sufficiently well for us to be able to evaluate the accuracy of our algorithms in these more difficult environments. Note, however, that this is an extremely naive solution to dealing with temporary losses of satellite locks. In the future, we plan to devise better, more robust ways of dealing with this problem, but for this phase of the project, we simply needed a way to keep the tracks moving to evaluate our technique under these dynamic conditions.

The entirety of this experiment involved placing three GPS nodes on top of a car and driving in a 12.2-km loop, where the course was broken up into two distinct parts. The first part involved driving at relatively low speeds (<50 km/h) between 2-4 story tall buildings and under numerous leafy trees; in other words, a slightly higher dynamic environment than in previous experiments with significantly more opportunities for multipath, cycle slippage, and losses of lock. This was followed by an extremely high-dynamic situation in which we drove on an interstate highway, where the main obstructions were the numerous overpasses that temporarily blocked satellite visibility. Finally, we exited the interstate and closed the loop to return back to our starting point.

In addition to the three mobile nodes on the roof of the car, we also set up a stationary node at the starting position to test the accuracy of our algorithm when a receiver is tracking multiple nodes many kilometers away (a maximum of 3.5 km in this case).

6.2.1 Driving in Obstructed Area

Three nodes were placed on top of a vehicle situated in a wide open parking lot with a clear view of the sky, two in the front approximately 1.04 m apart and a third on the back left side approximately 1.35 m behind the front left node. After initialization, the car was driven slowly through a very narrow alleyway with buildings on either side and significant tree cover. The car then drove through a one-lane, suburban-type road with occasional tree cover, followed by a main road (at approximately 50 km/h) with tree cover. The total length of this portion of the experiment was 1.478 km, which took 5 minutes to complete including a few stops due to traffic. Table 2 summarizes the results as they accumulated over time, where "RegTrack" indicates the pairwise node ranges as computed with reference to the stationary node, and "RegTrack-Direct" indicates the results as computed directly (pairwise) from each of the mobile nodes on the vehicle relative to one another, excluding the stationary node.

Somewhat surprisingly, the overall RegTrack results were only marginally less accurate than those from the running track, even though this experiment included a much more difficult GPS environment. We would have expected multipath and losses of satellite locks to have more of an impact, but it is possible that the close proximity of the receivers to one another meant that any multipath effects were actually quite similar for all receivers, and therefore canceled out.

It is interesting to note that the direct application of RegTrack from each of the roving nodes to one another resulted in less accurate results than when viewed from the stationary node by about a factor of 3. The most likely reason for this is that the stationary node had a clear view of the sky, meaning it was more likely to have a larger number of visible satellites in common with each of the mobile nodes at any given time than they did with one another. In either case, RegTrack outperformed the A2R method by a factor of 2 for the direct case, and a factor ranging from 4.5-6.5 when using the stationary node as a reference.

6.2.2 *High-Speed Driving*

For this portion of the driving test, we entered an interstate highway with a clear view of the sky, obstructed only by occasional overpasses. It is important to note here that we did not stop and re-initialize the RegTrack algorithm, but rather continued on from the end of the previous portion of the driving experiment. Therefore, any error that had accumulated during that time was also present to begin this test.

The total length of the path traversed during this experiment was 7.027 km, taking 4.75 minutes to complete. The receivers were moving an average speed of 90 km/h during this time. The results for two of the mobile node pairs are summarized in Figure 10:

Clearly, the improvement of RegTrack over A2R in the mean error graph for mobiles nodes #1 and #2 looks significantly better than the results from nodes #2 and #3. We included both sets of results to emphasize an important point, namely to show how crucial it is that the initial relative positions of the nodes be set properly. Nodes #1 and #2 correspond to the front two receivers on the car, which, from looking at both GPS tracks and analyzing the result data, accrued only a modest amount of error over the first part of the driving experiment. Node #3 was the node on the back of the car directly behind node #2, and it was apparent that this node had accumulated more error than the other two in the directional sense (in other words, the reported ranges between the nodes were quite close to the actual ranges, however the direction vectors from node #3 to the other nodes were slightly incorrect). As such, the tracking algorithm could have been working flawlessly and the comparison to ground truth would still show significant error since the initial positions at the beginning of this portion of the experiment had already accumulated error. Again, this just serves to show the importance of correct position initialization in any tracking algorithm.

Since the initial positions of nodes #1 and #2 were shown to be more closely representative of the ground truth, the results in the first graph are more indicative of the performance of the RegTrack algorithm. Once again, RegTrack outperformed A2R by a significant margin, only this time the direct localization approach (i.e. the positions of the mobile nodes as seen from one other, excluding the stationary node) performed slightly better than the stationary node case (as expected). This again furthers our theory that low satellite visibility in the first part of the experiment was to blame for the decrease in accuracy.

Method	Distance Traveled	Mean Error	Standard Deviation
RegTrack	500 m	15.2 cm	10.5 cm
RegTrack-Direct	500 m	50.7 cm	24.0 cm
A2R	500 m	93.6 cm	36.5 cm
RegTrack	1 km	15.0 cm	10.2 cm
RegTrack-Direct	1 km	48.4 cm	24.1 cm
A2R	1 km	97.5 cm	36.5 cm
RegTrack	1.48 km	25.3 cm	24.8 cm
RegTrack-Direct	1.48 km	62.2 cm	36.4 cm
A2R	1.48 km	113.4 cm	55.6 cm

Table 2: **Cumulative accuracy for one of the node pairs while driving through a difficult GPS environment.**

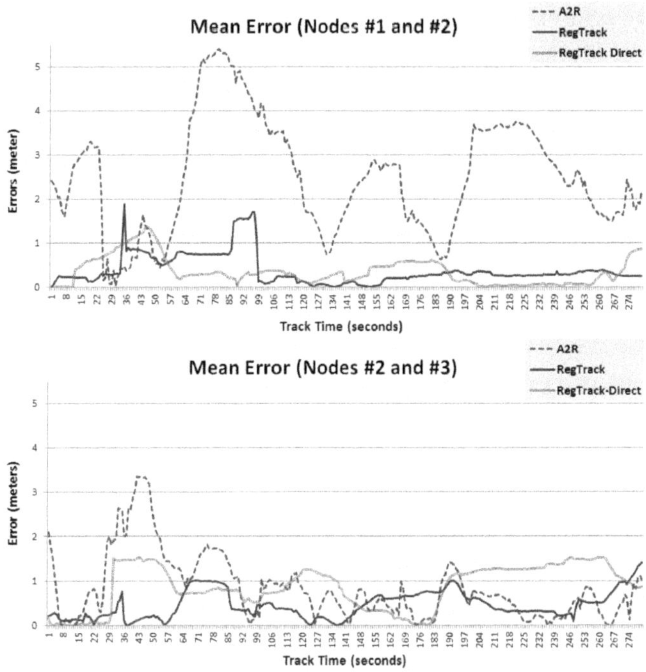

Figure 10: **Mean errors over time for two of the mobile node pairs attached to the roof a car driving along the interstate.**

For numerical comparison, the mean error of the A2R method was 2.47 m with a standard deviation of 1.29 m, whereas the mean error of the RegTrack method was 37.6 cm with a standard deviation of 34.5 cm, and the mean error of the RegTrack-Direct method was 34.8 cm with a standard deviation of 31 cm. As a frame of reference, this level of accuracy allows for quite obvious feature extraction of important driving events such as lane-changing as shown in Figure 11, approximately 1 km into the experiment. For a video of the entire experiment, go to `http://tinyurl.com/bvelw4c`.

Figure 11: **Track of car carrying out a lane change.**

6.2.3 *Closing the Loop*

At the very end of the interstate experiment, our vehicle passed under a wide overpass while at the same time subtly changing directions. Also, each of the nodes re-acquired satellite locks at slightly different times. As a result, the simple velocity extrapolation method used throughout the rest of the experiment failed in this case, with the 3 mobile receivers emerging from the overpass with tens of meters of distance between them as seen from the stationary reference node.

One node, however, was able to re-acquire its satellite locks quickly enough to have only accrued a minimal amount of error, enabling us to continue to track its position relative to the stationary node as we closed the loop and returned back to the starting position. This required an additional 3.696 km of driving over 5.2 minutes. At this point, the remaining node appeared 2.3 m away from its starting position. While this number by itself is quite impressive, considering RegTrack relies on dead reckoning and the entire experiment lasted 15 minutes and covered 12.2 km of moderate to difficult GPS terrain, we expect that the result may have even been better had the final overpass not temporarily disabled the RegTrack algorithm.

The final important thing to note about this driving experiment is the level of accuracy that was able to be maintained relative to a stationary reference node, even though the range to that node varied up to 3.5 km away. This shows that our error analyses and the corrections used in RegTrack produce precise enough satellite observations that accuracy is largely independent of the pairwise distances between the mobile nodes being tracked. As a summary, the following table shows the results of all experiments described in this section:

Experiment	Method	Mean Error	Standard Deviation
Track: *Stationary*	RegTrack	9.1 cm	6.1 cm
	A2R	168.4 cm	77.3 cm
Track: *9-ft Pole*	RegTrack	16.8 cm	8.4 cm
	RegTrack-Direct	14.2 cm	7.8 cm
	A2R	89.0 cm	68.5 cm
Track: *Triangle*	RegTrack	23.2 cm	17.6 cm
	A2R	112.0 cm	63.2 cm
Driving: *Obstructed/ Multipath*	RegTrack	25.3 cm	24.8 cm
	RegTrack-Direct	62.6 cm	36.4 cm
	A2R	113.4 cm	55.6 cm
Driving: *High-Speed*	RegTrack	37.6 cm	34.5 cm
	RegTrack-Direct	34.8 cm	31.0 cm
	A2R	247.0 cm	149.0 cm

Table 3: **Summary of experimental results for all nodes in each experiment. Note that in the stationary case, the RegTrack and RegTrack-Direct methods of evaluation are synonymous.**

7. FUTURE WORK

Before we can fully realize our vision of a complete standalone localization system, RegTrack needs an additional component to compute the instantaneous relative positions of any of the nodes participating in the localization process following a temporary loss of all satellite locks. This is also necessary to initialize the tracking at start-up time and because any complete loss of satellite locks resulting in fewer than four visible satellites will necessitate a complete re-initialization of the tracking algorithm. To tackle this problem, we have a very clear idea for the continuation of our work. Aside from the obvious advantage of being able to accurately track a set of receivers through time, the centimeter-scale results obtained from our algorithm are useful because they enable us to mathematically reverse the relative motions of a receiver such that an initial receiver-receiver baseline can be estimated *as if both receivers had remained stationary*. That is, it will be possible to estimate the relative positions of two receivers at any given time based on data from multiple epochs.

To make this clearer, assume that a node exists with a general idea of its (reference) location on Earth and is trying to localize a second roving node. Since only a general idea of the absolute location of a node is required to produce an extremely accurate satellite direction vector, it can be assumed that the reference location is precisely known and does not change over time; likewise, this paper has demonstrated that the relative motions of a roving node can be tracked very accurately, leaving only the coordinates of the initial baseline vector to be determined. Thus, a system of range equations can be written as a function of the initial baseline coordinates with respect to the "stationary" reference at some arbitrary time. Using this model as a basis for our future work, our next research step will be to determine a way to use it to provide centimeter-scale relative positions *without* requiring tracking initialization.

A final natural extension to RegTrack that has the potential to improve the overall results is to perform a network-wide localization step using the the individual location vectors computed by the nodes. In surveying terms, this is referred to as "closing the loop," whereby the addition of any number of relative vectors which form a closed-loop from one receiver back to itself should equal 0. In a network of n nodes, $(n - 1)$ such vectors are sufficient to compute the relative locations of any of the nodes. In our system, we will have far more than this required number, resulting in an overdetermined system. Any number of optimization approaches could be used to estimate the node locations while minimizing overall error.

8. CONCLUSION

This paper presented a novel approach to GPS-based differential tracking of mobile nodes. The evaluation of the technique under various conditions clearly showed the feasibility of achieving an order of magnitude improvement in localization accuracy over the traditional absolute positioning algorithms provided by standard GPS while relying on low-cost, single frequency receivers alone.

Unlike most GPS-based navigation solutions, our approach does not snap positions to maps or try to use a dynamic model for the motions of the receivers (other than during satellite losses of lock). Also unlike other high-precision GPS localization techniques used in applications for which our system may have utility in its current tracking-based state (e.g. Differential GPS, Real-Time Kinematic navigation, or any number of post-processing methods used in applications such as land surveying, precision agriculture, temporal feature extraction, or multiple sensing-modality localization apps), our approach does not require a stationary calibration phase, using only instantaneous relative node locations for tracking initialization.

By allowing a network of GPS receivers to share their raw satellite measurements with one another, we were able to achieve centimeter-scale tracking accuracy via:

- Better modeling and correction of the error sources unique to the two-receiver localization case,

- Creation of a new observation model called the *Dual-Epoch, Double-Differenced* model which is able to use independent satellite observations from two receivers through time to create a set of unambiguous, highly-accurate carrier phase equations representing the relative satellite-receiver changes in range, and
- Integration of this new model into a tracking algorithm that produces pairwise 3D location vectors between a local node and any number of remote receivers.

In three different walking experiments, we were able to achieve improvements ranging from 7-20x better than the corresponding "standard" GPS positioning techniques, and sub-meter accuracy was likewise achieved while driving at various speeds, with varying baseline lengths, and under difficult GPS conditions. *The demonstrated high-accuracy of RegTrack is notable because the approach uses a form of dead reckoning in which errors accumulate over time.*

Likewise, our experiments included receiver-receiver baseline lengths ranging from 0 m all the way up to 3.5 km, with little to no impact on the precision of the results. We conclude, therefore, that our method is quite robust to changing baseline lengths (within reason), and the limiting factor may be the various mathematical assumptions mentioned in Section 4.3 regarding use of the Dual-Epoch, Double-Differenced model in tracking. As such, we anticipate similar levels of accuracy to be achievable for baselines up to $\sim$1000 km in length.

Finally, we note that our method has several unique characteristics that make it attractive for a wide array of use cases. First, since our tracking algorithm works on pairwise sets of satellite data, its computational complexity does not grow with the addition of GPS receivers to the network. In fact, with modern processing speeds, the primary bottleneck is the communication bandwidth required to broadcast the raw satellite measurements among a potentially large number of receivers. Since the amount of data transmitted from a single node every second is actually quite low (on the order of 500 bytes/second), there are better ways (than the naive multicast approach used in our experiments) of approaching this problem if and when communication scalability becomes a problem. Secondly, since each and every node considers itself to be the "reference node" in our technique, the system is symmetric and contains no single point of failure. If any node experiences problems, it will simply drop out of localization participation until the problem is resolved.

The approach presented in this paper represents a large first step toward our ultimate goal of a complete standalone relative localization system using only low-cost, commercial GPS receivers. The research in its present state already has significant utility in the realm of precision tracking, which currently has a notable lack of simple, low-cost solutions. While our technique is elegant in its simplicity, we truly believe that it has the ability to open doors for further research and applications that are either difficult, out of reach, or prohibitively expensive given the current state of the art.

9. ACKNOWLEDGMENTS

The research presented in this paper was supported in part by the National Science Foundation under the CNS-NeTS program (Grant #1218710), a Google Research Award, the DARPA Transformative Apps program, Vanderbilt University, and Project #TAMOP-4.2.2.A-11/1/KONV-2012-0073 of the European Union and the European Social Fund. Additionally, we would like to thank Thyagarajan Nandagopal for his helpful suggestions regarding our research. Finally, we are very grateful to our anonymous paper reviewers and shepherd, Marco Gruteser, for their collective input. Any opinions, findings, conclusions, or recommendations expressed in this material are those of the authors and do not necessarily reflect the views of the sponsors.

10. REFERENCES

[1] Neil Ashby. The Sagnac effect in the Global Positioning System. *Relativity in Rotating Frames*, 2012.

[2] Chaminda Basnayake, C. Christopher Kellum, James Sinko, and Joseph Strus. GPS-based relative positioning test platform for automotive active safety systems. In *ION GNSS 19th International Technical Meeting of the Satellite Division*, ION GNSS International Technical Meeting, pages 1457–1467, Fort Worth, TX, USA, September 2006.

[3] K. Borre, D.M. Ákos, N. Bertelsen, P. Rinder, and S.H. Jensen. *A Software-Defined GPS and Galileo Receiver*. Springer Verlag, 2007.

[4] Eniuce Menezes de Souza, Joao Francisco Galera Monico, and Aylton Pagamisse. GPS satellites Kinematic Relative Positioning: Analyzing and improving the functional mathematical model using wavelets. *Mathematical Problems in Engineering*, 2009, June 2009.

[5] Christopher Hegarty Elliott D. Kaplan. *Understanding GPS: Principles and Applications*. Artech House, 2.00 edition, 2005.

[6] Jay Farrell and Tony Givargis. Differential GPS reference station algorithm – Design and analysis. *IEEE Transactions on Control Systems Technology*, 8:519–531, May 2000.

[7] Jgroups: A toolkit for reliable multicast communications. `http://www.jgroups.org`.

[8] Raja Jurdak, Peter Corke, Dhinesh Dharman, and Guillaume Salagnac. Adaptive gps duty cycling and radio ranging for energy-efficient localization. In *Proceedings of the 8th ACM Conference on Embedded Networked Sensor Systems*, SenSys '10, pages 57–70, New York, NY, USA, 2010. ACM.

[9] Lao-Sheng Lin. Application of GPS RTK and total station system on dynamic monitoring land use. In *Proceedings of the ISPRS Congress Istanbul 2004, Commission VII*, ISPRS Congress, Istanbul, Turkey, July 2004.

[10] J. Liu, B. Priyantha, T. Hart, H.S. Ramos, A.A.F. Loureiro, and Q. Wang. Energy efficient gps sensing with cloud offloading. 2012.

[11] RTKLIB: An open source program package for GNSS positioning. `http://gpspp.sakura.ne.jp/rtklib/rtklib.htm`, 2011.

[12] Eric Sutton and Rockwell Collins. Calibration of differential phase map compensation using single axis rotation. In *Proceedings of the 11th International Technical Meeting of the Satellite Division of the Institute of Navigation*, ION GPS 1998, pages 1831–1840, Nashville, TN, USA, September 2008.

[13] TxDOT survey manual - GPS RTK surveying. Texas Department of Transportation, http://onlinemanuals.txdot.gov/txdotmanuals/ess/gps_rtk_surveying.htm, April 2011.

[14] Péter Völgyesi, Sándor Szilvási, János Sallai, and Ákos Lédeczi. External smart microphone for mobile phones. In *Proceedings of the International Conference on Sensing Technology*, ICST, 2011.

[15] What is differential GPS. Rose India Technologies, http://www.roseindia.net/technology/gps/what-is-Differential-GPS.shtml, February 2008.

[16] Yang Yunchun, Ronald R. Hatch, and R. T. Sharpe. Minimizing the integer ambiguity search space for RTK. *Wuhan University Journal of Natural Sciences*, 8:485–491, 2003.

Guoguo: Enabling Fine-grained Indoor Localization via Smartphone

Kaikai Liu, Xinxin Liu, and Xiaolin Li
Scalable Software Systems Laboratory
University of Florida, Gainesville, FL 32611
kaikailiu@ufl.edu, xinxin@cise.ufl.edu, andyli@ece.ufl.edu

ABSTRACT

Using smartphones for accurate indoor localization opens a new frontier of mobile services, offering enormous opportunities to enhance users' experiences in indoor environments. Despite significant efforts on indoor localization in both academia and industry in the past two decades, highly accurate and practical smartphone-based indoor localization remains an open problem. To enable indoor location-based services (ILBS), there are several stringent requirements for an indoor localization system: highly accurate that can differentiate massive users' locations (foot-level); no additional hardware components or extensions on users' smartphones; scalable to massive concurrent users. Current GPS, Radio RSS (e.g. WiFi, Bluetooth, ZigBee), or Fingerprinting based solutions can only achieve meter-level or room-level accuracy. In this paper, we propose a practical and accurate solution that fills the long-lasting gap of smartphone-based indoor localization. Specifically, we design and implement an indoor localization ecosystem Guoguo. Guoguo consists of an anchor network with a coordination protocol to transmit modulated localization beacons using high-band acoustic signals, a realtime processing app in a smartphone, and a backend server for indoor contexts and location-based services. We further propose approaches to improve its coverage, accuracy, and location update rate with low-power consumption. Our prototype shows centimeter-level localization accuracy in an office and classroom environment. Such precise indoor localization is expected to have high impact in the future ILBS and our daily activities.

Categories and Subject Descriptors

C.2.1 [**Network Architecture and Design**]: Wireless communication; H.5.5 [**Sound and Music Computing**]: Signal analysis, synthesis, and processing

Keywords

Localization, Smartphone, Anchor Network, Acoustic Signal

MobiSys'13, June 25-28, 2013, Taipei, Taiwan

1. INTRODUCTION

Current coarse-grained (room-level or meter-level) indoor localization on a smartphone has enabled a lot of mobile services, such as location-based services, indoor maps, and indoor navigation systems. However, these services are severely limited due to low resolution. Indoor users can hardly navigate like using outdoor GPS services. The major difference is as follows: meter-level (e.g. GPS with five-meter accuracy) localization is sufficient to navigate a car (meter-level footprint) on a street (several-meter footprint); but it is far from sufficient to navigate a user (foot-level footprint) in a library (with half-meter-wide isles and inch-level books) or a shopping mall (with inch-level items). Smartphone-based accurate "indoor GPS" or IPS (indoor positioning system) has long been waited to improve indoor mobile services and enable new services. Despite significant efforts on indoor localization in both academia and industry in the past two decades [2, 3, 4, 5, 23, 26], highly accurate and practical smartphone-based indoor localization remains an open problem. Some accurate localization solutions cannot be readily converted to smartphone-based ones due to various constraints.

The technology that enables centimeter or decimeter level location accuracy and integrates with context-aware mobile services has the potential to revolutionize users' mobile experiences. Using ranging, angle, displacement or fingerprinting based sensing is required for accurate indoor localization. However, none of existing solutions could achieve desired performance at low cost and low complexity. Time-of-Arrival (TOA) based ranging approaches, e.g., special devices using ultra-wideband or ultrasound signals, are more reliable and accurate. However, the increased complexity and additional devices make them not practically useful for conventional users. Other low-complexity approaches rely on existing sensors in smartphones to infer current location, e.g., WiFi, fingerprinting, compasses and accelerometers. However, their low accuracy and prerequisites like site survey or pairing limits their applications.

Recent research on leveraging ubiquitous microphone sensors in a smartphone introduces a convenient approach of ranging by using the audible band acoustic signal (less than 20kHz). A microphone sensor is inexpensive and has potential for high accurate ranging due to the low transmission speed of acoustic signals. However, the limited bandwidth of a microphone, strong attenuation of aerial acoustic signals, as well as various interferences in the audible band, poses significant challenges in using acoustic signals for indoor localization. Although using acoustic signal to perform ranging-based localization suffers from various issues, such as short operation distance, low update rate, and sound pollution, the potential of centimeter-level localization accuracy motivates us to design better solutions to overcome its drawbacks.

In this paper, we propose an indoor localization system called "Guoguo" [1], and further improve its performance in terms of coverage, accuracy, update rate, and sound pollution. We make its acoustic beacons imperceptible to humans and improve detection sensitivity for better location coverage. Rather than simply using "Beep" signals, to enable passive sensing for multiple smartphone users, we design the transmission waveform, wide-band modulation, and one-way synchronization and ranging schemes. We design a transmission scheme of the acoustic beacon that follows the high-density pseudo-codes to enable anchor node identification without radio assistance on a smartphone. We propose a *symbol-interleaved* beacon structure to overcome the drawback of the low transmission speed of acoustic signal and improve the *location update rate*. To improve the accuracy of ranging, we propose a fine-grained adaptive time-of-arrival (TOA) estimation approach that exploits the details of the beacon signal and perform Non-line-of-sight (NLOS) identification and mitigation. By combining all these techniques together, we implement the prototype system with anchor nodes and localization processing app in a smartphone, and make it work in realistic environment.

The rest of the paper is organized as follows. Section 7 summarizes the related work. Section 2 introduces the design consideration and system architecture. Section 3 presents the acoustic beacon and anchor network design. Section 4 presents the ranging and localization approaches by using smartphone. Section 5 presents the experimental evaluation of our proposed approach. Section 9 discusses the future work. Section 8 concludes the paper.

2. SYSTEM DESIGN

2.1 Motivation

Various existing localization solutions rely on different assumptions and are dedicated to specific applications. For most existing solutions using only built-in sensors in a smartphone, rough position information can be obtained for building- or room-level navigation. For indoor mobile services for shelf-to-shelf navigation, location-aware and context-aware information recommendation and virtual-reality interaction, fined-grained indoor localization with the foot-level accuracy is critical.

In terms of system complexity, users' side is more stringent especially in hardware requirement. It is very hard to persuade the consumers to purchase special devices for indoor localization. Even with special devices, the integration with the mobile services provided by smartphone is also a difficult problem. To enable centimeter or decimeter level localization accuracy, and only require smartphone on the user side, the investment on indoor infrastructure is necessary and potential for other interesting applications, e.g., surveillance and monitoring. For normal retail stores, several hundred dollars investment on indoor infrastructure to enable indoor "smart" shopping, could attract more consumers to enjoy the mobile services, and in turn boost their business.

With these two points in mind, we focus on developing a fine-grained smartphone-based indoor localization system leveraging indoor low-complexity anchor network.

2.2 Design Challenges and Consideration

To meet the localization accuracy, TOA-based ranging is more appropriate [21]. Limited by the smartphone, using acoustic signal for TOA-based ranging is the only solution. However, making the acoustic signal for ranging and localization in real situations has a lot of challenges.

First, the coverage of the anchor network should be sufficient for a room or a retail store with less than 10 anchor nodes placed to minimize the infrastructure cost. The possible solution is to increase the transmit power or detection sensitivity. However, increase the transmit power could cause sound pollution and high energy cost. [17, 22] all suffer from sound pollution caused by the audible signal. H. Liu et al. [14] achieves less pollution, but only works within 3 meters. Maintaining a low transmit power and keeping the acoustic beacon unnoticeable are the two prerequisites in the anchor network design. Thus, improving the detection sensitivity in the smartphone by using advanced signal processing technique is the feasible solution to ensure sufficient coverage.

Second, sufficient update rate is required to track users' movement. If the localization update rate is too sluggish, no user could be patient enough to wait their location results. There are also not enough time margin for mobile services. Existing acoustic ranging solution proposed in [14] shows 7.8s delay in one location calculation; authors in [19] perform localization for desktop and calculates the running time for 5 nodes in the range of 3.7s to 285s. Possible solutions for improving the location update rate includes better design of the anchor network protocol, real time implementation of the algorithm, and eliminate the use of WiFi assistance (takes about 2s for one scan).

Third, the system should support multiuser simultaneously. However, solutions used in [22, 14, 19] utilize the two-way approach for ranging. Two-way ranging eliminates the synchronization requirement, but suffer from the limitation of only allowing one user to access at one time. Sound source localization [25] is another way to eliminate the synchronization by using active transmit mode for users, however, the random access time of the user making the sensor network could only handle limited users at the same time. One-way passive ranging should be utilized to maximize the multiuser capacity, which could support unlimited number of users in theoretical.

2.3 System Architecture

In order to meet the requirements mentioned in Section 2.1 and 2.2, we propose to the develop an anchor network with better coverage and make the beacon unnoticeable. With several low-complexity anchor nodes mounted on indoor places, the smartphone can localize itself by receiving more than three beacon signals from the anchor nodes. The simplified architecture of our proposed localization system is shown in Fig. 1. In the receiver side, we implement advanced signal processing and ranging algorithm in smartphone to achieve accurate localization in passive mode. The cloud server provides mobile services, e.g., localization, naviga-

[1]"Guoguo" means katydid/bush-cricket in Mandarin Chinese. Guoguo, famous for its beautiful sound, represents a pet culture in ancient China for thousands of years

tion, for the accessed users in real-time response mode and minimize the computation and storage cost in the smartphone.

Specifically, the anchor network transmits modulated acoustic beacon signals based on the token of the controller periodically. By detecting and extracting the desired information bits embedded in beacon signals, the smartphone demodulates the symbols and calculates the relative TOA. The algorithm in smartphone eliminates erroneous measurements using statistical pruning methods, and access the anchor position by matching the pseudocodes. Finally, the smartphone can be aware of its fine-grained position by accessing the localization results.

3. ANCHOR NETWORK DESIGN

3.1 Design Criterion

In our anchor network design, an anchor transmits the spatial beacon signal to inform its unique location to a smartphone without relying on additional radio communication devices. Such basic design criterion requires the anchor network to support acoustic communication in addition to ranging. Moreover, anchor nodes and mobile phones are distributed without explicit connection or pairing, and use acoustic communication to realize synchronization. Compared with systems using a radio signal for synchronization and communication to assist acoustic ranging, e.g., Cricket [23] and Beep [17], our system implements both acoustic communication and localization. With acoustic communication and ranging, our solution features the following salient advantages: no need of special radio signal (e.g. ZigBee) that is not available on a smartphone; no need of special devices for ranging assistance; enabling one-way passive ranging to support massive users like the outdoor GPS. Ranging based on the acoustic communication channel improves efficiency and scalability, and reduces the hardware requirements of system implementation. Using such configuration, we can simply extend our system to other devices that contains a microphone and computation resources rather than limited to the smartphone platform.

3.2 Transmitter Waveform Design and Modulation

Using audible-band acoustic signal as beacon for ranging and communication, we must contend with a variety of noises to ensure its accurate ranging due to the highly populated frequency band below 20kHz. The ranging accuracy direct depends on the signal-to-noise ratio (SNR) and effective bandwidth. However, higher transmitter signal bandwidth and power will generate sound noise that disturbs to users. The standard microphone in mobile phone can only support bandwidth of 200Hz $\sim$ 20kHz. To minimize the sound noise while perform ranging, we choose 15kHz $\sim$ 20kHz as the operating band. The reason is that our ear is less sensitive to the high frequency signal, while the microphone in smartphone could still receive signal in this boundary band. With well controlled transmitter signal power, the acoustic beacon could be unnoticeable to humans while still detectable for smartphone. We use spread-spectrum and ultra low-duty-cycle pulse sharping techniques to ensure the proper operation of the acoustic beacon under realistic environment, as well as improving the ranging accuracy. Unlike the less sophisticated single-frequency acoustic signal used in Cricket and Beep, the beacon signal used in *Guoguo* is wide-band modulated and unnoticeable to humans.

The task of anchor nodes that transmitting modulated acoustic sharp pulse to the mobile receiver is to realize synchronization and ranging, as well as inform its unique pseudocode $\mathbf{p} = [p_{m,i}]$, $m = 1, \ldots, M$, $i = 1, \ldots, L$, where M is the number of the anchor nodes; L is the pseudocode length. The pseudocode $\mathbf{p}_{m,i} = 0, 1$ is also the information bits carried by the beacon signal. For the symbol waveform, we choose to use the second derivative of the Gaussian (Doublet) Pulse [24] and multiple it to the carrier wave. The waveform could be written as

$$g(t) = \frac{A}{\tau}\left[1 - 4\pi\left(\frac{t}{\tau}\right)^2\right]\exp\left[-2\pi\left(\frac{t}{\tau}\right)^2\right]\cos(2\pi f_c t) \quad (1)$$

where τ is the pulse width parameter, f_c is the carrier wave frequency. We truncate the Doublet pulse by their 3τ to approach the real-time condition.

The center frequency f_c of the modulated pulse is controlled by the on-chip timer and working at 18kHz. In addition to f_c, τ is tuned to ensure the effective bandwidth of (1) lies in between 15kHz $\sim$ 20kHz. The multiplication with the carrier wave in (1) is also a spread spectrum process that extend the initial narrow band f_c to wide band signal $g(t)$ by using the Gaussian Doublet Pulse sharping. The use of ultra low-duty cycle pulse (1) has the feature of higher data rate, higher location refresh rate, better multipath resolution, lower energy consumption and smaller sound pollution. To balance between the system complexity and the sophisticated modulation scheme, we choose to perform 2-PAM modulation with symbol duration as T_s; i.e., transmit sharp pulse $g(t)$ represents symbol '1', no pulse for symbol '0'.

3.3 Pseudocode Selection

One design challenge faced in selecting the pseudocode is to utilize the proper pseudo-codes with enough code distance redundancy to separate different anchor nodes, e.g., utilize orthogonal codes. In addition to communication, every symbol '1' in $\mathbf{p}$ will contribute to one ranging measurement, thus the high density bit '1' could improve the location update rate.

Conventional communication process relies on the preamble part of a frame to perform synchronization, then follows the data bits. For our designed anchor network, the beacon signal should only contain the pseudocodes and transmits cyclically to save round time for higher location update rate. The stringent requirement on efficiency making the remove of unnecessary part of bits especially important for Guoguo due to the low transmission speed of acoustic signal. However, most orthogonal pseudo-codes are not cyclic orthogonal; it will loss orthogonality due to the cyclical transmission. Using Walsh-Hadamard codes, for example, only $L+1$ codes with length L are orthogonal to each other in all phases among Hadamard Matrix $H(2^L, L)$. Moreover, the balanced '1' and '0' in these pseudo-codes does not comply with our requirement on high '1' density sequence.

In order to meet the special requirement of pseudocode for our anchor network, we select three distinct maximum sequence as $\{ms_1, ms_2, ms_3\}$ with length of 2^L, L is the pseudocode length. To increase the '1' density, we perform plus and decision process to combine these three m-sequences as

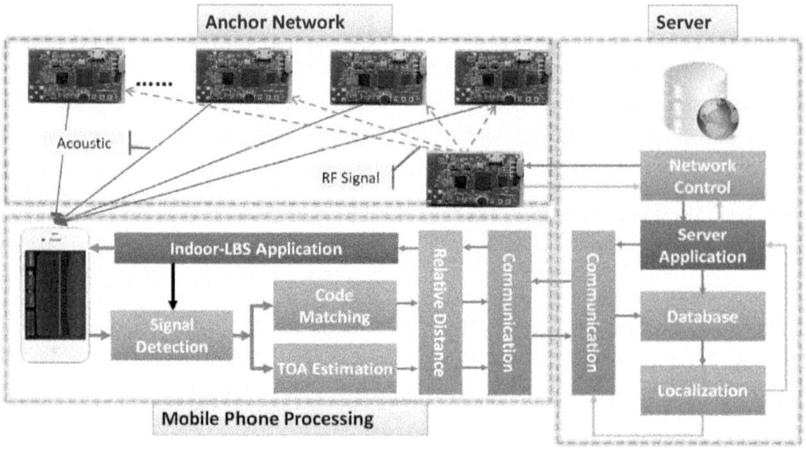

Figure 1: Conceptual Architecture of the Guoguo System.

a new sequence ms', as

$$ms' = \{ms_1 + ms_2 + ms_3\} \gtrless_0^1 0.5 \quad (2)$$

where the length of ms' is 2^L. Reshape ms' into a (L', L) matrix as $\mathbf{m} = \{m_{a,b}\}$, with $L' = 2^{(L-1)}/L$, $a = \{1, \dots, L'\}$, $b = \{1, \dots, L\}$. L is the code length, and total L' sequences in $\mathbf{m}_{a,b}$. To maintain the minimum code distance d_{tol} between each sequences, we only select sequences in $\mathbf{m}$ that satisfy the conditions in any phases that

$$\begin{aligned} p_{m,i} = \arg_{\hat{a}}\{p_{\hat{a},i} | \min ||m_{a,i} - p_{k,i+\triangle_i}||_1 \geq d_{tol}\}, \quad (3) \\ \forall k = \{1, \dots, m-1\}, \forall \triangle_i = \{1, \dots, L\} \\ \hat{a} \in \{1, \dots, 2^{(L-1)}/L\}, m = m+1 \end{aligned}$$

where $|| \cdot ||_1$ calculates the code distance between $m_{a,i}$ to the selected sequences $p_{k,i+\triangle_i}$, $i + \triangle_i$ performs cyclic phase change for the sequence. (3) filters sequences in $\mathbf{m}$ that meet minimum distance d_{tol} among selected sequence sets and add into $p_{m,i}$. When $L = 16$, among total $2^{(L-1)}/L = 2048$ sequences, only 12 sequences satisfy (3). These sequences can be assigned to M anchors, where $M = 9$ for a micro-cell in our system.

3.4 Anchor Network Protocol

The anchor network structure is shown in Fig. 1, with several anchor nodes and one controller. The controller provides basic timing via radio beacon passing for the whole network; and all the anchor nodes are synchronized to the controller by receiving the radio beacon passively and periodically. Such scheme can guarantee that the transmitted signal from anchor nodes are synchronized to a common timing source. There are two kind of beacons in Guoguo, the first kind of beacon is transmitted by the controller, which synchronizes all the anchor nodes to the controller's clock based on message passing; the second kind of beacon is transmitted by the anchor nodes from the acoustic speaker, which provide ranging and synchronization information to the smartphone.

The controller beacon is realized by using the existing radio chips, e.g., Zigbee. The data domain contains the anchor token, and current beacon index. The anchor node performs its own processing, i.e., transmit its own acoustic beacon, when the anchor token is received. Denote the controller beacon interval is T_p, if every anchor node executes the similar processing, the delay can be viewed as fixed and making the acoustic beacon timing equals to T_p.

Due to the reason that there is no commercial acoustic communication physical layer in mobile devices, we need to design our own processing to realize the communication capability. The ranging and synchronization capabilities of the anchor-smartphone pair are all based on the acoustic communication channel, while a good beacon structure can improve the overall throughput and data rate.

Denote the guard time between each beacon is T_g; the frame duration is $T_f = LT_s + T_g$. One beacon period of anchor can be written as $T_p := T_f = LT_s + T_g$. Using the Time Division Multiple Access (TDMA) to avoid the collision between each beacon, the total round period T_r equals to $T_r = MT_p = M(LT_s + T_g)$. The mobile phone can differentiate all the anchor nodes after T_r, thus the synchronization time between the anchor network and smartphone is $T_{syn} = M(LT_s + T_g)$. The localization process after synchronization also needs M beacons to obtain ranging information from all the anchors, i.e., update rate is $T_{up} = T_{syn} = M(LT_s + T_g)$. When $M = 9$, $L = 16$, $T_s = 0.0781s$, assume $T_g = T_s$, then $T_{up} = T_{syn} = 11.9493s$. Such a long time of synchronization and position update is caused by the low transmission speed of acoustic signal, and it is not sufficient fast enough for tracking the movement of humans. One possible way to increase the update rate is to lower the symbol duration T_s, with faster symbol transmission rate. However, symbol duration is restricted by the delay spread or coherence bandwidth of channel, and could not be further reduced without sacrificing the multipath resistance. To improve the speed of localization without relying on the compression of the symbol interval, a new beacon structure should be developed.

3.5 Symbol-Interleaved Beacon Structure

One possible solution is interleaving the L length symbols into the different beacon period; we call it *symbol-interleaved* acoustic beacon structure. Unlike the conventional TDMA that transmits the whole frame within a beacon period, i.e., $T_p := T_f = LT_s + T_g$, we divide the whole frame into symbols. By transmit one symbol in each beacon period without T_g, the beacon period T_p can be decreased to $T_p := T_s$.

With reduced T_p, the anchor network can achieve higher accuracy by receiving more radio beacons from the controller for every second. In the receiver side, the adjacent received symbols are from different anchors. The receiver maintains L length pipeline, and performs code matching in an iterative way. When the symbols in the pipeline matched with one sequence in $\mathbf{p}$, the anchor node can be identified. Using *symbol-interleaved* beacon structure, the initial synchronization time T_{syn} cannot be lowered, but the following *update time interval* can be reduced to $T_{up} = MT_s = 0.7029s$. The refresh of the location data for every 0.7029 second is sufficient for tracking slow-moving humans.

Using *symbol-interleaved* beacon structure, the transmitted beacon sequence from the anchor network in j-th period can be written as $p_{c(j)}(a(j), b(j))$, where $a(j) \equiv [j \mod M]$ is the index of the anchor node; $b(j) \equiv \lfloor j/L \rfloor$ is the index of the pseudocode in one frame; $c(j) \equiv \lfloor j/(ML) \rfloor$ is one round measurement.

Using *symbol-interleaved* beacon structure, the transmitted beacon from the anchor network can be modeled as

$$g_t(t) = \sqrt{\varepsilon} \sum_{j=0}^{N_s-1} p_{c(j)}(a(j), b(j)) \cdot g(t - jT_s) \tag{4}$$

$g(t)$ is the acoustic sharp pulse designed in (1); ε is the signal energy. The number of total transmitted symbol is N_s.

4. SMARTPHONE LOCALIZATION

4.1 Design Work flow

In the smartphone, the *Signal Detection and Demodulation* module performs audio signal recording and filtering, detect and extract the embedded beacon signal. The detection result is the digital symbols. *Code Matching* module matches the demodulated digital symbols to determine the anchor ID and its predefined location. The *TOA Estimation* module obtains pseudo-ranges by measuring the arrival time of the signal. *Relative Distance* module accumulates all the distance from different anchor nodes until sufficient number of measurements available for localization. *Localization* module performs location calculation by using the measured pseudo-distance pairs and available anchor positions. The technical details of all these modules are elaborated in the following subsections.

4.2 Symbol Detection and Demodulation

In the receiver side, i.e., the smartphone, we need to detect the signal and demodulate the information bits in the received signal $r(k)$. The received signal constitutes ξ_j multi-paths, and these multi-paths can be utilized to extract the symbol. Thus, the detection problem can be written as to detect the signal present or not in the j-th symbol. The received signal waveform in the j-th symbol period could be written as

$$r_j(k) = \sqrt{\varepsilon} \sum_{l=0}^{\xi_j-1} A_j^l g_j(k - k_j^l) + n_j(k) \tag{5}$$

Assume the sampling rate is F_s, for symbol duration T_s, the total sampling point in one symbol is $M_o = T_s \times F_s$. For the low-duty-cycle pulse used in (1) as the symbol waveform, the actual signal length is shorter than the total symbol length. Assume the multi-path delay spread coefficient is α, the average sampling points for the signal region is $M_p = \alpha \times (3\tau) \times F_s$. Thus, the two conditions of the hypothesis for detecting the signal can be written as

$$\begin{cases} H_0: & \mathbf{r}_{j,k} = \mathbf{n}_{j,k} \quad k = 1 \cdots M_o \\ H_1: & \begin{cases} \mathbf{r}_{j,k} = \sqrt{\varepsilon}\mathbf{s}_{j,k} + \mathbf{n}_{j,k} & k = k_j^0 \cdots k_j^0 + M_p - 1 \\ \mathbf{r}_{j,k} = \mathbf{n}_{j,k} & k = 1 \cdots k_j^0 - 1, k_j^0 + M_p \cdots M_o \end{cases} \end{cases} \tag{6}$$

where $\mathbf{n}_{j,k}$ is the matrix form of the noise $n_j(k)$, $\mathbf{s}_{j,k}$ is the k-th sampling point for the signal in j-th symbol. The symbol synchronization process is to detect the signal region in the noise background, i.e., detect H_1 condition out of H_0, while the TOA estimation is to detect the first path of signal and its delay k_j^0.

To detect the signal region (H_1 condition), the decision vector $\mathbf{z}_j$ can be obtained by using generalized likelihood ratio test (GLRT) [10]. The decision vector could be derived as the form of $\mathbf{z}_{j,k} > \eta_{syn}$, with j-th symbol declared present if the inequity condition is satisfied and return an estimated value of the signal region k_p. The threshold η_{syn} is chosen to maintain a constant false alarm rate (CFAR) [10], and written as the form of $\beta\sigma$, where σ is the noise variance, β is calculated in experiment by using the given false alarm rate. Then $\hat{p}_{c(j)}(a(j), b(j))$ in the receiver will be set to '1', otherwise $\hat{p}_{c(j)}(a(j), b(j)) = 0$, where $c \equiv \lfloor j/(ML) \rfloor$. $\hat{p}_{c(j)}(a(j), b(j))$ is one estimated version of $p(a(j), b(j))$, c is one round measurement.

4.3 TOA Estimation

After detected the symbols in Section 4.2, more detailed time-of-arrival (TOA) estimation should be performed to estimate the first path sample k_j^0 in the whole symbol duration. The TOA estimation provides ranging information that needed for localization, and its accuracy directly affects the overall position resolution. The TOA estimation problem can be written as to detect k_j^0 in j-th symbol of (5) as

$$\hat{k}_j^0 = \min_k(k | r_j(k) > \eta_{toa}), k \in [k_p - J_p, K_p + M_o] \tag{7}$$

where k_p is the obtained rough signal region during signal detection; J_p is the step length used for Jump-Back-and-Search-Forward (JBSF) [8]; η_{toa} is the TOA estimation threshold; $\hat{k}_j^0$ is the estimated TOA path of k_j^0. The challenges of dynamically change the TOA estimation threshold η_{toa} to balance between the false alarm and miss detection is addressed in [15] by maximizing the *TOA Detection Probability*.

4.4 Synchronization and Code Matching

Perform code matching between predefined pseudo-codes $p_{m,i}$ and the estimated information bits $\hat{p}_{c(j)}(a(j), b(j))$, the m-th anchor node can be identified if these two sequences matched. When symbols with total $M \times L$ length have been received, the code matching process can be utilized to synchronize between the anchor node and the smartphone by

$$[\Delta_a, \Delta_b] = \tag{8}$$
$$\arg\min_{\Delta_a, \Delta_b} ||\hat{p}_{c(j)}(a(\hat{j}) + \Delta_a, b(\hat{j}) + \Delta_b) - p_{m,i}||_1 < d_{tol}$$

where the beacon period index $j \in [j_0, j_0 + ML]$, $j_0 = c(j) \times (ML)$ is the starting index of the symbol sequence, ML is the total length of symbols that used to perform (8), $\hat{j} =$

$j - j_0$. $c(j)$ can be used to illustrate the index number of code matching. $a(j)+\Delta_a$ and $b(j)+\Delta_b$ is the cyclic shifting in $\hat{p}_{c(j)}(\cdot)$.

With the offsets Δ_a and Δ_b available for the anchor node index and pseudocode sequence index, the mobile phone can aware the the anchor node index ($\hat{m}$) and sequence index ($\hat{i}$) of the current received symbol j as

$$\begin{aligned} \hat{m} &= [(j - j_0) \mod M] + \Delta_a \\ \hat{i} &= [(j - j_0) \mod L] + \Delta_b \end{aligned} \tag{9}$$

where $j_0 = \lfloor j/ML \rfloor \times (ML)$.

4.5 Distance Update

After the synchronization in Section 4.4, and obtained $\hat{m}$ and $\hat{i}$ in (9), then every M symbols can obtain one distance measurement group with the same pseudo sequence index $\hat{i}$. Such group of measurements is the minimum tuple of ranging for one position update, and every measurement in such a group is from different anchor nodes. For j-th symbol, the index of group is $j_g = \lfloor j/M \rfloor$ with each element represents the TOA value obtained in (7). Denote the TOA estimation matrix as $\mathbf{r} = r_{m,j_g}$, $m = [1, M]$. For notation convenience, one group of measurements from all anchor nodes can be represented as $\mathbf{r}_g = r_{m,j_g}$, where j_g is a fixed value, $\mathbf{r}_g$ is a measurement vector.

Due to some symbol-miss in real situations and none distance measure during '0' symbols, the TOA value is not fully available for all M anchor nodes in one round time, i.e., the obtained ranging value $\mathbf{r}_g$ is a sparse vector. To improve the reliability of ranging results, we perform sliding window for the TOA estimation matrix $\mathbf{r}$ with an appropriate length of W, and obtain a new version of $\mathbf{r}_g$. The rational of the sliding window is to use the historical data to represent current sparse measurement. However, different symbol index corresponds to its own starting index of the TOA measurement, e.g., the TOA value in j-th symbol is larger than $(j-1)$-th TOA value by N_k. Thus, for the extracted length of W and width of M matrix, i.e., the latest W column of the matrix $\mathbf{r}$, $\mathbf{r}_g = [r_g(m)]$ can be calculated by

$$r_g(m) = \frac{1}{N_d(m)} \sum_{\Delta_g=0}^{W-1} \left[r_{m,(j_g-\Delta_g)} + \Delta_g \times N_k \right] \tag{10}$$

where $r_{m,(j_g-\Delta_g)}$ only counts when it contains TOA measurement, $N_d(m)$ is the total number of effective measurements available in the W length matrix $\mathbf{r}$, m represents the m-th row. Thus, vector $r_g(m)$ can be used as the current distance measurement, with each TOA value indicates the pseudo-range from the m-th anchor to the mobile device.

The measured pseudo-ranges between the anchor nodes to the mobile phone is $\hat{r}_m = \mathcal{C} \times r_g(m)$, where $\mathcal{C}$ is the speed of the aerial acoustic signal. Denote the true distances are r_m, $m = [1, \ldots, M]$, the unknown starting point is δ_r, $\hat{r}_m$ can be written as

$$\hat{r}_m = r_m + \delta_r + n_m \tag{11}$$

where n_m is the distance measurement noise for $\hat{r}_m$.

4.6 Location Estimation

With the measured distance from M anchor nodes available, multilateration can be performed to localize the smartphone. Assume the real position of the smartphone is $\mathbf{p} = (x, y)$, the position of the anchor node is $\mathbf{p}_m = (x_m, y_m)$, then the real distance from the smartphone to the anchor node m can be written as $r_m = \sqrt{(x-x_m)^2 + (y-y_m)^2}$. We define the vector of unknown parameter as $\theta = [x \quad y \quad \delta_r]^T$. The localization purpose is to obtain estimated value of θ from observations, where $[\hat{x}, \hat{y}]$ in $\hat{\theta}$ is the estimated position.

However, (11) contains the nonlinear term, rather than estimate θ directly, we select one of the M measurements as the reference f, and using this reference to cancel out the nonlinear term. The selection of this reference could be random or based on the code-matching quality (the mis-match residues). To better illustrate this process, we can square the both sides of (11) and minus the reference measurement f as

$$\begin{aligned} &[(x_m^2 + y_m^2 - \hat{r}_m^2) - (x_f^2 + y_f^2 - \hat{r}_f^2)] + 2\hat{r}_m\widetilde{n}_m - 2\delta_r n_m \\ &= 2(x_m - x_f)x + 2(y_m - y_f)y - 2\delta_r(\hat{r}_m - \hat{r}_f) \end{aligned} \tag{12}$$

where $\widetilde{n}_m$ is differential noise term of $n_m - n_f$. Equation (12) can be expressed in matrix form as

$$\mathbf{A}\theta = \nu + \mathbf{p_n} \tag{13}$$

where $\mathbf{A} = \begin{bmatrix} x_m - x_f & y_m - y_f & \hat{r}_f - \hat{r}_m \\ \cdots & & \\ \cdots & & \cdots \end{bmatrix}$, $\theta = \begin{bmatrix} x \\ y \\ \delta_r \end{bmatrix}$ and $\nu = \frac{1}{2}[(x_m^2+y_m^2-\hat{r}_m^2)-(x_f^2+y_f^2-\hat{r}_f^2)]_{(M-1)\times 3}$, $m = 1, \ldots, M$ when $m \neq f$. $\hat{r}_m$ is the measured distance obtained from (11). $\mathbf{p_n} = 2\hat{r}_m\widetilde{n}_m - 2\delta_r n_m$ is the noise term with its first moment as $\mathrm{E}(\mathbf{p_n}) = 0$ and the covariance matrix of vector $\mathbf{p_n}$ as $\widetilde{\mathbf{\Sigma}} = \mathrm{Cov}(\mathbf{p_n})$. The diagonal element of the covariance matrix are $2\hat{r}_m(\sigma_m^2 + \sigma_f^2) + 2\delta_r\sigma_m^2$, with other elements in the matrix as $2\hat{r}_m\sigma_f^2$.

Then (13) can be formulated as a Least-Square (LS) problem, and we can obtain the solution as

$$\hat{\theta} = (\mathbf{A}^T\widetilde{\mathbf{\Sigma}}^{-1}\mathbf{A})^{-1}\mathbf{A}^T\widetilde{\mathbf{\Sigma}}^{-1}\nu \tag{14}$$

Initially, the value of the covariance matrix $\widetilde{\mathbf{\Sigma}}$ is unknown, we could initialize $\widetilde{\mathbf{\Sigma}}$ with all '1' in its diagonal and '0' for other elements. For the following snapshots, $\widetilde{\mathbf{\Sigma}}$ could be estimated, and we can substitute $\widetilde{\mathbf{\Sigma}}$ into (14) to improve estimation accuracy.

4.7 Error Pruning Techniques

Error pruning techniques are essential for the correct operation of the indoor localization system. The source of potential errors could be the sound noise, blockage, indoor Non-light-of-sight (NLOS) transmission, anchor network failure. In real system, applying too strong criterion in error pruning would lower the location update rate, thus the parameters used in the following techniques should balance between the accuracy and location update rate.

Signal Level Resistance. To deal with the signal noise issues, we perform spread spectrum in transmission and correlation processing in the receiver to obtain noise resistance. We use the the Gaussian second derivative pulse as the waveform, which has the properties of high multipath and timing resolution, low energy consumption, robust to noise, and low spectrum emission.

NLOS Identification and Mitigation. Compared with the noise, indoor harsh environment with blockage and high-dense multi-paths is more challenge. The blocked localization beacon could either be attenuated or introduces additional delay that prolonged the obtained ranging distance, we call it NLOS bias effects. Using these problematic ranging results could cause over-fitting in localization calculation, or even make the final results diverge. Thus, how to identify and mitigate these prolonged or problematic ranging measurement is crucial in localization.

One of the superiority of using acoustic signal for ranging lies its high timing resolution and the full access of the acoustic channel information. Extract features from estimated channel condition, the goodness of transmission could be evaluated. For example, if the delay spread of the estimated channel is significant larger than normal conditions, the ranging result from this channel has high probability of blockage, i.e., NLOS condition. By lowering the weighting efficient of these ranging measurements during localization, overall location result could be more stable. We use the combined metrics of RMS delay spread, Kurtosis, and Mean excess delay to identify the NLOS channel condition, and assigns lower weight for the measurements from NLOS channel during localization processing.

Anchor Level Error Mitigation In subsection 4.4, the demodulated pseudocode is matched to identify the anchor node. In real situations, these exists some bit-error for our implemented acoustic communication physical layer. When designing the pseudocode, some extent of redundancy is embedded. The code matching process has some tolerance of d_{tol} for the bit-error. However, if the bit-error for one anchor node is higher than the design redundancy, then the measurements from this anchor node should be mitigated in this round. This process could eliminate some extent of large errors.

5. PERFORMANCE EVALUATION

In this section, we perform system performance evaluation by using Apple's iPhone 4S and iPod Touch 5 (iTouch5) without any modification of the hardware or jailbreak of the operating system. First, we provide quantified results of the sound pressure level of our acoustic beacon in subsection 5.1. Second, we evaluate the localization performance of our proposed system in two typical environments: office (Subsection 5.2) and classroom (Subsection 5.3).

The 3dB pulse width of the transmitted signal as in (1) is chosen with $T_w = 1.5ms$ to meet the bandwidth constraint. A sharper pulse results in better multipath robustness and time-domain resolution, but with increased bandwidth occupancy. Restricted by the bandwidth of a microphone, the effective pulse energy and operating distance would be decreased when more frequency components outside the receiver band. The symbol duration is chosen as $T_s = 0.0781s$, resulting in the pulse duty cycle of $R = 1.92\%$. Shorter symbol duration leads to a higher data rate and location refreshing rate, but restricted by the multipath environment. The choice of these parameters is a tradeoff between the achievable resolution and maximum operating distance.

5.1 Sound Pressure Level Measurement

Guoguo system uses audible-band signal as beacon, making it user-friendly and widely applicable for many indoor location services and applications. However, users might be concerned about the noise effect of the acoustic signals in indoor environments.

To make our transmitted acoustic signal unperceptible to users, we tuned the waveform of the beacon signal with appropriate transmission power. To quantify the results, from the perception curve of human ears (*A-weighting* coefficients, we derive the *sound pressure level* (SPL) value as a metric of noisiness of the environment. We place four anchor nodes very close to a smartphone (the most noisy case), and measure the difference of SPL. The normal sound background case is named ("Normal"); the environment that filled with our beacon signal is called ("Beacon"). The SPL values for these two conditions in four different environments are shown in Fig. 2b. From Fig. 2b, we observe that the difference in average SPL level of the "Normal" and "Beacon" is under the level of randomness: different measurement of the SPL in different time has some sort of randomness (near 2dBA). The maximum difference of the SPL caused by the "Beacon" is 0.85dBA, which is below the perception level of human's ear. Therefore, we can conclude that our transmitted acoustic beacon signal is completely ignorable and *disturbance-free* even in extreme cases.

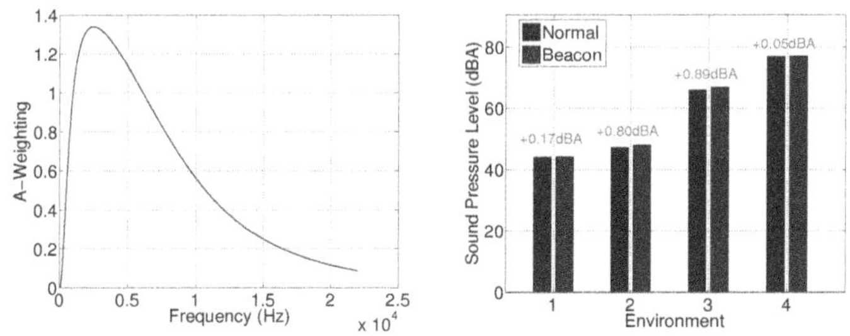

(a) A-weighting curve (b) Sound Pressure Level

Figure 2: (a) The perception level of human ears; (b) comparison of sound pressure level in four scenarios.

5.2 Exp I: Office Environment

Experiment Setup. We deploy 9 anchor nodes in a typical office environment to evaluate the performance of Guoguo as shown in Fig. 3. The maximum distance between anchor nodes is larger than 10 meters.

Total 12 cases have been tested: 6 of them are tested under quite environment for theoretical performance; other 6 cases are tested under simulated realistic environment (simulate human talking by playing video sound near the mobile device). The experiment configuration is summarized in Table 1. The term *Length* represents the measurement lasting time in seconds, which is randomly chosen. The last term is the effective number of accessed anchor nodes (N_{eff}) during localization calculation. The number of real accessed anchor nodes is less than total number of deployed anchors. This is often caused by interference, blockage, and NLOS during localization process.

Localization Accuracy in Quite Environment. The scatters of the localization results for users in different locations in a normal office environment are shown in Fig. 4. In this case study, to support quantitative analysis, we localize a smartphone when its user stands still at different spots. We can get the error surface of localization from Fig. 4. Note that, our system is not limited to localize a standing subject. Localization traces of a moving subject are demonstrated in the next section.

Figure 3: Experiment setup in an office environment

Table 1: Experiment configuration in an office environments

ID	Use Cases	Length (s)	Background	N_{eff}
1	Env1	60.91	Quite	6.86
2	Env2	60.97	Quite	6.15
3	Env3	60.61	Quite	8
4	Env4	60.64	Quite	7.77
5	Env5	60.53	Quite	8.24
6	Env6	60.64	Quite	8.72
7	P4snoise1	522.97	Sound	5.03
8	P4snoise2	300.48	Sound	6.11
9	P4snoise3	346.35	Sound	5.99
10	Touchnoise1	398.79	Sound	5.97
11	Touchnoise2	461.03	Sound	6.13
12	Touchnoise3	582.14	Sound	6.07

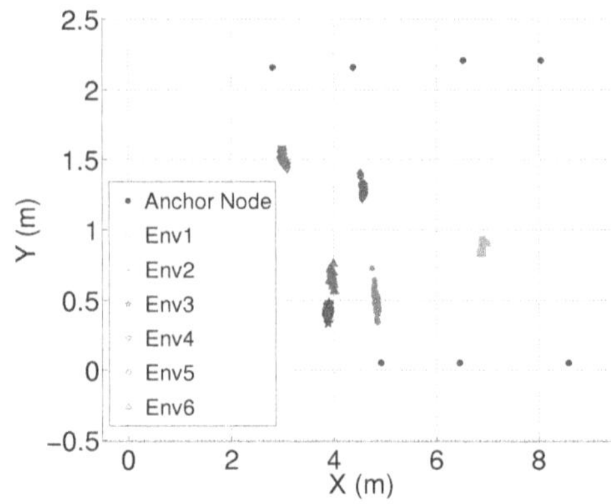

Figure 4: Scatters of the localization results in an office environment.

The cumulative distribution function (CDF) of the localization error (LE) are shown in Fig. 5. If using 80% probability, the localization error for all the cases is in the range between $4cm$ to $8cm$. These localization results are very accurate and sufficient for fine-grained indoor location-based services.

Localization Accuracy under Background Sound. To evaluate the localization performance in realistic environment, we add artificial sound by playing high volume videos. The CDFs of the added sound are shown in Fig. 6. The measured sound pressure level (dBA) is calculated from the received acoustic signal at a smartphone during localization.

Fig. 7 shows the CDF of the localization error (LE) in an office environment. In these six cases with background sound, the final localization accuracy is still within $10cm$, with less than 10% results slightly affected. From another point of view, the number of effective accessed anchors under background sound is slightly lower than the normal cases from the N_{eff} value in Table 1 because some of the acoustic beacons have been mitigated. Since we use more anchors than the minimum requirement (three anchors), these additional anchors can improve our system's availability under realistic environment.

Localization Metrics. Other metrics that used to evaluate the system performance are the *Ranging Rate*, localization *Miss Rate*, and location *Average Update Time*. The definition of the *Ranging Rate* is N_{TOA}/N_s, where N_{TOA} is the total Number of TOA measurements, N_s is the total number of symbols transmitted. Higher *Ranging Rate* means better ranging detection probability. The maximum theoretical value of *Ranging Rate* depends on the '1' density of the pseudo-code rather than 1. From Fig. 8a, we know that the *Ranging Rate* is larger than 0.5 for most cases, which is contributed by using our derived high '1' density pseudo-codes.

The localization *Miss Rate* evaluates the quality of obtained location values. The definition of *Miss Rate* is N_{loc}/N_{pos}, where N_{loc} is the number of obtained location results; N_{pos} is the number of refined location results after the post-processing module. Lower *Miss Rate* means better localization results. The *Miss Rates* for all the cases in Fig. 8b show very small value, i.e., the localization results have a very good quality.

Another important metric is the *Average Update Time*, representing the refreshing rate of the localization process. If the refreshing rate is too slow, it is hard to keep up with the moving traces of subjects. Due to the low transmission speed of acoustic signal, minimizing *Average Update Time* is nontrivial. From Fig. 8c, we observe that the *Average Update Time* for Guoguo is less than one second, sufficient for capturing the traces of moving subjects at modest speed. This rate is significantly faster than other existing approaches that also use acoustic signal for localization.

Overall Localization Accuracy. Using 50-percentile, 80-percentile, and 90-percentile probability to evaluate the localization accuracy, the results of all 12 cases are shown in Fig. 9. The achieved localization accuracy is in the centimeter-level even for the cases with added interference. Such results could push the current coarse-level LBS into fine-grained level in an effective way.

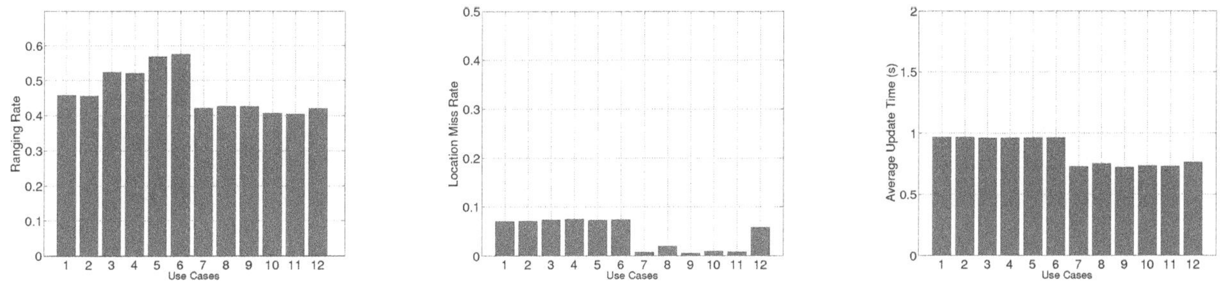

(a) Ranging Rate (b) Miss Rate (c) Average Update Time

Figure 8: Measured performance metrics of Ranging Rate (a), Miss Rate (b), and Average Update Time (c) for different measurements in an office environment.

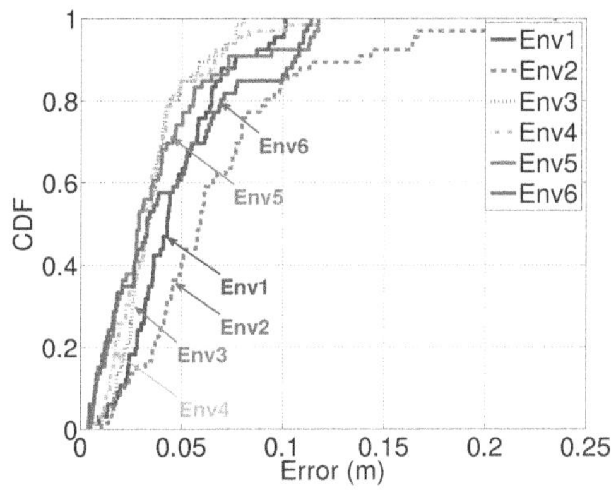

Figure 5: CDF of the localization results in an office environment.

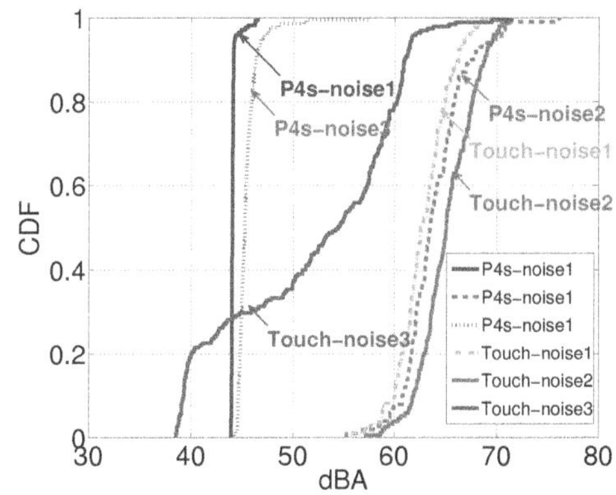

Figure 6: CDF of the added background sound level in an office environment.

5.3 Exp 2: Classroom Environment

Experiment Setup. Similar to subsection 5.2, we deploy 9 anchor nodes in a multimedia classroom environment to evaluate the performance of Guoguo as shown in Fig. 10, with maximum distance larger than 15 meters.

The experiment configuration in this classroom environment is summarized in Table 2.

Table 2: Experiment configuration in a classroom

ID	Use Cases	Length (s)	Background	N_{eff}
1	Env1	590.43	Quite	6.98
2	Env2	408.70	Quite	6.80
3	Env3	459.76	Quite	7.0
4	Env4	676.39	Quite	6.99
5	Env5	270.49	Quite	5.9
6	Env6	599.47	Quite	7.0
7	P4snoise1	279.38	Sound	6.94
8	P4snoise2	641.74	Sound	7.96
9	P4snoise3	240.40	Sound	7.72
10	Touchnoise1	599	Sound	7.0
11	Touchnoise2	88.79	Sound	5.38
12	Touchnoise3	347.5	Sound	5.0

Localization Accuracy under Quite Environment. The scatters of the localization results for users in different locations in a classroom environment are shown in Fig. 11. Similar to Fig. 4, the error surface of achieved location results is very small.

The CDF of the localization results for the measurements in Fig. 11 is shown in Fig. 12. For most of the cases, e.g., using 80% probability, the localization accuracy is very high and in the range from $5cm$ to $10cm$.

Localization Accuracy under Background Sound. To evaluate the localization performance under interference, we added artificial sound in the classroom environment by playing the lecture videos. The CDF of the added different background sound is shown in Fig. 13. The CDF of the localization results under background sound on classroom environment is shown in Fig. 14. One interesting observation from Fig. 14 is that the iPhone4s achieves much better performance than the iTouch5. The reason could be the build-in multi-microphones and noise-canceling mechanisms in iPhone4s; while the iTouch5 is only equipped with one microphone and no noise-canceling hardware.

Localization Metrics. The *Ranging Rate* for the measurements in a classroom environment is shown in Fig. 15a, while two cases of iTouch5 suffers from low *Ranging Rate* under background sound. The *Miss Rates* in Fig. 8b shows very small value. The *Average Update Time* for the environment of classroom is near 0.8 second, and sufficient for mobility cases.

Figure 10: The experiment setup in a classroom environment

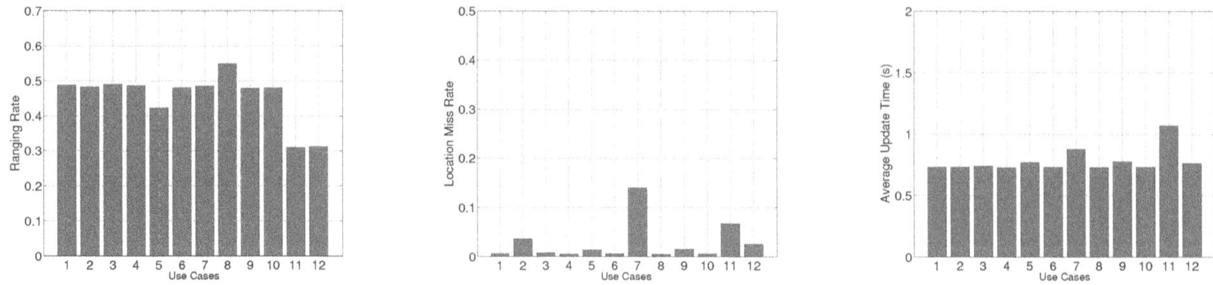

(a) Ranging Rate (b) Miss Rate (c) Average Update Time

Figure 15: Measured performance metrics of Ranging Rate (a), Miss Rate (b), and Average Update Time (c) for different measurements in a classroom environment.

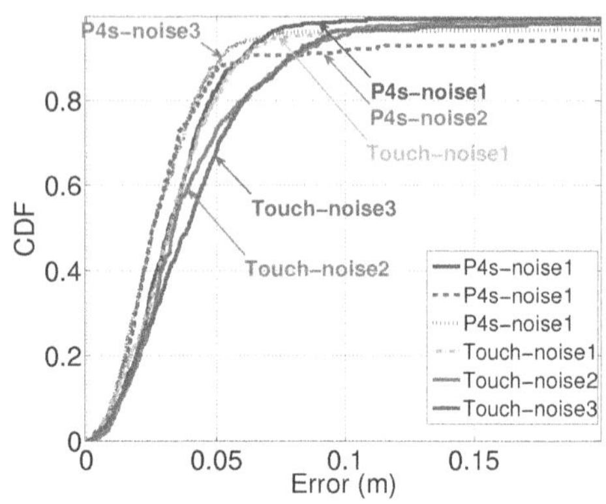

Figure 7: Localization accuracy (LE) in an office.

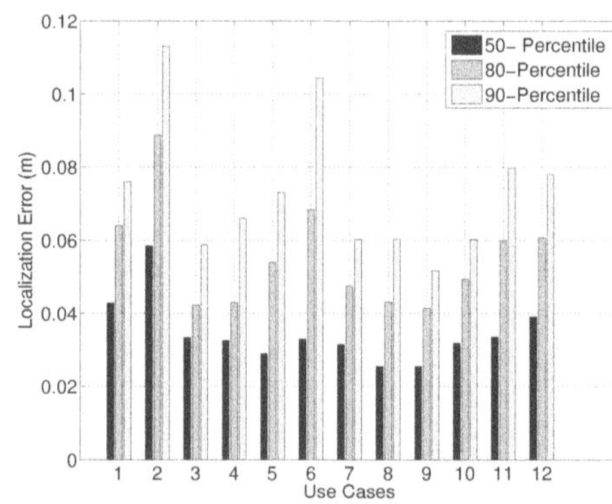

Figure 9: Localization error for different measurements in an office environment

Overall Localization Accuracy. The 50-percentile, 80-percentile, and 90-percentile localization accuracy results are summarized in Fig. 9. Except the iTouch5 under background sound, other cases achieves localization accuracy under $10cm$ for most cases. The localization results of iPod Touch5 are slightly worser than iPhone4s, but still sufficient for indoor location-based services.

6. PUTTING IT ALL TOGETHER

Our proposed smartphone-based indoor localization system achieves centimeter localization accuracy by leveraging the anchor network and processing on smartphone. To make the real system applicable and suitable for real deployment, significant efforts should be made to design the anchor network and implement the algorithm into the smartphone.

Anchor Node Design. Targeting at fine-grained indoor location-based services, e.g., retail store, museum, office and classroom, several hundreds investment on the anchor infrastructure to enable centimeter-level location related services could be profitable. To minimize the infrastructure cost and promote the real system deployment, we designed our own hardware for the anchor node with low-complexity and additional features, e.g., solar powered, battery charging, pluggable sensor board, remote program upload, wireless speaker/microphone. The comparison of our "Guoguo" hardware vs. two quarters is shown in Fig. 17. The total BOM price for the anchor node is less than \$10. With one anchor every 10-20 meters deployed in an indoor space (e.g. museum, shopping center) and minimum of four anchors,

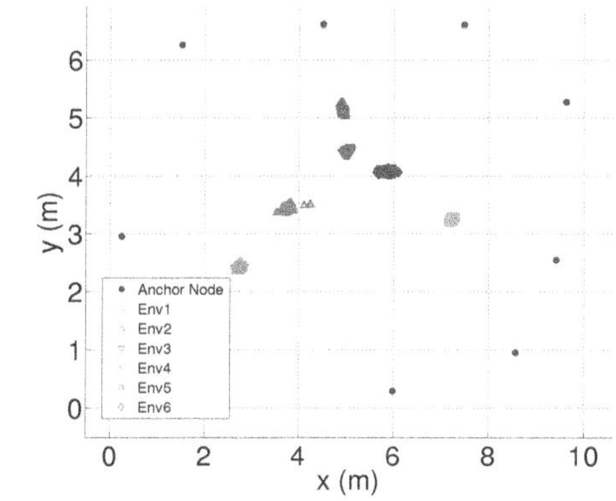

Figure 11: Scatters of the localization results in a classroom environment.

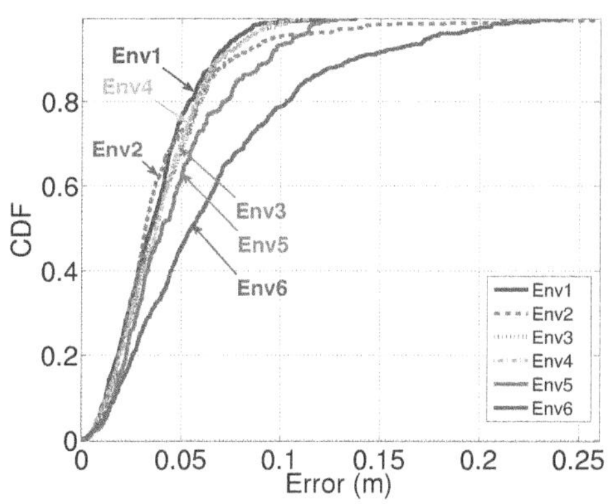

Figure 12: CDF of the localization results in a classroom environment.

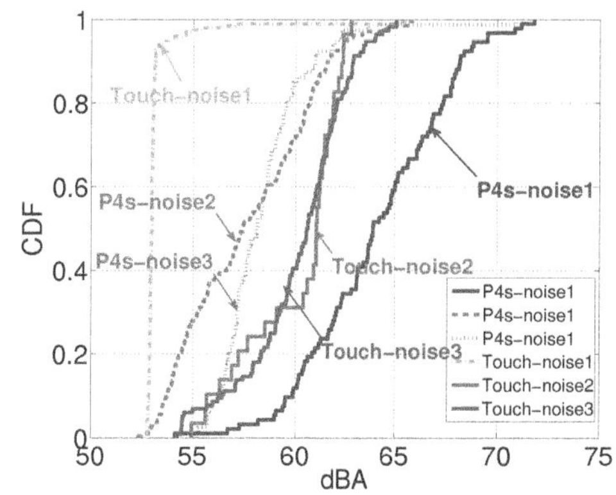

Figure 13: CDF of the background sound in a classroom environment.

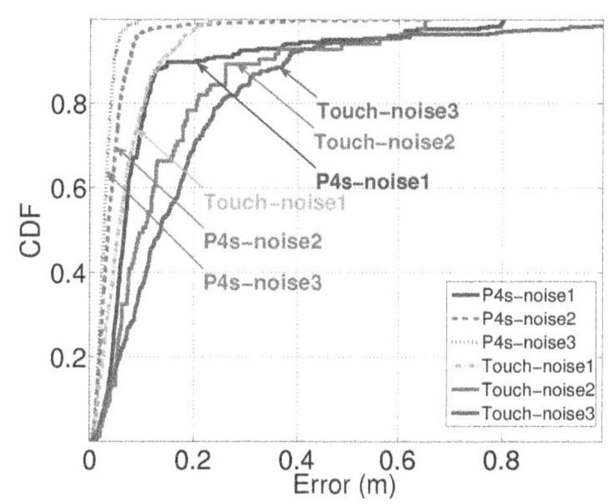

Figure 14: Localization error of the background sound in a classroom environment.

it is feasible and cost effective to deploy such systems in many indoor environments. For example, with marginal investment on the indoor infrastructure, a retail store can enable "smart" shopping experiences for smartphone users with fine-grained shelf-to-shelf navigation, location-aware recommendation and advising, and physical items searching and navigation.

Smartphone Processing. We implemented the algorithms from audio recording and pre-processing, signal detection, TOA estimation, code matching, and NLOS mitigation into the smartphone app. All the processing was put in the iOS Grand Central Dispatch (GCD) queue to enable concurrency with the mobile application without slowing down the smartphone's responsiveness. To ensure efficiency of the smartphone processing, we use the vDSP portion of the Accelerate framework in iOS. Other complex computation was executed in the server to minimize the computation cost in the smartphone. Once the smartphone publishes a ranging result to the server, the process on the server side performs localization and returns the result to the smartphone asynchronously. Such configuration balanced the communication and computation cost: the smartphone extracts ranging information from the audio raw data and greatly reduces communication overheads; the server handles concurrency and serves multiple localization requests from smartphones.

Moving Traces Demo. To demonstrate the performance of "Guoguo" in real situations, three typical moving traces captured by the Guoguo system are shown in Fig. 18. The moving traces demonstrate the localization accuracy and feasible update rate of our system.

7. RELATED WORK

Localization schemes can be classified into three categories: angle-based, fingerprinting-based, and ranging-based. An angle-based approach relies on the directional antenna scan to achieve angle resolution. But a narrow-beam directional antenna is very expensive and unsuitable for consumer applications. Fingerprinting-based approaches [3, 5, 2, 4] or other proximity approaches [20, 9, 6, 1] feature lowest complexity without any requirement on additional infrastructure. However, they achieve only room-level resolution and require the site-survey to build fingerprinting databases at the cost of intensive labors. Ranging-based approach is more straightforward. Measuring the radio signal strength (RSS) and time-of-arrival (TOA) are the two typical ranging solutions. Compared with TOA, RSS information is widely available and lots of work are dedicated to use the RSS of WiFi, bluetooth, or cellular signal, for indoor localization [27, 7, 11, 13]. However, the need of the prior information of the radio attenuation model, and the time varying

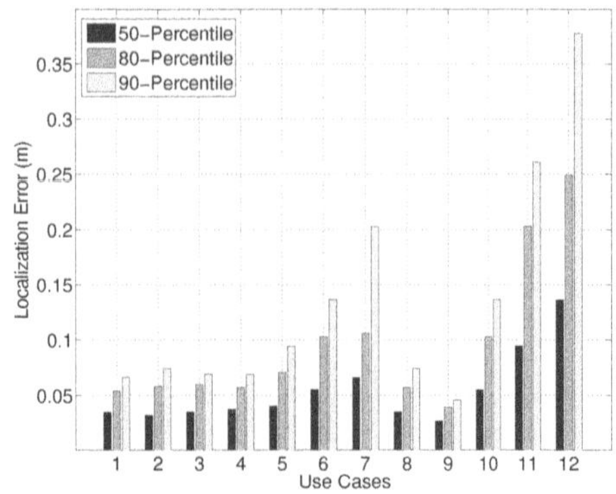

Figure 16: Localization error for different measurements in a classroom environment

Figure 17: Guoguo anchor node vs. quarters

features of channel make these approaches only suitable for applications with low location accuracy needs.

TOA-based ranging is more accurate and robust. The Cramér-Rao Low Bound (CRLB) of TOA ranging is inversely propositional to the effective bandwidth of signal, it is also why Ultra-wideband (UWB) signal received special attention for its high accuracy on ranging and localization. However, current UWB techniques are still under development and not available on current smartphones. Another option is to use the acoustic signal for TOA ranging due to its low transmission speed. MIT Cricket[23], Active Bat [26] and DOLPHIN [18] are well-known systems that use ultrasound for localization. However, normal smartphones cannot receive ultrasound. In addition, they require radio signal for synchronization, e.g., ZigBee for Cricket. Dependence on

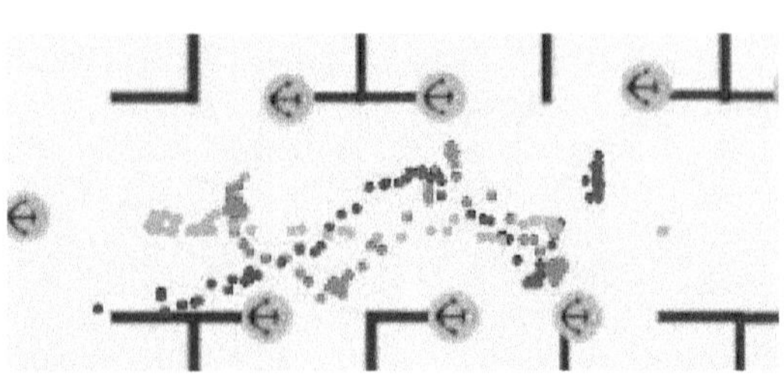

Figure 18: Moving traces obtained by indoor localization

special devices and non-applicability on smartphones greatly limits their adoption in daily indoor activities.

Recent research on leveraging the ubiquitous microphone sensors in a smartphone introduces a convenient and low-complexity approach. A. Mandal et al. [17] used a PDA to transmit noticeable 4kHz acoustic signal. C. Peng et al. [22] proposed to transmit low-attenuation 2-6kHz acoustic signal for better coverage, but their solution causes sound pollution due to the audible signal. H. Liu et al. [14] used a smartphone to transmit high-band audible sound to assist WiFi localization. Authors in [19] performed localization using desktop PCs and laptops, achieving location accuracy of several meters. In addition, these solutions are not scalable and feature low location update rates. Due to the use of two-way ranging and simple acoustic "Beep" signal, only one user can be handled and localized at a time. Adopting time-divided coordination among users could be a partial solution. However, random concurrent access patterns of many users in real situations make their solutions hard to support multiple users.

To compare the performance of Guoguo with other existing indoor localization approaches, we summarize their key features in terms of principle, accuracy, cost, scalability, pros and cons in Table 3. The scalability refers to how many end users can be supported simultaneously. From Table 3, we observe that Guoguo achieves better balance in terms of cost and performance over other acoustic/ultrasound based approaches. Ranging in the passive receiving mode in a Guoguo-enabled smartphone makes it highly scalable while other ranging methods in the active transmitting mode limits the scalability due to interference of signals. Guoguo only requires a smartphone for a user, along with low-cost anchor nodes preconfigured by a service provider. Compared with other low cost approaches (mainly smartphone-based), e.g., RSS and fingerprinting based approach, Guoguo significantly outperforms other approaches in accuracy. Existing smartphone-based approaches achieve only room-level or several-meter-level accuracy. As far as we know, Guoguo outstands as a practical smartphone-based solution with foot-level accuracy without special hardware extensions on users' phones.

8. CONCLUSION

We proposed the Guoguo algorithm and ecosystem to realize the smartphone-based fined-grained indoor localization. For the first time, we can locate a smartphone user at the centimeter-level, which has significant implication for potential indoor location services and applications compared with existing meter-level localization solutions. To address the challenges of utilizing the audible-band acoustic signal in smartphone localization, i.e., strong attenuation, interference-rich, high sound disturbance and difficulty in synchronization, we proposed comprehensive schemes to improve the localization accuracy and extend coverage without sound disturbance. Significant improvements were achieved in terms of accuracy, cost, and scalability, compared with other existing approaches. Experimental results demonstrated that the achieved average localization accuracy is about 6 $\sim$ 25cm in typical office and classroom environments. Guoguo represents a leap progress in smartphone-based indoor localizations, opening enormous new opportunities for indoor location-based services, positioning and navigation systems, and other commercial, educational, or entertainment appli-

Table 3: Comparison of Guoguo with existing localization techniques

System	Signal Type	Technique	Accuracy	Cost	Scalability	Pros	Cons
Guoguo	Modulated acoustic signal (17-20kHz)	Passive-mode ranging	High (6 $\sim$ 25cm)	Low	High	No dedicated device for users, high accuracy and scalability, disturbance-free	Low-complexity anchor nodes
Cricket[23]	Ultrasound, radio-assistant	Ranging based	High (10 cm)	Medium	High	High accuracy	Need dedicated devices
Beep [17]	Acoustic signal (4kHz)	Active-mode ranging	High (60cm)	Medium	Limited	High accuracy	noticeable acoustic signal, complex anchors, limited users
Active Bat [26], DOLPHIN [18]	Ultrasound	Active-mode ranging	High (centimeter)	Medium	Limited	High accuracy	Need dedicated devices, need dense anchor nodes, limited scalability
Ultra-wideband [12, 16]	Impulse-radio Ultra-wideband signal	Ranging based	High	High	High	High penetrating ability, high accuracy, high multi-path resolution	Need dedicated devices, expensive devices
Radio RSS [7, 11, 13, 27]	WiFi, bluetooth, or cellular signal	Ranging based	Low	Lowest	High	No dedicated devices, existing infrastructure, low cost	Need a prior of the radio attenuation model, low accuracy, need calibration
Fingerprinting [2, 3, 4, 5]	WiFi, Cellular, Bluetooth, FM and ambient sound	Fingerprint matching	Low (room-level)	Lowest	High	No need of additional infrastructure, low cost	Need war-driving, time-varying, low accuracy
Proximity [1, 6, 9, 20]	RFID, NFC and acoustic signal	Proximity based	Low	Medium	High	Low cost sensor nodes, support multi-users	Low accuracy, and needs dense sensors

cations. We will build Guoguo-enabled indoor LBS applications, and plan to deploy such ILBS applications in museums and libraries, and further push the envelope of high-resolution indoor localization.

9. FUTURE WORK

Anchor Coverage and Maximum Operation Distance. In this paper, we only demonstrated that the Guoguo works in two typical indoor environments. A more comprehensive study regarding the maximum operation distance of the anchor and the coverage of the anchor network should be conducted. In real environments with blockages, e.g., big shelves or human walking, the effective coverage of the anchor network would be much smaller. Different schemes of anchor node placement, and the guideline for real deployment should be developed for better coverage and easy installation.

Optimized Localization Approach. The localization algorithm used in Guoguo is a normal least squares (LS) based approach. When the pseudorange measurements are non-convex, LS approach would converge to local optimal values. In the future work, we will apply global location optimization approaches, e.g., Semidefinite Programming, to jointly estimate the location and delay (δ_r), and avoid the calculation of the matrix inversion operation in (14).

Interference-robust Scheme. The inherent interference in the crowded audible-band would impede the appropriate operation of Guoguo. Ambient noise causes the in-band interference, and has much large bandwidth and energy than the acoustic beacon of Guoguo. In addition to the approaches proposed in this paper for signal detection, TOA ranging and localization, sophisticated error and interference mitigation schemes should be developed to improve the robustness.

Human and Animal Exposure. In this paper, we made the beacon unnoticeable to human to minimize the potential healthy risk. For the effect caused by long term exposure of the acoustic beacon, related professional studies should be cited. Moreover, we are not sure whether some animal species can actually hear the beacon sound. Further studies should be conducted to analyze the reaction of the animal or pets when exposed to the acoustic beacon. It is very important to make the system pet friendly.

10. ACKNOWLEDGMENTS

We would like to thank our reviewers and our shepherd Anthony LaMarca for all of their great input. The work presented in this paper is supported in part by National Science Foundation under Grant No. CNS-0709329, CNS-0923238, CCF-0953371, CCF-1128805, and CNS-0940805 (BBN subcontract).

11. REFERENCES

[1] Sonitor system website. http://www.sonitor.com/.

[2] M. Azizyan, I. Constandache, and R. Roy Choudhury. Surroundsense: mobile phone localization via ambience fingerprinting. In *Proceedings of the 15th annual international conference on Mobile computing and networking*, pages 261–272. ACM, 2009.

[3] P. Bahl and V. Padmanabhan. Radar: An in-building rf-based user location and tracking system. In *INFOCOM 2000. Nineteenth Annual Joint Conference of the IEEE Computer and Communications Societies. Proceedings. IEEE*, volume 2, pages 775–784. Ieee, 2000.

[4] G. Borriello, A. Liu, T. Offer, C. Palistrant, and R. Sharp. Walrus: wireless acoustic location with room-level resolution using ultrasound. In *Proceedings of the 3rd international conference on Mobile systems, applications, and services*, pages 191–203. ACM, 2005.

[5] Y. Chen, D. Lymberopoulos, J. Liu, and B. Priyantha. Fm-based indoor localization. In *Proceedings of the 10th international conference on Mobile systems, applications, and services*, pages 169–182. ACM, 2012.

[6] I. Constandache, X. Bao, M. Azizyan, and R. Choudhury. Did you see bob?: human localization using mobile phones. In *Proceedings of the sixteenth annual international conference on Mobile computing and networking*, pages 149–160. ACM, 2010.

[7] I. Constandache, S. Gaonkar, M. Sayler, R. Choudhury, and L. Cox. Enloc: Energy-efficient localization for mobile phones. In *INFOCOM 2009, IEEE*, pages 2716–2720. IEEE, 2009.

[8] D. Dardari, C. Chong, and M. Win. Threshold-based time-of-arrival estimators in UWB dense multipath channels. *IEEE Transactions on Communications*, 56(8):1366–1378, 2008.

[9] G. Jin, X. Lu, and M. Park. An indoor localization mechanism using active rfid tag. In *Sensor Networks, Ubiquitous, and Trustworthy Computing, 2006. IEEE International Conference on*, volume 1, pages 4–pp. Ieee, 2006.

[10] S. Kay. *Fundamentals of Statistical Signal Processing, Volume 2: Detection Theory*. Prentice Hall PTR, 1998.

[11] M. Kjærgaard, J. Langdal, T. Godsk, and T. Toftkjær. Entracked: energy-efficient robust position tracking for mobile devices. In *Proceedings of the 7th international conference on Mobile systems, applications, and services*, pages 221–234. ACM, 2009.

[12] J. Lee and R. Scholtz. Ranging in a dense multipath environment using an UWB radio link. *IEEE Journal on Selected Areas in Communications*, 20(9):1677–1683, 2002.

[13] K. Lin, A. Kansal, D. Lymberopoulos, and F. Zhao. Energy-accuracy trade-off for continuous mobile device location. In *Proceedings of the 8th international conference on Mobile systems, applications, and services*, pages 285–298. ACM, 2010.

[14] H. Liu, Y. Gan, J. Yang, S. Sidhom, Y. Wang, Y. Chen, and F. Ye. Push the limit of wifi based localization for smartphones. In *Proceedings of the 18th annual international conference on Mobile computing and networking*, pages 305–316. ACM, 2012.

[15] K. Liu, X. Liu, and X. Li. Acoustic ranging and communication via microphone channel. In *Proc. IEEE Globecom '12*, Anaheim, California, USA, 2012. IEEE.

[16] K. Liu, H. Yin, and W. Chen. Low complexity tri-level sampling receiver design for uwb time-of-arrival estimation. In *Communications (ICC), 2011 IEEE International Conference on*, pages 1–5. IEEE, 2011.

[17] A. Mandal, C. Lopes, T. Givargis, A. Haghighat, R. Jurdak, and P. Baldi. Beep: 3d indoor positioning using audible sound. In *Consumer Communications and Networking Conference, 2005. CCNC. 2005 Second IEEE*, pages 348–353. IEEE, 2005.

[18] M. Minami, Y. Fukuju, K. Hirasawa, S. Yokoyama, M. Mizumachi, H. Morikawa, and T. Aoyama. Dolphin: a practical approach for implementing a fully distributed indoor ultrasonic positioning system. *UbiComp 2004: Ubiquitous Computing*, pages 347–365, 2004.

[19] R. Nandakumar, K. Chintalapudi, and V. Padmanabhan. Centaur: locating devices in an office environment. In *Proceedings of the 18th annual international conference on Mobile computing and networking*, pages 281–292. ACM, 2012.

[20] L. Ni, Y. Liu, Y. Lau, and A. Patil. Landmarc: indoor location sensing using active rfid. *Wireless networks*, 10(6):701–710, 2004.

[21] N. Patwari, J. Ash, S. Kyperountas, A. Hero III, R. Moses, and N. Correal. Locating the nodes: cooperative localization in wireless sensor networks. *Signal Processing Magazine, IEEE*, 22(4):54–69, 2005.

[22] C. Peng, G. Shen, Y. Zhang, Y. Li, and K. Tan. Beepbeep: a high accuracy acoustic ranging system using cots mobile devices. In *Proceedings of the 5th international conference on Embedded networked sensor systems*, pages 1–14. ACM, 2007.

[23] N. Priyantha, A. Chakraborty, and H. Balakrishnan. The cricket location-support system. In *Proceedings of the 6th annual international conference on Mobile computing and networking*, pages 32–43. ACM, 2000.

[24] J. Taylor. *Ultra-wideband radar technology*. CRC, 2001.

[25] J. Valin, F. Michaud, J. Rouat, and D. Létourneau. Robust sound source localization using a microphone array on a mobile robot. In *Intelligent Robots and Systems, 2003.(IROS 2003). Proceedings. 2003 IEEE/RSJ International Conference on*, volume 2, pages 1228–1233. IEEE, 2003.

[26] R. Wand, A. Hopper, V. Falcao, and J. Gibbons. The active bat location system. *ACM Transactions on Information Systems*, pages 91–102, 1992.

[27] J. Yang and Y. Chen. Indoor localization using improved rss-based lateration methods. In *Global Telecommunications Conference, 2009. GLOBECOM 2009. IEEE*, pages 1–6. Ieee, 2009.

Avoiding Multipath to Revive Inbuilding WiFi Localization

Souvik Sen, Jeongkeun Lee, Kyu-Han Kim, Paul Congdon
Hewlett-Packard Labs
{souvik.sen, jklee, kyu-han.kim, paul.congdon}@hp.com

ABSTRACT

Despite of several years of innovative research, indoor localization is still not mainstream. Existing techniques either employ cumbersome fingerprinting, or rely upon the deployment of additional infrastructure. Towards a solution that is easier to adopt, we propose *CUPID*, which is free from these restrictions, yet is comparable in accuracy. While existing WiFi based solutions are highly susceptible to indoor multipath, CUPID utilizes physical layer (PHY) information to extract the signal strength and the angle of only the direct path, successfully avoiding the effect of multipath reflections. Our main observation is that natural human mobility, when combined with PHY layer information, can help in accurately estimating the angle and distance of a mobile device from an wireless access point (AP). Real-world indoor experiments using off-the-shelf wireless chipsets confirm the feasibility of CUPID. In addition, while previous approaches rely on multiple APs, CUPID is able to localize a device when only a single AP is present. When a few more APs are available, CUPID can improve the median localization error to $2.7m$, which is comparable to schemes that rely on expensive fingerprinting or additional infrastructure.

Categories and Subject Descriptors

C.2.1 [**Network Architecture and Design**]: Wireless communication; H.3.4 [**Information Storage and Retrieval**]: Systems and Software

General Terms

Design, Experimentation, Performance

Keywords

Wireless, Localization, Cross-Layer, Application,
Indoor positioning

MobiSys'13, June 25Ð28, 2013, Taipei, Taiwan

1. INTRODUCTION

Extensive interest in location-aware services has driven many novel indoor localization techniques [1], yet it is hard to find a solution that is widely deployable. While existing approaches try to address the problem by using several techniques, solutions based on pervasive WiFi systems have remained the dominant theme of localization. Several innovative approaches have employed WiFi fingerprints to design a precise indoor localization system [2–4]. However, the accuracy comes at the cost of expensive, and meticulous war-driving. Such war-driving is not a one time cost because the indoor RF environment can change due to change in layouts and objects, or due to frequent and automatic wireless configuration changes [5, 6]. Attempts to *eliminate* the war-driving requirement have been successful [7–9], but at the expense of performance, or widespread applicability. Realizing this difficulty, there has been efforts to reduce the overhead of war-driving by using crowdsourcing techniques [10, 11]. Apart from being slow to adapt to frequent RF changes, they remain unattractive because of a lack of clear user incentive to share sensor and location information. Thus, despite decades of studies, the tradeoff between accuracy, pervasiveness, and cost has remained the primary challenge in designing a widely deployable indoor localization system. This paper is tasked to break away from this tradeoff, and achieve the accuracy of a fingerprinting-based system, without any war-driving, or crowdsourcing. Although this is a high bar, we demonstrate its feasibility by utilizing wireless physical layer(PHY) information, available from off-the-shelf wireless chipsets.

We explore the candidate solution-space using WiFi, since an approach based on pervasive WiFi will be easier to adopt. Existing WiFi-based approaches typically rely on distance, or angle as the major metric for indoor localization. It is possible to estimate distance using signal strength(RSSI), but RSSI performs poorly indoors primarily because of multipath reflections. Existing *angle-of-arrival(AoA)* estimation algorithms also have similar shortcomings. The key problem is that it is difficult to discriminate between multipath reflections and the *direct path*, i.e., the signal component traversing along the straight line joining the client to the AP (figure 1). Whenever the direct path is relatively weak, RSSI, or AoA is biased by stronger reflected components, which traverses longer distance, and perhaps a different angle than the direct path. If we can somehow accurately estimate the distance, and the angle of the mobile device from only the direct path, localization performance will improve significantly. Our system, *CUPID* distinguishes the direct path from multipath reflections by leveraging PHY layer information along with natural human mobility. CUPID accurately determines the

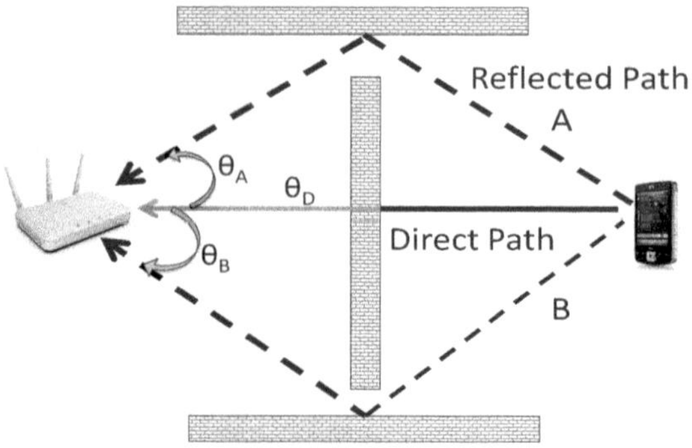

Figure 1: Wireless signal traverses through multiple paths, a direct, and a few reflected paths.

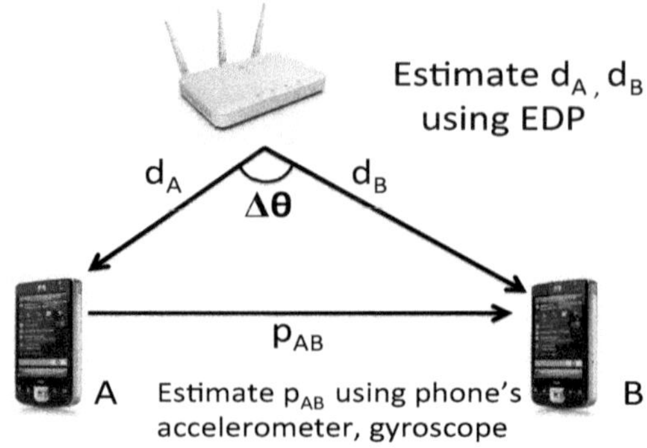

Figure 2: Change in ANDP ($\Delta\theta$) can be computed from the estimated distances – d_A, d_B, and p_{AB}.

distance, and angle of the mobile device from her AP, ultimately yielding her location. CUPID requires no crowdsourcing, or additional hardware, but relies on multiple antennas present in today's commodity wireless APs. Furthermore, it can achieve reasonable accuracy with only a single AP, not to mention multiple APs.

Estimating distance: CUPID relies on only the *energy of the direct path (EDP)* to estimate distance. We find that a PHY layer information called *channel state information (CSI)* exported from Atheros 9390 cards can be used to estimate the EDP of a received signal. Further, we find that it is possible to estimate the propagation characteristics of the signal based on the EDP. Consequently, while converting the energy estimate to distance, CUPID can correctly choose critical parameters such as path-loss exponent. Our experiments show that EDP outperforms RSSI, reducing the mean distance estimation error to $4m$ from $10m$.

Estimating angle: Angle-of-arrival (AoA) techniques, such as MUSIC [12], can estimate the angles at which the transmitted signal arrives at the receiver. Figure 1 shows three such angles. However they cannot determine which of these angles corresponds to the *angle of the direct path(ANDP)*. CUPID leverages human mobility to identify the ANDP, from MUSIC's AoA estimates. We explain our key idea using figure 2. In this example, as the user walks from location A to B, CUPID can track the change in ANDP ($\Delta\theta$). The AP uses the EDP to estimate the distance of the mobile client, d_A, and d_B, when it is at location A and B respectively. It estimates the user's displacement between location A, and B (p_{AB}), by using her phone's inertial sensors – a method called *dead reckoning*. Since d_A, d_B, and p_{AB} are known, CUPID can estimate $\Delta\theta$, which captures the change in ANDP. From MUSIC's AoA estimates at location A, and B, the angle that undergoes a similar change is the actual ANDP. We show that by employing the CSI from the 3 antennas of the Atheros 9390 chipset, CUPID can achieve a mean ANDP estimation error of $20°$.

CUPID combines the client's distance, and angle estimates, yielding her location. By systematically addressing the key issues with WiFi, CUPID enables indoor positioning even with a single AP, making it a practical yet widely deployable solution. Ofcourse, translating the above high level ideas into a working system entails a large number of technical challenges: (1) How does CUPID accurately calculate distance from EDP? (2) How does CUPID deal with errors from EDP, and dead-reckoning, while estimating angle? (3) How does CUPID deal with poor resolution offered by commodity wireless cards? (4) Will CUPID even work if the direct path is very weak? (5) Finally, will CUPID consume a lot of energy? This paper addresses these challenges, and prototypes the system using HP laptops, and Android Nexus S phones. Testbed results from a 4500 square meter building confirm our claim. With a single AP, CUPID can achieve a median localization error of $4.5m$. Ofcourse, with $2-3$ additional APs, CUPID can reduce the error to $2.7m$, remaining robust to dynamic environmental changes. We believe that this could be a promising direction, and with rigorous testing and tuning, a potential candidate for the real-world.

Our main contributions are summarized as follows:

- **We identify the opportunity to utilize PHY layer information to eliminate the effect of multipath reflections in WiFi based localization systems.** We distinguish, and harnesses only the direct path to find the user's location.
- **We demonstrate how the energy of the direct path (EDP) can be a reliable indicator of distance:** Our solution is the first to identify the relationship between EDP and path loss exponent.
- **We combine existing AoA techniques with user mobility to find the angle of the direct path(ANDP):** CUPID is the first to reliably identify the ANDP by leveraging natural human mobility.
- **We implement, and demonstrate our solution using commodity wireless cards:** Our algorithm exploits the CSI information from the 3 antennas of Atheros 9390 wireless chipsets.

In the following sections, we elaborate on our key intuitions, perform controlled measurements, and develop insights to design the CUPID system, followed by performance evaluation. We end the paper with a discussion on open questions, opportunities, and the scope for future work.

2. BACKGROUND AND OBSERVATIONS

This section presents the relevant background material on PHY layer information. Along with wireless propagation foundations, we present our ideas related to extracting the direct path energy.

2.1 Distance Estimation using Wireless Path Loss Equation

A wireless signal traverses in all radial directions, and reflects off walls, furnitures, and other objects. Due to reflections, multiple copies of the same signal arrives at the receiver, each undergoing different delay and attenuation – a phenomena which is commonly called multipath. We define the *direct path* as the straight line joining the transmitter and the receiver. A wireless signal is composed of a direct path, and other reflected components, and suffers attenuation as it propagates from the transmitter to the receiver. Indoors, wireless attenuation is mainly caused by path-loss, and multipath reflections. It is possible to estimate a crude distance between the transmitter and the receiver by using the received energy at the receiver (P_R) in the path-loss equation:

$$P_R = P_0 - 10\gamma log(d) \quad (1)$$

where P_0 is the received energy at a distance of $1m$ from the transmitter, d is the distance between the transmitter, and the receiver in meters; and γ is the path loss exponent. γ depends on the propagation characteristics of the received signal. Earlier approaches have typically used RSSI as the received energy (P_R) in the above path loss equation. However, RSSI is an union of the energy of all the signal paths – direct as well as multipath reflections. If we use RSSI as P_R, we will need to estimate the propagation characteristics of all the signal paths, to correctly choose the path-loss exponent. Unfortunately, today's WiFi cards do not expose any specific multipath information, making it difficult to choose the correct path-loss exponent. Rather than trying to model the aggregate signal (RSSI), we show that it is easier to only use the *energy of the direct path or EDP*. Since EDP is not sensitive to the energy of the reflected paths, it can be a robust indicator of distance, even in dynamic indoor environments.

Extracting the Direct Path Signal: In search of a mechanism to extract the direct path signal, we found that Atheros 9390 chipsets can export the Channel State Information (CSI) from the PHY layer to the driver. The delay, and attenuation of different signal paths are captured in the CSI. If a transmitter transmits a symbol X, the quality of the received symbol at the receiver, Y, depends on the CSI H:

$$Y = H * X + n \quad (2)$$

where n captures noise. The CSI is reported as a matrix of complex numbers representing the channel gain for every subcarrier and for every transmit-receive antenna pair. By an appropriate Inverse Fast Fourier Transformation (IFFT), the frequency-domain CSI can be translated into the time-domain *power-delay profile (PDP)*. PDP captures the energy of the different paths incident at increasing delays. Since, the direct path traverses the minimum distance amongst all the received paths, it's energy will likely appear in the earliest component of the PDP. Figure 3 shows the PDP at two different clients which are equidistant from the AP. For the first client (figure 3(a)), the direct path does not pass through obstructions, and thus yields the strongest component. However, for the second client (figure 3(b)), the direct path's trajectory is blocked by a human standing between the client and the AP. Thus the direct path is attenuated, and appears weaker than stronger reflected paths. RSSI cannot discriminate between these scenarios. It will use the same path-loss exponent (in Eq. 2) to measure the distance of both the clients, resulting into large errors. We will show how *CUPID can mitigate the distance error due to multipath by using only the energy of the direct path.*

2.2 Angle-of-arrival Estimation

A wireless transmission from the client arrives at several angles at the AP. If we can determine the *angle of the direct path or ANDP*, it is possible to combine the angle of the client with her distance,

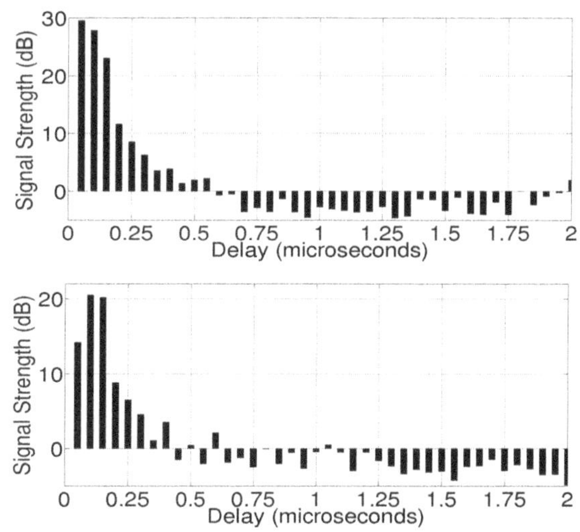

Figure 3: Power delay profiles of two different indoor transmissions: (a) Client has line-of-sight path to the AP, hence its direct path signal is stronger than the reflected, and delayed components. (b) Client's direct path is blocked, hence EDP is also weaker.

ultimately yielding her location. Existing AoA estimation algorithms analyze the received signal on multiple antennas to find out the angular components of the signal [12]. The key idea is to analyze the phase of the received signal, a quantity which changes linearly by 2π for every wavelength (λ) traversed by the signal. For the simplicity of explanation, consider a single path between the transmitter and the receiver. Let us consider that the AP has only two antennas, placed at a distance of $\lambda/2$ (figure 4(a)). Let θ be the angle at which the signal arrives at the two antennas. The signal travels an extra distance before reaching the second (left) antenna. This extra distance(Δd) can be approximated as:

$$\Delta d = \lambda/2 \sin(\theta)$$

We know that an extra distance Δd will result into a phase difference($\Delta\phi$):

$$\Delta\phi = 2\pi\Delta d/\lambda$$

Thus, by observing the phase difference ($\Delta\phi$) of the arriving signal, we can find the angle-of-arrival as:

$$\theta = \arcsin(\Delta\phi/\pi)$$

The above explanation assumes that the arriving signal has only one angular component. In reality, a wireless signal will propagate through multiple paths. AoA estimation algorithm can identify the angles of multiple paths by using many antennas. In the interest of space, we omit the details here, but point the reader to [12] for a detailed explanation of a representative AoA estimation algorithm called MUSIC. The output of the MUSIC algorithm is a pseudospectrum(figure 4(b)). Each peak in the pseudospectrum is an estimated *angle-of-arrival(AoA)*. Multiple peaks in figure 4(b) implies incoming signals from different directions, including the direct path, and a reflected path.

Angle Estimation using AoA: How can we locate the peak which corresponds to the direct path in MUSIC's pseudospectrum? The height of a peak may be proportional to the amount of energy incident on the receiver from the corresponding angle [13, 14]. When the receiver is visible to the transmitter, the direct signal path may often be the strongest component. Secureangle [13] uses this intuition. It declares the AoA of the strongest peak of the pseudospectrum as the client's angle. However, this scheme

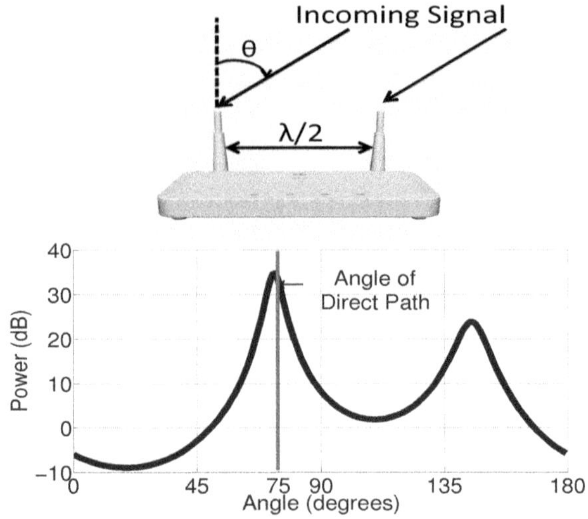

Figure 4: (a) A signal arriving at an angle θ at an AP with two antennas. (b) Output of MUSIC algorithm.

breaks down in indoor environments, where the direct path is often blocked, and hence weaker than a reflected signal. Moreover, a stronger reflected signal may arrive from any random direction, which may be totally unrelated to the angle of the direct path (ANDP). CUPID should only use the ANDP to estimate the location of the client. Otherwise, it will perform poorly whenever it is confused by a stronger reflected component. In this paper, we demonstrate how *human mobility can be combined with MUSIC's AoA estimates to correctly determine the ANDP.*

3. MEASUREMENTS AND SOLUTIONS

In this section, we report measurements from a busy office environment to verify our observations made in the previous section. First, we briefly describe our measurement infrastructure, followed by measurement based analysis of RSSI and AoA. Finally, we develop our key solutions using EDP and ANDP.

3.1 Measurement Infrastructure

We use HP laptops running Linux OS as APs. To enable per-packet CSI measurements at the laptops, we replaced the internal wireless card with Atheros AR9390 chipset. We further attached 3 antennas to the laptop. Ideally, the mobile client should be a smartphone with sensors which can track the user's mobility. The AP should extract the CSI values from the mobile phone's upload packets. However, we found that Atheros AR9390 chipsets export the CSI for packets which have the 802.11n sounding flag turned on in the PHY header. We could not modify the android wireless device driver to add this functionality, and thus could not extract the CSI from regular phone to AP transmissions. To address this challenge, we tape the phone to a laptop and modified the ath9k driver on the laptop to set the sounding flag for uplink transmissions. At the AP, we extract the CSI from the laptop client's transmission, as well as the accelerometer, and gyroscope readings as reported by the phone. We conducted experiments at 500 locations, and analyzed the data to develop our key algorithms.

3.2 Limitations of RSSI-based Distance Estimation

As explained in §2.1, RSSI is the aggregated energy of all the signal paths – direct, as well as multipath reflections. Thus, while translating RSSI to distance, choosing the appropriate path-loss exponent(γ) becomes difficult because γ depends on the time-varying propagation characteristics of the signal. For instance, in a *line-of-sight (LoS)* environment like corridor, the path loss exponent (γ in equation 2) will be close to 2. On the other hand, for complex indoor scenarios the path loss can go upto 4. Figure 5(a) shows the distribution of path loss exponents from 500 known locations in our building Clearly, there is a large range. Even at a single location, we found that the per-packet path loss exponent can vary between 2.1 to 3.4. Since RSSI does not capture any information regarding wireless propagation, choosing the right path-loss exponent for each received packet is difficult. Measuring the path loss exponents at a few locations and using the average of them to estimate distance will likely lead to poor performance (figure 5(b)). We observed up to 100m error while the maximum client-AP distance was 40m.

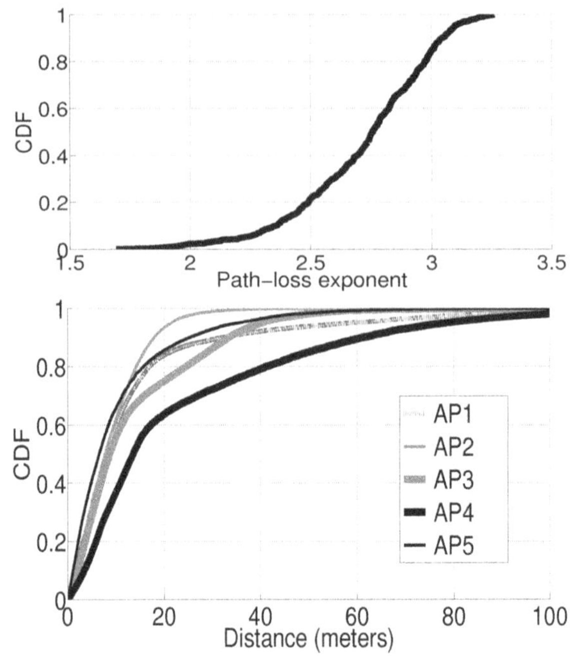

Figure 5: (a) CDF of path loss exponents from 500 known locations. (b) RSSI-based distance estimation error.

3.3 Distance Estimation using EDP

While it is impossible to capture multipath characteristics of a signal using RSSI, the power-delay-profile (PDP) obtained from the CSI information can estimate the same. Due to bandwidth limitations, it is not possible to distinguish every signal path from the PDP. E.g., the resolution of PDP with a 20MHz 802.11n OFDM reception is approximately $50ns$. However, as discussed in § 2.1, the first component of the PDP is likely to contain the direct path signal. The first component may also contain a few other reflected paths, which arrives at almost the same time as the direct path. However, the later arriving components in the PDP correspond to reflected paths which have traversed significantly longer distance (more than $15m$ than the direct path, due to the $50ns$ resolution). Hence these reflected components should be ignored while computing the distance between the transmitter and the receiver. We approximate the energy of the first component of the PDP as the energy of the direct path (EDP). Though not perfect, EDP based distance estimation is more robust than RSSI, since it is much less susceptible to multipath reflections.

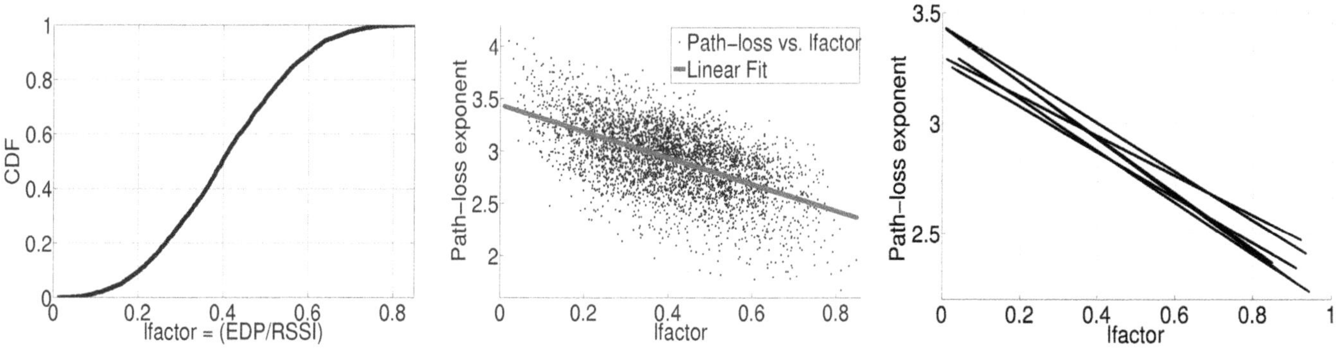

Figure 6: (a) CDF of lfactor values at 500 locations. (b) path loss exponent vs. lfactor at 500 known locations. (c) Relationship between path loss exponent and lfactor for 5 APs.

However EDP is susceptible to shadowing. For example, the direct path between an AP and the mobile device may be blocked by the human carrying the phone. At the same location, the estimated EDP will be higher when the user faces the AP with the phone (*line-of-sight or LoS*, figure 7(a)), versus when she is back-facing it (*non line-of-sight or NLoS*, figure 7(b)). Here, we observe that a blockage on only the direct path may not affect the other reflected components [1]. We use this observation to quantify the likelihood of LoS by computing the *LoS factor (lfactor)* as:

$$lfactor = \frac{EDP}{RSSI} \tag{3}$$

Figure 6(a) demonstrates that a wide range of lfactor values can occur in an indoor setting. A high lfactor will imply that most of the received signal arrives along the direct path, like in a corridor scenario with LoS. On the other hand, if the direct path is blocked, we will witness a low lfactor value. Thus, we expect that the path loss exponent for the direct path will be inversely proportional to lfactor. Figure 6(b) shows the EDP path loss exponent with increasing lfactor for transmissions to a single AP. The trend is clear, and we further observed that the result looks similar at other APs. From these measurements *we can apply linear fitting to establish a relationship between path loss exponent and the lfactor.* We believe we are the first to propose a systematic approach of finding the correct *per-packet path loss exponent* using EDP and lfactor.

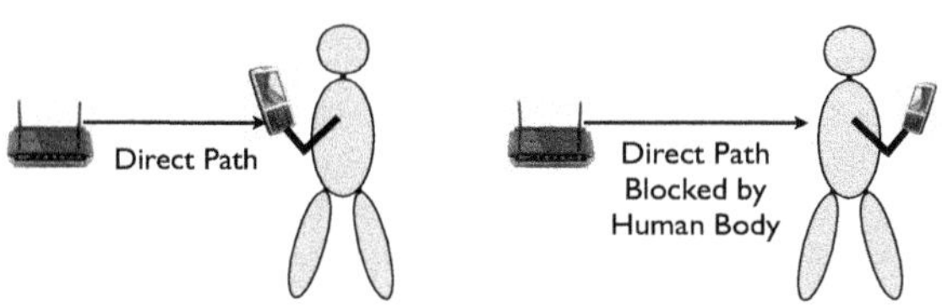

Figure 7: User orientation w.r.t AP: (a) facing (b) blocked

The path loss vs. lfactor relationship may not depend on a particular AP, or even environment. Figure 6(c) plots the path-loss exponent vs. lfactor relationship for 5 different APs. The lines are similar because lfactor directly estimates the environmental factors affecting the EDP, which ultimately governs the path-loss exponent. Hence the relationship between path-loss exponent (γ) and lfactor does not vary much over different environments. Measurements from a few known locations can adequately establish the relation, and we could apply the same relation to other environments as well (§4.4). Of course the lfactor vs. path-loss exponent relationship may not be as straightforward in complex environments, e.g., crowd gathering. However, lfactor may still capture sufficient details of wireless propagation in most scenarios. Later in our evaluation section we will show how lfactor can reduce the distance estimation error in office environments.

[1] Blockage of all signal components will likely weaken RSSI, which can be separately identified.

To summarize, the AP calculates the EDP and lfactor from the CSI of a client's transmission, and thereafter uses the lfactor-to-γ relation to select a correct path loss exponent for each received packet. The AP then calculates the distance to the client using the path loss equation (Eq. 2) with EDP and path loss exponent as inputs. Note that by choosing the correct path-loss exponent, our solution allows distance estimation to adapt to fast fading on a per- packet basis. Later in our evaluation we show that EDP, along with the use of lfactor, can reduce the median distance estimation error to $4m$, in comparison to $10m$ while using RSSI.

3.4 Limitations of existing AoA Algorithms

In addition to distance, angle is also important for location estimation. Existing angle-of-arrival(AoA) techniques can estimate the angles at which the signal arrives, but cannot determine which of these angles correspond to the angle of the direct path (ANDP). We study the limitations of a representative AoA estimation technique, MUSIC. As discussed in § 2.2, the angle of the highest peak in MUSIC's pseudospectrum may correspond to the ANDP in LoS scenarios. However, whenever the direct path is blocked, the highest peak may correspond to a stronger reflected path, resulting into large errors in angle estimation(figure 8).

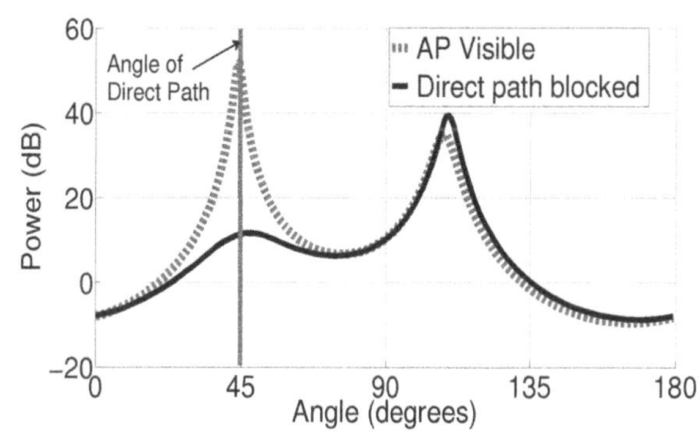

Figure 8: MUSIC's pseudospectrum output at the client when the AP is visible, and when the direct path is blocked by a human. In the later case, MUSIC will mistakenly declare the AoA of a reflected path as the ANDP.

How often does this simple scheme fail, and what is the associated error? In figure 9(a), we plot the angle estimation error, if the strongest peak in MUSIC's pseudo spectrum is used for ANDP computation. The estimation error is more then 60° for 40% measurements. Analyzing the data, we found that large errors indeed happen due to a stronger reflected component. To explain this further, figure 9(b) shows that the ANDP estimation error reduces with increasing lfactor. If the lfactor is low, the direct path is weaker than a stronger reflected path, and hence choosing the strongest peak results in large errors. The median lfactor in our measurements is approximately 0.4 (figure 6(a)), indicating rich multipath. Hence, we need to address the multipath issue before we can exploit existing AoA algorithms. However, before exploring such solutions, we need to understand whether any of the AoA peaks actually captures the ground truth ANDP, the actual angle toward the client location. Due to estimation noise, and poor angle resolution due to only 3 antennas, none of the AoA values may exactly match with the ground truth ANDP. Figure 9(a) plots the estimation error if the peak closest to the ground truth is chosen as the estimated ANDP. Clearly, there is opportunity. If we could identify the best peak, the estimation error will decrease to median 20°, contributed mainly by poor angle resolution. We show how it may be possible to identify the best peak by leveraging natural human mobility. We develop our ANDP estimation scheme in conjunction with MUSIC. However, our approach is generalizable to other AoA estimation algorithms as well.

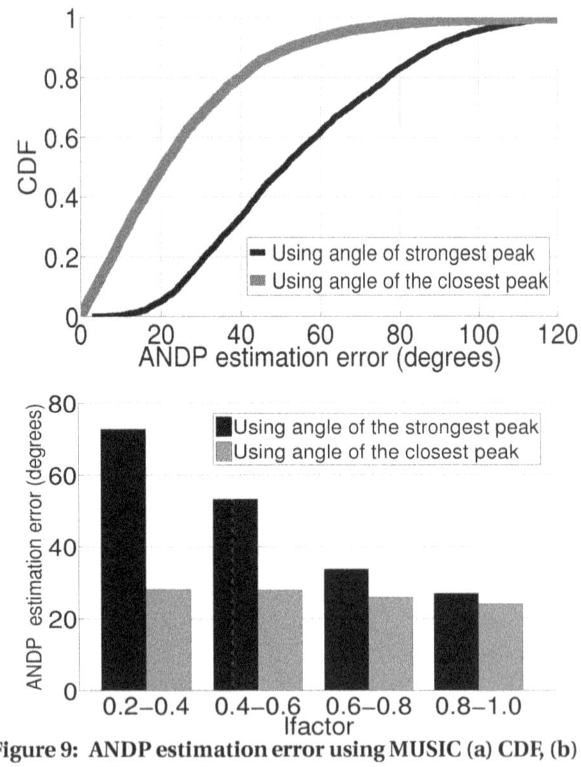

Figure 9: ANDP estimation error using MUSIC (a) CDF, (b) with increasing lfactor value

3.5 Angle Estimation Using Human Mobility

We leverage the observation that by analyzing the AoA values at two different locations that the user has walked through, it is possible to identify the ANDP. The AP computes the AoAs by by employing MUSIC on the CSI estimates of the received uplink packet

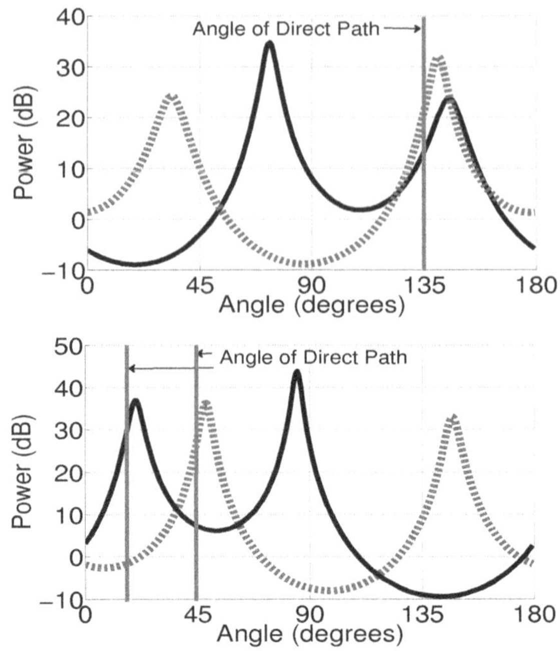

Figure 10: MUSIC pseudospectrum when the client is at two different locations: (a) The ANDP is stable at both the locations, however the reflected angles are different (b) Both ANDP and reflected path angles are different.

from the user's mobile device. By analyzing the AoA values from two different locations, we find that two different scenarios may occur (as shown in figure 10). First, it is possible that although the reflected paths are stronger at two different locations, their angles are different. Rather, the weaker direct path is consistent,and hence the ANDP can be approximated as the AoA which remains stable in the pseudospectrums. Second, none of the AoAs in the pseudospectrums from the two locations may closely match. In this scenario, CUPID identifies the ANDP using dead reckoning, and EDP-based distance estimation as described next.

We explain our key idea using figure 11. Let us assume that the received signal arrives at two different angles; one component of the signal due to the direct path and another due to a reflected path. When the user is at location A, let the AoA estimates be θ_{A1} and θ_{A2}. When the user moves to position B, let the corresponding estimates be θ_{B1}, θ_{B2}. For the purpose of explanation, let us assume that the signal component which arrives at an angle of θ_{A1} at location A, incidents at an angle of θ_{B1} at location B, and likewise for θ_{A2} and θ_{B2}. Let the EDP-based distance estimate of the client at location A and B, be d_A and d_B respectively. When the user walks from location A to B, we can compute the physical distance between the two locations (p_{AB}) by consulting her phone's accelerometer and gyroscope – a method called *dead reckoning*. The change in ANDP ($\Delta\theta$) is nothing but the angle formed at the AP by the two locations. From the properties of a triangle, $\Delta\theta$ can be computed as:

$$\Delta\theta = \arccos \frac{(d_A^2 + d_B^2 - p_{AB}^2)}{2 * d_A * d_B}$$

The angular change of the ith AoA (ϕ_i), between locations A and B is $\theta_{Bi} - \theta_{Ai}$. We can now identify the AoA (θ_{Bk}) which has experienced the same change as the estimated change in ANDP (($\Delta\theta$)):

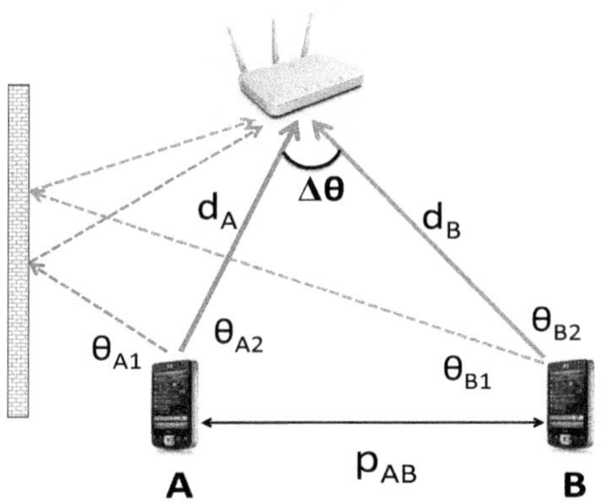

Figure 11: Detecting ANDP exploiting mobility.

$$ANDP = \theta_{Bk}$$
$$\forall i \neq k \, |\Delta\theta - \phi_k| \, < \, |\Delta\theta - \phi_i|$$
$$\forall i \, \phi_i \, = \, \theta_{Bi} \, - \, \theta_{Ai}$$

To identify the ANDP, the AP tracks the AoAs measured at a location, at all subsequent locations the user walks through. We observe that the pseudospectrums from two nearby locations (within $2m - 3m$ distance) have similar AoA values. Thus, we can pair an AoA measured at a location, with the closest angle measured from a subsequent location. As the user walks, we can use this correspondence to track each AoA in the pseudospectrum. [2] The AoA which undergoes the same angular change as the direct path is CUPID's estimate of ANDP.

How long does the user have to walk before her ANDP can be identified? If we compare the pseudospectrums at two nearby locations, the change in ANDP ($\Delta\theta$) will be small. A reflected path's angle difference may be similar to $\Delta\theta$ due to estimation noise. To avoid this confusion, ANDP estimation is triggered only when the change, $\Delta\theta$, is more than $20°$. Of course, if only a particular AoA value remains stable, the estimate is safely used as the ANDP. Figure 12 shows that the user has to walk only a reasonable distances before her ANDP can be appropriately identified. Observe that, mobility estimation is required only until the ANDP is identified. Once the ANDP is identified it can also be tracked. The AoA close to the previous ANDP estimate can be used as the new ANDP. Although rare, it may be possible that at a new location none of the AoA estimates matches with the previous ANDP. In such scenarios, a fresh round of dead-reckoning and ANDP estimation can be triggered. To our knowledge, we are the first to utilize user mobility to identify the ANDP. Once the ANDP is known, the AP can combine it with the estimated distance to locate the user.[3]

4. DESIGN AND IMPLEMENTATION

Translating the above high level ideas into a functional prototype entails two additional tasks: (1) How to process CSI values from multiple antennas to compute the EDP and AoA values? (2) How to estimate user's mobility to identify the ANDP from the AoA values? The AP can find the location of the client by using the estimated distance, and angle. If multiple APs collaborate, localization performance can be improved. We propose a simple algorithm which can leverage multiple APs. In the next section we will present detailed results on the performance of our scheme.

[2]To deal with estimation noise, we find all the AoA estimates in a window of 2 seconds, and group them based on similarity.

[3]We assume that the location of the AP is known beforehand.

Figure 12: CDF of physical distance walked by the user before the ANDP can be appropriately estimated.

4.1 CSI Processing

802.11n defines a channel sounding mechanism where the transmitter can trigger CSI estimation at the receiver by setting an appropriate flag in the transmitted packet. The receiver can thereafter feedback the estimated CSI to the transmitter for the purpose of calibration, or beamforming. We use this mechanism to extract CSI. We modify the device driver of Atheros 9390 cards to appropriately set the sounding bit of a transmitted packet. On the receiver side, the CSI is estimated for each receive and transmit antenna pair. The Atheros 9390 reports one complex number per subcarrier for 56 out of the 64 available subcarriers, and we only use these for our scheme.

Figure 13 shows the magnitude and phase of the CSI reported for 10 consecutive packets. Since the chipset is MIMO and beamforming capable [4], the three MIMO transceivers are time synchronized and phase locked to run at the same frequency. As a consequence, we find that the reported CSI does not include random phase errors across different receive antennas. The phase difference between the antennas remain stable within the coherence time of the channel, making it appropriate for AoA computation. There might be some error due to downconversion in the PHY layer, which can be mitigated using communication between two APs [17]. We do not apply this optimization in our system. Apart from CSI, we also aggregate the RSSI values from all the antennas as today's WiFi drivers do.

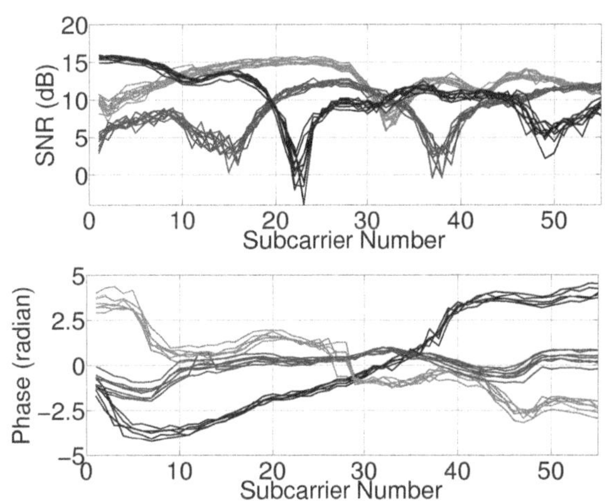

Figure 13: (a) Magnitude and (b) phase of CSI reported for 10 **consecutive packets.**

[4]Standard for 802.11n and 802.11ac systems [15, 16]

4.2 Location Estimation

CUPID uses the estimated EDP in the path-loss equation (Eq. 2), to determine the distance of the client. We use the highest observed EDP in our measurements as P_0 in equation 2. The AP runs MUSIC algorithm on the CSI to identify the angular components of the received signal. It exploits the mobility pattern of the user to identify the ANDP from the multiple angles reported by MUSIC. We co-opt dead-reckoning techniques to estimate the user's mobility, as described next.

Mobility Estimation using Dead Reckoning

Dead reckoning involves computing the user's displacement from accelerometer, and tracking the direction of movement using the compass. To calculate user's physical displacement, CUPID identifies a human-walking signature from the accelerometer readings, as shown in Figure 14(a). This signature arises from the natural bounce of the human body for each step taken. To identify the steps, we pass the accelerometer readings through a moving average filter, and identify two consecutive local minimas. A legitimate step will cause a significantly strong local maxima between two local minimas. We track the number of steps the user has taken by counting the local maximas. In our experiments, we could achieve a 98% accuracy in step detection. The physical displacement of the user can be computed by multiplying step count with the user's step size, which can be automatically tracked [11].

To estimate ANDP, CUPID calculates the distance between a past location of the user and her current location. Thus apart from physical displacement, orientation information is also required. Past work has demonstrated the feasibility of estimating orientation using smartphone compass. However, compass is vulnerable to indoor magnetic fiends created by metallic and electrical objects. Fortunately, CUPID is only interested in the distance between two locations, the absolute direction is not required. Thus, it only needs to track the angular changes as the user walks from one location to another. Smartphone gyroscope is appropriate for this purpose. It remains unaffected by changing magnetic fields [18], and computes the relative angular velocity. This yields the relative angular displacement of the user when multiplied by the time interval. CUPID can thereafter translate the physical and angular displacement into distance between two locations. Figure 14(b) shows the dead reckoning based distance estimation error between two locations. Errors in step size, along with noisy gyroscope readings increases the error for large distances. However, it is still reasonable (<5m) for up to 50m actual distance, which is the typical range of WiFi APs. In contrast, absolute location estimation using dead-reckoning will require compass angles, which might be erroneous indoors. Thus, in figure 14(b) location estimation error using dead-reckoning increases quickly. We conclude that although dead-reckoning may not be enough for localization, it is adequate for our purpose.

Side Ambiguity with Linear Antenna Placement

CUPID can find the ANDP from MUSIC's AoA estimates by estimating user's mobility using dead-reckoning techniques. In our implementation, we use laptops as APs, which has 3 antennas placed in a straight line, analogous to a linear antenna array. However, a linear antenna array can differentiate between signals from one array side only. This is because the AoA range of a linear array is between 0 and 180. Clients on the two sides of the line formed by the antennas are not differentiable. A circular antenna array type can differentiate signals from all directions. However, it requires almost double the number of antennas to achieve the same accuracy as a linear array. Thus with a linear antenna placement, CUPID needs to address the side ambiguity issue, before it can find the exact client location. We address this by observing the user's turns.

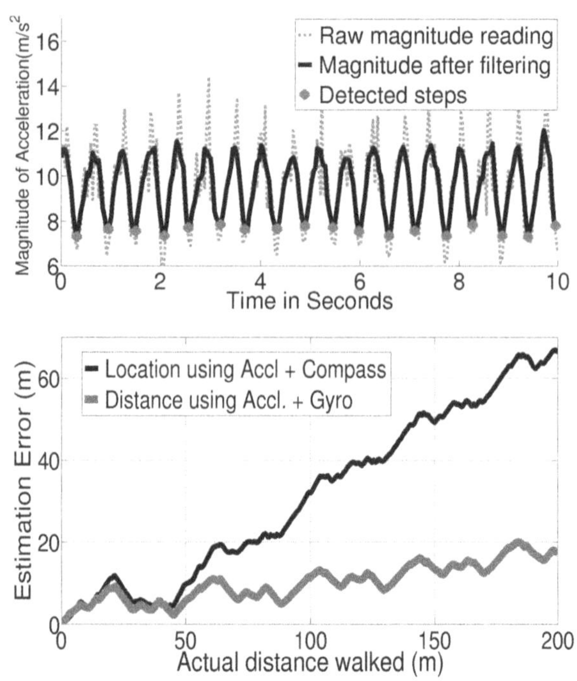

Figure 14: (a) Identifying steps from accelerometer readings. (b) Error from dead-reckoning for increasing distance between two locations.

We explain the key idea using figure 15. Let us assume while walking from location A to C, the user takes a turn at B. The angle of the user (ANDP) increases as he walks from A to C. The linear array cannot distinguish between angles on its two sides. Hence, the change in angle (θ) will be the same if the user walks through ABC or $A'B'C'$. However, the tie between ABC, and $A'B'C'$ can be broken by observing the turn the user undertook. If the gyroscope of the user's phone registered a right turn, she is indeed located in the front of the antenna array. On the other hand, if the user took a left turn, she was walking through $A'B'C'$. In general, it is possible to find out whether the user is located

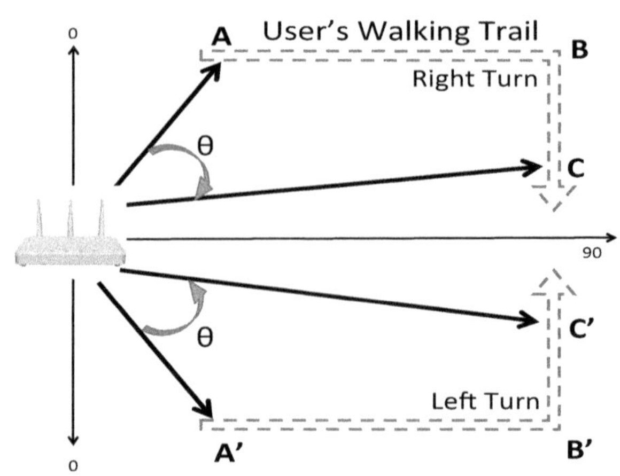

Figure 15: Side ambiguity due to linear antenna array.

in the front, or back side of the antenna array by observing the change in ANDP, and the nature of turn undertaken from her gyroscope (Table 1). The estimated ANDP remains the same if the user is in front. However, if the user is in the back of the array, we use $(-ANDP)$ as the actual angle. Once the angle of the client is determined, the AP can combine the angle with the distance estimate to find the location of the client.

Table 1: Addressing side ambiguity using user turns.

Change in ANDP	Gyroscope Reading	Final Angle
Positive	Right turn	ANDP
Positive	Left turn	- ANDP
Negative	Right turn	- ANDP
Negative	Left turn	ANDP

4.3 Leveraging Multiple APs

An AP can determine the location of all its associated clients by estimating their distances, and angles. However, if multiple APs can overhear a client's upload transmission to it's own AP, they can also independently estimate the location of the client. Of course, it is possible to utilize other APs on different channels if the client performs active 802.11 AP probing over multiple channels. Such active probing is not desirable because it can create throughput degradation and battery drain. Thus, CUPID combines the location estimates across only those APs which can overhear client's transmissions to it's own AP as described next.

Let the d_i be the distance, and θ_i be the angle estimate of a client from an AP (located at $AP_{i,x}, AP_{i,y}$). The AP can utilize the estimated distance, and angle to find the location of the client (x_i, y_i):

$$x_i = AP_{i,x} + d_i \cos\theta_i \tag{4}$$

$$y_i = AP_{i,y} + d_i \sin\theta_i \tag{5}$$

If more than one AP is available, CUPID combines the location estimates across them using a weighted centroid approach:

$$C_x = \frac{\sum x_i EDP_i}{\sum EDPi}, C_y = \frac{\sum y_i EDP_i}{\sum EDPi} \tag{6}$$

where EDP_i is the EDP estimated at AP_i from the client's upload transmission. CUPID announces the weighted centroid (C_x, C_y) as the location of the client. We observe that far away APs may cause large errors in location estimation. For the same angle estimation error, and perfect distance estimation, positioning error is proportional to the distance between the client and the AP. Thus, we optimize the system by ignoring the APs which receives the client's packet at less than $15dB$ signal strength. In this way, CUPID also mitigates distance error due to shadowing effect that is not captured by lfactor, to some extent.

If the client is stationary at the beginning of a new localization attempt, her accurate ANDP information won't be available at every AP. In this case, CUPID solves a system of non-linear equations involving the unknown location of the client (L_x, L_y) and its estimated distance from different APs:

$$|| < AP_{i,x}, AP_{i,y} > - < L_x, L_y > || = d_i \tag{7}$$

i = 1 ... n, where n is the number of APs. Observe that to solve the above multilateration problem, CUPID requires atleast 3 APs which are in range of the client.

4.4 Points of Discussion

Figure 16 presents the overall architecture of CUPID, showing how the distance calculation, ANDP estimation and ANDP database modules collectively mitigate the multipath, LoS/NLoS and side ambiguities to compute the client location. CUPID calculates the distance between the AP and the mobile device using EDP, and lfactor. It also calculates the AoA values of the mobile device using MUSIC. The mobile device shares with the AP its dead-reckoning based distance estimates, as well as past turn information. If the AP had a previous ANDP record for the same mobile device, it declares the AoA which is closest to the past ANDP as the current ANDP. Otherwise, it compares the current AoA with past recorded AoA values to find the ANDP. Whenever the user takes a turn, the AP corrects her ANDP according to the observed gyroscope reading (table 1). If the AP could estimate both distance, and ANDP of the mobile device, it computes an estimated location by using equation 4, and forwards the same to a location server [5]. Otherwise, if the ANDP is not available, the AP sends only the estimated distance value. The location server combines the distance, and ANDP from multiple APs and further refines the user's estimated location. We cover some additional discussion points below in building the real system of CUPID.

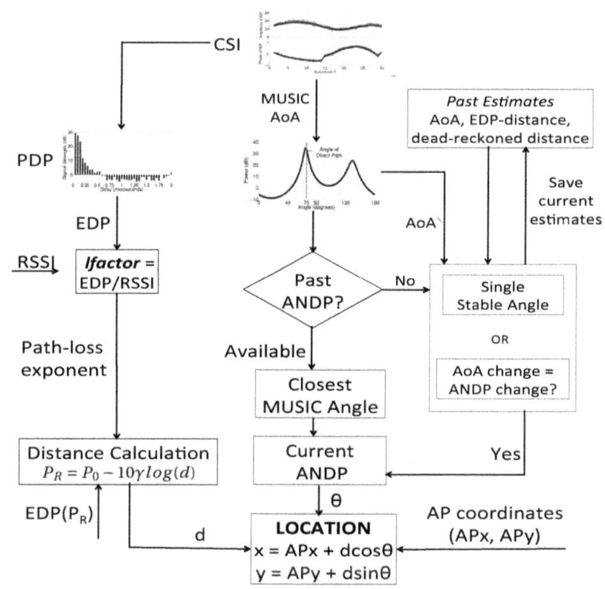

Figure 16: CUPID Architecture

CUPID uses measurements from a few known locations to construct the lfactor to path-loss exponent relation – is this not fingerprinting? We argue that this is certainly not fingerprinting because finding this relationship is a one time effort. Unlike fingerprinting, the relationship may not vary across different locations and environments. We find that a different building within our campus exhibit a very similar lfacor vs. path-loss relation (figure 17). Therefore, we postulate that once the relation is adequately established from any particular building, it can be used in all other locations. Vastly different environments (open desert vs. shopping malls, cold storage vs. indoor office) may show different relation due to the big difference of material or temperature; profiling the relations for such a few representative environments incurs very little cost. In contrast, fingerprinting has to be triggered whenever the environment changes, or the AP changes

[5]One of the APs can participate as the location server.

its channel, or power settings, which can happen very frequently (4 mins) [6].

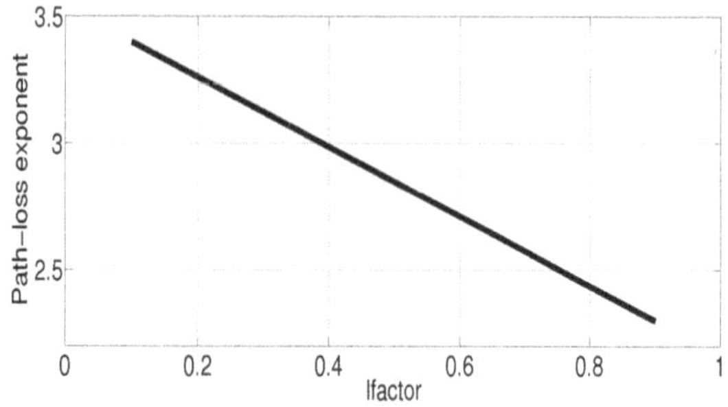

Figure 17: Relationship between lfactor and path-loss exponent for a single AP, estimated from a different building.

CUPID depends on the presence of a direct path signal. Will the direct path signal exist at most locations? It is difficult to evaluate whether the direct path signal exists in all our measurements. However, later we find that the ANDP estimation accuracy falls sharply when the signal strength of a client at the AP is below $15dB$. From this observation, we postulate that for weak clients, it might be difficult to identify the direct path signal. However, if multiple APs are available, CUPID will be able to leverage the nearby APs. Considering the dense AP deployments in typical indoor settings, it's reasonable to expect to have one or more neighboring APs with signals above $15dB$.

Will CUPID work if the user is static? CUPID can still estimate the location of a static client by leveraging her distance estimations. Of course, if the user was walking before becoming stationary, CUPID can estimate her angle from the past ANDP values. In such scenarios, CUPID can find the location of a static user even with a single AP.

Will CUPID consume a lot of energy? CUPID is designed with energy efficiency in mind. Contrary to existing schemes that require power-hungry channel scanning (fingerprinting) or active AP probings (AoA), CUPID can find the location of the client using only a few APs available on the same channel. Further, CUPID uses the client's accelerometer, and gyroscope readings only until her ANDP is known. Thus by eliminating the need of costly AP probing, and continuous scanning, CUPID limits the energy overhead, making it a practical proposition.

5. EVALUATION

We implement CUPID using laptops with Atheros 9390 wireless card and Google Nexus S phone. The phone is time synchronized for timestamping and physically attached to the laptop. It samples the accelerometer at $24Hz$, and the gyroscope at the highest permissible rate, and sends the dead-reckoning based relative location estimate to the AP. The client laptop uses only a single antenna, and it broadcasts packets at $20MHz$ bandwidth in a $5GHz$ band. The APs are also laptops with Atheros 9390 wireless cards, but uses all 3 available antennas. The location estimation logic at the AP is implemented using C in driver, and MATLAB.

5.1 Methodology

We design real-life experiments in an office environment with 5 APs installed at known locations, as shown in figure 18. The APs calculate the distance, and ANDP of a client, and sends them to the location server. The server knows the location of the APs, and can combine the information gathered from multiple APs to estimate the location of the client. We walked around arbitrarily in the building for an hour during normal office hours covering approximately $4500m^2$. As we walked, the client broadcasted 5 packets per second, unless differently specified, and the APs calculated the distance and angles to the client using the received packets. APs use a moving average filter on the distance, and angle estimates to deal with noise. The width of the filter is fixed as the number of packets received in the last 2 seconds; 10 packets by default. We made separate arrangements to collect ground truth (GPS is not availble indoors). Briefly, we pasted markers at known locations (red circles in figure 18). Each marker had a number on them, whenever the user walks through a marker, she records the number. The locations of the markers are known, and between two markers we did interpolation using step-count as the ground truth; we used approximately 1800 ground truth locations. The distance between the ground truth and the estimated location, is CUPID's instantaneous localization error.

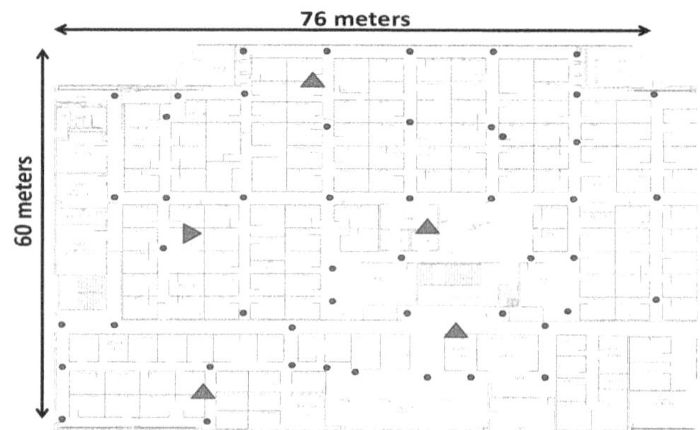

Figure 18: Floorplan of our office building. AP locations are shown as blue triangles, and markers as red circles.

5.2 Distance Estimation Performance

Figure 19(a) shows the distance estimation error of the client at 5 different AP. CUPID greatly reduces distance error compared to the conventional RSSI-based ranging in figure 5(b). It precomputes the lfactor to path-loss exponent mapping function from a few known locations. The accuracy of the function affects the distance estimation process because CUPID uses the path-loss exponent to compute distance. Figure 19(b) shows that even with a few known locations used to generate this function, CUPID performs well. However, the performance is poor at a few client locations. Upon analyzing the data we found that the error is high for weak links (figure 19(c)). This is because of the low fidelity of the CSI estimation process at weaker signal strengths [4].

5.3 Angle Estimation Accuracy

CUPID combines AoA estimation with user's mobility pattern to calculate the angle of the client (ANDP). It further exploits the user's gyroscope to address the side ambiguity introduced by linear antenna placements. Figure 20(a) shows that by using only the angle of the direct path, CUPID's median angle estimation accuracy is 20°. The error in CUPID's angle estimation is mostly due to the poor resolution driven by using only 3 antennas, that commodity 802.11n cards support. We further postulate that some high errors are due to weak links as shown in figure 20(b). Weak links may not have significant energy on the direct path, and hence

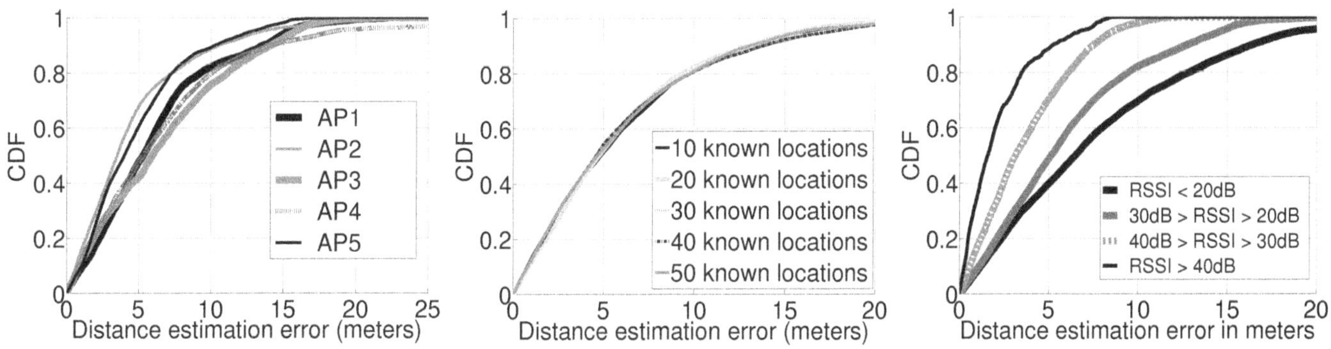

Figure 19: CDF of EDP-based distance estimation error (a) at different APs, (b) for different number of known locations used to find the lfactor-to-γ mapping. (c) Distance estimation error reduces as signal strength increases. Client-AP distance is <= 40m (Fig 19(b)).

are more prone to errors. This led us to exclude weak APs in the design of CUPID.

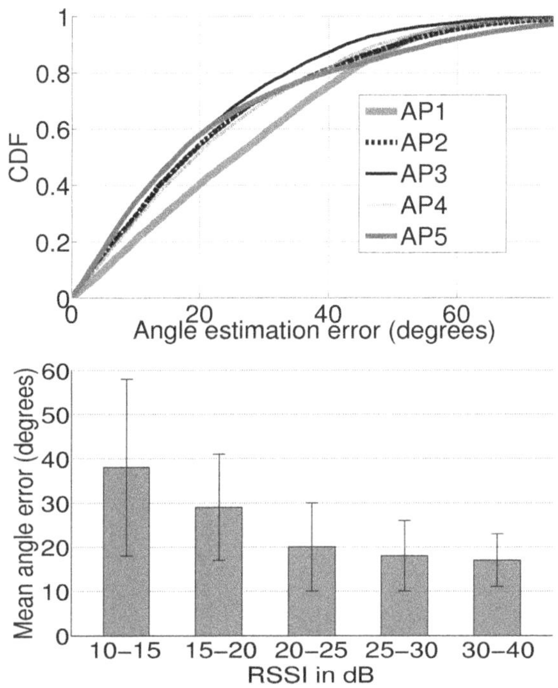

Figure 20: (a) CDF of angle estimation error. (b) Angle estimation error for different RSSI values.

5.4 Localization Performance

By combining the distance, and angle of a client, an AP can find her location. First, we present the localization performance in a single AP scenario. Thereafter we discuss how performance can be improved by leveraging multiple APs.

Single AP Performance

Figure 21(a) demonstrates CUPID's location estimation error by employing only the AP that the client associates with. We plot the distribution of the actual client-AP distance in figure 21(b). Figure 21(a) also demonstrates the effect of number of client's broadcast packets on positioning accuracy. As the client transmits more packets, the moving-average filtering process can be more effective in dealing with noise. However, even with 2 packets per second from the client (total 4 packets in 2 seconds), median localization error is $5m$. We also find that the localization error is large ($> 10m$) at a few locations. To understand this better, we plot the error as a function of RSSI in figure 21(c). We find that most of the errors can be attributed to locations where the strongest AP is less than $15dB$ strong. Thus, while CUPID might be able to locate most of the clients reasonably well, its single AP localization performance degrades at the edge of the wireless network. However, we believe that this is still a significant improvement over previous indoor localization schemes which rely on many APs to attain a reasonable accuracy.

Performance by Leveraging Multiple AP

If multiple APs can overhear the client's upload transmission, CUPID can combine the location estimates from them to further improve the performance. If the user is static, the APs can only find her distance (and not angle). CUPID computes the user's final location by using the per-AP distance estimates in equation 7. As the user moves, accurate ANDP becomes available, and hence CUPID can further refine the user's location. Figure 22(a) shows the comparison of these two forms of localization - evidently the advantage of user mobility is appreciable. Mean localization error reduces from $7m$ when the user is static (thus EDP only), to $2.7m$ when the user has walked a reasonable distance (EDP+ANDP). While the system can use up to 5 APs, we observe that the weak APs can inject large errors in our distance and angle estimation. Hence for better accuracy for mobile users, CUPID uses the location estimate from an AP only if the AP sees signal more than $15dB$ strong; EDP+ANDP plots this case. In our experiments only upto 3 APs satisfied this criteria in 80% of test locations. If CUPID indiscriminately uses all the 5 APs (EDP+ANDP w/o AP selection), localization error may increase - as evident from figure 22(a).

Impact of number of APs: We further analyze CUPID's performance for varying number of APs. We divide the locations into different categories depending on how many APs are visible ($> 15dB$) at each location. Even when a single AP is visible, CUPID can locate the client with an accuracy of $4.4m$ for 50% and $6m$ for 90% (figure 22(c)). As the number of APs increases, the median error quickly goes down to $2m$. Notably, CUPID can locate the client with only 2-3 APs at reasonable accuracy, thus eliminating the need of probing APs across different WiFi channels to use more APs.

Comparison with existing RSSI and AoA: We evaluate if previous RSSI, and AoA-based schemes can achieve similar accuracy as ours. For the RSSI based multilateration, we use RSSI based

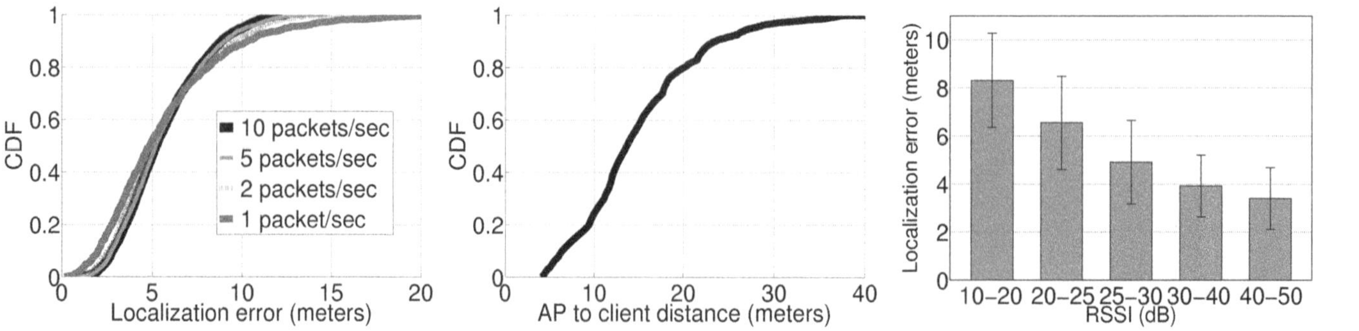

Figure 21: Performance using single AP: (a) CDF of localization error with varying upload traffic. (b) CDF of distance of the client locations from the AP. (c) Localization accuracy increases with signal strength.

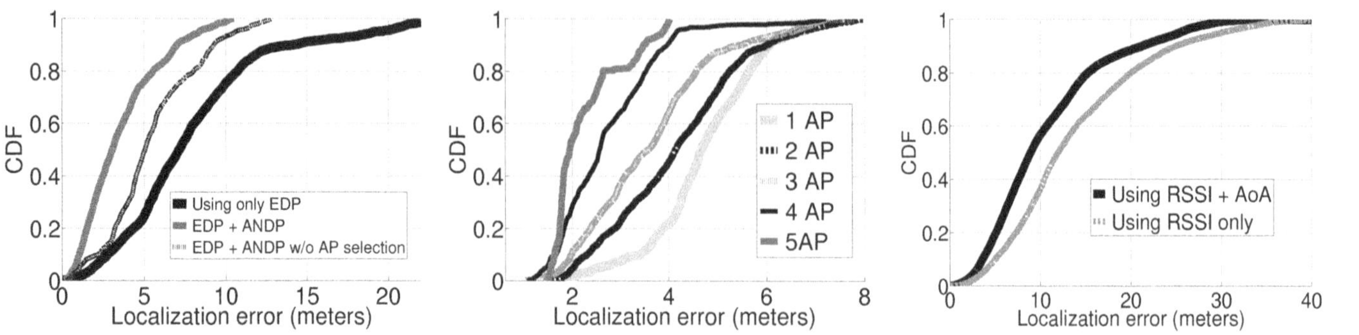

Figure 22: Performance using multiple APs: (a) Localization error in static and mobile scenarios. (b) Localization error with increasing number of APs. (c) Performance of existing RSSI, and AoA schemes.

distance, instead of EDP, in equation 7. The path loss exponent was set to the measured average on a per-AP basis. Since RSSI is a poor estimator of distance, RSSI based multilateration leads to large errors of median $11.5m$ and $> 25m$ for 90% (figure 22(c)). We also explore the possibility of combining RSSI with AoA. The strongest peak in the AoA pseudospectrum was selected as the angle to the client as done by [14]. The previous AoA algorithm cannot address the side ambiguity issue of the linear antenna array. To compare, we sidestep the issue by assuming that the AoA algorithm somehow knows which side the client is in. The combination of RSSI and the strongest AoA does not perform well either (median $9m$ error), confirming the importance of avoiding multipath ambiguity in AoA estimation.

6. RELATED WORK

The indoor localization literature is vast [1, 19]. In the interest of space, we heavily sub-sample this literature, focussing on systems related to CUPID.

RF fingerprinting based localization has been the dominant theme of localization. RADAR [2] was the first to perform detailed site surveys to build a location fingerprint database, based on the AP SSIDs and RSSI reported by wireless devices. Horus [3] proposes enhancements to RADAR by exploiting the structure of RSSI. Place Lab [20] and Active Campus [21] attempt to reduce the overhead of calibration by combining WiFi and GSM signal information. PinLoc [4] demonstrates that by utilizing high resolution CSI fingerprints, it is possible to localize a device with meter scale accuracy. WiFi fingerprints are amenable to environmental changes and periodic WLAN maintenance and configuration changes, requiring frequent wardriving which is expensive, and may not scale over wide areas.

Calibration-free localization: Recent approaches advocate the use of crowdsourcing to reduce the cost of wardriving [10, 11, 18]. However, crowdsourcing either requires a strong user incentive model, or leads to coarse grained fingerprint information which reduces their accuracy. Crowdsourcing further cannot adapt to frequent, and automatic configuration changes as adopted by recent WLAN APs; the default update time settings found in [5, 6] are 10mins and 4mins. Map based particle filtering [9, 22] relies on unique indoor walking paths such as long corridors, making them ineffective in open areas such as airport, auditorium etc. *EZ* [8] was among the first to attempt WiFi based indoor localization without any fingerprinting. Their key intuition is that RSSI based distance estimations from several overheard WiFi APs can find the user's location, provided the mobile device can obtain a few GPS fixes. While GPS can be erratic inside a building, the precise RF signal propagation may also vary over time due to fading. In contrast, CUPID identifies and uses only the direct path, and automatically adapts to environmental variations.

Ranging-based techniques localize nodes by computing the distances between them using a variety of techniques. RSSI-based ranging [23–26] computes inter-node distances based on the observed signal strength. Although appropriate wide-open outdoors, RSSI is susceptible to multipath, resulting into large errors indoors. FILA [27] attempts to utilize the CSI to reduce the error from RSSI based ranging, but stops short of identifying the key issues with multipath and LoS/NLoS ambiguities. Centaur [7] combines RSSI and acoustic ranging. PinPoint [28], and work by Werb et. al. [29] utilize time delays in signal propagation to estimate distances between wireless nodes. TPS [30] uses difference in time of arrival of multiple RF signals from transmitters at known location. Similarly, PAL [31] uses time difference of arrival between UWB signals at multiple receivers to determine location. Cricket [32] and AHLoS [33] utilize propagation delays between ultrasound and RF signals to estimate location of wireless devices. Such solutions require tight time synchronization and/or additional ranging hardware, limiting their applicability.

Angle-of-arrival based techniques use multiple antennas to estimate the angle at which the signal is received, and then employs geometric relationships to locate the wireless transmitter [13, 14, 34–36]. Even with access to raw signal information and using 8 antennas [13, 14], they can be derailed in multi-path rich indoor environments where the direct signal path is often blocked. To address this problem, some AoA based techniques require 6-7 sophisticated antenna systems [14, 37, 38], not possible with low resolution commodity WiFi hardware. Recently the ArrayTrack system [39] achieves high localization accuracy by utilizing the AoA computed from a rectangular array of 16 antennas. Arraytrack uses spatial smoothing, and time-based AoA grouping to suppress the effect of multipath on AoA based location estimation. While these techniques will certainly improve the accuracy of CUPID, Arraytrack stops short of identifying the actual ANDP, particularly under the constraints of linear antenna arrays offered by commodity WiFi hardware. SpinLoc [40] and Borealis [41] requires the user to make a full 360° turn to find her angle. CUPID's reliance on WiFi alone, along with the ability to extract distance, and angle information from off-the-shelf chipsets, makes it attractive for immediate deployment.

7. LIMITATIONS AND DISCUSSION

Dependence on particular hardware cards: CUPID relies on the availability of CSI information from the wireless chipset. This is not a difficult proposition because the CSI information is already calculated in the hardware for channel estimation, calibration, and beamforming purposes. Moreover for 802.11n, and 802.11ac wireless systems CSI estimation and reporting is a mandatory operation [15, 16]. Hence, although we use a specific a wireless card in our evaluation, we believe that with minor modifications, CUPID can be deployed on other platforms as well.

Phone orientation effect: We have experimented with the phone in hand. Handling arbitrary phone orientations, and their effect on the reported sensor values is an important direction for future research. While magnitude of acceleration may be an orientation-independent feature, gyroscopes may be further leveraged to map an arbitrary orientation to a specific frame of reference.

Localizing clients with heterogeneous hardware: While angle estimation may only depend on the wireless propagation, distance computation using the path-loss equation (Eq. 2), is not independent of the client's transmission power(*txpower*). Mobile devices may use different txpower settings with up to $10dB$ of difference [8]. One way to address this is to let the mobile device report its txpower to the AP. While this requires a minor platform modification, CUPID can employ commercial solutions [42] to identify the type of the device to infer its txpower. In addition, if multiple APs are available, CUPID can utilize existing techniques [8, 24] to infer the location of a mobile device with unknown transmission power.

Angle estimation with only 3 antennas: Since CUPID uses commodity off-the-shelf (COTS) chipsets, it suffers from the poor resolution offered by only 3 antennas. CUPID's performance will certainly improve if additional antennas can be leveraged at the AP. A few recent WiFi APs have several antennas, but, they also tend to have multiple radios, such that the number of antennas per radio is around 3. It is extremely difficult to combine the CSI from multiple COTS radios because of the tight phase-synchronization requirement, that is only possible by utilizing raw signals (like in [13, 17]). The upcoming IEEE 802.11ac standard allows up to 8 antennas. However AP vendors tend to mix different antenna polarizations (vertical vs. horizontal), and placements (linear, rectangular, or circular) to maximize the network coverage. Thus, it is reasonable to assume that even in near future, the achievable angle resolution will be similar to that of a linear array of 3 – 4 antennas. CUPID is an attempt to improve the capability of WiFi positioning in such practical settings.

Modeling Path-loss: We did not explore sophisticated path-loss models [43] in our system. Our goal was to identify practical heuristics that capture multipath and LoS information directly from each received packet's CSI, instead of trying to tune sophisticated path-loss models at every different location and environment.

8. CONCLUSION

Although attractive for its simplicity, multilateration and triangulation has traditionally suffered from the randomness of multipath reflections, leading to proposals which advocates fingerprinting, or crowdsourcing for the purpose of indoor localization. This paper is an attempt to revisit basic multilateration, and triangulation based techniques using PHY layer information. We find that CSI information, when combined with natural human mobility, can accurately estimate the distance, and angle from only the direct path, ultimately yielding the location of the client from her AP. Our solution system, CUPID, identifies and harnesses only the direct path, avoiding the affect of multipath reflections. Experiments using off-the-shelf Atheros chipsets, and Google Nexus S phones confirm feasibility, demonstrating accuracy comparable to that of expensive fingerprinting based techniques. We believe that CUPID tackles the fundamental issue of multipath ambiquity and can be applied to the other RF-based localization systems that suffer from multipath such as urban outdoor cellular.

9. ACKNOWLEDGMENT

We sincerely thank Prof. Guoliang Xing for shepherding our paper, as well as the anonymous reviewers for their valuable comments and feedback.

10. REFERENCES

[1] Y. Gu et al. A survey of indoor positioning systems. *IEEE Communications Surveys & Tutorials*, 2009.

[2] V. Bahl et al. RADAR: An in-building rf-based user location and tracking system. In *INFOCOM*, 2000.

[3] M. Youssef and A. Agrawala. The horus WLAN location determination system. In *MobiSys*, 2005.

[4] S. Sen et al. Spot localization using phy layer information. In *MobiSys*, 2012.

[5] Cisco. Radio resource management under unified wireless networks. Cisco Whitepaper.

[6] Aruba Networks. Configuring adaptive radio management (arm) profiles and settings. Aruba Whitepaper.

[7] R. Nandakumar et al. Centaur: locating devices in an office environment. In *MobiCom*, 2012.

[8] K. Chintalapudi, A. Iyer, and V. Padmanabhan. Indoor localization without the pain. In *MOBICOM*, 2010.

[9] F. Li et al. A reliable and accurate indoor localization method using phone inertial sensors. 2012.

[10] Z. Yang et al. Locating in fingerprint space: wireless indoor localization with little human intervention. In *MobiCom*, 2012.

[11] A. Rai et al. Zee: Zero-effort crowdsourcing for indoor localization. In *MobiCom*, 2012.

[12] R. Schmidt. Multiple emitter location and signal parameter estimation. *Antennas and Propagation, IEEE Transactions on*, 1986.

[13] J. Xiong et al. SecureAngle: improving wireless security using angle-of-arrival information. In *HotNets*, 2010.

[14] J. Xiong and K. Jamieson. Towards fine-grained radio-based indoor location. In *HotMobile*. ACM, 2012.

[15] E.H. Ong et al. Ieee 802.11 ac: Enhancements for very high throughput wlans. In *IEEE PIMRC 2011*.

[16] Y. Xiao. Ieee 802.11 n: enhancements for higher throughput in wireless lans. *Wireless Communications, IEEE*, 2005.

[17] H.C. Chen et al. Determining rf angle of arrival using cots antenna arrays: A field evaluation. In *MilCom*, 2012.

[18] H. Wang et al. Unsupervised indoor localization. MobiSys, 2012.

[19] J. Hightower and G. Borriello. Location systems for ubiquitous computing. *Computer*, 2001.

[20] Yu-Chung et al. Accuracy characterization for metropolitan-scale wi-fi localization. In *MobiSys*, 2005.

[21] William G. Griswold et al. Activecampus: Experiments in community-oriented ubiquitous computing. *Computer*, 2004.

[22] J. Hightower and G. Borriello. Particle filters for location estimation in ubiquitous computing: A case study. *UbiComp 2004*.

[23] K. Whitehouse et al. A practical evaluation of radio signal strength for ranging-based localization. *ACM MC2R*, 2007.

[24] S. Yang, J. Yi, and H. Cha. Hcrl: A hop-count-ratio based localization in wireless sensor networks. In *SECON*, 2007.

[25] N. Banerjee et al. Virtual compass: relative positioning to sense mobile social interactions. *Pervasive Computing*, 2010.

[26] K.K. Chintalapudi et al. Ad-hoc localization using ranging and sectoring. In *INFOCOM 2004.*, 2004.

[27] K. Wu et al. Fila: Fine-grained indoor localization. In *INFOCOM, 2012*, 2012.

[28] M. Youssef et al. Pinpoint: An asynchronous time-based location determination system. In *ACM Mobisys*, June 2006.

[29] J. Werb and C. Lanzl. Designing a positioning system for finding things and people indoors. *IEEE Spectrum*, 35(9), September 1998.

[30] X. Cheng et al. TPS: A time-based positioning scheme for outdoor sensor networks. In *IEEE Infocom*, March 2004.

[31] R.J. Fontana et al. Commercialization of an ultra wideband precision asset location system. In *ICUWB*, 2003.

[32] N. B. Priyantha. *The cricket indoor location system*. PhD thesis.

[33] A. Savvides and M. Han, C.C. Srivastava. Dynamic fine-grained localization in ad-hoc networks of sensors. In *ACM MobiCom*, 2001.

[34] D. Niculescu and B. Nath. Ad hoc positioning system (APS) using AoA. In *IEEE Infocom*, 2003.

[35] L. Cong and W. Zhuang. Hybrid tdoa/aoa mobile user location for wideband cdma cellular systems. *Wireless Communications, IEEE Transactions on*, 1(3):439–447, 2002.

[36] A. Tarighat et al. Improved wireless location accuracy using antenna arrays and interference cancellation. In *ICASSP*, 2003.

[37] D. Niculescu and B. Nath. VOR base stations for indoor 802.11 positioning. In *ACM MobiCom*, September 2004.

[38] I. Jamil et al. Improved method for estimating angle of arrival in multipath conditions using music. In *IEEE APWC 2009*.

[39] J. Xiong and K. Jamieson. Arraytrack: A fine-grained indoor location system. In *USENIX NSDI*, 2013.

[40] S. Sen et al. Spin once to know your location. In *Hotmobile*, 2012.

[41] Z. Zhang et al. I am the antenna: accurate outdoor ap location using smartphones. In *ACM Mobicom*, 2011.

[42] ARUBA Networks. Bring your own ipad to work. Aruba Whitepaper.

[43] Theodore S. Rappaport. *Wireless Communications: Principles and Practice (2nd Edition)*. Prentice Hall, 2002.

Spartacus: Spatially-Aware Interaction for Mobile Devices Through Energy-Efficient Audio Sensing

[1]Zheng Sun, [1]Aveek Purohit, [2]Raja Bose, and [1]Pei Zhang
[1]Electrical and Computer Engineering, Carnegie Mellon University, Pittsburgh, PA
[2]Microsoft Silicon Valley, Sunnyvale, CA
{zhengs, apurohit, peizhang}@cmu.edu, {raja.bose}@microsoft.com

ABSTRACT

Recent developments in ubiquitous computing enable applications that leverage personal mobile devices, such as smartphones, as a means to interact with other devices in their close proximity. In this paper, we propose Spartacus, a mobile system that enables spatially-aware neighboring device interactions with zero prior configuration. Using built-in microphones and speakers on commodity mobile devices, Spartacus uses a novel acoustic technique based on the Doppler effect to enable users to accurately initiate an interaction with a neighboring device through a pointing gesture. To enable truly spontaneous interactions on energy-constrained mobile devices, Spartacus uses a continuous audio-based lower-power listening mechanism to trigger the gesture detection service. This eliminates the need for any manual action by the user.

Experimental results show that Spartacus achieves an average 90% device selection accuracy within 3m for most interaction scenarios. Our energy consumption evaluations show that, Spartacus achieves about 4X lower energy consumption than WiFi Direct and 5.5X lower than the latest Bluetooth 4.0 protocols.

Categories and Subject Descriptors

C.3 [**Special-purpose and application-based systems**]: Signal processing systems

Keywords

Interaction; audio sensing; device pairing; spatial interaction; gesture; mobile system; context aware

1. INTRODUCTION

Recent developments in ubiquitous computing enable applications that leverage personal mobile devices, such as smartphones, as a means to interact with other devices in their close proximity. Numerous application scenarios are either commonly observed or can be foreseen in the near future, ranging from *Person-to-Person* interactions – For example, conference attendees exchanging contact information, or friends playing multi-player pass-the-parcel mobile games, to *Person-to-Device* interactions – For example, a student printing out a document by interacting with a nearby printer, remote control of projectors, accessing product information in stores, controlling digital display screens, or changing thermostat settings.

Establishing such an interaction requires that the device initiating the interaction makes the target device aware of its intent and sets up a connection, without any prior configuration. While users themselves can intuitively know and identify the nearby target device based on its relative location, the existing methods require additional manual effort or prior configuration to translate this *spatial-awareness* to an identifier understandable by the device.

For example, device discovery features in Bluetooth or Wi-Fi can be used to initiate the interaction, where the user must scan for nearby devices and select the target from a list. Similarly, other methods have been proposed where users (the initiator and the target) must share information a priori [3] or perform synchronized actions [6].

Recent work, Point & Connect [15], has proposed a novel system that uses a pointing gesture to initiate interactions between a mobile device and its target. However, the system requires an initial channel of communication such as a local Wi-Fi or Bluetooth network to exist beforehand to enable a device to *point-and-connect* to the target device. In addition, due to the energy-constrained nature of mobile phones, the system service cannot be run continuously in the background and requires users to manually trigger it, on all nearby devices.

In this paper, we propose Spartacus, a mobile system that enables spatially-aware neighboring device interactions with zero prior configuration. First, Spartacus uses a novel acoustic technique based on the Doppler effect to enable users to accurately initiate an interaction with a particular target device in their proximity through a pointing gesture. Second, Spartacus uses a continuous audio-based low-power listening service that runs in the background and automatically triggers the relatively power hungry gesture detecting service. This enables Spartacus to run continuously in the background and removes the need for any manual user actions prior to the interaction. The system can be implemented as a software application on commodity mobile devices without any special hardware or software requirement.

As a proof of concept, we implemented the Spartacus

MobiSys'13, June 25—28, 2013, Taipei, Taiwan

system on the Android smartphones, and tested the system using various device models under different interaction scenarios. Our experimental results show that Spartacus support spontaneous device interactions with an average of 90% device selection accuracy within 3m for most interaction scenarios. Evaluation results of energy consumptions show that, Spartacus consumes about 150mW power. As a reference, we also compare energy consumption of Spartacus with the state-of-the-art peer-to-peer scanning techniques, and show that Spartacus achieves about 4X lower energy consumption than WiFi Direct and 5.5X lower than the latest Bluetooth 4.0 protocols, respectively.

The key contributions of this paper are as follows:

1. We proposed a novel acoustic technique based on the Doppler effect to enable spatially-aware interactions between devices that provides high accuracy and supports numerous natural human gestures.

2. We developed a novel undersampling audio signal processing pipeline that achieves better accuracy without increasing computational complexity, allowing the method to be used on commodity mobile devices.

3. We designed and implemented a low-power listening protocol using periodic audio sensing to trigger gesture detection that reduces energy consumption and enables the system to run continuously in the background. This enables the interaction to be truly spontaneous without any manual actions on part of the user.

4. We analyzed and experimentally validated the design tradeoffs in achieving low latency and power consumption given hardware and software limitations of commodity mobile devices.

The rest of the paper is organized as follows. Section 2 gives a system overview of Spartacus. We describe the design of algorithms in Section 3 and discuss implementation details in Section 4. Section 5 shows evaluation results. Related work is shown in Section 6. Finally, Section 8 concludes the paper.

2. SYSTEM OVERVIEW

Spartacus supports spatially-aware device selections in close proximity (i.e. within 5m), using intuitive pointing gestures. As illustrated in Figure 1, when a user wants to initiate an interaction with a nearby device, she makes a pointing gesture towards the device using her mobile phone. Then the interaction with the target device is automatically initiated.

To select the target device, Spartacus emits a continuous audio tone at a known frequency during the course of the pointing gesture. Other devices that are close to the user's phone will be able to capture the tone via their microphones. Due to the motion of the gesture, a Doppler frequency shift is observed in the received audio deviating from the original frequency, which is a monotonically increasing function of the gesture velocity [4]. Therefore, since the gesture is made in the direction of the target device, the target device can be isolated by finding the *peak frequency shift* among nearby devices.

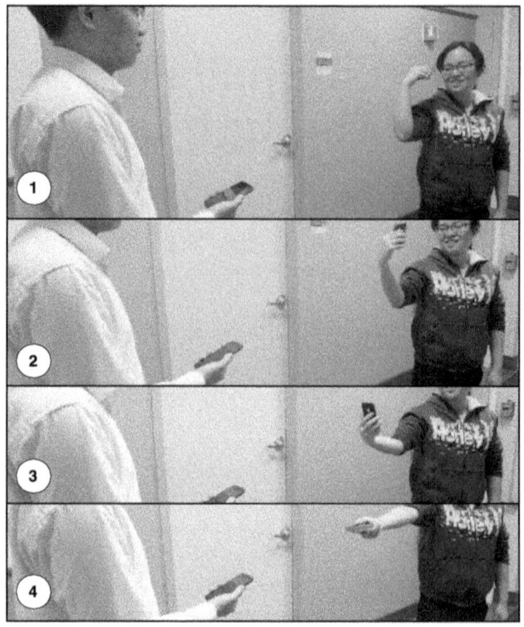

Figure 1: An interaction scenario of the Spartacus interaction system. A user selects a nearby device for interaction by quickly pointing her mobile phone towards the targeting device.

To eliminate any configurations from users in the entire interaction process, Spartacus needs to automatically trigger the gesture detection service on nearby devices before the gesture. Previous work adopts a continuous listening approach [15]. Given the limited energy budget on mobile devices, this approach becomes impractical to be active all the time and users are required to manually turn on the gesture detection service before the interaction. In contrast, Spartacus solves this problem by providing a zero-configuration interaction trigger mechanism, whereby mobile devices running Spartacus continuously perform a periodic low-power listening using their built-in microphones. Before a user issues the gesture, an audio beacon with a short duration (i.e. a couple of seconds) is emitted. Nearby devices that successfully capture this beacon trigger their gesture detection service and begin listening for the gesture tone from the initiator. After the gesture is over, the gesture detection service is turned off to conserve energy. Our experimental results show that, the low-power listening protocol is more energy-efficient than other state-of-the-art peer-to-peer scanning techniques, such as WiFi Direct and Bluetooth 4.0. (Detailed in Section 5.5)

We have implemented the Spartacus system on the Android mobile platform (Detailed in Section 4). The entire system is implemented in software, and runs as a mobile phone app, without any change to the existing mobile operating system and APIs. Since Spartacus leverages existing built-in microphones and speakers on commodity mobile devices, such as smartphones, it does not require any extra hardware.

2.1 Design Challenges of Spartacus

To support spatially-aware device selections and zero-configuration interaction triggers, the Spartacus system addresses a number of major technical challenges:

1. **High Resolution Doppler-Shift Detection** – Spartacus selects the target device through the analysis of peak Doppler frequency shifts in the pointing gestures. However, pointing gestures of average users are usually transient (i.e. generally shorter than 0.5s), and the gesture velocity is low, which leads to limited Doppler frequency shifts. Thus, accurately detecting the transient peak velocities requires digital signal processing techniques with a high frequency resolution, without sacrificing the time resolution. Spartacus addresses this challenge by utilizing an undersampling technique, and increases the frequency-domain resolution by 5X as compared to traditional FFT-based approaches. This translates to a 2X increase in angular resolution. (Detailed in Section 3.1)

2. **High-Accuracy Device Selection** – To successfully select the target device, Spartacus needs to accurately estimate the peak frequency shifts observed by each nearby device, and to select the one with the maximum peak shifts. To address this challenge, we design and implement a bandpass audio signal processing pipeline in Spartacus, which is robust against ambient and intermittent high frequency acoustic noises. (Detailed in Section 3.2)

3. **Energy-efficient Interaction Trigger** – To trigger interactions on nearby devices without user configurations, mobile devices need to be *always* ready to capture the pointing gestures, while keeping the energy consumption low. Spartacus addresses this challenge by designing a low-power audio listening protocol that periodically detects incoming interaction triggers. (Detailed in Section 3.3)

3. SYSTEM DESCRIPTION

Using Spartacus, a user initializes a device interaction process by pointing her mobile phone towards a target device, during which an audio tone with a known frequency is emitted. Spartacus utilizes audio signal processing techniques to detect the frequency shifts in the audio tone, such that the target device can be selected by searching for the maximum peak frequency shifts among multiple candidate devices. This section provides detailed system description of this process.

3.1 Detect Doppler Shift with High Resolution

To select the target device, Spartacus emits a continuous audio tone at a known frequency f_0 during the course of the pointing gesture. According to the Doppler effect, the frequency of the received tone can be calculated as $f = (\frac{c+v_R}{c-v_S})f_0$, where c, v_R, and v_S are the speed of sound, of the gesture receiver, and of the gesture sender, respectively [4]. In our case, assuming the receiver is stationary during the course of the gesture (i.e. $v_R = 0$), and the speed of sound c is constant, the observed frequency becomes a monotonically increasing function of v_S. Since the user made the gesture directionally towards the target device, the target device would be able to observe the maximum Doppler shift. Thus, by comparing the peak frequency shift among nearby devices, the target device can be selected.

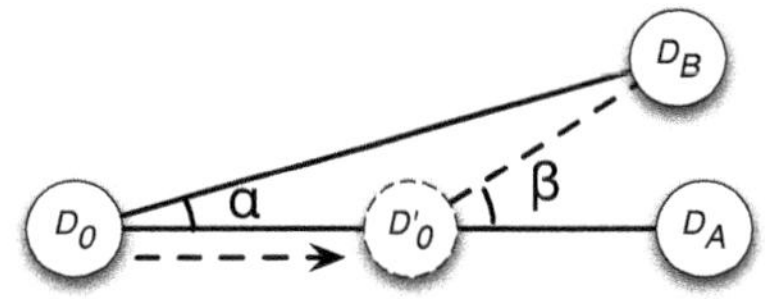

Figure 2: Geometry of tone transmission between mobile devices. When D_0 is moved towards the target device D_A during the pointing gesture, the phone displacement increases the directional difference from α to β.

3.1.1 *Deriving Angular Resolution*

Spartacus selects the target device D_A by measuring the time-varying Doppler frequency shifts. This is accomplished by running an audio signal analysis process over a series of overlapped audio frames. Applying the FFT transform on each audio frame, the quantity of the frequency shift in this audio frame of D_A can be calculated as $\Delta n_A = (f_A - f_0) \cdot \frac{N_{FFT}}{F_s}$, where f_A is the observed tone frequency of D_A, f_0 the frequency of the original tone, F_s the sampling rate, N_{FFT} the number of FFT points, and Δn_A the calculated frequency shift expressed in terms of FFT points. Assume the target device is stationary during the course of the gesture, i.e. $v_R = 0$, given the equation of the Doppler effect, Δn_A can also be expressed as $\Delta n_A = \frac{c}{c-v_S} \cdot \frac{f_0 \cdot N_{FFT}}{F_s}$, where c and v_S are the speed of sound and the gesture sender, respectively. As shown in Figure 2, suppose another device D_B is in close proximity to the target device D_A. Let the angle between the three devices be α, then the velocity observed at D_B will be $v_S \cdot \cos\alpha$. Therefore, correctly selecting D_A to be the target device requires Δn_A is at least one FFT point larger than Δn_B through the FFT analysis, i.e. $\Delta n_A - \Delta n_B > 1$. Given that c is constant and the maximum velocity of a particular gesture is fixed, this requirement can be expressed as $(\frac{1}{c-v_S} - \frac{1}{c-v_S \cdot \cos\alpha}) \cdot \frac{c \cdot f_0 \cdot N_{FFT}}{F_s} > 1$. Reorganizing this inequality, the minimum differentiable α_{res}, i.e. the angular resolution, can be expressed as

$$\cos\alpha_{res} < \left(c - \frac{1}{\frac{1}{c-v_S} - \frac{Q}{c}}\right)/v_S, \qquad (1)$$

where $Q = \frac{F_s}{f_0 \cdot N_{FFT}}$. Using Equation 1, we can compute the achievable angular resolution of Spartacus. For example, suppose a user used audio tones at 20KHz, and pointed her phone with an average 3.4m/s peak velocity. At the receiver device, the audio signal was sampled at 44100Hz, utilizing a 2048-point FFT, then the angular resolution would be 26.7°. Suppose a target device is 5m away, this translates to 2.3m spatial resolution, which is too large to conduct practical interactions! We will evaluate the velocity variance of the pointing gestures in Section 5.1.

3.1.2 *Improving Resolution using Undersampling*

To improve the angular resolution, Equation 1 indicates that α_{res} is a monotonically increasing function of Q, which implies three options to reduce α_{res}: 1) increasing the original tone frequency f_0, 2) increasing the number of FFT points N_{FFT}, or 3) decreasing the sampling rate F_s.

The first two options both have drawbacks. For the first option, audio tones with higher frequencies experience stronger energy degradation, which consequently reduces the supported interaction range (We will evaluate the effect of energy degradation of sound in Section 4.2). For the second option, increasing the number of FFT points would involve a higher computational burden. Our experimental results indicate that, using 10ms audio frames and 2048-point FFT, processing one second audio takes 7 seconds on modern mobile devices, which is too slow for any interactions that require high responsiveness, such as mobile gaming.

To avoid these drawbacks, Spartacus exploits the last option, which is to decreasing the sampling rate F_s. This option seems to be impractical because Nyquist sampling theorem states that the sampling frequency has to be larger than twice the maximum signal frequency, to perfectly reconstructed the original signal, otherwise the sampled signal would be aliased [14]. However, if the bandwidth of a bandpass signal is significantly smaller than the central frequency of the signal, it is still possible to sample the signal at a much lower rate than the Nyquist sampling rate, without causing the alias.

This technique is called undersampling, which has been used in RF communication and image processing systems, for analyzing bandpass signals [5, 20]. In Spartacus, since the tones are transmitted at a very high frequency (i.e. above 18KHz), whereas the frequency shifts of tones are only a few hundred Herz, the entire received audio tone can be seen as a bandpass signal. Therefore, using the undersampling technique can significantly reduce the required sampling rate. The effect of the undersampling technique to the spectrums is shown in Figure 4.

Denote the lowest and the highest band limits of the received frequency-shifted tone as f_L and f_H, respectively, then the bandwidth of the signal is $B = f_H - f_L$. According to the undersampling theorem, the condition for an acceptable new sampling rate is that shifts of the bands from f_L to f_H and from $-f_H$ to $-f_L$ must not overlap when shifted by all integer multiples of the new sampling rate $F_s^\star$ [5]. This condition can be interpreted as the following constraint:

$$\frac{2 \cdot f_H}{n} \leq F_s^\star \leq \frac{2 \cdot f_L}{n-1}, \forall n: 1 \leq n \leq \lfloor \frac{f_H}{B} \rfloor, \quad (2)$$

where $\lfloor \cdot \rfloor$ is the flooring operation, B the signal bandwidth, and $n = F_s/F_s^\star$ the undersampling factor. In our experiments, we observe that average users can generate pointing gestures with an average peak velocity of 3.4m/s, which equals to 200Hz frequency shift. Considering the edge effect of FFT transforms, we conservatively assume the bandwidth of the received tone signal is 2KHz, which is sufficient to avoid spectrum aliasing for human pointing gestures. Take this value of the bandwidth into Equation 2, we get a list of possible $F_s^\star$ and n combinations, as shown in Table 1.

3.1.3 Determining Undersampling Parameters

These parameter combinations provide rich options for us to design our system. However, when choosing undersampling parameters, there are a number of design considerations: 1) A higher n is generally favored, as it leads to a lower new sampling rate, which results in a better angular resolution. 2) Since the central frequency of the tones is $f_L + \frac{B}{2}$, a higher f_L increases the central frequency of the tones. During our experiments, as will be shown in Section 4.2, higher tone frequencies generally cause greater energy degradation of sound, which would significantly reduce the interaction range and the accuracy of tone detection. In practice, to support sufficient interaction range and achieve optimal device selection accuracy, we empirically avoided using f_L higher than 19KHz (i.e. the entire bandwidth of the audio tone resides between 19KHz and 21KHz). However, we would note that, thought this general design consideration holds, the frequency of the audio tones could also be varied according to the specific frequency response performance of the microphones and speakers. 3) Commodity mobile devices support a limited choices of audio sampling rates, which generally include 8KHz, 16KHz, 32KHz, 44.1KHz, and 48KHz, etc. This means the original audio sampling rate can not be arbitrarily set, which consequently limits the choices of $F_s^\star$ and n.

After examining all these design considerations, we found that, only when n=5, 6, or 7 given F_s = 44.1KHz, or when n = 4 given F_s = 48KHz, the parameter combinations satisfy the central frequency requirement. Furthermore, among these parameter combinations, most of the cases lead to a low undersampling factor n, except the case where $n = 7$ given F_s = 44.1KHz. Thus, we finally choose this pair of parameters in Spartacus, which yields a new sampling rate $F_s^\star = 44.1/7 = 6.3$KHz. Given this lower sampling rate, based on Equation 1, the theoretical angular resolution is improved to 10°. As compared to the original angular resolution of 26.7° discussed in Section 3.1.1, this is more than 2.5X better than the original resolution.

3.2 Select Target Device with High Accuracy

3.2.1 Bandpass Signal Processing Pipeline

Using the undersampling technique, we set the central tone frequency at 20KHz and use a bandwidth of 2KHz, which satisfies the f_L requirement shown in Table 1. This design choice also avoids stronger energy degradations. Using the undersampling process, the spectrum of the original audio samples is essentially mapped from 19KHz-21KHz to a much lower spectrum from 0.58KHz-2.58KHz with a central frequency at 1.58KHz. However, since the new sampling rate is much lower than the Nyquist rate, aliasing arises in the original sampled audio signals. This makes the audio tone buried under ambient noises and makes frequency shift detection impossible.

Table 1: Candidate combinations of undersampling parameters. "$\star$" is finally chosen.

F_s (KHz)	n	$F_s^\star = F_s/n$ (KHz)	Supported f_L (KHz)
44.1	5	8.8	(17.7, 20.0)
44.1	6	7.3	(18.4, 20.0)
44.1	7	6.3	(18.9, 20.0) $\star$
44.1	8	5.5	(19.3, 20.0)
48	4	12	(18.0, 22.0)
48	5	9.6	(19.2, 22.0)
48	6	8	(20.0, 22.0)
48	7	6.9	(20.6, 22.0)

To solve this problem, we designed and implemented an audio signal processing pipeline, as shown in Figure 3, to recover the frequency shifts. First, each mobile device receives and samples audio data at the default 44.1KHz rate. As will be discussed in Section 5.1, our experimental results show that the peak velocities of pointing gestures only lasts tens of milliseconds, we split consecutive audio samples into 10ms analysis windows, with a 75% overlapping ratio, achieving a high time-domain resolution. Then, a 10-order Butterworth

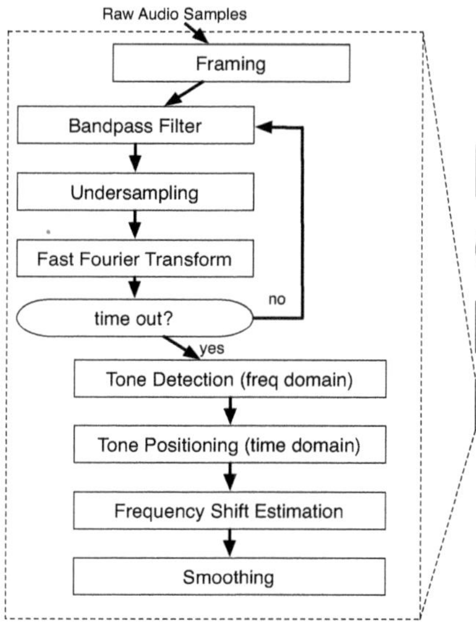

Figure 3: Signal processing pipeline.

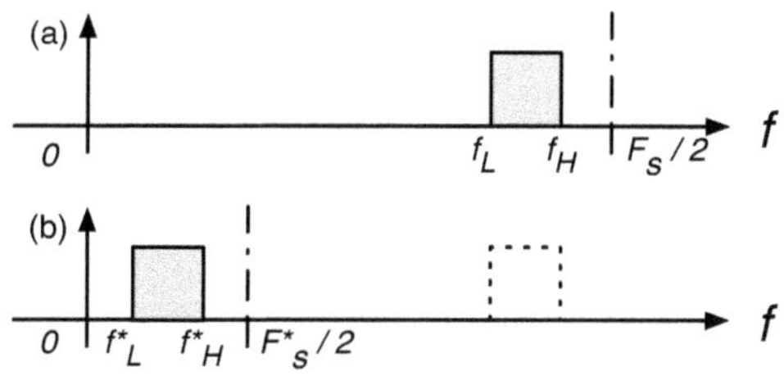

Figure 4: Illustration of the effect of undersampling to the spectrums. (a) The originally received audio tone is located from f_L to f_H. (b) After undersampling the audio samples, the tone is shifted to lower frequencies.

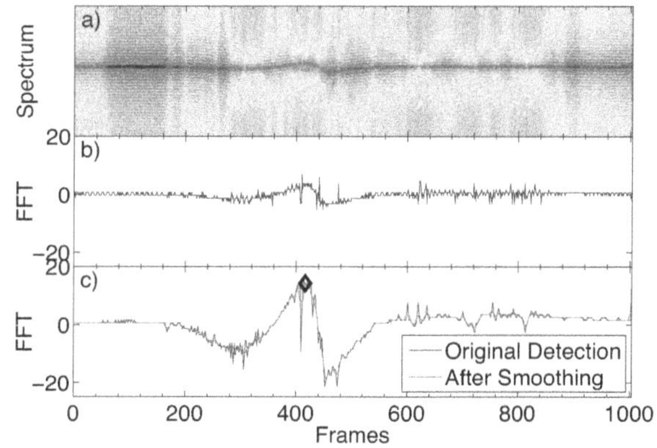

Figure 5: Effect of the undersampling analysis. (a) Spectrogram of the original audio. (b) Frequency shift detection using the traditional FFT approach. (c) Frequency shift detection using the proposed undersampling technique. The detected peak frequency shift is marked as "◇".

bandpass filter is used to attenuate out-of-band signals lower than 19KHz or above 21KHz. Then, the filtered audio samples go through the undersampling filter, which uses the new sampling rate F_s^*. With $n = 7$, this filter essentially keeps every 7th sample and deletes other samples. Note that although this process reduces the number of samples being analyzed, it still preserves the necessary frequency-domain information due to undersampling. The entire bandpass-filtering and undersampling operations process audio samples as a streamline, with a total time complexity of only $O(N)$ time, which is efficient for responsive interactions.

To estimate frequency shifts, each undersampled audio frame is processed using a 2048-point FFT transform, and FFT transforms of multiple consecutive audio frames are processed altogether to find the frequency shift. Specifically, an energy-based tone detector first compares energy of the spectrum of each frame from 1.08KHz to 2.08KHz (i.e. corresponds to 19.5KHz to 20.5KHz of the original spectrum before undersampling) to that of the entire 0Hz to 3.15KHz (i.e. $F_s^*/2$) spectrum. If the former energy is M times greater than the latter energy, this audio frame is set to "1", otherwise "0". Second, a tone positioning operator determines the frequency bin with the highest energy for each frame that have been set to "1", and links these frequency bins through a moving-average smoothing operation. This operation eliminates intermittent high frequency spikes caused by acoustic noises, such as clangs of metals.

Finally, the peak frequency shift is determined by finding the maximum frequency shift among all the frequency bins. During our experiments, we found that $M = 1.5$ led to robust performance in various indoor environments. The effect of this process is shown on Figure 5. Note that, by using the undersampling technique, the amount of frequency shifts has been significantly increased as compared to the traditional FFT approach.

After each device detects the Doppler frequency shifts, all the devices that detect a positive shift value report their frequency shift to the sender device, along with the device's ID information. The sender device then compares all the received Doppler shifts and determines the target device.

We would like to note that, when Spartacus is used in a crowded indoor scenarios, such as an airport, where numerous devices might be interacting with each other, contentions may occur. However, due to the intrinsic rapid energy degradation of audio signals, as will also be shown in Section 4.2, different interaction sessions can be automatically separated if they are spatially far away from each other (i.e. more than 5m). If many interactions take place in close proximity, a coordination mechanism could be used to create a contention window that conditionally accepts the reports of the Doppler shifts, so that different interaction sessions can be separated in the time domain. Previous research provides various contention-control schemes, however, this is out the scope of the current work.

3.2.2 Angular Gain through Pointing Gestures

Spartacus uses the bandpass signal processing pipeline to estimate frequency shifts in audio tones. However, due to geometric constrains, the condition of whether a nearby device would be selected as the target device is determined by the angular resolution α_{res} of the system. As indicated in Section 3.1, when the number of FFT points is 2048, the smallest angular resolution is 10° when the undersampling factor n is equal to 7. However, during our tests in practice, we found that when candidate devices are close to the user (i.e. within 3m), the device selection accuracy is better than the analysis. This improvement is caused by

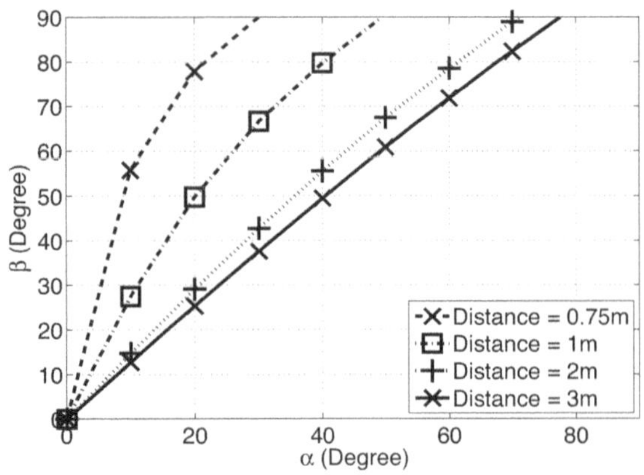

Figure 6: Angular gains caused by the stretch of user arms during the pointing gestures. These gains improve the device selection accuracy of Spartacus.

the increased directional difference, as illustrated in Figure 2. During a pointing gesture, since the user stretches her arm toward the target device D_A, the phone displacement makes the effective directional difference α increase. This angular change is significant when the candidate devices D_A and D_B are close to D_0. As shown in Figure 6, when D_A and D_B are 0.75m away and $\alpha = 10°$, the two devices are supposed to be barely differentiable. However, assuming the user's arm is 60cm, the effective angular difference β is increased to 55°, which makes the two devices much easier to be differentiated. Clearly, this angular gain diminishes when the distance between D_0 to the two devices increases, as well as when the user does not fully stretch her arm during the pointing gestures.

3.3 Energy-efficient Interaction Triggering

Spartacus seeks to enable spatially-aware interaction between an initiating device and receiving devices in its neighborhood. This requires that the receiving devices are *listening* to gesture broadcasted by the initiator. However, such continuous listening for gestures consumes a significant amount of energy and is a challenge to realize on energy-limited mobile devices. Therefore, in Spartacus we leverage a low-power audio listening protocol to save energy. This section describes the design details of this protocol.

3.3.1 Low-Power Audio Listening

The audio based low-power listening protocol has the following advantages:

1. Ubiquitous Hardware Support – Microphones and speakers are ubiquitous on most devices such as mobile phones, laptops, smart-TV sets, etc. No extra hardware modifications are need to implement this protocol. In addition, the cost of commodity audio hardware is very low.

2. Limited Range – The objective of this protocol is to initiate interaction strictly with devices in close proximity to the sender, typically line of sight and single space scenarios. Audio has a limited range and attenuates considerable when passing through walls. This makes the medium better suited for detecting neighboring devices within the same space, unlike radio based discovery such as WiFi and Bluetooth. This advantage also helps the Spartacus system to automatically separate concurrent interaction sessions that are spatially apart.

3. Energy Efficient – The continuous periodic listening and beaconing protocol using audio is orders of magnitude more energy efficient than discovery schemes using WiFi or Bluetooth, partly because these communication protocols are not designed for continuous discovery. Moreover, fine grained control or modification of WiFi and Bluetooth device discovery schemes is not possible on consumer hardware devices.

The audio based protocol has two major modes:

1. Periodic Listening – All devices periodically wake up (every T_{rx}) and record sound for a duration d_{rx}. The time d_{rx} is the amount of audio required to detect if a specific beacon tone frequency is being broadcasted by an initiating node.

2. Beaconing – Whenever a sender node wishes to broadcast a gesture, it first emits a beacon tone for a duration d_{tx}. This guarantees that all the receiving devices in range will receive the beacon and switch to continuous listening mode to record the gesture.

The theory of low-power listening states that, to guarantee every beacon will be successfully detected by nearby devices, the beacon duration d_{tx} must be at least as large as T_{rx} [16]. This relationship indicates that, the shorter the duration of the beacons, i.e. T_{rx}, the shorter the user needs to wait before starting the gesture, thus the more natural the gesture can be accomplished. However, a short beacon duration requires increasing the duty cycles of the interaction listening on the receivers, which consequently consumes more energy. We will evaluate the tradeoff between energy consumption vs. duty cycles in Section 5.5.

To identify the sender, Spartacus encodes the device ID using the Reed-Solomon coding, and sends the ID in a transmission immediately succeeding the beacon transmission. In the current implementation of Spartacus, the device ID is modulated using a 16 Frequency Shift-Keying (FSK) scheme with a central frequency at 19KHz. Keys are separated in the frequency domain using a 50Hz guard band. Note that, since the central frequency of the tone emitted during the pointing gesture is 20KHz, the transmission of the device ID is at least 200Hz lower than the gesture tone, thus will not cause ambiguities.

3.3.2 Dealing with Wakeup Jitter

The low-power listening protocol relies on the assumption that the duration of the beacon (d_{tx}) transmitted by the gesture transmitter is greater than the maximum interval (T_{rx}) between adjacent listening events on the receiving devices. However, since mobile platforms, such as Android, are not real-time operating systems, wakeup jitters can be observed between when an API starts recording sound and when the system actually begins recording. We empirically measure the latency of an API call on Galaxy Nexus Android phones. As shown in Figure 7, the average jitter in the wakeup timer is about 70ms, with a standard deviation of 15ms. This result indicates that, using the original beacon duration will cause the receiving devices to miss interaction triggers, which leads to a failure of capturing the upcoming gesture tone. To solve this problem, as shown in Figure 8, we include an additional guard band in the beacon length based on empirical measurements to account for the wakeup jitters.

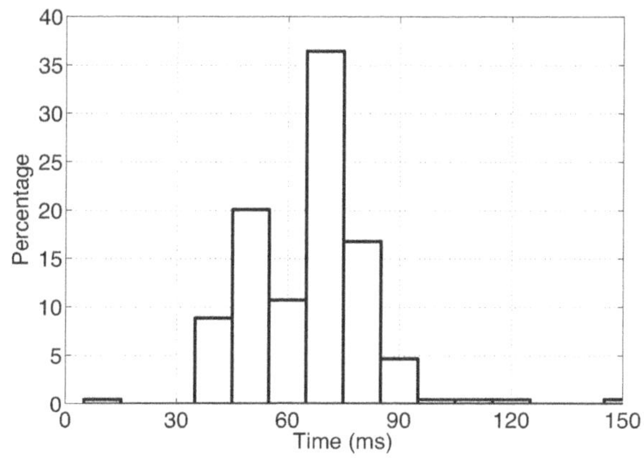

Figure 7: Distribution of wakeup jitters.

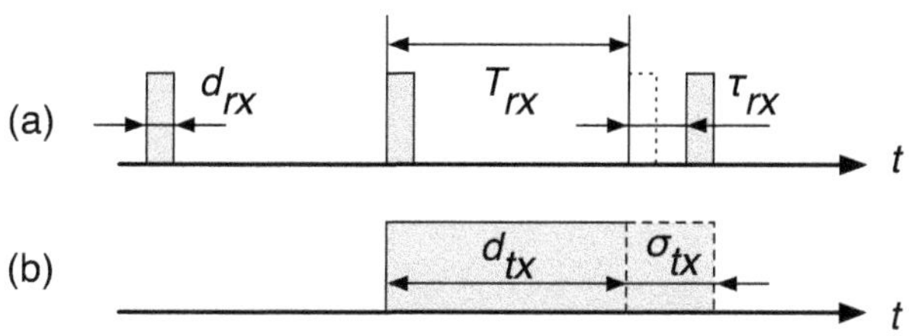

Figure 8: The graph shows the relationship between the wakeup period T_{rx} and the wakeup duration d_{rx} of the gesture receivers, and the beacon duration d_{tx} of the gesture transmitter. Note that, due to the existence of the wakeup jitter τ_{rx}, an additional guard band σ_{tx} is used in the beacons.

4. IMPLEMENTATION

To evaluate the interaction system, we implemented the Spartacus system on the Android platform, and tested it on various phones, including Galaxy Tab, Nexus 7, Galaxy Nexus, and HTC One S. This section discuss the implementation details of Spartacus.

4.1 Software Implementation

To evaluate the interaction system, we implemented the Spartacus system on the Android platform, and tested it on various phones, including Galaxy Tab, Nexus 7, Galaxy Nexus, and HTC One S. The current Spartacus has a client end and a server end. The client end runs as an Android app, which has 4 components: `GestureSensing`, `LowPowerListening`, `AudioModem`, and the GUI. The design of Spartacus strictly follows the Object-Oriented programming paradigm, such that each component is standalone, and can be easily incorporated into any existing apps as an add-on interaction support. For example, if an app needs to conduct the low-power audio listening, it simply calls the `LPL.start()` to start the listening thread, and a message handler is used to receive notifications in case an interaction request is detected. Similarly, for issuing gestures, an app could simply call `GestureSensing.makeGesture()`, then an audio tone at a predefined frequency will be generated during the gesture; on the receiver's end, a counterpart `GestureSensing.analyzeGesture()` will trigger a background thread that runs the signal processing pipeline described in Section 3.2 to compute the frequency shifts. The entire Spartacus project contains a total of 3500+ lines of Java code, including both the server and the client.

4.2 Hardware Limitations on Mobile Devices

To generate and receive audio tones emitted during the course of the gestures, Spartacus leverages the built-in speakers and microphones on mobile devices, and use software-implemented digital signal processing algorithms to detect the gestures. In our implementation process, we conducted experiments to understand the limitations of modern mobile devices in emitting high frequency audio tones.

Previous research has found that microphones on commodity mobile phones supports sampling rates up to 48KHz, which enables the use of tone frequencies as high as 24KHz [4, 7, 8]. In Spartacus, we use tone frequencies higher than 20KHz, which is inaudible [8]. However, a downside of using high frequency tones is the potential stronger energy degradation of sound. To investigate this effect on mobile devices, we model the transmission of audio tones as three consecutive processes, as shown in Figure 9. Similar to a RF communication system, the degradation of signal energy occurs inside of the speakers and the microphones, as well as during the transmission in the acoustic channel. We investigate each of these processes.

First, to quantize the energy degradation of sound, we benchmarked the frequency responses of speakers and microphones on various mobile devices. A Sennheiser MKE 2P microphone and a Yamaha NX-U10 speaker are used as references. As shown in Figure 10(a) and 10(b), we observe that, due to the characteristics of the hardware, a significant energy degradation exists for audio tones higher than 15KHz. This phenomenon is not surprising considering that the hardware of mobile phones are designed intentionally for human conversations and music, which feature dominant energies generally lower than 15KHz. We also found that, as tone frequencies go up, the degradation becomes even larger. To be specific, as the tone frequency increases every 1KHz, the degradation of sound energies increases 5dB on speakers, and 3.3dB on microphones, respectively. Second, we investigate the degradation of sound energy caused by the transmission through acoustic channels. As shown in Figure 10(c), we observe that there is an average 3.2dB/m energy decrease of sound from 1m to 6m, irrespective of the tone frequency.

In summary, we found that the energy degradation of sound is collaboratively caused by the frequency responses of the speakers, the microphones, and the transmission through acoustic channels. For interactions in close proximity, the degradation largely comes from the frequency responses of the hardware. These results indicate that, to reduce energy degradation and increase interaction range, audio tones with lower frequencies should be leveraged.

5. EVALUATION

In this section, we evaluate the performance of Spartacus given different interaction scenarios. Spartacus leverages the pointing gestures of users to accurately select the target device, without user configuration. To understand the boundary of system performance, we first conduct experiments to investigate trajectory and velocity variances of the pointing gestures of average users. Then we provide performance analysis of Spartacus, by discussing the device selection accuracy and the interaction range. Finally we discuss the

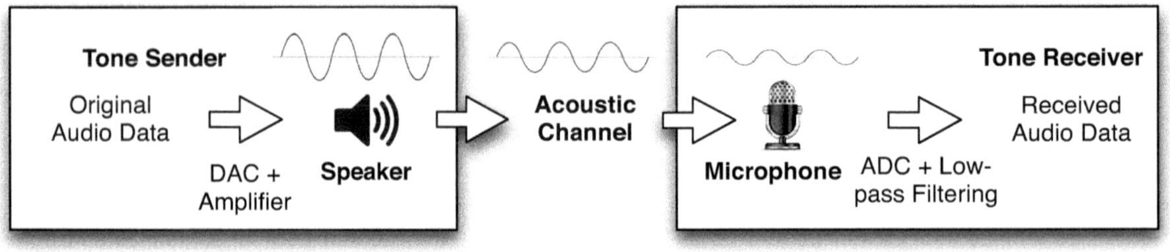

Figure 9: Audio tone transmission between mobile devices.

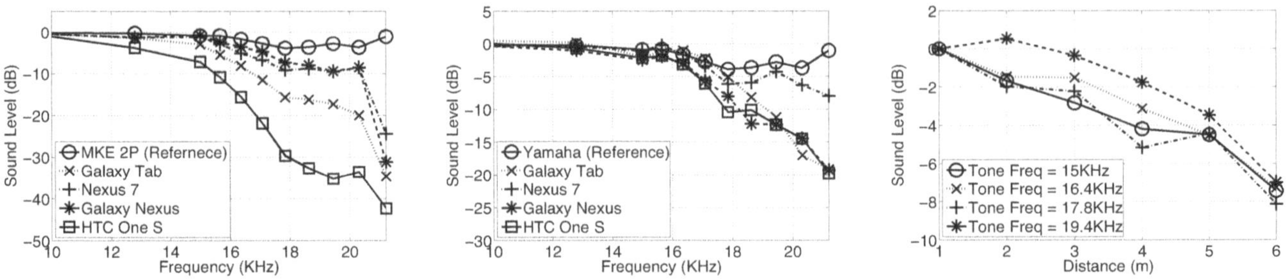

(a) (b) (c)

Figure 10: A graph showing frequency responses of various mobile devices (1/16 octave band-filtered from 15KHz). (a) Frequency responses of speakers as a function of the tone frequency. (b) Frequency responses of microphones as a function of the tone frequency. (c) Attenuation of sound energy vs. distance.

interaction latency, and present the power consumption of Spartacus as compared to other state-of-the-art techniques.

5.1 Evaluation of Pointing Gestures

To accurately select the target device, Spartacus makes an assumption that when a user points her phone towards the target device, the target device will always observe the largest Doppler frequency shift. However, in practice, user gestures can be significantly diverse in terms of directional precision, velocity, and trajectory. Such diversities make accurately estimating the peak frequency shift significantly challenging.

In order to investigate what factors may affect the performance of Spartacus, we conducted experiments to fully understand the characteristics of pointing gestures of average users. Some fundamental questions that we would want to investigate include:

1. *How diversely do users point their phones, and how fast can a user point?*
2. *If the user points fast enough, how often does the target device observe the highest frequency shift, thus the highest velocity, of the gesture?*
3. *If we want to estimate the frequency shifts, how much frequency- and time-domain resolution do we need to successfully capture the peak frequency shift inside of a gesture?*

To answer these questions, we conducted experiments with 12 participants (6 females) and investigated their pointing gestures. To capture the gesture trajectories, we attached a video recorder on the ceiling right above the participants, and videotaped the entire experiment. The video we took recorded complete 2D trajectories of the gestures. Before doing the experiment, we briefed the participants on the idea of Spartacus, and let them to freely choose any *natural* gestures they wanted. During the experiment, each participant performed 10 gestures towards a target device 2m away from them, using a Galaxy Nexus phone. A red marker was attached to the participants' hands for motion-tracking. After the experiment, we detected hand trajectories of the participants using image processing techniques. Then, we estimated the velocities of the gestures given the frame rate of the video. We summarize our findings as below:

Finding 1: As shown in Table 2, three types of gesture trajectories were seen during the experiments. Among the three gesture types, a majority of the participants (10 out of 12) predominantly utilized a vertically downward pointing movement. To further analyze the Doppler frequency shifts, we plotted the spectrogram of each gesture and correlated the spectrogram with the recorded video. As shown in Figure 11(a) and 11(b), we found that the arm trajectory variance of the participants who performed this gesture was limited – in most cases, the velocity of users' arms increased during the process of stretching out the users' arms (i.e. Frame #30), and the peak velocities predominantly occurred close to the end of this process (i.e. Frame #31). Then the arm reached a full stretch, and the velocity diminished quickly. We found most of the participants fully stretched out their arms in the experiments, which translates to a 55cm to 75cm phone displacement and angular gains, as discussed in Section 3.2.2. We will show how this factor affects the performance of Spartacus in Section 5.3.1. Since gesture trajectories can be easily differentiated using built-in inertial sensors of the mobile devices, as a proof of concept, we focus on evaluating this vertically downward gesture trajectory in the current design of Spartacus.

Finding 2: To investigate how often the target device

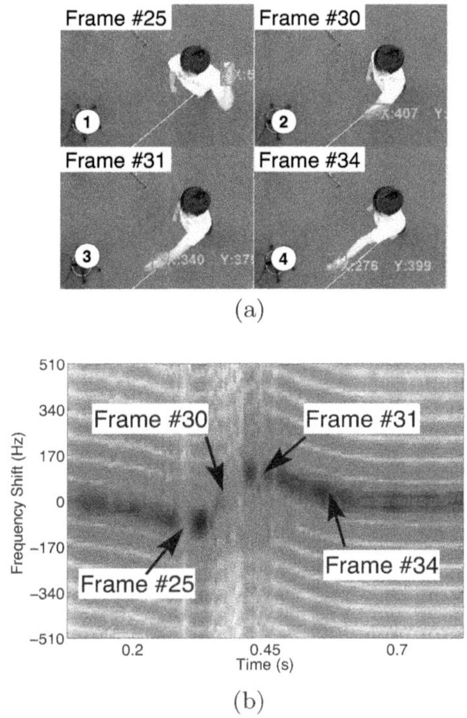

Figure 11: The graphs show (a) a vertically downward pointing gesture performed by one student and (b) the corresponding Doppler frequency shifts of each frame. The yellow line indicates the direction of the target devices.

Table 2: Trajectory variations of gestures

Gesture Type	Total Count (Male/Female)
Vertically downward	10 (6/4)
Vertically upward	1 (0/1)
Horizontally outward	1 (0/1)

could successfully observe the maximum velocity of the gestures, we computed directions of the highest 70% velocities of the gestures, and calculated the angular deviation from the direction towards the target device. As shown in Figure 12(b), we found that in most cases, the highest velocities were predominantly facing towards the target device, with an average $\pm 7.5^\circ$ angular bias. When interacting with a device 3 meters away, this bias translates to 0.38m. This result indicates that participants are able to precisely point the phones towards the target device, and selecting the target device using the maximum velocity is appropriate.

Finding 3: The peak velocity of the gestures of all participants was 3.4m/s on average, as shown in Figure 12(a). This is similar to results reported in related work [4]. Using an audio tone at 20KHz and assuming the speed of sound is 343m/s, this translates to a maximum Doppler frequency shift of 200Hz. Moreover, we found that the peak velocity is transient. As shown in Figure 12(c), most of the gestures lasted less than one second, and the peak velocities appeared and diminished within 25ms. These findings indicate that to accurately estimate the peak velocity, Spartacus needs a high time-domain resolution to position the peak frequency shifts, as well as a high frequency-domain resolution to estimate the quantity of the shift.

After understanding the variances of the pointing gestures, we evaluate the performance of Spartacus under different indoor scenarios.

5.2 Experimental Setup

The first set of experiments was done in a student lounge in our university, in which multiple ambient noise conditions were tested. The other two sets of experiments were done in a student cubicle area and along a hallway. During each experiment, a target device was placed in front of a student with distance d; another device was placed at α° apart from the direction of the target device, with the same distance. For each test, a student pointed a Galaxy Nexus phone 25 times towards the target device, with a peak velocity of about 3m/s. To guarantee each individual gesture was not made too fast or too slow, after the experiments, we manually investigated the duration of each gesture, and selected 20 from the 25 gestures that achieved the closest peak velocity for analysis. To compute the frequency shift, audio tones were captured at the two candidate devices at 44.1KHz, undersampled 7 times to 6.3KHz, and then processed using the signal processing pipeline discussed in Section 3.2. A 2048-point FFT was applied for each 10ms analysis window, with a 75% overlapping ratio. These parameters were used throughout the entire evaluation process.

5.3 Device Selection Accuracy

5.3.1 *Performance with Distances and Angles*

Spartacus selects the target device by comparing the detected peak velocity of user gestures among nearby devices. As shown in Figure 15, as the distances between devices increase, the device selection accuracy drops gradually. This is consistent with our analysis of sound energy degradation. As described in Section 3.2, Since Spartacus leverages an energy comparison method for tone detections, the energy difference between tones and other frequency bands decreases as the distances increase. Moreover, due to the performance gain caused by the stretch of arms, for all tested device directions, Spartacus achieved 90% accuracy within 4 meters, and 80% within 5 meters.

To evaluate how directional changes affect the performance, we keep the devices at fixed distances, and change α. As shown in Figure 14, as α decreases, the accuracy of device selection drops. For interactions within 3 meters, the device selection accuracies are above 90% when devices are at least 30° apart. When the devices are at least 45° apart, the accuracies are above 90% within 5 meters.

It is worthing noting that, although the theoretical angular resolution of Spartacus is 10°, we still achieved high device selection accuracy (i.e. above 90%) when the directional difference between devices are lower than 20° and the interaction range is within 1 meters. This is because when the interaction range is short, the angular gain due to the stretch of arms is significant. These evaluation results show that the performance of Spartacus is robust against directional and distance changes for interactions in close proximity. However, as distances keep increasing (i.e. above 5 meters), the performance drops gradually due to the decrease of sound energy and the resultant difficulty in detecting the audio tones. This observation justifies the close-range interaction scenarios of Spartacus, where various ubiquitous applications take place.

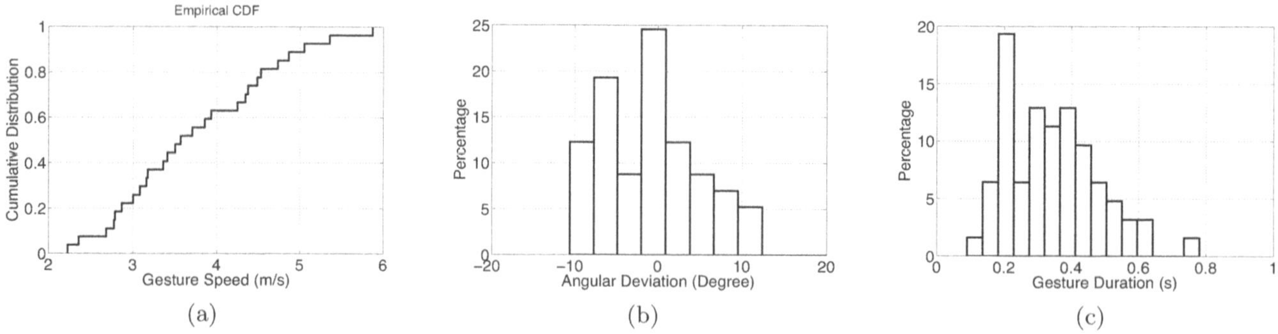

Figure 12: Characteristics of pointing gestures. (a) Speed distribution. (b) Directional precision. (c) Duration variance.

Figure 13: The three different indoor scenarios where we conducted experiments.

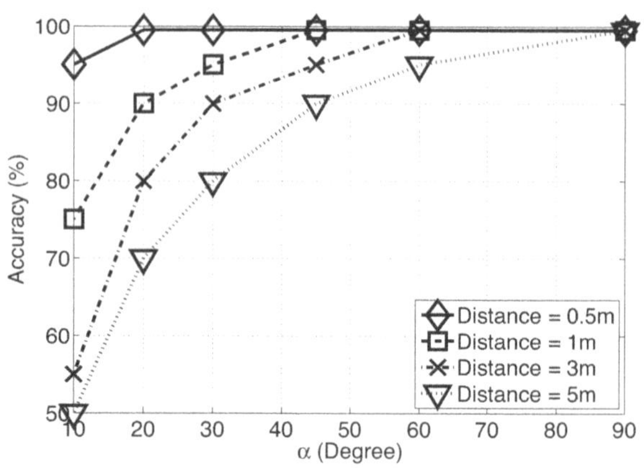

Figure 14: Performance of device selection when device directions change.

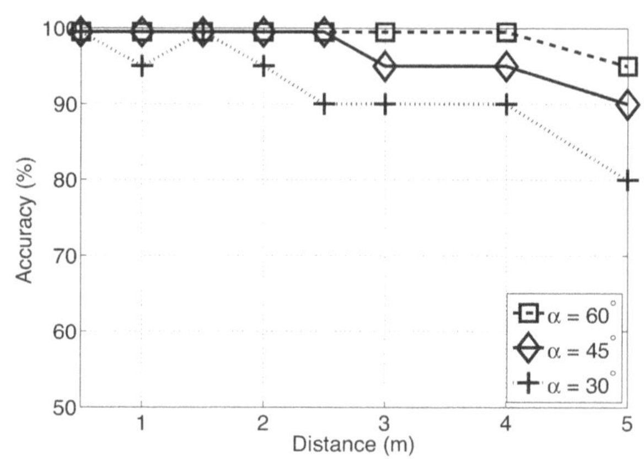

Figure 15: Performance of device selection when device distances change.

5.3.2 *Performance Under Noisy Conditions*

To evaluate the performance of Spartacus against different noise backgrounds, we conducted experiments in the student lounge at different times. The first experiment was done when a couple of students were having a group discussion in the lounge, resulting human conversations in the background. Previous research has shown that the sound of clanging metals would generate high frequency noise [8]. To evaluate this effect, we purposely played a piece of rock music (i.e. "Burn It Down" of Linkin Park) in the background, which features rich clangs of metal instruments. In both experiments, we changed the distance from 1m to 2m. The experimental results of the lounge are used as a comparison. As shown in Figure 17, the experimental results show that under 1m distance, the performance for all three cases for all tested directions are constant, with higher than 95% accuracy. When the distance is increased to 2m, except the 30° case under human conversations, all the three cases achieved above 90% accuracy. Audio spectrum indicates that, as shown in Figure 16, metal clangs can hardly reach frequencies above 18KHz, which has limited effect to Spartacus. These experimental results indicate that the performance of Spartacus is robust against common indoor noises.

5.3.3 *Performance with Different Scenario*

To evaluate the performance under different indoor scenarios, we conducted experiments in cubicle areas and a hallway, as shown in Figure 13. Due to limited space in these scenarios, we only tested performance up to 1.5m with 30°. Figure 18 shows the results. For the distance of 0.5m, all three cases had 100% device selection accuracies. As the distance increases, the performance of the cubicle area and the hallway is seen to have slight decreases. This is primarily

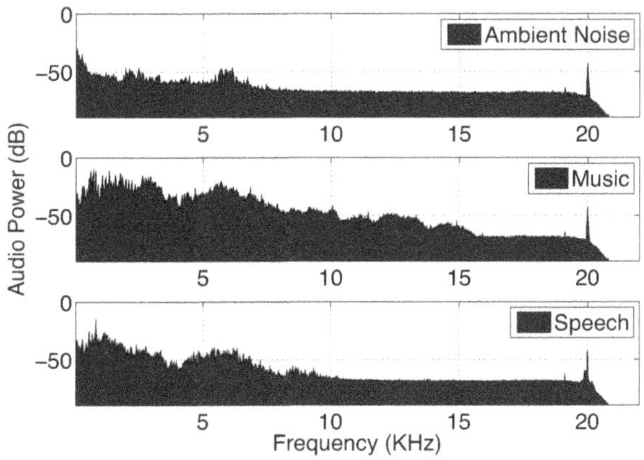

Figure 16: Spectrums of the three noise cases measured at 1m. Note that, in all cases, the audio tone at 20KHz (i.e. the spikes on the spectrums) for the pointing gestures is easily detectable.

due to the stronger multi-path effects in the two scenarios as compared to the student lounge. However, in all three cases, Spartacus has achieved higher than 85% accuracy.

5.4 Interaction Latency

Using the undersampling technique, Spartacus reduces the number of audio samples that need to process, without decreasing the time-domain resolution. As discussed in Section 3.1, if undersampling technique was not used, Spartacus would have to increase the number of FFT points to achieve the equivalent angular resolution, which as a consequence, involves longer processing time. To evaluate this performance, we tested the processing latency of Spartacus using different FFT points. As shown in Figure 19, Spartacus leverages a 2014-point FFT processing, which takes 1.5s to process a 1-second gesture audio. To achieve the same angular resolution, a traditional FFT approach would have to use at least an 8192-point FFT processing, which takes 8.7s! Such a processing latency is impractical for any responsive interactions, such as mobile gaming. These results justify the use of undersampling in Spartacus.

5.5 Power Consumption

Spartacus leverages a low-power audio listening technique to automatically sense the potential interaction requests from nearby devices, so as to eliminate any user involvement. In this section, we evaluate the performance of Spartacus in terms of power consumption in low-power listening. To compare the performance under different duty cycles, we fixed the duration of each listening session to 200ms, and changed the periods. To eliminate hardware variations, all the experiments were done on the Galaxy Nexus mobile phones. In the experiment, the screens and the CPUs of the mobile phones were completed shut off, and the power consumption was measured using an oscilloscope. For each test, we measured the power consumption by running Spartacus's low-power listening task for 5min, and we compute the mean and the standard deviation of the collected data.

The experimental results are shown in Figure 20. As a baseline, we first measure the power consumption of the devices being idle, i.e. turning off the screen and shutting down all the application processes. This yields the baseline power consumption at 75mW. Then we evaluate the performance of Spartacus. When the duty cycle is 5% (i.e. the period equals 4s), Spartacus consumes 120mW power. As the duty cycle increases, the power consumption goes up gradually. At the maximum 25% duty cycle, Spartacus consumes 250mW. As a comparison, we tested the state-of-the-art peer-to-peer scanning techniques, and found that WiFi Direct consumes 460mW of power, and Bluetooth 4.0 consumes 670mW. These results indicate that on average, Spartacus achieves about 4X lower energy consumption than WiFi Direct and 5.5X lower than the latest Bluetooth 4.0 protocols, respectively.

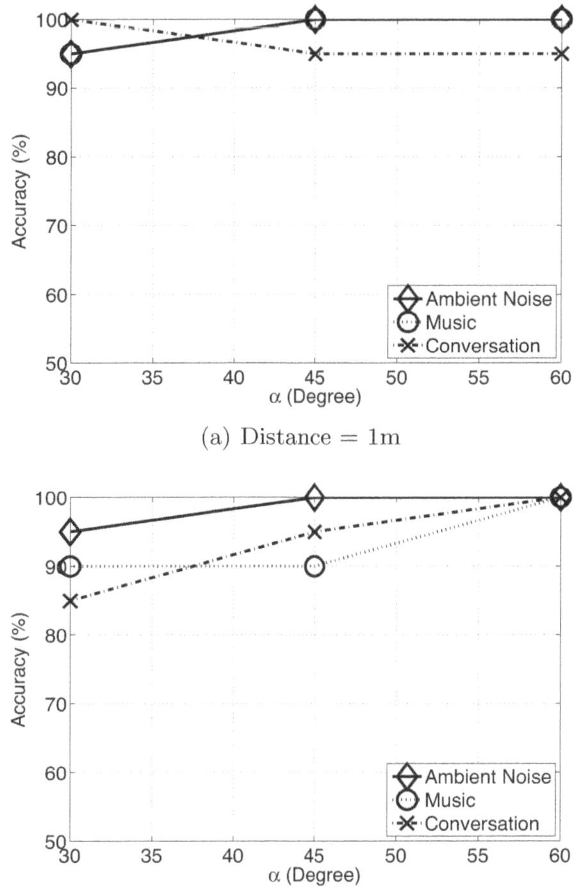

(a) Distance = 1m

(b) Distance = 2m

Figure 17: Performance of device selection with various background noise conditions.

6. RELATED WORK

Spartacus leverage built-in microphones and speakers on commodity mobile devices for both active device interaction and passive listening for potential interaction requests. In this section, we compare Spartacus with previous work that leverage audio signals in two main categories: mobile sensing and device interaction.

6.1 Audio Processing in Mobile Sensing

Microphones have been widely used in mobile sensing applications to capture audio data. For example, Miluzzo et al. has used human conversation snippets for analyzing

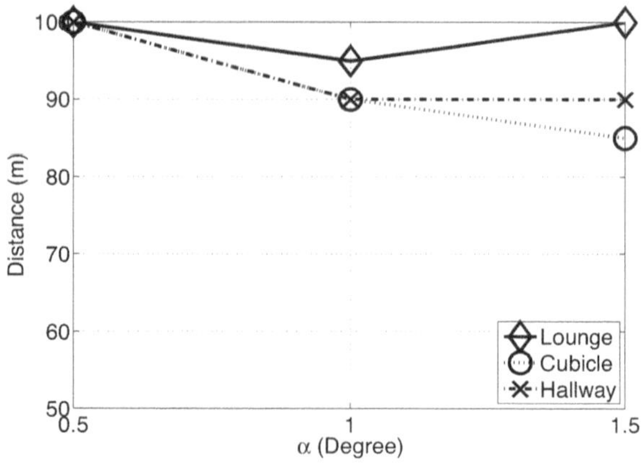

Figure 18: Performance of device selection in different indoor scenarios. α is fixed at 30°.

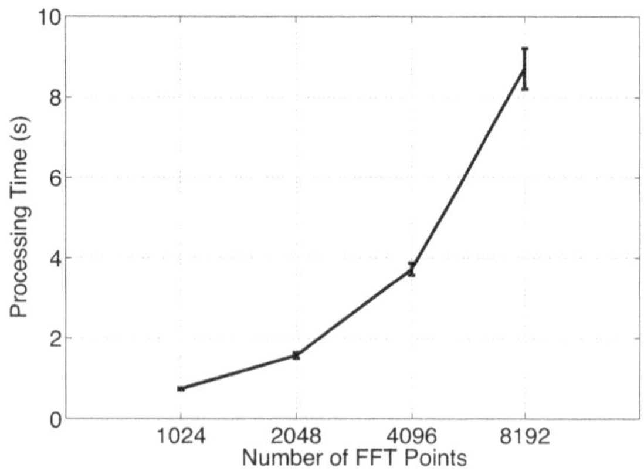

Figure 19: The processing time of a 1-second audio recording using different number of FFT points.

social activities [12]. SurroundSense also utilized audio data, combined with data from other sensing modalities, such as accelerometers, cameras, and magnetometers to detect locations of users for social context inferences [1]. Similarly, Lu et al. has provided a tailored signal processing pipeline for audio sensing and learning, such that unknown social events can be automatically identified and easily labeled [9]. These early projects have largely focused on the knowledge discovery tasks of using audio data, while assuming a fixed or default audio sensing mechanism.

For energy-efficient continuous audio sensing, some more recent work has been published. JigSaw and Darwin Phones focused on enabling energy-efficient continuous sensing and collaborative learning techniques [10, 11]. MoVi presented an approach of using collaboratively sensed audio data from multiple participants to create integrated social event records [2]. SwordFight provide a continuous and accurate distance ranging technique using time difference of sound arrivals [22].

All the previous work mentioned above leveraged microphones in a continuous manner. Spartacus differs from them by proposing a low-power audio listening technique for passive interaction sensing. Since interaction requests from nearby devices can happen spontaneously, it requires Spartacus to coordinate the tradeoff between detection latency and

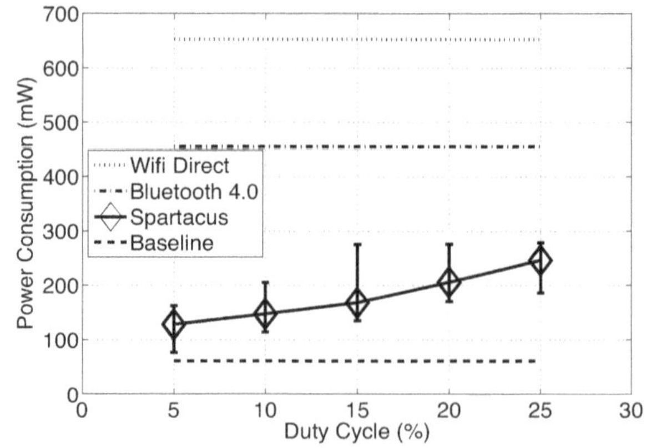

Figure 20: Power consumption of Spartacus under different duty cycle settings. As references, power consumptions of scanning of Bluetooth 4.0 and WiFi Direct are also shown.

energy efficiency. Other papers have also presented systems using audio tones [7] for indoor counting or localization [8]. Differing from them, Spartacus leverages tones at high frequency to generate Doppler effect for device interaction.

6.2 Spatially-Aware Device Interactions

Interactions through mobile devices generally require two pieces of functionalities, i.e. device selection and interaction detection. For selecting devices, previous work has shown that touching, scanning, and pointing are the most common interactions when performing user-mediated object selection and indirect remote controls [17]. Point & Connect (P&C) proposed an interaction technique based on time difference of sound arrivals. Both Spartacus and P&C can be used for device interactions in close proximity. However, the two systems differ significantly in several aspects. First, P&C requires users to manually set up a dedicated broadcast WiFi channel or start discoverable mode of their Bluetooth. Enabling P&C may prevent the users from using their default WiFi networks. In contrast, Spartacus runs in the mobile devices as a system service, and the periodic interaction detection mechanism automatically detects potential interactions. Second, P&C was focused on providing the device selection solution, while making an assumption that the surrounding devices have already launched the related service and continuously waiting for interaction requests. In practice, this continuous audio listening would consume significant energy. Therefore, Spartacus uses the duty-cycled audio listening mechanism, and our evaluation results have shown this mechanism is energy-efficient, as compared to the traditional peer-to-peer communication techniques, such as WiFi Direct and Bluetooth 4.0.

SoundWave leverages the Doppler effect to sense user gestures for close-range (i.e. within 1m) single-device interactions [4]. As the Doppler effect is made by moving user arms in front of a laptop, and the laptop is both the transmitter and the receiver, the generated frequency shift is doubled. This significantly increases the detection accuracy of the frequency shifts and makes detection easier. In contrast, Spartacus selects the target device by comparing the peak frequency shifts between multiple devices, which requires higher frequency- and time-domain resolution. We solve these problems by proposing a bandpass signal processing pipeline to increase Doppler shift estimation accuracy.

To detect nearby devices and interaction requests, various techniques can be used. However, existing techniques either required extra infrastructure (i.e. laser tags and pointers [13]), or did not provide spatial accuracy sufficient for supporting device interactions (i.e. WiFi-based indoor localization [21]). Other work involved extra effort from users to initiate interactions (e.g. the simultaneous shaking required by the Bump app), or is not energy efficient (e.g. WiFi or Bluetooth techniques). PANDAA provided an automatic device locationing service using ambient sound generated in indoor environments, without requirements of extra infrastructures or extra manual effort, and has achieved centimeter-level locationing accuracy [18]. However, PANDAA only supports devices in stationary placements, thus if moving users are involved in interactions, other mechanisms would have to be used. More recent work in Polaris provided an indoor orientation determination technique that could support spatially-aware indoor device interactions [19]. However, since Polaris dealt with only absolute directional relationships of devices (i.e. relative to the earth's magnetic field), nearby devices can hardly be differentiated if their relative orientations change, such as in the interaction scenarios that involve moving users. In this paper, we describe the low-power audio listening technique used in Spartacus to detect nearby interaction requests, which periodically wakes up the CPU and microphones on mobile devices, and detects audio beacons emitted by nearby devices. We also present experimental results that show the low-power audio listening technique is much more energy-efficient than other state-of-the-art techniques, such as WiFi Direct or Bluetooth 4.0.

7. DISCUSSION

In the current stage, the Spartacus system focuses mainly on the signal processing techniques and prove the novel interaction concept through the use of the Doppler effect. This section addresses a number of related system issues and discusses their possible solutions.

7.1 Energy-Efficient Interaction Triggers

To support automatic interaction triggers without user involvement, Spartacus leverages energy-efficient audio sensing to automatically detect interaction intents from nearby devices. This makes the system more appropriate to be used on mobile devices with limited energy budgets. While the current system adopts the continuous low-power audio listening technique, we would note that, if the energy constraint is not a major concern in particular applications, the system could also be enabled on demand. Moreover, in addition to the proposed energy-efficient audio sensing technique, the system could also be triggered by other traditional communication schemes, such as Bluetooth or WiFi Direct.

When choosing between different interaction triggering mechanisms, there are a few design tradeoffs. On one hand, as we have pointed out in Section 5.5, the proposed low-power audio listening technique is more energy-efficient than the Bluetooth 4.0 and the WiFi Direct techniques. On the other hand, due to the intrinsic slow data rate of audio signals, the user has to wait for a couple of seconds for a "warmup beacon" before doing the gesture. As a comparison, this issue can be solved, given that the relatively faster wireless communication schemes could be used, such as the Bluetooth and the WiFi techniques.

7.2 Security Issues

Spartacus leverages the Doppler effect to support spatially-aware device interactions. This interaction may be vulnerable to security attacks. For example, when a user generates a pointing gesture, a malicious device standing close by could pretend to have detected higher Doppler shifts than other devices, so that it deceives the sender into thinking it was the receiver; similarly, the same trick could also be used to prevent other receivers from being connected with the sender. To avoid these issues, a secured connection mechanism could be used, so that only trusted and authenticated devices are allowed to report their Doppler shifts. Alternatively, knowledge from the users could also be used to reduce the possibility of malicious recipients. For example, after the user's device determines the potential receiver who has reported the maximal Doppler shifts, the name and identity of receiver's owner would be shown on the user's device. Then the user would be able to determine the correctness of the interaction recipient.

7.3 Contentions Among Interaction Sessions

When the Spartacus system is used in a crowded scenario, e.g. an airport, where many users would use the system concurrently, contentions could be an issue for device pairing techniques. However, since Spartacus leverages an audio sensing mechanism for close-range interactions, concurrent interactions can be automatically separated if they are far away from each other (i.e. beyond 5m), due to the fast degradation of sound energy. If the interactions do occur with close proximity, a contention coordination mechanism (e.g. a contention window that receives the Doppler shift measures) could also be leveraged to solve the problem.

8. CONCLUSION

This paper presents Spartacus, a spatially-aware interaction system that allows users of mobile devices to establish spontaneous interactions with high accuracy, low latency, and low energy consumption. Spartacus does not require extra hardware. Leveraging sensors ubiquitous in most commodity smartphones, Spartacus enables users to use intuitive pointing gestures to select target devices with zero prior configuration. We provide a comprehensive evaluation of the Spartacus system in various use conditions. Our experimental evaluations show that Spartacus performs significantly better than existing device interaction systems in terms of intuitiveness, accuracy, latency, and energy consumption. This new paradigm of mobile interactions will enable natural, fast, and seamless interactions in numerous emerging applications.

9. ACKNOWLEDGEMENT

This work was partially the results of the generous support from Intel Inc., and National Science Foundation grant number CNS-1135874. In addition, the authors would like to thank our shepherd Prof. Shyam Gollakota for providing valuable guidance during the process of finalizing the camera-ready version of the paper. Moreover, the authors would also like to thank Prof. Ian Lane of CMU for clarifying audio-related concepts and for lending us the reference microphones and speakers for doing the experiments.

10. REFERENCES

[1] M. Azizyan, I. Constandache, and R. Roy Choudhury. SurroundSense: mobile phone localization via ambience fingerprinting. In *Proceedings of the 15th annual international conference on Mobile computing and networking*, MobiCom '09, pages 261–272, New York, NY, USA, 2009. ACM.

[2] X. Bao and R. Roy Choudhury. MoVi: mobile phone based video highlights via collaborative sensing. In *Proceedings of the 8th international conference on Mobile systems, applications, and services*, MobiSys '10, pages 357–370, New York, NY, USA, 2010. ACM.

[3] M. T. Goodrich, M. Sirivianos, J. Solis, G. Tsudik, and E. Uzun. Loud and Clear: Human-Verifiable Authentication Based on Audio. In *Distributed Computing Systems, 2006. ICDCS 2006. 26th IEEE International Conference on*, page 10, 2006.

[4] S. Gupta, D. Morris, S. Patel, and D. Tan. SoundWave: using the doppler effect to sense gestures. In *Proceedings of the 2012 ACM annual conference on Human Factors in Computing Systems*, CHI '12, pages 1911–1914, New York, NY, USA, 2012. ACM.

[5] H. Harada and P. Ramjee. *Simulation and Software Radio for Mobile Communications*. Boston: Artech House, 2002.

[6] K. Hinckley. Synchronous gestures for multiple persons and computers. In *Proceedings of the 16th annual ACM symposium on User interface software and technology*, UIST '03, pages 149–158, New York, NY, USA, 2003. ACM.

[7] P. G. Kannan, S. Padmanabha, M. C. Chan, A. Ananda, and L.-S. Peh. Low Cost Crowd Counting using Audio Tones. In *The 10th ACM Conference on Embedded Networked Sensor Systems (SenSys 2012)*, pages 155–168, 2012.

[8] P. Lazik and A. Rowe. Indoor Pseudo-ranging of Mobile Devices using Ultrasonic Chirps. In *The 10th ACM Conference on Embedded Networked Sensor Systems (SenSys 2012)*, pages 99–112, 2012.

[9] H. Lu, W. Pan, N. D. Lane, T. Choudhury, and A. T. Campbell. SoundSense: scalable sound sensing for people-centric applications on mobile phones. In *Proceedings of the 7th international conference on Mobile systems, applications, and services*, MobiSys '09, pages 165–178, New York, NY, USA, 2009. ACM.

[10] H. Lu, J. Yang, Z. Liu, N. D. Lane, T. Choudhury, and A. T. Campbell. The Jigsaw continuous sensing engine for mobile phone applications. In *Proceedings of the 8th ACM Conference on Embedded Networked Sensor Systems*, SenSys '10, pages 71–84, New York, NY, USA, 2010. ACM.

[11] E. Miluzzo, C. T. Cornelius, A. Ramaswamy, T. Choudhury, Z. Liu, and A. T. Campbell. Darwin phones: the evolution of sensing and inference on mobile phones. In *Proceedings of the 8th international conference on Mobile systems, applications, and services*, MobiSys '10, pages 5–20, New York, NY, USA, 2010. ACM.

[12] E. Miluzzo, N. D. Lane, K. Fodor, R. Peterson, H. Lu, M. Musolesi, S. B. Eisenman, X. Zheng, and A. T. Campbell. Sensing meets mobile social networks: the design, implementation and evaluation of the CenceMe application. In *Proceedings of the 6th ACM conference on Embedded network sensor systems*, SenSys '08, pages 337–350, New York, NY, USA, 2008. ACM.

[13] B. A. Myers, R. Bhatnagar, J. Nichols, C. H. Peck, D. Kong, R. Miller, and A. C. Long. Interacting at a distance: measuring the performance of laser pointers and other devices. In *Proceedings of the SIGCHI Conference on Human Factors in Computing Systems*, CHI '02, pages 33–40, New York, NY, USA, 2002. ACM.

[14] A. V. Oppenheim and R. W. Schafer. *Digital Signal Processing*. Prentice Hall.

[15] C. Peng, G. Shen, Y. Zhang, and S. Lu. Point & Connect: intention-based device pairing for mobile phone users. In *Proceedings of the 7th international conference on Mobile systems, applications, and services*, MobiSys '09, pages 137–150, New York, NY, USA, 2009. ACM.

[16] A. Purohit, B. Priyantha, and J. Liu. WiFlock: Collaborative group discovery and maintenance in mobile sensor networks. In *Information Processing in Sensor Networks (IPSN), 2011 10th International Conference on*, pages 37–48, Apr. 2011.

[17] E. Rukzio, K. Leichtenstern, V. Callaghan, P. Holleis, A. Schmidt, and J. Chin. An experimental comparison of physical mobile interaction techniques: touching, pointing and scanning. In *Proceedings of the 8th international conference on Ubiquitous Computing*, UbiComp'06, pages 87–104, Berlin, Heidelberg, 2006. Springer-Verlag.

[18] Z. Sun, A. Purohit, K. Chen, S. Pan, T. Pering, and P. Zhang. PANDAA: physical arrangement detection of networked devices through ambient-sound awareness. In *Proceedings of the 13th international conference on Ubiquitous computing*, UbiComp '11, pages 425–434, New York, NY, USA, 2011. ACM.

[19] Z. Sun, A. Purohit, S. Pan, F. Mokaya, R. Bose, and P. Zhang. Polaris: getting accurate indoor orientations for mobile devices using ubiquitous visual patterns on ceilings. In *Proceedings of the Twelfth Workshop on Mobile Computing Systems & Applications*, HotMobile '12, pages 14:1—-14:6, New York, NY, USA, 2012. ACM.

[20] P. Vandewalle, L. Sbaiz, J. Vandewalle, and M. Vetterli. How to take advantage of aliasing in bandlimited signals. *IEEE Conference on Acous- tics, Speech and Signal Processing*, 3:948–951.

[21] H. Wang, S. Sen, A. Elgohary, M. Farid, M. Youssef, and R. R. Choudhury. No need to war-drive: unsupervised indoor localization. In *Proceedings of the 10th international conference on Mobile systems, applications, and services*, MobiSys '12, pages 197–210, New York, NY, USA, 2012. ACM.

[22] Z. Zhang, D. Chu, X. Chen, and T. Moscibroda. SwordFight: enabling a new class of phone-to-phone action games on commodity phones. In *Proceedings of the 10th international conference on Mobile systems, applications, and services*, MobiSys '12, pages 1–14, New York, NY, USA, 2012. ACM.

ViRi: View it Right

Pan Hu, Guobin Shen, Liqun Li, Donghuan Lu
Microsoft Research Asia, Beijing, 100080, China
{v-pah, jackysh, liqul, v-donlu}@microsoft.com

ABSTRACT

We present ViRi – an intriguing system that enables a user to enjoy a frontal view experience even when the user is actually at a slanted viewing angle. ViRi tries to restore the front-view effect by enhancing the normal content rendering process with an additional geometry correction stage. The necessary prerequisite is effectively and accurately estimating the actual viewing angle under natural viewing situations and under the constraints of the device's computational power and limited battery deposit.

We tackle the problem with face detection and augment the phone camera with a fisheye lens to expand its field of view so that the device can recognize its user even the phone is placed casually. We propose effective pre-processing techniques to ensure the applicability of face detection tools onto highly distorted fisheye images. To save energy, we leverage information from system states, employ multiple low power sensors to rule out unlikely viewing situations, and aggressively seek additional opportunities to maximally skip the face detection. For situations in which face detection is unavoidable, we design efficient prediction techniques to further speed up the face detection. The effectiveness of the proposed techniques have been confirmed through thorough evaluations. We have also built a straw man application to allow users to experience the intriguing effects of ViRi.

Categories and Subject Descriptors

C.3.3 [**Special-Purpose and Application-based Systems**]: Signal processing systems; I.4.0 [**Computing Methodologies**]: General Image Displays

General Terms

Algorithm, Design, Experimentation, Performance

Keywords

Fisheye camera; fisheye image; viewing angle estimation; perspective distortion correction; face detection; device-user awareness; light sensor; continuous sensing

MobiSys'13, June 25-28, 2013, Taipei, Taiwan

(1) Slanted View (2) ViRi Effect

Figure 1: Our fisheye camera prototype on a Galaxy Nexus smartphone, and a comparison of the various effects at the 60° slanted viewing angle.

1. INTRODUCTION

A human vision system ensures the best visual quality when viewing from a frontal view, i.e., facing squarely to the display content. People make every effort (mostly subconscious) to have a frontal view, for example by adjusting the screen or properly holding the device. In real life, however, there are plenty of situations where we end up viewing a device's screen from a slanted viewing angle. For example, a person may put a mobile phone on the desk next to the keyboard while working on a PC. When there are prompts such as reminders or push notifications (e.g., SMS, emails, etc.) on the phone screen, the user will be viewing them at a slanted angle; a tablet user may not always hold the device for viewing. She may instead rest the device on a table and continue reading in a more relaxed posture. Additionally, the fact that people desire displays with large viewing angles is also evidence of the high likelihood of viewing screen content at a slanted viewing angle.

Visual content is difficult to consume at a slanted viewing angle. Even though the user may actually see the pixels of the content clearly, recognition is difficult due to the perspective distortion and the smaller effective viewing area. In the above example, the user may have to pick up the phone to read the prompt, which leads to an unnecessary interruption to ongoing work, especially when the prompt is of little or no importance (e.g., spamming SMS/emails, etc); a tablet user may have to accept lower viewing quality or change to a less relaxed posture, or as many others do, purchase a stand for their tablet. The Microsoft Surface actually comes with a kickstand to ensure a better viewing experience.

In this paper, we present *ViRi*, an intriguing system that enables a mobile user to enjoy a frontal view experience in natural viewing situations. With ViRi, from no matter what angle the user is viewing the display, she will always see the content as if she were viewing the content squarely from the front. Figure 1 illustrates such an effect, as well as the original slanted view for comparison. In the above example, a ViRi mobile phone user would not be interrupted as she can clearly see the prompts even at a glance, and a ViRi tablet user can continue reading from a relaxed position without resorting to any stand to hold the device.

ViRi tries to restore the frontal view effect by augmenting the graphics rendering pipeline with a geometry correction module. The module counteracts the negative effects caused by the slanted viewing angle, i.e., the perspective distortion and reduced effective viewing area. Evidently, the necessary prerequisite is an effective and accurate estimate of the actual viewing angle under natural device usage. This is extremely difficult, as the natural usage implies that the device may be held or placed in a nearby stand, and that the user will not make any special signal to facilitate viewing angle detection. In addition, this has to be achieved under the constraints of the device's computational power and limited battery reserve.

Among all the sensors a mobile phone is equipped with, only the camera, with its remote sensing capability, might be feasible for our target scenario, i.e., sensing the user even when the device is placed away from the user. If we can detect the face and eye positions, we can estimate the viewing angle and make corrections accordingly. However, the current phone camera has a very limited field of view (FOV), and is thus not very helpful because when the camera can see the user, she is already at an almost frontal view.

We propose equipping mobile devices with a fisheye camera that features an extremely large FOV. In our prototype (see Figure 1), we augment the existing phone camera by adding a commercial off-the-shelf fisheye lens. However, using a fisheye lens creates new challenges. First of all, the images captured with a fisheye lens are severely distorted, suffering from both radial distortion and perspective distortion. Secondly, a large FOV can easily include light sources, which leads to harsh lighting conditions (e.g., strong backlight and underexposed faces) that typical face detection applications would carefully avoid. Thirdly, our target scenario requires quick adaptation of the display to the actual viewing angle. Hence ViRi needs to quickly detect the viewing angle (mainly the face detection). Unfortunately, face detection is of high computational complexity and usually takes a long time. This implies significant power consumption and would increase the tension caused by a limited battery charge.

We address all these challenges with ViRi. Instead of developing new face detection algorithms specifically for fisheye images, we properly pre-process the fisheye image and leverage existing face detection tools. In particular, we perform an offline camera calibration process to obtain the camera model, with which we can effectively rectify a fisheye image into a planar one to fix the radial distortion. We perform camera reorientation to fix the perspective distortion, and adopt an auto exposure algorithm to handle harsh lighting conditions.

To reduce energy consumption, we identify different viewing situations (Hand-Held and Off-the-Body) and leverage system states (i.e., screen on/off and if there are pending prompts), low power sensors (accelerometer, light sensor, and proximity sensor) to rule out impossible viewing situations and maximally skip face detection in real viewing situations. For situations in which face detection is indeed necessary, we have developed effective prediction methods to reduce the face detection time without compromising detection accuracy. More concretely, in Hand-Held viewing situations, we perform face detection only when the accelerometer indicates a new (quasi-)stationary state after significant device attitude changes. We have designed an angle-based prediction scheme that extracts the Euler angles between the attitudes before and after the change and predicts the most likely face position from that in the previous attitude. In Off-the-Body viewing situations, a large viewing angle change is usually associated with significant posture changes. We leverage the light sensor to detect such situations. Based on the fact that the device does not move while the user's head will move slightly (even if a person may not sense the movement, the device detects it), we have designed a motion-based prediction scheme that takes two pictures at a short interval (say 300 ms) and predicts the face position according to the differences between the two images using an effective integral-image based technique.

We performed thorough evaluations of each component technique. Our proposed preprocessing techniques boost the face detection ratio by 21%, and angle-based prediction and motion-based prediction achieve accuracy of 90% and 85% , respectively, in component evaluations where the test cases are more stressed. In system evaluation of natural phone usage, performance is even better. The average view angle detection error is usually within 10 degrees. We have also built a straw man application in which the user can provide a picture and experience the effect after viewing angle correction at arbitrary slanted viewing angles. A small-scale informal user study suggests that ViRi provides an appealing viewing experience, but also reveals new issues such as smart content selection (due to the reduced effective viewing area). Also, supporting a wide spectrum of applications requires seamless integration with the graphics pipeline of the operating system. We leave these issues for future study.

Contributions: In brief, we have made the following contributions in this paper:

- We identify the slanted viewing phenomena and advocate a consistent front-view experience; We study the feasibility of using a fisheye camera for perpetual user sensing;
- We design effective pre-processing techniques to ensure robust face detection with existing face detection tools, and design effective angle-based and motion-based prediction techniques to speed up the face detection task in natural viewing situations;
- We leverage system events and low power sensors to avoid unlikely viewing situations and further identify opportunities where face detection can be skipped. We conduct an in depth study of the light sensor, which has not been well explored before.

2. MOTIVATION AND THE PROBLEM

2.1 Motivation

When viewing a device from a frontal view, we face the display squarely (or at least the portion of the screen being viewed when the screen is large). This offers the best viewing quality because, humans have a small depression from 2.5 to 3 mm in diameter at the center of the retina known as the yellow spot or macula, which offers the best vision resolving power. In addition, our eyeballs and head naturally rotate to adapt the viewing angle so that the content being viewed will be imaged at the macula area. In fact, people strive (mostly subconsciously) to maintain a frontal view, by for example adjusting the screen or properly holding the device.

However, in real life, we often encounter situations where the front-view experience is hard to maintain all the time. We may be forced to look at the screen from a *slanted viewing angle*, as in the following common scenarios:

- People often put their phone beside the objects (e.g., laptop, book) they are using. When new information or prompts are received, such as an SMS or a pushed email, it is desirable to be able to peek at the content first before deciding to pick up the device and respond, as the action will interrupt their ongoing activity.
- People often read ebooks or watch videos on their devices such as a tablet. It is very hard to keep a single viewing posture for a long time, and thus highly desirable to continue reading comfortably in relaxed postures that may change from time to time.
- Most mobile devices can automatically switch between portrait and landscape display mode using the accelerometer. This works effectively when the user's view orientation is upright, but will mess things up if the user is watching horizontally such as while lying on a bed [7].
- People prefer large displays for higher productivity or better visual effect. However, the larger display is usually adjusted so that the center area corresponds to the eye height of the user. This ensures a perfect front-view for the center area, but leads to possible slanted viewing angles for side areas.
- People usually place the TV opposite to the sofa. But sometimes people may watch TV from a location other than the sofa, say the dinner table.

The fact that people unanimously require displays with large viewing angles also implies a high likelihood of viewing screen content at slanted viewing angles. Modern display technologies typically support a wide viewing angle. For example, IPS panels can offer a viewing angle up to 178 degrees. With a wide viewing angle display, and the proper orientation of the head and eyeballs, we are almost ensured of receiving clearly displayed content, even at very slanted viewing angles. Nevertheless, although it might be clear, the slanted viewing angle results in a distorted image and a reduced effective viewing area. This will cause an uncomfortable viewing experience and people might find the content is hard to interpret.

2.2 Problem Statement

Our goal is to improve the viewing experience at slanted viewing angles by compensating for distorted images and better utilizing the reduced effective viewing area. This will enable users to consume display content as if they were viewing from the front-view, regardless of a device's resting position. To this end, the necessary prerequisite is an accurate estimation of the user's viewing angle under natural phone usage.

While it is possible to ask the user to manually activate viewing angle detection, it would hurt the user experience, especially when both hands are occupied. Thus, it is more desirable to perform continuous sensing of the user's viewing angles. This is also a first step towards continuous, real-time, and in-situ detection of user attention. With ViRi, several other interesting scenarios can easily be enabled:

- Healthy posture monitoring: it could be desirable to monitor the working posture of users and alert them when they have stayed in the same posture for a long time to avoid problems such as neck pain or myopia. This is generally a difficult task for mobile phones without resorting to wearable peripherals.
- Forgotten device alarm: Alert the user to bring the device when leaving. This can be a highly desired feature, as forgetting a mobile device can cause a great deal of inconvenience and may raise the concern of privacy leaks.

Problem Statement: We hope to design an effective means for a mobile device to perform *continuous*, *real-time* and *in situ* detection if the user is looking at the device, and further estimate the actual viewing angle of the user without changing the user's habits. We focus on solving the problem for mobile devices because the viewing angle detection problem for a fixed display (e.g., a Desktop PC) is a special case. The solution needs to work in a number of real situations such as when the device is being held by the user or is resting nearby. It also needs to respect the constraints of the device's computational power and limited battery reserve.

3. SOLUTION IDEA AND CHALLENGES

3.1 Solution idea

Design Considerations: The *in situ* requirement implies that we cannot depend on an infrastructure aid for the sake of user mobility. The constraint of not altering a user's habits implies that we cannot ask the user to have any special gadgets (such as Google Glasses), nor make any special signal (e.g., manual activation) to facilitate the detection. Thus we have to completely rely on existing phone sensors. Considering the possibility that the device may be away from the body, only the microphone and camera may be viable options. While a microphone can sense the user via voice detection, it is not dependable as a user does not speak all the time, nor will voice detection be able to determine a user's viewing direction.

The only remaining possibility is to use the camera. If we can capture and detect a user's face and eyes, we can estimate the viewing angle. Camera have become pervasive on commodity smartphones. Advances in face detection and increasing availability of public face detection SDKs and web services make it practical to explore many camera-based face-aware applications. However, existing phone cameras usually have a rather limited field of view (FOV). Without careful placement, it is very likely the user's face will fall outside of the FOV. Figure 3.1 shows an image taken by the front camera of a Galaxy Nexus placed near the keyboard

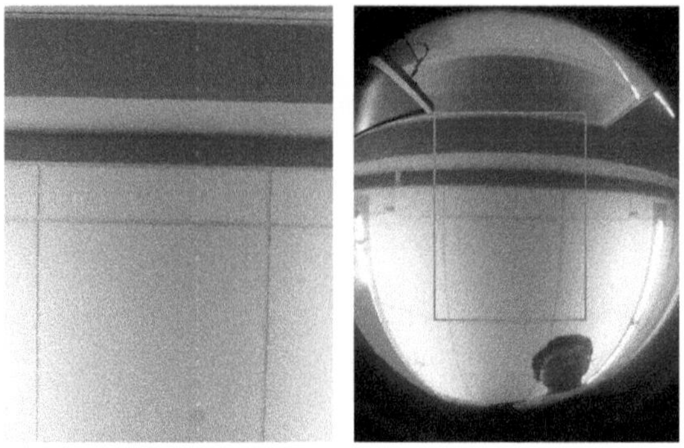

(a) Normal View (b) Fisheye View

Figure 2: Fisheye lens significantly expands the FOV. Images were taken with the front camera on a Galaxy Nexus, with a COTS fisheye lens.

while the user is sitting in front of a PC. Obviously, the user is not captured in the image. The camera cannot be a viable solution unless we can expand its FOV.

Leverage Fisheye Lens: Fisheye lenses can achieve ultra wide FOV of 180-degrees or even wider. There are commodity fisheye lens accessories for mobile phones such as Olloclip [4]. We can concatenate a fisheye lens to an existing phone camera system to expand its FOV.[1] The effect is shown in Figure 3.1. The view covered by the original image is highlighted with the rectangle. As can be seen, the viewing angle is greatly increased and the user is now captured in the image. Quantitatively, the resulting FOV increases from the original 45 and 60 degrees (horizontal and vertical directions) to about 120 and 140 degrees, respectively, after putting on the fisheye lens. The difference in horizontal and vertical FOVs are due to the aspect ratio of the image sensor.

One special merit of fisheye lens is its very large depth of field – the distance between the nearest and farthest objects in a scene that appear acceptably sharp in an image, due to its extremely short focal length. Essentially, the complete scene, near to far, is sharp. Fisheye lens can take sharp images even without focusing. This is a very favorable feature as face detection algorithms desire sharp face images.

3.2 Challenges

A fisheye lens greatly increases the FOV and provides the possibility of achieving our goal, but it also creates new challenges. The adoption of face detection also leads to new issues for resource-constrained mobile devices.

Face Detection in Highly Distorted Images: Fisheye lenses achieve ultra wide angles of view by forgoing straight perspective lines (rectilinear images), opting instead for special mapping (e.g., equisolid angle) to create a wide panoramic or hemispherical image. As a result, they produce highly distorted images with both radial distortion and perspective distortion. A fisheye image is more distorted in the peripheral areas than in the central area due to the view compression. This can be clearly observed from images in Figure 3.1, as well as Figure 3 that shows a set of fisheye

[1]Such a simple concatenation actually sacrifices the FOV of the fisheye lens. We envision future mobile phones may equip a genuine fisheye or ultra-wide FOV camera by design, as there are many other advantages in having such a system to be explored.

Figure 3: Example of fisheye images at different viewing angles and distances. Left to right: viewing angles are 60, 45, 30, 15 and 0 degrees. Top to bottom: viewing distances are 30, 50, and 70 cm.

images taken from different viewing angles and distances in a typical office environment. As a large portion of the scene is imaged in the peripheral areas of the resulting image, this leads to low pixel density for the objects that appear in the peripheral areas (see Figure 3) and becomes more obvious when rectified into planar pictures (see Figure 8). Figure 3 also presents cases in which only a partial face may be captured, especially at large viewing angles.

In actual daily usage, the mobile device usually faces upwards. Due to the extra wide FOV of the fisheye lens, it is very likely to include light sources in the view, especially in indoor environments where the lights are mostly on the ceiling. The phone camera adopts a central weighted average exposure measurement. It can easily be fooled and yields severely underexposed images.

Fast Detection Speed on The Device: Face detection algorithms commonly adopt a binary pattern-classification approach. The content of a given part of an image is first transformed into features by matching against a series of templates. Then a classifier trained on example faces decides whether that particular region of the image is a face or not. This process is repeated at all locations and scales using a sliding window [20]. Thus, face detection time is closely related to image size.

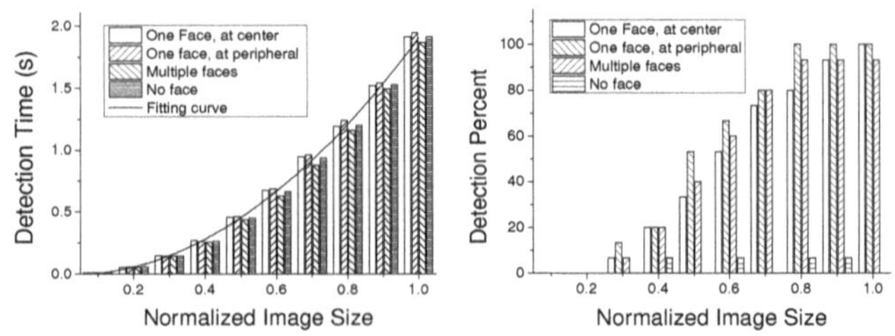

(a) Detection Time (b) Detection Accuracy

Figure 4: Detection time and corresponding accuracy at different image sizes. The size is normalized against the largest input, which is 1280×960.

We measured the face detection time at different input image sizes, where an input image may contain no, one, or multiple faces and may appear in the center or peripheral areas, on a Galaxy Nexus using Android FaceSDK. Figure 3.2 shows the results, where the x-axis is the image size ratio normalized against the highest resolution 1280×960. From the figure, we can see that the detection time indeed increases with the image size, quadratically to the size ratio and linearly to the area ratio. The detection time seems content independent, as it varied little no matter whether there was one or more faces in the image or no face at all.

However, while leading to faster detection speed, smaller images impair the detection ratio as well. This is confirmed by the detection rate for the same set of images shown in Figure 3.2. There is a tradeoff between face detection accuracy and detection speed, and one cannot achieve a fast detection speed by simply reducing the image size. It is therefore a challenge to achieve both high detection accuracy and fast detection speed.

Energy Consumption: As phones are usually battery operated, we need to reduce energy consumption as much as possible. To understand energy consumption, we measure the energy footprints for different device states that a face detection application may undergo: standby mode (screen off), CPU idle, previewing, image capture. and face detection. Figure 5 shows the measurement results. The image size for capturing and processing is 1280×960. WiFi and Bluetooth are turned off, the screen is lit up but kept at a minimum brightness unless otherwise explicitly stated. The energy consumption for standby mode and for a screen with max brightness is also measured for reference purposes.

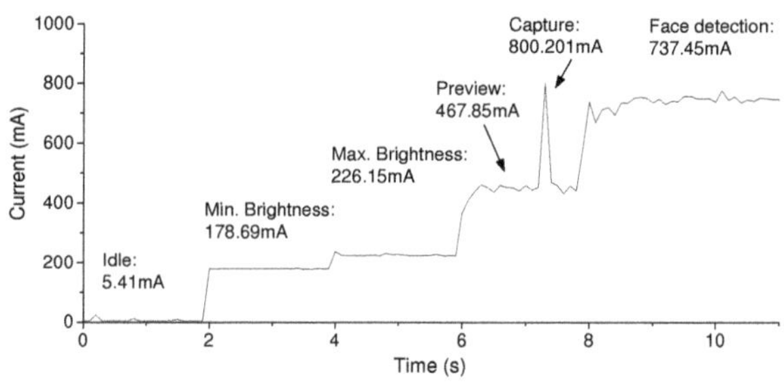

Figure 5: Energy consumption (measured in current strength) at different stages during face detection.

Note that current mobile devices commonly activate a preview state before taking a picture or recording a video. While it is necessary to let the user frame the scene and specify the focus point, such a preview stage can be safely avoided for a fisheye lens because of its extremely large depth of field, and there is no need for framing in our scenario. Therefore, the net energy consumption mainly consists of the power consumed by image capture and face detection, which is around 340 mA and 270 mA (after subtracting the power for preview, which takes about 290mA), respectively, as shown in Figure 5.

4. VIRI SYSTEM DESIGN

4.1 ViRi Overview

ViRi augments existing phone cameras with an external off-the-shelf fisheye lens, and relies on face detection to detect the viewing angle. Instead of developing a new face detection tool specially optimized for fisheye images, we try to leverage existing face detection SDKs [1, 3, 5] by developing effective pre-processing techniques to convert fisheye images into planar ones. In ViRi, a face detection module is treated as a *black box*. As the user's viewing angle on the device may change at any time, ViRi needs to perform continuous monitoring. This can lead to a severe waste of scarce battery resources.

To mitigate the problem, ViRi leverages the free system states and events, and low power sensors (accelerometer and compass, light sensor, proximity sensor) to filter out unlikely viewing situations and aggressively seeks further opportunities to skip face detection in real viewing situations. As a result, viewing angle detection is performed only when there is a significant situation change, such as a device attitude change, the user approaching or leaving, or a significant posture change. To further speed up face detection and reduce energy consumption, ViRi applies various prediction schemes to estimate possible face positions in the newly captured image based on context-aware hints. Intuitively, if a viewing situation change is caused by a device attitude change, then the angle between attitudes (measured using an accelerometer and compass) can be used for prediction. If it is due to a user posture change, we can predict the face area from the differences between neighboring image capture. We then use the small, predicted area of the image for face detection.

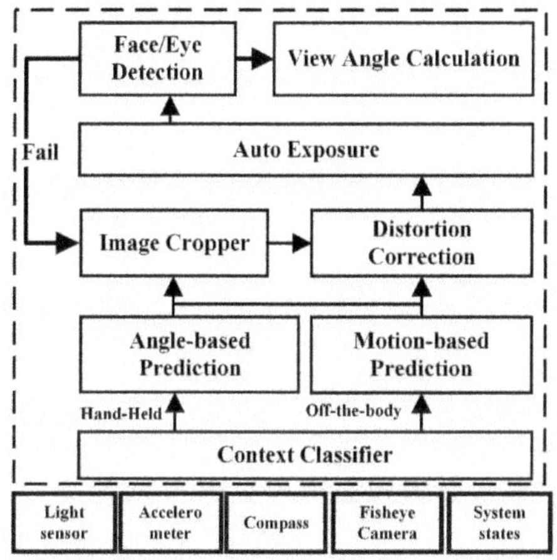

Figure 6: System architecture of ViRi.

4.2 ViRi Architecture and Workflow

ViRi runs as a background service on mobile devices (smartphone and slates), attempting to seamlessly adapt the display to the viewing angle of the user. The architecture of ViRi is shown in Figure 6.

First, ViRi uses a context classifier that takes input from system states, the accelerometer, light, and proximity sensors to identify the interested viewing situations including Hand-Held and Off-the-Body (e.g., on a desk), in which face detection might be conducted. In a Hand-Held viewing situation, when the device's attitude changes from one (quasi-)stationary state to another, we trigger face detection and further leverage the device attitude change angle to make a prediction. In an Off-the-Body viewing situation, face detection is triggered by significant posture changes, which are detected using the light sensor. The motion-based predictor

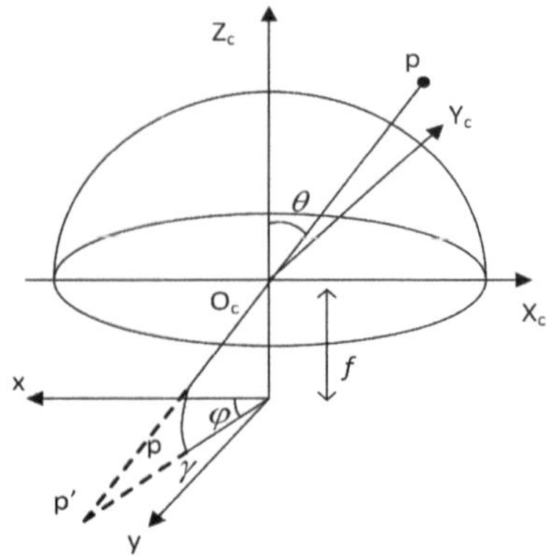

Figure 7: Fisheye lens model.

is then called upon. The predicted face area is then cropped and fed into the distortion correction module. It further goes through the auto exposure module to equalize the lighting. Finally, face detection is conducted on the resulting image using existing face/eye detection SDK.

In the following sections, we will elaborate on the proposed techniques and present component evaluations.

5. FACE DETECTION AND VIEWING ANGLE ESTIMATION

Due to the view compression characteristic of fisheye lens, a face may be heavily distorted, especially when imaged in the peripheral area. Direct application of face detection tools developed for planar images suffers from low detection accuracy. As aforementioned, we hope to use existing face detection tools through proper pre-processing, including geometry distortion correction and harsh lighting handling.

5.1 Geometry Distortion Correction

Parametric Camera Model with Fisheye Lens: The calibration of a fisheye lens has been well studied. In this paper, we adopt a simplified version from [10]. The fisheye lens model is illustrated in Figure 7. Since the camera is rotationally symmetric, an incoming light ray is uniquely identified by the two angles θ and φ. Let $\mathbf{\Phi} = (\theta, \varphi)^T$. Let $\vec{p} = (p_u, p_v)^T$ and $\vec{m} = (m_x, m_y)^T$ be the pixel coordinates in the image and the ideal Cartesian coordinates in the sensor plane, then the simplified fisheye lens model can be described as

$$\vec{p} = \mathcal{A} \circ \mathcal{F}(\mathbf{\Phi})$$

where $\mathcal{F}(\mathbf{\Phi}) = \mathbf{r}(\theta)(\cos\varphi, \sin\varphi)^{\mathbf{T}}$ is the transform from ray direction $\mathbf{\Phi}$ to the ideal Cartesian coordinates, and $\mathcal{A}$ is the affine transform that forms the final pixel image from the projected image through alignment and scaling, i.e.,

$$\mathcal{A}(\vec{m}) = \mathbf{S} \cdot (\vec{m} - \vec{m}_0)$$

with $\vec{m}_0$ being the possible misalignment between the center of the sensor plane and the light axis of the lens, and $\mathbf{S}$ is the scaling matrix that scales the size of the sensor plane to the actual image dimension in pixels.

Different choices of $r(\theta)$ lead to different camera models. For a fisheye lens model, we use a fourth-order polynomial $r(\theta) = \sum_{i=0}^{4} a_i \theta^i$. The calibration process then identifies all the parameters. We envision the fisheye lens is fixed in the device, so we perform an offline, once-for-all calibration process using a checkerboard and obtain the intrinsic model parameters of the fisheye lens. The procedure is an iterative process that fixes one set of model parameters ($\mathcal{A}$ or $\mathcal{F}$) and optimizes the other, and vice versa.

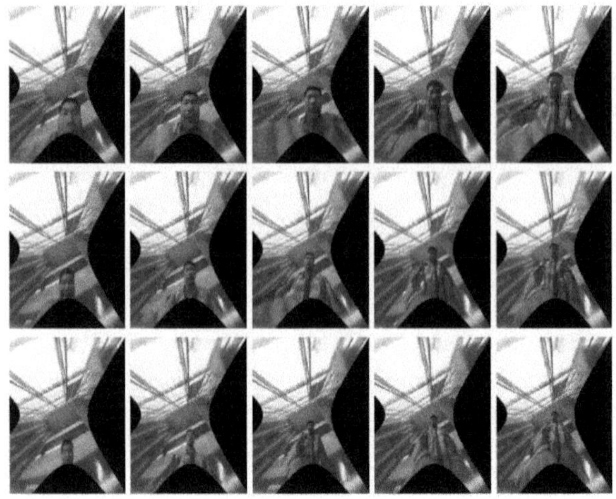

(a) Rectified Images

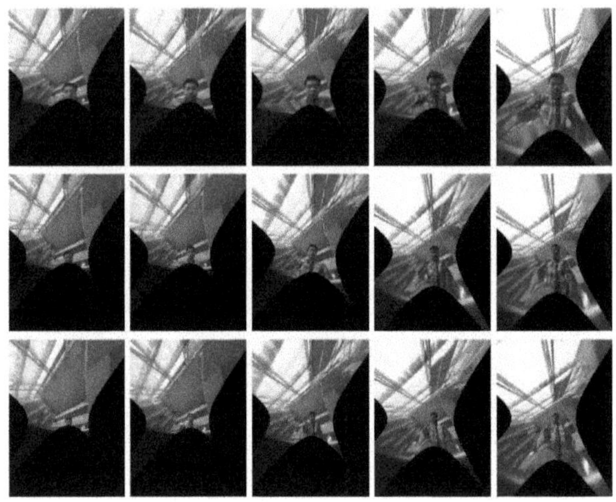

(b) Reoriented Images

Figure 8: Fisheye images after geometry distortion correction. Same set of images as shown in Figure3.

Radial Distortion Correction: The first pre-processing step is to rectify a fisheye image into a planar one to correct the radial distortion. Having learnt the parameters of the camera model, we find the mapping between a pixel $\vec{p}$ in a fisheye image and the corresponding pixel $\vec{p}'$ in the rectified image. The mapping is achieved by first resolving the incoming angle for $\vec{p}$ using the fisheye camera model, and then projecting it to another image using the pinhole model $r(\theta) = f \tan\theta$. Because the mapping is fixed for a given pixel position, this process can be effectively implemented via table lookup.

Figure 8-(a) shows the effect of radial distortion correction for the set of images shown in Figure3. From the figures, we can see that all the straight lines that were warped to curves in fisheye images have become straight again.

Perspective Distortion Correction: For many cases in which the face is in a peripheral area of the fisheye image, the perspective distortion stretches the face heavily, which may render the face detection templates pre-trained from normal face images invalid. To handle this, we reorient the camera, i.e., rotate the fisheye image to center around the face, and achieve the effect as if the image were taken with the camera facing straight to the face. Suppose the face is at the incoming angle $\mathbf{\Phi}$, we simply rotate along the Z-axis by φ first and then rotate the resulting image along the Y-axis by θ. Note that, in real applications, this would create a *paradox*: we hope to rotate the image to center around the to-be-detected face position which is unknown yet. As detailed in Section 7, we will overcome this paradox through prediction: we predict the most likely face location and reorient the camera to center around that.

The effect of camera reorientation is shown in Figure 8-(b). From the figures, we can see that after camera reorientation, the view is centered around the face. Both radial distortion and perspective distortion are fixed and the face looks normal.

5.2 Harsh Lighting Handling

Due to the ultra wide FOV of the fisheye lens, light sources are often captured by the camera. This may lead to strong backlighting and underexposed faces, which usually needs to be intentionally avoided in face detection applications. In our settings, we do not alter a user's usage habits and the device can rest unattended. Hence we cannot manipulate the positioning of the faces nor exclude the light sources. The only possibility is to adjust the exposure and rely on signal processing.

As the face itself can never be a light source, therefore, we first overexpose by one stop (on the basis of the camera's center weighted light measurement results) when capturing images. We further adopt an auto-exposure technique [18] that better equalizes the resulting picture. In brief, it divides the whole image into regions with different exposure zones (borrowed from Ansel Adam's Zone theory), and estimates an optimal zone for every region while considering the details in each zone and the local contrast between neighboring zone regions. It then applies a detail-preserving S-curve based adjustment that fuses the global curve obtained from zone mapping with local contrast control.

5.3 Effectiveness of Pre-processing Techniques

To evaluate the effectiveness of pre-processing techniques, we invited 5 volunteers to help with data collection. For each volunteer, we captured 35 images from various viewing angles (0, 15, 30, ... 60 degrees) and various viewing distances (30, 40, ..., 70 cm). The images are captured in a discussion room with harsh lighting conditions. We plot the face detection rates using different processing techniques in Figure 9, where the X-axis represents different users.

From the figure, we can see the original (i.e., without pre-processing) detection rates vary from 40% to 71%. We applied auto-exposure and distortion correction separately to the raw image to determine their effectiveness in improving face detection rate. We can see that applying a single pre-processing technique already increased the detection rate for most cases. But the improvements were sometimes minor, such as for user 4 and 5. We then combined both techniques and found that there was significant improvement, 21% on average. In our implementation, we treated face detection as a black-box, and are thus unable to tell the exact reason

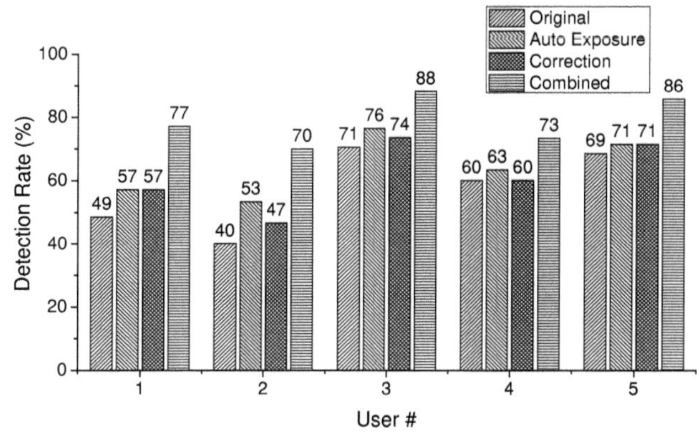

Figure 9: Effectiveness of geometry correction and the harsh lighting condition handling techniques.

for this observation. To our understanding, applying both techniques highly increases the probability of passing the face detection filters.

5.4 Viewing Angle Estimation

Once we have detected the face, we next find the position of the eyes. Most existing face SDKs provide eye positions as a side product because they are typical feature points in the matching templates in face detection. We then take the middle point of the two eyes and reverse calculate the viewing angle using the camera model. We actually build up a mapping table during the calibration phase and perform simple table lookup when resolving viewing angles.

6. CONTEXT SIFTING

Energy consumption of ViRi mainly consists of two parts: the fixed overhead of image capture and the dynamic consumption of face detection that is dictated by its execution time. Thus, our strategy to save energy is two-fold: to skip unnecessary face detection situations as much as possible, and to reduce the face detection time if we have to.

In this section, we present context sifting that seeks to leverage the system states and low power sensors to rule out all situations of no interest, and to further identify opportunities to safely skip both image capture and face detection. For viewing situations that deserve new face detection, the sifting process also provides hints for face location prediction, which can speed up face detection, as will be elaborated on in the next section.

6.1 Ruling Out Situations of No Interest

Interested Viewing Situations: In typical viewing scenarios, users either hold the device or put the device on a table or stand. We refer to these two situations as *Hand-Held* and *Off-the-Body* viewing situations hereafter for the sake of clarity. In general, in whatever viewing situation, the device is stationary or quasi-stationary and the user always tries to maintain a stable relative position to the device for a better viewing experience. There are cases in which both the user and the device are moving (e.g., viewing while walking or on a moving bus), but these are rare cases and not encouraged as they are harmful to eyesight.

Detection of Interested Viewing Situations: We detect interested viewing situations via simple logical reasoning from several information sources, including system states

Situation	System state	Light sensor	Proximity sensor	Accelerometer	Reasoning logic
No interest	screen off AND no pending prompts	small or zero (<20)	close (<20cm)	motion	OR
Hand-Held	screen on	non-zero (>20)	far (>20cm)	quasi-stationary	AND
Off-the-Body	screen on OR pending prompts	non-zero (>20)	far (>20cm)	stationary	AND

Table 1: Interested normal viewing scenarios and their detections via sensors.

(screen is on, or is off but with pending prompts), IMU sensor (accelerometer and compass, for motion state sensing), light sensor (for environmental lighting), and proximity sensor (closeness to body). All these information sources have very low energy footprints.

The reasoning is presented in Table 1. We first leverage the system states, the proximity sensor and the light sensor to exclude some obvious non-interesting cases in which the user is definitely not viewing the screen. For instance, when the screen is off and there is no content pending to display, or the device is put very close to the face/body (via the proximity sensor), or in a pocket (via the light sensor), or the device itself is in a motion state (via accelerometer) etc., all these are impossible reading situations.

When all the sensors indicate a possible viewing situation, we then leverage the accelerometer to detect if the device is held in a hand or is resting on a table, which corresponds to a quasi-stationary or stationary state, respectively. Using the accelerometer to detect motion states is a well-studied topic [11]. In ViRi, we simply use the variance of the magnitude of acceleration to classify the device's motion states into three categories: motion, quasi-stationary, and stationary.

6.2 Skipping Unnecessary Detections

In real viewing situations, a user subconsciously tries to stabilize the relative position between her face/eyes and the device's screen. Even though the relative position cannot be completely stable and there are subtle variations, such small variations are usually compensated for by the human visual system. Therefore, there is no need to re-estimate the viewing angle in a stationary viewing state. When a large change in the relative position happens, the estimation of the new viewing angle is needed when it enters another stationary viewing situation. Frequent adaptation to small viewing angle changes will lead to a flickering display and actually impair the viewing experience.

A large relative position change is usually associated with a device attitude change or significant head/body movement such as a posture change. The attitude change would only happen in the Hand-Held case. It can be trivially detected using the accelerometer and compass, which may also tell the extent (in Euler angles) of change. For the Off-the-Body situation, posture changes will incur significant change in the lighting condition (seen from the device's view). We can use a light sensor to detect such changes, as elaborated below.

Leverage The Light Sensor: Figure 10 shows a trace of the light sensor for over 8 hours in a working day with normal phone use. Labels 1-4 indicate various zoomed-in situations in the sub-figures below. In particular:

- ◇ When the user moves closer to or away from the device, there is an apparent valley with gradual changes [Sub-figure (1)]. Similar effects are observed for people walking by at a close distance (less than 0.5 meter).

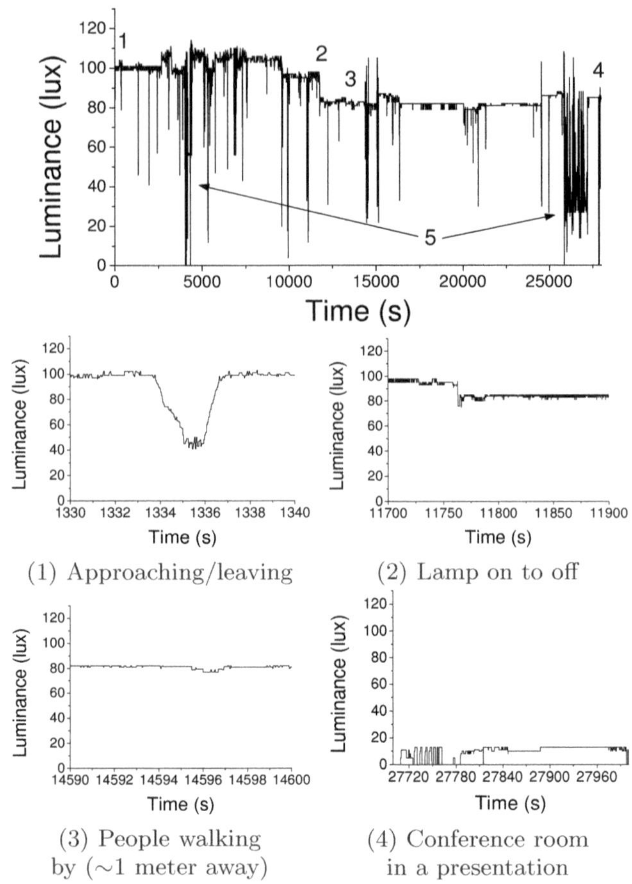

(1) Approaching/leaving (2) Lamp on to off (3) People walking by (~1 meter away) (4) Conference room in a presentation

Figure 10: Lighting sensor traces observed by a device for over 8 hours in a typical working day.

- ◇ Turning off the luminance lamp causes a sudden drop in light sensor readings [Sub-figure (2)].
- ◇ When people are walking by at a distance over 1 meter, there is almost no impact on the sensed luminance [Sub-figure (3)].
- ◇ Small fluctuations are observed in a conference room with the projector showing some slides [Sub-figure (4)].

From the figures, we can see that the lighting conditions are mostly stable when there is no significant state change. Label 5 indicates the light sensor readings when the device is put in a pocket. The readings are mostly low but not always zero, because the light sensor resides on one end of the phone, which accidentally captures some light when in the pocket.

Our goal is to detect interested viewing situation changes such as when the user approaches/moves away from the device or changes her viewing posture significantly. Due to the various luminance conditions that the device may undergo, any single threshold-based triggering method, using either absolute luminance or relative luminance changes, will not work. However, our observations show that a user's posture change, such as approaching/leaving, causes a continuous and monotonous change, in contrast to a sudden change such as turning on/off a lamp. Therefore, in our design, we use the increasing or decreasing trend to trigger face detection. The detection is simple conditioned the continuous increase/drop in light sensor readings for at least 500 ms.

In summary, we exploit the system states and the lower power sensors to filter out unlikely viewing situations, and identify two possible reading situations, Hand-Held and Off-the-Body, using the accelerometer and the light sensor. We perform new face detection only when the viewing situation becomes stationary again after the viewing angle changes.

7. FACE POSITION PREDICTION

The speed of face detection not only affects system energy consumption, but also has an essential impact on the user experience. As aforementioned in Section 3.2, the key is to reduce the size of the image that feeds into the face detection module, which is treated as a black-box in ViRi. This can be achieved via prediction of the potential face area. Due to the very different properties of Hand-Held and Off-the-Body situations, we design different prediction schemes for the two situations.

7.1 Angle-based Prediction: Hand-Held

If the contextual change is caused by the motion states or attitude of the device, we may exploit the relative orientation changes of the device, which can be obtained from the IMU sensor (accelerometer and compass) readings. We always record the orientation of the device when it enters a quasi-stationary state. If the device is manipulated and becomes stationary again, we calculate the relative rotation angles (Euler angles). If there is a face detected in the previous state, we predict where the face is likely to reside using the resulting rotation angle.

We now describe the general prediction process. We use $\vec{p}$ and $\mathbf{\Phi}$ to denote the pixel coordinates and the ray direction in the lens coordinate system C as shown in Figure 7. Then we have $\vec{p} = \mathcal{A} \circ \mathcal{F}(\mathbf{\Phi})$ (refer to Section 5.1). Thus, given the pixel $\vec{p}$ and ϕ (shown in Figure 7), we can calculate θ of the ray direction $\mathbf{\Phi}$. Suppose that the phone coordinate system changes to C' due to pitch, yaw, and roll. Assume that the origin of the coordinate system does not change (rotate around the optic center O_C in Figure 7). The new pixel coordinates of $\mathbf{\Phi}$ (denoted as $\vec{p}'$) are determined by θ' and ϕ', which are the angles between $\mathbf{\Phi}$ and the new $Z_{C'}$ and $X_{C'}$ axes, respectively. To calculate θ' and ϕ', we measure the Euler angles for pitch, yaw, and roll (illustrated in Figure 11) of the relative attitude change using the accelerometer and compass. The details of the calculation are omitted here due to space limitations. They can be found in [2].

In practice, when the user is holding the phone and viewing the display, it is unlikely that the phone is intentionally yawed or rolled (relative to the user) except when changing the device's orientation. The Euler angles of a yaw or roll are thus relatively small. We assume that the origin O_C is fixed, which may not hold in real situations. However, the relative position between the user and the device (held-in-hand) usually does not change significantly in a short time. Therefore, the proposed angle-based prediction can still work in practice.

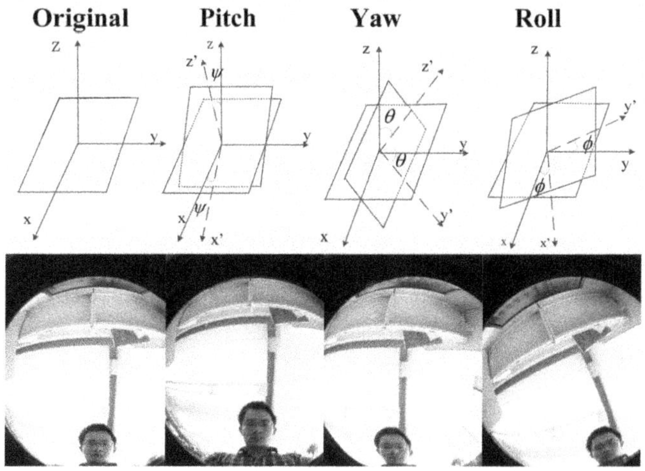

Figure 11: Illustration of Pitch, Yaw, and Roll changes between different stationary attitudes and their effects.

We have described the process of mapping one pixel in the previous image to the new image. We will now discuss how to generate the prediction window based on the face detected in the previous image. The algorithm is illustrated in Figure 12. We use $\vec{p_l}$ and $\vec{p_r}$ to denote the left and right eye in the previous image, respectively. First, $\vec{p_l}$ and $\vec{p_r}$ are mapped to $\vec{p_l}'$ and $\vec{p_r}'$ in a new captured image. Then, the prediction window's size is set heuristically with width $|\vec{p_l}' - \vec{p_r}'|$ and height $\frac{4}{3} \cdot |\vec{p_l}' - \vec{p_r}'|$, where $\frac{4}{3}$ considers the shape of the face.

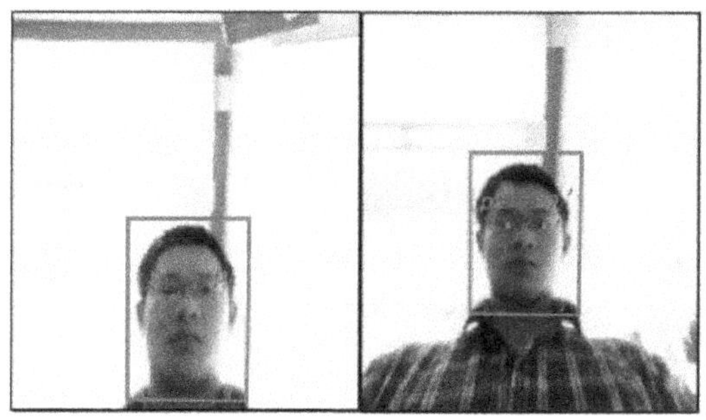

Figure 12: Prediction window generation based on eye feature points mapping.

7.2 Motion-based Prediction: Off-the-Body

When the phone is put away from the body, e.g., on the table next to the user, the accelerometer will fail to capture the user's movement. Recall that we use the changing trend of the light sensor to detect any situation change. While the omnidirectional light sensor can trigger a state change, it cannot be exploited for prediction purposes. We have designed a motion-based prediction method employing the image sensor.

In such situations, the device is still, the user might be moving, slightly or significantly, and the background generally remains stationary. This is quite common from our user studies involving 10 volunteers. The part of the scene in motion is most likely just the user. Therefore, we have proposed a lightweight, motion-based prediction scheme, which takes two consecutive images captured at short intervals and performs motion detection to identify potential face areas. One should note that motion-based prediction is inappropriate for when the device is hand-held as the background is also shifting. Applying more advanced motion detection algorithms such as those adopted in video coding systems may solve this problem, but will certainly add greatly to the computational costs. In contrast, we desire lightweight algorithms that better suit mobile devices.

We have designed an *integral-subtraction* image-based prediction scheme. Integral images are widely used to compute rectangle features [20]. The scheme includes three steps. First, we subtract two consecutive images in a pixel-wise fashion and obtain a subtraction image. The parts in motion will have large values in the subtraction image whereas the parts that are still will mostly have zero or small values. Second, an integral image is calculated based on the subtraction image. Third, a sliding window traverses through the integral subtraction image. The sum of the pixel values falling into the window is calculated. The window corresponding to the maximum value is the motion area and used as the prediction results.

Figure 13 shows the intermediate processes of the integral-substraction scheme. Two images are captured when the user was in front of a laptop with the phone beside the keyboard. The interval was 300 ms. The subtraction image is shown in Figure 13-(b). We can see that the subtraction image successfully captures slight posture changes. An integral image (shown in Figure 13-(c)) is then generated based on the subtraction image. The pixel at (x, y) stores the sum of all pixels from the subtraction image whose coordinates (x', y') satisfy $x' \le x, y' \le y$. We then traverse the integral subtraction image with a sliding window $[(x_1, y_1), (x_2, y_2)]$, where (x_1, y_1) and (x_2, y_2) are the left top and right bottom corners. The sum of all pixels within the window can be computed with $I(x_2, y_2) - I(x_1, y_2) - I(x_2, y_1) + I(x_1, y_1)$ where $I(x, y)$ represent the element (x, y) in the integral image. The execution complexity of the two-step scheme is proportional to the size of the image. In our implementation, the sliding window size is set to 320×320.

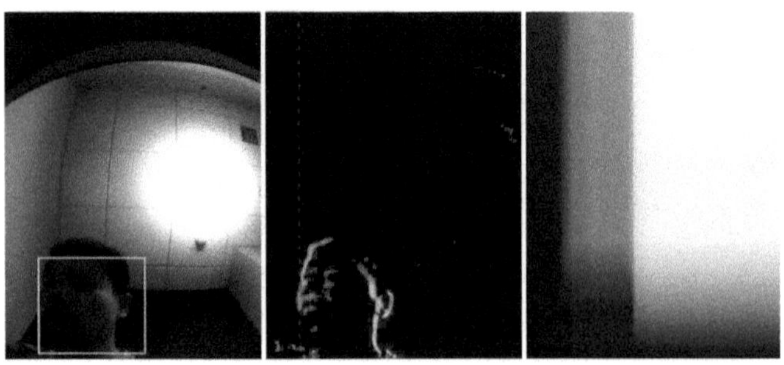

(a) Original (b) Subtraction(300 ms) (c) Integral

Figure 13: Exemplar original, subtraction, and integral of the subtraction images.

7.3 Prediction Effectiveness: Benchmarks

Angle-based Prediction: We collected 80 images from 2 users, each with around 40 images, at random device attitudes. We recorded the accelerometer readings when the images were taken. The maximum angle difference in our experiments reached 60 degrees. We manually labeled the eye positions for each image. We then randomly picked a pair of images (each represents one quasi-stationary state) to test the angle-based prediction scheme. The prediction accuracy is quantified by the pixel distance between the middle point of the predicted and the actual eye locations. We have plotted the cumulative distribution function (CDF) of the prediction errors in Figure 14.

We can see that over 90% of all prediction errors fall below 20 pixels. In practice, the size of the face in the image is typically larger than 60×100 pixels when the user was within a reasonable distance (say less than 1 meter). Thus, an error of 20 pixels is relatively small. Moreover, Figure 14 shows the error between pairs of randomly selected images. The actual rotation angles should be smaller in real viewing situations due to gradual natural transition. Therefore, we plot the prediction errors versus rotation angles in Figure 15. We can see the error is small ($\le$ 10 pixels) when the rotation angle is below 40 degrees. The error exceeds 20 pixels only when the rotation angle is larger than 50 degrees, which rarely happens in practice.

Motion-based Prediction: We evaluated our motion-based prediction system using traces from 10 users. All traces were collected when users were sitting in their cubicle, using a laptop with their phone on the desk ($\sim$ 40 cm from the camera to the user's face). For each user, we recorded a video clip of 10$\sim$20 seconds and then extracted frames from the clip. The frame rate was 30 FPS. To calculate the subtraction image, we used two consecutive images interleaved by 300 ms (or 10 frames). This interval was sufficient to capture the user's motion while short enough to avoid ambient light change. We collected a total of 1400 test cases. For each prediction, we compared the predicted results with human labeled groundtruth. The successful rates are shown in Figure 16. The overall success rates are high. The worst case is observed for user 3. The reason is that during the video recording, the user's face moved out of the FOV for a while. In cases where the user's face remained in the FOV the whole time, the successful rates were all over 85%.

7.4 Prediction Failure Handling

Angle-based prediction depends on a previously detected face position, while motion-based prediction does not. Therefore, if there is no such face position recorded, angle-based prediction is always skipped. In rare situations that meet the criteria for interested viewing situations, but lack a face in the fisheye images (e.g., the phone is put on the desk and the user is away, with new prompts pending), we will end up with one vain prediction and detection. Prediction may fail. If this indeed happens, we would perform face detection over the entire frame. We notice that this is a limitation because of the black-box approach. Ideally, we would continuously expand the search area from the predicted area, to avoid repeated examination of the predicted area.

8. SYSTEM EVALUATION

8.1 Implementation

We built the ViRi engine on a Samsung Galaxy Nexus phone running Android 4.0. The executable file size was 1.11 MB with a memory footprint of 39 MB. One issue we faced in our implementation was the restriction imposed by the OS in terms of camera usage: we have to turn on the screen and enter the preview mode before we can take a image. That is, we are forbidden to automatically take a

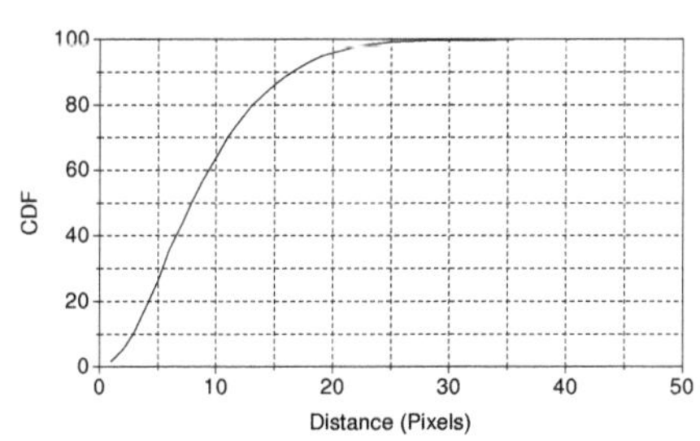

Figure 14: Angle-based prediction accuracy for different users.

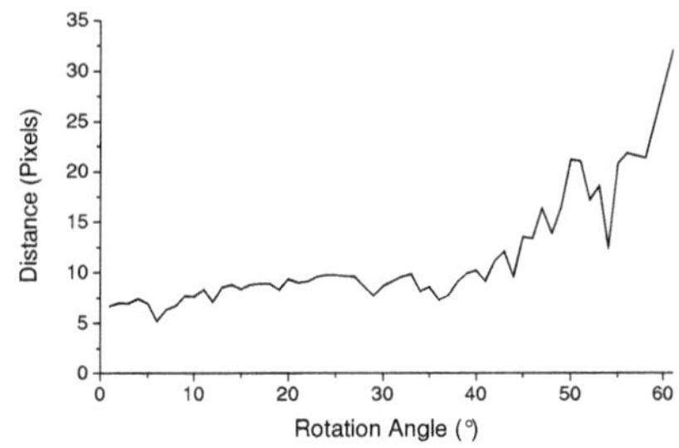

Figure 15: Angle prediction error vs actual rotation angles.

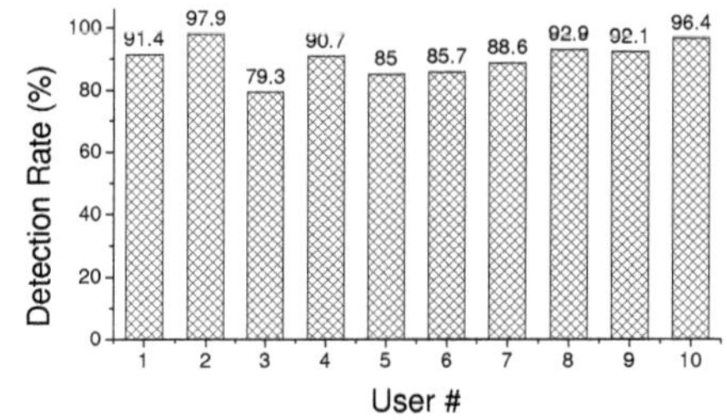

Figure 16: Motion-based prediction rates for 10 users.

photo without activating the screen and previewing. This brings significant overhead in energy consumption.

Perspective Distortion Correction: Due to perspective distortion, the effective display, which is perpendicular to the line connecting the eye and the screen center, has the shape of a *trapezoid*, as depicted in Figure 17, where the phone is laying on a surface and the effective display is shown by in dashed lines. ViRi seeks to properly adjust the

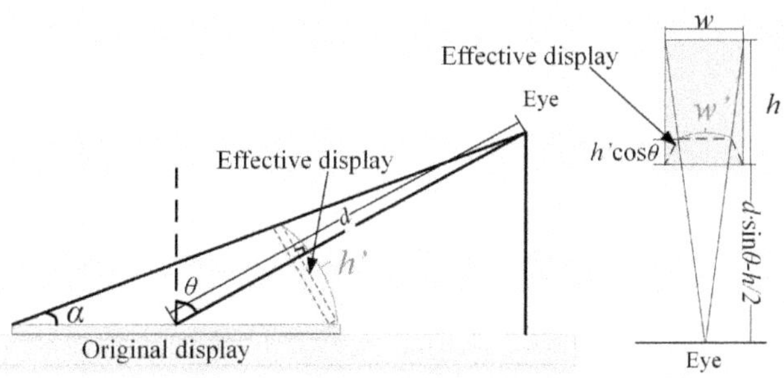

Figure 17: Illustration of the perspective distortion correction process.

to-be-displayed content to generate a normal looking image on the effective display. Obviously, the key task is to find the actual size of the effective display. Assume the distance between the eye and the center of the physical display is d, which is typically set to within the range of 0.3m-1m.

Given the estimated viewing angle θ, we calculate the dimensions of the effective display as follows: let h and w be the height and the width of the physical display. Evidently, the length of the bottom edge of the effective display is w, and we only need to find the length of the top edge (w') and the height (h') of the effective display. According to the Sine Theorem, h' is calculated by

$$h' = h \cdot \frac{\sin\alpha}{\sin(\pi - \theta - \alpha)}$$

where α is the angle shown in Figure 17. Note that α can simply be derived once d and θ are fixed. After obtaining h', w' can be calculated by

$$w' = w \cdot \frac{d \cdot \sin\theta - h/2 + h' \cdot \cos\theta}{d \cdot \sin\theta + h/2}$$

as illustrated in the right part of Figure 17. Once h' and w' are calculated, we can manipulate the to-be-shown content and fit it to the effective display.

8.2 System Evaluation

We have already evaluated component technologies. In this section, we evaluate the overall system performance, including end-to-end face detection accuracy, detection speed, and resource consumption.

Methodology: We separated the two common viewing scenarios and evaluated them separately. We invited different users and recorded their behavior via a camcorder, from which we manually identified the viewing angle changes and compared them with our system detection.

8.2.1 Effectiveness of Prediction in Face Detection

Hand-Held Situation: We invited five volunteers to try our prototype phone in typical usage scenarios, e.g., ebook reading, web browsing, and movie playback. The accelerometer triggered image capture when there was a transition between two quasi-stationary states as described in Section 7.1. The accelerometer readings were continuously recorded. The data collection for each volunteer lasted for tens of minutes with 30~60 images captured. For each state transition, we applied angle-based prediction. The predicted face area was cropped out and fed to the face detection module. If a face was detected, we counted a successful hit. Otherwise, we performed face detection using the whole image. We present the prediction success rates in Figure 18.

We can see the overall prediction success rates varied from 0.78 to 1.00. The right bar in each cluster in Figure 18 shows the detection rate for the whole image without prediction. This accounts for the limitation of the face detection SDK. Note that the actual prediction success rates were higher than those shown in Figure 18, because a prediction should be concluded is a failure only when the face was not detected in the cropped image but successfully detected in the whole image. Thus, taking volunteer 4 as an example, the actual prediction success rate was $78/92 \approx 0.85$. One may notice that the results shown in Figure 18 look much better than those in Figure 9. The reason is that the data collections for Figure 18 were under normal reading conditions, whereas those for Figure 9 were under more stressful conditions, e.g., with harsher lighting.

Recall that the goal of prediction is to reduce the processing time by feeding the face detection black box with a small image. The size of a full image in our system is 768×1024 pixels. We observed the cropped image sizes varied from 0.16~0.21 of the full size. The processing time decreased quadratically with the image size ratio as shown in Figure 4-(a). Therefore, the face detection after a successful prediction took only 1/25 or even less time than that for a full-sized image. Figure 19 shows the average processing times with prediction, including the handling of prediction failure. The right bar in the figure shows the average processing time for full-sized images. We found that the average

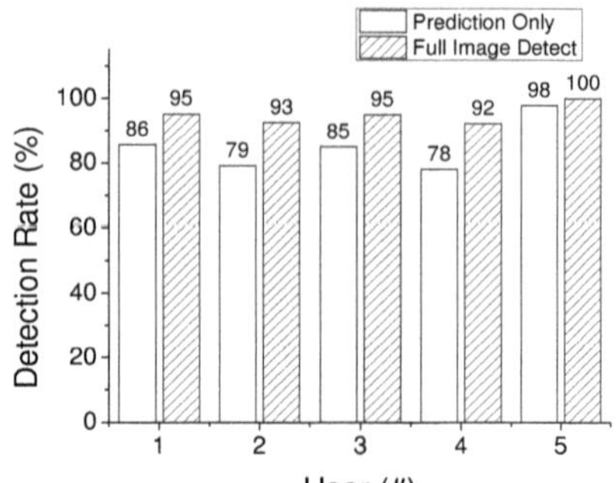

Figure 18: Prediction and full detection rates for 5 volunteers under normal device usage.

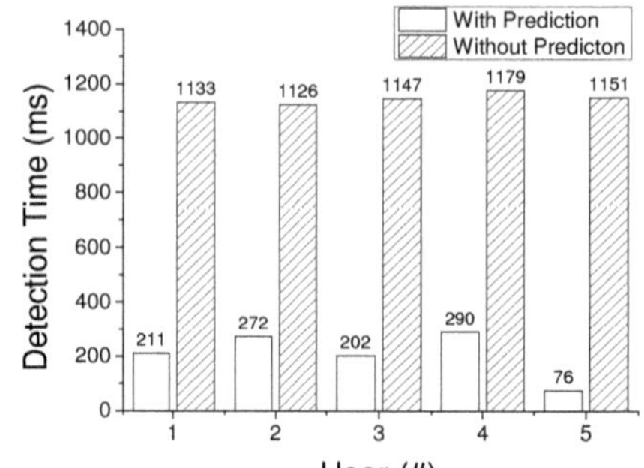

Figure 19: Average face detection times for 5 volunteers, with and without prediction.

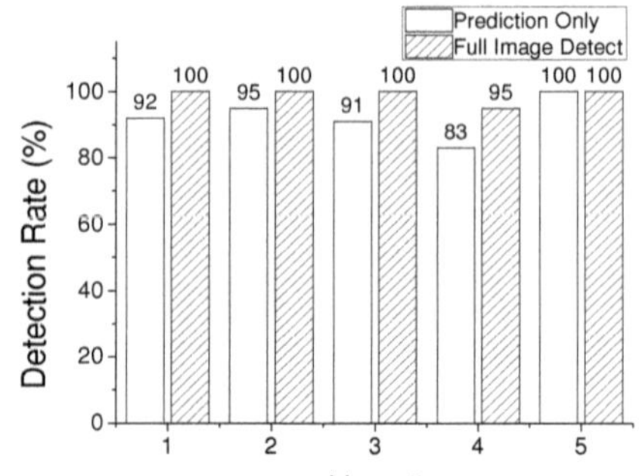

Figure 20: Prediction rates and detection rates for 5 volunteers in Off-the-Body scenarios.

processing time dropped to 76ms when the successful prediction rate was 98%. Though fail predictions led to full image processing, the average processing time with prediction still significantly outperformed those without prediction.

Off-the-Body Situation: We carried out similar experiments when the device was away from the body. We had 5 volunteers put the phone beside their keyboard when they were sitting in their cubicles. The phone invoked a face detection each time the light sensor detected an event such as when the user leaned towards the phone or the phone received notifications. For each volunteer, the light sensor triggered 7∼15 times during half a day usage. We observed the phone successfully captured all intentional events with only a small fraction of false alarms (10% ∼ 30% depends on the actual position of the phone).

For each prediction, the predicted area is cropped and fed into the face detection module. If a face was detected, we counted it as a successful prediction. Otherwise, a full scan was carried out to find the face. If a face was detected, we counted it as a successful detection. We show the prediction success rates and detection rates in Figure 20. We can see that the prediction rates varied from 0.83 to 1.00 across different volunteers. The mean processing times with and without prediction showed similar trends with Figure 19, which is therefore omitted due to space limitations. In conclusion, motion-based prediction significantly reduces the execution time of face detection in Off-the-Body scenarios.

8.2.2 *Evaluation of Viewing Angle Detection*

The view direction is determined by two angles θ and ϕ, as defined in Section 5.1. As the two angles are independent, we evaluated them separately for easy acquisition of ground truths. We first evaluated the detection of θ. We obtained 5 groups of images, each of which was from a volunteer. Each group contained images at 6 different viewing angles, i.e., 45°, 40°, 30°, 20°, 10°, and 0°.

We plot the mean estimated viewing angles versus the actual ones in Figure 8.2.2. The dashed line represents the ideal case, where the detected viewing angles equal actual ones, and the error bars show the max and min calculated angles among different image groups. We can see that the calculated results fit well with the ideal line. The errors seem independent from the actual viewing angle. The maximum error across all test cases was less than 8 degrees, which means our viewing angle detection algorithm satisfies moderate application requirements. We also evaluated the detection of ϕ in the same way as that for θ. The results

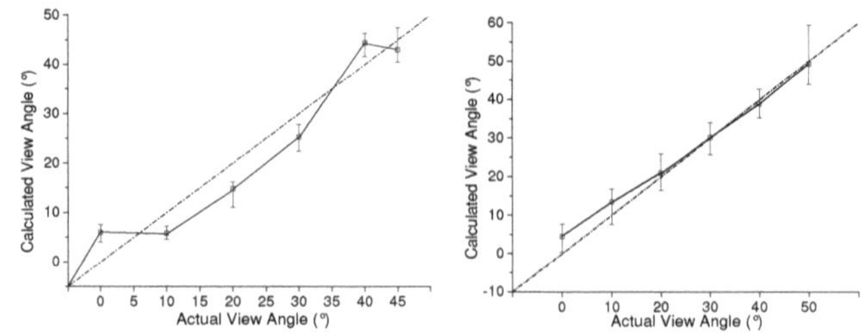

(a) Pitch θ (b) Roll ϕ

Figure 21: Viewing angle detection accuracy.

are shown in Figure 8.2.2. From the figure, we can see that average estimated angles fit well with the actual ones, and the max-min variation is within 10 degrees.

8.2.3 *Energy Consumption*

In ViRi, we need to monitor the viewing situations continuously, and we have exploited free system states and low power sensors (accelerometer, compass, proximity sensor, and the light sensor) to trigger more energy expensive camera sensors and face detection. The sensors themselves consume negligible energy. For example, the popular LSM330DLC accelerometer consumes about 11uA at its highest rate, and it drops to 6uA in low power mode, and the AK8975c compass consumes about 0.35mA at a high sampling rate.

However, in current smartphones, such background sensing needs to activate the main CPU and thus consumes more energy than necessary. We profiled all the low power sensors used by ViRi, and there are only a few mA differences when using those sensors at the highest sampling rate or not using them at all. Notice that the computational complexity of sensor sampling and processing are very simple. A low power MCU such as MSP430 series can do the job, and consumes only a few milliamperes. Actually, given the high demand of continuous sensing of user contexts by many mobile applications, future mobile phones may have more energy-efficient peripheral sensory boards [13, 14] or may adopt new CPU designs (e.g., [17]) that can dedicate one core for all the low energy sensing tasks.

Besides the energy consumption of the low power sensors, most of the energy consumed by ViRi is spent on image capture and face detection, which would depend on the actual usage pattern of different users. Recall that ViRi is triggered only when there are substantial contextual changes (motion, pending notifications, and lighting). To obtain a real understanding of the energy consumption of ViRi, we surveyed 10 mobile phone users by checking the number of prompts, including SMS, push emails, reminders, and push notifications from their favorite social network applications (WeChat and Weibo). For push notifications coming in a batch, we treated them as a single event. So did the instant message sessions.

To account for different usage patterns, we conducted conservative estimation by assuming all the predictions would fail, and used the actual energy profiling results of the current implementation. As mentioned in Section 8.1, we have to go through the preview stage in the current implementation and thus consume more energy than necessary. According to the survey results, a user receives on average 30.4 events per day, with the standard deviation being 17.9 events. For each such event, in the worst case where all predictions fail, Viri consumes about 644mA on average for about 3 seconds, including the preview, image capture, prediction, and fail over to full-image face detection. Then the energy consumption for each detection is 0.54mAh. Multiply this by 84, the sum of average and three-times deviation, and the energy consumption is 45.1mAh, which is about 2.5% of a typical 1800mAh battery.

ViRi also executes when the user actually views the screen. In such cases, we perform viewing angle estimation only when the device changes from one (quasi-)stationary attitude to another significantly different one. In addition, the CPU and the screen are already on. Thus the CPU overhead for accelerometer sensing and the energy consumed by lighting up the screen should be excluded. Let's assume a user views the screen for three hours a day and the attitude changes every one minute, and assume a 90% prediction success rate (from Section 8.2.1). Under these settings, ViRi would consume about 10.45mAh, about 0.6% of a 1800mAh battery. Therefore, with a conservative estimate, the energy overhead of ViRi in typical usage is about 3.1% of total battery charge.

8.3 An Strawman App and Early Feedbacks

We have built a straw man mobile application that incorporates all the proposed viewing angle detection techniques. With the application, a user can provide a picture of interest and see the effect of viewing angle correction at arbitrary slanted viewing angles by either holding the phone and changing its orientation or resting the phone on a desk and changing her own viewing posture.

We performed a small-scale, informal user study. All users found that ViRi provides an intriguing viewing experience, especially when the tilting angle is large. Images with a black background showed better results than white ones. We think this is partially due to the OLED screen that remains completely dark for black pixels. The user trial also revealed some issues, some of which were expected. For example, ViRi's perspective correction could lead to either a full but smaller image or partial but larger image, due to the reduced effective viewing area. Figure 22 shows two such examples. The full but smaller one will sacrifice fine details of the original image, whereas the partial but larger one may only show a portion. All users suggested studying smart content selection, i.e., to show full or partial (full or partial what), and to show which portion when showing partial content. Some users were further concerned that if ViRi were applied on a larger display, then the top and bottom pixels would have different viewing angles, which might require luminance compensation. As could be expected, all users want ViRi to be an OS feature and support all applications.

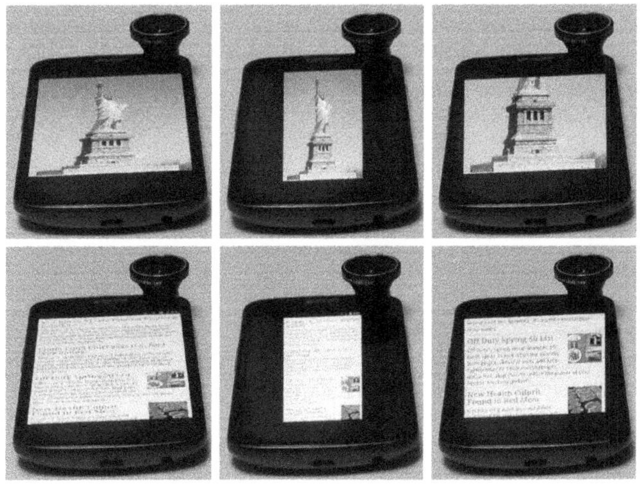

Figure 22: ViRi effects of full frame content. From left to right: original content at slanted view, ViRi with full but smaller image, ViRi with partial but larger image.

9. DISCUSSION

The effective working range of our prototype is only about 2 meters (1 meter to each side of the lens). We conjecture this is partially due to the concatenation of the fisheye lens and the existing phone camera system, which actually reduced the effective FOV of the fisheye lens, and also partially due to the low resolution of the front-camera of the phone we used. We expect if a high resolution, genuine fisheye camera were used, the working range and detection ratio would increase significantly.

The adoption of a fisheye camera in ViRi opens up new opportunities and challenges for many computer vision technologies such as face detection. We have adopted existing face detection tools and focused on various pre-processing techniques in order to use them directly. There are two possible improvements to improve face detection. First, we can apply super-resolution technologies to mitigate the view compression problem of fisheye cameras to increase the face detection rate. Second, we may directly perform face detection on fisheye images.

The high computation complexity of face detection makes Cloud services an appealing solution. We chose not to use the Cloud because it would create dependency on the network infrastructure. Moreover, pictures are usually of large size and wireless communication is also energy hungry, sending pictures to the Cloud may consume more energy than local processing, putting aside the long transmission latency.

The wide FOV of a fisheye lens makes it possible to include multiple faces in certain situations such as in a meeting. This may confuse the motion-based prediction. We have not properly addressed this issue. One strategy is to detect the largest face area and track the user or to simply disable this function if multiple faces are detected. After all, a mobile device is a personal device.

We have mainly focused on perspective correction for on-axial slanted viewing angles, i.e., our sight line is perpendicular to one of the device's boundary frames. In real world situations, we may end up with off-axial slanted viewing angles. In principle, as previously shown, we can detect the actual viewing angles (θ and ϕ), it is more challenging to show perspective corrected content on the screen, as the effective viewing area decreases at the order of $\cos\theta \cdot \cos\phi$.

10. RELATED WORK

Fisheye Image Correction: Several efforts [6, 19, 21] have been made to build a more natural view for a fisheye captured image. In [19], a fisheye photo is divided and projected onto multiple planes, leaving sharp seams between joint scenes. Users can specify where to put the seams in order to make them unnoticeable. In [6], the properties to be preserved are controlled by the user, and the mapping from the view sphere to the image plane is performed via weighted least-squares optimization. These schemes improve distortion correction performance at the cost of human intervention and a high computation cost, which are not desirable for our scenario. Thus, we use a simplified single global mapping to preprocess each image before face detection. The global mapping allows efficient computation via simple table lookup.

Mobile Applications Exploiting Face Detection: It is natural to have face detection on mobile phones for biometric unlocking, self-portrait, and mood sensing [15]. The key constraints for applying face detection on mobile phones are the limited computational resources (memory and CPU) and variable environments [8]. As a result, existing face detection libraries are ported carefully to mobile platforms to minimize memory usage and do hardware specific optimization. Examples [5] include OpenCV4Android, OpenCV iOS, and FaceDetection WinPhone (OpenCV in C#). The latest Android OS already provides native APIs for face detection. In ViRi, we simply leverage existing SDKs instead of developing special face detection algorithms for fisheye images.

Eye Tracking: Eye tracking has recently gained the attention of researchers. In [12], the authors proposed using eye blinks to activate a smartphone app. To this end, they tracked and mapped the user's eye to the smartphone display. Another piece of recent work [9] focused on detecting the blink rate of the user using a Samsung Galaxy Tab. A key challenge in their work was to track the eye in spite of camera motion. They developed an accelerometer-based eye position prediction algorithm that exhibits some similarity to our angle-based prediction scheme. As a salient feature of the Galaxy SIII, Samsung introduced SmartStay, which maintains a bright display as long as the user is viewing the screen [16]. The key differences are that we cover both Hand-Held and Off-the-Body situations and we avoided unnecessary detection using low power sensors to trigger image capture, which significantly reduces power consumption.

11. CONCLUSION

In this paper, we have mainly studied the viewing angle estimation problem of ViRi, which aims to achieve an all-time front-view viewing experience for mobile users in realistic viewing situations. We propose augmenting an existing phone camera system with a fisheye lens and use face detection tools to detect the actual viewing angle. We have come up with effective preprocessing techniques to correct the severe distortion of fisheye images. We have designed and evaluated several techniques for energy savings, including context sifting using low power sensors to maximally skip unnecessary face detection, and efficient prediction techniques to speed up face detection when there is a real need. We have also built a straw man application to allow users to experience the effect of viewing angle correction.

We think ViRi represents an initial step towards a more general direction of mobile sensing: allowing the device to gain perpetual awareness of it user, making mobile devices more intelligent and serving its users better. It is an extremely difficult task under normal usage styles and worth more study. For ViRi, our next step is to further study and integrate the display adjustment to the graphics pipeline of the operating system to support all applications.

12. REFERENCES

[1] Android Face Detector. `http://developer.android.com/reference/android/media/FaceDetector.html`.

[2] Euler Angles. `http://mathworld.wolfram.com/EulerAngles.html`.

[3] Microsoft Face SDK. `http://research.microsoft.com/en-us/projects/facesdk/`.

[4] Olloclip. `http://www.olloclip.com/`.

[5] G. Bradski. The OpenCV Library. *Dr. Dobb's Journal of Software Tools*, 2000.

[6] R. Carroll, M. Agrawal, and A. Agarwala. Optimizing content-preserving projections for wide-angle images. In *SIGGRAPH '09*, 2009.

[7] L.-P. Cheng, F.-I. Hsiao, Y.-T. Liu, and M. Y. Chen. irotate: Automatic screen rotating based on face orientation. In *CHI 2012*, 2012.

[8] A. Hadid, J. Heikkila, O. Silven, and M. Pietikainen. Face and eye detection for person authentication in mobile phones. In *ICDSC '07*, 2007.

[9] S. Han, S. Yang, J. Kim, and M. Gerla. Eyeguardian: a framework of eye tracking and blink detection for mobile device users. In *HotMobile '12*, 2012.

[10] J. Kannala and S. S. Brandt. A generic camera model and calibration method for conventional, wide-angle, and fish-eye lenses. *IEEE Trans. Pattern Anal. Mach. Intell.*

[11] F. Li, C. Zhao, G. Ding, J. Gong, C. Liu, and F. Zhao. A reliable and accurate indoor localization method using phone inertial sensors. In *UbiComp'12*.

[12] E. Miluzzo, T. Wang, and A. T. Campbell. Eyephone: activating mobile phones with your eyes. In *MobiHeld '10*.

[13] B. Priyantha, D. Lymberopoulos, and J. Liu. Littlerock: Enabling energy-efficient continuous sensing on mobile phones. *Pervasive Computing, IEEE*, 2011.

[14] M.-R. Ra, B. Priyantha, A. Kansal, and J. Liu. Improving energy efficiency of personal sensing applications with heterogeneous multi-processors. In *UbiComp '12*, 2012.

[15] N. D. L. Robert LiKamWa, Yunxin Liu and L. Zhong. Moodsense: Can your smartphone infer your mood? In *PhoneSense workshop*, 2011.

[16] Samsung. Galaxy S3 Smart Stay. `http://www.samsung.com/global/galaxys3/smartstay.html`.

[17] Texas Instruments Inc. TMS320C6472 Datasheet. `http://www.ti.com/lit/wp/spry130/spry130.pdf`.

[18] L. Yuan and J. Sun. Automatic exposure correction of consumer photographs. In *ECCV'12*, 2012.

[19] L. Zelnik-Manor, G. Peters, and P. Perona. Squaring the circles in panoramas. In *ICCV '05*, 2005.

[20] C. Zhang and Z. Zhang. A Survey of Recent Advances in Face Detection. In *TechReport, MSR-TR-2010-66*, 2010.

[21] D. Zorin and A. H. Barr. Correction of geometric perceptual distortions in pictures. In *SIGGRAPH '95*.

ScreenPass: Secure Password Entry on Touchscreen Devices

Dongtao Liu
Duke University
Durham, NC, USA

Eduardo Cuervo
Duke University
Durham, NC, USA

Valentin Pistol
Duke University
Durham, NC, USA

Ryan Scudellari
Duke University
Durham, NC, USA

Landon P. Cox
Duke University
Durham, NC, USA

ABSTRACT

Users routinely access cloud services through third-party apps on smartphones by giving apps login credentials (i.e., a username and password). Unfortunately, users have no assurance that their apps will properly handle this sensitive information. In this paper, we describe the design and implementation of ScreenPass, which significantly improves the security of passwords on touchscreen devices. ScreenPass secures passwords by ensuring that they are entered securely, and uses taint-tracking to monitor where apps send password data. The primary technical challenge addressed by ScreenPass is guaranteeing that trusted code is always aware of when a user is entering a password. ScreenPass provides this guarantee through two techniques. First, ScreenPass includes a trusted software keyboard that encourages users to specify their passwords' domains as they are entered (i.e., to tag their passwords). Second, ScreenPass performs optical character recognition (OCR) on a device's screenbuffer to ensure that passwords are entered only through the trusted software keyboard. We have evaluated ScreenPass through experiments with a prototype implementation, two in-situ user studies, and a small app study. Our prototype detected a wide range of dynamic and static keyboard-spoofing attacks and generated zero false positives. As long as a screen is off, not updated, or not tapped, our prototype consumes zero additional energy; in the worst case, when a highly interactive app rapidly updates the screen, our prototype under a typical configuration introduces only 12% energy overhead. Participants in our user studies tagged their passwords at a high rate and reported that tagging imposed no additional burden. Finally, a study of malicious and non-malicious apps running under ScreenPass revealed several cases of password mishandling.

Categories and Subject Descriptors

C.2.4 [**Distributed Systems**]: Network Operating Systems

General Terms

Security

Keywords

OCR, Passwords, Phishing, Smartphone security, User interface design, User study

1. INTRODUCTION

Users routinely access cloud services such as Facebook and Twitter via third-party applications (i.e., "apps") on touchscreen devices. To interact with these services, an app must provide a user's password to one or more remote servers. Passwords are highly sensitive data and handing them over to third-party apps raises the following question: how can users be sure that an app properly handles their passwords? The recent discovery of password-stealing apps and other vulnerabilities in Android demonstrates that users have reason to be concerned [10, 21].

A trusted information-flow monitor such as TaintDroid [6] can track the propagation of password data, but data must be *tagged* before it can be tracked. Past systems have tagged sensitive user input via a *secure attention sequence (SAS)*, such as "@@", to indicate the beginning of a password [12, 16]. Trusted software (i.e., a keyboard driver) must monitor the incoming character stream for the SAS and, when it appears, must treat subsequent characters as password data.

However, recognizing SASes in the text-input stream of a touchscreen device is difficult because of *software keyboards*. Trusted code such as the touchscreen driver and user-interface manager receive taps on a touchscreen as a set of coordinates, and can only understand the intended meaning of a user's taps when they understand the content of the screen.

The platform could reserve part of the screen for secure gestures, but modern devices' small screens make screen real estate a precious resource. Important third-party apps such as games, media players, and web browsers need write access to the entire screen. Unfortunately, a malicious app can abuse this privilege to *spoof* a platform's user interface, including its trusted software keyboard. Under a spoofing attack, a user may input an SAS meant for the trusted platform without realizing that the input was delivered directly to a malicious app.

To ensure that passwords are input securely, we have developed a system called ScreenPass. ScreenPass provides a special-purpose software keyboard for entering sensitive text such as passwords that allows a user to *tag* her input with a domain (e.g., Google, Facebook, or Twitter). ScreenPass uses these tags to taint-track the user's password data as it propagates through the app.

Tags can subsequently be used to enable a number of useful policies. For example, the system may want to know when plaintext password data is written to disk or when password data is shared between apps via IPC. Similarly, if an app tries to write password data to the network, a guard can check the write's safety by reasoning about features of the network endpoint (is the destination port associated with unencrypted traffic?), the taint tag's domain (is the destination IP address in the appropriate domain?), or a password's usage history (is the app adhering to the OAuth specification and only sending a password once?). If an action is considered unsafe, then the guard can either block the data from being released, or it can raise an alert.

ScreenPass's primary goal is ensuring that password data is only entered through a trusted keyboard so that it can be tagged before it is given to an app. To achieve this goal, ScreenPass performs dynamic optical character recognition (OCR) on regions of the screen where users expect a software keyboard to appear. If text in this region of the screen is sufficiently similar to the "qwerty" text of a keyboard and the foreground app has not yielded control of the screen to the trusted keyboard, the OS can kill the foreground process or raise an alert.

This paper makes the following contributions:

- Previous secure UIs have restricted *where* untrusted code can write to the screen [8, 19], but ScreenPass is the first system designed specifically for the limited screen real estate of a mobile device; ScreenPass protects sensitive input by restricting *what* untrusted code may write to sensitive parts of the screen.
- ScreenPass is the first system to prevent UI spoofing through efficient and robust online computer vision. Software-only computer-vision techniques such as OCR minimize ScreenPass's hardware requirements and allow our approach to generalize to any modern touchscreen device.
- We have implemented a ScreenPass prototype for Android and evaluated its robustness to attack as well as its energy and performance overheads. Our attack study found that ScreenPass is robust to a wide range of static and dynamic attacks while generating zero false positives. ScreenPass only failed to detect spoofed keyboards with noisy backgrounds that look significantly different than a standard system keyboard.

  ScreenPass consumes no additional energy when the screen is not updated or tapped. Under a typical configuration, ScreenPass introduces 12% energy overhead in the worst case. It consumes far less for apps that infrequently update the screen or require little user input. ScreenPass also had negligible impact on interactivity; under a typical configuration, no workload experienced a statistically significant drop in frame rate under ScreenPass.
- We have also conducted two in-situ user studies with ScreenPass-like software keyboards. Our initial 18-user, three-week user study showed that tagging passwords imposes little additional burden on users, and showed that users will tag passwords at a high rate when prompted. A smaller, follow-up study demonstrated that integrating a password manager with ScreenPass incentivizes users to tag their passwords at a high rate even when they are not prompted.

The rest of the paper is organized as follows: Section 2 describes ScreenPass's trust and threat model, Section 3 provides an overview of ScreenPass's approach to securing passwords on mobile devices, Section 4 describes the design and implementation of ScreenPass, Section 5 describes our evaluation, Section 6 describes related work, and Section 7 gives our conclusions.

2. TRUST AND THREAT MODEL

We assume that a user trusts the mobile platform running on her device, and relies on the operating system's existing mechanisms to thwart attacks against the platform itself. We assume that the trusted computing base (TCB) consists of any code that sits behind the standard set of APIs on which a mobile app is implemented.

For example, the essential components of Android's security model are a Linux kernel, user-space daemons called services running under privileged UIDs, and an IPC mechanism called Binder. Each Android app is signed by its developer and runs as a Linux process with its own unique, unprivileged UID. Apps access protected resources such as the software keyboard through Binder IPC calls. Apps and services can limit interactions with other code by specifying access-control policies to the Binder dispatcher.

An information-flow monitor such as TaintDroid cannot track important data unless it is properly tagged and cannot protect tagged data without release policies. However, even though these tags can allow a monitor to provide stronger security for a user's passwords than is possible today, some classes of attacks are difficult or impossible to prevent with existing monitors.

For example, like many monitors, TaintDroid does not prevent data from leaking through covert channels such as a program's control flow or timing information. Recent work on selectively tracking implicit flows using information from the symbolic execution of a program is promising [11], and such techniques may be applicable to existing monitors. We consider attacks against the taint-tracker to be outside the scope of this paper; our goal is to ensure that password input is always tagged. Furthermore, ScreenPass is not designed to prevent passwords from leaking via covert channels like a device's motion sensors [3, 13]. These vulnerabilities have straightforward solutions, such as disabling access to motion sensors whenever a password is input.

ScreenPass's taint tags associate data with a coarse-grained domain. As a result, ScreenPass alone cannot prevent attacks in which passwords are leaked within a domain. For example, untrusted code could log into a service using credentials that are hardcoded into the app binary or accessed from an external server. Once logged in, the untrusted code could leak another user's password through the original account (e.g., by writing the user's password on an attacker's Facebook wall). Alternatively, an untrusted app could encode a user's Facebook password as a world-readable message on the user's own wall, wait for an external machine to read the post, and then delete the post before the user noticed anything strange.

These attacks are challenging, but allowing a system to monitor which domains have access to a password make it more likely that problems can be detected than if passwords continue to be shared without restriction. For example, many services maintain detailed records of all user actions. If a service detects a same-domain attack on mobile users' passwords, then it may be able to use its logs and identify how many other users were affected.

Finally, this work assumes that passwords are input through a "qwerty" English keyboard, though we believe that our techniques can be generalized to more specialized keyboards, such as numeric keyboards or non-English keyboards. We assume that users will not trust apps that require passwords to be input through a keyboard with a non-standard layout or an unusual set of keys.

3. APPROACH OVERVIEW

ScreenPass must ensure that the TCB intercepts all password input so that it can be tagged and tracked by an information-flow monitor like TaintDroid. The original TaintDroid prototype [6] tracks sensitive data that is accessed through a small number of

API calls with well-defined semantics. By interposing on these taint sources, TaintDroid can tag several important classes of sensitive data before they are accessed by untrusted code. Once this data has been released, TaintDroid tracks its propagation by integrating dynamic taint analysis (taint-tracking) into Android's Dalvik VM, native system libraries, file system, and Binder IPC mechanism. Tagging sensitive data as it enters a program by interposing on API calls with well-defined semantics is sufficient for many classes of sensitive data (e.g., a device's location and IMEI number), but this approach is not a good fit for passwords.

Apps access passwords through character-stream interfaces that do not distinguish between sensitive and non-sensitive data. Previous approaches to identifying password inputs have required users to explicitly identify their passwords through a *secure attention sequence (SAS)* [12, 16]. An SAS is a well-known sequence of characters (e.g., "@@") that labels bytes in the stream as password data. As long as trusted code can identify individual characters, it can look for the SAS and tag password data. Unfortunately, on touchscreen devices with software keyboards, untrusted apps can circumvent the SAS by hiding text input from the TCB.

Software keyboards translate touchscreen gestures to characters by correlating the screen location where a user tapped or gestured with what was displayed at that location. Well-behaved apps allow trusted code to map gestures to characters by invoking the platform's standard software keyboard. When invoked, the trusted software keyboard assumes control of the lower half of the screen, where it displays a virtual keypad. The keypad receives the coordinates of taps from the touchscreen driver, translates those inputs into characters, and returns the characters to the app. In addition, well-behaved apps using a platform's standard library of widgets can put text-input boxes into "password" mode by manipulating its attributes. For example, Android apps can set the "android:password" attribute of a text-input widget to explicitly notify the TCB when input to the text box is a password.

Unfortunately, touchscreen platforms cannot force apps to yield control of the screen to the trusted UI. An untrusted app can bypass the trusted keyboard by retaining control of the screen, displaying a keypad that is visually indistinguishable from the trusted one, and translating touchscreen gestures to characters by itself.

Under such a spoofing attack, trusted code such as the touchscreen driver and UI manager would only see taps and swipes on the screen and cannot interpret the semantics of those gestures. Trusted code would have no way of knowing that a user's taps and swipes were meant to be text inputs, and a user would have no way of knowing that the TCB was oblivious to her password input.

To address these challenges, we developed ScreenPass while keeping the following design considerations in mind:

Minimize hardware assumptions. ScreenPass should work on as many touchscreen devices as possible. There are hundreds of touchscreen devices with a wide range of hardware configurations. However, because of the minimalist industrial design of modern smartphones we conservatively assume that all interactions with a user occur through the touchscreen. Furthermore, ScreenPass should not re-purpose already overloaded inputs such as a home or power button for an SAS, or rely on a non-touchscreen output such an external LED to signal the user.

Maximize display utilization. Screen real estate is a precious resource for mobile apps. Prior approaches to secure UIs [8, 19] have reserved part of the screen for messages from the TCB to the user, but this is inappropriate for consumer touchscreen devices. Android, iOS, and other mobile platforms provide a bar at the top of the screen for system information and notifications, but allow apps such as games, media players, and web browsers to hide this bar when in full-screen mode. To preserve the functionality of these important apps, ScreenPass should also support full-screen mode.

Minimize users' responsibilities. ScreenPass should avoid burdening users' with easy-to-ignore and error-prone new responsibilities. For example, ScreenPass could display a secret image, known only to ScreenPass and the user whenever it detected password input. If the image was absent during password entry, a user would be expected to notice and not provide her password. We did not pursue this approach because (1) ScreenPass would have to rely on users to choose images that could not be guessed by untrusted code, and (2) the secret image would have to be managed through additional layers of UI (e.g., for setting and resetting), each of which would need to be secured.

Furthermore, Schechter's 2007 study of site-authentication images (SAIs) found that these secrets provide very little security in practice [17]. This study found that 92% of participants logged in to a banking site when their secret image was replaced with a generic maintenance message. Schechter's study also found that 100% of participants logged in when the secure-connection indicator (i.e., a red "https" string) was absent. Other studies of web-based systems have found that relying on users to heed warnings or notice the absence of a visual signal are often ineffective [4, 5, 20].

The main observation behind our approach to securing password input is that a keyboard consists of a unique and predictable sequence of characters. Thus, ScreenPass uses efficient optical character recognition (OCR) to search for text in the portion of the screen where a user would expect a keyboard (i.e., the lower half). If the OCR engine detects character sequences that are close to those of a keyboard (e.g., "qwerty" or "qvvrty"), it checks whether the trusted software keyboard has been invoked. If not, ScreenPass can take a variety of actions, such as killing the foreground process or warning the user.

4. ScreenPass

ScreenPass is a realization of the approach to secure password entry for Android touchscreen devices outlined in Section 3.

4.1 Background

The Android mobile platform includes a Linux kernel, Java programming environment, and several layers of trusted middleware. ScreenPass also relies on TaintDroid for taint-tracking. We briefly describe the most relevant of these subsystems below.

4.1.1 Android

Application Framework An Android app consists of three components. An *activity* defines the app's UI, and controls all of an app's widgets (called "views" in Android). Activities interact with background services and content providers. An application's *background service* is a separate thread that contains the application's core logic and soft state. An app's *content provider* offers an interface to persistent storage such as the file system or a SQL database.

Dalvik Virtual Machine App components are written in Java, and this code is compiled into Dalvik Execution (DEX) byte codes. The Android team developed their own Dalvik Virtual Machine (VM), which is optimized for mobile devices. Android apps execute within separate VM instances, and VM instances are managed as processes by the underlying Linux kernel. Apps use Android's custom IPC protocol (Binder) to communicate with processes outside of their own.

Input Method Framework The Input Method Framework (IMF) provides a way to invoke and manage input methods such as on-screen software keyboards. When a user selects a text-input box, the widget makes a request to the IMF for an Input Method Engine

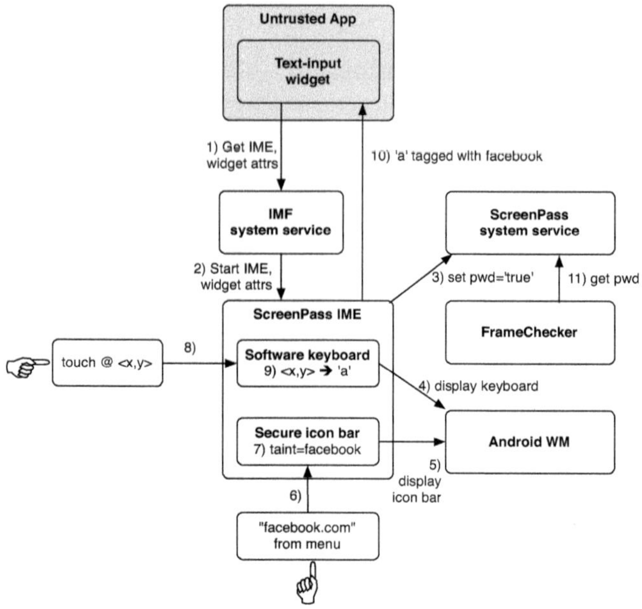

Figure 1: Overview of the ScreenPass architecture.

(IME) that can receive input from the user. The IME runs in a separate process from the requesting app and writes user input to a string field in the text-input widget via IPC.

Frame Buffer The Linux frame buffer (FB) is an abstraction that provides access to the graphical output of the device. Android's FB device is found at /dev/graphics/fb0 and can be accessed by only the root user and the graphics group. The FB has a front and back buffer: the front buffer contains the pixel data currently displayed on the screen, and the back buffer is used for composition by the SurfaceFlinger.

SurfaceFlinger The SurfaceFlinger (SF) is Android's system-wide surface composition engine, and is responsible for managing surfaces and the virtual frame buffer device. When an activity creates a widget, it asks the SF to allocate a new surface. The SF allocates a back and front buffer for the surface and returns a handle to the requesting process. As the owner of this surface, the requesting process is free to update the back buffer as needed. The back buffer is used by the activity for rendering new frames. Once a process has finished rendering, it swaps the front and back buffers and asks the SF to draw the new frame to the screen. The front buffer is used by the SF for composition.

4.1.2 TaintDroid

TaintDroid is a system-wide taint-tracking extension for Android [6]. TaintDroid associates tags with sensitive data that is released to untrusted code via *taint sources* such as requests for a device's current location. Taint tags are 32-entry bit vectors that can be associated with program variables, IPC messages, and files. TaintDroid implements a tag-propagation logic to capture data dependencies as the system executes.

4.2 Capturing and tainting passwords

Figure 1 shows a high-level overview of how ScreenPass captures and tags a user's password. Arrows in the diagram represent IPC calls across components. All components in the figure are trusted except for the untrusted app in gray.

The first step in tagging a user's password is for the untrusted app to request an IME from the IMF system service. The request contains attributes describing the target widget so that the software keyboard can be appropriately configured. For example, if a text field is an email address, the software keyboard can display an "@" key along with the usual alphabetical keys. The IMF assigns the app to the ScreenPass IME and passes along the target widget's attributes. The IME checks these attributes to see if the widget is in password mode.

If a widget says that it is in password mode, the secure keyboard first contacts the ScreenPass system service to put the device in password mode. The ScreenPass system service acts as a central repository for ScreenPass state. IPCs to access this state can be controlled using Android's code-signing framework. Only code that has been signed by a trusted entity is allowed to communicate with the ScreenPass system service.

A malicious app could claim that the target widget was not in password mode, while still obfuscating text input as a user would expect of a password field. If this happens, the ScreenPass IME will not prompt the user to tag their password, and the user must either (1) avoid entering their password, or (2) use an area at the bottom of the secure keyboard to actively tag their password and put the device in password mode. We call this a *silent-widget attack*. We will return to this attack shortly.

Once the device is in password mode, the keyboard makes a request to the Android Window Manager to display the secure keyboard and domain chooser. Figure 2 shows the software keyboard and chooser. The tag list allows a user to associate an administrative domain with her password. This association must be set *before* a user inputs her password or else characters may not be properly tagged. As a result, the software keyboard ignores input until the user has chosen a tag, and the secure keyboard immediately prompts the user for a domain when triggered. Figure 2 shows the prompt a user sees after the keyboard is displayed. ScreenPass uses an integrated password manger to incentivize users to tag their passwords when they are not explicitly prompted (e.g., during a silent-widget attack).

Once the user has chosen a domain, the keyboard looks up the associated taint tag and applies the tag to all subsequent character inputs (whether input by the user using the keypad or loaded from the password database). It should be noted that once a user has chosen a tag, there is no way to change the tags that have been previously applied. However, our prototype allows users to choose from a preset list of domains or to define a new tag.

As described earlier, TaintDroid's taint tags are 32-bit bit vectors. The original TaintDroid design treats tags as bit vectors so that data derived from multiple sensitive sources can be represented. However, this approach leaves ScreenPass with too few bits to represent all of the services a user might use. As a result, ScreenPass reserves the highest 10 bits of each tag and treats those bits as a 10-bit namespace. Passwords do not need to be associated with multiple domains, and 1023 domains should be sufficient for most users.

When a user taps on the secure keyboard, it maps the coordinates of the taps to characters, and uses TaintDroid to tag the IPC message back to the untrusted app that contains password data. Once the untrusted app receives the tainted IPC message, TaintDroid propagates its tags as the app uses the password. When the app attempts to send a password over the network, to the file system, or over an IPC channel, TaintDroid inspects the buffer's tags and can enforce a system-defined policy.

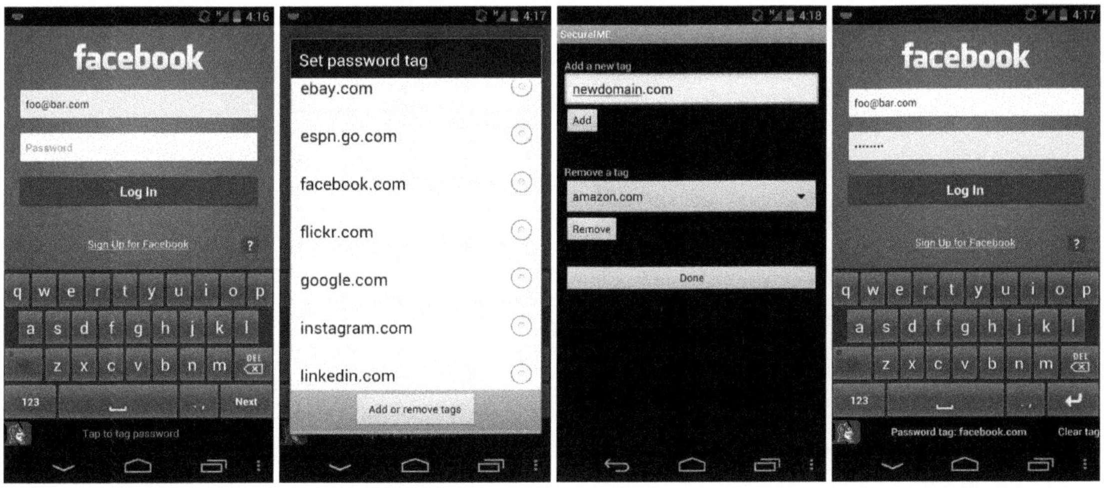

Figure 2: When a user taps on a password field, ScreenPass's secure keyboard prompts the user to tag their password, and then applies the tag to each character using TaintDroid.

4.3 Preventing spoofing attacks

The FrameChecker is responsible for detecting attempts to spoof the software keyboard. The FrameChecker is a thread running within the SF. The SF's main thread composes the system's surfaces together and posts the resulting frame to the frame buffer's (FB's) front buffer. Implementing the FrameChecker as a separate thread keeps spoof detection out of the critical path of the SF's main work.

At a high-level, a typical working cycle of the FrameChecker consists of three stages: (1) capturing the screen, (2) performing OCR to detect software keyboards, and (3) sleeping for a random, short amount of time. The random sleep time helps ScreenPass reduce its energy overhead to an acceptable level. As we will show in Section 5, performing OCR without resting could quickly drain a user's battery under certain workloads. Our current implementation sleeps for a randomly chosen time between 0ms and 1,000ms; that is, the expected sleep time is 500ms.

4.3.1 Screen capture

Upon waking up, the FrameChecker first checks with the ScreenPass system service to see if the device is in password mode, if the touchscreen has not been tapped, or if the screen has not changed since it went to sleep. If any of these conditions are true, then the FrameChecker does not need to analyze the screen and can go back to sleep. The SF maintains information about which regions of the screen are dirty, which allows the FrameChecker to avoid inspecting the FB if it has not changed since the last scan. In addition, a thread runs alongside the FrameChecker to detect touchscreen inputs. It detects all touch events by polling the device file /dev/input/event0 and maintains a status variable indicating whether a touch event occurred. After the FrameChecker wakes up, it checks this status variable.

The vast majority of the time, the screen will not have changed. Furthermore, only analyzing the screen while a user is interacting with it avoids performing analysis when the screen is updating but the user cannot be inputting her password. This is common for games that are primarily controlled by a device's motion sensors and for watching videos.

If the FrameChecker finds that the device is not in password mode, that the screen has been updated, and that the user is interacting with it, then the FrameChecker must perform OCR. However, taking a single instantaneous screen capture would leave ScreenPass vulnerable to dynamic attacks. Under a dynamic attack, malicious code rapidly alternates between frames of a partial keyboard so that a user viewing the screen sees a complete keyboard, but no single frame contains one. To combat this attack, another thread in the SF computes a "squashed image" composed of all instantaneous screen captures between FrameChecker requests. The squashed image contains the average pixel values over a period of time, and, as we will see in Section 5, closely approximates what a user perceives under a dynamic attack.

To reduce the computational load of computing the squashed image, ScreenPass takes two steps. First, we only target the bottom two-fifths of the screen where a keyboard may appear. Our Nexus S prototype has a screen resolution of 800×480 pixels, and our squashed image is 320×480 pixels. This not only reduces the effort needed to compute the squashed image, but the work of the OCR engine as well. Second, we used the NEON 128-bit SIMD instruction available on the Nexus S's ARM processor. This instruction allows us to add up to 16 8-bit integers in a single instruction, and greatly increases the efficiency of computing a squashed image.

One danger of computing squashed images is that, for periods containing a transition from a non-keyboard scene to a keyboard, the averages will be polluted by pre-keyboard pixels. However, as we will see in Section 5.2 users type passwords much more slowly than ScreenPass checks the screen. If a user starts to type her password, ScreenPass will have computed a "clean" squashed image well before she finishes.

4.3.2 OCR Analysis

The FrameChecker analyzes screen content using OCR. Our current implementation uses the well-known TesseractOCR package [18]. OCR converts images of text into machine-encoded characters, and is widely used to digitize a number of paper-based data sources including books, documents, receipts, and checks. A typical OCR process integrates techniques from computer vision, pattern recognition, and artificial intelligence. Usually, the steps include locating and segmenting the characters from input images, preprocessing the images to remove noise, extracting patterns from the characters for classifiers, organizing the identified characters

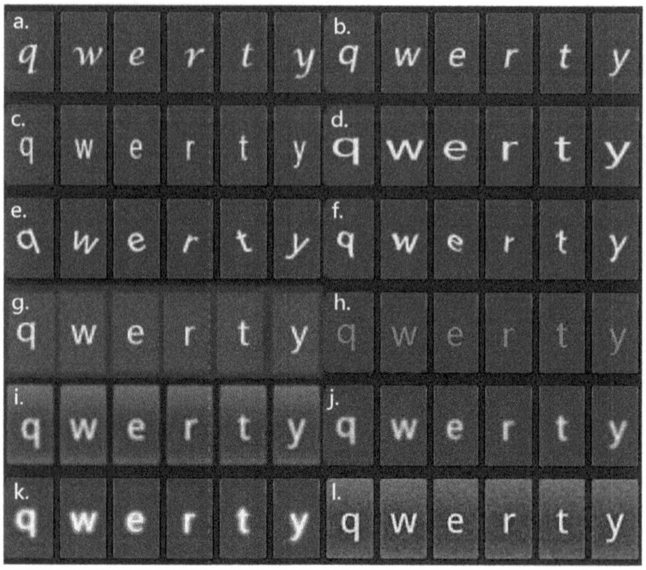

Figure 3: Static attack images tested: a. Scripted typeface, b. Italicized typeface, c. Narrowed typeface, d. Widened typeface, e. Rotated characters, f. Warped characters, g. Colored background, h. Colored characters, i. Blurred background, j. Blurred characters k. Shiny characters, l. Random noise

to reconstruct original words, and postprocessing to correct OCR errors by checking the context.

One of the advantages of using OCR to detect keyboards is that the analysis does not have to be completely accurate. The FrameChecker only needs to identify fragments of text that are sufficiently similar to the character sequences expected of a keyboard. Furthermore, attackers have no room to alter the character sequences on a spoofed keyboard, since a user will become instantly suspicious of a keyboard in which the keys have been moved around.

A keyboard is usually divided into three areas: the characters, the keys, and the background. The keys cover the majority of this area. To improve character identification, we apply preprocessing to the screen captures to highlight the characters and reconcile the color of the key and background. The keys cover more pixels than the characters and the background, so we can determine the color of the keys by identifying the peak color for all pixels. Then we refill the background with the same color of the keys so that the characters are highlighted against a pure color background. The preprocessing algorithm is fast and traverses all pixels twice. In the first traversal, we count the number of pixels in gray scale and identify the color for the peak. Then we change the color of the background pixels in the second traversal.

It is also worth pointing out that TesseractOCR itself can tolerate some color differences between the keys and background. We apply preprocessing only to handle some extreme cases, such as a black background and white keys, and to better facilitate character recognition. Finally, we use the training data for the English language from the TesseractOCR official site. When the FrameChecker starts, it loads the training data and initiates the OCR engine.

5. EVALUATION

To evaluate ScreenPass, we sought answers to the following questions:

- How robust is ScreenPass to spoofing attacks?
- What is the perceived burden of tagging passwords?
- How likely are users to tag their passwords?
- How often should ScreenPass check for spoofing attacks?
- What is the performance and energy overhead of ScreenPass?
- Can taint-tracking detect when apps mishandle passwords?

Figure 4: Sample frame from a dynamic-attack keyboard that ScreenPass could not detect by analyzing individual frames. ScreenPass detected the attack by analyzing a squashed image.

To answer the first question, we subjected our ScreenPass prototype to a variety of attack keyboards. To answer the next two questions, we performed two user studies. The first was a three-week, in-situ user study with 18 participants; the second was a one-week, follow-up study with eight of the initial participants. To answer the next two questions, we measured the performance and energy characteristics of our prototype using a mix of representative apps. To answer the final question, we ran 31 Android apps (30 benign and one malicious) on our ScreenPass prototype. Our prototype implements ScreenPass on top of Android 2.3.4, uses TaintDroid for taint-tracking, and runs on an HTC Nexus S smartphone.

5.1 Robustness to spoofing attacks

To measure ScreenPass's robustness to various kinds of spoofed keyboards, we created 12 static attacks and four dynamic attacks.

For the static attacks, we applied the following modifications classes to the stock Android keyboard: transformations, color changes, and special effects. Each class can be applied to the keyboard's background, its characters, or both. Figure 3 shows the upper-left corner of each static attack keyboard used in our experiments with the character sequence "q w e r t y".

Transformation To generate the transformed attack keyboards, we altered the shape of each character in the stock keyboard. These transformations included changing the font, italicizing the font, altering the font width, rotating characters, and warping characters.

Color Color attacks altered the background or character color of the stock keyboard.

Effects We also created attack keyboards by applying special effects to parts of the stock keyboard, such as a blurred background, blurred characters, "shiny" characters, and adding random noise.

If ScreenPass only performed OCR on individual frames it would be vulnerable to dynamic attacks in which a malicious app rapidly alternated partially complete frames. ScreenPass's squashed images smooth out visual differences between frames over a period of time to approximate what a user sees.

For our dynamic-attack experiments, we were interested in knowing (1) how incomplete frames needed to be before analyzing individual frames became insufficient, and (2) how robust our squashed-image approach was to these attacks. Each frame in our dynamic attack keyboards consisted of a checkerboard pattern of alternating empty blocks and keyboard-image blocks. Consecutive frames in an attack sequence swapped empty and keyboard-image blocks, so that when alternating frames were displayed at 30 FPS, a user saw a legitimate keyboard on the screen.

When the alternating blocks were only 1×1 pixel, OCR still detected the keyboard on individual frames. However, when blocks were 4×4 and 8×8 pixels large, OCR failed on individual frames but succeeded on the squashed image. The only dynamic attack that ScreenPass could not defeat was a keyboard with a flowery background. Figure 4 shows an example frame from the attack. The reason that ScreenPass failed to detect this keyboard is that the characters on the keyboard blended in with the noisy background in our squashed image. Nonetheless, this attack keyboard was clearly non-standard and would be easy for users to detect.

5.2 User studies

To better understand ScreenPass's usability, we designed two in-situ user studies. In both studies, participants were asked to (1) replace the software keyboard of their personal Android smartphone with a ScreenPass-like study keyboard, and (2) use their smartphones to complete a series of online surveys.

5.2.1 Study designs

Both study keyboards provided a high-fidelity simulation of using ScreenPass. The keyboards' default behavior was to immediately prompt the user to tag their password when the keyboard received a password-input request from an app. The prompt included a list of alphabetically-ordered pre-loaded tags, as well as an option to add a new tag. As with ScreenPass, the keyboard allowed users to tag any text input, even in the absence of an explicit prompt. The keyboard also included hooks for remotely turning explicit prompting on and off. The main difference between the keyboards used in our initial study and our follow-up study was that the initial-study keyboard did not include a password manager, whereas the keyboard in the follow-up study did. In both studies, each participant was instructed to disable the "password remembering" feature of their phone's web browser and to set the study keyboard as their phone's default input method. Each time an app requested password input the keyboard uploaded a timestamped record with the following information:

- whether the user was prompted to tag their password
- whether the user tagged their password
- a cryptographic hash of the tag (i.e., a domain name)
- a timestamp of when the keyboard received the password-input request
- a timestamp of when the keyboard displayed the tag prompt
- a timestamp of when the tag prompt stopped being displayed
- a timestamp of when the keyboard stopped being displayed

This data allowed us to measure how often users tagged their passwords (with and without prompting), how many unique tags a user used, how long users took to tag their passwords, and how long users took to type in their passwords. In the initial study, the keyboard did not log individual keystrokes or unhashed tags. In the follow-up study, the keyboard stored passwords to a local database so that they could be loaded automatically at a later time.

In addition to logging this data, we also asked participants to complete online surveys on their smartphones, as well an initial demographic and exit questionnaire on a PC. Surveys could only be accessed after logging in with a username and password, which increased the number of study-keyboard logins we could observe. In the initial study, we asked participants to complete three surveys, and in the follow-up study, we asked participants to complete two surveys.

Each of the online surveys (i.e., pre-study, mid-study, and post-study for the initial study and pre-study and post-study for the follow-up study) consisted of three questions. Each question was presented as a statement, and users were instructed to select their level of agreement with each statement on a scale from one ("Strongly disagree") to seven ("Strongly agree").

The first two survey statements were *"I worry that websites and mobile apps may steal my passwords"* and *"Before I log into a website, I make sure that the connection is secure."* These statements were intended to gauge a user's awareness of security threats, and were identical in all pre-study, mid-study, and post-study surveys.

The third statement asked participants to indicate how difficult they felt logging into apps and websites on a smartphone is. For the pre-study surveys, we presented the statement *"Before beginning the study, logging into websites and mobile apps on my smartphone was difficult."* For the mid-study and post-study surveys, we changed the start of the statement from *"Before beginning the study"* to *"Since beginning the study"*, while leaving the remaining wording the same. The change in phrasing allowed us to compare the perceived difficulty of inputting passwords on smartphones with and without the study keyboard.

For the first 20 days of the initial study, users were always prompted to tag their passwords. However, we turned off prompting before releasing the post-study survey. Because users were instructed to complete the post-study survey from their smartphones, turning off prompting at the end gave us a sense of how users would react to a silent-widget attack after 20 days of experience with the study keyboard. We similarly turned off prompting after a training phase in our follow-up study.

5.2.2 Recruitment and training

After receiving approval for our initial study from the university Internal Review Board (IRB), we recruited candidate participants by posting a call for participation on Facebook and Google Plus, and by sending emails to several university mailing lists. Interested users were instructed to complete a demographic questionnaire on our study website. As an incentive to participate, we offered each participant a $20 Amazon Gift Card, to be given after completing all study tasks.

46 individuals registered and completed our demographic questionnaire. We selected 20 participants from these candidates. We rejected candidates who used a non-Android smartphone or lived too far from campus to sign a consent form in person. From our initial set of 20 participants, two did not install the keyboard in a timely manner, and we have excluded them from our results. Thus, our reported results from the initial study are from 18 participants who installed our study keyboard on their personal Android smartphone for a period of three weeks during November and December, 2012.

From the initial demographic questionnaire, the average age of the 18 participants was 24 years old. Participants had owned an Android smartphone for an average of 1.5 years, spent an average of two hours each day browsing the Internet on their phone, and spent an average of five hours each day using the Internet on a PC. 15 of the participants were undergraduate or graduate students, one was a professor, one was a doctor, and one worked for local technology company. Four participants were female.

After notifying participants that they had been selected for the study, each signed a consent form in person. After signing the consent form, we installed the study keyboard on their personal Android smartphone and set it as the default keyboard. We also disabled the remembering-passwords option in their web browser settings. Lastly, we showed each participant how to tag their passwords and how to add a new password tag. The list of pre-loaded tags did not include one for the study website. We repeated this set-up procedure in our follow-up study.

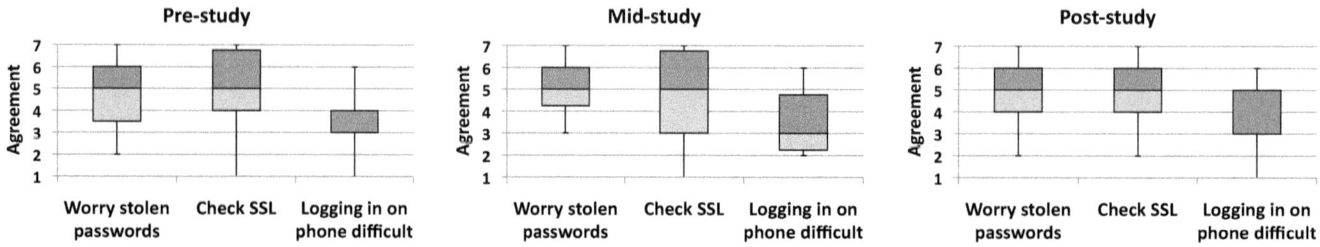

Figure 5: At the beginning, middle, and end of our initial user study, participants were asked to rate how much they agreed with statements that (1) they are worried that malware will steal their passwords, (2) they make sure SSL is enabled before logging into a website, and (3) logging into apps and websites on a smartphone is difficult. Pre-study responses reflect users' experiences before participating in the study. Mid-study and post-study responses reflect users' experiences during the study. The agreement scale ranges from one ("Strongly disagree") to seven ("Strongly agree"). The top edge of each dark-gray box represents the 75th percentile response, the bottom edge of each dark-gray box represents the median response, and the bottom edge of the light-gray box represents the 25th percentile response. The top whisker extends to the maximum response, and the bottom whisker extends to the minimum response. Note that an absent light-gray box indicates that the 25th percentile response was equal to the median response.

5.2.3 Results and analysis

In analyzing our study results, we were primarily interested in characterizing the qualitative and quantitative burden of using ScreenPass, and users' willingness to tag passwords with and without explicit prompting.

Tagging burden

Figure 5 shows the results of our pre-study, mid-study, and post-study surveys for the initial study. These graphs have two noteworthy features. First, the median level of worry about stolen passwords and the median level of diligence about checking for SSL remained constant throughout the study. It is hard to draw any conclusions from the slight fluctuations of the 25th and 75th percentile responses to the first two survey questions. These results show that, in general, our participants thought of themselves as being fairly security conscious, and that this self perception did not change over the course of the initial study.

The median reported difficulty of logging into apps on a smartphone also remained constant throughout the initial study. However, the 75th percentile response rose slightly in the mid-study and post-study surveys of the initial study, which cover the period when users were asked to tag their passwords with the study keyboard. This indicates that tagging a password imposed only a minor additional burden on users beyond the existing inconveniences of typing in a password on a smartphone.

The timing numbers collected whenever participants input a password are consistent with our survey results. Figure 6 shows that during the initial study the median time to tag and enter a password was 23.3 seconds, the median time to tag a password was 4.9 seconds, and the median time to type in a password was 18.6 seconds. Note that the median tag and password values do not sum to the median total value because the median total time was taken from a different event than the median tagging time and median password-entry time.

The slowness of inputting passwords on a smartphone has three implications for ScreenPass. The first is that the time to tag and type in a password is dominated by typing. Thus, it is not surprising that users did not report a significant increase in the burden of logging into apps during the study. The second implication is that integrating a system-wide password manager into ScreenPass (as we did in our follow-up study) should make logging in significantly faster. Integration would essentially make entering a password as fast as tagging; a user would only have to choose a tag, and the keyboard would send the password characters to the requesting app.

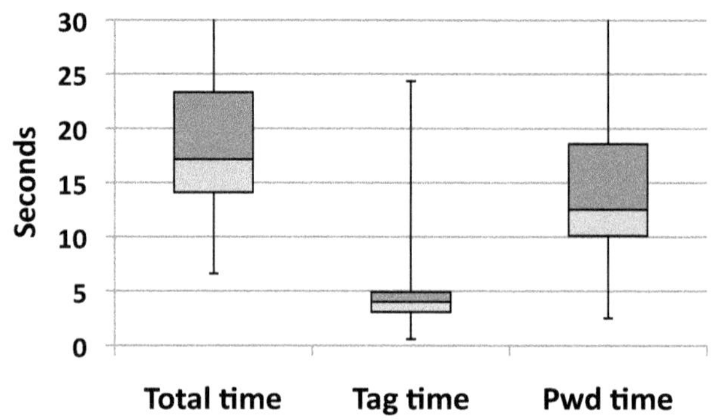

Figure 6: When a participant tapped on a password field, we recorded the total time the keyboard was displayed ("Total time"), the time spent tagging the input ("Tag time"), and the time spent typing in a password ("Pwd time"). The top edge of each dark-gray box represents the 75th percentile time, the bottom edge of each dark-gray box represents the median time, and the bottom edge of the light-gray box represents the 25th percentile time. The top whisker extends to the maximum time, and the bottom whisker extends to the minimum time. Note that the top whiskers for "Total time" and "Pwd time" have been cut off to improve readability. The maximum login time was 117 seconds, and the maximum time to enter a password was 116 seconds. These results are for the initial study only.

Finally, even with an integrated password manager, ScreenPass users will occasionally have to input new passwords. However, the long latency of entering a password gives ScreenPass a large window for detecting spoofing attacks. This large window affords ScreenPass the opportunity to safely throttle the frequency with which it performs OCR. We will return to this issue in Section 5.3.

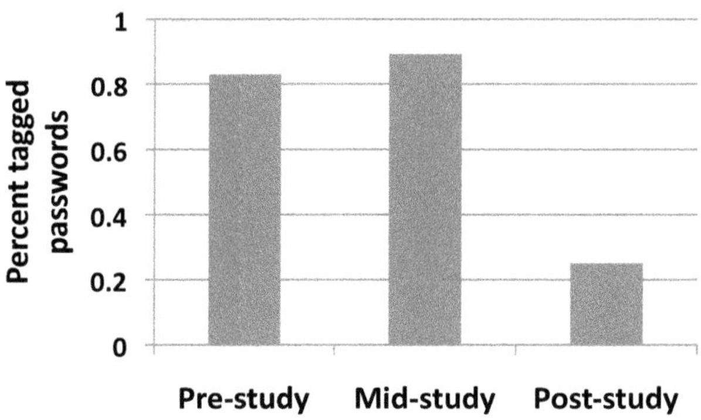

Figure 7: The first bar ("Pre-study") depicts data for the period starting with the beginning of the study and ending before the first mid-study survey was completed. The second bar ("Mid-study") depicts data for the period starting with the completion of the first mid-study survey and ending before the first post-study survey was completed. The third bar ("Post-study") shows data for the period beginning with the completion of the first post-study survey and ending with the end of the study. During the pre-study and mid-study periods, users were immediately prompted to tag their password. During post-study period, users were not prompted to tag their passwords. These results are for the initial study only.

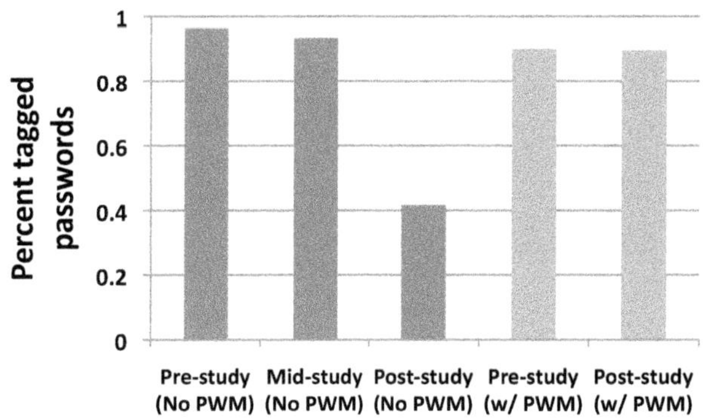

Figure 8: This graph compares the tagging rates for the eight users who participated in our initial user study and our follow-up user study. The first three bars depict tagging rates for those users during the three phases of the first study, when the study keyboard did not include a password manager ("No PWM"). The last two bars depict the tagging rates for those users during the two phases of the follow-up study, when the study keyboard included a password manager ("w/ PWM"). Explicit prompting was turned off during the "Post-study" phase for both studies.

Willingness to tag

During the initial study we recorded data from 134 logins. The average number of logins per user was 7.2 (with a maximum of 20), and the median number of unique tags per user was 2.5 (with a maximum of 6). Despite our instructions, some participants did not complete the surveys on their smartphones, although most users did as we asked.

Figure 7 shows how frequently participants tagged passwords over the course of the initial study. During the first period of this study, beginning from the start of the study until the time when the first mid-study survey had been completed, participants tagged their passwords 83% of the time (i.e., 49 out of 59 passwords were tagged). During the second period of the study, beginning from completion of the first mid-study survey until the first post-study survey was completed, participants tagged their passwords 89% of the time (i.e., 42 out of 47 passwords were tagged). We suspect that the rise in tagging rate is due to users becoming more comfortable with the study keyboard. Thus, the overall tagging rate for prompted logins was 86% (i.e., 91 out of 106 passwords were tagged). However, disabling prompting during the final period of the initial study had a major impact on the observed tagging rate. With prompting off and without a password manager, only 25% of passwords were tagged (i.e., 7 out of 28 passwords).

The low tagging rate for unprompted logins demonstrated that ScreenPass must give users a strong reason to tag their passwords without being prompted. If not, users will likely fall victim to silent-widget attacks. Thankfully, as mentioned earlier, integrating a password manager into ScreenPass provides precisely such a reason. In a silent-widget attack, users still interact with the secure keyboard, but are not prompted to tag their password because a malicious app does not set a password flag in its input request. Telling the secure keyboard to load a password from a ScreenPass-maintained database effectively tags the password and prevents the attack.

To test our hypothesis, we ran a small, IRB-approved follow-up study with eight participants from our initial study over one week in April, 2013. We recruited volunteers for the follow-up study by reaching out to the pool of participants from the initial study. Seven of the eight were graduate students, one was a professor, and two were female. Each volunteer received a $20 Amazon gift card for participating.

As before, participants were prompted to tag their passwords during an initial training phase lasting six days, and prompting was turned off during the final phase to simulate a silent-widget attack. However, unlike the initial study, the keyboard in the follow-up study included an integrated password manager that saved passwords the first time they were entered, and automatically loaded a saved password according to the tag specified by the user. In the interest of clarity, we only present the tagging rates from our follow-up study.

Figure 8 shows the tagging rates during the initial and follow-up studies for the eight volunteers who participated in both. First, users who chose to participate in both studies had higher tagging rates than the broader population that only participated in the initial study. For example, these eight participants tagged passwords at rates of 96%, 93%, and 42% during the initial study's pre-study, mid-study, and post-study phases, respectively. Importantly, as with the the larger population in the initial study, the eight who participated in both studies exhibited a sharply lower tagging rate when prompting was turned off.

As Figure 8 shows, the unprompted tagging rate increased dramatically when users were given a keyboard with an integrated password manager. With prompting on during the pre-study phase, users tagged their passwords at a rate of 90% (i.e., 27 out of 30 passwords were tagged). With prompting off during the post-study phase, users tagged 89% of their passwords (i.e., 17 out of 19 passwords were tagged). This tagging rate is more than double the rate of those same volunteers in the post-study phase of the initial study. Because the sample sizes are relatively small, it is hard to precisely cross-compare the phases of each study. Nonetheless, the trend for unprompted tagging is striking and strongly suggests that inte-

Workload	*App version*	*Description*
General	Android 2.3.4 Settings	Scrolled and browsed through system settings.
App Drawer	Android 2.3.4 App Launcher	Vigorously scrolled through app icons.
Video	YouTube, version 4.4.11	Played the "Fast Five" movie trailer in HD.
Labyrinth	Version 1.5.2	Loaded and started a game.
Winds of Steel	Version 2.2	Loaded and started a game.
Email	Android 2.3.4 email client	Read a sequence of emails from the inbox.
PDF Reader	Adobe Reader, version 10.5.2	Resized and read a research paper (occasionally scrolling to recenter the text).

Table 1: App workloads used for energy and performance experiments.

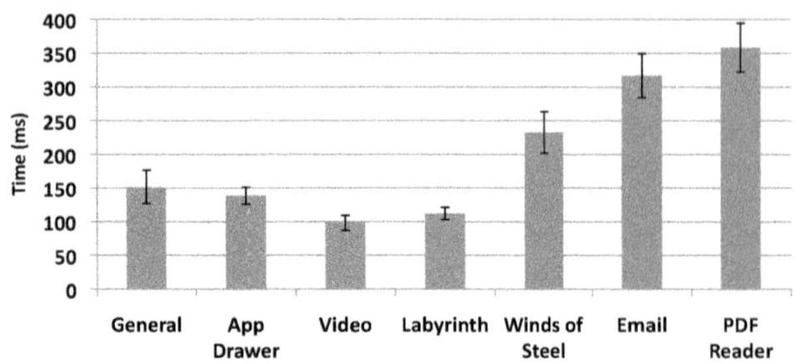

Figure 9: The average time taken by the FrameChecker to scan a single frame.

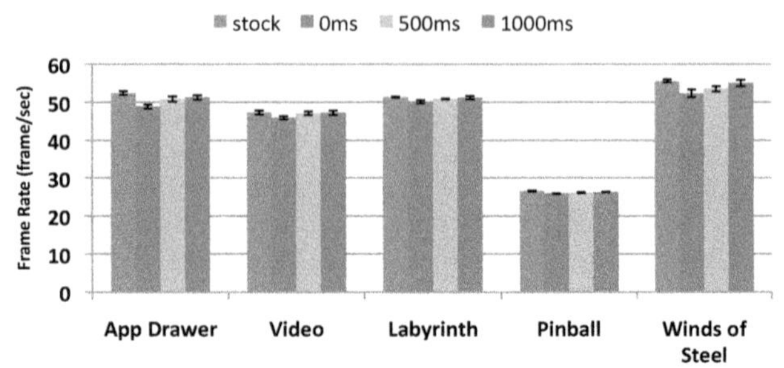

Figure 10: The average frame rates observed while running several applications.

grating a password manager into ScreenPass makes users far less vulnerable to silent-widget attacks.

5.3 OCR performance

Because users react to screen updates slowly, ScreenPass performs OCR periodically rather than on every frame displayed. We expect the system to notify the user of an attack within one second of being drawn on the screen, which should be before she has given the app her password. The time the FrameChecker takes to analyze a frame determines how often it can run. The faster the FrameChecker is, the more frequently it can check for attacks.

To characterize the performance of analyzing a frame, we used a variety of representative app workloads: exploring Android's system-preference menus ("General"), scrolling the App Drawer ("App Drawer"), playing a YouTube video ("Video"), playing two popular games from the Android Market ("Labyrinth" and "Winds of Steel"), browsing email ("Email"), and reading a PDF document ("PDF Reader"). Table 1 summarizes each app and our interactions with it. We ran each app for at least one minute and averaged the times to analyze all frames within a run. For these experiments, the FrameChecker did not skip any frames and did not pause between scans.

The results of our experiments are in Figure 9 with error bars representing standard deviations. The high standard deviations we observed while running resource-intensive apps like games were expected, since the FrameChecker thread must contend for the CPU with the app itself. This also explains why analyzing Winds of Steel, which has a high CPU utilization, was relatively slow. None of the other workloads require much CPU time.

The text-heavy workloads of Email and PDF Reader were the slowest to analyze, requiring an average of 317ms and 358ms, respectively. Their high standard deviations are due to the difference between analyzing a frame containing static text, which was slower, and analyzing a (squashed) frame generated while scrolling and zooming, which was faster. For example, during the Email workload, we read a sequence of emails from Android's stock email client. Scrolling within a message and moving to new message caused text to move and change on the screen, but these events were infrequent relative to the amount of time spent reading static text.

We suspect that the times to scan General and App Drawer frames were also relatively high because of the amount of text displayed on the screen. These numbers indicate that the OCR engine's analysis time is strongly correlated with the amount of text in a frame. Thankfully, as we will see in Section 5.4, text-heavy apps require infrequent OCR analysis since they update the screen and are tapped infrequently relative to FrameChecker wake ups.

As noted earlier, experiments with our ScreenPass prototype were run on a Nexus S smartphone, which has a single-core CPU. A multi-core mobile processor would help ease the CPU contention observed with Winds of Steel, and a device with a newer, faster CPU should significantly improve OCR performance. However device screens are also growing in size and pixel density. For example, the Nexus 4's screen has a resolution of 1280×768 and contains over two and a half times more pixels than the Nexus S, whose screen resolution is 800×480. It is unclear how well ScreenPass will continue to perform given these competing trends, and we leave an investigation of this question to future work.

Finally, we note that for all workloads, our ScreenPass prototype generated zero false positives.

5.4 Sampling Rate

Though OCR is fast enough to sample frequently, we would like to choose a sampling rate that best balances the overhead of running ScreenPass and its security guarantees. To characterize the tradeoffs, we configured ScreenPass with three sleep-time ranges: no sleep (0ms), 0 to 500ms (500ms), 0 to 1,000ms (1000ms). *Note that the expected rest time for the 500ms configuration is 250ms,*

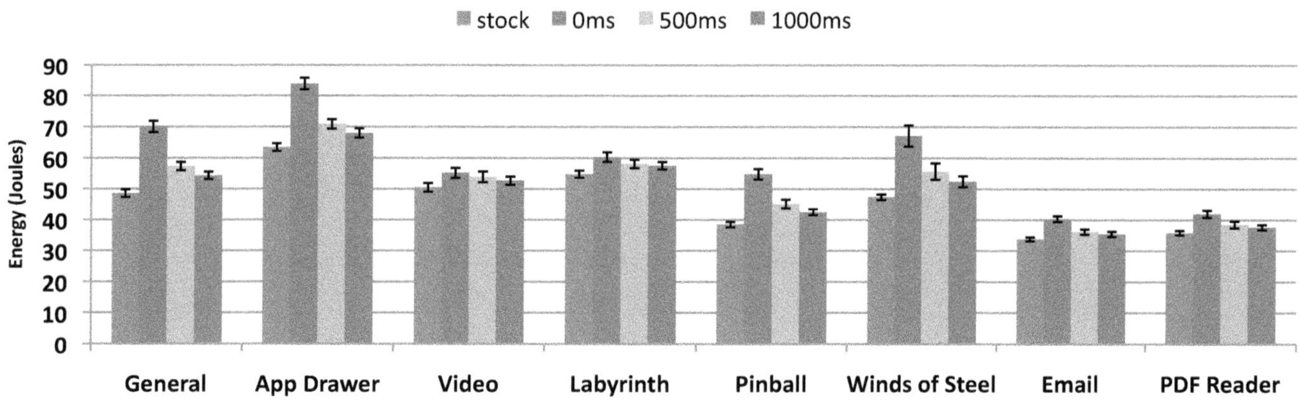

Figure 11: The average energy consumed over one minute while running several applications.

and that the expected rest time for the 1000ms configuration is 500ms.

To understand the sampling-rate tradeoff, we used the same apps as before plus another game (PinBall, version 1.3.2), and measured their frame rates and energy consumption. Frame rate captures ScreenPass's impact on device responsiveness. However, because the FrameChecker runs in parallel with an app, ScreenPass could still drain the battery without affecting responsiveness.

5.4.1 Frame Rate

UI responsiveness is important for mobile devices and can be captured by measuring an app's frame rate. We should note that Android supports two frame-rendering modes: *continuous* and *render when dirty*. In *continuous* mode, the system continuously renders frames, regardless of whether anything on the screen has changed. In contrast, *render when dirty* mode only renders frames when on-screen changes occur. *Render when dirty* mode is not useful for measuring the effect of ScreenPass on frame rate, and we focused on apps that use Android's *continuous* rendering mode. For this reason we do not include our frame-rate results for the General, Email, or PDF Reader workloads.

Similar to our OCR-performance experiments, we recorded the frame rates of a variety of apps while running ScreenPass. In particular, we looked at video playback and resource-intensive games, since frame rate is extremely important for these apps. We ran our apps on an unaltered version of Android 2.3 and ScreenPass using three sleep ranges. Each app ran for one minute. We measured the frame rate by periodically logging the frame rate for a small time slice of approximately 250ms throughout the experiment. We then averaged the logged frame rates for that run. Note that for these experiments, we conservatively analyzed the screen even if the user had not tapped the screen.

Figure 10 shows our results. Continuous analysis has the most significant impact on frame rate due to CPU contention. Most apps experienced little to no slowdown when the FrameChecker slept between 0 and 500ms. Video playback, Pinball, and Labyrinth were all within 1-3 frames/sec of the unaltered system. In the worst cases (App Drawer and Winds of Steel under 0ms), the frame rates dropped by approximately 3.5 frames/sec, but both were close to 50 frames/sec overall. This is a relatively small performance hit that we would not expect to users to notice.

5.4.2 Energy

We were also interested in characterizing ScreenPass's effect on energy and battery life. To measure energy overhead we attached a hardware power meter and power source to our Nexus S prototype's battery. We measured current at 5000 Hz and assumed a constant voltage. Using all of the apps from this section under the stock, 0ms, 500ms, and 1000ms configurations, we ran each app continuously for five minutes. To measure energy, we separated the samples into minute-long intervals. Finally, we averaged each interval for a given app and system configuration.

Figure 11 shows our results. The energy overhead of running the FrameChecker continuously is too great. The General workload experienced the greatest energy overhead of 44%, due to its high interactivity and frame-update rate. However, 500ms and 1000ms required far less energy. For 500ms, the maximum overhead was 18% for General, while the interactive games of Pinball and Winds of Steel exhibited overheads of 17%. All other apps were 10% or less under 500ms. For 1000ms, all apps exhibited overheads of less than 12%. Of course, ScreenPass has no impact on either performance or energy when the screen is not updated or when the user does not tap the screen. For example, playing a YouTube video and the game Labyrinth require infrequent user tapping and have low energy overhead across all configurations. This is also true of our two text-heavy workloads, Email and PDF Reader; both imposed 7% overhead for 500ms and 5% overhead for 1000ms.

Recall that in our user study 75% of passwords took 10.1 seconds or longer to enter, and that the minimum time to enter a password was 2.5 seconds. Recall too that under a 500ms configuration, the FrameChecker expects to pause for 250ms between analyses. The FrameChecker expects to pause for 500ms between analyses under a 1000ms configuration. Thus, with a maximum analysis time of around 350ms, either a 500ms or a 1000ms configuration would provide a good balance of safety and energy efficiency; 500ms would provide better safety, and 1000ms would provide better energy efficiency.

Though several in-situ app-usage studies have been published in recent years [2, 7, 14], it is difficult to use these studies to precisely quantify the impact ScreenPass would have on overall battery life. The worst-case workload for ScreenPass is one that is highly interactive and frequently updates the screen, as in the General workload and interactive games.

None of these studies found that users spend much time browsing their phone's settings. However, a study of iPhone users found

Application Behavior	*# of Applications and type*
Sent the password through the network	28 (1 business, 1 comics, 1 communication, 1 entertainment, 4 finance, 1 music, 3 productivity, 1 shopping, 13 social, 1 tools, 1 malicious)
Stored the password in the file system	12 (1 entertainment, 1 finance, 3 productivity, 7 social)

Table 2: App types grouped by their password handling (saving to the file system or sending over the network). App categories are shown in parenthesis.

Observed Behavior (# of apps)	*Details*
Password to third party servers (4)	Fake NetFlix, one Financial, and two Social sent the password for the requested services to the application developer's server.
Password through the network in plaintext (4)	Fake NetFlix, one Entertainment, and two Social sent the password in plaintext.
Password stored in plaintext (4)	Two Entertainment and two Social stored the password in the phone's local storage in plaintext.

Table 3: Problematic password handling practices in eight of the studied apps. One of the apps stored and sent passwords in plaintext.

that social networking apps accounted for 8% of overall app usage, while games accounted for approximately 5% of app usage [14]. A study of Android users found that users have their screen on for an average of 60 minutes each day and that the average game session lasts 114 seconds [2]. An earlier study of Windows Mobile users found a wide range of usage, with screens on between 30 minutes and 500 minutes each day. Among Windows Mobile users, mapping apps and games tended to have the longest sessions, lasting approximately 120 and 110 seconds, respectively, on average [7].

A common conclusion across all three studies is that phone usage can vary significantly from user to user. Thus, we suspect that ScreenPass under a 500ms configuration would scarcely impact light and average phone users, while heavy users may prefer running ScreenPass under a 1000ms configuration. Either configuration would provide strong security against keyboard-spoofing attacks.

5.5 App study

To better understand how existing apps handle passwords, we ran 30 apps from the Android Market and one malicious credential-stealing app from the Android Malware Genome Project [21] under ScreenPass. We are unaware of any malicious apps in the wild that mount keyboard-spoofing or silent-widget attacks.

The non-malicious apps were chosen from a pool of the top 20 free applications in the following categories: finance, communication, education, media and video, shopping, social, comics, and productivity. To broaden our pool we also added the top 20 apps returned after searching for the following keywords: password, auctions, and online games.

From this larger pool, we required apps to be in English, to request a password without requiring the username to be validated first (as most banking apps do), to not use native libraries (since TaintDroid does not support native libraries), and to have been installed at least 100,000 times (most of our apps had more than 250,000 installations). Finally, we tried to create a diverse range of apps by choosing apps in less well-represented categories over apps with more installations in categories that were already represented. All apps in our study either stored a user's password locally in the file system or sent it over the network. Table 2 shows the distribution of apps, organized by how they handle passwords.

Our malicious app was a fake NetFlix app provided by the Android Malware Genome Project. The fake NetFlix app poses as a legitimate NetFlix app and requests a user's NetFlix login credentials. However, rather than sending a user's password to NetFlix servers, it posts it to the hard-coded URL `http://erofolio-.no-ip.biz/login.php`. We should note that since this host is no longer active, we manually changed the hardcoded URL to one under our control to run the app. The fake NetFlix app is the only app in the Android Malware Genome Project archive that attempts to steal a user's password.

Our findings are summarized in Table 3. ScreenPass found that four apps sent passwords to a third-party server controlled by the app developer, four apps sent passwords over the network in plaintext, and four stored passwords in the local file system in plaintext.

Sent to third-party servers: Four of the 28 applications that sent passwords over the network sent them to a server controlled by the app's developer. We have already discussed the fake NetFlix app above. The remaining three non-malicious apps aggregate credentials for the user's convenience: two are multiprotocol IM clients, while the other aggregates a user's financial information from her credit and investment accounts. To the credit of the financial app, its user agreement clearly states that it stores passwords on its servers and that they are used solely to provide functionality. Unfortunately, the IM clients do not discuss how users' passwords are handled in their user agreements.

Sent in plaintext over the network: We found that four of the 28 applications that sent passwords through the network did so in plaintext. ScreenPass tracked both SSL and non-SSL connections. We examined the contents of flagged non-SSL connections and found plaintext passwords in three of them. One of these apps was the fake NetFlix app, two are first-party clients for widely-used dating networks, and another was an online game and instant messaging client.

Stored in plaintext in the file system: Out of the 12 applications that stored passwords in the file system, four saved them in plaintext in the phone's file system. All kept passwords inside a preferences xml file. We manually inspected all flagged accesses to the file system, and only reported those in which the file persisted after the app was closed.

6. RELATED WORK

The problem of securely delivering sensitive data from a user to trusted software is not new. Similar problems on PCs have been addressed through a secure attention sequences (SAS), such as "@@" or the `F2` in Bumpy [12] and PwdHash [16], respectively. The well-known `ctrl-alt-delete` command on Windows machines is also an SAS.

Relying on an SAS requires on a secure path from a user to the OS, usually through a trusted keyboard driver. Unfortunately, recognizing an SAS on a modern mobile platform is more challenging than on a PC, since nearly all popular devices lack a physical keyboard. Mobile operating systems can interpret taps on a touchscreen only as a set of coordinates with opaque semantics. Non-touchscreen inputs are scarce by design and typically have well-established functionality (e.g., the home button of the iPhone or the menu button on Android devices).

Previous attempts to create secure user interfaces on desktop machines [8, 19] have restricted *where* applications may write on the screen rather than *what* they may write. The general approach of these systems is to partition the display into regions that are writable by untrusted application and regions that are writable only by the trusted computing base. This approach is not appropriate on small-screen mobile devices, where screen real estate is at a premium. For example, mobile games would be much less usable if regions of the display were off limits.

Using visual similarity to prevent spoofing has been previously used to identify phishing attacks [1, 9]. These projects compile training databases of well-known websites and then analyze unknown email and web sites to determine how visually similar they are to entries in the training database. The primary difference between our proposal and this prior work is that OCR can detect spoofed keyboards more accurately and efficiently than general purpose computer vision can identify logos and other iconography. In addition, performing similarity analysis continuously on the display of a mobile device imposes additional performance constraints not faced by the network proxies used to detect phishing emails and web sites.

As mentioned previously, many studies have shown that security indicators are ineffective on web users [4, 5, 17, 20]. However, our user study results suggest that integrating a password manager into ScreenPass provides a strong incentive for users to tag their passwords.

OAuth (currently version 2) is an emerging standard for web APIs that allows users to delegate privileges to software at a fine grain. Previously, when a third-party application wanted to access a user's cloud-based data, it required access to her username and password. OAuth allows cloud services to give applications a token, making it easier to restrict and revoke privileges. Tokens are very similar to web cookies. However, in order to acquire an OAuth token, apps still require users to authenticate themselves with their username and password to the cloud service before the token can be delivered.

Android and iOS provide integrated account services for various services such as Google, Twitter, and Facebook. However, these account services do not prevent malicious apps from asking a user for her login credentials.

Finally, [15] proposes a new way for users to assign and monitor permissions to their apps through ACGs (access control gadgets). If a user grants an app permission to access a resource, such as a camera, the system embeds the appropriate ACG within its UI. ACGs are a useful way to make apps' permissions explicit and visible to users. Unfortunately, ACGs cannot solve the problem of spoofed keyboards on mobile devices, because mobile platforms must support full-screen mode.

7. CONCLUSION

In this paper we have presented ScreenPass, which allows users to securely tag their passwords before handing them to third-party mobile apps. ScreenPass provides users with a trusted password-entry UI and prevents spoofing of the trusted UI through OCR.

Our evaluation of a ScreenPass prototype demonstrates that ScreenPass is robust to both static and dynamic attacks, and our energy and performance results show that running ScreenPass imposes modest overhead in the common case. Our user studies show that users are willing to tag their passwords when prompted, and that integrating a password manager into ScreenPass gives users a strong incentive to tag their passwords when they are not prompted.

Acknowledgements

We would like to thank our shepherd, Jason Nieh, and the anonymous reviewers for their helpful comments. Our work was supported by Intel through the ISTC for Secure Computing at UC-Berkeley as well as the National Science Foundation under NSF awards CNS-0747283 and CNS-0916649.

8. REFERENCES

[1] D. S. Anderson, C. Fleizach, S. Savage, and G. M. Voelker. Spamscatter: characterizing internet scam hosting infrastructure. In *USENIX Security*, 2007.

[2] M. Böhmer, B. Hecht, J. Schöning, A. Krüger, and G. Bauer. Falling asleep with Angry Birds, Facebook and Kindle: a large scale study on mobile application usage. In *MobileHCI*, 2011.

[3] L. Cai and H. Chen. TouchLogger: inferring keystrokes on touch screen from smartphone motion. In *HotSec*, 2011.

[4] R. Dhamija, J. D. Tygar, and M. Hearst. Why phishing works. In *CHI*, 2006.

[5] S. Egelman, L. F. Cranor, and J. Hong. You've been warned: an empirical study of the effectiveness of web browser phishing warnings. In *CHI*, 2008.

[6] W. Enck, P. Gilbert, , B. gon Chun, L. P. Cox, J. Jung, P. McDaniel, and A. Sheth. TaintDroid: An information flow tracking system for realtime privacy monitoring on mobile phones. In *OSDI*, 2010.

[7] H. Falaki, R. Mahajan, S. Kandula, D. Lymberopoulos, R. Govindan, and D. Estrin. Diversity in smartphone usage. In *MobiSys*, 2010.

[8] N. Feske and C. Helmuth. A Nitpicker's guide to a minimal-complexity secure GUI. In *IEEE Computer Security Applications Conference*, 2005.

[9] A. Y. Fu, L. Wenyin, and X. Deng. Detecting phishing web pages with visual similarity assessment based on earth mover's distance (EMD). *IEEE Transactions on Dependable and Secure Computing*, 3, October 2006.

[10] X. Jiang. Smishing vulnerability in multiple android platforms. `http://csc.ncsu.edu/~jiang/smishing.html`.

[11] M. G. Kang, S. McCamant, P. Poosankam, and D. Song. DTA++: Dynamic taint analysis with targeted control-flow propagation. In *NDSS*, 2011.

[12] J. M. McCune, A. Perrig, and M. K. Reiter. Safe passage for passwords and other sensitive data. In *NDSS*, 2009.

[13] E. Owusu, J. Han, S. Das, A. Perrig, and J. Zhang. ACCessory: password inference using accelerometers on smartphones. In *HotMobile*, 2012.

[14] A. Rahmati, C. Tossell, C. Shepard, P. Kortum, and L. Zhong. Exploring iPhone usage: the influence of socioeconomic differences on smartphone adoption, usage and usability. In *MobileHCI*, 2012.

[15] F. Roesner, T. Kohno, A. Moshchuk, B. Parno, H. J. Wang, and C. Cowan. User-driven access control: Rethinking permission granting in modern operating systems. In *IEEE Security and Privacy*, 2012.

[16] B. Ross, C. Jackson, N. Miyake, D. Boneh, and J. C. Mitchell. Stronger password authentication using browser extensions. In *USENIX Security*, 2005.

[17] S. E. Schechter, R. Dhamija, A. Ozment, and I. Fischer. Emperors new security indicators: An evaluation of website authentication and the effect of role playing on usability studies. In *IEEE Security and Privacy*, 2007.

[18] R. Smith. An overview of the Tesseract OCR engine. In *ICDAR*, 2007.

[19] S. Tang, H. Mai, and S. T. King. Trust and protection in the Illinois browser operating system. In *OSDI*, 2010.

[20] M. Wu, R. C. Miller, and S. L. Garfinkel. Do security toolbars actually prevent phishing attacks? In *CHI*, 2006.

[21] Y. Zhou and X. Jiang. Dissecting Android malware: Characterization and evolution. In *IEEE Security and Privacy*, 2012.

Accounting for Roaming Users on Mobile Data Access: Issues and Root Causes

Guan-Hua Tu, Chunyi Peng, Chi-Yu Li, Xingyu Ma, Hongyi Wang,
Tao Wang[+], Songwu Lu
UCLA Computer Science, Los Angeles, CA 90095, USA;
CECA, School of EECS, Peking University, Beijing 100871, China[+]
{ghtu, chunyip, lichiyu, maxy12, hywang, slu}@cs.ucla.edu, wangtao@pku.edu.cn[+]

ABSTRACT

In this paper, we study how mobility affects mobile data accounting, which records the usage volume for each roaming user. We find out that, current 2G/3G/4G systems have well-tested mobility support solutions and generally work well. However, under certain biased, less common yet possible scenarios, accounting gap between the operator's log and the user's observation indeed exists. The gap can be as large as 69.6% in our road tests. We further discover that the root causes are diversified. In addition to the no-signal case reported in the prior work [23], they also include handoffs, as well as insufficient coverage of hybrid 2G/3G/4G systems. Inter-system handoffs (that migrate user devices between radio access technologies of 2G, 3G, and 4G) may incur non-negligible accounting discrepancy.

Categories and Subject Descriptors

C.2.1 [**Computer-Communication Networks**]: Network Architecture and Design—*Wireless Network*; C.4 [**Performance of Systems**]: *Design Studies*

General Terms

Measurement, Experimentation, Performance

Keywords

Cellular Networks, Mobile Data Services, Data Accounting

1. INTRODUCTION

Mobile data accounting records the data usage volume for each roaming user over wireless cellular networks. It has become an increasingly important problem in recent years. On one hand, most cellular carriers use metered accounting, which charges mobile users based on the data volume they consume. It thus departs from the typical, flat-rate based charging over the wired Internet and requires accurate accounting. On the other hand, user mobility is prevalent in reality and mobile data traffic increases with the popularity of smartphones [22, 27]. The global mobile data traffic grew 2.3 times in 2011, and is expected to double over the next four years [3]. To meet the rapidly increasing demand, mobile operators have been accelerating the deployment of higher-speed 3G/4G (third-generation/fourth-generation) cellular infrastructure from the legacy 2G/3G networks [2].

Although the cellular network accounting system has been generally working well, recent studies [23] have shown that, accounting gap, which measures the difference between data usage accounted by operators and data volume recorded at mobile devices, does exist under certain extreme conditions in reality. Overcharging may occur when a mobile user enters a no-signal or weak-signal zone, in which the device does not receive data packets but the operator charges the user for the undelivered volume. [23] models the accounting gap for no-signal scenarios with the packet lost/undelivered volume being $s \times t$, where s is the data transmission speed and t is the duration the user stays in the no-signal zone, and shows that the accounting gap is up to 450 MB. However, prior work studies indoor, static scenarios only, and the impact of user mobility is not explored. In this work, we examine how *mobility* affects data accounting in operational 2G/3G/4G systems. We focus on *outdoor, roaming* scenarios. Note that, it is quite common that cellular users access data services "on the go," e.g., searching Google Map for route directions while driving on the road.

At a first glance, we think that mobility seems a non-issue for data accounting. Anyway, seamless mobility support has been an appealing highlight of cellular networks. In fact, it is the only large-scale, wide-area mobility management solution deployed in practice. After two-decade technology evolution, it has been operating pretty well. The network-initiated handoff solutions in 2G/3G/4G systems remain intact despite the evolution trend toward all IP-based design of the overall architecture. Data losses due to handoff may occur but the volume is expected to be generally negligible. However, our experiments contradict our initial belief and reveal some interesting, yet not necessarily common cases.

We address three aspects in mobility-oriented accounting: (1) Can non-negligible accounting gap be ever observed in the mobility scenario? (2) What are the root-cause factors beyond the known no or weak signals [23]? (3) Which factor plays the dominant role if new factors are indeed uncovered? To this end, we run experiments and perform analysis in two large cities over three major US carriers. Before proceeding with experiments and results, we rush to clarify what this work is not about. Our study does not seek to characterize the common cases. We identify what *possible* cases, even rare/worst cases, may go wrong in accounting for mobility. Though we tested 13 routes and hundreds of runs in two major areas, they may not capture the average-case performance in the statistical sense. Our results are biased to certain degree. Moreover, though we discover quite large gaps in certain settings, these

MobiSys'13, June 25–28, 2013, Taipei, Taiwan

somewhat biased results should not be interpreted as the failure of operational cellular systems. On the contrary, we show that current systems are generally successful despite few observed glitches.

Our study yields several findings. First, we discover that accounting gap indeed exists for the mobility scenario. The gap can be as large as 69.6% in our road tests. The volume discrepancy is route dependent and operator specific. Second, we further find that, the root causes are also diversified. Accounting gap is observed even with strong signal (measured in RSSI) settings. The key factor is the associated handoff, which may play a dominant role in certain scenarios. Third, various types of handoffs are triggered in operational 2G/3G/4G networks with distinctive quality of packet delivery. Operators have been using all deployed systems simultaneously whenever they can, and thus various handoffs are triggered. This practice is partly for offloading traffic from the high-end 4G/3G systems, partly due to partial deployment of high-end technology. As expected, intra-system handoff (across cells with the same radio access technology) works well and incurs little or no loss in 3G/4G systems. However, inter-system handoff (across radio technologies, e.g., between 3G and 2G, 4G and 3G) is problematic for data accounting. It leads to visible overcharging in many test routes; we observe the accounting gap ratios greater than 5% in 9 test routes. In one discovered setting, a popular handoff implementation, which uses buffering to improve wireless link performance, may negatively increase the observed accounting gap (in the range of tens to hundreds KBs). Fourth, low mobility speed may incur more occurrence of inter-system handoff (e.g., three times of that observed at high mobility speed), which leads to a larger accounting gap than the high-speed case. Fifth, we uncover a slightly new case for insufficient coverage. Certain regions are covered by legacy 2G/3G networks but not by high-end 3G/4G systems. The observed gap thus differs from that in the no-coverage case. Finally, we see the average accounting gap ratio between 0.0-40.1% when using five real applications: Web browsing, Email, FTP, Youtube and PPS Streaming, and 0.0-3.6% for a few mobile-phone users in their daily commute.

The rest of the paper is organized as follows. Section 2 introduces the data accounting process and mobility support in cellular networks. Section 3 describes the study methodology. Sections 4 and 5 summarize the results and root causes. Sections 6 and 7 discuss the root causes of accounting gap observed in handoff and insufficient coverage, respectively. Section 8 describes other factors contributing to the accounting gap. Section 9 provides possible solutions to the accounting gap. Section 10 compares with the related work, Section 11 concludes this paper and Appendix documents the trace processing details.

2. BACKGROUND

We now introduce the cellular network architecture, and its accounting and mobility management.

Cellular network architecture: Figure 1 illustrates a conceptual architecture for packet-switched cellular networks [19], which are widely used in the 3G and 4G systems. It consists of core network (CN), radio access network (RAN), and mobile devices. The major components in RAN are base stations (BSes)[1], which provide wireless access to the mobile devices and relay packets between CN and mobile devices. CN is composed of three network elements: (1) gateway (GW), which forwards packets between external networks and RAN, acting like routers in the Internet, as well as records per-device data usage and transfers accounting records to the charging

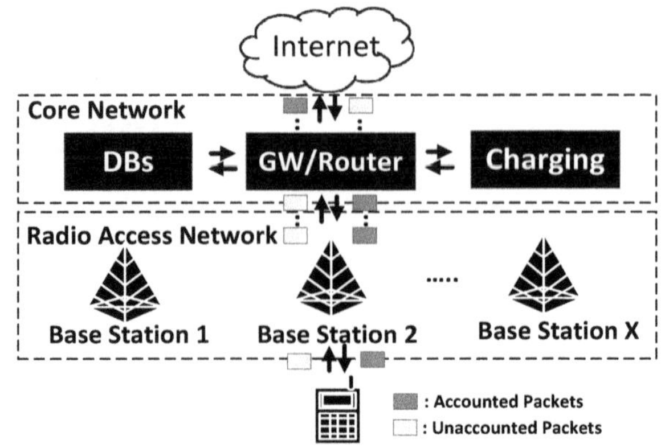

Figure 1: Packet-Switched cellular network architecture and its accounting system.

Acronym	Term	Generation	Predecessor	MaxRate
GSM	Global System for Mobile communications	2G	-	9.6Kbps
GPRS	General Packet Radio Service	2.5G	GSM	56-114 Kbps
EDGE	Enhanced Data Rates for GSM Evolution	2.5G	GRPR	384 Kbps
UMTS	Universal Mobile Telecommunications System	3G	EDGE	2 Mbps
HSPA	High Speed Packet Access	3.5G	UMTS	14.4-42 Mbps
HSPA+	Evolved HSPA	3.5G	HSPA	84 Mbps
cdmaOne	Code Division Multiple Access One	2G	–	14.4 Kbps
EVDO	Evolution-Data Optimized or Evolution-Data Only	3G	cdma2000	2.4 Mbps
eHRPD	Evolved High Rate Packet Data	3.5G	EVDO	tens of Mbps
LTE	Long Term Evolution	4G	HSPA/eHRPD	150-300 Mbps

Table 1: Major cellular network technologies.

server; (2) Databases (DBs), which store the mobile device's registration, location and profile information (e.g., the used data plan); (3) Charging server, which charges mobile users based on their data usage.

In the past two decades, cellular networks have been evolving to provide higher speed, e.g., from 9.6 Kbps (2G GSM) to 2 Mbps (3G UMTS) and further to 300 Mbps (4G LTE). Different generations of cellular networks mainly vary in their RAN technology. Table 1 summarizes the major operational cellular technologies [13, 19, 20, 28]. In practice, an operator continues to upgrade its cellular network technologies; a hybrid network is usually deployed at any given time. In our measurement, all 2G/3G/4G technologies are observed in the same area, and all technologies except GSM/cdmaOne are observed in use.

Accounting: Accounting is a critical management feature to enable the cellular operators to realize their profit. Most cellular operators adopt a usage-based scheme to charge mobile users. As shown in Figure 1, the core gateways record the volume of data packets that traverse them in both uplink (i.e., from the mobile device to the Internet) and downlink (i.e., from the Internet to the mobile device) directions. The status of data packets turns from "unaccounted" to "accounted" after they pass those gateways.

Mobility support: The transmission range of one BS is limited (e.g., ranging from several hundred meters to several kilometers). To provide seamless mobile access, the cellular operator deploys a large number of BSes, each covering a small area. When a mobile device roams from the coverage of one BS to another, it performs a handoff (HO) to switch its associated, serving BS. It is one crucial technique for mobility support. The handoff procedure works as follows. It is first triggered by the mobile device or the serving BS when needed (e.g., when the perceived signal strength is too weak); then, the serving BS (say, BS1) finds another BS (say, BS2) that probably provides better performance (e.g., with stronger signal strength); it sends BS2 a handoff request to reserve radio

[1] In practice, there shall be BS controllers. BSes in this work also provide functions that BS controllers offer.

resources for the mobile device. After that, the mobile device disconnects from BS1 and connects to BS2. During this process, internal gateways also update mobile location and adjust the forwarding path accordingly. The ultimate goal for HO is to not disrupt ongoing services. Though its concept is relatively straightforward, the implementation in reality is quite complex. With various cellular technologies and BS types involved, there are multiple types of handovers. We will address their performance impact, design issues and accounting effect later in this work.

3. EXPERIMENTAL METHODOLOGY

We now describe our experimental methodology to study the impact of mobility on data accounting.

Experiment setting: We test all three major US operators, which serve about *243 million* mobile subscribers and cover *75.3%* of the US market [18]. We denote them as OP-I, OP-II and OP-III for privacy concerns. Hybrid 2G/3G/4G networks are used in these carrier networks. For instance, all three technologies of LTE (4G), UMTS (3G) and EDGE (2G) are observed in the same area.

We perform experiments in two largest metropolitan areas in the US, New York (NY) and Los Angeles (LA). The test area covers 16 towns and 4 major freeways in two 29×64 square kilometers and 48×58 square kilometers regions. We have tested with 13 routes, which cover four types of roads: (1) *local* in *rural* areas, (2) *local* in *urban* areas, (3) *freeway* in *rural* areas and (4) *freeway* in *urban* areas. The basic route information is shown in Table 2. The first five routes are located in NY while the others are in LA. The route distance ranges from 1.9 to 40.9 km, with the median value being 15 km. The short route (i.e., 1.9-km Route-10) is explored because of its interesting network deployment. Difference also exists between the routes in NY and those in LA. The NY routes are located in the rural area around a medium-sized town (north NYC). Six routes in LA are close to the downtown area, and the other two are near the mountain and coastal areas. We select routes mainly by their importance to mobile users, e.g., roads with heavy traffic or necessary pathways between a rural area and an urban area. For example, Routes 7 and 13 are major freeways connecting north/south and west/east LA areas, respectively. Route 12 is a major route between Malibu city and Westwood area.

Note that, we do not intend to use these 13 routes to represent all possible cases (i.e., the statistics may be biased). Constrained by the time spent on each experiment (we need to wait for the data volume charged by the operators before we continue another experiment), we use real traces to analyze a few cases and demonstrate what happens for accounting on the go. These routes sample diverse geographic regions and different network deployment, thus shedding light on how mobile accounting works in reality.

We have run driving tests during three months (from August 1 to October 31, 2012). While driving on a test route, we establish a data session from the mobile device to our deployed server (via UDP or TCP) or popular Internet services (e.g., Youtube and PPStream). We then collect the data volume recorded by operators and mobile devices, as well as log network status traces. In our tests, we use six Android phone models, including Samsung Galaxy S1/S2/Note/Stratosphere, and HTC Incredible S/Sensation that run on 2.3.5, 2.3.6, 4.0.3 or 4.0.4 OS versions. To ensure clean runtime environment (i.e., no more background services), we conduct factory reset first and disable "Background data" and "Auto-sync" features before each test [23, 24].

Collected results: For each test, we record data volume observed by different parties. In particular, we collect (1) V_{ue}, the data volume perceived by mobile devices, (2) V_{op}, the data volume accounted by the operator, and (3)V_{sr}, the one recorded by our deployed server if used. To ensure that the V_{ue} is accurately recorded, the mobile data usage is collected from two tools. One is Traffic Monitor [9], an Android application in Google Play to collect data usage for WiFi and cellular interfaces. It records data volume for each application with 0.01 KB accuracy. The other is our developed tool that uses the TrafficStates class [10] in Android SDK to retrieve the data volume of mobile devices on a per-application basis. Note that the data volume recorded by both tools contains the headers of both network layer (i.e., IP) and transport layer (i.e., TCP/UDP) in our experiments. We use both to record the mobile data volume and verify whether the volume is consistent or not.

Name	City	Area	Type	Distance (km)
Route-1	NY	Rural	Freeway	28.5
Route-2	NY	Rural	Freeway	19.8
Route-3	NY	Rural	Local	11.7
Route-4	NY	Urban	Local	8.8
Route-5	NY	Rural	Local	9.8
Route-6	LA	Rural	Freeway	31.7
Route-7	LA	Urban	Freeway	19.2
Route-8	LA	Urban	Local	9.4
Route-9	LA	Urban	Freeway	7.2
Route-10	LA	Urban	Local	1.9
Route-11	LA	Rural	Freeway	15.0
Route-12	LA	Rural	Local	28.3
Route-13	LA	Urban	Freeway	41.0
Total				232.3

Table 2: Route information.

The data volume V_{op} charged by the operator is obtained via two methods [23]. One is to dial a special number to retrieve the current monthly data usage and calculate the used data volume during experiments. It usually takes 5–30 minutes for the operators to update the usage record. We disable the network access (i.e., packet-switched service) of mobile devices until they update data records. To further mitigate the impact of the updating latency, we have multiple mobile user accounts (e.g., multiple sim cards) for each operator. Before the operator finishes updating data usage of mobile user account A, we use another mobile user account B to run experiments. The other is to log onto the operators' Web sites and access itemized data usage records. All three operators support the DIAL-IN method, while OP-I and OP-III also support the second online method. All three support data usage with 1 KB accuracy. [14] specifies that the data usage recorded by operators covers both application data volume as well as network-layer and transport-layer headers.

In order to verify the accuracy of traffic monitor tools and how the operators account data usage (whether they consider network layer and transport layer headers or not) in current practices, we conduct an experiment to send/receive several UDP datagrams, each of which carries 1 byte UDP payload. If carriers do not account IP/UDP headers, the data usage recorded by operators should increase by 1 KB after 1024 UDP datagrams are sent/received. However, we observe that the recorded data usage already achieves 1 KB after tens of UDP datagrams are sent/received. The data usage collected by both TrafficMonitor and our tool also exceeds 1KB; the volume is consistent with those accounted by operators.

In addition to data volume, we also collect real-time cellular network status and packet delivery logs at the phone. In the network trace, we *periodically* log the following information: *timestamp*, *operator*, *network type*, *cell identifier*, *signal strength*, and *location* (i.e., GPS latitude and longitude). The record interval is 250 ms. Table 3 shows an example of mobile network traces using OP-I

TIME(ms)	OP	TYPE	CID	RSSI	LAT	LON
7590	OP-I	EDGE	37605	-103	34.0513862	-118.50484915
8777	OP-I	UMTS	58873657	-109	34.05124171	-118.50496962
...	...	...	...	...	...	...
72194	OP-I	UMTS	56645543	-113	34.04644347	-118.50847563
73221	OP-I	UMTS	588735920	-113	34.04644347	-118.50847563
...	...	...	...	...	...	...
157982	OP-I	unknown[a]	n/a	-113	34.03924701	-118.50924827

Table 3: An example of cellular network trace.

[a]It can be "search for ⋆". Both imply that the phone perceives no networks (no coverage) and we use "unknown" to denote both cases hereafter.

network. We use relative time[2] to record *timestamps*. The *network type* (TYPE) denotes the used radio access network, and our data set covers eight 4G/3G/2G technologies: LTE, HSPA+, HSPA, HSDPA, UMTS, EVDO, EDGE and GPRS, introduced in Section 2. The *cell identifier* (CID) is the associated cell ID. We use TYPE and CID to determine whether a handoff occurs; details are given in Section 4. The *signal strength* (RSSI) records the strength of perceived radio signals from the associated cell; it may vary greatly upon a handoff.

The packet delivery trace is logged in an *event-triggered* manner. When a new packet is sent/received, the mobile phone logs the following attributes: *timestamp*, *sequence number* of the packet received/sent, and the accumulative delivery information including the number of received/sent bytes or packets. To obtain the sequence number and timestamp of sent packets, we insert them in each packet that is sent from our deployed server. For popular Internet services, packet traces do not contain such information.

4. ACCOUNTING GAP FOR ROAMING USERS

In this section, we first offer an assessment of the mobility impact on accounting over all tested routes. We then use an example to illustrate where the charging gap occurs. We seek to answer two key questions:

- Does nonnegligible accounting discrepancy exist for roaming users?
- Is there any other factor contributing to such gap beyond the no-signal factor identified in prior work [23]?

4.1 All Tested Routes

We first run simple experiments to study whether accounting gap exists over test routes or not. We download UDP datagrams from our deployed server at a constant rate (say, 200 kbps). Note that, our test does not seek to capture the common-case scenario, but identify accounting issues in simple mobility settings. We drive at the full speed (e.g., 104 km/h (65 mph) on freeways or 56 km/h (35 mph) at local) in the absence of heavy vehicle traffic. The results depend on several factors, e.g., the adopted applications, source rate, driving speed and operator policy. We will address their impacts in later sections. We run experiments at least three times on each route. For those routes with small or even no gap (< 1MB), we observe that the gap results are stable. For the routes of interest, e.g., those with large accounting gap, we repeat 10-15 runs and still observe that the gap be consistently large. Figure 2 plots the median accounting gap ($V_{OP} - V_{ue}$), gap ratio (Gap/V_{OP}) and unit-distance gap (Gap/Distance) from top to down. Note that it only shows results under the given experiment setting (i.e., the mobile device is constantly transferring data during the test runs) and does not plot results for all mobility scenarios and real applications. The other experimental settings and applications, e.g., Youtube, will be elaborated in Section 8.

[2]The time starts recording once the experiment begins.

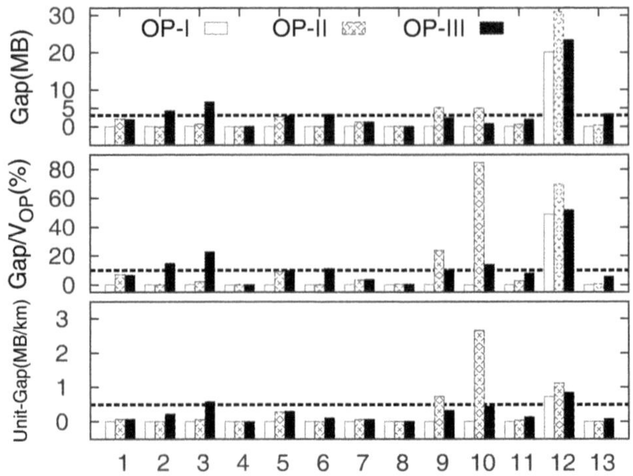

Figure 2: Median accounting gaps, ratios and unit-gaps on all the routes in preliminary experiments. The dash lines denote 3 MB gap, 10% ratio and 500 KB gap per km.

We make three observations. First, our experiments show that *the accounting gap caused by user mobility indeed exists and may affect many people.* The gap is observed in both rural and urban areas, and on local roads and freeways with heavy traffic (e.g., annual average daily traffic reaches 374,000 vehicles). In some routes, the accounting gap ratio even reaches up to 69.6%. For instance, on Route 12, the data volume accounted by OP-II is 44.3 MB while that recorded by the mobile device is only 13.5 MB.

Second, *the accounting gap is route dependent.* For example, in OP-I, the accounting gap varies from 0.0 MB to 20.2 MB (49.0%). The unit-distance gap ranges from zero (or several KB) to 2.7 MB per km (OP-II, Route-10). Significant accounting gaps do not exist in most routes. For instance, only 6 out of 39 cases (i.e., route plus operator) have more than 500 KB gap per km or 10 cases have the gap ratios larger than 10%. However, large accounting gap does exist in certain routes, e.g., Route 12 for all the three operators, and Routes 9 and 10 for OP-II and OP-III.

Third, *the accounting gap is operator specific.* For example, on Route 3, the accounting gaps and ratios for OP-I, OP-II and OP-III are 0.06 MB (0.2%), 0.7 MB (2.4%) and 6.6 MB (22.7%), respectively. Nine routes have ratio differences larger than 5% among three operators. They are Routes 1, 2, 3, 5, 6, 9, 10, 12 and 13 in our test. In terms of the accumulative volume gap on all test routes, OP-I, OP-II and OP-III yield the gap as large as 20.6 MB (5.3%), 48.9 MB (12.7%), and 52.4 MB (13.4%), respectively. OP-II and OP-III perform worse than OP-I.

4.2 Case Study on An Example Route

To better understand what is going on, we first use an OP-I trace on Route-12 for a case study. The route takes about 30-minute drive. Our measurement shows that OP-I charges the mobile user of $V_{op} = 41.1$ MB while the phone only sends and receives $V_{ue} = 21.0$ MB. The accounting gap reaches 20.1 MB, about 49.0% of the accounting volume. For OP-II and OP-III, the measured discrepancy turns into 30.8 MB (69.6%) and 23.4 MB (51.9%), respectively.

We seek to find answers to three issues: (1) Why does accounting

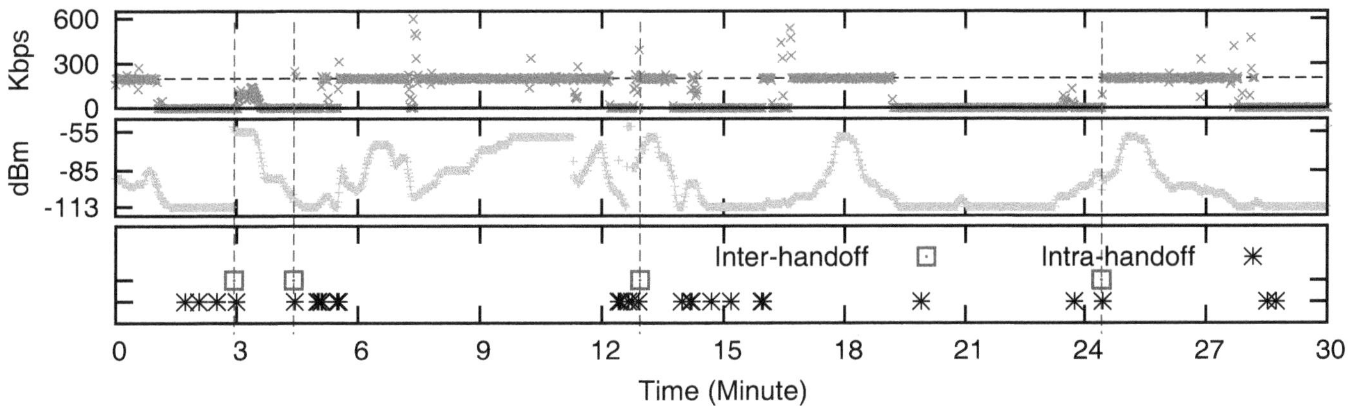

Figure 3: An example of network status trace and packet delivery log on Route 12 using OP-I.

gap occur? (2) What factors contribute to the gap? (3) Are there other factors in addition to the no-signal case discovered before [23]? To this end, we plot the phone traces of packet reception, RSSI and detected events over time (minute) in Figure 3.

The top plot of Figure 3 shows the reception rate at the phone in one-second bin. We find that, the accounting gap is incurred by the failure in packet delivery, which is the norm rather than an exception in the mobility setting. In the case, the client reception rate is expected to be 200 kbps, the same as the source. However, the actual link rate fluctuates and even falls to zero occasionally. For example, packet delivery pauses more than six times (e.g., during [1, 3] and [19.4, 24.5] minutes). Unfortunately, our prior study shows that the accounting system is based on the local view at the core network [23]. Operators count the data packets traversing the core network gateway, no matter whether those packets have been successfully delivered to end users or not. Failure to deliver those packets that have been accounted by the core network results in accounting gap.

The next issue is on which factor leads to failure of packet delivery in the mobility scenario. We first observe that packet loss occurs when the RSSI is low. The middle plot of Figure 3 shows that RSSI fluctuates along the route. The minimal observed RSSI value is -113 dBm, which infers that the phone enters into a dead zone[3]. As expected, the time window of low (or no) packet reception matches well with the one with low RSSI, for example, during the intervals of $[1.5, 3]$, $[14.5, 16]$, $[19.4, 23.2]$ and $[28, 30]$ (min). This finding also confirms the no-signal/weak-signal case of [23].

However, we find that the accounting gap may also occur with relatively high RSSI setting, e.g., during the interval of [3, 4.5]. Our trace analysis shows that the decisive factor is handoff. Surprisingly, even though handoff generally works well in 2G/3G/4G networks, it may occasionally incur large amount of packet delivery loss. The bottom plot of Figure 3 marks all the handoff events learned from the network trace. It turns out that handoff can be classified into two categories: intra-system handoff and inter-system handoff. Upon an intra-system handoff, the mobile device still uses the same RAN and CN, but different base stations. In contrast, the mobile device switches to different RAN and CN after an inter-system handoff. In this example, we observe 4 inter-system handoffs and 31 intra-system handoffs. We also note that the events of weak-signal, no-signal coverage and handoff are not orthogonal. Handoff often occurs when the RSSI value is small (e.g., around -113 dBm). It is usually triggered in a weak-signal or no-signal zone. A phone performs handoff to another base station with stronger RSSI when it leaves the coverage of its original base station.

[3] [15] indicates that the lowest signal strength measured at phones is -113 dBm, which is too weak to enable data links.

	Handoff (HO)	Non-Handoff (NH)
RSSI	various HO types	**SC**: RSSI > -105 dBm **WC**: RSSI $\in (-113, -105]$ dBm **NC**: RSSI $= -113$ dBm or network TYPE is "Unknown"

Table 4: Event classification.

5. DIVERSIFIED ROOT CAUSES

In this section, we show that the root causes for overcharging are more diversified beyond the no-signal/weak-case factors identified in prior work [23]. We further identify which factor plays a dominant role.

5.1 Root-Cause Event Classification in Traces

To identify root cause events and their impact, we classify all events into two nonoverlapping categories: *Handoff* (HO) and *Non-Handoff* (NH), based on the occurrence of handoff. In the *HO* category, more sub-events are defined based on the handoff type (Section 6). The *NH* category is further divided into three sub-cases based on RSSI values: strong coverage (SC), weak coverage (WC) and no coverage (NC). Table 4 lists our event classification. We mainly use two RSSI thresholds, -113 dBm and -105dBm. -113 dBm is the minimal RSSI observed on test phones, or when the network operation mode turns into "UNKNOWN"; regarding weak signal strength, there is no agreed definition in the literature. We define it based on the end-user perception. When RSSI is smaller than -105 dBm, the signal strength icon on the test phones is retreated to the weakest signal strength level, e.g., Level 1 of four levels.

We next seek to compute the accounting gap for each event. Based on the operator's record, it is easy to calculate the *total* accounting gap between mobile users and the operator. To further understand which factor or event is more crucial, we need to learn the accounting gap during each cause event. There are two methods to do that. The first is to re-do experiments for each event. To this end, we first identify when and where each event happens; for

	SC		WC		NC		HO	
	Dur	Ratio	Dur	Ratio	Dur	Ratio	Dur	Ratio
OP-I	190.4	90.7%	5.3	2.5%	0.9	0.4%	13.4	6.4%
OP-II	202.8	88.1%	3.8	1.7%	15.5	6.7%	8.0	3.5%
OP-III	201.0	86.9%	3.0	1.3%	1.1	0.1%	27.2	11.8%

Table 5: Time durations (minute) for four events.

	SC		WC		NC		HO	
	Gap	Ratio	Gap	Ratio	Gap	Ratio	Gap	Ratio
OP-I	1.5	7.1%	0.6	2.8%	1.9	9.4%	16.6	80.4%
OP-II	13.0	26.5%	0.7	1.5%	25.4	51.9%	9.8	20.0%
OP-III	15.1	28.7%	0.0	0.0%	0.0	0.0%	37.4	71.3%

Table 6: Accounting gaps (MB) for four events.

example, the first inter-system handoff happens at the 3rd minute in the example of Section 4.2; then we re-run this experiment only on this sub-route. This method looks reasonable but not feasible in practice. First, it is hard and even impossible to guarantee to cover only a single event in any experiment. The start and end of the experiments cannot be accurately controlled; some events only last several seconds (e.g., the intra-system handoff around the 13th minute). Moreover, the action depends on the historical status. The phone performs handoff at certain time instant because it is associated with another BS before but the signal strength from that BS degrades later. By repeating experiments only around handoff, the phone may not even connect to the original BS. The second method is to decouple the accounting gap for each event from the complete route trace. This is our processing choice. There are two steps. We first extract all time windows of each event, and single out those for handoffs and non-handoffs. We then classify them according to RSSI values or handoff types, and finally calculate the accounting gap (i.e., packet loss) during each event window based on the packet reception log. The details are given in Appendix.

5.2 Findings

Table 5 shows the total time duration for four events on all thirteen test routes. Note that, the number of experimental runs differs on each route. Thus, for each single event, we calculate the average time duration in all experiment runs performed on one route. It shows that these three operational cellular networks have good coverage; SC occupies more than 86-90% of the test time and OP-I is slightly better than OP-III in this test case. WC and NC are rare for OP-I and OP-III, because they usually trigger handoffs when signal strength degrades and both operators have good BS deployment coverage. For OP-II, NC time is longer because of the dead zone where the phone cannot connect with any OP-II base station (more details will be discussed in Section 7). OP-III has longer handoff duration; this is due to its radio access technology. It will be further discussed in Section 6.

Table 6 summarizes the accounting gap for four events on all test routes. From this table, we can find out which event plays an important role to affect accounting gap for mobile users. We observe that major root-cause events for the accounting gap vary with operators. For OP-I and OP-III, HO contributes to the majority of

	SC	WC	NC	HO
OP-I	0.0	0.1	2.1	1.2
OP-II	0.1	0.2	1.6	1.2
OP-III	0.1	0.0	0.0	1.4

Table 7: Unit-time gap (MB/min) for four events.

the accounting gap (80.4% and 71.3%). For OP-II, in addition to HO, NC contributes to the main portion (51.9%). It is deployment specific and OP-II fails to provide sufficient coverage for mobile users. It is not surprising to see that the SC event also contributes a relatively large portion of the accounting gap (about 26-28% for OP-II and OP-III). In most times, mobile users stay in the SC zone, even when driving. In terms of unit-time gap (Gap/duration), the gap is much smaller in SC, see Table 7. Moreover, we see that NC and HO have higher unit-time gap than the other two events. This is not difficult to understand. Mobile users experience their worst packet delivery when there are no signals, or handoffs are triggered when signals fluctuate. However, three more issues remain to be addressed: (1) How do HO and NC events affect packet loss and thus accounting misalignment? (2) Are there hidden mechanisms or insights to improve the current system? (3) How do other factors, such as mobility speed, traffic types/source rates, and network deployment, affect the result? We next elaborate on these aspects.

6. WE PAY FOR HANDOFF

In this section, we explore how handoff affects accounting gap and leads to overcharging for users. We identify different cases and their root causes. Handoff incurs accounting gap because data transmission suspends during it. The mobile device must disconnect with the serving BS to connect with another BS, because the device is usually unable to concurrently connect to both BSes. The data transmission suspension starts from the time when last packet is received before a handoff, and continues until a new packet is received after a handoff. Different types of handoffs result in distinctive suspension durations.

6.1 Impact of Handoff Types

Handoff can be broadly classified into two categories: *intra-system* handoff and *inter-system* handoff. During an intra-system handoff, the mobile device still uses the same RAN and CN. In contrast, after an inter-system handoff, the mobile device switches to different RAN and CN. Using this criterion, we have four network sets: $S_{2G} = \{EDGE, GPRS\}$, $S_{3G1} = \{HSPA, UMTS\}$, $S_{3G2} = \{EVDO\}$, and $S_{4G} = \{LTE\}$. Inter-system handoff implies that users move from one set to another. For intra-system handoff events, there are two cases: (1) users move from one network to another network within the same set, e.g., from EDGE to GPRS; (2) users stay at the same network but move to another cell, e.g., within GPRS RAN.

Handoff Occurrences: From the traces of the 13 test routes, we have discovered 22 inter-system handoffs (OP-I: 5, OP-II: 9, OP-III: 8) and 554 intra-system handoffs (OP-I: 46, OP-II: 50, OP-III: 458). Note that the number of handoff occurrence is the average of all DL-UDP-200kbps experimental runs performed on each test route. The number of handoff occurrence is influenced by other factors to be discussed in Section 8.

We make two observations. First, most handoff events are intra-system handoffs. The number of intra-system handoffs represents 90.2%, 84.7%, 98.3% of the total number of handoffs within OP-I, OP-II and OP-III, respectively. Therefore, inter-system handoff events are not widely observed, since operators deploy the same radio access networks in most of 13 test routes.

Second, the number of intra-system handoff events within OP-I and OP-II is much smaller than that in OP-III. We find that, our test phones are mainly using OP-I and OP-II's 3G HSPA networks on Routes 2, 3, 6-11 and 13. When 3G HSPA networks are used, the cell identifier is not going to be changed. However, this scenario is not observed on other radio access technologies including 4G LTE, 3G EVDO/UMTS and 2G EDGE/GPRS. It may be caused by

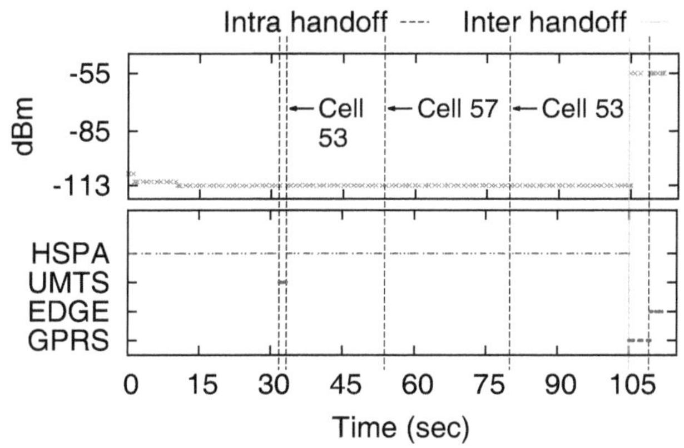

Figure 4: An example of composite handoff (1 inter-HO, 5 intra-HOs).

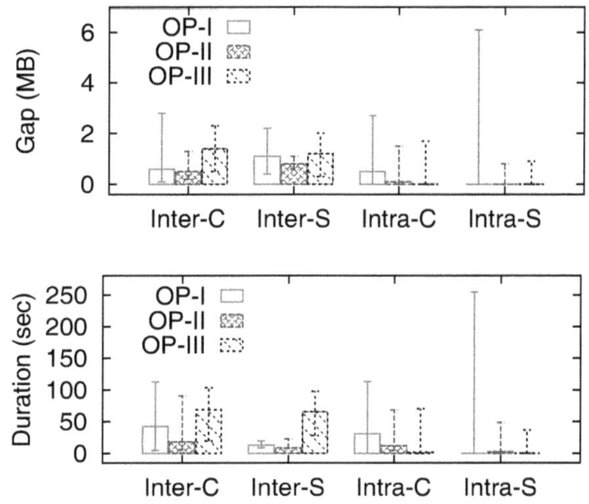

Figure 5: Accounting gap (MB) and time duration (s) with handoff types.

specific implementations of phone vendors or operator deployment policy. [12] states that HSPA operators such as Telstra in Australia are reporting mobile broadband downlink speed of 2.3 Mbps with the range up to 192 km from the cell site. Our longest test route is 41 km and the sending rate of UDP is 200 kbps. Thus, this observation may be caused by operator deployment policy. In Section 8, we conduct another experiment to study the root cause.

Composite Handoff: From our experimental results, we find that more than one handoff may be performed within the same data transmission suspension period. We define it as a composite handoff. In contrast, if only one handoff occurs, we denote it as a single handoff in this work.

We observe that the composite handoff occurs in three scenarios: (1) RSSI is close to (or equal to) -113 dBm; (2) high mobility speed; (3) upgrade or downgrade of RAT. For the first scenario, we find that when the phone is unable to associate with a cell that has strong signals, it keeps switching RATs within the same cell, e.g., alternating between HSPA and UMTS, or switching among a set of cells (e.g., two or three cells) using the same RAT. When users are stuck in such a "jumping" scenario, users do not receive any packets and incur large accounting gap until they move away from this area. We illustrate this scenario in Figure 4, which plots the RSSI and network type of a 112.9s composite handoff. It contains one inter-system handoff and five intra-system handoff events. The RSSI degrades to -113 dBM during [10, 104] seconds. The phone is initially stuck in the "jumping" scenario between HSPA and UMTS networks during [32,35] seconds, followed by in two HSPA cells (53 and 57) within [35, 78] seconds. This situation disappears when the phone moves away from this area and uses the GRPS networks at the 105th second. In the second scenario, a user moves to the next new cell and triggers another handoff before data suspension incurred by the previous handoff completes.

In the third scenario, we find that the inter-system handoff between 3G HSPA and 2G EDGE networks does not always directly move users to the target RAN. For example, users may traverse some intermediate RANs before reaching the final RAN. An inter-system handoff from 3G HSPA to 2G EDGE may go through HSPA, UMTS, GPRS and EDGE networks. The sequence of traversed RANs is highly dependent on operator deployment history. Most operators would upgrade their existing GPRS and UMTS base stations to EDGE and HSPA BSes, respectively, to offer higher rate. Users are thus able to access four RATs at the same place. The selection of RANs is determined by the signal strength of each RAN measured at the mobile device.

In this paper, we further define a composite handoff as a composite inter-system handoff if an inter-system handoff is observed among the associated handoff events; otherwise, we denote it as a composite intra-system handoff.

6.1.1 *Accounting Gap and Duration of Single/Composite Handoff*

In addition to the regular three experimental runs on each test route, we perform the DL-UDP-200kbps experiments on where inter-system handoffs occur with extra 10 runs. For intra-system handoffs, we only analyze the results collected from three runs, since the number of intra-system handoffs observed for each operator is more than 120. Figure 5 plots the accounting gap and the transmission suspension time for single/composite inter-system and intra-system handoffs, which are denoted as inter-S/inter-C and intra-S/intra-C, respectively. The bar, upper line, and lower line mark the median, maximum, and minimum values of accounting gap or transmission suspension duration in each case, respectively.

We make three observations. First, the accounting gap is always observed when inter-system handoffs occur no matter they are single or composite handoffs. The minimum gaps for single and composite inter-system handoffs within in OP-I, OP-II and OP-III are 1.3 MB, 0.1 MB, 0.2 MB, 0.6 MB, 0.5 MB and 0.3 MB, respectively. Second, the accounting gaps for most intra-system handoffs are almost zero, i.e., the median accounting gaps for single intra-system handoffs within OP-I, OP-II and OP-III are all 0.0 MB and those for composite intra-system handoffs within OP-I, OP-II and OP-III are 0.5 MB, 0.1 MB and 0.0 MB, respectively. Third, the time duration of most inter-system handoffs is longer than that of most intra-system handoffs. For example, the median time durations of single and composite inter-system handoffs within OP-I are 13.2s and 42.6s, respectively, but those of single and composite intra-system handoffs are merely 0.0s and 0.1s, respectively. Hence, we believe that the inter-system handoffs play an important role in terms of accounting gap.

6.1.2 *Accounting Gap and Duration of Handoffs with Same or Different RATs*

To understand why inter-system handoffs cause larger accounting gap and longer time duration than most intra-system handoffs,

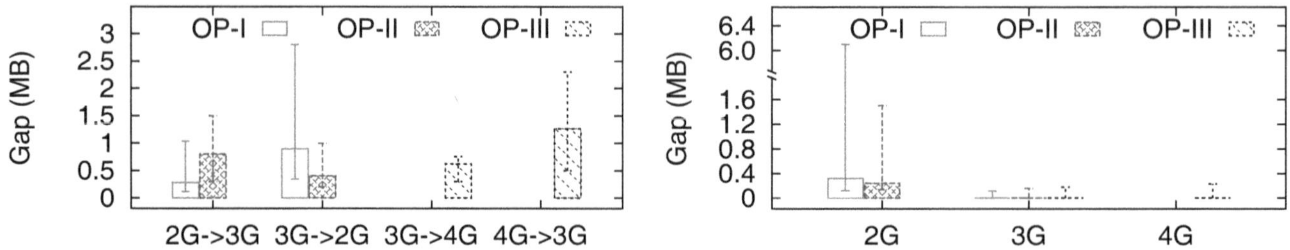

Figure 6: Accounting gap varies with handoff types. Left: Inter-system handoff; Right: intra-system handoff.

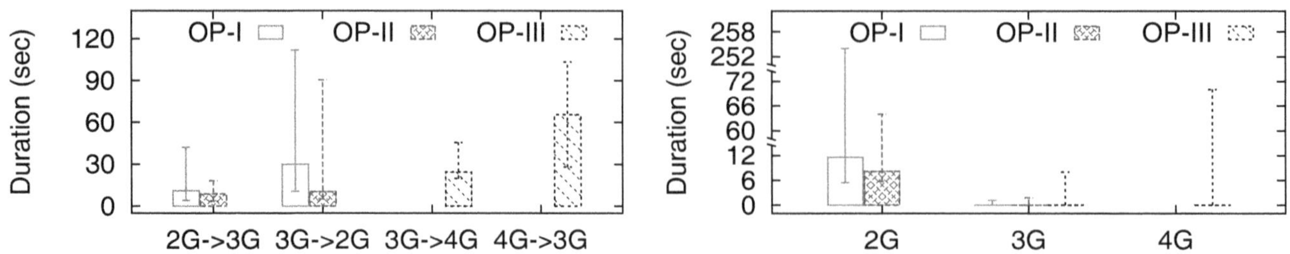

Figure 7: Suspension duration varies with handoff types. Left: Inter-system handoff; Right: intra-system handoff.

From \ To		4G	3G			2G	
		LTE	HSPA	UMTS	EVDO	EDGE	GPRS
4G	LTE	OP-III	×	×	OP-III	×	×
3G	HSPA	×	OP-I,II	OP-I,II	×	OP-II	OP-I, OP-II
	UMTS	×	OP-I,II	OP-I	×	OP-II	×
	EVDO	OP-III	×	×	OP-III	×	×
2G	EDGE	×	OP-I,II	OP-I,II	×	OP-I, OP-II	×
	GPRS	×	×	×	×	OP-I, OP-II	×

Table 8: List of handoff types observed.

we further study handoff events with the same or different RATs. Table 8 lists the observed handoff types in terms of RATs[4]. Both OP-I and OP-II support S_{2G} and S_{3G1} networks, but GPRS is not observed in OP-II. Handoffs are observed within and between LTE and EVDO networks for OP-III, but OP-III does not deploy S_{2G} and S_{3G1} networks. Though both OP-I and OP-II claim to support LTE (S_{4G}), we do not observe it due to phone hardware constraint.

Figures 6 and 7 plot the accounting gap and the duration of data transmission suspension with respect to different handoff types. The bar, upper line, and lower line denote the median, maximum and minimum values, respectively. Note that we do not differentiate single or composite handoffs, since they have similar behaviors in terms of accounting gap and time duration of inter-system and intra-system handoffs. The composite handoffs only contribute 21.1%, 16.9% and 3.4% of all handoff events in OP-I, OP-II and OP-III, respectively. Our results show that they may significantly affect the maximum accounting gap, but not the median value, for each handoff type.

We make three observations. First, we find that most 3G/4G intra-system handoffs do not incur accounting gap and have almost zero data transmission suspension duration. However, 2G intra-system handoffs contradict this finding. Second, the accounting gap with an inter-system handoff is larger than that with an intra-system handoff. For example, for OP-II, the accounting gap for inter-system handoff from 2G to 3G networks is about 1 MB while the intra-system handoff within 2G networks is about 0.22 MB. The intra-system handoff within 3G network even does not incur any volume gap. Third, longer data transmission suspension time usually leads to larger accounting gap. For instance, for OP-III, the data transmission durations for inter-system handoff from 3G to 4G networks and from 4G to 3G networks are about 24s and 66s, leading to 0.61 MB and 1.34 MB volume gap, respectively. However, there exists an exception and counter-intuitive finding in OP-I. The data transmission suspension for inter-system handoff from 2G to 3G networks is longer but the gap is smaller.

Based on the above findings, we would like to ask three questions: (1) Why do all intra-system handoffs within 2G networks have accounting gap while most intra-system handoffs within 3G and 4G network have no gap? (2) Why do all inter-system handoffs cause accounting gap? (3) Why may shorter data transmission suspension time create larger accounting gap?

6.2 Certain Intra-System Handoff Incurs Accounting Gap But Others Do Not

Table 9 shows the accounting gap and data transmission suspension for eight intra-system handoffs. We make two observations. First, for the intra-system handoffs within 4G LTE, 3G EDVO, 3G HSPA and 3G UMTS networks, no accounting gap is seen in OP-I, OP-II and OP-III. The data transmission suspension time is around 0.04 to 0.05 seconds, close to the packet inter-arrival time at the sending rate of 200 kbps with 1KB packet size, i.e., 1/(200/8) = 0.04s. The underlying reason is that current 3G/4G standards support soft handover/handoff [20], which enables to simultaneously connect to multiple base stations and send/receive data to/from them. In contrast, in hard handoff, the mobile device breaks the connection to the original base station before the connection to the new base station is established. The soft handoff consequently provides seamless access to the original and new base stations. How-

[4]In the current practice, carriers deploy several RATs simultaneously, which affect what types of handoffs are observed.

	Type	OP-I		OP-II		OP-III	
		Gap	Dur	Gap	Dur	Gap	Dur
4G	LTE<>LTE	n/a		n/a		0	0.04
3G	EVDO<>EVDO	n/a		n/a		0	0.04
	HSPA<>HSPA	0	0.04	0	0.04	n/a	
	HSPA<>UMTS	0	0.05	0	0.05	n/a	
	UMTS<>UMTS	0	0.04	0	0.04	n/a	
2G	EDGE<>EDGE	0.19	7.95	0.23	8.12	n/a	
	EDGE<>GPRS	0.5	18.71	0.28	8.16	n/a	
	GPRS<>GPRS	n/a		n/a		n/a	

Table 9: Median accounting gap (MB) and data suspension duration (second) for intra-system handoffs.

ever, soft handoff requires extra signal processing and radio resources. For example, the UMTS soft handoff [20] requires different codes for downlink transmissions, so that the mobile device is able to distinguish signals from different base stations. In summary, 3G/4G mobile devices are able to connect to multiple base stations simultaneously. The data suspension duration during intra-system handoff is thus significantly reduced.

However, in some exception cases, intra-system handoffs within 3G/4G networks still incur accounting gap. Since soft handoff cannot be applied to two base stations using different frequency bands [20], mobile users suffer from the issues similar to the inter-system handoff. In practice, to improve the spatial diversity of cellular networks, operators configure base stations to use different frequency bands. If the mobile device is moving to a new base station using a different frequency band, it has to disconnect with the current base station and then connect to the new base station. Accounting gap is thus observed in this scenario.

Moreover, intra-system handoffs within 2G networks lead to larger accounting gap and longer data transmission suspension than those within 3G/4G networks. 2G networks are using TDMA [29], where a mobile device only sends or receives packets at given time slots over a specific frequency band, and soft handoff is not supported. The 2G mobile device cannot receive packets from multiple base stations concurrently. Moreover, GPRS and EDGE adopt different Modulation and Coding Schemes [29] so that the device requires extra time to synchronize with new base stations. In summary, the intra-system handoff between EDGE and GPRS networks takes longer time than that within pure EDGE or GPRS networks.

6.3 Inter-System Handoff Always Incurs Accounting Gap

Table 10 shows the median accounting gap and data transmission suspension for three types of inter-system handoffs. We can see that inter-system handoffs always incur larger accounting gap than its intra-system counterparts. For example, the accounting gap of inter-system handoff between 3G HSPA and 2G EDGE within OP-II is 0.6 MB, whereas the accounting gap of 3G HSPA and 2G EDGE intra-system handoffs is 0.0 MB and 0.23 MB, respectively. The major cause is that the mobile device uses different radio access technologies, such as 3G EVDO and 4G LTE for OP-III, TDMA-based 2G and CDMA-based 3G for OP-I and OP-II. Most mobile devices cannot connect to two base stations using different RATs due to hardware constraints (e.g., only a single antenna to receive data on one frequency). They have to disconnect with the original BS during handoff. This leads to inevitable suspension time. Another reason is that the core network also varies. It takes time to update/modify states in core network components before establishing a new radio access bearer [17].

	Type	OP-I		OP-II		OP-III	
		Gap	Dur	Gap	Dur	Gap	Dur
4G<>3G	LTE<>EVDO	n/a		n/a		1.3	65.6
3G<>2G	HSPA<>EDGE	0.5	17.5	0.6	10.8	n/a	
	UMTS<>EDGE	0.5	18.0	0.6	10.5	n/a	

Table 10: Median accounting gap (MB) and data suspension duration (second) for inter-system handoffs.

6.4 Shorter Suspension Time May Incur Larger Accounting Gap

Table 10 further shows a counter-intuitive result: shorter suspension time may incur larger accounting gap. According to the related work [23], the accounting gap would be given by *data_suspension_time* × *application_sending_rate* in principle. However, this equality does not hold for the mobility scenario. Its root cause is related to buffering and the operator's policy on buffer management.

We first verify that buffering indeed exists in 2G/3G networks. We set the sending rate at our UDP server slightly higher than that can be accommodated by the receiving mobile device, and observe the reception behavior at the mobile. Figure 8 (Left) and (Middle) plots the sequence number of received packets and packet travel time (that measures the time spent from the server to the device during the packet travel process) using an OP-II 3G network, respectively. At the beginning, the device receives packets without any loss and the packet travel time gradually increases, possibly due to queueing delay at the buffer. It then receives packets intermittently (since the buffer becomes full) and the packet travel time is limited by the receiving speed and stabilizes around 10 seconds. If the buffer were nonexistent, packets would be received intermittently since the beginning. We thus infer that buffering does exist.

We next show that buffering does not help data accounting during inter-system handoffs. To analyze the impact of buffer management during an inter-system handoff on accounting gap, we repeat the experiment in the inter-system handoff area and configure the sending rate of our UDP server at 400kbps and 800kbps. Intuitively, the buffer cannot be observed if the receiving rate at the mobile device is higher than the sending rate of UDP server. Before the experiment, we use the Speedtest.net [8] to measure the maximum transmission rate at the mobile device. If the rate is higher than 800 kbps, we go to the place with weaker signal strength within the coverage of the same base station. Once an experiment starts, we wait for 5 seconds (to ensure full buffer) and drive through the handoff area. Figure 8(Right) plots packet reception before and after an inter-system handoff. We make two observations. First, the buffer is full when the inter-system handoff occurs. The mobile device receives all packets without loss before the 180th packet. Upon receiving the 180th packet, the mobile device starts receiving packets intermittently until the 885th packet is received. Based on the packet reception trace, we infer that the buffer is full when data transmission suspension starts. Second, the user does not receive the packets that are stored in the buffer at the time of the inter-system handoff occurrence. The data suspension starts from the time when the 885th packet is received to the instant when the 1400th packet is received. The mobile device does not receive any packets from 886 to 1399. If the packets in the buffer were not lost, the mobile device would intermittently receive packets from 886 to 1399. However, we do not observe such events after data transmission suspension completes. We believe that the user has lost all packets stored in the buffer when the inter-system handoff occurs.

The mobile user loses all packets in the buffer when the inter-system handoff occurs, even though the data transmission suspen-

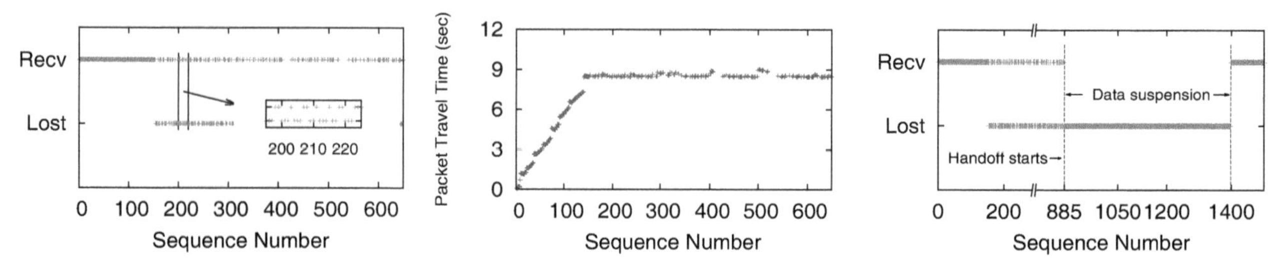

Figure 8: Packet reception. Left: during buffer experiment; Middle: packet travel time during buffer experiment; Right: with an inter-system handoff.

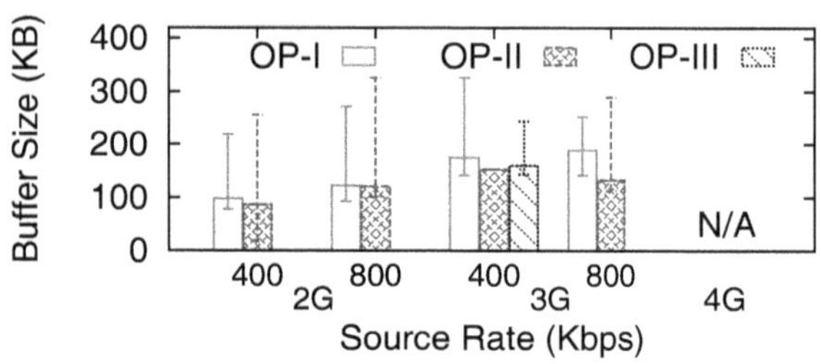

Figure 9: Buffer size in 2G, 3G and 4G networks

sion is short. This is the reason why shorter data transmission suspension may incur larger accounting gap. It depends on how many packets are buffered within the RAN when an inter-system handoff occurs. Along this direction, the buffer size does affect the accounting gap. Larger buffer can potentially store more packets, thereby incurring larger accounting gap upon inter-system handoffs.

We further quantify how bad the accounting gap due to buffering can be in practice. Figure 9 shows that, the estimated buffer size varies from 18KB to 356KB in operational networks. Such a buffer size also offers a worst-case upper bound for the accounting gap. The buffer size for 4G is not observed because we do not find a spot where the rate in 4G is lower than 800kbps[5].

Note that the accounting operations specified by the standard [14] do not take into account the buffer drops triggered by the inter-system handoff events. Therefore, operators should not be held accountable for the incurred accounting gap. The handoff of a mobile device is triggered when its signal strength is weak. During the handoff, it may be charged for the packets that it does not receive. Although carriers may be aware of such handoff-incurred accounting gap, they are unable to avoid billing users based on current accounting operations without new mechanisms, which will be discussed in Section 9.

7. INSUFFICIENT COVERAGE

Insufficient coverage is commonly observed [4, 6], and hybrid networks (e.g., 2G and 3G) in the same region are also common practice in reality. We now study their impact on data accounting for mobile users.

Insufficient Coverage: Prior work demonstrates that accounting gap exists in no-signal zones in static cases [23]. It also holds true in mobility scenarios. Due to insufficient coverage, mobile users may cross no-signal zones on a regular basis while driving. For example, on Route 12, we discover no coverage on an 8-km sub-route in a residential area near mountains; RSSI is -113 dBm and no handoffs occur within OP-II. The no-coverage area contributes 71.1% of accounting gap on Route 12 using OP-II. Among all three operators, OP-II experiences severe issues due to insufficient coverage (shown in Section 5.2).

Hybrid Network: One more interesting case is insufficient coverage due to hybrid network deployment, where both high-speed (e.g., 3G/4G) and low-speed (e.g., 2G) cellular technologies coexist. Uncovered by high-speed networks, but covered by low-speed networks, mobile users might experience accounting gap due to the improper switching between these two networks. When users leave the coverage of the high-speed network, operators migrate them to the low-speed network through inter-system handoff. If the application source rate is higher than that can be accommodated by the low-speed technology, packets have to be dropped, thus incurring accounting gap. Our tests show that, the accounting gap strongly depends on how long the user stays in the low-speed network and the receiving rate at the mobile device. We present the results in OP-II, and the other two carriers are similar. Figure 10 shows the average accounting gap of different rates and durations. We make two observations. First, given the same application source, longer duration leads to larger accounting gap. For instance, the accounting gap for 1-min and 2-min is 2 MB and 4 MB, respectively, when the rate is 400kbps. Second, given the same duration, faster application source leads to larger accounting gap. For example, the accounting gap of 400kbps and 800kbps is 2 MB and 4.9 MB, respectively, when the duration is 1 minute.

We note that the root cause differs from the conventional case of insufficient coverage. In this case, the gap ratio grows faster than the source rate increase. For example, the accounting gap increases to 245% (i.e, $(800-123)/(400-123) = 2.45$) if the application source rate increases from 400kbps to 800kbps. The reason is that, the mobile device is able to receive packets in the low-speed network. Thus, we have to consider the receiving rate in this example. In this experiment, the average transmission rate in OP-II is about 123kbps. We find that the accounting gap is roughly given by (*Application Source Rate- Mobile Receiving Rate*) $\times$ *duration.*

The accounting gap caused by hybrid networks is not as large as that with insufficient coverage. However, it is more often observed than the former case, and it may last for longer time. In current practice, even 4G LTE device still makes a voice call through the legacy 2G network.

8. FACTOR IMPACT

We assess how six factors affect mobile data accounting.

Real Applications: We now quantify the impact of applications on the accounting gap. We conduct experiments with five applications including Web browsing (Webkit [11]), Email (Gmail [5]),

[5]This is the maximum transmission rate supported by our ISP.

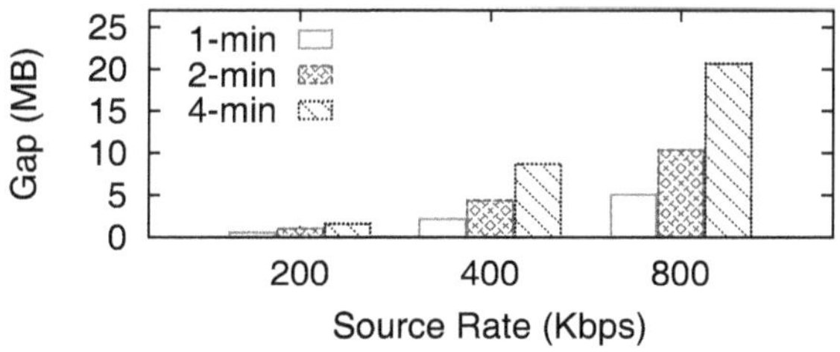

Figure 10: Accounting gap in OP-II hybrid network

	Web Browsing	Email	FTP	Youtube	PPS
OP-I	0.0%	0.0%	0.6%	0.7%	24.8%
OP-II	0.0%	0.0%	0.6%	1.6%	40.1%
OP-III	0.0%	0.0%	0.6%	0.7%	21.3%

Table 11: Average accounting gap ratio ($Gap/V_{op}(\%)$) with real applications on Route 12.

FTP (AndFtp [1]), Youtube and PPS [7], on Route 12. The first four applications are running over TCP, whereas the last one, a popular peer-to-peer video streaming application [7], is using UDP. During driving, we keep on fetching the homepage of CNN.com in Webkit and refreshing the inbox in Email. For the FTP test, we download a 2.9GB file. We play a 1-hour 360p video in both Youtube and PPS. The applications are stopped once we arrive at the destination. Each application is performed three runs.

Table 11 shows the average accounting gap ratio (Gap/V_{op}) for real applications. We make three observations. First, there is no accounting gap observed on both Web browsing and Email applications for all three operators. The reason is that, the downlink data traffic is triggered by the phones' request messages. If the requests are not successfully delivered to the Web or Email server, web pages or emails will not be sent to the phones. Second, only small accounting gap exists for both FTP and Youtube applications. This is because they rely on the TCP flow and congestion control to adapt their sending rates. The reason that the gap still exists is that the ongoing session is not immediately stopped when a handoff occurs or a no-coverage area is encountered. Moreover, prior to the inter-system handoff event, as the signal strength gets worse, the TCP sender congestion window and transmission rate become smaller and slower, respectively. It thus leads to a smaller number of packets stored in the buffer than that in UDP. Mobile users do not experience severe accounting discrepancy like UDP. We also observe that the frozen session is then resumed by the TCP retransmission mechanism. Figure 11 shows the traces of one FTP test over time for OP-I. They include the TCP sequence numbers observed at the phone, RSSI, and network type. We see that a handoff does suspend the data transmission, which is during [210, 290] seconds. However, the accounting gap is very small, since the FTP server does not keep on sending packets during handoff. Third, the accounting gap ratios incurred by PPS are 24.8%, 40.1%, 21.3% for OP-I, OP-II and OP-III, respectively. We discover that the ratios are much smaller than those in our DL-UDP-200kbps experiments, though the PPS streaming rate is higher than 200 kbps. Despite a rate control mechanism, PPS responds much slower than those TCP-based applications, thus leading to larger accounting gap. The volume gap is closely related to the application/transport-layer control, so applications with an inert rate control may degrade. This is consistent with the results in the static scenarios [23].

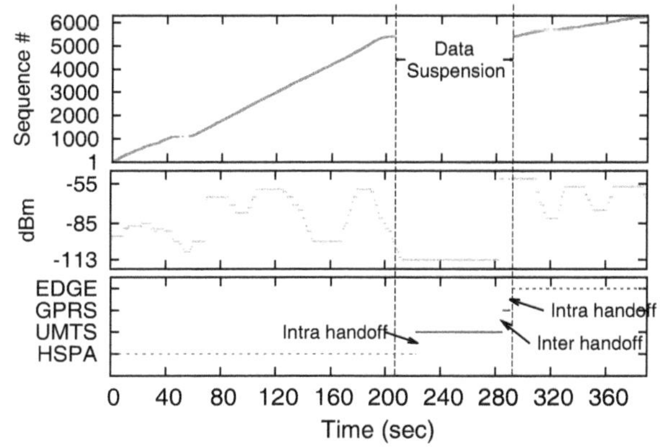

Figure 11: TCP sequence numbers with handoff occurrences in time scale (s).

	OP-I		OP-II		OP-III
User	1	2	3	4	5
Apps	LINE Gmail	Whatsapp, Gmail WeatherChannel	FaceBook Messenger, PPS, LINE, Gmail	Pandora Radio, Gmail Whatsapp, Stock	Facebook, Whatsapp Skype, LINE, Gmail
Route Dis.	41.9 km	75.5 km	89.6 km	76.8 km	18.8 km
V_{UE} (MB)	37.2	198.7	1204.3	387.2	73.9
V_{OP} (MB)	37.2	199.6	1249.7	389.8	74.3
Gap (MB)	0.0	0.9	48.2	2.6	0.4
Gap Ratio	0.0%	0.4%	3.6%	0.6%	0.5%

Table 12: Accounting gap for driving commuters during March 18-29, 2013.

Real Mobile Users: We also study the impact of mobility on data accounting for five commuters who drive in the LA area (driving distance ranges from 18.8 km to 89.6 km) and have data plans with OP-I, OP-II and OP-III. We record the data usage measured at the mobile devices and the one accounted by operator for two weeks (March 18-29, 2013) in Table 12. In this field trial, we only focus the accounting gap observed during daily commute. Since these five commuters have WiFi access in office or at home, we thus configure their mobile devices to disable cellular networks (packet-switched services only) and use WiFi networks whenever WiFi networks are available (i.e., commuters arrive at offices or homes). To quantify the accounting gap on real commuters, except TrafficMonitor and our traffic capture tool, we retain those applications on their devices already and do not install other new applications. Note that, we do not claim that these samples well represent the daily usage for average commuters in all scenarios. Instead, we show that mobile accounting gap exists for real mobile users. Among these users, the most popular applications are Gmail and messaging services, e.g., Whatsapp, LINE or Skype (not for video/voice services here). We see that the accounting gap of User 3 is 48.2 MB (3.6%), whereas that of Users 1, 2, 4 and 5 is below 2.6 MB and 0.6%. User 3 takes his children to preschool and occasionally plays cartoon movies to his kids via PPS during his daily commute. This scenario may be quite common for family commuters but not for those who remain single.

Application Source Rate: We now discuss how application source rate affects accounting gap in the test routes. Due to space limit, we present only the results of Routes 1 and 2 with three different source rates. Figure 12 plots the accounting gap of these two routes. We observe that the accounting gap increases with the application source rate. For example, in OP-II, the overall accounting differences of Route 1 are 0.05 MB, 2.6 MB and 9.6 MB for the 200kbps, 400kbps and 800kbps sources, respectively.

We also observe that the source rate may affect the number of

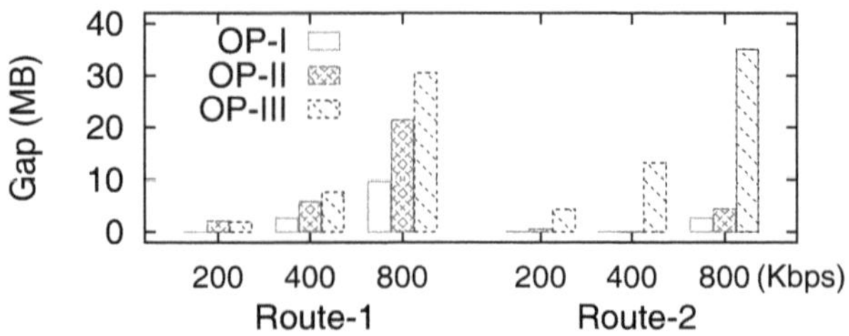

Figure 12: Accounting gap with source rate.

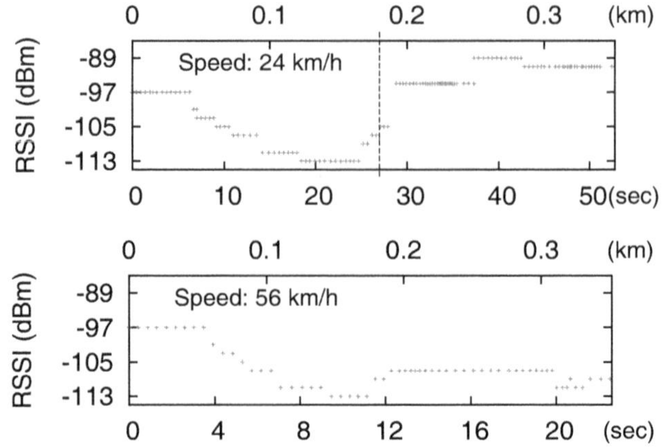

Figure 13: Handoff occurrence with mobility speed.

intra-system handoff occurrences. On Route 7 (19.2 km), we observe only one intra-system handoff for both OP-I and OP-II, but 76 times for OP-III, when the source rate is 200kbps. However, when the source rate decreases to 1.6kbps, the numbers of handoffs for OP-I and OP-II increase to 14 and 15, respectively. Similar results are observed on our all Samsung and HTC phones. We think that this phenomenon may be induced by the operator's network deployment or its packet forwarding mechanism similar to Mobile IP [25], which is used to reduce handoffs and packet losses during an ongoing data session. Unfortunately, due to lack of information on the practices by OP-I and OP-II, we are unable to verify our conjecture.

Mobility Speed: We now examine how mobility speed affects the accounting gap incurred by handoff. There are two findings. First, low mobility speed incurs more inter-system handoffs. We perform the DL-UDP-200kbps experiments on our test routes in the absence of no-coverage areas but in the presence of hybrid networks, e.g., Route 1 or 10, at three speeds: low, medium and high. In local routes, the low, medium, and high speeds are 24 km/h, 40 km/h and 56 km/h, respectively. In freeway routes, they are 72 km/h, 88 km/h and 104 km/h, respectively. We find that the speed will not directly affect the accounting gap caused by handoff. Note that our speed does not exceed the speed limit for a roaming terminal that cellular networks support (e.g., 560 km/h over LTE [26]). We observe that lower mobility speed leads to more inter-system handoff occurrences.

To understand the root cause, we use an example (in OP-II) to illustrate what happens at both low and high speeds. In Route 10, we observe 6 and 2 handoff occurrences for low mobility speed and high mobility speed, respectively. To illustrate the impact of mobility speed on handoff occurrence, we look into the first 0.35 km of Route 10, when the first inter-system handoff is observed during driving at low speed mobility. Figure 13 shows the RSSI changes over time and distance on the test route. The dash line specifies when and where inter-system handoffs occur at low and high speeds, respectively. When a mobile device stays longer in the zone with weak RSSI (i.e., $<$ -106 dBm), an inter-system handoff is more likely to be observed. For example, the RSSI within the distance range of [0.08, 0.16] on the route is around -108 dBm to -113 dBm. The mobile device stays in this area for 13 seconds and 4 seconds at low and high speeds, respectively. An inter-system handoff occurs at the distance of 0.18 km when the mobility speed is low. The RSSI improves to -93 dBm at the distance of 0.19km due to this handoff. In contrast, the mobile device does not have any inter-system handoff triggered at the same spot at high mobility speed. However, its RSSI quickly improves to -106 dBm at the distance of 0.19 km. The mobile carrier does not initiate an inter-system handoff unless the mobile device stays in the zone with weak signals longer than a pre-specified time threshold. We have not fully analyzed the precise, triggering threshold for an inter-system handoff. Based on our experimental estimate, the time threshold is about 5 to 15 seconds and varies with operators.

Second, we observe that the 3G radio access technology adopted by OP-III is not as dependable at high mobility speed as that used by OP-I and OP-II. When we remain static, the transmission rate of EVDO is around 452 kbps with the RSSI being -95 dBm. We then configure phones to use 3G networks only and perform the DL-UDP-200kbps experiment on Route 13 at the speed of 104 km/h. We find that the average transmission rate of 3G EVDO for OP-III is reduced to 160 kbps (with the RSSI being between -75 dBm and -95 dBm). Accounting gap is observed and mostly due to the SC events. In contrast, the average transmission rate is close to 200 kbps for both OP-I and OP-II, and there is no visible accounting gap (i.e., the gap ratio below 1%).

Vehicle traffic: In order to gauge the impact of vehicle traffic on the accounting gap, we perform the DL-UDP-200kbps experiments on Route 13, which traverses the LA downtown area. The experiments are conducted during both rush hours (6pm-7pm, weekdays) and non-rush hours (9pm-10pm, weekdays), during the two-week period (from October 1st to October 12th, 2012). We do not observe any inter-system handoff occurrence for both OP-I and OP-II. However, in OP-III, we observe that two inter-system handoffs were triggered during non-rush hours when traffic jam was observed on October 5th, and six inter-system handoffs occurred during rush hours on Oct-1st, Oct-2nd and Oct-12th. Since the RSSI is strong (i.e., from -75 dBm to -85 dBm) at the spot where inter-system handoffs are triggered, there is no reason for OP-III to migrate users to another system (e.g., 3G EDVO) due to low RSSI. Therefore, we presume that this migration is mainly due to its system capacity limit. However, an inter-system handoff is not always observed within OP-III even during rush hours, though heavy vehicle traffic implies more roaming users and may potentially consume more capacity. We speculate that vehicle traffic may not have strong correlations with the inter-system handoff occurrence. Not all vehicles during rush hours use OP-III networks and request radio resources for data transfer or voice calls. Consequently, heavy vehicle traffic does not imply that all carriers always experience resource shortage.

Gray Zone: We observe gray zones similar to the spots shown in [4] on some test routes. On Route 4, there is 0.5-km road nearby a shopping mall. When we drive through it, we do not receive any packets, and an accounting gap thus occurs within OP-I. However, the interesting thing is that the RSSI of the road is from -76 dBm to -87 dBm and no handoff occurs. Moreover, this is also observed on Route 11 for OP-III. Although gray zones are not commonly observed (i.e., there are only two zones within 232 km for all three operators), they may affect a large number of users. The first one is nearby a shopping mall in city, and the second one is on the freeway with the heaviest traffic in LA. Both zones observe many users on a daily basis.

9. POSSIBLE SOLUTIONS

In this section, we discuss several possible solutions to mitigating the accounting gap caused by handoff or insufficient coverage. Each solution has its pros and cons. Which one is more appropriate highly depends on the usage scenario.

Suspend Accounting: Stop accounting incoming packets until handoff is completed. The merit of this approach is that, users completely eliminate the accounting gap caused by handoff. However, it does not reduce the accounting gap incurred by insufficient coverage. The perceived quality for data transfer is worse due to longer data transmission suspension time.

Report Unsent Packets: The RAN records the volume of packets that are not successfully sent to the phone, and reports this volume to internal routers (i.e., accounting elements). Then internal routers deduct the unsent data volume from the user's data usage. The merit of this proposal is to minimize the accounting gap caused by both handoff and insufficient coverage. However, its prerequisite is that reliable delivery mechanism, e.g., acknowledgement mode [16], is enabled in RAN. Without the feedback from the mobile device, RAN does not know whether packets are delivered or not. Therefore, if the unreliable delivery mechanism, e.g., unacknowledged transmission mode [16], is used, RAN cannot provide such information to internal routers.

Client-Based: Each application server shall effectively control its sending rate when delivering data to the mobile device depending on the mobile device's feedback. In the absence of feedback from the device, the application server shall immediately decrease its rate. Accounting gap is then mitigated (i.e., little data will be sent to the mobile during handoff). However, it is not quite practical to expect all applications to implement efficient rate control mechanisms.

Proxy-Based: Setup a proxy for mobile devices. All packets for such devices shall be relayed to this proxy and then forwarded to mobile devices. The proxy can dynamically enable/disable packet forwarding to mobile devices through cellular networks. The merit of this proposal is that users are able to control packet forwarding at the proxy depending on the network status (e.g., when approaching handoffs or insufficient coverage areas), and reduce the accounting gap without modifying current applications. Unfortunately, deployment and operations of the proxy raise concerns. In current practice, carriers distribute user data traffic to various deployed middle-box (e.g., http proxy or NAT) machines. If our proxy-based solution can be combined with these middle-box functionalities at the deployed servers, the maintenance cost will be reduced.

10. RELATED WORK

In 3G/4G cellular networks, subscribers are charged based on the traffic volume of mobile users. A recent work has studied the discrepancy of the 3G accounting system [23]. It reported several scenarios where users are charged for what they do not receive. It identifies the root cause as open-loop operations in 3G accounting without taking proper feedback from users. In contrast, our work focuses on data accounting under the mobility scenario, where users handover from one network to another. It complements the scenarios studied in [23].

Mobility-related performance issues in cellular networks have been reported in several earlier studies. [27] offers comprehensive mobility performance assessment of a commercial HSPA network. Regarding handoffs, it notes that the triggers and the consequences of handoffs are not predictable and favorable in many cases. It shows that in nearly 30% of all handoffs, selecting a base station with poorer signal quality has happended. [21] states that the maximum time for handover is 114 to 140 seconds and the average time is 20 to 30 seconds. The instability and unpredictability of handovers on performance is observed, but accounting-related issues are not addressed.

11. CONCLUSION

With rapid deployment of 3G/4G cellular infrastructure, more users have data access while roaming around. Unlike the wired internet, most operators adopt usage-based charging, rather than flat-rate charging. Users are thus concerned about whether their data usage is correctly accounted for or not. In this work, we conduct experiments on three US carriers to study how accounting works for users on the go.

Our study shows that roaming users do not receive packets but are charged by operators during inter-system handoffs (across 2G, 3G, and 4G systems) and when driving through no-signal zones. This is mainly because packet drops during handoff events are not taken into consideration during the standardized accounting operations. The problem is that, data accounting is not halted when handoff is performed and buffered packets are dropped. Consequently, mobile users pay for what they do not receive during inter-system handoffs. Despite being operator specific and route dependent, the accounting gap is largely predictable since handoffs and insufficient coverage can be traced and gauged over time. Our ongoing effort seeks to build an accounting map that logs the observed gap volume for roaming users. Once constructed, users can prefetch it and act accordingly to minimize the potential overcharging.

12. ACKNOWLEDGMENTS

We greatly appreciate the insightful and timely comments from our shepherd, Dr. Matt Welsh, and the anonymous reviewers for their constructive feedback. We also thank all participants in the mobile accounting experiments.

13. REFERENCES

[1] AndFTP - LYSESOFT, v2.9.8. http://www.lysesoft.com.
[2] At&t coverage viewer. http://www.wireless.att.com/coverageviewer/.
[3] Cisco visual networking index: Global mobile data traffic forecast update, 2011-2016. http://www.cisco.com.
[4] Dead Cell Zones. http://www.deadcellzones.com/.
[5] Gmail. https://play.google.com/store/apps/details?id=com.google.android.gm.
[6] Open Signal. http://opensignal.com/coverage-maps/US.
[7] PPS. http://www.pps.tv/.
[8] Speedtest.net - Ookla. https://play.google.com/store/apps/details?id=org.zwanoo.android.speedtest.
[9] Traffic Monitor - RadioOpt GmbH. https://play.google.com/store/apps/details?id=com.radioopt.widget.
[10] TrafficStats. http://developer.android.com.
[11] WebKit, Defatult Web Browser in Android. http://developer.android.com/reference/android/webkit/package-summary.html.

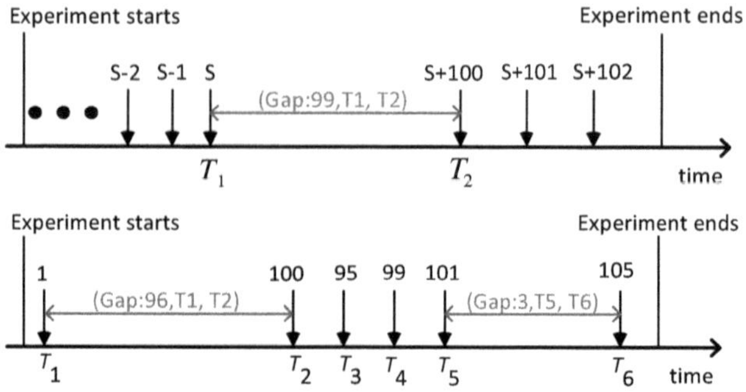

Figure 14: Accounting gap processing with packets arrival in order and out of order.

[12] 4g americas - 3gpp white paper for release 7 and release 8, 2008. http://www.4gamericas.org/documents/3GPPRel-7andRel-8_White_Paper07-08-08.pdf.

[13] 3GPP. TS23.060: GPRS; Service description; Stage 2, Dec. 2006.

[14] 3GPP. TS32.298:Telecommunication management; Charging management; Charging Data Record (CDR) parameter description, Sep. 2007.

[15] 3GPP. TS27.007: AT command set for User Equipment (UE), Dec. 2011.

[16] 3GPP. TS25.322: Radio Link Control (RLC) protocol specification, Sep. 2012.

[17] 3GPP. TS43.129: GSM/EDGE Radio Access Network; Packet-switched handover for GERAN A/Gb mode, Sep. 2012.

[18] CNET. Competitive wireless carriers take on at&t and verizon, 2012. http://news.cnet.com/8301-1035_3-57505803-94/competitive-wireless-carriers-take-on-at-t-and-verizon/.

[19] H. Holma and A. Toskala. *WCDMA FOR UMTS - HSPA EVOLUTION AND LTE*. Wiley, 2007.

[20] H. Holma and A. Toskala. *LTE for UMTS: Evolution to LTE-Advanced*. Wiley, 2011.

[21] X. Liu, M. Seshadri, A. Sridharan, H. Zang, and S. Machiraju. Experiences in a 3g network: Interplay between the wireless channel and applications. In *ACM Mobicom*, 2008.

[22] U. Paul, A. P. Subramanian, M. M. Buddhikot, and S. R. Das. Understanding traffic dynamics in cellular data networks. In *INFOCOM'11*, April 2011.

[23] C. Peng, G. hua Tu, C. yu Li, and S. Lu. Can We Pay for What We Get in 3G Data Access? In *ACM MOBICOM*, 2012.

[24] C. Peng, C.-y. Li, G.-H. Tu, S. Lu, and L. Zhang. Mobile data charging: new attacks and countermeasures. In *ACM CCS*, pages 195–204, 2012.

[25] RFC2002: IP Mobility Support, 1996.

[26] I. T. S. Sesia and M. Baker. *LTE - The UMTS Long Term Evolution: From Theory to Practice*. Wiley, 2009.

[27] F. P. Tso, J. Teng, W. Jia, and D. Xuan. Mobility: A double-edged sword for hspa networks. In *ACM MobiHoc*, 2010.

[28] A. D. V. Vanghi and B. Vojcic. *The cdma2000 System for Mobile Communications: 3G Wireless Evolution*. Pearson Education, 2004.

[29] I. C. Yi-Bing Lin. *Wireless and mobile network architectures*. Wiley, 2001.

APPENDIX

A. Event Detection: We first extract time windows for handoffs and non-handoffs. After that, we classify them according to RSSI values or handoff types. We induce the occurrence of handoff based on the change of TYPE or CID in network traces. Say, one network trace has TYPE_X and CID_X at the x-th timestamp. Therefore,

$$HO \Leftarrow \text{TYPE}_X \neq \text{TYPE}_{X+1} \,|\, \text{CID}_X \neq \text{CID}_{X+1},$$

For instance, Table 3 shows two examples: one handoff from 2G EDGE to 3G UMTS and the other handoff within 3G UMTS. Note that the network trace only indicates when a handoff completes. In fact, the handoff starts before that and its impact lasts longer. So we define the time window of an handoff as the one between the timestamp (t_{start}) that the last packet is received before handoff and the timestamp (t_{end}) that the first packet is received after handoff. Given the timestamp of handoff occurrence, we look for these two time (t_{start} and t_{end}) in its packet delivery log. This time window is also called handoff suspension time.

For the remaining time, we use RSSI thresholds to distinguish non-handoff events: NH/SC, NH/WC and NH/NC, defined in Table 4. The handoff classification will be described in Section 6.1.

A1. Handoff type detection: Broadly, handoff can be classified into two categories: intra-system handoff and inter-system handoff. When an intra-system handoff finishes, the mobile device still uses the same RAN and CN, but different base stations. In contrast, the mobile device switches to different RAN and CN after an inter-system handoff is completed. Say, one network trace has he network trace has TYPE_X and CID_X at the x-th timestamp. Therefore,

$$\begin{aligned} HO &\Leftarrow \text{TYPE}_X \neq \text{TYPE}_{X+1} \,|\, \text{CID}_X \neq \text{CID}_{X+1}, \\ \text{Intra-HO} &\Leftarrow HO \,\&\, \text{TYPE}_X \equiv \text{TYPE}_{X+1}, \\ \text{Inter-HO} &\Leftarrow HO \,\&\, \text{TYPE}_X \neq \text{TYPE}_{X+1}. \end{aligned}$$

The equivalence of two network types will be extended in Section 6. For instance, Table 3 shows two examples: one is an inter-system handoff from 2G EDGE to 3G UMTS and the other is an intra-system handoff within 3G UMTS.

B. Gap Calculation: Now the key question is to learn how much packets are not received in each specific time window. These packet loss finally contribute to the accounting gap as discussed before. The challenge we have is that packet delivery is logged in an event-driven way. Constrained by this, we can only induce the packet loss in the time period starting and ending with packet reception. As shown in Figure 14 (above), we receive packet S at T_1 and packet $S + 100$ at T_2. We can induce the packet loss in $[T_1, T_2]$, but not in a smaller time window part of $[T_1, T_2]$. We will address it in the following mapping (Step C).

Now we investigate how to calculate the gap from the packet delivery log. Say, the phone receives a packet with sequence number S_X at time T_X. If there is no packet loss between two continuous timestamps, that is, $S_{X+1} - S_X \equiv 1$, the gap in $[T_X, T_{X+1}] = 0$. In other words, the gap in $[T_X, T_{X+1}]$ is calculated as $S_{X+1} - S_X - 1$. For example, the packet loss in the above plot of Figure 14 is 99 in $[T_1, T_2]$. But the actual packet delivery can be out-of-order. As shown in the bottom plot, Packets 95 and 99 may arrive after packet 100. To handle packet out-of-delivery problem, we update the highest sequence number S_{higest} in the process and look forward to check if any packets have been received latter. We only calculate the volume gap if the sequence number is larger than S_{higest}. For those packets that will be received later, we exclude them in the accounting gap. Take the example in Figure 14 (below), we receive Packets 1, 100, 95, 99, 101 and 105 in order. When Packet 100 is examined, we retrieve the accounting gap in $[T_1, T_2]$ as 97 packets, i.e., Packets 2-94 and 96-98. We then set S_{higest} to 100. Thus, we will not calculate accounting gap when we examine Packets 95 and 99. Note that the packet log might fail to record the last packet reception, for example, Route 12 ends in no coverage zone and phones do not receive any packet at the end. In this case, we determine the last accounting gap using the V_{OP} and V_{UE}.

C. Event and Gap Mapping: We now need to map the accounting gap within each event. By compare each gap time period and event time period, we are able to find out which event happens during gap time period. In most cases, the gap time window is much smaller than the event one, and we will sum up all the gaps for one single event. In case more than one event crosses the same gap time window, e.g., NC and SC, we treat this accounting gap into the category NC+SC, instead of NC or SC. Our measurement shows that less than 60KB accounting gap are contributed by multiple events, no more than 0.3% of the total gap. Due to space limit, we do not discuss the accounting gap caused by multiple events in this paper.

Comparison of Caching Strategies in Modern Cellular Backhaul Networks

Shinae Woo
KAIST
shinae@ndsl.kaist.edu

Eunyoung Jeong
KAIST
notav@ndsl.kaist.edu

Shinjo Park
KAIST
pshinjo@ndsl.kaist.edu

Jongmin Lee
SK Telecom, Inc.
jminlee@sk.com

Sunghwan Ihm*
Princeton University
sihm@cs.princeton.edu

KyoungSoo Park
KAIST
kyoungsoo@ee.kaist.ac.kr

ABSTRACT

Recent popularity of smartphones drives rapid growth in the demand for cellular network bandwidth. Unfortunately, due to the *centralized* architecture of cellular networks, increasing the physical backhaul bandwidth is challenging. While content caching in cellular networks could be beneficial, little is known about the traffic characteristics to devise a highly-effective caching strategy.

In this work, we provide insight into flow and content-level characteristics of modern 3G traffic at a large cellular ISP in South Korea. We first develop a scalable deep *flow* inspection (DFI) system that can manage hundreds of thousands of concurrent TCP flows on a commodity multicore server. Our DFI system collects various HTTP/TCP-level statistics and produces logs for analyzing the effectiveness of conventional Web caching, prefix-based Web caching, and TCP-level redundancy elimination (RE) without a single packet drop at a 10 Gbps link. Our week-long measurements of over 370 TBs of the 3G traffic reveal that standard Web caching can reduce download bandwidth consumption up to 27.1% while simple TCP-level RE can save the bandwidth consumption up to 42.0% with a cache of 512 GB of RAM. We also find that applying TCP-level RE on the largest 9.4% flows eliminates 68.4% of the total redundancy. Most of the redundancy (52.1%~58.9%) comes from serving the same HTTP objects while the contribution by aliased URLs is up to 38.9%.

Categories and Subject Descriptors

C.2.3 [**Computer-Communication Networks**]: Network monitoring; C.2.m [**Computer-Communication Networks**]: Miscellaneous

General Terms

Measurement, Performance

Keywords

Deep Flow Inspection, Cellular Networks, Caching, Redundancy Elimination

*Current affiliation: *Google, Inc.*

MobiSys'13, June 25-28, 2013, Taipei, Taiwan

1. INTRODUCTION

Recent popularity of smartphones and tablet PCs drives the rapid growth of the mobile data in cellular networks. The global cellular data traffic is predicted to increase by 18 times in the next five years, which is 3 times faster than the growth rate of the fixed IP networks [20]. While many cellular ISPs are planning to invest tens of billions of dollars to prepare their infrastructure [43], it is unclear if the physical capacity will meet the future demand. As a status quo, cellular ISPs curb the demand using pay-per-usage service plans or by throttling access speed [45].

With increasing deployments of high-speed base stations and femtocells [40], the wireless channel bandwidth to radio access networks (RANs) has improved over time. However, cellular networks typically have a *centralized* architecture where all user traffic has to traverse one of a few gateways at core networks (CNs) before reaching the wired Internet [16, 22]. Centralization is necessary for tracking the location of mobile devices, billing, and handovers, but high traffic concentration at CNs could lead to potential congestion as the number of base stations rapidly grows.

Caching popular contents in the backhaul networks is a cost-effective solution that could increase the effective bandwidth. It is especially attractive since deploying IP-based caching equipment is getting easier in packet-switched 3G/4G networks [1]. While there have been many works on the effectiveness of Web caching in cellular backhaul links [22, 23] and at mobile devices [37, 38], relatively little is known about the effectiveness of protocol-independent redundancy elimination (RE) [13, 28, 42] or prefix-based Web caching [15, 34, 35] in the cellular networks. Prefix-based Web caching can address the redundancy from aliased Web objects in addition to regular objects, which is increasingly popular for caching aliased multimedia contents in the Internet. In this work, we compare the efficacy of these caching strategies. Specifically, we explore (a) the characteristics of modern cellular traffic that can impact the caching strategies, (b) the fraction of redundancy that can be addressed by each caching scheme and the source of the redundancy, and (c) system overheads of caching strategies in terms of cache size and concurrent flow counts.

To find the answers to these questions, we analyze the TCP flow and content-level characteristics of commercial 3G traffic at a 10 Gbps backhaul link at one of the largest ISPs in South Korea for one week. We choose to do online analysis as dumping packet contents at high speed to disk for offline analysis is prohibitively expensive. We develop Monbot, a scalable deep *flow* inspection (DFI) system, that analyzes the network-level behavior and content-level redundancy of *every* TCP flow in real time. One challenge in Monbot lies in how it handles millions of packets per second, maintaining hundreds of thousands of concurrent flows. We address this problem by balancing the flow management and content analysis loads among multiple CPU cores with *symmetric* receive-side scaling (symmetric RSS). Similar to RSS [33], symmetric RSS distributes the incoming packets to multiple CPU cores while ensuring the packet order in each flow. But unlike RSS, it maps the packets in the same TCP connection (*i.e.*, packets in both upstream and downstream flows) to the same CPU core, obviating the need to share the TCP context across different cores. This promises high scalability on a multicore system by avoiding cross-core synchronization or shared lock contention. Monbot also implements per-core memory management for flow buffers and timeout-based buffer recycling, which effectively reduces the memory footprint for a large number of concurrent flows. With these techniques, we could monitor 375.5 TBs of packets (8.3 billion flows) without a single packet drop on a 12-core commodity server.

Our contributions are summarized as follows. First, we show the design and implementation of Monbot that scalably manages 100Ks of active TCP flows at a 10 Gbps link. Monbot can be easily extended to work as high-performance middleboxes such as stateful firewalls, intrusion detection systems, or transparent RE nodes. Second, we develop symmetric RSS that evenly distributes the packets by their TCP connection at line rate. Symmetric RSS can be applied to any commodity hardware-based system that needs to maintain TCP flows in the high-speed networks. Third, we analyze the characteristics of commercial 3G traffic both in the network and content level using Monbot. Our findings are summarized as follows.

- Commercial 3G traffic shows heavier dominance of HTTP and TCP than in the wired Internet. 95.7% of the downlink traffic uses TCP, and the HTTP traffic constitutes 74.6% of all downstream bytes.
- Most TCP flows are small, but the majority of the transferred bytes belong to large flows. That is, only 9.4% of the flows are larger than 32 KB, but these flows contribute to 93.7% of the transferred bytes. Monbot processes as many as 1.3 million new TCP connections per minute, and up to 270K concurrent flows at any given time.
- The 3G traffic usage exhibits a strong diurnal pattern as in the wired Internet. We see local bandwidth peaks in the morning rush hour (8 - 9 am) and lunchtime (12 - 1 pm) every working day. The daily bandwidth peak happens around 11 pm - 12 am, mostly driven by video contents.
- With infinite cache, we find that up to 59.4% of the traffic is redundant with TCP-level redundancy elimination (TCP-RE). While standard Web caching achieves only 21.0~27.1% of bandwidth savings despite with infinite cache, TCP-RE achieves 26.9~42.0% bandwidth savings with only 512 GB of memory cache. Prefix-based Web caching sits in between, producing 22.4~34.0% of bandwidth savings with infinite cache.
- Unlike for enterprise traffic [13], TCP-RE for the 3G traffic effectively lowers the bandwidth peaks in the morning time and lunchtime. It also provides significant bandwidth savings (30.7~36.9%) during the peak usage in the night time.
- The chunk popularity follows strong Zipf distribution. The LRU cache replacement is slightly better than FIFO in terms of bandwidth savings.
- 52.1%~58.9% of the redundancy is from serving the same HTTP objects. Aliased objects contribute to 30.4%~38.9% of the redundancy.

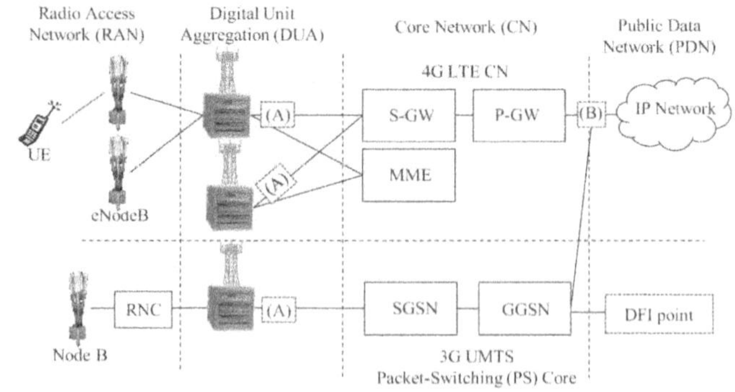

Figure 1: Overall 3G/4G cellular network architecture. (A) and (B) are candidate locations for deploying caching middleboxes.

To the best of our knowledge, we analyze and report the largest amount of the 3G cellular traffic on commodity hardware. We believe our findings are useful in designing a middlebox-based TCP-RE system with tunable parameters that control the level of bandwidth savings and system overheads.

2. BACKGROUND

In this section, we provide the background on the structure of cellular networks, and popular redundancy elimination approaches.

2.1 Modern Cellular Networks

Figure 1 shows the overall architecture of 3G Universal Mobile Telecommunications System (UMTS) and 4G Long Term Evolution (LTE) cellular networks. A radio access network (RAN) consists of a set of base stations (called Node B in UMTS, and eNodeB in LTE) and User Equipments (UEs). A UE communicates wirelessly with a base station and the data is forwarded to a regional digital unit aggregation point (DUA). There are tens to hundreds of DUAs per ISP in South Korea that are connected to a cellular core network. A S-gateway (S-GW) in LTE acts as a mobility anchor for UE handovers between eNodeBs (or between LTE and other 3GPP networks), and forwards packets to P-gateway (P-GW), which serves as a gateway router to IP networks (called public data networks (PDNs)). A mobility management entity (MME) is in charge of many control-plane tasks such as tracking and paging UEs, performing handovers between LTE core networks (CNs), authenticating users, etc. Similar functionality is found in 3G UMTS where a Serving GPRS Support Node (SGSN) takes the role of S-GW and MME, and a Gateway GPRS Support Node (GGSN) acts as a P-GW in LTE. Since 3G/4G networks use IP packets via GPRS Tunneling Protocol (GTP) throughout its packet-switched domain, it is easy to deploy IP-based caching/monitoring systems.

2.2 Available Caching Techniques

As shown in Figure 1, cellular networks have a *centralized* architecture where all packets are concentrated at a few P-GWs or GGSNs in a country. With the improvement of RAN technologies and wider deployments of cell towers, it is predicted that the backhaul links to CNs could become the next bottleneck[6, 9]. If we can reduce redundant data transfers between DUAs and a CN, we can increase the effective bandwidth in the backhaul networks. We consider Web caching and protocol-independent RE as possible caching solutions here.

Web caching is a popular technique that suppresses redundant Web transfers. Since a large portion of the cellular traffic uses

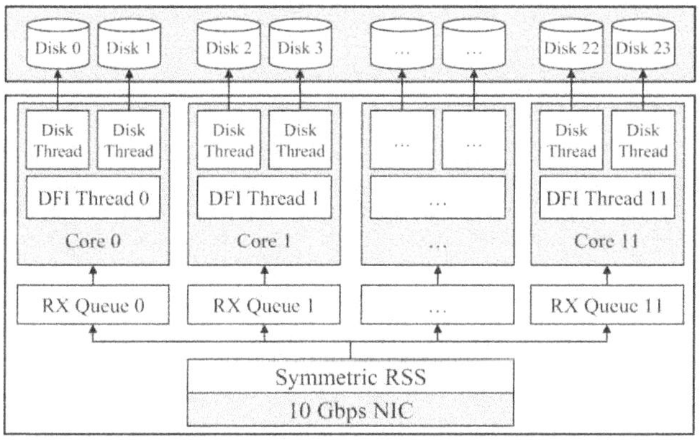

Figure 2: Overall architecture of Monbot

HTTP [22], we expect significant bandwidth savings as well as fast response if Web caches are deployed at DUAs ((A) in Figure 1), or near the gateways ((B) in Figure 1). However, it poses two problems. First, standard Web caching cannot suppress duplicate objects that are uncacheable or that have different URLs (*i.e.*, aliases). It cannot suppress the partial content overlap in similar objects as well. Second, it is challenging to handle UE handovers across DUAs while the content is being delivered. If a UE moves its attachment point to another DUA, content from a Web cache at one DUA should be re-routed to the new location, which is difficult since the route is centrally managed by MME or SGSN.

Prefix-based Web caching alleviates the first problem of Web caching by suppressing the aliased or duplicate objects that are uncacheable. A typical approach is to confirm an alias by comparing the hash of the first N bytes of an object (called `prefix key`), and the `content-length` fields. It assumes that two HTTP objects of the same size have the same content if their prefix keys match. While this potentially presents a correctness issue especially if N is small, it is already widely used in the wired Internet to serve aliased multimedia contents (e.g., aliased videos) [15, 34, 35]. Unfortunately, little is known about its effectiveness and false positives, which we study in Section 6.2.

Protocol-independent RE can address both of the problems of Web caching at the cost of high engineering complexity and computational overheads. It assumes two middleboxes deployed at (A) and (B) in Figure 1. (B) divides incoming content into small chunks, and sends a stream of chunk hashes to (A). (A) reconstructs the original content with those hashes, and delivers it to UEs. If any chunks are cache misses at (A), (A) fetches the original content from (B), and caches them for future references.

There are many variants of RE, but we use TCP-RE to compare the effectiveness with other caching strategies. Unlike packet-level RE, TCP-RE works over the content of each TCP flow. We reassemble the segments in the same TCP flow and divide them into smaller chunks (either fixed-sized or variable-sized) that serve as the unit of caching. While TCP-RE has additional overhead to manage TCP flows, it allows scalable cache management as well as flow-based caching policies. We discuss packet-based RE and TCP-based RE approaches in more detail in Section 6.4.

3. SCALABLE ANALYSIS OF REDUNDANT TRAFFIC

In this section, we describe the design and implementation of Monbot, a high-performance DFI system on commodity hardware. At a high-level, Monbot produces three types of log data in real time for later analysis – (1) TCP flow statistics, (2) HTTP request / response statistics, and (3) SHA-1 hashes of content chunks. We primarily focus on the TCP and HTTP traffic since they take up the majority of the total traffic volume.

While there are many high-end DPI solutions that produce various protocol-level traffic statistics or dump packets to disk [2, 4, 8], we do not know of any system that analyzes the content-level redundancy in the high-speed 10 Gbps network. Dumping packets to disk is not an option since our traffic volume for a week would require more than 120 3 TB disks, not to mention the enormous time for offline analysis. Instead, we focus on online analysis, which requires high-performance packet capture, scalable flow management and content hash calculation, and parallel disk I/O for writing the log data. Monbot supports this goal on a pure commodity server without any dedicated packet capture cards such as [3, 7].

One challenge of Monbot is to process a large amount of concurrent flows without a packet drop. Indeed, our measurement shows that the system should handle 1.4 million packets per second and 270K concurrent TCP connections at peak. To cope with this scale, Monbot exploits processing parallelism in modern multicore systems, making each core handle a partition of flows in parallel. To avoid expensive inter-core communication, we also develop symmetric RSS that assigns both upstream and downstream packets that belong to the same TCP connection to the same core. Our current prototype has two 3.47 GHz hexacore Xeon X5690 CPUs in dual-NUMA nodes with 144 GB of RAM and a dual-port 10 Gbps NIC with the Intel 82599 chipset, and has 24 3TB SATA disks for storing log data.

3.1 Parallel Flow Monitoring Architecture

Figure 2 shows the overall architecture of Monbot. Monbot transparently receives IP packets from the monitored 10 Gbps link (*e.g.*, via port-mirroring), and distributes them to CPU cores with symmetric RSS. For high-speed packet reception (RX), we use PacketShader I/O engine (PSIO) [26]. PSIO is known for achieving multi-10 Gbps packet I/O even for 64B packets by batch processing of RX packets and efficient CPU cache usage.

The central goal of the Monbot design is to achieve high core scalability. Given that the majority of the TCP flows are small (in Section 5), it is important to efficiently handle small TCP control packets in the same CPU core without any lock contention [27, 36]. Each CPU core in Monbot runs one DFI thread and two disk threads pinned to it. The DFI thread is responsible for packet RX with PSIO, and for producing TCP/HTTP flow statistics and content hashes. Each disk thread buffers the logs passed from the DFI thread, and writes them to its dedicated disk in batches. This way, all 12 CPU cores and 24 disks are utilized in parallel completely independent of each other.

To efficiently manage buffers for a large number of concurrent flows while dealing with packet reordering from packet losses or retransmissions[1], Monbot also implements per-core memory pools with different buffer sizes. Dynamically adjusting buffer sizes with `realloc()` is prohibitively expensive as it incurs lock contention across cores, and having a uniform buffer size risks either packet losses or out of memory. Instead, each DFI thread pre-allocates $\frac{1}{N}$-th of the total memory where N is the total number of cores, and creates a set of memory pools with different buffer sizes (*e.g.*, 32 KB, 64 KB, ..., 2 MB). A new flow is assigned to the smallest buffer, and moves to a larger buffer as more space is needed. Based

[1]When a flow with a large receive window (*e.g.*, we see as large as 16 MB) sees burst packet losses, a large gap in the buffer is inevitable.

Algorithm 1 RSS Hash Computation Algorithm

```
function RSS_HASH(INPUT, RSK)
  u_int32 ret = 0;
  for each bit b in INPUT
    if (b == 1) then ret = ret xor (left-most 32 bits of RSK);
    shift RSK left by 1 bit;
  end for
  return ret;
end function
```

INPUT Field	INPUT Bit Range	RSK Bit Range
Source IP (32 bits)	1 .. 32	1 .. 63
Destination IP (32 bits)	33 .. 64	33 .. 95
Source port (16 bits)	65 .. 80	65 .. 111
Destination port (16 bits)	81 .. 96	81 .. 127
Protocol (8 bits)	97 .. 104	97 .. 135

Table 1: RSK bit ranges that affect the portions of an IPv4 header for RSS hash calculation

```
0x6d 0x5a 0x6d 0x5b 0x6d 0x5a 0x6d 0x5b
0x6d 0x5a 0x6d 0x5a 0x6d 0x5a 0x6d 0x5a
0xc6 ...
```

Table 2: Sample RSK that satisfies Equation (3)

on our observation that 90.6% of the total TCP flows are smaller than 32 KB and short-lived, we assign 90% of the total memory to 32 KB buffers, and proportionally decrease the size of the memory pools for larger buffer sizes. This way, Monbot can process 40K concurrent flows per DFI thread, handling 480K concurrent TCP flows with 12 cores.

3.2 Symmetric Receive-Side Scaling

RSS is a modern NIC feature that balances the packet processing load across multiple CPU cores. It distributes incoming packets into multiple hardware receive queues (RX queues) that are mapped to each CPU core by running the Toeplitz hash function [30] on the five tuples of IP packet headers (src/dest IPs, ports, and a protocol). This way, packets in the same flow are accessed exclusively by a core without lock contention.

However, RSS is not suitable for high-performance DFI middleboxes that monitor TCP connections in *both* directions, as the packets in the same connection may end up in two different RX queues, one for upstream packets and another for downstream packets, and accessing them requires acquiring locks. While one can re-run hashing and distribute packets in software [5, 44], it not only wastes CPU cycles but also loses the benefit of hardware-supported RSS.

To overcome this limitation, we develop symmetric RSS that maps the packets in the same connection into the same RX queue regardless of their directions, by leveraging the existing RSS feature. More importantly, symmetric RSS does not modify the RSS algorithm itself, thus it can still distribute the packets at line rate. The basic idea is to produce the same RSS hash value even if the src/dest IPs and ports are swapped.

Algorithm 1 shows the pseudo code of the Toeplitz hash function that takes INPUT and RSK as inputs. INPUT is typically five tuples of the IP header, and RSK is a 320-bits random secret value that gets mixed with INPUT. Since the value of RSK can be configured when activating NICs, we can craft the value of RSK that satisfies the following condition where s and d represent source and destination (*e.g.*, sIP is a source IP), and p represents a one-byte protocol field (*e.g.*, TCP or UDP).

$$\begin{aligned} &RSS\_Hash(sIP : dIP : sPort : dPort : p, RSK) \\ &= RSS\_Hash(dIP : sIP : dPort : sPort : p, RSK) \end{aligned} \quad (1)$$

We can further limit the scope of Equation (1) with the following observation, which derives Table 1 that shows RSK bit ranges affecting each IP header field in RSS hash calculation.

OBSERVATION 1. *For calculation of the nth bit of INPUT, only the nth to $(n+31)^{th}$ bit range of RSK is used.*

Plugging Table 1 into Equation (1) yields the following condition where $RSK_{A..B}$ represents a bit range of RSK from the Ath bit to the Bth bit.

$$RSK_{1..63} = RSK_{33..95}, \quad RSK_{65..111} = RSK_{81..127} \quad (2)$$

By removing the overlapping regions from Equation (2), we obtain the final condition as follows.

$$\begin{aligned} &i)\ RSK_{1..15} = RSK_{17..31} = RSK_{33..47} = RSK_{49..63} \\ &\quad = RSK_{65..79} = RSK_{81..95} = RSK_{97..111} = RSK_{113..127} \\ &ii)\ RSK_{16} = RSK_{48} = RSK_{80} = RSK_{96} = RSK_{112} \\ &iii)\ RSK_{32} = RSK_{64} \end{aligned} \quad (3)$$

One such example of RSK for IPv4 packets is shown in Table 2 where each byte is alternating except for the 4th, 8th, and 17th bytes. This is because Equation (3) requires that each group of 16 bits should be identical except for the 32nd and the 64th bit positions. Similarly, we can further tweak this RSK to be used for both IPv4 and IPv6 packets with the following observation.

OBSERVATION 2. *For calculation of the nth byte of INPUT, only the nth to $(n+4)^{th}$ byte range of RSK is used.*

This implies that if every odd byte of RSK has the same value, and so does every even byte, we can ensure the byte-level symmetry in RSS hash calculation.[2] For example, we only need to replace `0x5b` with `0x5a` in Table 2 to support IPv6 packets.

Evaluation. To confirm if symmetric RSS evenly balances TCP connections, we analyze the number of flows handled by each core on Monbot during the week-long measurement. Figure 3 presents the maximum deviation, which is the maximum difference in the number of flows processed by each core divided by the per-minute average. We find that both algorithms behave almost the same. In fact, as long as the IPs and ports are randomly distributed, we can prove that the level of load balancing in symmetric RSS is not worse than that in the original RSS [46].

The maximum deviations look somewhat high (9.5%) in both algorithms because the distribution is skewed since the number of CPU cores (12) is not a power of two. In fact, the first eight cores receive about 9% more flows than the remaining four cores. The deviation among the first 8 cores is less than 0.2% and so is for the remaining 4 cores. Our simulation on 16 CPU cores confirms that symmetric RSS bounds the deviations within 0.2% across all cores.

One concern with symmetric RSS is that one might craft an attack such that all traffic is veered onto one or a few CPU cores. While more thorough cryptanalysis is required, we think that brute-force attacks are non-trivial since trying all 24-bit key space for RSK is

[2] More details can be found in our technical report [46].

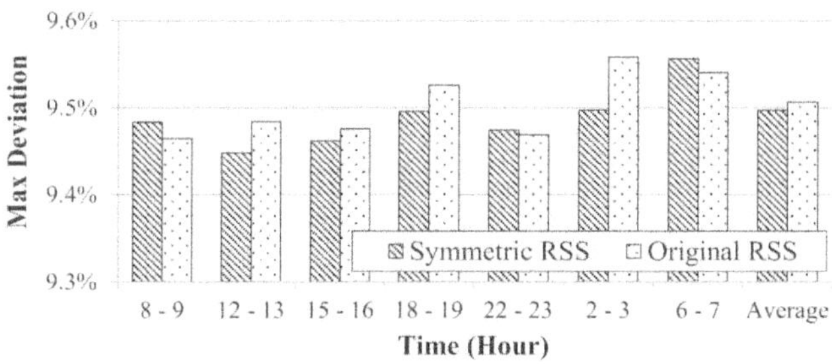

Figure 3: Maximum deviation in the number of flows per core

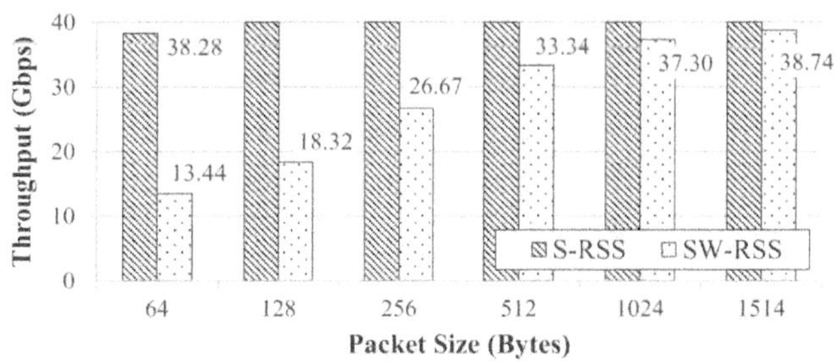

Figure 4: Packet RX performance of PSIO+S-RSS (S-RSS) vs. PF_RING+S/W hashing (SW-RSS)

time consuming and the attacker may not know how many cores are employed for the system. We leave it as our future work.

Next, Figure 4 compares the packet RX performances of PSIO with symmetric RSS (S-RSS), and PF_RING 5.5.1 with software hashing (SW-RSS) that distributes the packets in the same connection to the same thread [5]. PF_RING uses RSS and distributes the packets to CPU threads by zero copy. Both libraries support interrupt and polling modes, and we use interrupt mode here. [3]

To gauge the maximum performance, we add an extra 10 Gbps NIC to the machine so that its maximum RX rate reaches 40 Gbps. We use our own packet generator that blasts packets at 40 Gbps regardless of packet size [26], and use only 8 CPU cores to avoid RSS load imbalance. IPs and port numbers are randomly populated in a packet, and for each packet, we send its corresponding ACK packet by swapping IPs and port numbers. Except for 64B packets, S-RSS achieves a 40 Gbps line rate for all packet sizes. In contrast, SW-RSS shows 1.5x~2.8x lower performance than S-RSS at 64B~256B packets, although its performance is close to 40 Gbps at larger sizes.

4. DATASET

This section describes our measurement environment and the limitations in our dataset.

Measurement Environment. We place Monbot at a core network switch on GGSN in Seoul (as shown in Figure 1), which serves as a gateway to IP networks. This point of presence (PoP) covers the 3G traffic from half of all regions in South Korea served by the ISP, which has 12.5 million 3G subscribers. Monbot monitored all IP traffic at a 10 Gbps link from 12 pm on July 7th (Saturday) to 2 pm on July 14th (Sunday) in 2012. During the period, it logged 8.3 billion TCP connections from 1.8 million unique client IPs and 4.5 million unique server IPs, which amounts to 370 TBs in volume or 590 billion packets. UEs use the shared private IP space (*e.g.*, 10.*.*.*) allocated by DHCP, and their IPs are NAT-translated to public IPs after our measurement point while the server-side IPs are seen as public at Monbot.

Monbot stores a log record for each TCP connection and HTTP request. A TCP connection log includes source and destination IPs and ports, start and end timestamps, amount of transferred bytes, connection setup RTT, etc. A HTTP log includes a request URL, host name, start and end timestamps of each request, `content-type`, `content-length`, `user-agent`, and other caching-related header fields. It also records SHA1 hashes of 8 different prefix sizes of the response body, from 1 KB to 1 MB, as well as the hash of the entire object to gauge the effectiveness of prefix-based Web caching. Furthermore, Monbot handles HTTP pipelining and persistent connections, and stores each HTTP session log.

[3]PF_RING polling mode did not improve performance.

For content-level analysis, Monbot logs SHA1 hashes of fixed 4 KB content chunks for all of the downlink TCP traffic, except for HTTP response headers. We exclude HTTP response headers since some fields (*e.g.*, `Date`) are dynamically regenerated regardless of content. For any chunk / content that is smaller than 4 KB, we hash the entire chunk / content. The total size of the logs is 1 TB for TCP session logs, 2.8 TB for HTTP logs, and 11.4 TB for the content chunk hashes.

Limitations. We summarize the limitations in our dataset here. First, the 10 Gbps link being monitored is one of the flow-level load-balanced links by equal-cost multi-path (ECMP). Due to this setup, our dataset cannot capture all flows from a specific UE, but all packets in the same connection are monitored. Also, we do not have UE identifiers such as IMSI for client-side IPs, and a private IP can be reused by another device. When we need to identify a client, we use a heuristic that compares the IPs and the OS versions in the HTTP `user-agent` field. This limitation, however, is only subject to false positives in Figure 18(b), and all other findings remain intact.

Second, while we did not see any packet loss at the NIC of Monbot, we observe packet losses from switch-based mirroring. We confirm this by seeing client-side ACKs for the packets that are not captured by Monbot. We skip the TCP buffer region with a hole for SHA1 hash calculation, and ignore the potential redundancy for prefix-based Web caching when the incomplete region happens within the prefix range. The skipped bytes due to incomplete regions constitutes about 1.92% of the downlink traffic.

Finally, we use 4 KB fixed-sized chunking, which may miss some redundancy that is otherwise observed with a smaller chunk size or variable chunking methods. This choice was inevitable given the limitation in the available storage space and CPU cycles. Since our primary focus is to find if we can suppress a reasonable level of traffic by a software-based RE system on commodity hardware for 10+ Gbps environments, we believe our findings are still useful for practical RE systems design.

5. FLOW-LEVEL CHARACTERISTICS

In this section, we analyze TCP and application-level characteristics of our traffic, and also discuss the performance requirements and trade-offs of flow management overhead, latency, and throughput, which shapes the design of caching middleboxes.

Protocol and Application Mix. We first analyze the overall protocol composition in Table 3. As observed in other mobile networks, the downlink traffic volume is much larger (13x) than the uplink traffic volume [29]. TCP accounts for 95.7% of the entire downlink traffic, implying most of the traffic is downloads of content from servers to mobile devices. The remaining traffic is

IP Version	Volume	Volume Ratio	# Packets	Protocol	Volume	Volume Ratio	# Packets	# Packet Ratio
IPv4 Downlink	343.5 TB	91.5%	341,920,148,702	TCP	328.7 TB	95.7%	318,498,981,294	93.2%
IPv4 Uplink	25.6 TB	6.8%	243,711,521,675	UDP	14.1 TB	4.1%	21,543,090,962	6.3%
Others	6.4 TB	1.7%	20,140,919,576	ICMP	6.5 GB	-	71,621,981	0.02%

Port	Application	Volume (TB)	Volume Ratio(%)	# Flows Ratio(%)	Port	Volume (TB)	Volume Ratio(%)	# Flows Ratio(%)		
									# Uniq Server IPs / 7 days	4,502,812
									# Uniq client IPs / 7 days	1,807,499
80	HTTP	256.2	74.6	78.1	≥ 1024	59.6	17.4	10.8	# Uniq server IPs / hour	119,460
443	HTTPS	10.2	3.0	10.4	17600	9.7	3.6	0.01	# Uniq client IPs / hour	922,631
110	POP3	0.37	0.14	0.04	8405	3.8	1.4	0.01	# TCP flows	8,307,724,934
995	POP3	0.16	0.06	0.03	9000	3.5	1.3	0.02	# TCP concurrent flows	174,322
993	IMAP	0.30	0.11	0.20	8012	2.3	0.9	0.00	Payload unmergeable ratio	1.92%
554	RTSP	0.17	0.06	0.01	8008	2.3	0.8	0.00	# Total 4K chunks	87,330,807,203

Content-type	Average Size	# Flows	Volume	Volume (%)	Cacheability (# Objects)	Cacheability (Volume)	Web Cache (Volume)	Prefix Cache (Volume)	TCP-RE (Volume)
HTTP Total	34.5 KB	7,738,867,184	248.3 TB	100.0%	53.9%	40.7%	23.7%	27.7%	32.7%
Video	1982 KB	45,457,010	83.9 TB	33.8%	19.8%	35.9%	18.7%	20.0%	28.4%
Image	19.9 KB	3,748,164,242	69.4 TB	28.0%	83.4%	93.1%	66.8%	67.5%	53.1%
App	45.8 KB	1,413,098,511	56.3 TB	22.7%	22.2%	62.2%	21.9%	28.3%	61.6%
Text	11.0 KB	2,047,840,830	20.9 TB	8.5%	30.4%	44.0%	33.7%	37.6%	43.4%
Audio	1073 KB	16,707,509	16.8 TB	6.8%	12.6%	18.3%	7.0%	32.4%	39.5%
Etc	2.60 KB	467,599,082	1.1 TB	0.4%	5.2%	18.4%	6.3%	6.7%	20.2%

Table 3: Overall statistics of the 3G traffic trace

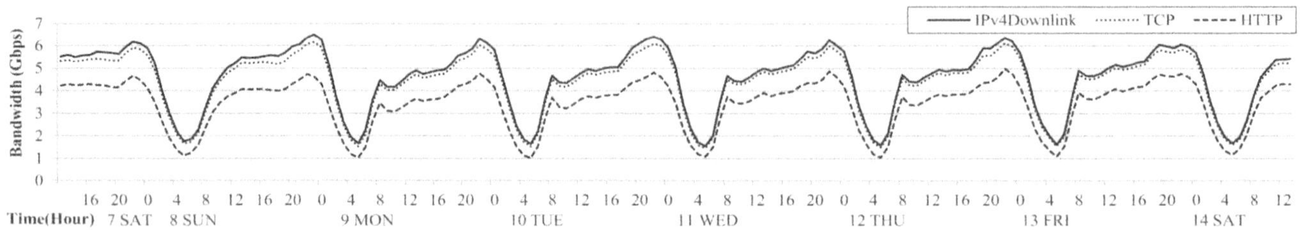

Figure 5: 3G traffic volume for seven days (each point is a 1-hour average)

largely UDP (4.1%) and a tiny amount of ICMP and GRE (less than 10^{-5}%) traffic.

Table 3 shows the contributions by various application protocols identified by server-side port numbers. We observe that HTTP (74.6%) and HTTPS (3.0%) dominate the traffic. However, the dominance of HTTP in the cellular network is much heavier than in broadband (57.6 %) [31]. We suspect that this is because most smartphone applications use HTTP as its communication protocol [32]. We also see the other traffic such as POP3, IMAP, RTSP, SSH, FTP, and TELNET, but their individual contribution is less than 1%, with the aggregate volume of only 3.7%. Remaining applications with ports larger than 1023 account for non-negligible 17.4% of the traffic. Further investigation shows that the top-ranked port (17600, 3.6%) is used for serving local P2P live video content [10]. We also find that other ports are used only by specific IP subnet ranges, implying that they are mainly custom protocols.

Figure 5 shows the hourly bandwidth consumption over the measurement period. We observe a clear diurnal pattern where most of the bandwidth usage happens during the daytime between 8 am and 11 pm. The peak bandwidth is about 6 Gbps at 11 pm (7.5 Gbps as per-minute average), and the lowest bandwidth is 2 Gbps at 4 am, 3x smaller than the peak bandwidth. Interestingly, the bandwidth demand during the weekend is slightly larger than that of the weekdays. We also observe small peaks every weekday in the rush hour (8 - 9 am) and during lunchtime (12 - 1 pm), which implies that people use smartphones for Internet access while commuting or having lunch. We further investigate the amount of traffic by their HTTP content types in Figure 6. Interestingly, the numbers (left plot) and byte volumes (right plot) of flows by each content

Percentile (%)	Concurrent Flows (# flows)	Created Flows (# flows/min)	Duration (sec)
1%	55,000	218,000	0.09
10%	67,000	288,000	0.17
50%	197,000	931,000	1.01
90%	237,000	1,087,000	11.01
99%	257,000	1,168,000	64.52
Average	174,000	812,000	6.52

Table 4: TCP flow statistics for a week. Flow counts are snapshotted every minute.

type remain stable regardless of the time of the day, exhibiting self-similarity [21]. Multimedia objects contribute to only 0.8% by the flow count, but its byte volume constitutes 40.6% of the traffic. This implies that caching solutions focusing on multimedia objects could deal with a significant portion of traffic at a small flow management cost.

TCP Flow Characteristics. We examine the characteristics of the TCP flows more in depth, which can suggest the performance requirements of middleboxes such as RE systems. Table 4 shows TCP flow-level statistics for the entire week. We observe that the number of concurrent flows changes dynamically from 50K (at 5 am) to 270K (at 11 pm), and the number of newly-created TCP flows per minute ranges from 0.2M to 1.3M. While most of the flows are short-lived (1 second as median, 11 seconds as 90th%-tile), the distribution has a long tail that spans more than one day.

Figure 7 analyzes the flow sizes by their number (left plot) and by their byte volume (right plot) over seven one-hour time slots,

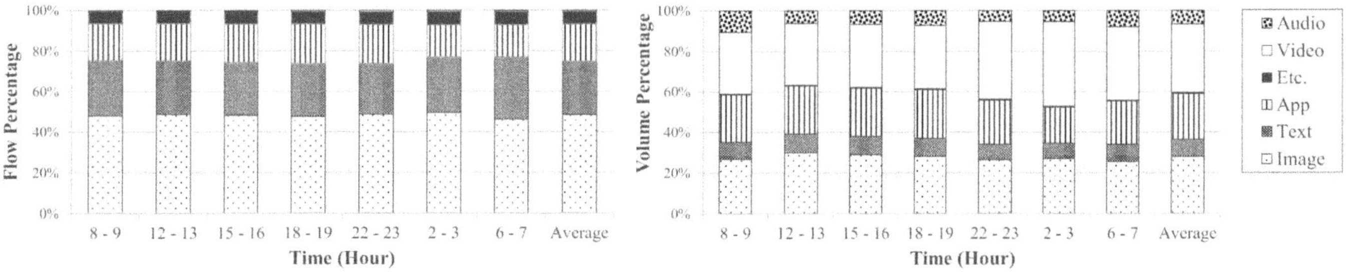

Figure 6: The percentage of flows and byte volume by the HTTP content type

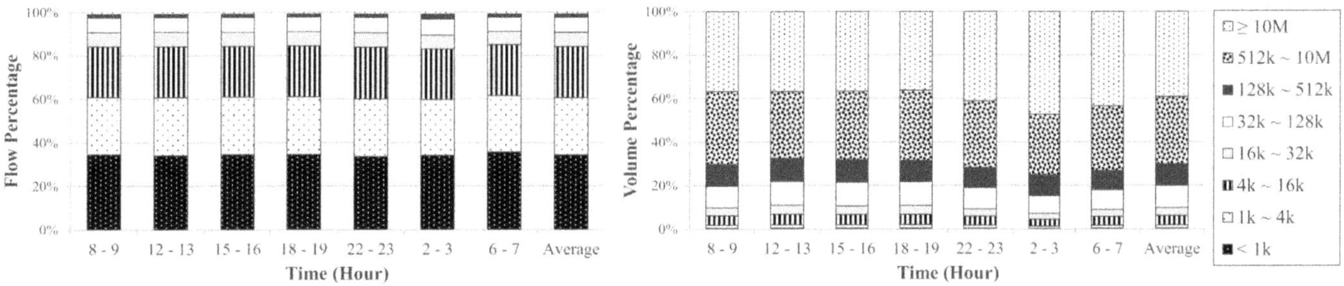

Figure 7: Distributions of TCP flows by flow size over various time slots

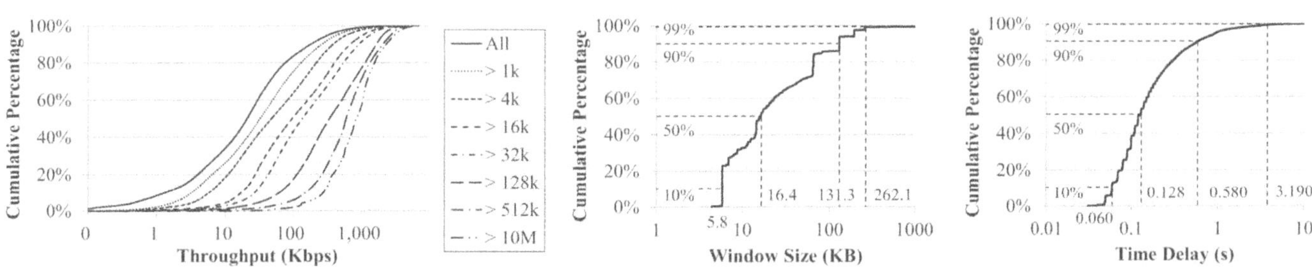

(a) Throughput by flow size (b) Advertised window size (c) Connection setup delay

Figure 8: Cumulative distribution of throughputs, advertised window sizes, and connection setup delays

aggregated for one week. On average, 60.6% of the flows are smaller than 4 KB and only 9.4% of the flows are larger than 32 KB. In contrast, the volume of the flows larger than 32 KB accounts for 90.3% of the total traffic. This implies that if TCP-RE systems bypass these small flows (*e.g.*, by checking the `content-length` field), we can reduce almost 90% of the flow management overhead while still covering more than 90% of the total volume. Similar to Figure 6, flow size distributions also exhibit self-similarity.

TCP Performance. Figure 8(a) shows the throughput distributions of individual TCP flows grouped by the flow size between 10 - 11 pm for one week. Overall, the median throughput is 21.1 Kbps, and even 90th%-tile is only 182.4 Kbps. The low throughput seems to be because most flows are short-lived, and thus do not leave the TCP slow-start phase. This is in line with Figure 8(b), which shows the median advertisement window as only 16 KB. On the other hand, for larger flows, we observe the maximum throughput of 13.6 Mbps and the window size of up to 16.0 MB. Figure 8(c) also shows the connection setup delay between client-side SYN and ACK, which includes the round-trip time and server-side connection creation overhead. We observe the minimum, median, and 99th%-tile delays of 39 ms, 128 ms, and 3.19 seconds, respectively.

6. REDUNDANCY IN THE 3G TRAFFIC

In this section, we compare the effectiveness of standard Web caching, prefix-based Web caching, and TCP-RE from various perspectives. We also discuss different RE designs for high-speed cellular backhaul networks, and study the origin and temporality of the redundancy.

6.1 Effectiveness of Web Caching

We measure the effectiveness of Web caching by simulating our HTTP log trace. We follow the HTTP 1.1 standard [24] for caching, and assume a log-based disk cache as in [17]. Overall, we find that 53.9% of the total objects are cacheable and they account for 40.7% of the downlink traffic (by the byte volume) during the period. With infinite Web cache, one can save 23.7% of the downlink bandwidth for the week by standard Web caching.

Figure 9(a) shows daily bandwidth savings with various cache sizes from 128 GB to 16 TB as well as infinite cache. The difference in bandwidth savings slowly grows over time, but the working set size is relatively small since even 512 GB cache, which fits in memory, can provide bandwidth savings ratio of 18.6%. Figure 9(b) shows the difference in bandwidth savings at different times of the day, averaged for seven days. Morning rush hour (8 - 9 am), lunch time (12 - 1 pm), and mid-afternoon (3 - 4 pm) produce relatively

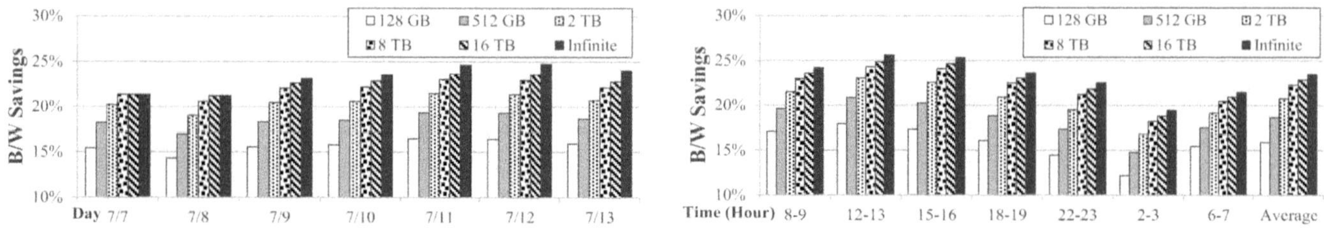

(a) Various Web cache sizes (b) Different times of a day, averaged for seven days

Figure 9: Bandwidth savings by standard Web caching

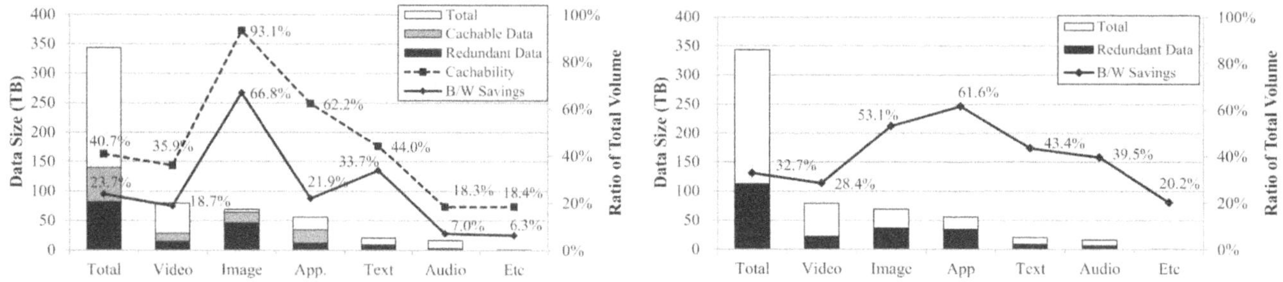

(a) Web cache (infinite size) (b) TCP-RE (512GB)

Figure 10: Redundancy by content type with Web caching and TCP-RE

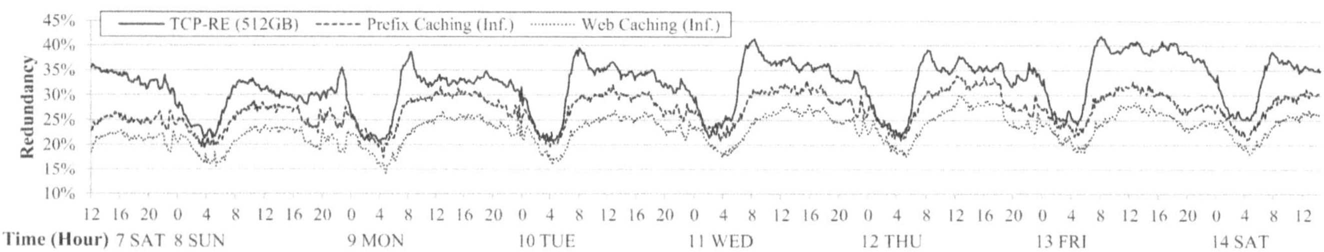

Figure 11: Comparison of bandwidth savings by Web caching, prefix-based Web caching, and TCP-RE

larger bandwidth savings, while early morning (2 - 3 am, 6 - 7 am) shows the smallest savings.

Figure 10(a) shows the breakdown of cacheability and cache hit ratios by content types. Images produce the largest bandwidth savings. 93.1% of the image bytes are cacheable, and 66.8% of them lead to bandwidth savings. Applications are highly cachaeable as well (62.2%), but their bandwidth savings ratio is limited to 21.9%. Video takes up the largest traffic, but only 35.9% is cacheable with 18.7% of bandwidth savings. Audio exhibits the lowest cacheability, and we suspect this is one of the reasons why rush hour peaks cannot be suppressed by Web caching as much as TCP-RE as shown in Figure 11.

6.2 Effectiveness of Prefix-based Caching

Prefix-based Web caching complements the weakness of standard Web caching by serving aliased, or redundant but uncacheable content. It operates as standard Web caching for the HTTP requests, but when a request is a cache miss, it compares the hash of the N-byte prefix and the length of the response to confirm an alias. If the aliased object is found in its cache, it stops downloading from the origin, and delivers the leftover from its cache instead.

Prefix Key Size vs. False Positives. The prefix key size is crucial for the effectiveness of prefix-based Web caching. In general, a smaller prefix key size would produce more bandwidth savings at the risk of having a higher false positive rate. On the other hand, a larger prefix key size cannot suppress aliased objects that are smaller than the key, so it produces smaller bandwidth savings, but with a lower false positive rate.

Table 5 shows the number of false positives over various prefix key sizes from 1 KB up to 1024 KB for *all* HTTP objects downloaded for the measurement period. Surprisingly, we find false positives in every prefix key size while the number of false positives decreases as the key size increases. We manually inspect some of false positives. For small prefix keys, we find that many of them are due to modifications on the texts (*e.g.*, HTML pages or scripts like CSS and Javascript) or metadata (*e.g.*, timestamps). We also find some large animated GIFs that have the same content up to the 1 MB prefix key size, but contain different image frames located beyond 1 MB.

Bandwidth Savings. Figure 13 shows the bandwidth savings with infinite cache across various content types. We choose 1 MB as the prefix key size as it minimizes the false positives in our trace. We perform similar simulations as in Web caching for 2 TB and infinite cache sizes. Prefix-based Web caching saves 27.7% of the downlink traffic (excluding the false positives) during the period, improving Web caching by only 4%. While audio, application, and video show 25.4%, 6.4%, 1.3% additional bandwidth savings than

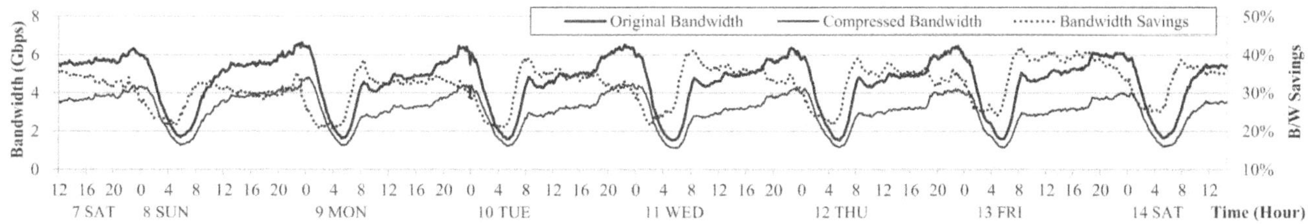

Figure 12: Original and estimated bandwidth usages by TCP-RE (512 GB cache)

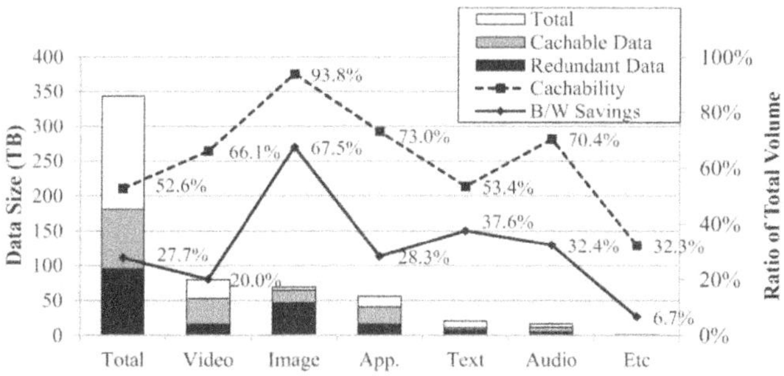

Figure 13: Bandwidth savings by prefix-based caching

Prefix Key Size	Number of FP Object	% of Total Object	Size of FP Object	% of Total Traffic
1 KB	52,936,642	0.68%	3.79 TB	1.10%
4 KB	14,993,908	0.19%	3.49 TB	1.02%
16 KB	4,173,023	0.05%	2.93 TB	0.85%
128 KB	277,039	0.004%	0.60 TB	0.18%
256 KB	102,689	0.001%	0.33 TB	0.10%
512 KB	39,519	0.001%	0.25 TB	0.07%
1024 KB	24,732	0.0003%	0.19 TB	0.05%

Table 5: False positives for prefix-based Web caching

standard Web caching, respectively, other types are typically smaller than 1 MB, and do not see further savings.

Finally, Figure 14 compares daily bandwidth savings of standard and prefix-based Web caching. On the first day, prefix-based Web caching with 2 TB cache shows slightly larger bandwidth savings than Web caching with infinite cache. The difference between standard and prefix-based Web caching with infinite cache stays more or less the same (3∼4%) over time. This implies that (a) the additional redundancy detected by prefix-based Web caching is limited by a large prefix key size, and (b) old content may not benefit from prefix-based Web caching as much as the new content does.

6.3 Effectiveness of TCP-RE

We present the effectiveness of TCP-RE over the measurement period in Figure 11 where we use the LRU cache replacement algorithm with 512 GB chunk cache size. Overall, we find 30∼40% of bandwidth savings most of the day (8 am - midnight) while it drops below 20% early in the morning (4 - 6 am).

Figure 10(b) compares bandwidth savings by HTTP content type. Video, image, application take up over 80% of the total HTTP traffic, and contribute to 85% of the total bandwidth savings. Image and application show high redundancy while the redundancy in video is relatively lower. Compared with Web caching, however, more redundancy is found for video since they are often uncacheable with `sessionID/userID` embedded in their URLs (*e.g.*, YouTube).

Redundancy at Peak Bandwidths. In general, the bandwidth savings shows a positive correlation with the bandwidth usage, but

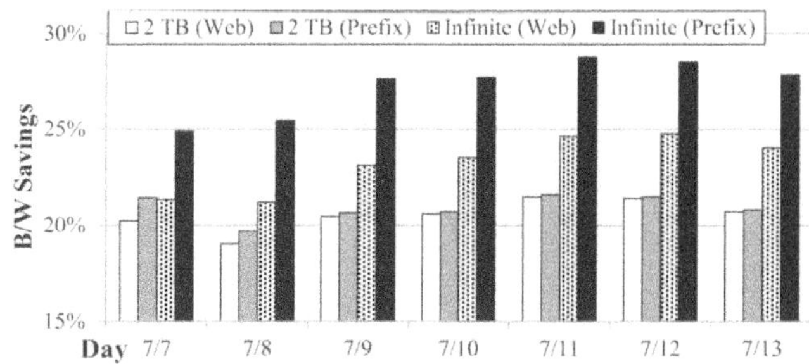

Figure 14: Comparison of daily bandwidth savings by standard and prefix-based Web caching

the peak times (10 - 11 pm) do not always yield higher redundancy. Figure 11 indicates that the periodic bandwidth peaks in the rush hour can be effectively suppressed by TCP-RE. The content types that drive the local peaks are audio and text, which implies that many users are listening to popular music or reading popular online news while commuting. In contrast, these periodic bandwidth peaks cannot be addressed by standard Web caching that saves 14.4∼18.2% less bandwidth than TCP-RE. Further investigation shows that many of those audio objects are from subscription-based music services, and are set uncacheable. Similar periodic bandwidth spikes during lunch time can also be effectively reduced by TCP-RE.

On the other hand, some bandwidth savings at 10 - 11 pm shows a slightly negative correlation with the bandwidth usage (*e.g.*, Mon., Tue., and Wed.) where a similar behavior is observed in enterprise traffic analysis [13]. Nevertheless, TCP-RE still promises 30.7∼36.9% bandwidth savings at the peak time in the 3G traffic. Figure 12 shows the estimated bandwidth usage for the seven days (called compressed bandwidth) after applying TCP-RE. Bandwidth fluctuation is much smaller with TCP-RE, which effectively curbs the usage below 5 Gbps.

Cache Size and Replacement Policy. We further investigate the effect of different cache sizes and cache replacement algorithms on bandwidth savings in TCP-RE. Due to the large volume of our traces and the limitation in the available memory (144 GB) of our machine, we divide the traces into 24 disks by chunk hash values and calculate the bandwidth savings on one partition.

First, Figure 15(a) shows bandwidth savings for the first five days [4] where each bar represents bandwidth savings for each day. We increase the cache size from 4 GB to infinite, and use the LRU cache replacement policy. Except for the infinite cache case, the bandwidth savings stays more or less the same. The infinite cache can find 48.9∼59.3% of the redundancy while even 4 GB cache reduces the traffic by more than 10%. As expected, the bandwidth savings grows as the cache size increases, but we observe diminish-

[4] Due to the the memory limitation, we could not simulate infinite cache beyond the first five days.

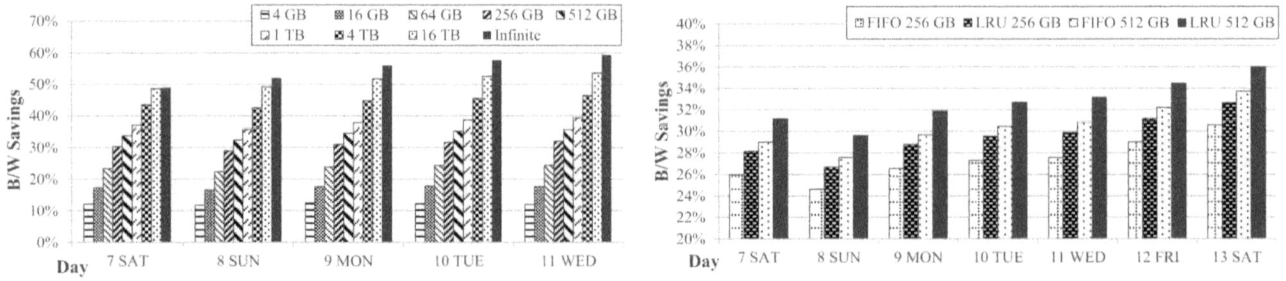

(a) Bandwidth savings over various cache sizes (b) Comparison of bandwidth savings between FIFO and LRU

Figure 15: TCP-RE bandwidth savings by cache size and cache replacement algorithms

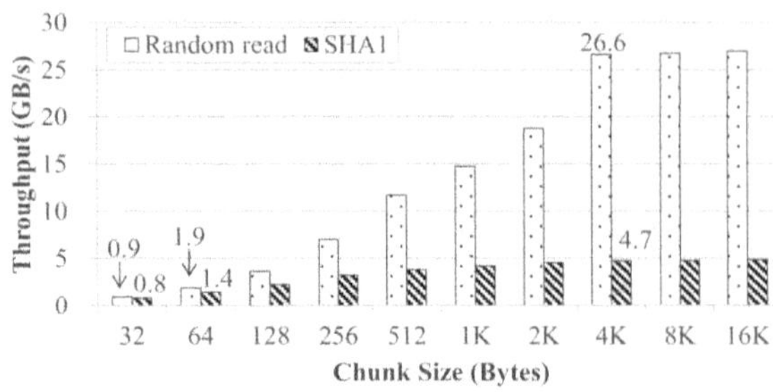

Figure 16: Memory I/O performance on Monbot

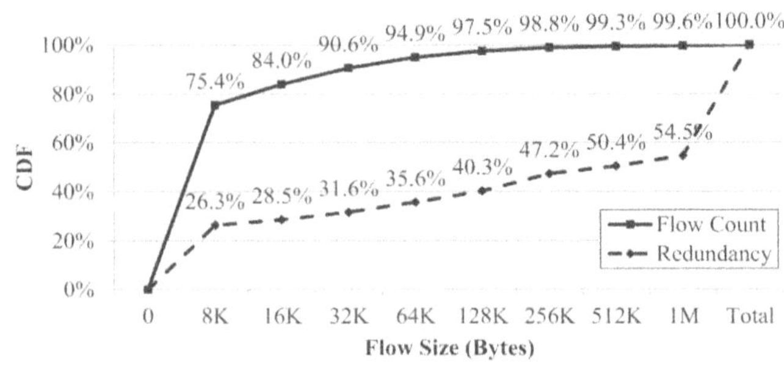

Figure 17: TCP-RE bandwidth savings by flow size

ing gains. This is because the popularity of the chunks follows the Zipf distribution, which we will discuss further in Section 6.5.

Next, we compare the impact of FIFO and LRU cache replacement algorithms on the bandwidth savings for two practical cache sizes that can be installed on currently available commodity servers. Figure 15(b) suggests that LRU is slightly better (2.1$\sim$2.3%) than FIFO for the same cache size. It implies that the redundancy comes mostly from temporal locality.

6.4 TCP-based RE vs. Packet-based RE

We discuss performance trade-offs of different RE system designs, and their suitability in high-speed cellular backbone networks. While we assume middlebox-based TCP-RE here, an alternative approach is packet-level RE [14, 42], which detects candidate fragments for RE within each IP packet, typically using content-based fingerprinting functions [11, 13, 39]. Packet-level RE is simpler because it does not manage TCP flows nor terminate the TCP connections at middleboxes. Also, it can potentially find more redundancy since it operates on smaller chunk sizes (*e.g.*, 32 to 64 bytes [11, 13, 42]).

However, there are a few drawbacks with packet-level RE in high-speed cellular backhaul networks. First, small chunks can easily explode the index sizes in a high-speed network. For example, a 64B average chunk size may require 64x more index entries than 4 KB chunks for the same cache size. Second, a small chunk size would incur a higher hashing and content reconstruction cost, and it stresses the memory system which is typically the performance bottleneck in memory-based RE. Figure 16 compares random memory read and SHA1 hashing performances over various chunk sizes when all 12 cores on Monbot do only the memory operations. We run the experiment five times and show the averages. Both random memory read and SHA1 performances increases as the chunk size grows and saturates at 4 KB. The 4 KB random read performance is 28.3x and 14.2x larger than those of 64B and 32B chunks, presumably due to much smaller TLB cache misses and page table operations. From the Figure, it looks very challenging to achieve 10 Gbps RE performance with 32B or 64B chunks on a single machine. Similarly, SHA1 performance of 4 KB chunks is 5.78x or 3.36x higher than those of 32B or 64B chunks. Some previous work [11] reduces the hashing overhead by maintaining a synchronized chunk cache, but it would be challenging to be applied to cellular networks since the packet routes can change abruptly due to user mobility. Finally, it is difficult to enforce flow-based policies with packet-level RE. Cellular ISPs may want to apply RE to only large file downloads or to specific content types that exhibit high redundancy with a small flow management overhead.

Instead, middlebox-based TCP-RE with fixed 4 KB chunks strikes a balance between memory I/O costs and bandwidth savings, which we think is reasonable for cellular backbone networks. It could even reduce the flow management cost while still offering a reasonable level of bandwidth savings by selectively processing flows. Figure 17 shows the cumulative distribution functions (CDFs) of the redundancy and the number of flows for the flow size. It shows that the largest 10% of the flows bring about 70% of the bandwidth savings. That is, bypassing any HTTP responses smaller than 32 KB could eliminate the cost of managing 90.6% of the flows while still providing 31.6% of the bandwidth savings.

6.5 Source of Redundancy

We study the source of redundancy to help determine the effective caching strategies and deployment options. First, we analyze the source of the HTTP object-level redundancy. Specifically, we measure the fraction of redundancy from serving the same object with the same URL (`intra-content`) and with different URLs (`alias`), partial content overlap in the objects with the same URL (`object update`) and with different URLs (`inter-content`). Second, we measure the fraction of the redundancy in the communicating node pair. We mark it `same-pair` if the redundancy is found from the same client and server pair, `same-server` if it comes from the same server but different clients, `same-client` if it comes from the same client interacting with different servers, and `diff-pair` if the redundancy is from different client and server pairs.

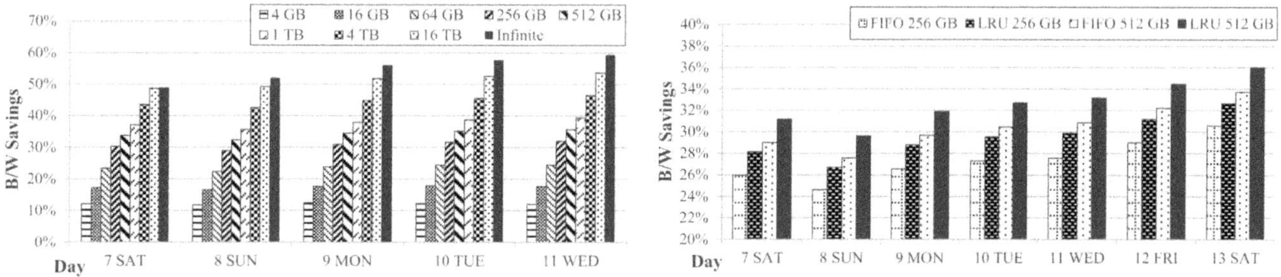

(a) Bandwidth savings over various cache sizes

(b) Comparison of bandwidth savings between FIFO and LRU

Figure 15: TCP-RE bandwidth savings by cache size and cache replacement algorithms

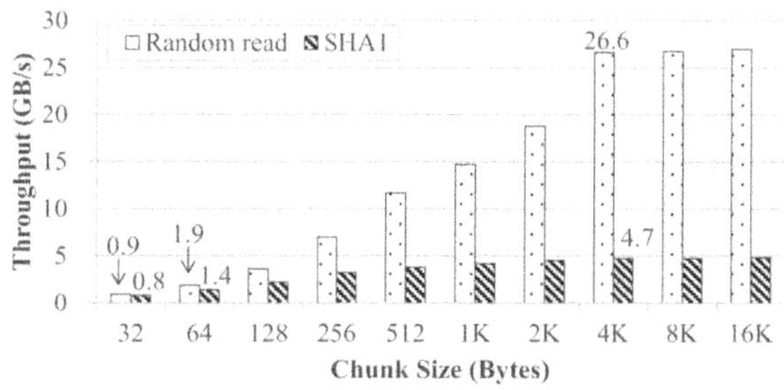

Figure 16: Memory I/O performance on Monbot

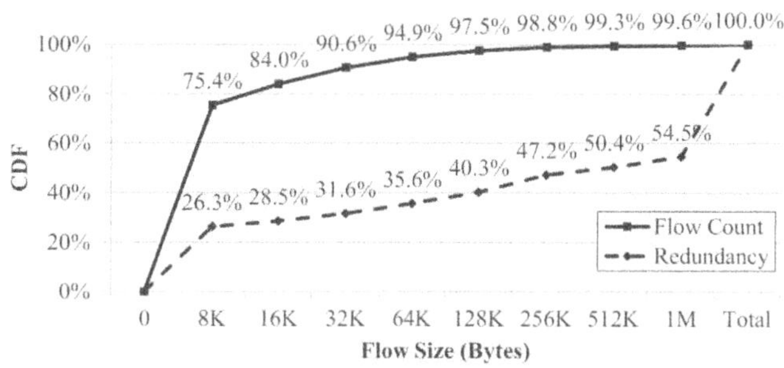

Figure 17: TCP-RE bandwidth savings by flow size

ing gains. This is because the popularity of the chunks follows the Zipf distribution, which we will discuss further in Section 6.5.

Next, we compare the impact of FIFO and LRU cache replacement algorithms on the bandwidth savings for two practical cache sizes that can be installed on currently available commodity servers. Figure 15(b) suggests that LRU is slightly better (2.1∼2.3%) than FIFO for the same cache size. It implies that the redundancy comes mostly from temporal locality.

6.4 TCP-based RE vs. Packet-based RE

We discuss performance trade-offs of different RE system designs, and their suitability in high-speed cellular backbone networks. While we assume middlebox-based TCP-RE here, an alternative approach is packet-level RE [14, 42], which detects candidate fragments for RE within each IP packet, typically using content-based fingerprinting functions [11, 13, 39]. Packet-level RE is simpler because it does not manage TCP flows nor terminate the TCP connections at middleboxes. Also, it can potentially find more redundancy since it operates on smaller chunk sizes (*e.g.*, 32 to 64 bytes [11, 13, 42]).

However, there are a few drawbacks with packet-level RE in high-speed cellular backhaul networks. First, small chunks can easily explode the index sizes in a high-speed network. For example, a 64B average chunk size may require 64x more index entries than 4 KB chunks for the same cache size. Second, a small chunk size would incur a higher hashing and content reconstruction cost, and it stresses the memory system which is typically the performance bottleneck in memory-based RE. Figure 16 compares random memory read and SHA1 hashing performances over various chunk sizes when all 12 cores on Monbot do only the memory operations. We run the experiment five times and show the averages. Both random memory read and SHA1 performances increases as the chunk size grows and saturates at 4 KB. The 4 KB random read performance is 28.3x and 14.2x larger than those of 64B and 32B chunks, presumably due to much smaller TLB cache misses and page table operations. From the Figure, it looks very challenging to achieve 10 Gbps RE performance with 32B or 64B chunks on a single machine. Similarly, SHA1 performance of 4 KB chunks is 5.78x or 3.36x higher than those of 32B or 64B chunks. Some previous work [11] reduces the hashing overhead by maintaining a synchronized chunk cache, but it would be challenging to be applied to cellular networks since the packet routes can change abruptly due to user mobility. Finally, it is difficult to enforce flow-based policies with packet-level RE. Cellular ISPs may want to apply RE to only large file downloads or to specific content types that exhibit high redundancy with a small flow management overhead.

Instead, middlebox-based TCP-RE with fixed 4 KB chunks strikes a balance between memory I/O costs and bandwidth savings, which we think is reasonable for cellular backbone networks. It could even reduce the flow management cost while still offering a reasonable level of bandwidth savings by selectively processing flows. Figure 17 shows the cumulative distribution functions (CDFs) of the redundancy and the number of flows for the flow size. It shows that the largest 10% of the flows bring about 70% of the bandwidth savings. That is, bypassing any HTTP responses smaller than 32 KB could eliminate the cost of managing 90.6% of the flows while still providing 31.6% of the bandwidth savings.

6.5 Source of Redundancy

We study the source of redundancy to help determine the effective caching strategies and deployment options. First, we analyze the source of the HTTP object-level redundancy. Specifically, we measure the fraction of redundancy from serving the same object with the same URL (`intra-content`) and with different URLs (`alias`), partial content overlap in the objects with the same URL (`object update`) and with different URLs (`inter-content`). Second, we measure the fraction of the redundancy in the communicating node pair. We mark it `same-pair` if the redundancy is found from the same client and server pair, `same-server` if it comes from the same server but different clients, `same-client` if it comes from the same client interacting with different servers, and `diff-pair` if the redundancy is from different client and server pairs.

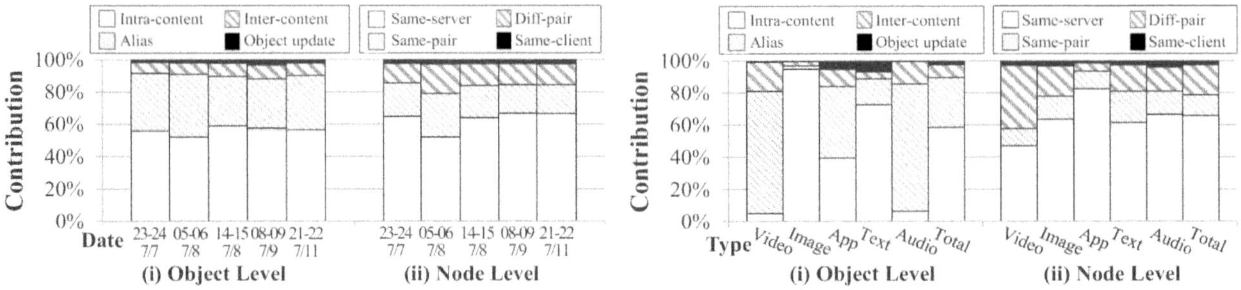

(a) By time slot

(b) By content type

Figure 18: Source of redundancy

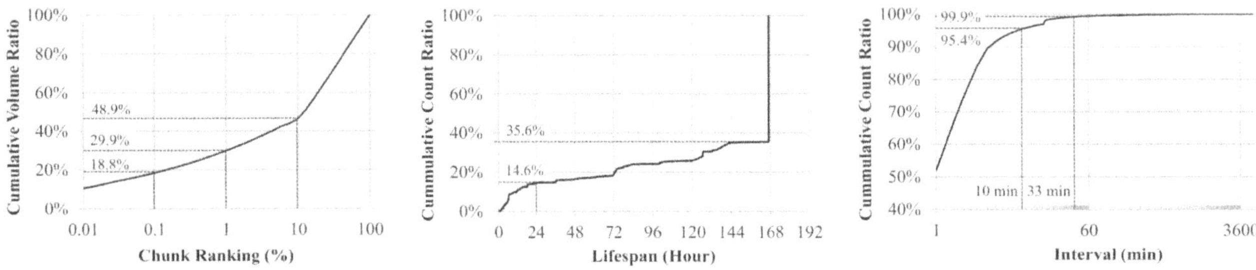

(a) Volume distribution by chunk popularity (b) Cache-hit interval distribution (c) Chunk lifespan distribution

Figure 19: Temporal analysis of the most popular 1000 chunks

Figure 18(a) shows the results for five one-hour time slots that are carefully chosen based on bandwidth usage. Each bar represents an average for seven days. Interestingly, the behavior is similar across all time slots. The intra-content redundancy shows 52.1~58.9% while alias contributes to 30.4~38.9%. The redundancy from partial content overlap is less than 9% most of the time. This implies that Web caching is effective in addressing a large portion of the redundancy while prefix-based Web caching with a small prefix key size could suppress most of the redundancy if it can avoid false positives.

For the node level analysis, we assume that it is the same client if it uses the same IP, the same mobile device model, and the same OS version in the user-agent field. If we detect the change of the device model or the OS version, we assume that the IP is reassigned and consider it as a different client. While this can bloat the actual redundancy from a client, we find that the redundancy from the same client (e.g., same-pair, same-client) is less than 21%, which implies the client-side RE would produce limited bandwidth savings. This is in contrast to the enterprise traffic where as much as 75% of the redundancy is attributed to the intra-host traffic [11]. The majority of the redundancy in our 3G traffic comes from downloading popular contents from the same server.

Figure 18(b) shows the source of redundancy by the content type. Overall, the major source of redundancy is from the same contents (intra-content, alias) and from the same server (same-server, same-pair). However, the contribution by aliases is much higher for media contents such as video and audio than other contents since they are usually served by multiple servers for load balancing. On the other hand, we find that the contribution by partial content overlap (inter-content, object update) and client-side RE (same pair, same-client) is limited.

The redundancy in the non-HTTP traffic is 2.8~12.9% in the time slots, which is lower than that of the HTTP traffic. The top traffic contributor is P2P video streaming that uses port 17600 [10] and the SSL traffic, taking up 3.6% and 3.4% of the downlink traffic each.

Data Type	10-11 pm 7/7	11 pm-12 am 7/7	5-6 am 7/8	8-9 am 7/8
Chunks	0.7441	0.7512	0.7177	0.7490
Web Objects	0.8820	0.8799	0.8798	0.8755

Table 6: Zipf's α values for one-hour time bins

We see that the P2P traffic with port 17600 significantly increases in early morning (up to 8.8% in 4-6 am), which partly explains why the bandwidth savings decreases during the time.

6.6 Temporality of Redundancy

We find that both HTTP objects and chunks follow the Zipf distribution. Table 6 shows that the Zipf α values of Web objects (0.88) are relatively larger than those of chunks (0.72~0.75), but we actually find that TCP-RE is more effective even with a smaller cache size. This implies that the cache duration and the cacheability of the HTTP objects set by the content providers may be suboptimal in terms of bandwidth savings.

We also analyze the temporal locality of the chunks in the first one hour of our measurement more closely. Overall, we find strong temporal locality of the chunks. During the first hour, the most popular 1% chunks represent 29.9% of the total downlink bytes in the hour and the top 10% chunks represent 48.9% of the hourly volume as shown in Figure 19(a). Figure 19(b) shows the distribution of hit intervals of the most popular 1,000 chunks in the first hour. 95.4% of all hits occur within 10 minutes while 99.0% of them are within 33 minutes. Lastly, Figure 19(c) shows the distribution of the lifespans (the time between the first and the last hits of the same chunk) of the most popular 1,000 chunks in the first hour for the remaining 7 days. We find that 64.4% of the chunks are accessed throughout the seven days while 14.6% of them are used only on the first day. We also find that there is no strong correlation between the lifespan and the hit-count rank.

Motivated by the high temporal locality of chunks, we simulate

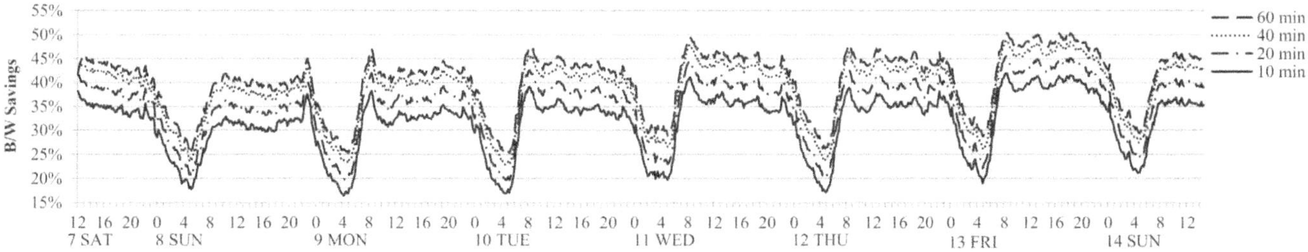

Figure 20: TCP-RE bandwidth savings for caching for the most recent N minutes

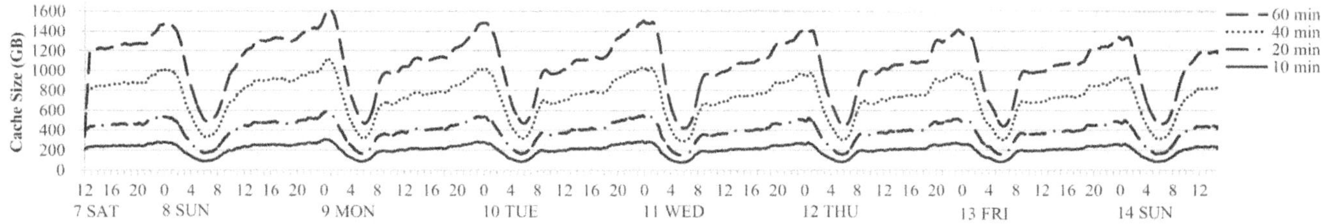

Figure 21: Required TCP-RE cache size for caching for the most recent N minutes

the effect of limited but realistic TCP-RE cache sizes. Figure 20 and Figure 21 show the bandwidth savings and required cache sizes when caching chunks only for the most recent 10 to 60 minutes. We achieve as much as 30∼40% of the bandwidth savings by caching chunks for the most recent 10 minutes while caching for 60 minutes increases the bandwidth savings by only 10% at the cost of linear increase in the required cache size. That is, the high temporality of the chunks greatly helps suppress the redundancy even with small cache size but larger cache size would yield a marginal increase in bandwidth savings.

One interesting finding is that the top two chunks consist of a stream of 0x00 (chunk with all 0's) and 0xFF (chunk with all 1s), and they are used for various content types like image, app, and even text. We suspect these are due to padding generated by commonly-used libraries.

7. IMPLICATIONS FOR CACHING MIDDLEBOXES

This section summarizes our key findings that could shape the design of caching middleboxes for high-speed cellular backhaul networks.

- Caching middleboxes should be able to efficiently manage a large number of concurrent flows in high speed links. In our data set, we observe up to 270K concurrent flows, 1.3M new flows per minute, and about 7.5 Gbps peak per-minute bandwidth usage.
- Unlike wired network traffic, our mobile network traffic incurs several periodic spikes in bandwidth usage related to user mobility during the day (*e.g.*, rush hour, lunch time, and midnight).
- Among different caching strategies, we find TCP-RE with 512 GB memory cache outperforms other approaches, and it is even effective for suppressing peak bandwidth usage. While prefix-based Web caching offers higher bandwidth savings than standard Web caching, it comes with false positives that severely limit its utility. Due to the Zipf-like distribution of chunk popularity, LRU slightly outperforms FIFO.
- Packet-based RE may be unsuitable for high-speed cellular backhaul links because of its high overhead on indexing and memory I/Os. We also find that an end-host based caching approach provides only limited bandwidth savings.
- Most flows are short-lived, but a small fraction of large flows (*e.g.*, video) dominate the entire traffic volume. This offers an optimization opportunity for RE systems to reduce the flow management cost while still providing a reasonable level of bandwidth savings.

8. RELATED WORK

Our work is built upon previous research in many areas. In this section, we relate our work to this previous work.

Scalable Traffic Analysis on Multicore Systems. Various efforts exploited processing parallelism in multicore systems for scalable packet/flow management [25, 36, 41]. Sommer *et al.* build a custom FPGA-based NIC that manages a large table indexed by five tuples of a packet header, and dispatches packets to core-pinned CPU threads based on the routing decision in the table entry [41]. For high scalability, they ensure the core affinity of packet processing but allow event queues to exchange information between threads. Fusco *et al.* present virtual capture devices for scalable packet analysis on a commodity NIC [25]. They use RSS to distribute incoming packets to multiple RX queues, and virtualize a physical NIC to provide multiple virtual devices for packet capture threads. Affinity-accept focuses on core-scalable `accept()` on an end node by removing lock contention and ensuring core affinity in incoming TCP packet processing [36].

In comparison, Monbot achieves scalable TCP flow processing in a middlebox using a commodity NIC. Monbot extends PacketShader I/O engine [26] to process all packets in the same TCP connection in the same core by symmetric RSS without lock contention or any sharing of flow context across different cores.

Network Redundancy Elimination. There have been many works that suggest redundancy suppression for WAN acceleration. Spring *et al.* first present packet-level RE based on Rabin's fingerprinting, and showed that 39% of the uncacheable Web traffic can be saved [42]. More recently, Anand *et al.* report 59% and 31% of potential bandwidth savings for small and large enterprise traffic [13]. They also find that over 75% of the savings are from intra-host matches. Drawing from this fact, EndRE suggests pushing the RE cache to clients [11]. Other proposals include deploying network-wide RE by carefully coordinating the router cache [14], and supporting RE as a primitive service in the IP-layer [12]. Furthermore, PACK [47] shows the power of chunk prediction in reducing the redundant traffic for cloud traffic. Ihm *et al.* find 42.0~50.6% of the redundancy in the CoDeeN content distribution network Web traffic [28].

We find that the cellular network traffic could also benefit from significant bandwidth savings by TCP-RE. Unlike the enterprise traffic, our measurements show that the redundancy in the intra-host traffic is rather limited, and the middlebox-based approach would bring higher redundancy suppression in the cellular backhaul networks. Furthermore, our work deals with one or two orders of magnitude larger traffic than previous works [13, 23], showing the daily redundancy pattern, flow dynamics, and detailed comparison of effectiveness of various caching strategies.

Web Caching in Cellular Networks. Erman *et al.* report 68.7% of the HTTP objects are cacheable with 33% of the cache hit ratio in their two-day measurements in a 3G cellular network in 2010 [22]. While the fraction of cacheable objects is smaller (53.9%) in our measurement, the cache hit ratio is similar (38.3%). Another work finds that 36% of the 3G traffic is attributed to video streaming, and 24% of the bytes can be served from HTTP cache [23]. Our numbers match the volume of the traffic (33.8%), but the video bandwidth savings in Web cache is smaller in our trace (18.7%). However, we show that TCP-RE could increase the bandwidth savings further by 9.7% for video. Qian *et al.* report that Web caching on smartphones (*e.g.*, browser or application cache) could be ineffective due to the lack of support for Web caching or library bugs [38]. More recently, Qian *et al.* measure the effectiveness of Web caching, file compression, delta encoding, and packet-level RE using packet traces collected from 20 mobilephone users for 5 months [37]. They find that combining all of the four methods could reduce the cellular traffic by 30%. In comparison, our middlebox-based TCP-RE provides the similar bandwidth savings without any modification of the server and the client. In addition, we believe packet-level RE that they use is difficult to deploy in practice since it is challenging to synchronize the RE cache due to device mobility.

Breslau *et al.* report that the popularity of Web objects follows the Zipf distribution [18]. We see the same trend in our 3G Web traffic with $\alpha = 0.88$. This suggests that even a small cache reduces a large amount of Web traffic, which is implied in Figure 9(a). Chunk-level popularity shows smaller α values, but it is more effective than Web caching even with a smaller cache size.

TCP Performance in Cellular Networks. The TCP performance of the live cellular networks has been measured in previous research. Chesterfield *et al.* report an average throughput of 350 Kbps and 200 ms of delays in early 3G UMTS networks in 2004 [19]. Later, Jurvansuu *et al.* report an effective bandwidth of 1 Mbps and 61 ms of delays in HSDPA networks in 2007 [29].

In contrast, our measurements show that the average throughput is only 111.92 Kbps because the majority of the TCP flows are small and they do not leave the slow start phase. For flows larger than 1 MB, however, the average bandwidth is 0.95 Mbps, and the maximum throughput we observe reaches 13.6 Mbps.

9. CONCLUSION

Caching in the cellular networks is an attractive approach that can address the backhaul congestion in core networks. By monitoring 8.3 billion flows of 3G backhaul traffic for one week, we have compared the benefits and trade-offs of promising caching solutions. We have found that TCP-RE is the most effective in terms of bandwidth savings and cache size overhead. It gives 14% additional bandwidth savings compared to standard Web cache, with only 512 GB memory. Prefix-based caching is effective with a small key size, but we find that it produces false positives even with a large prefix size such as 1 MB. We have also shown the flow-level characteristics of modern 3G traffic, which should be useful for provisioning the capacity of the networks or for designing various middleboxes for cellular networks. Finally, we have presented Monbot, a high-performance DFI system on commodity hardware that scalably manages hundreds of thousands of concurrent flows by balancing the load across CPU cores with symmetric RSS. We believe Monbot and symmetric RSS could serve as a basis for flow managing middleboxes in high-speed networks.

10. ACKNOWLEDGMENTS

We appreciate many valuable comments from the anonymous reviewers of ACM MobiSys 2013. We also thank our shepherd, Morley Mao, for her help in improving the paper, and Vivek S. Pai for providing comments and insights on the early draft of the paper. We thank Kyoungjun Lee who greatly supported setting up the measurement environment in the ISP. We thank Marc Fiuczynski who helped catch numerous editorial errors in the final version. This project is supported in part by the grant from SK Telecom and by the National Research Foundation of Korea (NSF) grant #2012R1A1A1015222.

References

[1] 3GPP LTE. `http://www.3gpp.org/LTE`, 2012.

[2] ComWorth SwiftWing SIRIUS. `http://www.comworth.com.sg/products/swiftwing-sirius-line-rate-capture-storage-system`, 2012.

[3] Endace DAG. `http://www.endace.com/endace-dag-high-speed-packet-capture-cards.html`, 2012.

[4] Endace Intelligent Network Recoder. `http://www.endace.com/endace-high-speed-packet-capture-probes.html`, 2012.

[5] Libzero for DNA: Zero-copy flexible packet processing on top of DNA. `http://www.ntop.org/products/pf_ring/libzero-for-dna/`, 2012.

[6] Mobile operators risk backhaul gap in LTE networks. `http://www.telecomstechnews.com/blog-hub/2013/feb/13/mobile-operators-risk-backhaul-gap-in-lte-networks/`, 2012.

[7] Napatech NT40/NT20. `http://www.napatech.com/products/capture_adapters/1x40g_pcie_nt40e2-1_capture.html`, 2012.

[8] NPulse HammerHead. `http://www.npulsetech.com/Products/HammerHead-Flow-Packet-Capture.aspx`, 2012.

[9] Perfecting policy control. `http://www.ericsson.com/res/docs/whitepapers/WP-e2e-policy-control.pdf`, 2012.

[10] AfreecaTV, Inc. `http://www.afreeca.com/`.

[11] B. Agarwal, A. Akella, A. Anand, A. Balachandran, P. Chitnis, C. Muthukrishnan, R. Ramjee, and G. Varghese. EndRE: An end-system redundancy elimination service for enterprises. In *Proceedings of the USENIX Symposium on Networked Systems Design and Implementation (NSDI)*, 2010.

[12] A. Anand, A. Gupta, A. Akella, S. Seshan, and S. Shenker. Packet caches on routers: The implications of universal

redundant traffic elimination. In *Proceedings of ACM SIGCOMM*, 2008.

[13] A. Anand, C. Muthukrishnan, A. Akella, and R. Ramjee. Redundancy in network traffic: Findings and implications. In *Proceedings of the ACM SIGMETRICS*, 2009.

[14] A. Anand, V. Sekar, and A. Akella. SmartRE: An architecture for coordinated network-wide redundancy elimination. In *Proceedings of ACM SIGCOMM*, 2009.

[15] ARA Networks, Inc. `http://www.aranetworks.com/`.

[16] ARS Technica. The State of 4G: It's All about Congestion, not Speed. `http://arstechnica.com/tech-policy/2010/03/faster-mobile-broadband-driven-by-congestion-not-speed/`, 2010.

[17] A. Badam, K. Park, V. S. Pai, and L. Peterson. HashCache: Cache storage for the next billion. In *Proceedings of the USENIX Symposium on Networked Systems Design and Implementation (NSDI)*, 2009.

[18] L. Breslau, P. Cue, P. Cao, L. Fan, G. Phillips, and S. Shenker. Web caching and zipf-like distributions: Evidence and implications. In *Proceedings of IEEE INFOCOM*, 1999.

[19] J. Chesterfield, R. Chakravorty, J. Corwcroft, P. Rodriguez, and S. Banerjee. Experiences with multimedia streaming over 2.5G and 3G networks. In *Proceedings of the International Conference on Broadband Communications, Networks, and Systems (BROADNETS)*, 2004.

[20] Cisco, Inc. Cisco visual networking index: Global mobile data traffic for 2011-2016. `http://www.cisco.com/en/US/solutions/collateral/ns341/ns525/ns537/ns705/ns827/white_paper_c11-481360_ns827_Networking_Solutions_White_Paper.html`, 2012.

[21] M. E. Crovella and A. Bestavros. Self-similarity in World Wide Web traffic: evidence and possible causes. *IEEE/ACM Transactions on Networking*, 5(6):835 – 846, 1997.

[22] J. Erman, A. Gerber, M. T. Hajiaghayi, D. Pei, S. Sen, and O. Spatscheck. To cache or not to cache: The 3G case. *IEEE Internet Computing*, 15(2):27–34, Mar. 2011.

[23] J. Erman, A. Gerber, K. Ramakrishnan, S. Sen, and O. Spatscheck. Over the top video: The gorilla in cellular networks. In *Proceedings of the ACM SIGCOMM Conference on Internet Measurement Conference (IMC)*, 2011.

[24] R. Fielding, J. Gettys, J. Mogul, H. Frystyk, L. Masinter, P. Leach, and T. Berners-Lee. Hypertext Transfer Protocol – HTTP/1.1. RFC 2616, 1999.

[25] F. Fusco and L. Deri. High speed network traffic analysis with commodity multi-core systems. In *Proceedings of the ACM SIGCOMM Conference on Internet Measurement Conference (IMC)*, 2010.

[26] S. Han, K. Jang, K. Park, and S. B. Moon. PacketShader: a GPU-accelerated software router. In *Proceedings of ACM SIGCOMM*, 2010.

[27] S. Han, S. Marshall, B.-G. Chun, and S. Ratnasamy. MegaPipe: a new programming interface for scalable network I/O. In *Proceedings of the USENIX Conference on Operating Systems Design and Implementation (OSDI)*, 2012.

[28] S. Ihm and V. Pai. Towards understanding modern web traffic. In *Proceedings of the ACM SIGCOMM Conference on Internet Measurement Conference (IMC)*, 2011.

[29] M. Jurvansuu, J. Prokkola, M. Hanski, and P. Perala. HSDPA performance in live networks. In *Proceedings of IEEE International Conference on Communications (ICC)*, 2007.

[30] H. Krawczyk. LFSR-based hashing and authentication. In *Proceedings of the 14th Annual International Cryptology Conference on Advances in Cryptology (CRYPTO)*, 1994.

[31] G. Maier, A. Feldmann, V. Paxson, and M. Allman. On dominant characteristics of residential broadband Internet traffic. In *Proceedings of the ACM SIGCOMM Conference on Internet measurement Conference (IMC)*, 2009.

[32] G. Maier, F. Schneider, and A. Feldmann. A first look at mobile hand-held device traffic. In *Proceedings of the Passive and Active Measurement (PAM)*, 2010.

[33] I. Microsoft. MSDN: Introduction to receive-side scaling. `http://msdn.microsoft.com/en-us/library/windows/hardware/ff556942%28v=vs.85%29.aspx`, 2012.

[34] Oversi, Inc. `http://www.oversi.com/`.

[35] PeerApp, Inc. `http://www.peerapp.com/`.

[36] A. Pesterev, J. Strauss, N. Zeldovich, and R. T. Morris. Improving network connection locality on multicore systems. In *Proceedings of the ACM European Conference on Computer Systems (EuroSys)*, 2012.

[37] F. Qian, J. Huang, J. Erman, Z. M. Mao, S. Sen, and O. Spatscheck. How to reduce smartphone traffic volume by 30%? In *Proceedings of the Passive and Active Measurement (PAM)*, 2013.

[38] F. Qian, K. S. Quah, J. Huang, J. Erman, A. Gerber, Z. M. Mao, S. Sen, and O. Spatscheck. Web caching on smartphones: Ideal vs. reality. In *Proceedings of the ACM International Conference on Mobile Systems, Applications, and Services (MobiSys)*, 2012.

[39] M. O. Rabin. Fingerprinting by random polynomials. Technical Report TR-15-81, Harvard University, 1981.

[40] E. Seidel and E. Saad. LTE home node BS and its enhancements in release 9. `http://www.nomor.de/uploads/fc/lp/fclpAIhtNJQ9zwyD957atQ/2010-05_LTE_HomeNB_Rel9_Overview.pdf`, 2012.

[41] R. Sommer, V. Paxson, and N. Weaver. An architecture for exploiting multi-core processors to parallelize network intrusion prevention. *Concurrency and Computation: Practice and Experience*, 21(10):1255–1279, 2009.

[42] N. T. Spring and D. Wetherall. A protocol-independent technique for eliminating redundant network traffic. In *Proceedings of ACM SIGCOMM*, 2000.

[43] The Cuttting Edge. U.S. could see $53 billion in 4G network investments in five years. `http://www.thecuttingedgenews.com/index.php?article=52617&pageid=28&pagename=Sci-Tech`, 2011.

[44] G. Vasiliadis, M. Polychronakis, and S. Ioannidis. MIDeA: A multi-parallel intrusion detection architecture. In *Proceedings of the ACM Conference on Computer and Communications Security (CCS)*, 2011.

[45] I. VerizonWireless. Verizon optimization deployment-terms & conditions. `http://support.verizonwireless.com/terms/network_optimization.html`, 2012.

[46] S. Woo and K. Park. Scalable TCP session monitoring with symmetric receive-side scaling. `http://www.ndsl.kaist.ac.kr/~shinae/papers/TR-symRSS.pdf`, 2012.

[47] E. Zohar, I. Cidon, and O. Mokryn. The power of prediction: Cloud bandwidth and cost reduction. In *Proceedings of ACM SIGCOMM*, 2011.

LEAD: Leveraging Protocol Signatures for Improving Wireless Link Performance

Jun Huang, Yu Wang and Guoliang Xing
Department of Computer Science and Engineering, Michigan State University, USA
{huangjun, wangyu3, glxing}@cse.msu.edu

ABSTRACT

Error correction is a fundamental problem in wireless system design as wireless links often suffer high bit error rate due to the effects of signal attenuation, multipath fading and interference. This paper presents a new cross-layer solution called LEAD to improve the performance of existing channel decoders. While the traditional wisdom of cross-layer design is to exploit physical layer information at upper-layers, LEAD represents a paradigm shift in that it leverages upper-layer protocol signatures to improve the performance of physical layer channel decoding. The approach of LEAD is motivated by two key insights. First, channel codes can correct more errors when the values of some bits, which we refer to as *pilots*, are known before decoding. Second, some header fields of upper-layer protocols are often fixed or highly biased toward certain values. These distinctive bit pattern signatures can thus be exploited as pilots to assist channel decoding. To realize this idea, we first characterize bit bias in real-life network traffic, and develop an efficient algorithm to extract pilot bits with assured prediction accuracy. We then propose a decoding framework to allow existing channel decoders to effectively exploit extracted pilots. We implement LEAD on GNURadio/USRP platform and evaluate its performance by replaying real-life packet traces on a testbed of 12 USRP links. Our results show that LEAD significantly improve wireless link performance, while incurring very low overhead. Specifically, LEAD reduces more than 90% bit errors for 48.9% packets, and improves the end-to-end link throughput by 1.43x to 1.93x over existing error correction schemes.

Categories and Subject Descriptors

C.2.1 [**Computer Communication Networks**]: Network Architecture and Design—*wireless communication*

Keywords

Cross-layer design, bit predictability, channel code, decoder

MobiSys'13, June 25–28, 2013, Taipei, Taiwan

1. INTRODUCTION

The last decade has witnessed a phenomenal penetration rate of 802.11-based Wireless LANs (WLANs). Nevertheless, as an important part of communication infrastructure, today's WLANs struggle to keep up with the ever growing user demands for higher data rate and coverage. The fundamental challenge for significantly improving WLAN performance lies in the fact that wireless links suffer from high error rate due to the effects of signal attenuation, multipath fading, and interference. To improve the resilience to transmission errors, wireless communication systems employ channel coding at the physical layer (PHY). However, when the number of errors exceeds the correcting capability of channel code, the original data cannot be fully recovered through channel decoding, leading to corrupted packets. The problem is exacerbated by user mobility, which becomes the common case due to the proliferation of portable wireless devices such as tablets and smartphones.

In this paper, we propose LEAD, Leveraging protocol signaturEs for pilot-Assisted Decoding, to reduce bit error rate (BER) of 802.11 links. LEAD is motivated by two key observations. First, 802.11 traffic carries numerous upper-layer protocol headers, and some particular fields in these headers are often fixed or biased toward certain values. For instance, the service type field of logical link control header is fixed to 0x0800 for packets that use IP at the network layer. Moreover, previous studies showed that network traffic is bursty in nature [17]. As a result, IP packets that target the same host will lead to temporal bias patterns in the destination field of IP header. Second, the channel decoder of wireless receiver can correct more errors when the values of some bits, which we refer to as *pilots*, are predictable at the receiver before decoding. This is due to the fact that the decoding success rates of adjacent bits are dependent on each other, and the predictable values of pilots may affect the decoding of adjacent bits, improving their decoding success rates.

The key idea of LEAD is to leverage protocol signatures as pilots to improve the performance of channel decoding. By capturing these protocol signatures, a LEAD receiver can 'guess' some values of received bits (before they are decoded), and then exposes them to the physical layer to guide the decoding of whole packet. We address several challenges in the design and implementation of LEAD. First, due to the inherent dynamics of network traffic, bit patterns of protocol signatures are time-varying, leading to possible pilot mispredictions and decoding errors. Second, protocol signatures are only present in packet headers and hence have limited impact on the decoding accuracy of packet payload.

Moreover, bits received at the physical layer are scrambled and encrypted, making it challenging to recognize pilots before decoding. In summary, we make the following main contributions in this paper.

1. We present LEAD, a novel cross-layer design to reduce bit errors in 802.11-based WLANs. While traditional wisdom of cross-layer design is to exploit physical layer information at the MAC layer or above, LEAD represents a paradigm shift in that it leverages upper-layer protocol signatures to improve physical layer channel decoding. LEAD offers several key advantages. First, the design of LEAD is independent of the underlying channel code. Thus the pilot-assisted decoding mechanism of LEAD can be exploited by all existing channel codes to reduce error rates of wireless links. Second, LEAD works with existing 802.11 encoders and requires minimum modifications to the 802.11 physical layer. Moreover, it is largely orthogonal to existing error recovery mechanisms (*e.g.*, partial packet recovery [16], link layer forward error correction [18], and block retransmission-based recovery [13]) and can be integrated with them to further reduce packet error rate.

2. We conduct a measurement study to characterize bit bias in real-life network traffic. Our results show that, although bit bias is prominent in upper-layer protocol signatures, it yields distinct patterns that significantly affect the predictability of bit values. We then design an efficient algorithm that classifies bit bias patterns and extracts "good" pilot bits with assured prediction accuracy.

3. We develop a decoding framework that consists of several key components to enable pilot-assisted decoding for existing channel codes: *link addressing* allows a decoder to recognize the link identity of a received packet, so that it can leverage the protocol signatures extracted on this link to assist decoding; *pilot spreading* interleaves extracted pilots across the whole packet so that the decoding of payload can leverage adjacent pilots; *pilot reshaping* deals with the impacts of scrambling and encyption on pilot-assisted decoding; and *pilot misprediction handling* detects faulty pilots to avoid decoding errors induced by mispredictions.

4. We develop pilot-assisted decoders for convolutional code, LDPC, and rateless Spinal code, and integrate them with LEAD to leverage protocol signatures. We implement LEAD on GNURadio/USRP platform and evaluate its performance by replaying real-life packet traces on a testbed of 12 USRP links. Our results show that LEAD significantly improve wireless link performance, while incurring very low overhead. Specifically, LEAD reduces more than 90% error bits for 48.9% packets and corrects all errors for 29.4% packets. Moreover, LEAD improves the end-to-end link throughput by 1.43x to 1.93x over the existing error correction schemes.

The rest of this paper is organized as follows. Section 2 summarizes related work. Section 3 introduces the background of convoloutional code. Section 4 motivates the design of LEAD. In Section 5 we characterize protocol signature and propose a simple method of pilots extraction. Section 6 introduce the details of LEAD design. Section 7 reports evaluation results and Section 8 concludes the paper.

2. RELATED WORK

Reducing decoding errors. Several mechanisms have been proposed to improve the performance of channel decoding for 802.11-based WLANs. For example, SoftCast [15], ParCast [19], and Joint source-channel decoding (JSCD) [8], exploit source redundancy to improve video qualities over wireless links. Different with these schemes that are designed for wireless video streaming, LEAD provides a general approach which exploits protocol signatures to improve the performance of channel decoding. This allows LEAD to work efficiently with diverse upper-layer protocols and applications.

Modern network standards, such as 802.11 and LTE, use pilot symbols explicitly inserted into the physical layer to improve the performance of demodulation. For example, current 802.11 OFDM PHY deploys four pilot subcarriers in each OFDM symbol to help the receiver track channel conditions. In comparison, LEAD uses pilots to help channel decoding, thus is complimentary to pilot-assisted demodulation. Moreover, LEAD extracts decoding pilots from protocol headers, thus avoids the extra bandwidth consumption for embedding pilot symbols.

Partial packet recovery. Partially corrupted packets can be exploited to improve the performance of wireless networks. Selective retransmission based protocols [16] [13] reduce packet recovery overhead by only retransmitting the bits that are likely to be wrong. Similarly, Zhang et al. [34] propose μACK, which sends ACKs for every few symbols on a separate feedback channel to enable in-frame recovery. Other protocols, such as ZipTx [18], use link layer FEC to correct bit errors. Unite [33] combines selective retransmission and link layer FECs to minimize error recovery overhead. Leveraging the broadcast nature of wireless channel, cooperative protocols [10] [20] [21] [32] coordinate multiple receivers that hear the same transmission to correct packet errors. Compared with these work, LEAD operates at the physical layer to improve the performance of channel decoding. Therefore, LEAD is orthogonal to existing partial packet recovery schemes, and can be integrated with them to achieve better performance.

Cross-layer design. Cross-layer design has been extensively studied in existing literature. Most prior work focus on leveraging physical layer information at the upper-layer, e.g., using decoding confidence to reduce link layer retransmission overhead [16], or exploiting the error structure at the PHY to provide unequal protection to upper-layer flows [25] [5]. Similarly, PHY-aware rate adaptation algorithms, such as EffSNR [11], AccuRate [28] and SoftRate [31], exploit different physical layer hints to facilitate bit rate adaptation. Compared with these work, LEAD features a different design which leverages upper-layer protocol signatures in channel decoding. LEAD can be integrated with previous cross-layer design to further improve wireless link performance.

Exploiting bit predictability. Prior work [1] [2] exploits bit predictability for compressing IP/TCP and IP/UDP headers. However, existing header compression protocols are exclusively tied with specific protocols, thus cannot be applied

state (m_1m_2)	Transition $m_0 = 0$	Transition $m_0 = 1$	Output $m_0 = 0$	Output $m_0 = 1$
00	00	10	00	11
01	00	10	11	00
10	01	11	10	01
11	01	11	01	10

Table 1: The transition and output table of a rate-1/2 convlutional encoder with a constraint length of 2. The two generator polynomials are $n_1 = m_0 \oplus m_1 \oplus m_2$, and $n_2 = m_0 \oplus m_2$, where m_0 is the input bit of the current round, m_1m_2 represents the encoder state.

Tx code	Rx code	PATH-1 Code	PATH-1 Bit	PATH-1 Cost	PATH-2 Code	PATH-2 Bit	PATH-2 Cost
00	01	00	0	1	11	1	1
00	11	00	[0]	3	01	[1]	2
00	00	00	0	3	01	0	3
00	00	00	0	3	00	1	3
00	10	00	0	4	10	0	3

Table 2: An example of using known bits to reduce decoding errors. The true message is 00000, which is encoded using the code defined in Tab. 1. The transmitted and the received codeword sequences are 0000000000 and 0111000010, respectively. The table shows the expected codewords, decoded bits and accumulated costs of the correct path (PATH-1) and a faulty path (PATH-2). If the second bit of the original message is known to be 0, then PATH-2 can be eliminated because its output at the second round is (shown in a box) 1, even though it has a lower cost than the correct path.

for signature extraction on other protocols. Moreover, the main objective of header compression is to save the transmission time of headers to improve bandwidth usage. This may work on low bit rate networks, such as Deep Space Networks where the typical bit rate is below 100Kbps. However, today's 802.11n-based WLANs offer a maximum bit rate of 600Mbps, which reduces the transmission time of a 60-byte IP/TCP header to 800 nano-seconds. Recent study shows that most bandwidth resources of 802.11 are consumed in error packet recovery [35] and channel contentions [26] [27]. As a result, the benefits of header compression diminish substantially. Compared with header compression protocols, LEAD aims at exploiting protocol signatures to improve the performance of physical layer channel decoding on high bit rate 802.11 links, where the overhead of error recovery is significantly higher than that of header transmissions. Another alternative for exploiting bit predictability is to replace predictable bits with parties, which are then decoded at the receiver to correct bit errors. Compared with this alternative, LEAD saves the computation overhead of removing predictability and decoding parities, while significantly reducing bit error rate.

3. BACKGROUND ON 802.11 CODING

In this section, we introduce the background of 802.11 channel coding that is necessary for understanding our approach. Although we focus on convolutional code in this section, our approach is also applicable to other channel codes (see Sec. 6).

Convolutional code is the default channel code used in 802.11. A rate-m/n convolutional code transforms each m-bit symbol of the original message into an n-bit codeword using n generator polynomials. Each polynomial defines how modulo 2 additions are performed on the current and the last k input symbols, which are buffered by the encoder using shift registers. The state of encoder is defined by the values of shift registers. Tab. 1 shows an example of a rate-1/2 code with $k = 2$. The transition table describes how an input bit triggers a state transition inside the encoder, and the output table gives the computation results of generator polynomials.

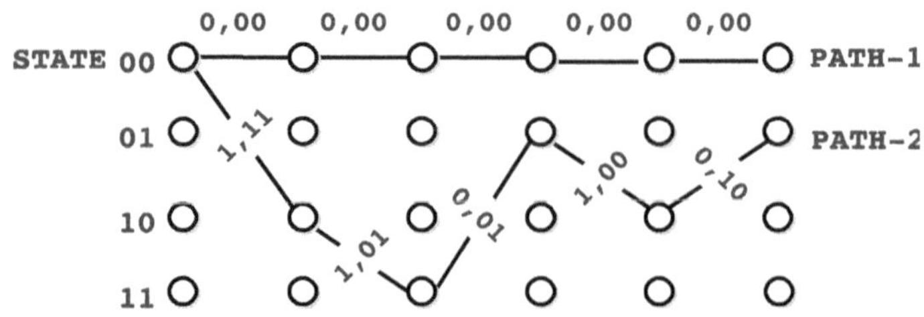

Figure 1: Illustration of convolutional encoding. Each branch is labeled by the input bit that triggers the transition, along with the output codeword.

Fig. 1 shows the encoding process using the code defined in Tab. 1. PATH-1 and PATH-2 show the traces of state transitions when encoding the messages of 00000 and 11010. The objective of decoding is to find the most likely path that yields the codeword sequence of minimum *distance* to the received codeword sequence. A common metric that quantifies the distance between two paths is the number of different coded bits, namely Hamming distance. For example, given a received codeword sequence of 0100000100, the costs of PATH-1 and PATH-2 are 2 and 5, respectively. In this case, PATH-1 is more likely the correct path.

4. MOTIVATION

The key observation that motivates the design of LEAD is that, *if some bits of a packet can be correctly predicted before decoding, then the receiver can exploit these predictions to identify the correct coding path, reducing decoding errors.* Tab. 2 shows an example. We compare the costs of the correct path (PATH-1) and a faulty path (PATH-2). Due to the large amount of errors in received codeword sequence, a conventional convolutional decoder will prune PATH-1 due to its higher cost, resulting in flipped bits in output. However, if the value of second bit (which equals to 0) can be correctly predicted, the receiver can eliminate PATH-2 where the second output is 1, therefore reviving PATH-1 in the subsequent steps of decoding. We refer to the bits whose values can be predicted by the receiver before decoding as *pilots*, and the process of using these pilots to identify correct coding path as *pilot-assisted decoding.* Although we use convolutional code in this example, we note that the idea of pilot-assisted decoding is also applicable to other channel codes. In Section 7, we will study the gains of pilot-assisted decoding for LDPC [9] and Spinal [22], which are typical examples of block code and rateless code, respectively.

To realize pilot-assisted decoding, a key question is how to obtain the pilots. We propose a novel algorithm that extracts pilots from real-life network traffic. This solution is motivated by the observation that, *upper-layer protocols of 802.11 link have unique signatures in their headers, which have distinct bit bias patterns.* The bit bias refers to the fact that a bit takes the value of 1 or 0 with high frequency, such that it can be predicted by the receiver with high accuracy. There are numerous examples of bit bias in network traffic. The link invariant bits, such as the bits located in MAC addresses, are fixed across all the packets transmitted on a link. In real-life traffic, the service type of logic link control header is biased to 0x0800 because most of packets use IP at the network layer. Moreover, bursty IP traffic [17] will cause a temporary bias in the address fields of IP header. Similarly, the retry flag of MAC header will be biased to 1 in the presence of interference caused bursty packet losses [29] [3].

The above observations motivate the design of LEAD, a cross-layer solution that leverages biased bits in upper-layer protocol headers as pilots to improve the performance of channel decoding. In the following, we first discuss how to extract pilots from protocol signatures, and then introduce the design of LEAD in detail.

5. EXTRACTING PILOTS FROM PROTOCOL SIGNATURES

In this section, we formalize the definition of bit bias, characterize bit bias in real-life network traffic, discuss the causes of bit bias, and present the pilot extraction algorithm. Our study focuses on data packets. Control packets such as ACKs, RTSs and CTSs have heterogeneous protocol headers. Applying pilot-assisted decoding to these packets is left for the future work.

5.1 Definition of Bit Bias

We define bit bias as *the high probability that a bit takes value of 0 or 1 in a window of packets.* Given a link, we use $\mathbf{T}_{m,n}$ to represent a window of its packets,

$$\mathbf{T}_{n,m} = \begin{bmatrix} b_{1,1} & \cdots & b_{1,n} \\ \vdots & \ddots & \vdots \\ b_{m,1} & \cdots & b_{m,n} \end{bmatrix} \quad (1)$$

where $b_{j,i}$=1 or 0 gives the value of the ith bit in the jth packet, and n defines the maximum packet size. If the size of jth packet is shorter than i, we define that $b_{j,i}$ takes 0 or 1 at equal probability. The bias of the bit i can be calculated as follows,

$$\beta_i(\mathbf{T}_{n,m}) = 2 \times \left| \frac{\sum_{k=1}^{m} b_{k,i}}{m} - \frac{1}{2} \right| \quad (2)$$

which gives the higher probability that 0 or 1 is observed on bit i. Specifically, in a window of m packets $\mathbf{T}_{n,m}$, if bit i is perfectly biased, i.e., fixed to 0 or 1, $\beta_i(\mathbf{T}_{n,m}) = 1$. If the bit is perfectly unbiased, i.e., takes 0 or 1 at equal probability, $\beta_i(\mathbf{T}_{n,m}) = 0$.

5.2 Bit Bias of Real-life Network Traffic

In the following, we present a measurement study to characterize bit bias in real-life network traffic. Our objectives are to validate the abundance of biased bits and to understand the temporal variations of bit bias.

Our measurement uses real-life traffic traces collected in WLANs that differ from each other in both scales and deployment scenarios. SIGCOMM'08 [24] and OSDI'06 [6] were collected in WLANs of hundreds of users attending the two conferences. PDX [23] includes traces collected in a library, an office building, and a cafeteria in a university. Our trace, named as APT, was collected in an apartment from an 802.11n WLAN that serves three laptops, one tablet, and two smartphones. For each packet in the above traces, application layer data was stripped out to preserve user privacy. Therefore, our measurements focus on the bit bias of the first 80 bytes of each packet, which include all protocol headers up to the transport layer.

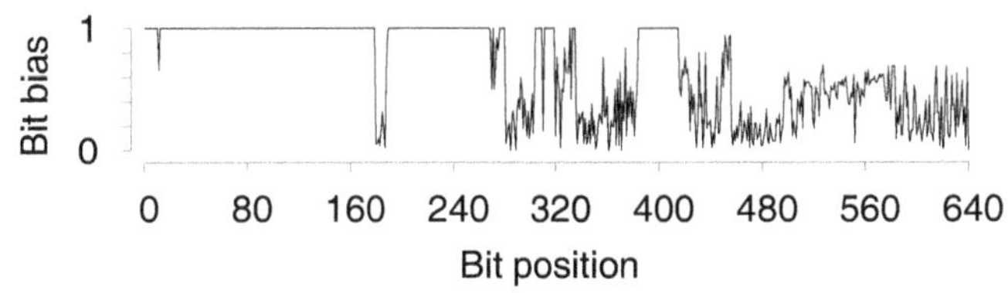

Figure 2: Bit bias measured in a window of 100 packets.

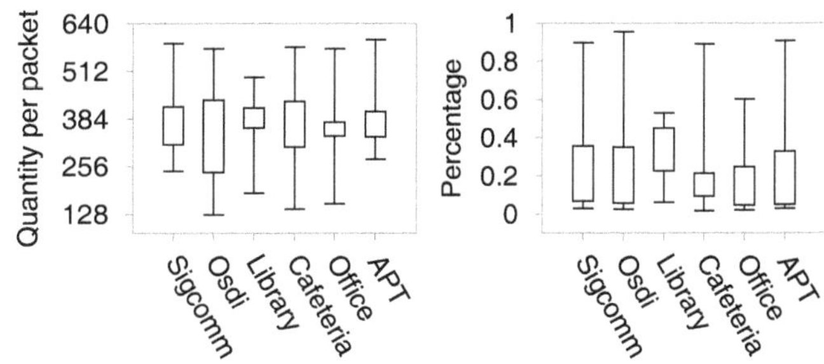

Figure 3: Quantities and percentages of fixed bits. Min, Max, 25th, and 75th percentiles are shown.

We first validate the abundance of biased bits. For each link in the datasets described above, we measure bit bias using the first 100 packets. Fig. 2 plots the result for a randomly selected link. Among the 640 bits studied, 314 are fixed, *i.e.*, have bias of one. Fig. 3 shows the quantities and percentages of fixed bits, where the percentage is computed as the ratio of fixed bits to the total traffic. Specifically, in the SIGCOMM'08 trace, each IP packet contains an average of 363 fixed bits, which account for 17.5% of the total traffic.

In Fig. 2 and Fig. 3, the bit bias is measured in a window of 100 packets. It is critical to understand how bit bias varies at different scales of windows. To this end, we collect bit traces using 5000 packets on an uplink (*e.g.*, packets are transmitted from a client to an access point) that uses IPv4 at the network layer. Fig. 4 plots the trace measured in the IPv4 header. We observe two distinct patterns of bit bias. First, some bits, such as the bits located in the destination and differentiated service (DiffServ) field, are *consistently* biased. While other bits, especially the bits in the source and time to live (TTL) field, experience *bursty* biases. Similar results were observed in other protocol headers on most links in the datasets.

5.3 Causes of Bit Bias

Bits in protocol headers have specific semantics. For example, the 11th bit of 802.11 MAC header is defined as the retry flag; the first four bits of IP header denote the version of IP protocol. In our measurements, we identified two classes of bit biases, namely *consistent bias* and *bursty bias.*

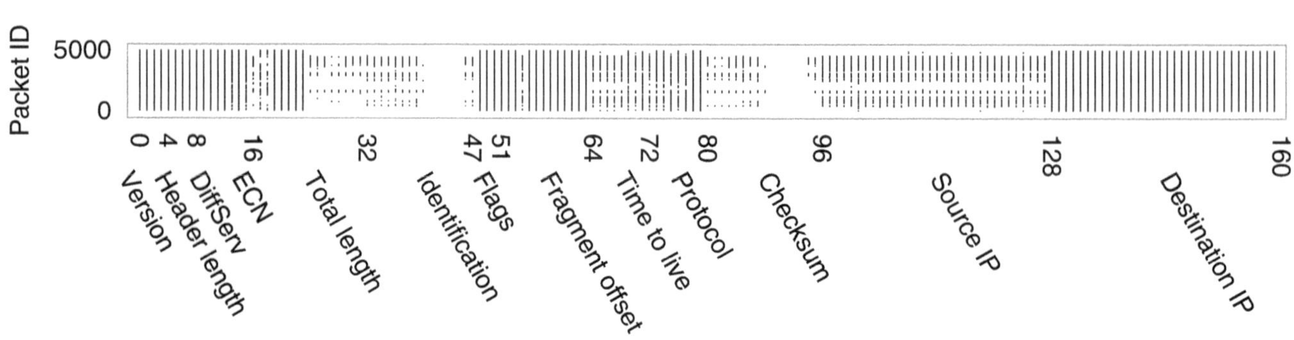

Figure 4: Temporal variations of bit bias in IPv4 header. A bar at a specific bit position indicates that the bit is fixed in the packets represented by the bar. For clear illustration, we only plot bars that contain more than 100 packets.

Pattern	Cause	Examples
Consistent bias	Link invariant data	MAC addresses, IP address of WLAN client.
	Uneven distribution of service types	Frame type in MAC header, service type in logic link control
Bursty bias	Network dynamics	MAC retry flag, IP TTL, IP explicit congestion control (ECN).
	Bursty traffic	IP destination of uplink, IP source of downlink, IP protocol number, source and destination port of TCP and UDP header.

Table 3: Causes of bit bias in 802.11 traffic.

In the following, we explain the causes of bit bias based on bit semantics. Tab. 3 summarizes our discussion.

- **Consistently bias.** Bits that describe link invariant protocol addresses, such as MAC addresses, the IP address of WLAN client, are fixed on each link. Bits that denote frame and service types are also consistently biased because of the uneven distribution of packet or service types in network traffic. For instance, most data packets use IP at the network layer, which is denoted by 0x0800 in the service type field of logic link control header.

- **Bursty bias.** Some bits experience bursty biases because of the burstiness of network traffic [17]. For example, on a link that uses IPv4 at the network layer, bursty TCP traffic causes the IP protocol number biased to 0x06, and leads to temporary biases on the bits located in the source and destination fields of the TCP header. Moreover, network dynamics, such as wireless channel variations and network congestions, may affect bit bias. For example, bursty packet losses [29] [3] may cause the retry flag of MAC header biased to 1. Similarly, the value of IP TTL is biased when many packets of an IP flow traverse paths of the same hop count through the Internet.

5.4 Pilot Extraction

In this section, we present an algorithm that leverages bit bias to extract pilots from the first 80 bytes of each packet, which include all protocol headers up to the transport layer. Since bit values of packet may appear random after encryption, the extractor works on decrypted bits to measure bit bias. The extractor design is driven by the following objectives.

Transparent to upper-layer protocols. The extractor should NOT be tied with specific upper-layer protocols, such that the extractor can be easily deployed on diverse wireless platforms where different protocols are operated at the upper-layers. Previous solutions [1, 2] predict bit values based on bit semantics of protocol headers. For example, as the first four bits in IP header denotes the version of IP protocol, their values can always be predicted by the receiver if the protocol version is known. However, existing solutions are exclusively rely on prior knowledge of protocol header structures, thus cannot be applied to other protocols. Moreover, as bits in protocol headers are coded during transmission, knowledge about upper-layer protocols is not available before the packet is decoded.

Maximizing pilot number while achieving assured prediction accuracy. Physical layer decoder can correct more bit errors with more predictable bits. However, due to the dynamics of network traffic, bit values in protocol headers are time-varying, making it challenging for accurate prediction. To maximize the performance gain of pilot-assisted decoding, the extractor should maximize the number of pilots while achieving assured prediction accuracy.

Extractor overview. Instead of relying on prior knowledge of bit semantics, we propose a simple extractor, which sniffs network traffic at run-time and selects bit i as a pilot if it is fixed in last k_i packets. Because different bits may have different bias levels and bias patterns, the extractor tunes k_i for each bit i to optimize pilot extraction performance. Given a sequence of n packets, for the ith bit, we use $\mathcal{N}_i(k)$ to denote the times that it is selected as pilot using a history size k. We have $\mathcal{N}(k_0) \geq \mathcal{N}(k_1)$, if $k_0 \leq k_1$. This is because $\mathbf{h}_i(t, k_0) \subset \mathbf{h}_i(t, k_1)$, where $\mathbf{h}_i(t, k)$ is the set of last k observations on bit i when packet t is received. Thus if bit i is selected using $\mathbf{h}_i(t, k_1)$, it will also be selected using $\mathbf{h}_i(t, k_0)$. Let $\mathcal{E}_i(k)$ to be the pilot misprediction rate. Our goal is to tune k_i for each bit i, such that,

$$k_i = \operatorname*{argmin}_t \{\mathcal{E}(t) \leq \Delta\} \tag{3}$$

where Δ is the pre-defined threshold on pilot misprediction rate. To reduce decoding errors, Δ should be lower than the BER of conventional decoder. Recent study [7] shows that the BER observed on commodity 802.11 radios typically

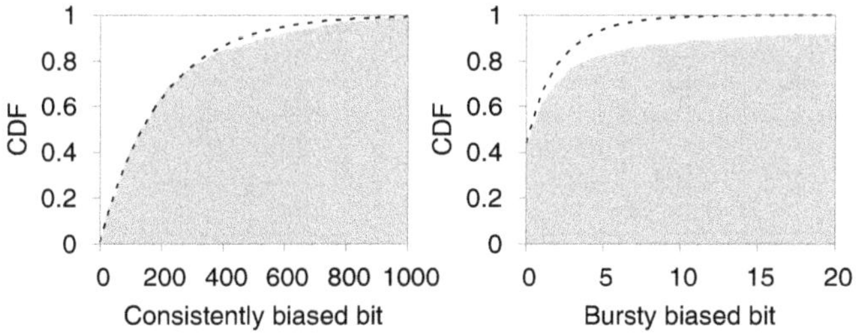

Figure 5: The burst length CDFs measured on a consistently biased bit and a bursty biased bit. The former is from the service type field of logic link control header. The latter is located in the IP source of a downlink. The dashed curves are the theoretical burst length distributions of the memoryless bits with the same biases. Difference between the distributions quantifies the burstiness of bit bias.

ranges from 0% to 10%. In this work, we adopt a threshold of 0.5%. We will study the effect of pilot misprediction in Section 7.4.

A key factor that affects the predictability of protocol signature is the pattern of bit bias. Fig. 5 compares the burst length CDFs for a bursty biased bit and a consistently biased bit, where the burst length is the size of packet window in which a bit is fixed. The dashed curves in the figure show the theoretical burst length CDFs of the memoryless bits with the same bias, which follow the Bernoulli distribution. As shown in the figure, the two bits have distinct probabilistic distributions, calling for different strategies to control the history size of pilot extraction. Specifically, a small history size should be used for a bursty biased bit to capture its temporal predictability. In contrast, a large history size should be used on a consistently biased bit to assure that the measured predictability is statistically significant. In the following, we first present a bias pattern classifier, and then discuss how to optimize the history size for different bias patterns. Finally, we discuss how the pilot extractor works in practice.

Classifying bias patterns. We propose a metric that formally models the busrtiness of bit bias. Let $\mathcal{P}_i(t)$ to be the CDF of burst length for bit i, and $\mathcal{Q}_i(t)$ to be the theoretical burst length CDF for the memoryless bit, which follows Bernoulli distribution. To quantify bias burstiness, we define μ_i as the Kullback-Leibler divergence between $\mathcal{P}_i(t)$ and $\mathcal{Q}_i(t)$ measured on bit i, which can be expressed as,

$$\mu_i = \mathcal{D}_{KL}(\mathcal{P}_i||\mathcal{Q}_i) = \left|\sum_t \mathcal{P}_i(t) \ln \frac{\mathcal{P}_i(t)}{\mathcal{Q}_i(t)}\right| \quad (4)$$

where $\mathcal{P}_i(t)$ can be measured using empirical observations of burst lengths. Our empirical study shows that a threshold of 2 is sufficient to classify bursty bias from consistent bias, *i.e.*, bit i is classified as a bursty biased bit if its bias burstiness satisfies $\mu_i \geq 2$.

Optimizing history size. The extractor selects bit i as a pilot if it is fixed in the history of last k_i packets. In the following, we discuss how to tune k_i to meet the objective of Eq. (3).

Consistently biased bits. When using a consistently biased bit as pilot, the misprediction rate can be computed as $0.5 - 0.5\beta$, where β is the bit bias. To satisfy Eq. (3), β must be larger than $1-2\Delta$. The extractor should use a large k such that if bit bias is lower than $1-2\Delta$, the probability that the bit is fixed in last k packets is small. This probability can be computed as $(0.5+0.5\beta)^k$. Using a confidence level of 95%, k should satisfy $(0.5+0.5\beta)^k < 0.05$. Therefore, we can calculate the minimum history size for a consistently biased bit as,

$$k = \frac{\log 0.05}{\log(1-\Delta)} \quad (5)$$

Bursty biased bits. Given a bursty biased bit which has been fixed in last t packets, the probability that it will not change in the next packet can be computed as $\Pr(t+1|t) = \frac{1-\mathcal{P}(t+1)}{1-\mathcal{P}(t)}$, which is the conditional probability that the burst length is longer than $t+1$, given that the length of current burst is t. $\mathcal{P}(t)$ is the burst length CDF. As a result, the minimum history size can be derived as,

$$k = \underset{t}{\operatorname{argmin}} \left\{ \frac{1-\mathcal{P}(t+1)}{1-\mathcal{P}(t)} > 1-\Delta \right\} \quad (6)$$

However, calculation of k requires a fine grained burst length CDF, which is difficult to obtain without a large number of samples. We address this problem by curve fitting. Observing that $\mathcal{P}_i(t)$ of bursty biased bit is featured by a long tail, we fit the measured burst length CDF to the power-law Pareto distribution, whose CDF is given by,

$$\mathcal{F}(t) = \begin{cases} 1-\frac{1}{t^\alpha}, & t>1 \\ 0, & \text{otherwise} \end{cases} \quad (7)$$

where α can be derived from on-line measurements using maximum likelihood estimation. Given n observations of burst lengths, denoted by $\{x_1, ..., x_n\}$, we have,

$$\hat{\alpha} = \frac{n}{\ln x_1 + ... + \ln x_n} \quad (8)$$

Therefore, we can calculate the minimum history size for a bursty biased bit as,

$$k = \frac{1}{1-\exp\left(\frac{\log(1-\Delta)}{\hat{\alpha}}\right)} - 1 \quad (9)$$

Putting them together. The extractor maintains a moving window of N correctly received packets, and updates the burst length CDF $\mathcal{P}(t)$ and the burstiness metric μ for each bit every T seconds. We observed that LEAD performance is not sensitive to the update period T, i.e., the measured burst length distribution is accurate enough to assure low misprediction rate even using long update intervals. This is because the burst patterns of header bits mainly depend on the bit semantics defined by upper-layer protocols, which do not vary over time. Motivated by this observation, we conduct offline measurements using real-life packet traces to find a long update interval, which minimizes the update overhead while assuring that the misprediction rates of extracted pilots are below the given threshold. Our empirical study shows that $T = 10s$ and $N = 600$ work efficiently in practice.

For each sender, the receiver allocates 160 bytes in the physical layer RAM to store its pilots. Each bit in the first 80 bytes takes two bits: one is used to indicate whether it is a pilot; the other is the pilot value. At the MAC layer, the extractor maintains a counter for each bit to monitor the length of its ongoing burst. A bit is selected as pilot to decode the next packet, if its counter is longer than the computed minimum history size. The physical layer RAM is updated when new pilots are extracted, or any existing pilots are removed.

6. EXPLOITING PILOTS TO IMPROVE DECODING PERFORMANCE

In this section, we present a decoding framework that allows existing channel decoders to effectively exploit the extracted pilots. In the following, we first present the design of LEAD framework, and then describe pilot-assisted decoding algorithms.

6.1 LEAD Framework

Several key challenges must be addressed to enable pilot-assisted decoding on 802.11 links. First, since extracted pilots differ on different links, LEAD needs to know the link address of a received packet for choosing pilots before decoding. Second, as bits are typically scrambled and encrypted during transmission, protocol signatures extracted at upper-layer cannot be directly used as pilots to direct physical layer decoding. Third, as pilots are extracted from packet headers, they have limited impact on the decoding accuracy of payloads. Fourth, due to the dynamics of network traffic, bit predictabilities are time-varying, which leads to possible mispredictions of pilots, causing decoding errors at the receiver.

We now introduce the framework of LEAD to address the above challenges. The framework is composed of four key components, including *link addressing*, *pilot reshaper*, *pilot spreader*, and *pilot misprediction handler*.

Link addressing. To identify the link address before decoding, LEAD adopts a link addressing scheme, where the sender and receiver MAC addresses are hashed into a one-byte identity, which is then appended after the 802.11 SIGNAL symbol. At the receiver, LEAD parses the identity before decoding, and then chooses the pilots that were extracted for this link to direct decoding. In practice, multiple links may be hashed to the same identity. Such identity collision can be easily detected by LEAD at the MAC layer. When collision occurs, LEAD falls back to the conventional decoding mode. Because the collision probability of two links is only 1/256 when a one-byte link identity is used, its effect on LEAD performance is negligible.

Pilot spreading. Since pilots are extracted from protocol headers, LEAD needs an interleaver to spread pilots over the whole packet, such that the decoding of payload bits can be benefited from adjacent pilots. Unfortunately, the default 802.11 interleaver cannot serve this purpose because of its limited interleaving depth. Specifically, it only permutates coded bits within each OFDM symbol to mitigate the bursty errors caused by frequency selective fading. In 802.11g, the maximum number of bits carried by an OFDM symbol is only 216 bits, while a packet can be as large as thousands of bits. As a result, using the default 802.11 interleaver, pilots extracted from protocol headers cannot be spread over the entire packet. To address this problem, LEAD employs an additional MAC layer interleaver to uniformly spread pilots

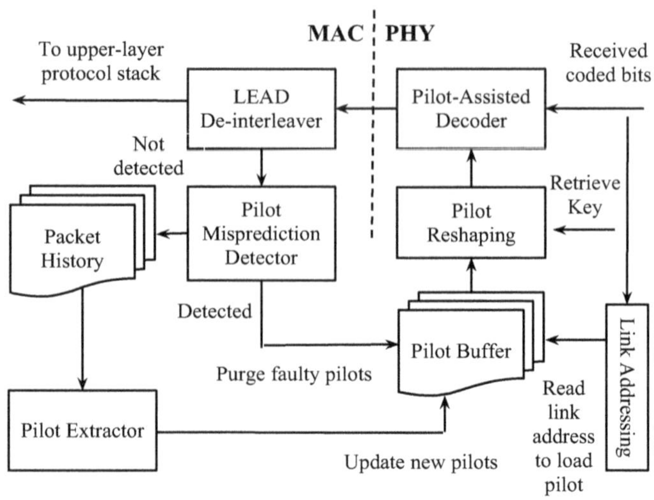

Figure 6: The architecture of LEAD receiver. Standard 802.11 operations such as OFDM demodulation, de-interleaving, and descrambling are not included.

to packet palyload. At the receiver, the reverse operation is performed to recover bit orders after pilot-assisted decoding.

Pilot reshaping. Bit values of a packet may appear random after encryption and scrambling. As discussed in Sec. 5, the pilot extractor of LEAD addresses this issue by extracting pilots after decryption and descrabmling. However, since the extracted pilot values may not match those received at the physical layer, the pilot cannot be directly applied in the physical layer decoding. LEAD addresses this issue in the pilot reshaping module. Specifically, before using pilots to decode a packet, the receiver first scrambles and encrypts the pilots, such that the values of reshaped pilots will match those received at the physical layer. To allow the pilot reshaper to use keystream for encryption before decoding, the LEAD sender appends the header of encryption protocol after the 802.11 SIGNAL symbol. When a packet is received, the receiver first decodes the encryption header to retrieve the keystream. A practical concern is the processing delay caused by reshaping. We will evaluate the delay in Section 7.4.

Handling pilot mispredictions. Pilot misprediction occurs when the pilot used in decoding does not match the value of a received bit, causing decoding errors. LEAD adopts a checksum-based method to detect pilot mispredictions. Ideally, the checksum should be calculated over only the pilot bits. However, this is difficult because pilots are extracted at the receiver at run-time, and notifying the sender of which bits are pilots may incur prohibitive messaging overhead. Another approach is to compute the checksum for the first 80-byte of the packet, from which the pilots are extracted. This approach is also inefficient because the checksum failure may be caused by the errors of non-pilot bits.

LEAD employs a block checksum mechanism to address this problem. Specifically, the sender divides the first 80 bytes into blocks and then calculate checksum for each block. If a checksum fails, the receiver stops using the pilots extracted from the corresponding block, until the pilots are updated using a correctly received block. This approach

Channel code	Decoder	Number of lines	
		Standard	Pilot-assisted
Convolutional	BCJR [4]	143	147
LDPC	BP [9]	87	97
Spinal code	Bubble [22]	158	181

Table 4: Pilot-assisted decoders of LEAD.

avoids using faulty pilots to decode a sequence of packets, therefore limiting the detrimental effect to a single transmission. In our implementation, we use two block checksums, and employ CRC-4 for checksum computation.

Putting them together. In the following, we describe the decoding process of LEAD by tracing the transmission and reception of an 802.11 packet.

At the transmitter, LEAD first uses a MAC layer interleaver to spread bits in protocol headers over the whole packet. After the packet is encrypted and scrambled, LEAD inserts its own header after the 802.11 SIGNAL symbol. The LEAD header contains the one-byte link identity, the two block checksums computed using CRC-4, and the encryption protocol header. To notify the receiver that the packet uses LEAD protocol for decoding, the sender flips the reserved bit in 802.11 SIGNAL symbol as the delimiter of LEAD packet.

Fig. 6 shows the architecture of a LEAD receiver. When a LEAD packet is received, the receiver first decodes the LEAD header, parses the link address to choose pilots, and retrieves keystreams to reshapes pilots through scrambling and encryption. The reshaped pilots are then fed into the pilot-assisted decoder. If decoding is successful, LEAD logs the first 80 bytes to the MAC layer packet history, and updates the physical layer buffer if new pilots are extracted. Otherwise, LEAD uses the two block checksums embedded in LEAD header to locate bad blocks that contain mispredicted pilots. If detected, all pilots in the bad blocks will be purged from the physical layer buffer to prevent further decoding errors.

6.2 Pilot-Assisted Decoders

The design of LEAD is independent with the underlying channel code. Thus LEAD can be exploited by all existing channel codes using their pilot-assisted decoders. In this work, we augment three decoding algorithms, including BCJR [4] of convolutional code, the belief propagation (BP) decoder [9] of LDPC code, and the bubble decoder of rateless Spinal code [22], to perform pilot assisted decoding. Tab. 4 summarizes our implementations of these pilot-assisted decoders. Due to space limitation, we only introduce the design of pilot-assisted BCJR. Details of other decoding algorithms are available in a technical report [14].

Pilot-assisted BCJR decoder. BCJR is a popular soft-output decoding algorithm for maximum *a posteriori* decoding. Given a sequence of k received codewords $o_{1:k}$, the BCJR decoder infers the coding input with the maximum *a posteriori* probability estimation. Specifically, the decoder performs forward recursion and backward recursion to compute the posterior marginals of all states for inference. During the forward recursion, the decoder computes the probability that the coder ends up at a particular state s at time t given the first t observations in received codeword sequence.

$$\alpha_t(s) = \Pr(s|o_{1:t}) = \sum_{s'} \alpha_{t-1}(s')\gamma_t(s,s') \tag{10}$$

where $\gamma_t(s,s')$ computes the probability of state transition from s to s' at time t, which depends on the distance between received codeword at time t and the expected codeword given the transition. During the backward recursion, the decoder computes the probability of observing the remaining codewords given a start point t.

$$\beta_{t-1}(s) = \Pr(o_{t:k}|s) = \sum_{s'} \beta_t(s')\gamma_t(s,s') \tag{11}$$

Based on the Bayes rule, the probability that the coder reaches state s at time t given the received codeword sequence $o_{1:k}$ can be calculated by

$$\lambda_t(s) \propto \Pr(s|o_{1:t}) \times \Pr(o_{t+1:k}|s) \tag{12}$$

Since the encoder starts and ends up at state 0, the BCJR decoder can be initialized as follows

$$\begin{aligned} \alpha_0(0) &= \beta_k(0) = 1 \\ \alpha_0(s) &= \beta_k(s) = 0 \quad \text{for all } s \neq 0 \end{aligned} \tag{13}$$

Let $\mathbf{s^0}$ and $\mathbf{s^1}$ denote the state where the starting bit is 0 and 1 respectively. The soft-output of the decoder is the log-likelihood for bit y_t, which is calculated as

$$\text{LLR}(y_t) = \log \frac{\sum_{s \in \mathbf{s^1}} \lambda_{t+1}(s)}{\sum_{s \in \mathbf{s^0}} \lambda_{t+1}(s)} \tag{14}$$

Pilot-assisted BCJR augments the standard BCJR by improving the estimation of $\lambda_t(s)$ in Eq. (12), where the $\gamma_t(s,s')$ in Eq. (10) and Eq. (11) equals to 0 if the bit that corresponds to the transition $s \rightarrow s'$ does not match the pilot bit. Therefore the pilot bits reduce the space of possible transitions and improves the estimation quality of adjacent data bits.

7. EVALUATION

LEAD is implemented atop the OFDM implementation of GNURadio/USRP platform. LEAD takes demodulated symbols as input, converts complex symbols on constellation to soft coded bits using a soft-output demapper [30], and then performs pilot-assisted decoding through the procedures illustrated in Fig. 6.

In this section, we evaluate the performance of LEAD. Our evaluation centers around four aspects. (1) How efficiently can LEAD extract decoding pilots from upper-layer protocols? (2) Compared with standard channel decoder, how much performance gain does LEAD yield on decoding 802.11 packets in real-life traffic? (3) How much is the overhead of LEAD? and (4) How does LEAD perform on different channel codes?

7.1 Pilot Extraction

We first evaluate the performance of pilot extractor proposed in Section 5.4. LEAD extracts a bit as pilot if it is fixed in the last k packets. Because bit predictability depends on the bias level and bias pattern, LEAD classifies bias patterns, and tunes the history size k for each bit to

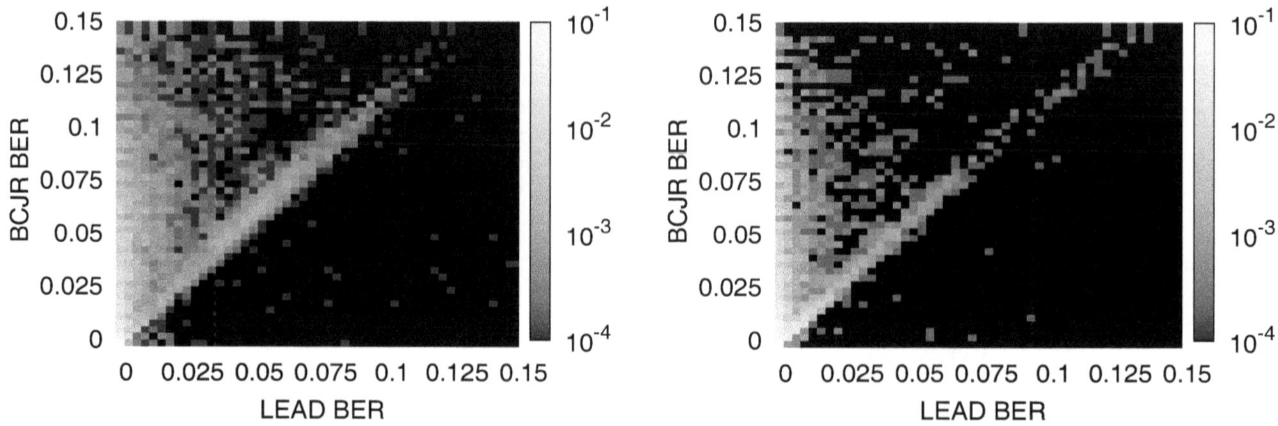

(a) QAM16, rate-1/2.

(b) QAM64, rate-2/3

Figure 9: Bit error rates of LEAD and BCJR when decoding the same 802.11 packet trace. Each point in the figure represents a packet. For clear illustration, we divide the two dimensional space into grids of 0.002×0.002, and use brightness to indicate the percentage of packets contained in the grid. Brighter grids contain more packets. As shown in the figure, compared with BCJR decoding, LEAD yields a significant BER reduction for most partially corrupted packets.

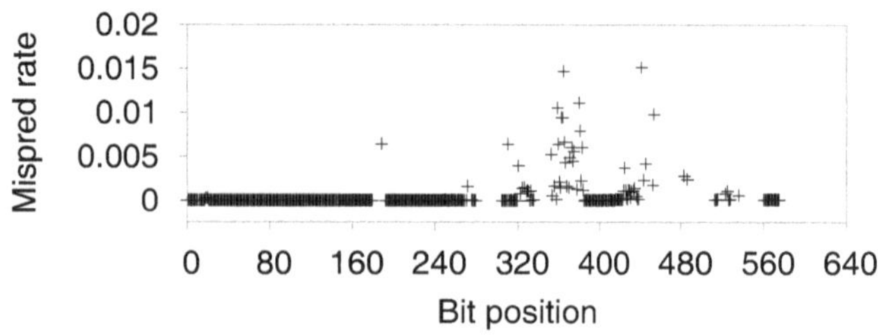

Figure 7: Misprediction rate of extracted pilots when using a threshold of 0.005.

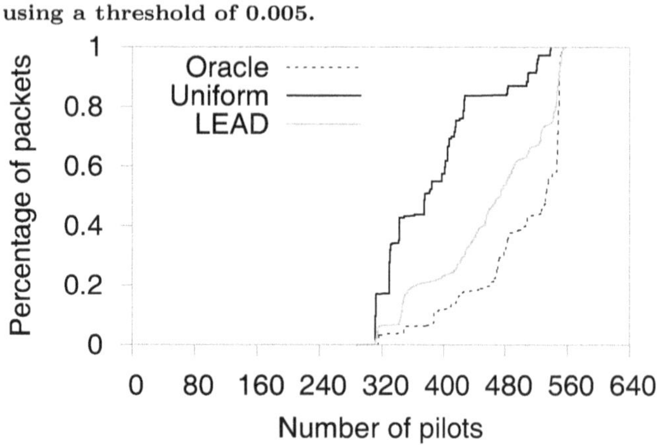

Figure 8: CDF of the number of extracted pilots.

maximize the number of extracted pilots while limiting the misprediction rate under a pre-defined threshold. In our implementation, we adopt a threshold of 0.005, and update the history size every 10 seconds. In the following, we first study how efficiently LEAD controls the pilot misprediction rate, and then evaluate the quantity of extracted pilots. Our evaluation is performed using five real-life traffic traces introduced in Section 5. Due to space limitation, we only present the results measured using the SIGCOMM'08 trace [24]. The results observed on other traces are similar.

Fig. 7 shows the average misprediction rates for the bits located in the first 80 bytes of packets wen using a misprediction threshold of 0.005. The results are measured using 14968 packets collected on a WLAN downlink. Among the first 80 bytes of packet, total 575 bits were used as pilots. Only 14 bits have an average misprediction rate higher than 0.005. This result shows that our history size estimation (described in Section 5.4) can effectively bound the misprediction rate. We further evaluate the quantity of pilots extracted by LEAD. Two baseline algorithms are employed for performance comparison. The first baseline, named Uniform, uses the same history size for all the bits. The history size is set as the minimum value that bounds the average misprediction rate below 0.005 on all the bits. The second baseline, named Oracle, chooses the optimal history size for each bit. For both baselines, the history sizes are updated every 10 seconds. To implement Oracle, we first run the extraction algorithm using all history sizes in each interval of 10 seconds, and then look back to choose the optimal history size that meets the misprediction bound. Fig. 8 shows the distributions of pilot quantity measured on 24 links. The average numbers of pilots extracted by Uniform, LEAD, and Oracle are 375, 477 and 522, respectively. LEAD outperforms Uniform by 27.2%, which validates the effectiveness of our per-bit history size optimization mechanism based on the level and pattern of bit bias.

7.2 Bit Error Reduction

Experiment setting. We now evaluate the performance of LEAD a convolutional code, which is the default channel code of 802.11. To quantify the decoding efficiency, we compare the BERs of packets decoded by the standard BCJR algorithm and LEAD, which uses the pilot-assisted BCJR algorithm described in Section 6.2. Our evaluation is conducted on a testbed of 12 USRP links deployed in an office building, on a 4MHz channel centered at 5 GHz. We observe that channel conditions differ substantially in our testbed, where the average signal-to-noise ratios (SNR) measured on USRP links range from 7 dB to 20 dB. To improve the realism of our evaluation, we replay the traffic trace collected in SIGCOMM'08 [24] on our USRP testbed. For each USRP link, we randomly select a link from the trace, and replay 10 minutes of traffic at the USRP transmitter. The experiment

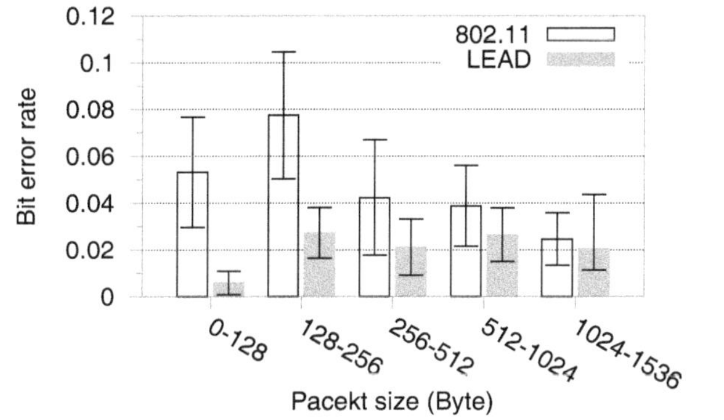

Figure 10: Effect of packet size on the bit error rates of 802.11 and LEAD.

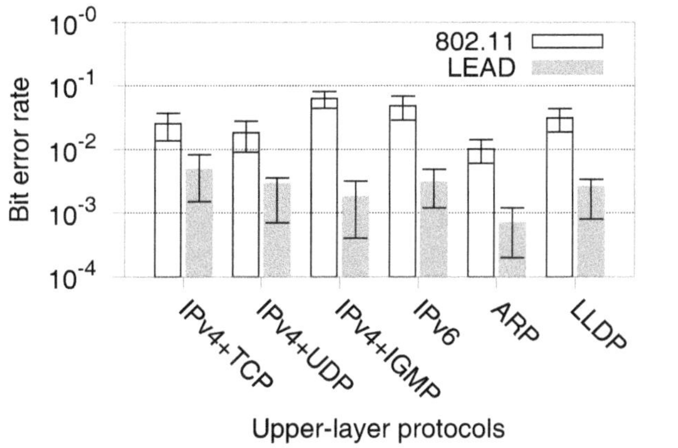

Figure 11: Decoding BERs of 802.11 and LEAD for different upper-layer protocols.

is repeated multiple times, each time using a different combination of modulation and coding rate. For a fair comparison over time-varying wireless channels, we log the demodulated symbols at the receiver, and decode them using LEAD and the standard BCJR to compare their BERs.

BER reduction. Fig. 9 compares the BERs of standard BCJR and LEAD at two bit rates, including QAM16 rate-1/2, and QAM64 rate-2/3. We observe that LEAD significantly reduces bit errors in both settings. Specifically, when QAM64 and rate-2/3 coding are used, LEAD reduces more than 90% bit errors for 48.9% packets. Moreover, LEAD mitigates all bit errors for 29.4% partially corrupted packets. Only in 1.4% packets, LEAD induces more bit errors due to pilot mispredictions. We observed similar results under other bit rates. Unless stated otherwise, we will use QAM16 and rate-1/2 in the following experiments.

Effect of packet size. Fig. 10 evaluates the effect of packet size on LEAD performance. We observe that LEAD achieves significant performance gain for packets that are shorter than 256 bytes. Specifically, when the packet size is shorter than 128 bytes, LEAD mitigates 89% bit errors. When the packet size is between 128 and 256 bytes, LEAD reduces the bit error rate from 0.077 to 0.027. This is because the ratio of pilots is higher for short packets. We note that short packets, which are used extensively by Internet telephony and gaming applications, account for a major fraction of real-life network traffic. For example, in the SIGCOMM'08 and our APT trace, 57.3% and 49.5% packets are smaller than 256 bytes. As a result, reducing the loss rates of short packets will significantly improve the channel utilization rate, leading to overall performance improvement on lossy wireless links.

Different upper-layer protocols. We further evaluate the gain of LEAD for different upper-layer protocols. Fig. 11 compares the BERs of packets decoded by LEAD and the standard BCJR. We observe that LEAD consistently outperforms BCJR for all protocols. LEAD is especially efficient for those protocols that extensively use short packets. For example, for IGMP, LEAD reduces 97.3% bit errors compared to the standard BCJR decoder.

7.3 Impact on Link Layer Performance

In the following, we evaluate the impact of LEAD on link layer performance. Due to the processing delay, USRP cannot support full-featured link-layer protocols (*e.g.*, real-time rate adaptation). Therefore, we turn to trace-driven simulations in this section to evaluate the end-to-end performance gain of LEAD. To collect fine-grained channel trace, we employ the tool introduced in [12] to sample channel state information (CSI) on a 20 MHz channel using a link of two Intel 802.11n NICs. During trace collection, the sender transmits UDP packets at a speed of 2,000 packets/second. Meanwhile, the receiver moves around the sender at normal walking speed. We then run our implementations of LEAD and standard 802.11 over this channel trace to compare their performance.

Link layer settings. To adapt bit rate over time-varying channel, we employ the algorithm proposed in [11], where the transmitter tunes its bit rate based on the effective SNR measured using receiver ACKs. We implemented the binary exponential backoff at the MAC layer, where the transmitter doubles its backoff window whenever a packet drop is detected. According to 802.11, the maximum retry limit is set to 6. To evaluate the impact of LEAD on link layer error recovery mechanisms, we implemented three protocols, including *Maranello* [13], *link layer forward error correction (FEC)* [18], and *partial packet retransmission (PPR)* [16].

- *Maranello.* Maranello [13] is a block retransmission based partial packet recovery protocol. Specifically, a partially corrupted packet is divided into blocks. For each block, a 32-bit checksum is computed and returned to the sender for identifying block(s) that contain bit errors. To reduce recovery overhead, Maranello only retransmits corrupted block(s). In our implementation, we use a block size of 64 bytes, which is compliant to the setting introduced in [13].

- *Link layer FEC.* To evaluate the impact of LEAD on link layer error correcting schemes, we implemented the protocol introduced in [18]. To correct bit errors, Reed-Solomon (RS) code is adopted at the link layer. RS code breaks each packet into n-bit symbols, and then groups each r symbols to a codeword, where $r \leq 2^n$. Two redundant symbols can correct up to one bad symbol in a codeword. In our implementation, we set n=8, which is the popular choice on byte-oriented systems. When an ACK timeout is detected, the transmitter sends the *optimal* amount of parity symbols, which is the minimum number of symbols that assures error correction.

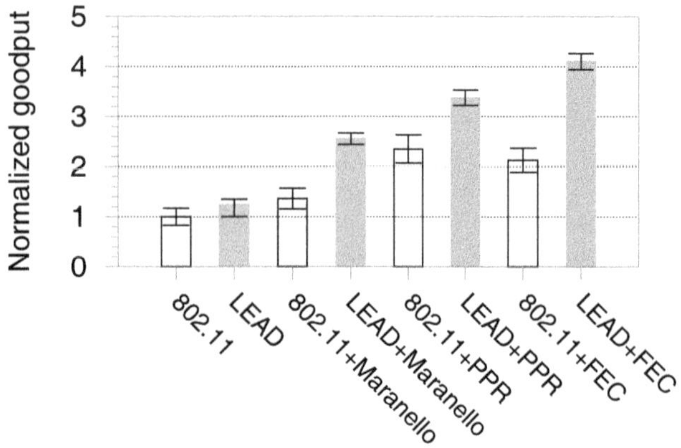

Figure 12: Link layer goodput gains of LEAD over 802.11 when different error recovery protocols are used at the link layer.

- *PPR.* PPR [16] exploits physical layer decoding confidence to estimate bit error probabilities. The sender only retransmits the bits of low decoding confidence to avoid the costs of retransmitting correct bits.

Evaluation results. We evaluate the impact of LEAD on link layer performance by replaying real-life traffic traces over our channel trace. Total 100 links are randomly selected from the SIGCOMM'08 trace. For each link, we replay a 10-minute traffic trace and measure the link layer goodput at the receiver. Higher layer factors, such as TCP reactions, affect how this link layer goodput translates to real system throughput.

We integrate LEAD with the above error recovery protocols, and evaluate their effects on link layer goodput. The results are shown in Fig. 12. The goodputs shown in the figure is normalized to 802.11 goodput. Our result shows that the performance gain of LEAD is significantly boosted with the support of link layer error recovery protocols. Specifically, when both 802.11 and LEAD are integrated with Maranello, PPR, and optimal link layer FEC, the performance gains of LEAD over 802.11 are 1.72x, 1.43x, and 1.93x, respectively. This is because LEAD enables error recovery protocols to better exploit partially corrupted packets to improve network performance. Since LEAD is able to significantly reduce bit errors, the error recovery protocols need to retransmit fewer bits, leading to higher system throughput. The results demonstrate that the bit-level error reduction achieved by LEAD results in a significant end-to-end performance gain at the link layer.

7.4 Overhead

In the following, we evaluate the overhead of LEAD, including the protocol overhead, the cost of pilot misprediction, and the processing delay of pilot reshaping.

Protocol overhead. For each data packet, LEAD requires two bytes for inserting its own protocol header. A question we aim to answer is if it is better off to use these two bytes to carry redundant information for error correction. To justify the protocol overhead of LEAD, we compare its performance to an error correction scheme, which adopts the Reed-Solomon (RS) code at the link layer to correct bit errors. In our implementation, we adopt the setting used in [18], where n=8 and r=255. For each packet, we randomly select a RS codeword to add two redundant symbols, which is equivalent to the protocol overhead of LEAD.

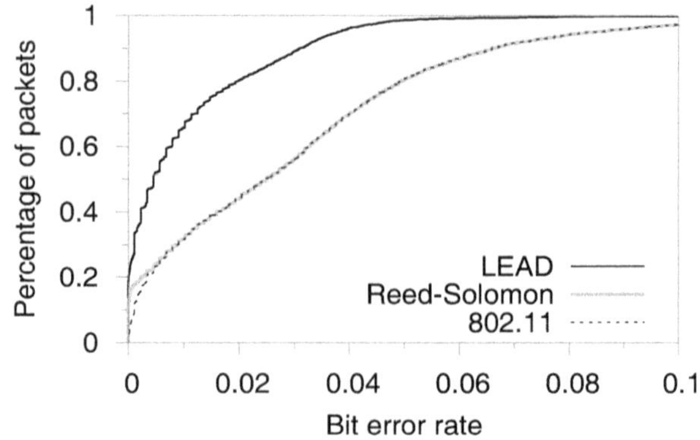

Figure 13: Bit error rate distributions of 802.11, LEAD, and link layer Reed-Solomon code.

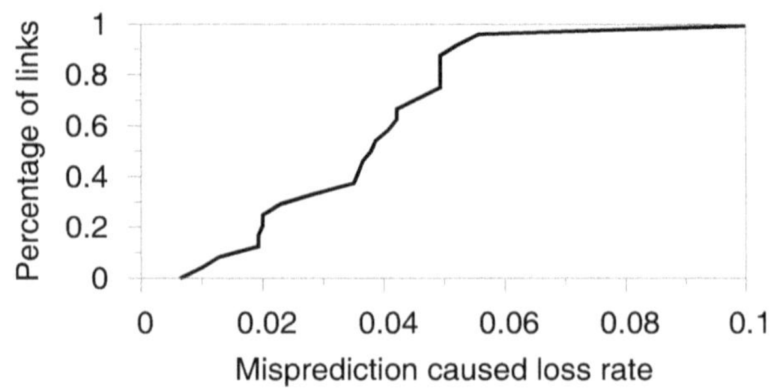

Figure 14: Packet loss rate caused by mispredictions.

Fig. 13 compares the BERs of 802.11, LEAD, and the link layer RS code. We observe that LEAD yields significant performance gains when compared with 802.11 and link layer RS code. This is because RS code cannot partially reduce bit errors when the number of flipped bits goes beyond its error correcting capability. In comparison, LEAD is able to significantly reduce bit errors, which can be transformed to a significant performance gain when error recovery protocols are available at the link layer, as discussed in Sec. 7.3.

Cost of pilot misprediction. During pilot-assisted decoding, LEAD eliminates the outputs that do not match the values of pilots. As a result, pilot misprediction may cause decoding errors. We evaluate this cost by studying the packet loss rate when replaying real-life packet traces on a wireless channel of good quality (average SNR=20dB) using the most robust bit rate (*i.e.*, BPSK with rate-1/2 coding). Fig. 14 shows the distribution of packet loss rate. The results are measured using 24 links randomly selected from the SIGCOMM'08 trace. We observe that the packet loss rates are lower than 5% for more than 90% links. When link layer retransmission is enabled, the impacts of misprediction on packet loss rate and link goodput are negligible.

Pilot reshaping delay. As bit values observed in upper-layer protocols usually differ from those received at the physical layer, protocol signatures extracted from packet headers cannot be directly used in decoding. Therefore LEAD receiver reshapes pilots through encryption and scrambling before using them in pilot-assisted decoding, which incurs a processing delay. To evaluate the processing delay, we implemented a software pilot reshaper for the WiFi Pro-

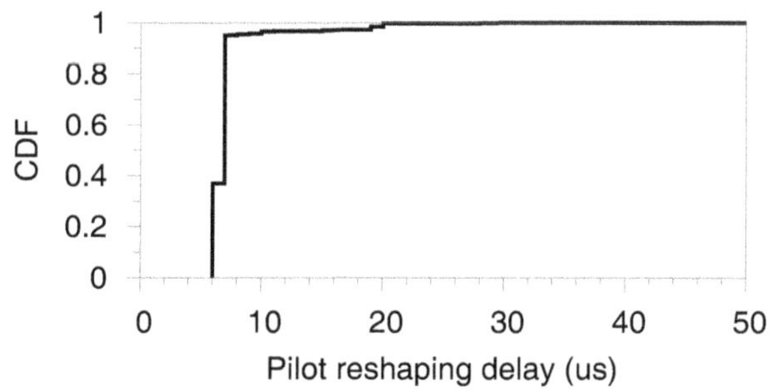

Figure 15: Delay caused by software pilot reshaping.

tected Access (WPA) protocol and the standard scrambler of 802.11. The reshaper follows the key mixing function defined in Temporal Key Integrity Protocol (TKIP) to combine the root key and the initialization vector into a 128-bit RC4 key, and then generates the keystream. The reshaper performs encryption and scrambling on 80 bytes, which is the upper bound on the length of bits used by LEAD to find bit bias. To measure the distribution of reshaping delay, we repeat this experiment 10000 times on a laptop equipped with a 2.9GHz CPU. Fig. 15 shows the distribution of reshaping delay. We observe that for more than 95% cases, the reshaping delay is below 7 *us*, which is shorter than the 10 *us* SIFS defined in 802.11g. As a result, the reshaping delay does not cause an 802.11 link to drop packets. We also note that such delay can be significantly reduced when the pilot reshaper is implemented in the firmware of WLAN NICs.

7.5 Pilot Availability and Other Channel Codes

Our measurements presented in Section 5 on five real-life traffic datasets show that the ratio of pilot bits typically ranges from 10% to 30%. However, the percentage of pilot bits in a particular network also varies substantially depending on the size of packet payload. Moreover, the efficiency of pilot-assisted decoding also depends on the specific channel codes.

We now evaluate the effect of pilot ratio on the decoding performance. We demonstrate the efficiency of pilot-assisted decoding for three channel codes, including the BCJR decoder of convolutional code, the belief propagation decoder of LDPC, and the bubble decoder of Spinal code. We augment these standard decoders to exploit pilots, and measure the percentage of error reduction. The spinal code is configured using the parameters introduced in [22]. For LDPC and convolutional code, we use a coding rate of 1/2 with QPSK for modulation and demodulation. We also conducted the same experiments under other physical layer settings. Similar results are observed.

We deployed a link of two USRP nodes in an office environment. The transmitter sends back-to-back packets using different transmission power levels. The receiver logs the trace of demodulated symbols, and decodes them using standard and pilot-assisted decoders, respectively. For each packet, a group of bits are randomly selected as pilots[1], whose values are made known to the pilot-assisted decoder. We then vary pilot ratios to study the impact on decoding performance. For each channel code, the performance gain of pilot-assisted decoding is measured using 10000 packets that are erroneously decoded by the standard decoder.

The results are shown in Fig. 16. We observe that pilot-assisted decoding significantly reduces BERs for all codes. Specifically, when the pilot ratio is 20%, bit error is reduced by 71% and 74% for convolutional code and LDPC, respectively. Using Spinal code, the transmitter keeps sending coded symbols round by round, until the receiver successfully decodes the packet. We hence compare the BERs of the standard and pilot-assisted decoders in different rounds. Using 30% pilots, the BER is reduced by 44%, 80%, and 94% in the second, fifth and tenth round. The results demonstrate the efficiency of exploiting pilots to reduce decoding errors across different channel codes.

8. CONCLUSION AND FUTURE WORK

We present a new cross-layer wireless error correction approach called LEAD. The key idea of LEAD is to predict the values of some received bits based on the signatures of upper-layer protocols, and then use them as pilots to improve the PHY decoding performance. We first characterize the bit bias of protocol signatures in real 802.11 traffic, and develop an efficient algorithm to extract pilot bits whose values have high predictability. We then develop several mechanisms to integrate LEAD with 802.11 protocol stack, including interleaving protocol signatures across a whole packet so that the decoding of payload can leverage adjacent pilots, handling scrambled and encrypted pilots, and detecting and handling mispredicted pilots. We augment three standard decoders, including the BCJR decoder of convolutional code, the belief propagation decoder of LDPC code, and the bubble decoder of the Spinal code to effectively exploit pilots. We implement LEAD on USRP platform and evaluate its performance by replaying real-life traffic traces on a testbed of 12 USRP links. Our results show that LEAD can reduce BER by more than 90% for half of the error packets while incurring very low overhead. Moreover, LEAD improves the end-to-end link throughput by 1.43x to 1.93x over the existing error correction schemes.

The performance of LEAD depends on the availability of "good" pilots whose values can be correctly predicted by the receiver. The pilot extraction algorithm of LEAD maximizes the number of pilots while limiting the misprediction threshold under a given threshold. When the wireless channel condition is good, it is desirable to set a lower misprediction rate to minimize the additional bit errors caused by pilot misprediction. In contrast, when the channel condition is bad, the threshold should be set higher to produce more pilots. In the future, we will develop an adaptive scheme which adjusts the bound dynamically according to the measurement of channel quality.

LEAD has important implications for the efficiency of several types of wireless protocols. The pilots extracted by LEAD can be utilized to estimate accurate channel BER at the receiver without resorting to probing packets. This can significant reduce the overhead of rate adaptation. Several cross-layer protocols such as PPR [16] utilize PHY information (e.g., decoding confidence) to estimate packet errors. LEAD can improve the decoding performance and hence helps error estimation accuracy. We will integrate LEAD with these protocols and study the benefits of pilot-assisted decoding on partial packet recovery and rate adaption.

[1]The random pilot selection strategy is consistent with our implementation where the pilots are uniformly spread over the entire packet by the interleaver.

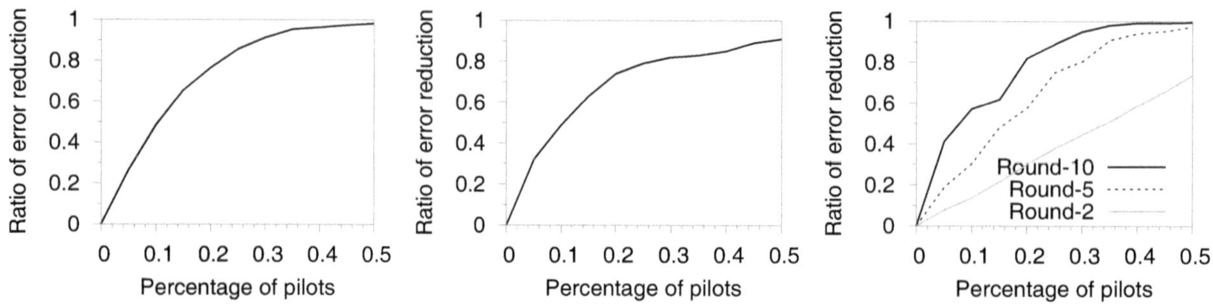

(a) Convolutional code. (b) LDPC. (c) Rateless spinal code.

Figure 16: Ratios of reduced errors when using pilot-assisted decoding for convolutional code, LDPC, and Spinal.

9. ACKNOWLEDEMENTS

This work was supported in part by U.S. National Science Foundation under grants CNS-0916576 and CNS-0954039 (CAREER). We thank the anonymous reviewers and the shepherd Dr. Suman Banerjee for providing valuable feedbacks for this work.

10. REFERENCES

[1] RObust Header Compression (ROHC): Framework and four profiles: RTP, UDP, ESP, and uncompressed. RFC 3095, July 2001.

[2] The RObust Header Compression (ROHC) Framework. RFC 4995, July 2007.

[3] D. Aguayo, J. Bicket, S. Biswas, G. Judd, and R. Morris. Link-level measurements from an 802.11b mesh network. In *ACM SIGCOMM*, 2004.

[4] L. Bahl, J. Cocke, F. Jelinek, and J. Raviv. Optimal decoding of linear codes for minimizing symbol error rate. In *IEEE Transactions on Information Theory*, 1974.

[5] A. Bhartia, Y.-C. Chen, S. Rallapalli, and L. Qiu. Harnessing frequency diversity in wi-fi networks. In *ACM MobiCom*, 2011.

[6] R. Chandra, R. Mahajan, V. Padmanabhan, and M. Zhang. CRAWDAD data set microsoft/osdi2006 (v. 2007-05-23).

[7] B. Chen, Z. Zhou, Y. Zhao, and H. Yu. Efficient error estimating coding: feasibility and applications. In *ACM SIGCOMM*, 2010.

[8] P. Duhamel and M. Kieffer. *Joint Source-Channel Decoding: A Cross-Layer Perspective with Applications in Video Broadcasting*. Academic Press, 2010.

[9] R. G. Gallager. Low-density parity-check codes, 1963.

[10] M. Gowda, S. Sen, R. R. Choudhury, and S.-J. Lee. Cooperative packet recovery in enterprise wlans. In *IEEE INFOCOM*, 2013.

[11] D. Halperin, W. Hu, A. Sheth, and D. Wetherall. Predictable 802.11 packet delivery from wireless channel measurements. In *ACM SIGCOMM*, 2010.

[12] D. Halperin, W. Hu, A. Sheth, and D. Wetherall. Tool release: Gathering 802.11n traces with channel state information. *ACM SIGCOMM CCR*, 2011.

[13] B. Han, A. Schulman, F. Gringoli, N. Spring, B. Bhattacharjee, L. Nava, L. Ji, S. Lee, and R. R. Miller. Maranello: Practical partial packet recovery for 802.11. In *NSDI*, 2010.

[14] J. Huang, Y. Wang, and G. Xing. Lead: leveraging protocol signatures for improving 802.11 decoding performance. Technical Report MSU-CSE-12-14, Computer Science and Engineering, Michigan State University, East Lansing, Michigan. `http://www.cse.msu.edu/cgi-user/web/tech/reports?Year=2012`.

[15] S. Jakubczak and D. Katabi. A cross-layer design for scalable mobile video. In *ACM Mobicom*, 2011.

[16] K. Jamieson and H. Balakrishnan. Ppr: Partial packet recovery for wireless networks. In *ACM SIGCOMM*, 2007.

[17] W. E. Leland, W. Willinger, M. S. Taqqu, and D. V. Wilson. On the selfsimilar nature of ethernet traffic. In *ACM SIGCOMM*, 1993.

[18] K. C.-J. Lin, N. Kushman, and D. Katabi. Ziptx: Harnessing partial packets in 802.11 networks. In *ACM MobiCom*, 2008.

[19] X. L. Liu, W. Hu, Q. Pu, F. Wu, and Y. Zhang. Parcast: soft video delivery in mimo-ofdm wlans. In *ACM Mobicom*, 2012.

[20] M.-H. Lu, P. Steenkiste, and T. Chen. Design, implementation and evaluation of an efficient opportunistic retransmission protocol. In *ACM MobiCom*, 2009.

[21] A. Miu, H. Balakrishnan, and C. E. Koksal. Improving loss resilience with multi-radio diversity in wireless networks. In *ACM MobiCom*, 2005.

[22] J. Perry, P. Iannucci, K. E. Fleming, H. Balakrishnan, and D. Shah. Spinal Codes. In *ACM SIGCOMM*, 2012.

[23] C. Phillips and S. Singh. CRAWDAD data set pdx/vwave (v. 2009-07-04).

[24] A. Schulman, D. Levin, and N. Spring. CRAWDAD data set umd/sigcomm2008 (v. 2009-03-02).

[25] S. Sen, S. Gilani, S. Srinath, S. Schmitt, and S. Banerjee. Design and implementation of an "approximate" communication system for wireless media applications. *ACM SIGCOMM*, 2010.

[26] S. Sen, R. Roy Choudhury, and S. Nelakuditi. Csma/cn: carrier sense multiple access with collision notification. In *ACM MobiCom*, 2010.

[27] S. Sen, R. Roy Choudhury, and S. Nelakuditi. No time to countdown: migrating backoff to the frequency domain. In *ACM MobiCom*, 2011.

[28] S. Sen, N. Santhapuri, R. R. Choudhury, and S. Nelakuditi. Accurate: constellation based rate estimation in wireless networks. In *NSDI*, 2010.

[29] K. Srinivasan, M. A. Kazandjieva, S. Agarwal, and P. Levis. The beta-factor: measuring wireless link burstiness. In *ACM SenSys*, 2008.

[30] F. Tosato and P. Bisaglia. Simplified soft-output demapper for binary interleaved cofdm with application to hiperlan/2. In *Communications, 2002. ICC 2002. IEEE International Conference on*, 2002.

[31] M. Vutukuru, H. Balakrishnan, and K. Jamieson. Cross-layer bit rate adaptation. In *ACM SIGCOMM*, 2009.

[32] G. R. Woo, P. Kheradpour, S. Dawei, and D. Katabi. Beyond the bits: cooperative packet recovery using physical layer information. In *ACM SIGCOMM*, 2007.

[33] J. Xie, W. Hu, and Z. Zhang. Revisiting partial packet recovery in 802.11 wireless lans. In *ACM MobiSys*, 2011.

[34] J. Zhang, H. Shen, K. Tan, R. Chandra, Y. Zhang, and Q. Zhang. Frame retransmissions considered harmful: improving spectrum efficiency using micro-acks. In *ACM MobiCom*, 2012.

[35] J. Zhang, H. Shen, K. Tan, R. Chandra, Y. Zhang, and Q. Zhang. Frame retransmissions considered harmful: improving spectrum efficiency using micro-acks. In *ACM MobiCom*, 2012.

PROTEUS: Network Performance Forecast for Real-Time, Interactive Mobile Applications

Qiang Xu
University of Michigan
Ann Arbor, MI
qiangxu@umich.edu

Sanjeev Mehrotra
Microsoft Research
Redmond, WA
sanjeevm@microsoft.com

Z. Morley Mao
University of Michigan
Ann Arbor, MI
zmao@umich.edu

Jin Li
Microsoft Research
Redmond, WA
jinl@microsoft.com

ABSTRACT

Real-time communication (RTC) applications such as VoIP, video conferencing, and online gaming are flourishing. To adapt and deliver good performance, these applications require accurate estimations of short-term network performance metrics, e.g., loss rate, one-way delay, and throughput. However, the wide variation in mobile cellular network performance makes running RTC applications on these networks problematic. To address this issue, various performance adaptation techniques have been proposed, but one common problem of such techniques is that they only adjust application behavior reactively after performance degradation is visible. Thus, proactive adaptation based on accurate short-term, fine-grained network performance prediction can be a preferred alternative that benefits RTC applications.

In this study, we show that forecasting the short-term performance in cellular networks is possible in part due to the channel estimation scheme on the device and the radio resource scheduling algorithm at the base station. We develop a system interface called PROTEUS, which passively collects current network performance, such as throughput, loss, and one-way delay, and then uses regression trees to forecast future network performance. PROTEUS successfully predicts the occurrence of packet loss within a 0.5s time window for 98% of the time windows and the occurrence of long one-way delay for 97% of the time windows. We also demonstrate how PROTEUS can be integrated with RTC applications to significantly improve the perceptual quality. In particular, we increase the peak signal-to-noise ratio of a video conferencing application by up to 15dB and reduce the perceptual delay in a gaming application by up to 4s.

MobiSys'13, June 25–28, 2013, Taipei, Taiwan

Categories and Subject Descriptors

C.2.1 [**Network Architecture and Design**]: Wireless communication; C.2.4 [**Distributed Systems**]: Client/server; C.4 [**PERFORMANCE OF SYSTEMS**]: Modeling techniques; Measurement techniques

General Terms

Design, Measurement, Performance

Keywords

Cellular network performance prediction; Interactive applications; Real-time communication (RTC) applications; Mobile applications

1. INTRODUCTION

One of the biggest trends today is the accelerated adoption of mobile devices, whose power is approaching that of PCs. The rapid adoption of mobile devices is resulting in the migration of real-time communication (RTC) applications from PCs to mobile devices. RTC applications include (i) multimedia real-time communication including VoIP/video conferencing applications such as Skype, FaceTime, and Google+ Hangout; (ii) interactive multi-player gaming applications such as Draw Something, Modern Combat 3, and Call of Duty; and (iii) application sharing, desktop sharing, and virtual desktop interface (VDI). RTCWeb (Real-Time Collaboration over Web) is an ongoing effort to enable RTC applications to run inside browsers without plug-ins [8].

Running RTC applications in mobile networks presents a major challenge since they require accurate short-term estimates of network metrics, e.g., loss rate, one-way delay (OWD), and throughput, whereas cellular network performance varies rapidly and widely [20, 24, 44]. Although performance adaptation solutions have been proposed [1, 2, 5, 7, 34, 40, 48], they are ineffective for RTC applications, where the end-to-end delay between content generation and content consumption is on the order of network latencies. Thus, techniques such as packet retransmissions or use of large client-side de-jitter buffers to absorb jitter variations, effective for web browsing and video playback, will lead to intolerable delays in RTC applications.

Instead, RTC applications need to rely on an appropriate amount of forward error correction (FEC) to account for packet loss and a small yet appropriately sized de-jitter buffer to absorb varying packet delay. Over-protection using FEC wastes precious bandwidth, while under-protection negates the effectiveness of FEC, as any unrecoverable packet loss will lead to severe quality degradation in voice calling and video conferencing. Similarly, if the de-jitter buffer size is too large, it adds to the application latency. If it is too small, late arriving packets will be considered lost, which also leads to significant quality degradation. Accurate throughput prediction is also necessary to allow bandwidth intensive applications to maximize throughput without incurring additional queuing delay. Thus, short-term, fine-grained network performance prediction on mobile networks is of great importance.

Existing work on mobile network performance measurement and prediction is of limited importance to RTC applications for several reasons: (i) the measurement or prediction approaches are carried out on coarse-grained time granularity or offline, which are not suitable for RTC applications; (ii) the performance adaptation techniques react to performance only after observing any degradation, when the user experience has already been negatively impacted; and (iii) the existing techniques used by RTC applications for network prediction are usually naïve such as using the previous performance,the average of previous performance, or linear regression techniques, which work well only for relatively stable wired networks.

In this study, we propose a system interface named PROTEUS designed to accurately predict fine-grained detailed network performance in real time over short time scales allowing applications to adjust their behavior to best optimize their performance. The fine-grained and accurate performance prediction in real time is necessary yet challenging from three aspects: (i) cellular network performance may be affected by a multitude of unobservable factors, such as radio resource scheduling, other users sharing the spectrum, and signal-to-noise ratio; (ii) network performance predictions on fine-grained time granularity is inherently noisier than coarse-grained predictions; and (iii) active probing is prohibitive for RTC applications due to significant resource consumption, while passive monitoring has limited visibility only based on traffic generated by applications.

To address the above challenges, PROTEUS utilizes a machine learning framework based on regression trees to learn the trend of network performance over short, fine-grained time windows using previous available observations. Even though past work has provided the evidence that cellular networks have a potential to have predictability for network performance, to our best knowledge, PROTEUS is the first system to forecast short-term network performance in real time, and the first to demonstrate the benefit of proactively adjusting the operating parameters in real time for use by mobile RTC applications. The key contributions of our paper are as follows:

- We characterize short-term network behavior and investigate the performance predictability in three major cellular networks of AT&T, T-Mobile, and Sprint based on more than 400 hours of traces across 3 locations. We identify the existence of strong predictability over short time scales for these cellular networks.
- We discover that loss rate, one-way delay, and throughput in cellular networks can be accurately predicted in real time from past measurements by feeding past network performance metrics into regression trees. For a following 0.5s time window, we can predict loss occurrence with 98% accuracy, late packet arrival with 97% accuracy, and throughput with a median error of 10kbps with average throughput ranging from 100–800kbps.
- We prototype PROTEUS, an efficient framework that forecasts achievable network performance in real time and evaluate its usage by a video conferencing system and an online game, i.e., Draw Something. By adapting its behavior through prediction from PROTEUS, the video conferencing system can improve its peak signal-to-noise ratio by up to 15dB over the state-of-the-art adaptation techniques. Utilizing PROTEUS, Draw Something can reduce the perceptual delay in viewing the stroke-by-stroke animation by up to 4s.

The rest of this paper is organized as follows. §2 identifies the potential factors that allow for short-term, fine-grained performance predictability in cellular networks. §3 overviews the infrastructure of PROTEUS, followed by §4 where we characterize short-term predictability of cellular networks. §5 applies PROTEUS into a video conferencing system and a multi-player gaming system and evaluates the benefits from PROTEUS. The related studies are discussed in §6 and we conclude our paper in §7.

2. CELLULAR NETWORK BACKGROUND

In this section, we examine the relevant network behavior in cellular networks to establish the time scale in which network performance may be predictable.

In UMTS, EV-DO, and LTE networks, a mobile device estimates the channel quality through the perceived signal-to-noise ratio of the pilot signal from the base station in every time slot, e.g., 1.67ms for EV-DO. The device determines the modulation and coding scheme (i.e., DRC) from the channel quality and reports back to the base station. Depending on the channel quality, the base station allocates time slots via proportional fair scheduling to fairly allocate radio resource while maximizing the overall radio resource utilization [18].

To precisely understand how the proportional fair scheduler works, let $\mathtt{W[n]}$ denote the exponentially averaged throughput at time slot $\mathtt{n}$ which is computed from $\mathtt{W[n]} = (1-\alpha)\mathtt{W[n-1]} + \alpha \cdot \mathtt{I[n-1]} \cdot \mathtt{C[n-1]}$, where $\mathtt{I}[\cdot]$ is the indicator function on whether the user is served in a given time slot, $\mathtt{C}[\cdot]$ is the function of channel quality report, and α is the discount factor controlling the aggressiveness for the base station switching time slots across users [28]. The proportional fair scheduler allocates time slot $\mathtt{n}$ to a user with the maximum value of $\frac{\mathtt{C[n]}}{\mathtt{W[n]}}$ to balance serving between the device with the best channel quality and the device consuming the most resources.

The average duration of staying in a DRC is hundreds to thousands of time slots for stationary devices and tens of time slots for moving devices [31]. Moreover, a device spends a large fraction of time in one dominant DRC, indicating the presence of a dominant channel condition [31]. Thus, the number of continuous time slots that a device can occupy is decided by $\frac{1}{\mathtt{W[n]}}$, which is affected by the discount factor α. To encourage a device to access a time slot in time [21] and to occupy enough continuous time slots to efficiently deliver a non-trivial amount of data, α is usually set to a small value (e.g., 0.001) [25]. This allows a device to occupy the order of $\approx \frac{1}{\alpha} = 1000$ time slots, which means that a device can occupy the channel with the same DRC on the order of ≈1.67s. Since the network performance on a wireless link between the device and base station is largely a function of the channel condition and the DRC value, we expect that it should be possible to predict network performance on a similar time scale, i.e., 1.67s. Note that we expect the presence of network predictability in other variants of 3G or 4G networks as well due to the consistent utilization of proportional fair scheduling and channel quality report schemes [27].

3. PROTEUS OVERVIEW

PROTEUS is designed to complement the underlying transport protocol and any performance optimization techniques (e.g., FEC, de-jitter buffers, congestion control) that are widely used by RTC applications. For example, video conferencing applications using UDP have their own congestion control based on delay and loss. Applications using TCP rely on TCP's congestion control algorithm. The goal of PROTEUS is to provide applications with prediction of delay, loss, and throughput, so that they can perform application-specific optimizations such as tuning source bit-rate, amount of FEC inserted, and de-jitter buffer size.

To avoid measurement overhead, PROTEUS does not actively probe the network. Instead, PROTEUS is designed as a library that relies on application traffic to collect network measurements. This is done by appending and recording the time and sequence numbers for outgoing and incoming packets. PROTEUS can be either in user space or inside the kernel. Inside the kernel, PROTEUS has lower overhead. As shown in Figure 1, applications (e.g., `app #1`) can call `send'()` and `recv'()`, which are PROTEUS's wrapped version of standard socket API's `send()` and `recv()`. The socket wrapper allows PROTEUS to transparently collect network statistics (one-way delay, loss, and throughput) by inserting sequencing and timing information into packet headers. However, there may be many applications that already append sequencing and timing information in their packet headers to compute similar network statistics, e.g., RTP packets used by many VoIP and video conferencing applications already contain sufficient information to accurately compute network statistics. These applications (e.g., app #2) can alternatively use the standard socket APIs and inform PROTEUS with network statistics.

PROTEUS provides applications and the socket wrapper another two sets of APIs: the inform API and the inquiry API. The inform API enables the socket wrapper (e.g., `app #1`) and applications (e.g., `app #2`) to inform PROTEUS with packet sequencing and timing information, whereas the application issues the inquiry API to obtain from PROTEUS the predicted future network performance, as depicted in Figure 1. Based on this fine-grained information of packet sequencing and timing provided by either the wrapped socket (e.g., `app #1`) or the application (e.g., `app #2`) through the inform API, PROTEUS can compute current packet loss rate, one-way delay, and throughput from which it can predict future network performance. PROTEUS uses a clock drift compensation technique [35] to adjust the remote timestamp to the local clock to compute one-way delay.

The overhead of adding timestamps and sequence numbers into packet headers is acceptable, which has been evaluated in previous research [3, 41]. The statistics of loss, delay, and throughput are collected over small non-overlapping time slices (i.e., time windows). This is the granularity over which statistics collection as well prediction are performed. Using the observed statistics from a certain number of previous time windows (i.e., information windows), PROTEUS trains regression trees to identify the dependencies across various network metrics and to forecast the network performance in future time windows. There could be more than one way to learn traffic histories. We resort to regression trees simply as it is one of the state-of-the-art approaches that have relatively low memory and computation overhead [17]. Another advantage of regression trees over other techniques is that it can provide a real-value prediction of a metric as opposed to simply a binary decision.

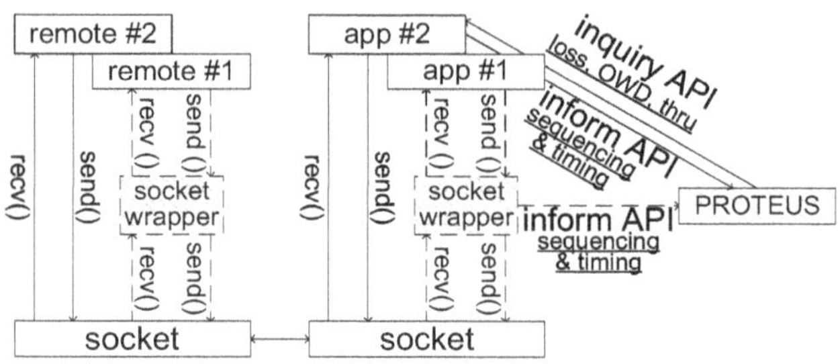

Figure 1: The overall design of PROTEUS. The details of its interaction with an application are shown in Figure 11.

The accuracy of PROTEUS's prediction is determined by two factors: (i) the inherent predictability of cellular network performance (described in §4.1), and (ii) the effectiveness of PROTEUS's forecasting technique (examined in §4.2).

The information exchanged through the inform API between applications and PROTEUS is common across applications. However, the information from the inquiry API and the resulting action taken by each application may be very different. In Table 1, we classify applications into four broad categories depending on how sensitive their performance is to the three network parameters of packet loss, one-way delay, and throughput and show how PROTEUS can be useful.

- Type 1 consists of applications whose performance is not sensitive to loss, one-way delay, or throughput. These are either non-real-time, low-bandwidth applications insensitive to network performance, or applications that do not benefit much from prediction. For example, the performance of Dropbox and other file transfer applications depends on throughput, but there is little adaptation in response to throughput prediction.
- Type 2 consists of applications whose performance is not sensitive to packet loss or one-way delay but is sensitive to throughput. These are non-real-time, high-bandwidth applications such as video on demand (VOD). Such applications can take steps to improve performance such as adapting the rate of the stream served to the client [5] in response to throughput prediction.
- Type 3 consists of applications whose performance is sensitive to packet loss and/or one-way delay, but not to throughput. These are real-time, interactive, low-bandwidth applications such as VoIP. For these applications, throughput prediction is of little benefit. However, loss prediction can be

type	description	example	inquiry API
1	non-real-time, low rate, or insensitive to performance	Weather, Calender, Reminder, Dropbox	N/A
2	sensitive to throughput	YouTube, NetFlix. Hulu	throughput
3	sensitive to loss and one-way delay (OWD)	Skype Call, Google Voice	loss, OWD
4	sensitive to loss, OWD, and throughput	Skype Video, Google+ Hangouts, Draw Something, online games	loss, OWD, throughput

Table 1: The types of applications based on the sensitivity to network loss, OWD, and throughput.

used to control the amount of FEC used [15]. The one-way delay prediction can be used to adjust the de-jitter buffer size for adaptive playout to reduce both late arrival induced loss [15] and de-jitter buffer induced delay.

- Type 4 consists of applications whose performance is sensitive to packet loss, one-way delay, and throughput prediction. These are real-time, interactive, high-bandwidth applications such as video conferencing, and real-time software applications such as desktop sharing. PROTEUS can be used for throughput prediction to control the source rate produced by the source. The number of FEC packets to insert can be inferred from loss prediction, and the de-jitter buffer size can be determined from one-way delay prediction.

Type 3 and Type 4 are real-time, interactive applications that can benefit from PROTEUS. Type 2 consists of *non-real-time* applications that can still benefit from throughput prediction.Although a coarse-grained predictor may work for Type 2 applications, it may not work for RTC applications. A coarse-grained predictor can be built upon a fine-grained predictor such as PROTEUS by simply averaging the prediction over multiple time windows.

Types 2, 3, and 4 applications are becoming increasingly popular and contribute to a majority of the traffic on the Internet [47]. This trend is readily visible by the increasing popularity of Skype, FaceTime, and Google+ Hangouts. The increasing push towards the cloud also makes other RTC applications such as online gaming and VDI (virtual desktop infrastructure) scenarios even more important. The broad industry interest in the performance of such applications is apparent from recent efforts around RTCWeb [8] and DASH (Dynamic Adaptive Streaming over HTTP) [6].

4. PREDICTION USING PROTEUS

In this section, we investigate the predictability of cellular network performance and evaluate the accuracy of PROTEUS's forecasting.

4.1 Characterizing Cellular Networks

Although the understanding of the channel estimation scheme on mobile devices and the radio resource scheduling algorithm at base stations, along with the performance predictability observations from previous studies [31] give us confidence that cellular network performance is predictable, it is still uncertain (i) how much predictability there is in cellular networks, particularly in the short term as is needed by RTC applications; (ii) what network features can be the best predictors; and (iii) how much overhead is required to achieve accurate prediction. These challenges have not been fully addressed by any previous research, but need to be studied to improve the performance of Type 3 and Type 4 applications in Table 1.

Autocorrelation for the same network metric. To quantify the predictability of cellular network performance, we first study the correlation across network metrics over time. A high correlation of a particular network characteristic would indicate that the feature should be predictable whereas a low correlation would imply difficulty in prediction. We take network measurements across non-overlapping time intervals, i.e., aforementioned time windows, and then compute the correlation coefficient between current time window with a time window $\mathtt{t}$ in the past, i.e., the time lag, using $\mathtt{R_t} = \frac{\mathtt{E[P_0 \cdot P_t] - E[P_0] \cdot E[P_t]}}{\sigma[\mathtt{P_0}] \cdot \sigma[\mathtt{P_t}]}$, where $\mathtt{E}[.]$ is the expectation operation, $\sigma[.]$ is the standard deviation operation, and $\mathtt{P}$ is the stochastic process of any network performance metric[1]. A high autocorrelation coefficient would indicate that the metric is predictable using a linear predictor.

device	carrier	network	down.[1]	up.[1]
iPhone 4	AT&T	UMTS	77(4)	42(4)
Captivate	AT&T	UMTS	159(N/A)	72(N/A)
Atrix	AT&T	HSPA	42(N/A)	20(N/A)
Nexus	T-Mobile	HSPA+	109(N/A)	108(N/A)
dongle	Sprint	EV-DO	44(N/A)	115(N/A)

[1] The number of UDP(TCP) flows, each lasting ≥1 hour.

Table 2: The devices and cellular networks covered by the experiments. FlowSet Refers to the AT&T flows.

To study if cellular network performance can be predicted using fine-grained time windows, e.g., 0.5s, we collect a large number of traces from various cellular networks in Table 2 and compute the autocorrelation of throughput using each trace choosing a time window of 0.5s, i.e., $\mathtt{tw} = 0.5$. We plot the distribution of the autocorrelation coefficient as a function of the time lag in Figure 2(a) for the flows in FlowSet, as defined in Table 2. Given a time lag, we show the distribution across flows via the 5th, 25th, 50th, 75th, and 95th percentiles.

In Figure 2(a), more than half of the time, the autocorrelation coefficient at a time lag of 0.5s is more than 0.6, indicating that the network performance using a time window of size 0.5s is indeed predictable to some degrees using previous time windows. From Figure 2(a), we also see that once the time lag is above 20s, the median autocorrelation coefficient is close to 0, and the 25-75th percentiles are in the range of [-0.05, 0.05]. Therefore, we expect that using the time windows that are within the last 20s is sufficient to predict network performance. The results presented here show the autocorrelation function for throughput. We see similar behavior for packet loss and one-way delay.

Time granularity of performance prediction. One parameter affecting the autocorrelation coefficient is the size of the time window. If the time window chosen is small,

[1]The value of the autocorrelation function lies in the range $[-1, 1]$, with 1 indicating perfect correlation, -1 indicating perfect anti-correlation, and 0 indicating no correlation.

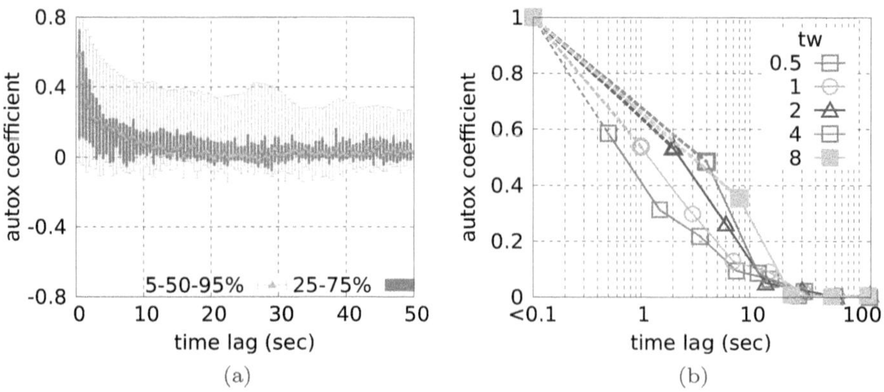

Figure 2: The autocorrelation coefficient of throughput under the impact of (a) the time lag and (b) the time window size ("tw").

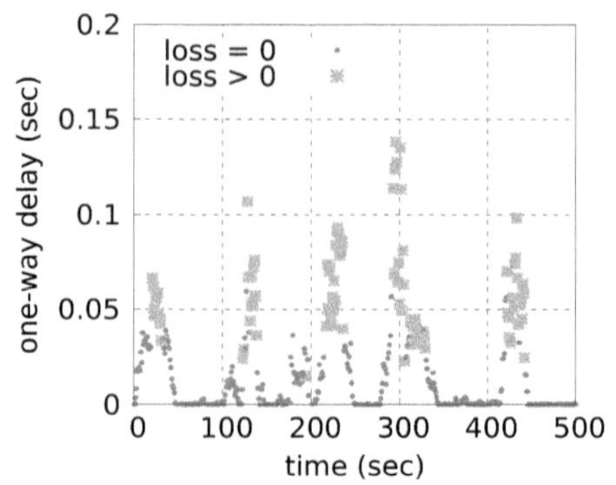

Figure 3: The one-way delay for the time windows with and without loss.

the measurements may show high variability, which may be more difficult to predict. However, if the time window chosen is large, the measurements may be affected by long term drift and cannot accurately reflect the fine-grained performance needed by RTC applications. To appropriately select a time window size, we study the effect of time window size on the autocorrelation function. Figure 2(b) shows the median autocorrelation coefficient for UDP throughput as a function of the time lag for various time window sizes, i.e., 0.5s, 1s, 2s, 4s, and 8s. We expect that as the time window size increases, the autocorrelation coefficient for a given time lag should also increase until it eventually converges. In Figure 2(b), "`tw` = 4" being close to "`tw` = 8" indicates that using time windows greater than 4s provides no additional benefit. However, we see that even with a window size of "tw = 0.5", the average autocorrelation coefficient at a time lag of 0.5s is above 0.6 and is similar to that using a larger time window. Thus, we conclude that we can indeed predict network performance from previous time windows using fine-grained windows, e.g., 0.5s, as needed by RTC applications.

In total, we have three observations from studying the autocorrelation function: (i) the current network performance is correlated with the network performance in the previous time windows; (ii) to predict the network performance, the time window size can be as short as 0.5s as required by RTC applications; and (iii) using information within the previous 20s should be sufficient for accurate prediction.

Cross correlation between network metrics. These three observations answer the question of whether network performance is predictable on cellular networks using previous values of a particular metric to predict future values of the same metric. However, the question of whether previous values of other metrics can also be used to improve prediction remains. To study this, we study the cross-correlation coefficient across various different network metrics.

Since packet loss and end-to-end network delay are commonly used as congestion signals by congestion control protocols as well indicate overbuffering in cellular networks [26], we expect that these metrics may be correlated. To confirm this understanding, we investigate the cross correlation between the various network performance metrics. The distribution of the cross-correlation coefficient as a function of the time lag is shown in Figure 4. From Figures 4(a) and (b), we find that throughput does not correlate well with either loss or one-way delay. The maximum absolute median cross correlation coefficient between throughput and loss is less than 0.1, and between throughput and one-way delay is less than 0.15. We believe that this is because the throughput is decided more by the DRC on the link between the device and the base station, while loss and one-way delay are affected more by the congestion along the path. However, from Figure 4(c), we see that loss rate and one-way delay do have a strong correlation with each other. When the time lag is close to 0, the median cross correlation coefficient is around 0.5. Figure 3 further shows this correlation by showing the average one-way delay for each time window as a function of time for time windows with loss and those without loss. We clearly see that for those windows where loss occurs, the average one-way delay is also significantly higher than for those where there is no loss. As a result, the forecasts of loss and one-way delay use both previous loss rate and one-way delay, while throughput prediction uses just the throughput from previous time windows.

4.2 Constructing the Regression Trees

We utilize a framework based on regression trees to automatically learn the correlation between previous network performance and current network performance [17]. Note that there could be more than one way to learn traffic histories and predict network performance, e.g., Markov chains. We resort to regression trees simply because it is one of the state-of-the-art approaches that has relatively low memory and computation overhead. We have tried to use a Markov chain to model the short-term network performance behavior, however, tuning the parameters for the model is ad hoc.

We construct a regression tree for each of the network metrics, with the target of the tree being the metric predicted and the attributes being the metrics used to perform the prediction. The loss regression tree predicts the loss rate in the next time window using the loss rate and one-way delay values from previous time windows. The delay regression tree uses the same attributes to predict the one-way delay in the next time window. The throughput regression tree predicts the throughput in the next time window using the throughput values from previous time windows and the sending rate from the immediate previous time window.

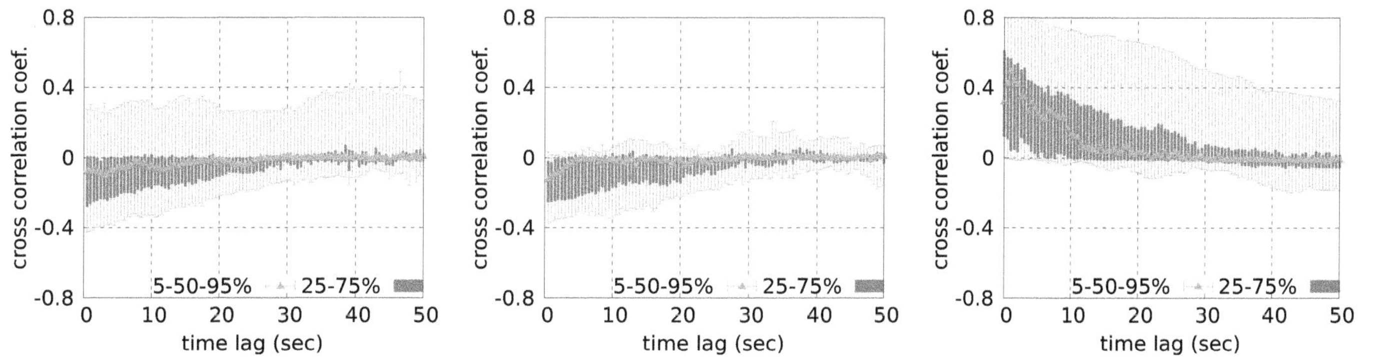

(a) throughput and loss rate. (b) throughput and one-way delay. (c) loss rate and one-way delay.

Figure 4: The cross correlation coefficient between performance metrics. The cross correlation is computed per flow and the distribution across flows of the correlation coefficient under a given time lag is presented as 5-, 25-, 50-, 75-, and 95- percentiles. The correlation coefficient is normalized so that the maximum value is 1 for each flow.

The sending rate is included to address the case in which the application is sending at a rate much below the throughput.

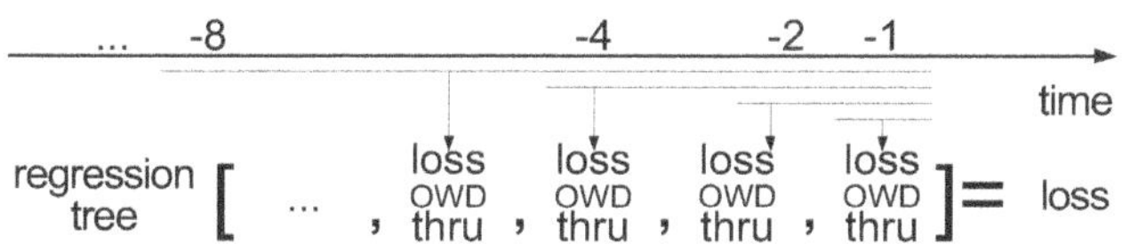

Figure 5: The attributes of the loss regression.

The number of attributes in the regression trees can be controlled by selecting an appropriate information window size from the correlation analysis (Figures 2 and 4). As illustrated by Figure 5, the attributes are computed using time windows in an exponential backoff fashion, i.e., the attributes are the average values of a given metric in the previous $1, 2, 4, 8, \ldots, 2^{\lceil \log_2(\mathtt{M}) \rceil}$ time windows, where M is the information window size. Creating attributes using this approach allows us to place greater importance on the more recent time windows as the more recent time windows are represented in multiple attributes. It also controls the number of attributes since we only have $\lceil \log_2(\mathtt{M}) \rceil + 1$ attributes for a given information window of M time windows instead of M attributes. With a time window of 0.5s and an information window of 20s, we have only 7 attributes referring to the average of previous 1, 2, 4, 8, 16, 32, 64 time windows. In PROTEUS, the time window size is 0.5s and the information window size is 20s by default without particular specification.

According to Figure 2(a), the correlation between the current network performance and the performance many seconds ago is too weak to be useful. Thus, PROTEUS does not perform offline training which can be inefficient and expensive. PROTEUS keeps feeding the regression trees with the most recent performance metrics, allowing the regression trees to perform hyper-correction internally. Based on the knowledge of performance histories, the regression trees output the respective performance predictions for the next time window.

4.3 Evaluating Forecast Accuracy

To evaluate the performance of PROTEUS, we carry out controlled experiments to measure its forecasting accuracy. The forecasting accuracy may be variable due to several aspects. When a mobile device is in communication over cellular networks, the network, the device, and even the different cellular technology generations under the same network can influence network predictability. Thus, we conduct the experiments using diverse setups as shown in Table 2. Table 2 lists the device, the network, and the cellular technology used. As TCP has built-in congestion control and retransmission, the objective of evaluating TCP is its direct impact to RTC applications, described in §5. To minimize bias, we repeat our experiments at different times in the day and at different locations. To directly control the sending rate and to easily observe loss, one-way delay, and throughput, we conduct most of our experiments over UDP. Even though most RTC applications operate directly over UDP, the applicability of PROTEUS is not limited by the transport protocol used by the application.

In the experiments, the mobile device communicates with a remote server in our campus in either the downlink or uplink direction and keeps the packet rate constant over the entire flow. To choose the sending rates, we saturate the end-to-end connection using UDP and estimate the bandwidth from the receiving rate. Based on the estimated bandwidth, the sending rate steps from 50% of the estimated bandwidth to 150% by 10% every time and each flow of a sending rate lasts at least one hour. On both the mobile and the remote server, we monitor packet traces using `tcpdump`. From the collected packet traces, we identify throughput, loss rate, and one-way delay. Here, we investigate one-way delay instead of round trip time because one-way delay is a more accurate measurement of network characteristics in a single direction and directly affects application performance. As mentioned in §3, PROTEUS performs clock drift compensation to compute one-way delay.

In the evaluation, we compare PROTEUS with general linear regression based prediction, representing the majority of on-demand prediction solutions [1, 2, 5, 7, 11]. Any given linear regression based prediction solution can be generalized as $\mathtt{P}[\mathtt{t}] = \lambda_1 \mathtt{P}[\mathtt{t}-1] + \lambda_2 \mathtt{P}[\mathtt{t}-2] + \cdots + \lambda_k \mathtt{P}[\mathtt{t}-\mathtt{k}]$, in which $\mathtt{P}[\mathtt{t}]$ is the network performance at time window t and $\lambda_{1,\cdots,k}$ are the linear regression coefficients. However, deter-

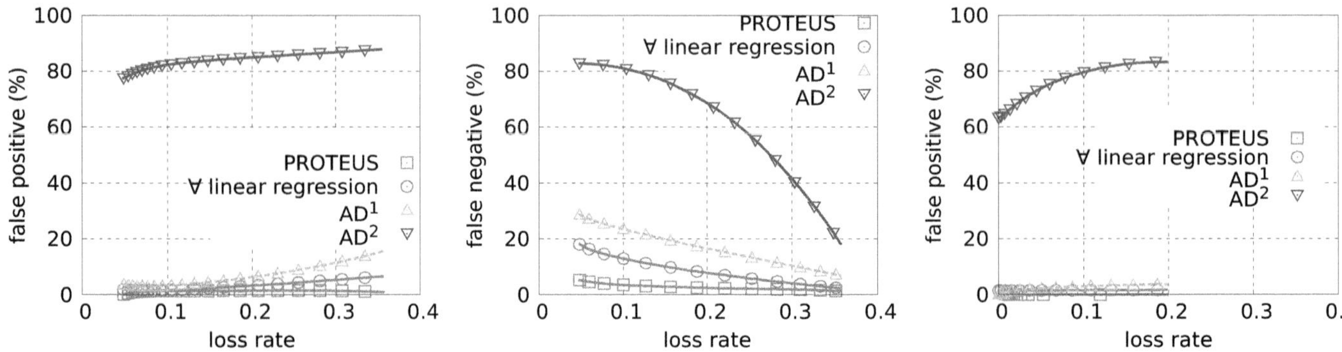

(a) downlink false positive. (b) downlink false negative. (c) uplink false positive.

Figure 6: The accuracy in loss prediction. The X-axis shows the loss rate of each flow in FlowSet. The loss rate can be high because UDP's sending rate is agnostic of highly variable cellular links, which could commonly occur for UDP based applications.

mining the best $\lambda_{1,\cdots,k}$ for real-time use is challenging due to the diversity of network condition. To compare with linear regression based prediction, we perform linear regression offline for each experiment to obtain the $\lambda_{1,\cdots,k}$ that can best fit performance estimation, and hypothetically assume that the best $\lambda_{1,\cdots,k}$ is known a priori, which is an upper bound for any linear regression based solution. Besides, a common walkaround in engineering (named as AD^1 and AD^2) is to use the most recent network performance as follows.

- AD^1 assumes the performance in the next time window is the same as the performance observed in the current time window.
- AD^2 is less aggressive than AD^1 to circumvent random variation in cellular networks. AD^2 assumes that the performance in the next time window is the average of the performance in the information window, i.e., the same as PROTEUS's information window.

Although AD^1 and AD^2 may seem simple and naïve, most existing RTC applications estimate loss rate and one-way delay using such methods since they work relatively well on wired networks where statistics are relatively stable.

PROTEUS's performance in loss prediction. We first investigate PROTEUS's accuracy in predicting the presence of any packet loss in the next time window by measuring the false positive and false negative rates in FlowSet. A false positive occurs when PROTEUS predicts a packet loss in the time window but there is none. False positives can cause inefficient usage of network resources. For example, an application may introduce unnecessary FEC, which would reduce the rate available for the actual coding of media. In contrast, a false negative occurs when PROTEUS predicts no packet loss but a packet is lost in a time window. For many applications, the false negatives may result in degraded application performance due to unrecoverable packet loss. This is especially true for RTC applications where retransmissions are not possible.

In Figures 6(a)-(c), we show the false positive and false negative rates as a function of the actual loss rate for downlink and uplink traffic. From Figure 6(a), we see that PROTEUS's false positive rate is consistently around <1% when the loss rate is in the range from 0.05 to 0.4, while AD^1's false positive rate is around 2-5% when the loss rate is less than 0.3 and increases to 20% after the loss rate grows to 0.35. AD^2 performs even worse with the false positive rates higher than 80%. The hypothetical upper bound for any linear regression based prediction ("∀ linear regression") is around 3%. Note that the loss rate can be as high as 0.35, because UDP's sending rate is agnostic of highly variable cellular network performance [14, 45], which could commonly occur for UDP based applications. There are two reasons that PROTEUS outperforms linear regression techniques: (i) PROTEUS uses cross statistics, e.g., the use of loss in delay prediction and vice versa; and (ii) regression trees have some amount of non-linearity. Consequenly, without fully capturing the performance trend in previous time windows, AD^1 and AD^2 can only achieve the accuracy as poor as random guessing by merely estimating based on the last time window or aggregated history information.

In Figure 6(b), we show the false negative rate of the flows in FlowSet. As mentioned, a false negative is more critical than a false positive, for RTC applications. From Figure 6(b), PROTEUS's false negative rate is consistently around 1-3%, AD^1's false negative is 5-30%, and AD^2's false negative is around 20-80%. The upper bound for linear regression based approaches is 5-20%, which is much worse than PROTEUS. When the loss rate is low, the running flow may not provide sufficient information of true positives, i.e., lost packets. Thus, as the loss rate decreases, PROTEUS, AD^1, and AD^2 all have increasing false negative rates. Although AD^2's false negative rate is only slightly worse than PROTEUS, PROTEUS's false positive rate is significantly better. Compared to AD^1, AD^2 has low false positive rate, but does not retain a low false negative rate at the same time.

Besides downlink traffic, we also investigate uplink traffic as uplink traffic is significant in applications such as Skype, FaceTime, and Google+ Hangouts. Similar to Figure 6(a), PROTEUS is slightly better than the hypothetical upper bound of linear regression solutions and AD^1, and much better than AD^2 in false positive rate according to Figure 6(c). PROTEUS's false positive rate is less than 2% over the flows in FlowSet, "∀ linear regression"'s and AD^1's false positive rates range from 1% to 3%, and AD^2's false positive is no less than 60%. Due to space limitation, we only include the false positive for uplink flows, but we observe similar perfor-

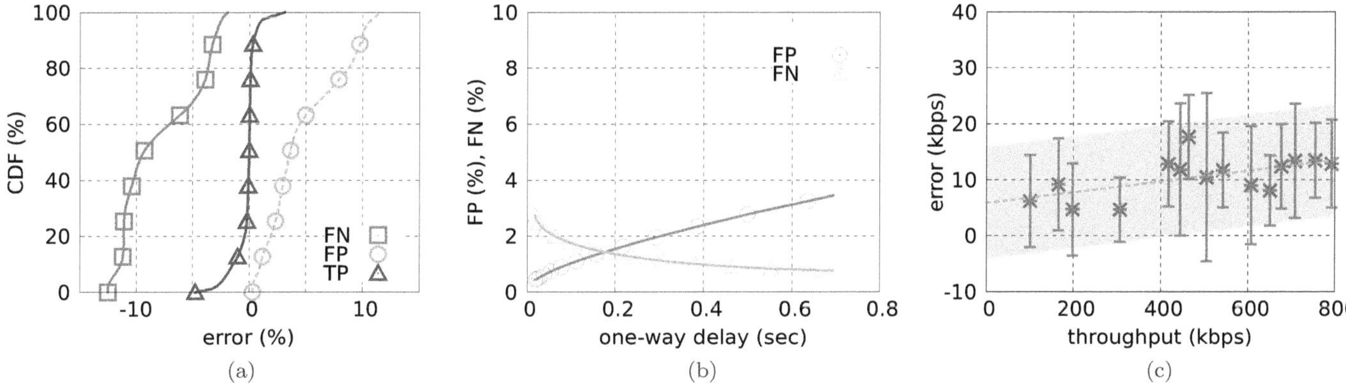

Figure 7: The quantitative accuracy on (a) loss rate, (b) one-way delay, and (c) throughput. In (c), only 15 randomly chosen flows are presented to avoid overlapping.

mance for PROTEUS, AD[1], and AD[2] in their false negative for uplink flows.

The false positive and false negative results for the packet loss presented above show the prediction accuracy. Moreover, the regression tree used in PROTEUS also predicts the packet loss rate quantitatively rather than giving a simple binary decision of whether there will be packet loss. In Figure 7(a), we show the accuracy of this quantitative prediction of packet loss rate. We show the error in packet loss rate prediction for each of the three categories according to the error type, i.e., false negative, false positive, and true positive. Only true negatives do not lead to error because both the predicted and the ground truth loss rate are zero. We show the cumulative distribution function (CDF) of the error for each of these three error types in Figure 7(a).

Among true positive predictions, PROTEUS could either overestimate or underestimate the loss rate. If the loss rate is overestimated, similar to false positives, applications may introduce unnecessary FEC. If loss rate is underestimated, similar to false negatives, applications may experience information loss, which may be more critical. In Figure 7(a), 70% of true positive predictions have no error or the negligible error of less than 0.1% and 99% of them have the error within 5%. PROTEUS's median false negative error is around 10%. With false positives, PROTEUS's median error is 2% and 95% of predictions are less than 10%, which indicates that our design will very unlikely make applications introduce unnecessary protection traffic.

PROTEUS's performance in delay prediction. Besides loss rate prediction, RTC applications can also benefit from one-way delay prediction. One-way delay prediction allows applications such as video conferencing and VoIP to appropriately set their de-jitter buffer sizes, which determines how long the application waits for a packet before declaring it to be lost. Most VoIP and video conferencing systems do not use a fixed de-jitter buffer. The de-jitter buffer starts at something small and grows to some maximum value if packets do not arrive in time. This maximum is set to something which is tolerable for the given application. For example, a 150-200ms end-to-end delay is the maximum that video conferencing systems can tolerate [16]. Once packets start to arrive in time, the de-jitter buffer size shrinks according to some schedule (e.g., 10% every 5s) to lower the end-to-end delay seen by the application. Usually, de-jitter buffer size adaptation is accomplished by using an adaptive rate playout (either speeding up or slowing down media playback) [15]. Accurately predicting one-way delay can allow an application to more intelligently control this adaptation to improve performance.

Inappropriate de-jitter buffer size selection can result in suboptimal performance. If it is set larger than needed to absorb the inherent network delay variation, the application suffers from larger delay than needed. Otherwise, if it is set too small, a large number of packets that arrive late will be declared lost which results in poor application performance. In Figure 7(b), we show the accuracy of PROTEUS in predicting if the delay in the following time window will exceed the tolerable end-to-end delay (i.e., 150ms [16]) as a function of the true one-way delay. This can answer the question whether we should grow the de-jitter buffer size. Note that the one-way delay is calibrated so that the one-way delay is 0ms if there is no congestion on the network [35]. Similar to before, a false positive occurs when we predict the delay to be larger than 150ms but in reality it is not. A false negative is when we predict the delay to be smaller than 150ms, but in reality it is larger. According to Figure 7(b), the false positive is around <3% and the false negative is around <2%.

PROTEUS's performance in throughput prediction. Predicting the throughput in the next time window is also important for certain bandwidth intensive applications such as video conferencing and VOD. For RTC applications such as video conferencing, throughput prediction can be combined with loss rate prediction to appropriately set the encoder bitrate and the FEC rate. For non-RTC applications such as VOD using chunked video streaming, throughput prediction can be used to appropriately assign bit allocation across video chunks to improve video quality. Overestimating the achievable throughput may lead to application-level information loss or increased delay, while underestimating the achievable throughput prevents applications from maximally utilizing the network.

Since PROTEUS passively monitors network traffic, it cannot predict the achievable throughput of the following time window at an arbitrary sending rate. PROTEUS makes the prediction assuming the sending rate of the next time window is the same as the previous one. We evaluate PROTEUS's accuracy in throughput prediction as a function of

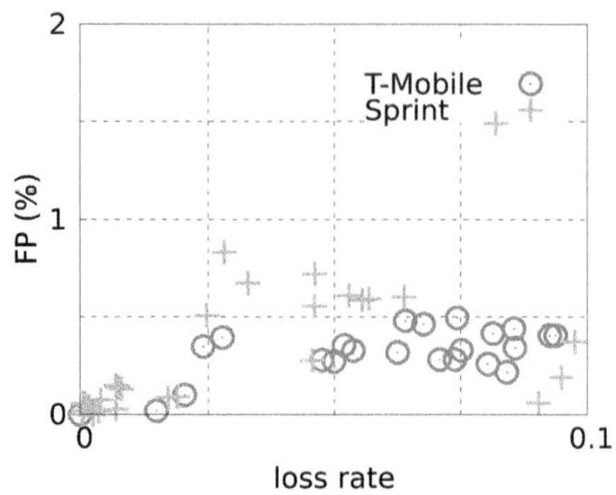

Figure 8: The impact of the cellular network.

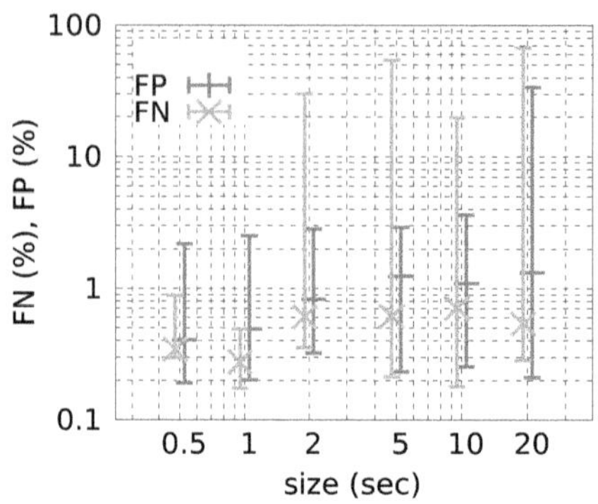

Figure 9: The impact of the time window size.

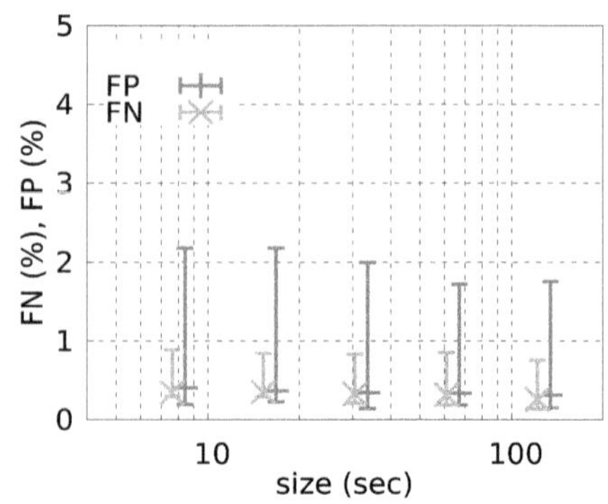

Figure 10: The impact of the information window size.

the actual throughput and show the results in Figure 7(c). To ensure Figure 7(c)'s readability, 15 flows in FlowSet are randomly chosen. Each flow corresponds to an error bar showing the median and standard deviation of the predicted throughput over all the time windows. We see that throughput prediction is fairly accurate across the entire range of throughput, i.e., the median error is around 10kbps with a standard deviation of around 10kbps.

PROTEUS's performance in other networks. So far, we have investigated the accuracy of using PROTEUS to predict the loss rate, one-way delay, and throughput for one particular cellular carrier. To be broadly applicable, we need to verify if PROTEUS's accuracy applies to other cellular carriers as well. Figure 8 shows the false positive rate of loss predictions for T-Mobile and Sprint, whose setup is described in Table 2. According to Figure 8, both T-Mobile and Sprint have even a lower false positive than AT&T. Due to space limitation, we only include the evaluation on false positive rate of T-Mobile and Sprint, but have verified that PROTEUS also has high prediction accuracy in terms of the false negative and false positive rates in one-way delay and throughput prediction.

PROTEUS's performance affected by the time and information window size. We also study the impact of the time window size and the information window size. We have investigated the impact of the time window size on autocorrelation coefficient in Figure 2(a). Here we investigate the impact of time window size on PROTEUS's prediction accuracy. Figure 9 shows the distribution of the false positive and false negative rates as functions of the time window size. Unlike Figure 2(a), PROTEUS's false positive rate is the minimum when the time window size is 0.5s, while PROTEUS's false negative is the minimum when the time window size is 1s. If the time window size further increases, the variation of the false positive can be extremely high (>50%). Using a large time window with a fixed information window size suffers from high performance variability due to the fact that only a few time windows are available. Using a small time window with the same amount of history allows predicting performance on a finer granularity and is preferred. We choose a time window of 0.5s as the lower bound since it is reasonable to keep the time window larger than typical network round trip time.

Another parameter is PROTEUS's information window size which in conjunction with the time window size determines the number of time windows used in the prediction. Similar to the autocorrelation results in Figure 2(b), we see from Figure 10 that prediction gains from larger information windows in PROTEUS are marginal. Thus we can achieve accurate prediction using time windows within the last 8s.

5. APPLICATION OF PROTEUS

Applications can take advantage of network metric prediction to improve their performance. The exact benefit will depend on how each application uses the information obtained from PROTEUS. Here we show the improvement PROTEUS can provide to two RTC applications: a video conferencing application and an interactive software application, i.e., Draw Something.

5.1 Video Conferencing System

Equivalent video conferencing emulation. We describe how we realistically evaluate the video conferencing application to make use of PROTEUS in a working system, considering all the overhead of the associated changes with the small difference of running the client software on a legacy laptop instead of a mobile device due to software constraints.

There are standard methods to evaluate video conferencing using the H.264/AVC reference software [4] on PCs. However, there is no such equivalent open-source encoding/decoding suite on mobile platforms. Thus, to best effectively evaluate video conferencing on mobile platforms, we take the following steps: (i) we modify the H.264/AVC reference software so that the H.264 encoder can adjust the video codec bitrate and FEC rate for each video frame rather than sticking to fixed codec bitrate and FEC rate for an entire video stream; (ii) we use a 2GHz dual core Thinkpad T60 with 2G RAM to run the H.264 decoder, with the computation performance as close to off-the-shelf mobile devices as possible; and (iii) we replay the packet traces collected in cellular networks (i.e., FlowSet) to emulate mobile network performance for H.264, which ensures identical, reproducible, and representative mobile network conditions.

The packet sequencing and timing information seen by PROTEUS is exactly the same as it is in FlowSet, enabling PROTEUS to make the same predictions as it does in cellular networks. The emulation setup results in only two overestimations in evaluating the perceptual video quality. One is due to the Thinkpad T60 being more powerful than a mobile device, and the other is due to the elimination of the

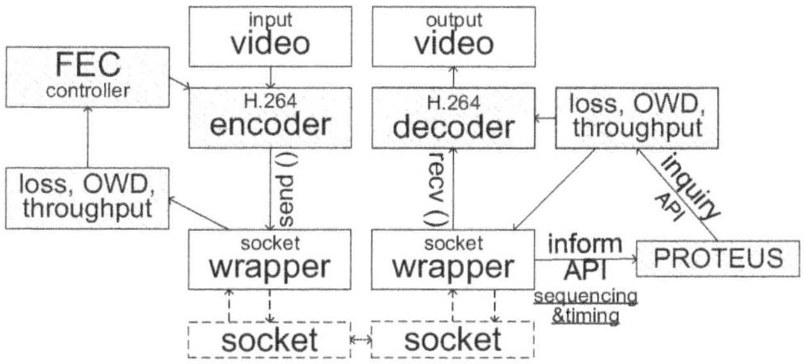

Figure 11: The platform setup to emulate mobile video conferencing. The dashed blocks and arrows are replayed using FlowSet to guarantee realistic mobile network condition.

cost for traffic transmitting over its network interface. The overestimations should be acceptable given that video conferencing applications such as Skype can work perfectly well on mobile devices with excellent network connections.

As depicted in Figure 11, we focus on evaluating the performance in downlink video conferencing, i.e., the video stream is adaptively encoded and sent from the server (either a content server or the other mobile device in P2P scenarios) to the client, where we can evaluate the perceptual quality of the received video stream. The H.264 decoder in Figure 11 represents the video conferencing application on the client, i.e., the mobile device emulated by the 2GHz dual core Thinkpad T60, while the H.264 encoder and FEC controller represent the counterpart on the server.

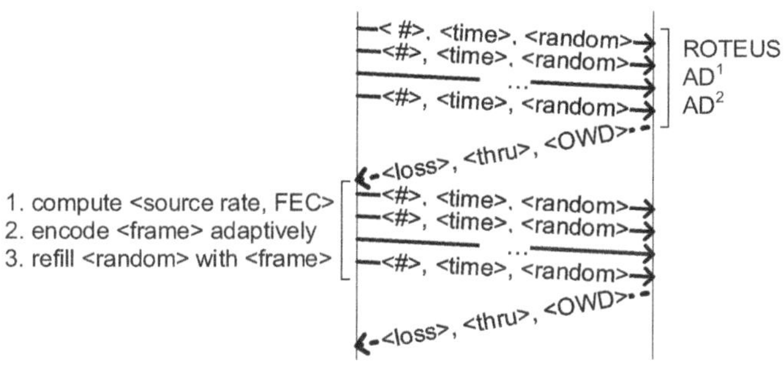

Figure 12: The packet trace replaying to guarantee reproducible mobile network conditions.

As shown in Figure 12, along a packet trace in FlowSet, each UDP packet from the sender includes a sequence number, a timestamp, and some random content. The receiver sends a placeholder packet at the end of every time window. When the packet trace is being collected, those placeholder packets are filled with random values. However, we refill these packets with the predicted performance metrics later in evaluating PROTEUS, AD^1, or AD^2. Once the sender sees a placeholder packet refilled with performance predictions, it computes the best source coding rate and FEC, and encodes the next frames accordingly. After the encoding, it refills the random content in UDP packets with newly encoded frames. Eventually, we decode the replayed packet trace on the receiver side and evaluate the perceptual quality.

By replaying network traces collected from the cellular network in FlowSet, we can reproduce representative mobile network conditions. We measure the video quality performance using standard video sequences shown in Table 3 (referred as VideoSet) [9]. As illustrated in Figure 11, given a video sequence in VideoSet, the H.264 encoder on the server translates the video sequence to a RTP network stream. To test the video quality under various and reproducible network conditions, for each flow in FlowSet, we replace its content with the encoded network stream respectively. On the client, the H.264 decoder decodes the received network stream and constructs the video for users. According to FlowSet, if a packet is lost or does not arrive in time at the de-jitter buffer, the corresponding frame may be corrupted so that the perceptual quality of the decoded video will be affected.

PROTEUS utilization in video conferencing. Based on past work, there are well established adaptations that applications take in response to changing network conditions. The quality of video conferencing is very sensitive to three network metrics, i.e., the packet loss, the one-way delay, and the throughput. To ensure good quality, the video conferencing application can tune several parameters.

- The video codec can adjust the compression ratio, trading source video quality with codec bitrate, by adjusting the quantization parameter (QP) of macroblocks [29, 30]. A smaller QP value results in better visual quality at the expense of a higher bitrate and higher bandwidth requirement.
- The application can insert an appropriate number of forward error correction (FEC) packets. This process allocates the total transmission rate amongst source bitrate and channel (error correction) bitrate.
- The application can adjust the de-jitter buffer size, which specifies how long the receiving end waits for data to arrive before it is played back. The de-jitter buffer size trades application latency with *late loss*. A larger de-jitter buffer size increases the chance that a packet will arrive in time for playback, but increases the end-to-end application latency. For video conferencing applications, the user cannot perceive an end-to-end delay (including propagation delay, network queuing delay, and time spent in the de-jitter buffer) lower than 200ms [10]. However, when the end-to-end delay is above this threshold, there is perceived degradation.

video	# of frames	sequence	resolution	size (MB)
akiyo	300	10/IPPP	QCIF,CIF	44
bowing	300	10/IPPP	QCIF,CIF	44
bridge(close)	2001	10/IPPP	QCIF,CIF	291
bridge(far)	2101	10/IPPP	CIF	305
foreman	300	10/IPPP	QCIF,CIF	44
highway	2000	10/IPPP	CIF	291

Table 3: The video sequences to reproduce video conferencing streams (VideoSet). The frame rate for all these video sequences is 30fps.

We denote the predicted packet loss rate, one-way delay, and throughput by the triplet with $(\epsilon, \delta, \mathtt{T})$. This is the predicted network performance obtained from the regression tree on the mobile device and delivered to the server. Given this network prediction, we set the application parameters as follows: (i) the video codec bitrate for a given frame is set to $\mathtt{R} = (1 - \alpha\epsilon)\mathtt{T}$ $(\alpha \geq 1)$; (ii) the FEC rate to $\alpha\epsilon\mathtt{T}$; and (iii) the receiver de-jitter buffer size to $\beta\delta$ seconds. α is a constant that determines the actual amount of FEC protec-

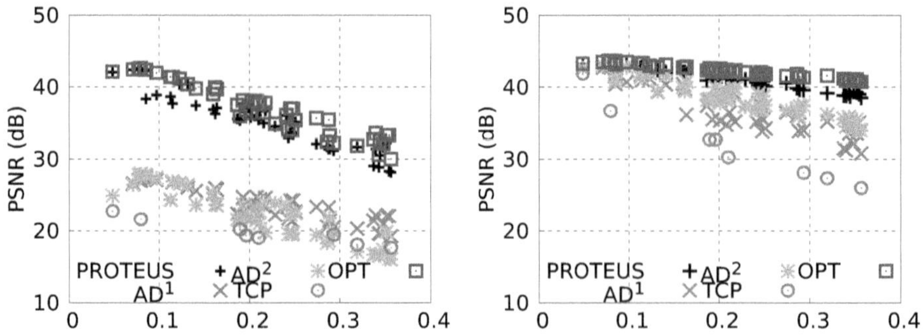

(a) 5th-percentile PSNR.

(b) 25th-percentile PSNR.

Figure 13: The PSNR for PROTEUS, AD[1], AD[2], TCP, and OPT, which assumes that we a priori know the exact loss rate.

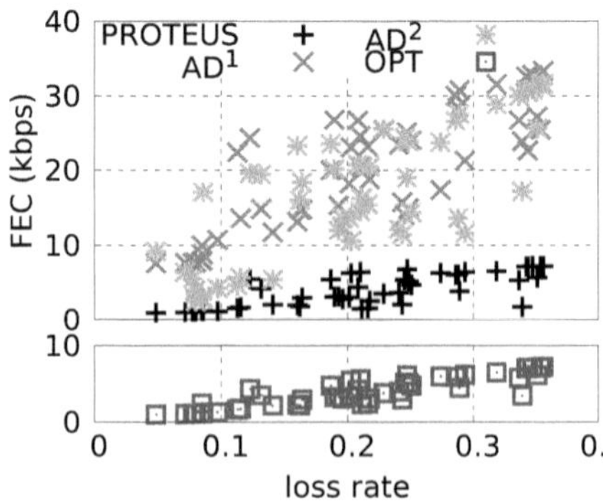

Figure 14: The FEC overhead. "OPT" shows the total FEC overhead in the optimal scenarios.

tion used. In the evaluation, $\alpha = 1$. The total estimated throughput T is divided amongst source rate and FEC rate. As an example, suppose T is estimated as 500kbps, the estimated loss rate is $\epsilon = 0.06$, and $\alpha = 2$ is used. With this, 440kbps should be used for source coding and 60kbps for FEC protection. With a video frame rate of 15fps and a packet size of 500 bytes, this approximately translates to 7 packets per frame of source coding and 1 packet per frame of FEC.

Once the video frames are coded into packets, the evaluation platform assumes that these packets go through a network that has characteristics obtained from the collected network trace. If the actual loss on the network is less than or equal to $\alpha\epsilon$T, the receiver has sufficient information to decode the frame, otherwise the frame is assumed to be lost. In addition to packet loss on the network, we also consider delay in the evaluation, assuming a de-jitter buffer size of $\beta\delta$ ($\beta \geq 1$), which is slightly larger than the estimated δ. In the above example, if two or more packets are lost or delayed later than $\beta\delta$, the respective frame is lost. In the evaluation, $\beta = 1$.

Perceptual video quality assessment. The H.264 decoder provides the ability to conceal lost frames. Upon decoding the sequence, which may potentially have some frames lost, we compare the decoded video sequence to the original and measure the peak signal-to-noise ratio (PSNR), which is a commonly used metric to measure video quality. This setup is used to repeatedly measure the video quality using the prediction obtained from PROTEUS, AD[1], and AD[2] over the various video sequences in VideoSet and over the various network traces in FlowSet.

If we underestimate ϵ (i.e., loss rate), then the application may add insufficient redundancy, which results in unrecoverable packet loss for the application. Otherwise, if we overestimate ϵ, then the application may add too much redundancy causing the video codec bitrate to be lower than needed, resulting in poorer video quality. Thus, both underestimation and overestimation of the future network performance can lower the perceptual video quality. We analyze the effect of network parameter mis-prediction on video quality for the three prediction techniques, PROTEUS, AD[1], and AD[2]. We also analyze the performance hypothesizing that we exactly know the loss rate and insert just the right amount of FEC to counteract any packet loss. It is possible as we have the network traces. This optimal scheme is denoted as OPT.

For each video sequence in VideoSet, we run all the network traces from FlowSet using each of the four methods (PROTEUS, AD[1], AD[2], and OPT). For each of the four methods, we compute a distribution of PSNR. In Figure 13, we show the 5th and 25th percentiles of the PSNR as a function of loss rate for each of the four methods. We purposefully show the low PSNR values in the distribution since this is what most affects overall user satisfaction and is a measure of how each of the three schemes performs in tough network conditions. In addition to the four adaptive methods using UDP, we evaluate the adaptive bitrate streaming over TCP as well assuming that the encoded bitrate is always adapted to the throughput in the current time window. To guarantee the network conditions for TCP and UDP experiments are comparable, for each TCP flow, we create UDP packets back-to-back lasting for the same duration. In Figure 13, the distribution of PSNR for TCP flows is represented as the function of the loss rate of the back-to-back UDP flow's loss rate.

In general, if a frame is lost, the PSNR of the other frames that reference the lost frame becomes very low, e.g., PSNR <25dB. Since PROTEUS can accurately predict loss rate with almost 99% accuracy, there are very few cases (i.e., <1%) where we see unrecoverable packet loss. Thus, as we see from Figure 13(a), even the 5th percentile PSNR shows no packet loss using PROTEUS. The only reason the 5th percentile PSNR is below OPT is due to over-protection, which reduces the video codec bitrate. This reduction in PSNR in PROTEUS when compared to OPT (due to over-protection) is on the order of 1dB, whereas the reduction in PSNR in AD[1] and AD[2] (due to unrecoverable lost packets) is on the order of 15dB. As loss rate increases, the PSNR using PROTEUS decreases but stays close to OPT. It is obvious that increasing loss rate results in decreased capacity. Since a larger portion of the total throughput has to be allocated to FEC, we see a reduction in PSNR. To show the visual effect of unrecoverable packet loss, we show representative frames in the 5th percentile of PSNR values in Figure 15 using the schemes AD[1,2], TCP, and PROTEUS. It is clear that unrecoverable packet loss results in substantial video quality degradation. As PROTEUS may overestimate the actual loss rate, there will inevitably be some cases where

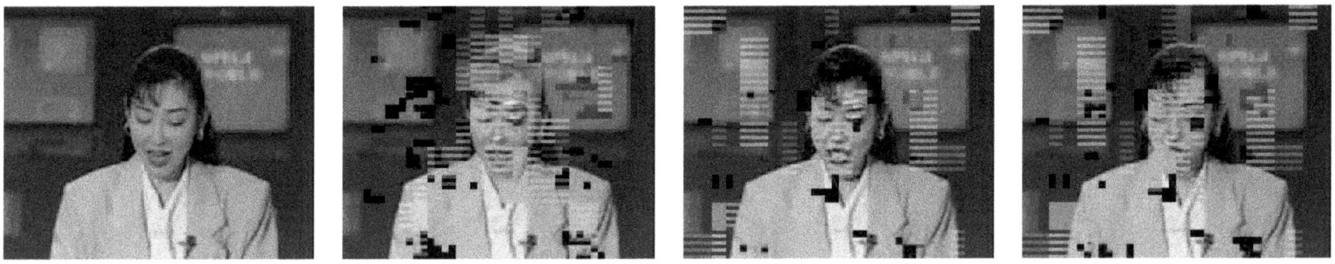

(a) 36dB – PROTEUS. (b) 23dB – AD^1. (c) 23dB – AD^2. (d) 20dB – TCP.

Figure 15: The perceptual video quality corresponding to the 5th-%ile PSNR (using "akiyo" in Table 3).

we over-protect. In Figure 14, we show the bitrate taken by FEC packets which are not used to correct any loss. The bottom plot shows the amount of needed FEC to correct for packet loss. As we see, as the loss rate increases, the amount of needed protection also increases. The top plot in Figure 14 shows the amount of additional FEC beyond the needed amount which is applied when using each of the three schemes to predict the loss rate. We see that indeed PROTEUS does add a certain amount of FEC overhead. However, it is fairly small, and as we have seen from Figure 13, it only results in about a 1dB reduction in PSNR. Even at high loss rates, this overhead is less than 10kbps. The overhead for AD^1 and AD^2 is actually much higher as it only reacts once loss has already started occurring. Just because there was loss in the previous time window does not guarantee that there will be loss in the future time windows. So not only do AD^1 and AD^2 suffer from unrecoverable packet loss, they also actually insert more FEC than PROTEUS.

5.2 Interactive Software Application

Many interactive software applications have bursty traffic patterns, e.g., the burst can consist of a screen update. A good measure of the performance of such interactive software applications can be the time taken to deliver the burst of data. However, as opposed to throughput sensitive applications such as file downloading, a burst is relatively small in duration and thus the latency caused by packet loss recovery becomes significant in determining performance. Therefore, an adaptive UDP based scheme that appropriately controls the throughput allocated to source and FEC becomes important in determining application performance [33], especially for the channels with packet loss such as wireless networks.

Here we consider a particular application, Draw Something, to show how PROTEUS can benefit interactive software applications such as desktop sharing and multi-player gaming. In Draw Something, two players alternate turns between drawing a picture to convey a guessword for the partner to guess. In each turn, the stroke-by-stroke drawing animation playing back to the partner results in a traffic burst. We rely on trace analysis to evaluate how PROTEUS can benefit such an application. We capture the application traffic via `tcpdump` on Android and identify the traffic bursts corresponding to drawing animations. The trace consists of a duration lasting five hours and consisting of hundreds of bursts.

To measure the improvement of an adaptive UDP scheme using PROTEUS over TCP, we replay the traffic using UDP plus PROTEUS (UDP/PROTEUS) and measure the time between the first packet of a burst being sent to the last packet in the burst being received. UDP/PROTEUS adds an appropriate amount of FEC if packet loss is anticipated. A poor prediction of loss rate can result in higher burst delivery time due to either retransmission or over-protection. To verify that the traffic replaying under UDP/PROTEUS experiences roughly the same network conditions as the Draw Something's original trace over TCP, we compare their median perceptual delay. Figure 16 shows the distribution of the perceptual delay over different burst size. As the median perceptual delay for UDP/PROTEUS is very close to TCP's, we expect that UDP/PROTEUS experiences similar network conditions. According to Figure 16, when the burst size is very small, TCP and UDP/PROTEUS perform equally at any percentile in the distribution. However, when the burst size grows to 10KB and larger (e.g., 20KB), UDP/PROTEUS performs much better, particularly in the 75-90th percentile perceptual delay, which may easily produce user dissatisfaction. UDP/PROTEUS reduces the 90th percentile perceptual delay by roughly 1s when the burst size is around 10KB. When the burst size is around 20KB, UDP/PROTEUS's 90th percentile perceptual delay is 2s while TCP's is up to 6s.

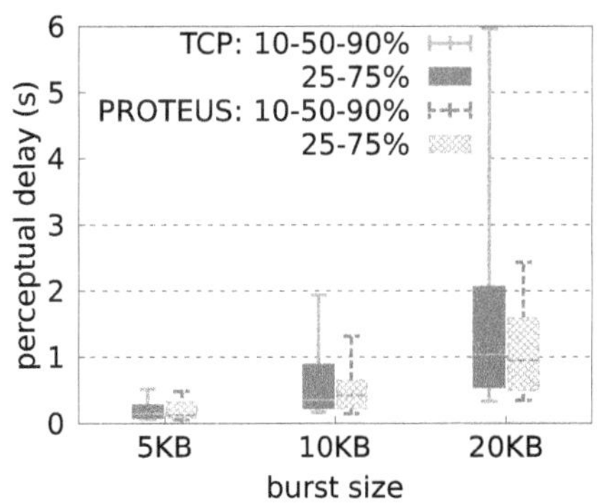

Figure 16: The perceptual delay in Draw Something.

6. RELATED WORK

There has been a significant amount of previous work proposing solutions for adapting to varying network performance [1, 2, 5, 7, 19, 22, 23, 34, 42, 48]. However, these proposed solutions adjust the application behavior based on the "current" network condition. By then, performance degradation may be observed already. PROTEUS is fundamentally different from these previous adaptation approaches in that PROTEUS proactively forecasts the achievable network performance rather than passively reacting to performance degradation. This allows applications to modify their behavior in anticipation of degrading network condition which can significantly improve performance.

The key to the effectiveness of PROTEUS is network performance predictability. There have been previous measurement studies to investigate the network behavior of cellular networks [13, 19, 20, 24, 31, 32, 44]. Among these measurement studies, the existence of network predictability has been indicated from certain aspects. For example, Liu et al. observed that the time for a mobile device to stay in any particular data rate state is on the order of hundreds of time slots (with each time slot being 1.67ms) in a EV-DO network [31]. Manweiler et al. found that in AT&T and T-Mobile networks, the network latency measured in a 15-minute time window has certain dependency on the latency of a previous time window [32]. Standing upon the shoulder of previous studies, PROTEUS answers the following three questions. First, how predictable are cellular networks? Second, what network features can be used for performance prediction? Third, how accurate is the prediction?

There has also been a significant amount of previous work that studies predictability in mobile (cellular) networks with the goal of improving application performance [32, 37, 39, 40, 46]. Access pattern predictability is investigated with the attempt to reduce connectivity overhead due to frequent user mobility in [36, 37] and with the attempt to switch to better access networks in [12, 38, 43]. PROTEUS distinguishes itself from these studies in two aspects. First, PROTEUS forecasts network performance at run time, rather than offline. As cellular networks are well-known to be highly variable, a one-time, offline prediction will not work well because it will be quickly out-dated. Second, PROTEUS's performance prediction is much more fine-grained. Unlike previous studies that usually attempt to improve performance for non-real-time bandwidth intensive applications, which are not sensitive to packet loss and one-way delay, PROTEUS targets a broad spectrum of applications including RTC applications that are sensitive to packet loss and one-way delay.

To the best of our knowledge, our study is the first one proposing a fine-grained, real-time solution for predicting future network performance over cellular networks, which allows applications to react before network degradation occurs.

7. CONCLUDING REMARKS

In this study, we systematically quantified the predictability of network performance metrics in three major cellular networks: AT&T, T-Mobile, and Sprint. For all three carriers, we identified the existence of strong predictability of network performance, even over a short term window e.g., 0.5s. To take advantage of this predictability, we proposed a system PROTEUS, which collects network performance information being observed by applications, employs regression trees to learn network performance patterns, and forecasts future network performance to benefit application performance. PROTEUS can predict the occurrence of packet loss within a time window for 98% of the time windows, occurrence of long one-way delay for 97% of the time windows, and the throughput within a median error of 10kbps with average throughput ranging from 100–800kbps. By using PROTEUS in a video conferencing scenarios, we can improve the PSNR of the perceived video by 15dB when compared against traditional performance adaptation techniques. Compared with the hypothesized optimal scenario in which the application knows exactly which packets will be lost, PROTEUS is only 1–2dB worse.

We believe that PROTEUS is a comprehensive and effective network performance forecasting framework for use by mobile applications especially for use over cellular networks. PROTEUS can also inspire the development of challenging applications on mobile devices.

8. ACKNOWLEDGMENTS

We would like to thank the reviewers and Koen Langendoen for shepherding the paper. This research was sponsored in part by NSF grants CNS-1059372, CNS-1050157, CNS-1039657, and CNS-0939707 and Navy award N00014-09-1-0705.

9. REFERENCES

[1] Adobe HTTP Dynamic Streaming. http://www.adobe.com/products/hds-dynamic-streaming.html.

[2] Apple HTTP Live Streaming. https://developer.apple.com/resources/http-streaming.

[3] Cisco TelePresence Secure Communications and Signaling. http://www.cisco.com/en/US/docs/solutions/Enterprise/Video/telepresence.html.

[4] H.264/AVC JM Reference Software. http://iphome.hhi.de/suehring/tml.

[5] IIS Smooth Streaming. http://www.iis.net/download/SmoothStreaming.

[6] ISO/IEC DIS 23009-1.2 Dynamic Adaptive Streaming over HTTP (DASH). http://www.iso.org/iso/iso_catalogue/catalogue_tc/catalogue_detail.htm?csnumber=57623.

[7] Octoshape Broadcasting Flash Media Multi-Bit Rate. https://support.octoshape.com/entries/20655458-broadcasting-flash-media-multi-bit-rate.

[8] RTCWeb Status Pages. http://tools.ietf.org/wg/rtcweb/.

[9] YUV Video Sequences. http://trace.eas.asu.edu/yuv.

[10] ITU-T recommendation G. 114, 2000.

[11] S. Akhshabi, A. Begen, and C. Dovrolis. An Experimental Evaluation of Rate-Adaptation Algorithms in Adaptive Streaming over HTTP. In *Proc. ACM MMSys*, 2011.

[12] A. Aljadhai and T. Znati. Predictive Mobility Support for QoS Provisioning in Mobile Wireless Environments. *IEEE J. Selected Areas in Communications*, 2001.

[13] N. Antunes, C. Fricker, P. Robert, and D. Tibi. Metastability of CDMA Cellular Systems. In *Proc. ACM MOBICOM*, 2006.

[14] A. Balasubramanian, R. Mahajan, and A. Venkataramani. Augmenting Mobile 3G Using WiFi. In *Proc. ACM MobiSys*, 2010.

[15] J.-C. Bolot and A. Vega-García. Control Mechanisms for Packet Audio in the Internet. In *Proc. IEEE INFOCOM*, 1996.

[16] A. Bouch, M. Sasse, and H. DeMeer. Of Packets and People: A User-Centered Approach to Quality of Service. In *Proc. IEEE IWQoS*, 2000.

[17] L. Breiman. *Classification and Regression Trees.* Chapman & Hall/CRC, 1984.

[18] T. Bu, L. Li, and R. Ramjee. Generalized Proportional Fair Scheduling in Third Generation Wireless Data Networks. In *Proc. IEEE INFOCOM*, 2006.

[19] R. Chakravorty, S. Banerjee, P. Rodriguez, J. Chesterfield, and I. Pratt. Performance Optimizations for Wireless Wide-Area Networks: Comparative Study and Experimental Evaluation. In *Proc. ACM MOBICOM*, 2004.

[20] M. Chan and R. Ramjee. TCP/IP Performance over 3G Wireless Links with Rate and Delay Variation. In *Proc. ACM MOBICOM*, 2002.

[21] M. Chuah, W. Luo, and X. Zhang. Impacts of Inactivity Timer Values on UMTS System Capacity. In *IEEE Conference on Wireless Communications and Networking Conference*, 2002.

[22] I. Haratcherev, J. Taal, K. Langendoen, R. Lagendijk, and H. Sips. Optimized Video-Streaming over 802.11 by Cross-Layer Signalling. *IEEE Computer Magazine*, 44(1):115–121, 2006.

[23] B. Higgins, J. Flinn, T. Giuli, B. Noble, C. Peplin, and D. Watson. Informed Mobile Prefetching. In *Proc. ACM MobiSys*, 2012.

[24] J. Huang, Q. Xu, B. Tiwana, Z. Mao, M. Zhang, and P. Bahl. Anatomizing Application Performance Differences on Smartphones. In *Proc. ACM MobiSys*, 2010.

[25] A. Jalali, R. Padovani, and R. Pankaj. Data Throughput of CDMA-HDR a High Efficiency-High Data Rate Personal Communication Wireless System. In *Proc. IEEE VTC*, 2000.

[26] H. Jiang, Z. Liu, Y. Wang, K. Lee, and I. Rhee. Understanding Bufferbloat in Cellular Networks. In *Proc. ACM SIGCOMM IMC*, 2012.

[27] N. Kolehmainen, J. Puttonen, P. Kela, T. Ristaniemi, T. Henttonen, and M. Moisio. Channel Quality Indication Reporting Schemes for UTRAN Long Term Evolution Downlink. In *Proc. IEEE VTC*, 2008.

[28] H. Kushner and P. Whiting. Convergence of Proportional-Fair Sharing Algorithms under General Conditions. *IEEE Trans. Wireless Communications*, 2004.

[29] H. Lee, T. Chiang, and Y. Zhang. Scalable Rate Control for MPEG-4 Video. *IEEE Trans. Circuits and Systems for Video Technology*, 2000.

[30] Z. Li, F. Pan, K. Lim, X. Lin, and S. Rahardja. Adaptive Rate Control for H. 264. In *Proc. IEEE ICIP*, 2004.

[31] X. Liu, A. Sridharan, S. Machiraju, M. Seshadri, and H. Zang. Experiences in a 3G Network: Interplay between the Wireless Channel and Applications. In *Proc. ACM MOBICOM*, 2008.

[32] J. Manweiler, S. Agarwal, M. Zhang, R. Roy Choudhury, and P. Bahl. Switchboard: A Matchmaking System for Multiplayer Mobile Games. In *Proc. ACM MobiSys*, 2011.

[33] S. Mehrotra, J. Li, and Y.-Z. Huang. Optimizing FEC Transmission Strategy for Minimizing Delay in Lossless Sequential Streaming. *IEEE Trans. Multimedia*, 2011.

[34] I. Mohomed, J. Cai, S. Chavoshi, and E. De Lara. Context-Aware Interactive Content Adaptation. In *Proc. ACM MobiSys*, 2006.

[35] S. Moon, P. Skelly, and D. Towsley. Estimation and Removal of Clock Skew from Network Delay Measurements. In *Proc. IEEE INFOCOM*, 1999.

[36] A. Nicholson, Y. Chawathe, M. Chen, B. Noble, and D. Wetherall. Improved Access Point Selection. In *Proc. ACM MobiSys*, 2006.

[37] A. Nicholson and B. Noble. Breadcrumbs: Forecasting Mobile Connectivity. In *Proc. ACM MOBICOM*, 2008.

[38] J. Pang, B. Greenstein, M. Kaminsky, D. McCoy, and S. Seshan. WiFi-Reports: Improving Wireless Network Selection with Collaboration. In *Proc. ACM MobiSys*, 2009.

[39] S. Schubert, F. Uyeda, N. Vasic, N. Cherukuri, and D. Kostic. Bandwidth Adaptation in Streaming Overlays. In *Proc. IEEE COMSNETS*, 2010.

[40] A. Schulman, V. Navda, R. Ramjee, N. Spring, P. Deshpande, C. Grunewald, K. Jain, and V. Padmanabhan. Bartendr: A Practical Approach to Energy-Aware Cellular Data Scheduling. In *Proc. ACM MOBICOM*, 2010.

[41] H. Schulzrinne. RTP: A Transport Protocol for Real-Time Applications. *IETF, Request For Comments 3550*, 2003.

[42] S. Sen, N. Madabhushi, and S. Banerjee. Scalable WiFi Media Delivery through Adaptive Broadcasts. In *Proc. USENIX NSDI*, 2010.

[43] L. Song, U. Deshpande, U. Kozat, D. Kotz, and R. Jain. Predictability of WLAN Mobility and Its Effects on Bandwidth Provisioning. In *Proc. IEEE INFOCOM*, 2006.

[44] W. Tan, F. Lam, and W. Lau. An Empirical Study on 3G Network Capacity and Performance. In *Proc. IEEE INFOCOM*, 2007.

[45] F. Tso, J. Teng, W. Jia, and D. Xuan. Mobility: A Double-Edged Sword for HSPA Networks: A Large-Scale Test on Hong Kong Mobile HSPA Networks. In *Proc. ACM MobiHoc*, 2010.

[46] R. Wolski, N. Spring, and C. Peterson. Implementing A Performance Forecasting System for Metacomputing The Network Weather Service. In *Proc. IEEE Supercomputing*, 1997.

[47] Q. Xu, J. Erman, A. Gerber, Z. Mao, J. Pang, and S. Venkataraman. Identifying Diverse Usage Behaviors of Smartphone Apps. In *Proc. ACM SIGCOMM IMC*, 2011.

[48] Z. Zhuang, T. Chang, R. Sivakumar, and A. Velayutham. A3: Application-Aware Acceleration for Wireless Data Networks. In *Proc. ACM MOBICOM*, 2006.

NuActiv: Recognizing Unseen New Activities Using Semantic Attribute-Based Learning

Heng-Tze Cheng, Feng-Tso Sun, Martin Griss
Electrical and Computer Engineering
Carnegie Mellon University
{hengtze, fengtso}@cmu.edu,
martin.griss@sv.cmu.edu

Paul Davis, Jianguo Li, Di You
Applied Research Center
Motorola Mobility
{pdavis, jianguo.li, di.you}
@motorola.com

ABSTRACT

We study the problem of how to recognize a new human activity when we have never seen any training example of that activity before. Recognizing human activities is an essential element for user-centric and context-aware applications. Previous studies showed promising results using various machine learning algorithms. However, most existing methods can only recognize the activities that were previously seen in the training data. A previously unseen activity class cannot be recognized if there were no training samples in the dataset. Even if all of the activities can be enumerated in advance, labeled samples are often time consuming and expensive to get, as they require huge effort from human annotators or experts.

In this paper, we present *NuActiv*, an activity recognition system that can recognize a human activity even when there are no training data for that activity class. Firstly, we designed a new representation of activities using semantic attributes, where each attribute is a human readable term that describes a basic element or an inherent characteristic of an activity. Secondly, based on this representation, a two-layer zero-shot learning algorithm is developed for activity recognition. Finally, to reinforce recognition accuracy using minimal user feedback, we developed an active learning algorithm for activity recognition. Our approach is evaluated on two datasets, including a 10-exercise-activity dataset we collected, and a public dataset of 34 daily life activities. Experimental results show that using semantic attribute-based learning, NuActiv can generalize knowledge to recognize unseen new activities. Our approach achieved up to 79% accuracy in unseen activity recognition.

Categories and Subject Descriptors

I.5.2 [**Pattern Recognition**]: Design Methodology—*Classifier design and evaluation*; C.3 [**Special-Purpose and Application-Based Systems**]: Real-time and embedded systems

MobiSys'13, June 25-28, 2013, Taipei, Taiwan

General Terms

Algorithms, Design, Experimentation, Performance

Keywords

Activity recognition, zero-shot learning, semantic attributes, active learning, machine learning, mobile sensing, wearable computing, context-aware computing

1. INTRODUCTION

The understanding of context and human activities is a core component that supports and enables various kinds of context-aware, user-centric mobile applications [10, 11, 14, 29]. Examples of application areas include user behavior modeling for marketing and advertising, health care and home monitoring, context-based personal assistants, context-enabled games, and social networks [14].

There has been extensive research on activity recognition using various sensors and various machine learning algorithms [2,18,21,25,40]. To recognize the context of a mobile phone user, most existing approaches require two steps: (1) collect and label a set of training data for every activity class that the system aims to detect, and (2) classify the current sensor readings into one of the pre-defined classes. However, labeled examples are often time consuming and expensive to obtain, as they require a lot of effort from test subjects, human annotators, or domain experts. Therefore, it has been reported that a fully supervised learning method, where labeled examples from different context are provided to the system, may not be practical for many applications [24,36,37]. More importantly, existing approaches to activity recognition cannot recognize a previously unseen new activity if there were no training samples of that activity in the dataset. According to the activity lexicon in the American Time Use Survey by U.S. Bureau of Labor Statistics [38], there are at least 462 different activities that people do in their daily lives. Considering the diversity of people and cultures that were not covered by the study, the actual number of activities is likely even larger. However, the fundamental problems in the existing activity recognition methods prevent the systems from recognizing any previously unseen activity and from extending to tens or hundreds of different human activity classes.

In light of existing problems, there are two major research questions we aimed to answer:

Q1. How to recognize a previously unseen new activity class when we have no training data from users?

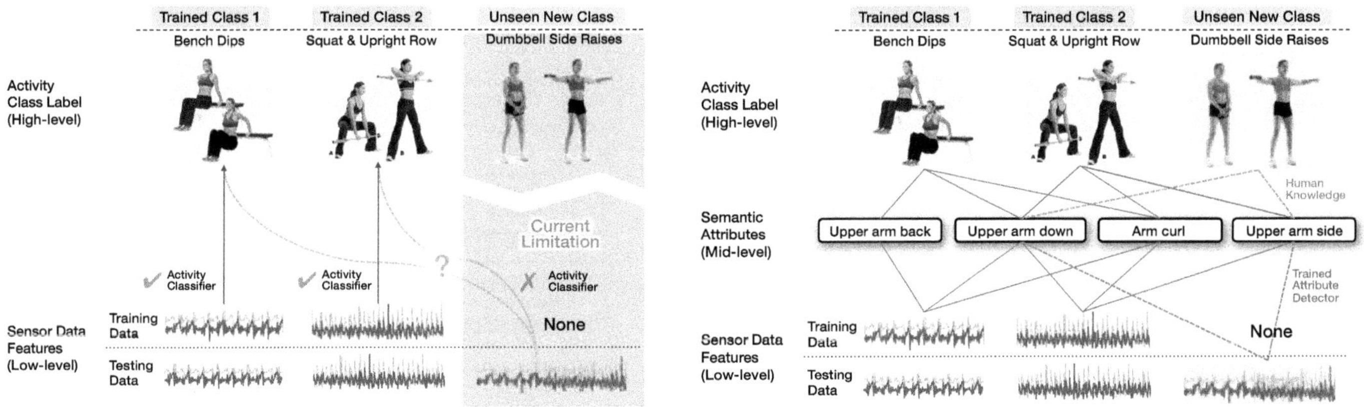

(a) Existing supervised-learning approaches. (b) Proposed semantic attribute-based learning.

Figure 1: Illustration of the comparison between existing supervised learning approach to activity recognition and the proposed semantic attribute-based learning approach.

Q2. If we have the opportunity to ask users for labeled training data, how to reinforce the recognition accuracy using minimal help from users?

In this paper, we present the *NuActiv* system to recognize human activity even when there are no training data for a particular activity class. NuActiv can generalize previously learned knowledge and extend its capability to recognize new activity classes. The design of NuActiv is inspired by the following observations:

- *Many human activities and context types share the same underlying semantic attributes*: For example, the attribute "`Sitting`" can be observed in the activities of both "having lunch in the cafeteria" and "working at a desk". Therefore, the statistical model of an attribute can be transferred from one activity to the another.
- *The limit of supervised learning can be overcome by incorporating human knowledge*: Rather than collecting sensor data and labels for every context, using nameable attributes allows humans to describe a context type even without the process of sensor data collection. For example, one can easily associate the activity "office working" with the motion-related attributes such as "`Sitting`," "`HandsOnTable`," and sound-related attributes such as "`PrinterSound`," "`KeyboardSound`," and "`Conversations`."

Based on these observations, we developed the NuActiv system to tackle the two research questions. The research question Q1 is often referred to as the *zero-shot learning* problem, where the goal is to learn a classifier that can recognize new classes that have never appeared in the training dataset [30]. While having been shown successful in the recent computer vision literature [13], zero-shot learning has been less studied in the area of human activity recognition.

There are several challenges when applying zero-shot learning to activity recognition. Firstly, while there exist some well-established attributes in the field of computer vision (such as shapes and colors), it has not been shown what kinds of representations or attributes are useful for recognizing human activities from sensor data. Secondly, most previous work on zero-shot learning focused on static image data, which is quite different from sequential sensor data in activity recognition.

To address these challenges, we designed a new representation of human activities by decomposing high-level activities into combinations of semantic attributes, where each attribute is a human readable term that describes a basic element or an intrinsic characteristic of an activity. The semantic attributes are detected based on the low-level features, which capture the temporal dynamics in the sequential sensor data. Using this representation, a two-layer attribute-based learning algorithm is developed for activity recognition. Figure 1 illustrates the difference between existing supervised-learning-based approach and our proposed semantic attribute-based learning approach, using exercise activities as examples.

For the research question Q2, to reinforce the activity recognition accuracy by leveraging user feedback, we extend the previous work in active learning [35] by designing an outlier-aware active learning algorithm and a hybrid stream/pool-based sampling scheme, which is suitable for the scenario of activity recognition using mobile or wearable devices. We integrated active learning in the framework of zero-shot learning for activity recognition, so that the system is able to not only recognize unseen activities but also actively request labels from users when possible.

The main contributions of the work include:

- The design and implementation of NuActiv, a new system to recognize human activity even when there are no training data for a particular activity class.
- The design and development of the semantic attributes as a representation for human activities, and the zero-shot learning algorithm to learn high-level human activities by decomposing them into combinations of semantic attributes.
- The design and development of the outlier-aware active learning algorithm to efficiently reinforce the recognition accuracy using minimal user feedback.
- The evaluation of the activity recognition system on two real-world human activity datasets, one in the daily life activity domain and the other in the exercise activity domain.

The paper is organized as follows. The system design and the algorithms are presented in Sections 2 and 3. We present

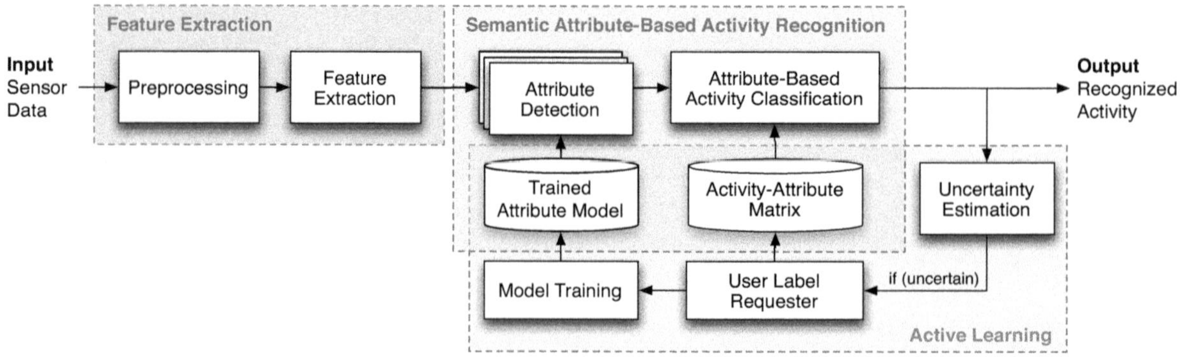

Figure 2: The architecture of the NuActiv activity recognition system.

the dataset collection, evaluation methodology, experimental results, and discussions in Section 4 and 5. In Section 6, we discuss and compare related work. The conclusion is presented in Section 7.

2. NUACTIV SYSTEM OVERVIEW

2.1 Scenarios and Design Considerations

NuActiv is designed for general human activity recognition in the field of mobile, wearable, and pervasive computing. The learning and recognition framework is independent of sensor data types or device types, so the source of sensor data does not limit to mobile phones but can also be wearable devices. Wearable mobile devices are becoming increasingly available in the commercial market [1]. Phones and devices can be worn as wrist watches (e.g. MotoACTV [27]), glasses (e.g. Google Glass [8]), and more. Advances in nanotechnology are further driving this trend by introducing flexible materials. These new wearable devices enable a wide range of context sensing, inference, and pervasive computing applications [14]. With these considerations in mind, in this work we choose phones and wristwatches with inertial sensors as examples to demonstrate two scenarios of activity domain: *daily life activities* and *exercise activities*.

The first scenario is daily life activity monitoring [9, 18]. Suppose we have the training data for two activities "`ReadingAtHome`" and "`Driving`". What if we want to detect if the user is "`ReadingOnTrain`"? Instead of hiring subjects to collect and label new sensor data, our goal is to directly recognize the new activity class "`ReadingOnTrain`" by reusing the model we already trained for "`ReadingAtHome`" and "`Driving`".

The second scenario is exercise activity detection. Detecting physical exercises and sports activities is useful for health and fitness monitoring applications [7, 28]. Through experiments on real-world sensor data, we will show that our semantic attribute-based learning applies well to this activity domain because many exercise activities are built up by the same underlying attributes, as illustrated in Figure 1.

Daily life activities are of bigger interest because they comprise the most part of people's lives. On the other hand, daily life activities are also arguably of much larger variation because different people do the same things differently. Even the same person can do one activity differently at different times. In this research, we started by testing our system and algorithms for the exercise activity scenario because the activities are well-defined, repeatable, and of lower variation among different people. After observing the effectiveness of our approach on exercise activities, we further generalized the approach to daily life activities.

2.2 System Architecture of NuActiv

The system architecture of NuActiv is shown in Figure 2. NuActiv consists of three main components:

(1) Feature Extraction: This component preprocesses the raw sensor data from various sensor inputs, and extract low-level signal features from the processed sensor data. (Section 3.1).

(2) Semantic Attribute-Based Activity Recognition: This component can be further divided into two part. The first part is *Attribute Detection*, which transform low-level features into a vector of human-readable semantic attributes. The second part is *Attribute-Based Activity Classification*, which classifies the detected attribute vector as one of the activity classes given the *activity-attribute matrix*, even if no training data exist for some of the target activity classes. (Section 3.2).

(3) Active Learning: Given the output recognized activity class, the active learning component estimates the uncertainty of the recognition result. Only when the result is estimated to be highly uncertain, the *user label requester* prompts the user for feedback or ground-truth labels. The labels are then used for re-training and updating models for attribute detection and activity classification. The function of this component is to reinforce activity recognition accuracy using minimal user feedback (Section 3.3).

All of the components can run on a mobile phone or sensor-enabled wristwatch in our system implementation. In cases where offline model training is needed, the attribute detection models can be pre-trained on a server and then be downloaded to a mobile device.

3. SYSTEM DESIGN AND ALGORITHMS

3.1 Feature Extraction

The NuActiv system is agnostic to input data type. Any kind of sensor data can be fed into the system for learning an activity recognition model. In this work, we select inertial sensor data from two activity domains—exercise activities and daily life activities—as examples to demonstrate the effectiveness of the system. The features we use include:

- The mean and standard deviation of sensor data in dimension x, y, and z.

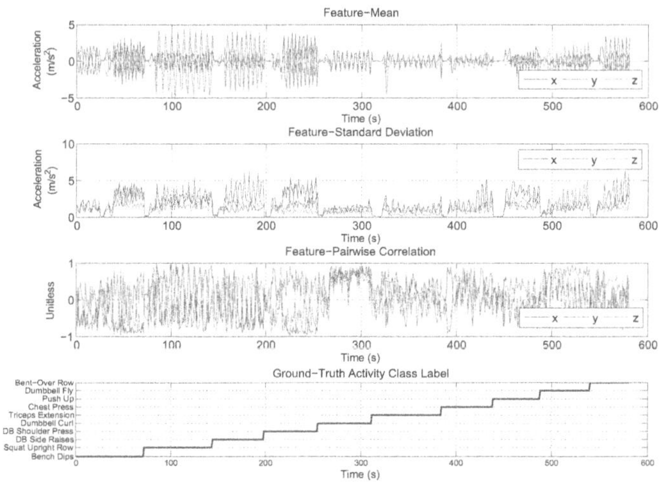

Figure 3: Examples of features extracted from acceleration data for each exercise activity.

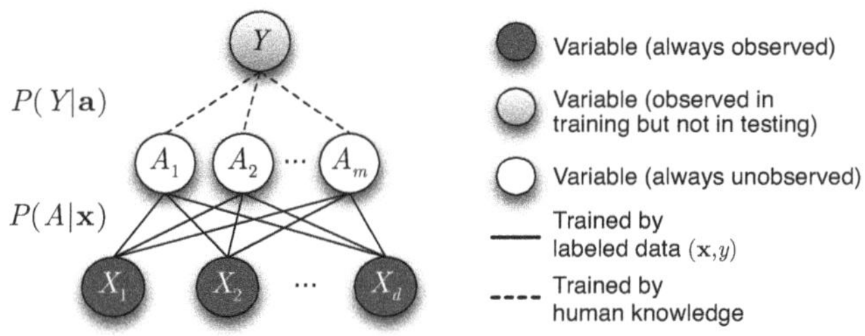

Figure 4: Graphical representation of semantic attribute-based activity recognition.

- Pairwise correlation between each pair of dimensions x, y, and z.
- Local slope of sensor data in dimension x, y, and z in using 1st-order linear regression.
- Zero-crossing rate in dimension x, y, and z.

Some examples of extracted features are shown in Figure 3. The sensor data and settings used in each dataset are described in Section 4.2. To capture the temporal changes of the features, we further include the nth-order temporal features. Specifically, we concatenate the feature vector at time t with those at time $t-1, t-2, ..., t-n$ (n is empirically set to 2 using a 10-fold cross validation on the validation set in our experiments). For the daily life activity dataset [9], we also include time of day as an additional input feature, as it carries important information about the daily life routines of a user.

3.2 Semantic Attribute-Based Activity Recognition

3.2.1 Background and Problem Formulation

In this section, we describe the background and formulation of the problem of activity recognition with unseen classes. The formulation is inspired by and adapted from previous work in attribute-based classification and zero-shot learning [13, 30].

The problem of activity recognition is formalized as follows. Let Y be the class label, a random variable that can be one of the k classes in the activity class space $\mathcal{Y} = \{y_1, y_2, ..., y_k\}$. $\mathbf{x} = [X_1, X_2, ..., X_d]$ is a d-dimensional vector containing d input features in the feature space $\mathcal{X}$. We want to learn a classifier function $f : \mathcal{X} \rightarrow \mathcal{Y}$ where the function outputs an estimate or prediction of the most likely class label y given an input feature vector $\mathbf{x}$. Most of the existing approaches in activity recognition train the classifier f using a training dataset $D_{train} = \{(\mathbf{x}_i, y_i) | i = 1, 2, ..., N\}$, which contains N pairs of input features and ground-truth output class labels. If we have training instances for every class in $\mathcal{Y}$, we are able to train a classifier f. However, if there are no training data for a subset of classes $\mathcal{Y}$, we are not able to predict those classes.

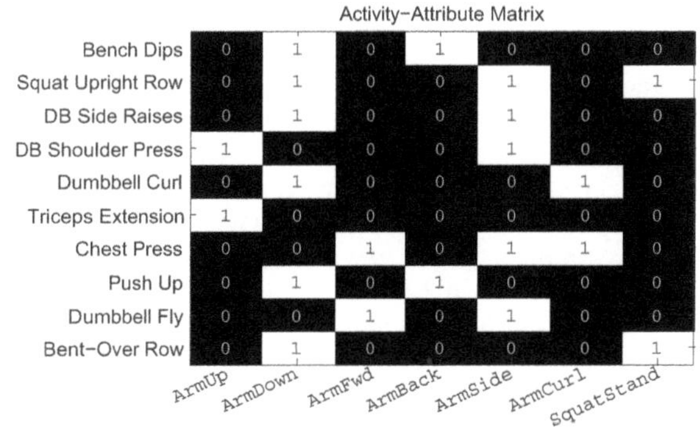

Figure 5: Activity-attribute matrix for exercise activities. The rows are the activities and the columns are the attributes.

In this work, we aim to solve the problem of recognizing previously unseen activity classes. Suppose $\mathcal{Y} = \{\{y_1, y_2, ..., y_s\}, \{y_{s+1}, ..., y_{s+u}\}\} = \mathcal{Y}_S \cup \mathcal{Y}_U$. $\mathcal{Y}_S$ is the set of *seen classes*, where there exists some training data for every class in $\mathcal{Y}_S$. $\mathcal{Y}_U$ is the *unseen classes* set where there are no training data for any class in $\mathcal{Y}_U$. The problem is: How to recognize an unseen class $y \in \mathcal{Y}_U$?

The idea is to first transform low-level features $\mathbf{x}$ into a vector of mid-level semantic attributes $\mathbf{a} = [A_1, A_2, ..., A_m]$ in the attribute space $\mathcal{A}$. Each attribute corresponds to an atomic physical motion or a specific characteristic of a complex activity. If every high-level activity in $\mathcal{Y}$ can be mapped to a point in the attribute space $\mathcal{A}$, then it is possible for us to recognize every activity class $y \in \mathcal{Y}$ given an accurately detected attribute vector $\mathbf{a}$. Since every semantic attribute in $\mathbf{a}$ is a human readable term, the mapping between y and $\mathbf{a}$ can be defined based on human knowledge without training data. Without this attribute layer, the direct mapping between y and $\mathbf{x}$ can only be trained with labeled sensor data, because the values in $\mathbf{x}$ low-level signal features that are hard for humans to interpret directly. The fundamental idea of semantic attribute-based learning is illustrated in Figure 4, where the edges represents $P(A|\mathbf{x})$, the probability of the attribute A given a feature vector $\mathbf{x}$, and $P(Y|\mathbf{a})$, the probability of the class label Y given an attribute vector $\mathbf{a}$. We will explain each step in details in the following sections.

3.2.2 Activity-Attribute Matrix

The Activity-Attribute Matrix encodes the human knowledge on the relationship between an activity and a set of semantic attributes that are associated with the activity. We designed the activity-attribute matrix by extending previous work in attribute-based object similarity and classification [12, 13]. For M activities and N attributes, the activity-attribute matrix is an $M \times N$ matrix where the value of each element a_{ij} represents the level of association between activity i and attribute j. We define each element as a binary value, indicating whether such an association exist ($a_{ij} = 1$) or not ($a_{ij} = 0$), although in general a_{ij} can be real-valued ($0 \leq a_{ij} \leq 1$), indicating the level or confidence of the association. An example of a binary activity-attribute matrix we manually defined for the exercise activity domain in our experiments is shown in Figure 5. In general, an activity-attribute matrix can be manually defined by common-sense knowledge or domain knowledge. Alternatively, the process can be automated using existing web text mining [31] or crowdsourcing platforms [34]. A user can also manually define a custom new activity by describing it using the attributes, which is equivalent to inserting a row in the matrix.

3.2.3 Attribute Detection

Given an activity-attribute matrix, the next step is to train a set of attribute detectors so that we are able to infer the presence/absence of an attribute from the sensor data features. However, collecting a separate training dataset for every attribute is not practical for several reasons. First of all, not all of the attributes are sub-activities themselves. Many attributes are descriptions, characteristics, or consequences of an activities rather than standalone sub-activities. Therefore, it may not be possible to collect data for an attribute "alone" without other interference or confounding factors. Furthermore, there can be a large number of possible attributes. If there were a need to collect many separate training dataset, the benefit of attribute-based learning would diminish significantly.

Since the goal is only to infer if an attribute is present or not given the feature vector (i.e. $P(A|\mathbf{x})$ in Figure 4), what we need is one set of positive samples and another set of negative samples. Therefore, to learn an attribute detector, we reuse the existing training data by merging the labeled data of all activity classes that are associated with the attribute as the positive set. Similarly, the negative set consists of the data of all activity classes that are not associated with the attribute.

After the training sets are constructed, a binary classifier is trained for each attribute. In general, any type of classifier can be used. We evaluated various classifiers and selected the Support Vector Machine (SVM) classifier [4] as the optimal implementation (the experiments are discussed in Section 4.4.3). SVM finds the hyperplane $\mathbf{w}^T\mathbf{x}_i + b = 0$ that maximizes the margin between the data points of different classes by optimizing the following Quadratic Programming problem:

$$\min_{\mathbf{w},b} \quad \frac{1}{2}||\mathbf{w}||^2 + C\sum_{i=1}^{n}\xi_i \qquad (1)$$

s.t. $a_i(\mathbf{w}^T\mathbf{x}_i + b) \geq 1 - \xi_i$ and $\xi_i \geq 0$, $\forall i$, where $\mathbf{x}_i$ and a_i are the feature vector and the attribute value for the i-th training sample, respectively. $\mathbf{w}$ and b controls the orientation and the offset of the hyperplane. The parameter C is a regularization term which controls overfitting and the tolerance on the degree of false classification ξ_i for each sample. After training phase, we have a trained attribute detector for each attribute specified in the activity-attribute matrix.

In some cases, we might only have positive or negative examples for an attribute. For example, this can happen when all of the seen classes in the training data exhibit a certain attribute. In such cases, we train the attribute detector using one-class SVM [23], which classifies a sample as one of the two classes given only training data of one class (positive or negative).

Algorithm 1 Hybrid Feature/Attribute-Based Activity Recognition Algorithm

```
Input: low-level feature vector x
Output: estimated activity class y
isUnseenClass ← unseenClassDetection(x);
if isUnseenClass = true then
    Keep only unseen classes in the attribute space;
    a ← attributeDetector(x);
    y ← attributeBasedActivityClassifier(a);
else
    Keep only seen classes in the feature space;
    y ← featureBasedActivityClassifier(x);
end if
return y;
```

3.2.4 Attribute-Based Activity Classification

After the attributes are detected, in the attribute space, a nearest-neighbor classifier is used to recognize the high-level activity given an attribute vector generated from attribute detectors [30]. Specifically, the activity recognizer takes an attribute vector $\mathbf{a} = [A_1, A_2, ..., A_m]$ as input and returns the closest high-level activity y^* represented in the attribute space $\mathcal{A}$ according to the activity-attribute matrix. In other words, the activity-attribute matrix essentially provides the information of $P(Y|\mathbf{a})$ shown in Figure 4.

3.2.5 Hybrid Feature/Attribute-Based Activity Recognition

While attributes are human readable and can be used to recognize previously unseen new classes, there are certain amounts of information in the low-level feature space that we do not want to discard. Transforming low-level features to mid-level attributes has the benefit for unseen class recognition, but there is an information loss associated with it.

Inspired by this thought, our idea is to keep the advantages of both feature-based and attribute-based activity recognition. Specifically, if we know that a sample belongs to a seen class where we had training data in the dataset, we can directly apply feature-based classifier to recognize the activity. On the other hand, if we think that a sample belongs to a new class that we have not had any training data associated with, we have to apply attribute-based activity recognition so that we can learn by reusing the known attributes.

Now the question is: How do we know if a sample belongs to a seen class or an unseen class? We draw an analogy between this problem and the problem of anomaly detection. A sample from a seen class is like a typical sample, which is similar to the other samples we had in the training data. In comparison, a sample from an unseen class is like an "anomaly" because it does not look like anything that the system has seen before. To approach this problem, we first train an unseen class detector using the one-class SVM classifier [6], where only the positive samples (all samples that belong to the seen classes) are given to the classifier. After using the unseen class detector, we then do a hybrid feature/attribute-based activity recognition using the algorithm described in Algorithm 1.

3.3 Active Learning: Reinforcing Activity Recognition Using Minimal User Feedback

So far we have focused on the scenario where no training data for the target class are available. What if we have the opportunity to acquire some ground-truth labeled data from users? Obviously, if we ask users to label every single sample, we can achieve the best recognition accuracy possible. However, it is impractical to ask a user to label his/her activity every single minute because it would be extremely intrusive. The more frequently we prompt the users for inputs, the more intrusive the system will be [35]. This observation motivates us to design a user feedback loop for the NuActiv system using active learning algorithms [35,37].

Our idea is simple: We ask a user for labels only when we are highly uncertain about our recognition result. To achieve this, we used the idea of uncertainty sampling in the field of active learning. The idea of active learning algorithms is that a machine learning algorithm can perform better with less training data if it is allowed to choose the data from which it learns [35].

3.3.1 *Sampling Scheme*

There are two types of selective sampling schemes in active learning [35]. The first one is *Stream-Based Sampling*, where an unlabeled instance is typically drawn one at a time from the input source, and the system must decide whether to query or discard it. The second scheme is *Pool-Based Sampling*, where a large pool of unlabeled data is available. Having observed all the unlabeled instances, the system can ask for the label of one instance at a time according to a certain decision criteria.

In this work, we use a hybrid stream/pool-based sampling scheme that is more suitable for the scenario of human activity recognition using mobile phones or wearable devices. The pool is not so big so that a user forgets what he/she did during the time interval asked by the system, yet large enough for the system to select a good sample to ask the user for a ground-truth label. The detailed settings are described in Section 4.6.

3.3.2 *Uncertainty Sampling Metrics*

In this work, we carefully evaluated several different widely used metrics [35,37] that measure the uncertainty of a sample to the classifier in order to seek an optimal solution:

Least Confident: Ask the user for a ground-truth label when the confidence score of the classifier output $\hat{y}$ given the input feature x of a sample is minimum:

$$x^*_{LC} = \underset{x}{\operatorname{argmin}}\, P_\theta(\hat{y}|x) \qquad (2)$$

Minimum Margin: Ask the user for a ground-truth label when the difference between the confidence of the first and the second likely classes ($\hat{y}_1$ and $\hat{y}_2$) is small:

$$x^*_M = \underset{x}{\operatorname{argmin}}\, [P_\theta(\hat{y}_1|x) - P_\theta(\hat{y}_2|x)] \qquad (3)$$

Maximum Entropy: Entropy, in information theory, is measure of the uncertainty associated with a random variable. $H_\theta(Y|x) = -\sum_y P_\theta(y|x) \log P_\theta(y|x)$ means that given a sample x and classifier model θ, how uncertain the classifier is about the value of class label Y. Therefore, we can ask the user for a ground-truth label when the entropy over Y given a specific sample x is the largest among all x in consideration:

$$x^*_H = \underset{x}{\operatorname{argmax}} - \sum_y P_\theta(y|x) \log P_\theta(y|x) \qquad (4)$$

The comparison between the performances using different metrics is reported in Section 4.

Algorithm 2 Outlier-Aware Uncertainty-Sampling Active Learning Algorithm for Activity Recognition

Input: A sequence of initial unlabeled instances $\mathcal{U} = \{x_i | i = 1, ..., N_\mathcal{U}\}$; A set of initial labeled instances $\mathcal{L} = \{(x_i, y_i) | i = 1, ..., N_\mathcal{L}\}$; An initial classifier model θ; A pool window length L_{pwin}
Output: Updated activity classifier model θ
/* $N_\mathcal{U}$: the number of unlabeled samples available in the pool window */
while Activity Recognition Service is running **do**
    while $N_\mathcal{U} < L_{pwin}$ **do**
        $d \leftarrow$ getCurrentSensorData();
        $x \leftarrow$ extractFeatures(d);
        insert x into $\mathcal{U}$;
        $N_\mathcal{U} \leftarrow N_\mathcal{U} + 1$;
    end while
    $maxScore \leftarrow -\infty$; $x^* \leftarrow x_1$;
    for i **from** 1 **to** L_{pwin} **do**
        $score \leftarrow$ getOutlierAwareUncertainty(x_i);
        if $score > maxScore$ **then**
            $maxScore \leftarrow score$;
            $x^* \leftarrow x_i$
        end if
    end for
    $y^* \leftarrow$ queryForLabel(x);
    insert (x^*, y^*) to $\mathcal{L}$;
    $\theta \leftarrow$ trainClassifier($\mathcal{L}$);
    Remove all samples in pool $\mathcal{U}$; $N_\mathcal{U} \leftarrow 0$;
end while
return θ;

3.3.3 *Outlier-Aware Uncertainty Sampling*

Using uncertainty sampling, however, can run the risk of choosing outliers as samples to query [35]. The reason is that outliers are away from the other samples of the same class in the feature space; therefore, for most uncertainty metrics we use, outliers are likely to receive higher uncertainty scores than other samples. Unfortunately, knowing the label of outliers does not help training a classifier because outliers are exceptions rather than representative examples that a classifier should learn from. As a result, actively choosing outliers for training can even "mislead" the classifier and end up degrading the accuracy.

To mitigate the negative affect of outliers, we used Outlier-Aware Uncertainty Sampling in tandem with the uncertainty sampling metrics. The idea is to select samples that are uncertain but not outliers, i.e., samples that are representative of the underlying distribution (e.g. in dense region of the feature space). To determine whether a sample is representative of the underlying distribution, we calculate the mean similarity between this sample and all the other samples. If a sample is close to many other samples in the feature space, its mean similarity with all the other samples will be high; on the other hand, for an outlier that is far from most samples, the mean similarity will be low. Incorporating this constraint into the uncertainty sampling metric, the new objective function is:

$$x^*_{OA} = \underset{x \in \mathcal{U}}{\operatorname{argmax}} \left(\phi(x) \cdot \frac{1}{N_{\mathcal{U}}} \sum_{x' \in \mathcal{U}} S(x, x') \right) \quad (5)$$

The first term $\phi(x)$ refers to one of the uncertainty metrics we described in Section 3.3.2. To be consistent with the argmax objective, for Lease Confident uncertainty metric, $\phi(x)$ is defined as $\exp(-P_\theta(\hat{y}|x))$. Similarly, $\phi(x) = \exp(-(P_\theta(\hat{y}_1|x) - P_\theta(\hat{y}_2|x)))$ for minimum margin metric, and $\phi(x) = H_\theta(Y|x)$ for the maximum entropy metric. The second term $\frac{1}{N_{\mathcal{U}}} \sum_{x' \in \mathcal{U}} S(x, x')$ measures the mean similarity, $S(x, x')$, between a sample x and all other samples x' in the unlabeled sample pool $\mathcal{U}$, where $N_{\mathcal{U}}$ is the total number of samples in $\mathcal{U}$. The complete algorithm is shown in Algorithm 2.

4. EVALUATION

To evaluate our approaches, we investigated and answered the following questions through system implementation, dataset collection, and experiments:

- What is the overall precision/recall of unseen activity recognition using NuActiv? How does the performance vary among classes? (Section 4.4.1)
- How does the recognition accuracy change with the number of unseen classes? (Section 4.4.2)
- How does the performance vary with the use of different classification algorithms for attribute detectors? (Section 4.4.3)
- How to select attributes based on their importance to unseen activity recognition? (Section 4.4.4)
- What is the cross-user performance, i.e. when the users in the training set are different from those in the testing set? Is the system able to generalize from one or a few users to many new users? (Section 4.4.5)
- How does the attribute detection accuracy vary with the position and combination of the devices and sensors? (Section 4.4.6)
- How does NuActiv perform on recognizing unseen daily life activities? (Section 4.5.2)
- How efficiently can the system reinforce its performance using active learning? How does the performance vary with different active learning algorithms? (Section 4.6.1)
- What is the effect of outlier-aware uncertainty sampling on active learning algorithms? (Section 4.6.2)

4.1 System Implementation

We have implemented and tested the system on Nexus S 4G phones and MotoACTV wristwatches [27]. A picture of our system running on these two types of devices is shown in Figure 6. The Nexus S 4G phone has a three-dimensional accelerometer and a gyroscope. The MotoACTV has a three-dimensional accelerometer, Wi-Fi, and Bluetooth radio.

For the software part, we have implemented the code for feature extraction and the classification algorithm in the Java programming language. The code runs on the Android Operating System installed on the Nexus S 4G phones and the MotoACTV. For the classification algorithm, the Support Vector Machine classifier is implemented using the

Figure 6: NuActiv running on MotoACTV wristwatch (left) and Nexus S 4G phone (right).

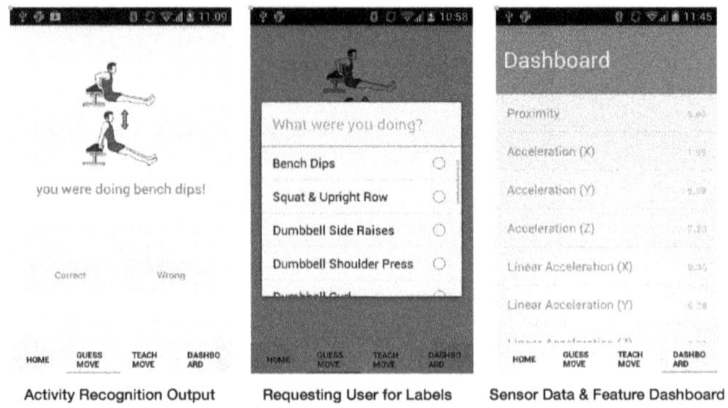

Figure 7: The screenshots of our mobile app running NuActiv activity recognition system.

LibSVM library [6]. The screenshots of several operations of the application are shown in Figure 7.

4.2 Datasets

4.2.1 *Exercise Activity Dataset*

We conducted an experiment involving exercise activities on 20 subjects. Each subject is asked to perform a set of 10 exercise activities as listed in Figure 5 with 10 iterations. Before the experiments, the subjects are given instructions on how to perform each of the 10 exercise activities. More information about these activities can be found in the literature [7,28]. During the experiment, each subject is equipped with three sensor-enabled devices: A Nexus S 4G phones attached to the arm using an armband, a MotoACTV wristwatch, and a second MotoACTV unit fixed at the hip position using a clip. A pair of three-pound dumbbells is also provided to the subject to perform some of the free-weight exercises (e.g. Dumbbell Side Raises, Dumbbell Curl, etc.). For sensor data collection, we collected accelerometer and gyroscope data using our mobile application with a sampling rate of 30 Hz. For feature extraction, the sliding window size is empirically set to 1 second with 50% overlap, based on a 10-fold cross-validation test on the validation dataset to find the optimal parameter.

4.2.2 *Public Dataset on Daily-Life Activities*

For the scenario of recognizing daily-life activities, we use a published and publicly-available dataset collected by Technische Universitat Darmstadt (TU Darmstadt) [9,36]. The dataset includes 34 daily life activity classes (including the *unlabeled* class) collected from one subject for seven days.

Table 1: **Attribute list for daily life activities.**

Type	Attribute Name
Basic	`Sitting`, `Standing`, `Walking`
Posture	`PostureUpright`, `PostureKneeling`
Hand/ Arm	`HandsOnTable`, `HandAboveChest`, `WristMovement`, `ArmPendulumSwing`
Motion Type	`TranslationMotion`, `CyclicMotion`, `IntenseMotion`
Relation	`WashingRelated`, `MealRelated`
Time	`TimeMorning`, `TimeNoon`, `TimeEvening`

The sensor data were collected using a wearable sensor platform with a three-axis accelerometer (ADXL330) worn on the wrist and the hip of the subject. The sampling rate is 100Hz, and the features are computed from a sliding window of 30 seconds with 50% overlap.

To apply NuActiv to the TU Darmstadt daily-life activity dataset, we defined a list of 17 attributes (as shown in Table 1) and an activity-attribute matrix[1] based on the 34 daily life activities in the dataset. It is to be noted that the list is not mutually exclusive or collectively exhaustive. We show that these semantic attributes defined by human knowledge can enable unseen activity recognition using NuActiv in Section 4.5.

4.3 Evaluation Methodology

We used leave-two-class-out cross validation, the most widely used validation method used in the literature of zero-shot/zero-data learning [15, 30]. The validation scheme is used for recognizing unseen classes that do not have any sample in the training set. The traditional 10-fold cross validation is not applicable to unseen class recognition because it does not leave out all samples of certain "unseen" classes in the training step, so that every class will have some samples in the training set.

The leave-two-class-out cross validation works as follows. Suppose there are a total of N classes. Each time we first train our system on $(N-2)$ classes, and then test the discriminative capability of the classifier on the remaining 2 classes that were "unseen" by the system during the training process. We repeat this test for all $\binom{N}{2}$ unseen/seen class combinations. Finally, the average performance over all tests is reported.

The results are reported in precision, recall, and F1-score. These metrics show different aspects of the performance of an activity recognition system. Specifically, the metrics are defined as follows:

$$precision = \frac{TP}{TP+FP} \qquad recall = \frac{TP}{TP+FN} \qquad (6)$$

$$F_1\text{-}score = \frac{2 \cdot precision \cdot recall}{precision + recall} \qquad (7)$$

where TP, FP, TN, and FN denotes true positive, false positive, true negative, and false negative, respectively. Precision indicates the percentage of times that a recognition result made by the system is correct. Recall means the percentage of times that an activity performed by a user is detected by the system. F_1-*score* is a integrated measure that combines both. For overall performance across all classes, the *accuracy* is computed as the number of correctly recognized samples divided by the number of all samples in the test set.

[1]The activity-attribute matrix can be downloaded from the supplemental materials at `http://www.ece.cmu.edu/~hengtzec/data/DLActivityAttributeMatrix.pdf`

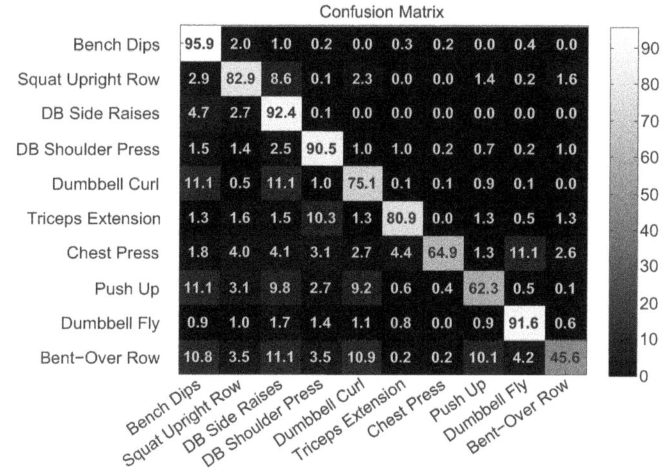

Figure 8: Confusion matrix of recognizing unseen activities using the 10-Exercise dataset. The rows are the ground-truth activity classes, and the columns are the estimated activity classes (classifier outputs). The numbers are shown as percentages.

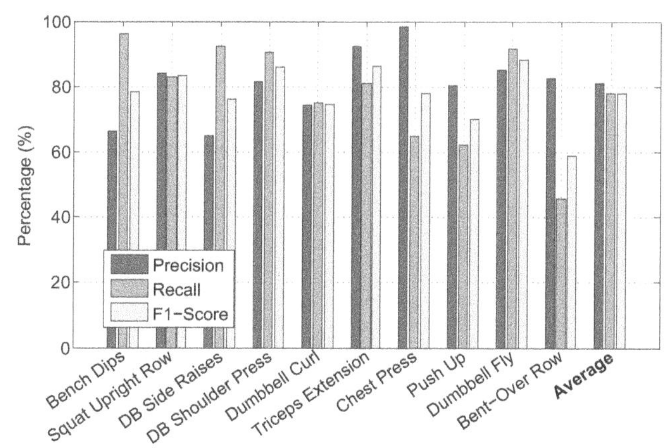

Figure 9: Precision and recall rate of recognizing unseen activities using the 10-Exercise dataset.

4.4 Case Study I: Exercise Activities

4.4.1 *Unseen Activity Recognition Result*

The confusion matrix of recognizing previously unseen exercise activities is shown in Figure 8. The average accuracy is 79% over all activities, among which the system achieved a promising recognition accuracy of 80-90% for five activity classes. It is to be noted that in these results, the target activities are recognized under the situation that no training data of any target activity class were given to or seen by the system during the training phase. The results support our hypothesis that unseen new human activities can be recognized with a reasonable accuracy using the proposed semantic-attribute-based learning approach in NuActiv.

One observation that we can draw from the experimental result is that misclassification usually happens when two activities only differ in one attribute. In this case, the success of recognition depends heavily on the detection accuracy

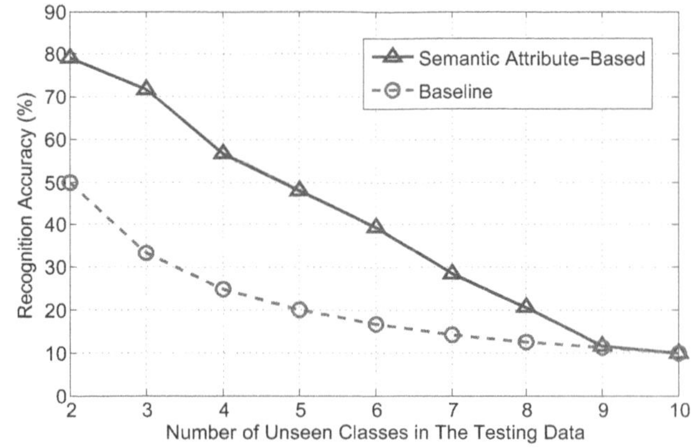

Figure 10: Accuracy vs. number of unseen classes in the testing dataset.

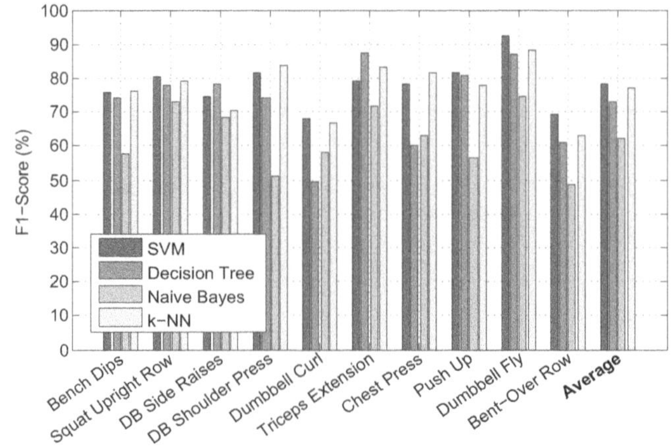

Figure 11: F1-score of unseen activity recognition vs. different classifiers for attribute detectors.

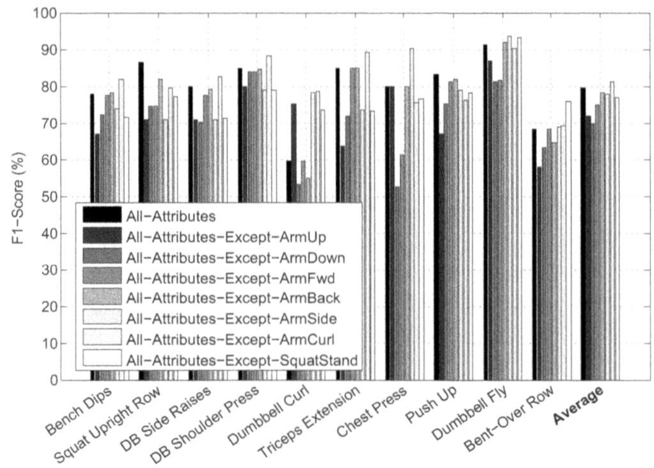

Figure 12: F1-score vs selected attributes. Each color represent an attribute that was unselected.

of the presence of that particular attribute. For example, "`DumbbellFly`" is classified as "`ChestPress`" because these two activities are inherently similar and are only different in the attribute "`ArmCurl`". The problem can potentially be overcome by including additional sensors/modalities so that other discriminative attributes can be used to further distinguish two similar classes.

4.4.2 The Impact of Number of Unseen Classes And Comparison with Baseline

The capability to recognize unseen new activity classes is built on the knowledge learned from the seen activity classes. As we can imagine, if all the classes were unseen, the system has nothing to learn from and thus is not able to recognize any activity with reasonable accuracy. To understand the capability and limitation of our approach, we conducted the following experiment: For a total of k classes, we vary the number of unseen classes (n_u) in the testing data from 2 to k, where the corresponding number of seen classes ($n_s = k - n_u$) in the training data varies from $k-2$ to 0. For each number of unseen classes, we repeat the test for all $\binom{k}{n_u}$ combinations and report the average results.

The result is shown in Figure 10. We observe that the recognition accuracy gradually degrades as the number of unseen classes in the testing data increases (i.e. the number of seen classes in the training data decreases). This is in accordance with the expectation, because it gradually becomes difficult for the system to generalize to a large number of unseen activity classes based on only a few seen classes. Furthermore, a successful unseen activity recognition relies on an accurate attribute detection. To accurately detect an attribute, it is important for the training classes to cover both positive and negative examples of the attribute. Therefore, the larger the seen-to-unseen class ratio is, the more likely that we can recognize unseen activities effectively.

We also compare our results with a baseline approach. The baseline approach is the random-guess prediction given the number of unseen classes, which is the best that a supervised learning-based activity recognition system can do. From Figure 10, we can see that our semantic-attribute-based approach is 20-30% better than the baseline for most cases, except for the cases where almost all the classes were unseen (when the system has seen zero to two classes in the training data). The results suggest that NuActiv is an viable approach to unseen activity recognition.

4.4.3 Comparison of Different Attribute Detectors

We also compare the SVM classifier with other classifiers that are widely used in the related work, including the Decision Tree classifier, Naive Bayes classifier, and k-Nearest Neighbor (k-NN) classifier [2,18,20]. For k-NN, the optimal result with $k = 3$ is reported.

The results are shown in Figure 11. SVM outperforms the Decision Tree and Naive Bayes classifier on average and for most of the classes if we break down the results by activity class. Overall, the accuracy using k-NN is comparable to the result using SVM. However, k-NN classification requires the storage and access to all the training data. Thus, k-NN is less scalable for a large dataset and less practical to run on mobile devices given their limited storage. Therefore, we used SVM for our experiments and implementation on the mobile devices.

4.4.4 Evaluation of The Importance of Attributes

We now investigate the importance of each semantic attribute and gain insights into attribute selection. The selection of attributes is important in two aspects. The first one is *discriminability*, meaning how well can an attribute discriminate between different high-level classes. The second

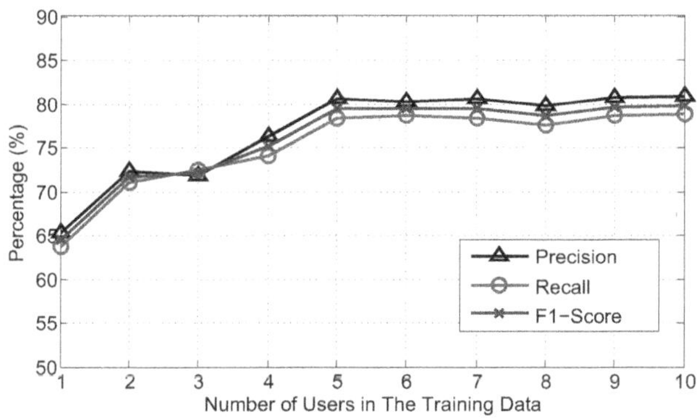

Figure 13: Cross-user recognition accuracy vs. number of seen users in the training data. The testing set includes 10 users that are different from those in the training data.

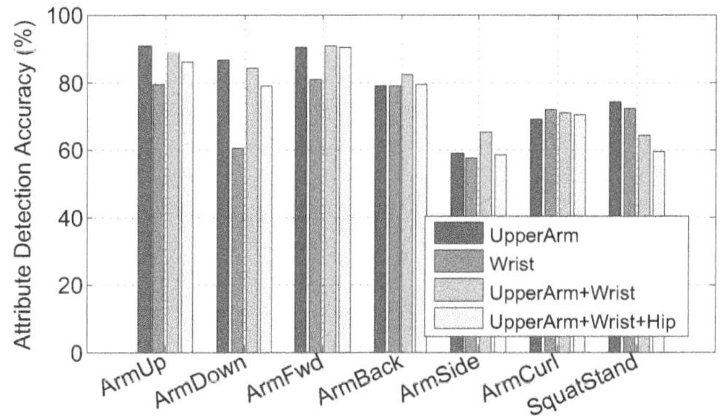

Figure 14: Attribute detection accuracy vs. device/sensor positions for each attribute.

one is *detectability*, namely how accurately can we detect the presence or absence of an attribute.

To test the *discriminability*, we conducted the following experiment: First, we run the unseen activity recognition test using all n_A semantic attributes ($n_A = 7$ for exercise activities). Then, we run n_A tests where each time we exclude one of the attributes and observe the change of the performance. If the performance drops significantly when an attribute is excluded, then being able to detect this attribute is important to accurately recognize the high-level activities. On the other hand, if the performance does not change much without an attribute, then the attribute is less likely to be important. To test the *detectability*, we compute the detection accuracy of each attribute. The accuracy is computed as the number of times an attribute is correctly detected divided by the number of times an attribute appears in the samples of the testing data.

The results of the discriminability and detectability test are shown in Figure 12 and 14, respectively. From the average F1-score (the rightmost bar group) in Figure 12, we can see that the attributes `ArmUp`, `ArmDown`, and `ArmFwd` have a higher impact on the activity recognition performance than other attributes. However, from the results broken down by activity class, we can see that an attribute may be important to some activity classes but not for other classes. Therefore, the selection of attributes also depends on the characteristics of the targeted classes. One reason for these phenomena is the inherent attribute-composition of an activity. Another possible reason is that some attributes are easier to detect than others. As shown in Figure 14, the system generally achieves higher accuracy detecting the first four attributes. These differences in detectability can be caused by the positions and types of the sensors used, the type of classifier used for detection, and the consistency of the presence of an attribute given an activity is performed.

4.4.5 *Cross-User Activity Recognition Results*

It is important for an activity recognition system to not only be able to recognize the activities of the users it has seen, but also be able to generalize to the activities of new users it has never seen before. To evaluate the generalizability and the limitation of our approach, we randomly divide the 20 users into two equal sets. While fixing the test set to be the 10 users in the first held-out set, we iterate the number of training users from 1 to 10, randomly chosen from the second set. For each test, we repeat the random choice for 100 times and report the average performance.

The results are shown in Figure 13. As we can see, the performance stays approximately constant when the number of seen users in the training data is equal to or greater than five. Furthermore, the precision, recall, and F1-score are almost the same as the case where the data of all the users exist in both the training set and the testing set, as shown previously in Figure 9. The F1-score decreases slightly when number of seen users in the training data falls below four, yet the system can maintain an F1-score of over 70% when having seen 2–4 users in the training data. The edge case happens when the system has only seen one user in the training set, where the F1-score is 60%. Overall, the system is able to achieve 70-80% accuracy after training on two or more users in the training set.

4.4.6 *Impact of Device Position on Attribute Detection Accuracy*

An attribute is often inherently associated with a characteristic of a human activity or a motion of a specific part of human body. Therefore, we conducted experiments to understand how the position or the set of positions at which the sensors are placed affects the attribute detection accuracy, which in turns affects the final activity recognition accuracy. When collecting the exercise activity dataset, we have placed sensor-enabled phones/devices on three different body positions of the users (as described in Section 4.2.1). The experimental results using sensor data from different body positions is shown in Figure 14. It is observed that while using the upper arm sensors (phone in an armband) usually achieves better and more stable accuracy than using the wrist sensors (wristwatch), combining these two data sources leads to improvement in accuracy in some cases. One possible reason is that while the movement of the wrist is of larger variation and less predictable, it complements the limitation of what can be observed by the upper arm sensors. Adding the hip sensor did not improve the accuracy, possibly because most attributes defined in our case study do not involve changes in lower-body postures. It is to be noted that the results do depend on the activity domains and sensor types.

4.5 Case Study II: Daily-Life Activities

4.5.1 *Reproduction of Results in Previous Work*

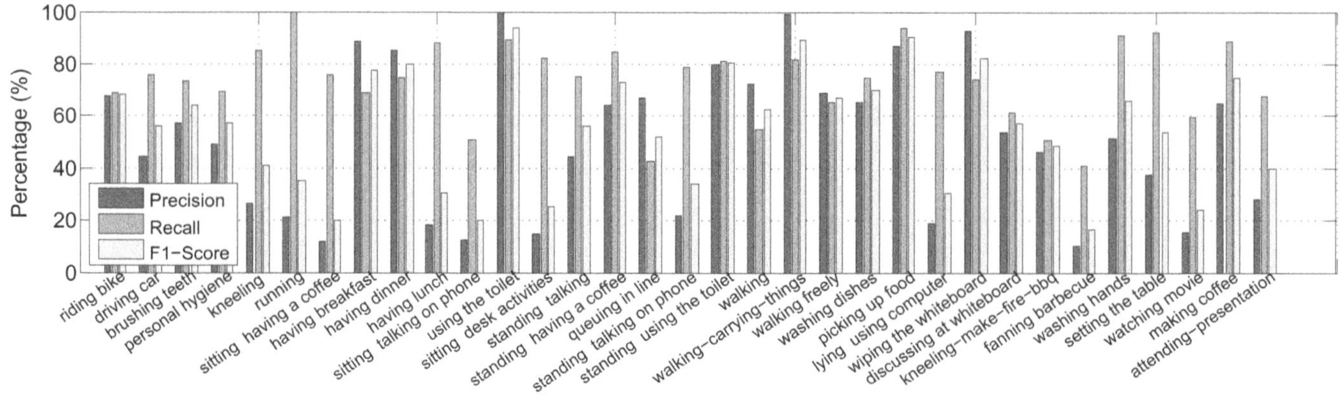

Figure 15: Precision, recall, and F1-score of recognizing unseen daily life activities in the TU Darmstadt dataset using NuActiv.

For the daily life activity recognition experiments, we used the public dataset of 34 daily life activities provided by TU Darmstadt [9], as described in Section 4.2.2. We first implement the supervised learning method closely following the experiment protocols in the paper of the dataset provider [9]. Given that all the classes were seen in the training set, our implementation achieved 71.2% accuracy, which is very close to 72.7% as reported in the previous work [9]. This reproduction of previous results confirms that our use and understanding of the dataset and features are valid.

4.5.2 *New Task: Recognizing Previously Unseen New Daily Life Activity*

After successfully reproducing the results in the previous work, we proceeded to a new problem—recognizing unseen daily life activities—which has not been addressed before in the activity recognition literature. We applied the NuActiv system and algorithms to the 34-daily-life dataset [9], and evaluated the performance using the evaluation methodology described in Section 4.3. The results are shown in Figure 15. We can see that for some classes the system can achieve high recall and lower precision, and vice versa for some classes. Overall, the system achieves 60-70% precision and recall rate for most classes. The mean precision and recall rate is 52.3% and 73.4%, respectively, averaged over all classes. Some classes, such as "sitting-desk-activities" or "sitting-talking-on-phone", do not have a clear difference in attributes since we only have inertial sensor data available in the dataset. Therefore, the system tends to have a low precision rate on these classes. This problem can be alleviated by incorporating extra sensing modalities such as ambient sound. While there is clearly room for improvement, the fact that our system is able to recognize an unseen daily life activity class with no training data with a reasonable accuracy is a new result in the field of activity recognition.

4.6 Active Learning Experiments

4.6.1 *Comparison of Active Learning Algorithms*

In addition to unseen activity recognition, we further evaluate how the system can improve itself using minimal user feedback. The active learning algorithms we used for the experiment are explained in Section 3.3.

Following the experiment protocols in the active learning literatures [35], our experiment setting is described as follows. The data set we used is the 34-daily-life dataset [9]. Each sample is a feature vector extracted from a window of 30 seconds of sensor data. An initial labeled set $\mathcal{L}$ of 50 samples from Day 1 of the dataset is provided to the system. Then, an unlabeled set $\mathcal{U}$ of 11087 samples from the rest of Day 1 to Day 5 is sequentially provided to the system in the order of time. Each time the system improves itself using the newly acquired labeled data, we evaluate its performance on a separate test set $\mathcal{T}$ of 5951 samples from Day 6 and 7. The active learning is performed as described in Algorithm 2, with $L_{pwin} = 100$ and SVM classifiers.

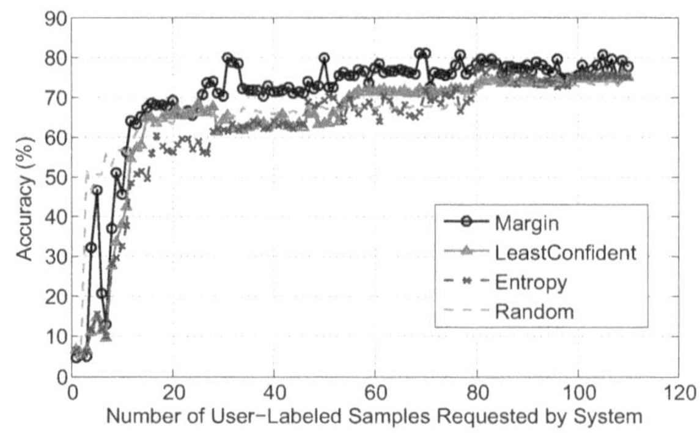

Figure 16: Recognition accuracy vs. user labels requested in the active learning experiment.

The results are shown in Figure 16. Using active learning, the classifier generally improves faster (using less labeled samples from the user) than the *random* baseline (randomly query the user without active learning). The margin-based uncertainty metric achieved 70% accuracy using only 30 labeled samples from the user and converged faster than other approaches. The entropy and least-confident metrics yielded comparable results.

4.6.2 *Outlier-Aware Uncertainty Sampling Results*

We further incorporate the outlier-aware uncertainty sampling as described in Section 3.3.3, and compare the results with those not using outlier-aware uncertainty sampling. The results are shown in Figure 17. It is observed that given the same amount of user-labeled samples requested by the system, using outlier-aware uncertainty sampling in general leads to comparable or better accuracy when compared to active learning algorithms without outlier-awareness. The

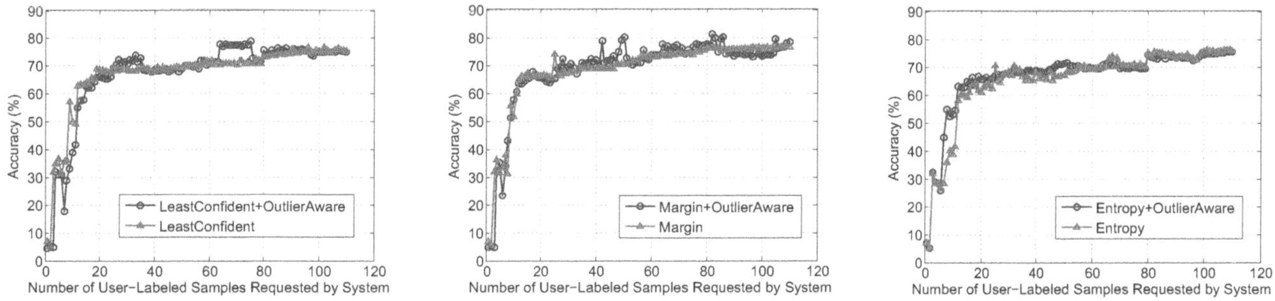

(a) Least-confidence-based sampling. (b) Margin-based sampling. (c) Entropy-based sampling.

Figure 17: Comparison between the learning curve of active learning algorithms with/without outlier-aware uncertainty sampling .

amount of improvement, of course, would depend on the relative weighting between the uncertainty term and the outlier-awareness term in Equation 5, and on whether there is a large number of outlier samples in the input data.

5. DISCUSSION

In this section, we discuss some assumptions and limitations of the current version of NuActiv, along with our ongoing work and potential future directions.

5.1 Semantic Attribute-Based Learning

In the current version of our semantic attribute-based learning approach, it is assumed that there exists a one-to-one mapping between an activity class label and a point in the attribute space, and that the associations between activities and attributes are fixed. This implies a fundamental limitation that the lower bound on the minimum number of attributes is $n_A \geq \log_2 n_Y$ for n_Y activity classes and n_A different attributes, assuming binary-valued attributes are used. As a future research direction, it is possible to overcome this limitation by incorporating continuous-valued attributes or relative attributes [32]. Further more, while we present an initial attempt to evaluate the attribute-based learning approach on two datasets, it would be beneficial to expand the study to more activity domains with a larger number of activities, attributes, and users in the future.

In the current implementation, the attributes are manually defined using common-sense knowledge and domain knowledge as an initial attempt towards zero-shot learning for activity recognition. To further reduce the effort of one-time manual definition per class, a potential future direction and part of our ongoing work is to automate the process using web text mining [31] or crowdsourcing [34] as explored in the zero-shot learning literature.

Our results suggest that the performance of the zero-shot learning model varies depending on the selected semantic attributes. Therefore, another future direction is to develop a systematic way for semantic attribute selection based on the discriminability and detectability of the attributes. Further, to truly exploit the advantages of both low-level features and mid-level attributes, future work and experiments are to be done to explore and compare various kinds of algorithms for hybrid feature/attribute-based activity recognition.

5.2 Active Learning for Activity Recognition

For the active learning experiment, it is assumed that the users are willing to provide the label and all the labels provided by the user are correct. Related study or future work on usability and interruptibility [33] can be further leveraged to adjust the frequency of requesting labels from users based on their preferences, and to improve the effectiveness of active learning in real practice. It would also be beneficial to study the ideal way (e.g. haptic, gestural, or audio-based interfaces) to engage users to provide labeled data for activity recognition using wearable and mobile devices.

6. RELATED WORK

6.1 Activity Recognition

6.1.1 Supervised Learning

In the field of mobile, wearable, and pervasive computing, extensive research has been done to recognize human activities (e.g. sitting, walking, running) [2,5,14,21,25,36,37,40]. In terms of the learning method, the majority of the research in this field used supervised learning approaches, including discriminative classifiers (e.g. Decision Trees, SVM) and generative models (e.g. Naive Bayes, Hidden Markov Model), where a classifier is trained on a large set of labeled examples of every target activity. [2,3,18,21,25,40]. There has also been prior study of representing high-level activities as a composite of simple actions, using a supervised layered dynamic Bayesian network [39]. While many promising results have been reported, a widely acknowledged problem is that labeled examples are often time consuming and expensive to obtain, as they require a lot of effort from test subjects, human annotators, or domain experts [36,37].

6.1.2 Semi-Supervised and Transfer Learning

To lessen the reliance on labeled training data and to exploit the benefit of abundant unlabeled data, previous work has incorporated semi-supervised learning into activity or context recognition systems [19,22,24,36,37]. Semi-supervised learning approaches can improve the recognition accuracy by refining the decision boundary based on the distribution of the unlabeled data, or by assigning highly-confident estimated labels to the unlabeled data. Recently, transfer learning has also been explored so that the model learned for one target class can be transferred to improve the recognition accuracy of another target class [5,41]. As a result, the amount of training data required for new applications can be reduced. While many promising results have been reported, most of the existing approaches can only recognize activity classes that were included in the training data. Inspired by previous study, our work presents an early attempt to recognize unseen human activities with no training data using attribute-based zero-shot learning.

6.1.3 Active Learning

Active learning has been used to improve the accuracy of human activity recognition [17, 19, 37] or to model the interruptibility of a mobile phone user [33]. We extend the previous work by incorporating active learning in the framework of zero-shot learning for activity recognition, so that the system is able to not only recognize unseen activities but also actively request labels from users when possible.

6.1.4 Unsupervised Learning

Another related research direction is unsupervised learning. Unsupervised learning focuses on clustering or pattern discovery rather than classification [9, 26]. Although labels are not required for unsupervised learning approaches, the output is a set of unnamed clusters which cannot be used for classification purposes. To perform classification, labels are still needed to connect the discovered patterns to the actual classes.

6.1.5 Human Activity Domain

In terms of the activity domain of interest, some previous work in the area of human activity recognition focused on daily life activities [9, 18, 36] and some focused on sports and exercise activities [7, 28]. In this work, we evaluated our system in both domains to validate its effectiveness in general unseen activity recognition.

6.2 Zero-Shot Learning

The idea of semantic or human-nameable visual attributes and zero-shot learning has recently been explored in the field of computer vision such as object recognition and has been shown to be useful [13, 16, 34]. Palatucci et al. presented an early study on the problem of zero-shot learning [30], where the goal is to learn a classifier that can predict new classes that were omitted from the training dataset. A theoretical analysis is done to study the conditions under which a classifier can predict novel classes. For case study, the authors study the problem of decoding the word that a human is thinking from functional magnetic resonance images (fMRI). There has also been some previous work on using zero-shot learning to solve computer vision problems [13, 34]. In [13], the system does object detection based on a human-specified high-level description (such as shapes or colors) of the target objects instead of training images. Compared to our work, these problem domains are inherently different from activity recognition because image data are static rather than sequential. Furthermore, the image attributes and description for visual objects cannot be directly applied to activity recognition. Inspired by these previous studies, we designed and implemented a new activity recognition system using the concept of attribute-based zero-shot learning.

7. CONCLUSION

In this paper, we have presented the design, implementation, and evaluation of NuActiv, a new activity recognition system. Existing machine-learning-based approaches can only classify sensor data as one of the pre-trained classes in the training data, and thus cannot recognize any previous unseen class without training data. NuActiv uses semantic attribute-based learning to recognize unseen new activity classes by reusing and generalizing the attribute model learned for other seen activities. An outlier-aware active learning algorithm is also developed to efficiently improves the recognition accuracy of the system using minimal user feedback. The system achieved up to an average of 79% recognition accuracy on the unseen activity recognition problem, which could not be solved using existing supervised or semi-supervised approaches. Experimental results also support our hypothesis that using outlier-aware active learning the system can converge faster to optimal accuracy using fewer labels from the user.

8. ACKNOWLEDGMENTS

This research is supported in part by Applied Research Center, Motorola Mobility. The views and conclusions contained in this paper are those of the authors and should not be interpreted as necessarily representing the official policies, either expressed or implied, of any funding body. We are grateful for the advice and help from Dr. Ying Zhang, Dr. Ole Mengshoel, Senaka Buthpitiya, Faisal Luqman, and Zheng Sun. We sincerely appreciate the suggestions and feedback from our shepherd, Dr. Junehwa Song, and from anonymous reviewers.

9. REFERENCES

[1] M. Azizyan, I. Constandache, and R. Roy Choudhury. SurroundSense: Mobile phone localization via ambience fingerprinting. In *Proc. Int'l Conf. Mobile Computing and Networking*, pages 261–272, 2009.

[2] L. Bao and S. S. Intille. Activity recognition from user-annotated acceleration data. In *Proceedings of The International Conference on Pervasive Computing*, pages 1–17. Springer, 2004.

[3] E. Berlin and K. Van Laerhoven. Detecting leisure activities with dense motif discovery. In *Proceedings of the 2012 ACM Conference on Ubiquitous Computing*, UbiComp '12, pages 250–259, New York, NY, USA, 2012. ACM.

[4] C. M. Bishop. *Pattern Recognition and Machine Learning*. Springer-Verlag Inc., 2006.

[5] U. Blanke and B. Schiele. Remember and transfer what you have learned - recognizing composite activities based on activity spotting. In *International Symposium on Wearable Computers (ISWC)*, pages 1 –8, Oct. 2010.

[6] C.-C. Chang and C.-J. Lin. *LIBSVM: a library for support vector machines*, 2001. Software available at `http://www.csie.ntu.edu.tw/~cjlin/libsvm`.

[7] K.-H. Chang, M. Y. Chen, and J. Canny. Tracking free-weight exercises. In *Proc. Int'l Conf. Ubiquitous computing*, UbiComp '07, pages 19–37, 2007.

[8] Google Inc. Google Glass, Apr. 2013. `http://www.google.com/glass/`.

[9] T. Huynh, M. Fritz, and B. Schiele. Discovery of activity patterns using topic models. In *Proceedings of The International Conference on Ubiquitous Computing*, UbiComp '08, pages 10–19, New York, NY, USA, 2008. ACM.

[10] S. Kang, J. Lee, H. Jang, H. Lee, Y. Lee, S. Park, T. Park, and J. Song. Seemon: scalable and energy-efficient context monitoring framework for sensor-rich mobile environments. In *Proceedings of The 6th International Conference On Mobile Systems, Applications, And Services*, MobiSys '08, pages 267–280, New York, NY, USA, 2008. ACM.

[11] S. Kang, Y. Lee, C. Min, Y. Ju, T. Park, J. Lee, Y. Rhee, and J. Song. Orchestrator: An active resource orchestration framework for mobile context monitoring in sensor-rich mobile environments. In *International Conference on Pervasive Computing and Communications (PerCom)*, pages 135–144, 2010.

[12] C. Kemp, J. B. Tenenbaum, T. L. Griffiths, T. Yamada, and N. Ueda. Learning systems of concepts with an infinite relational model. In *Proceedings of the 21st national conference on Artificial intelligence - Volume 1*, AAAI'06, pages 381–388. AAAI Press, 2006.

[13] C. H. Lampert, H. Nickisch, and S. Harmeling. Learning to detect unseen object classes by between-class attribute transfer. In *Proceedings of the IEEE Conference on Computer Vision and Pattern Recognition*, pages 951–958, 2009.

[14] N. D. Lane, E. Miluzzo, H. Lu, D. Peebles, T. Choudhury, and A. T. Campbell. A survey of mobile phone sensing. *IEEE Comm. Magazine*, 48:140–150, September 2010.

[15] H. Larochelle, D. Erhan, and Y. Bengio. Zero-data learning of new tasks. In *Proc. Conf. on Artificial intelligence*, AAAI'08, pages 646–651, 2008.

[16] J. Liu, B. Kuipers, and S. Savarese. Recognizing human actions by attributes. In *Conf. Computer Vision and Pattern Recognition*, pages 3337–3344, 2011.

[17] R. Liu, T. Chen, and L. Huang. Research on human activity recognition based on active learning. In *International Conference on Machine Learning and Cybernetics (ICMLC)*, volume 1, pages 285–290, 2010.

[18] B. Logan, J. Healey, M. Philipose, E. M. Tapia, and S. Intille. A long-term evaluation of sensing modalities for activity recognition. In *Proc. Int'l Conf. Ubiquitous computing*, UbiComp '07, pages 483–500, 2007.

[19] B. Longstaff, S. Reddy, and D. Estrin. Improving activity classification for health applications on mobile devices using active and semi-supervised learning. In *International Conference on Pervasive Computing Technologies for Healthcare*, PervasiveHealth'10, pages 1–7, 2010.

[20] H. Lu, W. Pan, N. Lane, T. Choudhury, and A. Campbell. SoundSense: Scalable sound sensing for people-centric applications on mobile phones. In *Proc. Int'l Conf. Mobile systems, applications, and services*, pages 165–178, 2009.

[21] H. Lu, J. Yang, Z. Liu, N. D. Lane, T. Choudhury, and A. T. Campbell. The Jigsaw continuous sensing engine for mobile phone applications. In *Proc. ACM Conf. Embedded Networked Sensor Systems*, SenSys '10, pages 71–84, 2010.

[22] M. Mahdaviani and T. Choudhury. Fast and scalable training of semi-supervised CRFs with application to activity recognition. In J. C. Platt, D. Koller, Y. Singer, and S. Roweis, editors, *Advances in Neural Information Processing Systems*, pages 977–984. MIT Press, Cambridge, MA, 2007.

[23] L. M. Manevitz and M. Yousef. One-class SVMs for document classification. *Journal of Machine Learning Research*, 2:139–154, Mar. 2002.

[24] E. Miluzzo, C. T. Cornelius, A. Ramaswamy, T. Choudhury, Z. Liu, and A. T. Campbell. Darwin phones: the evolution of sensing and inference on mobile phones. In *Proc. Int'l Conf. Mobile systems, applications, and services*, pages 5–20, 2010.

[25] E. Miluzzo, N. D. Lane, K. Fodor, R. Peterson, H. Lu, M. Musolesi, S. B. Eisenman, X. Zheng, and A. T. Campbell. Sensing meets mobile social networks: the design, implementation and evaluation of the CenceMe application. In *Proc. ACM Conf. Embedded network sensor systems*, SenSys '08, pages 337–350, 2008.

[26] D. Minnen, T. Starner, I. Essa, and C. Isbell. Discovering characteristic actions from on-body sensor data. In *In Proc. International Symposium On Wearable Computing*, pages 11–18, 2006.

[27] Motorola Mobility. MotoACTV, Apr. 2013. `https://motoactv.com/`.

[28] M. Muehlbauer, G. Bahle, and P. Lukowicz. What can an arm holster worn smart phone do for activity recognition? In *Proc. International Symposium on Wearable Computers*, ISWC '11, pages 79–82, 2011.

[29] S. Nath. ACE: exploiting correlation for energy-efficient and continuous context sensing. In *Proc. Int'l Conf. Mobile systems, applications, and services*, MobiSys '12, pages 29–42, 2012.

[30] M. Palatucci, D. Pomerleau, G. E. Hinton, and T. M. Mitchell. Zero-shot learning with semantic output codes. In *Proceedings of the Neural Information Processing Systems (NIPS)*, pages 1410–1418, 2009.

[31] D. Parikh and K. Grauman. Interactively building a discriminative vocabulary of nameable attributes. In *Proc. Int'l Conf. Computer Vision and Pattern Recognition*, pages 1681–1688, 2011.

[32] D. Parikh and K. Grauman. Relative attributes. In *IEEE International Conference on Computer Vision (ICCV)*, pages 503–510, 2011.

[33] S. Rosenthal, A. K. Dey, and M. Veloso. Using decision-theoretic experience sampling to build personalized mobile phone interruption models. In *Proc. International Conference on Pervasive Computing*, Pervasive'11, pages 170–187, Berlin, Heidelberg, 2011. Springer-Verlag.

[34] O. Russakovsky and L. Fei-Fei. Attribute learning in large-scale datasets. In *Proceedings of the 11th European Conference on Trends and Topics in Computer Vision*, ECCV'10, pages 1–14, Berlin, Heidelberg, 2012. Springer-Verlag.

[35] B. Settles. *Active Learning.* Morgan & Claypool, 2012.

[36] M. Stikic, D. Larlus, S. Ebert, and B. Schiele. Weakly supervised recognition of daily life activities with wearable sensors. *IEEE Trans. Pattern Analysis and Machine Intelligence*, 33(12):2521–2537, 2011.

[37] M. Stikic, K. Van Laerhoven, and B. Schiele. Exploring semi-supervised and active learning for activity recognition. In *Proc. International Symposium on Wearable Computers (ISWC)*, pages 81–88, 2008.

[38] U.S. Bureau of Labor Statistics. American time use survey activity lexicon. *American Time Use Survey*, 2011.

[39] S. Wang, W. Pentney, A.-M. Popescu, T. Choudhury, and M. Philipose. Common sense based joint training of human activity recognizers. In *Proceedings of the 20th international joint conference on Artifical intelligence*, IJCAI'07, pages 2237–2242, San Francisco, CA, USA, 2007. Morgan Kaufmann Publishers Inc.

[40] Y. Wang, J. Lin, M. Annavaram, Q. A. Jacobson, J. Hong, B. Krishnamachari, and N. Sadeh. A framework of energy efficient mobile sensing for automatic user state recognition. In *Proc. Int'l Conf. Mobile systems, applications, and services*, MobiSys '09, pages 179–192, 2009.

[41] V. W. Zheng, D. H. Hu, and Q. Yang. Cross-domain activity recognition. In *Proc. International Conference on Ubiquitous Computing*, Ubicomp '09, pages 61–70, New York, NY, USA, 2009. ACM.

SocioPhone: Everyday Face-to-Face Interaction Monitoring Platform Using Multi-Phone Sensor Fusion

Youngki Lee[1], Chulhong Min[2], Chanyou Hwang[2], Jaeung Lee[3], Inseok Hwang[2,4], Younghyun Ju[2], Chungkuk Yoo[2], Miri Moon[3], Uichin Lee[5], Junehwa Song[2]

[1]School of Information Systems, Singapore Management University
[2]Computer Science Department, KAIST, [3]Web Science and Technology Division, KAIST,
[4]Center for Mobile Software Platform, KAIST, [5]Knowledge Service Engineering Department, KAIST

[1]youngkilee@smu.edu.sg,
{chulhong, chanyou, leejai, inseok, yhju, ckyoo, miri.moon, junesong}@nclab.kaist.ac.kr, [5]uclee@kaist.edu

ABSTRACT

In this paper, we propose SocioPhone, a novel initiative to build a mobile platform for face-to-face interaction monitoring. Face-to-face interaction, especially conversation, is a fundamental part of everyday life. *Interaction-aware applications* aimed at facilitating group conversations have been proposed, but have not proliferated yet. Useful contexts to capture and support face-to-face interactions need to be explored more deeply. More important, recognizing delicate conversational contexts with commodity mobile devices requires solving a number of technical challenges. As a first step to address such challenges, we identify useful *meta-linguistic contexts* of conversation, such as turn-takings, prosodic features, a dominant participant, and pace. These serve as cornerstones for building a variety of interaction-aware applications. SocioPhone abstracts such useful meta-linguistic contexts as a set of intuitive APIs. Its runtime efficiently monitors registered contexts during in-progress conversations and notifies applications on-the-fly. Importantly, we have noticed that *online turn monitoring* is the basic building block for extracting diverse meta-linguistic contexts, and have devised a novel *volume-topography*-based method. We show the usefulness of SocioPhone with several interesting applications: *SocioTherapist*, *SocioDigest*, and *Tug-of-War*. Also, we show that our turn-monitoring technique is highly accurate and energy-efficient under diverse real-life situations.

Categories and Subject Descriptors

K.8 [**Personal Computing**]: General; C.3 [**Special-Purpose and Application-based Systems**]: Real-time and embedded systems

Keywords

Interaction, Conversation, Social, Platform, Volume Topography

1. INTRODUCTION

Face-to-face social interaction is an integral part of human life; everyday, people dine with family, have meetings with colleagues, and spend time with friends. A promising new direction for mobile sensing lies in capturing and utilizing sophisticated social contexts during daily face-to-face interactions. Early *interaction-aware applications* have been emerging and show its potential usefulness [22][27]. For example, *MeetingMediator* [22] displays the skew of individuals' verbal participations to promote group brainstorming. Another application helps a user remember the name of the person he is talking with, to help avoid the awkward experience of forgetting a name [27]. However, building interaction-aware applications involves severe challenges without system-level support. First of all, such applications are still in an early stage and most developers do not know which contexts to leverage during daily conversations. Furthermore, monitoring conversations requires implementing complicated inference logics, repetitive learning and testing to improve recognition accuracy, and significant optimization of battery use.

In this paper, we propose *SocioPhone*, a mobile platform for face-to-face interaction monitoring. Ideally, a full-fledged interaction monitoring platform would capture a variety of communicative cues expressed during face-to-face interaction such as verbal cues (spoken words and sentences), aural cues (tones, pitch), and visual cues (gesture, eye contact). As a first step, SocioPhone focuses on monitoring *meta-linguistic contexts* that provide useful information about conversations without requiring computation-intensive semantic inference on conversation contents. SocioPhone provides applications with a set of intuitive APIs to monitor rich meta-linguistic contexts on the fly (See Section 2); applications can submit simple monitoring requests to obtain contexts of interests. The SocioPhone runtime monitors registered contexts in a highly-efficient and precise manner, based on our new *volume-topography-based turn monitoring* technique (See Section 4).

In its core, SocioPhone monitors *conversational turns,* the basic unit of conversation; a *turn* is a continuous speech segment where a person starts and ends her speech [3][10]. We have noticed that monitoring turns is a first crucial step to deriving many interesting aspects of a conversion, e.g., how long and often one talks, how quickly she responds, who talks more or less, and how fast a conversation progresses. More interestingly, turn analysis enables high-level social inference, such as one's role in a conversation and problematic situations [9][16][35]. Future mobile applications will be tightly interwoven with sophisticated interactions, e.g., dynamic conversational flows and relational behaviors, in-situ; this will enrich and broaden the set of potential applications, from interaction facilitations to collaborative decision making, and even to psychological care. In a broader view, monitoring turns can also serve as the prerequisite for speaker-specific vocal inference and content analysis in real-time, such as assessing a speaker's emotional state and performing deep semantic analysis.

Online turn monitoring is a primitive building block, but it is challenging to implement it on everyday personal mobile devices. Existing voice recognition techniques such as speaker recognition

[1] This work was done while this author was at KAIST.

MobiSys'13, June 25–28, 2013, Taipei, Taiwan.

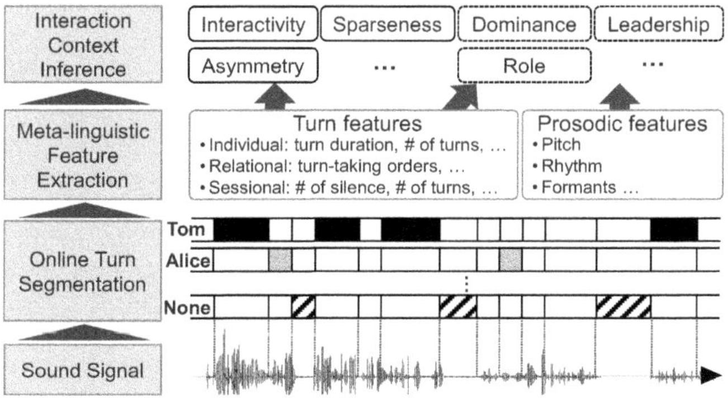

Figure 1. Online turn segmentation and meta-linguistic conversation monitoring

[7] and speaker diarization [2][4] rarely consider the challenges of mobile environments, e.g., unconstrained acoustic situations, real-time monitoring, and battery limitations. A potential approach to turn monitoring would be to continuously execute crafted speaker recognition logic, as in SpeakerSense [27] (See Section 3.1). However, this has a number of shortcomings. First, short-lasting turns (1-2 seconds) are common in casual conversations [2], but cannot be detected reliably. Existing techniques mostly require long speech segments (e.g., 3-8 seconds.) for reliable recognition to ensure statistical confidence of the windowed voice samples with respect to the speaker-specific pre-constructed spectral model [27][40]. More challenging, daily conversations do not occur in an ideal setting; dynamic ambient noises inevitably distort one's vocal signatures, leading to poor recognition accuracy. Furthermore, running speaker recognition on smartphones consumes significant power, (> 400 mW) for high-rate sound sensing and heavy computation [27][31].

To address the challenges for online turn monitoring, we propose an *on-the-spot multi-phone sensor fusion* approach; multiple smartphones work together to detect turn changes and associated speakers, along with a short in-situ training. Naturally placed phones belonging to conversation group members simultaneously sense a speaker's voice signals, but capture the signals with different strengths depending on their positions. Such relative sensory readings can be fused in realtime to form a *volume topography*, i.e., a signature vector of volume values sensed over different phones. Our key observation is that such a topography is unique to each speaker, showing enough discrimination power to identify turns and associated speakers. With a short training period, e.g., 30-60 seconds at the beginning of a conversation, frequent turn-taking of speakers can be very quickly and precisely traced through simple vector matching.

Our volume-topography-based technique has important advantages for online turn monitoring. First, volume parameters can be instantly and reliably estimated, even with a very short sensing window, e.g., 0.3 seconds; this allows us to monitor dynamic turn-taking behavior in a highly agile way. Second, volume-topography is less susceptible to diverse environmental noises as it is built in-situ to reflect the current noise characteristics. Third, our approach is computationally much lighter than existing techniques [7][27]; it does not require complex signal processing such as MFCC extraction and GMM matching. Finally, we note that the method works well even at very low sampling rates (as low as 500 Hz), which has the potential to reduce users' privacy concerns.

SocioPhone shows the potential to transform a personal mobile device into a social device that is aware of fine-grained face-to-face interaction contexts. So far, a number of mobile sensing systems have been proposed; yet, most of them focus on sensing personal status [25][28][29]. A few systems aim at capturing social contexts to facilitate interaction, but they provide only coarse-grained contexts such as encounters or presence of conversation [11][27].

We now summarize the contribution of this paper. First, we propose SocioPhone, a novel mobile interaction monitoring platform; it provides useful APIs to monitor '*turn*' and turn-derived meta-linguistic contexts. Second, as a key building block, we propose a new online turn-monitoring technique based on the volume topography constructed on the spot by collaborative sound sensing. In addition, we adopt and craft other supporting components to build SocioPhone as a working platform. Third, we prototype three promising applications, *SocioTherapist*, *SocioDigest,* and *Tug-of-War* on SocioPhone, and show their potential use. Finally, through extensive experiments, we show that our technique outperforms the state-of-the-art techniques in terms of accuracy, noise-resiliency, and resource usage.

The rest of the paper is organized as follows. Section 2 motivates face-to-face interaction monitoring and introduces the SocioPhone API and our applications. Section 3 presents the technical challenges of daily conversation and online turn monitoring. Section 4 describes the volume-topography-based technique in detail, and Section 5 presents the platform implementation. In Section 6, we show the effectiveness of our technique, and discuss potential issues in Section 7. We present related work in Section 8, and conclude the paper in Section 9.

2. SOCIOPHONE API And APPLICATIONS

2.1 Meta-Linguistic Interaction Monitoring

Developing a mobile platform to monitor everyday face-to-face interaction opens a broad spectrum of design considerations. First of all, it is important to identify core system requirements for interaction monitoring and abstract them as common interfaces. In addition, we need to devise techniques to support diverse real-life interaction situations that are often disorderly, noisy, and dynamic. Unconstrained mobile environments make it difficult to simply adopt existing technologies that were mostly developed for rather orderly and lab-like environments. Finally, the issues of computation- and energy-efficiency are further intensified in mobile environments.

In this paper, we take a first step toward an *online conversation monitoring platform*; it supports diverse applications with *meta-linguistic conversational contexts* in unconstrained mobile environments. While there has been much work on conversation analysis from various angles [3][10][17][35], it is important to note that they focus on offline analysis of collected records. The challenges of online monitoring have not been thoroughly explored yet. Figure 1 shows the high-level process of meta-linguistic conversation monitoring composed of two layers: online turn segmentation and meta-linguistic context inference.

Online turn segmentation: Online turn segmentation forms a common basis for any conversation-monitoring system. As the core technical effort, we focus on executing online turn segmentation using smartphones. As a conversation progresses, it identifies turns continually; each turn is annotated with a triple, (*speaking person, start time, end time*).

Table 1. Key APIs of SocioPhone

Monitoring conversation sessions and turns
registerSessionStartListener (callback(Session), conditions) *registerTurnChangeListener* (callback(Turn)) * conditions = TARGET_PERSON | TARGET_PLACE class Session{ /* seeTable 2 */}; class Turn{ /* see Table 3 */};
Monitoring prosodic features & interaction characteristics
enableProsodicFeature (session_id, /* features to enable */) * Feature ={energy_avg, energy_var, pitch_avg, energy_var, ...} *getSparsity* (window_time | window_turns) *getInteractivity* (window_time | window_turns) *getAsymmetry* (window_time | window_turns) *registerDominanceListener* (callback(Interactant), Inferrer) *registerLeadershipListener* (callback(Interactant), Inferrer)
Querying interaction history
getOnGoingSessionHistory("SQL_Query_Statement"); *getPastInteractionHistory*("SQL_Query_Statement");

Table 2. Session table

sID	Interactants	start_time	end_time	place	...
1	Sheldon, Leonard	Nov-6 19:20	Nov-6 21:05	Office	...
2	Wife	Nov-6 22:50	Nov-6 23:08	Home	...
...	...	...	...	...	...

Table 3. Turn table

sID	tID	speaker	start_time	end_time	prosodic_ptr	...
1	1	Sheldon	19:20:35	19:20:39	pointers to Prosodic table entries	...
1	2	Myself	19:20:39	19:21:04		...
1	3	NOBODY	19:21:04	19:21:11		...
...	...	...	...	...	...	...

Meta-linguistic conversation monitoring: Based on the online turn segmentation, we also develop a *light-weight meta-linguistic interaction monitor* that tracks non-verbal elements during conversations such as voice tone and speaking style. Such elements are combined with turn information to infer behavioral and relational characteristics of the conversation participants.

To be more specific, the monitor extracts a number of useful *turn features* from identified turns and complementarily *prosodic features* from sound samples to infer high-level interaction contexts. First, turn features are largely classified as those describing individual participants (e.g., speaking length, number of turns, duration statistics), relations among participants (e.g., turn taking orders, pair-wise turn-taking frequencies), and the whole interaction session (e.g., duration of speaking and non-speaking turns). *Prosodic features* are also useful indicators of social behavior [38] and complement the turn features. Example features are pitch, energy, loudness, rhythm, as well as spectral features like formants, bandwidths, spectrum intensity.

When these simple features are combined, high-level interaction contexts can be further inferred, which are essential for delivering rich interaction-aware applications. For example, a fast-paced conversation can be identified from turn durations. Also, the sparseness of a conversation could be measured from the length and the distribution of the non-speaking turns, which an application may correlate with the progress or troublesome status of the on-going interaction. More complicated inference can be performed using the features. For example, one can understand the most (or the least) dominant person, the roles of participants, their role-playing patterns, and emergent leaders (See Section 5).

2.2 SocioPhone API

Table 1 shows the key SocioPhone APIs to facilitate monitoring rich meta-linguistic information in daily face-to-face interactions.

Monitoring sessions and turns: The two key primitives are *registerSessionStartListener*() and *registerTurnChangeListener*(), with which applications can trace conversational sessions and turns on-the-fly. Once the former is registered, SocioPhone notifies applications of the Session structure upon the start/end of a conversation and join/leave of a participant. See Table 2 for the Session structure. Applications may designate people or places of interest with the "CONDITION" clause. Upon notification of a session start, applications can further request turn monitoring with *registerTurnChangeListener*(). Then, SocioPhone provides the Turn information (Table 3) continuously upon each turn-taking event, i.e., alternation of a speaker or occurrence of pause.

Monitoring meta-linguistic interactions: Applications also can retrieve rich prosodic features associated with each turn using *enableProsodicFeatures*(); such features are provided only with explicit requests to save resources. The API currently provides volume, energy, and pitch features with their means and variances. SocioPhone also provides a set of convenient APIs for informative turn features and their patterns. For example, *getSparsity*() returns how far the speaking turns are separated by non-speaking turns. *registerDominanceListener*() encapsulates complex social inference to find someone with dominance over the conversation. Note that applications can replace the built-in inference engine with custom implementations.

Querying interaction history: In addition to real-time monitoring, SocioPhone supports querying the interaction history of a user. Applications can use *getOnGoingSessionHistory*() to query the on-going session, and *getPastInteractionHistory*() to query completed sessions. Example queries are "*How many turns has John taken within last 10 minutes*" and "*Which three friends has John spoken to the most this week?*" SocioPhone provides a conventional SQL interface to support flexible and easy querying of stored *Session* and *Turn* information.

2.3 Example Applications on SocioPhone

To demonstrate the usefulness of SocioPhone and its APIs, we designed and prototyped three interaction-aware applications.

SocioTherapist: Nonverbal social interaction and turn-taking deficits are a specific characteristic of young autistic children [32]. In speech therapy sessions for autistic children, the therapist often employs a stimulus, e.g., a toy, to evoke verbal turn-takings from a child. Upon a successful response, the child is reinforced with small rewards such as verbal encouragement or a snack [24].

SocioTherapist is a smartphone application for children with a mild degree of autism, and is designed to mimic stimuli and reinforcements *in-situ* during daily social interactions. The motivation and design have been largely advised by a local kindergarten in collaboration with us [18]. The symptoms of those mildly autistic children are not so severe to require full-time treatment in a special education facility. Instead, they attend regular kindergartens as well as periodic dedicated sessions with a speech therapist. However, in daily interactions out of the clinic without the therapist's guidance, they often experience difficulties with turn-taking when chatting or playing with other non-autistic children. Delayed or failed turn-taking may discontinue their interactions, or even result in eventual social isolation.

Figure 2. Daily report by SocioDigest. (a) Cumulative conversation time within the user's social circle (b) Relative per-person talking times in a session (c) Relative number of turns exchanged in a session

We prototyped SocioTherapist on top of SocioPhone APIs; a callback is triggered for every turn-taking event, i.e., when the speaker has been switched. Through the Turn instance, SocioTherapist easily obtains the properties for the newly started turn, e.g., its speaker, the timestamp it started, etc.

To implement a few basic criteria for desirable turn-taking behaviors, we consulted a speech therapist for autistic children. Accordingly, our initial prototype of SocioTherapist looks for *initiations*, *long-lasting turns*, and *rapid responses*. An initiation is a newly begun turn breaking a long silence. A long-lasting turn indicates a completed turn which lasted for a sufficient duration of time, ruling out short utterances like "Wow!" or "I got it." A rapid response is a newly begun turn immediately after another person's turn. When such turn-takings occur, SocioTherapist displays small rewards on the phones, i.e., well-known robotic characters for children gradually upgraded upon desirable turn-takings.

Our pilot deployment was encouraging. A group of three children played together for 15 minutes with SocioTherapist, including one with a mild degree of autism. The deployment was entirely supervised by a child education professional, who acknowledged clearly noticeable increases of utterances from the autistic child in both frequency and duration of turns.

SocioDigest: The ubiquity of mobile sensing allows us to digitally capture and archive what we see and what we do everyday. This is also known as *life-logging* [36]. As highly social beings, we believe that it is a natural expansion of life-logging to archive our fine-grained interactions around our daily social circles.

In this light, we have been developing SocioDigest, an application providing daily report on a user's 24/7 face-to-face conversations. Figure 2(a) shows a daily report for a PhD student, illustrating relative times he talked to his colleagues and family. SocioDigest further reports the detailed anatomy of each conversation session. Figure 2(b) shows the relative total time durations for which each participating person talked in a conversation session. Based on the report, SocioDigest gives the user a small suggestion as well. SocioDigest is implemented with SocioPhone APIs and easily retrieves the turn-wise durations from the timestamp attributes of the Turn instances. Figure 2(c) reports even more details, the turn-taking graph. Each vertex denotes a participant of the conversation, and the edge thickness denotes the numbers of turns exchanged between the pair. A thick edge implies that this person would be the most respondent to me, or I was to him/her as well.

Figure 3. Turn-taking patterns in a sample conversation case

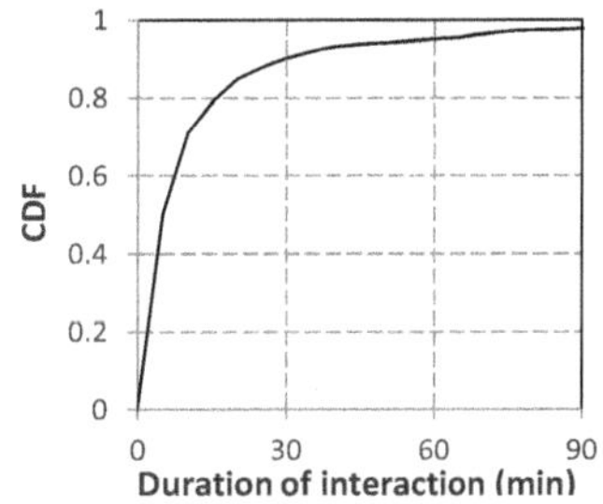

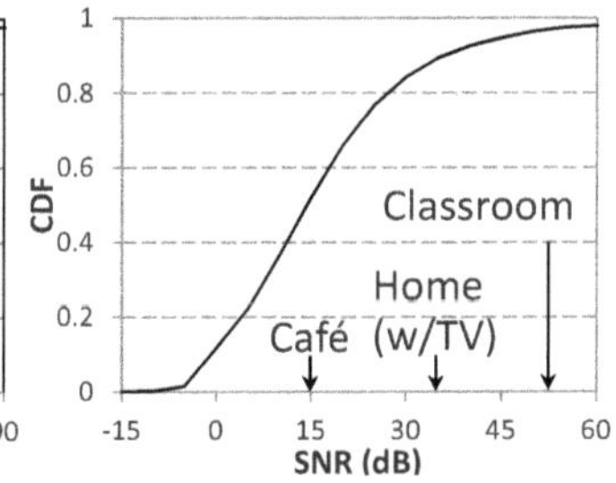

Figure 4. Distribution of daily conversation durations (left)
Figure 5. SNR distribution during daily conversations (right)

We conducted a mini-deployment study of a preliminary version of SocioDigest; Section 6.4 discusses the settings and lessons.

Tug-of-War: In group meetings or brainstorming, the level of participation of each individual may vary greatly; there might be someone who mostly remains silent, whereas a few might talk excessively, unwantedly giving others few chances to talk. It was reported that encouraging balanced participations from all individuals yields better outcomes in brainstorming [22].

Tug-of-War is a smartphone application that monitors turn-takings of participants and provides in-situ graphical feedback of how long each has talked so far. It is inspired by SensibleOrb [33], which employed dedicated wearable sensors called Sociometric Badges to monitor individuals' utterances. While we do not claim that its design is novel, the objective is to provide the key features of SensibleOrb on commodity mobile devices in everyday group-meeting setting. Using SocioPhone APIs and the participants' own smartphones enables convenient, rapid, and low-cost development of the monitoring functionalities of SensibleOrb. The lines of code of our prototype is only 75 (without counting those for GUI), demonstrating the effectiveness of SocioPhone to facilitate the development of interaction-aware applications.

3. CHALLENGES IN DAILY CONVERSATION MONITORING

We studied characteristics of daily conversations in real-life settings to understand the key requirements for our platform. To this end, we collected real-life conversation data using a custom smartphone logger that continuously recorded sound and performed off-line extraction of conversation through a voice-activity detection tool [37]. We deployed the software to five university students and collected data for ten days (total 753 user-hours). Although our dataset is limited in size and population, analyzing such real-life data gives us valuable insights into the challenges of daily-interaction monitoring.

Interaction patterns: The following observations strongly influenced the design of SocioPhone. First, we found that participants spend 4.5 hours a day, on average, in face-to-face conversations. This shows that new mobile applications to support our daily interactions have the potential to appeal to many developers and users. Also, we can see that conversation monitoring should be performed in an energy-efficient way to support such long interaction times. Second, conversations consist of many short speaking turns. Figure 3 illustrates a turn-taking history of speakers in a sample conversation that we collected using throat microphones

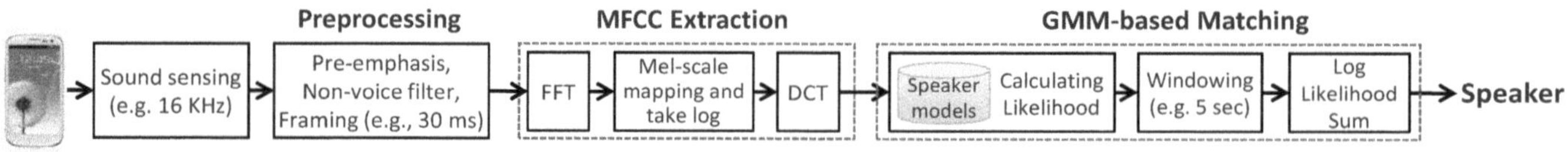

Figure 6. Typical speaker recognition pipeline

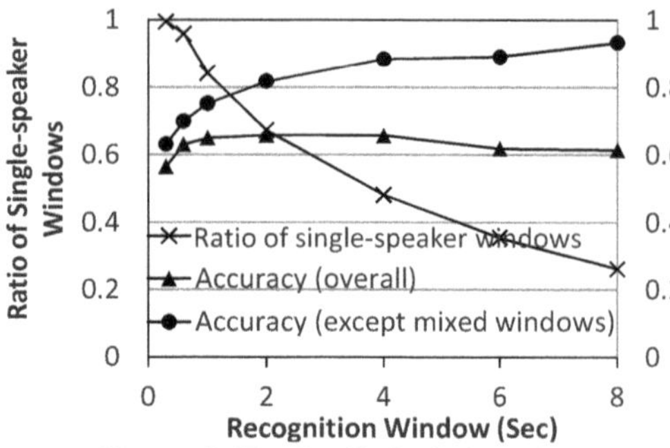

Figure 7. Tradeoff of window size

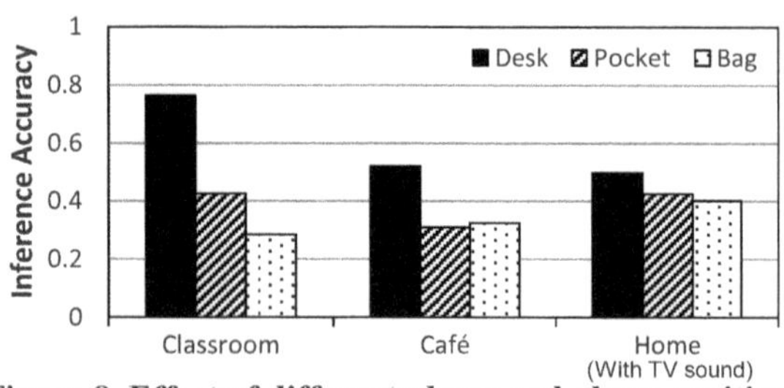

Figure 8. Effect of different places and phone positions

Table 4. Power cons. of speaker recognition on Galaxy Nexus

Component	Idle	Sensing	Preprocessing	MFCC	GMM	Total
Avg. power (mW)	13.5	160.9	4.0	54.2	204.2	437

(see Section 6.1). In the figure, we find that short, spontaneous turns dominate the conversation. Thus, daily-conversation monitoring must capture such short turn-takings. Third, Figure 4 shows that more than 50% of conversations last more than 5 minutes. Moreover, conversations lasting longer than 5 minutes account for 83% of the total conversation time, and conversations longer than 10 minutes do for 70% of the total time. Separating the short, active learning phase and the long, energy-efficient monitoring phase is a key aspect of our design. We will describe this in Section 4.2.

Environmental characteristics: Real-life acoustic environments are largely different from ideal lab environments, especially in terms of noise, making everyday conversation monitoring challenging. To understand these noise characteristics, we initially analyzed Signal-to-Noise Ratios (SNRs) during conversations; we measure the SNR values by applying the WADA-SNR library [21] to the conversation periods. Figure 5 shows the broad range of SNR values in real-life situations, mostly from -5 dB to 45 dB. The quality of recorded sound could vary greatly according to place (e.g., a silent meeting room, a noisy coffee shop), phone positions (e.g., on a table, in a pocket), and performance of microphones. This implies that conversation monitoring should be robust enough to handle noisy real-life environments.

3.1 Limitations of Existing Techniques

As a baseline approach, we can consider a representative speaker-recognition method [7][27] that has been well-established over several decades. Figure 6 shows its processing pipeline. It first splits continuous sound data into fixed frames, extracts cepstral features (MFCC) from each frame, and matches them with pre-built Gaussian mixture models (GMM) of MFCCs, containing unique vocal features of speakers. We now summarize key limitations of this approach for daily conversation monitoring.

Slow, inaccurate speaking turn detection: The baseline speaker-recognition pipeline hardly detects the highly-interactive turn-takings of daily conversations. This is because it generally requires 3-8-sec windows for reliable recognition, while turn-taking events often occur within smaller windows; note that a study reports two seconds of average turn length [2]. Figure 7 shows that as the window size increases, a window is more likely to contain multiple people's speech, degrading the accuracy of speaker recognition. (see Section 6 for the definition of accuracy) One may consider reducing the window size, but the accuracy drops significantly when a window size is too short. As the pipeline relies on the spectral signature of a person's speech, it must listen long enough to obtain statistically representative spectrum from the speaker and thereby identify who he is reliably. Instantaneous spectrum largely varies even for a single speaker, depending on his intonation and which consonants he pronounces [40]. With a short window, such so-called "atypical" sounds easily dominate the overall spectrum, making model matching difficult.

Vulnerability to real-life acoustic environments: The accuracy of a speaker-recognition pipeline can be easily compromised by background noises and phone positions in real-life situations. Figure 8 shows the effect of noise in different places, i.e., a quiet classroom, a noisy café, and a living room with TV sound, as well as different phone positions, i.e., on the desk, in the pocket, and in the bag (see Figure 5 for SNR of each place); we used a 4-second window, which provides the highest overall accuracy. The results are mainly attributed to several factors, namely poor SNR, noise-vulnerability of MFCC [5], and GMM-mismatch in real, distorted data. While there are solutions to handle these problems such as noise cancellation, in-situ model building, and collaborative sensing [4][31], their improvements are known to be limited.

High energy consumption: The baseline pipeline consumes a significant power. As shown in Table 4, the overall recognition process consumes 437 mW on a Galaxy Nexus phone; its 1750 mAh battery will drain in about 14 hours to only perform the recognition. In particular, MFCC extraction and GMM matching require 54 mW and 204 mW, respectively. A system could filter out non-voice parts to avoid frequent execution of resource-demanding recognition logic [27][29]. However, the logic still needs to examine entire conversations, which are long enough (e.g., 4.5 hours a day) to significantly impact the battery life.

Limitation of existing collaborative sensing approaches: Recent work exploits collaboration opportunities with nearby phones for effective context monitoring [26][31]. These approaches can be applied for conversation monitoring. One may execute the recognition pipeline on co-located phones and aggregate their inference results for better accuracy [31]. Alternatively, for resource saving, only one phone may run the pipeline and share the results with the others [26]. However, since these systems still use a conventional approach to speaker recognition, they suffer from low accuracy when detecting frequent, short turn-takings.

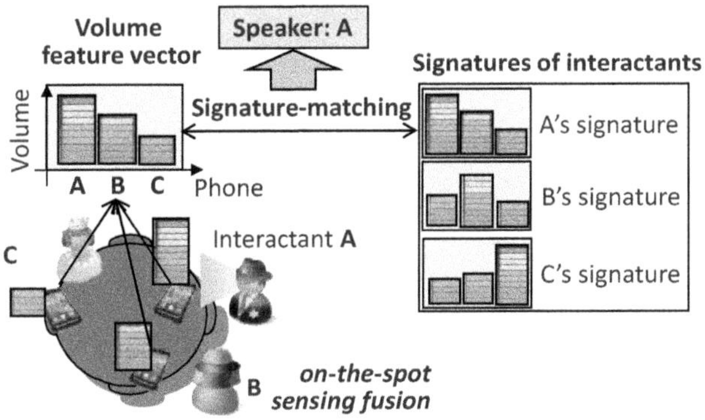

Figure 9. Illustration of online turn monitoring

4. IN-SITU TURN MONITORING

To address aforementioned challenges, we devised a novel turn monitoring technique. In this section, we present the details of our turn-detection algorithm and practical implementation issues.

4.1 Overview

Consider a group conversation scenario with three people as in Figure 9. When a person speaks, multiple phones acting as wireless receivers can capture the sound signals that the person (or transmitter) generates. Each phone measures a speaker's voice signal strength (or volume in μPa). When a speaker's phone is placed right next to the speaker (mostly true in practice), this phone is likely to measure the strongest signal strength among all the neighboring phones. A simple approach to speaker recognition is then to select a phone (and its owner) that has the strongest signal strength; this naïve method is called a *Volume-peak-based algorithm*. In real-life situations, however, this approach has the following limitations: (1) location and placement of phones are not controllable (e.g., a phone may be placed in a pocket), (2) some of the phones may not be available (e.g., due to limited resources or poor recording quality), and (3) peak detection is susceptible to background noise.

To handle such limitations, we devise a *Volume topography-based method* that leverages the relative difference of recorded signal strengths over multiple phones. As in Figure 9, speaker A's voice has been recorded over three phones with different volumes (represented as a volume vector). Due to relative position differences, each speaker will have a unique volume signature (or topography) over three phones. These phones can collaboratively build a topography database a priori (say during a learning phase), and we can identify the speaker by matching a newly measured volume vector with the topography database.

Our method is advantageous in several ways. First, it is much lighter than existing speaker recognition systems like [27], since we limit complex signal processing only in the learning phase. Second, volume vectors can be reliably obtained even with a very short sensing window, e.g., 300 ms, and thus enable turn-taking monitoring in a highly agile way; a turn is simply extracted by aggregating consecutive results. Third, the volume topography is less vulnerable in noisy acoustic environments; the background noises easily distort the users' voice spectra, but the topography itself is mostly consistent as long as the spatial placements of the phones and the speakers are consistent. In addition, the volume topography can be quickly re-trained in-situ to update phone positions and noise characteristics. Such in-situ topography also enables our method to work even when some phones may not be available (i.e., number of monitoring phones < number of users).

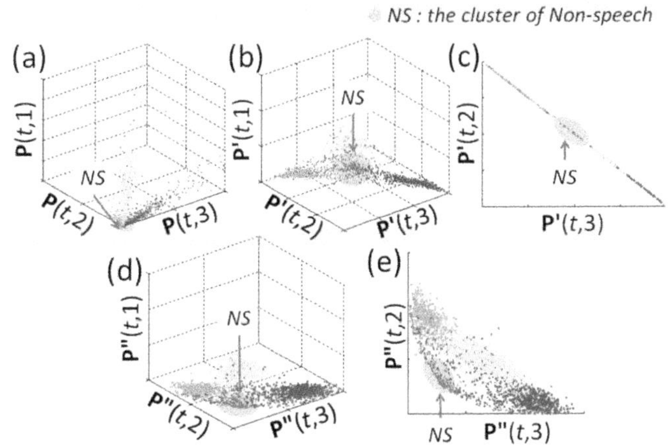

Figure 10. Distribution of feature vectors

4.2 Volume Topography-based Algorithm

Training data collection: During the learning phase, each phone samples the incoming sound at the rate of 8 kHz. The sampled audio stream is segmented into 300 ms-frames (i.e., 2,400 samples). For a given time t, each phone i calculates $p(t,i)$, the power of the frame from phone i at time t, i.e., the average of the square of the audio signals. Thus, we have a feature vector, $\mathbf{P}(t) = (p(t,1), p(t,2), \ldots, p(t,n_p))$, where n_p is the number of monitoring phones; note that n_p may not be equal to the group size. For adequate learning, phones collect the feature vectors for L seconds, where L is a system parameter for a learning period. We use L=60 seconds in three-user experiments, obtaining 200 vectors in total.

Feature vector transformation: One of the key challenges is to define the feature vector so that it has discrimination power. Our initial approach was to simply use $\mathbf{P}(t)$ itself. Figure 10(a) plots $\mathbf{P}(t)$ for a three-user group as in Figure 16(a). In this case, we were able to differentiate three users, but we found that this approach performs poorly in discriminating non-speech turns (or silent turns). Our alternative was to normalize the vector as $\mathbf{P'}(t) = \mathbf{P}(t) / \mathrm{E}(t)$, where $\mathrm{E}(t)$ is an average of a vector $\mathbf{P}(t)$. Figure 10(b) plots $\mathbf{P'}(t)$ for the same situation. This approach distinguishes human speech from non-speech well. However, we find that discrimination is weak when the number of phones is less than the group size due to loss of degrees of freedom (i.e., the sum of $\mathbf{P'}(t)$ is always 1). Figure 10(c) shows $\mathbf{P'}(t)$ with one fewer phone.

To overcome this, we define the feature vector as the product of $\mathbf{P'}(t)$ and the decibel measured on phone i, i.e., $\mathbf{P''}(t) = \{\mathrm{D}(t,1) \times \mathrm{p}(t,1) / \mathrm{E}(t), \ldots, \mathrm{D}(t,n_p) \times \mathrm{p}(t,n_p) / \mathrm{E}(t)\}$, where $\mathrm{D}(t,i)$ is defined as follows

$$D(t,i) = 20 \log_{10} {}^{p(t,i)}/_{p_{ref}},$$

where p_{ref} is the standard reference sound pressure level, i.e., 20 μPa. In addition to the second approach, it discriminates better even with fewer phones. Figure 10(d) and (e) show $\mathbf{P''}(t)$ using three and two phones, respectively.

Topography generation: From the training dataset, we build a set of audio-signal signatures, i.e., *volume topographies*, for each group member plus the non-speech case (the moment when no member speaks). For an n-member group, we use k-means clustering where k is set to n+1.

Classifier training and classification: The input dataset collected during the learning phase is used, namely feature vectors labeled with a cluster-ID. We select a multi-class SVM classifier, known as

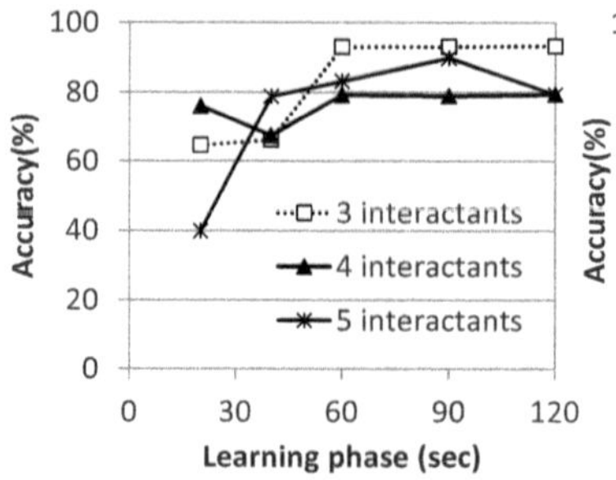

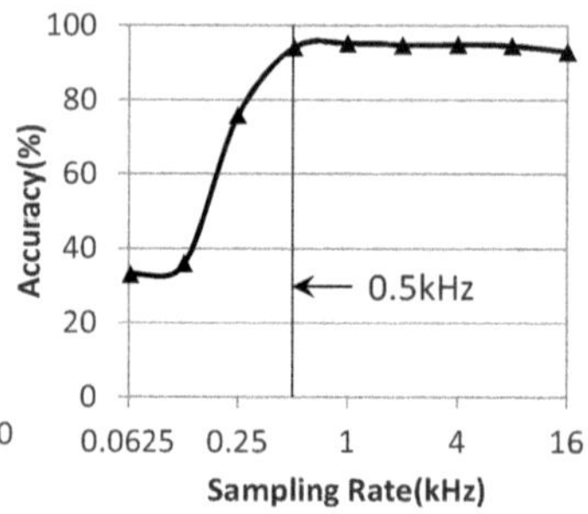

Figure 11. Effect of learning phase duration (left)
Figure 12. Effect of sampling rate (right)

one of the best performing classifiers [1]. After training has completed, SocioPhone segments turns online by simply mapping incoming frames into cluster-IDs using this classifier. According to our experiences, training duration is short (around one minute), and turn monitoring can start shortly after a conversation starts.

Turn recognition: A turn is detected if two consecutive frames belong to different clusters. We do not consider non-speech turns in a user's speech of less than 300ms; they are regarded as small pauses and often ignored [2].

Mapping audio signatures (cluster-IDs) to group members (member-IDs): In the learning phase, we also build a mapping table that converts cluster-IDs to member-IDs. We use a conventional speaker recognition technique [27]. Each phone trains the recognition algorithm for its owner a priori by building a reference speech model. At the end of learning phase, each phone uses all original frames that belong to each audio signature to generate MFCC and compute GMM likelihood. The cluster head collects the GMM likelihoods from its members and determines the mappings of cluster-IDs onto member-IDs.

4.3 Other Practical Issues

Energy-efficient conversation detection: The first step of turn monitoring is to detect whether a group conversation has started. Given that a conversation starts when people talk with one another, SocioPhone periodically monitors ambient sound to detect voice activity (e.g., analyzing about 2-sec-long audio signals in every 30 seconds). To be precise, the incoming sound wave is sampled at the rate of 8 kHz and the samples are segmented into frames. The duration of a frame is 2,048 ms (i.e., 16,384 samples per frame). For a given frame, we calculate two metrics, root mean square (RMS) and zero-crossing rate (ZCR). Then, we decide whether the sound is human speech using an offline-trained decision tree, which is commonly used in human-speech detection [27].

Group formation and head selection: Upon the detection of voice activity, SocioPhone discovers nearby friends by performing Bluetooth scanning. It retains MAC addresses of a user's friends; the list can be collected using conventional peer introduction mechanisms (only once per friend) [13]. If it finds any registered friends, a group network is formed. In a group, one phone is selected as a head and coordinates the collaborative turn detection; it collects volume features from other phones, matches them to the topography, and shares the results. The head is randomly selected; the difference of resource consumption between a head and a member is marginal (See Section 6.3).

Duration of a learning phase: Each user should speak at least once in a learning phase. To determine the proper duration, Figure 11 shows the accuracy while varying group sizes and learning durations. For the group sizes of three or four, accuracy tapers off around the 60 seconds, whereas it tapers off around the 90 seconds for group sizes of five. Reasonably assuming that the learning duration is proportional to the group size, we set the duration to the group size $n \times 20$ seconds; our experiment shows 95% of speaking turns are shorter than 20 seconds (see the details in Section 6.2). During the learning phase, the topography-based turn monitoring will not be available on-the-fly. SocioPhone can apply the volume-peak-based algorithm in parallel, which does not require any training a priori. Also, it is worth noting that many daily conversations last quite long as discussed in Section 3.

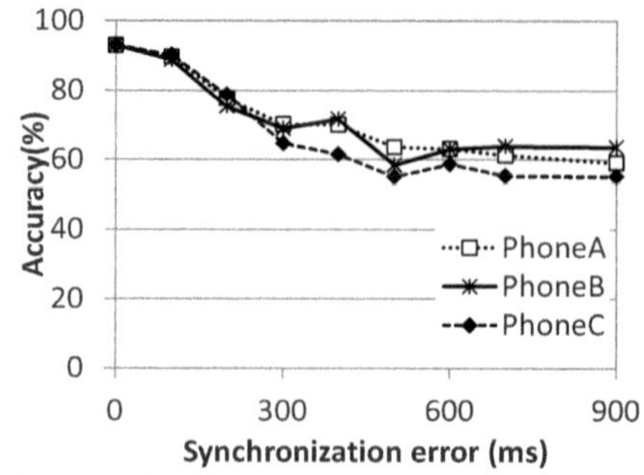

Figure 13. Effect of synchronization error

Sampling rate selection: Figure 12 shows that SocioPhone achieves highly stable accuracy at sampling rates as low as 500 Hz (see Section 6 for configurations). Using low sampling rates has two major benefits: energy saving by reduced computation and privacy preserving even if the sampled speech is temporally stored. We elaborate the latter one. By the Nyquist sampling theorem, with the speech signal sampled at 500 Hz, we can reconstruct only the signals whose frequencies are no higher than 250 Hz, i.e., half the sampling frequency. Then, we refer to the *articulation index* (AI), a value quantifying the intelligibility of a given speech signal [14], where AI = 1 for most intelligible, zero for completely unintelligible. For example, AI is 0.9 for a low-passed speech signal cut off at 5000 Hz, 0.1 at 500 Hz and zero at 250 Hz or lower. Therefore, the speech that SocioPhone samples is largely unintelligible, which potentially preserves users' privacy.

Time synchronization: To align feature vectors at the same time, we synchronize the phone clocks by well-known means (e.g., GPS or NTP). Note that phones may be out of sync by 1-2 seconds in WCDMA network. To investigate the required level, we performed an experiment with a 3-user group by deliberately making synchronization errors in one of the phones. Figure 13 shows that our algorithm tolerates about 100ms of errors. SocioPhone periodically checks the availability of GPS (once a day when a user is outdoors) and fixes the time from the GPS receiver whose time is accurate to 200 nanoseconds.

4.4 Discussion on Potential Improvements

Detection of a conversation group: In our current design, SocioPhone simply identifies conversation group members by an initial Bluetooth scan. We assume a single-group interaction among collocated friends. This assumption holds in many daily life situations, but sometimes groups may be partitioned into subgroups. We admit that further study is required to enable robust and practical detection of conversation groups, especially to deal with such multiple sub-group situations. One possible way would be to dynamically divide the sub-groups by analyzing overlapping speech patterns [6]; note that overlapping speech is limited within a single conversation group as people often speak once at a time whereas

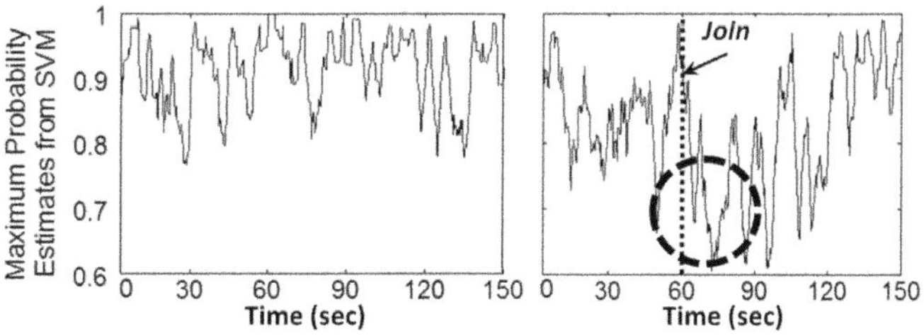

(a) w/o dynamic event (b) w/ dynamic event

Figure 14. SVM probability estimates over time

overlapping frequently occurs among different conversation groups within a place.

Selection of monitoring phones: In real situations, participation from all available phones does not always guarantee the best accuracy; excluding a phone may achieve higher accuracy if that phone shows poor recording quality. However, it is challenging to estimate the expected accuracy in advance. One possible approach is to check if the signal-to-noise ratio (SNR) is above a certain threshold, but reliable SNR calculation is difficult and also consumes much power. Another alternative approach is to leverage phone placements. For example, from our empirical studies, we observe that turns are monitored more accurately by excluding phones in bags. To apply this method, we need to incorporate phone-placement detection, such as [30]. Besides accuracy, we can further consider the available power of phones to select the monitoring phones. For example, SocioPhone can exclude phones with little battery remaining, e.g., < 10%, if the number of phones is greater than three and most are qualified.

Noise reduction: Our technique is resilient to some forms of noise such as *ambient noise* that may persist or fluctuate but uniformly applies to all participating phones. An example is the background human utterances in a restaurant where people at the surrounding tables are chatting in similar tones. However, volume-topography may be vulnerable to nearby *point-sourced noise*; for example, an announcement from a nearby loud speaker or a cup rattling next to a specific phone. Given such a point-sourced noise, the large variance of phone-to-source proximity significantly distorts the volume topography. To improve robustness against such point-sourced noises, pre-filtering of non-human vocal spectrum at the recording stage would narrow down the vulnerable bandwidth. Techniques like spectral subtraction and Wiener filtering [8] could be leveraged for this purpose.

Handling dynamic situations: Our technique properly operates when the relative positions of users and their phones are mostly fixed. However, diverse events may dynamically occur during a conversation, e.g., join and leave of a new member, moving phones, turning on a TV, which potentially compromises the monitoring accuracy. First, if the topography is successfully built in the learning phase but such dynamic events appear during the monitoring phase, we believe that the probability estimates of the SVM classifier can be used to handle the events. Figure 14 shows empirical behaviors of the probability estimates in the case of a group conversation with three users. The value mostly remains above 0.8 without any dynamic event (Figure 14(a)). When a fourth person joined the group and started speaking (at the 60 second mark), the values dropped to around 0.6 for about 10-20 seconds, as shown in Figure 14(b). For such a sudden drop within a predefined duration, the topography can be retrained in the background (during which the old ones are still used). Second, the topography training and associated classification can be spoiled when dynamic events occur during the learning phase. In such a case, the clues suggesting a retraining may be found from multiple sources, e.g., erratic turn-taking patterns which are unlikely in normal conversations, considerably low probability estimates, etc.

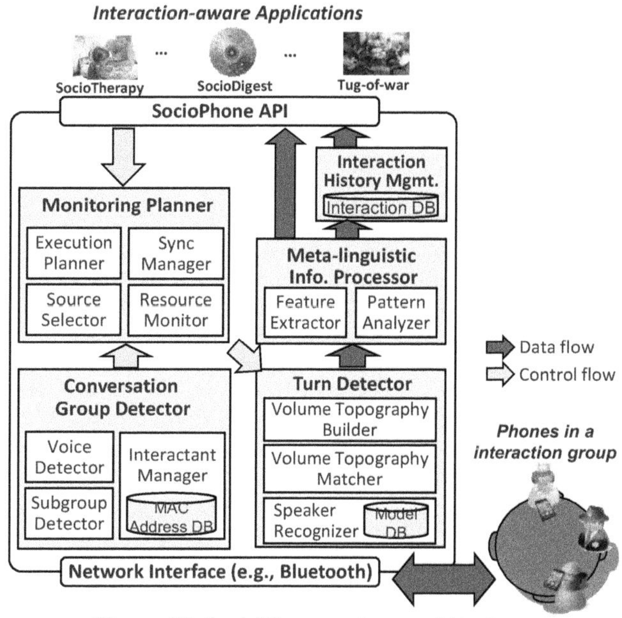

Figure 15. SocioPhone system architecture

Detection of overlapping speeches: As our technique classifies each speech frame into a single speaker, it fails to detect overlapping turns in which the multiple speakers talk at the same time. However, the portion of such overlapping speeches is not significant in our daily conversation. From our experiment with three people in a café (Figure 17 (c)), the total time of overlapping speech is under 10% of the total conversation time; a study also reports the overlapping ratio from 6% to 14% [39]. Also, most overlapping speeches are short, less than 2 seconds. Accordingly, meta-linguistic features can be extracted properly regardless of the overlap. For some applications, however, overlap detection can be useful; for example, the successful interruptions are considered to infer the leadership in the group discussion [35]. Note that even in field of speech diarization, identifying overlapping speech and the associated speakers remains an on-going challenge.

5. PLATFORM IMPLEMENTATION

We have implemented a SocioPhone prototype in Java using Android SDK 4.0. It runs as a middleware and fully supports the SocioPhone APIs. Figure 15 shows the system architecture of the prototype. We implemented *Turn Detector* and *Conversation Group Detector* using the techniques introduced in Section 4. Here, we briefly explain the role of other system components.

Monitoring Planner decides how to perform turn monitoring. Its key role is to determine the feasibility of collaborative turn detection. *Source Selector* first figures out how many phones participate; it checks if the phone has sufficient battery power and if its sound signals are clear enough for discriminative volume topography. If there are sufficiently many sources available, *Execution Planner* performs turn monitoring with the volume-topography-based method. Otherwise, it performs conventional speaker recognition. Note that SocioPhone may ask users to place their phones in a better position when the collaborative method is not possible.

Table 5. SocioPhone evaluation parameters

Parameters	Default values	Other values used
# of interactants	3	4, 5
Place	Seminar room	Home, café
# of avail. phones	3	2, 4, 5
Phone Position	On a table	In a pocket / a bag
Mic. Direction	To the owner	Reversed

Meta-linguistic Information Processor computes rich meta-linguistic contexts, based on the turns computed by *Turn Detector*. Additionally, *Feature Extractor* processes prosodic features such as volume, pitch, and their variation over segmented sound signals. *Pattern Analyzer* infers a number of meaningful social contexts by combining turn information and prosodic features. In the current prototype, it supports the following contexts: dominance and leadership in a conversation group, conversation asymmetry, interactivity, and sparseness. To infer the dominance and leadership, *Pattern Analyzer* applies a supervised SVM over the turn and prosodic features [3][17]. It also identifies interactivity, sparseness, and skewness, applying heuristic metrics as follows:

- *Level of interactivity*: # of speaking turns per minute
- *Level of sparseness*: # of non-speaking turns over three seconds per minute
- *Level of skewness*: standard deviation of # of speaking turns for all participants

Besides the above examples, *Pattern Analyzer* can flexibly incorporate other algorithms to infer diverse contexts. For example, emergent leaders in a conversation group can be further inferred using the method in [35]. Another method can infer expressiveness from volume and pitch [38]. We leave detailed evaluation of these derived contexts as a future work.

Interaction History Manager supports SQL queries from applications. To support the queries, it stores 'conversation session' and 'turn' information in an internal database. For efficiency, SocioPhone holds the turn information for the on-going session in the memory, while flushing it to persistent storage when the conversation completes. Internally, it is implemented using SQLite, a light-weight database in Android.

Network Interface: SocioPhone uses Bluetooth for peer discovery and communication. We considered using Wi-Fi Direct since it provides adequate features such as ad-hoc peer discovery and message broadcasting. However, it consumes too much power to use in everyday monitoring, as it is designed for short-term high-bandwidth communication. According to our measurements, exchanging messages every second through Wi-Fi Direct requires about 413 mW of power. For the same, Bluetooth communication requires only 138 mW.

6. EXPERIMENTS

Our goal is to fully evaluate SocioPhone's performance under a range of real-life situations. However, since real-life sound sensing is affected by a number of factors simultaneously, a direct, fully unorganized deployment would make isolating the root causes of performance changes extremely challenging. As an initial step, we carefully select representative real-life scenarios, and we identify independent parameters that may largely affect SocioPhone's performance, as shown in Table 5. Then, we rehearse diverse variants of the scenarios by applying different combinations of the parameters to understand the causality of performance inclines or declines. Based on such understanding, we also describe our experiences and lessons learned from subsequent unorganized real-world deployments of SocioPhone.

Figure 16. Experimental setup

6.1 Experimental Setup

Scenarios and parameters. For performance evaluation of SocioPhone, we consider three conversation situations in different places, i.e., seminar room, home, and café (See Figure 16(a)-(c)). We vary the following parameters to reflect diverse real situations: the group size, the number of available phones, the phone positions, and the direction of microphones. By default, we assume a casual conversation with three participants. Each participant's phone is placed on a table and the microphones are directed to their owners. Table 5 lists the default values and variations. Each conversation is 15 minutes of unscripted, free talking. For all experiments, we use Galaxy Nexus phones.

Alternative techniques we developed for comparisons:

SinglePipe is a conventional speaker recognition system, as shown in Figure 6. Each phone runs its own recognition pipeline and uses the results separately. The performance is reported as the average value measured over all phones.

CombinePipe is developed based on DarwinPhones [31]. It runs SinglePipe on every phone and makes the final inference by combining GMM likelihoods to improve accuracy.

SharePipe applies the idea from CoMon [26]. Among multiple phones, only a single phone runs SinglePipe and shares the results with other phones to save energy. We omit the inference accuracy of SharePipe, since it is expected to be the same as SinglePipe.

All the alternatives are built on conventional speaker recognition methods. We attempt to carefully select their parameters to show their best performance. First, from the previous lessons [31], we apply well-crafted speaker models for each situation and use only the models of the interactants participating in the conversation session. Also, as these methods generate results over a fixed-size sensing window, we apply a four-second window by default, which provides the best accuracy in our experiments.

Evaluation metrics: We adopt two key evaluation metrics: accuracy and resource efficiency in terms of energy and CPU. We measure energy consumption using a Monsoon PowerMeter.

Turn-monitoring accuracy: We adopt the duration-weighted accuracy used for speaker diarization [2]. It is the ratio of correctly

Table 6. Monitoring result in default situation

System	Monitoring accuracy (%)		
	Accuracy	Precision	Recall
SinglePipe	76.3	76.3	85.9
CombinePipe	80.4	80.4	90.6
SocioPhone	92.9	97.1	94.1

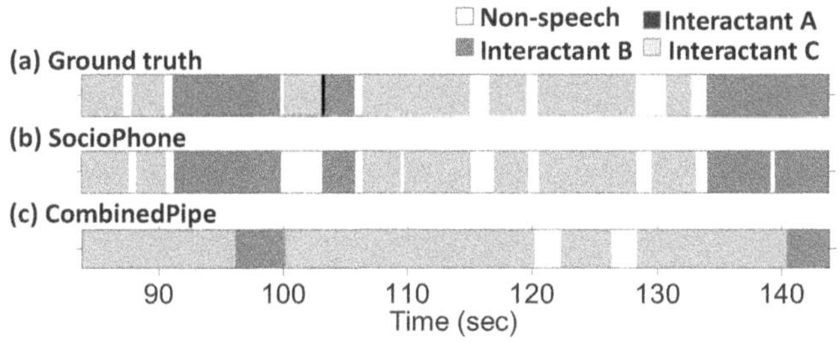

Figure 17. Turns over time

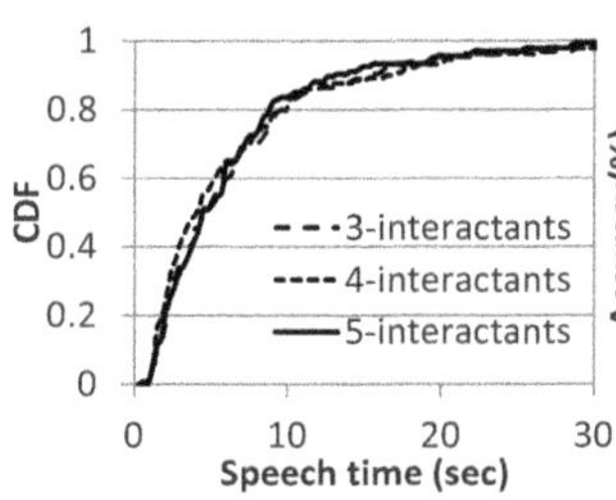

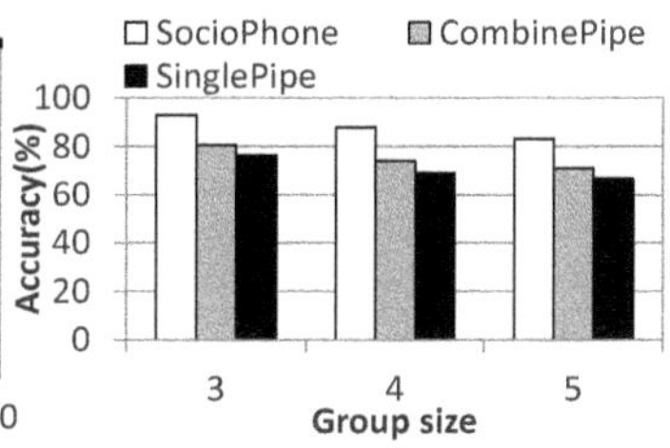

Figure 18. CDF of speech duration (left)
Figure 19. Accuracy with different group size (right)

inferred time to the total time of the conversation. A conversation session is segmented by the start and end times of the turns that are either annotated in ground truth or inferred by the evaluating technique. Each segment is labeled as true-positive (TP), false-negative (FN), false-positive (FP), and true-negative (TN). If the speaker of a segment in ground truth is identical to the inferred one, it is labeled as *TP*; in the case of non-speech, *TN* is tagged. *FN* means a speaker in ground truth is not found or incorrectly inferred. *FP* means a speaker by the inference is not in the ground truth. Based on the label and the segment duration, we define three metrics as followings:

- Accuracy = {D(*TP*) + D(*TN*)} / total time
- Precision = D(*TP*) / {D(*TP*) + D(*FP*)}
- Recall = D(*TP*) / {D(*TP*) + D(*FN*)}

where D(*tag*) is the total time of segments labeled as *tag*.

Ground-truth annotation: Correct ground truth is a precondition for the integrity of monitoring accuracy. For accurate and fine-grained annotation, we use throat microphones (See Figure 16(d)). The throat microphone records only its wearer's voice while suppressing external sound; it directly senses throat vibrations instead of vibrating air molecules. We also videotaped all conversations for post-hoc analysis. Note that manual tagging did not work properly due to the highly interactive nature of real-life conversations and difficulty of accurately tagging the start and end of a turn. Also, manual tagging was inconsistent across persons.

6.2 Turn-Monitoring Accuracy

We investigate turn-monitoring accuracy at the default setting. Table 6 summarizes the results. SocioPhone shows the highest accuracy, 92.9%; it accurately and quickly detects turn-takings by inspecting volume vectors every 0.3 seconds. The others show around 80%. They hardly segment the turns precisely due to their larger 4-second window for reliable inference. Note that CombinePipe slightly outperforms SinglePipe, since phones are in a similar situation and the combined inference benefit is marginal.

To see the detailed differences, we plot partial results from SocioPhone and CombinePipe over the ground truth as in Figure 17. SocioPhone captures the overall turn-taking pattern well. CombinePipe also recognizes speakers well in long-speaking turns, but often misses short, interactive turns. Figure 18 plots the CDF of speaking-turn durations. 45% of turns are less than four seconds, which is the window size of SinglePipe-based pipelines. More than 80% of speeches are less than 10 seconds, implying the importance of fine-grained turn segmentation for casual conversation. We find similar patterns in the 4- or 5-interactant conversations. Note that the topic or type of conversation could change the distribution, but the general trend would remain stable.

We observe that the interactants' speaking turns are sometimes overlapped. In our experiments, overlapped speech accounts for 1%-10% of the whole session time; the average duration of overlapped turns is 0.8-1 second. Interestingly, all the techniques mostly choose one speaker among the actually speaking speakers.

6.2.1 Effect of Number of Phones

We investigate the effect of the group size and the number of available phones on the turn-monitoring accuracy. In addition to the default setting, we consider two more situations with four and five interactants. Figure 19 shows the results with different group sizes. SocioPhone outperforms the others regardless of the group size by 12-19%. Even with 5 interactants, it shows the accuracy of 83%, while the accuracies of other techniques are below 70%.

We further examine the accuracy while varying the number of phones actually monitoring. We report the average accuracy over all possible combinations; e.g., in the case of three phones for five interactants, we calculate the average accuracy for all 10 combinations. We exclude SinglePipe since it runs on one phone. As shown in Figure 20, SocioPhone outperforms CombinePipe except when only two phones are available. This shows that the volume topography-based method works well even if a small portion of phones is unavailable, e.g., 78% accuracy with only three phones and five interactants. When the number of available phones is much smaller than the group size, our method performs worse than CombinePipe, e.g., two available phones for a 5-interactant conversation. In these cases, SocioPhone had better use the conventional speaker recognition method.

6.2.2 Effect of Phone Placement and Direction

We then investigate the effect of phone placement and direction. To equalize external variables such as noises and conversation patterns, we simultaneously deploy multiple phones on each interactant (Figure 16(d)). In this section, we omit the results with 3 and 4 interactants since their results are similar to a 5-interactant.

Effect of phone placement: Figure 21(a) depicts the accuracy in 5-interactanat conversation by increasing the number of phones in pockets. Except the case of (5,0) and (0,5), we report the average accuracy over all possible combinations. SocioPhone shows around 75% of accuracy even with three phones placed in a pocket and two phones on a table. This is similar to the accuracy of CombinePipe with all five phones on the table. CombinePipe also outperforms SinglePipe since a few phones with better sound quality disproportionately contribute to the results.

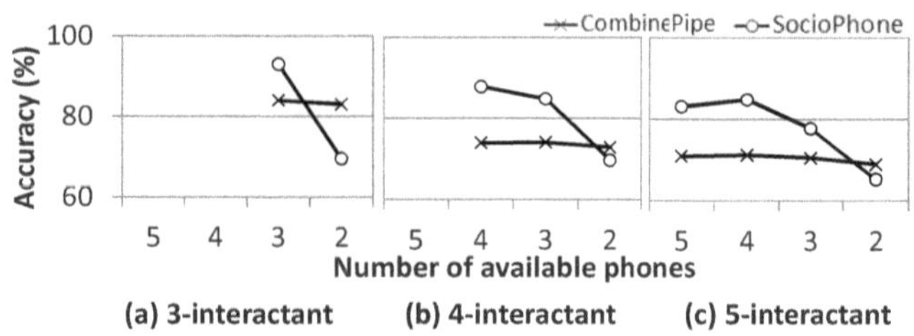

Figure 20. Effect of number of available phones

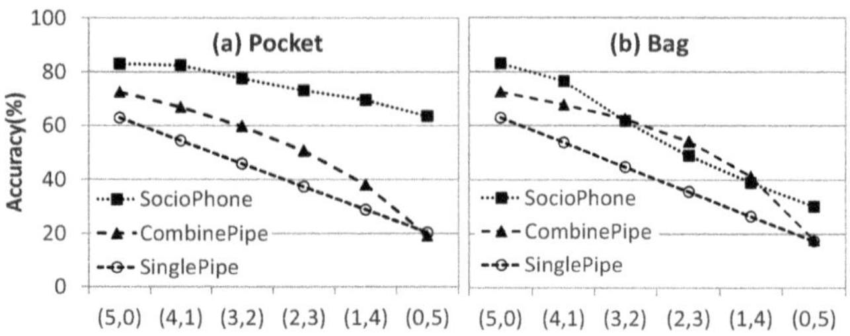

Figure 21. Effect of phone position; (X,Y), X: number of phones on a desk, Y: number of phones in a pocket or in a bag

We find an interesting result in the 3-interactant conversation (see Figure 23 for the setting). Figure 22 shows that the F1 score of each interactants depends on which phone is placed in a pocket. An F1 score is the harmonic mean of precision and recall. When a user *B* in Figure 23 puts his phone in his pocket, the accuracy is much higher and F1-score of interactants are more balanced, compared to other cases. From the video review, we find that the relative distances between interactants are different. The distance between *A* and *C* is much shorter than B. Interestingly, it is unexpected that uniformly distributed phones on the table will be more helpful. We speculate that an imbalance of recoding volume makes inference more difficult for users with relatively close positions such as A and C when C's phone is in C's pocket. This implies that the relative position of interactants as well as the phones will be a key to estimating the expected accuracy.

Figure 21(b) shows the accuracy putting some phones in a bag. In some cases, CombinePipe outperforms SocioPhone, but the overall trend is similar to the previous experiment. The accuracy of all pipelines is much lower than the previous experiment due to lower quality audio.

Effect of phone direction: We next measure the accuracy by varying phones' direction. The direction hardly affects accuracy. This is because the length of the smartphone is much shorter than the relative distance among smartphones, and thus the volume level or frequency-domain features are well maintained.

6.2.3 Effect of Places

We next examine the effect of background noise on turn-monitoring in different places: seminar room, home and café. In a café, background music is played and other guests are chattering. For home, we experimented in a living room with a TV turned on. To quantify the sensed audio quality, we use the SNR, with the method presented in Section 3.

Figure 24 depicts the average SNR in the three places. As expected, the SNR in the classroom, 40.7, is much higher than those in the home and café, 28.4, and 11.8, respectively. The SNR in home is also different from that in café. It might be due to the directivity of the microphone as well as the ambience of the noise. Café noise is spread out, whereas TV sound at home has more directivity.

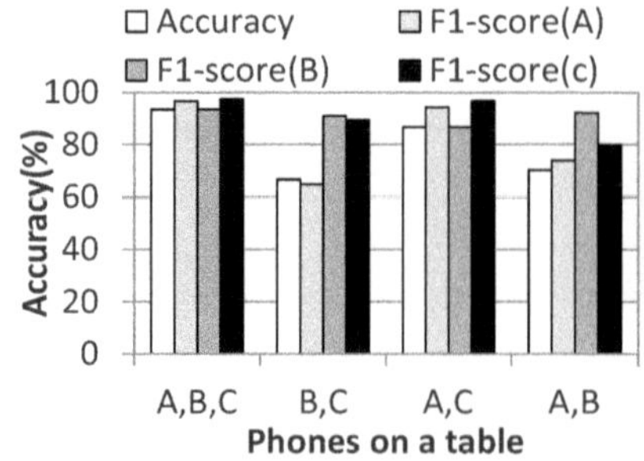

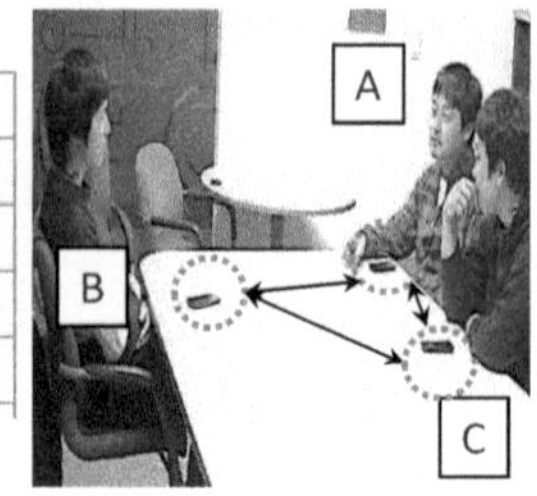

Figure 22. Effect of phone position (left)
Figure 23. Relative position of interactants and phones(right)

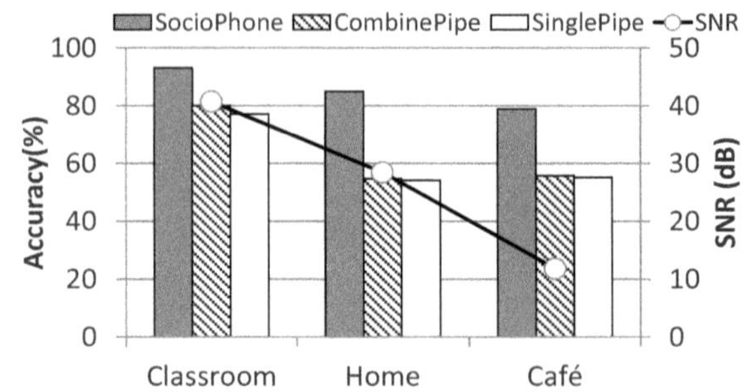

Figure 24. Accuracy on different places

Due to the degradation in audio quality, the monitoring accuracy at home or in the café drops compared to the seminar room, for all techniques. However, even in the café, which is an uncontrolled, noisy situation, we could observe that SocioPhone performs effectively at about 80% accuracy, whereas SinglePipe and CombinePipe show accuracy under 60%. The reason why SocioPhone is more robust against background noise may result from the different characteristic of MFCC features and the volume topography. Due to the logarithms, MFCC is easily influenced by low energies from noise. However, even in a noisy situation, people tend to speak louder than the background noise. Thus, a phone can still record an interactant's voice louder and thus, the volume topography will be maintained more stably.

6.3 Resource Usage for Turn Monitoring

6.3.1 Cost of Turn Monitoring

We evaluate the system cost for turn monitoring in terms of power consumption and CPU utilization. Table 7 shows the results of SocioPhone and the other techniques with the default setting in Table 5. All techniques but SinglePipe operates in two modes, head and member. A head takes charge of the coordination and final inference. A member transmits the required information to the head. Overall, SocioPhone consumes much less power at higher accuracy in turn monitoring; it consumes about 280 mW, whereas others range from 436 to 512 mW; a 1750 mAh battery would last about 23 hours with SocioPhone and 12-14 hours with others. The difference of power consumption between a head and a member on SocioPhone is marginal because of the light-weight matching. For SharePipe, a member consumes much less power, i.e., 89.3 mW since it performs no recognition-related processing. Interestingly, CombinePipe's member consumes 35.3 mW more than the head, since Bluetooth consumes more power for transmission than for reception. SocioPhone also uses much fewer CPU cycles by avoiding complex speaker recognition.

Table 7. Energy consumption and CPU utilization

Pipeline	Head		Member	
	Power(mW)	CPU(%)	Power	CPU
SinglePipe	436.8	15	N/A	N/A
SharePipe	481.9	17.3	89.3	< 2
CombinePipe	476.8	19.2	512.1	18.3
SocioPhone	282.1	< 2	278.6	< 2

Table 8. Power breakdown

Operation	Power(mW)	Ratio
Idle	13.5	0.05
Recording	160.9	0.57
Feature computation	5.7	0.02
Classification	3.5	0.01
Communication	98.6	0.35

Table 9. CPU time in the learning phase

# of interactats	3	4	5
(1) Clustering	3.4 ms	13.6 ms	15.2 ms
(2) SVM training	89.0 ms	125.8 ms	147.2 ms
(3) Speaker labeling	4624.8 ms		

6.3.2 Cost Breakdown of Turn Monitoring

For turn monitoring, SocioPhone continuously performs three common operations: (1) sound recording, (2) feature computation, and (3) feature and result transmission. A head performs extra operations for learning and matching.

Table 8 shows the power breakdown of SocioPhone. The top power consumer is sound recording, i.e., 57% of the entire power. The sound recording includes acquiring the wake lock in Android, about 30 mW. Bluetooth communication consumes about 98.5 mW due to frequent messaging every 0.3 seconds. However, logging applications such as SocioDigest may not need instantaneous turn results, and messages can be buffered and bulk-transmitted. We measured that Bluetooth consumes only 58.7 mW when messaging every 10 seconds. We omit the CPU breakdown since the total CPU usage is less than 2%.

We measure the training time of a *head* of SocioPhone. In the learning phase, a *head* performs the following three operations: (1) K-means clustering, (2) SVM model generation, and (3) speaker labeling using MFCC and GMM. Table 9 shows the CPU time for different group sizes. Since speaker labeling is executed on every phone for the same workload, we report the average value. Interestingly, (1) and (2) take only 160 ms even with 5-interactant data for 60 seconds. The bottleneck is (3), mapping the clusters onto speakers, which takes four seconds. Offloading such complex processing into the server might be useful to further optimize SocioPhone.

6.4 Deployment Experience

We conduct additional experiments to observe SocioPhone's performance under more natural interaction situations. Here, we do not attempt to show general performance characteristics but present notable lessons on the performance and user experiences.

6.4.1 Deployment in Natural Situations

For experiments, we recruited four frequently-interacting graduate students (P_1, P_2, P_3, and P_4) who did not know about SocioPhone in advance, and installed SocioPhone on their own smartphones; all the subjects were males in their twenties. For a natural setting, we let them freely have conversation sessions at school for a weekday. For ground truth, we asked them to wear throat microphones upon the start of a conversation and also to video-record the conversation sessions by themselves using a tripod; each participant was compensated with KRW 50000 (about USD 45) to participate in the study.

Table 10. Precision and recall in a natural situation

	Precision(%)	Recall(%)	Time(sec.)
P_1(on the desk)	96.4	89.0	244
P_2(on the desk')	97.4	63.1	190
P_3(in the pocket)	98.0	54.0	98
P_4(in the bag)	98.5	76.4	199
Non-speaking	19.2	88.8	48
Total	97.4	74.1	779

We first look at a case in which they go to a seminar room for brainstorming. We could see that P_1 and P_2 put their phones on the desk, P_3 put his in his pant pocket, and P_4 put his in his backpack; in the case of P_2's phone, the microphone was not facing towards him. In this natural brainstorming, the overall accuracy of SocioPhone is about 75%. This is 13% lower than the case of four phones on the desk as in Section 6.2.1 (88%). Table 10 shows the results per participant including non-speaking turns. Interestingly, while the precision for speaking turns is very high overall (> 96%), the recall is not as good, especially for P_3 and P_4 whose phones are not in open-air positions; SocioPhone often misses their speaking turns. In the case of P_2, the recall is also quite low, 60%, even though his phone is on the desk; this is different than our previous observations, indicating that the direction of the microphone hardly affects the accuracy. From our video review, we strongly suspect that this is because P_2 speaks in a calm tone so that his turn is often identified as non-speaking turns; interestingly, others asked him several times to speak again.

We investigate another case of three of the participants going to a café to have a casual conversation. Unlike when brainstorming, all participants comfortably put their phones on the coffee table. Unfortunately, in this setting, the ground truth collected by throat microphones was not accurate as the participants did not wear them tight enough. Instead of investigating accuracy, from the video recordings and SocioPhone logs, we found several scenes that cause notable performance problems. In brief, very short, instantaneous noises often led to misclassification. First, after taking a sip of coffee, putting the cup on the table makes a loud noise, especially to the nearby phone. Second, P_3 sometimes shakes his leg and his leg touches the table. In addition, we notice that when P_2 uses his phone to check his Facebook (we asked him afterwards), his screen taps also create loud noises to the very phone, causing instant misclassification. We expect that the noise reduction techniques discussed in Section 4.4 can be further incorporated to filter out such instantaneous noises.

6.4.2 Experiences with SocioDigest

We conducted a mini-deployment of SocioPhone for three consecutive days, to encompass a broader set of our daily interactions and find lessons regarding further in-the-wild issues and user experiences. We recruited 15 users for SocioDigest introduced in Section 2.3, many of whom are within the same social circle, i.e., lab members.

This mini-deployment enlightened us about future considerations for SocioPhone to work fully robustly in-the-wild. For example, SocioPhone did not perform well under some conditions, such as when everyone keeps their phones in their pants pockets. This often occurred when participants make unplanned small talk while standing. To circumvent it, we distributed wind vests to the participants and recommended that they put their phones in its chest pocket instead of the pants one. Besides, SocioPhone needs to be further improved to isolate the true conversation groups in some situations such as multiple independent conversation groups talking at the same time very closely.

On reviewing his daily conversation report, a user who is 31-year-old Ph.D. student, was surprised that most of his daily talks are concentrated on a few people. An interesting observation is that, on the first day SocioDigest reported that his wife is not highly ranked in terms of conversation length. On the next day, the total length did not change much but his wife and he exchanged quite more turns; he said it was his small effort to make better use of his limited amount of time at home.

7. DISCUSSION

Privacy: Privacy is a primary concern when audio recording is involved. Our SocioPhone design addresses privacy issues as much as possible. As SocioPhone works on mobile devices only, it does not provide any raw audio recording or rich features like MFCC to the third-party servers from which original speech can be inferred. More importantly, SocioPhone limits its sample frequency to 500 Hz and shares only simple volume features from which it is almost impossible to recover the original linguistic contents. Within a conversation group, partial exposure concerns still remain, such as the size of a conversation group or emotional tone of speech. We expect sharing of this kind of information would be reasonably acceptable among people in the same group.

In addition, malicious applications running on SocioPhone have the potential to secretly report any private meta-linguistic contexts. SocioPhone provides users with an access control interface by which users can easily ensure that only trusted applications access SocioPhone. We also expect future mobile OSs would incorporate real-time information tracing facilities to monitor unexpected usage of private data, as proposed in TaintDroid [12]. Finally, regardless of its privacy-preserving techniques, we admit the inherent limitations that nearby people might perceive intrusive from being audio-recorded itself [23].

Beyond meta-linguistic contexts: SocioPhone can incorporate existing speech recognition techniques to additionally provide semantic information like topics. For example, an application can recommend YouTube videos based on what a group has talked about so far. Supporting these advanced functions requires a better understanding of the resource requirements involved. The basic interaction awareness provided by SocioPhone can be an initial clue to determine when to selectively conduct heavy speech recognition given a device's limited resources.

We can further extend SocioPhone to capture visual cues such as gesture or eye contact. It is possible to adopt a gesture monitoring system like *E-Gesture* featuring energy-efficiency and resilience to activity-generated noises [34]. An interesting direction would be capturing eye contacts with new hardware like Google Glass.

8. RELATED WORK

Conversation analysis: Everyday social interaction has been a long-studied area in sociology. They studied formal models and methods to understand everyday interactions, such as video-taping a conversation and structuring a schematic by turns and their orders [15]. Our platform can provide a way to bring these research efforts and findings onto real-life services, enabling a variety of useful interaction-aware applications.

Interaction-aware applications: Initial applications are emerging to leverage social contexts during face-to-face interactions. For example, Pentland et al. infers meaningful social relationships by analyzing large volumes of daily social interaction data collected by mobile devices (e.g., Bluetooth scanning). Also, they propose several applications such as Sensible Orb [33] and Meeting Mediator [22] for workplace meeting situations. As a mobile platform, SocioPhone facilitates such applications in real-time.

Speaker recognition and diarization: In the fields of artificial intelligence, there have been significant efforts to infer diverse information from sound signals, including speaker, words, and emotions [2][4][7][8][17][39][40]. However, daily conversation monitoring on mobile devices imposes new requirements such as highly-interactive turns, dynamic acoustic situations, real-time processing, and the resource limitations of the mobile devices.

We may also consider using speaker diarization techniques to extract fine-granule "who spoke when" information [2][4]; example applications include conversation-structure analysis for meeting records or automatic index building on media contents. However, it is difficult to directly apply these techniques in our environments. First, they are designed for post-conversation analysis; they hardly support real-time monitoring, which is the key to enable timely interaction-aware services as in *Tug-of-War* and *SocioTherapist*. For applications based on offline profiling such as *SocioDigest*, diarization techniques might be useful but requires careful consideration. It requires huge power and storage (2.5 GB per day at 16-bit 16kHz PCM) to capture and store raw sound data. Also, the error rates of such techniques needs to be further investigated in daily-interaction situations, as most of the previous studies are based on highly quality-controlled sounds.

Mobile context monitoring systems: Some previous works propose mobile platforms to facilitate monitoring of user contexts on-the-fly [19][20][25][28][29]. Most work focuses on efficiently monitoring personal contexts such as location, activity, and emotion. SocioPhone expands the scope of context-awareness toward daily face-to-face interactions.

9. CONCLUSION

In this paper, we propose the design and implementation of *SocioPhone*, a mobile interaction-monitoring platform. It provides a set of APIs to monitor *turn* and turn-derived meta-linguistic contexts during conversations in progress. In its core, it incorporates highly-efficient online turn-monitoring techniques based on the volume topography collaboratively created by conversation participants' phones. We built several interesting applications on top of SocioPhone: *SocioTherapist*, *SocioDigest*, and *Tug-of-War*. Moreover, we showed that our turn monitoring technique offers significant advantages over comparative techniques in terms of both accuracy and battery usage. We believe SocioPhone is a first crucial step to build a full-fledged mobile platform for daily face-to-face interaction monitoring.

10. ACKNOWLEDGEMENT

We thank our shepherd, Prof. Landon Cox, for his valuable comments to improve the quality of this paper. We also thank Taiwoo Park, Haechan Lee, Yuhwan Kim, and Changhoon Lee, for their great help on building and demonstrating interesting applications, and Dr. Hyojung Shin for his valuable inputs for the project. This work was supported by the NRF of Korea grant

(MEST) (No. 2012-0005733) and the SW Computing R&D Program of KEIT(2012-10041313, UX-oriented Mobile SW Platform) funded by the Ministry of Knowledge Economy of Korea.

11. REFERENCES

[1] Alpaydin, E. *Introduction to Machine Learning, 1st edition*. The MIT Press, 2004.

[2] Anguera, X., Bozonnet, S., Evans, N., Fredouille, C., Friedland, G., and Vinyals, O. Speaker Diarization: A Review of Recent Research. In *IEEE Transactions on Audio, Speech, and Language Processing*, vol. 20, issue 2, pp. 356-370. 2012.

[3] Aran, O., and Gatica-Perez, D. Analysis of Group Conversations: Modeling Social Verticality. *Computer Analysis of Human Behavior*, pp. 293-322. 2011. Springer London.

[4] Barras, C., Zhu, X., Meihner, S., and Gauvain, J. Multistage Speaker Diarization of Broadcast News. *IEEE Transactions on Audio, Speech, and Language Processing*, Vol. 14, Issue 5. 2006.

[5] Boil, S., Suppression of acoustic noise in speech using spectral subtraction. *IEEE Trans. Acoustics, Speech, and Signal Processing*. Vol 27, Issue 2, pp. 113-120. 1979.

[6] Brdiczka, O., Maisonnasse, J., and Reignier, P. Automatic Detection of Interaction Groups, In *ICMI*, 2005.

[7] Campbell, J.P., Jr. Speaker recognition: a tutorial. *Proc. of the IEEE*, Vol. 85, Issue 9, pp. 1437-1462. 1997.

[8] Chen, J., Benesty, J., Huang, Y., and Doclo, S. New insights into the noise reduction Wiener filter. *IEEE Transactions on Audio, Speech, and Language Processing*, Vol. 14, Issue 4. 2006

[9] Choudhury, T, and Pentland, A. Sensing and Modeling Human Networks using the Sociometer. In *ISWC*, 2003.

[10] Cowley, S. J. Of timing, Turn-Taking and Conversations, *Journal of Psycholinguistic Research*, Vol. 27. Nov. 5. 1998.

[11] Efstratious, C., Leontiadis, I., Picone, M., Rachuri, K. K., Mascolo, C., and Crowcroft, J. Sense and Sensibility in a Pervasive World. In *Pervasive*, 2012.

[12] Enck, W., Gilbert, P., Chun, B., Cox, L. P., Jung, J., McDaniel, P., and Sheth, A. N. TaintDroid: An Information-Flow Tracking System for Realtime Privacy, In *OSDI*, 2010.

[13] Ford, B., Strauss, J., Lesniewski-Lass, C., Rhea, S., Kaashoek, F., and Morris, R. Persistent Personal Names for Globally Connected Mobile Devices. In *OSDI* 2006.

[14] French, N. R. and Steinberg, J. C. Factors Governing the Intellligibility of Speech Sounds. Journal of the Acoustical Society of America, vol. 19, no. 1, pp.90-119. 1947.

[15] Goffman, E. The Interaction Order. *American Sociological Review*, vol. 48, pp. 1-17. 1983.

[16] Hawkins, K. Some Consequences of Deep Interruption in Task-oriented Communication. In *Journal of Language and Social Psychology*, vol. 10, no. 3, pp. 185-203. 1991.

[17] Hung, H., Huang, Y., Friedland, G., Gatica-Perez, D. Estimating Dominance in Multi-Party Meetings Using Speaker Diarization. In *IEEE Trans. Audio, Speech, and Language Processing*, vol. 19, no. 4. 2011.

[18] Hwang, I., Jang, H., Nachman, L., and Song, J. Exploring Inter-child Behavioral Relativity in a Shared Social Setting: a Field Study in a Kindergarten. In *UbiComp* 2010.

[19] Ju, Y., Lee, Y., Yu, J., Min, C., Shin, I., and Song, J. SymPhoney: A Coordinated Sensing Flow Execution Engine for Concurrent Mobile Sensing Applications, in *SenSys*, 2012.

[20] Kang, S., Lee, Y., Min, C., Ju, Y., Park, T., Lee, J., Rhee, Y., and Song, J. Orchestrator: An Active Resource Orchestration Framework for Mobile Context Monitoring in Sensor-rich Mobile Environments, in *PerCom*, 2010.

[21] Kim, C., and Stern, R. M. Robust Signal-to-Noise Ratio Estimation Based on Waveform Amplitude Distribution Analysis. In *InterSpeech*, 2008.

[22] Kim, T., Chang, A., Holland, L., and Pentland, A. Meeting Mediator: Enhancing Group Collaboration using Sociometric Feedback. In *CSCW*, 2008

[23] Klasnja, P., Consolvo, S., Choudhury, T., Beckwith, R., and Hightower, J. Exploring Privacy Concerns about Personal Sensing. In *Pervasive* 2009.

[24] Koegel, R. L., O'Dell, M. C., and Koegel, L. K. A Natural Language Teaching Paradigm for Nonverbal Autistic Children. *Journal of Autism and Developmental Disorders*, vol. 17, no. 2, pp. 187-200, 1987.

[25] Lee, Y., Iyengar, S. S., Min, C., Ju, Y., Park, T., Lee, J., Rhee, Y., Song, J. MobiCon: Mobile Context Monitoring Platform, in *Communications of ACM* (*CACM*), 2012.

[26] Lee, Y., Ju, Y., Min, C., Kang, S., Hwang, I., and Song, J. CoMon: Cooperative Ambience Monitoring Platform with continuity and benefit awareness. In *Mobisys*, 2012.

[27] Lu, H., Brush, A. J. B., Priyantha, B., Karson, A. K., and Liu, J. SpeakerSense: Energy Efficient Unobtrusive Speaker Identification on Mobile Phones. In *Pervasive*, 2011.

[28] Lu, H., Pan, W., Lane, N. D., Choundhury, T., and Campbell, A. T. SoundSense: Scalable Sound Sensing for People-Centric Application on Mobile Phones. In *MobiSys*, 2009.

[29] Lu, H., Yang, J., Liu, Z., Lane, N. D. Choudhury, T., and Campbell, A. T. The Jigsaw continuous sensing engine for mobile phone applications. In *SenSys*, 2010.

[30] Miluzzo, E., Papandrea, M., Lane, N. D., Lu, H., and Campbell, A. T. Pocket, Bag, Hand, etc. – Automatically Detecting Phone Context through Discovery. In *PhoneSense* 2010.

[31] Miluzzo. E., Cornelius, C. T., Ramaswamy, A., Choudhury, T., Liu, Z., Campbell, A. T. Darwin Phones: the Evolution of Sensing and Inference on Mobile Phones. In *MobiSys*, 2011.

[32] Mundy, P., Sigman, M., Ungerer, J. and Sherman, T. Defining the Social Deficits of Autism: The Contribution of Non-verbal Communication Measures. *Journal of Child Psychology and Psychiatry*, vol. 27, no. 5, 1986.

[33] Olguin, D, O., Waber, B. N., Kim, T., Mohan, A., Ara, K., and Pentland, A. Sensible Organizations: Technology and Methodology for Automatically Measuring Organizational Behavior. *In IEEE Transactions on Systems, Man, and Cybernetics*, Vol. 39, Issue 1, pp. 43-55. 2009.

[34] Park, T., Lee, J., Hwang, I., Yoo, C., Nachman, L., and Song, J. E-Gesture: A Collaborative Architecture for Energy-efficient Gesture Recognition with Hand-worn Sensor and Mobile Devices, In *SenSys*, 2011.

[35] Sanchez-Cortes, D., Aran, O., Mast, M. S., and Gatica-Perez, D. Identifying emergent leadership in small groups using nonverbal communicative cues. In *ICMI* 2010.

[36] Sellen, A., and Whittaker, S. Beyond Total Capture: A Constructive Critique of Lifelogging. *Communications of the ACM*, vol. 53, no. 5, pp. 70-77. May 2010.

[37] Sohn, J., Kim, N. and Sung, W. Statistical model-based voice activity detection. *IEEE Signal Processing Letters*, Vol. 6, Issue 1, pp. 1-3. 1999.

[38] Wang, D. and Narayanan, S. S. Robust Speech Rate Estimation for Spontaneous Speech. In *IEEE Transactions on Audio, Speech, and Language Processing*, Vol.15, Issue 8. Pp. 2190-2201. 2007.

[39] Wrigley, S. N., Brown, G. J., Wan, V., and Renals, S. Speech and Crosstalk Detection in Multichannel Audio. *IEEE Transactions on Speech and Audio Processing*, Vol. 13, Issue 1, pp. 84-91. 2005.

[40] Wyatt, D., Choudhury, T., Bilmes, J., and Kitts, J. A. Inferring Colocation and Conversation Networks from Privacy-sensitive Audio with Implications for Computational Social Science. *ACM Trans. Intelligent Systems and Technology*, vol. 2, 2011.

MoodScope: Building a Mood Sensor from Smartphone Usage Patterns

Robert LiKamWa[†‡], Yunxin Liu[‡], Nicholas D. Lane[‡], Lin Zhong[†]
[†]Rice University, Houston, TX [‡]Microsoft Research Asia, Beijing, China

ABSTRACT

We report a first-of-its-kind smartphone software system, *MoodScope*, which infers the mood of its user based on how the smartphone is used. Compared to smartphone sensors that measure acceleration, light, and other physical properties, MoodScope is a "sensor" that measures the mental state of the user and provides mood as an important input to context-aware computing.

We run a formative statistical mood study with smartphone-logged data collected from 32 participants over two months. Through the study, we find that by analyzing communication history and application usage patterns, we can statistically infer a user's daily mood average with an initial accuracy of 66%, which gradually improves to an accuracy of 93% after a two-month personalized training period. Motivated by these results, we build a service, MoodScope, which analyzes usage history to act as a sensor of the user's mood. We provide a MoodScope API for developers to use our system to create mood-enabled applications. We further create and deploy a mood-sharing social application.

Categories and Subject Descriptors

H.1.2 [**Models and Principles**]: User/Machine Systems - human factors; J.4 [**Social and Behavioral Sciences**] – Psychology; I.5.2 [**Pattern Recognition**] – Design Methodology - *Classifier design and evaluation, Feature evaluation and selection, Pattern analysis.*

General Terms

Design, Experimentation, Human Factors.

Keywords

Smartphone usage; mood; machine learning; affective computing; mobile systems

1. Introduction

Mood is an affective state that plays a significant role in our lives, influencing our behavior, driving social communication, and shifting our consumer preferences. But in the digital realm of mobile devices, there is a distinct lack of knowledge about mood unless manually provided. While devices have many sensors to understand the physical world around them, they are unable to develop insight about the object that matters the most: the user. We consider the implementation of a mood sensor as a vital next step in enhancing the context-awareness of mobile devices.

There are numerous ways to employ mood information. Video and music recommender systems such as Netflix or Spotify would benefit from using mood as an input to their recommendation algorithms. By knowing the user's mood and building preferences based on previously selected items, these providers could recommend different media to match the user's current mood. While the system can ask the user to supply their mood, an automatic mood sensor will significantly improve the system's usability.

More importantly, mood sensing can build an interesting digital social ecosystem as users' devices automatically share their moods with close friends and family. Privacy concerns aside, these moods would enhance social networks by allowing users to share mood states automatically. Users would be able to know better how and when to communicate with others. For example, parents of a son in a bad mood could decide to call to cheer him up. When text messaging an upset boss, a user could be cautious of speaking brashly. Mood sensing can enable users to digitally communicate closer to the way they would in real life. For mood sharing, an automatic mood sensor will not only improve the usability but also more importantly, lower the social barrier for a user to share their mood: we do not directly tell others our mood very often, but we do not try to conceal our mood very often either.

To enable these scenarios, we consider a system that recognizes users' mood from their smartphone usage patterns. We call the system *MoodScope* for its ability to peer into usage data and infer a user's mood. Common observations inspire our approach. Our smartphones have rich information about us: where we have been, with whom we communicate, what applications we use, and even more. Furthermore, people use their smartphone differently when they are in different mood states. MoodScope attempts to leverage these patterns by learning about its user and associating smartphone usage patterns with certain moods.

MoodScope's approach is not invasive to users; it does not require users to carry any extra hardware sensors or rely on the use of the microphone or camera. Instead, MoodScope passively runs in the background, monitoring traces of users' smartphone usage. Because of this, MoodScope is also lightweight and power efficient; it does not rely on computationally intensive or power expensive data processing of video, audio or physiological signals. Furthermore, MoodScope works with the general patterns of smartphone usage, making it application-independent. Consequently, MoodScope is easy to deploy on existing smartphones without any modification to the OS and applications.

To validate the approach of MoodScope, we conducted user studies with 32 participants. We carried out focus group discussions to learn how mood plays a role in device interactions, and finished a two-month field study to collect daily smartphone usage logs and self-reported mood data from the participants. Based on the collected users' data, we build statistical mood models to infer the participants' mood states from their smartphone usage patterns.

In this paper, we find that smartphone usage correlates well with our users' moods. Users use different applications and communicate with different people depending on their mood. Using only six pieces of usage information, namely, SMS, email, phone call, application usage, web browsing, and location, we can build statistical usage models to estimate mood.

We build a general mood model to infer all participants' daily-average mood with 66% accuracy. However, when we personalize the system, building and testing a model only on a single participant's data, we report 93% accuracy on average after two months of training. This result suggests that a mood inference classifier should be trained on personal data. We also use a hybrid model that allows a user to gradually incorporate their personal data with a model instantiated from others' training data. This allows the model to attain higher accuracies faster than by using personalized models alone. After only 10 days of personal training, while personalized model training only performs with 40% accuracy, the hybrid model performs with 72% accuracy.

We provide an implementation of MoodScope as a system background service on both iPhone and Android and describe an API to be used by mood-enabled applications. We also develop an example of such an applications to show how to provide mood-sharing services. Our implementation operates with only 3.5 milliWatt-hours over a day, which roughly equates to 20 minutes of lost standby time and does not affect the performance of other applications.

Overall, our experience suggests that it is possible to build a *mood sensor* from smartphone usage patterns. Our main contributions of this paper are as follows:

- We demonstrate the feasibility of inferring mood from smartphone usage, paving the way for energy-efficient, privacy-preserving systems that automatically infer user mood. Validated with a two-month dataset collected from 32 users, our system, MoodScope, estimates users' daily mood averages with an accuracy of 66% which gradually grows to 93% over two months of training.
- The data from 32 users also allows us to make novel discoveries regarding mood and mood inference: We show that how mood affects smartphone usage is personal; a general model performs significantly worse than personalized models. We show that categorized application usage and phone calls are strong indicators of mood for our participants.
- We design a user-friendly mood journaling tool to effectively collect user mood data. Beyond data collection, it provides useful functions for users to review their mood history and thus encourages them to provide accurate ground truth.
- We describe a lightweight, power-efficient, and easy-to-deploy realization of MoodScope, consuming only 3.5 milliWatt-hours over a day. We also include an API for developers to interface with mood, which we use to develop and deploy a sample mood-sharing application.

The rest of the paper is organized as follows. In Section 2, we provide background on how mood is measured in psychology research and describe motivational applications. In Section 3, we survey the related work. In Section 4, we describe and evaluate our user studies and how we collect field data. In Section 5, we present the design of MoodScope and how we build mood models for users. We demonstrate how to build a mood inference engine and provide a mood API in Section 6 and showcase a mood-based application in Section 7. We discuss limitations of the paper and future work in Section 8 and conclude in Section 9.

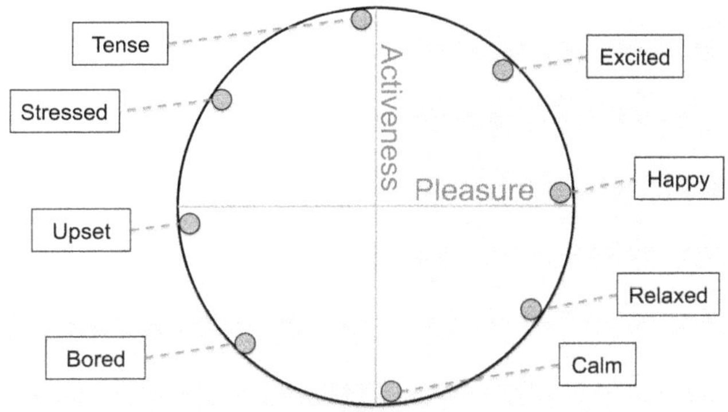

Figure 1: The circumplex mood model

2. Background and Motivational Applications

In this section, we provide background regarding how mood is measured in psychology research and describe motivational applications that can be enabled or enhanced by inferring the mental state of a human user.

2.1 The Science of Mood

Mood is an affective state and has been extensively studied in psychology [2, 31]. Mood is related but different from another important affective state, *emotion*, in several important aspects [31]. First, mood is typically less intensely felt by an individual and tends to last longer than emotion, e.g., persisting for days or hours instead of minutes or seconds. Second, mood is normally a reaction to a cumulative sequence of events while emotion is a more spontaneous reaction or feeling caused by a specific event. Finally, mood is more internal, while emotion is more visible to others. Due to its long-lasting and private nature, mood reflects the underlying feelings of people.

Psychology research has proposed and extensively validated several models to describe and measure affect. For our goal, we have considered three popular approaches, described below, and eventually employ the Circumplex mood model [1].

The Circumplex mood model employs a small number of dimensions to describe and measure mood. As shown in Figure 1, the model consists of two dimensions: the pleasure dimension and the activeness dimension. The pleasure dimension measures how positive or negative one feels. The activeness dimension measures whether one is likely to take an action under the mood state, from active to passive. As demonstrated in [1], users are able to accurately and consistently place discrete affects in the two-dimensional space. The Circumplex model has also been well validated and widely used in other studies [5-9].

Another common approach to describe affect is through the use of discrete categories [3, 4]. For example, a very popular example is Ekman's six basic categories: happiness, sadness, fear, anger, disgust, and surprise [3]. This approach is intuitive and matches people's daily experience well. However, basic categories fail to cover a full range of people's affect displays and it is hard to decide on a common set of independent discrete mood categories. It is also difficult to quantify affect with discrete categories.

Yet another approach used in psychology is the Positive and Negative Affect Schedule (PANAS) [10, 11] model. The PANAS model is based on the idea that it is possible to feel good and bad at the same time [12]. Thus, PANAS tracks positive and negative affect separately. To perform a measurement, the PANAS model uses a checklist to measure affect from various aspects. A typical checklist often consists of more than 20 items [10]. The PANAS model's complexity makes it difficult for participants to provide frequent mood inputs in field studies and in practical deployment.

We choose to utilize the Circumplex model because it is simple, quick to administer, and describes a wide range of mood states. This makes it suitable for our extensive field study, where the participants are asked to input their moods multiple times a day.

2.2 Motivational Applications

Automatic mood sensing can enable various new applications and enhance many existing ones. Next we describe some example applications that have motivated us to conduct the work of this paper.

Mood logger and browser. With automatic mood sensing, a new application can be built to log user moods and browse mood history. For example, users can view past mood states, filtered by location or time, e.g., daily, weekly, and monthly. This application could increase user awareness of mood changes and help users recall valuable moments in their life. Possible extensions of this application could allow users to understand the influence of various factors on their mood, detect abnormal mood states, and help improve mental health.

Mood sharing. Many users share their mood with friends via social networks but need to manually input mood states. With mood sensing, one can build a mood sharing application to automatically share a user's mood with friends. This application could convert mood states into a single sentence describing how users feel and automatically post single sentences on social networks, such as "I'm excited!" or "A bit upset today…". Similarly, an instant message application or video-chat application could also allow users to passively share their mood during a chat or voice call conversation, e.g. through a colored icon.

Mood-enhanced applications. Many existing applications could be enhanced with mood as a context to provide personalized services. For example, music players could automatically create mood-based playlists for users, matching how they feel. Smartphones could change their theme, wallpaper or ringtone settings according to user mood. Web, image, and/or video search could filter results to best match the user's current mood.

3. Related Work

In this section we survey existing automated approaches for affect recognition. These methods are mostly sensor-based techniques, often relying on mining speech or facial expressions.

Recognizing emotions from voice and video. Existing work in affect recognition focuses primarily on the recognition of emotions [13, 14], and does so largely by leveraging the visual [15-17] and acoustic [18, 19] signals found in the speech, actions, and faces of people. While the authors sometimes use emotion and mood interchangeably, they almost always measure transient affective states, not moods. For example, Mood Meter [32] detects smiles using campus video cameras. But momentary smiles tell us little about long-term mood states unless the larger temporal dynamics of such signals are considered. Moreover, the facial or spoken expressions of people may not reflect their true feelings due to professional or social reasons, e.g., to be polite. Finally, video and audio are not suited to the objectives of MoodScope due to the sensing and computational burden they place on a smartphone. Even monitoring and classifying audio alone can consume around 335 mW continuously, comparable to continuously sampling raw GPS data [40].

Alternative physiological signals. Physiological indicators offer a more direct signal of how we feel. For example, skin conductance, heart rate, breath rate, blood pressure, and skin temperature all offer difficult-to-fake indications of our affective states. A variety of prototypes have been developed that leverage such signals, e.g., [21-22]. The key limitation in this approach is that it requires additional hardware. This limits the range of applications to only those that users believe are high utility, such as medical applications, to compensate for the burden.

Leveraging signals from smartphones. Smartphones offer a rich set of user signals that only recently are beginning to be explored for affect recognition. For example, EmotionSense [23] proposes a complete end-to-end smartphone platform by performing audio-based emotion recognition. However, to the best of our knowledge, no existing smartphone system leverages a broad set of features based on user/smartphone interaction to recognize affective states. The most closely related systems to MoodScope thus far are [24, 33, 39]. The authors of [24] classify users emotions based on their typing characteristics. However, the relationships identified in the typing study have not been clearly validated as only a single user is studied. The authors of [33] use smartphone usage patterns to model personality. While we exploit the same source of data, MoodScope infers completely different user characteristics with different modeling challenges – unlike personality, which is constant for each user, moods change frequently. In [39], we present early results on inferring users' mood from smartphone interactions. MoodScope goes significantly further in its methodologies, realization, and evaluation.

The bulk of existing smartphone affect-related research uses the phone as a data collection tool. A variety of applications have been developed and released as part of large-scale projects to better understand affect in non-laboratory settings. For example, researchers in the UK are investigating user geospatial happiness with the "mappiness" application, released for Apple iPhones [25]. Another iPhone application, "gottaFeeling", allows users to track and share their feeling to improve their relationships [26]. These and other emotion-related smartphone applications do not study automated mood or emotion inference. However, they do provide considerable motivation for MoodScope as they highlight the willingness and interest of the public to track and share their affective states.

Comparison to MoodScope. Rather than sampling new high-density signals and/or requiring additional equipment, MoodScope exploits pre-existing usage patterns of an individual. By avoiding invasive image and audio data we are able to design a mood recognition engine on current smartphone OSes; this also allows us to run continuously in the background without compromising phone battery life.

4. User Study and Field Data Collection

In order to distill the design requirements of MoodScope and to collect user data under realistic settings, we conducted a longitudinal user study with 32 jailbroken iPhone users from China and the

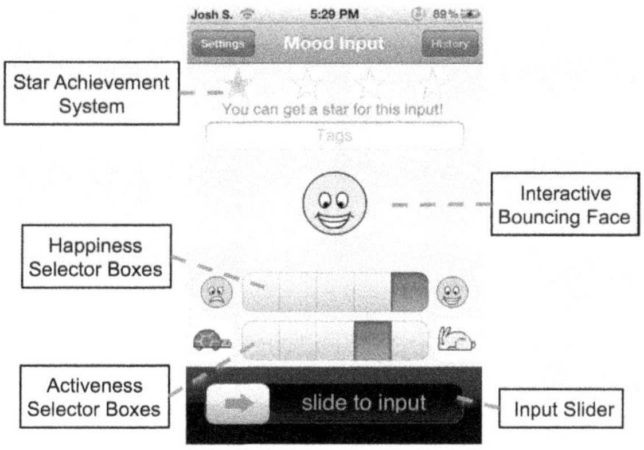

Figure 2: Mood journaling application view

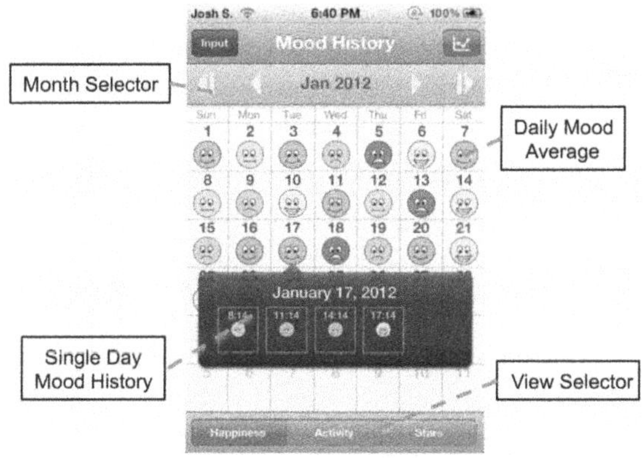

Figure 3: Mood calendar application view

USA. The user study consisted of one field study and two focus group discussions. The field study lasted more than two months in which we collected the users' moods and their smartphone usage patterns. Two focus group discussions, before and after the study, were conducted to gain subjective insights.

4.1 Participants

We recruited 32 participants for our user study. All are existing iPhone users. 24 of the users are college and graduate students but the rest covers a diverse set of occupations including two software engineers, one web editor, one salesman, and one teacher. They aged between 18 and 29 with 11 females. 25 of the participants were recruited in Beijing, China with advertisements on online forums. The remaining seven participants were recruited at a US university. Only the participants from Beijing took part in the two focus group discussions. Every participant was compensated with RMB500 or $75 USD and became eligible for an iPad 2 raffle after completion of the study.

4.2 Pre-Study Focus Group

We designed a two-part pre-study focus group to gain motivation and intuition of automatic mood inference and to gather insight into what data we should collect from the phones. The first part dealt with the impact of mood changes on smartphone usage habits. To this end, we asked the participants whether they use different applications or communicate with different people depending on their mood.

The second part of the focus group asked for the participants' opinions on mood sharing. We asked how they would publish their mood, with whom they would share their mood, when they would like others to see their mood, whose moods they would be interested in seeing, how they would like their phone to automatically adapt to their mood, and how sharing mood would affect their life.

4.2.1 Results: Mood Changes/Mood Sharing

Results from the pre-study focus group show that users believe that smartphone usage patterns change with mood changes. All but one of the participants told us that they use different applications and/or communicate with different sets of people depending on their mood. They also reported several mood-driven smartphone usage changes that were not logged in our field study, such as altering ringtones and wallpapers. All but one of the participants indicated that they would like their smartphone to automatically change with their moods, e.g., changing the color scheme, reordering the applications, and notifying them when their mood changes.

The focus group also showed that most of the participants thought that mood sharing would be valuable. All but one of the participants responded that they would like to publish their mood through micro-blogs, instant messenger, or other applications. All of the participants indicated that they would like to share their mood within certain social circles, e.g., friends or co-workers. All participants were interested in seeing others' mood, particularly the mood of their friends. One participant even responded that he would like to know everyone's mood, including the mood of strangers around him. Most participants mentioned that sharing mood would have very positive impacts on their lives, e.g., sharing happiness with friends or getting rid of bad moods with help from friends.

The results are highly motivational for automatic mood inference, using usage data already available in smartphones. Because smartphone usage patterns fluctuate as mood changes, it should be feasible to infer users' mood changes by observing their smartphone interaction patterns. The results also highlight that users do want to use their mood information in various ways, such as sharing mood with friends and changing smartphone settings based on mood. Therefore, it is valuable if our system can automatically infer users' mood so that users do not need to manually share their mood or change the settings of their smartphone.

4.3 Field Study

The field study collected real-world data from all 32 participants for over two months so that we could study the correlation between mood and smartphone interactions in order to build MoodScope. The study involves two pieces of custom developed software: a mood journaling application and a background logger.

4.3.1 Mood Journaling Application

We developed an iPhone application that allows users to report their mood conveniently. Figure 2 shows the primary GUI of the Mood Journaling Application. Two input bars allow the user to set their mood along the previously described Circumplex pleasure and activeness dimensions. For sake of simplicity, each bar limits the users to one of five options; and to prevent confusion, we intentionally omit showing numbers. The bar is also intentionally unselected at the beginning so as to prevent users from overselecting a default value. As the user inputs a mood, it is represented as a bouncing cartoon face in the center of the screen. As the pleasure bar is changed, the facial expression and color of the face changes. As the activeness bar is changed, the speed of the bouncing movement changes. We allow users to see their previous inputs through a calendar mode, shown in Figure 3, and also through a

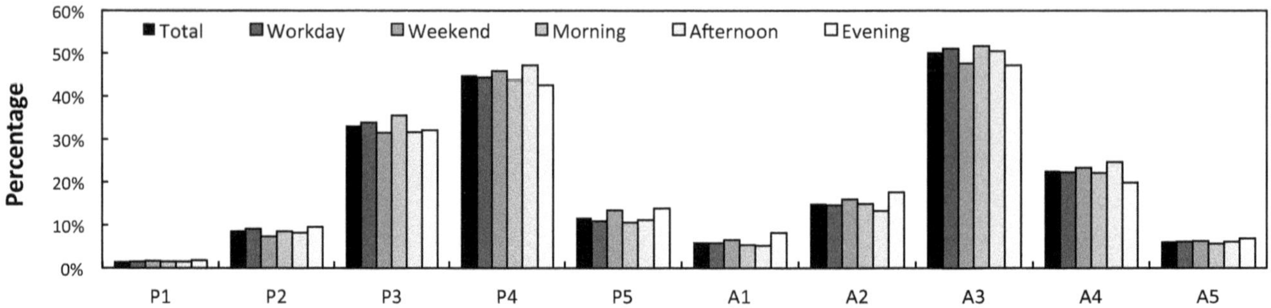

Figure 4: Distribution of user mood entries, grouped by different times-of-day. P1-P5 are moods entered as "very displeased" to "very pleased", while A1-A5 signify "very inactive" to "very active."

chart mode. To minimize the influence of previous inputs on users' mood, the input history is shown in a different GUI and not provided to users when they input their mood.

Users are asked to input their mood at least four times a day, with at least three hours between each input. This is motivated with a star achievement system, which gives a user a star for an input if their last star was given more than three hours prior. The user can gather up to four stars per day and is notified through smartphone alerts when a star is available. This star system enables us to regularly capture a user's self-reported mood.

4.3.2 Smartphone Interaction Logger

We created a logger to collect a participant's smartphone interaction to link with the collected moods. Our logger is based on the one reported in [27]; it captures user behavior by using daemons operating in the background, requiring no user interaction. The data is archived nightly to a server over a cell data or Wi-Fi connection.

Using this tool, we gather relevant information with the intention of creating feature tables for our mood models. Application usage, phone calls, email messages, SMSes, web browsing histories, and location changes are collected as user behavior features. We ensure that user privacy is properly protected, hashing all private user data, e.g., contact identifiers used in phone calls and SMSes.

4.4 Post-Study Focus Group

After the field study, we conducted another focus group discussion with the Beijing participants to ask for their opinions regarding the usability and effectiveness of our mood journaling application. We asked them whether the application is easy to use, whether four mood inputs per day is too frequent, and how likely they immediately input their mood upon receiving an input reminder.

In the focus group we received positive user feedback, which demonstrated the effectiveness of our field study in collecting users' daily mood data. Overall, participants found our mood journaling application to be user-friendly. All but one of the participants told us that the mood journal application is easy to use. The other participant had suffered a bug of our application, which we fixed once it was reported. Users felt that the mood journaling application imposed very little burden and felt they were able to provide accurate and timely mood data. Only three of the participants reported that prompting for four mood inputs per day was too frequent. Two of them explained that their mood didn't change quickly and preferred fewer inputs per day. These participants suggested other approaches, such as inputting mood only when the system thinks the mood has changed. All but one of the participants stated that they entered their mood immediately after receiving a reminder at least 50% of the time. The main reasons for non-immediate inputs were that the participants were busy or that it was not convenient to input their mood when they received a reminder.

We observed one significant limitation of our mood journaling application. Some participants reported that entering mood with our system could not cover their affective changes; sometimes their affective state could change faster than every three hours. While we realized that some users might occasionally have such rapid affective changes, we chose the three-hour mood input interval because our primary focuses were to minimize participant burden of entry and capture long-lasting mood states. From the focus group consensus, our mood journaling tool was highly effective at achieving these specific goals.

4.5 Characteristics of User Mood Entries

Although the user response to our mood journaling system was highly positive, we wanted to quantitatively understand the user response to our mood journaling system. This would further prove the effectiveness of our collection as well as motivate the design of our mood modeling. We investigate various aspects of the self-reported mood system, including the response rate of the users and the distribution of the moods entered.

As shown in the user interface of Figure 2, users indicate their mood states with two five-level scores representing the two mood dimensions. For the pleasure dimension, scores of 1-5 indicate very displeased (P1), displeased (P2), neutral (P3), pleased (P4), and very pleased (P5). For the activeness dimension, scores of 1-5 indicate very inactive (A1), inactive (A2), neutral (A3), active (A4), and very active (A5).

Although our participants are from two very different countries, we do not observe any culture difference among their mood entries and smartphone usage data. Thus, unless otherwise stated, we present the aggregated results from all the participants in this paper.

4.5.1 Response Rate

We first calculated the response rate of the overall mood input, confirming the reliability of user input into our journaling system. Although we asked users to enter their mood four times a day, we expected some absence of mood entry due to the extensive nature of our study. We calculated the daily response rate of our users and found that over all of the user's days, 6.6% had only one mood entry, 8.2% had two entries, 10.2% had three entries, and 75% had

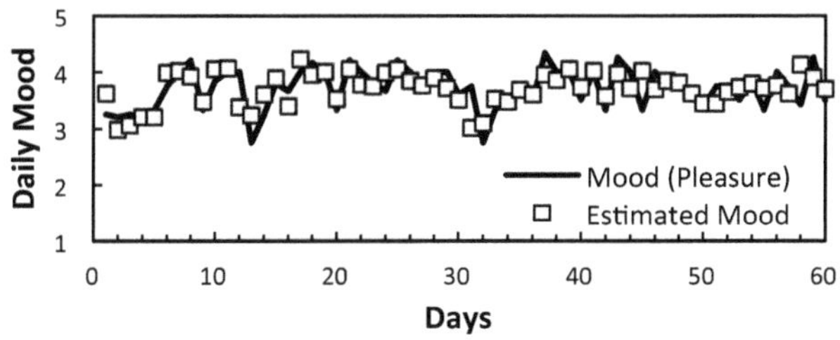

(a) Pleasure averages and estimations

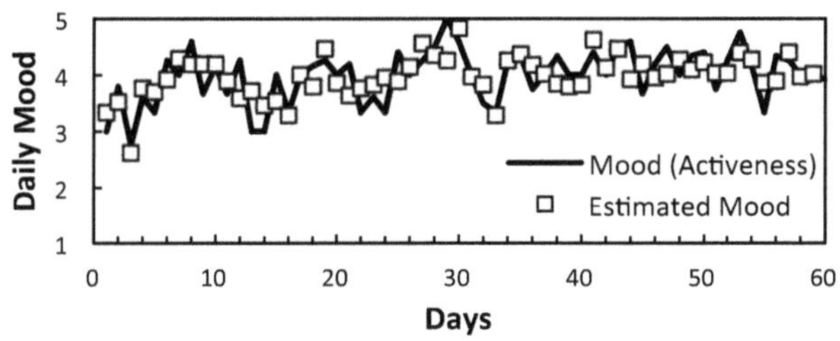

(b) Activeness averages and estimations

Figure 5: Daily mood averages and model estimations

four or more entries. We consider this response rate to be acceptable for our study. This again demonstrates the effectiveness of our mood journaling application.

4.5.2 *Daily Mood Persistence*

We next study the persistence of daily user mood to validate the background research in Section 2, which defines mood as a slowly changing affect. We consider the standard deviation of a user's mood entries within each day of our dataset. The average standard deviation of 0.41 within a single day supports the existence of an underlying mood, as it indicates that the mood typically does not heavily waver between any two adjacent mood levels. That said, we found the maximum standard deviation within a day to be 1.73, indicating that there are days when large mood swings do occur. For the most part, however, our persistence finding is consistent with the background psychology research that states that mood is fairly constant and slow-to-change.

4.5.3 *Mood Distribution*

We also analyze the distribution of moods that users enter into the system to analyze the variation our system would be challenged with estimating. As we expected, neutral mood states (P3 and A3) occupy a significant percentage of our dataset. 33.2% of mood entries reported neutral pleasure (P3), and 50.2% of the mood entries are neutral activeness (A3). Users were generally happy rather than sad. 44.8% of the total mood entries are pleased (P4) and 11.7% of total mood entries are very pleased (P5), while only 8.7% and 1.6% of the total mood entries are displeased (P2) and very displeased (P1).

When considering mood as a two-dimensional vector with 25 possible values, i.e., (P#, A#), we find that a plurality of 25.6% of reported moods are neutral at (P3, A3). The next two most common moods are (P4, A3), and (P4, A4) at 18.5% and 13.9% respectively. It was approximately twice as common for pleasure and activeness to be positively correlated; (P4-5, A4-5) and (P1-2, A1-2) occurred 20.1% and 4.4% of the time, while (P4-5, A1-2) and (P1-2, A4-5) occurred 8.3% and 2.4% of the time respectively.

The mood distributions were fairly consistent during different times, seemingly unaffected by whether the entry was during workdays, weekends, mornings, afternoons or evenings. Users were slightly happier during the weekend than on workdays. The full distribution of moods is presented in Figure 4. The response rate, mood persistence, and distribution of the entered moods show MoodScope's efficacy in collecting a wide variety of moods from the users, and provide insight into the design of MoodScope.

Table 1: Feature table of usage histograms (and previous mood averages)

Data Type	Histogram by:	Dimensions
Email contacts	# Messages	10
	# Characters	10
SMS contacts	# Messages	10
	# Characters	10
Phone call contacts	# Calls	10
	Call Duration	10
Website domains	# Visits	10
Location Clusters	# Visits	10
Apps	# App launches	10
	App Duration	10
Categories of Apps	# App launches	12
	App Duration	12
Previous 2 Pleasure and Activeness Averages	N/A	4

4.6 Smartphone Usage Data

In total we have collected 15,683 phone calls, 36,989 SMSes, 13,476 emails, 142,633 instances of application usage, 27,411 Web visits, and 1,146 unique clustered location records from all the participants. 1,678 unique applications were used during the whole field study. We use these smartphone usage data and the self-reported mood entries to train mood models in MoodScope.

5. The Design of MoodScope Models

The crux of MoodScope is in its ability to estimate a user's mood, which we discuss in this section. The data collected from the field study and analysis results presented in Section 3 provide a foundation for us to explore the design of MoodScope's models. We use various supervised machine learning techniques to investigate how a user's mood can be inferred from usage log analysis. We discuss the construction of daily mood samples and a usage log feature table. We then construct and evaluate various mood inference models from our collected mood journals and usage logs.

5.1 Daily Averages as MoodScope Output

As explained in Section 2, we wish to estimate mood as an underlying affect, changing slowly over long periods of times. Thus, rather than directly using single mood inputs, we first separate the mood inputs into their two dimensions and average all inputs in a calendar day. The resulting average moods for each of the sixty days of training act as sixty pairs of labels for our mood model.

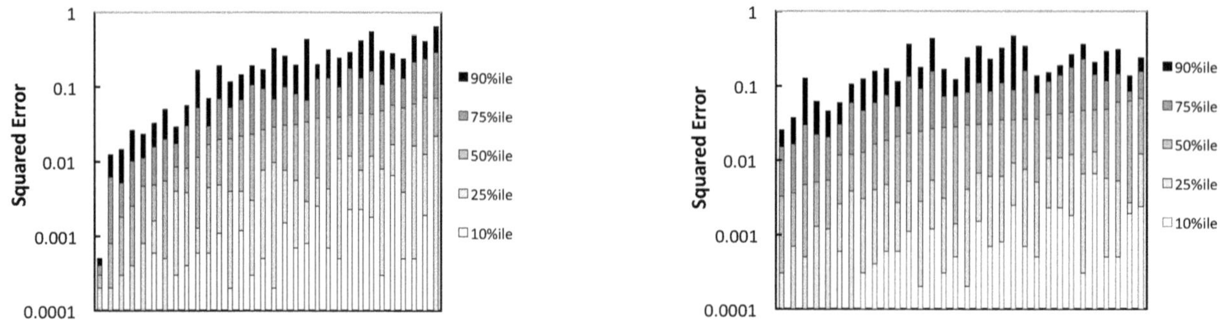

(a) Squared error for pleasure model training

(b) Squared error for activeness model training

Figure 6: Distributions of squared error in training. Each stack represents a user's percentile distribution of errors.

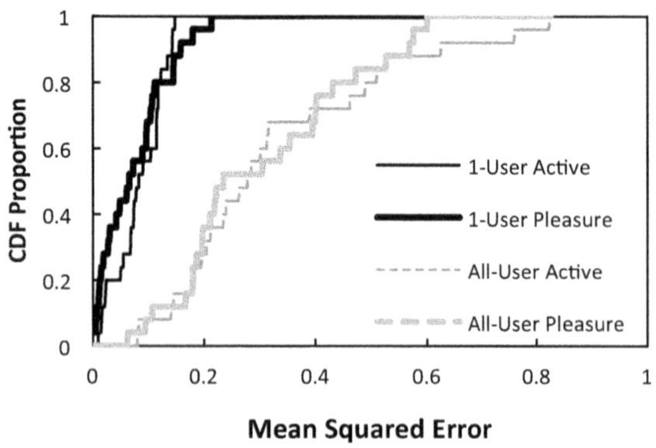

Figure 7: Cumulative distribution functions of Mean Squared Error of pleasure and activeness in both the personalized (1-User) and generalized (All-User) models

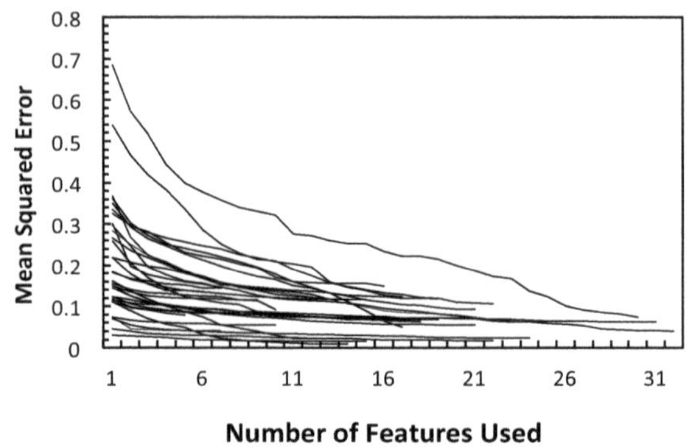

Figure 8: Decrease of Mean Squared Error of pleasure model as features are added. Each line represents a different user. A user's line ends when SFS terminates.

These daily mood averages, if predictable, can serve a number of purposes. In addition to simply indicating the current mood of a user, a trend of sliding daily mood averages can indicate when a user's mood is shifting from normal. A robust estimation of daily mood averages serves as the output of MoodScope's Mood Inference Engine.

5.2 Usage Records as MoodScope Input

We build MoodScope's inference feature table on the usage records collected by our logger. Literature suggests that mood is strongly correlated with the social interactions [28] and daily activities [29] of an individual. In our feature table, we focus on these two categories of mood-sensitive behavior: social interaction and routine activity. Our collected data allows us to indirectly observe these patterns through a variety of social interaction and routine activity relative frequency histograms.

5.2.1 Social Interaction Records

Collectively, phone calls, text messages (SMS) and emails signal changes in social interactions. We treat these three types of data separately, but identically, counting the number of exchanges the user has with their ten most frequently interacted contacts. For each day, we form a histogram of the exchanges over a 3-day history window and use the normalized frequency count as samples in the feature table. In addition to counting the number of exchanges, we also use the length of time of phone calls and number of words used in text messages and emails to form an additional histogram for each data type. Thus, we create 6 social interaction 10-dimensional histograms in the feature table.

5.2.2 Routine Activity Records

Similarly, we use patterns in browser history, application usage and location history as coarse indicators of routine activity. Applications are monitored based on the usage of the ten most frequently used applications, while browser activities are grouped by unique URL domains. We cluster our time-series of location estimates using the DBSCAN [30] clustering algorithm, which allows us to count user visits to each approximate location. We form three-day normalized histograms for the top ten used applications, website domains, and location clusters on the frequency of usage/visitation. We also form histograms based on the duration of time an application was used. These four routine activity histograms are each entered as 10-dimensional vectors in the feature table.

We also group applications by type, categorizing them as one of {Built-in, Communication, Entertainment, Finance, Game, Office, Social, Travel, Utilities, Weather, Other, or "cannot categorize"}. This allows us to use a larger set of applications, as many users will use applications beyond their top ten. To label the applications in our dataset, we executed a categorization task on Amazon Mechanical Turk. We create two application histograms grouped by the 12 categories; one histogram is a normalized count of categorized application usage instances, while the other is the proportion of time spent in applications of a specific category. These become 12-dimensional vectors in the feature table.

We also add a time-series component to our feature set by including the two most recent pleasure-activeness pairs of previous mood averages as features. With 6 social interaction histograms, 6 routine activity histograms, and 2 pairs of time-series components, our initial feature table has a total of 128 dimensions, as shown in Table 1.

5.3 Internal Model of MoodScope

With our daily mood averages as labels and usage records as a feature table, we apply a regression algorithm to our data on each dimension of mood to discern an inference model. We also use Sequential Forward Selection (SFS) to choose relevant features, reducing the dimensionality of our feature table. We evaluate the performance of our training of personalized mood models and a one-size-fits-all mood model on each dimension of mood. Unless otherwise indicated, our results are listed for the pleasure dimension. In all cases, model training for the activeness dimension is done identically, and performs similarly, within 1% of the pleasure model training.

5.3.1 Multi-Linear Regression

Because the daily averages of mood are non-integer numerical values, performing a regression along each mood dimension is a natural choice. In particular, we use a least-squares multiple linear regression to perform the modeling. This form of analysis requires no additional preparation for our data; we simply apply the regression to our usage feature table, labeled by the daily averages of mood.

A cross-validation of our regression assesses the robustness of the algorithm. Because we only have 60 samples per user, we use Leave-One-Out-Cross-Validation (LOOCV). LOOCV trains the model on all but one of the samples and validates the model on the remaining sample. As a result, each sample from the original data set is used for validation once. During any iteration of LOOCV, the cross-validation trains the model on 59 samples, allowing for robust model training on our study's small dataset.

5.3.2 Sequential Forward Selection of Features

Because of the large dimensionality of features compared to the number of samples, we choose a subset of relevant features to accelerate the learning process. For this task, we use Sequential Forward Selection (SFS) [36].

In SFS, our system attempts to pick a subset Y of the feature table that will give the best regression. In the SFS algorithm, Y starts out as an empty set. SFS then iterates, finding the feature x which is not already in Y that provides the best fit to the data, minimizing the mean error of the fit. It then adds x to Y and continues to iterate. SFS will stop running when it reaches a local minimum; at this point, adding any of the remaining features will increase the error. Through this process, SFS appropriately selects the data's most representative features, reducing the dimensionality of our table.

5.3.3 Personalized Mood Model

We create a personalized model for each user by performing multi-linear regression on each user's data individually. Using individualized multi-linear regression to train the pleasure dimension of the models, we report an average mean squared error (MSE) of 0.075 across all users, with a standard deviation of 0.050, a minimum MSE of 0.002, and a maximum MSE of 0.176. We received similar numbers when training the activeness dimension: 0.085, 0.062, 0.001, and 0.215 respectively. The standard deviation reveals that mood modeling works better for some users than others, but the MSE numbers are low enough to suggest that mood can be accurately inferred from smartphone interactions in our dataset; it takes a squared error of 0.25 to move from the center of one mood label halfway towards another label. On average, 93.1% of the daily pleasure averages and 92.7% of the activeness averages have a squared error under 0.25. The distribution of error for each user is shown in Figure 6. The CDFs in Figure 7 show the distribution of mean-squared-error across all users.

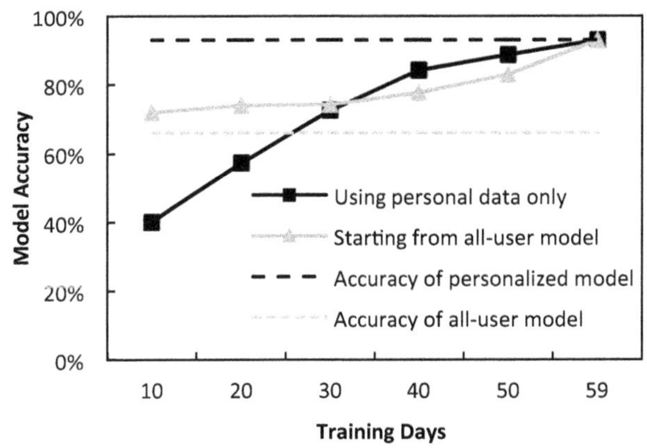

Figure 9: Pleasure training accuracy vs. training data size

On average, SFS chose 16.3 features per user. Some users used as few as 5 features, while others used 32 features to strengthen the model. Figure 8 shows how SFS improves the robustness of our algorithm as it adds more features.

5.3.4 All-User Mood Model

While personalized models report high accuracy, they require individual training over a long period of time. We attempt to reduce the amount of training required by the training by forming a "one-size-fits-all" mood model created from an aggregate of all of the users' data. If successful, this model can be used as an initial model for a new user, bootstrapping the training procedure.

To test the feasibility of an all-user mood model, we remove a user's data from our dataset and perform a multi-linear regression on the remaining data to create a model. We then apply the model to the user's data and compute the mean-squared-error of the computed mood.

After training, we found that the general model performed surprisingly well for some users. On pleasure model training the minimum mean-squared-error across our users is 0.069. However, for many users, the mean-squared-error is quite high, as our dataset had an average mean-squared-error of 0.296, with standard deviation of 0.175. The maximum mean-squared-error from our dataset is 0.79. On average, only 66% of pleasure estimates are off by less than 0.25 squared-error. Activeness estimation performs similarly, with average mean-squared error of 0.289. 67% of activeness estimates are off by less than 0.25 squared-error. The CDFs in Figure 7 show the distribution of accuracy across all users.

5.3.5 *Hybrid Mood Model Approaches*

An ideal mood model would blend together the respective strengths of the personalized (high accuracy) and all-user (no user training) modeling approaches. We investigate hybrid mood model design choices that combine a small amount of user-specific training data with larger amounts of training data collected from the general user population. To test a hybrid approach, we fit a multi-linear regression model with a modified objective function that prioritizes reducing residual errors related to personalized training data above errors related to training data sourced from the rest of the population. As a result, the hybrid model is able to incorporate unique characteristics in how an individual user's smartphone data relate to their mood while also capturing the coarse-grain patterns that are common across all people. Through our experiments we find the accuracy of the hybrid model is naturally sensitive to the weighting, i.e., prioritization, placed on personalized data residual errors relative to data from the general population; we determine this weighting term empirically by per forming a conventional grid parameter search that minimizes MSE error.

Figure 9 examines the MSE accuracy of our hybrid model when incrementally trained with increasing amounts of user-specific training data. In this figure, we compare the hybrid approach with user training data to an incrementally trained personalized model with no prior training data. We also represent the accuracy of the all-user model (66%) and personalized model (93%) as reference points. We find that even with only 10 days of personalized training data, the hybrid model has higher MSE accuracy than the incremental personalized by 31% and the all-user model by 6%. After 30 days, the personalized model outperforms the hybrid model and can be used with greater than 75% accuracy.

5.3.6 *Comparison to Strawman Models*

As shown in Section 4.5.3, P4 and A3 are the most common moods. However, guessing those as the mood would only result in 44.8% or 50.2% accuracy, respectively. Thus, simply using the overall most common mood as an estimate would not perform well. Instead, we compare our models with three simplistic strawman models that assume prior knowledge of a user's personal usage patterns. This reinforces the necessity to perform complicated model training and collect smartphone usage feature tables.

Model A, an average mood model, assumes that the mood never deviates from the average mood of the user. Model B, a slowly varying mood model, assumes that the mood is the same as the last-entered mood. Model C, the no-features model, performs leave-one-out multi-linear regression with the previous two mood pairs as input features alone.

The average MSE and accuracy of the strawman models are shown in Table 2. Of these methods, the average mood method works best, with an average MSE of 0.242 and accuracy of 73%, performing only slightly better than our all-user model. Thus, even with the full set of two months' training data, these simple strawman models compare unfavorably against personalized mood models and are insufficient for use in long-term mood estimation. Note that the hybrid model described in 5.3.5 achieves 72% accuracy but with much less personal training data, i.e., 10 days. While the strawman models leverage prior knowledge about each individual user, the hybrid model exploits prior knowledge about general users.

Table 2: Strawman model performance comparison

Model	Pleas. MSE	Pleas. Acc.	Activ. MSE	Activ. Acc
Model A: average mood	0.242	73%	0.229	74%
Model B: slow-varying mood	0.354	61%	0.318	65%
Model C: no phone features	0.258	70%	0.277	71%
All-user Model	0.296	66%	0.289	67%
Personalized Model	0.075	93%	0.085	93%

5.3.7 *Predicting Two-Dimensional Mood*

Our training process predicts mood along each dimension individually. We find that with two months of personalized training data, each dimension is within 0.25 squared error for 93% of the days. After predicting each dimension, we found that 85% of the estimated two-dimensional daily moods are within 0.25 squared error. This performs significantly better than random guessing, at 4% accuracy, or choosing the most common mood (P4, A3), at 25.4% accuracy.

5.4 Feature Table Characteristics

In this section, we explore characteristics of our feature table in mood model training. In particular, we discuss the relative importance of feature categories in discriminating mood. We also track the correlations of the feature types with pleasure and activeness. These characteristics allow us to draw several key insights into the efficacy of the data types we collect.

5.4.1 *Discriminative Features*

While SFS's primary function is to reduce the feature table to a reasonable dimension, it comes with the side benefit of highlighting which features are useful in detecting mood. There are several ways to determine which features are useful for discrimination. We consider a few of these approaches with our personalized models.

Count number of occurrences in reduced feature table: After SFS reduces the feature table, we count the number of features of each type of data that appear in all reduced tables. Figure 10 shows the results. Phone calls, *Calls*, and categorized applications, *Apps (Cat.)*, are the two most used features after SFS completes the feature selection.

Count number of statistically significant features: With the features used in the SFS, we perform Pearson Product-Moment Correlation on the data to obtain p-values. We used p-values less than 0.05 to indicate statistically significant features and present this data as the solid bars in Figure 10. Phone calls and categorized applications, which are the most commonly selected features, also show up as among the most common significant features. However, they are joined by significant features from emails, SMS, and ungrouped applications.

Count number of most discriminative features: Sequential Feature Selection selects features in order of how much they help the training. We look at the first chosen as the most discriminative feature and count the number of times they occur in Figure 11. For Activeness model training, phone calls and categorized applications again appear on top, in addition to SMS features, and followed closely by email features. However, for pleasure model training, email and SMS features are the common most-discriminative features, followed closely by phone calls. Amongst our users, categorized applications are only selected once for Pleasure model training.

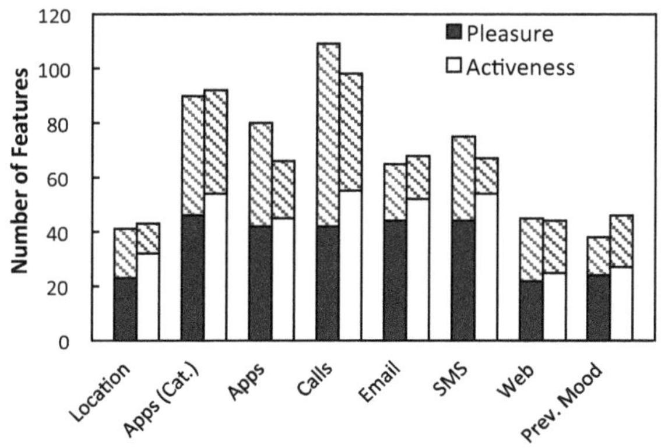

Figure 10: Number of features in SFS-reduced tables. Solid bars represent statistically significant features ($p < 0.05$).

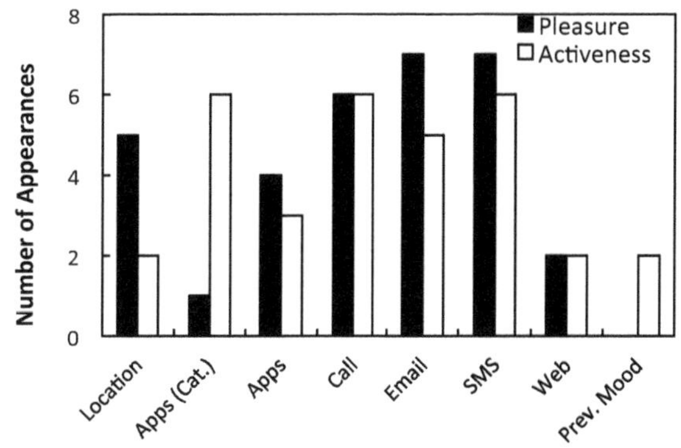

Figure 11: Number of times a category appears as a *most discriminative feature*

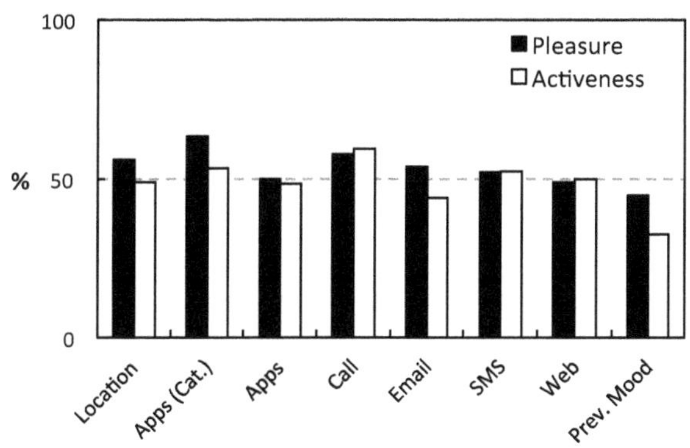

Figure 12: Percentage of features that positively correlate

Overall, phone calls invariably appear as a discriminative feature for determining mood. Categorized applications also appear very frequently and significantly. Emails and SMS follow closely as the next most discriminative features. Thus, while all features are used in varying combinations to predict mood, *communication history* and *categorized application usage logs* are the discriminative features that are most linked to mood.

5.4.2 Positively and Negatively Correlated Features

In addition to seeing which selected features are the most helpful, we also track which types of features' coefficients appear positively or negatively more often than other features. We count the percentage of positive coefficients for each type in our personalized multi-linear regression models and display the results in Figure 12.

Previous Mood is frequently negative for both Pleasure (55% negative) and Activeness (67% negative). This is likely because many users have a strong tendency towards neutral. In other words, a highly negative mood is often followed by a more-positive mood towards neutral and vice versa.

During pleasure model training, phone calls, categorized applications, and locations are often positive indicators of pleasure, appearing 55% of the time as positive. In activeness model training, Phone call features again appear for positive activeness, appearing 59% of the time as positive. A high value in many selected email features tended to indicate lower activeness, as only 44% of email coefficients were positive when used in activeness model training.

5.5 Summary of MoodScope Design

To predict the daily average of mood from histograms of interactions, we use multi-linear regression, tuned by a Sequential Forward Feature Selection. Personalized models report high accuracy for most users, while generalized all-user models perform worse. However, MoodScope can use the all-user model to predict moods until it collects enough training data from a new user.

We also used our model training to discriminate which features were more aligned with mood. Categorized application usage and communication history, especially phone calls, were the most useful features in determining a user's mood. However, amongst all the users, all features were significantly used to determine mood.

6. Mood Inference Engine

Guided by our mood modeling study, we design and implement a *Mood Inference Engine* capable of inferring the mood of a user based on their smartphone usage history. As shown in Figure 13, the mood inference engine consists of two software components, one residing in the phone and the other in the cloud. The phone-side software, written for iPhone and Android systems, collects smartphone usage logs and user mood labels, on behalf of the cloud. The cloud is responsible for training a predictive mood model using these data, which is provided back to the smartphone. By applying this model, the phone is able to locally infer user mood – without aid of the cloud.

In the remainder of this section, we discuss the internal design of the Inference Engine, and provide performance measurements of our prototype implementation. Later, in Section 7, we describe how we build an application that encourages users to input their mood states to bootstrap the mood inference model.

6.1 Training on the Cloud

Cloud-side software performs a combination of SFS and multi-linear regression, as described in Section 4, to train models for each user. The server processes usage logs with a collection of Unix bash scripts and Perl scripts. In total, this amounts to 815 lines of code. Models are trained using calls to MATLAB scripts that perform multi-linear regression with feature selection. Our system uses the Hybrid Mood Model from 5.3.5 to bootstrap the training mechanism. On a QuadCore 2.4 GHz Intel i7 processor, these two stages take on average 12 minutes at 100% computation to train a single mood model.

Table 3: Performance characteristics of MoodScope phone deployments. Tasks run in the background.

	iPhone 4	Galaxy S2
Logging (once/hour)		
Lines of Code	361	213
Computation Time	130 ms	102 ms
Power Consumption	---	177 mW
Pre-processing (once/hour)		
Lines of Code	1012	502
Computation Time	13.3 s	2 s
Power Consumption	---	182 mW
Inference (once/hour)		
Lines of Code	5	5
Computation Time	~0	~0
Power Consumption	---	~0
Communication (once/evening)		
Data Upload	1.0 MB	1.0 MB
Data Download	3.2 KB	3.2 KB
Time to send/receive	2 s	2 s
Power Consumption	---	1709 mW

6.2 Inference on the Phone

Although model training is offloaded to the cloud, mood inference is performed entirely locally on the smartphone. Feature extraction is lightweight, only involving the update of continuously maintained histograms describing select phone usage patterns, along with a lookup of the current location within a table of clusters discovered by running DBSCAN. Similarly, inference itself only requires performing a dot product multiplication between features.

6.2.1 Implementation and Performance

Our smartphone implementation prototypes are based on the LiveLab logger [27]. We implement the phone backend software on a jailbroken iPhone 4 running iOS 5.1 and a Samsung Galaxy S2 running Android 4.0.1. The iPhone 4 service implementation is written in 1378 lines of bash script, while the Android background service implementation uses 720 lines of Java code. Statistics regarding the code size, computation time, and power performance are displayed in Table 3.

The iPhone 4 performs all logging, feature, and inference stages in roughly 15 seconds. This process repeats once an hour to update the current estimated mood for the user. Running on a Galaxy S2, the processes take 3 seconds, also repeating each hour. Both implementations run silently in the background with no noticeable impairment to the user.

We obtain the system power consumption of the Galaxy S2 by measuring the voltage across a resistor put in series with the phone battery. Our measurements of the power consumption on the Android service reveal that we consume less than 400 mW during the logging and data processing. In total, over a day, the engine consumes approximately 3.5 milliWatt-hours, or less than 0.5% of a phone's battery capacity.

6.2.2 Communication Overhead

The complete user log for a whole day is typically around 1MB after compression is applied. Because many features require the frequency of usage across multiple days to be considered such as the top 10 SMS contacts spanning multiple days, we must transmit the entire log rather than just a summary.

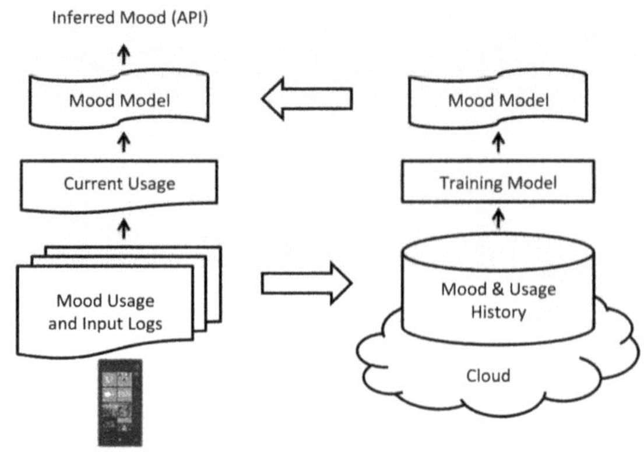

Figure 13: The Mood Inference Engine

A mood model can be represented as a series of coefficients, selected features and location clusters. An uncompressed plaintext encoding requires less than 5 KB to be downloaded to the phone. This compresses down to less than 3 KB.

The one-time cost of daily transmission and reception amounts to 2 seconds of 1709 mW power consumption and thus has negligible impact on the user. To further reduce the impact, this process is only performed at night, when users typically charge their phones and are connected to household Wi-Fi networks.

6.3 Application Programming Interface

Our Inference Engine system service exposes a simple API for developers to use. Developers are abstracted away from any concerns related to machine learning or mood psychology, leaving them free to innovate. As shown in Table 4, the API is very simple. An application can retrieve a user's current or historical mood state with two scores of pleasure and activeness. The application can also set the user's current mood state to update the mood model.

7. MoodScope Social Sharing Application

With the API provided by MoodScope, application developers can enable various mood-based applications for more personalized services, increasing the usability of the phone and lowering the social barrier of sharing mood.

We design a MoodScope Social Sharing App on top of our iPhone Mood Inference Engine as an end-to-end demonstration of a fully functional mood-aware application. Every night, this application determines the user's mood simply with an API call to the Inference Engine. Current user mood is then visualized using a pair of thermometer bars, one for each mood polarity, accessible to the user as a smartphone application. Users are able to manually correct errors in inferred mood by altering the temperature of either thermometer. If desired, inferred mood can be shared automatically to the user's Facebook Timeline.

When first used our application must rely on the generic All-User Mood Model, and potentially suffer from unreliable performance. However, as users correct inaccurate mood inferences this feedback is provided back to the Engine by the application. The MoodScope Engine incorporates these new observations into the model through hybridized model training. Over time, the model will be personalized to specific mood indicators that represent the usage logs of the user. Once the accuracy of the mood prediction stabilizes, the application provides settings for the automatic shar-

Table 4: Mood Inference Engine API specification

Interface	Description
`MoodState class`	Data structure containing two floats to represent pleasure and activeness.
`GetCurrentMood()`	Returns current `MoodState`.
`GetPastMood(time)`	Returns the `MoodState` at a given timestamp
`SetMood(mood)`	Sets the current `MoodState` to *moodstate*. Also updates the model on the cloud.

ing of mood with certain social circles of friends and/or family. We envision that easy sharing of everyday moods will enhance online communication, which lacks many of the subtle non-verbal signals presented in face-to-face interactions.

We deployed our application on three university students from the original 32 participants after their 2 months of training models in the field study and received positive feedback. During their 4 days of usage, users reported that the application performed reasonably well, especially with the users who had diligently journaled his mood for the 2 months. While not all participants wished to share their mood publicly on Facebook, they all enjoyed seeing the device estimate their mood and were excited about the potential of using the mood in other applications.

8. Discussion and Future Work

Our findings show MoodScope is a promising and practical approach for inferring mood with smartphones. However, a number of limitations in our study must be overcome before MoodScope is ready for widespread usage.

We evaluate MoodScope with a small-scale user population that is fairly homogenous. We have only tens of participants from two cities and most of them were young students. We do not claim that our results will generalize to other user groups. Large-scale validation of our results remains as future work.

Entering mood four times daily can be too burdensome for public adoption. Our future work seeks to reduce the frequency of mood entry, prompting the user for the mood only when the system has low confidence. Ideally, mood inference should be a largely unsupervised process, especially in the long-term. This again requires a large-scale longitudinal user study.

Not every factor that impacts user mood can be captured by a smartphone. MoodScope is currently oblivious to factors well known to alter mood, such as face-to-face arguments, stressful traffic conditions or even the weather. The aim of our study is to investigate the relationship between smartphone usage patterns and user moods. We acknowledge that some external factors can go undetected with this approach. Similarly, user smartphone behavior can change in ways that suggest dramatic shifts in mood – even when the cause is in fact unrelated to mood. Example situations include travel or critical work deadlines. At these times, routine patterns of social contact or daily activities, e.g., exercise, may sharply decline, even if the underlying mood of the person remains the same. In future studies we will attempt to detect these inflection points in user lifestyle to reduce the rate at which false positives/negatives occur. Our initial approach will be to selectively engage the user to ask when these situations are suspected. We also plan to investigate how user interactions across multiple devices and services – in addition to their smartphone – can collectively determine if user behavior change is driven by mood or some other confounding factor.

The privacy preserving mechanisms found within the existing MoodScope design are insufficient for a release to the general public. Nevertheless, we take privacy concerns seriously and adopt a variety of data anonymization techniques when capturing user-to-smartphone interactions. However, unintended leakage of information when handling rich high-dimensional personal data can easily occur [37]. Careful study still remains to understand what types of unintended information an adversary might infer from the specific data we utilize. MoodScope can operate locally on the phone, and so does not need to record or share the sensitive underlying information – but this does not solve the privacy problems faced during model training. In the future we will explore how mood models can be trained using data from multiple people while still providing sufficient guarantees of privacy to each user.

9. Conclusions

We foresee mood inference as a vital next step for application context-awareness. Such inference would improve the utility of the smartphone and lower the social barrier for sharing mood.

To approach this goal, we study the possibility of mood-inference from smartphone usage analysis. We collect 2 months of usage data and self-reported mood from 32 users. Using statistical regression techniques, we robustly regress the daily average of mood. Furthermore, our analysis also provides the ability to discern which features contribute most to mood detection. Phone calls and categorized applications strongly predicted mood.

Based on our findings, we build a Mood Inference Engine that can apply mood models to smartphone user data in real time. The engine leverages the cloud as needed to create the model efficiently, while the smartphone tracks and processes usage data to accurately and efficiently determine the mood. The smartphone component runs silently as a background service, consuming minimal power and does not impact other smartphone applications. We design a MoodScope API for application developers to use the outputs of our mood inference system to build and enhance their own custom mood-enabled applications.

Acknowledgments

The authors thank Clayton Shepard for his LiveLab Logger source code, Junyuan Xie for his assistance with the hybrid mood model training experiments, Melik Yuksel for iOS software development assistance, and Juliana Gomez, Aaron Roe, and Peter Washington for Android development assistance. This work was supported in part by NSF Awards #1054693, #1012831, and #0923479. The authors are grateful for the useful comments made by the anonymous reviewers and the paper shepherd, Dr. Rajesh Balan.

REFERENCES

[1] J. A. Russell. A circumplex model of affect. *Journal of Personality and Social Psychology*, 39(6), pp. 1161–1178, 1980.

[2] C. D. Batson, L. L. Shaw and K. C. Oleson. Distinguishing affect, mood and emotion: toward functionally-based conceptual distinctions. *Review of Personality and Social Psychology*, 13, Newbury Park, 1992.

[3] P. Ekman. Universal and cultural differences in facial expressions of emotion. In *Proc. Nebraska Symp. Motivation*, 1971.

[4] S. S. Tomkins. *Affect, Imagery, Consciousness.* Springer, 1962.

[5] J. A. Russell. Affect grid: a single-item scale of pleasure and arousal. *Journal of Personality and Social Psychology,* 57(3), 1989.

[6] J. Tao and T. Tan. Affective computing: a review. *Affective Computing and Intelligent Interaction*, LNCS 3784, Springer, 2005.

[7] M. Yik, Studying Affect among the Chinese: The circular way. *Journal of Personality Assessment*, 91(5), 2009.

[8] K. Church, E. Hoggan and N. Oliver. A study of mobile mood awareness and communication through MobiMood. In *Proc. NordiCHI*, 2010.

[9] A. Gluhak, M. Presser, L. Zhu, S. Esfandiyari and S. Kupschick. Towards mood based mobile services and applications. In *Proc. European Conference on Smart Sensing & Context (EuroSSC),* 2007.

[10] D. Watson, L.A. Clark, and A. Tellegen. Development and validation of brief measures of positive and negative affect: The PANAS scales. *Journal of Personality and Social Psychology*, 54, pages 1063-1070, 1988.

[11] J. R. Crawford and J. D. Henry. The positive and negative affect schedule (PANAS): construct validity, measurement properties and normative data in a large non-clinical sample. *British Journal of Clinical Psychology*, 43, pages 245-265, 2004.

[12] J. T. Larsen, A. P. McGraw and J. T. Cacioppo, Can people feel happy and sad at the same time? *Journal of Personality and Social Psychology*, 81(4), 1988.

[13] Z. Zeng, M. Pantic, G. I. Roisman and T. S. Huang. A survey of affect recognition methods: audio, visual, and spontaneous expressions. *IEEE Transactions on Pattern Analysis and Machine Intelligence*, 31(1), 2009.

[14] A. Vinciarelli, M. Pantic and H. Bourlard. Social signal processing: survey of an emerging domain. *Image and Vision Computing*, 2009.

[15] J. F. Cohn. Foundations of human computing: Facial expression and emotion. In *Proc. ACM Int'l Conf. Multimodal Interfaces (ICMI)*, 2006.

[16] M. Pantic and M.S. Bartlett. Machine analysis of facial expressions. *Face Recognition*, K. Delac and M. Grgic, eds., pages 377-416, I-Tech Education and Publishing, 2007.

[17] P. Ekman, W.V. Friesen, and J.C. Hager. Facial action coding system. *A Human Face*, 2002.

[18] C.M. Lee and S.S. Narayanan. Toward detecting emotions in spoken dialogs. *IEEE Trans. Speech and Audio Processing*, 13(2), pages 293-303, 2005.

[19] B. Schuller, R.J. Villar, G. Rigoll, and M. Lang. Meta-classifiers in acoustic and linguistic feature fusion-based affect recognition. In *Proc. IEEE Int'l Conf. Acoustics, Speech, and Signal Processing (ICASSP '05)*, pages 325-328, 2005.

[20] R. W. Picard. *Affective computing*, MIT Press, 1997.

[21] The Affectiva Q sensor, http://www.affectiva.com/q-sensor/.

[22] A. Gluhak, M. Presser, L. Zhu, S. Esfandiyari and S. Kupschick. Towards mood based mobile services and applications. In *Proc. European Conference on Smart Sensing & Context (EuroSSC)*, 2007.

[23] K. K. Rachuri, M. Musolesi, C. Mascolo, P. J. Rentfrow, C. Longworth and A. Aucinas. EmotionSense: a mobile phones based adaptive platform for experimental social psychology research. In *Proc. ACM Int'l Conf. on Ubiquitous Computing (UbiComp)*, 2010.

[24] H. Lee, Y. Choi, S. Lee and I. P. Park. Towards unobtrusive emotion recognition for affective social communication. In *Proc. IEEE Consumer Communications & Networking Conference (CCNC)*, 2012.

[25] The mappiness application, http://www.mappiness.org.uk/.

[26] The gottaFeeling application, http://gottafeeling.com/.

[27] C. Shepard, A. Rahmati, C. Tossell, L. Zhong and P. Kortum. LiveLab: measuring wireless networks and smartphone users in the field. *ACM SIGMETRICS Perform. Eval. Rev.*, 38(3), 2010.

[28] J. P. Forgas, G. H. Bower and S.E. Krantz. The influence of mood on perceptions of social interactions, *Journal of Experimental Social Psychology*, 20(6), 1984.

[29] L. A. Clark and D. Watson. Mood and the mundane: Relations between daily life events and self-reported mood. *Journal of Personality and Social Psychology*, 54(2), 1988.

[30] M. Ester, H.-P. Kriegel, J. Sander and X. Xu. A density-based algorithm for discovering clusters in large spatial databases with noise. In *Proc. Second International Conference on Knowledge Discovery and Data Mining*, 1996.

[31] C. J. Beedie, P. C. Terry and A. M. Lane. Distinctions between emotion and mood. *Cognition and Emotion*, 19(6), 2005.

[32] Hernandez, Javier, et al. Mood meter: counting smiles in the wild. In *Proc. ACM Int'l Conf. on Ubiquitous Computing (UbiComp)*, 2012.

[33] G. Chittaranjan, J. Blom and D. Gatica-Perez. Who's who with Big-Five: Analyzing and Classifying personality traits with smartphones. In *Proc. Int'l Symposium on Wearable Computers (ISWC), 2011.*

[34] L. Lu, D. Liu and H. Zhang. Automatic mood detection and tracking of music audio signals. *IEEE Transactions on Audio, Speech and Language Processing*, 14(1), 2006.

[35] N. Japkowicz and S. Stephen. The class imbalance problem: A systematic study. *Intelligent Data Analysis,* 6(5), 2002.

[36] A. Jain and D. Zongker. Feature selection: Evaluation, application, and small sample performance. *IEEE Transactions on Pattern Analysis and Machine Intelligence*, 19(2), 1997.

[37] A. Narayanan and V. Shmatikov. Myths and fallacies of Personally Identifiable Information. From *Commun. ACM* 53(6), pages 24-26, June 2010.

[38] N. D. Lane, Y. Xu, H. Lu, S. Hu, T. Choudhury, A. T. Campbell and F. Zhao. Enabling large-scale human activity inference on smartphones using community similarity networks (CSN). In *Proc. ACM Int'l Conf. on Ubiquitous Computing (UbiComp)*, 2011.

[39] R. LiKamWa, Y. Liu, N. D. Lane and L. Zhong. Can your smartphone infer your mood? In *Proc. PhoneSense Workshop*, 2011.

[40] Hong Lu, A. J. Bernheim Brush, Bodhi Priyan-tha, Amy K. Karlson, and Jie Liu. SpeakerSense: energy efficient unobtrusive speaker identification on mobile phones. In *Proc. Int'l Conf. on Pervasive Computing,* 2011.

Auditeur: A Mobile-Cloud Service Platform for Acoustic Event Detection on Smartphones

Shahriar Nirjon[1], Robert F. Dickerson[1], Philip Asare[1], Qiang Li[1], Dezhi Hong[1], John A. Stankovic[1], Pan Hu[2], Guobin Shen[2], and Xiaofan Jiang[3]
[1]Department of Computer Science, University of Virginia, USA
[2]Microsoft Research Asia, Beijing, China
[3]Intel Labs China, Beijing, China
{smn8z, rfd7a, pka6qz, lq7c, dh5gm, stankovic}@virginia.edu, {v-pah, jacky.shen}@microsoft.com, fred.jiang@intel.com

ABSTRACT

Auditeur is a general-purpose, energy-efficient, and context-aware acoustic event detection platform for smartphones. It enables app developers to have their app register for and get notified on a wide variety of acoustic events. Auditeur is backed by a cloud service to store user contributed sound clips and to generate an energy-efficient and context-aware classification plan for the phone. When an acoustic event type has been registered, the smartphone instantiates the necessary acoustic processing modules and wires them together to execute the plan. The phone then captures, processes, and classifies acoustic events locally and efficiently. Our analysis on user-contributed empirical data shows that Auditeur's energy-aware acoustic feature selection algorithm is capable of increasing the device-lifetime by 33.4%, sacrificing less than 2% of the maximum achievable accuracy. We implement seven apps with Auditeur, and deploy them in real-world scenarios to demonstrate that Auditeur is versatile, 11.04% – 441.42% less power hungry, and 10.71% – 13.86% more accurate in detecting acoustic events, compared to state-of-the-art techniques. We present a user study to demonstrate that novice programmers can implement the core logic of interesting apps with Auditeur in less than 30 minutes, using only 15 – 20 lines of Java code.

Categories and Subject Descriptors

C.3 [**Special-Purpose and Application-Based Systems**]: Real-time and embedded systems

General Terms

Design, Experimentation

Keywords

Acoustics, Soundlets

MobiSys'13, June 25-28, 2013, Taipei, Taiwan

1. INTRODUCTION

Being able to deliver smartphone apps quickly to customers is crucial in today's highly competitive app market. Developers depend heavily on APIs provided by their smartphone platform for common tasks, but when it lacks necessary functions for their application, it costs developers weeks of time for implementation. Beyond just time, many developers do not have the necessary technical background to implement these functions correctly or efficiently. Because of this, there is a growing trend where smartphone apps are paired with numerous web services by other providers to get access to specialized or computationally demanding tasks. Microsoft's Hawaii [1], for example, supports path prediction, key-value storage, translator, relay, rendezvous, OCR, and speech-to-text services. Google provides services such as web search, maps, play, YouTube, cloud drive, and Gmail. Other providers give access to data sources such as weather, financial data, airline information, and parcel tracking.

Smartphones have begun to use their microphones for various acoustic processing tasks, but most of the apps are special purpose acoustic event detectors. Examples of voice and music based systems include: speaker identification [16], speech recognition [31], emotion and stress detection [18, 28], conversation and human behavior inference [20, 21], music recognition [32], music search and discovery [3], and music genre classification. There are other types of apps that fall into the non-voice, non-music category, such as a cough detector [14], a heart beat counter [23], and logical location inference [4, 6]. These examples are limited in number and acoustic sensing is often one of multiple sensing modalities in these works. There are existing works [17, 19] that consider multiple types of acoustic events. SoundSense [17] considers speech, music and ambient sound, and provides a mechanism to label clusters of ambient sounds to extend the set of classes. Jigsaw [19] considers speech and sounds related to activities of daily living. These systems still lack in providing tools and mechanisms to easily extend detection capabilities and effectively support development process. They are limited for general purpose acoustic event detection service for smartphones and in exploiting the promising opportunities given by already prevailing smartphones equipped with microphones.

To address this need, we have built a general-purpose acoustic event detection platform called *Auditeur*. Compared to the previous works in the literature, we position Auditeur as a developer platform rather than just a system detecting a set of sounds. Auditeur provides APIs to developers to enable their app to register for and get notified on a wide variety of acoustic events such as speech, other types of man-made sounds, such as emotional or physiological sounds, music, environmental sounds, sounds observed in households, offices, or public places, sounds of vehicles, tools and so forth. Auditeur achieves this capability of classifying general-purpose sounds by utilizing its *tagged soundlets* concept which are crowd-contributed, short-duration audio clips recorded on a smartphone along with a list of user given tags and automatically generated contexts. The cloud hosts the collection of tagged soundlets and provides a set of services, which are used by the smartphones, to upload new soundlets and to obtain a detailed *classification plan* to recognize sounds specified by the list of tags as parameters. Typically a plan contains one or more acoustic processing *pipeline configurations*, corresponding to different energy-requirements and user-contexts, specifying the required acoustic processing units, their parameters, and how they are connected.

Several salient features when taken in combination make Auditeur unique. First, Auditeur provides a simple yet powerful API which novice developers with basic object-oriented programming skills can learn easily. Second, Auditeur supports both personalization and generalization. It is possible to manage personal sounds and classifiers as well as obtain sounds and classifiers that were created by other users of the system. Third, the acoustic processing pipeline inside the phone is flexible and extensible. The phone contains a wide range of acoustic processing primitives. However, only the ones that are required to recognize the desired sounds (as mentioned in the classification plan from the cloud) are dynamically instantiated and wired to form the pipeline. Addition of a new primitive is easy since the processing units have a generic structure and are dynamically wired. Fourth, the sound recognition service running on the phone is adaptive. Apps are notified on a change of context or at a specific battery level, and a new pipeline configuration is loaded to adapt to the change. Fifth, Auditeur is designed for efficiency in communication, computation, and energy consumption. The phone needs to connect to the cloud only once to obtain the classification plan. Hence an uninterrupted Internet connectivity is not a requirement. Acoustic processing in Auditeur is efficient as only the necessary components run within the phone. An energy-aware acoustic processing plan to be executed by the phone is generated at the cloud to increase the lifetime of the device while maintaining high accuracy.

Partitioning the planing and execution between the cloud and the phone let Auditeur have the best of both of an in-phone [17, 16, 18] sound recognizer and a cloud-assisted [28, 32, 14] one. In-phone recognizers perform all of the processing inside the phone. Typically, they are highly tuned to the application scenario, and use a fixed set of features and an offline-trained, fixed classifier. Thus, they are rigid and are not usable if either the application or its context changes. Cloud-assisted recognizers, on the other hand, send unprocessed or partially processed data to a server, and rely on web services to perform further processing and classification. This approach is more flexible, but has several limitations such as the requirement for an uninterrupted Internet connectivity, high bandwidth, and the expense of sending a large chunk of data over the cellular network. Our approach for Auditeur takes the best of these two strategies. Auditeur performs the signal processing and feature classification completely inside the phone, but uses the cloud to store user contributed sound clips, build new classifiers, and obtain an energy-aware classification plan. Once the smartphone receives the classification plan from the cloud, it dynamically instantiates the components required to execute the plan, and keeps detecting acoustic events efficiently and locally.

Auditeur and its energy and context-aware classification planning architecture are different from existing context monitoring and mobile sensing platforms [11, 12, 13, 7, 20]. SymPhoney [11] requires developers specify their hand-tuned processing pipelines, whereas the acoustic processing pipeline in Auditeur is generated automatically. SeeMon [12] maintains an essential set of sensors to optimize the sensing and transmission cost associated with the sensors. Orchestrator [13] provides a plan-based execution framework with policy-based system optimization which dynamically adapts to the changing system and application situations. It opportunistically changes its execution plan based on the current status of resources under a specified policy such as minimum accuracy or minimum overall energy cost. Unlike [12, 13], Auditeur maintains an informative set of acoustic features and takes a deterministic approach in maximizing its classification accuracy while satisfying the developer specified minimum lifetime goal. Certain aspects of Kobe [7] such as the API to create a classifier, the search for an optimum configuration, and runtime adaptation are conceptually similar to Auditeur's, however, they are quite different in design and technical details. For example, Kobe requires explicit declaration of the processing pipeline, performs an exhaustive search, and offloads code to server, whereas Auditeur generates pipelines automatically, applies dynamic programming instead of a search, and does not offload code to satisfy its energy constraint. DarwinPhones [20] proposes a collaborative approach of exchanging classifiers and classification results among phones. Auditeur's shows it collaborative nature at the data level via its crowd-contributed tagged soundlets.

We evaluate Auditeur with four types of experiments. First, we measure CPU and memory footprints, and energy consumptions of different processing units. Second, we perform an empirical study on different categories of sounds to demonstrate the efficacy of our energy-aware feature selection algorithm. Third, we describe case studies on seven apps, implemented with Auditeur, to demonstrate the versatility of Auditeur, and to quantify their energy efficiency, accuracy of event detection, and context awareness. Fourth, we describe a user study on developers evaluating the usability of the Auditeur API.

The contributions of this paper are the following:

- A versatile, general-purpose, flexible, extensible, context-aware, and efficient end-to-end acoustic event detection platform for smartphones, backed by the cloud.
- A sound recognition service on the smartphone, capable of dynamically wiring acoustic processing units, and running an app-tailored and context-aware classification plan on the phone, and an API to register and get notified on specific sound events.
- A collection of crowd-contributed, admission controlled, and contextually-tagged short sound clips in the cloud available to the developers, and an API to upload and manage them.
- A dynamic programming based acoustic feature selection algorithm that generates energy-aware acoustic event detection plans for smartphones. Our empirical evaluation shows that the algorithm is capable of increasing the device-lifetime by 33.4%, sacrificing less than 2% of its maximum achievable accuracy.
- We implement 7 apps with Auditeur, and deploy them in real-world scenarios to demonstrate that Auditeur is versatile, $11.04\%-441.42\%$ less power hungry, and $10.71\% - 13.86\%$ more accurate in detecting acoustic events, compared to state-of-the-art techniques. A user study demonstrates that novice programmers can implement the core logic of interesting apps with Auditeur in less than 30 mins, using only $15 - 20$ lines of Java code.

2. USAGE SCENARIOS

We describe three scenarios to illustrate the use cases of Auditeur.

Auditeur is for Developers. Alice is a smartphone app developer who has an exciting idea for an app. Her envisioned app listens to a piece of music, determines its genre, and suggests similar music to the user. But the problem is, Alice does not know the technical details of how to classify music based on their acoustic features. She finds Auditeur helpful which has a collection of short music clips and their genre. She uses Auditeur's API to obtain a music genre classifier by specifying the music-types she wants to recognize, uses Auditeur's API to perform the classification on the phone, and uses Auditeur (or, any other online music databases) to get a list of songs of the same genre.

Auditeur is for Researchers. Bob is a behavioral researcher who wants to perform a quick study on how people interact socially. For his study, he gathers some volunteers and collects samples of their voice, laughter, and yelling sounds using a custom app powered by Auditeur. At first, he uses Auditeur's API to record the audio and add proper tags, e.g., voice, laughter, yell, context, and recording environment, to it. Then he uses Auditeur' API to upload the samples, and obtains a classifier from the cloud which detects speaker id, laughter, and yelling sounds in different environments and contexts. Finally, he uses Auditeur API to continuously listen to the microphone and log social interactions of his study subjects.

Auditeur is for End-users. Cathy is a busy housewife, a mother of a newborn, and a smartphone user. Recently she installed a smartphone app that monitors her sleeping baby when she is busy working downstairs. During the configuration of the app, the GUI asks her to record sound samples of her baby crying, whining, coughing, and doing baby-talks as well as other possible sounds that might occur in the room, e.g., the sound of the air conditioner, hanging toys, door squeaking, and noise made by the pet. She records all of these sounds using the app, protects them with a password, and selects the ones she wants to be notified of. Once the configuration is completed, she keeps the phone on a table within the suggested distance from the baby and starts the app. The app keeps monitoring the baby and whenever a sound of interest occurs, the phone alerts her by calling the phone in the kitchen.

3. THE TAGGED SOUNDLET CONCEPT

A *tagged soundlet* is a short-duration ($3 - 30s$) audio clip, recorded on a smartphone along with two types of contextual information: user given tags and phone generated context.

3.1 Tags

The logical tags associated with a soundlet are the user given identifiers that describe its content and the surrounding environmental context. Examples of tags are in Table 4 of Section 8.3.

Content and Container Tags. While the user chooses the tags that he wants to use to describe a soundlet, we require him to enlist two kinds of tags: *content*, and *container* tags. The content tags describe what the sound *is*, and the container tags describe the background which contains the sound. For example, a $15s$ recording of Alice's voice at her office should have `{voice, female, Alice}` in the list of content tags, and `{office}` in the list of container tags.

Lookfor and Within Tags. The content tags are used in two different ways during the training of a soundlet classifier. The *lookfor* tags describe a class of soundlets that the user wants to recognize, and the *within* tags describe the class of soundlets that represents the universe of sounds, i.e. the set of sounds that might be present in the environment along with the sound that he wants to recognize. For example, when creating a training set for a classifier that detects Alice's voice at her office: the lookfor tags should have `{voice, Alice}` on the list, the within tags should include `{voice, printer, phone}`, and the container should be `{office}` as before.

3.2 Phone Contexts

The phone context refers to additional information about the soundlets which may or may not be conveyed by the tags. These are similar to the tags in the manner they are used by the recognition algorithm, but they are different in the manner they are generated. The phone context is either automatically generated by an algorithm using information from the on-board sensors, or they are assumed. The developer of the app specifies whether an automatically generated context or an assumed context – whichever is more suitable to the app – should be used.

Aside from basic audio information such as the sampling rate, encoding, duration, and timestamp, Auditeur generates three other types of contexts, which are: (1) the location of the phone, (2) the position of the phone with respect to body, and (3) the environmental noise level. Section 6.2 provides an elaboration of phone contexts. Note that, the developer of an app can always override the context generation process. We keep this provision in Auditeur as context generation has its overhead and in many cases an app is used only in a few specific presumed contexts. For example, an app that detects vehicle sounds can assume that the location is outdoors instead of periodically getting it computed.

3.3 Public and Private Spaces

The space of soundlets is logically partitioned into two subspaces from a user's point of view – *public* and *private*. A *user* of Auditeur is anyone who has an account in Auditeur. Typically, the user is an app developer, who uses the public space by default, but may use a private space with proper permissions from an end-user.

3.3.1 Public Soundlets

The public space contains shared soundlets, contributed by all users of Auditeur. This is visible to everyone, and does not require any authentication to access. However, there are two constraints that must be met by each soundlet.

Tag and Sanity constraints. There is a predefined fixed set of tags that can be attached to public soundlets. The user cannot create, modify or delete any tag. The set of tags is maintained by the system admin of Auditeur. Although, at present, there are over 1000 different tags, we admit that no fixed set is ever sufficient to cover the enormous possibilities of tags. However, limiting the tags in the public space keeps the space manageable and provides us a way to ensure the confidence in sound recognition.

Every public soundlet goes through a sanity check to ensure that it is not an outlier with respect to other soundlets with the same tags. Thus, a public soundlet is not immediately made visible to everyone until it passes an outlier detection test. This is to ensure that no attacker can mess up the public space by filling it up with soundlets with non-representative tags. A service running on the cloud automatically detects non-conforming soundlets using distance based outlier detection technique [5] which is described in Section 7.2.

3.3.2 Private Soundlets

Private soundlets are user specific and are not shared. The user has to access his private space using proper authentications. Unlike public soundlets, the private ones are not limited by the tag and sanity constraints, i.e. a user can upload any sound he likes into his private space and attach whatever tag he wants to describe it. However, the list of content and container tags has to be the same (in number of tags and the spelling of tags) in order for two soundlets to be treated as belonging to the same class.

We keep provision for private space in our design in order to complement the public space which is limited by the choices of tags and has a high degree of sanity requirement. The private space is more flexible, tailored to the specific needs of a user, and if properly used, an infinite number of possible sounds can be stored and recognized by our system making it highly extensible.

4. AUDITEUR SYSTEM OVERVIEW

The design of Auditeur is two-tiered: the phone contains the mechanism for sound capture, sound processing, and sound recognition, while the cloud provides the logic for building classifiers and tuning the parameters for the sound processing modules on the phones.

4.1 In-Phone Processing

4.1.1 Tagging and Uploading Soundlets

Auditeur provides an API to record, add tags, and upload soundlets to the cloud. The API provides an interface for the default sound capture device, however the developer may choose a different one (such as a Bluetooth microphone) or an already recorded sound clip. After the sound is captured, the tagging process automatically generates the phone contexts, and the user can review and change it prior to uploading. The sound clip is then uploaded to the cloud. At this stage, the upload of the public soundlet could fail if it violates the tag or sanity constraints.

Uploading soundlets to the cloud is energy consuming. However, this is done only once and is used to create classification plans for several apps. An alternative to uploading the sound clips is to extract the features locally and then upload the acoustic features only. But we do not follow this approach to keep our design simple and extensible. By uploading only the features we lose the opportunity to explore the possibility of considering new acoustic features and creating more sophisticated classification plans.

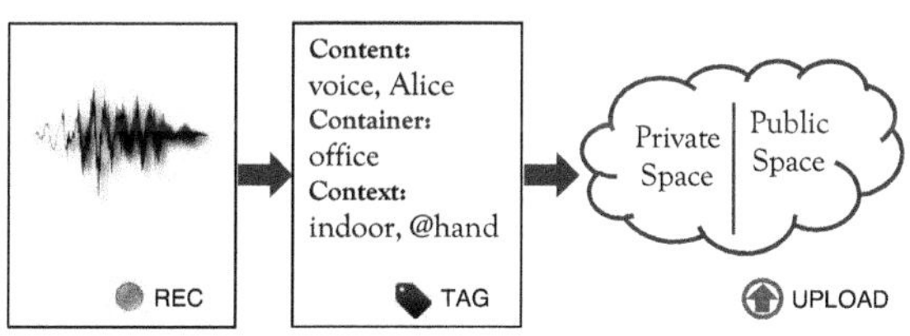

Figure 1: Recording, tagging, and uploading soundlets to the cloud.

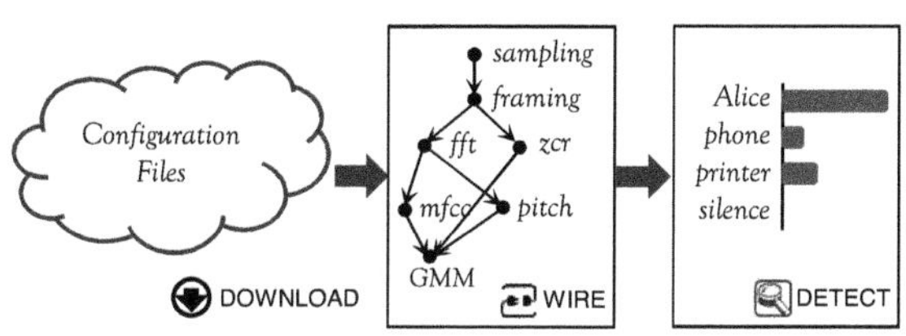

Figure 2: Downloading configuration, wiring components, and sound event detection.

4.1.2 Acoustic Event Detection

The cloud generates an app tailored acoustic event detection plan that directs the phone on which components should be instantiated on the phone and how they should be wired together to form an *acoustic processing pipeline*. The plan could contain more than one pipeline configuration, corresponding to different contexts or energy-requirements. The phone reads the plan from an XML file, instantiates and initializes the processing units with the specified parameters, and wires them together to form a pipeline. Once the pipeline is ready, an API call starts reading audio samples from the microphone, and pushes data down the pipeline. The app is issued a callback once the desired sound event is detected. A change in context, such as moving from indoors to outdoors, or putting the phone inside the pocket, automatically loads a different pipeline configuration by default, however, the developer can override this behavior.

4.2 In-Cloud Processing

An energy-aware acoustic event detection plan is generated in the cloud upon receiving a request from the phone. A request contains: sounds the app is looking for, other unwanted sounds that might occur in the environment, contextual information, and energy constraints. The tags and contexts are then used to create a comprehensive training set using a subset of the currently available soundlets in the desired space. To meet the energy constraint, the dimensionality of the training set is reduced by selecting a subset of features, considering the energy consumptions of different acoustic processing units. Finally, a number of classifiers are trained, and the one showing the highest accuracy during cross-validation tests while meeting the energy criteria is chosen. The sound processing pipeline, feature set, the classifiers, and their parameters altogether form the contents of a downloadable configuration file.

Since communication to the cloud and training classifiers on-the-fly is costly, the cloud packs a set of pipeline configurations, corresponding to different contexts and energy requirements, into one classification plan.

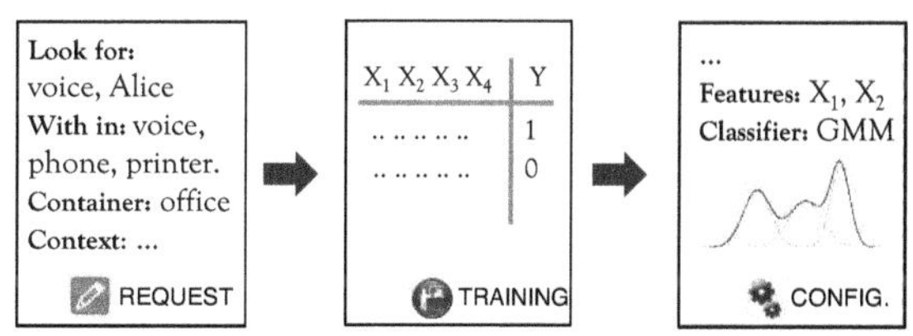

Figure 3: Request for a classifier, training the classifier, and generating configuration file for download.

4.3 API Example

Figure 4 shows a code snippet which demonstrates the usage of Auditeur API for recording, tagging, and uploading soundlets to the cloud, and obtaining and using a classification plan from the cloud. Lines 2 – 3 create a `SoundletRecorder` to record a $16s$ audio and obtain a `Soundlet`. Lines 4 – 5 create the content and container tags, and lines 6 – 7 set the tags and make the soundlet private. Lines 8 – 10 grab the `SoundletManager`, and upload the soundlet to the cloud. Lines 12 – 13 create the lookfor and within tags. Line 14 creates a `SoundletDetector` and registers the application as a listener. Line 15 obtains a classification plan and initializes the detector, and line 17 starts the continuous sound event detection process.

```
//Record and upload a soundlet.
SoundletRecorder recorder = new SoundletRecorder();
Soundlet soundlet = recorder.recordSoundlet(16);
String[] content = {"voice", "female", "Alice"};
String[] container = {"office"};
soundlet.setTags(content, container);
soundlet.setSharing(false);
SoundletManager manager = new SoundletManager(
    getSystemService("SoundletService"));
manager.uploadSoundlet(soundlet);
//Get a classifier and register for a match event.
String[] lookfor = {"voice", "Alice"};
String[] within = {"voice", "printer", "phone"};
SoundletDetector detector = new SoundletDetector(this);
detector.setPipeline(manager.getConfig(
        lookfor, within, container));
detector.start(SoundletDetector.CONTINUOUS);
```

Figure 4: An example code snippet to create, tag, upload, get classification plan, and detect soundlets.

5. KEY FEATURES OF AUDITEUR

5.1 People in the Loop

The person who contributes a soundlet knows it the best. Auditeur provides an API to let people record their own sounds, and tag them appropriately. An alternate approach, such as automated tagging, might help the user with some suggestions, but is not sufficient since a whole bunch of different sounds is often indistinguishable. For example, aerosol spray, steam, waterfall, and white noise sound almost the same. The tagging process in Auditeur is guided by the concept of the content and container tags, which keeps the background explicit from the sound of interest. The sound recognition process is guided by the *lookfor* and *within* tags, which specify the sound of interest as well as other possible sounds in the environment – the best way to identify these is to engage the end-user.

5.2 Personalization as well as Generalization

Auditeur has provision for both personalization and generalization in sound recognition. This is achieved by the two logical spaces: public and private spaces, which are used to store soundlets and create classifiers. The public space contains soundlets that are shared by everyone, and hence this collection is enormous, and the classifiers created using these soundlets have more generalization ability in sound recognition tasks. The public space is for developers who want to build and test an app quickly, and for apps that do not require personalization. The private space, on the other hand, ensures privacy, and the classifiers created using the private soundlets are tailored to meet the end-user's need.

5.3 Cloud-Directed On-Device Processing

Sound recognition on the phone is not a one-size-fits-all problem. Every problem is unique and involves different sets of tasks along the pipeline. This is why, in Auditeur, we keep provision for dynamically creating a chain of tasks for a specific problem. An algorithm running on the cloud decides which set of tasks are appropriate for a given problem, and creates a configuration file describing the tasks and parameters required to solve it. The phone downloads the configuration file, constructs the chain of tasks, and executes them locally. Communication with the cloud is not continuous, rather the phone is required to connect to the cloud only once to get the execution plan.

5.4 Designed for Efficiency

Mobile phones are limited by their processing capability and battery life. A novel feature of Auditeur is that, it provides the smartphone with an API to obtain energy-aware classification plans from the cloud. For this to work, we profile the energy consumption of all the tasks that are involved in the sound recognition process on the phone. The cloud uses this profile to formulate a dynamic programming problem that selects the set of acoustic features required to recognize desired soundlets, under a given energy constraint. That means, a smartphone having 30% remaining battery life can use a classifier which is aware of its current condition and is different from the one being used since the battery was full.

5.5 Context Awareness

Auditeur considers the contexts in which the sound is recorded and is matched. Keeping contextual information such as the location, body position, and environmental noise level makes the sound matching adaptive to change. This is where we exploit the mobility of the device to make our solution elegant when compared to standard sound matching algorithms. Contexts increase the adaptability of our system in different ways. For example, the physical location of the device greatly eliminates a large number of unlikely sounds from consideration during the sound matching process. Body position of the phone is used to normalize the received signal strength, and the environmental noise level guides the noise reduction process. We describe a set of experiments to demonstrate the benefits of using contextual information.

6. IN-PHONE COMPONENTS

The implementation of in-phone processing is modular and layered as shown in Figure 5. At the bottom, we have three services that are running in the background. The *Sound Engine* service is the one that performs the actual sound recognition task, while the other two manage contexts and communications to the cloud. These services, along with some internal APIs, support the public API layer, which interacts with the applications.

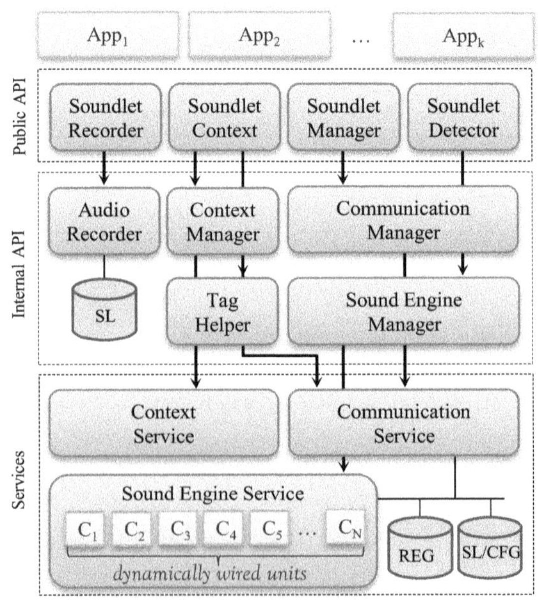

Figure 5: In-phone processing components.

6.1 The Sound Engine

The `SoundEngine` is a singleton, persistent service that is responsible for instantiating and initializing the acoustic processing units, forming a processing pipeline that detects sound events, and providing registration and notification services to the running applications.

6.1.1 *Acoustic Processing Pipeline*

Acoustic processing in Auditeur is divided into a five stage pipeline: (1) preprocessing, (2) frame level feature extraction, (3) frame level classification (frame admission), (4) window level feature extraction, and (5) window level classification. Each stage involves multiple tasks, and each task is performed at an *acoustic processing unit* (APU).

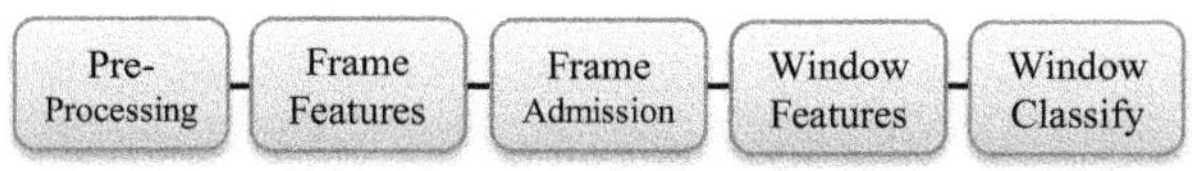

Figure 6: The acoustic processing pipeline in Auditeur.

Figure 6 shows the high level structure of the pipeline. The process starts with a *preprocessing* stage which captures audio from microphone, converts the byte stream into a stream of fixed sized frames, and applies filtering, windowing, and noise compensation as needed by the application. Each frame then passes through a *frame level feature extraction* stage. We have implemented a total of 25 time and frequency domain features, but not all of them might be used in single sound recognition task. These frames are then classified using a *frame level classifier* which acts as an admission controller, and decides whether or not to process a frame any further. If a frame is admitted to the *window level feature extraction* stage, a fixed number of consecutive frames are gathered to form a window, and up to 12 statistics are computed per feature per window, resulting in a maximum of 121-element feature vector. This number is less than 25×12 since not all statistical functions are applicable to all features. Each window is then classified by a *window level classifier*.

Table 1 shows the list of APUs that are implemented on the phone. We have implemented 5 preprocessors, 25 feature extractors, 12 statistical units, and 7 classifiers. We have put more emphasis on the frequency domain features as they are more robust to noise. We have implemented the classifiers that are commonly known to solve sound recognition problems, and implemented only their classification logic inside the phone as their training happens in the cloud.

APU	List
Preprocessor	Sampling, Framing, Filters, Windowing, Noise Compensation.
Features	FFT, ZCR, RMS, 13-MFCCs, Low Energy (Weak) Frame Rate Spectral {Entropy, Energy, Flux, Rolloff, Centroid}, Bandwidth, Phase Deviation, Pitch.
Statistics	Mean, Stddev, Geometric Mean, Harmonic Mean, Range, Moment, Zscore, Skewness, Kurtosis, Median, Mode, Quartile.
Classifiers	Naive Bayes, Decision Tree, GMM, MLP, SVM, kNN, HMM.

Table 1: Acoustic processing units in Auditeur.

6.1.2 *Forming the Pipeline*

The acoustic processing units (APUs) are the building blocks of the acoustic processing pipeline. APUs are dynamically instantiated and wired at runtime to form the pipeline. Each APU keeps a list of its immediate successor APUs, and implements two methods: `process` and `forward`. The `process` method performs its intended work, and the `forward` method pushes its output to its children. Instantiation of the APUs and the wiring process is guided by an XML-complaint configuration file that is obtained from the cloud. The configuration file is essentially the description of a directed acyclic graph where the nodes are the APUs and the directed edges denote the wiring among them.

```
<?xml version="1.0" encoding="utf-8"?>
<nodes>
    <node id="1" label="frame" />
    <node id="2" label="rms" />
    <node id="3" label="fft" />
    <node id="4" label="zcr" />
    <node id="5" label="entropy" />
    <node id="6" label="flux" />
    <node id="7" label="DT" parents="2" >
          <params> ... </params> </node>
    <node id="8" label="admitter" window="32" />
    <node id="9" label="stat.mean" window="32" />
    <node id="10" label="stat.mean" window="32" />
    <node id="11" label="aggregator" parents="3" />
    <node id="12" label="GMM" >
          <params> ... </params> </node>
    <node id="13" label="HMM" >
          <params> ... </params> </node>
</nodes>
<edges>
    <edge source="1" target="2" />
    ...
</edges>
```

Figure 7: Example of an XML file, describing the APUs and wiring to create the processing pipeline.

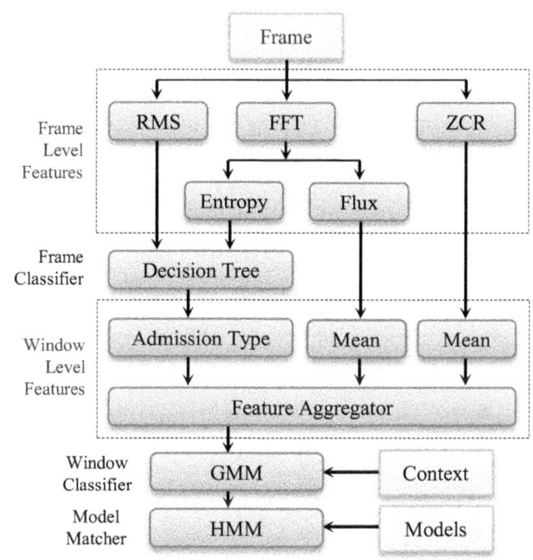

Figure 8: An instance of a dynamically wired pipeline corresponding to the XML file in Figure 7.

Example: Figure 8 shows an example of dynamically created pipeline based on the configuration file in Figure 7. This is similar to the sound processing as in [17], except that we show only a subset of features due to space limitation. In this example, 2 frame level features (RMS and spectral entropy) are used to admit frames using a decision tree classifier, and 2 window level features (spectral flux and zero crossing rate) are used to classify the window using a GMM. Finally, a HMM smoothens the classification results.

6.1.3 *Registration and Notification*

The sound engine internally maintains a register which keeps records of applications, desired sound events, and notification logic. Whenever an event, registered by a running application is detected, it broadcasts a notification according to the notification logic. Currently we support three types of notification: continuous (always notify), counter-valued (up to a number of events), and timed (up to a time duration after the registration or the first event).

6.2 Phone Context Generation

Auditeur provides three types of contextual information: location, position, and noise level. The location context refers to the GPS coordinates and whether the location is indoors or outdoors. While uploading a soundlet, we store the GPS coordinate if it is available. The availability means – we are getting a location fix and also the app has permission to use GPS. However, the current version of Auditeur only uses indoors or outdoors information. Yet we kept the GPS coordinates to investigate more fine grained location aware sound matching which we leave as a future work.

We adopt a simplified version of [34] to detect indoors or outdoors using only the accelerometer and cellular signals. The position context refers to the position of the phone with respect to human body which could be either direct (i.e. the sound source is close to the microphone), in pocket, or at a distance. This is similar to the phone contexts used in [17], and is estimated by the same principle. The noise level refers to the environmental noise level in dB scale.

Auditeur provides APIs to specify an action to be taken whenever there is a change in context. For example, when a person comes home from outside, the context engine would detect the change, and take actions that the developer programmed for, which is by default – loading a different pipeline configuration from the classification plan that is appropriate for home environment.

Auditeur provides APIs to enable and disable context checking, and to control the frequency of monitoring the change in each context. As context checking is costly, the developer of the app should choose an appropriate duty cycle to check and balance its benefit over cost.

6.3 Communication to the Cloud

Applications communicate to the cloud via the communication service, which submits new soundlets to the cloud through a Web HTTP interface. We implement a basic web application using JAVA and the Spring 3 Framework for this purpose. For hosting, we use the Amazon web services infrastructure by running our application in a Tomcat 7 web container on an Amazon EC2 instance. Soundlets, along with their tags and contexts, are serialized in JSON format and are submitted to the Web. Afterwards, the data is committed to the database as described in Section 7.3.

When an app requests a classification plan, the communication service issues a GET request to the web interface on its behalf with search parameters such as the tags, contexts, and energy constraints. In response, the cloud creates the classification plan, serializes it as a JSON object, and sends it to the phone.

6.4 Public and Internal API

Four components constitute the public API layer. The `Soundlet Recorder` records audio from the microphone, converts it to a Soundlet, and stores them locally. The `SoundletContext` uses the `ContextManager` to get the current context, and the `TagHelper` to get a list of matching tags from the cloud. The `SoundletManager`, with the help of `CommunicationManager`, manages the communication between the phone and the cloud to upload soundlets and to download classification plans. The `SoundletDetector` registers the running application as a listener for desired sound events, initializes the `SoundEngine`, and notifies the application at desired sound events.

7. IN-CLOUD COMPONENTS

The primary job of the cloud service is to generate an energy-aware acoustic event detection plan which we describe in detail. Other services such as tag suggestion, storage and caching are described briefly.

7.1 Energy Aware Classification Plan

Given a set of tags and phone context, a service in the cloud creates an energy aware acoustic event detection plan.

7.1.1 *Training Set Generation*

The cloud creates a training set by choosing a subset of the soundlets in the cloud. First, it selects the soundlets having all of the *container* tags – indicating that the training is environment specific. It then filters out soundlets that do not contain any of the *lookfor* or *within* tags assuming that those are not present in the acoustic environment. Among the remaining soundlets, the ones having all of the *content* tags are marked as positive examples, and the rest are marked as negative examples. Finally, all 121 acoustic features are extracted to form an extended training set, which is then reduced by a feature selection algorithm.

7.1.2 *Feature Selection Algorithm*

Unlike feature selection [9] in the machine learning literature, where the criterion is to minimize the *number* of features, Auditeur's goal is to minimize the total *energy consumption* of feature extraction on the phone, while maximizing their ability to retain enough information for an accurate classification. A brute force approach that enumerates all 2^{121} subsets is not feasible; hence we take a dynamic programming approach to this problem. A formal description of the problem and its solution are described next.

Given a training set T of size $n \times m$, where n is the number of samples and m is the dimension of the feature space, the target class labels C of size $n \times 1$, the energy cost of computing each feature on the phone $E = \{e_1, e_2, \ldots e_m\}$, and an energy budget B, the goal is to select a subset of features that uses no more than B units of energy while maximizing their ability to retain enough information for an accurate classification.

Since we are selecting a subset of the features, we need a metric to measure the goodness of a feature. A feature is *relevant* if it is correlated to the target class, and is *non-redundant* if it is not highly correlated to other features. In Auditeur, we take an information theoretic approach in measuring the correlation, which is based on the concept of *entropy*. The entropy of a feature X is defined as

$$H(X) = -\sum_i P(x_i)\log(P(x_i)), \tag{1}$$

and the entropy of X, after observing Y is defined as

$$H(X|Y) = -\sum_j P(y_j)\sum_i P(x_i|y_j)\log(P(x_i|y_j)), \tag{2}$$

where $P(x_i)$ and $P(x_i|y_j)$ are the prior and posterior probabilities of X, respectively. The difference between Equation (1) and (2) denotes the *information gain* [26], indicating how much is the added value of taking feature X, given that Y is already selected. In our algorithm, we use the normalized information gain, which is called the *symmetrical uncertainty* [24], to limit its value in the range $[0,\ 1]$.

$$SU(X|Y) = 2\left[\frac{H(X) - H(X|Y)}{H(X) + H(Y)}\right], \tag{3}$$

We now formulate a recurrence relation which is solved using

Processing Unit	Parameter	Choices
Sampling	rate (KHz)	8, 22.05, 44.1
Framing	length (ms)	32, 64
Window Size	length (sec)	1, 3, 5
Feature Extraction	discretization (level)	8, 16

Table 2: Choices of parameters for APUs.

dynamic programming technique. Let $f_j(b)$ be the optimal subset of features within an energy bound of b, considering the first j features, for $(0 < j \leq m)$. Based on the decision on X_j, there can be two cases:

$$f_j(b) = \begin{cases} f_{j-1}(b) & \text{if } X_j \text{ is not taken} \\ f_{j-1}(b - e_j) \cup \{X_j\} & \text{otherwise} \end{cases}$$

This is because, if X_j is taken, the bound b is reduced by e_j, the amount of energy required to compute X_j. The decision on X_j depends on the symmetrical uncertainties. X_j is taken only if $SU(X_j|C, f_{j-1}(b-e_j)) < SU(X_j|C, f_{j-1}(b))$, and not taken otherwise. The recurrence is solvable for $f_m(B)$ by beginning with the knowledge of $f_0(b) = \phi$ for all $b > 0$.

There are two implementation issues that require further explanation. First, our algorithm assumes that energy is integer valued; The definition of entropy also requires nominal values. To handle this, we quantize both of them to fit into our algorithm. Second, the energy budget B is for feature extraction only. It is derived by subtracting the energy cost of other APUs and services, e.g., pipeline overhead and context generation service, that run on the phone from the total budget for acoustic processing.

7.1.3 APU and Parameter Selection

The energy consumption and the classification accuracy depend on the choices of parameters for other APUs as well. Table 2 describes the choices of parameters considered in Auditeur for the sampling rate, frame size, window size, and number discretization levels for feature quantization. The higher the sampling rate the more energy it consumes, but provides better classification results. Frame size, window size, and discretization levels are problem dependent, and have effect on accuracy. The choice of classifier is also problem dependent, and their parameters are computed by analyzing the training set using standard practices. Considering all 36 combinations of these units and 7 classifiers, the cloud generates 252 different execution plans (all within the total energy budget), and selects the one that results in the highest accuracy in 10-fold cross validation test.

7.2 Tag Matching Service

The tag matching service is used in two scenarios: (1) admission control of a public soundlet, and (2) finding matching tags for an untagged soundlet. Both of these are done using a distance based outlier detection technique [5], i.e., extracting the feature vector of the soundlet, computing similarity scores of the feature vector against a subset of the existing soundlets, and returning the top k tags in the order of decreasing similarity. For admission control, one or more of the user given tags must be in the list of k tags, and for tag-suggestions, the list of k tags is sent to the phone.

The collection of soundlets against which the similarity is measured is selected using the phone contexts. For example, location (indoors or outdoors) and position contexts are used to eliminate any unlikely soundlets from considerations. If GPS coordinates are available, soundlets that are recorded within the vicinity of the untagged soundlet are always considered for a similarity match.

7.3 Storage and Caching

The cloud stores thousands of tagged soundlets and their acoustic features, therefore fast search and retrieval of items are paramount. We choose to use MongoDB which is a NOSQL database over a relational database for many reasons. First, the number of features for an instance can vary considerably depending on the processing configuration used at the time therefore a schema would be too rigid for our purposes. Secondly, NOSQL databases are optimized for write once, read many times situations and tend to scale linearly using replicas in the cloud infrastructure. For efficient queries into the training set, we create an index on the tag and context attribute set.

When a classification plan is requested from a client, the local cache of prepared classifiers is first searched. If a classifier for the particular tag combination and context are not found, a new classifier is generated from the set of matching instances in the training set and committed to the cache. If a new sound instance is added with the same tag combination as existing classifiers, the cache entry is marked dirty allowing an updated classifier to be created. Our default strategy uses on-demand creation of classifiers since many queries are very specific, however we also allow the cloud to preemptively create new classifiers on a daily basis from popular search queries.

8. EVALUATION

We describe four types of evaluations. First, we measure CPU and memory footprints, and energy consumptions of different processing units of Auditeur (Section 8.2). Second, we perform an empirical study on different categories of sounds to demonstrate the efficacy of our energy-aware feature selection algorithm (Section 8.3). Third, we implement seven apps, each in three ways: in-phone, in-cloud, and using Auditeur, and compare their energy consumption (Section 8.4.1), accuracy (Section 8.4.2) and context awareness (Section 8.4.3). Fourth, we perform a usability study of Auditeur API (Section 8.5).

8.1 Experimental Setup

We collect data from two sources. The first one is our own collection, obtained from a total of 35 participants from two different regions (Virginia and Beijing), collected over nine months, resulting in a database of about 5000 tagged soundlets with contextual information. The group of participants is comprised of undergraduate and graduate students, researchers, professionals, and their family members. Their ages are in the range of $10 - 60$, and they have diversities in speaking-style, life-style and ethnicity. The smartphones we have used during the data collection are Galaxy Nexus phones running Android 4.0 OS, each having a 1.2 GHz TI OMAP4460 dual core processor, 1 GB RAM, 32 GB internal storage, and 28 GB USB storage.

The other source of data is mainly websites including findsounds.com and grsites.com, yielding another 2000 tagged soundlets. The web crawled data is used only in the empirical evaluation, not in case studies. We use only those sound clips whose file format, number of channels, bit resolution, and sampling rates are the same as our phone recordings. We do not mix up web crawled data with data from phones in most cases. For example, sounds that are tagged 'monkey' are all from the web, we do not have any phone recorded monkey sounds. For some rare sounds in the empirical study, we re-recorded some of the web-audios with a smartphone. For example, we play the 'siren' sounds loudly on a laptop and then record that on a smartphone.

	CPU	Memory
Auditeur (silence)	6%	6.5 MB
Auditeur (active)	16% (42%)	11.8 MB (22 MB)

Table 3: CPU and memory footprints.

8.2 System Measurements

8.2.1 CPU and Memory Footprint

We measure the CPU and memory footprints of Auditeur when used in an app with a simple GUI. The GUI is used to select different sound recognition tasks that are run during the experiment. We use two utility apps (Norton and OS Monitor) to measure the CPU and memory usages. Table 3 shows the average (and the maximum in brackets) CPU and memory usages of the apps. The CPU usage is only 6% during silence when the system is duty cycling, 16% on average, and could reach up to 42% in the worst case if all of the processing units are used in an app (which is unlikely). The memory usage is about 6.5 MB during silence, but reaches 11.8 MB for an average app, as heap space is allocated for the dynamically instantiated units. However, this is not so high when compared to services such as Maps (62.7 MB), Music (54.9 MB), and Calendar (18.9 MB) on Android. The total size of the binary is only 596 KB.

8.2.2 Energy Measurements

We measure the energy consumption of each acoustic processing unit on the phone with a high precision power monitor [2]. Prior to the experiment, we kill all background services and running apps, disable wireless connectivity, and set the screen brightness to its minimum. We use two minute long audio files recorded at 44.1 KHz, and measure the total energy consumption.

Figure 9 shows the average energy consumption to process a 32 ms frame for each unit. We observe that, the most expensive units are the frequency domain feature extractors. However, all of these components (marked with an asterisk (*)) use the same FFT which is computed only once per frame to save energy. Despite this, the extraction of frame level features, together with the computation of window level statistics, account for 98.48% of the total energy consumption of the processing pipeline. This signifies why Auditeur emphasizes carefully choosing the features to increase the lifetime of the device. The sum of individual energy consumptions however is not an accurate estimate of the actual energy consumption; but from our experience with Auditeur we have seen that, this is a conservative estimate, and the phone lasts longer than the estimated lifetime in practice.

8.3 Empirical Evaluation

We analyze the trade-off between the accuracy and energy savings, compare the feature selection algorithm with a greedy heuristic, illustrate the energy efficiency, and measure the processing delay.

We use our empirical dataset in these experiments, which is segmented into 10 categories of sounds as described in Table 4. In this study, we are showing intra-category sound recognition accuracy within each dataset. Note that, these are very demanding datasets with many similar sounds in different categories within the same dataset to stress the accuracy metric, and even for humans these are hard to distinguish. However, later in our case studies (Section 8.4), we consider real-world scenarios where we have sounds from different classes.

8.3.1 Lifetime and Accuracy Trade-off

Auditeur's feature selection algorithm trades off less informative features for a longer lifetime of the device. The goal of this experiment is to quantify how much accuracy Auditeur compromises to achieve this.

ID	Dataset	Count	Subcategories
D1	Alert	334	alarm, bell, horn, siren, whistle.
D2	Animal	145	cat, cow, dog, horse, monkey, tiger.
D3	Household	453	air conditioner, doorbell, doorslam, fan, spray, vacuum, water tap, and more.
D4	Instruments	309	drum, guitar, piano, violin, flute.
D5	Music	1253	country, folk, indian, jazz, rap, rhymes, rock, spiritual, and more.
D6	Non-speech	783	asthma whizz, chew, clap, cough, cry, foot-steps, laughter, whistle, yell.
D7	Office	653	deskbell, keyboard typing, mouse clicks, phone, printer, sharpener, stapler.
D8	Speech	1725	female, male, child, speaker ID.
D9	Tools	439	broom, chain saw, drill, grinder, hammer, lawnmower.
D10	Vehicles	815	airplane, ambulance, bus, car, subway.

Table 4: Description of the empirical dataset.

Figure 10 shows the classification accuracy of Auditeur for different datasets. For each dataset, the first bar corresponds to the highest achievable accuracy considering no energy bound, and the other three bars correspond to minimum lifetime requirements of 300, 400, and 500 mins, respectively. The number on top of each bar denotes the number of selected features. We see that, for an unbounded energy, Auditeur would use all 221 features and achieve the highest average 10-fold cross validation accuracy of $65.4\% - 97.2\%$. The accuracy is below 70% for some datasets, such as D7, D3, and D9, which contain varieties of similar sounds. However, in an actual app, not all of these might be used or they might be representing the same class; hence the accuracy will be higher in practice as evident from Section 8.4.2. The tighter the energy bound becomes, i.e. the larger the minimum lifetime requirement is, Auditeur selects less number of features to maintain the lifetime goal. For a 500 min (8.3 hours) lifetime, Auditeur chooses only 18 features on average to keep the system running, sacrificing about 8.17% accuracy. However, for a moderate lifetime of 400 mins (6.67 hours), the difference in accuracy is $< 2\%$.

8.3.2 Evaluating Feature Selection Algorithm

We compare Auditeur's energy-aware feature selection algorithm with Weka's [10] symmetrical uncertainly attribute evaluator. Since Weka does not consider energy, we choose the first few highest ranked attributes as long as the sum of their energy costs remains within the bound. Figure 11 compares the average accuracy of a classifier for different minimum lifetime bounds, when the classifier uses these two feature selection methods. When the energy bound is lower, i.e. the minimum lifetime is as high as $500 - 600$ mins, less number of features are chosen by both of the algorithms. But Auditeur selects the subset that is optimal within the bound, whereas the greedy algorithm performs poorly. The gap between these two however gets closer as the bound becomes loose since both algorithms then select enough number of features to classify the sounds properly. Therefore, applications that require long term ($8 - 10$ hours) continuous sound recognition, Auditeur would provide $8\% - 14.9\%$ higher accuracy than the greedy algorithm.

8.3.3 Illustration of Energy Efficiency

We illustrate the energy efficiency of Auditeur with a simple example scenario. In this scenario, we run the same workload on two

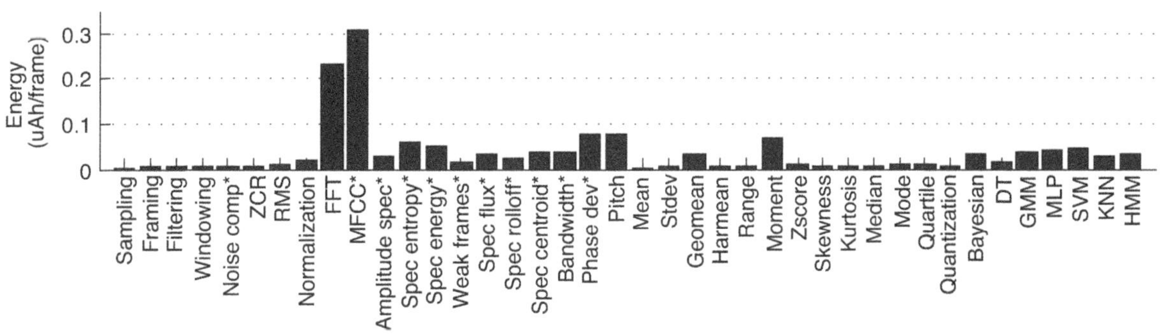

Figure 9: Feature extraction accounts for 98.48% of the total energy consumption of the processing pipeline.

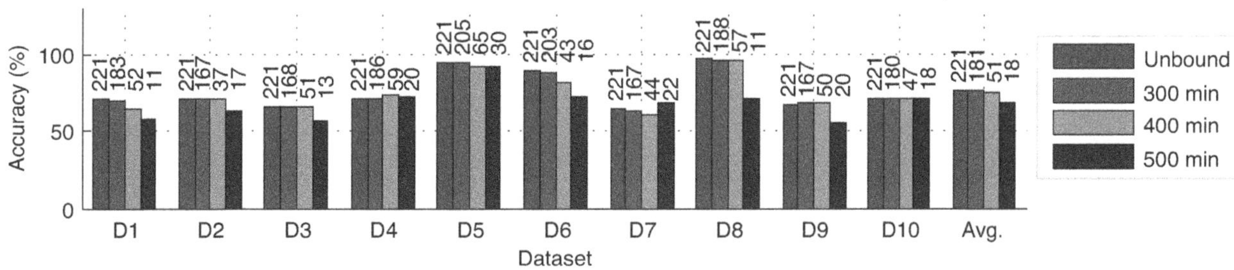

Figure 10: Auditeur increases the lifetime by $33.4\% - 66.7\%$, sacrificing $2\% - 8.17\%$ accuracy.

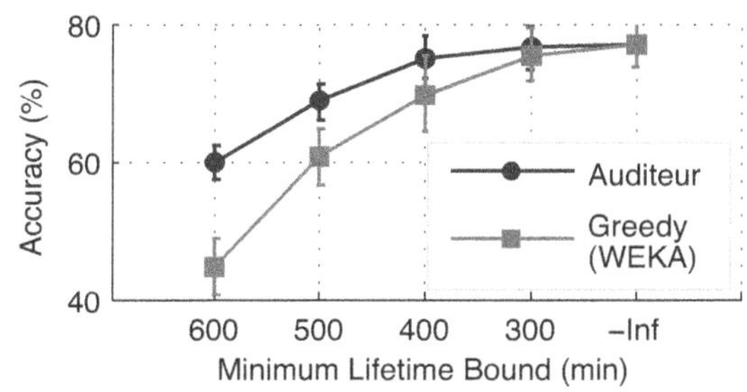

Figure 11: Auditeur achieves $8\% - 14.9\%$ higher accuracy than WEKA for long running apps.

identical Android phones for about 9 hours. Both of the phones run Auditeur, but one assumes an infinite energy bound, and the other one changes its classification plan after two hours to last longer.

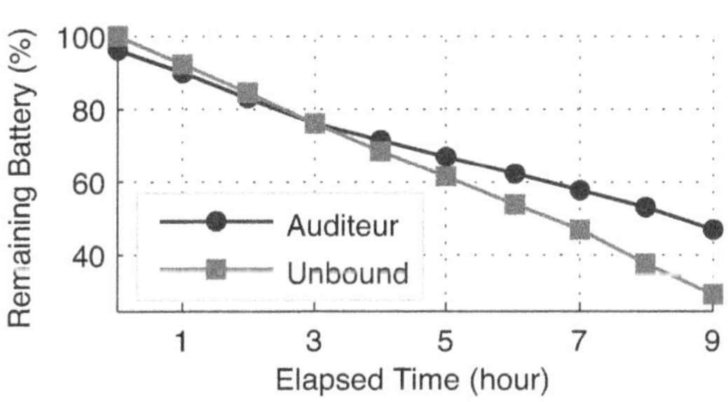

Figure 12: Auditeur's remaining battery is 18.12% higher than the unbounded one after 9 hours.

Figure 12 plots their remaining battery life at each hour mark. We see that, the phone with unbounded energy drains battery at the rate of 7.89% per hour, and after 9 hours, it's remaining charge is only 29%. The other one (denoted by Auditeur) initially drains battery at the rate of 6.67% per hour, but this rate is reduced to 4.81% after reducing the energy bound by 15% at hour 2. After 9 hours, Auditeur's remaining battery is 47.12%, which is 18.12% higher than the unbounded one. That means, Auditeur would last for 31 hours, whereas the unbounded one will die after 19 hours.

8.3.4 Processing Delay

We measure the processing delay, i.e., the average duration of a $1s$ long frame inside the pipeline. To obtain this, we capture $60s$ audio, and process it with 300 different pipeline configurations, each having a different minimum lifetime bound. The total time to process the frames is normalized to compute the processing delay of a frame.

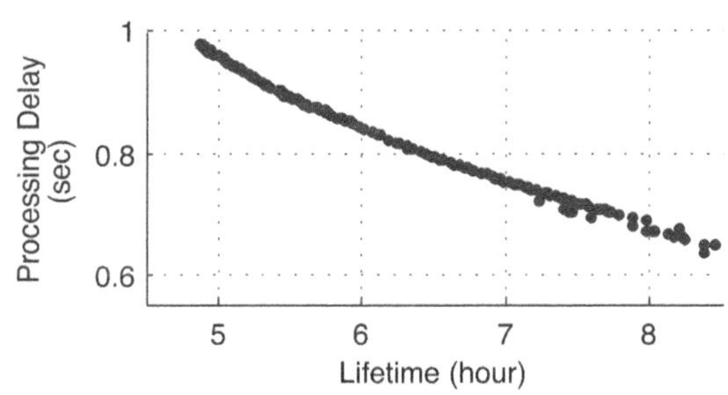

Figure 13: Processing delay for $1s$ frames is always $< 1s$.

Figure 13 shows processing delays of $1s$ long frames for different lifetime bounds, ranging approximately $5 - 8$ hours. We observe that, the delay is higher ($0.98s$) at the beginning, and drops below $0.7s$ as the bound crosses the 8-hour mark. This is because, at tighter bounds, Auditeur extracts a small number of features to meet its lifetime goal, which results in shorter processing delays. However, overall the delay is always $< 1s$ for a $1s$ frame.

8.4 Case Studies

We implement and evaluate seven apps with Auditeur and compare their energy efficiency, accuracy, and context awareness against two baselines: the in-phone and the in-cloud implementations of the apps. The features and parameters for the baselines are taken from corresponding existing works. Both baselines extract features on the phone, but the in-cloud version sends them to the cloud in real-time to get the classification results, while the in-phone version does everything on the device. The definitions of in-phone and in-cloud implementations thus consider any hybrid approach (such as – partitioning or offloading computation to the cloud at runtime [7]) as an in-cloud implementation. For communication, WiFi is used indoors and 3G outdoors. Auditeur however downloads all of its classifier configurations, corresponding to different location and position contexts, at the beginning and does not use wireless connectivity afterwards.

Five Android phones and a tablet are used at the same time during these experiments. Two phones run the baselines, one runs Auditeur, one runs Auditeur with only location context enabled, and one runs Auditeur with only position context enabled. The tablet is used for recording the ground truth and bookkeeping purposes. Each phone stores the timestamp, detected events, and the battery level.

App	Detected Events
Sound Sense	male, female, music.
Speaker Sense	person identification.
Musical Heart	heart beats.
Music Match	music genre recognition.
Vehicle Sense	car, bus, subway, trolley.
Kitchen Sense	door, blender, pots, stove, microwave, tap.
Sleep Monitor	talk, cough, steps, bathroom door, fan.

Table 5: Apps in case studies.

Table 5 shows the list of apps that we study. We replicate the first three apps from existing literature [17, 16, 23], and add four more to demonstrate Auditeur's performance in different real-world scenarios. Ground truths for Speaker Sense and Sound Sense are obtained from six volunteers, by logging who is talking and what music is played with a tablet. These experiments are done in ten $15 - 120$ minutes long sessions at indoors and outdoors. Musical Heart uses the dataset of [23] which is read from files. Music Match is trained on 200 English songs of different genre, and then the tablet randomly chooses and plays them at regular intervals, while the phones listen and classify them. Vehicle Sense and Kitchen Sense are trained on samples collected from members of two two-person families, and are tested on them separately in $3 - 5$ hours long experiments. Two volunteers participate in the Sleep Monitor experiment separately for two consecutive days where each session lasts for about $6 - 8$ hours. We record the entire sleep duration with a tablet, and perform a post-facto analysis, with visualization and manual classification, to identify the events.

8.4.1 Power Consumption

We compare the power consumptions of Auditeur with in-phone and in-cloud implementations. The power consumption is obtained from the total energy consumption, which we calculate using the values that are logged periodically into the phone, i.e. the remaining battery life, voltage, running time, and the battery capacity.

Figure 14 shows that, power consumptions of in-cloud implementations are $3.3 - 6.8$ times higher than the other two, as they continuously send and receive data over the Internet. Especially, for outdoor experiments where 3G is used (Vehicle, Sound, and Speaker), the mean is 4093 mW. Power consumption of in-phone version is comparatively closer to Auditeur. For long running experiments (Sound, Speaker, Vehicle, Kitchen, and Sleep), in-phone ones consume 19.56% more power than Auditeur, as unlike Auditeur, they do not have energy bounds. For short duration experiments (Heart and Music), in-phone versions are slightly more energy efficient than Auditeur. However, this is not a problem for Auditeur because of two reasons: (1) when sufficient energy is available, Auditeur uses slightly more power to achieve a higher detection accuracy, and (2) even in such cases, developers can specify a tighter energy bound to achieve a lower power consumption. Overall, the power consumption of Auditeur is on average 11.04% less than the in-phone version.

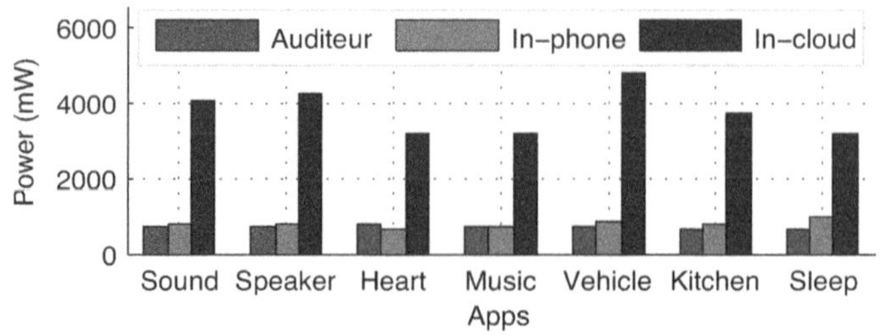

Figure 14: On average, Auditeur is 11.04% and 441.42% less power hungry than in-phone and in-cloud versions.

An Auditeur-powered app's lifetime can be further extended by duty cycling. However, this has to be done by the app developers by explicitly specifying the cycling interval for their app using the API (see line 17 of the code snippet in Figure 4). Since none of the baseline apps in this experiment implement duty cycling, for a fair comparison of energy consumption, we do not perform duty cycling in Auditeur as well.

8.4.2 Detection Accuracy

The accuracy of event detection is the percentage of events that are detected and classified correctly. All three implementations use the same silence vs. non-silence detection method whose accuracy is almost perfect (98.72%). Hence, we consider the classification of non-silent, fixed length time windows as the overall accuracy.

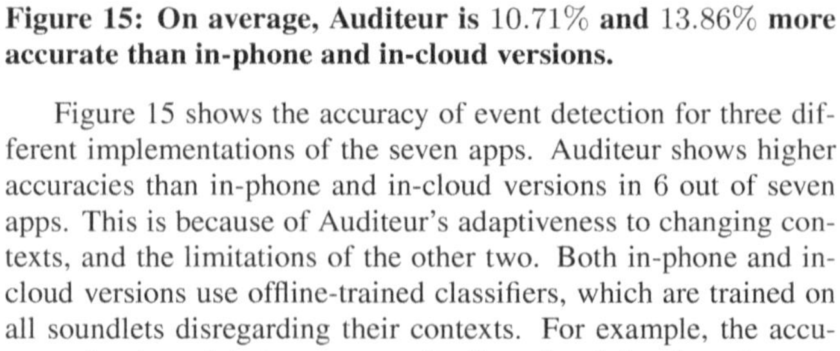

Figure 15: On average, Auditeur is 10.71% and 13.86% more accurate than in-phone and in-cloud versions.

Figure 15 shows the accuracy of event detection for three different implementations of the seven apps. Auditeur shows higher accuracies than in-phone and in-cloud versions in 6 out of seven apps. This is because of Auditeur's adaptiveness to changing contexts, and the limitations of the other two. Both in-phone and in-cloud versions use offline-trained classifiers, which are trained on all soundlets disregarding their contexts. For example, the accuracy of voice related apps, e.g., the Sound and Speaker, depends on the location (indoors vs. outdoors) due to the presence of reverberation. Auditeur being aware of such contextual information are capable of handling them separately, which the other two cannot. Furthermore, the in-cloud versions lose $14.3\% - 26\%$ accuracy in outdoor scenarios (Vehicle, Sound and Speaker), due to long communication delays in a 3G network. The accuracy of Auditeur in case of Heart app however is similar to the other two versions. This is because, the Heart app, which is one of our previous works [23], uses a highly sophisticated algorithm for heart rate detection and has a very high accuracy. It is hard to beat such an algorithm using Auditeur especially when the accuracy is close to 100%. Overall, Auditeur shows 10.71% – 13.86% higher accuracy than the other two versions.

8.4.3 Context Awareness

Auditeur uses different pipeline configurations for different location (indoors vs outdoors) and body position (direct, pocket, or distant) contexts to boost its accuracy. In this experiment, we measure their individual effects on accuracy.

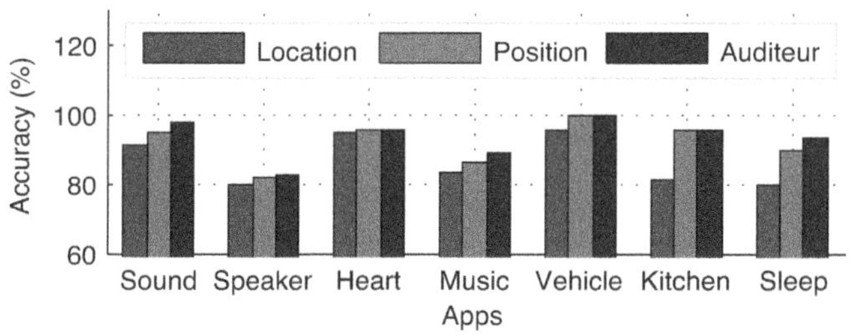

Figure 16: Position context is in general more effective than location context.

Figure 16 compares Auditeur with two other versions of it: (1) only location, or (2) only position context enabled. A combination of the two always results in a higher accuracy, but their individual contribution varies with apps. Location context is ineffective in Heart, Vehicle, Kitchen, and Sleep, since these are performed entirely indoors or outdoors. For other apps, location alone improves accuracy over baselines (of Figure 15) by 4.08% – 7.93%. Position contexts are more effective than location contexts in environments where the phone may be in any of the three position contexts, such as in Sound, Speaker, Music, Kitchen (pocket and table), and Sleep (table and under pillow), contributing 6.45% more accuracy over the location only version.

8.5 User Study

We perform a user study to evaluate the usability of Auditeur API, i.e. how easy or hard it is to learn and use the API. Another motivation is to observe what application ideas burgeon when such an API is made available to the public.

A total of 15 undergraduate students from 3 universities participated in this study. We recruited them by posting an online advertisement and their participation was voluntary. Their experience-levels in Java and Android programming are 0 – 5 years (avg. 16.6 months), and 0 – 12 months (avg. 4.73 months), respectively. We provided them with a documentation explaining the API and an example code snippet. Each of the participants was asked to read the documentation to learn the API, think of an app scenario, code it, and then comment on their overall experience.

Since developing a fully functioning application involves other non-sound recognition tasks, such as, programming the GUI and handling events, which are not part of our study, we ask the participants to code only the portion of the app that is Auditeur-specific, while the rest of the app has already been coded for them. This is done to remove any biases that originate from sources unrelated to learning or coding with the Auditeur API. Figure 17 shows the learning time and coding time as they have reported in their answers. About 75% of the participants take less than 15 mins to learn the API, and about 60% of them program the core logic in just 10 mins using only 15 – 20 lines of Java code. The worst case learning time is as high as 30 mins, while the highest of the coding times is about an hour. This indicates that, Auditeur is very easy to learn and code.

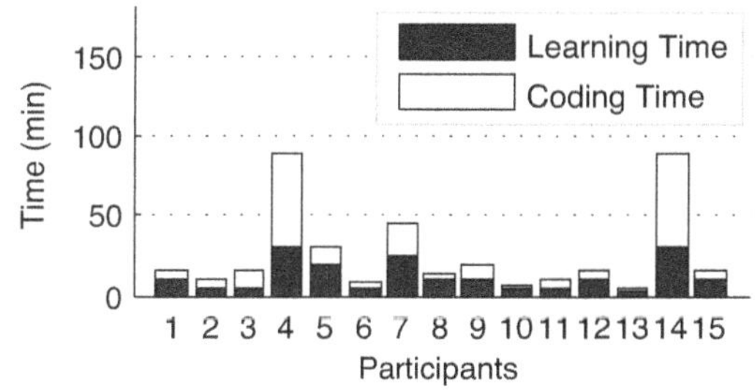

Figure 17: Learning and coding time.

It is interesting to observe how our participants have come up with a number of fascinating app ideas and have been able to realize them with Auditeur. Table 6 describes some of the ideas that we find more interesting than others.

App	Short Description
Snore	Detect snoring and vibrate the phone until he stops.
Honk	Detect car honks on road and alert inattentive user.
Asthma	Detect asthmatic wheezing sound and alert the caregiver.
Subway	Detect the arrival of a train in subway.
Dog	Detect pet dog barking while the user is away from home.

Table 6: Interesting app ideas found in our study.

We also ask our participants to comment on the Auditeur API. Some of those comments turn out to be helpful and are actually incorporated in the system. For example, the participant who implemented the Dog app, asked if we could provide an API to get the last few seconds of audio, so that she knew what caused her dog to bark (e.g. an intruder came). Another participant asked if we could provide a confidence of a match instead of just the detected event. These comments have led us to expose some internal API to obtain last few minutes of audio and the probability distribution of the detected events from the application layer.

9. DISCUSSION

Auditeur is capable of detecting sound events that are recognizable from short-term time and frequency domain features. Recognizing sounds that depend heavily on temporal variations, such as recognizing long spoken sentences, are not suitable for it. Especially, speech recognition is a complex, well-studied problem having several well-known services, and hence we leave it out of the scope of Auditeur.

To make sure that people do not upload soundlets with wrong labels, Auditeur performs sanity checks and discards the sound if there is a lack of similarity. This was not an issue in our experiments since the data were uploaded by our trusted users and we only had to deal with unintentional human errors. However, this could be a big issue when the system is open to the public. A more sophisticated sanity checking mechanism will be required at that moment. This is a limitation of our current implementation and we leave it as future work.

Lack of sufficient training examples, specially for private spaces, is another issue. To cope with this, we suggest developers to utilize sounds from public spaces as long as the private space is small, while keep adding new soundlets to the private space. Auditeur provides an API to retrieve last few minutes of audio; developers should use this facility and upload new soundlets via user-feedback.

The features and classifiers used in Auditeur are shown to recognize varieties of sounds, but yet no such list is ever exhaustive. However, Auditeur is an extensible system where addition of a new feature extractor or a new classifier unit is easy since APUs have a generic structure and are dynamically wired. Hence, such extensions do not require any change to the framework.

The energy consumption and lifetime depend on the phone model and battery capacity. The relative energy costs of the processing units are, however, implementation dependent, and remain the same. This is, therefore, a scaling problem, and the lifetime bound for such cases should be considered as power levels instead of an absolute value. We leave it as a future work to remotely profile energy consumption of the device to provide device tailored lifetime values.

Scalability of the services running on the cloud is not addressed in this paper which is by itself a well-formed problem. Our current implementation is a proof of concept which runs on an Amazon EC2 instance. However in future we plan to move our server to Google App Engine which provides automatic scaling of apps without requiring us to manage the machines by ourselves.

10. RELATED WORK

Acoustic sensing on smartphones has been used in several works. Examples of voice and music sensing applications are, speaker identification [16], speech recognition [31], emotion and stress detection [18, 28], conversation and human behavior inference [20, 21], music recognition, search and discovery [32, 3]. There are some limited number of applications that consider other types of sounds. MusicalHeart [23] uses a special-purpose microphone to count heart beats, [14] counts coughs, Nericel [22] detects horns, Ear-phone [29] monitors noise pollution, SurroundSense [4] and CSP [6] infer logical location. All these systems detect only one specific type of sound. SoundSense [17] distinguishes voice from music and noise, and cluster other sounds. But unlike Auditeur, none of these systems aim at solving the general purpose acoustic event detection problem.

There are several web services available for smartphone developers. Hawaii [1] provides social mobile sharing (SMASH) service for rapid prototyping of social computing apps, service to predict user's destination using current route, key-value storage for app-wide state information, text translation service, providing relay point in the cloud for apps' communication, optical character recognition service (OCR), and English speech-to-text services. But Hawaii does not have an acoustic event detection service. Google provides services such as: web search, Google maps, app store (Google play), video streaming (YouTube), Google cloud drive, and email service (Gmail). Other providers give access to data sources such as weather, financial data, airline information, and parcel location tracking. Unlike Auditeur, none of these provide a sound recognition service and API to the developers.

Feature selection is a problem studied by many; [9] provides a survey. WEKA [10] implements several of these attribute selection methods. But our problem is different as our selection criterion is to minimize energy consumption, not to minimize the number of features. Like Auditeur, symmetrical uncertainty has been used in [33] as a goodness measure, but their approach is greedy whereas we apply dynamic programming principle.

There are several works that deal with resource aware sensor data classification on smartphones. Kobe [7] is tool to generate energy and latency aware classifiers, but unlike Auditeur, it requires uninterrupted mobile-cloud communication for adaptive code-offloading (so is required for MAUI [8] and Odessa [27]), it is not sensitive to user context, and their set of features is predetermined and fixed by the developer. Orchestrator [13] enables multiple applications to effectively share resources (e.g. sensors) whose availability changes dynamically. The optimum plan selection problem in Orchestrator is similar to the acoustic feature selection problem in Auditeur. However, unlike Auditeur, their selection algorithm is not scalable as they enumerate an exponential number of plans while Auditeur uses a polynomial time dynamic programming algorithm to eliminate the need for enumeration of exponential number of subsets of features and thus limits the total number of plans to consider. [30] proposes a heuristic algorithm to select a subset of sensors and their tolerance levels so that they can infer multiple contexts in an energy efficient manner. Their solution is efficient, but is not optimum, whereas feature selection in Auditeur is both optimum and efficient.

Some works are technically similar to Auditeur, but solve different problems. TagSense [25] senses people, activity and context in a picture, and creates tags on-the-fly, whereas Auditeur involves people in the sound tagging process, but provides automated tag suggestions. Sphinx [31] uses generic processing units which are similar to the APUs in Auditeur, but they have a simpler pipeline, highly tuned to solve speech recognition problem. Pickle [15] creates privacy preserving classifiers on the cloud whereas we preserve privacy by providing the user with private spaces, and classifiers in Auditeur are trained for energy efficiency.

11. CONCLUSION

This paper presents the design, implementation, and evaluation of Auditeur which is a general-purpose, energy-efficient, and context-aware acoustic event detection platform for smartphones. This is a useful platform and would save months of development time for developers who want to build apps that act upon acoustic events. Aside from its ability to recognize a wide variety of sounds, the platform is shown to be energy efficient and accurate. We provide empirical evidence that Auditeur's energy-aware algorithm is capable of increasing the device-lifetime by 33.4%, sacrificing less than 2% of the maximum achievable accuracy. Seven apps have been implemented with the Auditeur API to demonstrate its versatility and to show that apps developed with Auditeur are 11.04% – 441.42% less power hungry, and 10.71% – 13.86% more accurate in detecting acoustic events compared to state-of-the-art techniques. A user study on 15 undergrads shows that even novice programmers can implement the core logic of interesting apps with Auditeur in less than 30 minutes, using only 15 – 20 lines of Java code.

Acknowledgments

This paper was supported, in part, by NSF grants CNS-1035771 and EECS-901686, and by DGIST via funding from the Ministry of Education, Science and Technology of the Republic of Korea.

12. REFERENCES

[1] Microsoft's Project Hawaii. http://research.microsoft.com/en-us/projects/hawaii/.

[2] Power Monitor. http://msoon.com/LabEquipment/PowerMonitor/.

[3] Sound Hound. http://www.soundhound.com/.

[4] M. Azizyan, I. Constandache, and R. Roy Choudhury. SurroundSense: mobile phone localization via ambience fingerprinting. In *MobiCom '09*, Beijing, China.

[5] S. D. Bay and M. Schwabacher. Mining distance-based outliers in near linear time with randomization and a simple pruning rule. In *KDD '03*, Washington, D.C.

[6] Y. Chon, N. D. Lane, F. Li, H. Cha, and F. Zhao. Automatically characterizing places with opportunistic crowdsensing using smartphones. In *UbiComp '12*, Pittsburgh, PA.
[7] D. Chu, N. D. Lane, T. T.-T. Lai, C. Pang, X. Meng, Q. Guo, F. Li, and F. Zhao. Balancing energy, latency and accuracy for mobile sensor data classification. In *SenSys '11*, Seattle, Washington.
[8] E. Cuervo, A. Balasubramanian, D. Cho, A. Wolman, S. Saroiu, R. Chandra, and P. Bahl. MAUI: making smartphones last longer with code offload. In *MobiSys '10*, San Francisco, CA.
[9] I. Guyon and A. Elisseeff. An introduction to variable and feature selection. *Journal of Machine Learning Research*, 3:1157–1182, Mar. 2003.
[10] M. Hall, E. Frank, G. Holmes, B. Pfahringer, P. Reutemann, and I. H. Witten. The weka data mining software: An update. *SIGKDD Explorations*, 11(1), 2009.
[11] Y. Ju, Y. Lee, J. Yu, C. Min, I. Shin, and J. Song. SymPhoney: a coordinated sensing flow execution engine for concurrent mobile sensing applications. In *SenSys '12*, Toronto, Canada.
[12] S. Kang, J. Lee, H. Jang, H. Lee, Y. Lee, S. Park, T. Park, and J. Song. SeeMon: scalable and energy-efficient context monitoring framework for sensor-rich mobile environments. MobiSys '08, Breckenridge, CO, USA.
[13] S. Kang, Y. Lee, C. Min, Y. Ju, T. Park, J. Lee, Y. Rhee, and J. Song. Orchestrator: An active resource orchestration framework for mobile context monitoring in sensor-rich mobile environments. In *PerCom '10*, Mannheim, Germany.
[14] E. C. Larson, T. Lee, S. Liu, M. Rosenfeld, and S. N. Patel. Accurate and privacy preserving cough sensing using a low-cost microphone. In *UbiComp '11*, Beijing, China.
[15] B. Liu, Y. Jiang, F. Sha, and R. Govindan. Cloud-enabled privacy-preserving collaborative learning for mobile sensing. In *SenSys '12*, Toronto, Canada.
[16] H. Lu, A. J. B. Brush, B. Priyantha, A. K. Karlson, and J. Liu. SpeakerSense: energy efficient unobtrusive speaker identification on mobile phones. In *Pervasive '11*, San Francisco, CA.
[17] H. Lu, W. Pan, N. D. Lane, T. Choudhury, and A. T. Campbell. SoundSense: scalable sound sensing for people-centric applications on mobile phones. In *MobiSys '09*, Poland.
[18] H. Lu, M. Rabbi, G. T. Chittaranjan, D. Frauendorfer, M. S. Mast, A. T. Campbell, D. Gatica-Perez, and T. Choudhury. StressSense: Detecting stress in unconstrained acoustic environments using smartphones. In *UbiComp '12*, Pittsburgh, PA.
[19] H. Lu, J. Yang, Z. Liu, N. D. Lane, T. Choudhury, and A. T. Campbell. The jigsaw continuous sensing engine for mobile phone applications. In *SenSys '10*, Zurich, Switzerland.
[20] E. Miluzzo, C. T. Cornelius, A. Ramaswamy, T. Choudhury, Z. Liu, and A. T. Campbell. Darwin Phones: the evolution of sensing and inference on mobile phones. In *MobiSys '10*, San Francisco, CA.
[21] E. Miluzzo, N. D. Lane, K. Fodor, R. Peterson, H. Lu, M. Musolesi, S. B. Eisenman, X. Zheng, and A. T. Campbell. Sensing meets mobile social networks: the design, implementation and evaluation of the CenceMe application. In *SenSys '08*, Raleigh, NC.
[22] P. Mohan, V. N. Padmanabhan, and R. Ramjee. Nericell: Using mobile smartphones for rich monitoring of road and traffic conditions. In *SenSys '08*, Raleigh, NC, 2008.
[23] S. Nirjon, R. Dickerson, Q. Li, P. Asare, J. Stankovic, D. Hong, B. Zhang, G. Shen, X. Jiang, and F. Zhao. MusicalHeart: A hearty way of listening to music. In *SenSys '12*, Toronto, Canada.
[24] W. H. Press, S. A. Teukolsky, W. T. Vetterling, and B. P. Flannery. *Numerical recipes in C (2nd ed.): the art of scientific computing*. Cambridge University Press, New York, NY, USA, 1992.
[25] C. Qin, X. Bao, R. Roy Choudhury, and S. Nelakuditi. TagSense: a smartphone-based approach to automatic image tagging. In *MobiSys '11*, Bethesda, MD.
[26] J. Quinlan. *C4.5: Programs for machine learning*. Morgan Kaufmann, 2002.
[27] M.-R. Ra, A. Sheth, L. Mummert, P. Pillai, D. Wetherall, and R. Govindan. Odessa: enabling interactive perception applications on mobile devices. In *Proceedings of the 9th international conference on Mobile systems, applications, and services*, MobiSys '11, Bethesda, Maryland, USA.
[28] K. K. Rachuri, M. Musolesi, C. Mascolo, P. J. Rentfrow, C. Longworth, and A. Aucinas. EmotionSense: a mobile phones based adaptive platform for experimental social psychology research. In *Ubicomp '10*, Copenhagen, Denmark.
[29] R. K. Rana, C. T. Chou, S. S. Kanhere, N. Bulusu, and W. Hu. Ear-phone: An end-to-end participatory urban noise mapping system. In *IPSN '10*, Stockholm, Sweden.
[30] N. Roy, A. Misra, C. Julien, S. K. Das, and J. Biswas. An energy-efficient quality adaptive framework for multi-modal sensor context recognition. In *PerCom '11*, Washington, DC, USA.
[31] W. Walker, P. Lamere, P. Kwok, B. Raj, R. Singh, E. Gouvea, P. Wolf, and J. Woelfel. Sphinx-4: a flexible open source framework for speech recognition. Technical report, Mountain View, CA, 2004.
[32] A. Wang. An industrial-strength audio search algorithm. In *ISMIR '03*.
[33] L. Yu and H. Liu. Feature selection for high-dimensional data: A fast correlation-based filter solution. In *International Conference on Machine Learning*, pages 856–863, 2003.
[34] P. Zhou, Y. Zheng, Z. Li, M. Li, and G. Shen. IODetector: A generic service for indoor outdoor detection. In *SenSys' 12*, Toronto, Canada.

Kwiizya: Local Cellular Network Services in Remote Areas

Mariya Zheleva, Arghyadip Paul, David L. Johnson and Elizabeth Belding
Department of Computer Science
University of California, Santa Barbara
{mariya, arghyadip, davidj, ebelding}@cs.ucsb.edu

ABSTRACT

Cellular networks have revolutionized the way people communicate in rural areas. At the same time, deployment of commercial-grade cellular networks in areas with low population density, such as in rural sub-Saharan Africa, is prohibitively expensive relative to the return of investment. As a result, 48% of the rural population in Africa remains disconnected. To address this problem, we design a local cellular network architecture, Kwiizya, that provides basic voice and text messaging services in rural areas. Our system features an interface for development of text message based applications that can be leveraged for improved health care, education and support of local businesses. We deployed an instance of Kwiizya in the rural village of Macha in Zambia. Our deployment utilizes the existing long distance Wi-Fi network in the village for inter-base station communication to provide high quality services with minimal infrastructure requirements. In this paper we evaluate Kwiizya in-situ in Macha and show that the network maintains low delay and jitter (20ms and 3ms, respectively) for voice call traffic, while providing high call Mean Opinion Score of 3.46, which is the theoretical maximum supported by our system.

Categories and Subject Descriptors

C.2 [**Computer-communication networks**]: Network architecture and design; C.4 [**Performance of systems**]: Design studies

Keywords

Mobile telephony, Rural area networks, Low-cost communication, OpenBTS, Cellular communication

1. INTRODUCTION

It is clear that mobile phone usage has become one of the most prevalent means of communication worldwide. 2011 statistics from the International Telecommunication Union indicate that, worldwide, there are 85.7 mobile-cellular subscriptions per 100 inhabitants [13]. This number has been steadily increasing over the last 10 years, with growth over the last five years primarily driven by subscriptions in the developing world.

While the statistics are encouraging, what they mask is the huge differential in cost and service availability and quality between the developed and the developing world. For instance, while residents of developed countries spend on average 2% of their monthly income on cellular service, the cost in developing countries is closer to 12% [13]. In addition, the ability of residents in developing regions to access cellphone technology is reduced by limited cellular deployments; while many residents own phones and buy either subscriptions or pre-paid plans, coverage may be spotty or non-existent within residential areas of low population densities[1], as is characteristic of the majority of the world's rural developing regions. Further, while 4G is rapidly becoming available throughout the developed world, in developing regions coverage is often limited to 2G, or 2G + EDGE at best. This discrepancy hints that despite technological advancements, there will always exist an economic challenge in deployment of high-end cellular technology in sparse rural areas. Thus, there will be recurring need for lower cost solutions to serve those areas.

Despite these limitations and high costs, mobile phones are critical for providing communication in developing regions due to limited or non-existent telecommunications infrastructure and poor roads, making quick distance travel difficult. In many developing communities, cultures are oral – communication is based on oral, as opposed to written, forms. Storytelling in such communities is vital to forming world views, maintaining trans-generational knowledge and teaching practical skills. Further, oral communication facilitates practical information exchange, such as crop prices, health care availability, and numerous others. In our own fieldwork in Macha, Zambia, we have witnessed that cellphone availability combined with Internet access can enable rapid information dissemination, whereby person(s) with Internet access serve as information gateways to other, disconnected interested parties.

Our work is in partnership with the LinkNet organization in Macha, Zambia. Our team has visited Macha over the past three years, most recently spending three weeks in the Macha community during June/July 2012. During these visits, through both informal conversations and structured

[1]The World Bank 2012 report on "Maximizing Mobile" notes that mobile network operators find it commercially infeasible to operate in rural areas.

MobiSys'13, June 25-28, 2013, Taipei, Taiwan

interviews, we have learned first hand of the deep desire of local residents for better cellular access. While every resident we encountered owns a cell phone, few have coverage at their homes. In fact, many residents own multiple phones to leverage any available coverage they come across as they travel. Further, the cost of cellular access is prohibitive. Residents rely on pre-paid access cards, which they can afford at unpredictable times due to unreliable income streams. Even the cost of frequent SMS is out of reach for many residents. Yet, the residents have enough experience with this technology to appreciate its value; 100% of our interviewees expressed a desire for better, more affordable cellular access. As a result of these costs, call durations are short, and conversations are quick and to the point. Many users simply carry phones, waiting for someone to call them, as incoming calls are free in the current cost structure.

Studies of locality of interest [14, 20] indicate that communication through technology largely appears between individuals in close physical proximity. Onnela et al. analyzed 72 million calls and 17 million text messages in Europe and found that probability of communication decreases by 5 orders of magnitude when distance between communicating parties increases from 1km to 1000km [20]. Our own prior work has demonstrated the propensity of rural users to communicate with those physically nearby: Facebook Instant Message analysis in Macha showed that, while only 35% of observed users were in the village, 54% of instant messages were between local users [14]. These statistics emphasize the need for solutions that support local voice communication in remote areas.

To address the lack of reliable and affordable cellular coverage in remote communities, we have endeavored to create a cellular access system that facilitates free local calls and SMS within a community. Our system, Kwiizya[2], leverages open-source software solutions, such as OpenBTS[3] and FreeSwitch[4], to provide local voice and text messaging services. In our recent trip to Macha, we deployed two Kwiizya instantiations and gave pre-registered SIM cards to project partners. As a result, we have had the opportunity to assess usage in a fairly unregulated, in-situ scenario. In an earlier work we outlined VillageCell, an idea for providing local calls within a community [5]. In contrast, our current solution utilizes different open-source software components, offers SMS and IM-to-SMS functionality, has been fully deployed and tested in-situ in Macha, Zambia, and opened to a set of test users in Macha.

This paper makes several contributions:

- design and integration of a *low-cost* cellular network alternative that is well suited for local communications in remote rural communities,
- evaluation of a fully operational instance of our system deployed in the field,
- modification of OpenBTS to support Instant Message to SMS functionality for SMS-based applications,
- evaluation of our platform for SMS-based applications, and
- discussion of infrastructure and sustainability-related aspects of alternative cellular network deployments.

[2]Kwiizya means "to chat" in Tonga, the native language in Zambia's Southern province.

[3]`http://wush.net/trac/rangepublic`

[4]`http://freeswitch.org/`

We begin by describing the current state of rural telephony in our partner communities, including results from our detailed interviews with Macha residents. We then describe the Kwiizya architecture, including voice and SMS functionality. In section 5 we describe our deployment within Macha, including some of the deployment challenges we faced in this remote community. We describe results from controlled field tests, as well as results from public usage, of Kwiizya in section 6. Based on our performance analysis and our experience in Macha and in maintaining the system remotely, we offer our thoughts for improvement and some general guidelines for work in remote regions in section 8.

2. VOICE COMMUNICATION IN RURAL ZAMBIA

Voice technologies are revolutionizing communication in remote areas. For example, access to cellphones in Macha allowed farmers to overcome what they call the "briefcase buyers problem", whereby businessmen who buy maize come to the village and often attempt to exploit farmers who are unaware of market prices, buying crops at extremely low prices. Farmers in Macha can now call the Zambian Food Reserve Agency (FRA) to get information about crops prices. Furthermore, a new communication structure of a combination of Internet and cellphones has emerged in Macha, whereby a farmer who has access to both the Internet and a cellphone can check crop prices online and send text messages to fellow farmers.

During our field work in Zambia, we visited Macha and three surrounding villages – Hamoonde, Chikanta and Mapanza. All of these villages use VoIP, cellular technology or both as a means for voice communication. Within the four communities the level of availability of these technologies varies widely, resulting in fundamentally different voice communications usage patterns. We summarize the current cellphone coverage and usage in these communities below.

Macha. Macha is a village in the Southern province of Zambia, located 70km from the closest city, Choma. There are 135,000 people in the area spread over a large radius of 35km. The village is connected to the national power grid; however, individual households rarely have access to electricity. This sparse availability of power results in creative solutions, such as travel to powered public spaces to charge cellphones; others charge their phones while at work. However, while power is technically available, the reality is that the availability and quality can vary on an hourly or daily basis.

Cellphone coverage in Macha was first introduced in 2006 by Celtel (now Airtel). By 2012, MTN was a second active cellphone provider in the village. Residents with a cellphone subscription can use plain voice and text messaging and, where available, low data rate GPRS service for Internet access. The coverage provided by the two operators is largely available in the central part of the village; coverage is inconsistent and spotty in residential areas. A large percent of the people we interviewed had subscriptions with both cellular providers to increase the likelihood they have cellphone coverage at any given time. Our first hand and anecdotal experience, however, indicates that the failures of both commercial networks are highly correlated and often coincide with power failures.

In terms of VoIP, Macha is connected to the Internet through one of Zambia's Internet service providers. A monthly subscription limited at 1GB traffic costs 30 USD. Together with electrical unavailability, this high price renders home Internet access impossible for most residents. A small subset, however, can access the Internet from work or from an Internet café in order to use VoIP services.

Hamoonde. In contrast with Macha, neighboring Hamoonde, only 5km away, has very sparse cellular coverage, no Internet access and no connection to the power grid. Villagers identified the lack of electricity as the main obstacle to computer and Internet access in the village. People we spoke with, however, owned cellphones and expressed their desire to have more widespread cellular coverage. Residents carry their phones for use when they enter an area where cellular access is available. We encountered a case where a cellphone was used as a voice gateway to the Internet, whereby one resident of the village regularly called a relative in the city with access to the Internet to ask her to lookup information online.

Chikanta. Chikanta has population of about 40,000 and is 25km away from Macha. There is no access to electricity within the village; commercial cellphone coverage was introduced in some areas of the village in the beginning of 2012. A commute of 2km is common for village residents to reach an area with cellphone coverage. Interestingly, Chikanta has been largely influenced by the technological innovations within Macha. In 2010, two years before commercial cellular coverage was available in the village, Chikanta obtained an Internet container kiosk[5] that connects the village to the Internet through a satellite link and that runs on solar power. This allowed people from the village to start gaining experience with VoIP before they had easy access to cellular technology.

Mapanza. Mapanza is 7km away from Macha and has population of about 2000 people. There is cellphone coverage in the central part of the village. Similar to Chikanta, Mapanza recently obtained an Internet container kiosk that operates as an Internet café and uses a slow satellite link to connect to the Internet.

3. SOCIAL SURVEYS

During our three week field trip to Zambia in June/July 2012, we conducted extensive interviews with local residents to better understand their usage and experience with voice communication technologies. Each interview was conducted privately with one interviewee, one interviewer and a translator if necessary. Part of the interview questions were of closed form (pre-selected answer options) while others were open ended to enable free discussion of voice communication topics. Interview participation was voluntary and no material incentive was associated with participation. While our method did not produce a random sample of interviewees, we made an effort to interview people across age, gender, occupation and income groups.

In the course of three weeks, we interviewed 26 people total from Macha, Hamoonde and Chikanta. Our interviewees were between 20 and 48 years old; 14 were female and 12 were male. All had owned a cellphone at some point; 96% owned a phone at the time of the interview. Those who did not wanted to recover access but did not have money to do so. People who owned a phone either bought the phone themselves (76%) or obtained it as a gift. Despite the high availability of cellphones among the group we interviewed, cellphones are very expensive relative to income; 68% of phone owners who bought their phone had to save between one month and one year to afford to buy that phone. Our interviewees shared that apart from buying the cellphone, the recurring cost for air time significantly adds to the financial burden for adoption of cellphone technology.

44% of our interviewees had more than one SIM card and most often identified one of two reasons for their subscription with multiple cellular networks. The first reason is associated with cost; inter-provider services cost more in comparison to intra-provider services. Thus, users often carry more than one SIM card and pick the one to use based on the network to which the person they are calling is subscribed. The second most popular reason for people having multiple SIM cards is reliability. As the quality of service often varies over time and space, users carry multiple SIM cards to increase the chance they will be able to use a cellphone network at any time. Despite this effort, a commute of 1-2km is typical for residents of Hamoonde and Chikanta to reach to an area with coverage and conduct a call.

When asked what is enjoyable about cellphone usage, 100% of our interviewees identified the opportunity to stay in touch with relatives, including those who live in other places. 80% indicated that they use the phone to obtain information, such as crop pricing for farmers, availability of goods for local businessmen who buy from the city and communication with regional authorities. Users with more advanced phones and data subscriptions identify the importance of staying connected to the Internet at all times. With the low rate GPRS connection in Macha, however, all users with cell phone Internet access indicated that browsing is slow and frustrating.

Our interview findings confirm the importance of cellphone technology for residents of remote areas. While the reasons for adoption of cellphone technology are not drastically different than these in the western world, the benefits for people in remote communities without infrastructure and with intermittent income is much more pronounced. Obtaining information via cell phone, as opposed to in person after travel, saves both critical time and money. Unfortunately, while the benefits and need of cellphone technology in remote areas are well understood, wide availability and affordability of such technology is still severely lacking.

4. KWIIZYA

Kwiizya is a low-cost cellular system that leverages existing, unmodified mobile phones and SIM cards to provide voice and text messaging for free within the network. We envision Kwiizya as an underlying infrastructure for low bandwidth applications that make use of short text messages and therefore enhance Kwiizya with functionality that enables such applications. In the following section we describe the voice and text messaging operation of Kwiizya, present the integration of Kwiizya's core components, and discuss the extensions we have implemented to facilitate SMS applications.

[5]`http://www.machaworks.org/en/projectwizard.html/project/25`

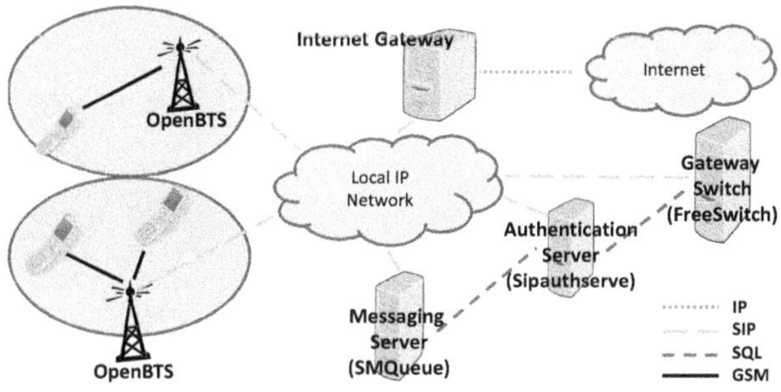

Figure 1: Kwiizya architecture.

4.1 Architecture

Depicted in Figure 1, Kwiizya utilizes free open-source software to provide voice and text message services. The base stations run OpenBTS, which implements the GSM stack and communicates with the associated cellphones using the standard Um radio interface for commodity 2G and 2.5G cellphones. OpenBTS is also responsible for translating GSM messages to SIP, which allows the use of low cost generic IP backbone infrastructure as opposed to an expensive commercial-grade GSM backbone. SIP translation enables the use of free VoIP server software to serve as a Mobile Switching Center for routing calls.

To route calls within and outside Kwiizya, we use FreeSwitch. FreeSwitch connects to OpenBTS via SIP and RTP and routes calls both in intra- and inter-BTS local scenarios. It has the capability to route calls outside of the network to commercial cellular, fixed line and VoIP networks using SIP and SS7. By the means of custom python scripts, FreeSwitch allows extension of the basic routing functionality to facilitate cellphone based applications. We describe in more detail the specific extensions we have implemented in section 4.2.

Kwiizya utilizes Sipauthserve and SMQueue to handle user authentication and text messaging, respectively. SMQueue is the SIP-based equivalent of an SMSC (Short Text Messaging Central) in a commercial-grade system. As such it interfaces with OpenBTS and makes use of commodity IP networks to transmit SMS (Short Message System). At the same time it can interface with commercial SMSCs using SS7 and SMPP. SMQueue implements a store and forward SMS queue functionality that allows messages to be delivered in a delay tolerant fashion. The latter is of great importance for areas with intermittent cellphone access and electric power availability as users are often either out of range or have their cellphone powered off. To handle user authentication and mobility, Kwiizya leverages Sipauthserve – a database server with an interface to process SIP REGISTER messages to track mobility. Both SMQueue and Sipauthserve are queried by other network elements (e.g. FreeSwitch and OpenBTS) through SQL.

4.2 Support for SMS-based applications

Because cellphone communication is an increasingly popular method for residents of remote areas to stay connected, cellphones are widely used for applications other than plain voice and text messaging. Low data rate applications that leverage 160-symbol text messages have been utilized in education [15, 24, 25], web browsing [8], agriculture [9, 22, 23] and health care [6, 10, 11, 16, 21].

In the design of Kwiizya we are inherently interested in enabling functionality that will support such applications. Beyond simple SMS, we need functionality that supports SMS broadcast and multicast, and in particular does so through an Instant Message (IM) interface. Our IM-SMS interface enables fast typing and rapid outreach to a large set of subscribers. This interface has a wide variety of uses. For instance, a health worker could use it to notify subscribers of a change in health post hours of operation, or of the availability of particular vaccinations during a health scare. Our solution exposes an API that allows development of applications that can leverage the text broadcasting functionality to automate message generation, obviating the need of an actual person to send IM messages. This capability facilitates a variety of automated services, such as automatic weather alerts, dissemination of crops prices, and health care availability updates. Our design unifies this IM extension with SMS to enable rapid distribution of instant messages from any packet data network. This unified mode of messaging is asynchronous by design to minimize resource waste and guarantees only best effort delivery. We have identified four key design considerations for such a unified mode of messaging to work seamlessly with Kwiizya in a rural setting:

- A small memory footprint of the IM client on the host device; the client is designed to work on unmodified commodity hardware available in rural areas.
- Usability across various operating systems to target a heterogeneous set of devices.
- Capability of exchanging packet data with Kwiizya remotely over the Internet.
- Ability to leverage the existing SIP switching/routing capability available in FreeSwitch to enable easy and accurate routing of IM messages to Kwiizya users in the form of SMS and vice-versa.

We implement our IM client using the open-source multimedia communication library PJSIP[6]. PJSIP implements the SIP protocol stack and supports all three NAT traversal functionalities, i.e. STUN, TURN and ICE. This facilitates routing of SIP traffic from various networks, including private IP networks such as home, office and enterprise LANs. It also exposes all functionality in suitable APIs for a wide variety of systems, including desktop and smart phones, and meets the key design goals identified above.

Figure 2 presents a typical usage scenario of our IM client. The client needs to be installed on a machine that can access the Kwiizya core network. The IM client then communicates directly with FreeSwitch when sending text messages to users associated with Kwiizya. FreeSwitch handles the delivery of a text message to the end user.

Provisioning a new user for Instant Messaging: Any new user of the IM service is manually provisioned with a valid SIP address of record [26] in the Kwiizya Subscriber Registry (Sipauthserve on Figure 2). An IM user in Kwiizya is identified by their SIP address of record (SIP user identity) and unique phone number. The SIP identity is used by internal subsystems in Kwiizya, i.e. FreeSwitch, SMQueue and OpenBTS, to validate and route any SIP traffic related to a particular IM user. The IM client's phone number is exposed to the other cellphone users of Kwiizya, so that the

[6] `http://www.pjsip.org/`

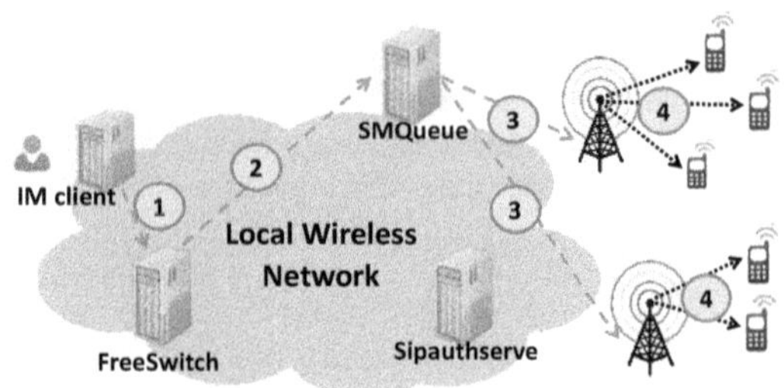

Figure 2: IM-SMS system architecture.

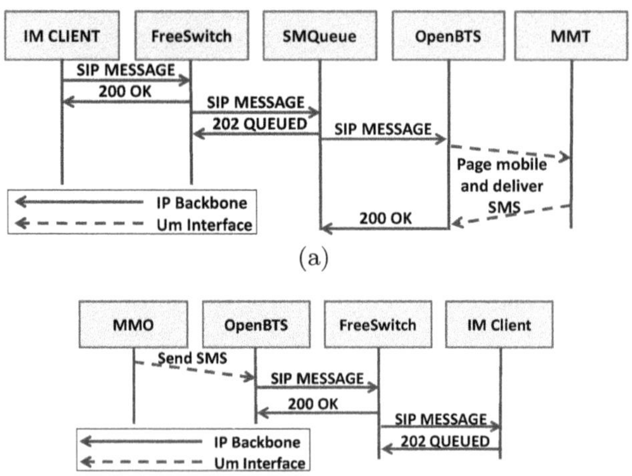

(a)

(b)

Figure 3: Message exchange between Kwiizya entities to send a SMS (a) from the IM client to a Kwiizya subscriber and (b) from a Kwiizya subscriber to the IM client.

sender of a message can be identified and the recipient can respond if needed. To reach the IM client, Kwiizya also stores the IP address of the host where the IM client is installed. Currently, this necessitates an IM user to utilize the IM service only from a pre-provisioned host address. This mechanism, however, can later be extended to a dynamic address binding scheme.

Routing an IM message: As illustrated in Figure 3(a), upon sending a message to a Kwiizya user (Mobile Message Terminator – MMT), the IM client generates a standard SIP MESSAGE request [7], that contains the message in plain text format as well as the SIP address of record of the recipient. This SIP MESSAGE is then sent to FreeSwitch, which forwards it to SMQueue after validating the identity of the sender. SMQueue stores the message in its store-and-forward queue and attempts best effort delivery to the Kwiizya base station where the recipient is registered. Because the entire SMS functionality in Kwiizya is asynchronous, a real time session is not required for transmission of the IM message to its recipient. This design makes Kwiizya messaging particularly suitable for rural environments, where a user is not likely to be associated with the network at the time the message is sent. If the user is not associated, SMQueue stores the message and regularly attempts delivery. This design avoids waste of resources typically associated with synchronous/session based messaging.

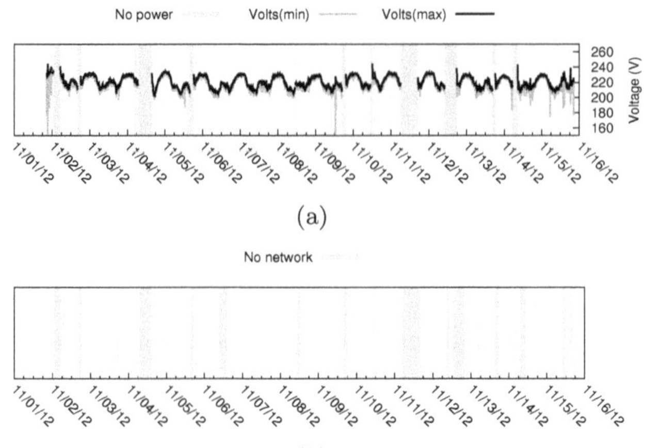

(a)

(b)

Figure 4: Power and network quality in Macha.

Our design enables a cellphone user (Mobile Message Originator – MMO) to send a message to a provisioned IM client using the SMS interface available in a legacy GSM phone. After receiving a SMS destined to an IM user, a Kwiizya base station constructs a new SIP MESSAGE request with the SMS content attached as a SIP message body in the SIP request and forwards it to FreeSwitch (Figure 3(b)). After validating that both the sender and the receiver are provisioned in Kwiizya, FreeSwitch sends a new SIP MESSAGE request to the IM client's host using the IP address it stored earlier in the Kwiizya Subscriber Registry. This exchange of messages between a Kwiizya user and an IM user also occurs asynchronously between all the participating entities.

5. MACHA DEPLOYMENT

During our trip to Macha in June/July 2012, we deployed an instance of Kwiizya. We chose Macha for our first field deployment, even though commercial cellphone coverage is available in the village center, because Macha is fairly well connected in terms of Internet access. This allows us to have remote access to our system for administration and performance evaluation purposes. In the following sections, we detail challenges we faced, many of which are not found in developed world deployments. We then describe how these challenges influenced our system deployment.

5.1 Design challenges

Power. Our Kwiizya base stations require 12VDC and draw a maximum of 3A, which can be supplied by a 12V power transformer powered by the main grid. Our deployment locations are connected to the national power grid; however, the quality of power varies drastically over time as shown in Figure 4(a). The figure represents a sample two week period. The x-axis of Figure 4(a) plots time in days and the y-axis plots voltage. The gray areas on the plot indicate periods of power outage. We measure power quality in Macha sampling every second; each plotted voltage value corresponds to five minutes and presents the minimum (green line) and maximum (black line) measured voltage within these five minutes. The supplied voltage in Zambia should be 220V; however, as Figure 4(a) indicates, the voltage varies from 150V to 240V with frequent power failures. Furthermore, there are long periods, for example November

(a) (b)

Figure 5: Our equipment in Macha: (a) the base station and (b) the power supply.

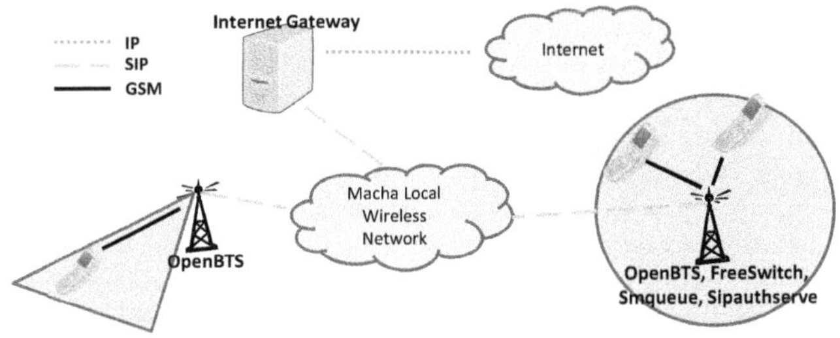

Figure 6: Kwiizya deployment in Macha.

(a) (b)

Figure 7: Kwiizya sites in Macha: (a) the water tower and (b) LITA.

15 and 16, of power brownouts in which electricity is available, but the voltage is continuously low. This is particularly harmful for computer equipment. Voltage tends to follow a diurnal pattern, typical for a system that is overloaded; the power quality is particularly poor during the day when the utilization of the power grid is higher. This poor power quality is harmful to equipment and makes remote access for administration and evaluation extremely challenging.

Internet access. The remote accessibility of the system is not only influenced by power availability but by network availability as well. Power is often available in the village; however, due to an outage in the upstream link, the village gateway cannot connect to the Internet. Figure 4(b) shows network availability over the same two week period in November. In comparison to power outages, there are many more network outages, which further reduce our ability to access Kwiizya remotely.

Logging and storage. Logging is important for system administration and troubleshooting; however, special attention should be paid when enabling logging to ensure it does not deteriorate system performance, as writing to disk can slow the system. We experienced an event where a combination of detailed logging and limited storage in the base station caused Kwiizya to malfunction.

We adapt our system design to meet these challenges. The following section provides technical details about our field deployment.

5.2 Technical details

Our Macha deployment operates in the GSM-1800 band. We chose this band for two reasons. First, most residents have basic dual band (900/1800) phones, so the use of GSM-1800 maximizes the number of people who will be able to use the system with their existing phones. Second, GSM-1800 does not interfere with commercial cellular providers, which operate at GSM-900 in rural areas.

Kwiizya consists of two self-contained RangeNetworks base stations[7] (Figure 5(a)), each of which covers a radius of up to 3km. Each base station unit includes a software-defined radio, a 1W power amplifier, a duplexer, and a small integrated PC with 4GB flash card that runs Ubuntu 10.04. Each unit can independently run all components of a GSM network. However, to scale the network to a wider physical area, we use one of the base station PCs as a network central server, running FreeSwitch, Sipauthserve and SMQueue; the second base station runs only OpenBTS and connects to the first one (Figure 6) for all other services. The connection between the two base stations is facilitated through a long distance Wi-Fi link that was readily available through the local wireless network in Macha.

To handle the problem of limited storage we attach a 1TB external hard drive to each base station. We check the internal disk utilization periodically and when it reaches 90%, we offload syslogs from the base station PC onto the external hard disk to free disk space and save logs for future reference. We use simple ping based monitoring to inform us when access to the village gateway is available from the outside, so that we can analyze network availability and know when our logs are accessible.

Determination of the most suitable power supply to resist the power fluctuations in Macha while providing stable 12V/3A to our base stations was an iterative process. We started with a complex of deep cycle car batteries and car battery chargers; however, within ten days we lost one charger due to poor power quality and two of the batteries started leaking due to overcharge. Eventually, we changed our power supply to the one shown in Figure 5(b), which includes a UPS, a 5A/12V monitor power supply and a wooden block with nails to keep the power cable terminals in place, so they do not short out.

The area of Macha is relatively flat with small hills, so providing coverage was a matter of installing the base stations on elevated locations. We installed one of the base stations on a 30m water tower with a 10m communication mast on top (Figure 7(a)). For this site we used an 11dBi omni directional antenna. Our second base station was installed close to the LinkNet IT Academy (LITA) on a 12m mast mounted on the ground (Figure 7(b)) and used an 11dBi 90 degree sector antenna. The distance between the two sites

[7]`http://rangenetworks.com/`

is 2.3km; each site is capable of providing coverage in up to 3km radius depending on terrain.

While Kwiizya supports open registration with existing cellphones and SIM cards, we opted for restricted registration during our initial field testing. We manually provisioned 20 SIM cards and distributed the cards to a small set of users comprised by our local partners and their families. This allowed us more control during the initial performance evaluation of our system, while still allowing our users unrestricted access. In the near future, we plan to deploy Kwiizya in neighboring communities with no existing cellphone coverage and enable open registration.

We placed two GSM modems in the field, which allows us to send SMS and conduct calls in the Kwiizya network in a controlled manner. We chose U-Blox quadband GSM/GPRS modems that can be powered and controlled through USB. The latter is important because it allows the modems to be powered by the server to which they are connected, thereby making them independent of an individual reliable power supply. We attached the modems to an Ubuntu server and were able to access and control them remotely using AT commands, which are a suite of specialized commands for remote control of GSM modems.

Each call in Kwiizya has two associated VoIP sessions – one for the mobile call originator (MCO) and one for the mobile call terminator (MCT). A VoIP session consists of a SIP control session and forward and reverse RTP streams that carry the actual voice traffic. The Kwiizya deployment in Macha supports four call scenarios depending on the locality of the MCO and the MCT. We describe these call scenarios in turn:

- *Water tower – Water tower.* This is a call scenario where both the MCO and the MCT are in the vicinity of the water tower base station. This setup does not utilize the backhaul wireless link; both VoIP sessions are established only through the water tower base station.
- *Water tower – LITA* and *LITA – Water tower.* In the first scenario, the MCO is associated with the water tower and the MCT with LITA; the opposite holds for the second call scenario. These two scenarios are identical in terms of resource utilization. In each of the cases one of the VoIP sessions utilizes the backhaul link and the other one is local at the water tower.
- *LITA – LITA.* In this case both the MCO and the MCT are attached at LITA. In this scenario, both the MCO and MCT VoIP sessions traverse the wireless backhaul.

6. EVALUATION OF KWIIZYA

Our evaluation of Kwiizya includes two parts – (i) controlled experiments and (ii) evaluation of system usage in the wild following our Macha deployment. Our controlled experiments take place in two testbeds: one located in our lab in UCSB and one in Macha. We first evaluate Kwiizya by running a number of controlled experiments that test the system's ability to provide services and the quality of these services. The second part of our evaluation assesses the actual deployment experience.

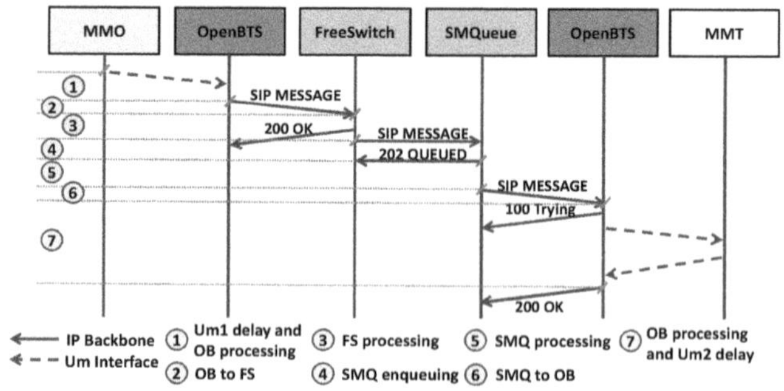

Figure 8: SIP messages transmission of a SMS from MMO to MMT.

6.1 Controlled experiments

We focus our controlled experiments on three aspects of the system: (i) text messaging, (ii) voice calls and (iii) instant messaging to SMS. In the process of evaluation we take into account OpenBTS' capabilities as well as limitations of the GSM modems to ensure the accuracy of our performance measurements. First of all, OpenBTS can handle at most 84 SMS messages per minute and 7 simultaneous calls, so we ensure we do not generate traffic at a higher rate so that delay and call quality are accurately measured. Furthermore, the GSM modems incur a delay of about 0.5 seconds to execute the commands associated with sending a single message. Finally, there needs to be an inter-message delay of 6 seconds to ensure the GSM modem does not become overloaded with outgoing messages. When overloaded, the modem fails to send messages to Kwiizya.

We conduct our controlled experiments in two testbeds, one located in our lab at UCSB and one located in Macha. Our lab setup includes one RangeNetworks SNAP unit, the same as the ones deployed in Macha. The unit operates as a self contained system running all four services – OpenBTS, FreeSwitch, Sipauthserve and SMQueue. Our testbed in Macha includes the base station installed at LITA and a second base station inside the IT room. The indoor base station runs FreeSwitch, Sipauthserve and SMQueue. LITA runs only OpenBTS and connects to the indoor base station for the other services. In this test setup we utilize the readily available network infrastructure in Macha to connect the two base stations. As a result, we use an existing wired connection for the backbone link between the indoor installation and LITA. All Kwiizya components are strictly time synchronized. This is achieved using NTP, where all machines in Kwiizya synchronize to a local server to maximize accuracy.

6.1.1 SMS and Voice Calls

To evaluate SMS and voice call quality through controlled experiments we use our testbed in Macha. We deploy two U-blox quadband GSM/GPRS modems in Macha and associate them with the LITA base station. Both modems are connected to a server that can be accessed from the Internet. We then automate SMS and voice calls between the two modems.

We evaluate the end-to-end delay for delivery of a single message and assess the delay components incurred by each element of Kwiizya. Figure 8 gives an overview of the SIP message exchange associated with delivery of a single

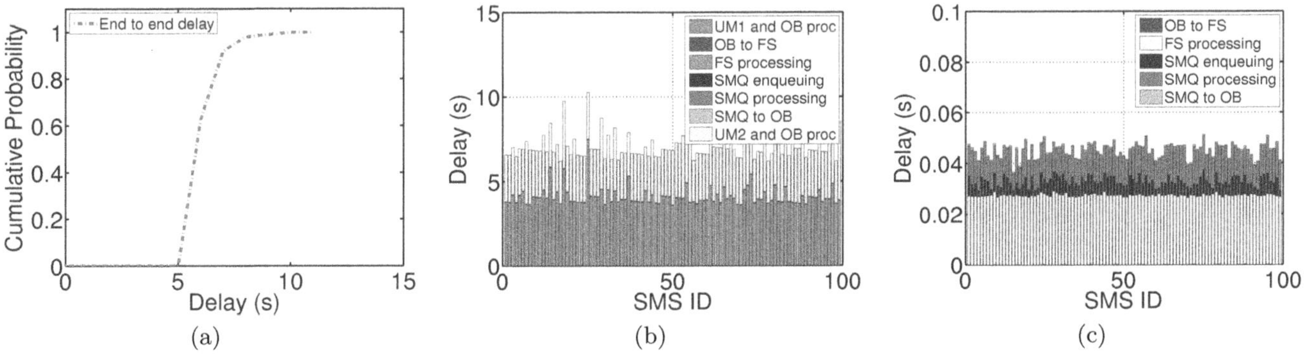

Figure 9: Evaluation of 100 SMS transmissions to associated users. (a) CDF of end to end delay; (b) breakdown of delay components per message; and (c) zoom of non-Um delay components.

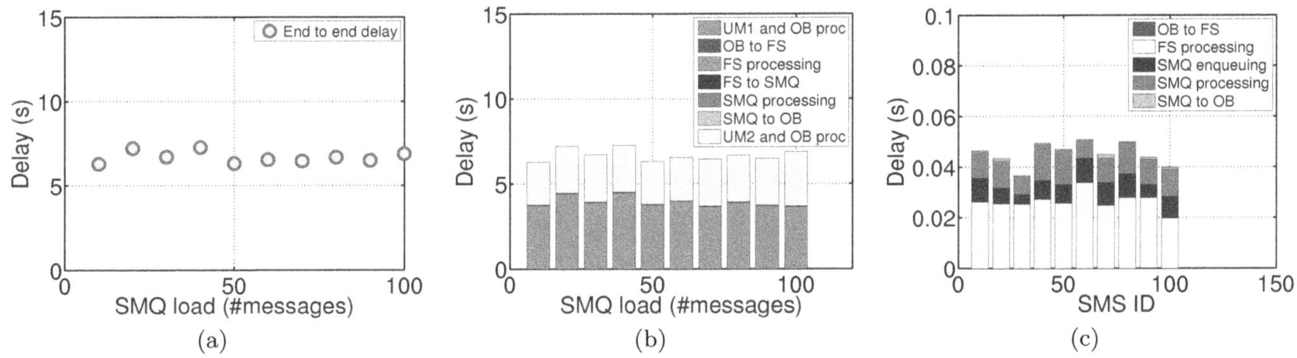

Figure 10: Impact of increasing SMQueue load on (a) the end to end delay; (b) the delay components; and (c) non-Um delay components.

SMS from a Mobile Message Originator (MMO) to a Mobile Message Terminator (MMT). If two components are coded with the same color, they run on the same physical machine. The figure also presents our approach to calculating the delay components. We calculate the end to end delay as a sum of each extracted delay component.

In our evaluation of SMS delivery we focus on two scenarios. First, we evaluate delay for delivery of messages to users associated with the network. We then evaluate the impact of SMQueue load on the end-to-end delay by increasing the number of transmitted messages to users that are provisioned but not associated with the network. The latter increases the load of pending messages in SMQueue. We then measure the time it takes for a message to be received by a registered user.

To evaluate the delay for message delivery to a user associated with Kwiizya, we sent 100 consecutive messages, with 6 seconds inter-message delay. 99 of these messages were received by Kwiizya; one message failed to depart from the sending GSM modem. Of the 99 messages that entered Kwiizya, all 99 were successfully delivered to the receiving modem. Figure 9 presents our results. In Figure 9(a) we plot a CDF of the end to end delay. As the graph shows, 99% of the messages were delivered to their destination in $6-9$ seconds; the maximum observed delay is 11 seconds. The average delay over all 99 messages is 7.06 seconds with standard deviation of only 0.7 seconds. Figure 9(b) presents a breakdown of delay incurred by the separate Kwiizya components for each text message. The major contributors to the end-to-end delay are the radio interfaces from the MMO to OpenBTS (Um1) and from OpenBTS to the MMT (Um2). Figure 9(c) shows a zoom of the delays of the non-Um components of Kwiizya. The contribution of the non-Um components together is at most 50ms with average over all messages of 45.4 ms. This performance is persistent over different messages, as the standard deviation for non-Um delay is only 2.9 ms.

Where users do not have continuous access to Kwiizya, the network stores text messages and aggressively attempts to deliver them every second. This incurs overhead in SMQueue in storing messages and reattempting delivery. We evaluate the impact of this overhead on the end to end delivery delay of messages to registered users. We increase the SMQueue load from 10 to 100 messages in steps of 10. At each step we send one message to a registered user and measure the delivery delay for this message. As Figure 10(a) shows, the end to end delay does not increase with the number of enqueued messages; thus it is not dependent on the SMQueue load for as much as 100 enqueued messages. This observation is further confirmed by Figures 10(b) and 10(c), which show delay components for each of the 10 delivered messages. Once again, Um1 and Um2 are the largest contributors to the end-to-end delay. Furthermore, each of the ten messages is delivered in less than 8 seconds, which is within the average delay range encountered on Figure 9(a).

Finally, in our test setup in Macha, we measure the call establishment time. As depicted in Figure 11, this is the time from when the first SIP INVITE message is sent by the MCO base station (informally from when the calling party hits "dial") to when the MCT starts ringing (or when the calling party starts hearing the "ring" tone). Again compo-

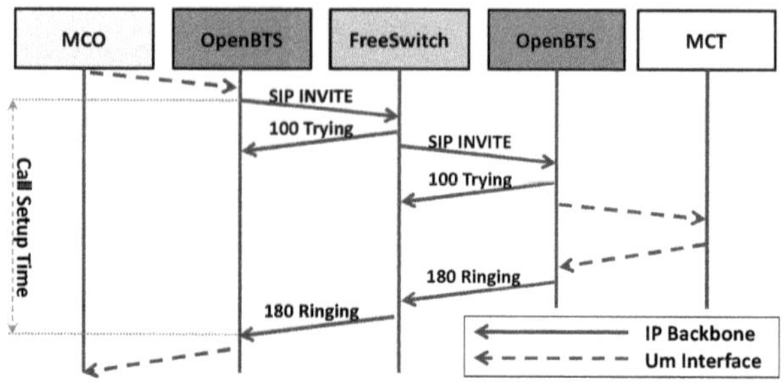

Figure 11: Call setup SIP message transaction.

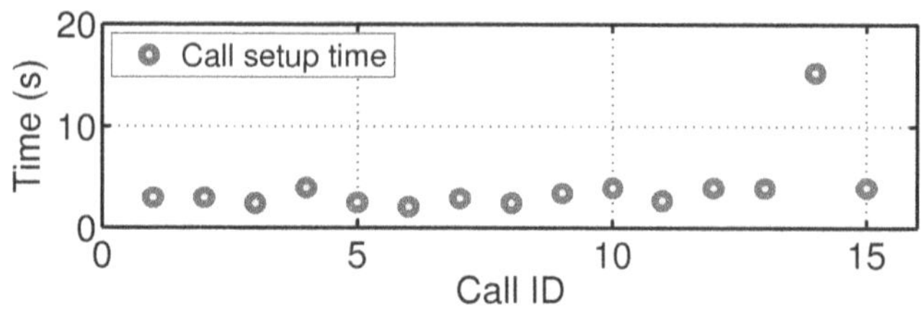

Figure 12: Call setup time.

nents with the same color run on the same physical machine. We run an experiment with 15 consecutive calls. Figure 12 presents our results; call ID is plotted on the x-axis and call setup delay in seconds on the y-axis. The figure indicates that with one exception, it typically takes between 2 and 4 seconds for a call to initiate. We examined the delay components of the outlier call 14; the 15 second setup time is caused either by delay in the Um radio interface between OpenBTS and the GSM modem or by a glitch in the GSM modem itself. We leave the evaluation of call quality to the calls placed by actual users; our findings are described in section 6.2.

6.1.2 Instant Messaging to SMS

As detailed in section 4, we extend Kwiizya's basic cellular network functionality to provide a platform for development of applications that utilize text messaging. This platform delivers an interface between an instant messenger and the cellular network and enables burst message transmission to users registered with the network.

We evaluate our Instant Messaging to SMS (IM-SMS) functionality in our lab setup at UCSB. We perform this evaluation at UCSB because of the need for multiple test receivers, for which we did not have the capacity in Macha. We installed our IM client on a server, running Ubuntu 12.04. We associate three HTC G1 phones with the test network to act as receivers during our experiments.

We conduct two sets of experiments to evaluate the end to end delay for message delivery from the IM client to users in Kwiizya. We also calculate the delay imposed by each Kwiizya component. Figure 13 presents the SIP message exchange for delivery of a SMS and breaks down each delay component. Again components that run on the same physical machine are coded with the same color.

Our first experiment evaluates the time for message delivery when the IM client sends bursts of messages to *associated users*. In particular, we are interested in the implications of the burst size on the end to end delay. We send bursts of messages of increasing size from the IM client to three users

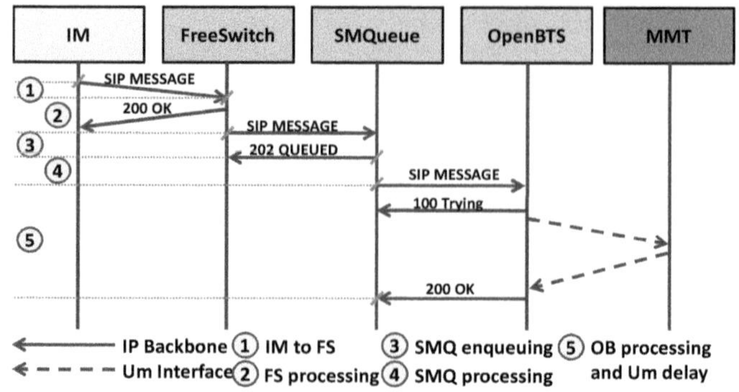

Figure 13: SIP messages transmission of a SMS from IM to a Kwiizya user.

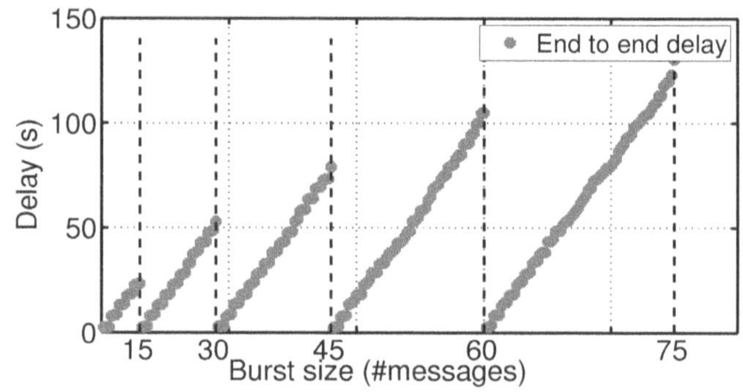

Figure 14: IM-SMS end to end delay when sending to registered users.

associated with Kwiizya with inter-burst time of 60 seconds. At each iteration 1/3 of the burst is sent to each of the receivers. It is important to note that each phone can only receive one message at a time. Thus, if five messages are sent simultaneously to the same phone, the first message should arrive in X seconds, the second in $2X$ seconds and so on. In our IM-SMS tests we used three phones to receive bursts ranging in size from 15 to 75 messages. Every message sent in this experiment was received at its destination.

Figure 14 plots burst size on the x-axis and end to end delay on the y-axis. Each point on the plot corresponds to delay for a single message and each vertical line indicates the burst size. In each segment of the graph there are $burstSize/3$ well established groups, each of which contains three plotted values, one for each receiver. On the plot these three values appear overlapped, which indicates that message delivery to all three phones is approximately the same. This separation in groups is due to the increasing delay for delivery of a burst of messages to the same user. Messages across different burst sizes take the same amount of delivery time, which demonstrates that Kwiizya is capable of handling bursts of variable size without incurring delay in message delivery. In a production network, it is unlikely that a single phone would need to receive large bursts. If the number of recipient phones corresponds to the size of message burst sent by the IM client, we will observe a constant delay across burst sizes, which will be close to the minimum measured delay – between 2 and 4 seconds.

In the second experiment we evaluate the impact of SMQueue load on the end to end delay during message

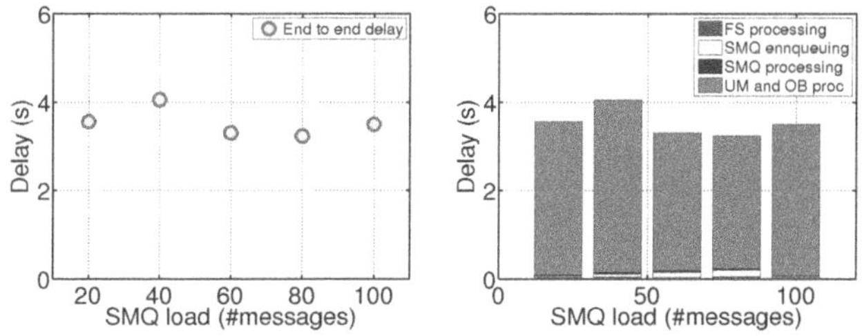

(a) (b)

Figure 15: Impact of SMQueue load on message delivery delay from IM to a Kwiizya user: (a) end to end delay and (b) breakdown of delay components.

bursts. To do so, we send bursts of messages to a mix of associated and non-registered users. To generate load in SMQueue, we transmit an increasing number of messages to a non-registered user, starting at 20 messages, and add 20 messages at each of five iterations. At each SMQueue load level we also send a burst of three messages – one to each of the three phones associated with Kwiizya. We measure the end to end delay and delay components for delivery of these three messages. Figure 15 presents our results. In 15(a) we plot the average end to end delay for the three deliverable messages sent at each iteration, as a function of SMQueue load. The delay does not increase with the increase of SMQueue load up to a hundred messages, which demonstrates Kwiizya's capability to deliver bursts of messages without negative impact from the number of enqueued messages in SMQueue. In Figure 15(b) we plot the delay components averaged over the three deliverable messages as a function of the SMQueue load. As we can see, the delay caused by the Um interface is still the largest delay component, while the one introduced by SMQueue is negligible.

6.2 Kwiizya field usage

We now present results from in-situ usage of our Kwiizya deployment in Macha from a period of two weeks in July 2012. We begin by describing our traffic collection system. We then evaluate call quality and compare with results from our controlled experiments. We note that the backhaul Wi-Fi link in our deployment in Macha carries live Internet traffic and thus there may be variability in results due to competing traffic. The impact of this background traffic on call quality was evaluated in our previous work [5].

6.2.1 *Kwiizya monitoring*

As noted in section 5, our deployment includes two base stations – water tower (WT), which runs OpenBTS, FreeSwitch, SMQueue and Sipauthserve; and LITA (LT), which runs only OpenBTS and connects to WT to use other services. To capture all system traffic, we installed three monitoring points and run tcpdump at each point to capture SIP and RTP traffic:

- *lo@WT* – the loopback interface at the water tower base station that captures all internal communication in WT between FreeSwitch, SMQueue and Sipauthserve. This monitoring point allows evaluation of calls where either or both the MCO and the MCT are in the vicinity of WT.
- *eth@WT* – the Ethernet interface at the water tower base station that connects to the Wi-Fi link from the water tower to LITA and captures all communication between WT and LT. This includes all SIP and RTP traffic related to calls where either one or both communicating parties are associated with LITA.
- *eth@LT* – the Ethernet interface at the LITA base station that connects to the Wi-Fi link from the water tower to LITA. This monitoring point captures the same traffic as *eth@WT*, however with different timing of packets. This allows us to assess timing related aspects of the system.

6.2.2 *Voice call quality*

Delay, Jitter and Packet Loss. Delay, jitter and packet loss are three characteristics of a VoIP session that are critical to voice quality. ITU recommendation G.114 mandates that tolerable one way delay is up to 150 ms [2]. The theoretical delay minimum that a system can provide is dependent on the used codec. Kwiizya uses GSM 6.10, for which the minimum delay is 20 ms. We evaluate these characteristics in our system by analyzing 52 VoIP sessions from Kwiizya users in Macha. Figure 16 presents our results. For each VoIP session, Figures 16(a) and 16(b) plot the average and standard deviation of delay and jitter. A single point shows the average delay or jitter and standard deviation across all packets within that VoIP session. Both delay and jitter are well below the tolerated thresholds for VoIP. At the same time, the average delay is close to 20 ms over all VoIP sessions. Furthermore, delay and jitter do not vary much over a single VoIP session as indicated by the standard deviation bars, which shows that Kwiizya has stable performance throughout a call. Finally, Figure 16(c) plots packet loss over the 52 VoIP sessions. Only three of all sessions suffered non-zero packet loss; however, these three were all less than 0.5%, which is within the limit for satisfactory call quality.

Mean Opinion Score. Mean Opinion Score (MOS) is a metric that describes the call quality as perceived by the communicating parties. The maximum MOS that a system can provide is dependent on the voice codec. We evaluate the MOS achieved by Kwiizya by utilizing the E-model [3]. This model takes into account the codec type as well as experienced packet loss during a call and outputs the MOS. According to the E-model, MOS is calculated as follows:

$$MOS = 1 + R.0,035 + R.(100 - R).(R - 60)).7.10^{-6} \quad (1)$$

where R is the *rating factor*, calculated as a function of the *effective equipment impairment factor* Ie_{eff}:

$$R = 93.2 - Ie_{\text{eff}} \quad (2)$$

The *effective equipment impairment factor* is packet loss dependent and can be found as follows:

$$Ie_{\text{eff}} = Ie + (95 - Ie).\frac{ppl}{ppl + bpl} \quad (3)$$

where Ie is the *equipment impairment factor* taken for zero packet loss; *bpl* is the *packet loss robustness factor* and *ppl* is the *packet loss probability*. Ie and *bpl* are given for different codecs in a recommendation by ITU [1]. For a single VoIP session consisting of two RTP streams (one forward and one

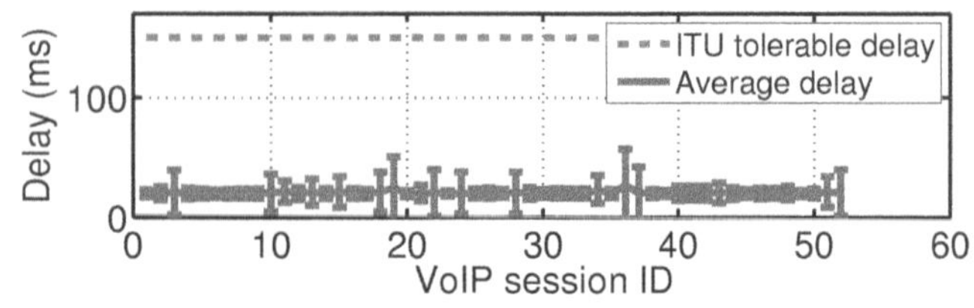

(a)

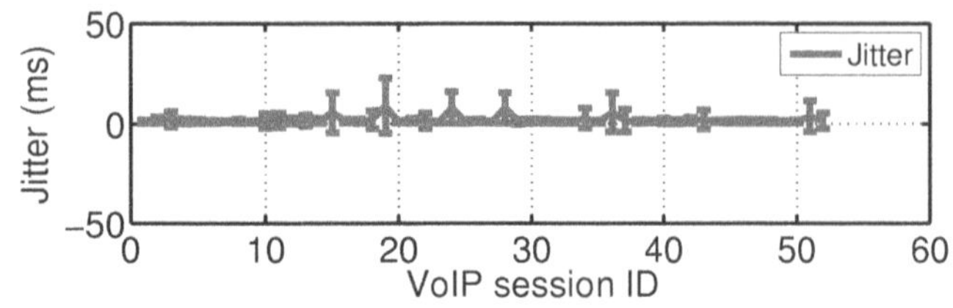

(b)

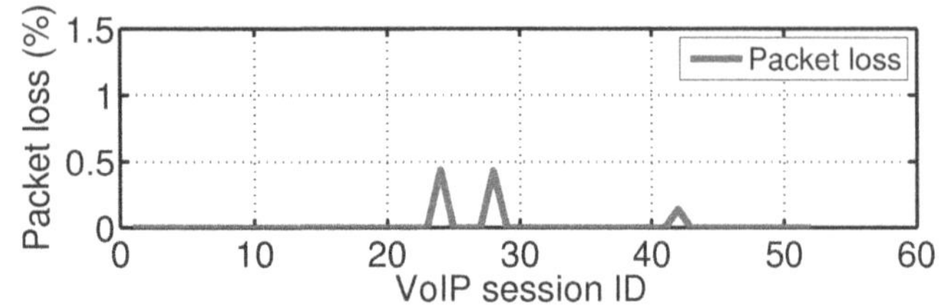

(c)

Figure 16: Field call (a) average delay; (b) average jitter and (c) packet loss.

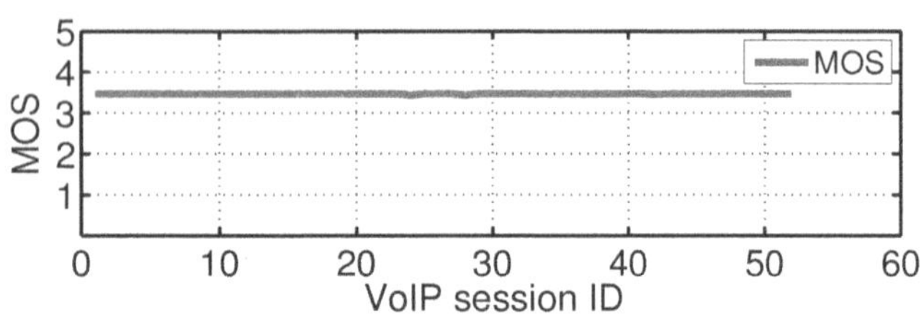

Figure 17: Mean Opinion Score.

reverse), the *ppl* value is calculated as follows:

$$totLoss = loss_{fwd} + loss_{rvs}$$
$$totSent = sent_{fwd} + sent_{rvs}$$
$$ppl = \frac{totLoss}{totSent} \quad (4)$$

FreeSwitch uses the GSM FR (6.10) codec, for which the *Ie* and *bpl* values are 26 and 43, respectively [1]. Given these, we can calculate that the maximum expected MOS provided by GSM FR (6.10) is **3.46** (effectively this is the MOS for $ppl = 0$).

Figure 17 presents our results for MOS for the 52 VoIP sessions. On the x-axis we have session ID, while on the y-axis we have MOS. The minimum measured MOS is 3.43 and the maximum (received by 49 of the 52 sessions) is 3.46 – equal to the maximum provided by the system.

Controlled vs real call. We compare the performance of a call conducted in our Macha testbed and one from a user in the network. Both calls are characterized by the same packet size and inter-packet timing of RTP packets

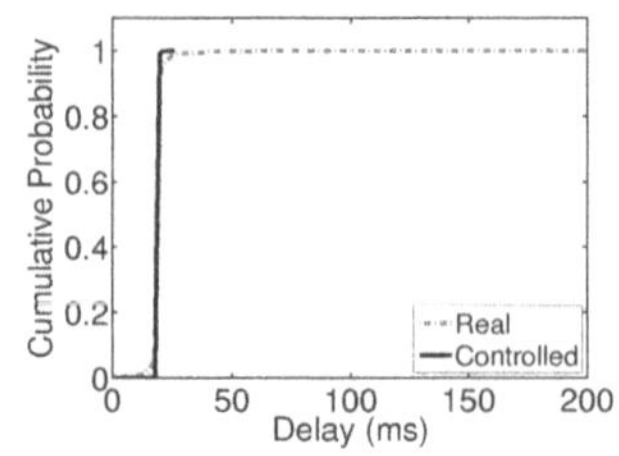

(a)

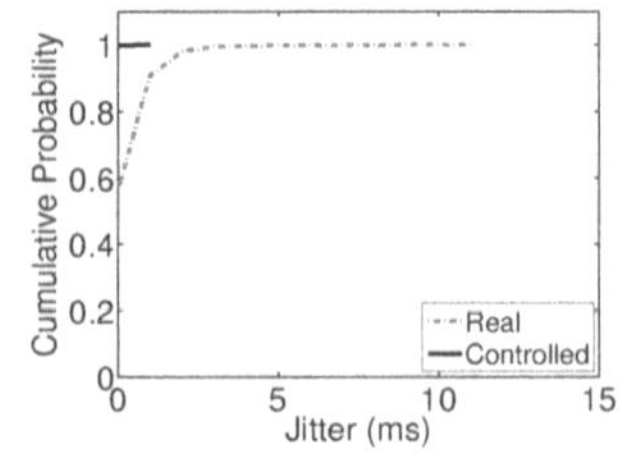

(b)

Figure 18: Controlled vs. actual user call: CDF of per packet (a) delay and (b) jitter.

in the media streams. There are two major differences between the Macha testbed and the actual deployment. First, the testbed uses a wired backhaul, whereas the actual deployment uses a long distance Wi-Fi link for inter-base station communication. The second difference is the distance between the users and the base stations to which they are connected; while in the testbed our GSM modems are only about 40m away from the base station, in the actual deployment phones can be anywhere in the range of a base station. Probabilistically, they are further than 40m since the transmission range is approximately 3km.

We present our comparison results in Figure 18. 18(a) and 18(b) plot CDFs of per-packet delay and jitter, respectively. The black solid line in both graphs presents results from our controlled call while the red dotted line presents results from a representative call from the actual deployment. We can clearly see the impact of the wireless link and the longer radio link to users' phones on the per-packet delay and jitter. While in our controlled call we experience a maximum delay and jitter of 26ms and 1ms, the actual call experiences slightly higher values. Nevertheless, more than 99% of the packets in the actual call experienced delay less than 30ms and jitter less than 3ms, which indicates that utilizing a long distance wireless backhaul link and realistic distance from users to base stations, Kwiizya can provide for delay and jitter well below the thresholds that threaten performance.

6.2.3 *Text messaging*

During our two week evaluation period, we observed only three text messages exchanged between Kwiizya users. From our conversations and interviews with cellphone users in Macha and the surrounding villages, we learned that residents typically use SMS more frequently in production cellular systems due to the lower cost of SMS in comparison with a voice call. When voice calls are more affordable, people prefer to call instead of text. This is in line with the oral communication culture within these communities, as well as high illiteracy rates. From our initial analysis of Kwiizya traffic, we observe the tendency of users to place voice calls instead of sending SMS messages because voice calls are free. However, it remains to be seen whether this observation would continue to hold once Kwiizya is opened to the general community.

7. RELATED WORK

The impact of cellphone technology on residents of developing countries has been widely studied [4, 9]. Examples from the literature show that cellphones have changed the way people learn and exchange knowledge, get access to health care and handle local government activities. There is increasing effort to develop applications that use plain text messaging and voice to leverage existing feature phones. These applications can be largely divided into those that use voice and those that use text messaging. In [23] for instance, the authors deploy a social network based on voice forums for farmers to exchange knowledge about crops and crop prices. [19] proposes a method for message exchange where messages are encoded as a sequence of missed call durations. Numerous applications use text messaging as a platform. Use cases include update of remote databases through SMS [16], attendance tracking [25], web search [8] and health care [6, 10, 15, 21].

The drawback of these solutions is that they all assume existence of an underlying cellphone network. However, ITU statistics show that 48% of the rural population in sub-Saharan Africa is still disconnected; this constitutes a large fraction of a population that benefits most from the outlined applications.

A few projects discuss alternative cellular network solutions for remote areas [12, 18]. Heimerl and Brewer were the first to propose the use of a PC and a SDR for cellphone coverage [12]. The paper describes an idea for providing intermittent cellular access to under-serviced areas, where the design focus is on minimizing the energy consumption for running a rural base station. Mpala et al. study the applicability of an OpenBTS based system in rural areas [18]. The paper describes a show case deployment of an OpenBTS and Asterisk-based cellular network with a limited range. These papers provide insight on design of such systems and discussion of obstacles to implementation; what they lack is holistic system design and large-scale evaluation of feasibility from a system point of view.

8. DISCUSSION AND CONCLUSION

The introduction of software-defined radios and software that converts GSM signals to voice over IP allows design of low-cost local cellular networks, which can notably improve communication in remote communities. We leverage these technologies and deploy the first large-scale prototype of such a network, Kwiizya, in the remote community of Macha in Zambia. While Wi-Fi is available in the community, access to the Wi-Fi service and Wi-Fi enabled user equipment is expensive. As a result, the majority of the people in the community only have access to feature cellphones. Kwiizya leverages unmodified cellphones to provide voice and SMS services; this capability is essential to covering large populations.

Kwiizya can scale to larger deployments through multiple options. It can use long-distance wireless links to physically connect communities that are a few kilometers apart. In cases where Internet is available, Kwiizya can use a globally accessible Private Branch Exchange server to connect individual installations through the Internet without the need of a physical connection between these installations.

Kwiizya can also interface with global services such as GoogleVoice, Skype or commercial operators, which allows Kwiizya users to call and text with other users who are outside the local network. We explored a configuration that uses GoogleVoice for outbound calls and text messaging; however, frequent changes in the GoogleVoice API as well as the inability to hide caller ID stopped us from opening outbound services to our users in this deployment. We plan to continue development of this option in the near future.

A reliable power supply is a major fraction of both capital and operating expenses in remote cellular deployments. Many remote deployments typically operate off the power grid, which requires alternative power sources such as diesel generators or renewable alternatives. 80% of the power consumption of a commercial cellphone network is induced by the base stations [17]; this constitutes a major fraction of the operation cost. This expense is further increased in the case of remote deployments due to the need for transportation of diesel or maintenance of renewable power sources. While this paper is not concerned with thorough evaluation of power consumption, we note that Kwiizya has significant advantages in power consumption in comparison with a commercial system. While a RangeNetworks SNAP unit such as the ones we use in Macha draws a maximum of 35W[8], a typical commercial-grade cellular base station[9] consumes 1.3kW. Thus, Kwiizya has great potential to reduce the operating expenses associated with power supply for small-scale local deployments.

While in this paper we focus on technology, there are several economic and regulatory factors beyond the scope of our work that influence the deployment of alternative cellular solutions in under-provisioned areas. Economic factors concern availability of financial resources to provision power, Internet access and equipment (software and hardware), while regulatory factors are largely related to licensing. Our partnership with LinkNet in Macha has helped us address economic aspects of Internet access and power availability. As opposed to a commercial-grade cellular system that uses licensed and costly software, Kwiizya relies entirely on free, open-source software. This, coupled with lower-cost hardware, reduces the cost for a singe base station by five to ten times in comparison with a commercial-grade counterpart. Licensing for experimental purposes is widely unregulated in sub-Saharan Africa. In Zambia, there is a national regulatory organization that governs the distribution of spectrum resources; however, there is no policy for granting experimental licenses [18]. Furthermore, pricing of commercial licenses is oblivious to the potential return of investment. We argue that lower pricing or subsidizing commercial licenses for economically unattractive areas such as rural areas would encourage entrepreneurs to seek alternative technologies and deploy in such areas. In this context, while Kwiizya has great technological potential to provide low-cost cellular infrastructure, the full potential of the system is yet to be realized. This realization largely depends on multi-faceted economic analysis of alternative solutions for cellphone access.

Deployments in remote areas require systems independent from factors such as power quality and availability, weather and network integrity. We have identified a few aspects of Kwiizya that need to be improved to make the system even more suitable for deployment in any remote community. First, a transition to solar power would facilitate deployment independent of the power grid and provide high quality power. A follow up evaluation would then help realize Kwiizya's potential to operate in the face of intermittent power availability. Second, it is very important to weather-

[8]`http://www.rangenetworks.com/store/snap-network`

[9]We compare with a Siemens BS-240 that supports 24 simultaneous calls and has a 40W output power amplifier.

proof a system that is installed in the field. For example, one of our base stations in Macha was damaged by lightning; we have learned first hand the importance of good insulation and lightning surge protectors. Lastly, to handle network integrity problems and provide continuous service, Kwiizya must be self-organizing, meaning a base station needs to sense whether access to central services is available and, if not, switch to another central server or fall back into self-contained mode.

Kwiizya is the first full scale deployment of an alternative, affordable cellular communications architecture for rural areas that lack cellular coverage. Through extensive evaluation, we demonstrated Kwiizya's capability to provide high quality services even through shared backhaul. Kwiizya reduces the capital expense by using free open-source software, SDR-based hardware and universal IP backbone. Kwiizya also reduces operation expenses by incurring much lower power consumption in comparison with a commercial cellular network. Kwiizya provides an efficient platform for SMS-based applications. Part of our ongoing work focuses on the design of such applications after careful consideration of specific needs in the community. We plan to continue to work with our partners within the Macha community to extend deployment of our solution to surrounding areas that lack cellular services, to both residential and public service areas, such as rural health posts, that are currently completely disconnected. Through longitudinal studies, we hope to provide further insights on the adoption and impact of our deployment on the local community.

9. ACKNOWLEDGEMENTS

This work was funded in part through NSF Network Science and Engineering (NetSE) Award CNS-1064821 and through a grant from the Bill and Melinda Gates Foundation. We are very thankful to our sponsors for enabling this work. We are also thankful to our partners from Macha: Gertjan van Stam, Consider and Pharren Mudenda, Austin Sinzala and Acent Milimo. We would also like to thank RangeNetworks for their support, Veljko Pejovic and David Kotz for their valuable feedback, and Kate Milosavljevic for her help with the interviews.

10. REFERENCES

[1] ITU, Estimates of Ie and Bpl parameters for a range of CODEC types.

[2] ITU-T Recommendation G.114, One-way transmission time. 2003.

[3] ITU-T Recommendation G.107, The E-Model, a computational model for use in transmission planning. 2011.

[4] J. C. Aker and I. M. Mbiti. Mobile Phones and Economic Development in Africa. In *Journal of Economic Perspectives*, volume 24, 2010.

[5] A. Anand, V. Pejovic, E. Belding, and D. L. Johnson. VillageCell: Cost effective cellular connectivity in rural areas. ICTD '12, Atlanta, GA, 2012.

[6] R. Anderson, E. Blantz, D. Lubinski, E. O'Rourke, M. Summer, and K. Yousoufian. Smart Connect: Last mile data connectivity for rural health facilities. In *NSDR*, San Francisco, CA, 2010.

[7] B. Campbell, J. Rosenberg, H. Schulzrinne, C. Huitema, and D. Gurle. Internet Engineering Task Force RFC3428: Session Initiation Protocol (SIP) extension for Instant Messaging. December 2002.

[8] J. Chen, L. Subramanian, and E. Brewer. SMS-based web search for low-end mobile devices. In *MOBICOM*, Chicago, IL, 2010.

[9] M. de Bruijn, F. B. Nyamnjoh, and I. Brinkman. *Mobile Phones: The New Talking Drums of Everyday Africa*. Langaa RPCIG, 2009.

[10] N. Dell, S. Venkatachalam, D. Stevens, P. Yager, and G. Borriello. Towards a point-of-care diagnostic system: automated analysis of immunoassay test data on a cell phone. In *NSDR*, Washington, D.C., 2011.

[11] B. DeRenzi, G. Borriello, J. Jackson, V. Kumar, T. Parikh, P. Virk, and N. Lesh. Mobile phone tools for field-based health care workers in low-income countries. *Mount Sinai Journal of Medicine: A Journal of Translational and Personalized Medicine*, 78(3):406–418, 2011.

[12] K. Heimerl and E. Brewer. The Village Base Station. In *NSDR'10*, San Francisco, CA, June 2010.

[13] International Telecommunications Union. The World in 2011; Facts and Figures. http://www.itu.int/ITU-D/ict/facts/2011/material/ICTFactsFigures2011.pdf, 2011.

[14] D. L. Johnson, E. Belding, and G. van Stam. Network traffic locality in a rural African village. ICTD '12, Atlanta, GA, 2012.

[15] M. Kam, D. Ramachandran, V. Devanathan, A. Tewari, and J. Canny. Localized iterative design for language learning in underdeveloped regions: the pace framework. In *CHI*, San Jose, CA, 2007.

[16] A. Kumar, J. Chen, M. Paik, and L. Subramanian. ELMR: Efficient Lightweight Mobile Records. In *MobiHeld*, Barcelona, Spain, 2009.

[17] V. Mancuso and S. Alouf. Reducing costs and pollution in cellular networks. *Communications Magazine, IEEE*, 49(8):63–71, 2011.

[18] J. Mpala and G. van Stam. OpenBTS, a GSM experiment in rural Zambia. Africomm, Yaounde, Cameroon, 2012.

[19] B. G. Omwenga and P. W. Githinji. Buzzenger: Asynchronous (Time-Sliced) Missed Call Duration Messaging. In *NSDR*, Boston, MA, 2012.

[20] J. Onnela, S. Arbesman, M. Gonzalez, A. Barabasi, and N. Christakis. Geographic constraints on social network groups. *PLoS ONE*, 6(4):e16939, 04 2011.

[21] M. Paik, J. Chen, and L. Subramanian. Epothecary: cost-effective drug pedigree tracking and authentication using mobile phones. In *MobiHeld*, Barcelona, Spain, 2009.

[22] T.S. Parikh, N. Patel, and Y. Schwartzman. A survey of information systems reaching small producers in global agricultural value chains. In *ICTD*, Bangalore, India, December 2007.

[23] N. Patel, D. Chittamuru, A. Jain, P. Dave, and T. Parikh. Avaaj otalo: a field study of an interactive voice forum for small farmers in rural India. In *CHI*, Atlanta, GA, 2010.

[24] N. Patel, S. Klemmer, and T. Parikh. An asymmetric communications platform for knowledge sharing using cheap mobile phones. In *ACM Symposium on User Interface Software and Technology (UIST)*, Santa Barbara, CA, October 2011.

[25] A. Reda, S. Panjwani, and E. Cutrell. Hyke: a low-cost remote attendance tracking system for developing regions. In *NSDR*, Washington, D.C., 2011.

[26] J. Rosenberg, H. Schulzrinne, C. Camarillo, A. Johnston, J. Peterson, R. Sparks, M. Handley, and E. Schooler. Internet Engineering Task Force RFC3261: SIP: Session Initiation Protocol. June 2002.

AdRob: Examining the Landscape and Impact of Android Application Plagiarism

Clint Gibler
UC Davis
cdgibler@ucdavis.edu

Ryan Stevens
UC Davis
rcstevens@ucdavis.edu

Jonathan Crussell
UC Davis
jcrussell@ucdavis.edu

Hao Chen
UC Davis
hchen@cs.ucdavis.edu

Hui Zang
Sprint Research
hui.zang@sprint.com

Heesook Choi
Sprint Research
heesook.choi@sprint.com

ABSTRACT

Malicious activities involving Android applications are rising rapidly. As prior work on cyber-crimes suggests, we need to understand the economic incentives of the criminals to design the most effective defenses. In this paper, we investigate application plagiarism on Android markets at a large scale. We take the first step to characterize plagiarized applications and estimate their impact on the original application developers. We first crawled 265,359 free applications from 17 Android markets around the world and ran a tool to identify similar applications (clones). Based on the data, we examined properties of the cloned applications, including their distribution across different markets, application categories, and ad libraries. Next, we examined how cloned applications affect the original developers. We captured HTTP advertising traffic generated by mobile applications at a tier-1 US cellular carrier for 12 days. To associate each Android application with its advertising traffic, we extracted a unique advertising identifier (called the client ID) from both the applications and the network traces. We estimate a lower bound on the advertising revenue that cloned applications siphon from the original developers, and the user base that cloned applications divert from the original applications. To the best of our knowledge, this is the first large scale study on the characteristics of cloned mobile applications and their impact on the original developers.

Categories and Subject Descriptors

D.4.6 [**Software**]: Security and Protection; K.4.1 [**Computers and Society**]: Public Policy Issues *Abuse and crime involving computers*

General Terms

Security, Economics

Keywords

Android; underground economy; plagiarism; advertising; mobile; measurement

1. INTRODUCTION

As mobile applications become more popular and lucrative, they also become a more likely target for criminals and other miscreants. A malicious activity unique to mobile application markets is large-scale application plagiarism [2]. This is because mobile applications, especially Android applications, are straightforward to reverse engineer and copy. We define a *cloned* application as an app that is a modified copy of another app, and thus shares a significant portion of its application code with the original. A *plagarized* application is a cloned app that was fraudulently copied from one developer to another. Prior studies showed that indeed there are many cloned applications on mobile markets [6, 28]. However, these studies leave many questions unanswered. From the plagiarists' point of view, what are their incentives From the users' point of view, how often do they run plagiarized applications From the original application developers' point of view, to what extent does the practice of application plagarism impact them The answers to these questions would have deep research, technical, and policy implications. For example, even if there were many plagiarized applications on the mobile markets, if users rarely download and run them, perhaps dealing with them is not a priority. On the other hand, if the plagiarized applications severely affect the economic interests of original application developers, we must deal with them swiftly and adequately to sustain interest in legitimate application development.

We take the first step toward answering the above questions. We use a technique that combines static application analysis with network analysis to bring a number of relevant insights into this problem. These techniques allow us to find cloned applications in the wild, to analyze the prominent properties among these clones, and to analyze the popularity and profitability of these clones. During the process, we face several challenges. First, we must download a large number of applications from various markets (because often the plagiarized and original applications appear on different markets) and detect clones among them using an automatic tool. Second, we must capture a large amount of live network data from mobile applications, allowing us to extract relevant advertising information to bring insight into each app's advertising revenue. Note that these traces must be from large numbers of real users unaffiliated with and unaffected by our study. This precludes generating traces in our lab, because the users aren't real, and capturing network traffic at our university, because the user population is not large or diverse enough. Finally, we must associate the original and plagiarized applications with their network traces to determine how much advertising revenue plagiarized applications receive relative to the original. For the purpose of this work, we attempt to distinguish *rebranded* apps (apps from the same developer with high code similarity) from truly plagiarized apps by merging developer accounts accross markets. We collectively refer to these techniques, along with the results presented, as *AdRob*.

1.1 Overview

The analysis used for AdRob consists of the following steps (Figure 1).

- We crawled 265,359 free Android applications from 17 markets around the world. Then, we ran a tool [6] to find clones within these applications, resulting in 44,268 cloned apps.
- We captured live HTTP advertising traffic generated by mobile applications at a tier-1 US cellular carrier for 12 days, resulting in 2.6 billion packets and 19,125,311 ad impressions.
- We link cloned applications detected in our lab to their network traffic by their *client IDs*. Most free Android applications include one or more advertising libraries. For each ad library, the application includes a client ID, which is sent along with the ad requests so that the ad provider can credit the application developer for ad impressions or clicks. We use static analysis to extract client IDs from the downloaded applications. Then, we extract client IDs for popular ad providers from captured HTTP traffic. Finally, we correlate these two sets of client IDs.

Using the data acquired in the above steps, we first examine properties of the cloned applications, including their distribution across different markets, application categories, and ad libraries. Next, we examine how cloned applications affect the original developers. We estimate a lower bound on the percent revenue that cloned applications siphon from the original developers, and the percent user base that cloned applications divert from the original applications. To the best of our knowledge, this is the first large scale study on the characteristics of cloned applications and their impact on the original developers.

We make the following contributions:

- We conduct a large scale study on the characteristics of cloned applications and their impact on the original developers. This serves as a first step toward understanding the incentives of application plagiarists.
- We combine static analysis with live network analysis to correlate the static properties of an application to its network characteristics. Using this methodology, we link applications crawled from major Android markets to their live traces in a tier-1 US cellular network carrier, which allows us to understand the impact of plagiarism broadly and deeply.
- We propose the use of client IDs in ad requests to correlate Android applications to their live network traces. We present approaches for extracting client IDs from both application code and network traces.
- We describe an approach to determine the *ownership* of apps using developer accounts, signing keys, and client IDs.

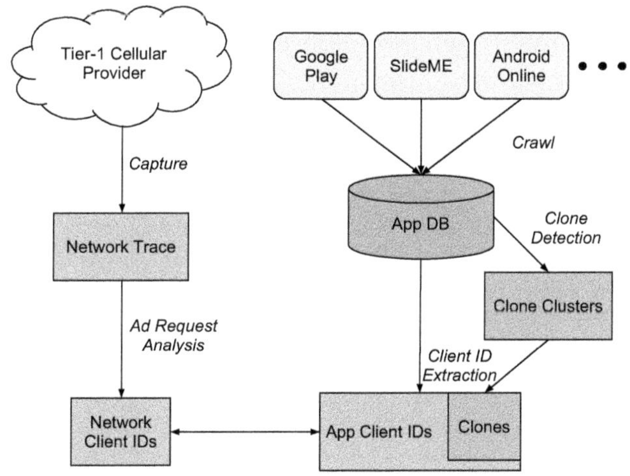

Figure 1: Overview of the AdRob methodology.

Non-Goal.

This work does *not* consider ad fraud. While app plagiarism detriments primarily the original developers of the plagiarized apps by siphoning their users and advertising revenue, ad fraud harms mainly the advertisers. Moreover, online ad fraud has been extensively studied [7, 11, 27]. Our work is the first to measure the impact of app plagiarism on the original developers.

2. BACKGROUND

2.1 Android Background

Android is a Linux-based smart phone operating system designed by Google that is designed to run Android applications (apps) that are downloaded from various Android app markets. An Android application is distributed as an `apk` file, which is similar to a Java `jar` file. The `apk` is a zip archive which contains all the code and data needed to install and run the app.

The largest and most popular app market is Google Play (also called the official Android market), which consists of over 550,000 applications by various developers [4]. In addition to Google Play, there are a number of third-party Android markets where users can go to download apps, for example the Amazon Appstore or SlideMe. There are various reasons developers would choose to release their apps on third-party markets: many do not charge to create a developer account and upload applications, they may have less stringent terms of service, or developers may simply want to increase the exposure of their apps across these different markets.

Before an app may be submitted to a market, it must be digitally signed by a certificate for which the developer owns the private key. This certificate is used by Android to determine authorship and trust relationships between apps [23]. Android phones and emulators will only install apps that are signed. Android developer certificates may be self-signed, so there is little barrier for a developer to create as many certificates as she wishes. However, for Android to allow an app to seamlessly update to the next version, the newer version must be signed with the same certificate. Otherwise, the user will be prompted to install the newer version as if it were a separate app.

An important file which is included with every app is the Android Manifest file. This XML document contains a number of parameters that the Android framework needs in order to run the app. This includes the names of the Activities, which are the different screens of the app, the permissions the app requires and the API version. Developers may also use this XML document to store any additional information the app may use; for example, advertising parameters are sometimes specified here.

2.2 Android Application Cloning

Android applications are written in Java and compiled into Dalvik bytecode in order to run on Android's Dalvik Virtual Machine. Dalvik bytecode is very well structured and clearly separates code from data which makes it much easier to reverse engineer than traditional machine code.

To protect their application from reverse engineering, prudent developers may use a tool called Proguard [16] to perform class and function name obfuscation. It can also be used to obfuscate the package name of included libraries. However, Proguard alone is not enough to protect apps from being reverse engineered or cloned. Open-source tools such as ApkTool [5] and smali [10] make it straightforward for unscrupulous individuals to reverse engineer, modify, and recompile the Dalvik bytecode of an Android application for distribution.

2.3 Advertising on Android

An Android developer who wants to make money by displaying advertisements as part of her application must sign up with an *ad provider* and download the provider's *advertising SDK*, which is a library (in the form of a `jar` file) that the developer includes in the app. The SDK provides an API for displaying an ad in the application, and abstracts away the complexity involved with fetching, displaying, and managing advertisements for the ad provider (an overview of which is shown in Figure 2).

In order to receive payment for ads shown in the application, the developer is given a *client ID* by the ad provider that uniquely identifies the app; this client ID is then specified in the application such that it is available to the ad library SDK. When it is time to display an ad, the SDK sends an *ad request* over HTTP to the ad provider's ad server. The ad request includes the client ID, a device identifier (for example, the IMEI), and other fields such as demographic information. The exact format of the ad request and the fields present differs between ad providers. Once the request is received, the ad server responds with the image URL of the ad to display and a click URL that opens in the browser

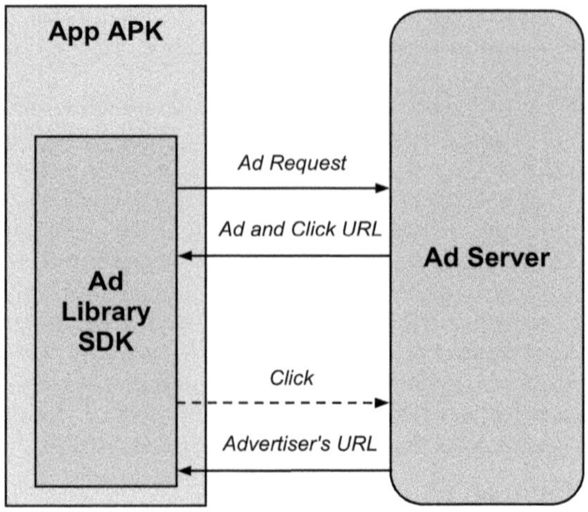

Figure 2: Overview of ad library SDK and ad server interaction.

app if the ad is clicked. A successful ad request and associated response is called an *impression* and represents one instance of an ad being displayed to the user. To track the clicks, the ad server generates a unique click URL for each impression which points to one of the provider's ad servers. When the browser opens this page the click is matched with its associated impression and recorded before the browser is redirected to the advertisement's landing page. Unlike ad requests, the click request does not contain the client ID of the application as the ad server can lookup the client ID once the click is matched with the impression that generated it. As we will explain in Section 4, this extra level of indirection prevented us from obtaining suitable click results.

3. DATASET

In this section we describe the data used in our study. The two main datasets are a large collection of downloaded Android applications, which we analyzed to find clones, and 3G network data from a tier-1 cellular carrier, which provided us insight into the advertising behavior of applications in our database.

3.1 Application Database

Our collection of Android applications consists of 265,359 Android apps from 17 markets around the world. Figure 4 shows these markets. The apps were collected via automated crawling and stored in a database along with any meta information provided by the market (such as developer name, number of downloads, and category). Only free applications are included in the collection. The breakdown across various markets is as follows: 73.7% of the apps are from the official Google Play market, 14.7% are from 9 third-party English markets, 13.8% are from 6 third-party Chinese markets, and 0.46% are from 2 Russian markets. Even though we may not have crawled all the markets or have downloaded all the applications from each market, our analysis in Section 4 indicates that our collection represents a significant portion of all the applications that include ads running on US cellular networks.

3.2 Plagiarized Applications

Using a more scalable tool based on DNADroid [6], we analyzed our application database to look for plagiarized applications. While DNADroid is highly precise because it is based on calculating subgraph isomorphism on PDGs, it is not scalable because it requires pair-wise comparison of apps. To avoid pairwise comparison, the tool used for this work converts each app into a set of semantic vectors, each of which represents a semantic feature of the program. Then, the tool clusters the semantic vectors of all the apps using LSH [1]. Finally, the tool considers a set of apps to be clones if they share a large number of semantic vector clusters and places these apps into the same *clone cluster*.

Each clone cluster contains applications published by different developers, as determined by their signing certificate. Each application appears in at most one cluster. In total, we investigate 5,431 clone clusters consisting of 44,268 unique applications. These clusters may or may not contain the victim of plagiarism, which we call the original app in this paper. Determining the original application is difficult and unreliable, as described in Section 6.2.1.

3.3 Network Data

We had access to live 3G network data from a tier-1 cellular network carrier, which consisted of a sample of all traffic that passed through a particular home agent in the southwest United States. Packets were tapped from the home agent and sent to the carrier's research lab for capture and analysis. The tap at the home agent was quarter-sampled at the flow level, so in theory all packets in a particular flow were available to be captured; however, packets were lost from limitations in bandwidth and capture speed of the tapping infrastructure. The network data included all 3G internet traffic sent from devices registered on the carrier's cellular network, including protocol headers and payload.

We captured HTTP traffic from the tap over the course of 12 days: from 28 June 2012 to 10 July 2012. Devices present on the network include both Android and iOS devices, as well as feature phones and wireless cards. The traffic characteristics are similar to those in [18]. To optimize the capture, only 32 bytes of the protocol header were captured along with the payload for each packet. Additionally, we performed IP filtering so that only packets with a source or destination IP address that corresponded with a known Android ad server were captured. In total, we captured 2.6 billions packets in our trace. We describe how we extract ad request data from the trace in Section 4.1.

4. METHODOLOGY

Figure 1 shows the procedure of our study. Our data came from two sources: (1) HTTP traffic generated by Android applications on a US tier-1 cellular network, and (2) Android applications downloaded from Android markets. We correlated the two datasets using advertising client IDs. In this section we explain how we extracted these IDs, both from the network and from applications.

4.1 Extracting Client IDs from Network Traces

We now explain how we extract client IDs from ad requests sent by Android applications. We extract advertising information from our cellular network trace (described in Section 3.3) by analyzing ad requests at the packet level as well as at the flow level. In order to identify ad requests, we manually ran a sample application for each Android ad provider and captured all traffic from the device so that we could characterize the format of each provider's requests. From each ad request, we record the ad provider, client ID, anonymized user identifier, and the application package name if available. We anonymize user identifiers to avoid recording any potentially sensitive device identifiers, such as the IMEI. We only record ad requests with an Android HTTP `User-Agent` field.

To get packet level data, we look at the HTTP header of each packet to determine if it is an ad request from a recognized Android ad provider and record relevant advertising information. To analyze ad requests at the flow level, we use the 32 bytes of protocol header to reconstruct each TCP flow, allowing us to observe both the ad request and the response from the server. The benefits of looking at ad requests at the flow level are twofold. First, we observed that ad requests for some ad providers are split across multiple packets, especially when the request uses HTTP POST, so it would be impossible to record the entire ad request in this case by only looking at packets individually. Second, the server response allows us to extract the click URL associated with each impression so that we can match the impression with any observed clicks in the trace. These clicks can be linked to an impression and thus a client ID by using the click URLs that we parse from each flow.

To extract client IDs, we first identify the ad provider by examining the host name in the HTTP request. For each ad provider, we create a pattern to identify its client IDs in the HTTP requests accurately.

4.2 Extracting Client IDs from Applications

We extract client IDs from Android applications via static analysis. Commonly, ad providers require developers to provide their client ID in one of five ways: declaring it in the application's manifest file, declaring it in a layout XML file, passing it to an ad object in the application code, specifying it as a constant string, or receiving it dynamically over the network.

4.2.1 In Android Manifest

The most straightforward client IDs to extract are those declared in the Android manifest file. *Admob*, for example, recommends that developers store their client IDs in a meta-data field with the name ADMOB_PUBLISHER_ID. Usually the client ID is directly included in the Manifest XML; however, in some cases there can be extra levels of indirection: Android allows developers to abstract values into constant files such as `string.xml`. In cases where the developer has abstracted the client ID using notation such as `@string/admob_id`, we resolve these abstractions accordingly.

4.2.2 In Layout XML

Some ad providers recommend that client IDs be included in one of the auxiliary XML files that developers generate for their application (not the manifest). Conveniently for us, these ad providers usually provide an example for developers to copy and replace the client ID with their own, which provides a common naming convention for each ad library. We take advantage of this convention by using XPATH to search XML files for specific XML elements known to contain

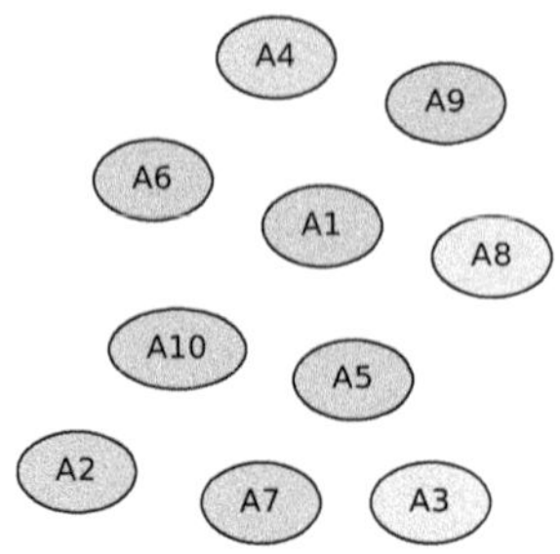

(a) Initial owners based on developer accounts (Phase 1)

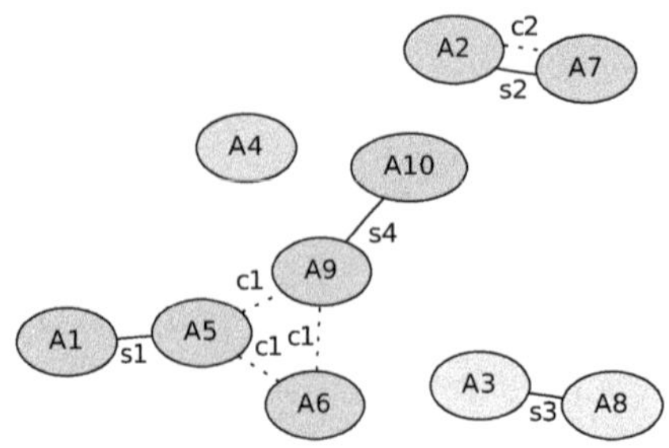

(b) Owners with edges based on shared certificates (s) and client IDs (c)

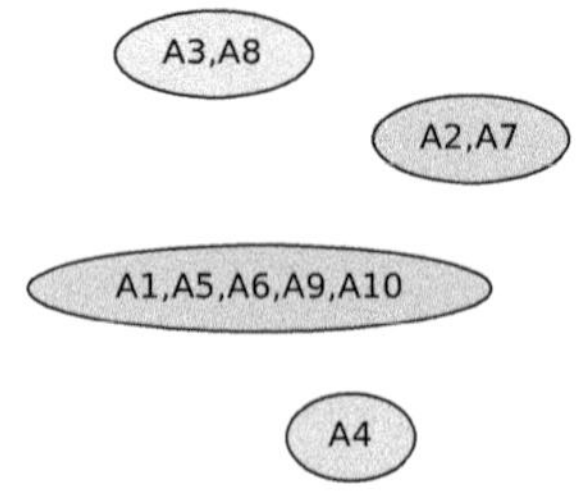

(c) Owners after merging (Phases 2 and 3)

Figure 3: Owner graph at various stages in owner merging.

client IDs. For example, *Jumptap* client IDs are usually in a field called `jumptaplib:publisherid`.

4.2.3 In Application Code

Client IDs that applications pass directly to ad library initialization methods are the most challenging to extract. The initialization may happen at any point in the code and the client ID may be instantiated in a number of ways, including being passed in as a constant, received over the network, generated dynamically, or read in from a file. We observed that the first two are the most common cases and focus on them accordingly.

Specified as Constants.

We dump values from the DEX string constants section in the application's `dex` file and search for strings that match the structure of client IDs for each ad library. This approach is effective for ad providers whose client IDs follow a distinctive pattern. To improve the precision of this analysis, we also implemented a static analysis tool that performs constant propagation to detect when constant values are passed to the client ID argument of ad library initialization methods. Unfortunately, we found it too slow to run on all of the apps in our dataset, as it took several minutes per app. We leave improving the precision of extracting constant-based client IDs in this manner to future work.

Received Over the Network.

In addition to ad libraries, many applications include Adwhirl's SDK. Adwhirl is not an ad provider, but rather offers a service that allows developers to dynamically decide which ad provider and client ID should be used in their ad requests. Before an application with Adwhirl makes an ad request, it queries Adwhirl with its Adwhirl client ID and receives a set of ad providers and client IDs, which the application then uses to send ad requests. This service allows developers to dynamically change the advertising behavior of their apps without having to push a new version of their app. We handle apps that use Adwhirl by first extracting Adwhirl client IDs from the application. Then, we query Adwhirl's server to obtain a mapping from an Adwhirl client ID to a set of client IDs and their ad providers. This allows us to obtain many client IDs not hardcoded in the applications.

From our application database, we extracted 1,386 unique Adwhirl client IDs, which mapped to 1,886 unique client IDs from one of the five ad providers we eventually used in this paper (described in Section 5.1). Of these, 1,539 (or 81.6%) were new client IDs that we had not extracted from our applications. Specifically, 764 were for *admob*, 523 for *millennial*, and 252 for *inmobi*.

4.3 Determining Ownership

As our goal is to measure the impact of plagiarism on developers, we must not regard as plagiarism similar apps from the same developer, known as *rebranded* apps. Rebranded apps may appear on the same or different markets. In this section we discuss how we determine app ownership by considering developer accounts, signing keys (represented by certificates), and client IDs. We make the following assumptions: first, each owner has her own unique set of certificates that are not shared with any other owner; second, each owner has her own unique set of client IDs that are not shared with any other owner. In Section 7.1.1 we discuss caveats associated with these assumptions. Note, however, that these caveats only cause us to merge owners more aggressively, resulting in lowering our measured cloning impact.

Merging owners consists of three phases. First, we build an owner graph where each node corresponds to a unique developer account that has uploaded an application that we crawled (Phase 1). Next, we merge owners based on shared certificates (Phase 2). Finally, we merge owners based on shared client IDs (Phase 3). An overview of the owner graph at various steps in the process is shown in Figure 3.

Phase 1: The first phase of merging owners is to create a graph with a node for each unique developer account. Each developer account is identified by the tuple of the market name and the developer's name and is associated with one or more apps in our database. Assuming that developer accounts are rarely compromised, then two apps from the same developer account must come from the same owner. Thus, developer accounts provide an initial mapping of apps to owners.

Phase 2: Next, we compute the set of certificates whose corresponding private keys were used to sign the apps uploaded by each developer account. As mentioned in Section 2, every Android app must be signed by the developer's private key before it may be uploaded to a market and then

Provider	Impressions	Clicks	Unique IDs
admob	9,288,333	920	348,275
airpush	3,212,878*	n/a	138,166
inmobi	220,982*	207	n/a
millennial	4,855,247	n/a	61,127
mobclix	1,547,871	1,080	32,751

Table 2: Number of observed impressions, clicks, and anonymized user identifiers in the network trace, broken down by ad provider. The report of impression counts uses packet level ad request analysis, unless otherwise noted (via *). Note that we were not able to measure clicks for all providers due to the format of their ad requests (for example, those with chunked HTTP encoding). Also note that inmobi does not include a user identifier in their ad requests.

installed on users' phones. Since private keys are supposed to be kept private (we discuss shared and stolen private keys in Section 7.1.1), two developer accounts that share a certificate must share the same owner so they are merged in the graph.

Phase 3: Finally, we merge any two owners whose applications share a client ID. Client IDs are used by ad providers to uniquely identify who should receive revenue for each ad shown or clicked. Therefore, if two developer accounts share a client ID, they are likely to be from the same owner.

We separate the merging of owners by certificates and client IDs into two phases because we have lower confidence about merges based on client IDs. This is because client ID extraction may have false positives while certificate calculation cannot. Other situations, such as a plagiarist who leaves the original developer's client ID intact, are discussed in Section 7.1.1.

5. EVALUATION

In this section we summarize the raw results of our analysis and determine the accuracy of our application client ID extraction.

5.1 Network Client ID Extraction

One important consideration of our work is which Android ad providers to include in our analysis. We started with 16 ad providers based on their popularity in our application database. Among these ad providers, seven[1] had very small number of ad requests in our captured traffic (some of them are Chinese but our traffic was captured in the US), and four had very little overlap between the client IDs observed on the network and client IDs extracted from our application database (Table 1)[2]. Therefore, we focus on the remaining five ad providers, whose number of impressions, clicks, and unique user identifiers are summarized in Table 2. These five ad providers are also among the top six most prevalent Android ad libraries reported by AppBrain [3]. Because our network capture was lossy, we were not able to record significant click results from the trace, as we could only measure clicks when the ad request, server response, and then click request did not experience any loss.

[1]Buzzcity, Mojiva, Quattro, Vdopia, Wooboo, Youmi, ZestAdz

[2]These four providers only represented 7% of the total number of ad requests we collected.

5.2 Application Client ID Extraction

While extracting client IDs from HTTP traffic generated by Android applications is highly accurate, extracting them automatically from Android applications themselves may not be as reliable, because client IDs may be provided in several different ways, some of which are unfriendly to program analysis (Section 4). Therefore, we would like to evaluate the accuracy of our client IDs extracted from Android applications. However, it is difficult to determine the ground truth, because doing so would require us to manually review all the applications, which is prohibitive given our large number of applications. One might suggest that we run each application in an emulator to extract the client IDs from its HTTP traffic. However, an application may contain multiple ad libraries, so we may not observe the client IDs from all these libraries during the execution of the application. Moreover, some ad libraries would not send ad requests if they detect that they are running in emulators.

Instead, we take advantage of the client IDs extracted from HTTP traffic to estimate a lower bound of the accuracy of our client ID extraction from applications. For each ad provider AP, let D_{AP} be the set of client IDs extracted from our application databases, and N_{AP} be the set of client IDs extracted from our captured HTTP traffic. The *network coverage*, $|N_{AP} \cap D_{AP}|/|D_{AP}|$, estimates a lower bound of the true positive rate of our client ID extraction from applications. The *database coverage*, $|D_{AP} \cap N_{AP}|/|N_{AP}|$, estimates the coverage our application database on all the Android applications running on the network where we captured traces.

The results of this analysis are summarized in Table 1. The database coverages for most providers are fairly high, indicating that our application database represents a significant portion of all ad-supported Android applications that are used in the geographic area where we collected the trace.

6. FINDINGS

6.1 Properties of Apps in Clone Clusters

There are a number of questions that come to mind when investigating our clone clusters: Which markets do apps in the clusters belong to Which markets have the highest proportion of apps involved in cloning What categories are most represented in the clusters What advertising libraries do cloners prefer In this section we seek to answer these questions by investigating common features of apps in our clone clusters. Note, at this point we do not yet speculate as to which app in each clone cluster is the original and which are clones.

6.1.1 Market Characteristics

Figure 4 shows which Android markets are most prevalent in our clone clusters. A significant percentage of apps in our clone clusters are from Google Play; intuitively this makes sense as Play is the most popular Android market. To compensate for this observation, we computed what percentage of all applications in our database from the market are present in a clone cluster. In this context, Play does not stand out more than other markets, but a number of other markets such as AndroidSoft, and the Chinese markets AndroidOnline, GoApk, and AppChina, have more than a quarter of their apps in our clone clusters. To better understand the cloning relationship between markets, we calculated the number of similar apps between each pair of

Ad Provider	Unique client IDs		Network coverage	Database coverage
	from databases	from network		
admob	51,434	19,718	21.2%	55.4%
airpush	8,728	8,829	36.9%	36.5%
inmobi	514	487	28.6%	30.2%
millennial	786	2,030	32.6%	12.6%
mobclix	2,994	1,781	38.0%	63.9%
adfonic	59,170	318	0.0%	0.0%
greystripe	59,616	212	0.3%	68.4%
jumptap	8	78	0.0%	0.0%
smaato	0	144	n/a	0.0%

Table 1: Percentage of extracted client IDs we observed in network traffic and percentage of observed network client IDs we also extracted from the application database, broken down by provider. The lower group of providers are ones which we did not include in our study because they did not have significant overlap with our application database.

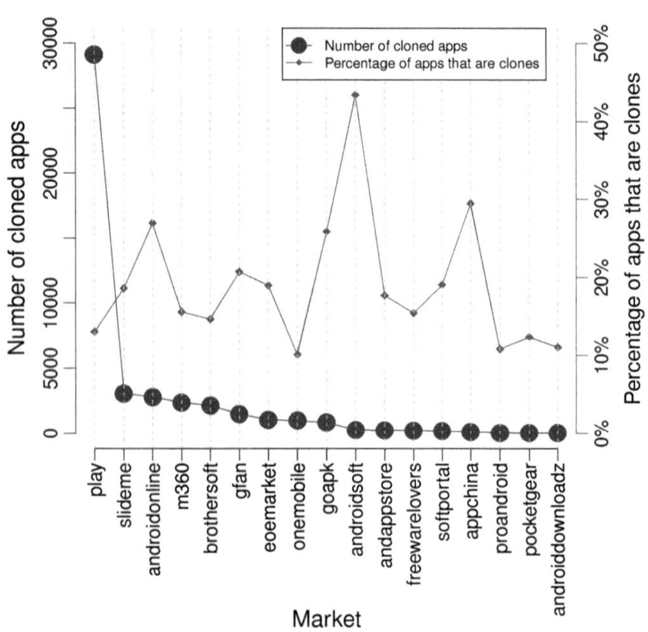

Figure 4: Plot showing the popularity of different app markets in our clone clusters. The absolute number of cloned apps from each market is represented by the axis labelled Number of cloned apps , whereas the axis labelled Percentage of apps that are clones represents the popularity of each market in our clone clusters normalized over the total number of apps from that market in our database.

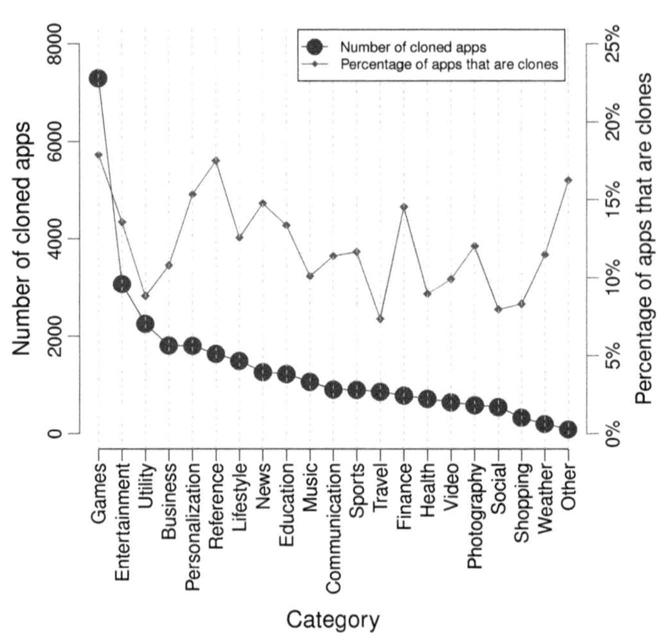

Figure 5: Plot showing the popularity of different app categories in our clone clusters. The absolute number of cloned apps in each category is represented by the axis labelled Number of cloned apps , whereas axis labelled Percentage of apps that are clones represents the number of cloned apps in each category normalized over the total number of apps in that category in our database.

markets in a clone cluster. Specifically, for the apps in given clone cluster and a pair of markets (I, J):

$$MarketSim_{cluster}(I, J) = \min(\text{apps from } I, \text{apps from } J)$$

Then, to get a global view of the amount of similar applications between markets we calculate the total $MarketSim(I, J)$ as follows:

$$MarketSim(I, J) = \sum_{c \in clusters} MarketSim_c(I, J)$$

In Figure 7, we plot the results of this calculation in an undirected graph. To reduce the complexity of the graph, we only show an edge between markets whose $MarketSim$ value is over 300 and remove unconnected markets.

We define a market as a cloning hub if it shares an edge with many different markets in the graph. Play is the largest cloning hub among all the markets, as it has a significant cloning relationship with almost every other market. Similarly, AndroidOnline is a cloning hub among the Chinese markets. The existence of these cloning hubs implies one of two things: either plagiarists prefer cloning from apps on these markets, or that plagiarists prefer these markets to publish their cloned apps. Since we do not speculate on which app in a cluster is the original, we leave the determining which of these cases is true to future work. Note that the

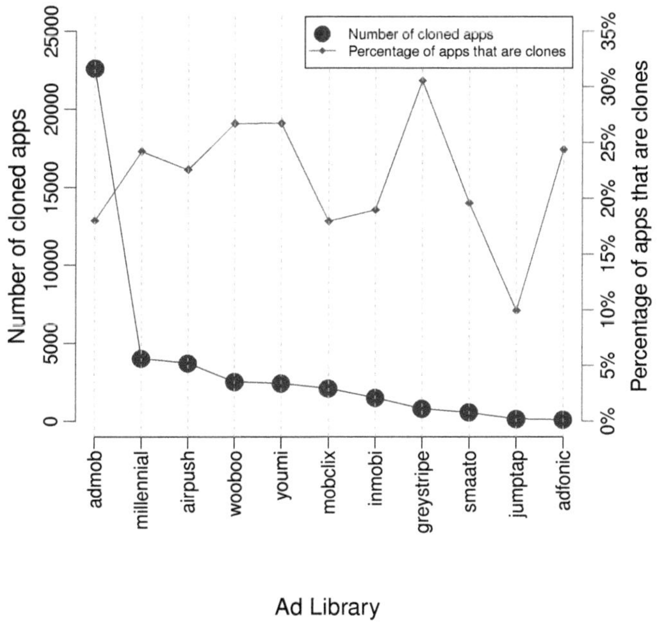

Figure 6: Plot showing the popularity of different ad libraries among apps in our clone clusters. The absolute number of cloned apps with each library is represented by the axis labelled Number of cloned apps , whereas axis labelled Percentage of apps that are clones represents the number of cloned apps with each library normalized over the total number of apps with that library in our database.

prevalence of Play as a cloning hub is likely influenced by the fact Play represents 73.7% of the apps in our database.

6.1.2 Category Characteristics

We now investigate which app categories are popular among apps in our clone clusters so that we can better understand what types of apps are involved in cloning. One difficulty with comparing categories among apps from different markets is that different markets use different category names to refer to the same type of application. To avoid this problem, we chose 21 meta-categories that represent the spectrum of different categories observed across all our markets (our mapping from category strings to meta-categories is presented in the Appendix). Figure 5 presents the number of applications in our clone clusters that belong to each meta-category. As we did for markets, we normalize the number of cloned apps in each category with the number of all apps in our database for that category to determine what percentage of apps in the category are involved in cloning. Interestingly, Games is the most popular category among apps in the clone clusters, but also has the highest prevalence of apps involved in cloning. Thus, markets that care about application cloning should focus on apps categorized as Games. Additionally, assuming that the original app and the clone belong to the same category, this implies plagiarists prefer applications categorized as Games. We hypothesize that this is because games are relatively complex, popular among Android users, and are often run for long periods of time, allowing more advertising revenue to be generated.

6.1.3 Ad Library Characteristics

Figure 6 gives a breakdown by ad provider of the applications in our clone clusters, as well as normalized across our entire application database. Admob is the most popular provider among cloned applications, but is also the most popular among all applications, and thus does not have a higher percentage of cloned apps compared with other providers. On the other hand, for our Chinese ad providers, Wooboo and Youmi, cloned applications represent a larger subset of the total applications that use these providers. Nonetheless, an alarmingly large percentage of applications for each provider are in our clone clusters, meaning that they either are clones of another app, or are a legitimate app that has been cloned. Note that we do not consider what percentage of ad traffic was generated by our clone clusters for each ad provider, as we do not speculate which app is the original and want to avoid any assumptions regarding how much traffic for a provider is a result of app plagiarism. In the next section, we estimate a lower bound for how much advertising revenue cloning siphons from legitimate applications.

6.2 Comparing Clones and Non-clones

In previous sections we examined a number of properties of apps in our cloned clusters without distinguishing the original apps from the clones. In this section, we wish to gain insight into the impact of cloning on developers. Specifically, we investigate the effects of cloning on the original authors' ad revenue and user install base. To do so, the original author in the cluster must be determined, which is surprisingly nontrivial.

6.2.1 Determining Original App

There are a number of intuitive approaches one could use to determine which application among a cluster of similar applications is the original. Unfortunately, most of these initial approaches are flawed. For example, one could use:

- Date first uploaded to the market
- Application popularity by number of installs or rating
- Code size by number of methods, instructions, or other metric

The date an application was first uploaded to the market is difficult to know as an external observer. Each market knows when the application was first uploaded, but unless an external observer has been crawling markets since their creation in both the free and paid sections, she cannot know for sure which app came first. Additionally, there have been cases where beta releases have been taken and uploaded to markets before the original developer's app. Application popularity may sometimes differentiate the clone from the original, for example in the case of Angry Birds, however, for less popular applications, users may be just as likely to download the clone as the original. Further, application popularity by both number of installs and ratings is vulnerable to sybil attacks which would be relatively easy to perform as most market accounts require only a valid email address. Lastly, the code size of applications can easily be distorted by plagiarists to make the plagiarized app appear larger or smaller.

Rather than rely on one of these flawed approaches, we instead use an approach that estimates a lower bound on

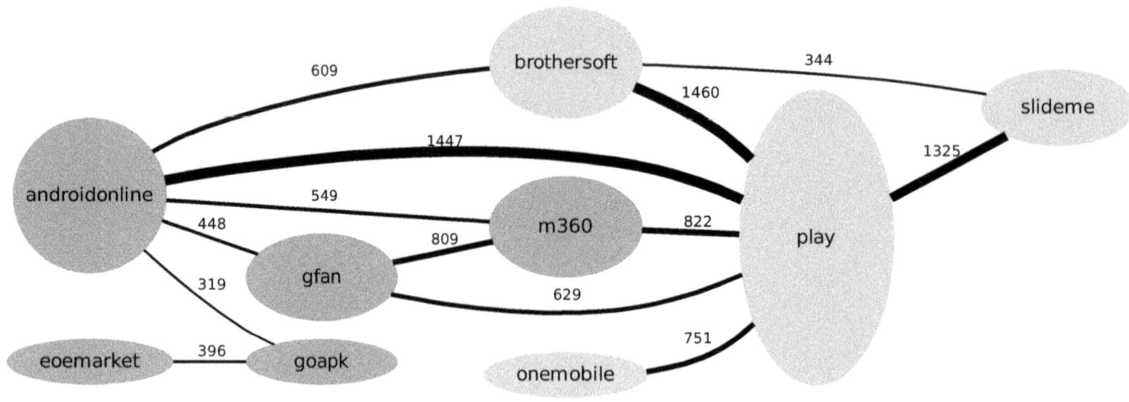

Figure 7: Markets which have a significant cloning relationship. The thickness of an edge is proportional to the *MarketSim* value between the markets, and the height of a node is proportional to the sum of the edge weights for a given market. Markets with nodes colored blue are US-based markets whereas markets with nodes colored red are Chinese-based markets.

	P1	**P2**	**P3**
Num Clusters	610	370	128
$LostImps_{total}$	1,764,609	1,076,614	56,884
$PercLostImps_{total}$	52%	51%	14%
$LostUsers_{total}$	166,534	122,718	3,808
$PercLostUsers_{total}$	49%	48%	10%

Table 3: Total amount of lost impressions and users across all of our clone clusters between each phase of developer merging. The value of Num Clusters represents how many clone clusters had more than one owner after each phase. P1, P2, and P3 represent Phase 1, Phase 2, and Phase 3, respectively.

our findings. For each cluster we deem the owner with the most observed impressions to be the original author and all other owners are treated as plagiarists. In the case where clones are more popular than the original, we will mislabel the original author as a plagiarist, but this is acceptable as we will only underestimate the percentage of lost advertising traffic. Indeed, this approach guarantees we will not overestimate the number of lost impressions from mislabeling the original as the above approaches might, as we only consider the least popular owners in a clone cluster as plagiarists (other caveats presented in Section 7.1.2). As we will see, merging developer accounts has significant impact over our results when app owners within a clone cluster are merged by certificate or client ID, and in some cases may attribute all apps within a cluster to the same merged owner. We do not consider such cases in our computations of lost revenue, as they do not represent fraudulent cloning.

6.2.2 How much revenue do clones siphon from the original authors?

In order to determine the impact of plagiarism on the advertising revenue of the original application, we first observe that hard dollar amounts are difficult to determine when looking at advertising network traffic alone. This is because an impression does not explicitly indicate how much it is worth in an ad request, as the ad provider does not want to disclose how much it or its affiliated developers are making. Instead, we show what percentage of lost ad traffic developers experience by comparing the ratio of impressions that belong to plagiarized applications compared with the total number of impressions we observed belonging to applications in our clone clusters. The number of lost impressions for a cluster is represented by $LostImps_{cluster}$, and the percentage of lost impressions for a cluster is this value divided by all impressions attributed to apps in the cluster, times 100 (represented by $PercLostImps_{cluster}$). Additionally, $LostImps_{total}$ represents the total number of plagiarized app impressions over all the clusters, and $PercLostImps_{total}$ represents what percentage of all impressions from all clusters that are a results of $LostImps_{total}$.

As previously stated, we consider the original author in a cluster as the app owner with the greatest amount of advertising traffic, thus the numerator is the number of impressions for all apps in the cluster not owned by this author. Additionally, we do not consider clusters with only a single owner. Figure 8a shows a CDF of the $PercImpsLost_{cluster}$ values across our clone clusters for each stage of application owner merging. When only considering developer accounts on their own (Phase 1 of the owner graph, see Section 4.3) nearly 25% of the clusters have exactly 50% lost revenue. This is a result of clusters having exactly two applications which belong to different developer accounts but which share a client ID. Intuitively, we would want to remove these anomalies by merging developer accounts where it makes sense. However, merging by certificates alone, which is very accurate, does not significantly change the distribution of lost revenue across our clusters (Phase 2 of owner graph). Thus, we use the results of Phase 3 of the owner graph where owners are merged by client IDs to ensure that our results do not overestimate the percentage of lost revenue. Figure 8b shows the impact of merging at each stage on the $PercImpsLost_{cluster}$ values, and Table 3 summarizes the total impact over all the clusters. Alarmingly, the value of $LostImps_{total}$ after all developer account merging is complete is 14%, meaning that authors who are the

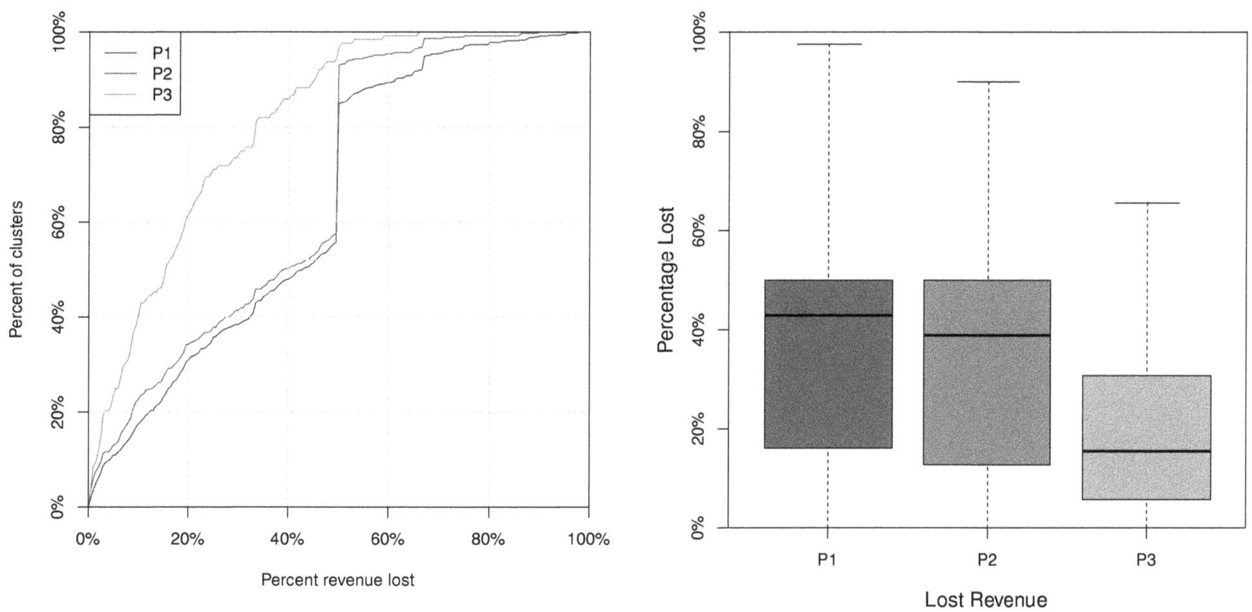

(a) $PercLostImps_{cluster}$ (b) $PercLostImps_{total}$

Figure 8: CDF and boxplot of percent impact to developers in terms of impressions for each phase of merging on the owner graph. P1, P2, and P3 represent Phase 1, Phase 2, and Phase 3, respectively.

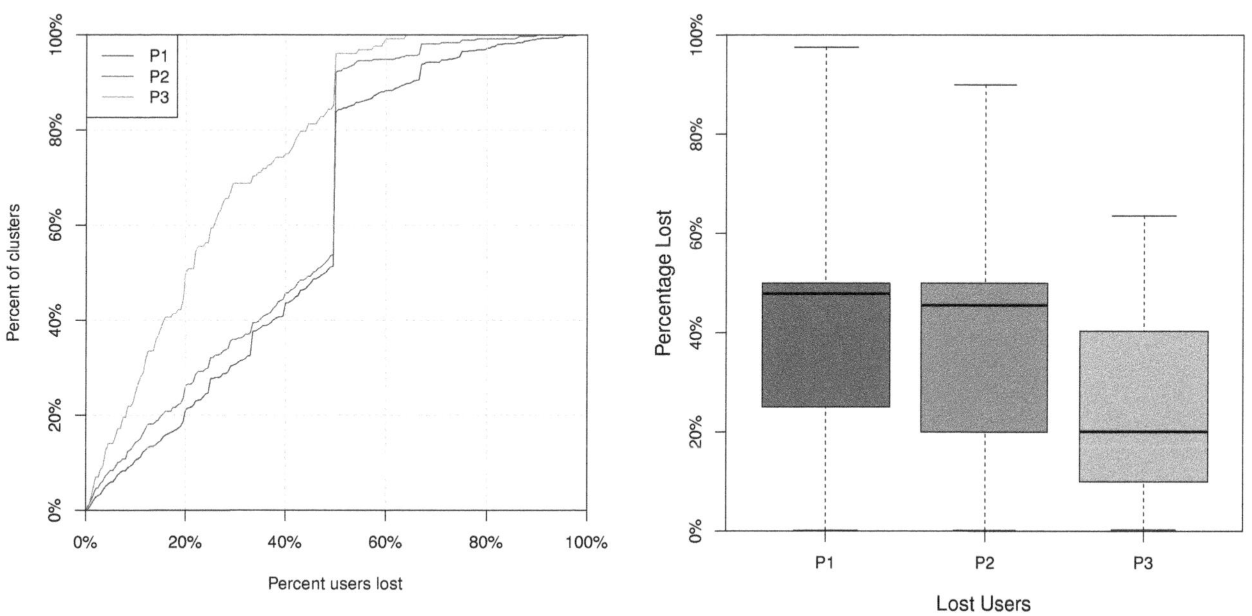

(a) $PercLostUsers_{cluster}$ (b) $PercLostUsers_{total}$

Figure 9: CDF and boxplot of percent impact to developers in terms of users for each phase of merging on the owner graph. P1, P2, and P3 represent Phase 1, Phase 2, and Phase 3, respectively.

target of cloning on average lost 14% of their advertising revenue to application plagiarism, assuming the users who downloaded the plagiarized versions would have used the original app instead.

6.2.3 How much of the user base do clones divert from the original app?

To determine how much user base application plagiarism siphons from the original authors, we used the anonymized device identifiers present in the ad traffic from our network trace to estimate the number of unique users per application. Similar to lost impressions, we compute the $LostUsers_{cluster}$ and $PercLostUsers_{cluster}$ values for each cluster and plot the distribution in Figure 9a. We also compute the total number of lost users across all our clusters as $LostUsers_{total}$ and the percentage lost across all the clusters as $PercLostUsers_{total}$. The value of these are summarized in Figure 9b and Table 3. We see that on average, 10% of the user base for an author in our clone clusters is siphoned due to plagiarism if we assume the users who downloaded the plagiarized applications would have used the original app if no plagiarism were present.

7. DISCUSSION

7.1 Limitations

7.1.1 Authorship Determination

During our exploration of potential methods for merging owners we encountered several challenges. All of these challenges could cause our analysis to merge developer accounts more aggresively, potentially causing us to underestimate lost impressions and users due to plagiarism.

Certificates Shared By Many Apps.

We found that some certificates are present on many apps that are associated with a large number of developer accounts on several markets. Eight certificates were present on apps from over one hundred developer accounts, the largest having 413. After manually reviewing the developer accounts associated with several of the most prevalent certificates, we decided that either one or several parties made a significant attempt to distribute their apps across many developer accounts or that the private keys were leaked or stolen. In fact, we discovered one of the certificates corresponds to a private key used in the Android Open Source Project[3] (AOSP). These keys are often used to sign custom ROMs. Apps signed with these keys can run with greater privileges when running on a custom ROM and some malware has been found to take advantage of this [21]. Regardless of why many developer accounts share a certificate, we were surprised to find that two apps sharing a certificate may not necessarily have the same owner.

Apps With Multiple Certificates.

Though it has not been discussed in the literature to the best of our knowledge and is only briefly mentioned in the Android documentation page on signing apps [23], Android apps may be signed with multiple developer keys. We found 667 apps in our dataset that have more than one certificate, with the largest having four. Android developers may do this as a means to collaborate with another developer or to ease the process of selling an app to a company [15, 19].

We hoped to use apps with multiple keys to merge owners in possession of at least one of the keys. Intuitively, if one app is signed by developer keys A and B, one would like to merge the owners of each key, as the developer of an app should have possession of each key that signed her app. We manually reviewed a number of cases where we tried to merge owners based on apps with multiple keys. While in several cases the developer accounts of each key seemed related, this was not always the case. Thus, in this work we ignore any app with multiple certificates as they may taint our results. Furthermore, these apps constitute a very small portion of our dataset (667 out of 265,359 apps).

Lazy Cloning.

We define lazy cloning to be cases when a cloner copies an app but does not change all of the client IDs in ad libraries contained in the original app. This would cause our analysis to merge the owners representing the original developer and the cloner, as they are responsible for apps that share a client ID. We believe this occurs infrequently in practice, as one of the major incentives behind cloning is financial gains.

7.1.2 Estimation on Lost Revenue and User Base

Since we cannot identify the original app in a clone cluster reliably, we choose the most popular app, measured by the number of ad impressions, as the original app. While this decision provides a lower bound estimation on the percent lost revenue and user base in most cases, it would fail in the following unusual cases.

Failure to merge owners.

When we fail to merge two different developer accounts of the same owner, we could inflate the number of unique owners in a clone cluster. This would happen when an owner publishes similar apps from different developer accounts using different certificates and different client IDs. Additional information, such as payment accounts and addresses, from app markets or ad providers could improve our app ownership determination.

Sharing of client IDs between different apps.

We assume that one client ID is specific to one family of similar apps. However, if a developer includes the same client ID in different apps but only some of them are in a clone cluster, we could inflate the number of impressions generated by the apps in the cluster. To verify this occurs rarely in practice, we calculated the total number of client IDs of which only a subset were in a cluster. Only 0.65% of our client IDs appear in apps both in and out of a cluster; thus, client ID sharing does not significantly impact our results.

Missing original apps.

If our database fails to include the original app for a cluster, we may overestimate the losses in cases where the missing original app is very popular. For example, we could find a large impression or user base differential between two Angry Birds clones, leading us to calculate a strong developer loss. However, by missing the original Angry Birds app we wouldn't see that it had many impressions, so the real loss

[3]http://source.android.com/

ratio is quite low. We believe this is unlikely to occur as our crawling focused on both newly published and popular apps.

Paid apps.

The estimated lost revenue and users is based on the assumption that if a clone app were unavailable, its users would have installed the original app and spent the same amount of time on it. Since we focus exclusively on free apps, it is reasonable to assume there is little difference between finding, installing, and running the original app and its clones. However, this assumption may not hold when considering paid apps.

7.2 Potential Steps to Reduce Cloning

A primary goal of our effort to gain insight into the current state of Android app cloning is to protect Android developers and users. Technical solutions such as the automatic plagiarism detection methods used for this work [6] should be employed by markets to improve the speed with which clones are caught and removed from markets. Reducing the lifetime of clones on markets limits their downloads and thus their impact.

However, as Android apps are straightforward to decompile, modify, and resubmit to markets, we do not believe technical solutions alone are sufficient. Detection tools can always continue to be improved, but it is unlikely that a tool can catch *every* clone, whether it's due to lack of access to every app across every market or significant code obfuscations. Instead, we believe reducing economic incentives is a more effective way to limit app cloning. For example, if all markets began charging at least a nominal registration fee then cloners would have to make back the registration cost from their clones before the account is banned or they will lose money. This also disincentives a plagiarist from creating many developer accounts, possibly making plagiarism detection easier. Similarly, ad providers could also charge a registration fee or delay ad revenue payout for some period of time to allow the developer's apps to be vetted. By increasing the time and/or cost to create developer accounts or sign up with ad providers, legitimate developers may be slightly affected but cloners wishing to create many developer or ad provider accounts can be significantly impeded.

We offer these potential solutions with caution, as one of the great advantages of the Android ecosystem is its openness and low barrier to entry. The associated costs must be carefully weighed to reduce cloning while not discouraging legitimate developers.

8. RELATED WORK

Malicious activities on Android.

Prior work examined information leaks within an application [9] and between applications [8]. Researchers discussed privacy violations in third-party libraries, especially advertising libraries [12, 22, 20, 24]. [29] characterized Android malware. DroidMOSS [28] and DNADroid [6] detected repackaged and cloned Android applications.

Examining the impact of malicious activities.

Kanich et al. investigated the underground economy of spam [14, 17]. Prior work examining the impact of malicious activities primarily focused on fraud that harmed the user, such as fake anti-virus software [26], keyloggers [13], and spam [25]. By contrast, application plagiarism detriments mainly the original developers of the plagiarized applications by taking away their users and advertising revenue. Online advertising fraud has been extensively studied in the literature [7, 11, 27]; however, application cloning does not necessarily imply advertising fraud because the advertiser still receives impressions and clicks from the users of cloned applications.

9. CONCLUSION

In this paper we presented AdRob, which is designed to be the first step towards understanding the economic incentives of application plagiarism on Android markets. We characterized application plagiarism and its impact on developers by crawling 265,359 free applications from 17 Android markets around the world and detecting clones among them. We captured live HTTP traffic generated by mobile applications at a tier-1 US cellular carrier for 12 days, and extracted client IDs from both applications and network traces to correlate the two datasets. Based on the data, we first examined properties of the cloned applications, including their distribution across different markets, application categories, and ad libraries. Next, we examined how cloned applications affect the origin developers. We estimated a lower bound on the revenue that cloned applications siphon from the original developers, and the user base that cloned applications divert from the original applications, and find an alarmingly high percentage of impressions is siphoned from developers who are victims of plagiarism. To the best of our knowledge, this is the first large scale study on the characteristics of cloned applications and their impact on the original developers.

10. ACKNOWLEDGEMENTS

We would like to thank Sharad Agarwal and the anonymous reviewers for their insightful feedback, as well as Liang Cai, Dennis Xu, Ben Sanders, Justin Horton, and Jon Vronsky for their assistance in obtaining Android applications. This paper is based upon work supported by the National Science Foundation under Grant No. 1018964.

References

[1] A. Andoni and P. Indyk. Near-optimal hashing algorithms for approximate nearest neighbor in high dimensions . In: *Foundations of Computer Science, 2006. FOCS'06. 47th Annual IEEE Symposium on.* Ieee. 2006, pp. 459–468.

[2] Jason Ankeny. *Feds seize Android app marketplaces Applanet, AppBucket in piracy sting.* Aug. 22, 2012. URL: `http://www.fiercemobilecontent.com/story/feds-seize-android-app-marketplaces-applanet-appbucket-piracy-sting/2012-08-22`.

[3] AppBrain. *Android Ad networks.* Mar. 2013. URL: `http://www.appbrain.com/stats/libraries/ad`.

[4] AppBrain. *Number of available android applications.* Nov. 2012. URL: `http://www.appbrain.com/stats/number-of-android-apps`.

[5] Brut.alll. *Android-Apktool.* URL: http://code.google.com/p/android-apktool.

[6] J. Crussell, C. Gibler, and H. Chen. Attack of the Clones: Detecting Cloned Applications on Android Markets . In: *Computer Security–ESORICS 2012* (2012), pp. 37–54.

[7] N. Daswani et al. Online advertising fraud . In: *Crimeware: Understanding New Attacks and Defenses* (2008).

[8] M. Dietz, S. Shekhar, Y. Pisetsky, A. Shu, and D.S. Wallach. Quire: lightweight provenance for smart phone operating systems . In: *USENIX Security.* 2011.

[9] William Enck, Landon P. Cox, and Jaeyeon Jung. TaintDroid: An Information-Flow Tracking System for Realtime Privacy Monitoring on Smartphones . In: (2010).

[10] Jesus Freke. *Smali/Baksmali.* URL: http://code.google.com/p/smali.

[11] Mona Gandhi, Markus Jakobsson, and Jacob Ratkiewicz. Badvertisements: Stealthy click-fraud with unwitting accessories . In: *Online Fraud, Part I Journal of Digital Forensic Practice, Volume 1, Special Issue 2.* 2006.

[12] M.C. Grace, W. Zhou, X. Jiang, and A.R. Sadeghi. Unsafe exposure analysis of mobile in-app advertisements . In: *Proceedings of the fifth ACM conference on Security and Privacy in Wireless and Mobile Networks.* ACM. 2012, pp. 101–112.

[13] T. Holz, M. Engelberth, and F. Freiling. Learning more about the underground economy: A case-study of keyloggers and dropzones . In: *Computer Security–ESORICS 2009* (2009), pp. 1–18.

[14] Chris Kanich et al. Show Me the Money: Characterizing Spam-advertised Revenue . In: *USENIX Security Symposium.* San Francisco, CA, Aug. 2011.

[15] *Keystore and Aliases - is there a use to multiple aliases?* Dec. 2012. URL: http://stackoverflow.com/questions/2667399/keystore-and-aliases-is-there-a-use-to-multiple-aliases.

[16] Eric Lafortune. *Proguard.* URL: http://proguard.sourceforge.net.

[17] Kirill Levchenko et al. Click Trajectories: End-to-End Analysis of the Spam Value Chain . In: *IEEE Symposium and Security and Privacy.* Oakland, CA, May 2011.

[18] H. Liu, C.N. Chuah, H. Zang, and S. Gatmir-motahari. Evolving Landscape of Cellular Network Traffic . In: *Computer Communications and Networks (ICCCN), 2012 21st International Conference on.* IEEE. 2012, pp. 1–7.

[19] *Multiple Signatures and Shared UIDs.* Dec. 2012. URL: https://groups.google.com/forum/?fromgroups=#!topic/android-security-discuss/LyyEWyFg5xc.

[20] P. Pearce, A.P. Felt, G. Nunez, and D. Wagner. AdDroid: Privilege Separation for Applications and Advertisers in Android . In: *Proceedings of the 7th ACM Symposium on Information, Computer and Communications Security.* ACM. 2012.

[21] *Security Alert: Malware Found Targeting Custom ROMs (jSMSHider).* Dec. 2012. URL: https://blog.lookout.com/blog/2011/06/15/security-alert-malware-found-targeting-custom-roms-jsmshider/.

[22] S. Shekhar, M. Dietz, and D.S. Wallach. Adsplit: Separating smartphone advertising from applications . In: *CoRR, abs/1202.4030* (2012).

[23] *Signing Your Applications.* Dec. 2012. URL: http://developer.android.com/tools/publishing/app-signing.html.

[24] R. Stevens, C. Gibler, J. Crussell, J. Erickson, and H. Chen. Investigating User Privacy in Android Ad Libraries . In: *IEEE Mobile Security Technologies (MoST), San Francisco, CA* (2012).

[25] B. Stone-Gross, T. Holz, G. Stringhini, and G. Vigna. The underground economy of spam: A botmasters perspective of coordinating large-scale spam campaigns . In: *USENIX Workshop on Large-Scale Exploits and Emergent Threats (LEET).* 2011.

[26] B. Stone-Gross et al. The underground economy of fake antivirus software . In: *Economics of Information Security and Privacy III* (2011), pp. 55–78.

[27] B. Stone-Gross et al. Understanding fraudulent activities in online ad exchanges . In: *Proceedings of the 2011 ACM SIGCOMM conference on Internet measurement conference.* ACM. 2011, pp. 279–294.

[28] W. Zhou, Y. Zhou, X. Jiang, and P. Ning. Detecting repackaged smartphone applications in third-party android marketplaces . In: *Proceedings of the second ACM conference on Data and Application Security and Privacy.* ACM. 2012, pp. 317–326.

[29] Y. Zhou and X. Jiang. Dissecting android malware: Characterization and evolution . In: *Security and Privacy (SP), 2012 IEEE Symposium on.* IEEE. 2012, pp. 95–109.

APPENDIX

Table 4: Mapping from market category strings to meta-categories. Meta-categories with just one market category are excluded.

Meta-category	Market category
Business	Business Enterprise
Entertainment	Comics Entertainment
Games	Arcade & Action Brain & Puzzle Cards & Casino Casual Fun & Games Games Racing Sports Games
Health	Health Health & Fitness Medical
Music	Music Music & Audio
News	News News & Magazines
Other	Developer / Programmer Home & Hobby Other Religion
Personalization	Personalization Wallpapers
Reference	Books & Reference E-books Ebooks & Reference Reference
Social	Collaboration Social Social Responsibility
Travel	Transportation Travel Travel & Local
Utility	Email & SMS Libraries & Demo Location & Maps Productivity System Tools Utilities
Video	Media & Video Multimedia

EnGarde: Protecting the Mobile Phone from Malicious NFC Interactions

Jeremy Gummeson[1], Bodhi Priyantha[2],
Deepak Ganesan[1], Derek Thrasher[1], Pengyu Zhang[1]
[1]University of Massachusetts Amherst, [2]Microsoft Research
{gummeson, dganesan, thrasher, pyzhang}@cs.umass.edu, bodhip@microsoft.com

ABSTRACT

Near Field Communication (NFC) on mobile phones presents new opportunities and threats. While NFC is radically changing how we pay for merchandise, it opens a pandora's box of ways in which it may be misused by unscrupulous individuals. This could include malicious NFC tags that seek to compromise a mobile phone, malicious readers that try to generate fake mobile payment transactions or steal valuable financial information, and others. In this work, we look at how to protect mobile phones from these threats while not being vulnerable to them. We design a small form-factor "patch", *EnGarde*, that can be stuck on the back of a phone to provide the capability to jam malicious interactions. *EnGarde* is entirely passive and harvests power through the same NFC source that it guards, which makes our hardware design minimalist, and facilitates eventual integration with a phone. We tackle key technical challenges in this design including operating across a range of NFC protocols, jamming at extremely low power, harvesting sufficient power for perpetual operation while having minimal impact on the phone's battery, designing an intelligent jammer that blocks only when specific blacklisted behavior is detected, and importantly, the ability to do all this without compromising user experience when the phone interacts with a legitimate external NFC device.

Categories and Subject Descriptors

C.3 [**Special-purpose and Application-based Systems**]: [Real-time and Embedded Systems]

General Terms

Security, Design, Algorithms, Experimentation, Measurement

Keywords

Near Field Communications, Passive Systems

MobiSys'13, June 25-28, 2013, Taipei, Taiwan

1. INTRODUCTION

Near Field Communication (NFC) has begun to make its way into major mobile phones, with several Android, Blackberry, and Nokia phones already providing such functionality. The proliferation of NFC on phones can open up a range of applications, from being able to interact with NFC-tagged smart posters to revolutionizing the payment industry, where phones are expected to replace credit cards as the most convenient way to pay for products at the point-of-sale.

These benefits of NFC come at a price — security becomes particularly challenging since phones are general-purpose computing devices that expose a relatively large attack surface that can be exploited by unscrupulous individuals. These issues were exposed in a recent security breach that leveraged the fact that NFC tags can be registered to open applications on a phone such as images, contacts, or web pages *without requiring user consent.* In this attack, a mobile phone was directed to a URL that hosted code that exploited a vulnerability in Android 4.1's web browser [16].

In addition to technical issues, there are also non-technical challenges at play — NFC mobile payments involve interaction between mobile phone manufacturers and OS vendors (Blackberry, Google), mobile phone operators (ATT, Verizon, etc), and banking organizations (VISA), leading to a complex and intertwined web of control. For example, viaForensics [21] announced a Google Wallet vulnerability almost a year ago, but it has yet to be patched because the fix would require a "change of agency" rather than a quick OS patch. Thus, the outcome of business interests and complex business dealings are likely to provide more opportunities for attacks that target the fuzzy boundaries between these entities.

Existing efforts attempt to address these security concerns in several ways. First, many mobile operating systems turn off the NFC interface when the screen is locked. But if the OS is compromised, a malicious rootkit can keep the NFC interface turned on when the screen is locked, thereby thwarting this defense. Second, mobile payments ask the user to provide a four digit pin before an NFC-initiated payment. However, this is also vulnerable to attacks such as the one demonstrated in [5], where the pin code was inferred by looking at data stored by an NFC payment application. Once the pin-code is cracked, a rootkit can potentially bypass user input entirely and make a mobile payment that the user is completely unaware of. Third, phones can use hardware (secure elements) that provides security guarantees for mobile payments ([14, 20]), but such hardware is not available for phones acting as readers. Thus, none of the mechanisms fully address the scope of security issues presented by NFC.

We argue that there is a need for a hardware-based "NFC guardian", *EnGarde*, that is perpetually attached to the phone, and acts as an NFC firewall that allows legitimate interactions to occur as normal, while blocking unwanted NFC interactions through jamming. While the idea of jamming unwanted interactions is reminiscent of RFID blockers [17], practical instantiations of such ideas are bulky systems with large power draw, and consequently not in wide use. In contrast, our design is small, passively powered, and can be fully integrated on a mobile phone, thereby making it entirely practical.

In addition to jamming, one of our goals is to design a tool that can be invaluable to security concerned individuals that seek more insight into the low-level behavior of their phone's NFC interface. For example, unexpected data usage by an official NFC application, Google Wallet, has been reported in several forums [1] but the lack of visibility makes it difficult to determine whether this is the result of interactions with external NFC devices. Creating a tool that puts the user in control of the interface, rather than the operating system, could satiate some of these concerns until the security implications of NFC on mobile phones are better understood.

Our design contributions are four-fold. First, *EnGarde* has the form-factor of a self-contained and self-powered thin pad that attaches to the back of the phone, and is agnostic of mobile operating system differences as well as idiosyncrasies of different dock connectors. Second, *EnGarde* is easy to use since it operates entirely through power scavenged from the NFC reader on mobile phones (or external readers accessing the phone). Thus, it requires zero effort on the part of user to change batteries, and only has a small effect on the phone in terms of overall harvesting needs. Third, *EnGarde* defends against a wide range of passive tag and active reader based attacks that cover the spectrum of NFC protocols and operational modes including those that target the phone a) in reader mode interacting with a malicious tag, b) in tag mode interacting with a malicious reader, and c) in active peer-to-peer mode interacting with a malicious phone. Fourth, *EnGarde* can be programmed to trigger upon detecting specific types of messages, protocols, or transactions that are indicative of security violations, and disrupt these interactions through jamming.

Our design presents a range of technical challenges that we address in this work. First, we dramatically reduce power consumption during jamming by requiring no active transmission in most cases; rather we leverage the NFC carrier wave to generate an interfering subcarrier while scavenging energy. Second, we design algorithms that maximize the energy scavenging efficiency from the phone while simultaneously minimizing the power footprint on the phone. Third, we design an early warning mechanism that detects presence or absence of an NFC device in the vicinity without any communication occurring between the phone and the device, thereby enabling *EnGarde* to stay out of the way when there is a legitimate transaction as well as to prime itself to thwart an illegitimate one. Fourth, we prototype the complete system and hardware, and demonstrate that all of the outlined capabilities can fit in a flat form-factor of roughly five square inches, demonstrating its practicality.

Our results show that:

- ▶ We can jam tag responses with 100% success rate while consuming only 6.4 μW of power, which is considerably more efficient than prior approaches that have used active jamming.
- ▶ We can accurately detect tag presence with an accuracy of 95% under a wide range of conditions, while having negligible impact on legitimate communications.
- ▶ We can continuously power *EnGarde* solely through NFC-based power scavenging, while being 4× more efficient than a naive harvesting approach that does not consider the host phone's power consumption.
- ▶ We can defend successfully against attacks similar to a known URL attack scenario, and show that we can detect and block a particular NDEF URL type with 100% accuracy, while allowing other NDEF messages to reach the phone unimpeded.

2. DESIGN REQUIREMENTS

In this section, we discuss some of the requirements that we used as the rationale for our design choices in *EnGarde*.

Protect all NFC Modes: A central design goal is protecting all NFC modes implemented on a mobile phone. This means that *EnGarde* should be able to block NFC messages between the phone and external entity whether the phone is acting as a reader or in tag emulation mode. The specific types of attacks *EnGarde* should protect against are:

- ▶ Malicious tags deployed in infrastructure (such as tags with URLs). When the phone discovers and interprets the tag's information, it is instructed to take some action that compromises the phone's security; this could be the phone being directed to a malicious web site. In this attack, we need to protect the phone while it acts as a reader and block communication before the phone receives the malicious data. This type of attack is well known in the security community as "fuzzing".
- ▶ A Phone encounters a malicious device in peer-to-peer mode. Since this type of interaction can support arbitrary file transfer, the phone is vulnerable to whatever content is transferred from its peer. *EnGarde* would need to detect and block these malicious data transfers.
- ▶ An external reader reads and discovers the ID used by the phone while in tag emulation mode. This would mean that an external entity would be able to track the location of a particular phone user each time the ID is read, compromising their privacy. Additionally, a similar attack could result in the user's financial information being compromised if it were sent in the clear. *EnGarde* should block the release of this information. This type of attack is well known in the security community as "identity theft".
- ▶ A user inadvertently installs an application on their mobile phone that uses the NFC interface for malicious purposes. The user's phone may then subsequently be used by an attacker to perform any of the attacks above.

Transparently Powered: *EnGarde* should integrate with a mobile phone in the most transparent way possible. For example, one way to power *EnGarde* would be to connect it via the phone's dock connector which could then be used to supply power. However, this would leave *EnGarde* completely unpowered if a user connects a different peripheral to the dock or charges the phone and forgets to plug in *EnGarde*; instead, we advocate a passively powered mechanism where *EnGarde* harvests power from the NFC interface while the phone is actively being used. We also note that powering the phone in this way would allow *EnGarde* to function independently from a *potentially* compromised operating system. Thus, *EnGarde* should be a physically separate piece of hardware that does not rely on a wired interface for power.

No impact on usability: We wanted *EnGarde* to be almost invisible, both in terms of physical form factor as well as in its effect on the usability of the phone for legitimate NFC transactions. This meant that *EnGarde* should be small enough that it can be a patch stuck on a phone (or eventually integrated with a phone's battery). Additionally, *EnGarde* should not diminish user experience for NFC transactions that a user wishes to make. In other words, there should be negligible effect in terms of packet loss rates or distance at which NFC transactions are possible if a legitimate NFC device is communicating with the phone.

Programmable Rules: Given that the types of NFC vulnerabilities will almost certainly evolve as new attacks are discovered and known attacks are patched, we want to have a fully programmable platform where the rules upon which to jam can be specified. These rules can range from blocking all exchanges of a certain type (e.g. payments), blocking exchanges with tags that contain a URL and use the browser, blocking when certain sensitive information is transmitted in clear text, and so on. Thus, *EnGarde* should be programmable, and block only those interactions that are known to be vulnerable, while allowing other messages to get through to the phone.

Fail Safe: Since *EnGarde* relies on energy scavenging, one question is what happens if it runs out of power; this may occur after a long period after the phone is idle. In particular, since *EnGarde* decodes messages and jams only when malicious interactions were detected, what would happen if the microcontroller that makes this decision is unable to operate? The duration when *EnGarde* is charging provides a window of opportunity to an attacker. Thus, a key requirement is that *EnGarde* should fail safely, i.e. when the MCU does not have sufficient power to make intelligent jamming decisions, it should default to a mode where it jams NFC interactions as soon as the phone initiates NFC discovery until the MCU is able to operate and make a more judicious decision. In this manner, the phone is protected whether or not *EnGarde* has charge.

3. AN OVERVIEW OF NFC

NFC is a relatively new technology. In this section, we give an overview of NFC by examining the underlying communication standards, protocols, and physical layer characteristics. The design of *EnGarde* is heavily influenced by these details.

3.1 NFC Communication Layer

NFC uses High Frequency (HF) RFID as its communication layer. The NFC standard requires that a compliant

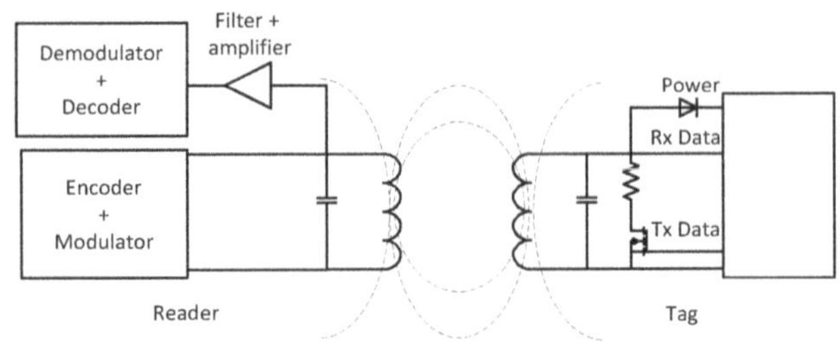

Figure 1: Functional block diagram of HF RFID reader and tag.

device be compatible with all existing HF RFID communication layer standards. HF RFID is used to communicate between a *tag* and a *reader*. The tag contains a globally unique ID and some data which is optionally writable by a reader. The tag is a passive electronic device which is powered by the reader during communication.

The reader powers tags in its vicinity using a magnetic field. Before communicating with a tag, the reader runs a discovery protocol to discover the tags in its vicinity. If multiple tags are found, a collision avoidance protocol is used to identify individual tags. Once a tag is discovered, the reader uses the tag ID to uniquely address the tag for reading and writing tag data.

Since the reader generates the magnetic field to power the tag, the communication is always reader initiated. During each interaction, the reader generates the field and sends a message addressed to a specific tag; the tag, after interpreting the reader message, sends a reply.

Figure 1 shows the basic components of the HF reader and tag. The reader generates a magnetic field at 13.56MHz using a tuned reader coil; the tag has a coil tuned to the same frequency. Due to the magnetic coupling between these coils, similar to the operation of an electrical transformer, the reader coil induces a voltage in the tag coil. This AC voltage is converted to a DC voltage to power the tag electronics. Since magnetic field strength decays rapidly with distance, NFC systems have a typical range of a few centimeters (with larger reader antennas and high-power readers, the communication range can go up to 1 meter).

Reader to tag communication: Reader to tag communications use Amplitude Modulation (AM) of the 13.56MHz carrier. The carrier amplitude variation causes a corresponding variation of the voltage induced at the tag's coil.

The tag decodes this signal variation using a simple circuit. Different communication protocol standards use AM as a primitive to encode data using different coding techniques. Table 1 shows various protocol standards and modulation formats.

Tag to reader communication: Tag to reader communications use load modulation, where the load across the tag coil is varied by switching on and off a parallel resistor (or a capacitor). Since the tag coil receives its power from the reader coil, the varying load causes a varying current and a voltage at the reader coil.

The load modulation is used to generate a 847.5kHz sub carrier which is encoded using different coding techniques (Table 1).

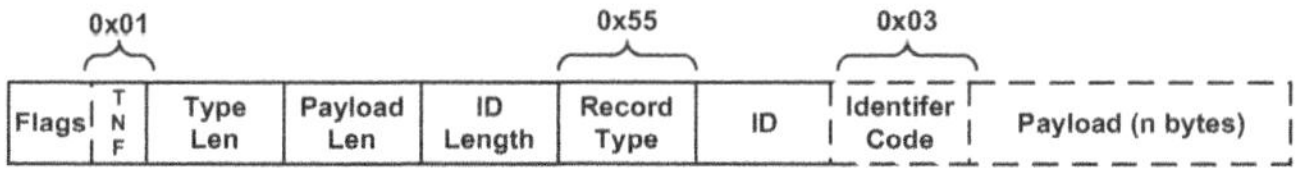

Figure 2: An NDEF message has a regular structure and holds an NDEF record. This one contains a URL that uses a prefix of "http://"

3.2 NFC Device-Level Interactions

Although NFC is based on HF RFID technology, NFC has more capabilities than discovery, reading, and writing of RFID tags by a reader.

Communication modes. Unlike a traditional reader or a tag, an an NFC-enabled phone can take on multiple roles:

Phone as a reader: In this mode, the NFC enabled mobile phone behaves as an RFID reader. The phone periodically runs a tag discovery loop to identify compatible tags in its vicinity, and establishes communication with them. This mode is typically used to scan QR-code like tags that contain a short piece of information such as phone numbers and URLs.

Phone as an emulated tag: In this mode, called *tag emulation* mode, the mobile phone behaves like an RFID tag – an external reader can discover and interact with the phone. Since the NFC-related circuitry is powered by the reader's magnetic field, this mode can be active even when the phone has no power. This mode is typically used for mobile payments in transit card-like applications.

Phone as a peer: Here the phone communicates in a peer to peer mode with another NFC enabled device such as a phone. In this mode, which is typically entered after one device discovers the other, both parties take turns generating the carrier. This communication mode supports the highest rate of communication and is used to share small files between mobile phones.

NDEF standard. The NFC Data Exchange Format (NDEF) provides a common language that enables HF RFID tags, which could be based on different HF standards, to exchange data. The well known NDEF message has a regular structure – In Figure 2, we show an example of one such NDEF message. This particular message contains a record that conforms to a well-defined type, as indicated by the TNF field being set to `0x01`. The ID field of the message increases the degree of specificity – the particular well defined type is a URI, as indicated by the Record Type field being set to `0x55`. The last field in an NDEF message contains the NDEF record; in a URI record, the first byte contains a prefix that is applied to the message. This particular URI uses an identifier code of `0x03` to apply the prefix `http://`; other options could have been `0x00` or `0x04` for example, which correspond to `no prefix` and `https://` respectively.

Platform support. In addition to the various protocols and messaging formats available, there are also differences in how NFC is supported across platforms. We summarize some of these differences in Table 2. All platforms we looked at disallow use of the phone as a reader while the screen is locked. A couple of key differences are that Blackberry 7

	Coding Forward	Coding Reverse	Bit Rate kbps
ISO 15693	1 out of 4/256	Manchester	1.65, 6.62, 26.48
ISO 14443-A	Mod. Miller	Manchester	106, 212, 424
ISO 14443-B	NRZ-L	BPSK	106, 212, 424
Sony FeliCa	ASK	Manchester	212, 424
ISO 18092	Mod. Miller Manchester	Manchester	106, 212,424

Table 1: Summary of NFC Forum Supported Protocols

Platform	Card Emulation Support
Android 4.1	While screen unlocked; only Google Wallet
Windows Phone 8	While screen unlocked/locked; Restricted applications
Blackberry 7	While screen unlocked/locked/off; Any user application supported

Table 2: The management of tag emulation mode varies across platforms.

and Windows Phone 8 allow card emulation mode to work while the screen is locked. In fact, Blackberry 7 allows any user application to access card emulation mode; however, only core applications have access to the secure element. *EnGarde* is designed to operate across all these platforms and operating systems.

4. IDENTIFYING NFC PROTOCOLS

One of our design requirements is that *EnGarde* supports programmable blacklisting rules, which implies that it should be able to both listen to, and interpret all possible NFC message exchanges in real time, and decide which ones to block and which ones to allow. However, this requires that *EnGarde* be able to decode a wide range of NFC modulation formats to determine which of the NFC protocols is being used so that it can determine the information content in them.

While this may seem similar to what an NFC reader does to read tags that support different NFC formats, there is a key difference. When an NFC reader establishes communication with another NFC device, it first goes through a discovery phase composed of multiple RFID protocol-dependent discovery messages. Hence, when a reader discovers a tag, the reader identifies and agrees upon the modulation protocol to be used with that tag. In contrast, *EnGarde* does not know what protocol is currently being used, and needs to search through all possible protocols to determine which one is correct.

One option to perform such a search might be to use a software radio, but this has significant limitations. The first column in Table 3 shows the modulation pulse width for different protocols varies by more than an order of magnitude; this implies that a software radio would need to sample the carrier at the highest rate required to decode all these protocols, and then search through the signal to identify the current protocol. However, this would result in considerable energy overhead, both because of the high rate of car-

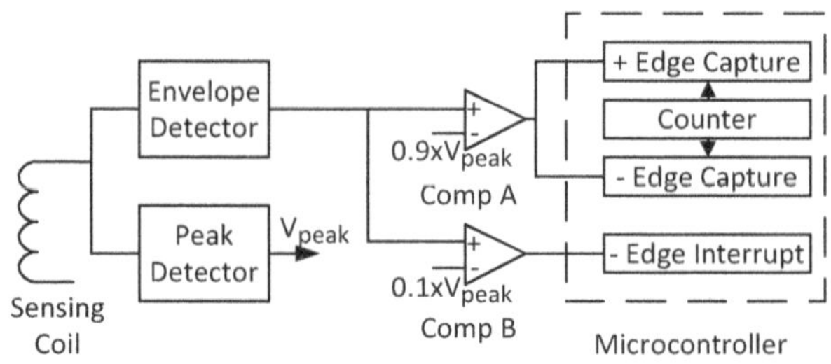

Figure 3: *EnGarde*classifies different NFC protocols by examing a signal's carrier pulse characteristics.

rier sampling (e.g. detecting NFC 15693 requires 31× lower sampling rate than for NFC 14443-A), and because of the substantial processing overhead of performing the search. Thus, it is critical to find a cheaper option for identifying the protocol.

Leverage reader-to-tag messages. Our key idea is to leverage the reader to tag portion of the each communication round. During each reader and tag interaction, the reader initiates the communication with an ASK modulated signal, while tags respond back with a subcarrier modulated signal. The ASK modulated carrier signal requires very limited energy resources to decode. We can simply examine the first pulse of the amplitude modulated carrier at the start of an NFC message to group the protocol into several categories. Table 3 shows how different pulse characteristics map to different protocols.

Low-power protocol detector. Figure 3 shows the HW implementation of such a detector that does the first level of protocol classification. *EnGarde* uses a small "sampling coil", consisting of a couple of turns, to sample the RF signal. Two comparators are used to detect the pulse edges and the modulation depth of the envelope of the modulated carrier signal. A HW timer-based capture units of a microcontroller enable the measuring of this pulse width with an accuracy of 0.5 μs; an interrupt pin captures the ASK modulation type. The power consumption of the analog portion of this circuit is only 34 μW.

Once the protocol is assigned to one of the subgroups, a lightweight software solution can uniquely identify the specific protocol by examining the first few starting bytes. Once the RFID protocol is identified, we use an off-the-shelf NFC reader chip for decoding the data.

5. JAMMING NFC COMMUNICATION

Once malicious activity is suspected by examining ongoing message exchanges, *EnGarde* should disrupt the communication by jamming. While past work on protecting RFID transactions has used active jamming techniques, this requires several 100 mWs of power, which is much higher than what we can afford on *EnGarde*. Our goal is to design a cheaper jamming mechanism, that operates within the constraints of the energy that we can scavenge.

Since NFC communication has two distinct phases — reader communication and tag response–we look at these cases separately, and design jamming primitives for each of them. We then show how these primitives can be used to effectively jam the different NFC protocols.

Pulse (μs)	OOK	ISO Protocol and speed (kbps)
0.29	N	14443A-848
0.59	N	14443A-424
1.18	N	18092-424, 14443A-212, Felica-424
2.36	N	18092-212, 14443B-424, Felica-212
2.36	Y	18092-106, 14443A-106
4.72	N	14443B-212
9.44	N	14443B-106, 15693
9.44	Y	15693

Table 3: Different protocols that map to given characteristics of the 1st carrier modulation pulse of a NFC data packet.

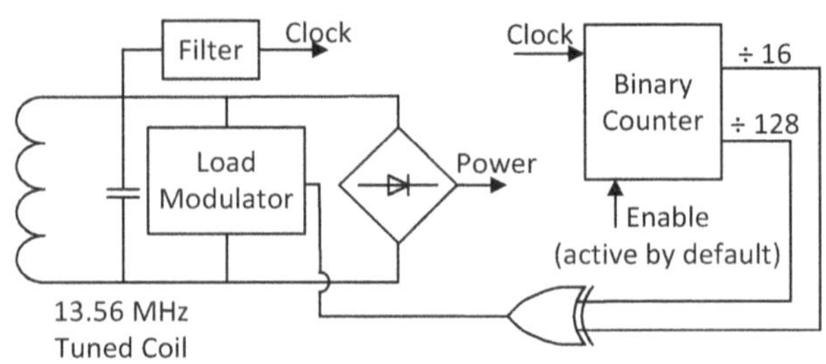

Figure 4: *EnGarde* harvests energy and blocks malicious tags using a load modulation-based tag jamming circuit.

5.1 Jamming Primitives

There are two jamming primitives, which we call *reflective jamming* and *pulse jamming* based on what communication modality is being jammed.

Reflective jamming. Tag-to-reader communication uses load modulation of the tag antenna using a subcarrier frequency. Our key observation is that all NFC protocols use a *common 847.5kHz subcarrier*, irrespective of the communication data rate used. Hence, to jam ongoing tag response communications, *EnGarde* only needs to generate a 847.5kHz subcarrier using load modulation of the tuned coil. Such a load-based modulation is particularly attractive since this is exactly what a typical NFC tag needs to perform, and hence can be easily done using energy scavenged from the ongoing communication that is being jammed.

A hardware implementation of such a subcarrier-based jammer is shown in Figure 4 (based on an NFC tag reference design in [9]). This circuit is similar to an NFC tag in that the jamming electronics are completely powered by the energy scavenged from the reader. The circuit has minimal components and therefore consumes little power. Our measurements show that subcarrier generation only consumes 6.4 μW of power.

Pulse jamming. Unlike jamming a tag response, jamming a reader (or a peer device) requires *EnGarde* to generate an active magnetic field transmission that interferes with an ongoing reader transmission. However, as we described earlier, generating active transmissions that are capable of swamping the signal from the reader would require 100s of mW of power (e.g. the TI TRF7970A RFID reader consumes as much as 250 mW). This would be almost an order of magnitude more power than what can be scavenged on *EnGarde*, making it infeasible for our purposes.

Our approach to address this problem is to generate a targeted pulse that disrupts an ongoing communication. Since different ASK-based carrier modulation schemes require carrier modulations at bit-time durations, a carrier pulse only needs to be $\simeq 20\ \mu s$ (2 bit durations at the lowest data rate) long in-order to corrupt the message. Such a pulse-based jamming mechanism is orders of magnitude shorter than the duration of the shortest valid NFC message, which means that it can easily be supported via scavenged energy.

Our pulse-based jamming approach has one drawback — it is possible that a high-powered NFC reader generates a strong enough signal that our attempts at corrupting the signal does not result in a sufficiently high signal-strength difference, and is therefore unsuccessful. While this is a weakness of the technique, we think that we would block a large fraction of reader transmissions, particularly because *EnGarde* would be much closer to the phone than an external NFC device that is initiating such a signal.

5.2 Jamming During NFC Communication

Given the two primitives, we now look at how to use them to jam different NFC communication modes.

- *Tag Reader Mode:* In this mode, the phone acts as an RFID reader and reads passive tag content. A possible attack could be a malicious tag that directs the mobile phone to a malicious website. In this mode, *EnGarde* uses subcarrier-based jamming to disrupt the data exchange with the tag.
- *Tag Emulation Mode:* Here, the phone acts as a tag and responds to queries from another NFC device (a phone or an infrastructure reader). In this mode, *EnGarde* can use the subcarrier-based jamming to prevent leakage of sensitive information from the phone.
- *Peer-to-Peer Mode:* During this mode, the phone and an external NFC device exchanges information by both actively transmitting signals. *EnGarde* needs to transmit a jamming pulse signal to block malicious interactions in this instance. While *EnGarde* may not be able to block malicious high power transmitters, we note that peer-to-peer interaction starts with a discovery step during which nearby devices are discovered. Hence, subcarrier-based jamming can be used at this stage to disrupt the establishment of a peer-to-peer communication thereby nipping such a transaction in the bud.

6. ENERGY SCAVENGING

Energy scavenging is central to the design of *EnGarde* since it allows the device to operate perpetually despite having a small energy buffer. Our approach is to leverage the same inductive coupling based harvesting mechanism that NFC tags use when communicating with the phone. This gives *EnGarde* the unique ability to jam communications while at the same time scavenging energy from the source.

Harvesting Strategy	Phone's NFC Duty Cycle	Phone Power Consumption Overhead	Energy Transfer Efficiency
Opportunistic	10.1%	0 mW	17.30%
Tag-Spoofing	33.3%	27.2 mW	19.16%
Subcarrier	86.6%	154.1 mW	12.49%
Full NFC	100%	287.4 mW	8.04%

Table 4: Several different harvesting strategies offer a tradeoff between harvesting rate and transfer efficiency between a phone and *EnGarde*. A completely opportunistic strategy harvests small amounts of power, but with no additional power consumption on the phone. In contrast, a strategy that keeps the phone's NFC interface active 100% of the time harvests the most power, but with significantly more power consumption on the mobile phone.

While NFC enables energy transfer, one question is how much power can be harvested by *EnGarde* from the phone, and how much power is expended by the phone for this transfer. To understand this, we measure the power draw of the phone using a Monsoon power meter on a Samsung Galaxy Nexus phone running Android 4.1 (Jelly Bean) when an NFC tag is in front of the phone vs when NFC is completely turned off. We also measure the peak AC power harvested on *EnGarde* during NFC activity. Our results show that the phone's carrier is continuously switched on, hence we are able to harvest 30 mW of power at *EnGarde*. This means that *EnGarde* can potentially have a fairly significant power profile. However, we also see that the phone consumes 301.5 mW of power during this process, i.e. the transfer efficiency is only 9.95%. In this section, we ask how to balance the need to buffer sufficient energy in *EnGarde*'s energy buffer while maximizing transfer efficiency so that *EnGarde* has only a small impact on the phone's battery.

6.1 Scavenging mechanisms

We now outline three scavenging alternatives that have better power transfer efficiency than the full-NFC mode for scavenging power from the phone.

Opportunistic. The first harvesting mode, which we refer to as *opportunistic*, is essentially for the tag to do nothing special, and just opportunistically harvest energy coming from discovery messages that are transmitted by the phone. When a phone is unlocked, the phone sends out discovery messages periodically (10% duty-cycle) to check for the presence of nearby devices. The advantage of this mode is that the phone incurs no additional overhead beyond what it is already incurring.

The transfer efficiency in this mode reveals a surprising result — the average power consumed by the phone increases only by 14.1 mW for transmitting discovery messages, which gives us a transfer efficiency of 17.3%, which is almost twice the transfer efficiency when the phone is in full NFC active mode. The likely cause for the difference in efficiency seems to be that the bulk of the NFC protocol is implemented on a dedicated NFC reader chip. Only valid responses from an NFC tag results in interrupts that are handled by the phone's operating system. Thus, when an NFC tag is transmitting valid responses, additional CPU cycles must be spent handling the read events, resulting in the extra power consumption. In summary, opportunistic harvesting is efficient but *EnGarde* only gets 10% of the power that it would have received were the phone's carrier is continually active.

Tag-Spoofing. The second harvesting mode, which we refer to as *tag-spoofing*, tries to trick the dedicated NFC chip into delivering more power without interrupting the Android OS as frequently as in full NFC mode. To implement this strategy, we look at how an NFC reader performs initial detection of tag presence. After sending energy to a potential tag, the first hint that a tag may actually be present is looking for a change in the voltage of the carrier it sent to a tag. A transponder influences this voltage by *modulating* its transponder coil. If a reader observes this change in voltage, it may decide to send additional energy for subsequent communications.

We test this theory by modulating the harvesting coil via a resistor using a short pulse that is 10 μs in length. Indeed, we found that this did result in the phone providing more power for a short period, after which it times out and reverts to discovery mode. The process can be repeated to ensure that the reader continues to provide additional power.

This harvesting strategy results in the phone's subcarrier being active for 33.3% of the time, so *EnGarde* gets about three times the power that was harvested in opportunistic mode, but it also incurs 41 mW of overhead on the phone (i.e. 27 mW more than for discovery messages). However, the transfer efficiency is high at about 19%, which is even higher than what was obtained in opportunistic mode.

Subcarrier. Our third harvesting mode, *subcarrier*, closes the gap between tag-spoofing and full-NFC in terms of amount of harvested power at *EnGarde*. As discussed in §??, jamming is performed by generating an 848 kHz subcarrier. Our measurements show that *subcarrier* is able to increase the amount of time the phone's transmitted carrier is active to 86.6%, and results in 168.2 mW of harvesting overhead on the phone. This yields a transfer efficiency of 12.49%, which, while not as good as the opportunistic and tag-spoofing modes, is about 50% better in efficiency than the full-NFC mode while giving *EnGarde* close to the maximum average power.

6.2 Demand Harvesting Algorithm

We now have three harvesting schemes that are more efficient than full NFC mode — opportunistic, tag spoofing, and subcarrier — that give us different options in terms of the amount of energy scavenged by *EnGarde*, as well as the efficiency of energy transfer.

We now describe a demand-based harvesting algorithm that runs on *EnGarde* and ensures that sufficient power is harvested from the phone to maintain its energy buffer at close to its maximum capacity, while minimizing the energy cost incurred by the mobile phone to transfer power. The algorithm works in two steps: First, it estimates the length of the next unlock interval by observing history of phone use. We use a simple EWMA filter over the history of unlock durations in our implementation. Second, it uses the estimated unlock duration to determine the fraction of time to use each harvesting mode. Intuitively, if the buffer can be filled up just using opportunistic harvesting, then this is the cheapest approach since discovery messages are transmitted by the phone whether or not *EnGarde* is harvesting this power. If this is not sufficient to replenish energy in the buffer, then the algorithm needs to decide how to use a combination of the other two harvesting modes to ensure that the buffer is filled while maximizing transfer efficiency.

We formally define the parameters described in the model as: a) T is the current estimate of unlock duration from an EWMA-based estimator, b) B is the current energy buffer level, and B_{max} is the desired energy level, c) $\{E_{opp}, E_{so}, E_{sub}\}$ are the Energy harvested from {opportunistic, tag-spoofing, subcarrier} modes if they were exclusively used for the time T, d) $\{C_{so}, C_{sub}\}$ represents the phone energy overhead for tag spoofing and subcarrier modes; note that the overhead in opportunistic mode, $C_{opp} = 0$, since the phone is expending this energy whether or not *EnGarde* is present, and e) $\{f_{opp}, f_{so}, f_{sub}\}$ are the fraction of time opportunistic, tag-spoofing and subcarrier modes are used within the interval T, where $f_{opp} + f_{so} + f_{sub} = 1$.

Our optimization problem can now be formulated as minimizing the overhead on the phone, where overhead is defined as the additional energy that the phone needs to use above and beyond what it is expended in opportunistic harvesting mode, given the constraints that the total energy harvested in time T should be sufficient to get the buffer to B_{max}.

$$\begin{aligned}
&\textit{min:} && Tf_{so}(C_{so} - C_{opp}) + Tf_{sub}(C_{sub} - C_{opp})) \\
&\textit{subject to:} && E_{opp}f_{opp} + E_{so}f_{so} + E_{sub}f_{sub} + B = B_{max} \\
& && f_{opp} + f_{so} + f_{sub} = 1 \\
& && f_{opp} > 0, f_{so} > 0, f_{sub} > 0
\end{aligned}$$

This linear optimization can be simplified using well-known approximation methods to run in real-time on *EnGarde*. The intuition behind the approximation is that $f_i, i = \{so, sub\}$ should be chosen to maximize the harvested energy E_i while minimizing the cost C_i. Thus, the ratio of $\frac{E_i}{C_i}$ determines the selection between tag-spoofing and subcarrier modes – since opportunistic mode has zero overhead, it will be used whenever possible.

7. NFC DEVICE DETECTION

The ability to detect the presence or absence of an NFC device in the vicinity of the phone is important in two ways: a) *EnGarde* can avoid disrupting legitimate interactions between the phone and an NFC device (smart tag, payment station, etc), and b) *EnGarde* can stop jamming when it detects that the offending device is no longer in the phone's vicinity, and is thus no longer a threat.

One approach to solving this problem would be to look at the message interactions to determine whether or not there is another NFC device present. The phone switches from discovery mode to active mode (or software tag emulation mode) once it starts communicating with another device in the vicinity. Since *EnGarde* has the capability to decode messages, it can detect a message that indicates the start of an interaction with another device.

However, this solution has a problem. If *EnGarde* is harvesting energy in any of the three modes, even if just harvesting opportunistically, it hampers the coupling between the phone and the external device. This means that we need to detect devices prior to communication occurring between them. Similarly, while we are jamming, we cannot decode messages to detect when the NFC device leaves the vicinity of the phone, and therefore when we should stop jamming.

Our solution to this problem has two key contributions: a) a reliable and fast NFC device detector that leverages changes in mutual coupling, and b) a dual-coil hardware design that includes a harvesting coil and a sampling coil that are tailored to different needs.

7.1 Mutual Coupling-based NFC Detection

Our key idea to detect the presence of an NFC device leverages the manner in which inductive coupling works when several coils are present. NFC coils operate using the property of electromagnetic induction *i.e.* one coil induces a voltage in the other coil (mutual inductance). If multiple coils are present in the vicinity of an inductor, then the mutual inductance is split across these two coils. Therefore, the voltage induced in each of the coils reduces. Our idea is to detect this change in voltage at the output of the rectifier, and use it as an indicator of the presence of another NFC device.

One drawback of such a detector is that nearby metallic materials that couple, may have the same effect on voltage. When a coil generating a magnetic field is brought near a conductive material such as aluminum, it induces eddy currents that reduce the amount of flux detected in *EnGarde*. However, we argue that false positives are not a significant concern since if *EnGarde* detects no NFC interaction for a time period, it can revert to harvesting mode.

To test this theory we attach a tuned coil and voltage regulator circuit to a Galaxy Nexus phone and bring tags of various technologies in proximity of the phone / harvester pair. In Figure 5, we plot the voltage across the rectifier. The plot shows two interesting observations. First, we see that the decrease in voltage is proportional to the amount of power the tag draws. A simple tag, such as an ISO 14443-A Charlie card transportation transponder, has a small impact, while a more complex tag, such as an ISO 14443-B EEPROM tag, has a much more noticeable impact. Second, we see that, as expected, other metallic objects (in this case a large aluminum plane) also causes large voltage changes.

To ensure reliable NFC device detection, we tune the detection threshold such that even a slight dip in the voltage compared to no tag being present causes *EnGarde* to backoff. To test our detector, we placed a set of tags (same as those used in Figure 5) in and out of the proximity of the phone and turned the phone's screen on and off. The results are over 100 such tag presence events, and we observe a detection accuracy of 95%, which shows that we only miss a small fraction of the cases. Note that even in these cases where a tag is not detected, *EnGarde* is still securing the phone since it is continuously listening for any message interaction that could be indicative of malicious behavior. The only downside of missed detection is a diminished user experience since the phone might need to be moved closer to the tag to ensure that *EnGarde* backs off and enables communication to occur.

7.2 Dual-coil Design

What should *EnGarde* do when an NFC device is detected in the vicinity? One option is to have a switch and detach the load from the coil, but in doing so, *EnGarde* loses the

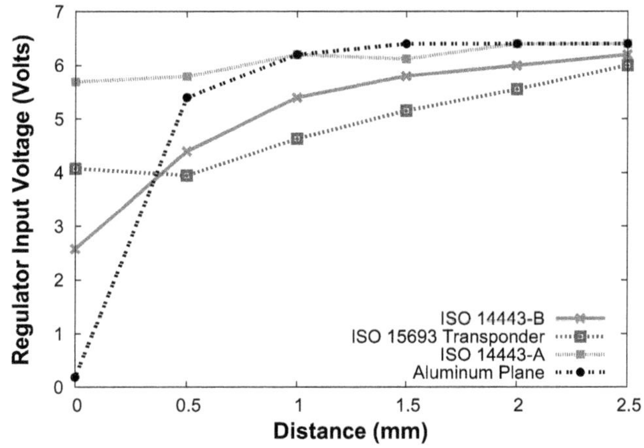

Figure 5: The presence of NFC transponders can be identified by observing a change in the output of a voltage rectifier; tag technologies that draw more power see a larger change in voltage. The presence of metal causes a huge change in voltage over a short range.

ability to listen to messages and decide when to jam based on message content.

Our key insight is that we can decode communications by using a small "sampling" coil that has fewer turns and is detuned to the carrier, and use a "harvesting" coil solely for harvesting and jamming purposes. The sampling coil would reduce the level of interference to be small enough not to impact communication between the tag and external device while still retaining the ability to decode messages.

To understand how well our dual-coil design works, we look at the cases when the coil is connected and disconnected from our harvesting circuit. With the harvesting coil disconnected, we measured an average communication latency of 20 ms across a set of ISO 14443-A, ISO 14443-B, and ISO 15693 tags. In all test cases, we found that the phone was able to read the tags even though *EnGarde* was physically present. We then connect it to our harvesting coil and repeat the previous experiment. We found that while harvesting power, tags had an increase in communication latency of 3 ms. We also found that in a handful of test cases (15% of the cases we tested), ISO 14443-B EEPROM based tags could not successfully read. This emphasizes the importance of the tag detection as described above.

8. ENGARDE IMPLEMENTATION

Figure 7 shows a prototype version of *EnGarde*; our current hardware implements all the design elements, except for pulse jamming, described in §5.1. The current prototype measures 2.0 by 2.6 inches, and is well within the form-factor of a typical smartphone. We believe that future revisions can shrink this even further. We now briefly describe the key hardware sub-components used in the prototype and describe its operation using a state machine abstraction that uses the hardware primitives to enable selective jamming.

8.1 Hardware

The goal of our *EnGarde* implementation was to build a form-factor prototype that can actually be attached to the

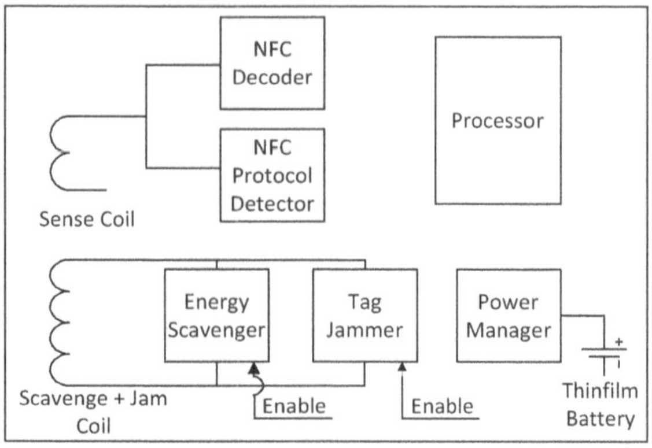

Figure 6: *EnGarde* is implemented across several subsystems that provide power, jam, and enforce a set of programmable blocking rules.

Figure 7: *EnGarde* is implemented as a low-profile printed circuit board with small form factor.

back of a mobile phone. We show how hardware subcomponents are interconnected in Figure 6.

The first key hardware element is a small "sensing" coil that is used to sense the magnetic field in vicinity of the phone. The NFC protocol detector module uses this coil's output to detect the active NFC protocol type. The NFC decoder block uses the sense coil's output and the Rx chain of a TI TRF7970A NFC reader; the reader is configured in software by the microcontroller to decode a particular RFID protocol. The sense coil's output is also used by the microcontroller for tag presence detection.

The next key design element is a tuned coil and a capacitor arranged in parallel; this coil is used for both jamming and energy scavenging. The jamming module is controlled by the onboard microcontroller and may be enabled or disabled depending on security or harvesting needs. One important characteristic of this circuit is that it fails safe if *EnGarde*'s energy buffer is depleted – this enables protection against malicious transactions and also improves the energy available via scavenging (Section 6).

A critical element of our hardware design is the energy scavenging module used to harvest energy from active reader transmissions. This module can be disabled to reduce the impact on the phone's NFC communications (Section 7). Since the microcontroller needs energy to boot, the scavenging module, much like the jamming module, defaults to active mode in the event that the energy buffer is depleted. Since jamming is based on load modulation, jamming is automatically disabled when the scavenging module is disabled.

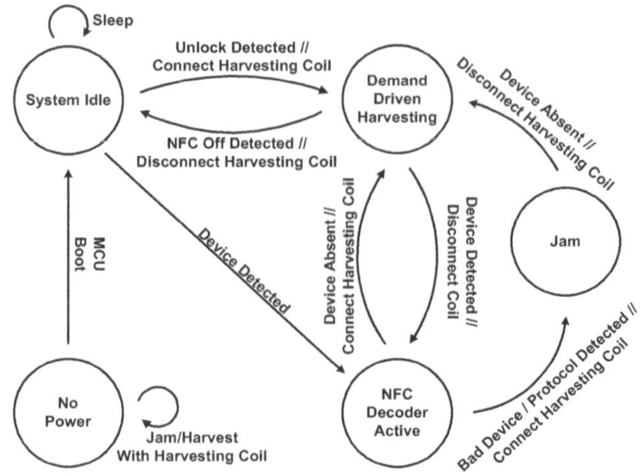

Figure 8: *EnGarde* switches between several different operational states to harvest energy, detect NFC devices, decode messages, and jam malicious NFC devices.

To condition harvested energy for storage, a MAX17710 battery manager chip manages the charging of the on-board Thinergy MEC201 1 mAH thinfilm battery. The use of a diminutive thin-film battery is particularly compelling, since *EnGarde* needs to minimize thickness in addition to length and width.

Finally, an MSP430F2274 16-bit low power microcontroller manages the various sub-components of *EnGarde*. This particular microcontroller was chosen because it has an ADC that enables tag detection, has low power operating modes and can transition between power states quickly.

8.2 State Machine

EnGarde follows the state machine shown in Figure 8. When *EnGarde* is drained of power or when its energy reserve is depleted, the device is in the state *no power* where the microcontroller is not active. However, our device fails safe, so the jamming module is used in conjunction with the tuned coil in this mode of operation. Whenever an NFC signal is seen either from the phone, or an external device, this circuit simultaneously jams the signal while increasing power transfer from the reader. After accumulating sufficient energy, control is relinquished to *EnGarde*'s microcontroller.

After the microcontroller boots, it enters a low power state referred to as *System Idle*; while in this mode, the microcontroller listens for interrupts from the sensing coil / tag presence detector. If an NFC device is found to be present, it uses the protocol detector module to decode reader-side messages.

If an external device has entered the vicinity of the mobile phone, *EnGarde* also switches on the decoder and enters its highest power state, *NFC Decoder Active*, where it decodes NFC transactions; before entering this state *EnGarde* detaches its harvesting coil and listens with the sensing coil.

After activating its NFC decoder, *EnGarde* decodes messages sent by the phone, as well as messages coming from the external device. It goes through its list of blacklisting rules, and if there is a match, it enters state *Jam*. If no such blacklist entry is matched, *EnGarde* will continue to listen to message exchanges until the external device exits the vicinity of the mobile phone at which point it reverts to demand-based harvesting using its tuned coil.

While in state *Jam*, *EnGarde* continuously generates a subcarrier that makes communication with external passive devices impossible for the phone to decode. If *EnGarde* detects a message from an active external device, as in peer-to-peer mode, it can generate an active subcarrier pulse for two bit durations per frame to disrupt active communications. As in the previous case, *EnGarde* continues to jam until it detects the external device has left the vicinity and returns to state *Demand Driven Harvesting*.

8.3 Blocking Rules

In addition to harvesting sufficient power and jamming effectively, *EnGarde* also needs to know when to block and when not to block particular NFC message exchanges. Since NFC is an emerging technology rather than a well established one, our work should be viewed as a preemptive mechanism that addresses potential threats rather than a reactive one that addresses existing attacks (NFC is one of the threat predictions for 2013 released by McAfee Labs [15]). Thus, instead of focusing on particular attacks, we provide a framework under which a rich sets of rules may be constructed.

Block protocol: The first level of rule-based filtering occurs in hardware – tag responses are sorted according to their respective protocols by using information provided by the protocol detection circuit presented in Figure 3 and subsequently handled by protocol-specific code. The highest granularity control a user has over *EnGarde* is to block all messages belonging to an entire protocol. An example where this might be used is where a more concerned user would like to prevent their phone's unique NFC ID from being read, so it blocks the entire ISO 14443-A protocol.

Block tag IDs: The next level of rule-based filtering occurs during the anti-collision phase of a particular protocol's anti-collision message exchange. During each of the protocols, a tag responds with a unique or pseudo-unique identifier that belongs to a particular tag. Thus, a user can block some subset of tag IDs that could correspond to a particular manufacturer or set of compromised tags.

Message content: The finest granularity of rule-based filtering occurs based on the content of the messages themselves. These rules are specified in a software graph structure using Aho and Corasick's keyword tree [2]. This structure has been used widely in pattern search algorithms and is also used in a popular packet tracing program, Snort [7]. We illustrate an example using this approach in Figure 9 – this rule definition logs all NDEF messages and proactively blocks those that correspond to well-known NDEF messages of the type URI that start with the substring "http://www.malware."

In our current implementation, these rule sets are decided at software compile time and programmed into the Microcontroller using a wired JTAG interface. In principle, these rules can be updated via NFC from a secure application, however we have not yet implemented this functionality on our current hardware.

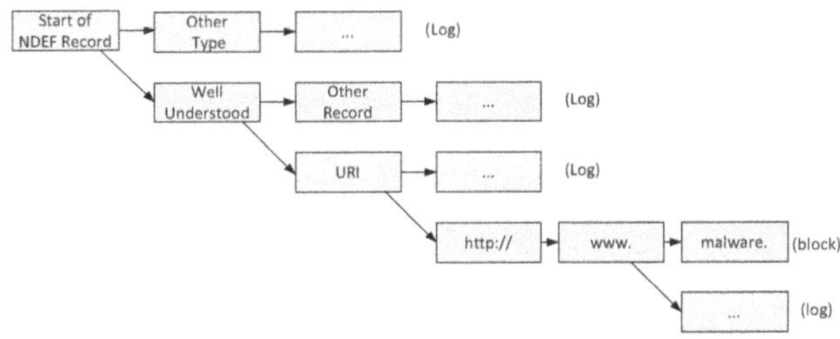

Figure 9: *EnGarde* implements a set of flexible rules based on a keyword tree structure specified in software. In this example, all well-understood NDEF messages corresponding to a URI type with prefix "http://www.malware.*" are blocked. Other sniffed tag responses are logged.

9. EXPERIMENTAL EVALUATION

Our evaluation covers three major aspects of our system: a) how effective is our jamming scheme in blocking interaction between the phone and other NFC devices, and b) a demonstration of *EnGarde*'s capability to perform targeted jamming of malicious tags while allowing benign ones to interact with the phone, and c) how well does our scavenging scheme perform over a long-term phone usage dataset,

9.1 Jamming Effectiveness

Figure 10: Our *EnGarde* prototype meets the form factor needs required for semi-permanent attachment to a mobile phone. Here, we show it on the back of a Galaxy Nexus

An understanding of how effectively *EnGarde* is capable of jamming NFC devices is critical towards showing that it sufficiently protects a mobile phone from external NFC threats. In particular, we want to understand what types of tags can circumvent our jamming signal and which types of tags the phone might be more vulnerable to. Figure 10 shows an image of our jamming effectiveness test setup.

Jamming malicious tags: We installed *EnGarde* on the back of a Galaxy Nexus phone and moved several different tags towards the phone, such that they were in direct contact with the back of the phone. The types of tags that we looked at were: ISO 14443-A. ISO 14443-B, ISO 15693, and a TI TRF7970 operating in ISO 14443-B tag emulation mode. We found that *none* of these tags could successfully communicate with the phone while the subcarrier was active. While we don't want to make any claims that communication with the phone is impossible, we haven't been able to find a tag that can get past our jamming signal.

Jamming malicious readers: Another important jamming on *EnGarde* is when an NFC reader, such as a mobile payment station, tries to read the mobile phone while in card emulation mode. We program a TRF7970 as a general purpose NFC reader, sending queries at its highest power level (200 mW). We found that when *EnGarde* is installed on the back of the phone, we effectively block 100% of the phone's ISO 14443-A response.

***EnGarde* Versus RFID Guardian [17]:** While a direct comparison against active jamming approaches, such as the RFID Guardian, would require designing another hardware platform, we briefly discuss the key differences. NFC Guardian actively generates two 424 KHz sub bands around the 13.56 MHz, which can block NFC tags within a half meter radius. Since we are only interested in protecting the mobile phone, we are able to passively generate a similar signal at negligible energy cost. For example, in the above experiments, if we change the setup by moving *EnGarde* some distance away from the phone, and place a tag directly on the back of the phone where *EnGarde* would normally be installed, we find that *EnGarde* blocks all communication provided that it is within 1.0 mm of the phone, but has limited effect after that distance. Thus, our jamming is extremely targeted, which improves our efficiency.

9.2 Targeted blocking of malicious interactions

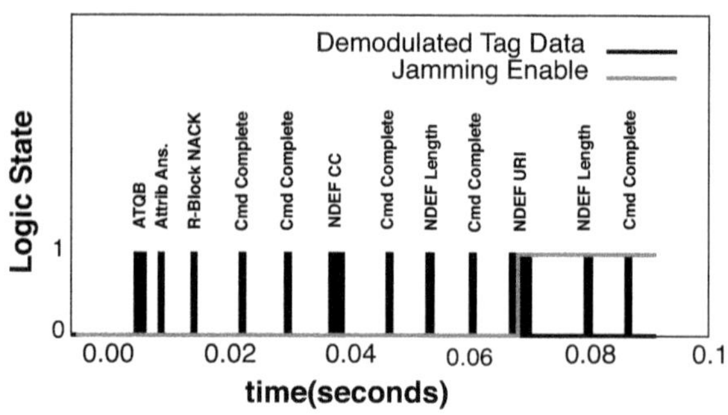

Figure 11: *EnGarde* monitors the messages sent from an emulated ISO14443-B tag, detects a malicious URL type and jams all subsequent communications

We now look at a case where there is a malicious tag and other non-malicious ones, and show that *EnGarde* can be programmed with blacklisting rules that allows real-time decoding of NFC interactions and targeted jamming of malicious ones. Specifically, we look at a case study where *EnGarde* is programmed to block a particular set of URLs on an ISO 14443-B NDEF tag.

In our study, we program a TRF7970A evaluation module to behave as an emulated ISO-14443-B NDEF tag. This emulated tag approaches a Galaxy Nexus phone; in a scenario when *EnGarde* is not present, the phone uses the discovery phase to identify a tag is present. The phone then sends a series of messages that select the NDEF message stored on the emulated tag, leading up to where the tag sends its reply that contains the requested NDEF message.

After successfully decoding the NDEF response, the phone takes action according to the contents of the NDEF message. In this case, the NDEF message has its TNF field set to 0x01, which means that it is a well understood type. After checking the ID type field, it finds that this message is a URI type message that contains a URL, Phone Number, or other address from a variety of different protocols. In the first byte of the NDEF record, the phone finds the value 0x01, which corresponds to the string "http://www." The subsequent characters correspond to the rest of the URL "malware.com". The phone automatically loads this webpage in its web browser.

Next let's look at the case where *EnGarde* is installed on the back of the phone. *EnGarde* decodes all of the bits corresponding to the emulated tag's reply; we show the bits actually decoded by *EnGarde* the time series shown in Figure 11. We can see that the tag first responds to the phone's REQB discovery message with an ATQB that contains the tags pseudo unique ID. After identifying the emulated tag, the phone sends an Atrrib message that indicates this particular tag has been selected for further communication, after which the tag replies with a standard Attrib answer message.

EnGarde next observes the sequence of messages corresponding to the NDEF message selection. After observing that the tag has sent its capability container (NDEF CC) and subsequent NDEF record length value, *EnGarde* knows where to find the NDEF message. It looks in the byte location that contains the URI identifier code 0x01, which corresponds to "http://www/" and immediately activates its subcarrier jamming circuit to block the rest of the message. It is also important to note that *EnGarde* will parse individual characters if the URI identifier code contains 0x00, which means that no compressed prefix is applied to the URI. If the characters correspond to "http://", again the rest of the message is blocked. We tried to get the phone to read the tag 20 times and the phone was never successful.

Finally, we show that *EnGarde* allows transactions that don't satisfy our blocking rules. To prove this, we use another emulated tag, but program it with the URL "https://www.cs.umass.edu". In this case, the URL is not blocked and the page opens in the phone's web browser. Again, we found that this was robust to various placements of the tag. While we did not quantify the impact *EnGarde* had on the benign tag's read range, it wasn't noticeably different than during a typical NFC interaction.

9.3 Scavenging performance

Our final evaluation looks at the performance of the scavenging subsystem. Since this evaluation depends on the actual time for which the phone is unlocked, and the duration between unlock events, we look at what impact these dynamics have on *EnGarde*. To accomplish this, we look at a set of traces provide by the LiveLab project at Rice University[18]. These traces were collected from 35 users over the span of a year and contain the screen unlock data needed to understand variability in available harvested energy.

Harvesting Study: Before looking at the behavior of the adaptive algorithm presented in §6.2, we first seek an understanding of the performance tradeoffs given the screen unlock interval dynamics present in the Livelab traces. In particular we ask the question: *What performance can EnGarde achieve despite variability in the amount of energy*

Simulation Parameter	Value
Quiescent Power Consumption	38.8 μW
Reader Power Consumption	32.7 mW
Opportunistic Power Harvesting	3.03 mW
Semi-Opp Power Harvesting	10.0 mW
Subcarrier Power Harvesting	26.0 mW
Thin-film battery capacity	14.4 J
Duration of NDEF exchange	0.56 seconds

Table 5: A summary of the parameters used in our simulation study

harvested from the mobile phone and what impact does this harvesting have on the mobile phone's battery lifetime? To answer this question, we look at how many messages *EnGarde* can sniff on a given day, as well as the impact *EnGarde* has on a mobile phone's battery irrespective of energy storage limitations on *EnGarde*. The CDFs we plot in Figures 12 and 13 are computed across all days and all users.

In Figure 12, we show *EnGarde*'s harvesting potential in terms of the number of NDEF interactions we sniff. To get a sense of how much each of these individual messages cost in terms of energy, we looked at the amount of time such an NDEF interaction takes to complete by measuring such an interaction between an Android Galaxy Nexus and an ISO 14443-A MiFare DESFire transponder card. We found that these interactions take 0.56 seconds, averaged across 20 trials; given the power consumption of *EnGarde*'s reader hardware, each interaction consumes 18.3 mJ of energy. Our three naive harvesting strategies – Opportunistic, Tag-Spoofing, and Subcarrier – are each capable of sniffing large numbers of these interactions. For example, the opportunistic harvesting strategy is capable of sniffing 100 such interactions for 86% of the days across all traces and 2413 interactions for 50% of the days; performance vastly improves when using the other two naive strategies.

Although *EnGarde* is capable of harvesting sufficient energy to sniff a substantial number of NDEF interactions, this comes at a cost. In Figure 13 we show the impact of NDEF sniffing on the phone's battery consumption for each naive harvesting strategy (We note that the x-axis % battery consumed is truncated to 100% because of the impact of several outlying data points; our goal is to show the impact on a single battery given no recharging). We note that the opportunistic-only strategy consumes 8.3% of the phone's battery in half the cases, while the more aggressive subcarrier-only strategy uses 95.7% of the phone's battery in half the cases. While we have shown that sufficient energy may be harvested to sniff substantial numbers of NFC transactions using all of the strategies, these naive strategies have a large impact on the phone's battery life. Thus, we need to show how this energy may be used for realistic workloads while also taking into account *EnGarde*'s energy buffer constraints.

Adaptive Harvesting Simulation: As a consequence of the issues raised in the prior study, we ask the question: *Does our demand driven harvesting algorithm achieve low NFC sniffing miss rates with a limited energy buffer, while simultaneously having minimal impact on its host phone's battery lifetime?* We answer this question through a trace-driven simulation of our adaptive harvesting algorithm; our simulator implements a complete *EnGarde* state machine, shown in Figure 8, and uses the measured values shown in Table 5. We compare the demand-driven harvesting algorithm against exclusively using one of the other three strategies. In the previous results, we showed *EnGarde*'s potential by removing restrictions on energy storage; however, in our simulation study, we simulate the behavior of a thin film battery with 14.4 Joules of energy storage capacity (same battery as used on *EnGarde* implementation). We look at *EnGarde*'s performance for a single workload that corresponds to 100 simulated NDEF interactions whose energy consumption is spread uniformly throughout the day; we do not simulate these interactions as discrete events, as no traces are currently available that show NFC user behavior. This workload is designed to be a reasonable approximation for a user that frequently interacts with NFC devices throughout the day.

Harvesting Strategy	% Missed NDEF interactions / day	% Phone battery consumed / day
Opportunistic	1.76	0.096
Tag-spoofing	0.68	0.281
Subcarrier	0.37	1.29
Adaptive	0.42	0.145

Table 6: Given a daily workload of 100 interactions with an NDEF tag, *EnGarde* is able to sniff most of these transactions with negligible miss-rate and with little impact on the host phone's battery across all users and all days by using an adaptive harvesting strategy.

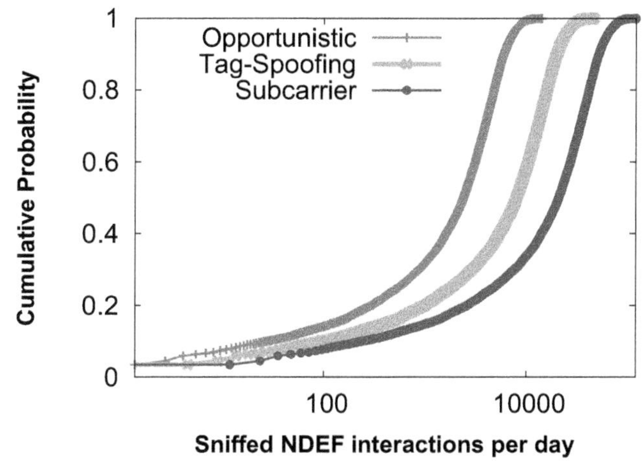

Figure 12: *EnGarde* harvests sufficient energy to sniff a large number of NDEF interactions between a mobile phone and passive transponder card.

We summarize the results of this study in Table 6 and show performance results in terms of the average % of simulated NFC interactions that *EnGarde* could not sniff given trace dynamics across all days and users; we also show the corresponding impact on the phone's daily % battery capacity. We note that the demand driven harvesting algorithm achieves a miss rate of only 0.42%, which is very close to the 0.37% miss rate achieved by the most aggressive, subcarrier-only strategy. We also note that the demand driven harvest-

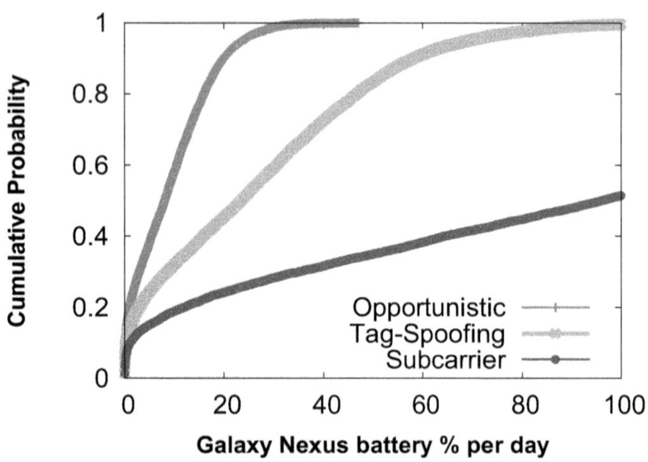

Figure 13: The energy harvesting strategies available on *EnGarde* use considerably different amounts of a phone's battery. The opportunistic harvesting mode consumes an average of 10% of the phone's battery, tag-spoofing consumes an average of 24%, while subcarrier mode would consume the phone's entire battery.

ing algorithm uses only 0.145% of the host phone's battery, which nearly matches the 0.096% consumed by the most efficient, opportunistic only strategy. These two metrics together show that our adaptive harvesting algorithm is effective at achieving low miss-rates while having minimal impact on a mobile phone's battery for a reasonably approximate workload.

10. DISCUSSION AND FUTURE WORK

Forensics: While this paper focuses on jamming unwanted NFC interactions, *EnGarde* can also be used to perform forensic analysis of mobile phone NFC interactions during normal use of a phone. Since little is currently known about NFC security in real-world settings, we think that this would be a valuable tool that will allow security researchers to have a better understanding of potential security threats and provide a means to bootstrap *EnGarde*'s blacklisting rules. One example of such forensic analysis is NFC malware — McAfee Labs' threat predictions for 2013 [15] highlights the risk of malware that spreads through peer-to-peer file transfer on mobile phones. Another forensic analysis may look at what data is sent over the phone's NFC interface encrypted versus plaintext. In particular, this would help in understanding whether or not information related to mobile payments (e.g. name, address, credit card number) is secured when sent over the NFC link.

Tighter phone integration: *EnGarde* makes the design choice that it needs to be physically decoupled from the phone, and therefore relies solely on harvested energy. However, an argument could be made that another approach might be to replace the back panel of a mobile phone with a replacement that contains elements of *EnGarde*. While this approach would achieve the objective of being decoupled from the mobile OS and therefore not vulnerable to malware running on the device, our solution is still far simpler for the average phone user who does not want to modify the device.

Long term evaluation: *EnGarde*'s power harvesting, detection, and jamming primitives all work together to protect a host phone's NFC interface. While our trace-driven studies have certainly made our approach towards power harvesting look promising, a longer-term real-world study would go a long way towards better understanding *EnGarde*'s effectiveness. We leave this evaluation as our future work.

11. RELATED WORK

Most similar to our work is the RFID Guardian [17]. The RFID Guardian monitors and jams specific NFC communication sessions in its vicinity. This longer range performance comes at a cost in form factor and power consumption. While useful for monitoring and protecting arbitrary sets of readers and tags, *EnGarde* is considerably more targeted and is designed to protect an individual mobile phone.

The Proxmark RFID tool [6] has been used extensively in NFC security research. It has the capability of decoding arbitrary protocols with an FPGA and additionally, it can emulate a tag. Since it uses an FPGA to decode and emulate tag responses, it can be programmed to decode any potential protocol. Two major drawbacks are its size and power consumption – while a valuable tool for debugging and security analysis, it is not suitable for continuous use on a mobile phone.

Another way to harvest energy from a mobile phone is through the audio interface [12]. Much like our NFC energy scavenger, the audio jack is universal across different phones. While a wired connection can harvest energy more efficiently, we instead opt to power *EnGarde* from the same power source as the attack surface.

Selective jamming devices are of particular interest in the area of implanted medical devices (IMD). One application is the implementation of zero power defenses [11]. *EnGarde* behaves much like a zero-power defense in that it generates a jamming signal completely passively. More recently, a non-invasive approach towards IMDs was proposed [10]. While the proposed IMDShield has parallels to our approach towards non-invasive jamming, they use a power-hungry software radio while ours operates entirely passively.

Other hardware and software systems that perform the task of packet filtering share much in common with our approach towards selective blocking of malicious NFC messages [4, 8]. While our approach towards filtering messages based on their contents is similar, we can relax our hardware requirements, since current NFC data rates are significantly slower than Gigabit Ethernet.

Security is also of critical importance to mobile health. One approach towards providing security for on-body sensors is to provide a security proxy with which they communicate through [19]. While not currently implemented as such, *EnGarde* could potentially be used as a similar security proxy.

Since NFC is a relatively new technology, new vulnerabilities are constantly being exposed [13, 16, 15]. *EnGarde* addresses these issues by providing a flexible set of security features that protect a mobile phone while remaining decoupled from platform vulnerabilities.

Finally, there have been significant efforts in securing RFID technology at the software level [3], and to place secure hardware elements in mobile phones [20]. We view our work as complementary. *EnGarde* serves as a hardware firewall that can augment software protection mechanisms to protect a mobile phone from potentially devastating attacks via NFC.

12. CONCLUSION

In this paper, we have outlined a practical, fully functional hardware shield, *EnGarde*, for phones that can intelligently protect phones from malicious NFC interactions while letting benign ones pass through. Our design is entirely passive thereby making our form-factor small enough to be placed as a patch on a phone or even integrated within a phones case. Perhaps the most compelling aspect of *EnGarde* is that it is widely deployable as-is on NFC mobile phones that are emerging in the market, thereby making our system market-ready.

While this paper focuses on jamming, *EnGarde* has immense potential in forensic analysis of NFC interactions. There is currently limited understanding of how NFC interactions work in practice — what information is sent in the clear? how do different phones implement mobile payments? and so on. *EnGarde* is a powerful tool that can log any NFC interaction that it decodes (including those in the vicinity of the phone), which can be used to perform such analysis. We defer such analysis to future work.

More information regarding *EnGarde* is available at: `http://sensors.cs.umass.edu/projects/engarde`

13. ACKNOWLEDGEMENTS

This research was partially funded by NSF grants CNS-0916577, CNS-1217606, and CNS-0855128. We thank our shepherd Justin Manweiler for providing guidance in preparing our final draft and the anonymous reviewers for their insightful comments.

14. REFERENCES

[1] xda-developers forum post. `http://forum.xda-developers.com/showthread.php?t=1980356`.

[2] A. V. Aho and M. J. Corasick. Efficient string matching: an aid to bibliographic search. *Communications of the ACM*, 18(6):333–340, 1975.

[3] V. A. Bhole, R. R. More, and N. C. Khadke. Security in near field communication (NFC) strengths and weaknesses. In *Proceedings of the 2nd National Conference on Emerging Trends in Information Technology: EIT-2007*, page 71. IK International Pvt Ltd, 2007.

[4] Y. H. Cho and W. H. Mangione-Smith. Deep packet filter with dedicated logic and read only memories. In *Field-Programmable Custom Computing Machines, 2004. FCCM 2004. 12th Annual IEEE Symposium on*, pages 125–134. IEEE, 2004.

[5] S. Clark. http://www.nfcworld.com/2012/02/09/313079/researcher-hacks-google-wallet-pin-on-rooted-android-phone/, Feb. 2012.

[6] G. de Koning Gans, J. Hoepman, and F. Garcia. A practical attack on the mifare classic. *Smart Card Research and Advanced Applications*, pages 267–282, 2008.

[7] N. Desai. Increasing performance in high speed NIDs. *A look at Snort's Internals*, 2002.

[8] S. Dharmapurikar, P. Krishnamurthy, T. S. Sproull, and J. W. Lockwood. Deep packet inspection using parallel bloom filters. *Micro, IEEE*, 24(1):52–61, 2004.

[9] K. Finkenzeller. *RFID handbook: fundamentals and applications in contactless smart cards, radio frequency identification and near-field communication.* Wiley, 2010.

[10] S. Gollakota, H. Hassanieh, B. Ransford, D. Katabi, and K. Fu. They can hear your heartbeats: non-invasive security for implantable medical devices. In *Proceedings of SIGCOMM*, 2011.

[11] D. Halperin, T. Heydt-Benjamin, B. Ransford, S. Clark, B. Defend, W. Morgan, K. Fu, T. Kohno, and W. Maisel. Pacemakers and implantable cardiac defibrillators: Software radio attacks and zero-power defenses. In *IEEE Symposium on Security and Privacy*, pages 129–142. IEEE, 2008.

[12] Y. Kuo, S. Verma, T. Schmid, and P. Dutta. Hijacking power and bandwidth from the mobile phone's audio interface. In *Proceedings of the First ACM Symposium on Computing for Development*, page 24. ACM, 2010.

[13] R. Lemos. http://www.eweek.com/c/a/security/android-phone-hacked-by-researchers-via-nfc-843123/, June 2012.

[14] H. Liu, S. Saroiu, A. Wolman, and H. Raj. Software abstractions for trusted sensors. In *Proceedings of the 10th international conference on Mobile systems, applications, and services*, pages 365–378. ACM, 2012.

[15] McAfee Labs. http://www.mcafee.com/us/resources/reports/rp-threat-predictions-2013.pdf, Dec. 2012.

[16] C. Miller. Exploring the NFC attack surface. In *Proceedings of Blackhat*, 2012.

[17] M. Rieback, G. Gaydadjiev, B. Crispo, R. Hofman, and A. Tanenbaum. A platform for RFID security and privacy administration. In *USENIX LISA*, pages 89–102, 2006.

[18] C. Shepard, A. Rahmati, C. Tossell, L. Zhong, and P. Kortum. Livelab: measuring wireless networks and smartphone users in the field. *ACM SIGMETRICS Performance Evaluation Review*, 38(3):15–20, 2011.

[19] J. Sorber, M. Shin, R. Peterson, C. Cornelius, S. Mare, A. Prasad, Z. Marois, E. Smithayer, and D. Kotz. An amulet for trustworthy wearable mhealth. In *Proceedings of the Twelfth Workshop on Mobile Computing Systems & Applications*, page 7. ACM, 2012.

[20] J. Sorber, M. Shin, R. Peterson, and D. Kotz. Plug-n-trust: practical trusted sensing for mhealth. In *Proceedings of the 10th international conference on Mobile systems, applications, and services*, pages 309–322. ACM, 2012.

[21] viaForensics. https://viaforensics.com/mobile-security/forensics-security-analysis-google-wallet.html, Dec. 2011.

AdRob: Examining the Landscape and Impact of Android Application Plagiarism

Clint Gibler
UC Davis
cdgibler@ucdavis.edu

Ryan Stevens
UC Davis
rcstevens@ucdavis.edu

Jonathan Crussell
UC Davis
jcrussell@ucdavis.edu

Hao Chen
UC Davis
hchen@cs.ucdavis.edu

Hui Zang
Sprint Research
hui.zang@sprint.com

Heesook Choi
Sprint Research
heesook.choi@sprint.com

ABSTRACT

Malicious activities involving Android applications are rising rapidly. As prior work on cyber-crimes suggests, we need to understand the economic incentives of the criminals to design the most effective defenses. In this paper, we investigate application plagiarism on Android markets at a large scale. We take the first step to characterize plagiarized applications and estimate their impact on the original application developers. We first crawled 265,359 free applications from 17 Android markets around the world and ran a tool to identify similar applications ("clones"). Based on the data, we examined properties of the cloned applications, including their distribution across different markets, application categories, and ad libraries. Next, we examined how cloned applications affect the original developers. We captured HTTP advertising traffic generated by mobile applications at a tier-1 US cellular carrier for 12 days. To associate each Android application with its advertising traffic, we extracted a unique advertising identifier (called the client ID) from both the applications and the network traces. We estimate a lower bound on the advertising revenue that cloned applications siphon from the original developers, and the user base that cloned applications divert from the original applications. To the best of our knowledge, this is the first large scale study on the characteristics of cloned mobile applications and their impact on the original developers.

Categories and Subject Descriptors

D.4.6 [**Software**]: Security and Protection; K.4.1 [**Computers and Society**]: Public Policy Issues—*Abuse and crime involving computers*

General Terms

Security, Economics

Keywords

Android; underground economy; plagiarism; advertising; mobile; measurement

MobiSys'13, June 25-âĂŞ28, 2013, Taipei, Taiwan
ACM 978-1-4503-1672-9/13/06.

CarSafe App: Alerting Drowsy and Distracted Drivers using Dual Cameras on Smartphones

Chuang-Wen You†*, Nicholas D. Lane‡, Fanglin Chen†, Rui Wang†, Zhenyu Chen†⊔, Thomas J. Bao†
Martha Montes-de-Oca⋈, Yuting Cheng†, Mu Lin†, Lorenzo Torresani†, Andrew T. Campbell†
†Dartmouth College, ‡Microsoft Research Asia, *Academia Sinica
⊔Chinese Academy of Sciences, ⋈National Autonomous University of Mexico
cwyou@citi.sinica.edu.tw, niclane@microsoft.com, {chentc, ruiwang, zhenyu}@cs.dartmouth.edu
thomas.j.bao@dartmouth.edu, martham@unam.mx, {yutingc, linmu, lorenzo, campbell}@cs.dartmouth.edu

ABSTRACT

We present CarSafe, the first driver safety application that uses dual cameras on smartphones to detect and alert drivers to dangerous driving conditions. CarSafe fuses events detected from cameras and readings from embedded sensors on the phone – such as the GPS, accelerometer and gyroscope – to detect and alert the driver of dangerous driving behavior in and outside of the car. Results from a 12-driver field trial show CarSafe can infer five of the most commonly occurring dangerous driving conditions with an overall precision and recall of 83% and 75%, respectively.

Categories and Subject Descriptors

H.4 [**Information Systems Applications**]: Miscellaneous

General Terms

Design, Experimentation, Performance.

Keywords

Driver safety, dual-camera sensing, smartphone sensing.

1. INTRODUCTION

Drowsy or distracted driving behavior not only increases the likelihood of serious accidents, injuries and fatalities but also is a serious problem for roadway safety. Drivers who drive while fatigued or inattentive to road conditions are typically unaware that they are tired or distracted. To raise drivers' awareness of drowsy or distracted driving behavior, the automobile industry is developing new driver safety technologies for their top end cars. However, these technologies are still considered too expensive to be incorporated into entry-level vehicles. To mimic the safety features found in many of the top-end cars, we developed CarSafe [1] (Fig. 1), the first driver safety app that uses dual cameras on smartphones. CarSafe uses computer vision and machine learning algorithms on the phone to monitor and detect whether the driver is tired or distracted using the front-facing camera, while, at the same time, tracking road conditions using the rear-facing camera. Because smartphones do not allow simultaneous dual-camera access, CarSafe incorporates an adaptive context-driven camera switching mechanism which also exploits always-on inertial sensors on smartphones to enable pre-emptive switching when the phone is "looking in the wrong direction".

MobiSys'13, June 25–28, 2013, Taipei, Taiwan.
ACM 978-1-4503-1672-9/13/06.

Figure 1: CarSafe, the first dual-camera sensing app, running on a Samsung Galaxy S3 mounted on the windshield of a car.

2. CARSAFE APP

CarSafe uses a context-driven camera switching algorithm to schedule processing between two different camera classification pipelines. The front camera pipeline classifies drivers' face directions and eye states to track driver attention and infer the drowsiness during driving, respectively. The rear camera pipeline estimates the "following distance" and lane trajectory categories (i.e., lane change or weaving). By fusing events inferred from both pipelines and readings from embedded inertial sensors, CarSafe can detect five of the most commonly occurring dangerous driving conditions: that is, drowsy driving, inattentive driving (e.g., when the driver is distracted and takes their eyes off the road), tailgating (i.e., getting too close to the preceding car), lane weaving or drifting, and ignoring blind spots during lane changes. However, camera switching means there are blind spots in the front or rear at any given time. To address this, CarSafe utilizes the "always-on" embedded sensors (i.e., inertial sensors) to provide blind spot hints that are used to enable pre-emptive switching for timely activating the rear camera to verify the car trajectory inference.

We developed a prototype of the CarSafe app using Samsung Galaxy S3 Android phones and evaluated CarSafe in a small-scale deployment under real-world driving conditions where 12 drivers used CarSafe in the wild. Results show an overall precision and recall of 83% and 75%, respectively, across all tested dangerous driving scenarios. For more information, check out the CarSafe video on YouTube: `http://youtu.be/tAd_sSfhZTw`.

3. REFERENCES

[1] C.-W. You, N. D. Lane, F. Chen, R. Wang, Z. Chen, T. J. Bao, M. Montes-de-Oca, Y. Cheng, M. Lin, L. Torresani, A. T. Campbell. CarSafe App: Alerting Drowsy and Distracted Drivers using Dual Cameras on Smartphones. In *ACM MobiSys '13*, 2013.

Keyword Programming for TouchDevelop

Vu Le
Univ. of California at Davis
vmle@ucdavis.com

Jonathan de Halleux
Microsoft Research, Redmond
jhalleux@microsoft.com

Sumit Gulwani
Microsoft Research, Redmond
sumitg@microsoft.com

Zhendong Su
Univ. of California at Davis
su@cs.ucdavis.com

ABSTRACT

This video demo features a new keyword programming environment for TouchDevelop, a popular touch-centric system for scripting mobile devices. The new environment allows users to simply enter a set of keywords, and its internal program synthesis engine automatically generates script snippets that most likely reflect the users' intent. Because the synthesis engine can be triggered anywhere in a script, it also exploits various contextual information, such as which variables/functions are in-scope, to guide the generation of snippets. Our new environment benefit both novice and experienced TouchDevelop users. It helps novice users to synthesize script snippets from keywords and explore unfamiliar TouchDevelop features. It also improves experienced users' productivity because they need to worry about fewer coding details and enter less code. The demoed feature has been released and deployed since TouchDevelop version 2.10.

Categories and Subject Descriptors

D.1.2 [**Programming Techniques**]: Automatic Programming; H.5.2 [**Information Interfaces and Presentation**]: User Interfaces—*Natural language*

General Terms

Algorithms, Design, Human Factors

Keywords

Program synthesis, keyword programming, TouchDevelop

Acknowledgements

We thank Dara Hazeghi for his voice narration. This work was supported by a Microsoft Research internship for the first author, and a consulting position for the last author.

MobiSys'13, June 25-28, 2013, Taipei, Taiwan.
ACM 978-1-4503-1672-9/13/06.

MoodScope: Building a Mood Sensor from Smartphone Usage Patterns

Robert LiKamWa[†,‡], Yunxin Liu[‡], Nicholas D. Lane[‡], Lin Zhong[†]

[†]Rice University, Houston, TX [‡]Microsoft Research Asia, Beijing, China

ABSTRACT

We present MoodScope, a software system which infers the mood of its user based on how the smartphone is used. Similar to smartphone sensors that measure acceleration, light, and other physical properties, MoodScope is a "sensor" that measures the mental state of the user and provides mood as an important input to context-aware computing.

We run a formative statistical study with smartphone-logged data collected from 32 participants over two months. Through the study, we find that by analyzing communication history and application usage patterns, we can statistically infer a user's daily mood average with an accuracy of 93% after a two-month training period. Motivated by these results, we build a service, MoodScope, which analyzes usage history to act as a sensor of the user's mood.

Categories and Subject Descriptors

H.1.2 [**Models and Principles**]: User/Machine Systems - human factors; I.5.2 [**Pattern Recognition**]: Design Methodology - Classifier design and evaluation, Feature evaluation and selection, Pattern analysis; J.4 [**Social and Behavioral Sciences**]: Psychology

General Terms

Design, Experimentation, Human Factors

Keywords

Smartphone usage; mood; machine learning; affective computing

1 Mood Sensing

Mood influences our behavior, drives our social communication, and shifts our consumer preferences. But in the digital realm of mobile devices, there is a distinct lack of knowledge about mood unless manually provided. While devices have many sensors to understand the physical world around them, they are unable to develop insight about the object that matters the most: the user. We consider the implementation of a mood sensor as a vital next step in enhancing the context-awareness of mobile devices.

There are numerous ways to employ mood information. Video and music recommender systems would benefit from using mood as an input to their recommendation algorithms, building preferences matched with the user's mood. Mood sensing can also build an interesting digital social ecosystem as users' devices automatically share their moods with close friends and family. Users would be able to better know how and when to communicate with others.

MobiSys'13, June 25-28, 2013, Taipei, Taiwan
ACM 978-1-4503-1672-9/13/06.

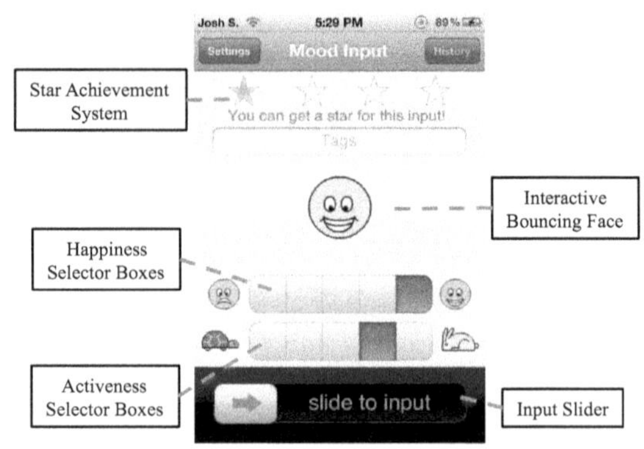

Figure 1: Mood entry application on iPhone

2 MoodScope System

To enable these scenarios, we build a system that recognizes users' mood from smartphone usage patterns. Our smartphones have rich information about us: where we have been, through location services; with whom we communicate, through e-mail, text messages, and phone calls; what applications we use; and what websites we visit. Furthermore, people use their smartphone differently when they are in different moods. MoodScope attempts to leverage these patterns by learning about its user and associating smartphone usage patterns with certain moods.

We collect smartphone usage logs with an adapted LiveLab Logger[2] on iPhone and Android. Our custom mood entry application prompts the user four times daily for their pleasure and activeness, the two dimensions of mood in the circumflex model[1]. The usage logs are aggregated into histograms to create a 128-dimensional feature vector. MoodScope estimates the mood by performing multi-linear regression with sequential feature selection. The mood is provided via an API to applications that wish to use the mood.

We have studied our system on a set of 32 users from China and the US using Leave-One-Out-Cross-Validation. After collecting two months of data, MoodScope estimates the pleasure dimension and activeness dimensions with 93% accuracy for each dimension.

3 References

[1] James A Russell. A circumplex model of affect. *Journal of personality and social psychology*, 39(6):1161–1178, 1980.

[2] Clayton Shepard, Ahmad Rahmati, Chad Tossell, Lin Zhong, and Phillip Kortum. Livelab: measuring wireless networks and smartphone users in the field. *ACM SIGMETRICS Performance Evaluation Review*, 38(3):15–20, 2011.

Energy Proportional Image Sensors for Continuous Mobile Vision

Robert LiKamWa[†,‡], Bodhi Priyantha[‡], Matthai Philipose[‡], Lin Zhong[†,‡], and Paramvir Bahl[‡]

[†]Rice University, Houston, TX [‡]Microsoft Research, Redmond, WA

ABSTRACT

A hurdle to frequently performing mobile computer vision tasks is the high energy cost of image sensing. In particular, modern image sensors are not energy proportional; for low resolution and low frame rate capture, the image sensor consumes almost the same amount of energy as it does at high resolutions and high frame rates.

We reveal two system-level energy proportional mechanisms: (*i*) using an optimal pixel clock frequency; (*ii*) entering low power standby mode between frames. These techniques can be implemented by the image sensor driver with minimal hardware adjustment. Further improvements can be made by designing sensors with heterogeneous hardware architectures. With energy proportionality, computer vision frameworks can be optimized for power consumption, continuously requesting low resolution frames with low energy while only occasionally using high energy to request high resolution frames. This will in turn enable low power continuous mobile vision applications.

Categories and Subject Descriptors

I.4.m [**Image Processing and Computer Vision**]: Miscellaneous; I.5.4 [**Performance of Systems**]: Modeling techniques, Performance attributes

General Terms

Design, Experimentation, Measurement, Performance

Keywords

Image sensor; energy efficiency; mobile systems; computer vision

1 Image Sensor Energy Consumption

An image sensor has two operational modes, T_{idle} and T_{active}, during which it consumes different amounts of power, P_{idle} and P_{active}[1, 2]. The energy consumption per frame depends on the power consumption of the operational modes and how much time the sensor spends in each mode. That is,

$$E_{frame} = P_{idle}T_{idle} + P_{active}T_{active} \quad (1)$$

T_{active} is determined by the number of pixels N and the clock frequency f, as one pixel is read out per clock period. The idle time T_{idle} is determined by the frame rate R of the video capture. Although the sensor mostly occupies T_{idle} for low resolution and low frame rate capture, P_{idle} is still significant, resulting in high energy capture for each frame.

MobiSys'13, June 25-28, 2013, Taipei, Taiwan
ACM 978-1-4503-1672-9/13/06.

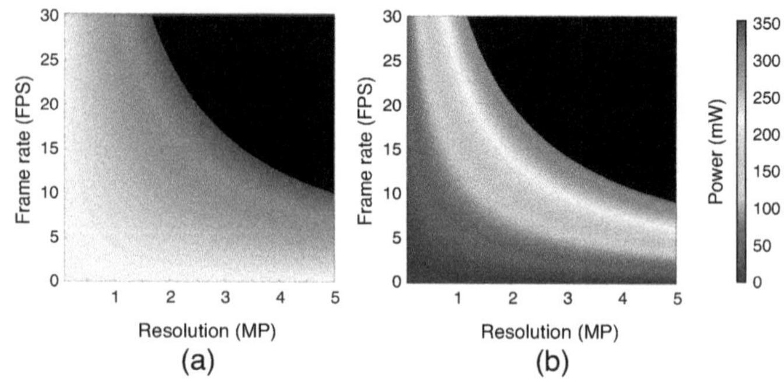

Figure 1: Power consumption at various resolutions and framerates for: (a) standard video capture; (b) with system-level energy proportionality optimizations, i.e. pixel clock frequency scaling and aggressive standby

2 Energy-Proportional Mechanisms

Using our understanding of image sensor power consumption, we can model image sensor power consumption, we devise a set of techniques that mobile systems can implement to create energy proportional image capture.

- **Pixel Clock Frequency Scaling** - As the clock frequency increases, the sensor consumes more power, but spends less time in T_{active}. The system can use this tradeoff to select an optimal clock frequency that minimizes energy consumption.
- **Aggressive Standby** - Most image sensors have a low power standby mode which retains the register states of the sensor. A sensor should enter standby mode as often as possible to reduce power. The sensor still must enter idle mode to allow for exposure before readout.
- **Heterogeneous Image Sensor Design** - Sensors should use heterogeneous analog signal chains for different bitrates of pixel readout. Because the power consumption of analog-to-digital converters is highly dependent on bitrate, low-bitrate analog signal chains would provide significant power savings over high-bitrate analog signal chains when capturing at low resolutions and/or low frame rates.

3 References

[1] J. Nakamura. *Image sensors and signal processing for digital still cameras*. CRC, 2005.

[2] J. Ohta. *Smart CMOS image sensors and applications*, volume 129. CRC, 2007.

CrowdAtlas: Self-Updating Maps for Cloud and Personal Use

Yin Wang
HP Labs, Palo Alto
yin.wang@hp.com

Xuemei Liu
Baidu Inc., Shanghai
liuxuemei01@baidu.com

Hong Wei
Shanghai Jiao Tong University
keith.collens@sjtu.edu.cn

George Forman
HP Labs, Palo Alto
george.forman@hp.com

Yanmin Zhu
Shanghai Jiao Tong University
yzhu@sjtu.edu.cn

ABSTRACT

Digital road maps have become essential to many aspects of our lives. Unfortunately, they have persistent quality issues, both in developing countries as well as in developed countries, evidenced by the recent Apple-Google map war. A survey of British drivers showed 26% have been directed by their GPS to go into no-entry areas, and the news periodically reports car accidents caused by or related to digital maps. In addition to correcting existing errors, maps need to be frequently updated to reflect the latest constructions, closures, and reconfigurations. TomTom estimates that roads change by as much as 15% each year. There are also growing demands for other types of maps, including off-road driving, cycling, hiking, and skiing maps. There are services for people to share GPS traces, but none creates navigable maps.

Getting maps up to date and maintaining them involves a great deal of effort and delay. Today's maps are built by expensive geological surveys, supplemented by manual editing work from aerial imagery or corrections submitted by aggravated map users. NavTeq (now Nokia) employs more than 7,000 employees worldwide in its Location Content team to update maps.

We present the CrowdAtlas system, which updates digital maps using the increasingly abundant GPS traces available as byproducts from a variety of sources: fleet management systems, telematics systems, and smartphone apps (e.g., navigation and location based services). We modified state-of-the-art *map matching* algorithms to accommodate the possibility that the existing map is incomplete. It uses the traces that match the map to monitor for road closures and fix road geometry. It uses tight clusters of trace segments from many vehicles that do not match the map in order to infer missing roads that connect to existing roads. The existing roads provide good segmentation of the traces to produce high quality clusters, enabling the automated (and even unsupervised) addition of missing roads. Using one week of traces from 70 taxis in Beijing, CrowdAtlas inferred 61 km of new roads, which we uploaded to OpenStreetMap and became its first set of computer generated roads.

To enable personalized maps, we also developed CrowdAtlas app based on OSMAnd, an open source navigation app. When acting as a GPS data source to CrowdAtlas server, it contributes data better optimized for map update with less communication. When acting in standalone-mode, it can add missing roads to its onboard navigation map. Instead of aggregating multiple GPS traces for high confidence, this app can add each new road immediately after the user traverses it, given user confirmation. We used our CrowdAtlas app in standalone-mode to map out major roads in a 4.5 km^2 area of Shanghai Pudong in less than 30 minutes and build the walking map of the SJTU campus in less than a day.

CrowdAtlas could fundamentally change the way people create and update maps. Together with incubating technologies that extract road metadata from street views and aerial imagery, modern cartography could be revolutionized, reducing or eliminating the expensive and slow manual mapping process used today.

The high-definition version of our video presentation is available at [1], and our accompanying full-length paper describes the technical details of CrowdAtlas [2].

MobiSys'13, June 25–28, 2013, Taipei, Taiwan.
ACM 978-1-4503-1672-9/13/06.

Categories and Subject Descriptors

C.2.4 [**Distributed Systems**]: Distributed applications; H.2.8 [**Database Management**]: Database Applications—*Data mining; Spatial databases and GIS*; H.4 [**Information Systems Applications**]: Miscellaneous; I.5.4 [**Pattern Recognition**]: Applications

Keywords

mobile systems; spatial data mining; GPS; map matching; map inference; road maps

1. REFERENCES

[1] CrowdAtlas video HD. `http://vimeo.com/62912005`.

[2] Y. Wang et al. CrowdAtlas: Self-updating maps for cloud and personal use. In *MobiSys*, 2013.

Video Streaming Using Whitespace Spectrum for Vehicular Applications

Tan Zhang, Sayandeep Sen, and Suman Banerjee
Department of Computer Sciences
University of Wisconsin-Madison, USA
{tzhang, sdsen, suman}@cs.wisc.edu

ABSTRACT

We present *Scout*, a communication system leveraging TV whitespaces to support robust and high–speed streaming services. *Scout* uses two key techniques to improve video performance. First, it extends network coverage through an asymmetric network architecture where whitespace transceivers are used for the downlink direction while a cellular path is used for the uplink. *Scout* further leverages some unique opportunities that arise in vehicular systems. In particular, it sends a front radio to lookahead and identify the best channel parameters when the rear radio eventually reaches the forward post. We demonstrate the performance of *Scout* by using a single base station to stream a high–quality video to a vehicle driving along a 1.3km road stretch.

Categories and Subject Descriptors

C.2.1 [**Computer-Communication Networks**]: Network Architecture and Design—*Wireless communication*

Keywords

TV Whitespaces, Vehicular Network, Video Streaming

1. DESCRIPTION

Video streaming is a vital on-board service that enables diverse road safety and infotainment applications for passengers. In this work, we explore using the emerging TV whitespaces spectrum for this purpose. This is not only because of the abundant spectral resource available for feeding the bandwidth-hungry video applications, but also for its excellent propagation characteristics especially suited for streaming to moving vehicles. To efficiently utilize TV whitespaces, we have recently developed a system called *Scout* [2] that consists of two key ideas.

(i) An asymmetric design for coverage improvement: *Scout* communicates the downlink traffic (usually the dominant fraction) primarily over the whitespace path while sending the uplink traffic primarily over existing cellular path as shown in Figure 1(a). The motivation of this design comes from the *asymmetric transmission power limit* in TV whitespaces. That is, the mobile client is allowed to transmit at *much lower* power–$100mW$ compared to the static base station allowed to–$4W$. The ubiquitous cellular connectivity allows *Scout* to circumvent the "weak" whitespaces uplink, in turn extending the coverage of each base station to a maximum.

(ii) A scouting radio for channel estimation: The operation of the asymmetric network is plagued by the *high feedback latency* in the cellular uplink. The delayed feedback leads to poor transmission decisions by the base station. To tackle this problem, *Scout* uses a scouting radio mounted at the head of the vehicle (Figure 1(b)) to "scout" the likely channel condition at the future reception location of the rear radio. By the time the rear radio reaches the same location l, the base station can use the channel observation previously made by the front radio at l to choose better transmission parameters for the rear radio. Built upon this estimation framework, we use multiple transmission techniques, i.e., rate adaptation, inter-packet FEC and traffic duplication, to enhance video delivery.

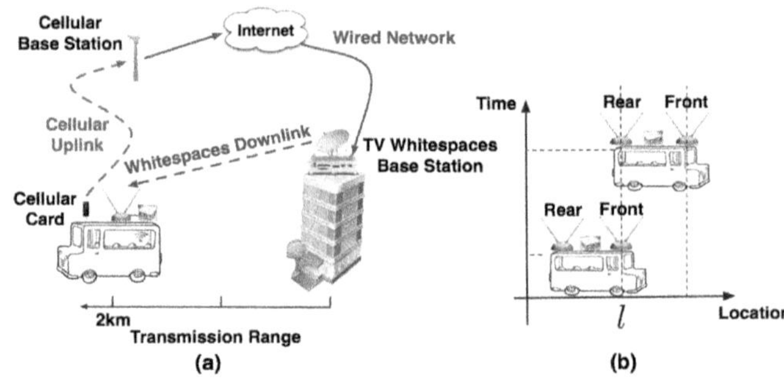

Figure 1: *Scout* design: (a) asymmetric architecture; (b) illustration of the "scouting" radio.

Video streaming using *Scout*: We showcase the video performance of *Scout* in [1] by streaming a high–quality (1080p) video from YouTube to a vehicle driving along a 1.3km road stretch. The setup consists of one base station and one mobile client. The base station is mounted atop a 8-floor building. It is equipped with an Ethernet connection for fetching video traffic from Internet and relaying it over the asymmetric network. It achieves extensive downlink coverage of several kilometers by using a whitespaces radio, a high-gain power amplifier, and directional antennas. As the mobile client, we mount two whitespaces radios on the vehicle for receiving downlink traffic, while using a 3G cellular card for uplink communications. The video playback over *Scout* is interruption–free.

Acknowledgments

The authors were supported in part by the US National Science Foundation via awards CNS1040648, CNS0916955, CNS0855201, CNS0747177, CNS1064944, and CNS1059306.

2. REFERENCES

[1] Scout demo - an asymmetric vehicular network design over tv whitespaces. `wings-www.cs.wisc.edu/projects/scout/`.

[2] T. Zhang, S. Sen, and S. Banerjee. An asymmetric vehicular network design over tv whitespaces. In *ACM HotMobile*, 2013.

MobiSys'13, June 25-28, 2013, Taipei, Taiwan.
ACM 978-1-4503-1672-9/13/06.

Sensing Device Co-location through Patterns of Silence

Wai-Tian Tan
Hewlett-Packard Labs
wai-tian.tan@hp.com

Mary Baker
Hewlett-Packard Labs
mary.baker@hp.com

Bowon Lee
Hewlett-Packard Labs
bowon.lee@hp.com

Ramin Samadani
Hewlett-Packard
ramin.samadani@hp.com

ABSTRACT

This document describes the technology behind the accompanying video, which gives a demonstration of determining the dynamic group membership of a meeting by matching patterns of relative audio silence, or *silence signatures*, sensed by mobile devices.

Categories and Subject Descriptors

H.5.3 [**Group and Organization Interfaces**]: Computer-supported cooperative work, Web-based interaction; I.5.4 [**Applications**]: Signal processing.

General Terms

Design, Experimentation.

Keywords

Mobile systems, mobile sensing, localization, co-location, audio, silence signatures, content sharing, mobile cloud services.

DESCRIPTION

A list of the dynamically changing group membership of a meeting supports a variety of meeting-related activities. These include effortless content sharing, providing business card information for attendees, feeding information into calendar applications to simplify scheduling of follow-up meetings, and populating the membership of collaborative editing applications, mailing lists, and social networks.

Our system uses audio sensing to maintain meeting membership automatically. Mobile devices carried by meeting attendees capture audio and convert it to *silence signatures,* which are sensed time-varying patterns of relative silence in the environment. The devices send these signatures to a cloud service that compares them. Those that match are very likely in the same acoustic environment, which means they are in the same physical location, or they may be participating in a teleconference or listening to the same broadcast audio. We use audio because hearing the same conversation provides a human-centric notion of attending the same gathering. It takes into account walls and other sound barriers between otherwise closely situated people. It can sense participants attending remotely by teleconference. It does not require attendees to perform any explicit action such as "tagging out" when leaving a meeting for which they should no longer have access to associated content. A signature based on simple silence patterns rather than a detailed audio characterization reveals less information about potentially private conversations and is also more robustly compared across devices that are not clock synchronized. The method works across a variety of meeting contexts, and in the video we demonstrate its use in both a teleconference and a noisy cafeteria lunch meeting. We require only the commonly available microphones on mobile devices to capture the audio for our silence signatures.

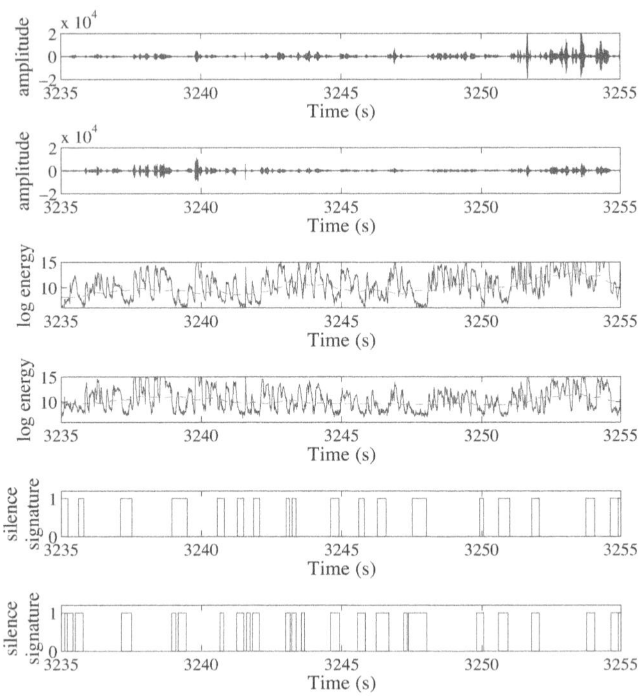

The figure shows sound signals versus our silence signatures. The top two graphs are audio recordings from the same 20 seconds of a meeting on two different mobile devices. Even though these recordings are from the same meeting, the relative amplitude of the sounds can be quite different and hard to compare. The middle two recordings show the energy of the sound over 10 ms intervals on a logarithmic scale. The dashed line is an adaptive silence threshold we use to quantize the signals into silence versus non-silence as compared to the (possibly changing) background noise. The bottom two plots show the silence signatures for these two recordings: 1 means silence and 0 means non-silence. The resulting silence signatures are relatively easy to match.

The accompanying video demonstrates an application using our silence signature matching service to display meeting participants coming and going. It also demonstrates using the information from the service to enable easy content sharing among meeting participants.

MobiSys'13, June 25–28, 2013, Taipei, Taiwan.
ACM 978-1-4503-1672-9/13/06.

RegTrack

A Differential Relative GPS Tracking Solution

Will Hedgecock
will.hedgecock@vanderbilt.edu

Miklos Maroti
miklos.maroti@vanderbilt.edu

Janos Sallai
janos.sallai@vanderbilt.edu

Peter Volgyesi
peter.volgyesi@vanderbilt.edu

Akos Ledeczi
akos.ledeczi@vanderbilt.edu

Institute for Software Integrated Systems, Vanderbilt University
Nashville, TN, USA

ABSTRACT

In many mobile wireless applications such as the automated driving of cars, formation flying of unmanned air vehicles, and source localization or target tracking with wireless sensor networks, it is more important to know the precise *relative* locations of nodes than their absolute coordinates. GPS, the most ubiquitous localization system available, generally provides only *absolute* coordinates. Furthermore, low-cost receivers can exhibit tens of meters of error or worse in challenging RF environments.

This video demonstration presents an approach that uses GPS to derive relative location information for multiple receivers [1]. Cooperating nodes in a network share their raw satellite measurements and use this data to track the relative motions of neighboring nodes as opposed to computing their own absolute coordinates. This is achieved via creation of a new error model that incorporates GPS localization errors specific to the multiple-receiver case, development of a new, highly accurate observation model that allows for the change in range between a single satellite and two receivers to be mapped through time, and the synthesis of these two models into a novel 3D pairwise tracking algorithm that uses the local GPS node as its own reference and requires only an approximate estimate of its own absolute position to achieve centimeter-scale relative tracking precision.

The system just described was implemented on a network of Android smartphones equipped with a Bluetooth-enabled, custom GPS node to provide raw measurement data. Several experiments were carried out to test our proof of concept in various GPS environments and under different types of dynamic conditions. Our evaluation shows that centimeter-scale tracking accuracy at an update rate of 1 Hz is possible under various conditions with the presented technique. This is more than an order of magnitude more accurate than simply taking the difference of reported absolute node coordinates or other simplistic approaches due to uncorrelated measurement errors.

The demo shown in this video represents one of the high-dynamic test cases in which we placed a stationary GPS receiver on a tripod in the middle of a parking lot and three additional nodes on top of an automobile. We proceeded to drive the automobile through various environments, including a multipath-rich alleyway, moderately benign suburban roads, and at high speeds on an interstate highway. The total length of the experiment was 15 minutes, spanning 12.2 km of terrain, with the baseline vector between the stationary node in the parking lot and the roving nodes on the automobile ranging from 0 to 3.5 km at any given time.

The visualization of the experimental results is taken from the point of view of the stationary node, enabling us to map the relative tracks of the roving nodes in an absolute coordinate space using Google Earth. The results of this experiment showed centimeter-scale tracking accuracy—a level of precision that enables clear distinction of driving features such as lane shifts and velocity changes—under various driving conditions, with only one problematic loss of satellite locks due to signal obstruction by a wide overpass while the vehicle was changing directions. This momentary loss of lock caused the tracking algorithm to resume after approximately 2 meters of error had already been accrued, and this error remained present and constant throughout the remainder of the experiment.

Future work involves solving for initialization and recalibration of the tracking algorithm on the fly, such that losses of lock and visibility obstructions do not degrade the accuracy of the system in the long run. In its present form, RegTrack already provides an order of magnitude better precision than complementary methods using low-cost, single-frequency commercial receivers, and the stage is set for further research to increase its robustness and utility for high-precision, low-cost applications.

MobiSys'13, June 25–28, 2013, Taipei, Taiwan.
ACM 978-1-4503-1672-9/13/06.

Categories and Subject Descriptors

C.3 [**Special-Purpose and Application-Based Systems**]: Real-time and Embedded Systems

Keywords

GPS, localization, differential tracking, relative localization

REFERENCES

[1] W. Hedgecock et al. High-accuracy differential tracking of low-cost GPS receivers. In *Proceedings of the 11th International Conference on Mobile Systems, Applications and Services*, 2013.

Pointer Wizard - A Remote Interaction User Interface

Jenq-Shiou Leu
Department of Electronic and Computer Engineering, National Taiwan University of Science and Technology, Taipei, Taiwan
jsleu@mail.ntust.edu.tw

Kuan-Wu Su
Department of Electronic and Computer Engineering, National Taiwan University of Science and Technology, Taipei, Taiwan
d10102107@mail.ntust.edu.tw

Tien-Yu Chu
Department of Electronic and Computer Engineering, National Taiwan University of Science and Technology, Taipei, Taiwan
m10102117@mail.ntust.edu.tw

Chen-Hsin Hsieh
Department of Electronic and Computer Engineering, National Taiwan University of Science and Technology, Taipei, Taiwan
b9802007@mail.ntust.edu.tw

Yu-Shan Athena Chen
Department of Business Administration, National Chengchi University, Taipei, Taiwan,
athena@nccu.edu.tw

Jui-Ping Ma
Graduate School of Creative Industry Design, National Taiwan University of Arts, New Taipei City, Taiwan
10035903@mail.ntua.edu.tw

ABSTRACT

In this video demonstration, we present a remote interaction user interface prototype – Pointer Wizard, to provide mixed reality experience with intuitive interaction afar. By identifying finger gestures and voice commands, it allows users to interact with appliances remotely, without the need of close proximity or even physical contact. It also brings information from the virtual world out into the real surrounding, thus creating the mixed reality experience. Due to the rapid improvement and development of smartphone and smart devices, we can now integrate the readily available hardware with micro-projection technology and quickly create prototypes that can be deployed rapidly. We designed image and speech recognition apps for smart devices in order to identify the figure gestures and target appliances, and through wireless transmission not only sending control signals to control relays for the appliances and receiving feedback information, but also gathering related information from the Internet,. The prompt control commands and related information are then projected out via portable light-weight projecting mechanism in real-time, hence users are seemingly able to operate and interact with the target from a distance. Through realizing this project, we hope to provide a more convenient way of life, and a more intuitive way of obtaining information or manipulating home appliances, like performing magic as wizards in a fantasy.

Categories and Subject Descriptors

H.5.2 [**Information Interfaces and Presentation**]: User Interfaces – *Ergonomics; Graphical user interfaces; Input devices and strategies; Interaction styles; Prototyping; User-centered design; Voice I/O.*

Keywords

Mixed Reality; Intuitive Interaction; Remote Interaction; User Interface; Smartphone; Micro-projection Technology; Prototyping; Pointer Wizard; Finger Gesture; Voice Control;

ACKNOWLEDGMENTS

The authors gratefully acknowledge the support by the National Science Council, Taiwan, under grants 101-2218-E-011-039.

And we also thank the National Federation of CPA Associations of the Republic of China for giving us permission to use their conference hall for field testing[1]. And also thanks for participants who joined the testing and questionnaires.

REFERENCES

[1] Mistry, P., Maes, P., Chang L. 2009. WUW - Wear Ur World - A Wearable Gestural Interface. In *CHI '09 extended abstracts on Human factors in computing systems.* Boston, USA.

[2] Mistry, P., Maes, P. 2009. Unveiling the "Sixth Sense," game-changing wearable tech. *TED 2009.* Long Beach, CA, USA.

[3] Baur, D., Boring, S., and Feiner, S. 2012. Virtual Projection: Exploring Optical Projection as a Metaphor for Multi-Device Interaction. In *Proceedings of the SIGCHI Conference on Human Factors in Computing Systems* (Austin, Texas, USA, May 5-10, 2012) CHI'12. ACM, New York, NY.

[1] On Mar 11 and Mar 18, 2013, at the National Federation of Certified Public Accountant Associations of the Republic of China, 9th Floor, No.1, Nanhai Road, Taipei, Taiwan

Kwiizya: Local Cellular Network Services in Remote Areas

Mariya Zheleva[1], Abigail Hinsman[2], Lisa Parks[2] and Elizabeth Belding[1]
[1]Department of Computer Science and [2]Department of Film and Media Studies
University of California, Santa Barbara
{mariya,ebelding}@cs.ucsb.edu and {abigail_hinsman,parks}@filmandmedia.ucsb.edu

ABSTRACT

Cellular networks have revolutionized the way people communicate in rural areas. At the same time, deployment of commercial-grade cellular networks in areas with low population density, such as in rural sub-Saharan Africa, is prohibitively expensive relative to the return of investment. As a result, 48% of the rural population in Africa remains disconnected. To address this problem, we design a local cellular network architecture, Kwiizya, that provides basic voice and text messaging services in rural areas. We deployed an instance of Kwiizya in the rural village of Macha in Zambia. In this video we present interviews with people from the Macha community talking about their use of cellphones. We also present footage from the installation of Kwiizya in Macha.

Categories and Subject Descriptors

C.4 [**Performance of systems**]: Design studies

Keywords

Mobile telephony, Rural area networks, Low-cost communication, OpenBTS, Cellular communication

1. PROBLEM DESCRIPTION

Despite low availability and high cost of cellphone services, mobile phones are critical for providing communication in remote developing regions due to limited or non-existent infrastructure. During our three week field trip to Zambia in June/July 2012, we interviewed local residents to better understand their usage and experience with voice communication technologies. All our interviewees had owned a cellphone at some point; 96% owned a phone at the time of the interview. People who owned a phone either bought the phone (76%) or obtained it as a gift. Despite the high availability of cellphones among the group we interviewed, cellphones are very expensive relative to income; 68% of phone owners who bought their phone had to save between one month and one year to afford to buy that phone. Apart from buying the cellphone, the recurring cost for air time significantly adds to the financial burden for adoption of cellphone technology.

When asked what is enjoyable about cellphone usage, 100% of our interviewees identified the opportunity to stay in touch with relatives. 80% indicated that they use the phone to obtain information, such as crop pricing for farmers, availability of goods for local businessmen and communication with regional authorities. Users with more advanced phones and data subscriptions identify the importance of staying connected to the Internet at all times. With the low rate GPRS connection in Macha, however, all users with cell phone Internet access indicated that browsing is slow and frustrating.

Our interview findings confirm the importance of cellphone technology for residents of remote areas. While the reasons for adoption of cellphone technology are not drastically different than these in the western world, the benefits for people in remote communities is much more pronounced. Unfortunately, wide availability and affordability of such technology is still severely lacking.

2. CHALLENGES

The challenges associated with deployments of alternative cellular networks can be largely divided in technical, economical and regulatory. In our work we address the technical challenges by demonstrating the feasibility of a system based on RangeNetworks[1] hardware and open source software. Such system costs five to ten times less than a commercial-grade counterpart and consumes orders of magnitude less power than a commercial base station.

Apart from the technical challenges there are economic and regulatory factors that also play an important role in alternative cellular network deployments. Economic factors concern availability of financial resources to provision power, Internet access and equipment, while regulatory factors are largely related to licensing. Our partnership with LinkNet in Macha has helped us address economic aspects of Internet access and power availability. Licensing for experimental purposes is widely unregulated in sub-Saharan Africa. Furthermore, pricing of commercial licenses is oblivious to the potential return of investment. We argue that lower pricing or subsidizing commercial licenses for economically unattractive areas such as rural areas would encourage entrepreneurs to seek alternative technologies and deploy in such areas. In this context, while Kwiizya has great technological potential to provide low-cost cellular infrastructure, the full potential of the system is yet to be realized. This realization largely depends on multi-faceted economic analysis of alternative solutions for cellphone access.

MobiSys'13, June 25–28, 2013, Taipei, Taiwan.
ACM 978-1-4503-1672-9/13/06.

[1]`http://www.rangenetworks.com`

Multi-Screen Social TV over Cloud-Centric Media Platform

Xiang Li, Tian Xie and Yonggang Wen
School of Computer Engineering, Nanyang Technological University
LIXI0044@e.ntu.edu.sg, xietian@ntu.edu.sg, ygwen@ntu.edu.sg

ABSTRACT

Multi-screen social TV is an innovative application for transforming the traditional "laid-back" video watching behavior with the emerging "lean-forward" social network experience. In this video, we demonstrate a set of use cases in which the multi-screen social TV, developed over our patent-pending cloud-centric media platform, is leveraged to change the way we work, study and play in future.

Categories and Subject Descriptors

C.2 [**Computer-Communication Networks**]: Distributed Systems

Keywords

Social TV, Multi-Screen, Mobile Cloud Media

1. INTRODUCTION

The multi-screen Cloud Social TV would transform the traditional "laid-back" video watching with a "lean-forward" social networking experience, marrying TV to the social networking lifestyle of today. In this video clip, we illustrate a few use cases of multi-screen social TV, built upon our patent-pending cloud-centric media platform (CCMP), to understand its power in shaping the way we work, study and play in future. This system, upon its debut in 2012, has been featured in more than 1600 news articles from over 29 countries.

2. USER FEATURES FOR SOCIAL TV

In the cloud-centric media platform, we have implemented the following user features, as illustrated in Figure 1, including:

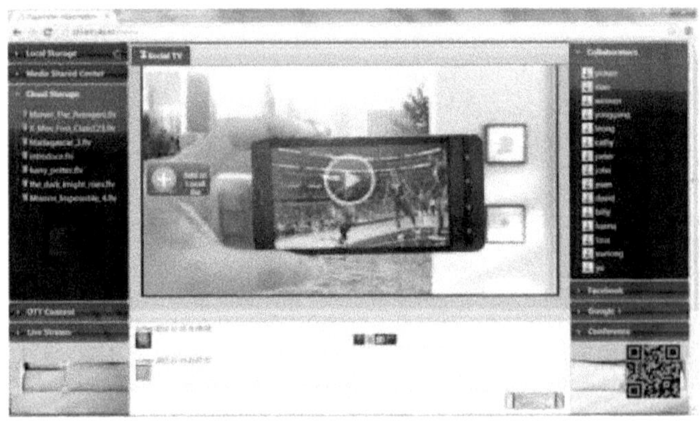

Figure 1: GUI for Multi-Screen Cloud Social TV

1. Content acquisition from diverse sources: the platform provides a "one-button" method, with flexible configuration capability, for the consumers to acquire video contents from different sources, including local DVRs, OTT content portals, shared resources from friend/family, and live TV streams.
2. Adaptive video streaming player: the video playback feature has self-adjusting capability to match the conditions in the network, screen size, content format, and user preference.
3. Communication by text, voice and video over private and public social networking: the platform allows the end users to communicate their friends from private group and public social networking profiles, while consuming the content of interest.
4. Video session migration across multiple screens: the platform leverages our proprietary video teleportation technique to enable the viewers to migrate video sessions across multiple screens with intuitive human-computer interaction (HCI) techniques, minimizing the learning process.
5. Collaborative content overlay: the system allows multiple viewers to edit the video program on the main screen collaboratively, and these changes are published for differentiated consumption.

3. CONCLUSIONS

This article presents the set of user features built into the cloud-centric media platform. We have designed and implemented an emerging multi-screen social TV application over the cloud-centric media platform, and the video clip illustrates potential use cases in changing the way we work, study and play.

MobiSys'13, June 25–28, 2013, Taipei, Taiwan.
ACM 978-1-4503-1672-9/13/06.

Rewriting an Android App using RetroSkeleton

Patrick Sheehan
University of California, Davis
pjsheehan@ucdavis.edu

Benjamin Davis
University of California, Davis
bendavis@ucdavis.edu

Hao Chen
University of California, Davis
chen@ucdavis.edu

ABSTRACT

This video demonstrates one potential application of RetroSkeleton [2], which is a system for specifying and applying transformations to Android apps via bytecode rewriting. These transformation policies are app-agnostic and can be applied to Android apps without any manual guidance. In this video, we show how RetroSkeleton can be used to automatically add custom fine-grained network access controls into an existing app, giving users more control over their apps. We also show the use of the RetroSkeleton web interface [1], available at `http://retroskeleton.com`.

Categories and Subject Descriptors

D.4.6 [**Operating Systems**]: Security and Protection

Keywords

Android; Dalvik; VM; bytecode; rewriting

1. ACKNOWLEDGMENTS

The content of this video is based upon work supported by the National Science Foundation under Grant No. 1018964.

2. REFERENCES

[1] B. Davis. RetroSkeleton: Android App Rewriting. `http://retroskeleton.com`.

[2] B. Davis and H. Chen. RetroSkeleton: Retrofitting Android Apps. In *11th International Conference on Mobile Systems, Applications and Services*, MobiSys '13, 2013.

Participatory Sensing and Crowd Management in Public Spaces

Tobias Franke
Paul Lukowicz
DFKI and University of Kaiserslautern
Germany
tobias.franke@dfki.de
paul.lukowicz@dfki.de

Martin Wirz
ETH Zurich
Switzerland
martin.wirz@ife.ee.ethz.ch

Eve Mitleton-Kelly
London School of Economics
UK
E.Mitleton-Kelly@lse.ac.uk

ABSTRACT

We present a smartphone app based system for crowd monitoring and management during large public events. The app has been deployed during a number of large scale public events including a large parade in London (Lord Mayor's Show), the Vienna marathon, the new Year's Eve celebrations in Zurich and the crowning ceremony of King Willem-Alexander in Amsterdam.

Categories and Subject Descriptors

C.2.4 [**Computer-Communications Networks**]: Distributed Systems—*Distributed Applications*

Keywords

Smartphones; Crowd Management; Participatory Sensing

1. MOTIVATION

Public safety and the management of emergencies in busy urban public spaces is a complex dynamic problem. In the long run, an understanding needs to be developed about how people use the space, where hot spots that can become potentially dangerous are located, and what signs of potential danger (e.g. dangerous crowd conditions) may look like. During concrete events a crowd of people and associated traffic need to be managed according to such an understanding. If a problem occurs in one area (e.g. extreme crowd density or panic) it needs to be quickly resolved through coordinated actions taking into account how these actions may impact the situation in other areas. Overall, the two key issues are situational awareness and the ability to efficiently execute coordinated actions potentially involving hundreds of thousands of people. Clearly, people-centric sensing [1], where users' personal devices provide data and peoples' mobility ensures the required coverage, is a promising approach to address these issues.

2. THE SOCIONICAL APP

As apart of the SOCIONICAL EU project we have developed a system that leverages the trend of using smartphone apps as the main information source for visitors to support crowd monitoring and management. Thus, the general idea is to (1) develop an app that provides enough information about an event to motivate a large number of people to use it, (2) build facilities for collecting relevant sensor data (assuming user informed consent) into the app and (3) delivering location and situation adapted messages in case of an emergency. Thus, our system consists of four parts. Firstly, there is a basic App kernel (currently running on Android and iOS with a Windows Phone version under development). Secondly, there is a web based tool that allows the App kernel to be quickly configured towards a specific event. Thirdly, there is a back-end that aggregates the sensor data into a representation of crowd density and state [2]. Finally there is a web front-end that allows the event organizers to access the density information during the event, to dynamically reconfigure the monitoring parameters and to issues messages to selected user groups. From the interviews with emergency services who have used the system during a variety of large events the following three benefits have been repeatedly highlighted. Firstly, the system provides an integrated, easily interpretable overview of the situation which is much easier to handle than many isolated CCTV cameras (which is the current state of the art). Secondly, the system allows predictions about the development of the crowd. Thirdly, the ability to send messages to users based on their location and state allows an unprecedented flexibility in terms of resolving potential problems. Finally, "post mortem" analysis of the data can provide important insight for the organisation of future events.

3. REFERENCES

[1] A. T. Campbell, S. B. Eisenman, N. D. Lane, E. Miluzzo, R. A. Peterson, H. Lu, X. Zheng, M. Musolesi, K. Fodor, and G.-S. Ahn. The rise of people-centric sensing. *Internet Computing, IEEE*, 12(4):12–21, 2008.

[2] M. Wirz, T. Franke, D. Roggen, E. Mitleton-Kelly, P. Lukowicz, and G. Troster. Inferring crowd conditions from pedestrians' location traces for real-time crowd monitoring during city-scale mass gatherings. In *Proc. IEEE WETICE 2012*, pages 367–372. IEEE, 2012.

MobiSys'13, June 25–28, 2013, Taipei, Taiwan.
ACM 978-1-4503-1672-9/13/06.

Demo: An Anonymous Matching System Based on Mobile Numbers

Jen-Hai Chou, Mi-Yen Yeh
Institute of Information Science, Academia Sinica, Taipei, Taiwan
jenhaic@gmail.com, miyen@iis.sinica.edu.tw

ABSTRACT

Many matchmaking applications help people find Mr./Ms. Right from people they might never meet. However, people usually tend to have a crush on someone in their daily life, such as classmates or colleagues. A big problem is: How to express love to your crush without hurting your original friendship? In response, we develop a mobile application, CrushList, to help people create a loving relationship with those around them based on an anonymous matching mechanism using mobile numbers as the user IDs. This is effective and efficient because mobile numbers are easy to access from one's mobile phone and the mobile contacts are usually those already known or met in one's daily life. The CrushList users can manage a *crush-list* by adding the mobile numbers of their crushes. Only when two users are in the *crush-list* of each other the system will notify both of them. Otherwise, a user always keeps anonymous to his/her crush.

Categories and Subject Descriptors

H.4[Information System Application]: Miscellaneous

Keywords

Mobile Number, Anonymous Matching

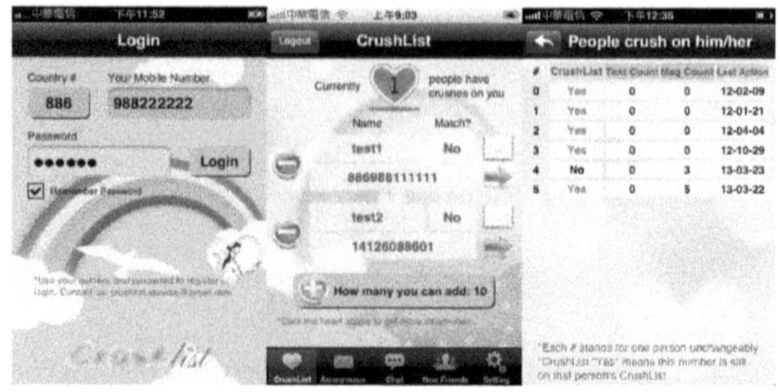

(a) Login interface (b) A crush-list (c) Distinct people

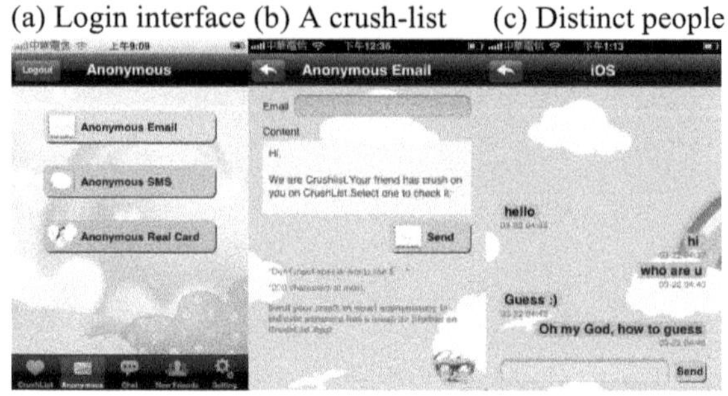

(d) Notifications (e) Anonymous email (f) Single blind chat

Figure 1: Screenshots of CrushList application

1. DEMONSTRATION SCENARIO

People use their mobile numbers to register as users in as shown in Figure 1(a). A user can add at most two mobile numbers at the same time from his/her mobile contacts to his/her *crush-list* as shown in Figure 1(b). Figure 1 (b) also shows the match results and how many people have a crush on this user. A user has default 12 quotas to change their *crush-list,* i.e., he/she can delete an old one and add a new one 12 times. If a user runs out of the default quotas, he/she can pay to have more quotas. A user can also add his/her crush's email to his/her *crush-list* to match other users. A user can press the heart icon or the green arrow in Figure 1(b) to to see more information about people having a crush on him/her or his/her crush as shown in Figure 1(c). Each row represents a fixed user, e.g., row 3 always shows information of the same user David. "Yes" in Figure 1(c) indicates that the row user still keeps his/her crush on his/her *crush-list*. The "Text Count" in Figure 1(c) stands for the number of SMS sent by the row user to his/her crush. The "Msg Count" stands for the number of messages sent within CrushList by the row user to his/her crush. A user can press the email icon in Figure 1(b) to check if his/her crush register on CrushList. If not, a user can go to Figure 1(d) to send his/her crush an anonymous notification that shows "someone has a crush you". There are three kinds of anonymous notifications: Anonymous Email, Anonymous SMS, and Anonymous Real Card. Figure 1(e) shows the template of an Anonymous Email. An Anonymous SMS/ Real Card is similar to an Anonymous Email, only sending a SMS/Real Card will be charged by CrushList. Figure 1(f) shows our special "single blind chat" function. CrushList users can chat on this application and only the one say "hello" first knows the other one. From our user study, users are curious and willing to chat with the one they do not know but has a crush on them. To the best of our knowledge, "CrushList" is the first system in the world to implement (i) *anonymous matching based on mobile numbers* and (ii) *single blind chat*. CrushList now can be downloaded on [1]. The demo video is on [2].

2. TECHNICAL CONTRIBUTIONS

When developing CrushList, we meet an issue to *identify the users' mobile numbers* when they forget the password. What the big companies such as Google and Facebook do is to send the password to the mobile number input by the users. However, this increases the cost of the companies. In contrast, we ask the users to send a text with their new password to us. Our way is more efficient and saves a lot of cost on sending SMS, which benefits startups or small companies

Besides, CrushList executes "*one device, one number*" policy. That is, once a user registers one mobile number successfully on his/her device, the device will get the same previously registered mobile number even if he/she deletes this application and re-install it. To implement this, we basically store the pair of a machine number and a mobile number in our database.

MobiSys'13, June 25–28, 2013, Taipei, Taiwan.
ACM 978-1-4503-1672-9/13/06.

REFERENCES

[1] Android & iPhone: http://goo.gl/aK6yL http://goo.gl/rbLci

[2] Demo Video: http://goo.gl/2p6Rh

Demo: Floodcasting, A Data Dissemination Service Supporting Real-Time Actuation and Control

Ye-Sheng Kuo, Pat Pannuto, and Prabal Dutta
Electrical Engineering and Computer Science Department
University of Michigan
Ann Arbor, MI 48109
{samkuo,ppannuto,prabal}@umich.edu

ABSTRACT

Packet collisions have gone from something to be avoided to something that can be embraced. We build upon recent results that employ intentional packet collisions for synchronized flooding to show how multi-hop wireless networks can support real-time actuation and control. First, we show how a network of nodes can synchronize their LED transmissions to extend the range of a visual light communication (VLC) system. Second, we show how buffer-free, streaming audio is possible over a multi-hop wireless mesh network.

Categories and Subject Descriptors

B.4.1 [**HARDWARE**]: Input/Output and Data Communications—*Input/Output Devices*; C.3 [**COMPUTER-COMMUNICATION NETWORKS**]: Special-Purpose and Application-Based Systems

General Terms

Design, Experimentation, Measurement, Performance

Keywords

Software-Defined Radio, IEEE 802.15.4, Wireless MAC Protocol, Constructive Interference, Real-Time

1. INTRODUCTION

Recent work exploited the concurrent transmission of hardware generated ACKs to achieve a low-power MAC layer protocol [1]. Follow-on work by Ferrari et al. debuted Glossy, a MAC protocol that attempted to exploit constructively interfering data packets to provide a cheap, efficient flooding protocol [2]. Practical Glossy implementation was stymied, however, by the inability of commercial radios to decode interfering full-length packets due to the envelope effect, severely limiting the data rate [3].

In this demo we present *Floodcasting*, a MAC protocol that provides a completely buffer-free, near real-time, high bandwidth, and tightly synchronized flood channel. We leverage our software defined radio platform, μSDR ([3]), to overcome the limitations of commercial radios and enable a continuous stream of constructively interfering full length IEEE 802.15.4 packets.

MobiSys'13, June 25–28, 2013, Taipei, Taiwan.
ACM 978-1-4503-1672-9/13/06.

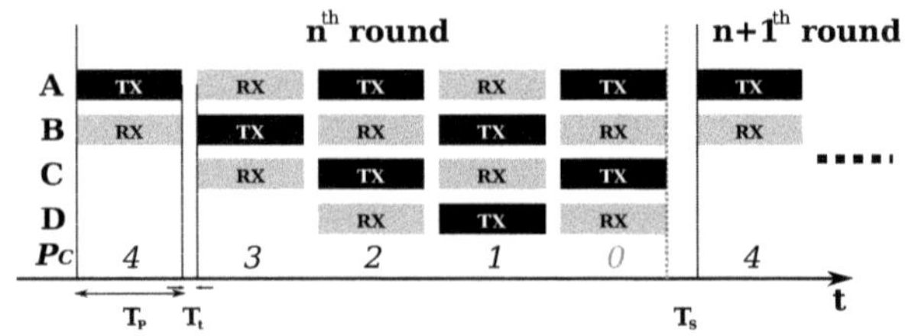

Figure 1: *Countdown Flooding*—Nodes A, B, C and D are all 1-hop from one another, connected linearly. In this example, node A initiates a countdown flood counting down from $P_C = 4$. At first, only node B receives the packet which it re-broadcasts after a turnaround time T_t with countdown value $P_C = 3$. This packet is then re-broadcast by nodes A and C with $P_C = 2$. This packet constructively interferes at node B and is simply received at node D. The re-broadcasting repeats until nodes A and C transmit a packet received by nodes B and D with $P_C = 0$. Upon completion of transmission/reception of the $P_C = 0$ packet, nodes A, B, C, and D simultaneously process the data packet.

2. DEMONSTRATION

To demonstrate the efficacy of Floodcasting, we demo two demanding applications built on our countdown flooding primitive (Fig 1) and deploy them on a testbed of μSDRs.

The first application is a tightly synchronized array of visual light communication (VLC) frontends. We show that by leveraging Floodcasting, the VLC drivers themselves can be made to generate constructively interfering waveforms to improve the range and coverage of VLC networks. We then build a buffer-free, real-time audio streaming application on top of a multi-hop wireless mesh network using Floodcasting. In this demonstration, we show that we can achieve sub-μs synchronization and high bandwidth communication across a multi-hop wireless mesh network.

3. REFERENCES

[1] P. Dutta, S. Dawson-Haggerty, Y. Chen, C.-J. M. Liang, and A. Terzis. Design and evaluation of a versatile and efficient receiver-initiated link layer for low-power wireless. In *SenSys '10*.

[2] F. Ferrari, M. Zimmerling, L. Thiele, and O. Saukh. Efficient network flooding and time synchronization with glossy. In *IPSN '11*.

[3] Y.-S. Kuo, P. Pannuto, T. Schmid, and P. Dutta. Reconfiguring the software radio to improve power, price, and portability. In *SenSys '12*.

Demo: Low-Cost Personal Air-Quality Monitor

Xiaofan Jiang, Ji Jia, Gansha Wu, and Jesse Fang
Intel Labs China
Beijing, P.R. China, 100190
fred.jiang@intel.com, ji.jia@ciilabs.org, gansha.wu@intel.com, jesse.z.fang@intel.com

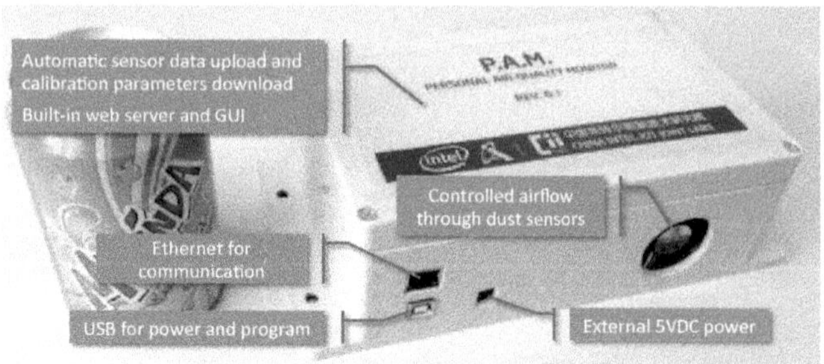

Figure 1: Personal air-quality monitor (PAM client)

ABSTRACT

We present the design, implementation, and preliminary results of PAM - a low-cost and portable personal air quality monitor that provides real-time air quality measurements for the user's immediate environment. PAM consists of a PAM client and a cloud-side PAM service. The PAM client utilizes two inexpensive dust sensors to obtain raw particulate concentration measurement, and two Arduino boards for local filtering, web services, and communication with PAM service. The cloud-side PAM service constructs a statistical model of air quality and provides PAM clients with context-dependent calibration curves. Together, PAM is able to approximate PM2.5, PM10, and AQI measurement for users in-situ and at low cost.

Categories and Subject Descriptors

H.4 [**Information Systems Applications**]: Miscellaneous

Keywords

Air quality, PM2.5, AQI, air pollution, particulate matter

1. PAM SYSTEM

Air quality is an integral part of our environment, and it affects our health on a daily basis. With increasingly deteriorating air in cities such as Beijing and New Delhi, residents are looking for better ways to monitor the air around them. There is growing number of smartphone applications that show air quality data such as PM2.5, PM10, and AQI, using publicly available data from regional air-quality stations. While this approaches gives the user a rough idea of city-level air quality, it cannot provide the user the actual air quality around her, which is much more relevant and valuable. Existing portable air quality monitors such as DustTrek II (5K USD) and Dylos (500USD) are still too expensive for personal use.

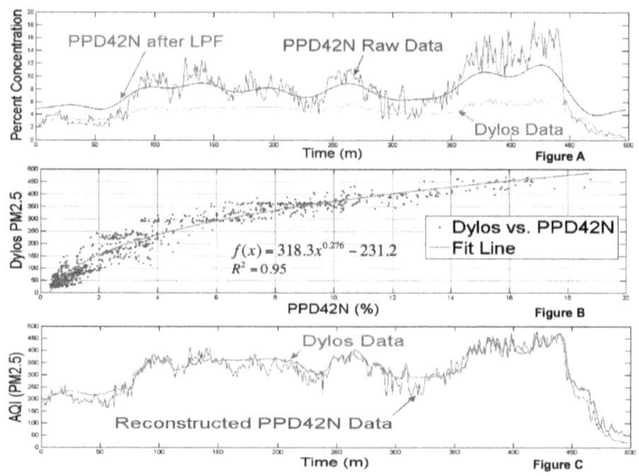

Figure 2: Data filtering (A), context-dependent calibration curve (B), and reconstructed AQI (C)

The PAM client, as shown in Figure 1, consists of two PPD42N dust sensors on each side of a wind conduit and two Arduino controllers. Raw particulate concentration data from PPD42N is filtered locally, as shown in Figure 2A, then sent to PAM service in the cloud via the Ethernet interface, together with contextual data such as location. PAM service continuously receives data from all PAM clients, and uses external data such as weather data, to construct a family of calibration curves, parameterized by temperature, humidity, pressure, and elevation, as shown in Figure 2B. Clients from similar locations are analyzed as a cluster. The selected calibration is then used to reconstruct the AQI, PM2.5, and PM10 estimations, as shown in Figure 2C. This data is finally sent back to the PAM client to be displayed to the user via the internal web server, shown in Figure 3.

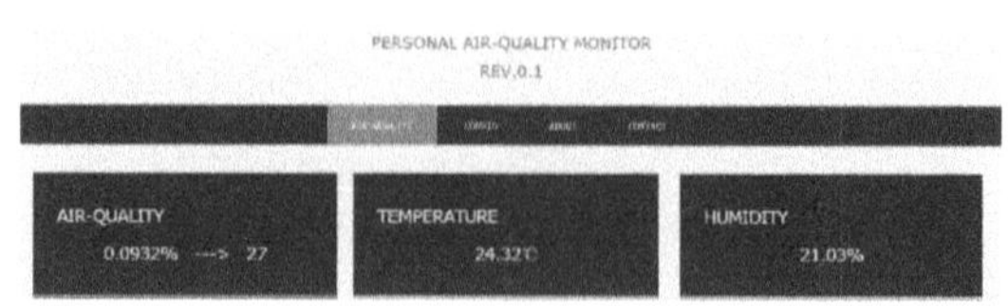

Figure 3: PAM client's embedded web server to display calibrated AQI information to the user

MobiSys'13, June 25–28, 2013, Taipei, Taiwan.
ACM 978-1-4503-1672-9/13/06.

DEMO: Power Management using Game State Detection on Android Smartphones

Benedikt Dietrich, Samarjit Chakraborty
Institute for Real-Time Computer Systems, TU Munich, Germany
{benedikt.dietrich, samarjit}@tum.de

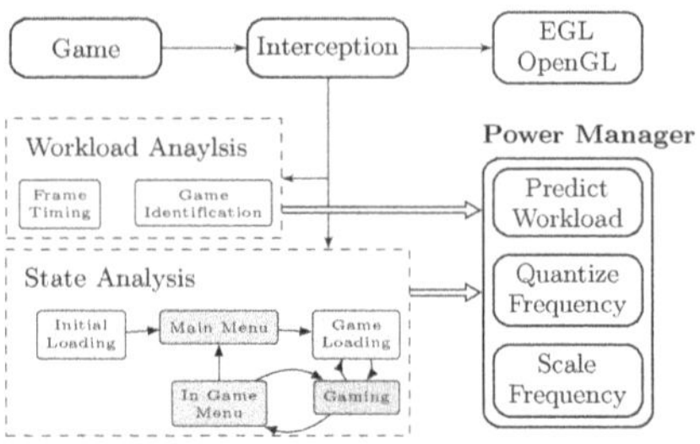

Figure 1: System Architecture Overview

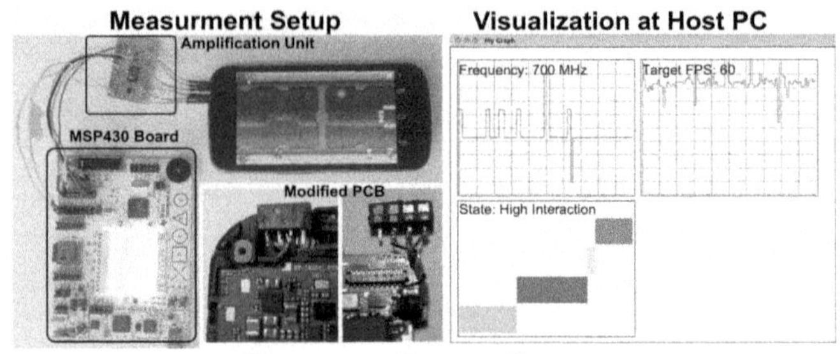

Figure 2: Demo Setup

Categories and Subject Descriptors

D.4.8 [**Operating Systems**]: Performance Measurements, Modeling and Prediction

Keywords

Android; Power Management; Workload Prediction; Mobile Games

1. INTRODUCTION

Compute intensive games currently represent the class of most popular and at the same time most power consuming applications on mobile phones. To reduce the power consumption of games we have developed a game state specific power management technique. Games typically consist of several *states* such as the game loading, main menu, in-game menu and gaming state. Each of these states has its specific processing requirements, e.g., the game loading state is likely to be memory bound and menu scenes are less interactive than gaming states and hence do not require high frame rates to satisfy the user's perception. Our `game state specific` governor (i) recognizes these game states by intercepting and analyzing calls made by the game application to the graphics library, and (ii) exploits these state-specific characteristics to enable power management strategies targeted to these individual states at runtime. Thereby, we achieve significant power savings of up to 50.8 % compared to Android's default `interactive` governor. In the following we describe the system architecture and the setup used during the demo.

2. SYSTEM ARCHITECTURE

We detect the game's current state based on the textures used to render the current frame. To identify the textures we intercept the game's texture related calls to the OpenGL library like shown in Figure 1. The gained state information is forwarded to our `game state specific` governor. To reduce the processor's power consumption we lower the processor's voltage and frequency whenever possible. If the current state is a memory bound loading state, the governor selects the processing frequency that minimizes the time the CPU is waiting for the memory. During interactive states like the gaming or menu state the governor maintains a state specific frame rate r_{state}. To predict the next frame's workload any suitable predictor can be used as the prediction is completely independent from the proposed technique to measure frame timings and detect states. In this work we predict the next frame's workload based on the timing of previous frames using an Autoregressive model. The frame timing of previous frames is measured by intercepting the `eglSwapBuffers()` call to the EGL library which is made by the game at the end of every frame. Based on the prediction result the governor selects a CPU frequency that allows finishing the processing of the next frame within $1/r_{state}$. As both, the state detection and the profiling mechanism are based on instrumenting Android's graphics libraries the game's source code is not required and hence the method can be applied to any Android based game.

3. DEMO SETUP

The demo setup consists of a Samsung Galaxy Nexus which has been modified to allow accurate CPU power measurements, a MSP430 based power measurement device and a monitor for live visualization purposes. During the demo we plan to invite the audience to play games like Cut the Rope, Jetpack Joyride or Temple Run using either the default `interactive` governor or our `game state specific` governor. While playing, the game's current state and the used processing frequencies are plotted. After the game the power measurement results for each game state and the total average power consumption are shown (see [1] for a video). This allows the audience to compare the performance of the two governors in terms of power savings and perceived gaming quality.

4. REFERENCES

[1] *Demo Video of Power Management using Game State Detection (http://www.rcs.ei.tum.de/en/staff/dietrich).*

MobiSys'13 June 25-28, 2013, Taipei, Taiwan
ACM 978-1-4503-1672-9/13/06.

Demo: Location-based Authentication System Using Space Dependent Information

Tatsuro Hachiya
Sophia University
hachiya@bandailab.org

Masaki Bandai
Sophia University
bandai@sophia.ac.jp

Categories and Subject Descriptors

C.2.1 [**Computer-Communication Networks**]: Network Architecture and Design—*Wireless Communication*

Keywords

Authentication, Location, Smartphone

1. INTRODUCTION

In this demonstration, we present SmartLocAuth: location-based authentication using space dependent information such as service set identifier (SSID) from WLAN access points. SmartLocAuth is a location-based authentication system. Figure 1 illustrates the concept of SmartLocAuth. SmartLocAuth can realize that an application can be unlocked within a predefined authentication area. There are three features on SmartLocAuth.

- Does not need GPS, unlike existing location-based authentication system [1]. Therefore, SmartLocAuth can be used indoor as well as outdoor environment.
- Can limit authentication area (within several meters).
- Not troublesome to unlock, unlike password.

2. SYSTEM DESIGN

SmartLocAuth uses Authentication list and Registration list. There are two processes in SmartLocAuth as follows:

- Process of registration
  1. Detect SSIDs around the device for T_A second.
  2. Add the detected SSIDs into its Registration list.
- Process of authentication
  1. Detect SSIDs around the device.
  2. Add the SSIDs into its Authentication list.
  3. Compare Registration list and Authentication list, then compute the concordance rate P.
  4. If P is equal or greater than the threshold of the concordance rate P_{th}, the authentication is succeed. If not, the authentication is failed.

P is defined as follows:

$$P = \frac{\text{Number of concordance}}{\text{Number of SSIDs in Authentication list}} \times 100$$

The number of concordance is defined as the number of SSIDs which are included in both Registration list and Authentication list.

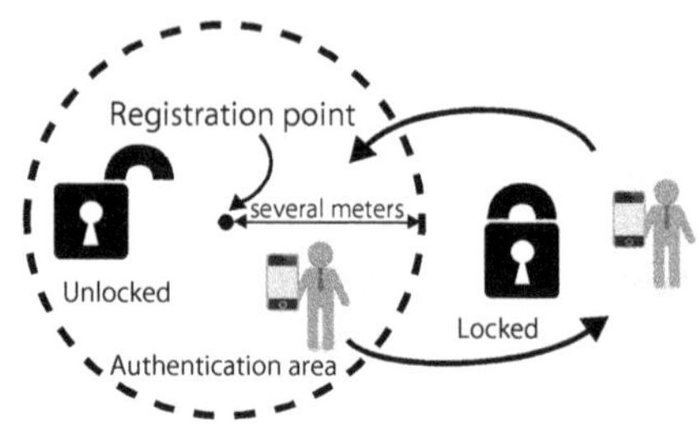

Figure 1: SmartLocAuth system

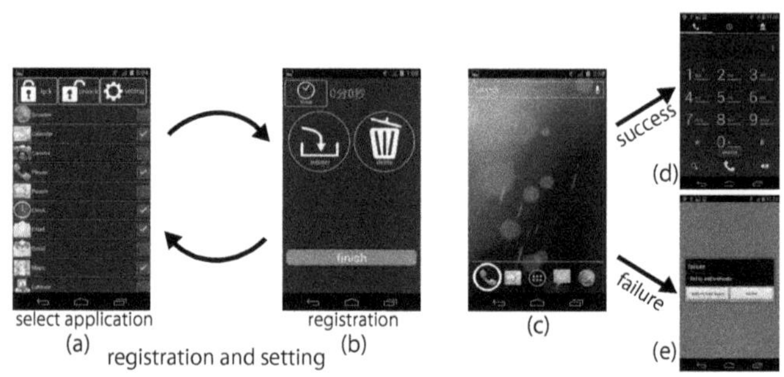

Figure 2: Screen shot of SmartLocAuth

3. IMPLEMENTATION

We implement SmartLocAuth in Galaxy Nexus (Android 4.0) and Nexus 4 (Android 4.2). Figure 2 shows the screen shot of SmartLocAuth. After selecting applications to lock (a), the process of registration starts (b). When a user launches the application (c), the process of authentication is called. If the authentication succeeds, the application is unlocked (d). If not, the application is still locked (e).

Note that an existing location-based authentication [2] can lock/unlock applications when the smartphone is connecting to a preregistered WLAN such as home. SmartLocAuth has an advantage that WLAN connections are unnecessary.

We have confirmed that SmartLocAuth can limit several meters of authentication area via indoor experiments.

4. REFERENCES

[1] H. Liao and P. Lee. "A Novel Vision-based Location Authentication Approach in a Ubiquitous Camera Environment," *Information Technology Journal*, 9, (8), pp. 1571–1584, 2010.

[2] Unlock With WiFi
http://benhirashima.com/unlockwithwifi/

Demo: Compass Fusion: High Precision Indoor People Localization and Identification

Wei-Chih Lin[a,b], Shih-Wei Sun[a,b,†], Wen-Huang Cheng[c,‡], Ya-Ting Chang[a,b], and Yu-Cong Lan[a,b]
[a]Dept. New Media Art and [b]Center for Art and Technology, Taipei National University of the Arts,
[c]Research Center for Information Technology Innovation, Academia Sinica, Taipei, Taiwan
[†]swsun@newmedia.tnua.edu.tw, [‡]whcheng@citi.sinica.edu.tw

Categories and Subject Descriptors

H.4.m [**Information Systems Applications**]: Miscellaneous

Keywords

Indoor Localization, Indoor Positioning, Compass, Mobile Device, Depth Camera, Fusion

1. INTRODUCTION

Indoor localization has attracted more and more attention with the growth of emerging location-based services (LBS) [1], e.g. microblogging, location-based content sharing, and interactive indoor multimedia display. In the literature, wireless-based indoor positioning for hand-held mobile devices is in meter-level precision, including WLAN (Wi-Fi), Bluetooth, and GSM-based approaches [2]. A smartphone-based LBS fusing various sensors, such as accelerometer, digital compass, Wi-Fi, and GPS, can achieve the localization at a better room-level accuracy [1]. In addition, the scanned Wi-Fi access point can determine the room-level identification for a mobile user. However, when multiple human subjects locating in the same coverage area for the same Wi-Fi access points, e.g. in the same room, the individuals often cannot be identified from each other.

Therefore, in order to achieve a high precision in a centimeter level for the indoor localization, we extended our head detection scheme of detecting people from depth camera [3], with an average estimation accuracy of 98.72%, and an average distortion of 2.06 cm. That is, because the compass of a mobile device can provide the orientation of how a human subject holds the mobile device, we proposed to fuse the orientation information analyzed according to the trajectory of a human subject obtained from depth cameras, for enhancing both the indoor localization and people identification accuracies to a centimeter level.

1.1 System Overview

Using the compass orientation history of a mobile device and the trajectory orientation history obtained from a depth camera, as shown in Fig. 1(a), we can observe that the different patterns of dynamic changes in the two modalities can help to reveal the identity of a user, as shown in Fig. 1(b). Therefore, when different users holding their own mobile devices (left part of Fig. 1(c)), the user ID login information sent with the compass sensor data to the cloud server can locate and identify the people in the same place with centimeter-level precision (right part of Fig. 1(c)).

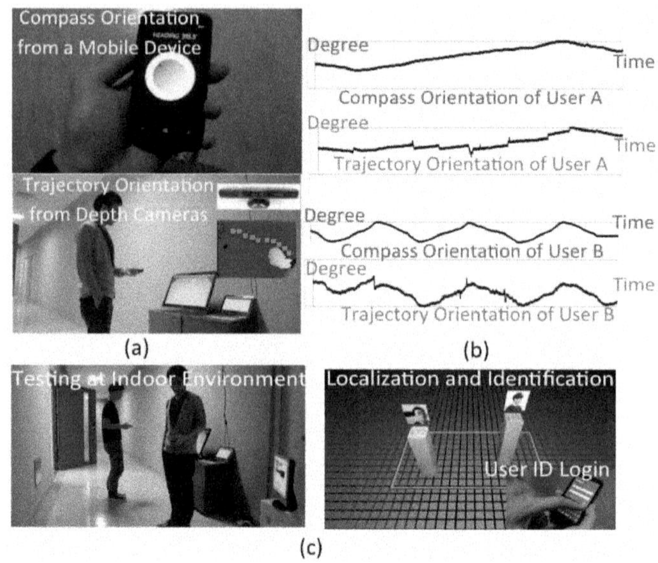

Figure 1: Compass fusion elements: (a) the compass orientation from a mobile device and the trajectory orientation calculated from depth cameras, (b) the measured orientations for two different users, and (c) real-time testing to locate and identify the users.

2. DEMONSTRATION

Our system (http://youtu.be/uKqklFYW6uQ) is deployed on three platforms of mobile devices: iOS, Android, and Windows phone. The depth data are obtained from a Kinect camera. In the real-time testing, multiple human subjects holding their own mobile devices can freely move in the Kinect camera's field of view. As shown in Fig. 1(c), the real-time results are presented by a 3D visualizaion, i.e. a located/identified user is placed in a virtual mapping of the physical space with the corresponding Facebook photo.

3. REFERENCES

[1] Y. Chon and H. Cha , "LifeMap: A smartphone-based context provider for location-based services," *IEEE Pervasive Computing*, 2011.
[2] H. Liu *et al.*, "Survey of wireless indoor positioning techniques and systems," *IEEE TSMC:C*, 2007.
[3] S.W. Sun *et al.*, "Whac-a-Mole: A head detection scheme by estimating the 3D envelope from depth image," *IEEE ICME*, 2013.

Demo- SocioPhone: Everyday Face-To-Face Interaction Monitoring Platform Using Multi-Phone Sensor Fusion

Youngki Lee[1], Chulhong Min[2], Chanyou Hwang[2], Jaeung Lee[3], Inseok Hwang[2,4], Younghyun Ju[2], Chungkuk Yoo[2], Miri Moon[3], Uichin Lee[5], Junehwa Song[2]

[1]School of Information Systems, Singapore Management University
[2]Computer Science Department, KAIST, [3]Web Science and Technology Division, KAIST,
[4]Center for Mobile Software Platform, KAIST, [5]Knowledge Service Engineering Department, KAIST

[1]youngkilee@smu.edu.sg, {chulhong, chanyou, leejai, inseok, yhju, ckyoo, miri.moon, junesong}@nclab.kaist.ac.kr, [5]uclee@kaist.edu

Categories and Subject Descriptors

K.8 [**Personal Computing**]: General; C.3 [**Special-Purpose and Application-based Systems**]: Real-time and embedded systems

Keywords

Interaction; Conversation; Social; Platform; Volume Topography

1. INTRODUCTION

In this demo, we introduce SocioPhone, a novel initiative toward everyday face-to-face interaction monitoring platform. Among diverse verbal, aural, visual cues expressed during face-to-face interaction, SocioPhone captures diverse *meta-linguistic* information from conversations and provides *interaction-aware applications* on-the-fly. Undoubtedly, conversations are a key channel for face-to-face interaction. Specifically, monitoring conversational turns, i.e., alternation of different speakers (including none speaking), is the first crucial step to derive diverse interesting aspects of conversations, e.g., who is talking right now, how long and often one talks, how quickly one responds to another, and so on. In this demo, we will show the core technique of SocioPhone, *volume-topography*-based *turn monitoring,* which is highly accurate and energy-efficient under diverse real-life situations. In addition, we will demonstrate several example applications running on SocioPhone.

2. CONVERSATION TURN MONITORING

With SocioPhone, multiple smartphones work together to detect turn changes and associated speakers, along with a short in-situ training. Naturally placed phones belonging to a conversation group simultaneously sense a speaker's voice signals, but capture the signals with different strengths depending on their positions. Such relative sensory readings can be fused in realtime to form a *volume topography*, i.e., a signature vector of volume values sensed over different phones (See Figure 1). Our key observation is that such a topography is unique to each speaker, showing enough discrimination power to identify turns and associated speakers. With a short training period, e.g., 30-60 seconds at the beginning of a conversation, frequent turn-taking of speakers can be quickly and precisely traced through simple vector matching.

Our volume-topography-based technique has important advantages. First, volume parameters can be instantly and reliably estimated, even with a very short sensing window, e.g., 0.3 seconds; this enables to monitor dynamic turn-taking behavior in a highly agile way. Second, volume-topography is less susceptible to diverse environmental noises as it is built in-situ to reflect the current noise characteristics. Third, our approach is computationally much lighter than existing techniques for speaker recognition and diarization; it does not require complex signal processing such as MFCC extraction and GMM matching. Finally, we note that the method works well even at very low sampling rates (as low as 500 Hz), which has the potential to reduce users' privacy concerns.

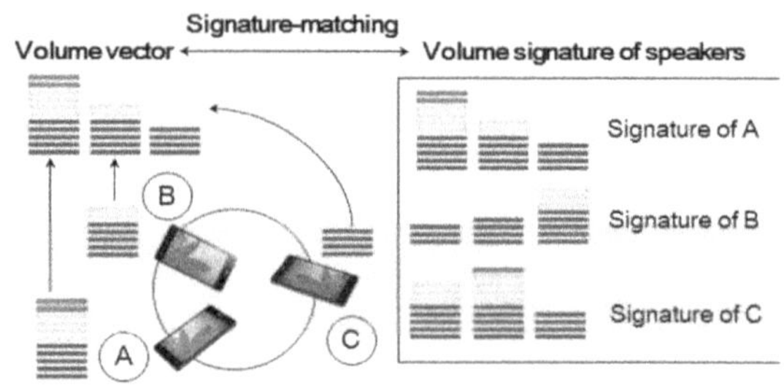

Figure 1 Illustration of in-situ turn monitoring

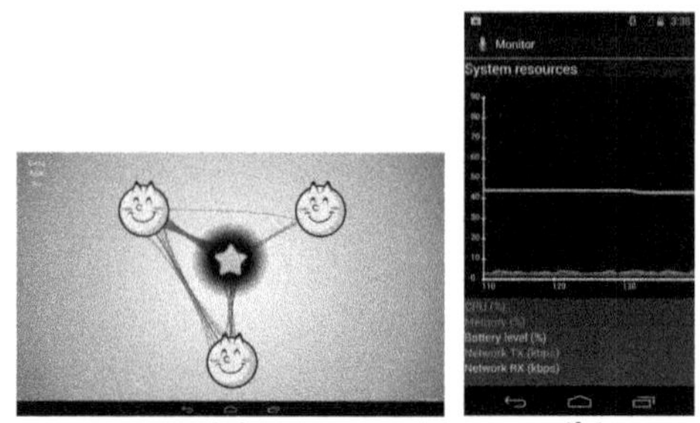

(a) (b)

Figure 2 Screenshots of applications

3. DEMONSTRATION

Turn Monitoring: We first demonstrate in-situ turn monitoring enabled by SocioPhone. We plan to setup a live visualization of the turn monitoring in the natural conversation between the guest and our staffs. Figure 2 (a) shows a screenshot of our conversation visualizer, denoting who are taking a turn from whom. In addition, we plan to demonstrate the resource feasibility of SocioPhone through our live resource monitor (see Figure 2 (b)).

Applications: We present a short video of everyday speech therapy for autistic children. This video delivers a concise digest of our field study at a local kindergarten with an autistic child. Following that, we show an initial deployment of our application designed to promote desirable conversation practices.

ACKNOWLEDGEMENT

This research was supported by the SW Computing R&D Program of KEIT(2012-10041313, UX-oriented Mobile SW Platform) funded by the Ministry of Knowledge Economy of Korea.

[1] This work was done while this author was at KAIST.

MobiSys'13, June 25–28, 2013, Taipei, Taiwan.
ACM 978-1-4503-1672-9/13/06.

Demo: A Mobile Live TV System for Taiwan High-Speed Rail

Hsin-Ta Chiao, Shih-Ying Chang, Yi-Ting Kuo, Ming Jing Li, Ming-Chien Tseng
Information and Communications Research Laboratories, ITRI
Chutung, Hsinchu, Taiwan
E-mail: {JosephChiao, itriA00550, ytkuo, itriA10324, MCTseng}@itri.org.tw

ABSTRACT

In Taiwan, because of the Doppler effects and tunnel shading, it is difficult to smoothly receive a live DVB-T channel inside a high-speed train by a laptop equipped with an ordinary DVB-T USB dongle. For providing live TV services inside a high-speed train, we develop a mobile live TV system for Taiwan High-speed Rail (THSR). The proposed system delivers live TV programs to a high-speed train through the mobile WiMAX network deployed along the THSR railway by the WiMAX operator VeeTime. Then, the received live TV programs are delivered to the terminal devices of high-speed rail passengers through Wi-Fi multicast. Using Wi-Fi multicast inside a high-speed train is necessary since there may be several hundreds of concurrent users on the same high-speed train. However, conventionally to provide a scalable Wi-Fi multicast streaming system is difficult because no extra reliability control mechanisms such as ARQ (Automatic Repeat-reQuest) are available for Wi-Fi multicast. Instead we overcome the difficulty of scalable Wi-Fi multicast streaming by using AL-FEC (Application Layer – Forward Error Correction). Hence, in the demo session of MobiSys 2013, we plan to show the whole mobile live TV system with a live TV input, especially focused on its capability of scalable Wi-Fi multicast streaming over a multi-hop Wi-Fi network that can emulate the real multi-hop Wi-Fi network inside a high-speed train.

Categories and Subject Descriptors

H.4.3 [**Communications Applications**], H.5.1 [**Multimedia Information Systems**].

Keywords

Wi-Fi multicast streaming; AL-FEC; high-mobility streaming.

1. SYSTEM ARCHITECTURE

Figure 1 shows the architecture of the proposed mobile live TV system for the demonstration over a real high-speed train. Both the VeeTime AV encoder and the ITRI head-end server are located in a server room of VeeTIME in Taichung city. In order to reduce the bandwidth consumption of the mobile WiMAX network, the VeeTIME AV encoder is responsible for trans-coding the program data of two live cable TV channels to meet the bandwidth requirement, which is about 600 to 900 Kbps for each channel in SD (Standard Definition) resolution. Then, the ITRI head-end server receives the audio and video data after trans-coding and encapsulates them into short file clips. For delivering the file clips through the mobile WiMAX network to the IPC (Industrial PC) inside a high-speed train, we develop a reliable FLUTE (File Delivery over Unidirectional Transport) protocol, which is a unicast file delivery protocol also based on AL-FEC to handle the packet losses due to high-mobility [1].

Inside a high-speed train, the multicast streaming server in the IPC delivers a multicast streaming service of two channels through the multi-hop Wi-Fi network across the 12 cars of the high-speed train, as shown in Figure 2. Here we use a scalable FEC framework to enhance the RTP multicast streaming service for compensating lost multicast packets [2]. In addition, we also provide fast channel switch capability because the protection period of AL-FEC is long (i.e., about 9.6 to 12.9 seconds).

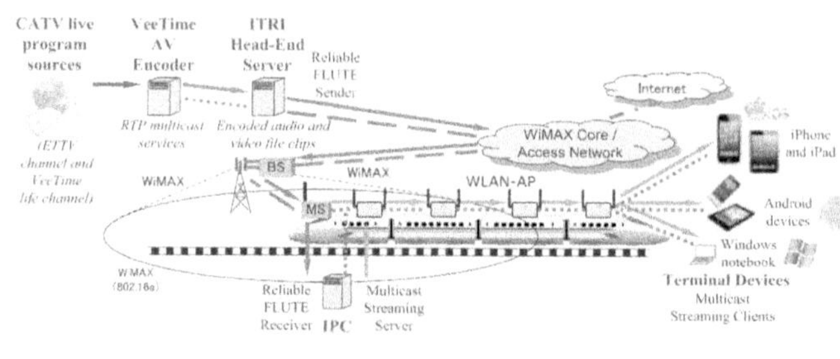

Figure 1. The architecture of the mobile live TV system.

For the demonstration in MobiSys 2013, we plan to move the head-end servers to the MobiSys demo site directly. Besides, an IPC and the equipments of a multi-hop Wi-Fi network will also be moved to the demo site for emulating the environment in Figure 2.

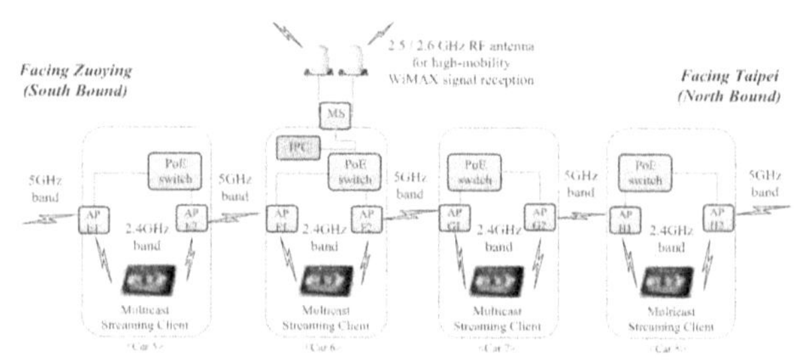

Figure 2. The multi-hop Wi-Fi network for a high-speed train.

2. REFERENCES

[1] Chang, S., Chiao, H., Yeh X., Tseng, M., 2013. UDP-Based File Delivery Mechanism for Video Streaming to High-Speed Trains. *Submitted to the IEEE PIMRC 2013*.

[2] Chiao, H., Chang, S., Li, K., Kuo, Y., Tseng, M. 2012. WiFi Multicast Streaming Using AL-FEC Inside the Trains of High-Speed Rails. In *Proceedings of the IEEE BMSB 2012*.

Demo: Indoor Geolocation on Multi-Sensor Smartphones

Chin-Lung Li
Cywee Corporation Ltd
Taipei, Taiwan
chinlung@cywee.com

Christos Laoudias
KIOS Research Center
University of Cyprus
laoudias@ucy.ac.cy

George Larkou
Dept. of Computer Science
University of Cyprus
glarko01@cs.ucy.ac.cy

Yu-Kuen Tsai
Cywee Corporation Ltd
Taipei, Taiwan
YKTsai@cywee.com

Demetrios Zeinalipour-Yazti
Dept. of Computer Science
University of Cyprus
dzeina@cs.ucy.ac.cy

Christos G. Panayiotou
KIOS Research Center
University of Cyprus
christosp@ucy.ac.cy

ABSTRACT

In this demo, we present an efficient hybrid indoor positioning solution that uses multi-sensory location-oriented observations, including WiFi, accelerometer, gyroscope and digital compass data, that are widely available on Android smartphones[1]. Our system mainly comprises three building blocks, namely the *WiFi Fingerprinting*, the *Inertial Measurement Unit (IMU) Positioning* and the *Location Fusion* components.

The *WiFi Fingerprinting* module relies on existing WiFi infrastructure and exploits Received Signal Strength (RSS) values from neighboring Access Points (AP) to infer the unknown user location. Specifically, it utilizes a number of RSS fingerprints collected a priori to build the so-called radiomap. Subsequently, the WiFi-based location is estimated with a state-of-the-art algorithm that exploits the currently measured fingerprint and fingerprints in the radiomap [1].

The *IMU Positioning* module performs multi-dimensional (i.e., 3-axis accelerometer, gyroscope and digital compass) motion sensor fusion for calculating the user orientation in real-time and implements an in-house pedometer algorithm for pedestrian trajectory tracking. An interesting feature in our implementation is the use of raw magnetic data to detect magnetic anomalies, which are common inside buildings, e.g. due to power cables, electrical appliances or metal surfaces, in order to refine orientation. Moreover, a map-matching submodule performs error correction in order to handle inaccurate IMU location estimates (e.g., showing a user passing through a wall or moving into a restricted area).

Finally, the WiFi-based and IMU-based location estimates and associated uncertainties are provided as inputs to the *Location Fusion* module that implements the hybridization scheme by means of a particle filter. Thus, our prototype system delivers a smooth final location estimate that is consistent with the actual travelled path; see Fig. 1.

We will demonstrate the real-time positioning capabilities of our hybrid system by allowing attendees to carry an Android smartphone running our tracking application and viewing their current location on a floorplan map, while walking around the demo area. In this interactive scenario, the participants will be able to appreciate the potential of our indoor geolocation system, which is reliable and attains a localization error below 3 meters through the integration and optimization of diverse technologies, while our software may run on any commercial Android smartphone.

Figure 1: Indoor localization using solely WiFi (left), solely IMU (middle) and location fusion (right) while a user walks several times along a rectangular path in a typical office environment.

[1]An early version of our prototype system was recently evaluated in a conference venue and the demo video is available at: `http://youtu.be/DyvQLSuI0OI`

Categories and Subject Descriptors

H.4 [**Information Systems Applications**]: Miscellaneous

Keywords

Indoor positioning, WiFi, Signal strength, Android, Sensors

1. REFERENCES

[1] C. Laoudias et al., "Localization Using Radial Basis Function Networks and Signal Strength Fingerprints in WLAN," in *IEEE GLOBECOM*, 2009, pp. 1–6.

MobiSys'13, June 25–28, 2013, Taipei, Taiwan.
ACM 978-1-4503-1672-9/13/06.

Demo: Yes, Right There! A Self-Portrait Application with Sensor-Assisted Guiding for Smartphones

Chi-Chung Lo, Sz-Pin Huang, Yi Ren, and Yu-Chee Tseng
Department of Computer Science, National Chiao-Tung University, Hsin-Chu, Taiwan
Email: {ccluo, sphuang, renyi, yctseng}@cs.nctu.edu.tw

1. ABSTRACT

Taking self-portrait on a smartphone is a lot of fun and can be easy when we know how (Fig. 1a). In addition, thank to self-timer, giving a delay between pressing the shutter release and the shutter's firing, we are able to take photos of ourselves when nobody on hand to take it (Fig. 1b). However, there are rare cases that we can get satisfied snapshots at our first try. The reason is that we usually had no idea whether we were in the right position of the camera frame (Figs. 1c, 2a and 2c). Although the front camera can help us to check position in the frame, its generated snapshot quality is much lower than that taken by the back camera. In this demo we will introduce a self-portrait App – "Yes, right there!" The App enables a camera to prevent faces from being cut out of the camera frame by giving suggestions to users until they are in a suitable position in the frame, as shown in Fig. 1d, Fig. 2b, and Fig. 2d. The suggestions are voice commands including "Raise your hand!", "Come closer!", "Please move to the left", and so on. They depend on the face's position in the camera frame [1] and the inertial sensing data on the phone. In the end, a good picture is then taken after the beep sounds.

More concretely, "Yes, right there!" supports two modes: *self-portrait mode* and *self-timer mode*. In self-portrait mode, our App initially asks users to take favorite photos as pre-training references. In the meantime, the application measures the yaw, pitch, and roll values from accelerometer, electronic compass, and gyro. Note that the users usually like to take photos with a special angle. Once a user wants to take self-portrait, she points the lens at herself so that her face is reflected in the camera frame. The App detects the face's position in the camera frame and measures the yaw, pitch, and roll values. Then the face's position and the inertial sensing data are being compared against the pre-training references while the App suggests the user to change her posture by voice commands. If the face moves to the right position and the yaw, pitch, and roll values are suitable, a good picture is then taken automatically; otherwise, the App repeats the suggestions. Note that the self-portrait mode can be easily extended for multiple users.

In self-timer mode, the user firstly specifies an area where she wants her face to appear in the frame. When the App works, it compares the position of her face against the area specified, and suggests the user to change her location by voice commands. As shown in Fig. 2a, the user's face is detected appearing in the grid 1 (outside the specified area in the frame). The voice interactive function is triggered to lead the user by saying "Please move to the left and then come closer, etc." until she moves to the suitable position (Fig. 2b). When the App works for multiple users, as shown in Fig. 2c, it detects that a user in the left side is not in the area specified (gird 5), and then the voice interactive function will give suggestions (e.g., The user in the right side please moves to the left, etc.) until all the users are appearing in the specified area in the frame (Fig. 2d). Fig. 3 shows our system model.

We will distribute Android phones to demo visitors, allowing real-time interaction with user interface on these phones. We will also show how "Yes, right there!" recommends users taking self-portrait without assistance from others. Moreover, users can set timer for different waiting intervals, and specify the number and range of the grid which is considered as suitable position. To the best of our knowledge, this is the first work that shows how to help users take self-portrait by detecting the face's position in the camera frame and measuring the inertial sensing data on the phone.

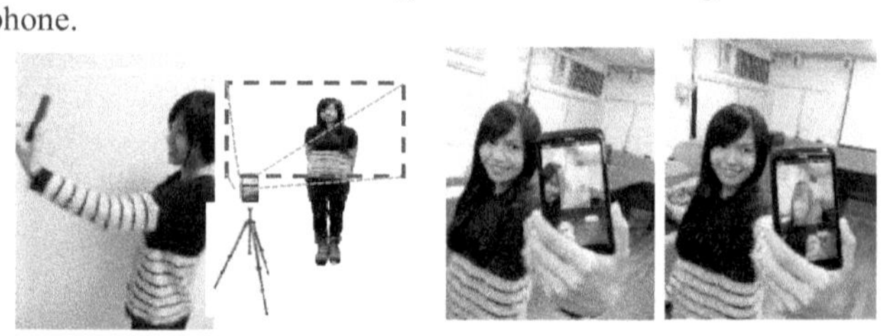

(a) (b) (c) (d)

Figure 1.: Examples of (a) self-portrait, (b) self-timer, (c) unsatisfied photo, and (d) satisfied photo for a single user.

(a) (b) (c) (d)

Figure 2.: Examples of (a) unsatisfied photo, (b) satisfied photo for a single user, (c) unsatisfied photo, and (d) satisfied photo for multiple users in the self-timer mode.

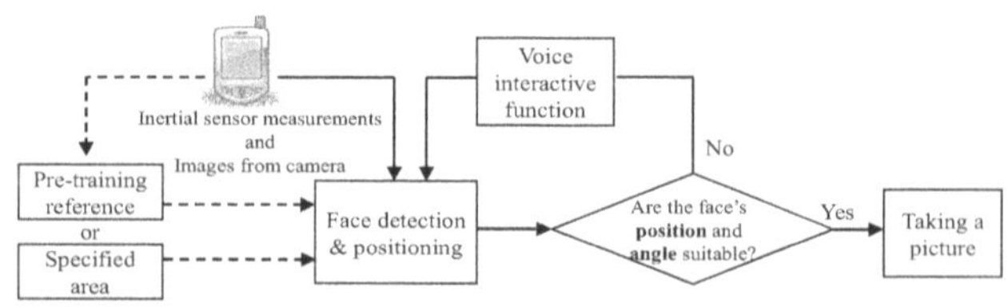

Figure 3.: The "Yes, right there!" system model.

Categories and Subject Descriptors

C.5.3 [**Computer System Implementation**]: Microcomputers - Portable devices, Personal computers

Keywords

Camera, Face Detection, Inertial Sensor, Smartphone

2. REFERENCES

[1] Suzuki, M. 2012. Image pickup apparatus for performing a desirable self-timer shooting and an automatic shooting method using the same. *U.S. Patent 8,194,140*, (Jun. 2012).

MobiSys '13, June 25-28, 2013, Taipei, Taiwan.
ACM 978-1-4503-1672-9/13/06.

Demo: BiFocus – Using Radio-Optical Beacons for An Augmented Reality Search Application

Ashwin Ashok[†], Chenren Xu[†], Tam Vu[†], Marco Gruteser[†], Richard Howard[†], Yanyong Zhang[†]
Narayan Mandayam[†], Wenjia Yuan[‡], Kristin Dana[‡]
[†]WINLAB, Rutgers University, [‡] Department of ECE, Rutgers University
{aashok, lendlice, tamvu, gruteser, reh, yyzhang, narayan}@winlab.rutgers.edu[†],
wenjiay@rutgers.edu[‡], kdana@ece.rutgers.edu[‡]

ABSTRACT

Augmented Reality (AR) applications benefit from accurate detection of the objects that are within a person's view. Typically, it is not only desirable to identify what is currently within view, but also to navigate the users view to the item of interest - for example, finding a misplaced object. In this paper we demonstrate a low-power hybrid radio-optical beaconing system, where objects of interest are tagged with battery-powered RFID-like tags equipped with infrared light emitting diodes (LED) that emit periodic infrared beacons. These beacons are used for accurately estimating the angle and distance from the object to the receiver so as to locate it. The beacons are synchronized using the radio link that is also used to convey the object's unique ID.

Categories and Subject Descriptors

C.2.1 [**Computer-Communication Networks**]: Network Architecture and Design—*Wireless Communication*

Keywords

Augmented Reality, Radio, RFID, Optical, Infrared, Angular Estimation, Ranging

1. INTRODUCTION

We often need to find a specific item in a rather chaotic setting – for example, a toy in a house, items in a office room, or a product in the grocery store. In this application it is not only desirable to identify what is currently within view, but also to direct the users view to the item of interest. The problem can be reduced to determining the angle of the object from a persons direction of view as well as the distance of the object from the viewer.

Presumably, the object that is closest to the direction of view (smallest angle) and closest to the viewer (smallest distance) is the one the person is looking at. When the right object is within the user's concentrated view (human eye has a concentrated vision within its fovea [3]), it is important that the angular resolution is sufficient to discriminate among these objects. With 50cm spacing between objects and a 3m distance between the user and the objects, the angular resolution required is about 10 degrees; with 10cm spacing and a 1-3m distance, the angle resolution required can be as small as 2 degrees.

Radio–Optical Beaconing Approach: Current barcode tagging approaches for augmented reality are very limited in reading range, while active RFID tags suffer from imprecise angle of arrival estimates [2]. To fill this void, we designed a low-power hybrid radio-optical beaconing system, where active RFID-like tags enhanced with a IR LED, emit a high energy light beacon which is detected and sampled by the photodiode elements at a receiver IR unit. The received IR signal energy is used to estimate the angle and distance between the transmitter and receiver with high accuracy, while the RF link provides tag ID and receiver synchronization of the extremely short IR pulses to lower energy consumption.

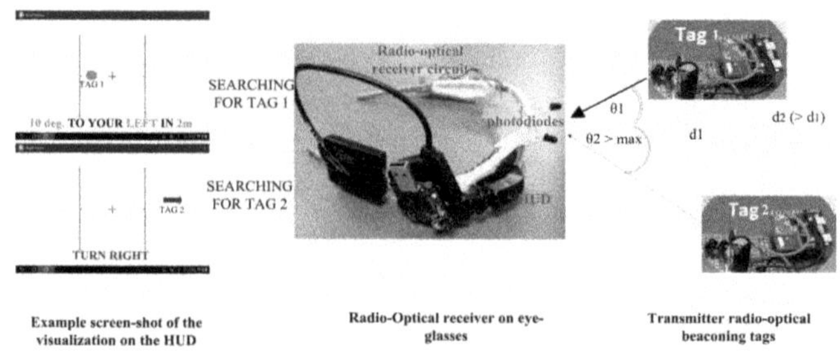

Figure 1: Illustration of the system demonstration

2. DEMONSTRATION SETUP

We will demonstrate our system using a receiver apparatus where the radio-IR receiver with two photodiodes is mounted onto eye-glasses along with a heads-up-display [1](HUD).

The radio transceiver also periodically uploads the object position data to a web-server. We will tag objects with our transmitter tags (each bearing a unique ID) and let the attendees find the object through the navigation aids we will provide through an app on the heads-up-display. We will also demonstrate the details of the system functions using a calibrated setup. Figure 1 shows an example screen-shot of the visualization along with the glasses and transmitter tags.

3. REFERENCES

[1] Recon mod-live heads-up-display. http://www.reconinstruments.com/products/snow-heads-up-display.

[2] Artag. http://www.artag.net/, 2009.

[3] C. Yuodelis and A. Hendrickson. A qualitative and quantitative analysis of the human fovea during development. *Vision Research*, 26(6):847 – 855, 1986.

Demo: Visible Light Communications for Scooter Safety

Shun-Hsiang You[1,2], Shih-Hao Chang[1†], Hao-Min Lin[1,2], and Hsin-Mu Tsai[1,2]
Intel-NTU Connected Context Computing Center[1] and
Department of Computer Science and Information Engineering[2]
National Taiwan University, Taipei, Taiwan
{r00922131,d00922003,hsinmu}@csie.ntu.edu.tw, jonhenry02@gmail.com[†]

ABSTRACT

Scooters are commonly used in many countries due to their low sale price, better fuel economy, and the ability to easily navigate through heavy traffic congestions. Today in Taiwan, approximately 70% of the registered vehicles are scooters. However, due to the low cost nature of the scooters, many safety technologies developed for cars cannot be adopted by them; statistics show that accidents involving scooters contribute to more than 80% of fatalities in traffic accidents in Taiwan, resulting in more than 2,000 deaths annually. It is therefore crucial to develop a new low-cost safety system that can be used by scooters. The enabling concept in this new safety system is *cooperation between vehicles*: scooters and cars sharing their current status and their observation of the neighboring environment via Vehicle-to-Vehicle (V2V) communications. However, how to implement this cost efficiently remains an open issue.

Visible Light Communications (VLC) use modulated visible light sources, *i.e.*, changing the intensity of the light emitted by the source, to transmit digital information, and Light Emitting Diodes (LEDs) are usually used as the transmission source. As LEDs become commonly used in automotive lighting, VLC appears as an attractive and cost-effective solution to implement V2V communications [1, 2]: no extra cost is needed for the main transmission component and the additional processing circuits have very low complexity.

Categories and Subject Descriptors

C.2.1 [**Network Architecture and Design**]: Wireless communication

Keywords

Scooter; V2V; Vehicle Safety; Visible Light Communications

1. DEMONSTRATION

We will present a scooter safety system utilizing VLC implemented with an off-the-shelf scooter taillight. The VLC-capable taillight periodically broadcasts messages with the current status of the scooter, including the engine revolution frequency, the speed, the brake signal, and the turn signals. After receiving a VLC message, the safety system in vehicles behind can either present the information directly to the driver or only present a warning to the driver when a collision is highly possible. We implements the former in this demonstration (See Figure 1). Demonstration video is available at: `http://goo.gl/lo1f9`.

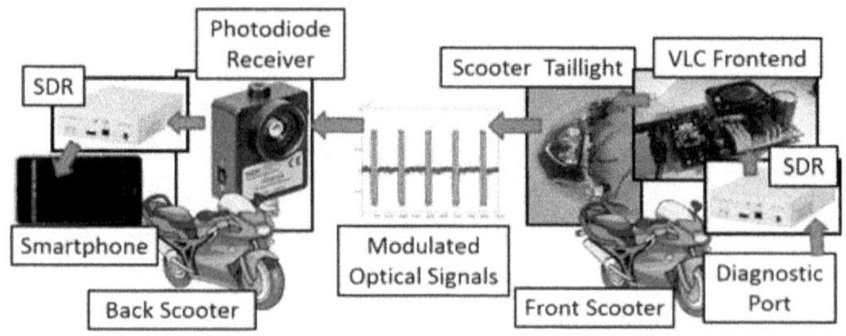

Figure 1: The demonstration scenario

The main technical contribution of this work includes: (1) to the best of our knowledge, this is the first integrated vehicle safety system that utilizes VLC to perform V2V communications, broadcasting live status information obtained from the scooter; (2) we implemented our system to be a flexible development platform, based on a commonly available software defined radio (SDR) platform, so that protocol and modulation designs can be easily modified for performance evaluations in the design process; (3) we used an unmodified off-the-shelf scooter taillight in our system, evaluating the feasibility of applying the VLC technology to today's product with minimum efforts. Our current implementation can transmit at a data rate of 10 Kb/s to a vehicle 20 meters away, sufficient for most vehicle safety applications.

2. ACKNOWLEDGEMENTS

This work is supported in part by National Science Council, National Taiwan University, and Intel Corporation under grants NSC101-2911-I-002-001, NSC101-2221-E-002-169, and NTU102R7501.

3. REFERENCES

[1] C. B. Liu, B. Sadeghi, and E. W. Knightly. Enabling vehicular visible light communication (V2LC) networks. In *Proc. ACM Intl. Workshop on VehiculAr Inter-NETworking (VANET)*, pages 41–50, 2011.

[2] A. Cailean, B. Cagneau, L. Chassagne, S. Topsu, Y. Alayli, and J-M Blosseville. Visible light communications: Application to cooperation between vehicles and road infrastructures. In *Proc. IEEE Intelligent Vehicles Symposium (IV)*, pages 1055–1059, 2012.

Demo: O'BTW- An Opportunistic, Similarity-based Mobile Recommendation System *

Mai ElSherief[†*], Tamer ElBatt[†*], Ahmed Zahran[†*], Ahmed Helmy[‡]
[†]Wireless Intelligent Networks Center (WINC), Nile University, Giza, Egypt
*Faculty of Engineering, Cairo University, Giza, Egypt
‡Dept. of Computer and Information Science and Engineering, University of Florida, Gainesville, USA

Categories and Subject Descriptors

C.2 [**COMPUTER-COMMUNICATION NETWORKS**]: Miscellaneous; K.4 [**COMPUTERS AND SOCIETY**]: Miscellaneous

Keywords

Mobile users, Opportunistic apps, temporal, Profiles, Similarity metrics, Proximity based Apps, Matrix vectorization

1. INTRODUCTION

Motivation and Objective: Earlier social studies, e.g., Homophily [Lazarsfeld and Merton (1954)], have shown that people tend to have similarities with others in close proximity. In our demo, coined O'BTW, we exploit the ubiquity of mobile phones and resource-rich users' social structure to develop opportunistic similarity-based mobile social networking applications. O'BTW exploits these key social insights to define new peer-to-peer networking regimes. O'BTW creates endless possibilities for highly personalized apps based on phone-to-phone communications, e.g., location-based services, targeted ads, dating and social networking apps and establishing trust.

System Overview: O'BTW demo hosts three major research components:

I. Introducing generalized mobile user profile structures that capture relevant factors in assessing user similarity. In O'BTW, we employ a general profile that incorporates different facets, like digital (e.g. visited websites) and physical footprints (physically visited sites), ratings, tips, etc. Additionally, our profile incorporates a temporal dimension that enriches the profile and improves the similarity assessment.

II. Developing novel similarity assessment tools that feature both high accuracy and low complexity. In O'BTW, we introduce Vectorized Cosine similarity metric for temporal profiles. This metric enjoys the computational simplicity of non-temporal similarity assessment for non-temporal profiles, e.g, Cosine similarity chosen for its superior performance and the richness brought in by incorporating the temporal dimension into the user profile, e.g., SVD-based similarity [1].

III. Designing DTN profile dissemination policies that compromise the tradeoff between forwarding overhead and delay. The optimal policy would maximize the information-theoretic "knowledge gain" metric (under investigation).

Other Apps that exploit the opportunistic encounters are iTrust and Shield. Highlight and Sonar are apps that connect people in proximity and share information, however, these apps reveal the complete identity of the users.

*This work was funded in part by a Google Faculty Research Award.

MobiSys'13, June 25–28, 2013, Taipei, Taiwan.
ACM 978-1-4503-1672-9/13/06.

2. O'BTW DEMO

The O'BTW demo is implemented using the Android SDK. The demo exhibits a "research-focused" use case in which user profiles are built on the spot through a friendly GUI where physical footprints are represented as the technical conferences attended over the past three years. O'BTW first establishes connection between devices in proximity using Bluetooth. Afterwards, it assesses pair-wise, temporal profile similarity using our Vectorized Cosine metric. In case of similarity, O'BTW exchanges the pre-stored tips representing this user's knowledge base.

Privacy is a major issue in profile-based communication systems that we are currently tackling via profile anonymization techniques as a first line of defense and is a major topic of a more comprehensive analysis and investigation.

O'BTW is proof-of-concept mobile app by which mobile users can readily, and anonymously, exchange knowledge, ratings and recommendations with others who are "alike" and happen to meet opportunistically. This, in turn, expands our knowledge base from the "legacy" O'BTW limited to "people we know and meet" to the digital O'BTW which leverages "people we encounter and do not know" and ultimately, with DTN forwarding to "people we do not know and have never encountered".

3. REFERENCE

[1] W. Hsu, D. Dutta, and A. Helmy. CSI: A paradigm for behavior-oriented profile-cast services in mobile networks. *Ad Hoc Networks*, 10:1586–1602, 2012.

Demo: Embedded NFC Protection and Forensics for Mobile Phones with EnGarde

Jeremy Gummeson[1], Bodhi Priyantha[2],
Deepak Ganesan[1], Derek Thrasher[1], Pengyu Zhang[1]
[1]University of Massachusetts Amherst, [2]Microsoft Research
{gummeson, dganesan, thrasher, pyzhang}@cs.umass.edu, bodhip@microsoft.com

ABSTRACT

Near Field Communication (NFC) on mobile phones presents new opportunities and threats. While NFC is radically changing how we pay for merchandise, it opens a pandora's box of ways in which it may be misused by unscrupulous individuals. This could include malicious NFC tags that seek to compromise a mobile phone, malicious readers that try to generate fake mobile payment transactions or steal valuable financial information, and others. In this demo, we show the capabilities of our hardware solution, *EnGarde*, that protects a mobile phone from these vulnerabilities.

Categories and Subject Descriptors

C.3 [**Special-purpose and Application-based Systems**]: [Real-time and embedded systems]

General Terms

Security, Design, Algorithms, Experimentation, Measurement

Keywords

Near Field Communications, Passive Systems

1. DEMO DESCRIPTION

This demo shows the capabilities of *EnGarde*, an embedded security tool that protects mobile phones equipped with near field communications (NFC). Our hardware implementation is completely passive in design and provides both forensic logging capabilities and selective tag blocking according to a user-defined set of blacklisting rules.

As shown in Figure 1, our hardware architecture comprises several elements that handle energy harvesting and management, tag detection, jamming, and forensics. We demonstrate each of these capabilities:

Energy Harvesting and Management: *EnGarde* harvests energy via inductive coupling with its *scavenge coil* from a mobile phone's NFC interface. By default, a phone's NFC interface is duty-cycled and does not output significant power. *EnGarde* increases the phone's power output by modulating a load with an 847.5 KHz subcarrier; a demand-driven harvesting algorithm uses this circuit to harvest energy while minimizing impact on the mobile phone's battery while achieving blocking and forensic security goals. *EnGarde* blinks LEDs to indicate the curent harvesting rate.

MobiSys'13, June 25–28, 2013, Taipei, Taiwan.
ACM 978-1-4503-1672-9/13/06.

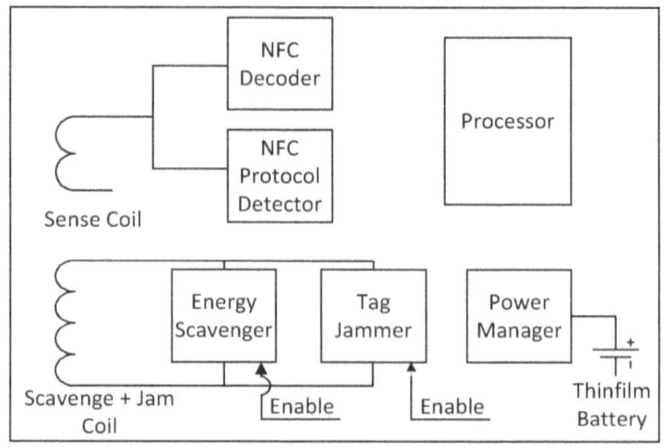

Figure 1: EnGarde System Architecture

Tag Detection: *EnGarde* determines when a tag approaches the mobile phone using a low power circuit that tracks the mutual inductance between the mobile phone and *EnGarde*'s *sense coil*. When a tag approaches *EnGarde*, an LED blinks to indicate that the tag has been detected.

Forensics: *EnGarde* uses a dedicated embedded NFC reader to sniff tags that respond to the phone's queries or the phone's response to an external reader. These sniffed responses are logged in the processor's flash memory and used to implement programmable response filtering. A serial interface to a PC shows the contents of these sniffed responses.

Jamming: *EnGarde* is able to block malicious tags using the same passive load modulation circuit used for harvesting. Using its embedded reader, *EnGarde* may block malicious tag responses using blacklisting rules. We demonstrate an example of a rule that only blocks tags belonging to a particular URL sub-domain known to be harmful; we show that similar tags with a different URL are allowed to communicate with the mobile phone.

Our demonstration shows that *EnGarde* is capable of protecting a mobile phone and provides valuable forensic data in-situ, while simultaneously having negligible impact on normal phone use.

2. ACKNOWLEDGEMENTS

This work was partially funded by NSF grants CNS-0916577, CNS-1217606, and CNS-0855128.

Demo: *PAUL* - Proactive Automated mobile User-centric content deLivery*

Mohamed A. Abd ElMohsen[1,2], Omar K. Shoukry[1,2], Hesham El Gamal[3], Tamer ElBatt[1,2], Nayer M. Wanas[4], Mohamed Abdel Raouf[4], Mostafa A. Zakaria[4], Ahmed I. Abdelkader[4], Hakem M. Zaied[4]

{massem, oshoukry}@inmobly.com [1]Nile University [2]Cairo University [3]Ohio State University [4]Inmobly

Categories and Subject Descriptors
C.2.3 [**Network Operations**]: Public networks

Keywords
Content pre-fetching, behavioral models, scheduling, smart phone traces, traffic offloading

1. INTRODUCTION

Motivation The wide adoption of bandwidth intensive multimedia applications on smart phones has been driving the growth of Mobile Data Traffic. The predictable mobile user behavior can be leveraged to retrieve content *before* demand to relieve cellular congestion [1].

Objectives In this demo, we exhibit the novel concept of proactive content delivery which performs "temporal" offloading to reduce congestion in cellular networks. *PAUL* is an Android Mobile App that showcases the proposed concept and system.

System Overview *PAUL* solves the cellular congestion problem via leveraging the users' predictable behaviors, which have tremendous impact on the traffic load. Moreover, it significantly enhances the user experience via eliminated download delays and reduced cost. *PAUL* proceeds through three major steps towards retrieving content before demand. First, it logs the behavior of the mobile users throughout the day, namely content consumption, Wi-Fi data rate and battery usage. Second, the logged traces are used to build probabilistic user behavioral models (profiles). These user profiles capture the resource-side (Wi-Fi data rate and battery conditions) and the demand-side (content consumption). Third, we propose a greedy, low-complexity, proactive scheduling algorithm. It utilizes the built profiles to create a schedule for retrieving content before demand over Wi-Fi connectivity opportunities throughout the day, resides on the cloud and constitutes the centerpiece of PAUL.

2. PAUL DEMO

Equipment We use several smart phones with Android 4.0 (or higher) OS, Wi-Fi connectivity and a laptop for illustrating user behavioral modeling. Demo setup requires less than five minutes.

Description The *PAUL* demo is based on an Android application hosting the logging and content fetching software modules on the smart phone, in addition to Python scripts running on the cloud server. The server side hosts the user behavioral modeling and proactive scheduling modules. The system demonstrates the following software modules and technologies: i) Logging module: records traces of the battery, Wi-Fi and content consumption on popular apps, ii) Probabilistic behavioral modeling: generates user profiles based on the logged data and iii) Proactive Scheduling: leverages the profiles to build content download schedules that are then used to retrieve content before demand. The demo also shows the direct impact the user profile has on pre-fetching opportunities, as targeted by the system to increase the probability of the user finding the content item already in its cache, when needed.

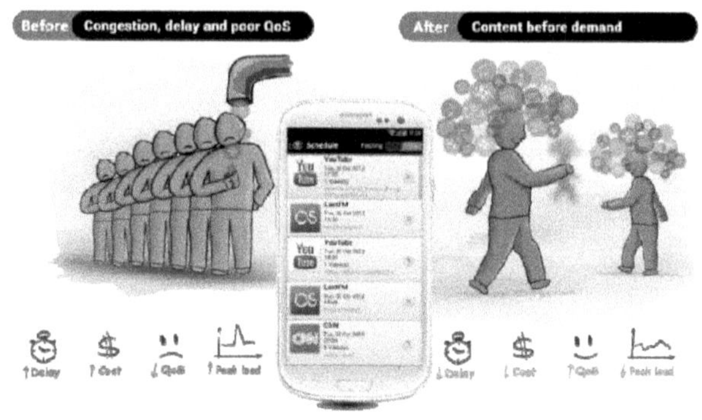

Figure 1: PAUL Concept

The demo hosts three major research components: i) A novel system architecture for proactive content delivery to mobile users with the core modules (behavioral modeling and proactive scheduling) residing on the cloud, ii) User behavioral modeling translates the logged data into representative histograms, for all time slots of the day. Three models are generated: a) The content model capturing the probability of consuming one of the content categories in each time slot, b) The battery model capturing the probability of being in one of three battery states (Charging, High and Low) in each time slot and c) The data rate model capturing the probability of having the average Wi-Fi download data rate in a certain range, in different time slots and iii) The proactive greedy scheduling algorithm decides which content item to assign to which slot of the day, depending on the resource availability and the probability of demanding this content in the future. The algorithm proceeds in N Rounds, where N is the number of slots per day, whereby a content item is assigned to a slot in each round. Within a single round, the algorithm assigns a content item based on its future demand and resource availability.

3. REFERENCE

[1] H. El Gamal, J. Tadrous, A. Eryilmaz, Proactive Resource Allocation: Turning Predictable Behavior into Spectral Gain, 48th Annual Allerton Conference on Communication, Control and Computing, Sept. 2010.

*This work was funded in part by a research contract with the Egyptian National Telecom Regulatory Authority (NTRA) and the Information Technology Industry Development Agency (ITIDA) under Round 9 Call For Proposals.

MobiSys'13, June 25–28, 2013, Taipei, Taiwan.
ACM 978-1-4503-1672-9/13/06.

Poster: Smartphone Sensing for Large DataSet Collection of Potholes

Saswat Raj
Indian Institute of Tech. Patna
saswat.cs11@iitp.ac.in

Ayush Jain
Indian Institute of Tech. Patna
ayush.cs11@iitp.ac.in

Dr. Rajiv Misra
Indian Institute of Tech. Patna
rajivm@iitp.ac.in

Categories and Subject Descriptors

H.3 [**INFORMATION STORAGE AND RETRIEVAL**]: Information Search and Retrieval; H.3.3 [**Information Search and Retrieval**]: Information filtering—*efficiency measures*

General Terms

Experimentation, Theory, Measurement

Keywords

crowdsourcing,smartphones,pothole data,large data sets

1. INTRODUCTION AND APPROACH

Crowdsourcing can be utilized for collection of large data sets.We have used standalone **implicit crowdsourcing** for collecting large data as it will add user incentive for providing data.Since most smartphones comes with the sensors needed for our work they become an ideal way for implementing crowdsourcing as they are an integrated part of the crowd.Due to large size of the data set, the data collected has to be stored centrally where it can be processed or aggregated according to the needs. Our approach to detect potholes was to record the value of acceleration along the z-axis of the device and specify a maximum value that this acceleration cannot cross i.e. the `z-threshold` value.For checking the sudden change of acceleration when a pothole is encountered we calculate the difference in the previous and the current value of acceleration and fix a threshold for this i.e. `z-difference threshold` value.

To solve the problem of the dynamically changing axis, the accelerometer event data was used to get the value of gravity.If the magnitude of acceleration recorded is larger than the threshold it is considered.

$$Ac = AccelerationOnDevice + G \tag{1}$$

$$A = Ac - G \tag{2}$$

$$ComponentofAalongG = \mod Acos\theta\hat{G} \tag{3}$$

$$cos\theta = \frac{A.G}{\mod A \mod G} \tag{4}$$

To differentiate a pothole and a speed breaker either 1 or -1 corresponding to the positive and negative values of component of A along G respectively is enqueued in a queue of size three.The queue is then checked for acceleration pattern of a pothole i.e. negative followed by zero followed by positive and the value of the threshold has crossed the specified value.If the pattern is matched and the condition is satisfied then pothole is recorded.

Moreover the threshold value would depend on environmental factors such as the suspension of the vehicle used for capturing the data.To remedy this we set a basic threshold which could be tuned by the user based on the conditions such as vehicle,hole size to be measured etc.When the threshold value was set to 1.2, according to our experimental results potholes,sink-holes and utility cuts of all sizes could be measured. On increasing the threshold to around 2, medium and large sized potholes were only recorded.Only large potholes were recorded at a threshold of around 3.3. A sample of experimental results is shown in `Table 1`.

The location of the pothole is recorded using GPS data from the smartphone. We then send this data of pothole to a cloud database.In our experiment we plotted the potholes on the google map of Bihar.

1.1 Experimental Data Collected

Table 1: Sample of Data Collected

Latitude	Longitude	Accuracy	Date
25.58918815	85.13504102	48	12/3/2013
25.58633017	85.13428625	54	12/3/2013
25.58637512	85.13424597	10	12/3/2013
25.58637512	85.13424597	18	12/3/2013

2. CONCLUSIONS

This paper describes a method to collect **Large Data Set** using smartphone sensing by **Implicit crowdsourcing** techniques.The experimental data that was taken from the crowd using smartphone sensing using our application for the detection of potholes in Bihar in India was 96.8% same when tested on the same area twice.Thus large data set with more than 96% accuracy can be collected by the method of crowdsourcing,thus verifying its reliability.The large amount of data collected could be used to model the roadway of an entire city by collecting real time data from the sensors of the smartphones.

3. ACKNOWLEDGMENTS

This work was supported by sponsored research project of DeitY and IIT Patna India.

MobiSys'13, June 25–28, 2013, Taipei, Taiwan.
ACM 978-1-4503-1672-9/13/06.

Poster: Authenticating and Tracing Biological Anonym of VANET Based on KMC Decentralization and Two-Factor

Fei Wang[1, 2], Yongjun Xu[1], Lin Wu[1, 2], Dan Liu[3] and Liehuang Zhu[3]

[1]Institute of Computing Technology, Chinese Academy of Sciences, P. R. China
[2]University of Chinese Academy of Sciences, P. R. China
[3]School of Computer Science, Beijing Institute of Technology, P. R. China
E-mail: {wangfei, xyj, wulin}@ict.ac.cn, {liudanking, liehuangz}@bit.edu.cn

Categories and Subject Descriptors

C.2.0 [**Computer-Communication Networks**]: General——*Security and Protection*;
C.2.1 [**Computer-Communication Networks**]: Network Architecture and Design——*Wireless communications*

Keywords

VANET; Privacy Preservation; Authentication; Two-Factor; Decentralization; Conditional Traceability

1. Motivation

Some previous privacy preserving authentication (PPA) schemes for vehicular ad-hoc network (VANET) are able to secure vehicle-to-vehicle (V2V) communication, and trace a vehicle conditionally. However due to centralized key management center (KMC), few could jump out scope of asymmetric key mechanism, thus corresponding cost is too high to suit broadcasting scenarios especially with high vehicle density. Plus, the tracing can't reach a single one of many biological drivers of one vehicle. So we consider an improved solution based on two ideas: 1) Decentralizing KMC by giving its duties to tamper-proof device (TPD); 2) Utilizing two-factor authentication (2FA) to integrate biological identifiers of drivers into messages. Overview is shown in Figure 1. The objective is to both authenticate anonymous drivers faster and provide enough evidences to trace any biological anonym driver.

2. Decentralizing KMC to improve efficiency

Cryptographic values and code are stored in TPD and can't be extracted in any circumstance. Thus vehicles can only do limited operations indirectly with system key. A vehicle registers itself to KMC to configure its TPD (system key and an initial pseudo identity (PID) written to TPD) and applies for access token of TPD. Before sending a message, a vehicle logs on TPD with access token and signs the message with PID generated by TPD based on initial PID. A receiver verifies received messages with matching PIDs. This benefits VANET PPA in 4 aspects compared with GSIS [1] and STAP [2]: 1) V2V authentication is 10^2~10^5 times quicker based on symmetric key mechanism or 2FA; 2) Bandwidth consumption decreases by 41.33% ~77.60%; 3) Cost of KMC's certificate revocation list is removed; 4) Mitigated role of roadside units (RSUs) makes it hard to reveal real identities even with all RSUs compromised.

MobiSys'13, June 25–28, 2013, Taipei, Taiwan.

ACM 978-1-4503-1672-9/13/06.

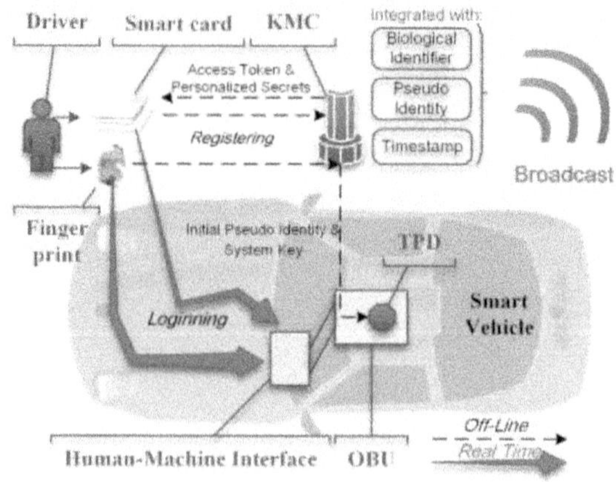

Figure 1. Overview of Proposed Solution.

3. Tracing Biological Anonym Utilizing 2FA

Multiple drivers of a vehicle might cause confusions when authorities need to reveal the real identities in case of accident investigation and other disputes. Moreover, smart vehicle is hot with advanced human-machine interface (e.g., tablet with fingerprint or iris scanner). Thus we uses 2FA which employs "something you have" (smart card) and "something you are" (biological identifier) to trace a single biological anonym driver conditionally. KMC utilizes submitted biological identifiers to generate personalized secret values and write them into a smart card. A driver needs to plug smart card and input biological identifier to pass the verification of human-machine interface. Then he is free to log on TPD and participate in VANET application. In V2V communication, PIDs are generated with initial PIDs by TPD, biological information and timestamps. Thus, any V2V message could be used by KMC to trace its biological author with privacy preserving. Moreover, 2FA is much faster than existing PPA schemes.

This poster shows an opportunity of using decentralized KMC to improve efficiency of PPA in VANET and using 2FA to trace any biological anonym.

4. REFERENCES

[1] X. Lin, X. Sun, P. Ho, X. Shen. GSIS: A Secure and Privacy-Preserving Protocol for Vehicular Communications. IEEE T VEH TECHNOL, 56, 6 (2007), 3442-3456.

[2] X. Lin, R. Lu, X. Liang and X. Shen. STAP: A Social-Tier-Assisted Packet Forwarding Protocol for Achieving Receiver-Location Privacy Preservation in VANETs. In *INFOCOM*, 2011.

Poster: Carrying My Environment with Me in IoT-enhanced Smart Buildings

Dawei Pan[*†] Abraham Hang-yat Lam[†] Dan Wang[†]
[†]The Hong Kong Polytechnic University, [*]Harbin Institute of Technology

Categories and Subject Descriptors

C.2.1 [**Computer-Communication Networks**]: Network Architecture and Design—*Wireless Communication*

Keywords

Internet of Things, Smartphones, BMS

Smart and intelligent buildings are proposed and heavily studied recently to increase building automation, reduce building operation and electricity costs, and enhance human comfort. With the development of infrastructure, standardization, wireless sensing systems, smart phones, etc, many top-up services that were difficult to realize in traditional buildings can be developed nowadays.

In this poster, we show a specific example. We design and implement "Carrying My Environment with Me" (CarryEn). The idea is that for human beings who are adapted to their surrounding environment in a building, e.g., their offices, when they move to other rooms, the configuration of their environment can be carried to next rooms. More importantly, such adjustment should be *non-intrusive*, i.e., people are not aware of the adjustment. The building management systems (BMS) should control the adjustment. (See Fig. 1)

Our design has three components: 1) a smart and open BMS (Internet-of-Things oriented); 2) smart phone based application, and 3) environment adjustment algorithms.

IoT-enhanced Building Management System:

Our IoT based BMS is designed for general purposes, yet CarryEn can become a specific example for using it. It has two features: 1) smart and wireless; and 2) open. Many new BMS are recently proposed, e.g., sMap [1]. Our design differs from them as we convert the traditional wired BMS into smart and wireless without modification of the upper layer building protocols. Thus, it does not need long time for re-standardization. Our design and real deployment can be found in [3]. We recently extend our BMS to make it open. As such, people can develop top-up apps which can interact with the BMS with public protocols. As an example besides CarryEn, Toshiba can monitor its air-conditioners in different buildings using different BMS. It can become part of cyber-physical search in the future as well. Intrinsically, we solve three problems: 1) a universal ID, 2) public protocols to communicate with the smart BMS, and 3) possible service providers to support the data communication. We choose IPv6 as the IDs. As IPv6 is heavy, we use 6LowPan. We choose CoAP as the protocol to integrate with building management protocols to offer information of the building devices. As IPv6 is not widely supported; a broker is needed. We choose SixXS to support IPv6 data communication. One interesting thing is that after we open our BMS system, Google spiders immediately scan our devices.

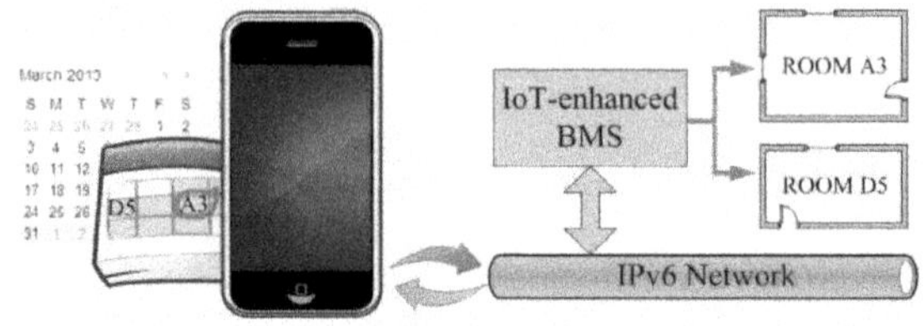

Figure 1: The framework of CarryEn

Smart Phone based Application:

The BMS will not record information of individual person or individual applications. It provides information and/or helps to control building operations/devices. We develop an Android app for CarryEn. When a person stays in a room, the app contact BMS (using open protocols) and records the ID of the room. When this person changes his room, the smart phone will contact the BMS to transfer the configuration of this room to the new room. Note that we do not need a localization algorithm. We also develop Google calender-based pre-scheduling. More specifically, the app extracts next room information from Google calender API and requests BMS to configure the room in advance. All these operations are non-intrusive.

Discussion:

The BMS only needs to copy the configuration between two rooms if there is only one person. If there are more people, an integration of different configuration is needed. There are recent studies on combined human comfort [2] and we plan to integrate their results into our work.

Acknowledgement

Dawei Pan, Abraham Hang-yat Lam and Dan Wang are affiliated to The Hong Kong Polytechnic University Shenzhen Research Institute, Shenzhen 518057, China. The work described in this paper was supported in part by the National Natural Science Foundation of China (No. 61272464).

1. REFERENCES

[1] S. Dawson-Haggerty et al. smap: a simple measurement and actuation profile for physical information. In *Proc. SenSys*, pages 197–210, 2010.

[2] V. L. Erickson et al. Thermovote: participatory sensing for efficient building hvac conditioning. In *Proc. Buildsys*, 2012.

[3] H. Luo et al. Demo abstract: Towards a wireless building management system with minimum change to the building protocols. In *Proc. ICCPS*, page 223, 2012.

Poster: Mobile User Clustering in Large Time-Scale Data Transfer Scheduling

Ting-An Lin[1], Yichuan Wang[2], Cheng-Hsin Hsu[1], and Xin Liu[2]
[1]Department of Computer Science, National Tsing Hua University, Taiwan
[2]Department of Computer Science, University of California, Davis, USA

Categories and Subject Descriptors

C.2.4 [**Distributed Systems**]: Distributed Applications

Keywords

Opportunistic transfers, scheduling, resource conservation, user clustering

1. LARGE TIME-SCALE SCHEDULING

Mobile data traffic has grown explosively in the past few years, largely due to the increasingly more smartphone users. A large portion of the mobile traffic, such as email and user-generated multimedia contents may tolerate delay to some extent. While there are existing works [1] proposing opportunistic data transfer in small time-scale, they do not leverage the much larger optimization room that is only achievable via large time-scale scheduling. In our previous work, we proposed two large time-scale scheduling algorithms: OSS and OSS_L using Markov decision theory [2]. While OSS and OSS_L lead to huge improvement on user-selected optimization criteria, such as throughput and energy consumption, they share two limitations, they: (i) need long profiles (e.g., 30 days) for accurate predictions, and (ii) may incur high training complexity (e.g., it takes OSS on average 457.2 sec and 3.96 GB memory to train the model for a single user). In the current work, we eliminate these two limitations via clustering mobile users by the optimization criteria, which is referred to as *contexts* throughout this abstract.

2. MOBILE USER CLUSTERING

We analyze user traces, referred to as *profiles*, of a large number of users, and cluster users with similar behaviors in the same groups. Then, we let users in the same cluster share the same model parameters (of OSS and OSS_L), so as to: (i) shorten the profile collection time and (ii) reduce the training complexity without scarifying the prediction accuracy. To our best knowledge, using clustering to address these two limitations has not been studied before.

We cluster mobile users by two contexts, energy consumption or network throughput, as follows. We collect the contexts and partition them into T-sec timeslots with a vector representation and save them in user profiles. The contexts are normalized to a range of $[0, 1]$. There are a wide spectrum of clustering techniques proposed in data mining literature. Our approach of mobile user clustering is general and can work with any clustering techniques. For concrete discussion, and as an initial step, we consider cosine distance and hierarchical clustering algorithm in the rest of the abstract. The cosine distance between any two users is defined as $\frac{\mathbf{V}_A \cdot \mathbf{V}_B}{\|\mathbf{V}_B\|\|\mathbf{V}_B\|}$, where $\mathbf{V}_A$ and $\mathbf{V}_B$ are timeslotted context vectors of users A and B. The hierarchical clustering has one input parameter: the number of clusters K. We define clustering ratio α as the ratio between K and number of users N, i.e., $\alpha = \frac{K}{N}$. The two system parameters, T and α, allow us to exercise the tradeoff between training overhead and prediction accuracy, as shown in the next section.

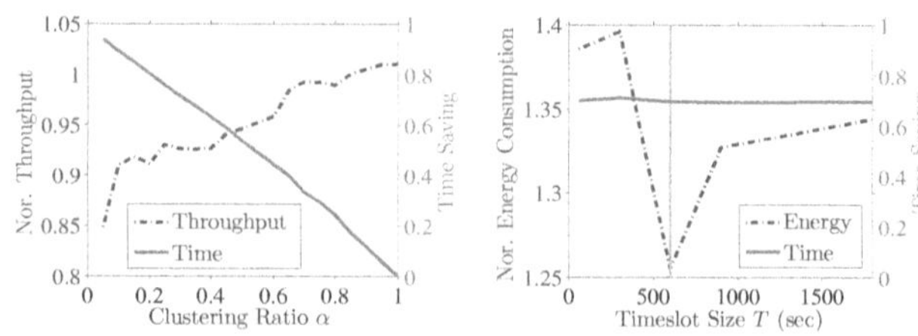

(a) (b)

Figure 1: Sample results of mobile user clustering by (a) network throughput, and (b) energy consumption.

3. TRACE-DRIVEN SIMULATIONS

To drive our simulator, we use 6 months of user profiles collected from 1041 users of an Android application we developed in [2]. The average profile length is 23.2 days. We have implemented a trace-driven simulator in Matlab to quantify the benefits of mobile user clustering. We have also implemented the hierarchical clustering algorithm with cosine distance in the simulator, but our simulator can be readily extended to support other clustering techniques. In Fig. 1, we show the results of OSS_L algorithm. The performance[1] and training time are normalized to the results of OSS_L without clustering. Our simulations reveal that mobile user clustering allows us to reduce the overhead of training prediction models yet achieving reasonable performance. For example. OSS_L with clustering achieves 95% of the original throughput with only 40% of original training complexity (Fig. 1(a)) and 600-sec timeslots lead to the minimum energy consumption with 30% of original training complexity (Fig. 1(b)). Last, we notice that although we use the optimization criteria as the context for clustering, other indirect contexts, such as WiFi availability may lead to better performance. Conducting more extensive simulations to systematically find the most *effective* clustering context is one of our future tasks.

4. REFERENCES

[1] A. Schulman, V. Navda, R. Ramjee, N. Spring, P. Deshpande, C. Grunewald, K. Jain, and V. Padmanabhan. Bartendr: A practical approach to energy-aware cellular data scheduling. In *Proc. of ACM MobiCom'10.*

[2] Y. Wang, X. Liu, A. Nicoara, T. Lin, and C. Hsu. SmartTransfer: Transferring Your Mobile Multimedia Contents at the Right Time. In *Proc. of ACM NOSSDAV'12.*

[1]We consider two performance metrics: energy and throughput.

Poster: Fusing Prefetch and Delay-Tolerant Transfer for Mobile Videos

Shu-Ting Wang[1], Ting-An Lin[1], Yichuan Wang[2], Cheng-Hsin Hsu[1], and Xin Liu[2]

[1]Department of Computer Science, National Tsing Hua University, Hsin-Chu, Taiwan
[2]Department of Computer Science, University of California, Davis, USA

Categories and Subject Descriptors

C.2.4 [**Distributed Systems**]: Distributed Applications

Keywords

Prefetching, Recommender System

1. FUSION OF OPPORTUNISTIC TRANSMISSIONS

People carry their mobile devices, such as smartphones and tablets, all the time, and generate tremendous amount of mobile video traffic. Per a Cisco report, mobile video represents 51% of mobile traffic in 2012, and mobile video users demand for short waiting time when clicking on a video. Unfortunately, network conditions are diverse and changing over time and locations, which leads to fluctuating throughput and thus degraded viewing experience. To cope with this issue, *opportunistic* transmissions may be leveraged, which come in different forms, including (i) prefetching and (ii) delay-tolerant transfer. Prefetching tries to download videos that are likely to be watched in advance, while delay-tolerant transfer attempts to postpone downloading videos. Both of them aim to *transfer videos under the best channel conditions*.

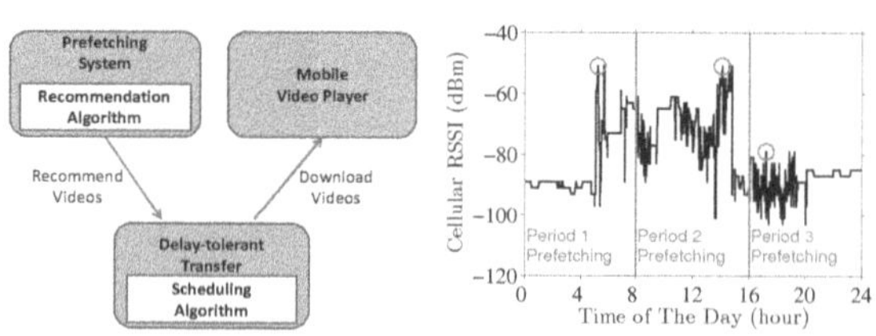

(a) (b)

Figure 1: (a) Architechture and (b) a sample day of our system.

This abstract answers the following question: *does fusing prefetching and delay-tolerant transfer enhance the user experience in mobile video streaming?* To answer it, we propose a new video download system (Fig. 1(a)) to minimize the waiting time and energy consumption for the best user experience. The system achieves this by periodically invoking a *recommendation* algorithm, once every prefetching period τ. The videos selected by the recommendation algorithm in the current period must be downloaded before the next period starts. That is, τ can be considered as a deadline of video downloads. Any recommendation algorithm can work in our system, and we let α be the prediction accuracy. Besides, the precise transfer time is determined by a delay-tolerant scheduling algorithm. While our system can work with any scheduling algorithm, we adopt a Markov Decision Process based algorithm [4] for concrete discussion. We consider large time-scale (in the order of hours and days) prefetching and delay-tolerant transfer algorithms, which result in larger optimization room compared to small time-scale (mins and secs) algorithms [2][3]. Fig. 1(b) shows a sample run of 3 prefetching periods, in which our system strives to download videos under the best network condition (marked by circles).

MobiSys'13, June 25-28, 2013, Taipei, Taiwan.
ACM 978-1-4503-1672-9/13/06.

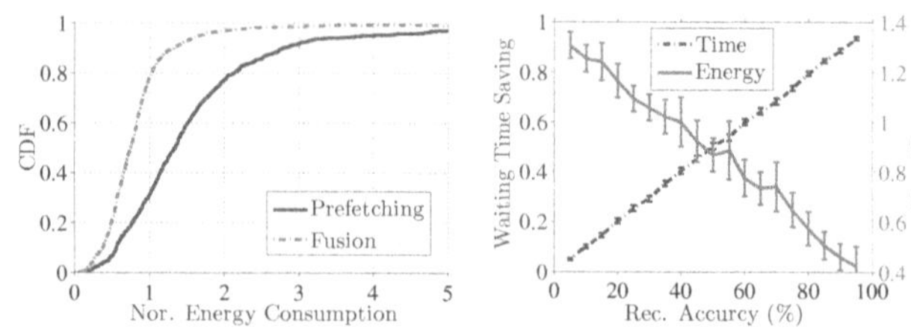

(a) (b)

Figure 2: (a) Energy consumption normalized to streaming and (b) implications of recommendation accuracy.

2. PRELIMINARY RESULTS

We implement a trace-driven simulator using Matlab, and employ real network traces collected from 1000+ real Android users to drive the simulator. We use Youtube video characteristics in the simulations, e.g., the video size follows a Gamma distribution [1]. We compare three video download schemes: (i) streaming, (ii) prefetching, and (iii) fusion of prefetching and delay-tolerant data transfer. We employ OSS_L (see [4]) as the scheduling algorithm, let τ = 24 hours and α = 0.50 if not otherwise specified.

Our simulation results show that compared to streaming: (i) prefetching and fusion save on average 51% of waiting time (figure is not shown), (ii) prefetching consumes 58% more energy while fusion saves 36% energy (Fig. 2(a)), and (iii) higher recommendation accuracy leads to less energy consumption and higher waiting time saving (Fig. 2(b)); in fact, when $\alpha \geq 40\%$, fusion consumes less energy than streaming.

3. REFERENCES

[1] A. Abhari and M. Soraya. Workload generation for Youtube. *Multimedia Tools Appl.*, 46(1).

[2] E. Jung, D. Gupta, N. Mastronarde, and X. Liu. Network-congestion-aware video streaming: A rest-and-download approach. In *Proc. of SECON'12*.

[3] A. Schulman, V. Navda, R. Ramjee, N. Spring, P. Deshpande, C. Grunewald, K. Jain, and V. Padmanabhan. Bartendr: A practical approach to energy-aware cellular data scheduling. In *Proc. of MobiCom'10*.

[4] Y. Wang, X. Liu, A. Nicoara, T. Lin, and C. Hsu. Smarttransfer: Transferring your mobile multimedia contents at the "right" time. In *Proc. of ACM NOSSDAV'12*.

Poster: WhereAmI: Image-based Positioning in Dense Urban Areas

Quoc Duy Vo, Klaus Mueller, Pradipta De
Dept of Computer Science, SUNY Korea
{rayvo, mueller, pradipta.de}@sunykorea.ac.kr

Categories and Subject Descriptors: H.3.4 [**Systems and Software**]: Distrbuted Systems

Keywords: Mobile, Locationing, OCR, Android

1. INTRODUCTION

Real time computer vision techniques, like OCR, on mobile platforms is opening new opportunities [4]. Image based locationing has traditionally focused on identifying well-known landmarks, like Eiffel Tower, in an image captured using a smartphone. However consider a user lost in the sprawling bazaars of a big city where a well-known landmark may be difficult to spot.

We propose a technique where texts appearing in names of shops, billboards, and road signs act as pseudo-markers to identify the location. Collection of different signs, which are keywords for the area, is often unique. For example, in Figure 1, the presence of "Indian Home Industries" and "Jain Gift House" together can be unique to an area. The texts in the image clicked by the user are extracted from the image to create a location signature. The signature is matched against a repository of signatures.

The repository of signatures is generated using geo-tagged images from online sources, like Flickr and Pinterest. Cities with CCTV or webcams, such as in Seoul or Singapore, can also feed images of different areas with geo-tag. The database of well-known signatures are populated by analyzing these pictures.

Unlike previous work on image based matching [1, 2], we are using *hints* embedded in the image. The cost of querying the location is minimized as few text strings need to be uploaded. Response time to the query will be faster as text matching may yield response quicker than image matching.

2. APPROACH

The design of the system, called *WhereAmI*, requires a frontend logic on the mobile phone to run OCR on image, and a backend service for matching signatures. The concept is described in Figure 1.

To extract text from an image, we are using the Tess4J OCR library [3]. While detecting the texts, we also assign weights to texts based on their relative size in the image. The weights help in guiding the search among large set of signatures. The bag of keywords is uploaded to a hosted WhereAmI service. WhereAmI service checks the repository of signatures, which are generated a priori by analyzing images with geo-tags. The effectiveness of the application hinges on fast matching of the correlated keywords.

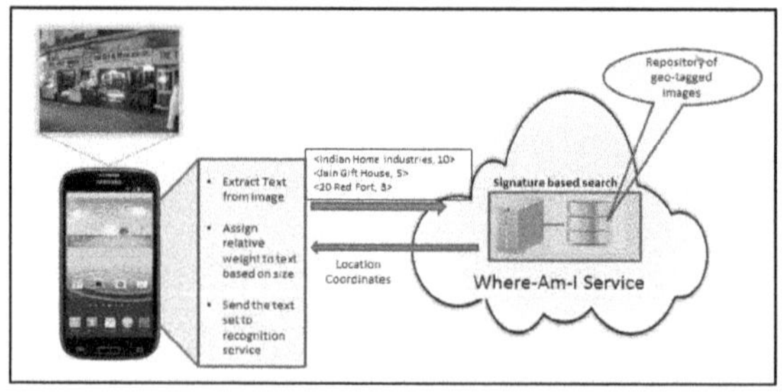

Figure 1: WhereAmI App and Service

There can be scenarios where the image does not contain enough distinguishing keywords. In this case, the user is given a feedback to snap another picture by guiding the user to point left or right.

Currently the work is exploring open source OCR tools on mobile platforms. The backend service will implement fast algorithms for matching against a database of signatures.

Acknowledgment

The work is (partially) supported by IT Consilience Creative Project through the Ministry of Knowledge Economy, Republic of Korea.

3. REFERENCES

[1] M. Cristani, A. Perina, U. Castellani, and V. Murino. Geo-located image categorization and location recognition. *Pattern Recognition and Image Analysis*, 19(2):245–252, Jun 2009.

[2] A. Mulloni, D. Wagner, I. Barakonyi, and D. Schmalstieg. Indoor positioning and navigation with camera phones. *IEEE Pervasive Computing*, 8(2), Apr 2009.

[3] Tess4j. http://tess4j.sourceforge.net/.

[4] G. Wang, Y. Xiong, J. Yun, and J. R. Cavallaro. Accelerating computer vision algorithms using OpenCL on the mobile GPU - a case study. In *International Conference on Acoustics, Speech, and Signal Processing (ICASSP)*, 2013.

MobiSys'13, June 25–28, 2013, Taipei, Taiwan.
ACM 978-1-4503-1672-9/13/06.

Poster: A Black-Box based Android GUI Testing System

Chao-Chun Yeh*‡ avainyeh@itri.org.tw
Shih-Kun Huang† ‡ skhuang@cs.nctu.edu.tw
Sung-Yen Chang* madchang@itri.org.tw

*Information and Communications Research Laboratories
Industrial Technology Research Institute
Hsinchu, Taiwan

† Information Technology Service Center
‡ Department of Computer Science
National Chiao Tung University, Hsinchu, Taiwan

ABSTRACT

In Android system, black box testing has risen to three key issues: S1: There is no source code and for tester to know the internal logic of the testing App. S2: There is no testing criterion for tester to know the correct behavior and testing scope of the testing App. S3: It is difficult to measure the testing coverage without instrumentation the testing App. In this paper, we provide an approach to analyze the GUI model during the testing process, implement the black-box based android GUI testing system and select 7 Apps for evaluation. Finally we compare our result of our system with the monkey tool [1] and discuss the inner App's properties that influence on the testing result.

Categories and Subject Descriptors

D.2.5 [**Testing and Debugging**]: *Testing tools*

Keywords

market App software, software testing, software quality.

1. System Prototype Design

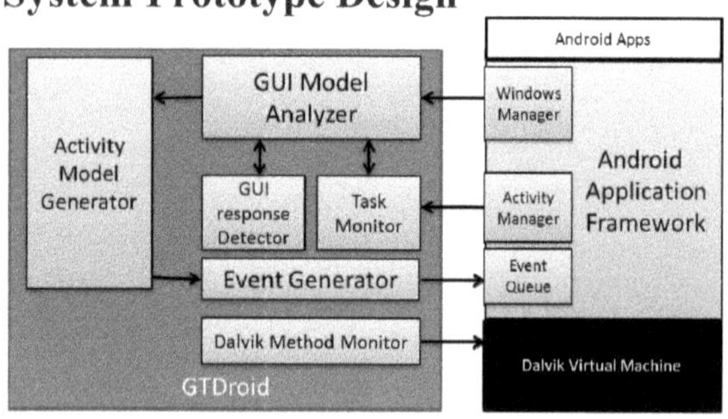

Figure 1. The Architecture of GTDroid

Figure 1 shows the architecture of our black-box Android GUI testing system– GTDroid, our proposed approach to address the issues, and explain the essential steps involved in testing an App with GTDroid. First, the App to be tested is installed and executed automatically in the emulator and then the GTDroid interacts with the android application framework modules and dalvik virtual machines. For S1, GUI model analyzer fetch GUI components information from windows manager and then analysis the layout of the current view. The analytic result sent to activity model generator for building the whole App Activity Model. For S2, the task monitor detect the current testing activity status such as task stack information and crash event with activity manager and event detector check the GUI based information from GUI model Analyzer such as ANR (Application Not Responding), exceptions and user define message. For S3, after event generator send events to the event queue and some dalvik methods might be executed by the related events. Dalvik method monitor inspects the executed methods with modified dalvik virtual machine and provide unique method count (UMC) for comparison with other test results.

2. EXPERIMENTS

Our experiment environment includes Ubuntu 11.04, Android emulator and we implement GUI model analyzer and event generator modules based on jython 2.5 and other modules on python 2.7. To evaluate GTDroid, we use 7 benchmark Apps from the bundle Apps in the emulator and the high download rate Apps in Google Play Taiwan Market [2]. We run each App in twenty minutes, collect UMC for coverage and compare the result with monkey tool. The results are presented in Fig. 2. In the result, we compare the UMC with GTDroid and Monkey tool. In average case, GTDroid can obtain more 27.02% UMC than Monkey with the base case (82.69%) and worse case (-1.82%).

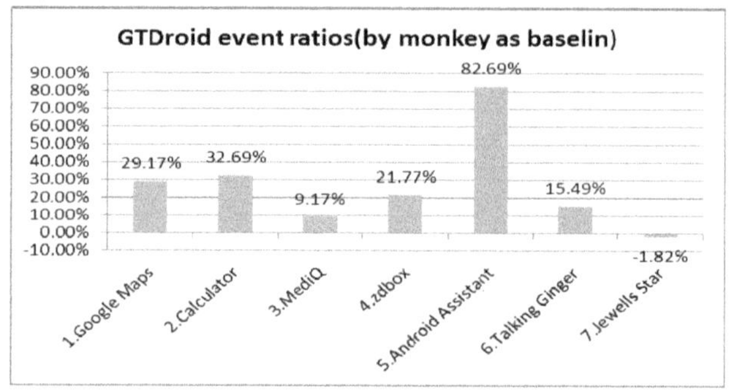

Figure 2 GTDroid UMC ratios

3. DISCUSSION & FUTURE WORK

In term of search strategy, Monkey is based on random events without any background knowledge such App module or the widgets in the top-most view. With this restraint, Monkey based test will case many duplicated tests. In GTDroid, we build App model and make cycle detection rule to prevent executing duplicated tests. In our 5th sample, we analysis the log and find there are many duplicated tests with Monkey tool like profile setting or data-filling in dialog. In our samples, some Apps (3th and 7th) are designed with single activity and simple control flow. There is no distinguished improvement between GTDroid and Monkey. While GTDroid demonstrates the results, it is still a prototype system and there are future work to overcome the limitations that it cannot detect user define widget and the coverage information should be more accuracy.

4. REFERENCES

[1] UI/Application Exerciser Monkey- http://developer.android.com/tools/help/monkey.html

[2] Android Apps on Google play- https://play.google.com/store

MobiSys'13, June 25–28, 2013, Taipei, Taiwan.
ACM 978-1-4503-1672-9/13/06.

This work is a partial result of Project No. C3522Q1200 conducted by Industrial Technology Research Institute under sponsorship of the Ministry of Economic Affairs, R.O.C., Taiwan.

Poster: An Approximation Algorithm of Orienteering Problems for Mobile Computing

Chen-Chih Liao and Cheng-Hsin Hsu
Department of Computer Science, National Tsing Hua University, Taiwan

Categories and Subject Descriptors

G.2.3 [**Applications**]

Keywords

Orienteering problems, approximation algorithms, mobile applications

1. ORIENTEERING PROBLEM AND ITS MOBILE APPLICATIONS

We study the orienteering problem with time window (OPTW), which is essentially a game in which users accumulate scores by getting to some geolocations during certain time periods [3]. Solving OPTW gives the optimal *path* for each user to maximize his/her score. OPTW can be leveraged to enhance many mobile applications (apps). For example, an app may solve OPTW problems to guide a user who is waiting for his/her train to nearby shops without missing the train. Another app may solve OPTW problems to adaptively compose a customized tour plan for an unfamiliar city or a theme park. Furthermore, a mobile crowdsourcing app may solve OPTW problems to compute the best detour paths for smartphone users, who have some time to spare and wouldn't mind to perform some tasks for small rewards [2]. While all these apps can provide better user experiences by solving OPTW problems, existing OPTW algorithm gives optimal solution at the expense of high computational overhead [3], and may not be suitable for real-time systems and resource-constrained smartphones.

This abstract aims to develop a *scalable* OPTW algorithm that allows users to tradeoff *complexity* and *optimality*. With the proposed algorithm, a user may opt to small (large) approximation gap with longer (shorter) running time, where the gap is controllable.

2. APPROXIMATION ALGORITHM: DPA

Our previous work [2] presents an optimal algorithm DP for the OPTW problem. In this abstract, we propose a (pseudo-)approximation algorithm DPA, based on DP. The main difference between them is that the running time of DPA depends on a user selected parameter $\epsilon \in (0, 1]$. We define a scaling factor $F = \frac{\epsilon p_{max}}{N}$, where p_{max} is the maximal score among all locations, and N is the total number of locations.

DPA works as follows. First, we scale the score p to $p'_n = \lfloor \frac{p_n}{F} \rfloor$ for all location n. Second, we apply dynamic programming to compute the path with the highest score. In particular, we iteratively expand the path from a user's source to his/her destination. For each location l, we record multiple subpaths from the source to itself. We only keep the potential *subpaths* that may become part of the optimal paths. We define *potential* subpaths as the subpaths that either reach fewer locations, spend less time, or achieve higher accumulated score, compared to any known subpaths at l. Upon reaching the destination, we return the best known path X.

In the DPA algorithm, larger F (larger ϵ) leads to more subpaths with the same score, which in turn allows us to drop more subpaths and thus achieve lower complexity. However, doing so affects the optimality of path X as well. Let X^* be the optimal path. We denote the total scores of X and X^* as $P(X)$ and $P(X^*)$, and we can derive $P(X) \geq (1-\epsilon)P(X^*)$ (the proof is similar to the one in [1]). This means that DPA achieves an approximation gap of ϵ, while higher ϵ leads to both lower complexity and higher approximation gap.

3. RESULTS AND CONCLUSION

We have developed a simulator for OPTW using C/C++. We ran the simulations on a PC with an AMD 2.6 GHz CPU. We have implemented DPA algorithm within the simulator, and compared it against DP [2] using datasets from Flickr. The preliminary results are given below. We consider two ϵ values: 0.2 and 0.8. Fig. 1(a) shows that DPA with $\epsilon = 0.8$ achieves almost optimal score (DP), while DPA with $\epsilon = 0.2$ slightly deviates from DP. Fig. 1(b) shows that, compared to DP, DPA with $\epsilon = 0.8$ and 0.2 achieve 3X and 2X speed ups, respectively. Fig. 1 demonstrates that the DPA algorithm successfully allows the users to tradeoff complexity and optimality. We are actively integrating DPA to a mobile crowdsourcing system [2] to verify its practicality and efficiency.

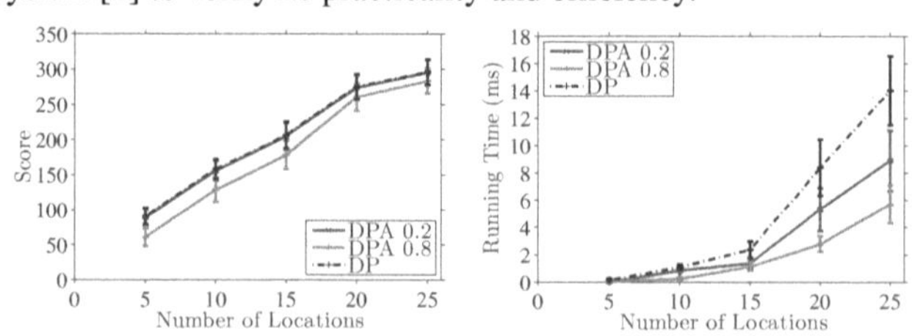

(a) (b)

Figure 1: Sample results from Taipei dataset: (a) score and (b) running-time.

4. REFERENCES

[1] K. Lai and M. Goemans. The knapsack problem and fully polynomial time approximation schemes (FPTAS). `http://math.mit.edu/~goemans/18434S06/knapsack-katherine.pdf`, 2006.

[2] C. Liao and C. Hsu. Detour planning algorithm in crowdsourcing systems for multimedia content gathering. In *Proc. of ACM MoVid'13*.

[3] P. Vansteenwegena, W. Souffriaua, and D. Oudheusden. The orienteering problem: A survey. *European Journal of Operational Research*, 2011.

Poster: Artistic Eye: Recognizing Key Viewing Points of Popular Sites

Chih-Hsiang Hsu[a], I-Chao Shen[a], Wen-Huang Cheng[a], and Shih-Wei Sun[b]
[a]Academia Sinica, [b]Taipei National University of the Arts, Taiwan
chih-hsiang.hsu11@imperial.ac.uk, joshshen@citi.sinica.edu.tw, whcheng@citi.sinica.edu.tw, swsun@newmedia.tnua.edu.tw

Figure 1. (a) [Left] We introduce cross domain image matching into our system, (b) [Middle] allowing camera parameters of artworks to be obtained and reconstructed together with photographs. Once reconstruction is done, we calculate the key viewing score additionally (the score values are encoded by intensity from low to high). This will then be completed by a navigation system (c) [Right] together, to direct users to these viewpoints.

Categories and Subject Descriptors
H.4.m [**Information Systems Applications**]: Miscellaneous.

Keywords
Photographs, Composition, Art, Cross-domain image match.

1. INTRODUCTION

Camera-enabled mobile devices (e.g. smart phones) are readily available for people to take photographs of historic or scenic sites conveniently. Any person with the right guidance will be able to take an aesthetically well-constructed picture. However, most people are not natural-born photographer. Taking a well-composed photograph is actually a challenging task. Consumer photographs that are available on the internet tend to have people being the subject, providing less relevant information to the actual site. On the other hand, numerous artworks by professional artists are widely available on the internet. These artworks inherent good aesthetic sense and clear perspectives, which can be utilized to provide useful guidances to take aesthetic photographs.

This work presents a system identifying the key viewpoints that are worth to be referencing for photographers/tourists around scenic sites; utilizing both online photograph datasets and artworks. Our system is motivated by the latest cross-domain image matching technique [1] which enables cooperation between realistic photographs and artworks. Moreover, by using the embedded GPS as a query, the site-related information will be downloaded. These information can provide real-time assist for users to reach key viewpoints to take photographs or recapture the existing artworks from the same viewpoints.

2. METHODOLOGY

The core concept of our system is that every photographs and artworks act as an assistant (i.e. voting for the key viewing points) for taking a photograph. Each user is treated as a non-professional photographer who does not have artistic sense and wishes to be navigated to reach the key viewpoints. Therefore, we take the similar approach to [2] that provides users a friendly image browsing and space navigation experience. We first get GPS information from the user's capturing devices, and use it as queries to retrieve massive amount of realistic photographs and artworks. Using well-known structure-from-motion technique, we reconstruct a 3D model of the site using the retrieved image data. In addition, we hypothesize that artworks constructed by artists, would have been created artificially in the most aesthetical composition. Consequently, these viewpoints would be the most relevant and give the best perspective of the site. To facilitate the 3D reconstruction which uses images of different domains (e.g. paintings, sketches), we propose to use cross-domain image matching technique [1] for the reconstruction process.

With the reconstructed 3D scene, we then evaluate each sample location according to two main factors: (1) whether any artworks was taken at the location, (2) the density of photographs that has been taken at nearby locations. Formally, we determine the importance of each location l by the following equation: $S(l) = \sum_{i=1}^{N} score(i)G(l)$, where N represents the total number of photographs/artworks taken/drawn near l, and the score ratio of artworks to photographs is 1000:1. $G(l)$ is a Gaussian kernel centered at l. Once we've done the importance computation for all the sample locations, we can start to give the navigation to the locations of key viewpoints. In our implementation, a backend server which stores precomputed data of some famous, historic sites and does online querying and computation of unknown sites. The users can use mobile devices with GPS as a query; the backend server then directs users to areas that are more appropriate for taking good view of the area.

MobiSys'13, June 25–28, 2013, Taipei, Taiwan.
ACM 978-1-4503-1672-9/13/06.

3. REFERENCES

[1] Hauagge, D.C. and Noah, S. 2012. Image matching using local symmetry features. *IEEE CVPR*, 206-213.

[2] Snavely, N., Seitz, S.M., Szeliski, R. 2006. Photo tourism: Exploring photo collections in 3D. *ACM Trans. Graphics*.

Poster - Instrumenting Thailand's Coastline: Mobile Devices for Environmental and Disaster Monitoring

Michael Nekrasov
University of California Santa Barbara
12737 Via Terceto
San Diego, CA 92130
+01 858 7549676
mnekrasov@cs.ucsb.edu

Sirilak Chumkiew
Walailak University
207/97 M.3 Thasala, Thasala,
Nakhon Si Thammarat 80160
+66 088 7622031
sirilak.chumkiew@gmail.com

Peter Shinn
University of California San Diego
9500 Gilman Drive
La Jolla, CA 92093-0436
+01 858 6997094
pshinn@ucsd.edu

ABSTRACT

This poster outlines ongoing work using mobile devices for communication and computation for environmental sensor networks in Thailand. This work is funded by a Fulbright scholarship spanning January to September 2013. The work is a partnership between the Center of Excellence for Ecoinformatics at Walailak University, the University of California Santa Barbara, and the University of California San Diego. It brings computer scientists and biologists together for the development of technology aimed at studying Thailand's costal ecosystems.

Bandon Bay, Surathani province, is home to mussel, cockle, oyster, and shrimp farmers. In March 2011, severe rainfall in the southern region of Thailand caused an influx of freshwater and sediment into the bay. Cockle and oysters were suffocated by a thick layer of sediment. The surge of water forced shrimp out into the open ocean. As a result, the aquaculture industry suffered immensely, with losses upwards of eight hundred million Baht. The aim of this project is to provide a valuable service to the region by giving farmers and locals a resource for assessing the water quality in Bandon Bay, as well as providing a warning system against possibly treacherous environmental patterns.

The system utilizes a Galaxy Nexus Android phone for real-time data collection and processing. The data is streamed to an Amazon EC2 server where it undergoes event-detection and archived for later study by ecologists. The system is deployed in the Gulf of Thailand, one mile off the coast. For power, the system uses a 40W solar panel. The data is transmitted using the phone's built in cellular modem. The system utilizes a SparkFun Electronics IOIO for interfacing to external sensors and power. The phone currently interfaces with a Vaisala WXT 520 meteorological station, with plans to extend the sensor suite to include water sensors for conductivity, dissolved oxygen, and pH.

The environmental conditions in the bay require a low power device that is capable of wireless communication. While there are industry devices capable of this, like the Campbell Scientific sensor suites, they are prohibitively expensive for developing nations and are heavily proprietary, impeding expansion and development. In contrast, a mobile device running open source software is a perfect candidate, as it is inherently capable of cellular communication, has a backup battery for intermittent power loss, and has the computing power necessary for data ingestion and onboard processing from a multitude of meteorological and aquatic sensors.

The system utilizes the Open Source Data Turbine streaming middleware [1] for real-time buffered data streaming and visualization. It builds upon the SensorPod [2] software stack developed at UCSD for interfacing with environmental sensors. For event detection, the system utilizes Esper for complex event processing. The mobile device collects and streams the data, which is captured by the cloud server and is run through a real-time event detection engine. Both the original data and the derived analysis are then made publically accessible and mirrored to universities in Thailand in real-time, using the DataTurbine middleware. Interested parties can visualize both the data and the derived analysis in real-time. In the event of connectivity interruptions, the mobile device buffers the data and retransmits when a connection is re-established.
Currently, the system is deployed in the bay, and we are in the process of writing the event detection logic. Once the system is determined to be stable, we will add water sensors necessary for flood detection. We are investigating transitioning some of the event detection logic onto the mobile device itself, but we are hesitant to use the Android compatible version of Esper, as it does not have ongoing support. If this project proves successful, we are considering mirroring the technology for use in coral observation and detection of coral bleaching.

Categories and Subject Descriptors

J.2 **[Physical Sciences and Engineering]**: Earth and atmospheric sciences

Keywords

Android; Real-time Analysis;, Environmental; Observing System; Water Quality; Event Detection; Mobile Computing

REFERENCES

[1] Fountain, Tony, et al. "Digital Moorea cyberinfrastructure for coral reef monitoring." *Intelligent Sensors, Sensor Networks and Information Processing (ISSNIP), 2009 5th International Conference on*. IEEE, 2009.

[2] Fountain, Tony, et al. "The open source Dataturbine initiative: empowering the scientific community with streaming data middleware." *Bulletin of the Ecological Society of America* 93.3 (2012): 242-252.

MobiSys'13, June 25–28, 2013, Taipei, Taiwan.
ACM 978-1-4503-1672-9/13/06.

Poster: CEGF- Corner Extraction by GPS Filtering for Power-Efficient Location Uploading

Shih-Yung Juan[1], Yi-Fan Chung[2], Chung-Ta King[1,2], Cheng-Hsin Hsu[2]
[1]Inst. of ISA, National Tsing Hua University, Hsinchu, Taiwan.
[2]Dept. of CS, National Tsing Hua University, Hsinchu, Taiwan.
[1] zoeh.ruan@gmail.com, [2] { YFChung, king, chsu }@cs.nthu.edu.tw

ABSTRACT

Over the past few years, personal sensing applications, such as travel path sharing and location recording, have been more and more popular. These applications use GPS sensors to record track points on smartphones and upload the track points to clouds in real time for information sharing. However, uploading a lot of GPS points may lead to heavy network traffic and much higher power consumption [1].

To address the problem, we present *corner extraction by GPS filtering* (CEGF) that extracts *corner feature GPS points* (CFGPs) from *GPS track points* (GTPs). Applications only need to upload the CFGPs to save the uploading energy on smartphones. CFGPs can be regarded as characteristic points of corners to represent the corresponding roads. To reduce the number of uploaded points, the problem is how to filter out the CFGPs from a large amount of GTPs.

Since a straight path can be represented by two end points, the problem of determining GTPs can be considered as finding *the turning points*, as illustrated in Figure 1 (a). We refer to these turning points as *corner feature GPS points*.

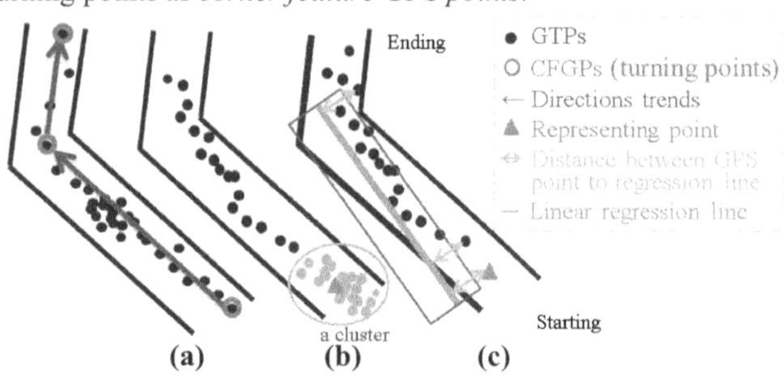

Figure 1. (a) CFGPs definition. (b) Finding representing points by DBSCAN clustering. (c) Rectangle method.

CEGF works as follows. First, we need to filter out the duplicated points at which the person stays for a long time. We use *DBSCAN* clustering algorithm [2] to extract a representing point for each cluster (see Figure 1 (b)). Second, we apply linear regression for a line to represent a series of points on the same path. Finally, as shown in Figure 1 (c), if there exists a GPS point that is far away from the regression line, we infer that it is a turn. We call this distance measurement method as *rectangle method*. This is because we assume a person's walking path would be bounded by the road width. Therefore, we use the rectangle block to approximate the road section. After finding the rectangle block, we can get the first and the last points which are in rectangle block as CFGPs. Repeating the rectangle method, we can get the complete CFGPs (see Figure 2).

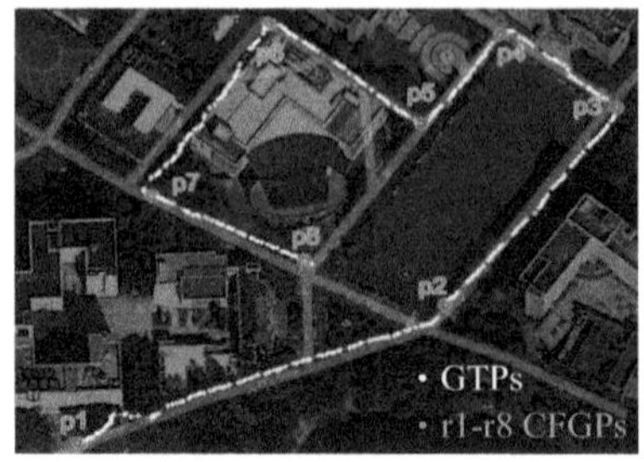

Figure 2. CFGPs result of experiment by using CEGF.

We implemented CEGF on Matlab, and collected GTPs at 1 point/sec on Samsung Galaxy Nexus phones. We walked on campus to record GTPs several times and used CEGF to extract CFGPs. The CFGPs are given in Figure 2. Finally, we measured uploading energy of data by GSam Battery Monitor. Table 1 shows our experimental results. This table shows that CEGF can save up to 14.9% of battery life time on a Samsung smartphone. We believe that CEGF can efficiently filter a large number of GPS track data into CFGPs and accurately represent the road sections. We are currently conducting more extensive experiments to demonstrate this.

Table 1. Experiment results

	Data size of GTPs (bytes)	Data size of CFGPs (bytes)	Filter rate (%)	Reduced power consumption (mJ)
Data1	13375	200	0.0150	7680.48 mJ
Data2	39210	205	0.0052	22738.32 mJ
Data3	26698	325	0.0122	15374.38 mJ
Data4	130044	1133	0.0087	75149.83 mJ

Categories and Subject Descriptors

I.5.5 [**Computing Methodologies**]: Pattern Recognition, Implementation

Keywords

GPS, Power-Efficient, Filtering

ACKNOWLEDGMENTS

This work was supported in part by MediaTek Inc. under Grant No.101F2211EA.

REFERENCES

[1] Liu et al., "Energy efficient GPS sensing with cloud offloading." In *Proc. 10th ACM Conf. Embed. Network Sensor Sys. (SenSys '12)*, Nov. 2012.

[2] Ester et al., "A density-based algorithm for discovering clusters in large spatial databases with noise". In *Proc. of the Second International Conference on Knowledge Discovery and Data Mining (KDD-96)*, Aug. 1996.

Poster: Mobile Code Offloading: Should it be a Local Decision or Global Inference?

Huber Flores
huber@ut.ee

Satish Nayarana Srirama
srirama@ut.ee

Institute of Computer Science, Mobile Cloud Lab
University of Tartu, Estonia
J. Liivi 2, Tartu

1. BASICS AND PROBLEM STATEMENT

Mobile and cloud computing are converging as the prominent technologies that are leading the change to the post-pc era. Mobile devices are looking towards cloud-aware techniques, driven by their growing interest to provide ubiquitous PC-like functionality to mobile users. These functionalities mainly target at increasing storage and computational capabilities. On one hand, storage limitations of the devices have been overcome by many cloud services provided in the Internet, which are built under different protocols (e.g. SyncML). On the other hand, binding computational cloud services such as Amazon EC2 to low-power devices such as smartphones have been proven feasible with latest mobile technologies [2, 1], mostly due to virtualization technologies and their synchronization primitives, enabling transparent migration and execution of intermediate code. Moreover, multiple research works have proposed different offloading strategies to empower the mobile application with cloud resources. Most of these solutions try to overcome the problem by granting the mobile, a local context logic, which is used to decide whether a mobile component is offloaded or not.

However, given this context, we can argue that much of the advantages of cloud computing are left unexploited and poorly considered. A cloud does not just mean a virtual machine or a pool of servers which are accessible from the Internet. It has its own intrinsic features like utility computing, fine-grained billing, parallelization of tasks, etc. So an ideal mobile cloud framework should take advantage of several of these features. Cloud computing may introduce many other dynamic variables to current code offloading models that could affect the overall offloading decision process. For instance, performance metrics (e.g. CPU load) of the instance/cluster at the cloud may be useful by the mobile in order to determine 1) whether a server is not that busy so that it can handle an incoming request and 2) a dynamic execution plan that allows to parallelize mobile operations in a single machine with multiple cores or in different machines, each with a single core. Consequently, a code offloading model should not just target mobility aspects, but also target oscillating changes in cloud infrastructure.

On the basis of these assumptions, we envisioned in this work, an "Evidence-based mobile code offloading approach" [3] that enables to transform raw code offloading traces, which are obtained by the huge amount of devices that connect to cloud, into knowledge that can be sent periodically in an asynchronous way to the handset in order to counter issues such as device diversity, adaptive application execution and unpredictable code profiling. Thus, fostering a strategy that continuously improves the offloading decision mechanisms that allow to increase performance and save energy.

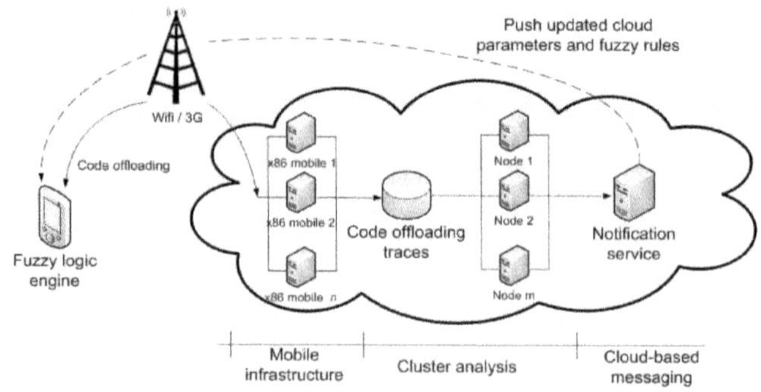

Figure 1: Evidence-based code offloading architecture

Moreover, unlike other approaches, we think that offloading is not a local decision process that happens just within the device's context, but rather offloading is a learning process that involves a global understanding of the infrastructure. Thus, we proposed an architecture (figure 1) which consists of 1) an offloading decision mechanism based on fuzzy logic, 2) a virtualized mobile infrastructure (Android x86), 3) a repository of offloading traces along with a cluster to analyze it and 4) a cloud-based messaging framework.

Categories and Subject Descriptors

C.1.3 [**Computer Systems Organization**]: Other Architecture Styles—*Cellular architecture (e.g., mobile)*

Keywords

Mobile Cloud, Code Offloading, Machine Learning

2. REFERENCES

[1] B.-G. Chun et al. Clonecloud: elastic execution between mobile device and cloud. In *EuroSys 2011*.

[2] E. Cuervo et al. Maui: making smartphones last longer with code offload. In *MobiSys 2010*.

[3] H. Flores et al. Adaptive code offloading for mobile cloud applications: Exploiting fuzzy sets and evidence-based learning. In *4th ACM MCS 2013*.

MobiSys'13, June 25-28, 2013, Taipei, Taiwan.
ACM 978-1-4503-1672-9/13/06.

Poster: Framework for Automated Power Estimation of Android Applications

Jemin Lee
Chungnam National University
Daejeon, South Korea
Leejaymin@cnu.ac.kr

Hyungshin Kim
Chungnam National University
Daejeon, South Korea
hyungshin@cnu.ac.kr

Categories and Subject Descriptors
D.2.5 [**Testing and Debugging**]: Testing tools

Keywords
Power Consumption, Smartphone, Automated Testing.

1. MOTIVATION

In spite of the incredible market penetration of smartphones and rapid growth of App markets, their utility has been restricted by their battery capacity. Smartphone users are frustrated by applications consuming too much power. For instance, energy bugs of applications cause unexpected amount of high energy consumption by the system as a whole [1]. To avoid this experience, they may have to profile energy consumption on the phone. However, it is difficult for a user to analyze energy consumption of his phone because the process requires deep understanding of the interaction between the hardware and software. Therefore, market curators need to examine applications for providing power consumption data before accepting them into App market. Unfortunately, current App markets mainly employ basic functional tests and checking policy on the submitted applications. Moreover, considering the exponentially increasing daily amount of new Apps posted on the App market, it is not feasible to perform the process manually. Therefore, if we can provide an automated energy estimation tool for App market curators, users can have energy consumption data in addition to the current functional description. We expect users may consider energy factor before they download the Apps.

2. FRAMEWORK

In this poster, we propose a framework for automated power estimation of android apps. The key features of our framework are as follows. First, in contrast to existing testing tools, our framework allows market curator to test apps without source code. Our framework decompiles app installers (.apk files) using APK Tools to obtain manifest.xml. Then, test scenarios are generated which are composed of the android component (activity, service, broadcast receiver, and content provider) and permission data by parsing manifest.xml file. Energy consumption is estimated while running apps with the scenarios. The process is performed as a black-box testing with the generated scenario and Monkey, which comes with the Android SDK. Second, our framework enables market curator to automate estimation of application power consumption. Energy consumption is measured from the current sensor on the phone or computed from the pre-generated power model. We perform each phase of testing by executing ADB (Android Debug Bridge) commands.

MobiSys'13, June 25–28, 2013, Taipei, Taiwan.
ACM 978-1-4503-1672-9/13/06.

Figure 1 shows the overall architecture of our framework. We have implemented our framework in Linux using python. Testing module is in charge of the whole estimation process. The module is executed on a Linux PC and connects to one or more target smartphones over Wi-Fi. The *Testing module* contains the following components: The *APK Dispatcher* imports APKs from marketplaces, installing apps to target smartphones. The *APK Decompiler* decompiles the app installers using APK Tools to obtain Android main component. The *Environment Set-Up* manipulates states of smartphone hardware such as GPS or Wi-Fi, so that testing scenario is applied with correct hardware setting. The *Event Generator* generates random or deterministic event sequences and feeds these events to an app of target smartphone. It is implemented by modifying Monkey. The *Logging* records read out values of the current sensor and completed events during the testing.

Key challenge for implementing this framework is to find representative usage pattern of the application to be applied to the Monkey Event Generator.

We believe that market curators should provide power consumption of apps in addition to other functional description. End-users should avoid energy problem from the estimated power data. App developers also should make an effort for reducing power consumption. With the support of our framework, we can guide users towards energy-aware usage of the mobile devices.

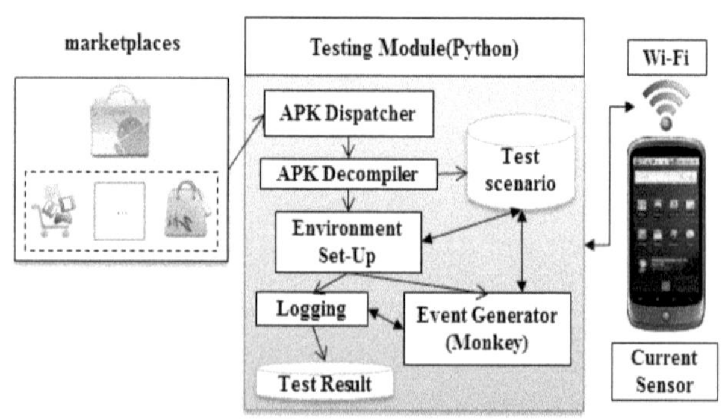

Figure 1. Our framework for automated power estimation of smartphone apps.

3. REFERENCE

[1] A. Pathak, Y. C. Hu, and M. Zhang, "Bootstrapping energy debugging for smartphones: A first look at energy bugs in mobile devices," in Proc. of Hotnets, 2011.

Poster: Solving Network Isolation Problem in Duty-cycled Wireless Sensor Networks

Haiming Zhang
Guangdong Uni. of Petrochemical Technology, China
haiming.zhang@live.cn

Lei Shu*
Guangdong Uni. of Petrochemical Technology, China
lei.shu@live.cn

Joel J.P.C. Rodrigues
University of Beira Interior, Portugal
joeljpcr@gmail.com

Han-chieh Chao
National Ilan University, Taiwan
hcchao@gmail.com

Categories and Subject Descriptors

C.2.3 [**Computer Systems Organization**]: Network Operations – *Network management.*

Keywords

Network isolation ; Network lifetime ; Sleep scheduling

1. The research problem

EC-CKN (*Energy Consumed uniformly Connected K-Neighborhood*) [1] is a sleep scheduling algorithm designed for duty-cycled wireless sensor networks (WSNs) based on Nath *et al.* proposed *Connected K-Neighborhood* (CKN) sleep scheduling scheme [1]. It inherited the key feature of CKN: "allow only a portion of sensor nodes to be awake to save energy while the global network is still connected by those awake nodes", and further focused on prolonging the network lifetime: "the residual energy owned by the awake nodes determined by the sleep scheduling scheme should be more than that of the asleep nodes determined by the algorithm". However, we discovered an important *Network Isolation Problem* in EC-CKN based WSNs as described in Fig. 1.

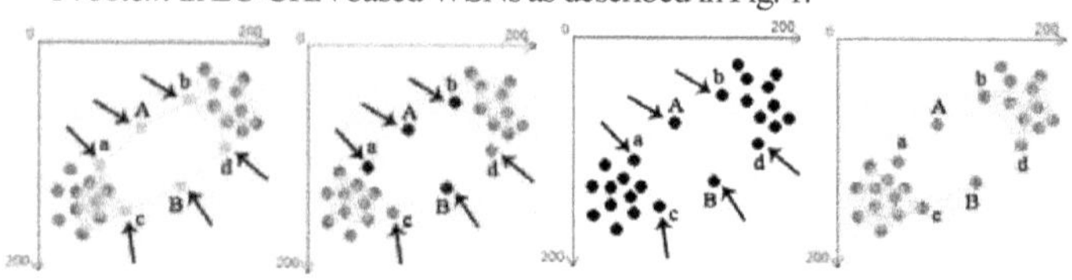

(a) Round = 1 (b) Round = 25 (c) Round = 46 (d) Round = 40

Figure 1. Blue nodes are normal working nodes, green nodes are sleeping nodes, and black nodes are dead nodes due to running out of energy. In figure, the is *K*-Neighborhood is 3 (K = 3). A, B in Fig.1(a) dissatisfy the condition of 3-neighborhood (K = 3), so that they cannot get any opportunity to sleep and save energy. In Fig.1(b) , after executing the EC-CKN algorithm for 25 rounds, nodes A, B, a, b run out of energy, which leads to two isolated network islands. All nodes run out of energy in the round of 46 as shown in Fig.1(c), which means these two network islands have been disconnected for 21 rounds. But our proposed method can avoid the network isolation problem and keep network connection even after 40 rounds as shown in Fig.1(d).

2. Proposed method

We propose a method called ATR-CKN to create sleeping opportunities for this kind of nodes, e.g., nodes A, B. Before executing EC-CKN, each node executes ATR-CKN as shown in Fig.2, in which the default transmission radius (TR) of all nodes is $DefaultT_r$ and the maximum TR supported by the node hardware is $MaxT_r$. Each time the transmission radius can be increased by $IncreaseT_r$ meters. (*Lei Shu is the corresponding author.)

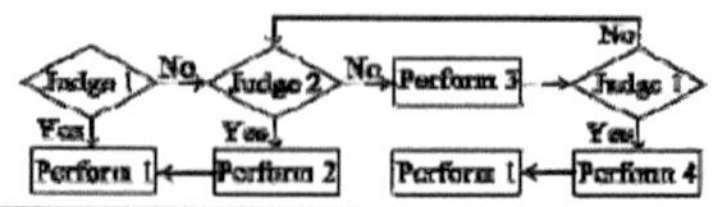

Judge 1	Does the node satisfy the condition of *k-neighborhood*?
Judge 2	Is the node using its $MaxT_r$?
Perform 1	Start to execute EC-CKN algorithm.
Perform 2	Set the transmission radius to $DefaultT_r$
Perform 3	Increase transmission radius of $IncreaseT_r$ meters.
Perform 4	Request its 1-hop neighbor nodes to increase their transmission radii to be the same as the current node.
Global Rule	Each node increase its TR based on the largest value, when receiving multiple requests for increasing its TR.

Figure 2. The method of Adjusting the Transmission Radius (ATR)

3. Simulation and result

In NetTopo [1], we conducted extensive simulation experiments. Fig.3 shows the simulation results of the average round of the first running out energy node and the whole network lifetime. The network lifetime is defined as the average time that sensor nodes in the network run out its energy from the beginning [1].

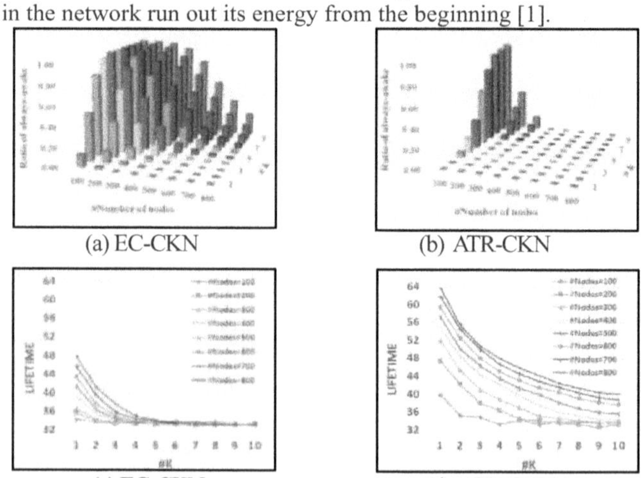

(a) EC-CKN (b) ATR-CKN

(c) EC-CKN (d) ATR-CKN

Figure 3. Observation of Fig.3: ATR-CKN gets more neighbor nodes can create sleeping opportunity for some nodes and increase the sleeping rate in the network, e.g. Fig3 (b), also avoid the *Network Isolation Problem* and prolong the network lifetime, e.g. Fig3 (d).

4. Acknowledgment

This research work is supported by the Guangdong Uni. of Petrochemical Technology's Internal Project No. 2012RC0106.

5. Reference

[1] Yuan, Zhuxiu, Wang, Lei, Shu, Lei, Hara, Takahiro, Qin, Zhenquan. "*A balanced energy consumption sleep scheduling algorithm in wireless sensor networks*". In Proceedings of IWCMC 2011.

Poster: An integrated System for Indoor and Outdoor Location-based Services (MapBiquitous)

Thomas Springer, Tenshi Hara, Gerd Bombach and Sina Grunau
TU Dresden, Chair for Computer Networks, 01062 Dresden, Germany
{thomas.springer|tenshi.hara}@tu-dresden.de

ABSTRACT

Within the last decade, outdoor location services have developed to be ubiquitous and generally available to the majority of users, be it on desktop pcs or on mobile devices such as smartphones and tablets. However, these types of services are limited to outdoor areas, e.g. navigation between two buildings. The logical next step was to expand to the indoor area, for which recently different indoor location services, especially navigation services, have emerged. Up to now, these solutions lack global coverage, since most of them operate in a proprietary and isolated manner.

This fact makes the integration of outdoor and indoor location based systems a very topical area of research. Major challenges are the provisioning of building information in an interoperable and scalable manner, the support of heterogeneous technologies (e.g. based on various technologies like Wifi, RFID, or smartphone sensors) for indoor positioning and the cross-building navigation with pathes inside and outside buildings.

MapBiquitous* addresses these challenges by providing an integrated system for indoor and outdoor location-based services. The basic principle envisages a decentralised client/server architecture with building servers providing the necessary building information, e.g. ichnography, floor plans and navigation information. Clients are able to discover building servers using a location-based directory service and load building information at the granularity of floor plans with separate layers for navigation and positioning.

To ensure interoperability of building information, open standards for accessing and representing building information are used. We particularly use the Web Feature Service (WfS) and the Geography Markup Language (GML) specified by the Open Geospatial Consortium (OGC). Floor plans contain geometric information representing rooms and floors as polygons as well as semantic information like room numbers and room descriptions.

Clients store that information in a local model and project floor plans onto the map information based on overlays. Since WGS 84 coordinates are used, no coordinate transformation is required to match positions provided by GPS.

To determine the position we support multiple positioning methods. In addition to GPS two modes are supported: On the one hand, multilateration based on WLAN access

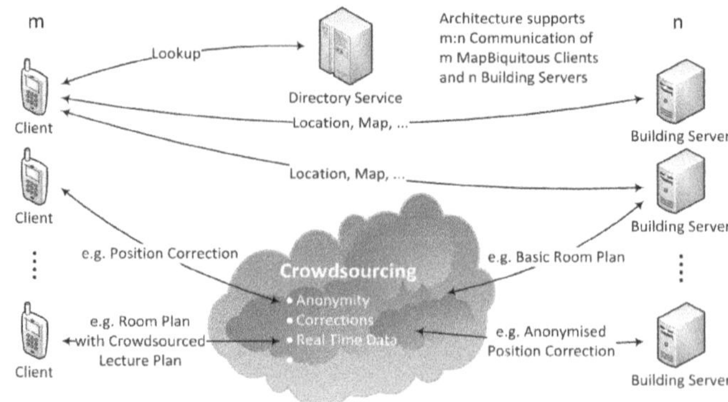

Functional showcase architecture of MapBiquitous

points can be utilised. On the other hand, building servers can provide a service for positioning based on WiFi fingerprints. Furthermore, mobile device sensors (particularly magnetometer, accelerometers and barometer) are used to determine orientation and distance of relative movements as well as the floor level.

The concept for calculating navigation paths is based on the shortest path algorithm by Dijkstra. The calculation is carried out by the involved building servers. For outdoor paths Google Maps Navigation API is used.

Ascertainment and correction of information is supported by a distributed crowdsourcing architecture that makes users and their submissions anonymous towards the building servers while maintaining retroactive cancellation of submissions as well as anonymous user ratings.

Building servers are implemented based on GeoServer and WfS. An Android App serves as MapBiquitous client. Crowdsourcing is ought to be a self-organising P2P network.

Our research includes feasible methods of positioning by smartphones, combination of different approaches (e.g. angulation with pace models) as well as possibilities of correcting data and ascertainment of real time information. The focus remains on mobile computing and offline availability.

Categories and Subject Descriptors

H.5.4 [**Information Interfaces and Presentation**]: Hypertext/Hypermedia *Navigation*; C.2.4 [**Computer Systems Organization**]: Distributed Systems *Client/Server, Distributed Applications*

Keywords

Location-based Services, Indoor Positioning, Building Model, Indoor Navigation, MapBiquitous

* Project description and comprehensive list of references at http://goo.gl/eqJkG

MobiSys'13, June 25–28, 2013, Taipei, Taiwan.
ACM 978-1-4503-1672-9/13/06.

Poster: How to Harmonize Wi-Fi and Bluetooth in a Mobile Device?

Wonhong Jeon, Byeong-Moon Cho, and Kyung-Joon Park
Department of Information and Communication Engineering
Daegu Gyeongbuk Institute of Science and Technology
Daegu, 711-873 Republic of Korea
Emails: {cwh4898, bmcho, kjp}@dgist.ac.kr

Categories and Subject Descriptors

C.2.1 [Network Architecture and Design]: Metrics-performance measures

Keywords

AHT, Bluetooth, Hybrid Arbitrator, WLAN, canceller, coexistence

1. INTRODUCTION

Wi-Fi and Bluetooth are two of the most widely used wireless technologies in mobile devices such as laptops, smart pads, and smart phones. We expect that the use of these two technologies will even more flourish with the forthcoming devices such as Google Glass and iWatch. However, Wi-Fi and Bluetooth share the same 2.4 GHz ISM band, which may result in severe self-interference when they coexist in the same device.

In this work, we show the possibility of resolving the in-device coexistence issue of Wi-Fi and Bluetooth without any change in the protocols. We expand the idea of self-interference cancellation in [1], which was originally proposed for full-duplex wireless communication. Our solution is highly practical in the sense that it only requires minimal change in the hardware circuitry without modifying wireless protocols.

2. PROPOSED SOLUTION

There exist several interference mitigating techniques between Wi-Fi and Bluetooth.In practice, the most widely used solution is adaptive frequency hopping (AFH), which measures the noise level over the entire channels. If the noise level of a channel is larger than a threshold, then AFH registers the channel as bad and excludes it from the hopping sequence.

However, AFH alone is often not enough to resolve the in-device coexistence issue of Wi-Fi and Bluetooth, especially with insufficient spatial isolation, which is exactly the case of mobile devices. In particular, the two cases when one is in transmission while the other is in reception are critical because the receive signal is much weaker than the transmit signal. When Wi-Fi is in transmission while Bluetooth is in reception without enough isolation, Bluetooth may not properly operate due to the insufficient number of good channels.

Hence, on top of the conventional AFH, we introduce a canceller that can cancel out the in-device interference when Wi-Fi and Bluetooth radios simultaneously operate in the same device. The idea of canceller is simple as follows: In order to remove the interference signal from the TX antenna, we place a reverse channel inside the circuitry as illustrated in Fig. 1 (a).

MobiSys'13, June 25-28, 2013, Taipei, Taiwan.
ACM 978-1-4503-1672-9/13/06.

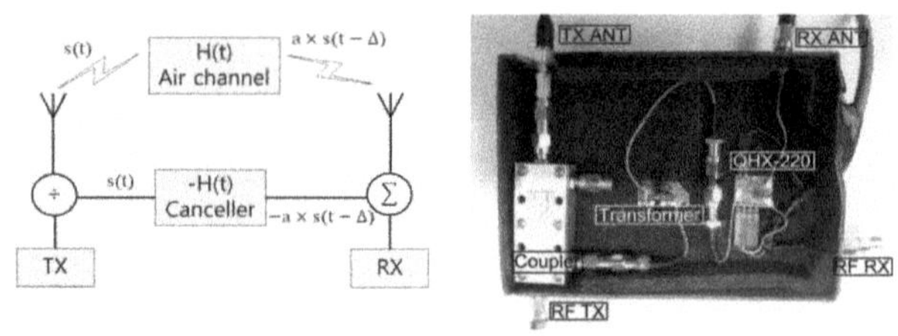

(a) Canceller mechanism (b) Canceller testbed

Figure 1: Canceller mechanism and our testbed.

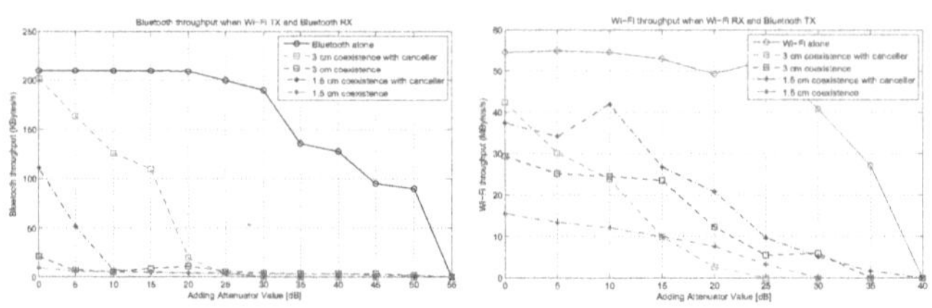

(a) Bluetooth throughput (b) Wi-Fi throughput

Figure 2: Throughput performance of Bluetooth and Wi-Fi.

3. EXPERIMENTAL RESULTS

In our testbed shown in Fig. 1 (b), the coupler divides the RF TX signal into two paths with 90% power and 10% power, respectively. Then, the 90% power path goes into the transmission antenna. In the meantime, the phase of the other path is inverted by the transformer, and the delay and the gain are further controlled by QHX-220 (which is a noise canceller).

In our experiments, we consider two values for the distance between two antennas, i.e., 1.5 cm and 3 cm, which are reasonable for consumer mobile devices. We consider the two cases when one is in transmission while the other is in reception as shown in Fig. 2. Our experimental results in Fig. 2 demonstrate that our scheme can introduce significant additional isolation between Wi-Fi and Bluetooth radios in a small mobile device without any transmission performance degradation.

4. REFERENCES

[1] M. Jain, J. Choi, T. Kim, D. Bharadia, K. Srinivasan, P. Levis, S. Katti, P. Sinha, and S. Seth, "Practical, real-time, full duplex wireless." in *Proc. ACM Mobicom*, 2011.

Poster: Odometer in the Pocket

Lin Wu[1,2], YongJun Xu[1], ZhuLin An[1], ChaoNong Xu[3] and Fei Wang[1,2]
[1]Institute of Computing Technology, Chinese Academy of Sciences
[2]University of Chinese Academy of Sciences
[3] Department of Computer Science and Technology, China University of Petroleum-Beijing

ABSTRACT
Some previous work has shown the feasibility of Pedestrian Dead Reckoning (PDR) using a mobile phone, but the estimation of length walked is still a big challenge. In this paper, we propose a formula for estimating walking velocity, which can be integrated to get distance.

Categories and Subject Descriptors
C.3 [**Special-Purpose and Application-Based Systems**]: Microprocessor/Microcomputer Applications; Signal Processing Systems

Keywords
Pedestrian dead reckoning, Mobile phone, Odometer, Length estimation

1. INTRODUCTION
PDR consists of length calculation and direction estimation. Our work focuses on length calculation. In this paper, we present an approach to estimate the length walked with accelerations collected by a mobile phone in a trouser pocket.

Researchers typically multiply stride length by stride number and the former is much more difficult to calculate. The method used by [1] for deriving stride length is to divide total length walked (obtained by RF fingerprinting and map matching) by stride number. The result will be used as an estimation of the pedestrian's stride length with random error. In [2], stride length was approximated through multiplying pedestrian's height by 0.413 (females) or 0.415 (males). An empirical equation was applied by [3], whose average error in total distance is 6% and can be reduced to 3% through calibration according to the author. In this paper, we propose a formula to estimate walking velocity directly without counting steps, and then integrate it over time to get distance. In this way, our approach has only one error source: error in estimating velocity.

2. APPROACH
First of all, we multiply 512 samples of acceleration by a hamming window. Then we make an 8192-point Fast Fourier Transformation (FFT) over the result to get the frequency spectrum (Vx(w), Vy(w) and Vz(w)) of acceleration. The gap W_{stride} between adjacent peaks is stride frequency. The formula to calculate walking velocity is as follows:

$$v = k * \left(\sum_{n=1}^{4} sqrt\left(V_x^{\frac{4}{3}}(n * W_{stride}) + V_y^{\frac{4}{3}}(n * W_{stride}) + V_z^{\frac{4}{3}}(n * W_{stride})\right) / n \,/ SampleCount^{2/3} - DC\right) \quad (1)$$

In the equation, k and DC varies slightly for different trousers and different people. The main reason may be that, the location of mobile phones is a little different in different trousers. Values of k and DC are about 2.8 and 0.2 respectively and they can be calibrated for different trousers and mobile phones automatically when combining PDR with absolute positioning methods. For convenience, the value of DC can be fixed and only adjust the value of k by the following equation:

$$k_{calibrated} = k_{original} * \frac{Distance_{true}}{Distance_{estimated}} \quad (2)$$

3. Evaluation
We evaluate our method with datasets recorded by an Android application running on mobile phones put in our left trouser pockets. For a sampling rate around 100 Hz (Huawei U8800 and Xiaomi M1) and walking speed from 4 km/h to 6 km/h, our method performs quite well with regard to standard deviation in estimating walking speed (standard deviation is around 2%) and total distance travelled (error is within 1%).

4. ACKNOWLEDGMENTS
This paper is supported in part by Important National Science & Technology Specific Projects under grant No.(2010ZX03006-002, 2010ZX03006-007), the National Basic Research Program of China (973 Program) (No. 2011CB302803), and National Natural Science Foundation of China (NSFC) under grant No.(61173132,61003307). The authors alone are responsible for the content of the paper.

5. REFERENCES
[1] Rai, A., et al. Zee: zero-effort crowdsourcing for indoor localization. In Proc. ACM MobiCom, 2012.

[2] Constandache, I., et al. Towards Mobile Phone Localization without War-Driving. In Proc. IEEE INFOCOM, 2010.

[3] Bylemans, I., et al. M. Mobile Phone-Based Displacement Estimation for Opportunistic Localisation Systems. In Proc. IEEE UBICOMM, 2009.

MobiSys'13, June 25–28, 2013, Taipei, Taiwan.
ACM 978-1-4503-1672-9/13/06.

HyCloud: A Hybrid Approach Toward Offloading Cellular Content Through Opportunistic Communication

Abouzar Noori
ETH Zurich
Communication Systems Group
Zurich, Switzerland
anoori@ethz.ch

Domenico Giustiniano
ETH Zurich
Communication Systems Group
Zurich, Switzerland
domenico.giustiniano@tik.ee.ethz.ch

Categories and Subject Descriptors

C.2.1 [**COMPUTERCOMMUNICATION NETWORKS**]: Network Architecture and Design

Keywords

Opportunistic Communication, Cellular Data Offloading, Cloud Computing

1. INTRODUCTION

The rapid proliferation of smartphones and the urge to offload mobile data is paving the way to blend the communication capabilities of cellular and opportunistic networks for delivering content. By exploiting the locality of users interested in the same content, the vision of HyCloud project[1] is to design and implement a hybrid architecture where content dissemination through opportunistic communication among several clients is controlled by the online cloud. Based on the foundation of our key theoretical findings, we are implementing a prototype architecture running on Windows Phone 8 mobile devices, taking advantage of the Windows Azure cloud platform.

2. DESIGN AND IMPLEMENTATION

The principle is that the cloud service *injects* content to some users through the cellular network and *coordinates* the opportunistic delivery from these users (e.g., via WLAN or Bluetooth) to other interested users upon meeting them, hence offloading the cellular network load. We have studied the optimal strategy for sending the content from the online cloud to mobile devices and designed an online scheduler to compute the optimal number and time of cellular deliveries to selected users based on the history of content deliveries.

In HyCloud, the content scheduler runs in Windows Azure Cloud Services while authentication, data storage and notification service are provided by Windows Azure Mobile Services. The main principles are illustrated in Fig. 1. Each device registers to subscription channels of its interest (such as popular news feed or video streams) and expects to receive the latest content stored in the online cloud. When the scheduler decides to send a content to a device, it communicates with the Microsoft Push Notification Service (MPNS), which notifies the device to download the content from Blob tables stored in Windows Azure SQL Database. Those mobile devices which own the latest data content take advantage of WLAN or Bluetooth interface to opportunistically disseminate the data to other subscribed devices in communication range. When the deadline for receiving the latest data content becomes close, each device which has not yet received the data content through either cellular network or opportunistic communication, pulls the content via cellular infrastructure. The beauty of HyCloud is that it is a highly scalable solution toward cellular traffic offloading which requires neither feedback of how many users have received the content (but only a report at the deadline time from those that have not received it yet) nor the estimation of intercontact rates.

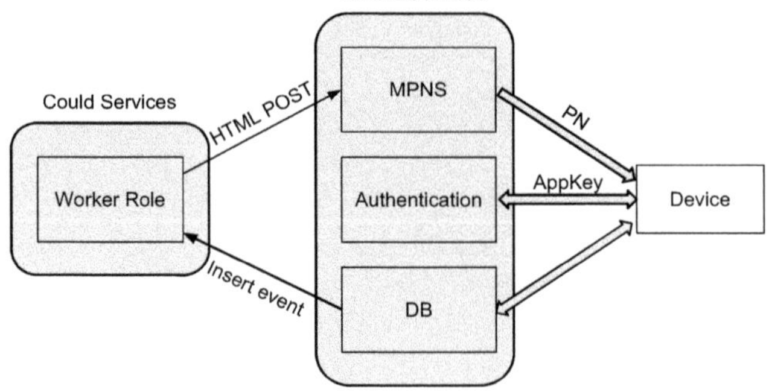

Figure 1: Design of HyCloud on Windows Azure cloud platform.

[1]The project is funded by Microsoft Research, as a part of ICES program.

MobiSys'13, June 25-28, 2013, Taipei, Taiwan.
ACM 978-1-4503-1672-9/13/06.

3. REFERENCES

[1] B. Han, P. Hui, V. A. Kumar, M. V. Marathe, G. Pei, and A. Srinivasan. Cellular traffic offloading through opportunistic communications: A Case Study. In *Proceedings of ACM CHANTS*, 2010.

[2] S. Ioannidis, A. Chaintreau, and L. Massoulie. Optimal and scalable distribution of content updates over a mobile social network. In *Proceedings of IEEE INFOCOM*, 2009.

[3] J. Whitbeck, M. Amorim, Y. Lopez, J. Leguay, and V. Conan. Relieving the wireless infrastructure: When opportunistic networks meet guaranteed delays. In *Proceedings of IEEE WoWMoM*, 2011.

Author Index

www.ingramcontent.com/pod-product-compliance
Ingram Content Group UK Ltd.
Pitfield, Milton Keynes, MK11 3LW, UK
UKHW051416290926
15471UKWH00009B/1636

9 781450 322881